Information Systems

A Management Approach

Information Systems

A Management Approach

Steven R. Gordon *Babson College*
Judith R. Gordon *Boston College*

THE DRYDEN PRESS
Harcourt Brace College Publishers

Fort Worth Philadelphia San Diego New York Orlando Austin San Antonio Toronto
Montreal London Sydney Tokyo

Acquisitions Editor	Robert Linsky
Developmental Editor	Elizabeth Hayes, Lisa Toftemark
Project Editor	Michele Tomiak
Production Manager	Eddie Dawson
Designer	Brian Salisbury
Permissions Editor	Adele Krause
Product Manager	Scott Timian
Proofreader	Leon Unruh
Indexer	Edwin Durbin
Compositor	GTS Graphics
Text Type	10/12 Bembo
Cover/Part Rug Designs	Tim Van Campen

Address for Editorial Correspondence
The Dryden Press, 301 Commerce Street, Suite 3700, Fort Worth, TX 76102

Address for Orders
The Dryden Press, 6277 Sea Harbor Drive, Orlando, FL 32887-6777
1-800-782-4479, or 1-800-433-0001 (in Florida)

ISBNs: 0-03-016314-5 (text)
0-03-097574-3 (text plus activities and cases)

Library of Congress Catalog Number : 95-67705

Printed in the United States of America

5 6 7 8 9 0 1 2 3 4 048 9 8 7 6 5 4 3 2 1

The Dryden Press
Harcourt Brace College Publishers

To our parents
Yvette and Herman Gordon
Elaine and Morry Rosecrans

our children
Brian, Laurie, and Michael

and the memory of
our son
Peter

The Dryden Press Series in Information Systems

Dean and Effinger
Commonsense BASIC: Structured Programming with Microsoft QuickBASIC

Forcht
Management Information Systems: A Casebook

Forrest
Multimedia: Issues in Interactive Communications

Gordon and Gordon
Information Systems: A Management Approach

Gary, King, McLean, and Watson
Management of Information Systems
Second Edition

Harrington
Database Management for Microcomputers: Design and Implementation
Second Edition

Harris
Systems Analysis and Design: A Project Approach

Head
An Introduction to Programming with QuickBASIC

Laudon and Laudon
Information Systems: A Problem-Solving Approach
Third Edition

Laudon and Laudon
Information Systems: A Problem-Solving Approach
(A CD-ROM interactive version)

Laudon, Laudon, and Weill
The Integrated Solution

Lawlor
Computer Information Systems
Third Edition

Martin
QBASIC: A Short Course in Structured Programming

McKeown
Living with Computers
Fifth Edition

McKeown
Working with Computers
Second Edition

McKeown
Working with Computers with Software Tutorials
Second Edition

McLeod
Systems Analysis and Design: An Organizational Approach

Millspaugh
Business Programming in C for DOS-Based Systems

O'Brien
The Nature of Computers
Second Edition

Parker
Computers and Their Applications
Fourth Edition

Parker
Understanding Computers: Today and Tomorrow
EXACT Edition

Simpson and Tesch
Introductory COBOL: A Transaction-Oriented Approach

Spear
Visual Basic

Sullivan
The New Computer User

Thommes and Carey
Introduction to CASE Using Visible Analyst Workbench v4.3 for DOS
CASE Tools: Using Visible Analyst Workbench for Windows

electronic learning facilitators, inc.

Stepping through Excel 4.0 for Windows
Stepping through Windows 3.1
Stepping through Word 2.0 for Windows
Up and Running with the Internet
Up and Running with Harvard Graphics 1.03 for Windows
Up and Running with PageMaker 5.0 for Windows
Up and Running with WordPerfect 5.2 for Windows
Up and Running with Quattro Pro 1.0 for Windows
Up and Running with Microsoft Works 2.0 for Windows
Up and Running with Lotus 1-2-3 Release 4 for Windows
Up and Running with Paradox 4.5 for Windows
Up and Running with DOS 6.0
Up and Running with Paradox 4.0 for DOS
Up and Running with DOS 6.0
Up and Running with Paradox 4.0 for DOS
Up and Running with Microsoft Works 3.0 for DOS
Up and Running with Excel 4.0 for the Macintosh
Up and Running with Word 5.1 for the Macintosh
Up and Running with PageMaker 5.0 for the Macintosh
Up and Running with WordPerfect 6.0 for Windows
Up and Running with Access 2.0 for Windows
Up and Running with Microsoft Works 3.0 for Windows
Working Smarter with DOS 5.0
Working with WordPerfect 5.0
Working with WordPerfect 5.1

Martin and Parker
Mastering Today's Software Series

Texts available in any combination of the following:

- *Microcomputer Concepts (chs. 1–5), 3e*
- *Extended Microcomputer Concepts (chs. 1–9), 3e*
- *Disk Operating System 5.0 (DOS 5.0)*
- *Disk Operating System 6.0 (DOS 6.0)*
- *Windows 3.1*
- *Windows 95*
- *Microsoft Office for Windows 95 Professional Edition*
- *Word Processing with WordPerfect 5.1*
- *Word Processing with WordPerfect 5.2 for Windows*
- *Word Processing with WordPerfect 6.0 for DOS*
- *Word Processing with WordPerfect 6.0 for Windows*
- *Word Processing with WordPerfect 6.1 for Windows*
- *Word Processing with Word 6.0 for Windows*
- *Word Processing with Word 7.0 for Windows 95*
- *Spreadsheets with Lotus 1-2-3 (2.2/2.3)*
- *Spreadsheets with Lotus 1-2-3 (2.4)*
- *Spreadsheets with Lotus 1-2-3 for Windows (4.01)*
- *Spreadsheets with Lotus 1-2-3 for Windows (5.0)*
- *Spreadsheets with Excel 5.0 for Windows*
- *Spreadsheets with Excel 7.0 for Windows 95*
- *Spreadsheets with Quattro Pro 4.0*
- *Spreadsheets with Quattro Pro 6.0 for Windows*
- *Database Management with dBASE III PLUS*
- *Database Management with dBASE IV (1.5/2.0)*
- *Database Management with dBASE 5 for Windows*
- *Database Management with Paradox 4.0*
- *Database Management with Paradox 5.0 for Windows*
- *Database Management with Access 2.0 for Windows*
- *Database Management with Access 7.0 for Windows 95*
- *Presentation Graphics with PowerPoint 7.0 for Windows 95*

Martin, Series Editor
Productivity Software Guide Series

- *Disk Operating System (DOS) 3.3/5.0*
- *Windows 3.1*
- *Word Processing with WordPerfect 5.1*
- *Word Processing with WordPerfect 6.0*
- *Word Processing with WordPerfect 5.2 for Windows*
- *Word Processing with WordPerfect 6.0a/6.1 for Windows*
- *Spreadsheets with Lotus 1-2-3*
- *Spreadsheets with Lotus 1-2-3 Release 5 for Windows*
- *Spreadsheets with Quattro Pro 4.0*
- *Spreadsheets with Quattro Pro 6.0 for Windows*
- *Database Management with dBASE III PLUS*
- *Database Management with dBASE IV*
- *Database Management with Paradox 4.0*
- *Database Management with Paradox 5.0 for Windows*
- *A Beginner's Guide to BASIC*
- *A Beginner's Guide to QBASIC*

The Harcourt Brace College Outline Series

Kreitzberg
Introduction to BASIC

Kreitzberg
Introduction to Fortran

Pierson
Introduction to Business Information Systems

Veklerov and Pekelny
Computer Language C

Preface

All people need and use information in their personal and professional lives. Most students, however, do not appreciate that they must *manage* information to maximize its usefulness. Although they are bombarded with information from an array of media, individuals generally feel able to select with ease the most important information to retain. They may use a relatively simple noncomputerized information system, such as a date book, checkbook, or address book, to assist them in dealing with the information. Sometimes they use computer-based systems, such as electronic calendars or computerized financial managers. But, at the organizational level, and sometimes even at the personal level, the volume or complexity of information being processed, its importance to the organization or individual, and the difficulty of sorting and interpreting the information require careful control, systematic processing, and refined analyses. Increasing the rigor of information management normally involves the development of more complex formal systems that collect, organize, retrieve, and communicate information. This book takes a *management approach to information systems;* it presents the subject matter in a way that managers and potential managers will find meaningful. Although the text includes detailed technical information, its presentation emphasizes the *use of information* by the student or prospective manager and the role of information systems in supporting this use.

This book is intended for use in a management information systems course in either undergraduate or graduate programs of business or management. Its goal is to prepare students for business settings where they will manage information needs and will use information systems to do so. It includes extensive examples of information management practices.

The Management Approach

This book takes a management approach to information systems. It presents a framework for thinking about and improving the management of information through the design and implementation of effective, high-quality information systems. The book offers a unique four-step approach to the process of managing information. This approach moves from a diagnosis of information needs, through an evaluation of options to meet the needs, to the design and eventual implementation of information systems. The book examines the nature of technology and issues related to its selection and development within the broader contexts of information management and information systems.

Organization of This Textbook

The organization of the book complements the four-step management approach. Chapters are ordered to encourage students to take a systematic approach to information management: students practice each step of the management approach before adding the next step. The content of later chapters, then, reinforces the performance of earlier steps of the management approach. If desired, this management approach can be deemphasized and the order of the chapters altered without significantly affecting the other learning objectives.

Part I sets the stage by introducing information systems and the management approach. Chapter 1 focuses on information itself—its definition, use, value, cost, and management; it provides an overview of information technology and information systems; it also presents the four-step management approach. Chapter 2 deals with individual needs, both work and nonwork related. Chapter 3 discusses the needs of managers—from first-line supervisors through executives, and in various parts of the organization—from functional areas to project management. Chapter 4 presents organizational information needs.

Part II provides an overview of the relevant information technology to enable students to evaluate options for managing information. Chapter 5 discusses software, and Chapter 6 describes hardware. Chapter 7 discusses database management systems. Chapter 8 concludes this part with a discussion of data communication. Because of the rapid and ongoing changes in information technology, these chapters focus on basic principles of hardware, software, database, and data communication design and selection that apply regardless of technological changes, rather than specific technologies that will be outdated by the time students are ready to apply their knowledge.

Part III examines classes or types of information systems that address the needs identified in Part I. It helps students understand the spectrum of information system designs so that they are able to select the appropriate ones for the information needs they will encounter. Chapter 9 deals with automation systems, and Chapter 10 addresses transaction processing systems. Chapter 11 discusses a variety of management information systems, including those commonly called management reporting systems, decision support systems, and executive information (or support) systems. Chapter 12 analyzes strategic systems.

Part IV presents the process and infrastructure necessary to support the design, development, implementation, and maintenance of information systems and manage the information resource. Chapter 13 discusses the process of systems planning, development, and implementation. Chapter 14 describes the infrastructure.

Features of the Textbook

This book provides an integrated presentation of each topic using text, case analyses, and exercises. It is designed to be versatile in its use, offering flexibility in the ordering of chapters and the selection of instructional materials. The major features include the following:

- The ***focus on information*** encourages students to diagnose their information needs and build, select, or buy computer systems to meet them.
- ***Issues of global information management,*** discussed throughout the text, extend the discussion beyond a national perspective to highlight the problems and dilemmas of using information technology in a multinational environment.
- The discussion of ***technology from a user's perspective*** helps students to more readily understand and apply the material presented to situations they face.
- The ***four-step management approach*** offers a systematic and analytical means of information management for students.
- ***Extensive pedagogical elements*** are included in each chapter. These include a chapter outline, learning objectives, chapter summary, key terms, review questions, notes, and recommended readings.
- A ***short case*** introduces each chapter. Key theories or concepts regarding a particular topic are then presented and applied to the opening case where appropriate.
- ***Extensive real-world examples*** illustrate key concepts. Their names are highlighted in the margin to allow students easy reference.
- ***Minicases,*** included in most chapters, allow students to experience real-life situations without leaving the classroom. The minicases encourage the application of the theoretical and conceptual perspectives to diverse situations.

- ***Videocases*** conclude each part of the text. Students can use the cases to analyze how others should have dealt with information management in a particular context. They can also compare others' approaches to their own prescription based on the management approach.
- ***Activities*** in each chapter provide students the opportunity to understand information needs, assess the effectiveness of information management strategies, and apply course concepts to developing aspects of information systems. These activities include short cases, role plays, debates, external contact activities, and hands-on computer simulations.

Instructional Support Materials

Activities and Readings in Information Systems

This supplement, which can be bound with the text as an appendix or ordered separately, includes cases and articles chosen to extend each chapter's discussion and study. Twenty-four full-length cases extend the opportunity for students to apply information management concepts to real-world settings. Through guided questions, students are encouraged first to list the facts of a case; second, to diagnose the information needs of the parties; third, to assess the approach used to meet these needs; fourth, to provide evidence that the approach used is either successful or unsuccessful; and finally, if appropriate, to develop a plan for effective information management.

Thirteen full-length articles present the thinking of writers and researchers in the field of information systems. The readings have been selected to provide critical elaborations of core concepts and to raise issues about the proper management of information. They include theoretical formulations, research reports, descriptions of information systems applications, and commentaries on the direction of management approaches to information. Discussion questions following each reading highlight these concepts and their contribution to managing information effectively.

Instructor's Manual with Transparency Masters

The detailed instructor's manual, written by M. Lisa Miller, includes chapter summaries, teaching tips, lecture outlines with key terms and transparency masters cross-referenced, and answers to review questions for each chapter of the book.

Each end-of-chapter activity and all the activities in the supplement *Activities and Readings in Information Systems* are given a full discussion in the instructor's manual. Each activity and reading is given an overview, teaching strategy, preparation time, and answers to the questions. The transparency masters are made up of chapter outlines, objectives, and key figures from each chapter.

Test Bank

The test bank, by Ellen Hoadley, is available in both printed and computerized forms. It includes more than 1,400 items including true/false, multiple-choice, fill-in-the-blank, and short essay questions for each chapter. Questions are keyed to learning objectives as well as level of difficulty.

The computerized test bank, available for IBM PC-compatible and Apple Macintosh computers, contains all the questions found in the printed test bank. It allows you to preview, add, delete, or edit test questions, as well as to output questions in any order and to print answer keys.

Videos

The Dryden Press Information Systems Video Series has been developed in response to a need for real business cases tailored to the educational market. Instead of borrowing corporate training tapes or using industry promotional videos, this series has been custom-developed, from the ground up, for classroom use.

The video segments range from 8 to 14 minutes in length, depending on the topic. Filmed on location, each contains interviews with each organization's key information systems executives, managers, and system users. Most of the video segments highlight a specific use of information technology as it supports the business enterprise; others present different types of technologies in more general context.

The series is accompanied by a detailed instructor's guide. For each video segment, the guide contains a brief description about the video's content, its length, a list of topics discussed in the video, additional background information relevant to the video material, and several discussion questions to stimulate classroom interaction after viewing.

Overhead Transparencies

This set of full-color transparencies, taken from figures in the book as well as new, is available to enhance lectures.

Electronic Transparencies

This CD-ROM includes the figures from the overhead transparency package in addition to PowerPoint lecture presentations created for each chapter of the book. Figures on the disk may be pulled into the PowerPoint presentations or used as is.

The Dryden Press will provide complimentary supplements or supplement packages to those adopters qualified under our adoption policy. Please contact your sales representative to learn how you may qualify. If as an adopter or potential user you receive supplements you do not need, please return them to your sales representative or send them to:

Attn: Returns Department
Troy Warehouse
465 South Lincoln Drive
Troy, MO 63379

Acknowledgments

The development book has been influenced by the contributions of many individuals. We would like to first thank the reviewers of this book, who made important contributions that significantly influenced its development and quality. We thank

Warren Boe
University of Iowa

Kent R. Burnham
Eastern Washington University

William R. Cornette
Southwest Missouri State University

Richard Fenzl
Syracuse University

Ellen D. Hoadley
Loyola College

John Landry
Metropolitan State University

M. Khris McAlister
University of Alabama–Birmingham

Ralph McCrae
University of Texas at El Paso

M. Lisa Miller
University of Central Oklahoma

Thomas C. Richards
University of North Texas

James B. Shannon
New Mexico State University

David C. Whitney
San Francisco State University

In particular, we thank M. Lisa Miller and Ellen D. Hoadley for their outstanding work on the instructor's manual and test bank.

We greatly appreciate the editorial and technical support provided by the professionals at The Dryden Press. In particular, Elizabeth Hayes, developmental editor, Robert Linsky, acquisitions editor, Scott Timian, product manager, and Michele Tomiak, project editor, provided invaluable assistance with this project. Shirley Webster was invaluable in finding excellent photographs and securing permissions for the book. We also thank Richard Bonacci, who acted as the first editor of this project, and Lisa Toftemark, who acted as the first developmental editor on the project, and wish them luck in their new endeavors.

We also wish to thank our colleagues at Babson College and Boston College for their enthusiastic support for this project. From Babson College, John Saber, Jerome Kanter, and the sponsors of the James E. Perry Term Chair deserve particular mention, as do John J. Neuhauser, Jean Bartunek, and Jean Passavant from Boston College.

Finally, our greatest thanks go to our extended families, whose enthusiasm has been greatly appreciated. We dedicate this book to our parents and our children, who motivate us to do our best work in their honor.

Contents in Brief

Contents

PART IV

Managing the Information Resource 389

Information Systems

A Management Approach

Part I

Perspectives on Information Management

We are an information society. People use information to perform basic job functions and make personal choices. Managers use information for planning, organizing, leading, and controlling. Organizations collect information, use it, sell it, and leverage it for strategic advantage. How do organizations diagnose their information needs and the needs of their employees? How do they determine the value and estimate the costs of information? Part I addresses these questions, focusing on the information needs of individuals, managers, and organizations.

Chapter 1

Using Information

OUTLINE

Managing Information in Four Organizational Settings

What Is Information?

- The Concept of Information
- The Uses of Information
- The Value of Information

The Cost of Information

- Acquiring Information
- Processing Information
- Storing Information
- Retrieving Information
- Communicating Information

Information Systems

- The Need for Information Systems
- Information Technology
- Types of Information Systems

Managing Information in a Global Environment

- Diagnosis
- Evaluation
- Design
- Implementation

Organization of This Book

LEARNING OBJECTIVES

After reading Chapter 1, students will be able to

1. Offer three definitions of information.
2. Describe three uses of information.
3. Describe three frameworks for determining the value of information.
4. Describe the costs of acquiring, processing, storing, retrieving, and communicating information.
5. Compare and contrast the relative costs of manual and computerized information acquisition, processing, storage, retrieval, and communication.
6. Define an information system and identify the various types of systems.
7. Identify three types of information needs.
8. List the components of information technology.
9. Describe four types of information systems.
10. Trace the four steps in the effective management of information.

Managing Information in Four Organizational Settings

Marcia Block is the manager of Daley's Department Store. Each day the store rings up more than 10,000 sales. The store carries more than 1,000 products in a variety of styles, colors, and sizes. How does Ms. Block determine which products are selling best, what styles and sizes are low in stock, and which products are earning the most?

Each evening, between 10:00 P.M. and midnight, more than 100 Federal Express aircraft arrive at Memphis, Tennessee, carrying packages destined for cities throughout the United States. Between midnight and 2:00 A.M., the aircraft depart carrying each package toward its final destination. How does the operations department match the incoming packages with the appropriate outgoing aircraft? How does the department schedule the aircraft and their crews to avoid bottlenecks and conflicts?

Ethan Heller is a recruitment specialist at Spaceway Electronics. The company planned to add a second shift at one of its manufacturing plants, requiring the hiring of 100 employees in a variety of positions including assembler, quality-control analyst, and production supervisor. More than 2,750 résumés and job applications were received. How does Mr. Heller proceed with the hiring process?

Steve Hanna is the chief of data management at California's Office of Environmental Protection (OEP). More than 2,000 companies report the locations of their facilities, by latitude and longitude, to the OEP so that it can selectively monitor the companies' hazardous waste management. A recent audit of the data showed that

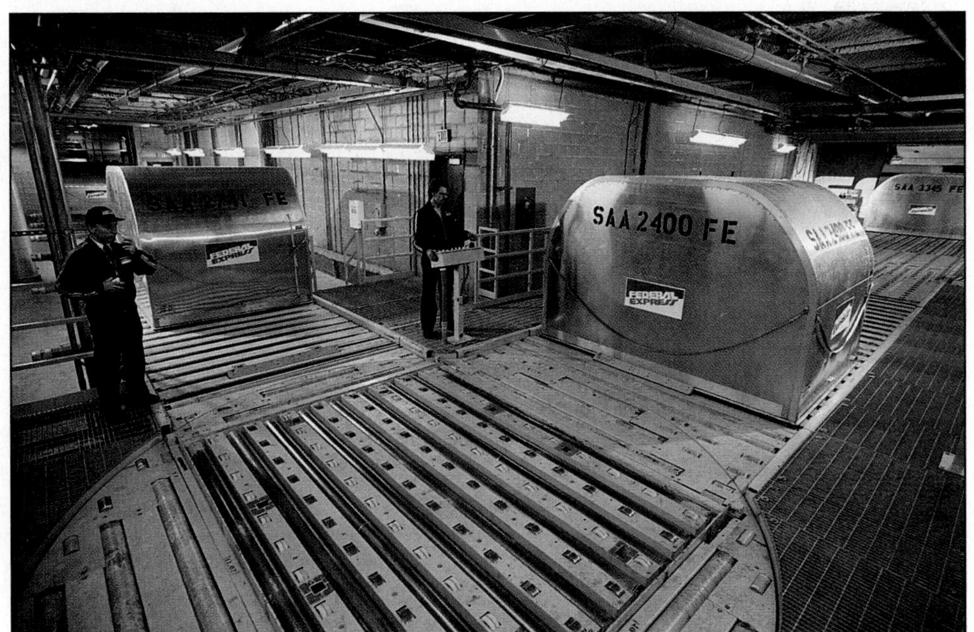

Containers at the Federal Express sorting center in Memphis, Tennessee, roll along an automated conveyor highway.

Tony Stone Images © John Riley.

more than 10 percent of the locations reported were not even in California, with some as far away as Africa, and one at the North Pole. What does Mr. Hanna do to ensure OEP's ability to perform its job? [1]

The answer to each question asked in the opening scenarios is the same: *Manage information effectively*. Marcia Block needs to collect and sort information about the store's sales to see what products are moving fastest, to combine information about sales, inventory, and order cycles to avoid or manage possible stock shortages, and to combine information about sales, profit margin, turnover, space requirements, and other factors to assess product profitability. The operations department at Federal Express needs to manage routing information on its incoming packages, information about flight schedules and aircraft capacity, and information about its worldwide facilities to turn around its incoming packages without delay. Ethan Heller needs to organize the information in the job applications so that they can be easily screened and so that qualifying applications can be easily matched to job positions. Steve Hanna of the California OEP needs to find better ways to capture the required facility information, to identify false information, and to organize hazardous work sites by type of hazard so that offending companies can be properly educated or punished.

In this chapter we introduce the concept of information and its management at all levels in the organization. We begin by defining information and discussing its use and value. The chapter continues with an examination of the cost of technology to individuals and organizations. We next present an overview of information systems, highlighting the needs for information, nature of information technology, and types of information systems. We conclude this chapter by considering a framework for managing information in a global environment.

What Is Information?

Are sales records information? Are flight and personnel schedules information? Are résumés and job applications information?

The Concept of Information

Information is a complex concept that has a variety of meanings depending on its context and the perspective in which it is studied. We describe information here in three ways—1) as processed data, 2) as the opposite of uncertainty, and 3) as a meaningful signal—to illustrate the richness of the concept of information.

Information as Processed Data. **Data** are generally considered to be raw facts that have undefined uses and application; **information** is considered to be *processed data that influence choices*, that is, data that have somehow been formatted, filtered, and summarized; and **knowledge** is considered to be an understanding derived from information. Such distinctions among data, information, and knowledge may be derived from scientific terminology. The researcher collects data to test hypotheses; thus, data refer to unprocessed and unanalyzed numbers. When the data are analyzed, scientists talk about the *information* contained in the data and the *knowledge* acquired from their analyses. For example, at Daley's Department Store in the introductory scenarios, the sales receipts from each of the 10,000 daily sales might be considered to be data, reports summarizing sales by product might be considered to be information, and an understanding of which products provide the greatest profit might be considered knowledge.

These definitions of data, information, and knowledge may blend or overlap in common usage because they ignore *point of view.* For example, John Smith's total rating on a performance evaluation form is data to a compensation analyst assigning pay raises but information to a manager who is attempting to improve John's performance. The confusion often extends to the information systems context, and the three terms may be used interchangeably.

Information as the Opposite of Uncertainty. A different perspective on information derives from economic theory and defines information as the *negative measure of uncertainty;* that is, the less information is available, the more uncertainty exists, and conversely, the more information is available, the less uncertainty exists.[2] In microeconomic theory the equilibrium of supply and demand depends on a market known as a *perfect market,* where all buyers and sellers have complete knowledge about one another and where uncertainty does not exist. Information makes a market perfect by eliminating uncertainties about supply and demand. In macroeconomic theory, firms behave according to how they read the economic climate. Economic signals that measure and predict the direction of the economy provide information about the economic climate. The firm reduces its uncertainty by decoding these signals.

In the introductory Federal Express scenario, each incoming aircraft has a scheduled arrival time. However, its actual arrival depends on unforeseen conditions at both its origin airport and Memphis. Data about when an aircraft departed from its destination is *information* in the economic sense because it reduces uncertainty about the aircraft's arrival time, thereby increasing Federal Express's ability to handle arriving packages.

Managers also define information in terms of its reducing uncertainty. Because managers must project the outcomes of alternatives in making decisions, the reduction of uncertainty about the outcomes of various alternatives improves the effectiveness of the decision-making process and the quality of the decision.

Information as a Meaningful Signal. **Information theory,** a branch of statistics concerned with measuring the efficiency of communication between people and/or machines, defines information as the *inputs* and *outputs* of communication.[3] Electronic, auditory, visual, or other signals that a sender and receiver interpret similarly convey information. For example, in the introductory scenario about recruiting specialist Ethan Heller, the résumés and applications for the open positions are information because they are signals sent by the applicants, received by Mr. Heller, and interpreted similarly by both.

Managers in their roles as communicators both generate and receive information. They receive reports that organize signals or data in a way that conveys their meaning. Reports of sales trends become information; so do reports about hazardous waste sites. Managers derive meaning from the information they see and hear as part of communication and use it to make decisions.

This definition of information requires a manager to interpret a given signal as it was intended. For example, a manager's incorrect interpretation of body language in a negotiation would not be considered to be information from this perspective, although we know that managers use both correct and incorrect perceptions as information in decision making and other managerial functions. Again, this view of information suggests the complexity of the concept and the value of a multifaceted definition.

The Uses of Information

Organizations may use information as a resource, as an asset, or as a commodity.

Information as a Resource. We generally think of organizations using money, people, raw materials, machinery, or even time as **resources**—inputs to the production of outputs. Information can also be viewed as a resource. Social workers use information about clients in helping them become more functional. Physicians use case histories of patients as inputs to diagnosis and prescription.

Resources can also substitute for one another to some degree.[4] Capital in the form of automated equipment can reduce labor required for production. Similarly, information can replace either capital or labor. Organizational members may also use information to decrease the cost or increase the quality of the final product or service. For example, in the introductory scenario about the California Office of Environmental Protection, information helped identify hazardous waste procedures to improve monitoring and management.

Information as an Asset. An **asset** is the property of a person or an organization that is used to produce a company's output and does not get used up as a resource does. Some resources are converted to assets that can be used over an extended period, such as the use of capital to purchase equipment that, in turn, becomes an asset. The information resource is similar, but not identical, to other resources in this respect. Information, even if used immediately, is rarely actually consumed. For example, when managers use data about a Daley's Department Store sale to determine whether inventory should be replenished, the sales data remain available as a resource for use in other analyses. In some cases, such as the Federal Express aircraft departures, the information quickly loses some value after its use, although it may have subsequent value as a resource for historical analyses. As a corporate asset, then, information is comparable to plant, equipment, and goodwill. It can even be viewed as inventory, with information considered as a raw material, work in process, or finished goods.[5]

The asset model of information encourages management to view information as an investment that managers can use strategically. Unlike resources, which managers seek to use efficiently to produce output, managers view assets as giving the organization an advantage over its competitors. For example, the information collected by Daley's Department Store about its sales may be extremely valuable to its suppliers and competitors.

DOW JONES

Information as a Commodity. Like corn, automobiles, washing machines, or other **commodities,** information is a saleable product. Some companies use information primarily to sell it. For example, credit bureaus collect information on your credit history to sell to your potential creditors. Dow Jones collects information on securities and companies to sell to potential investors. In our service-oriented economy, an increasing number of organizations are adopting a commodity view of information—viewing it as a saleable product.

The Value of Information

How often do you throw away old magazines, books, letters, or notes? Perhaps you use a rule such as "if I haven't looked at it in a year, I really don't need it." Consciously or not, you are making a decision about the value of the information contained in these items relative to the cost of storing them. Although the cost may be very small for any one item, the cumulative cost is significant and may far outstrip the value.

Recall the situation of Ethan Heller and the 2,750 résumés and job applications he received. What value does information have for him? What value would additional information have? How can he determine the value of the information he already has? Does he have too much data and not enough information? Consider again the situation faced by Marcia Block at Daley's Department Store. She likely has a large amount of information about the details of each sale. Is the detailed information useful to her, or does she value summaries? How much information should she save, and for how long should she save it? Does the value of the sales information change when it is organized into another form, such as averages, frequencies, or other summary data? Companies should constantly assess the *value* of their information relative to the cost of acquiring and storing it. Economic theory, decision theory, and game theory offer frameworks for the *valuation of information.*

Economic Theory. According to economic theory, perfect information yields a perfect market, where no uncertainties exist about supply and demand—a goal in economic practice. The value of information to society, then, is the lowered price that buyers pay as they acquire additional and better information. Similarly, the value of information to an individual or organization is the decrease in the price paid or reduction in the cost of searching among prices for the best deal, and hence an increase in competitiveness.

We can evaluate the value of information in terms of its effectiveness in creating a more perfect market; it "levels the playing field" for individuals and organizations to compete in buying and selling. The information received by Heller, the recruitment specialist, for example, could be evaluated from this perspective. What would be the financial impact on a company if it hired people without prescreening résumés or job applications? The information received saves a good deal of time and money in completing the search for employees.

Decision Theory. Information also has value according to the extent to which it helps management make better decisions. Based on the management science concept of the **expected value of information,** it is the difference between 1) the expected value of a sequence of optimal decisions when information is obtained and 2) the expected value of a sequence of optimal decisions made without the benefit of information.[6]

The value of information defined in this way is difficult to calculate except in very simple decisions. Consider Marcia Block's need to decide what products to stock. For her the value of information is the difference between the expected value of the decisions she makes using a complete set of data drawn from sales and purchase records and the expected value of the decisions she would have made without such data.

Game Theory. Game theory models an environment in which the players, either individuals, groups, or organizations, make decisions according to a strategy that accounts for the actions and strategies of competitors.[7] The payoff for a particular strategy depends upon how competitors react. For example, the payoff of increasing the price of a product may be greater if a competitor also increases its price than if the competitor decreases its price; or the opposite may be true. The pricing of products, determination of production quantities, and labor–management or trade bargaining situations illustrate applications of game theory.

Information plays a crucial role in these theoretical games, as it does in the real world. Players may or may not know the actions of their competitors in prior rounds, the strategy used by competitors, the payoff for each player for any combination of actions, the payoffs for each player in past rounds, or other information. Players may have equal amounts of information, or some may have an inherent advantage because they have more information than others. Players can also buy, sell, or leak information.[8]

The Cost of Information

Although information can be valuable, it is costly to use. Acquiring, processing, storing, retrieving, and communicating information each have costs.

Acquiring Information

The acquisition of information is a first step in its use. We can obtain information from either formal or informal sources, as shown in Figure 1-1. **Formal sources** provide information in a relatively organized and predictable fashion, for example, business forms; electronic monitoring equipment such as digital thermometers; and machine-readable purchased data such as an encyclopedia on a compact disc. **Informal sources** provide information in a less structured way and include conversations with customers, suppliers, and other employees, as well as general observations of personal and organizational activities. Generally, acquiring information through informal sources costs less, but the information acquired may be harder to organize and use effectively.

Data acquisition can occur manually or electronically. Managers often hand-write evaluation reports or salespeople maintain written records of customer orders. Increasingly, managers can enter evaluation data directly into the computer, and salespeople can use point-of-sale terminals to record detailed sales information electronically. Experts estimate that electronic forms for capturing data cost at least 70 percent less to design, purchase, use, carry, and revise than the equivalent paper forms.[9]

Processing Information

KFC

Processing information describes transforming it into a usable form. Processing typically occurs at two times: first, between the acquisition and storage of information, and second, between its retrieval and communication. The processing that occurs between acquisition and storage generally requires a large amount of personal labor. Manual processing, for example, involves duplicating, sorting, and filing data. Electronic processing, such as with electronic scanners, involves transforming and entering the data into an electronic form. KFC Corporation, for example, has a pilot project that integrates form processing, such as performance appraisals, job descriptions, employee information requests in the human resources area, and customer complaints and supply tracking forms in the administrative area, with its electronic mail system.[10] Information about a new employee is entered at the site of employment, transferred electronically to stored data files in the human resources department, and then transferred to the payroll department for appropriate action. Although both manual and com-

FIGURE 1-1 Examples of Information Sources

Formal Sources	Informal Sources
Business forms	Conversations with employees
Electronic monitoring equipment	Interviews with customers, and suppliers
Machine-readable purchased data	Observation of activities
Information databases	
Personnel records	
Corporate annual reports	
Summarized transaction histories	

KFC Corporation facilitates information flow by using electronic forms for applications such as employee performance appraisals and customer complaints.
Courtesy of Kentucky Fried Chicken.

puterized processing may require significant clerical time and incur high costs, electronic processing can reduce these costs, as described in Chapter 6.

Processing occurs between storing and communicating information for both manual and computerized systems. In manual systems, filing clerks typically perform the processes of retrieval, formatting, and display. When summaries or special analyses are required, analysts with special skills, such as skills in finance or accounting, may process the data. Manual information processing involves high labor and time costs but low equipment costs. Manual processing of large volumes of data tends to be more expensive than computer processing.

In computerized systems the processing between retrieval and communication allows more analysis and display possibilities in a shorter time. The costs of computerized processing include rental or depreciation of computer equipment, the labor costs of operating the equipment, and the costs associated with programming software to retrieve, format, and display information. Computerized processing involves lower labor and time costs but higher equipment costs than manual processing.

Storing Information

The primary cost of storing information is the cost of the storage medium and space. Noncomputerized storage uses paper, microform, or both. These media require much more physical storage space than electronic media and typically incur a greater cost for leasing or buying space than do electronic media. Computerized storage uses a variety of media, including hard disks, diskettes, and CD-ROM, depending on the amount of information to be stored and the desired speed of retrieval. The organizational overhead to monitor and control information storage, including staff salaries and physical equipment, adds to the cost of information storage.

Most large companies keep duplicates of their electronically stored information at a secure site remote from their processing facilities to ensure that the data can be retrieved in the event of a disaster such as a fire or flood. In addition, most companies keep duplicate paper or microform copies of much of their data. The cost of the media, physical facilities, and staff for these backup systems also contributes to the storage costs.

Both document and electronic storage have an ancillary cost for storing the documentation needed to locate information. Storing large amounts of data calls for simultaneously developing and storing an index or map that assists in locating the data.

Retrieving Information

Retrieving desired data from manual systems can be time consuming and expensive. Executives spend approximately six weeks a year on average looking for misplaced material.[11] Secretaries may spend as much as 30 percent of their time looking for paper documents and approximately 20 percent of that time searching for misfiled items.[12] Because paper files require large amounts of space, managers may store the data on a different floor or even in a different building. The labor costs of retrieving even small amounts of information exceed those for retrieving information electronically unless the organization can create small and compact storage for its paper records.

Electronic systems provide rapid and inexpensive access to information stored electronically in an organized fashion. The costs incurred are only those of using the computer equipment for a fraction of a second, particularly when retrieval is part of ongoing processing. If an individual requests the retrieval, it may require additional processing to translate the retrieval request from a form understood by the person to a form understood by the computer. When the information is stored in a different place from where it is requested, the request must be transmitted electronically to where the data are stored, and the retrieved data must be transmitted back. Communication costs are relatively low for small amounts of information, but the communication equipment and infrastructure can be expensive unless amortized over a sufficiently large volume of data communication. Companies that have small communication needs can pay to use the infrastructure of third parties, such as telephone companies.

Communicating Information

Manual transmission of information occurs frequently and easily in most organizations. Most organizational members rely on face-to-face communication in formal or informal settings or on written publications for much of the information they require to do their jobs. But face-to-face communication requires extensive amounts of time, a scarce resource in most organizations. Written media, such as memos, reports, advertisements, or other documents, can effectively transmit small amounts of information to large numbers of people.

Transmitting information long distance or exchanging large volumes of data can occur more effectively by electronic communication. Telephone, television, videoconferencing, fax, or other electronic data transmission can instantaneously establish communication links among individuals, groups, organizations, or data repositories. For each unit of information transmitted, electronic media are much less expensive than written or oral media. Figure 1-2 summarizes the relative costs of manual and computerized processes for each of the five information functions we have discussed so far. Note, however, that significant variations in cost, speed, and appropriateness may occur in different situations.

Information Systems

An **information system** combines information technology with data, procedures for processing data, and people who collect and use the data. A human resources department might have an information system that tracks all employees' work and salary history, training experiences, and performance evaluations and regularly provides reports to managers summariz-

Comparison of Costs of Manual and Computerized Processing

Function	Component	Processes	
		Manual	Computerized
Acquisition	Time:	High	Low
	Labor:	Moderate	Low
	Facilities/Equipment:	Low	High
Processing	Time:	Low	Low
	Labor:	High	Low
	Facilities/Equipment:	Low	High
Storage	Time:	Low	Low
	Labor:	Low	Low
	Facilities/Equipment:	High	Low
Retrieval	Time:	High	Low
	Labor:	High	Low
	Facilities/Equipment:	High	Moderate
Communication	Time:	High	Low
	Labor:	Moderate	Low
	Facilities/Equipment:	Low	Moderate

ing the data. An operations department might have an information system that incorporates an array of information about equipment, staff, and product or service requirements and provides ongoing comparisons and other analyses of the data. In this section we introduce the concept of an information system by commenting on its use, discussing the role information technology plays in information systems, and describing the types of information systems that facilitate the management of information.

The Need for Information Systems

Individuals, organizations, and society need to use a variety of systems to organize the collection, storage, processing, retrieval, and communication of information. Personal needs tend to be simple as individuals deal with relatively small amounts of data. Organizations collect extensive amounts of information, have a great need to share information among their members, and so generally have more formal and extensive systems for information management than do individuals. Individuals and companies use a variety of systems to satisfy these needs.

Individual Needs. Individuals need information systems both at work and at home (see Chapter 2). At work, individuals use file folders or piles on a desk to organize information stored on paper, directory systems to organize files on a computer disk or diskette, and calendars to organize information about future events. Increasingly, individuals use laptops or other portable electronic equipment to meet their information needs. Case workers at some public housing agencies, for example, use a portable computer office, which incorporates a small computer and cellular telephone to enable case workers to enter data on-site and then transfer it later at the agency's headquarters to a larger machine for processing.[13] Executives at Matsushita Electric of Canada have given portable technology to their staff and managers to allow them to work outside the traditional workplace, such as when visiting prospective and actual clients.[14] At home, individuals employ systems such as posting memo-notes on a refrigerator, setting alarm clocks, or scheduling regular times to share information with family and friends. An individual who lacks such aids combined into a personal information system may miss important appointments or fail to accomplish important tasks. Although systems for information management by individuals generally have few components and even fewer procedures, increasingly individuals are using sophisticated personal financial managers for personal budgeting, investment tracking, and bill paying.

MATSUSHITA ELECTRIC

Managerial Needs. Most managers require significant amounts of information to perform their jobs. They typically maintain information about employee performance, customer preferences, industry trends, and other subjects (see Chapter 3). The New York Giants' head scout and his staff, for example, use scouting databases that maintain information about each college senior playing football in the United States.[15] The coach uses an information system that analyzes team tendencies in various game situations to help the coach identify appropriate plays. Increasingly managers use computerized systems to assist with obtaining, maintaining, and using information; motivating, developing, and communicating with other organizational members; and making decisions, negotiating agreements, and managing resources. As managers become more sophisticated in performing their tasks, they require increasingly sophisticated systems to help them meet their information needs.

NEW YORK GIANTS

Organizational Needs. Because of the value of information to organizational performance, most organizations develop procedures to ensure that important information is collected, captured accurately, and organized effectively (see Chapter 4). Individual job holders, various types of computer equipment, and an array of computer software facilitate such information management. For example, some employees may collect information while others process it or analyze it. The University of Idaho, for example, introduced a computerized

UNIVERSITY OF IDAHO

Until recently, the only way to contact the conductor of one of Conrail's trains was to wave him or her down. Now, pen-based computers in each locomotive are connected by a cellular communications system to the national customer service center. Customers are pleased with the way the system has improved Conrail's response time in getting cars in and out of their plants; crew members are pleased by the way the system has reduced paperwork.

Courtesy of Conrail.

CONRAIL

financial aid management system that helped the university increase the timeliness and accuracy of its financial aid awards.[16] Conrail has outfitted more than 200 locomotives with computers linked by radio to its customer service center in Pittsburgh, Pennsylvania, as a way of meeting organizational needs for communication.[17]

Organizations that lack quality information systems may experience problems in accessing the data they need for executive decision making, lose important data during a relocation or power failure, perform redundant activities in dealing with customers or suppliers, or fail to respond quickly to changes in the marketplace or industry. Recall the scenario of Federal Express presented earlier in this chapter. Without a quality information system, Federal Express may have massive data about package pickups but lack the procedures to translate these data into efficient systems for package delivery. Many organizations even establish a special group that manages and develops information systems for the entire organization.

Information systems also make global news and information quickly available. They allow businesses to operate internationally by making information about transactions available to managers and other workers in any country.

Information Technology

Modern technology provides many tools to help managers acquire, process, store, retrieve, and communicate information. In this book, you will learn how to manage information to improve an organization's functioning. You will learn what type of information managers need, how managers use information, how managers can use computing and telecommunication equipment to assist them in their duties, and how organizations can use information to achieve strategic goals.

The Role of Information Technology. Information technology has allowed individuals, groups, and organizations to manage information *effectively* and *efficiently*. Consider the large networks of data available to financial analysts, marketing experts, or human resources professionals. Think about the availability of encyclopedias, texts, supermarket prices, airline schedules, and other information through data services. Now consider the ability to telephone or send mail electronically almost instantly from the United States to Europe and Asia.

Significant advances in information technology have made large quantities of information available to organizational members and other individuals at a relatively low cost. Many homes have personal computers and household devices with computer microchips. This widespread availability of computer technology has dramatically changed the way people process, store, and retrieve information. In this book, we will explore what this means for how we work and live.

Components of Information Technology. Information technology includes computer software, hardware, database management systems, and data communication systems. How does the computer system at Daley's Department Store know how to process sales information? What tells the computer system at Federal Express how to record the arrival or departure of aircraft? Computer **software** (see Chapter 5) provides the instructions, in the form of computer code and its accompanying documentation, for processing data electronically. Systems software directs the functioning of the computer machinery. Applications software assists in the acquisition, processing, storage, retrieval, and communication of information. Software development tools such as computer languages and screen generators facilitate creating or modifying software to respond to an organization's information needs. Individuals and organizations can purchase an array of software products. Off-the-shelf software is mass-produced software made for a variety of generic uses such as word processing. Sometimes managers and other organizational members require experts to write customized software because they have a unique need that no off-the-shelf software adequately meets. In some circumstances these same employees may develop their own software that they modify over time to meet their changing work or personal needs.

Computer **hardware** (see Chapter 6) refers to the equipment used in electronic information processing. Significant strides have occurred in the development of hardware in the last decade. While processing power has increased, the size of the hardware has decreased considerably. Today desktop and portable computers costing under $3,000 can outperform the room-sized, million-dollar computers of ten years ago. Input hardware captures raw data and information from interactive uses. Processing hardware converts or transforms data. Storage hardware includes removable and fixed media that allow rapid access to information. Output hardware provides copies of data on paper, microform, and video screens; it offers varying quality for graphics, print, voice, or other effects.

How can organizations such as Daley's Department Store easily maintain complete data on products, customers, and suppliers? How can they make available to managers information about new and current employees? How can executives secure data about the retail industry in general and their competitors in particular? **Database management systems** (see Chapter 7) offer a vehicle for storing and supporting the processing of large quantities of nonscientific information, such as data on employees, products, customers, and suppliers. This technology allows managers to easily access, sort, and analyze databases of information along a variety of dimensions.

Finally, **data communication technology** (see Chapter 8) has dramatically improved the communication of information across short and long distances. Managers and other employees can easily send data from one plant location to another or access data located halfway around the world using dial-in options, computer networks, video conferences, and other electronic media. Advances in communication technology occur frequently, reducing the cost and increasing the accuracy and speed of data transmission.

Types of Information Systems

Although we can classify information systems in several ways, in this book we classify them according to how information is used. As a result, technologies such as database management systems, expert systems, and parallel systems do not appear as special types, even though their names include the term *systems*. Of course, classifying information systems in this way ignores to some extent the interrelationship of information uses and the unclear boundaries in such systems. Nevertheless, for purposes of this discussion, we have drawn loose, somewhat artificial boundaries.

INTERNAL REVENUE SERVICE

Automation Systems. **Automation systems** (see Chapter 9) are those that use information technology to perform tasks that would otherwise be done manually. Office automation systems speed information processing and aid in time management, communication, document preparation, and filing. The Internal Revenue Service expects by 1996 to introduce a system that optically scans incoming returns and then converts the data into computer data for processing.[18] Automation of manufacturing and design via computer-aided design and computer-aided manufacturing systems often improves product quality, worker efficiency, and organizational performance. Automation of education and training through the use of computer-aided instruction can make large amounts of diverse information available to students inexpensively and easily. **Expert systems** automate functions that require highly specialized knowledge, such as product design, medical diagnosis, or equipment repair. Such automation systems may be linked to or part of a transaction processing system or management system, as described in the next sections.

Transaction Processing Systems. A **transaction processing system,** or **TPS** (see Chapter 10), records and processes an organization's routine business activities. These systems address questions such as the following: From whom does a company buy its supplies? How much has been bought? What has been delivered? Where has it been stored? How much are its suppliers owed? How much of that has been paid? How many hours have employees worked? How much should they be paid? How much should be deducted from their paychecks for taxes and benefits? Businesses cannot function without the ability to answer questions such as these and perform routine operations such as paying suppliers and employees.

Typically, transaction processing includes activities such as recording, filing, retrieving records, and filling out forms such as order forms and checks. Components of TPSs include systems for payroll, accounts payable, accounts receivable, general ledger, inventory control, fixed asset accounting, reservations, and billing, among others. Transaction processing systems have not eliminated the need for clerical and other low-level employees. Instead, they have transformed the nature of this work. For example, data entry clerks transfer data from paper documents, such as checks, into a computerized form. Increasingly, clerks input data directly into electronic form. For example, an airline agent uses a TPS to record or modify a reservation or to answer a question about the on-time performance of a flight; a salesclerk in the neighborhood retail store uses a computerized terminal to record sales; an employee at the license bureau prints out and records your auto registration or renews your license electronically. Such employees need not be computer literate but must be trained to use the specific TPS for the function they perform.

Management Systems. **Management systems** (see Chapter 11) have been designed and developed to facilitate the management of an organization by supplying the information management needs to function better or by assisting managers to communicate more effectively. Examples of management systems include management reporting systems, decision support systems, groupware, and executive information systems.

Management reporting systems provide management with information about business operations. For example, managers need to know which customers do not pay their bills on time. An aged accounts receivable report, for example, organizes and summarizes information contained within a company's accounts receivable system, the TPS that records bills sent to and payments received from customers. The aged receivable report should identify companies that have been delinquent and that require management attention to secure payment.

In making decisions, managers should be able to analyze the impact of decisions on the future. To do this they should move beyond the historical information provided by transaction processing systems. **Decision support systems (DSSs)** are systems designed to help managers evaluate the impact of alternative decisions and make the best possible choice.

FINIVEST SERVIZI

Finivest Servizi, a multibillion dollar Italian conglomerate, uses a decision support system called *progetto magnetto (project magnet)* to help the managers of its publications subsidiary to plan improved media strategies for their clients.[19] To support decisions, a decision support system should integrate information from a variety of internal and external information sources. In addition, it should incorporate models that managers can use to analyze the data, such as trend forecasting and projection, optimization, and sophisticated scheduling algorithms. Such models can assist managers in calculating optimal stock reorder points or scheduling employees for projects at the lowest cost. Since a DSS cannot anticipate all modeling needs, it should include model-building tools, such as spreadsheets, simulation languages, and statistical packages. Managers trained in the use of such tools can simulate their environment and evaluate the impact of alternative decisions.

In addition to gathering and analyzing information, managers must communicate with their peers, subordinates, and superiors. **Groupware,** which includes electronic mail, electronic notes, bulletin board systems, and electronic meeting systems, facilitates the sharing or communication of information. Groupware also includes group decision support systems; these systems provide DSS functions as well as facilities to assist managers in reaching a consensus among group members.

Executives have different information needs from those of most other managers in an organization. They often focus outside rather than inside the organization, hold a longer-term view of the organization and its environment, rely on less formal sources of information, deal with more ambiguous questions, and emphasize both problem identification and problem solution. **Executive support systems (ESSs)** or **executive information systems (EISs),** which support executive activities, often are specifically designed for a particular executive and reflect his or her style and information requirements. They usually allow an executive easy access to his or her favorite reports and an ability to focus quickly and easily on interesting features in more detail. Because executives perform nonrepetitive tasks, ESSs attempt to eliminate any need for training by incorporating a self-training, easy-to-use interface in the system. This interface often includes computer software that can understand questions posed in a natural language such as English and touch-screen hardware to reduce or eliminate typing. EISs typically incorporate groupware features such as electronic mail and notes and may include systems that scan news and wire services, automatically identifying news reports that are most likely to be of interest to the executive.

Strategic Systems. **Strategic systems** (see Chapter 12) extend the systems concept beyond organizational borders, seeking to make customers, suppliers, and distributors that are strategic partners part of the information system. They implement or strongly support the implementation of an organizational strategy. To the extent that parties outside the organization become dependent on the information supplied by the organization, the organization exercises a form of control that can develop into a sustainable competitive advantage. Providing unique information that competitors lack expands this competitive advantage. Strategic information systems may also function as transaction processing systems. The SABRE reservation system developed by American Airlines and supplied to its distributors (travel agencies) keeps the distributors dependent on American for their information.

AMERICAN AIRLINES

Managing Information in a Global Environment

Organizations today function in a global environment. They buy and sell products outside their home country, open subsidiaries, plants, or distribution centers around the world, and communicate worldwide. The current state of information technology has facilitated the expansion of organizational boundaries. In this book we acknowledge the role of information management in increasing the global competitiveness of organizations. We address the way it facilitates the communication required to ensure a global marketplace. We comment about its impact on organizational structures that encourage collaboration between companies and countries. Significant differences may exist in the computer technology and systems commonly used in different countries. One recent study of computer-based information systems in 72 companies in the People's Republic of China, for example, suggested that most of these firms rely on stand-alone microcomputers and use computer applications for support functions rather than such pivotal functions as order entry or billing.[20] This usage differs significantly from that found in many United States companies.

Now recall the situations described in the introduction to this chapter. How can Marcia Block manage the information she needs to determine the sales effectiveness of various products? How do top executives at Federal Express ensure that their employees match incoming packages to appropriate outgoing aircraft? How can Ethan Heller process the information he needs to make informed hiring decisions? How can Steve Hanna use information effectively to monitor the hazardous waste sites? In this section we propose an analytical model, which we call the **information management model,** to facilitate the effective use of information in managerial decision making. This model involves four steps, as shown in Figure 1-3: diagnosis, evaluation, design, and implementation. This model has some of the same characteristics as the systems development life cycle (see Chapter 13). The information management model, however, is intended to complement the systems development life cycle; the four-phase model is directed at *users* of information systems rather than information systems professionals or other systems designers.

Diagnosis

Managers, employees, and other individuals must begin by assessing their *needs* for information within a particular situation they face. **Diagnosis** requires a description of the existing problem, the context in which it occurs, the type of information available, the type of information required to solve it, and the possible ways of securing the needed information. Marcia Block, for example, must determine precisely the types of information she needs for making good product choices. Executives in her organization must determine the particular information they need for making organizational decisions, such as those regarding strategic direction, general marketing policies, or human resources practices.

Diagnosis of information needs can occur at the individual, managerial, or organizational levels. Individuals must assess their information needs at work and home. Managers often have needs for transaction processing, financial control, project management, and communication, among others. Organizations use information to increase their competitive advantage, such as by improving customer service, cost control, or quality monitoring. They also must identify the information they need for developing and implementing their organizational strategy. Society, too, uses information for communication, economic development, and generally improving the quality of life. Specifying in detail the information needs at each of these levels is the first step in the effective management of information.

FIGURE 1-3 The Information Management Model

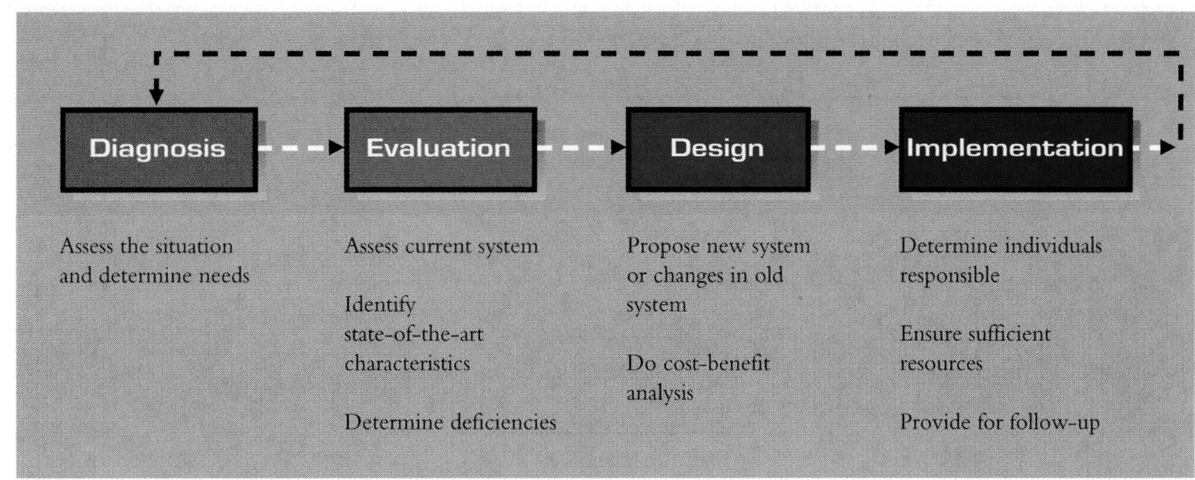

Evaluation

Evaluation of the methods, techniques, and systems for handling information follows the diagnosis of needs. This step begins with an assessment of the current manual or computerized systems for handling information. A manager, for example, might first describe or identify the components of the information systems and technology used to acquire, process, store, retrieve, or communicate information. Next he or she might compare these components to available systems. How well does the current system respond to the information needs? Are systems available that would significantly improve the handling of information? What consequences will result with a change in the way information is handled? Finally, the manager or other user might determine what aspects of his or her information needs are not handled and which cannot be handled, regardless of the information technology or information systems used. Figure 1-4 offers a list of questions the manager might ask as part of the evaluation step.

Design

A manager, staff specialist, information systems professional, or other organizational member combines information about individual, managerial, or organizational needs with the assessment of current information systems and technology and then **designs** coherent systems for information management. How does Ethan Heller design a coherent approach to managing the information he needs for personnel decisions? How does Marcia Block design a coherent system for the management of sales information?

Design involves correcting deficiencies in existing systems and integrating state-of-the-art practices and technology into them. Ethan Heller might determine that the manual processes for storing information about job applicants does not provide the necessary information for making informed hiring decisions; he might propose buying database management software that works on the department's personal computers. Alternatively, if he expects that the information management needs might increase and that individual managers might require access to data they currently lack, he might design a system that incorporates additional computer equipment and communication software. Marcia Block, on the other hand, might determine that the current point-of-sales terminals provide sufficient information for making the product decisions that comprise her job if she alters the software to provide one or two additional pieces of information.

FIGURE 1-4 Questions for Evaluating Information Systems and Technology

1. What are the current systems for handling information?
2. Are they manual or computerized?
3. What are the components of the information systems and technology used to acquire, process, store, retrieve, or communicate information?
4. How do these components compare to available state-of-the art systems?
5. How well does the current system respond to the information needs?
6. Would other systems better respond to the information needs?
7. Would state-of-the-art systems significantly improve the handling of information?
8. What consequences will result from a change in the way information is handled?
9. What information needs are not handled and cannot be handled, regardless of the information technology or information systems used?

The design phase involves making decisions about computer hardware and software, as well as about computer systems. It typically involves a cost-benefit analysis to ensure that the new design provides a sufficient return for the additional costs incurred. It also involves determining the responsibility for design and implementation, as described in the next section. System users and skilled professionals often collaborate to ensure the best design. The precise responsibility varies according to the degree of expertise required in the design process (see Chapter 13).

Implementation

The final step, **implementation,** focuses on issues associated with putting the new or altered systems to use. Who will be responsible for overseeing the implementation? How will it occur? What additional resources will be required for implementation? What types of follow-up will occur? How will the change affect other aspects of an individual's or organization's functioning? Identifying the parties' responsibility for implementation involves determining the roles individual managers, information systems staff, or specialists from outside the organization will play. Specifying the timetable for implementation typically follows. Top management must ensure that sufficient resources are available for the implementation as well as for dealing with changes that occur as a result of the implementation. They must also assess whether the information systems professionals function effectively throughout the four phases. Recognizing that the new system and technology likely will have unanticipated consequences should be a key aspect of planning; monitoring such effects and providing solutions for problems that arise should be part of the implementation. Implementation also includes ensuring that the new systems perform as expected and that they result in the predicted costs and savings.

Organization of This Book

This book discusses the *management of information.* Part I, which includes Chapters 1 through 4, defines information and information systems, introduces the four-step information management model used throughout the text, and assists students in diagnosing individual, managerial, and organizational information needs. Part II, Chapters 5 through 8, explores the technologies that can be used to help manage information. Part III, Chapters 9 through 12, addresses how information technologies can meet the varied information management needs of organizations and individuals. Part IV, Chapters 13 and 14, concludes the book by discussing how systems for managing information are designed, implemented, and themselves managed.

Summary

The effective management of information is essential to individual and organizational performance. This book discusses the management of information. We can describe information as processed data, as the opposite of uncertainty, or as a meaningful signal. It can be used as a resource, asset, or commodity. Information has value for reducing uncertainty in the marketplace, assisting managers in making better decisions, and increasing the payoff of actions vis-a-vis competitors. Information also has costs associated with acquiring, processing, storing, retrieving, and communicating it.

Information systems combine data, procedures for processing data, and people who collect and use the data with information technology. Information systems help meet individual, managerial, and organizational needs for information. Information technology, in the form of computer software, computer hardware, database management systems, and communication technology, facilitates meeting these needs. We can combine information technologies into automation, transaction processing, management, and strategic information systems.

Managing information in a global environment can be facilitated by using a four-step analytical model. Managers first assess their situation and their information needs. Next, they evaluate the quality of their existing information systems for meeting their information needs. Third, they propose modifications in the systems to better meet the needs. Fourth and finally, they deal with issues of implementation and follow-up.

Key Terms

Asset
Automation system
Commodity
Data
Data communication technology
Database management system
Decision support system (DSS)
Design
Diagnosis
Evaluation
Executive information system (EIS)
Executive support system (ESS)
Expected value of information
Expert system
Formal sources of information
Groupware
Hardware
Implementation
Informal sources of information
Information
Information management model
Information system
Information theory
Knowledge
Management reporting system
Management system
Resource
Software
Strategic system
Transaction processing system (TPS)

Review Questions

1. Give one definition of *information*.
2. How does information differ from data and knowledge?
3. Describe three uses of information.
4. What is the value of information from the perspective of decision theory?
5. What are three examples of formal sources of information? How do they differ from informal sources?
6. What are the primary costs of storing information? Are they greater for computerized storage or noncomputerized storage?
7. What are the primary costs of retrieving information? Are they greater for computerized storage or noncomputerized storage?
8. Define an information system and identify the various types of systems.
9. Identify three types of information needs.
10. List the components of information technology.
11. What is the primary function of automation systems? Describe two applications of automation systems.
12. What is the primary function of transaction processing systems?
13. Explain why transaction processing systems have not eliminated the need for clerical employees.
14. What is the primary function of management systems? Identify three types of management systems.
15. What is the primary function of strategic systems?
16. How does diagnosis differ from evaluation?
17. Identify several issues that must be addressed in implementing new or altered systems.

Notes

[1] Adapted from J. King, Cleanup efforts target 'dirty' data, *Computerworld* (October 28, 1991): 59.

[2] K. J. Arrow, Information and economic behavior, in *Collected Papers of Kenneth J. Arrow: The Economics of Information* (Cambridge, MA: The Belknap Press of Harvard University Press, 1984): 138; see also J. Hirshleifer and J. G. Riley, The analytics of uncertainty and information: An expository survey, *Journal of Economic Literature* 17 (1979): 1375–1421.

[3] The seminal work in information theory was done by C. Shannon, A mathematical theory of communication, *Bell Systems Technology Journal* 27 (1948): 379–423, 623–656. For an intelligible lay interpretation, see J. Singh, *Great Ideas in Information Theory, Language, and Cybernetics* (New York: Dover Publications, 1966): 12–21.

[4] D. Salvatore, *Microeconomics* (New York: HarperCollins, 1991).

[5] B. Ronen and I. Spiegler, Information as inventory: A new conceptual view, *Information & Management* 21(4) (1991): 239–247.

[6] D. R. Anderson, D. J. Sweeney, and T. A. Williams, *An Introduction to Management Science*, 6th ed. (St. Paul, MN: West, 1991).

[7] E. Rasmusen, *Games & Information* (Cambridge, MA: Basil Blackwell, 1989).

[8] See, for example, E. Bolder, Generalized equilibrium results for games with incomplete information, *Mathematics of Operations Research* 13 (1986): 265–276.

[9] M. Bragen, Form fitting, *Computerworld* (September 14, 1992): 105–107.

[10] Bragen, Form fitting, op. cit.

[11] A. Karr, The checkoff, *The Wall Street Journal* (August 4, 1992): 1.

[12] G. Curry, How color coding can aid records managers, *The Office* (July 1990): 70–71.

[13] Marilyn J. Henry, The computerized, portable office: Can it work for PHAs? *Journal of Housing* 49(2) (March/April 1992): 81–84.

[14] Mark Wessel, Power + portability = productivity, *Sales & Marketing Manager Canada* 32(11) (November 1991): 17–18.

[15] Christopher Lindquist, Giants use high-tech strategy to design winning game plan, *Computerworld* (August 5, 1991): 33.

[16] Joseph J. Geiger, Management implications of installing a modern financial aid system, *Journal of Systems Management* 43(3) (March 1992): 6–9.

[17] Thomas Hoffman, Conrail makes pen-based connection, *Computerworld* (March 14, 1994): 55, 61.

[18] Mitch Betts, IRS goes digital to speed returns, *Computerworld* (March 7, 1994): 8.

[19] Janette Martin, Synergy at Fininvest, *Datamation* (October 1, 1989): 72-15–72-16.

[20] M. Lu, Y. Qui, and T. Guimaraes, A status report on the use of computer-based information systems in PRC, *Information & Management* 15(5) (1988): 237–242.

Recommended Readings

Gilder, G. *Microcosm: The Quantum Revolution in Economics and Technology* (New York: Simon and Schuster, 1989).

Gorry, G. A. and Scott Morton, M. S. A framework for management information systems, *Sloan Management Review*, 13(1) (1971).

Hammer, M. Reengineering work: Don't automate, obliterate, *Harvard Business Review*, (July–August 1990): 104–112.

Johnson, R. A., Kast, F. E., and Rosenzweig, J. E. *The Theory and Management of Systems* (New York: McGraw-Hill, 1970).

Tom, P. L. *Managing Information as a Corporate Resource* (Glenview, IL.: Scott, Foresman, 1987).

Weinberg, G. *An Introduction to General Systems Theory* (New York: John Wiley & Sons, 1985).

Chapter 2

The Individual Perspective

Outline

Information Needs of Services International's Employees

Selecting and Organizing Information

- The Components of Perception
- Humans Versus Computers

The Individual at Work

- The Information Needs of Individual Job Holders
- Challenges of Information Management
- Information Management Requirements
- The Home Office
- Personal Computing in the Global Environment

Personal Information for Home and Leisure

- Typical Information Needs
- Information Management Requirements
- Personal Uses of Advanced Information Technology

Learning Objectives

After completing the reading and activities for Chapter 2, students will be able to

1. Describe the process of perception and how it affects the use of information.
2. Identify the advantages and disadvantages of computers compared with humans in processing information.
3. List and illustrate the types of information needs individual job holders might have.
4. Specify three challenges of information management for the individual job holder.
5. Describe the nature of information technology available for personal use in the work place and at home.
6. Cite two uses and types of home offices.
7. Identify five possible job-related information management needs of a telecommuting worker.
8. Describe the benefits and drawbacks of working at home for individuals and their employers.
9. Outline the issues for personal computing in a global environment.
10. Describe the characteristics of personal information systems.

Information Needs of Services International's Employees

Casey Jennings had been promoted to regional sales manager at Services International, a distributor and reseller of office equipment, one year ago. In this position she directly supervises six area sales managers and, through them, 20 salespeople. Jennings had taken this new job enthusiastically. She had a wealth of ideas that she had planned to implement. Looking back on the year, she realized that she had initiated fewer changes than she had expected, not enough to have made a noticeable impact on the image of the company nor on its total sales volume. Despite working at least 60 hours every week, Casey did not seem to have time to assimilate the information she needed to make even routine decisions. Casey knew that she had secured a lot of information about the sales function, but she seemed unable to translate it into new and productive initiatives.

Janice Grander reports directly to Casey Jennings. Janice directly supervises ten copier salespeople. She monitors their success in meeting the product needs of current customers as well as in identifying and selling to potential customers. Janice has held this position for three years and has experienced reasonable success in increasing the sales volume in her group. Three months ago she gave two of her salespeople portable computers to use on sales calls; these computers had software that described a variety of the company's products as well as software for recording information about clients.

Jake Martin, a copier salesman, reports to Janice. He has a cadre of existing customers to whom he sells copier supplies. He also tries to interest them in buying larger copiers with more features. Jake spends a significant amount of time identifying potential customers and then meeting with them to try to sell them copier equipment.

Joanne Eberly serves as one of five administrative assistants in Casey's region. Joanne maintains basic information about changes in the products sold in the region. She also collects data about sales and sales prospects from all salespeople in the region to ensure that Services International's salespeople do not compete with one another for sales to a particular customer.

Each of these employees also has a busy and complex home life. Some have children; others have elderly parents for whom they are responsible. Casey, for example, shares household chores with her husband but has the main responsibility for organizing the household. Janice serves as treasurer of a community group to which she belongs. Jake and his wife share a passion for stamp and coin collecting and have built an impressive collection over the past ten years. Joanne is also active in community activities and in meeting family responsibilities; she is currently looking for a new home to help reduce her commuting time.

These employees spend most of their work time dealing with information. Casey, for example, uses it in analyzing problems and developing strategies. For Janice to accomplish her goals, she must effectively acquire information and share it with the salespeople she supervises. Jake, too, needs detailed information about his current and potential clients. Joanne collects information about activities in the region.

Casey also spends time at home dealing with information; for example, she uses it to monitor her household budget. Janice uses information in her role as treasurer to ensure that the community organization remains solvent and has funds for its programs. Jake uses information to track his stamp and coin holdings and to help determine what additional purchases to make. Joanne uses information about the real-estate market during her house hunting. What information do members of the regional sales office at Services International need at work and at home?

This chapter concentrates on the first step of the four-step management model—*diagnosis.* We focus on the *personal information needs* of individuals such as Casey Jennings, Janice Grander, Jake Martin, and Joanne Eberly as well as on the ways they manage this information at work and home. (Chapter 3 discusses the managerial needs of workers such as Casey and Janice.) First we look at the way individuals process information. Next we consider the information function in the work arena, including a discussion of the home office. We then examine the role of information at home, including information needs and information management requirements. We conclude the chapter with a description of the ways personal information systems help meet these needs.

Selecting and Organizing Information

How do Casey and her associates begin to determine what information they should pay attention to, use, or discard? Deciding what information is important and necessary is the first and perhaps most important step in diagnosing and solving problems. In the stories of Sir Arthur Conan Doyle, the great detective Sherlock Holmes sees everything that the reader sees, but he is successful and wins our admiration because he recognizes what is important—perhaps the fact that a dog did not bark. The employees in Services International's regional sales office also need to identify the most important information for performing their jobs.

The Components of Perception

Perception is an active process by which an individual *attends* to certain stimuli and then *organizes* them in a meaningful way, as shown in Figure 2-1. Individuals attend to certain features of a situation or select specific pieces of information to see or hear because of their needs, personality, or experiences. The information itself may also influence whether attention occurs: Individuals select stimuli that are more intense, repetitive, in motion, novel, very familiar, or in contrast with their background.[1] People tend not to see information that they are exposed to repeatedly without consequence. Try to recall, for example, the pictures and shapes on the back of a five- or ten-dollar bill. Also, people tend to ignore information that runs counter to deep or long-held beliefs.[2] Consider why companies such as IBM or Digital Equipment Corporation failed to recognize the changing nature of the computer market in the late 1980s. Clearly, the subjectivity of perception limits the processing of information.

The Perceptual Process

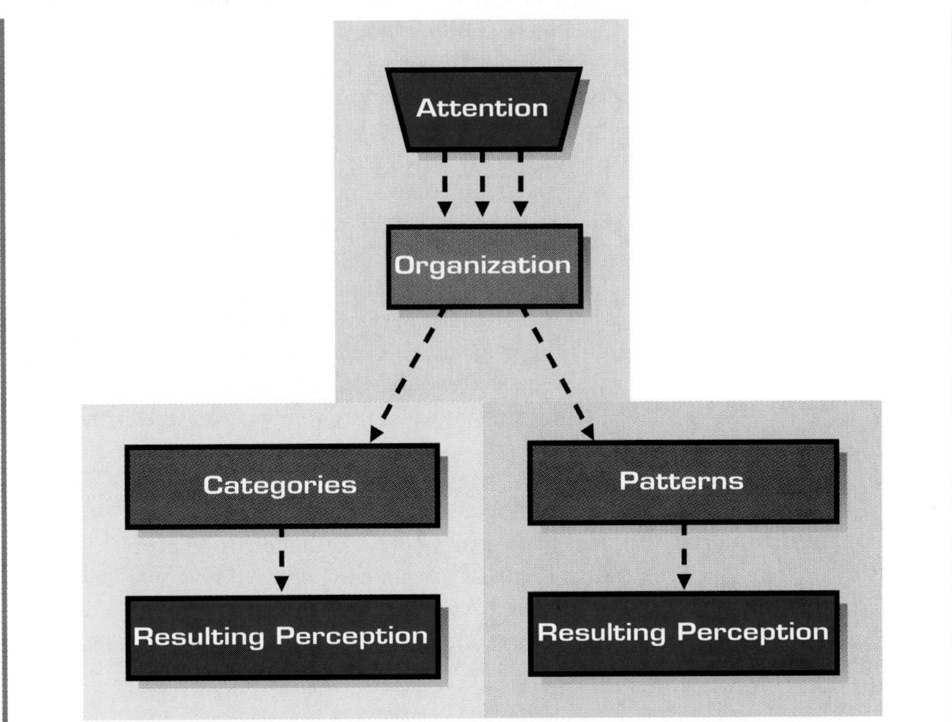

Once individuals attend to information about a situation, they organize it in several ways.[3] They may try to fit it into prototypes or categories that represent typical aspects of similar situations. They may match it to concrete examples. They may view it against a background, for example, within an environmental or situational context. Finally, they may group stimuli into patterns, trying to form a complete picture, sometimes even trying to do so using incomplete information.

An understanding of how people select and organize information is critical to designers of information systems. Managers rely on information systems to collect and summarize data about their organization, so systems designers must present information in ways that have the greatest chance of being seen and remembered to ensure that users select the most important information and organize it in the most effective way. Extensive research in information systems has addressed questions such as how much information to put into a single table, what type of data to present as tables and what type as charts, and how best to use color to convey information and facilitate quality decisions.[4]

Managers and other job holders also have a responsibility to ensure that they receive and select the information they need in order to operate effectively. Some managers may receive insufficient information for decision making; others obtain so much information that they cannot separate the important from the unimportant. Individuals who hold jobs that require extensive coordination with other job holders, as well as those who have a high ability and desire to communicate more frequently, experience overload more than those who do not.[5] This overload can be particularly problematic: Decision quality declines as the amount of relevant information increases beyond a manageable limit.[6]

Humans Versus Computers

Humans and computers are complementary in their ability to filter and save information, as shown in Figure 2-2. Humans can effectively decide what is important; computers cannot. Computers generally can retain much more information and collect it faster than humans. For example, computers at stores such as Toys "R" Us can maintain a complete, instantaneous, accurate inventory on the thousands of items in a store; manual tabulation by a store clerk would take weeks. Also, computers often process information more accurately than individuals. Marine biologists obtain the information they require by counting fish, checking maps, and diagnosing equipment flaws under water; underwater personal computers could make the data collection easier.[7]

TOYS "R" US

People can think easily in terms of symbols, objects, and concepts that have *meaning.* They can draw conclusions from data. Increasingly computers are able to think in this way, but they still have only a primitive ability to draw conclusions. Although physicians can use computer programs to help organize disparate symptoms into a pattern that assists with diagnosis, few patients would want a computer acting alone to treat their life-threatening disease.[8]

Computers can perform computations much more quickly and accurately than people: They can add a column of 50 ten-digit numbers in less than a second, whereas such addition would take even the most facile individual several minutes. They can sort a list of one million addresses by ZIP code to prepare envelopes for bulk mailing; to do so manually in a timely fashion would take hundreds of people. Elf Atochem North America, a chemical manufacturer, is using a computerized system to reimburse salespeople immediately for their expenses and verify the accuracy of the expenses afterward.[9] In this chapter we describe ways computers can help individuals meet their needs for various types of information.

ELF ATOCHEM NORTH AMERICA

The Individual at Work

Individuals assume a variety of roles on the job. Although these roles all require various types of information, the specific information needs vary considerably. Compare the needs of the four employees of Services International—Casey, Janice, Jake, and Joanne. How similar would they be? How would they differ? Now compare the needs of these salespeople to those of hospital employees such as an operating room nurse, admissions clerk, or food services manager. Do they have the same or different needs? Now compare the needs of two or more job holders in an organization you know. The manager of manufacturing has different infor-

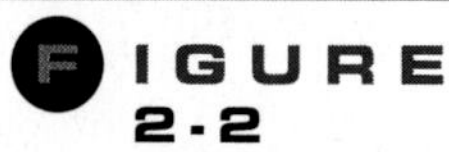

FIGURE 2-2 Humans Versus Computers

Human Assets	Computer Assets
Identify important information	Retain large quantities of information
Think symbolically	Collect information quickly and accurately
Evaluate information	Perform extensive computation rapidly and accurately
Recognize patterns	
Draw inferences and conclusions	Sort information rapidly and accurately
	Select information meeting preconditions

mation needs from the manager of finance; the accounts receivable clerk needs different information than the accounts payable clerk. The key challenge for individuals on the job is to diagnose their particular information needs. In the next section we identify several types of information needs. Note, however, that this selection is representative rather than exclusive. *Diagnosis of information needs must occur for each individual job at a specific time.*

The Information Needs of Individual Job Holders

Consider the job of Jake Martin, the copier salesman who works for Janice Grander at Services International. What information needs do he and his supervisor have? Jake uses an array of information to meet his customers' needs. Janice uses a variety of information to manage her salespeople. We can arbitrarily categorize the needs as related to task, time management, performance, and career.

Task-Related Needs. Jake uses information to perform a variety of tasks associated with his job. To identify potential customers he uses leads provided by his sales manager, data published in trade journals and newspapers about the sales volume and number of employees in specific companies, and stories he hears from contacts with prospective customers and from salespeople in other fields. To build a rapport with sales prospects and existing customers, Jake acquires information about their birthdays, the names of their family members, their favorite restaurants, and the types of entertainment they prefer. He also must know a great deal about his company's and his competitors' products. Sales representatives at Helene Curtis Industries, a manufacturer of hair-care and cosmetics products, had similar needs for access to constantly updated customer and product information so that they could react quickly to market changes.[10] The company introduced a retail information system to meet these needs and increase the sales representatives' business analysis capabilities. This computerized system replaced the use of written reports by sales representatives across the United States for tracking product sales.

HELENE CURTIS INDUSTRIES

The nature of information required for performing tasks associated with various jobs obviously differs. In an assembly-line job, for example, workers may focus on specifying the required parts, identifying defects, or counting completed products. An engineer may emphasize information about technical specifications of new products or the extent of new technological developments that aid their production. At the Texas Employment Commission, for example, tax collectors were required to enter tax-status changes directly into the computer because other Commission employees required that information to perform their jobs effectively.[11] Brokers at Robinson-Humphrey, an investment firm in Atlanta, needed information about minute-to-minute changes in the Dow-Jones average.[12] The company introduced a system that shows each company's relative contribution to the Dow-Jones average.

TEXAS EMPLOYMENT COMMISSION

ROBINSON-HUMPHREY

The Robinson-Humphrey brokerage firm depends upon computers to obtain timely and accurate information about the prices of securities it trades on behalf of its customers.

Courtesy of the Robinson-Humphrey Company.

Time Management Needs. During a normal work day Jake constantly makes decisions about the best way to handle his clients, for example, whether to spend his time trying to close a new deal with a likely prospect or trying to appease an unhappy customer. He uses the information about sales history and customers' businesses to help make these decisions. Jake also requires geographical information to be most productive; because northern Texas is a large territory, Jake is most productive when he minimizes his travel time. Janice Grander makes similar time-related decisions. She must determine how much time to spend meeting with subordinates, directly contacting customers, and investigating new products.

Performance-Related Needs. Not only do employees at all levels require information about the tasks they perform, they also can provide information to management about ways to improve task performance. Janice Grander, for example, in her supervisory role, might track the time her sales staff spends on various tasks so that she can propose ways of reordering those tasks or reallocating staff effort to increase efficiency. She might also determine that salespeople need new or better information about products to perform their jobs more effectively. Computer technology can also meet the needs associated with ensuring quality in the work place. Individuals involved in quality efforts require ongoing and updated information about customer needs and product defects.

Career-Related Needs. Many individuals view their jobs in the context of a career. Personal information needs include lists of personal skills, job opportunities inside and outside the organization, and specifications for transfers or advancements. Employees might also maintain logs of their own performance during a week, month, or year to incorporate into discussions about their personal training needs and career development. The members of the regional sales office might maintain such records to help with their personal planning and advancement.

Challenges of Information Management

In identifying their information management requirements, individuals face four major challenges in addition to securing the most appropriate information. First, they must deal with large quantities of information that may create overload. Second, they may face insufficient or conflicting information. Third, they must find ways to enhance their personal productivity. Fourth, they must acquire and maintain the technical skills needed for effective personal information management.

Dealing with Quantities of Information. The gap between the amount of information that an organization can collect and the ability of its employees to make sense of that information has been widening rather than narrowing. The early fear that computers would so improve a person's ability to process and manage information that a job holder would need only one-third to one-half the time to do his or her job has been dispelled: The reverse has occurred. Often employees face an **infoglut,** an overload of information.[13] For example, universal product code scanners provide 100 to 1,000 times as much information about product sales as was previously available. As individuals move higher in the organizational hierarchy and assume more managerial responsibility, information overload becomes an even more significant challenge. To avoid such overload individuals must carefully assess their information needs and then find effective ways of managing the required and available information. They must also find ways to manage data better.[14]

Facing Insufficient or Conflicting Information. Although computers can make large quantities of information available to individuals, such information may not address their needs. For example, Joanne Eberly may generate long lists of potential clients for salespeople in the region but lack information about the level of their interest in Services International's products. Or, Joanne may wish to do some library research about competitors' products. In spite of the large amount of information in the library's electronic catalog, she may not be able to secure the precise information she needs. Because computers process input from diverse sources, users may also obtain conflicting information if one source updates information more frequently than another.

Enhancing Personal Productivity. Employees in any organization increasingly use information technology to improve their personal productivity. To ensure high productivity, employees must know how to use computers to facilitate, not hinder, their performance. They must know how to access the information they require and recognize when manual data collection and processing is adequate. Often employees must lobby their employers to add new technology that will help increase personal productivity. The ability to show the cost-effectiveness of additional expenditures for diagnosing and meeting information needs is critical. Employees must also understand and demonstrate when advanced technology is a detriment rather than an asset.[15]

Maintaining Technical Skills. Finally, using information technology effectively requires continuous updating of technical skills. Although many companies provide training to their employees, others do not. Ensuring that employees have the appropriate skills has both financial and time cost implications. As a result, employees may find their mobility and productivity limited by the extent to which they can learn new technical skills independently of their employer.

Information Management Requirements

Individuals must accurately and quickly determine the information needed to respond to the demands of a changing environment and to ensure personal productivity. Personal information needs focus on managing time, records, and personal documents. In particular, workers must acquire, store, retrieve, and communicate information; they must also ensure the privacy and security of the information.

Acquiring Information. A variety of information industries, such as the newspaper, magazine, radio, television, and advertising industries, assist people in *acquiring* information for use at work. Many industries publish directories, indices, and evaluations of products and services in either or both paper and electronic form, as shown in Figure 2-3. For example, complete airline schedules are available in printed form as the *Official Airline Guide* and in electronic form from various for-profit and free sources. Other information available electronically includes current and past stock prices, the best prices and vendors for a variety of goods and services, and computerized bulletin boards of information.

Examples of Electronic Directories

Business headlines	Recipes
Consumer Reports	*Scott's Catalogue of Stamps*
Corporate annual reports	Software guide
Economic indicators	Sports—schedules
Encyclopedia	Sports—scores
Film reviews	Stock market quotations
Mobil Travel Guide	Weather forecasts around the world
Hit music charts	*Zagat Restaurant Guide*
Official Airline Guide	

A salesperson uses a portable computer to help close a sale. The computer makes a wealth of corporate information directly available to the consumer and allows the salesperson to generate quotations and customize designs and progarams on the spot. Because the salesperson can respond immediately to the customers' information needs, the competition may not even get a chance to make its pitch.

Courtesy of International Business Machines Corporation.

Storing Information. Individuals also keep significant amounts of information in files at work. They may keep copies of past correspondence, project documents, sales contacts, or a myriad of other details. Federal, state, or local regulations may call for the maintenance of specific corporate records for varying periods of time. Computerizing some of this information can reduce the amount of paperwork and facilitate retrieval.

Retrieving Information. Manual filing systems satisfy many personal needs for organizing and retrieving information. But, in these systems we typically can store information in only one location (unless we reproduce copies). Not only do computerized systems assist in storing information, but they may also facilitate its retrieval by supporting quick, repeated searches of data, potentially at multiple or off-site locations. For example, individuals or companies that require patent information for scientific inventions can use software to perform sophisticated and rapid patent searches.[16]

Communicating Information. Although direct speech and writing are the simplest means of communication, information technology has made it possible for individuals to communicate with one another more quickly and effectively. The telephone, invented in the nineteenth century, is still one of the most widely used information technologies. In recent years, it has become increasingly sophisticated: People can dial foreign countries without the assistance of a telephone-company operator, multiple parties can communicate simultaneously through conference calling, the caller's telephone number can appear on a display screen, and individuals can leave messages without using a separate answering machine. Currently, facsimile (fax) technology allows the transmission of written documents and pictures over telephone lines. Soon, the telephone system will routinely communicate moving pictures as well as words.

L. L. BEAN

Word processing, desktop publishing, and graphics capabilities of computers have affected the ease of producing and the appearance of written communication. Employees responsible for publishing catalogs for companies such as L. L. Bean could use electronic publishing to make their catalogs available to potential customers in computerized, rather than paper, versions.[17] Workers must also prepare, handle, and store personal documents. They may use dictation or rough notes to record the information. Sophisticated software for word processing, desktop publishing, and graphics arts (see Chapter 5) has enticed workers to create and modify their own documents, enabling them to immediately redesign documents to meet changing information needs.

Ensuring Privacy and Security. Recall Jake Martin, the copier salesperson described earlier in this chapter. Jake keeps large amounts of information about his clients on his personal computer. How can he ensure the integrity of the data? Users and developers of personal computer information systems are often lax in their attention to issues of security and privacy (see Chapter 14). This is particularly true if their organization lacks norms that encourage security-related behavior.[18] However, computer files are highly susceptible to theft and sabotage, particularly because these security breaches are not easily noticeable.

A variety of techniques can be used to protect against the theft and destruction of valuable personal information, as shown in Figure 2-4. Although most personal information systems are not meant to be shared, occasionally sharing some personal information, such as a calender or address list, may be desirable. Levels of security can be placed on information systems so that specified information can be shared with others who use the same computer or who are attached to the computer by an electronic network.

FIGURE 2.4 Directions for Encouraging Security

1. Keep all diskettes in a secure, fireproof location, such as a locked file cabinet, away from heat and magnetism.
2. Store a backup, second set of diskettes at a different site from the first set.
3. Develop a key lock and/or a password security system for your computer so that only a person having a key or the appropriate password can turn on the computer. Note that information thieves can bypass the key lock relatively easily by disassembling and reassembling the computer case.
4. Consider using encryption software when dealing with highly confidential material such as psychological records. Encryption software uses a secret code to scramble (and unscramble) data you have entered so that it cannot be read even by a thief who manages to physically remove the magnetic storage device from your computer.

Protecting personal privacy has also become a key issue as computer information systems can maintain large amounts of data about individuals without their knowledge.[19] Privacy advocates call for policies and procedures to protect individuals' privacy, such as ensuring the legal collection of only correct and up-to-date data that are relevant to the organization's goals.[20]

The Home Office

Information technology has made it possible for many people to perform their job functions using their home as an office. Many of the salespeople in Casey Jennings's organization, for example, may spend most of their time working from home because they require minimal interaction with the corporate office. Computer programmers increasingly work at home because they essentially require only a computer, modem, and telephone line to perform their job. These and other forms of **telecommuting,** where an individual works from home and typically communicates extensively with the corporate office using electronic media, have increased in popularity. In 1991, for example, the National Association for the Cottage Industry estimated that 38 million Americans spend a significant amount of time working out of a home office.[21] Experts estimate that about 75 percent of all information workers, encompassing more than 55 percent of the U.S. workforce, are potential telecommuters.[22]

APPLE COMPUTER

AT&T

J.C. PENNEY

PACIFIC BELL

The Value of Telecommuting. A home office offers a worker increased flexibility in work hours, increased ability to deal with family issues, less time spent in commuting, and the ability to purchase less costly homes distant from city centers; it also increases personal autonomy and control.[23] An organization that allows employees to spend most of their time working from a home office may hire or retain talented and unique employees who avoid a more traditional work location. Apple Computer, AT&T, J.C. Penney, and Pacific Bell exemplify the growing number of companies whose policies include telecommuting as an accepted corporate practice.[24] Many professionals who deal in foreign markets or with foreign companies maintain an office in their home in addition to or instead of an office at their company. This remote location permits them to work more easily throughout the night to stay in touch with key clients and branch offices and to monitor key market information as it evolves.[25]

The major disadvantage of telecommuting is a decrease in face-to-face communication with others in the organization. A group of female computer professionals polled in Singapore, for example, wanted to telecommute only one to three days a week to avoid such

TELLURIDE, COLORADO

problems.[26] In the near future, however, the increasing availability and lower cost of teleconferencing equipment that permits transmission of video images across the phone lines may reduce this problem.[27] Some small cities are trying to attract telecommuters as residents by significantly upgrading their communication capabilities; Telluride, Colorado, for example, initiated a project called InfoZone, which provides residents with direct links into various electronic networks.[28] Managers may oppose telecommuting because they fear a loss of control over workers, are concerned about an employee's legal obligations to the company when off-site, or fail to understand the benefits of this arrangement to the organization.[29] Improvements in telecommunication, greater acceptance of employee autonomy, and a greater number of successful home offices may address this problem.

Other Remote Options. Some individuals perform only part of their work at home, rather than doing the majority of it at home on a computer during regular work hours. Joanne Eberly, for example, may spend several hours a day working at home so that she can travel in off-peak hours. Workers such as Joanne may participate in *after-hours telecommuting,* where they perform their work on the computer at home outside regular office hours.[30] This type of alternative work arrangement potentially increases workers' flexibility by helping them handle multiple responsibilities, spend more time with children, and control the pacing of work. Although this flexibility should reduce the conflict between work and family, research suggests that the reverse has occurred.[31] In particular, after-hours telecommuting has two consequences. First, it increases role overload because of the increase in the number of hours spent per week working. Second, it interferes with workers' performing multiple roles because work spills into family time and intrudes on nonwork responsibilities.

Satellite offices, established away from the city center and near employee residences, offer an alternative to the home office. Employees can share time between a home office, one or more satellites, and the main office. This option retains the flexibility of the home office, reduces commuting and traffic problems, and increases the opportunities for face-to-face contact. TRW and GTE in California are experimenting with this approach.[32]

TRW

GTE

Office Equipment. The typical home office is equipped with a telephone, a telephone answering machine, a copier, and a variety of computer equipment. A personal computer, often portable, aids in composing documents and receiving data in electronic form. A **modem** receives and transmits data between computers over the telephone line. **Facsimile (fax) machines** transmit and receive images over telephone lines. One prediction suggests that 50 percent of home offices will be equipped with fax machines by 1995 and that 95 percent will have this equipment by the year 2000.[33]

Personal Computing in the Global Environment

Workers like those at Services International plan, track, and organize their time using such tools as calendars, alarm clocks, time cards, and diaries; they may keep telephone numbers of colleagues and customers on an indexed file such as a Rolodex and organize other information into folders in file cabinets. Computer software known as a **personal information manager (PIM)** automates many of these functions.[34] As shown in Figure 2-5, most PIMs offer such features as a personal telephone directory, a phone dialer, diary maintenance, note taking, outlining capability, an office appointment scheduler with an "alarm clock" to remind users of appointments, a calculator ability, and a generic "card" file that can be organized by topic and searched in a variety of ways. Although they primarily run on personal computers, some PIMs also can transfer data to other computers across a computer network.

FIGURE 2-5 Examples of Functions Performed by PIM

Personal telephone directory	Office appointment scheduler
Telephone dialer	Alarm clock
Daily/weekly/monthly diary	Calculator
Note taking and recording	Generic card file
Outlining	Data transfer

Portable technology—laptop computers, fax machines, and cellular telephones—support the management of information. Facilitating the use of spreadsheets, report writing, and telephone calls to clients, they allow insurance agents, for example, to support their client service at remote locations.[35]

The success of personal computing depends on the availability of computing capability. Although many European countries have comparable computing capacity, many other countries outside the United States are experiencing a growing, but still limited, capability. For example, the United Kingdom has seen a significant growth in telecommuting.[36] In contrast, one estimate suggests that the number of E-mail users in Poland increased from 50 people in 1987 to more than 30,000 in 1992.[37] Where personal computers are available, they seem to have a positive effect on satisfaction and performance. A study of 85 professionals in Saudi Arabia, for example, showed a positive relationship between the use of personal computers and job satisfaction, particularly on tasks with high variety, identity, autonomy, and feedback.[38]

Personal Information for Home and Leisure

Many home activities are information intensive and require information management. In 1993 Americans bought 5.85 million personal computers, resulting in a 24 percent increase in sales.[39] The complexity of home life has increased significantly in the past two decades. Now that women account for more than 45 percent of the U.S. workforce, the percentage of two-career couples has reached new highs.[40] Managing the interface of work and leisure poses significant challenges. In this section we illustrate information needs at home and then discuss approaches for managing the information.

Typical Information Needs

At first glance, Casey Jennings's information needs at home may seem relatively simple and straightforward: For example, she or her husband must remember family birthdays, social engagements, and schedules. But they may also budget and track home finances, plan vacations, decide how to invest the family's savings, search for the best mortgage, plan and shop for meals or parties, decide which movies to see, find a friend's telephone number, or even help organize their own or their child's baseball card or stamp collection.

Janice, Jake, and Joanne may have similar information needs at home. In addition, they also have needs unique to their special interests or circumstances. Janice needs financial information in her role as treasurer of a community group. Jake wants data about stamps and coins available for sale as well as current prices for various offerings. Joanne wants information about homes available for purchase that meet her criteria. Adding the information requirements at home to those at work increases the need for information management for working individuals.

Information Management Requirements

Individuals such as Casey Jennings, Janice Grander, Jake Martin, and Joanne Eberly must acquire, store, retrieve, and communicate information at home as well as use it for personal decision making. While these requirements resemble those of the work arena, the computer capabilities for supporting and facilitating information management differ in the home arena.

Information Acquisition. Individuals also use published directories at home. Prospective home buyers or their agents can access either the paper or electronic versions of the Multiple Listing Service (MLS) directories of homes for sale. Stamp collectors can obtain information about the value of precious stamps from the paper or electronic versions of *Scott's Catalogue.* Casey and her coworkers may access any of these guides or directories when planning a vacation, making financial decisions, or monitoring current national and international news.

Information Storage. Most individuals must also maintain household records for financial or social purposes. Some financial records ease transaction processing; for example, to write checks responsibly, a person must know how much money he or she has in a checking account; a check ledger stores information about to whom and in what amount checks were written as well as the size of the remaining balance. The U.S. government requires individuals to maintain records about their wages and other income. Individuals such as Jake Martin and his wife keep records about their stamp, coin, or other collections.

Information Retrieval. Have you ever spent hours looking for a letter, receipt, magazine article, or photograph that was not where it was supposed to be? Perhaps you cannot find the receipt for payment of an old automobile repair because you looked for it in the automobile service file rather than in the insurance file; or perhaps you filed it with your taxes, under casualty losses. Computerized filing systems reduce loss by enabling you to search for information in a variety of ways. You could easily search the automobile service, insurance, and tax files for information about specific automobile repairs. At the same time, converting most personal information to a form suitable for computer storage is a daunting, time-consuming task; hand-held scanners and other technology should make this task easier in the future.

Communicating Information. Individuals use the telephone and word processing systems for communicating from home. They use computers for writing personal correspondence, designing invitations, and preparing school reports and assignments. Increasingly, facsimile machines, electronic mail capabilities, and other interactive means of communication are becoming common for home and leisure use.

Personal Decision Making. Almost any type of personal decision making also requires information management. In deciding where to go for dinner, you need to know the restaurants in the vicinity, the types of food they serve, their price ranges, and the type of food you and your friends prefer. You may acquire some of this information on an ad hoc basis and secure other information from storage. Most individuals will not use electronic media to support these types of everyday decisions until the accessibility of information databases is simpler and quicker. Individuals are more likely to use computer models to assist in making complicated decisions; models that support financial decisions about how and where to invest savings, how to depreciate personal property, or how large a mortgage to seek, for example, are now available in commercial products such as Quicken or Managing Your Money.

Personal Uses of Advanced Information Technology

In the past five years, information technology has become common in the home. Experts expect this trend to continue and accelerate. Appliances are among the most common applications of microprocessor and sensor technologies. For example, some new televisions being tested in Japan now collect information about the brightness of the room and adjust the brightness of the television accordingly. They can also monitor the distance of the viewer and adjust the volume accordingly.[41] Because at current prices a personal computer is not much more expensive than most major home appliances, people are buying computers as if they were appliances. Automated home systems can now create **smart houses,** which include security components to automatically lock doors, turn on outside lights at dusk, or sprinkle the yard; emergency alert systems to check on children or the elderly; appliance systems that monitor appliance usage; and voice-activated communication and entertainment systems.[42] Estimates suggest that by the year 2000, 84 percent of all households will own computers.[43]

The direct purchase of information services by individuals is also increasingly popular. Subscribers communicate over telephone lines and access lists of stock prices, news and weather reports, sports scores, catalogs, encyclopedias, directories, and other sources of information. Subscriptions to Prodigy, for example, a product developed and offered by IBM and Sears, increased by 60 percent from 1990 to 1991 to 1.25 million subscribers.[44] Projections suggest that 17.7 million households will subscribe to at least one on-line service by 1998.[45]

HUNTINGTON BANCSHARES

AT&T

Information technology has also reduced the amount of time necessary to perform such personal financial chores as banking and bill paying. Huntington Bancshares of Columbus, Ohio, and AT&T formed a partnership to introduce a *smart phone,* a telephone with a built-in modem and touch-sensitive 4-inch by 6-inch screen that customers can use to pay bills, purchase tickets, conduct banking business, or shop at home.[46] People worldwide already use automatic teller machines (ATMs) to speed their banking; ATMs perform certain transactions more quickly than human tellers and offer greater convenience because of their 24-hour availability at multiple sites. The availability of powerful financial investment software for the home market also facilitates stock selection and other financial planning.

HOME SHOPPING NETWORK

CRATE & BARREL

US ORDER

Shopping from the home has also been made easier. In addition to using computerized home shopping services, individuals can shop using only the telephone. The Home Shopping Network broadcasts special offers over television channels in many major U.S. markets and receives almost 200,000 orders each day. Shoppers can fill their orders without ever talking to a sales agent simply by pressing the keypad of their touch-tone telephones in response to a computer-directed message system.[47] Crate & Barrel, a retail home furnishings store, recently provided a test group with the facility to order and pay remotely for catalog goods.[48] Customers use a product code reader wand for scanning the catalog and entering data into a computer terminal at US Order, the software vendor and intermediary, for an inventory check and computation of the bill; the customer then runs a credit card through a slot in the terminal for payment, and this sends the order and a transfer of funds to Crate & Barrel, who then ships the order.

Computer technology can also offer unique opportunities and provide valuable information for individuals. By using modified computers to compensate for disabilities, disabled

Crate & Barrel, a national retailer of household furniture and accessories based in Northbrook, Illinois, was the first company to test a US Order system to automate remote shopping.
Courtesy of Crate & Barrel.

individuals can continue to function effectively in the home and work arenas.[49] Similarly, a new technology called the Intelligent Vehicle/Highway Systems could provide motorists information about traffic conditions remotely.[50]

Summary

The first step in effective management of information is a careful diagnosis of information needs. Individuals process information by first attending to certain stimuli and then organizing them in a meaningful way. Humans and computers can play different roles in this process, with computers much more able to handle large volumes of data quickly and humans able to deal more effectively with symbols or objects that have meaning.

Individuals at work require various types of information for the roles they perform. These information needs include task-related, time management, performance-related, and career-related needs. Meeting these needs poses challenges for information management that include dealing with quantities of information, enhancing personal productivity, and maintaining technical skills. Information management to meet these needs involves managing time, records, and personal documents. The home office plays an increasingly important role in workers' lives. Telecommuting and satellite offices provide additional flexibility for employees. Significant variations exist in information needs and in the use of personal computing to meet these needs when viewed from a global perspective.

Individuals also have needs for information at home and in leisure pursuits. Information management at home involves the acquisition, storage, retrieval, and communication of information, and personal decision making.

Key Terms

Facsimile machine
Fax
Infoglut
Modem
Perception
Personal information manager (PIM)
Satellite office
Smart house
Telecommuting

Review Questions

1. What is meant by *perception*? How does perception affect the use of information?
2. What are the components of perception? How do individuals organize what they perceive?
3. Identify the advantages and disadvantages of computers compared with humans in processing information.
4. List and illustrate the types of information needs individual job holders might have.
5. Specify three challenges of information management for the individual job holder.
6. What is *infoglut*? How can you avoid it?
7. List five information management requirements of individuals.
8. Describe two techniques that can be used to protect against the theft and destruction of valuable personal information.
9. Why has privacy protection become an important issue for managers of computerized information systems?
10. Describe the benefits and drawbacks of telecommuting for both individuals and their employers.
11. What are two alternatives to telecommuting?
12. Identify five possible job-related information needs of a telecommuting worker.
13. Outline the issues for personal computing in a global environment.
14. What office equipment is typically required for a home office?
15. What is a personal information manager? List five functions performed by a PIM.
16. What is meant by a *smart house*?

MINICASE

Information for the Farmer

When Delbert Westphalen uses his portable computer in the field, he does so literally. A corn and soybean farmer, Westphalen says up-to-date information is critical for the business decisions he has to make to run his 400-acre farm in Atlantic, Iowa.

Before Westphalen got his Apple Computer Inc. Newton MessagePad PDA (Personal Digital Assistant) seven months ago, he had to handwrite crop records, such as whether he fertilized a field, how much fertilizer he used and when. Then he had to re-enter the information into his Gateway 2000 Inc. desktop PC later that day. Now he enters the data once into the Newton, then transmits it to the PC via a hard-wired serial cable at night.

"I find it indispensable," said Westphalen of his Newton MessagePad and Infielder crop records software from Monsanto Co., St. Louis, which also runs on his desktop PC. He uses the software to record historical records such as crop yields, pesticide use and soil conditions.

Westphalen is a test site for Infielder, which is being promoted by a consortium of 17 companies, including Apple, Monsanto and Deere & Co., Moline, Ill. The program, which runs on both the Newton and IBM compatibles using Windows 3.1 or higher, costs $999, including the Apple hardware and access to the Infielder database called Best Crop Practices.

Infielder's menu includes information on fields, such as total acreage, acreage planted and more than 3,000 soil types, as well as pesticide application, seeds planted, weather patterns, nutrient application, equipment purchased, and irrigation and harvest details. Currently, Infielder contains data on only soybean and corn fields in five Midwest states.

Farmer in the Dell of Red Tape

Westphalen has found mobile computing indispensable. Farmers are under increasing pressure from the U.S. government to keep detailed records on finances and crops. This can be complicated. Often a farm has multiple fields, and one 40-acre field could have two or three different soil types, each requiring different fertilizers. And each farm must cope with a variety of federal agencies.

For example, the Environmental Protection Agency requires farmers to keep reports on when they spread pesticides, which product they used, which field it was put on, the time of day, wind direction, wind velocity and temperature. "In the future I may have to make monthly or semi-annual reports to them," said Westphalen.

Also, legislation from the U.S. Department of Agriculture now requires him to keep reports on when he tilled a field and how much residue was kept on top of the field to prevent soil erosion. "This is the first year we must keep close track of this," said Westphalen, a fourth-generation farmer who runs his fields with his wife and two sons. "The paperwork and bureaucracy is terrible. The agencies even do aerial surveys to see if we are growing what is allocated," he said. Penalties for noncompliance are severe: The government can withhold loans or other financial aid.

Westphalen's and other new mobile computing applications are "client/server computing, but this is the first time we are seeing the client being a very mobile device in the hands of a nontraditional user," said Lou Clarke, project leader for advanced technology at Monsanto. "We will start to see this more and more," said Clarke, whose group helped develop Infielder.

SOURCE: Extracted from Lori Valigra, The new road warriors, *Client/Server Computing* (October 1994): 98–104.

Monsanto did plenty of research at its test farms before deciding on the Newton as the platform for Infielder. The criteria: light weight (Newton weighs less than one pound), small size and a day's worth of battery life so farmers wouldn't run out of juice in the field. In addition to Infielder, Monsanto used Omnis 7 from Blyth Software Inc., Foster City, Calif., to develop the database that is simultaneously updated when a farmer plugs the Newton into a desktop PC.

Farmer Westphalen plans to buy Infielder once his test is complete. "I like the portability and durability of it. I can get fresh information at the time it is happening. And fresh information is accurate information," he said. He noted, however, that the look of some of the screens and the handling of certain information have had to be modified to be more useful for farmers.

Case Questions

1. What information does Mr. Westphalen need in order to perform his work?
2. How does computer technology help Mr. Westphalen and other farmers address government requirements?
3. What alternatives does Mr. Westphalen have to using a PDA to collect and store the information he needs? What are the advantages and disadvantages of these alternative methods?

ACTIVITY 2-1 Outfitting an Architect's Office

short case

STEP 1: Read the following scenario.

Kim Peterson runs her architectural practice from a small office in her home. She has always had a small personal computer that she uses for billing clients and making notes about meetings with them. Kim also is responsible for managing her household; she pays the bills, schedules appointments, and generally assures that the household runs smoothly. Kim recently built a large addition to her house that includes a new office. She plans to equip her office to meet both her work and personal needs.

STEP 2: Individually or in small groups, develop an outline of needs that Kim can submit to contractors and vendors making bids on equipping her new office. Be sure to discuss her information needs in detail and then identify one or two possible ways of meeting each one.

STEP 3: In small groups or with the entire class, share the proposals you have developed. Then discuss and answer the following questions:

1. What do the various proposals have in common?
2. What are Kim's information needs?
3. How can you best meet these needs? ●

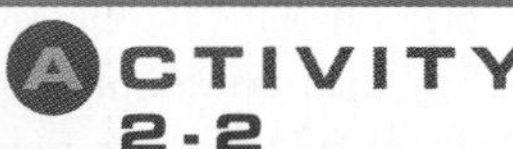

ACTIVITY 2-2 Telecommuting Debate

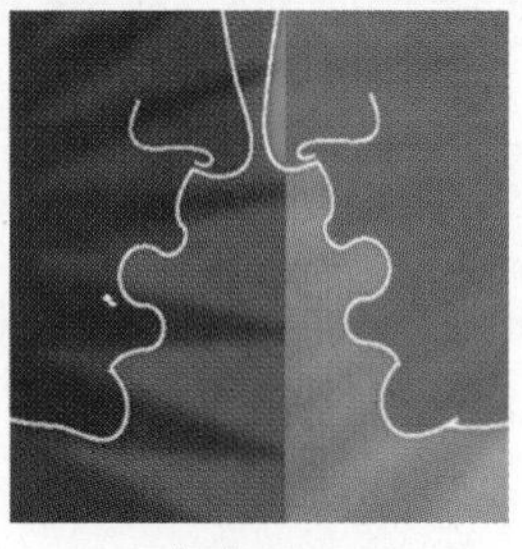

debate

Resolved. All companies should institute a telecommuting option for their workers.

STEP 1: Your instructor will assign you to teams that will debate either the pro or con side of this issue.

STEP 2: Prepare your position.

STEP 3: Conduct the debate with the opposing team.

STEP 4: In small groups or with the entire class, discuss and answer the following questions:

1. Which side was more convincing?
2. What should organizations consider before introducing a telecommuting option? ●

ACTIVITY 2-3 Using a Personal Information Manager

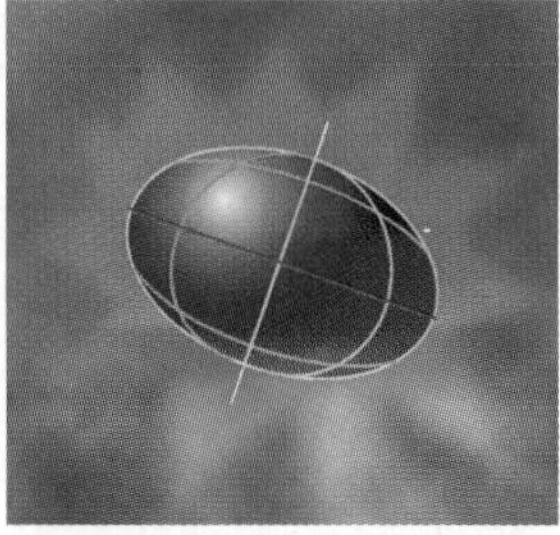

external contact

STEP 1: Select a personal information manager that is available at your computer center, that a friend has purchased, or that a local store will allow you to preview.

STEP 2: Evaluate this PIM by reviewing the trade press about it, reviewing any advertising information provided by the manufacturer or supplier, and then testing its features.

STEP 3: In small groups or with the entire class, compare and contrast the various PIMs evaluated. What features should a PIM have? What personal information needs do the PIMs that you tested meet? ●

ACTIVITY 2-4 Security in the Psychiatric Practice

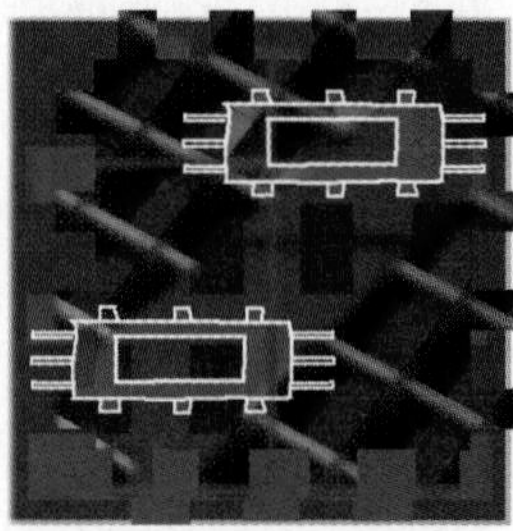

short case

STEP 1: Patrick Jameson runs a psychiatric consulting practice from two offices, one in a small medical building and the second in his home. Until three years ago, he kept all his notes about his clients in locked file cabinets. Then he bought two personal computers, primarily to assist him with billing. However, he also began to use the computer as a word processor to help type and organize his notes. In addition, he learned how to use database software on the computer to keep track of the status of his patients, the procedures and techniques he was using, and their outcomes. He backed up his files on diskettes, which he kept in boxes on the shelf above his computer. One day he noticed that one of the boxes was gone.

STEP 2: Individually or in small groups, offer a strategy to help Patrick avoid this problem in the future.

STEP 3: Interview five classmates who use a personal computer at work or for their school work about the security provisions they use to ensure that no one tampers with their computer files.

STEP 4: In small groups or with the entire class, share your strategies for dealing with Patrick's problem. Then share the strategies your classmates use to ensure the security of their personal computers. ●

Notes

[1]M. B. Howes, *The Psychology of Human Cognition* (New York: Pergamon, 1990).

[2]K. M. Bartol and D. C. Martin, *Management* (New York: McGraw-Hill, 1991): 529.

[3]J. R. Pomerantz and M. Kubovy, Theoretical approaches to perceptual organization. In K. R. Boss, L. Kaufmann, and J. P. Thomas, eds., *Handbook of Perception and Human Performance,* vol. 2 (New York: Wiley, 1986); I. Rock, The description and analysis of object and event perception. In Boss *et al.,* op. cit.; D. J. Schneider, Social cognition. In M. R. Rosenzweig and L. W. Porter, eds., *Annual Review of Psychology* 4(2) (1991): 527–561.

[4]I. Benbasat, A. S. Dexter, and P. Todd, An experimental program investigating color-enhanced and graphical information presentation: An integration of the findings, *Communications of the ACM 29* (11) (1986): 1094–1105; G. W. Dickson, G. DeSanctis, and D. J. McBride, Understanding the effectiveness of computer graphics for decision support: A cumulative experimental approach, *Communications of the ACM* 29(1) (1986): 40–47; E. D. Hoadly, Investigating the effects of color, *Communications of the ACM* 33(2) (1990): 120–125, 139; and J. K. H. Tan and I. Benbasat, Processing of graphical information: A decomposition taxonomy to match data extraction tasks and graphical representations, *Information Systems Research* 1(4) (1990): 416–439.

[5]J. W. Gibson and R. M. Hodgetts, *Organizational Communication: A Managerial Perspective,* 2d ed. (New York: HarperCollins, 1991).

[6]I. Iselin, The impact of information diversity on information overload effects in unstructured managerial decision making, *Journal of Information Science Principles & Practice* 15(3) (1989): 163–173.

[7]Ruth Coxeter, 10,000 PCs under the sea? *Business Week* (November 22, 1993): 137.

[8]Darlene Shura, Is there a doctor in this computer? *Computing Canada* 18(15) (July 20, 1992): 33.

[9]Peter Coy, The new realism, *Business Week* (June 15, 1992): 128–133.

[10]Maryfran Johnson, Making waves at Helene Curtis, *Computerworld Client/Server Journal* (1993): 27–30.

[11]Coy, op. cit.

[12]Paul Karon, Beyond number-crunching, *Computerworld* (January 17, 1994): 97–98.

[13]T. Harbert, Drowning in data, *CIO* 4(2) (November 1990): 96–106.

[14]E. J. Muller, Information overload, *Distribution* 90(4) (1991): 26–32; G. Buckler, Making the right moves, *Canadian Datasystems* 23(4) (1991): 22–25, 47; and C. E. Meglio and B. H. Kleiner, Managing information overload, *Industrial Management & Data Systems* 1 (1990): 23–25, address this problem and offer some strategies for dealing with too much information.

[15]See, for example, Too many computers spoil the broth, *Economist* 320 (August 24, 1991): 30; and J. Falvey, Computers: Literacy or lunacy? *Sales & Marketing Management* 143(3) (March 1991): 8, 10.

[16]Lynda Radosevich, Patent searching gets faster, *Computerworld* (November 8, 1993): 61.

[17]Evan I. Schwartz, This magazine could be on your PC screen, *Business Week* (June 28, 1993): 56.

[18]J. Frank, B. Shamir, and W. Briggs, Security-related behavior of PC users in organizations, *Information & Management* 21(3) (1991): 127–135.

[19]Louise Benjamin, Privacy, computers, and personal information: Toward equality and equity in the information age, *Communications & the Law* 13(2) (June 1991): 3–16.

[20]Michael H. Agranoff, Protecting personal privacy exposed in corporate data bases, *Information Strategy: The Executive's Journal* 7(4) (Summer 1991): 27–32.

[21]Greg Matusky, An international empire in your home, *World Trade* 4(6) (October 1991): 52, 54.

[22]K. Burger, Offices without walls: Remote computing in the '90s, *Insurance & Technology* 17(8) (1992): 46–50.

[23]R. Leider, Home work: A study in the interaction of work and family organizations, *Research in the Sociology of Work* 4 (1988): 69–94.

[24]N. D. Cosgrove, The office at home has inviting sound, *Office* 115(4) (April 1992): 42–43.

[25]Matusky, op. cit.

[26]C. S. Yap and H. Tng, Factors associated with attitudes toward telecommuting, *Information & Management* 19(4) (1990): 227–235.

[27]W. S. Mossberg, Hi Sis. What have you done with your hair? *Telephone Engineer & Management* 96(18) (1992): 10; and Carol Wilson, ASDL: A high-bandwidth hope for copper, *Telephony Supplement* (October 5, 1992): 40–41.

[28]Sandra D. Atchison, The care and feeding of 'lone eagles', *Business Week* (November 15, 1993): 58.

[29]C. Currid, Workers warm to telecommuting; middle managers stay cold, *InfoWorld* 14(11) (March 16, 1992): 59.

[30]This discussion of after-hours telecommuting is based on L. E. Duxbury, C. A. Higgins, and S. Mills, After-hours telecommuting and work-family conflict: A comparative analysis, *Information Systems Research* 3(2) (1992): 173–190.

[31]Duxbury *et al.,* op. cit.

[32]The eternal coffee break, *Economist,* 322 (March 7, 1992): 71.

[33]L. K. Vanston, W. J. Kennedy, and S. El-Badry-Nance, Forecast for facsimile, *Telephone Engineer & Management* 95(18) (September 15, 1991): 48–52.

[34]See John A. Murphy, Personal information managers: Putting your thoughts on disk, *Today's Office* 25(9) (February 1991): 30–33; M. A. Cox and W. Cummings, Personal information managers: Useful tools for accountants, *Journal of Accountancy* 170(4) (1990): 124–134, for examples of commercial products.

[35]G. Davis, The mobile insurance agent, *Rough Notes* 135(1) (January 1992): 10–11, 44.

[36]F. Kinsman, Home sweet office, *Accountancy* 108 (November 1991): 118.

[37]Ruth Ryan, International connectivity: A survey of attitudes about cultural and national differences encountered in computer-mediated communication, University of Alaska Southeast, unpublished paper, August 1992.

[38]J. A. Ghani and A. R. Al-Meer, Effect of end-user computing on job satisfaction: An exploratory study, *Information & Management* 17(4) (1989): 191–195.

[39]David Kirkpatrick, How PCs will take over your home, *Fortune* (February 21, 1994): 100–104.

[40]*The National Data Book,* U.S. Department of Commerce, Economics and Statistics Administration, Bureau of the Census, 111th ed., Table 657 (1990): 400.

[41]Norman C. Remich, Jr., Fuzzy logic now across most appliance lines, *Appliance Manufacturer* 40(4) (April 1992): 45–48.

[42]Heather Millar, Smart houses: Getting switched on, *Business Week* (June 28, 1993): 128–129.

[43]Marketplace: Home-office PC growth won't affect business sales, *Purchasing* 109(8) (1990): 93.

[44]Paul Miller, Prodigy trims the catalog "fat," *Catalog Age* 9(3) (March 1992): 7.

[45]Aaron Zitner, No space in cyberspace? *The Boston Sunday Globe* (February 6, 1994): A-1.

[46]Penny Lunt, Are customers finally ready to bank at home? *ABA Banking Journal* 84(2) (February 1992): 79, 81.

[47]Tom Mikol, Home shopping network: The technology channel, *Telemarketing Magazine* 10(8) (February 1992): 60–61.

[48]J. M. Angelo, From mail to phone to fax to . . . wand? *Catalog Age* 9(1) (1992): 16.

[49]K. Crane, PC gives counselor second career chance, *Computerworld* (November 25, 1991): 65.

[50]F. K. Plous, Smart roads, smart cars, *Planning* 58(1) (January, 1992): 12–15.

Recommended Readings

Christensen, K. (ed.) *The New Era of Home-Based Work: Directions and Policies.* Boulder, CO: Westview, 1988.

Fisher, D. *Communication in Organizations,* 2d ed. St. Paul: West, 1993.

Howes, M. B. *The Psychology of Human Cognition.* New York: Pergamon, 1990.

Kleyle, R. M. and De Korvin, A. A Belief Function Approach to Information Utilization in Decision Making. *Journal of the ASIS* 41(8) (December 1990): 569–580.

Swanson, Burton E. The Information Loop as a General Analytic View. *Information & Management* 20(1) (January 1991): 37–47.

Huws, Ursula, Korte, W. B., and Robinson, S. *Telework: Towards the Elusive Office.* New York: Wiley, 1990.

Chapter 3

The Managerial Perspective

OUTLINE

Watching the Payroll at Unum
The Manager's Job in a Global Environment
Information and Levels of Management
- Executive Management
- Middle Management
- First-Line Supervision

Information Required for the Process of Management
- Planning
- Organizing
- Leading
- Controlling

Functional Information Needs
- Accounting
- Finance
- Marketing
- Engineering
- Operations
- Human Resources

Managers and Information Systems
- Diagnosing Information Needs
- Applying Information Technology
- Interactions with Information Systems Professionals

LEARNING OBJECTIVES

After completing the reading and activities for Chapter 3, students will be able to

1. Describe the use of information by global managers.
2. Compare and contrast the information needs of top-, middle-, and lower-level managers.
3. Describe the use of information in performing the classic management functions of planning, organizing, leading, and controlling.
4. Highlight the information needs of six types of functional managers.
5. Diagnose the information needs of a particular manager in an organization.
6. Describe managers' use of information systems to perform their jobs.
7. Describe the interactions of managers and information systems professionals.
8. Cite three ways computerization of information has an impact on managers' job performance.

During a recent cost-cutting drive, James Orr, chair and chief executive of Unum Corporation, an insurer in Portland, Maine, asked for a daily count on the number of company employees. He was told he couldn't get it. Some data were kept by divisions and so were difficult to gather together in one place. Some were in a payroll database accessible only to programmers.

Orr persisted, however, and now the answer is at his fingertips whenever he wants it: A specially designed executive information system links personnel data to a personal computer in his office. "Management knows I'm watching the count very closely," he says. "Believe me, they don't add staff carelessly."[1]

Why does James Orr need information about the current number of company employees to do his job? What other types of information does he need to perform effectively as the chairman and chief executive of Unum Corporation? What information do the managers who report to him need? How does it differ from the information required by first-line supervisors?

In this chapter we examine the information needs of effective managers. The chapter begins with a discussion of the nature of global management. Next we examine the management activities of top-, middle-, and lower-level managers. The chapter continues with a description of the use of information in executing the classic management functions of planning, organizing, leading, and controlling. The next part of the chapter examines the information needs associated with six major functional areas in organizations: accounting, finance, marketing, engineering, operations, and human resource management. The chapter concludes with a brief introduction to managers' use of information systems and interactions with information systems professionals.

The Manager's Job in a Global Environment

Management is the process of achieving organizational goals by planning, organizing, leading, and controlling organizational resources. What does a typical manager's job look like, and what information does he or she need to perform that job? Managers face a variety of challenges in performing their work in a global environment. They must deal with increasing competition, decreasing resources, and rapidly changing technology. They must understand and respond to dramatic cultural differences, imposing legal constraints, and dynamic customer requirements.

Managers at all levels cope with less-than-perfect information in an uncontrollable environment. For example, managers at companies doing business in the former East Germany after the fall of the Berlin Wall initially experienced repeated difficulties with telephone service, which caused significant problems with voice communication and data processing.[2] Top executives attempt to analyze the economic, political, and technological aspects of the environment and plot a strategy to meet such changes. Often, however, they cannot anticipate changes in money rates, political upheavals in distant locations, or the speed of technological advancement. Middle-level managers may have information about production deadlines, sales forecasts, or hiring practices that proves to be unreliable or dynamic and that requires them to handle emergencies, reconsider the best way to perform their jobs, or change their priorities in unexpected ways. Dealing globally increases the likelihood that managers will have unreliable information and intensifies any existing deficiencies in the information because both distance and cultural diversity affect information quality. First-line supervisors may even experience delays in receiving up-to-date information from their bosses who must check directives from a distant corporate headquarters. How do managers perform effectively under such conditions?

Managers perform a great quantity of work at an unrelenting pace.[3] This level of activity involves a manager's continually seeking and then quickly processing large amounts of information, generally without time for leisurely reflection. Managers also participate in a variety of brief activities that result in significant fragmentation of their time. They become accustomed to the rapid exchange of information with others and hence must have the needed information readily available. Because time is precious and managers tend to deal with issues that are current and specific, they seek ways to secure information as efficiently as possible. James Orr, for example, wanted a daily count of the number of employees in his organization; in addition, he likely wanted easily accessible information about other labor, materials, and equipment costs, as well as data about sales and revenues. Managers also spend extensive amounts of time communicating with other managers both inside and outside the organization. As more information becomes available to them, managers seem to want and need even more information to perform effectively. Increasingly managers will spend more time interpreting historical data, anticipating future trends, setting accurate goals, measuring performance against goals, identifying variances quickly, allocating resources dynamically, and adapting to unanticipated events.[4]

Information and Levels of Management

Managers at different hierarchical levels in the organization have special concerns, as shown in Figure 3-1. At the highest level, managers are concerned with setting long-term goals and directions for the organization. At the lowest level, managers are concerned with supervising the conduct of day-to-day activities. As one moves up the corporate ladder, decisions have a longer term and wider ranging impact on the organization. These differences affect the characteristics of managers' information needs. In this section we illustrate the types of information needed by different levels of management. Note that at all levels managers cope with less-than-perfect information in an uncontrollable environment. They use information systems to help them bring as much order and completeness to the available information as possible.

Executive Management

Top-level managers establish the overall direction of an organization by setting its strategy and policies. They may decide that cost cutting requires reducing the number of employees or that introducing a new product line calls for hiring more workers. They typically develop a mission, reflected in a mission statement that defines the basic character and characteristics of the organization, that is, who the organization is, why the organization is in business, and what the organization is in the business to do. These executives also develop programs and activities in line with stated profit or service objectives.

Top executives typically have both an internal and external orientation: They must ensure that work gets done within their particular subsidiary or division while they interact with

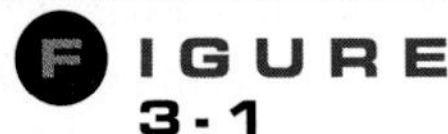

Concerns of the Three Management Levels

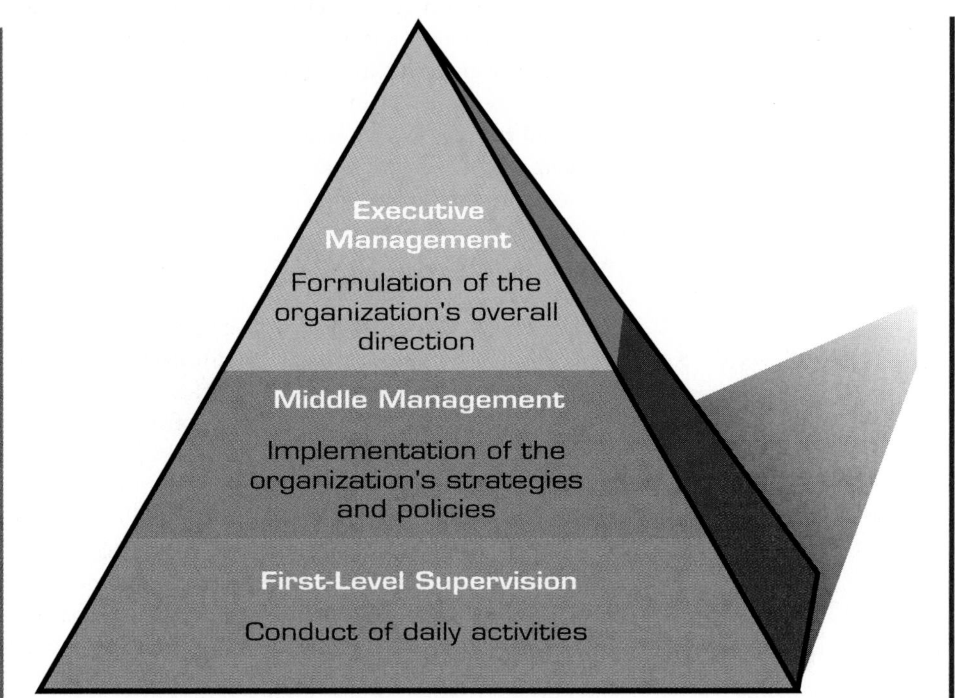

executives in other organizations and with the general public. Increasingly, such interactions span regional and national boundaries, requiring executives to have large repositories of information about an array of global issues. They may need to know the cost of labor in Taiwan and zoning laws in Detroit. Top executives may also spend large amounts of time in ceremonial roles, representing their company to the public. They must have knowledge of the customs and rituals of different cultures to perform these responsibilities effectively.

What types of information do top-level managers typically need? Top executives often need performance-related information about results of various divisions or product groups; they may require summary data about sales, production levels, or costs to assess the organization's performance. Top executives also use information about new technology, customers, suppliers, and others in the industry to gain a competitive advantage over other firms. As organizations increase their international focus, top executives require economic, legal, and cultural information about other countries in which the organization operates. Top-level managers may combine these various types of information to formulate a strategy for the organization (see Chapter 4) and a plan for implementing it. Of course, they never have complete information and try to use the available information as effectively as possible.

GEORGIA POWER

BANK OF BOSTON

Some managers, such as James Orr, want detailed information about particular aspects of their organization, such as the total number of employees or sales at any particular time; they may want general information that focuses on a division's profitability, market share, return on investment, or trouble spots. For example, the chairman of Georgia Power Company needs to know the current status of the utility's plants. The executive vice-president of Bank of Boston needs current information about the bank's exposure to third-world debt.[5] The information needs of top executives thus can vary considerably.

Consider the job of a senior marketing manager in the hair-care products division of a large company. She must determine the best mix of products for the company, authorize advertising and marketing research expenditures, and supervise a staff of managers responsible for accomplishing the department's goals. What types of information might she require? Now compare her information needs with those of a senior financial manager or even with those of a senior marketing manager in a computer software firm. Clearly these three managers have some needs in common, but they also have needs unique to their job, organization, and industry. Diagnosing the particular information needs of senior executives requires tracking their organizational and job goals and then assessing the information that helps accomplish those goals.

Middle Management

Unlike top executives, middle managers focus primarily on implementing the policies and strategies set by top management. Plant managers, regional sales managers, directors of staffing, and other middle managers almost always deal with internal organizational issues, such as finding ways to increase productivity, profitability, and service. Middle managers must meet production schedules and budgetary constraints while still acting independently. They also participate actively in various personnel decisions, including the hiring, transfer, promotion, or termination of employees. Middle managers serve as the interface between executives and first-line supervisors: They disseminate top management's directives to lower levels of the organization and communicate problems or exceptional circumstances up the hierarchy. They may work in the United States or abroad, directly managing one or more work teams, coordinating interdependent groups, or supervising support personnel.

Middle managers require more detailed information than executives about the functioning of the groups or workers they supervise, although generally they do not require as detailed information as a first-level supervisor requires. Often middle managers need detailed budget data, extensive information about workers' performance, schedules, and skills, and data about their group's products or services to perform their jobs well and to ensure that their work group focuses on organizational goals. Often they cannot obtain perfect information and must use the best information they can secure.

Middle managers who act as **project managers** might be responsible for one or more unique projects, such as the development of new spreadsheet software or a new computer chip, or ongoing projects, such as the provision of accounting services to a small business. Project managers typically supervise teams of workers who must accomplish a specific goal: Ten to twelve employees working on the same assembly line may compose a team; three to five accountants who work on a client's audit may make up a team. Note that some project managers have a smaller scope of responsibility and could be classified as first-line supervisors. Organizations consist of multiple, overlapping teams, only some of which are formally recognized by group or departmental boundaries. The manager must ensure that the project team works together effectively toward its common goal. He or she must have information about the project's goal, tasks, and timetable. The manager must know each team member's job responsibilities as well as the member's skills, abilities, and knowledge. The manager must also have information about the individuals, group, organization, and its environment to help in leading, motivating, resolving conflicts, and coordinating activities.

Middle managers might also serve as links between their own work groups and others in the organization. Occasionally these links may extend beyond local or regional boundaries, posing additional challenges for the manager. The middle manager, too, might require special knowledge about managing a multicultural workforce or conducting business internationally. DuPont, for example, charged five managerial teams around the world with ensuring employee retention in their areas; they use conferencing by telephone to share ideas.[6]

DUPONT

Consider the facilities manager responsible for siting a new manufacturing plant. What types of information does she need? Now consider the manager of training and development in a small financial services company. What types of information does he need? Accurately diagnosing the information needs of middle managers relies on understanding the characteristics of their particular work situations and the problems they encounter.

First-line Supervision

First-level managers have the most direct responsibility for ensuring the effective conduct of their organization's daily activities. The supervisor of long-distance telephone operators handles any problems that arise in servicing customers; the customer services manager in an insurance company oversees the interactions between customer service representatives and policy holders. Such supervisors might plan work schedules, modify a subordinate's job duties, train a new worker, or generally handle problems employees encounter. They ensure that their subordinates accomplish their daily, weekly, and monthly goals and regularly provide workers with feedback about their performance. They screen problems and may pass particularly significant, unusual, or difficult problems to middle managers for handling. First-line supervisors also spend large amounts of time in disturbance-handling roles, such as replacing absent workers, handling customer complaints, or securing repairs for equipment. They, too, may experience imperfections in the information they receive; they must recognize these deficiencies and respond accordingly.

Consider the night-shift nursing supervisor in the pediatrics ward of a hospital. What information must she have to perform her job? Certainly she requires detailed information about pediatric nursing procedures, knowledge about the skills of the nurses on the shift, and detailed listings of the nursing services required for each patient. If the staff is unionized, she should also know the provisions of the union contract. The head nurse might also require information about daily and vacation schedules as well as the ability to secure temporary employees. She should have a basic knowledge about the equipment on the floor as well as how to obtain repairs for it. What information does she need to solve an understaffing or absenteeism problem? Does she need the same information to answer questions about administration of medications or delivery of meals to patients on the floor? The night-shift supervisor in a manufacturing plant might require comparable information about the tasks, workers, and equipment. Of course, the specific details will differ as a function of the setting. Both the nursing supervisor and the plant supervisor may encounter special problems that require unique information. Diagnosis of information needs must be ongoing and responsive to the particular situations these managers face.

Information Required for the Process of Management

Collecting and disseminating information serve as the cornerstone of management activity. The manager gathers information from the environment inside or outside the organization. He or she reviews written information about the company and its industry, attends meetings that present information about the organization, or participates in task forces or committees that provide additional information about organizational functioning. What specific information might the new manager of a neighborhood restaurant seek? What information might the manager of customer service for Tyco Toys monitor in the organization or the environment? Monitoring the environment provides particular challenges for the global manager, who must scan worldwide for large amounts of diverse information.

TYCO TOYS

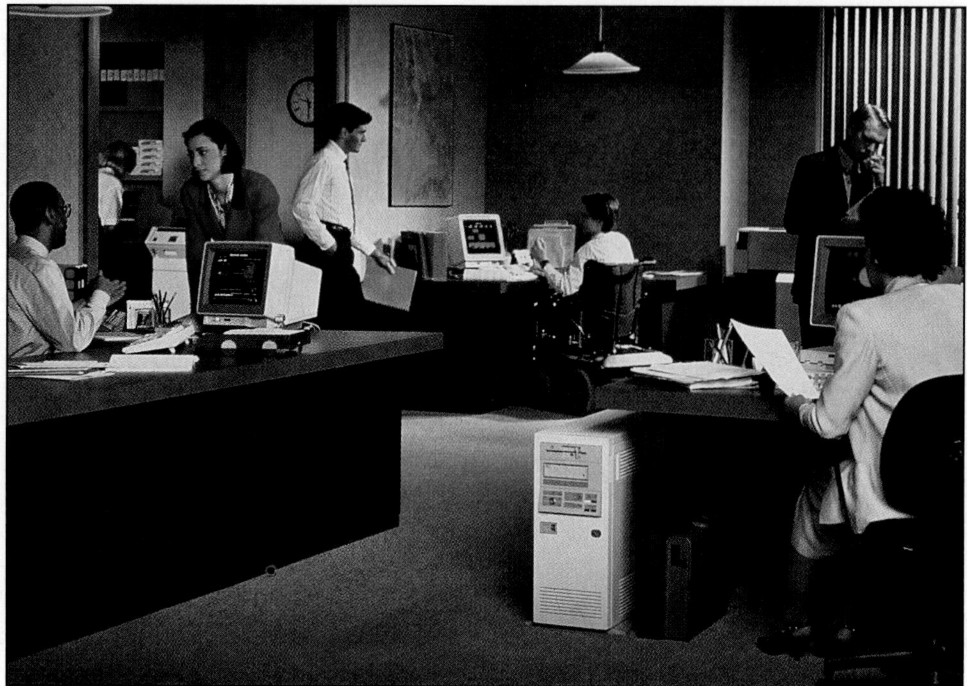

Managers collect and disseminate information in informal, face-to-face conversations, through written and electronic media, and in formal meetings.

Courtesy of International Business Machines Corporation.

Having collected information about the organization's functioning, the manager then disseminates it to subordinates, peers, supervisors, or individuals outside the organization. Such distribution may occur in face-to-face conversations, through electronic media, or at meetings.

The manager must have information about the environment in which the organization functions; this information may include data about industry trends, technological developments, and market requirements. The manager should also have a strong knowledge of the organization—its structure, goals, resources, and culture. The manager should know the needs of various organizational members so that he or she can choose the most appropriate information to convey and the most appropriate way to disseminate it; for example, the manager may give bad news to subordinates and superiors in different ways.[7] At the same time, the manager must consider his or her own information needs in performing the four basic management functions of planning, organizing, leading, and controlling, as shown in Figure 3-2. We incorporate a discussion of the roles managers perform into the presentation of these basic functions.[8]

Planning

Managers engage in a variety of planning activities that occur over short-, medium-, and long-term time frames. Driven in part by the need to respond to competition, the changing environment, and customer demands, managers develop the organization's mission and goals and the means to accomplish them. **Planning** usually refers to both the specification of goals and the blueprint for achieving them. It can occur at the individual, group, organizational, or extra-organizational level. Managers may engage in strategic, tactical, or operational planning, as shown in Figure 3-3. They also engage in decision making, in which they allocate resources and act as negotiators, problem solvers, change agents, and disturbance handlers.

The top managers at Unum, for example, likely decide which insurance products to sell and how to sell them as part of their **strategic planning**—the long-term planning for

Process of Management

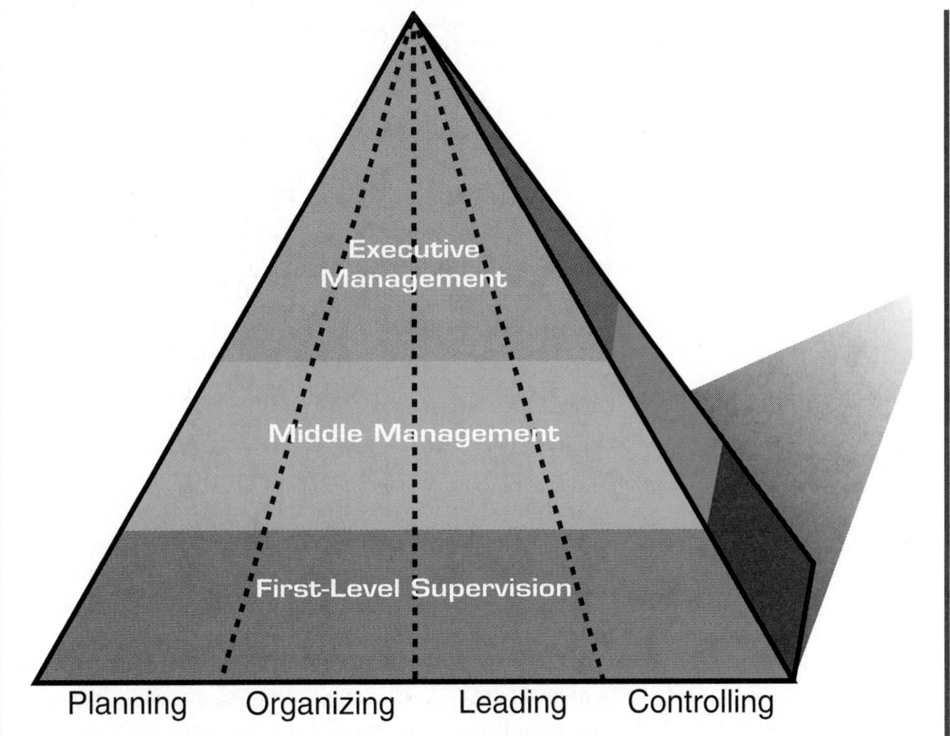

accomplishing the organization's mission. Information about Unum's capabilities, its competitors' competencies, and customer demands is essential for determining the organization's goals and its **strategic plan**—long-term activities the organization must undertake to accomplish its mission. James Orr must have information about potential changes in the environment in which his organization does business to help set strategic goals. Knowledge about technological developments and their applicability to the insurance company, as well as about the supply of various types of workers, constitutes additional information incorporated into the strategic plan.

In most organizations middle managers more often engage in medium- or short-term planning known as **tactical planning. Tactical objectives** describe what units within an organization must do to accomplish strategic objectives, and **tactical plans** refer to the steps for attaining the tactical objectives. Tactical plans may focus on decisions about staffing, advertising, and pricing, for example; or they may reflect other financial, marketing, or human resource decisions. Consider the types of information a manager needs in order to make staffing decisions. James Orr believed that he needed to know exactly how many people the company employed at any particular time. He might also need to know how many employees are required to perform specific activities or what an optimal span of control is for managers. What types of information would a manager need to determine the best advertising campaign for his or her products? The manager might need to know what competitive products exist, the nature of advertising for those products, and the cost of various media.

Operational planning, or planning for the issues of implementation, often accompanies strategic and tactical planning. The public works director of a small town must plan the monthly work schedules for the road crews she supervises. The shipping supervisor in a large manufacturing company must determine how often to schedule a third shift of workers. The

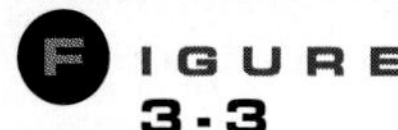

Types of Planning

Strategic	Long-term Focus on organization's mission Top executive involvement
Tactical	Medium-term Focus on organization's tactical objectives Middle-management involvement
Operational	Short-term Focus on implementation Middle-management or first-level supervisory involvement

program chairperson must schedule the particular events that compose the national meeting of the Academy of Management. In each case, these managers require an array of information about their subordinates, their clients, and their jobs to design the operational plan. What information does the public works director need, for example, to meet the objective of clearing snow within two hours of a snowfall? She needs to know the availability of crews and equipment, requirements for de-icing, and the possibility of additional snowfall.

All managers act as decision makers. James Orr, for example, determines his organization's goals and the strategy for accomplishing them. His subordinates make decisions about the number and types of employees necessary to accomplish the organization's goals. Marketing managers decide which insurance products the company should offer and at what price they should be sold. Managers at various levels determine the best way to reduce costs.

A manager determines the assignment of people to tasks, the allocation of money and materials to individuals, departments, and other work groups, and the scheduling of various organizational members' time. Effective allocation requires the manager to have information about individuals' existing work assignments, capabilities, and vacation schedules. The manager must also know the costs of various projects or products. He or she must understand the tradeoffs of various scheduling or budgeting alternatives. Consider the situation faced by the manager of a product development team for a new shampoo at Procter and Gamble. He or she must know how much overtime to budget into labor expenses to ensure a timely product launch.

PROCTER AND GAMBLE

Managers frequently negotiate with their subordinates or other managers about the allocation of resources or the best way to accomplish various group or organizational goals. What information, for example, should a manager have to handle his subordinate's complaint that he received an inadequate salary raise? The manager who negotiates the pay raise of a longtime employee needs information about current salary rates, the employee's performance, and industry pay standards to do a good job. The manager who serves on the negotiating team for a new labor contract should have information about the current contract, expected company performance, labor costs, competitors' labor agreements, both sides' bargaining ranges, and the union's wish list of demands. What specific information, for example, does the negotiator for management need when the head of the union's negotiating team calls for a strike within a week? Obviously, the particular negotiation determines the precise information required. Negotiators facing managers from countries outside the United States need specific information about how the cultural differences affect negotiating style,[9] the impact of variations in exchange rates, and acceptable standards in each country.

In conjunction with resource allocation and negotiation, the manager as a problem solver defines problems in a situation, analyzes them, and then proposes solutions. When the problems can be handled in a relatively long time frame, the manager acts as a change agent. When problems must be solved in a short time frame, the manager engages in disturbance handling.

To plan effectively, managers often need forecasts about likely future conditions. For example, they might need answers to questions such as the following: What will the prevailing interest rates be when we need our next infusion of cash? Will the new plant be finished and operating in time for the peak summer demand? How will the demand for our product change when our competitor's new product hits the market? Answers to questions such as these typically affect key decisions, and wrong choices could cost millions of dollars. For example, prevailing interest rates may affect whether a company should raise cash through the sale of debt or equity. The timing of a company's plant opening can affect whether the company will purchase a component of its product from a wholesaler or whether it will manufacture the component itself. The forecasted market share of a competitor's product should influence a company's production levels and possibly affect hiring and capacity decisions. No manager can be correct 100 percent of the time. Part of decision making involves assessing the risks of being wrong versus the rewards of being right. Managers may cushion the impact of incorrect foresight with contingency plans. Nevertheless, managers can increase their chances of correctly assessing future conditions by using quality forecasts.

Planning in organizations that function globally may pose special challenges. Managers may need to account for significant currency fluctuations, unpredictable political conditions, or an unknown labor pool; they may need to consider variations in national customs, worker expectations, and product acceptance. Consider the information needs of a manager who must close the company's manufacturing plants in Mexico. He or she must know, for example, the legal provisions that govern the sale of assets as well as the legal regulations for compensating terminated workers. The information needs of global managers in these circumstances are extensive and particular to the special business problems they must solve.

Decision making also involves significant information needs. Managers require information about individuals, groups, and organizations involved in or affected by the problem situation. They need information about the alternatives available and the costs and benefits associated with each. Managers as change agents also need data about workers' and management's attitudes toward change, the resources available for the change, and the consequences of similar changes in other situations. Managers should diagnose each decision situation to identify its unique information needs.

Consider the decision that a manufacturer of outdoor clothing must make about whether to purchase a small manufacturing plant in Taiwan. What information does the manufacturer require in order to make that decision? Now consider the decision that the head of social work services at a family services center must make about whether to add special adolescent counseling programs. What information does this manager need in order to make a quality decision? Managers must diagnose their information needs in each particular situation and then seek ways to obtain the required data.

Organizing

Managers must structure their organization and coordinate the organization's resources to accomplish its goals. **Organizing** generally means establishing a formal reporting structure and a system of accountability among workers; it means forming employees into meaningful work groups with appropriate supervision. Defining the hierarchy of authority, determining the location of decision making, and providing for coordination all contribute to the organizing process. First-line supervisors and middle managers generally establish a network

James Orr, Chairman and Chief Executive Officer of UNUM Corporation.

Courtesy of UNUM Corporation.

of contacts within and even outside the organization to gather information. The managers may use interactions with coworkers or colleagues in other organizations to improve their job performance.

Coordinating the activities of a group is a complex task shared by the manager and the group members. Middle managers at Unum, for example, must determine how to group employees into departments or work teams, how much authority to delegate to them, and what processes or activities to implement to best accomplish the organization's goals. Managers at all levels attempt to build effective work teams by encouraging cooperation and handling conflict that arises. Managing work groups generally calls for the open exchange of information and ideas. Managers and workers may jointly develop group goals congruent with organizational goals and orchestrate collaborative activities. Increasingly managers must supervise multicultural teams of workers; managing these heterogeneous groups requires special information about the impact of cultural differences on job performance and the techniques for handling them.

Managers need to know the status of group activities so that they can modify schedules and resource allocations. Group members must receive and share information about the status of their activities and thought processes. Organizing effectively requires information about the content of jobs, the skills of workers, and the availability of resources in the organization.

Managers must also understand the assets and liabilities of various structural forms, such as functional structures, project structures, alliances, or networks. The options for organizing become increasingly complex as managers deal internationally. Securing sufficient and appropriate information to coordinate globally challenges managers to diagnose their information needs effectively so that they do not obtain too much, too little, or irrelevant information. Chapter 4 addresses the needs associated with the organizing function in greater detail.

Leading

Leading generally refers to taking actions that direct and motivate employees to accomplish personal and organizational goals. Top executives, middle managers, and first-line supervisors help subordinates develop the skills, knowledge, materials, equipment, and time to perform their jobs. They offer guidance to subordinates about the best way to perform various job-related activities. Managers also evaluate their subordinates, and sometimes even peers and superiors, as part of their leadership responsibilities.

The manager acquires information about how individuals view the goals the manager has set and seeks information about what would encourage subordinates to accept these goals and work hard to achieve them. What information does a manager need to handle the problem of a poorly performing worker? The manager might need data about the employee's skill level and attitude, the job's requirements, and any job-related goals set. The manager might also need information about unusual factors, such as family illness or defective equipment, that might have affected the worker's performance. The manager might also need information about training programs in which the worker has participated. Subordinates also acquire information about how the manager perceives their efforts and adjust their performance and priorities accordingly. In many organizations, formal human resource management systems provide mechanisms for this feedback.

What types of information do managers require in order to lead effectively? They first need a clear understanding of the organization's goals and of their responsibilities for accomplishing them. They also benefit by having information about their boss's needs and goals. Managers need data about the skills, abilities, knowledge, needs, and experience of subordinates; they must also regularly secure information about their subordinates' performance. Managers must also have a comprehensive understanding of the situation to select the most appropriate leadership style for influencing workers to perform effectively. Researchers suggest that they need information about workers' needs and maturity, the leader's relationship with the subordinates, the task's structure, the organization's structure, and the organization's environment.[10]

What information needs are inherent in the interpersonal roles required for leading? Managers must know the nature of the tasks being performed, the expected standards of performance, and the potential barriers to their accomplishment. They must also have detailed information about the skills, experiences, and expectations of the workers they supervise. In addition, managers must have information about colleagues from whom they might gather information for the organization, listings of professional organizations, and data about colleagues employed by competitors. Effectively motivating and developing subordinates as well as influencing others and building relationships likely requires extensive situation-specific information that a manager should diagnose. Managers also should diagnose the information required to solve employee-related problems. Effectively leading a multicultural workforce creates both specific and generic information needs for managers functioning in the global arena.

Controlling

Managers must also monitor the quality and impact of managerial actions. **Controlling** means ensuring that performance meets established standards, that workers' activities occur as planned, and that the organization proceeds toward its established goals. Controlling requires comparative information about the optimal way to implement organizational processes and their actual implementation. In the control process, as shown in Figure 3-4, managers establish standards and methods for measuring performance, assess performance, and then compare performance with the standards. They require information about the organization's functioning to help them anticipate and handle organizational problems and challenges.

Managers commonly use information provided in budgets and financial controls to guide and constrain organizational activities. They also use cost information to maintain profitability. James Orr uses data about employee head count to ensure that labor costs fit with the company's goals. Managers use such information to take corrective actions that encourage goal attainment. The vice-president and controller of Boulevard Technical Services was hired to streamline information at Boulevard Bancorp in 1989.[11] He analyzed the organization's financial processes to ensure that standardized accounting processes existed for all banks in the organization and that employee's responsibilities were allocated to encourage maximum efficiency. This analysis led to a standardization of processes and software that resulted in

BOULEVARD TECHNICAL SERVICES

BOULEVARD BANCORP

FIGURE 3-4 The Control Process

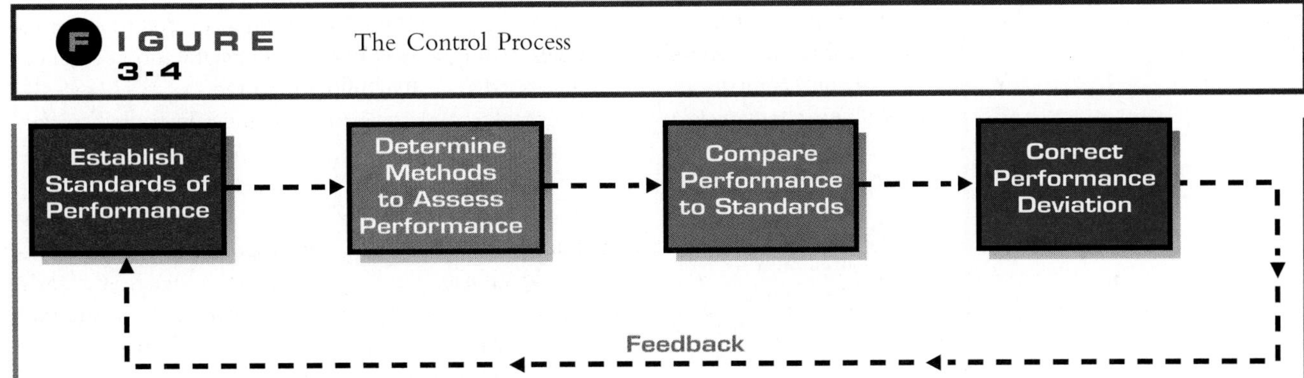

RUSSELL REYNOLDS ASSOCIATES

eliminating six days from the 20-day closing cycle. Executives at Russell Reynolds Associates, Inc., an executive search firm with offices worldwide, determined that top management required consistent and more detailed information from all offices. The director of international finance there led a design project that resulted in standard accounting procedures that conformed to U.S. and international regulations.[12] The discussion of accounting later in this chapter elaborates on the information needs related to the controlling function.

Functional Information Needs

Managers require a broad range of information to perform their day-to-day functional roles. Diagnosing information required to perform specific functional activities is an early step in effective information management. In this section we discuss examples of information needs in the areas of accounting, finance, marketing, engineering, operations, and human resource management; these functional areas are not intended to be exhaustive but to portray commonly occurring functional needs.

Accounting

Accounting is the process of recording, classifying, and summarizing the financial activities of an organization.[13] Originally used to create a historical record of the firm, managers now regularly use accounting information in making decisions. **Financial accounting** deals with preparing accounting information for users outside the organization, such as regulatory bodies, investors, shareholders, and tax assessors. **Managerial accounting** refers to the provision of financial information that managers within the organization need for their decision making. Accounts receivable, accounts payable, payroll, fixed asset management, and general ledger describe types of accounting information, as shown in Figure 3-5.

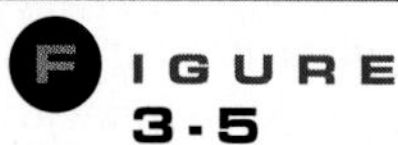

FIGURE 3-5 Types and Examples of Accounting Information

Accounts Receivable
- Names and addresses of customers
- Invoice information
  - Amounts owed
  - Due dates
  - Discounts available

Accounts Payable
- Names and addresses of suppliers
- Invoice information
  - Amounts owed
  - Due dates
  - Discounts available

Payroll
- Labor rates
- Hours worked
- Employee benefit classifications
- Withholding rates and amounts

Fixed Asset Management
- Properties owned
- Depreciation schedules
- Depreciation taken
- Mortgage/rental renewal dates

General Ledger
- Transaction type and amount
- Account codes affected
- Account balances

Managers working in the functional area of accounting must keep track of money owed to the organization. They require data about unpaid invoices, payments against these invoices, payment histories of customers, and additional credit information that helps managers decide how much credit to extend to customers. For companies such as utilities that have many customers and operate largely on credit, accounts receivable management is crucial not only for generating collections but also for addressing customer questions. **Accounts receivable systems** generally include such accounting information.

Managers in the accounting function must also monitor money owed by their organization. Such tracking requires detailed data about bills received from suppliers and other creditors as well as information necessary for approval of the payment of such bills. At many companies, for example, a supplier's bill must match an outstanding **purchase order,** which authorizes the purchase, and a **receiving document,** which verifies receipt of the purchased goods. Managers must also have access to information that helps them time payments, allowing them to benefit in the tradeoff between taking early-payment discounts and retaining sufficient cash in the organization. Managers also need information about checks written so that they can determine the amount still owed and respond to questions from suppliers. **Accounts payable systems** perform many of these functions for determining the money the organization owes to individuals or other organizations.

Accounting managers must also maintain and have access to employee information and tax information necessary to pay employees. James Orr specifically considered this information as critical to cost containment activities in his company. Accounting managers and staff must know employees' pay rates, deductions, tax withholdings, vacations, and hours worked so that the organization can generate payroll checks and forms for government taxing bodies.

Managers must also know the value of an organization's assets. Because many assets depreciate, or lose value, over time, the value of the organization that owns them will change as well; such changes typically have consequences for the price of stock in the company. In addition, organizations may keep funds that are used to renew or replenish the value of such assets; managers should know the availability of such funds. **Fixed asset systems** organize the information about a firm's assets and any funds maintained for their renewal.

Top executives, particularly the corporate controller, must have up-to-date information about the organization's profit or loss to help determine the company's financial worth. They must be able to classify expenses and revenues in ways that allow managers to attribute profits and losses to departments or individual products. **General ledger systems** use information generated by accounts payable, accounts receivable, payroll, and fixed asset systems to provide such profit and loss information. Managers also use the information generated by general ledger systems to plan their expenses and revenues for the future, a process called **budgeting.** Managers use budget information as part of their controlling activities, as described earlier in this chapter.

Managers in global organizations face peculiar information needs in their accounting practices because the relative value among the currencies of different countries changes constantly.[14] Managers may need access to data from uniquely international sources of information, such as bills of exchange. As a result, global accounting systems offer this information as well as information about the amount, nature, and origin of financial transactions. In addition to these generic information needs, accounting managers may have a set of needs specific to their job responsibilities and particular situations. Increasingly, managers require unique accounting information for various customer markets. At Johnson Wax, for example, managers in Johnson's Consumer Products Worldwide Innovation and Worldwide Service divisions discovered they needed information for their special financial environments.[15] Diagnosing these needs involves clearly specifying the problems or issues and the information required to deal with them.

JOHNSON WAX

Finance

Financial managers focus their activities on the acquisition and use of money. They periodically estimate the flow of funds into and out of the business, continuously monitor the use of funds within the organization, identify and evaluate alternative sources of outside funding, and describe and assess alternative uses of excess capital. Managers in global companies also use information about exchange rates and currency futures to keep their cash and other assets in countries where they have the greatest return or the least depreciation. Figure 3-6 illustrates types and examples of information financial managers use.

Managers use financial information for both planning and control. They need to know the financial position of their company before they can make decisions about how to allocate financial resources. They create budgets for each function of the company based on such factors as the company's financial status, the history of spending in prior years, operational plans and priorities, forecasts of revenue, and projections of cash flow. At the departmental level, first-line supervisors or middle managers create budgets in a similar fashion; senior management then uses the departmental budgets in its development of a corporate budget; departmental managers, in turn, modify their original budgets to reflect the parameters of the corporate budget. In the General Foods' Corporate Financial Planning and Control department, for example, managers supervised analysts who used microcomputers to consolidate financial data from 17 worldwide divisions and then report the data to upper management for its use.[16] Reebok, Inc. wants to shorten the time required for closing its books so that the finance department can spend more time in data analysis for managerial improvements.[17]

GENERAL FOODS

REEBOK

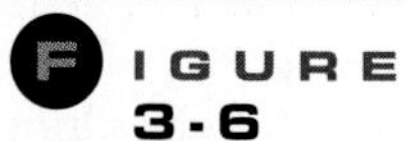

FIGURE 3-6 Types and Examples of Information Used in Managing the Financial Function

Budgeting
- Prior uses of funds
- Projected need for funds
- Availability of funds

Investment
- Short- and long-term cash needs
- Projections of cash availability
- Expected risk and return in security instruments

Securitization
- Company's bond rating
- Short- and long-term cash needs and availability
- Recent trends in stock offerings
- Laws and regulations regarding financial instruments

Hedging
- Stability in prices of key suppliers
- Risk in factors affecting price of company's product
- Margin requirements
- Market premium to protect price of supply or output

Foreign Exchange
- Exchange rates
- Foreign investment market returns

Managers must also constantly monitor the flow and allocation of expenses and income to identify potential deviations from the budgeted plan. James Orr, for example, might want to know how corporate labor expenses compare with the budget; or he might want to compare actual with projected sales revenues. This monitoring identifies and minimizes potential financial problems; it also flags potential problems with operations, marketing, quality, employee performance, or other factors that may affect the company's ability to implement its plans.

Analytical computer systems support diverse types of investment management.[18] Portfolio accounting systems provide both inventories and analyses of diverse types of assets. Financial managers must continuously diagnose the specific information they require for performing their job responsibilities and dealing with problem situations.

Marketing

Marketing is a social process involving the activities necessary to enable individuals and organizations to obtain the products and services they need and want through exchanges with others.[19] The concept of marketing derives from the idea of a marketplace where buyers and sellers meet to trade their goods and services for money or other goods and services. Marketing managers seek to ascertain consumers' needs and preferences. This knowledge helps them guide product development, distribution, pricing, presentation, and promotion so as to maximize the appeal to the consumer of an organization's products and services. Marketing managers also use sales information to improve interactions with suppliers as well as monitor business performance.[20] Marketing activities that offer potential for decision support systems include sales forecasting, budgeting, pricing, and product design.[21] Figure 3-7 presents examples of information used by the marketing function.

Market research is the process of gathering information about what consumers want and need. Marketing managers and their market research staff monitor what consumers buy; relate buying patterns to consumer characteristics such as income, family size, and geographic location; conduct surveys about hypothetical or real products; and test consumer responses to price, packaging, or other product or service characteristics. Managers can also purchase market research information from market research firms. For example, Nielsen, a division of Dunn & Bradstreet, and the Arbitron Company sell information about what consumers watch on television; such information can help managers decide whether to purchase air time to advertise a particular product. Managers also use information generated by market research to support product design and manufacturing decisions, as described later in this chapter.

NIELSEN

ARBITRON

Marketing may include additional activities, such as planning and budgeting for advertising, participating in product design, and forecasting future trends. Each of these has associated information needs. Marketing managers must diagnose the information they need to handle particular marketing problems. For example, marketing managers at General Mills need information about the cost and impact of various media to determine the components of an advertising campaign for Cheerios; they may need demographic information about consumers to determine whether to show television ads during the Superbowl or a weekday soap opera.

GENERAL MILLS

Engineering

As shown in Figure 3-8, information used for engineering includes product specifications; engineering designs or drawings; data concerning the physical, chemical, and electrical characteristics of materials; inputs and outputs of models that evaluate alternative designs; and blueprints for manufacturing. In a typical engineering environment, design groups work on different aspects of a common product.[22] Each design group may develop multiple designs

FIGURE 3-7 Types and Examples of Marketing Information

Market Research
- Product evaluation surveys
- Results of test market promotions
- Coupon usage data
- Lists of consumers of related products

Promotion
- Impact of past advertising promotions
- Price of advertising by medium
- Impact of shelf space and placement
- Sales and rebates offered by competitors

Pricing
- Impact of price and volume changes on profit
- Price elasticity of product
- Price/performance curves for similar products
- Market segmentation information

Product Design
- Engineering drawings and mock-ups
- Packaging alternatives

Distribution Channel Development
- Relationships with distributors
- Franchising laws and regulations

Market Intelligence
- Competitors' activities and strategies
- Information about new and existing products

so that a range of alternatives can be evaluated. In addition, as the design team combines the results of individual groups, the designs may undergo further modifications. Design group managers require technical information about product components and marketing information about customer requirements.

GENERAL MOTORS

NORTHROP

Modern management practices require designers and manufacturing managers to share information. Using this approach, for example, contributed to General Motors shaving its product-development time for the 1992 Buick LeSabre from 49 months to 34 months.[23] Similarly, Northrop's management found that using such collaboration could reduce the number of engineering changes by 70 percent and decrease both labor costs and the time between design and production by between 30 and 50 percent.[24]

BELLCORE

In most organizations, product engineering and design precede planning for manufacturing the product. Note, however, that some organizations have a separate research and development department whose activities accompany or even precede those of engineering and design by focusing on the original development of new products and processes. Bellcore, the research and development arm of the seven telephone holding companies, required information that would result in faster product development; to do this the president of Bellcore reduced bureaucracy, sped up decision making, improved quality, and instituted more information sciences research.[25]

Manufacturing managers need information in the engineering designs to plan the avail-

Examples of Engineering Information

Product Specifications
- Performance requirements
- Weight and shape (dimensions)

Engineering Drawings
- Part requirements
- Alternative component replacements
- Assembly implications

Material Properties
- Physical—hardness, strength, malleability, color
- Chemical—toxicity, reactivity
- Electrical—resistance, capacitance, inductance

Prototype/Simulation Information
- Conformance to specifications
- Market reaction
- Manufacturing cost estimation

Manufacturing Blueprints
- Estimates of component and assembly costs
- Machine time requirements
- Staffing requirements

MARTIN MARIETTA

NYPRO

ability of parts and materials, to design and schedule processes for materials handling, and to schedule production. However, when engineering is completed before the manufacturing plan is developed, the engineering designs may be more difficult or unreliable to manufacture than designs differing in minor ways. Increasingly, engineering and manufacturing are joining in concurrent or simultaneous engineering, which reduces or eliminates walls between the two functions.[26] This collaboration alters the information needs of all involved; it requires giving engineering and manufacturing personnel access to design, financial, marketing, and manufacturing data. Martin Marietta Aero and Naval Systems division, for example, uses teams of design, manufacturing, procurement, product support, and quality managers who share computerized product design.[27] Nypro, Inc., a precision injection molder, includes both customers and manufacturing on management teams and shares manufacturing process information with all team members so that they instantly know the quality of products and can modify processes as required.[28]

Operations

Operations management refers to the processes of planning, organizing, directing, and controlling the physical operations of an organization. By operations, we mean the transformation of an organization's resources into the goods and services that are its sources of revenue. Operations can encompass both manufacturing and the provision of services. Manufacturing managers need information that will allow them to integrate manufacturing with customer service and sales, control systems, back-office operations, and engineering.[29] For example, systems that take electronic orders and use them to automatically trigger the manufacturing process will become much more common. Increasingly, manufacturing also

Boeing introduced design/build teams that accelerated the design and manufacturing of the Boeing 757 aircraft. Information systems helped support this collaboration.

Tony Stone Images © Matthew McVay.

requires information to incorporate into quality programs. Other systems integrate engineering data into the management process.

The physical operations of a manufacturing organization include not only the manufacturing process, but also the processes of transporting and warehousing and the process in which finished goods or services are exchanged for money. The factory of the future may combine services with products, causing manufacturing managers to have more direct contact with customers.[30] This contact will expand their information requirements to include data about customers and their needs. Group Technologies, a maker of electronic components in Tampa, requires weekly updating of customer requirements and uses these to effectively schedule production facilities.[31] The physical operations of retail service organizations include most of the same processes except that manufacturing is replaced by product acquisition. For service organizations that deal primarily in information, such as law and accounting firms, the physical processes relate to acquiring information, assembling it into the proper form, and presenting it to the client. Despite these differences, the major components of operations management and associated information needs are alike, as listed in Figure 3-9.

GROUP TECHNOLOGIES

Transaction processing describes the recording and filing of data about a company's transactions and serves as a source of much of a company's internally generated information. It can be a major component of the operations function, although it can exist in other functional areas as well. A **transaction** describes a business event such as the sale of a product, receipt of a payment, hiring of an employee, or taking of a reservation. Hospitals process transactions as part of their system for charging for medical coverage; in one case, switching to a diagnosis-related reimbursement (DRG) system called for acquiring and processing new information about a patient's illness and treatment.[32]

Managers require information about transactions for several reasons. First, a transaction may affect the company's income statement or balance sheet. Laws in the United States and abroad require such financial information as an audit trail to support a business's tax statements and to account properly to the business's stockholders and investors. Second, managers use information about transactions in making marketing, financial, production, and human resource decisions. For example, managers seek information about customers' payments because the payments affect the company's cash position, which, in turn, influences the schedule of payments to suppliers as well as the company's credit decisions. Managers need infor-

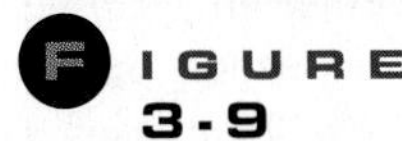
FIGURE 3-9 Components of Operations Management and Examples of Their Information Needs and Uses

Transaction Processing
Feeds information to all management functions

Product and Service Planning and Design
Product costs
Product prototypes
Engineering options

Capacity Planning
Loading dock space
Warehouse shelf space
Machine throughput rates
Forecasted production requirements

Process Design
Facility layout
Machine set-up time
Machine reliability
Forecasted production requirements

Scheduling
Staff expertise
Forecasted production requirements
Equipment maintenance schedules

Inventory Control
Current inventory levels by product and location
Holding costs: space, insurance, and capital
Implications of stock-out
Status of back-orders

Quality Control
Product specifications
Physical and operational measurements on product
Testing equipment technology

mation about hiring because it affects the organization's payroll, work schedule, production capacity estimates, and subsequent hiring decisions.

Low-level managers often secure information from transaction processing in making routine decisions. Consider, for example, a hotel manager who faces an irate customer claiming to have a reservation that the desk clerk cannot find. What information does the manager require to solve the customer's problem? The manager needs information about the hotel's bookings and the customer's record. Learning that the penthouse suite is unused and that the customer is a frequent guest, the manager might decide to offer the customer the suite at the price of the discount room.

Product and service planning and design generate ideas, test them for feasibility, and finalize them into the design of a product or service. Feasibility analysis typically requires the input and review of managers at various levels and specialties throughout the company. For example, the managers explore the financial, marketing, and distribution implications as well as available capacity, physical resources, and financial resources to bring the plan to market. At this stage, the ability to share information is critical. Also, productivity can be increased if designers and analysts can incrementally modify the designs without re-entering them.

Capacity planning refers to the process of determining how much to produce in the short and long term. It requires information about demand and available organizational resources for meeting the demand. Managers must translate the capacity decision into specific requirements for raw inputs, employee time, and machine time. Capacity planning often uses sophisticated models of the relationship between capacity needs and forecasts as well as sensitivity analyses on the assumptions used to make capacity decisions.

Process design involves identifying the technologies to be used in producing the product or service; selecting specific equipment, software, and so on to be used in production; specifying how the product or service should flow through the production system; selecting facilities and locations where the product is to be manufactured or the services rendered; making decisions about how to lay out the facilities to maximize throughput and minimize nonproductive activities; and designing the jobs that need to be performed in carrying out production plans. Managers secure much of the information needed to perform these tasks from outside the company, for example, from trade literature or vendors. In making decisions on the location of facilities, operations managers use information from market studies or data about transportation costs. Work flow, layout, and job design decisions require the knowledge of experts who have designed the same or similar processes at other locations or companies in the past.

Scheduling involves the process of matching equipment and employees to work processes. Inputs to scheduling include process flow; equipment needs; personnel availability, expertise, and preferences; and information about constraints such as those relating to work rules, safety, equipment, and maintenance. Managers must have information to schedule multiple orders through sequential manufacturing processes. To do this scheduling, they must determine the availability of equipment and materials resources, including their location, applicability for multiple use, and prior commitments or schedules. They must be able to prioritize objectives such as minimizing costs and time, providing inventory as required, and encouraging total quality.[33]

Inventory control is the management of raw materials, partially completed goods and services, and completed but unshipped goods. Ideally, to minimize inventory carrying costs, managers maintain only an inventory sufficient for completing the final product. Operations managers must know current levels of inventory, the rate at which inventory can be replenished, and the rate at which inventory is depleted to control inventory size and costs. Purchasing managers at retail chains such as Toys "R" Us use inventory information from all stores to determine the size of additional toy orders.[34] How can the purchasing manager assist a store manager whose customers complain that an item is regularly out of stock? The purchasing manager can check inventory information to determine the item's availability in other stores, its anticipated arrival date, and whether it regularly goes out of stock.

TOYS "R" US

Quality control manages each stage of the production process to minimize or eliminate defects and errors. Effective quality control includes carefully monitoring the production or service processes. Managers need information for quickly identifying problems or defects, proposing solutions, and implementing corrections. In manufacturing, equipment operators and their managers also need to monitor and detect problems with the manufacturing process quickly and easily. They need enough information to solve minor problems quickly and autonomously without calling on engineers or other personnel for assistance. Manufacturing managers also need information to identify and solve recurring problems.[35] What information do they need to solve the problem of an assembly line with more down-time than up-time? What information do they need to reduce the number of defects due to a faulty soldering joint? Diagnosis of information to solve specific problems is key to effective information management.

Human Resources

Human resource management refers to the deployment, development, assessment, rewarding, and management of individual organizational members and worker groups. The functions of human resource management include planning, staffing, training and development, performance management, compensation, labor–management relations, and administration, as shown in Figure 3-10. Human resource managers engage in the design of organization systems to perform these functions; they assist line managers with implementing the human resource policies, programs, and practices.

Human resource planning involves determining the demand and supply for various categories of workers. James Orr wanted a daily count of the number of employees in his organization; he could compare this supply with the requirements for workers to do various

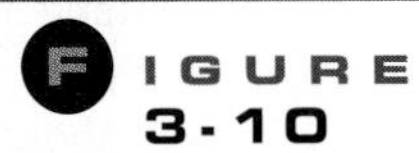

Human Resource Functions and Examples of Their Information Needs and Uses

Human Resource Planning
- Market rates and availability of types of labor
- Forecasts of staffing needs
- Position descriptions

Staffing
- Résumés of prospective employees
- Position descriptions
- Evaluation criteria

Training and Development
- Employee skills and credentials
- Position skill and credential requirements
- Availability of training staff and facilities
- Costs of outside training services
- Training materials

Performance Management
- Evaluations of past performance
- Objectives for future performance

Compensation
- Industry and organizational wage levels
- Federal and state tax regulations
- Insurance costs and options

Labor-Management Relations
- Grievance procedures
- Industry and organizational wage levels
- Industry and organizational productivity

Administrative
- Affirmative action plans and targets
- Safety and health procedures
- Government-requested information

jobs before making downsizing decisions. Effective planning also requires information about other potential sources of workers, such as high schools, colleges, and competitors.

Staffing describes the recruiting and selecting of individuals for job positions. **Recruiting** requires communicating information about job openings and the organization to those best qualified for the positions. National Semiconductor Corp. offers employees extensive information about job openings: Employees can review job openings by job code, title, division, department, location, or posting date; they can screen openings for required qualifications; and then they can enter their names, qualifications, and desired positions if they want an internal transfer.[36] **Selection** involves matching job candidates to job openings. This process passes detailed information about the position to the applicant and information about the applicant to the hiring manager, often through a human resource professional who screens applicants. Coors, for example, increases the availability of such information with a computerized system.[37] The hiring managers enter the requirements of the job and their relative importance into a computer system. A human resource manager rates applicants on each requirement based on history and skill. The computer then generates a screening list. The hiring manager interviews applicants from this list and adds to and updates the ratings.

NATIONAL SEMICONDUCTOR

COORS

Training and development addresses deficiencies in skills, knowledge, or experience required for quality job performance or advancement in the organization. Managers must assess individuals' training needs, determine the training opportunities and programs available to meet these needs, and choose the training options that best address the workers' needs. Managers require extensive information about workers' skills, abilities, knowledge, job requirements, and training programs already undertaken. When a manager encounters a poorly performing worker, the manager might wish to know whether the worker participated in any training programs to help assess the causes of the performance problem.

Performance management involves providing evaluation data for administrative and training decisions and development activities. Managers assess past performance and offer ways to improve it in the future. They may use observations, behavior checklists, or output measures as part of the appraisal. They provide counseling and discuss job opportunities as part of development. Data about an individual's actions, results, and attitudes, as well as about his or her job's requirements and goals are essential information for performance management. Managers use information collected in the appraisal for making staffing, training and development, and compensation decisions.

Compensation design and administration includes determining wages, benefits, and other forms of compensation, such as bonuses or stock options. Effective compensation management requires information about industry and organization wage levels as well as job and individual characteristics. In designing compensation programs, human resource managers must also know federal tax regulations and other relevant legislation. This information can help answer questions such as whether the company should offer a flexible benefits program, whether it should introduce on-site day care, or whether it should offer one-time bonuses or salary increases for good performance. In global organizations managers must know the differences in currency rates, living conditions, and expectations about compensation in countries throughout the world. A manager who has difficulty finding employees willing to work abroad for two years may need information to assess whether the compensation package provides enough incentives for the relocation.

The term **labor-management relations** typically refers to the interaction between union and management. This area of human resource management comprises unionization, collective bargaining, and dispute resolution. Human resource managers often lobby against unionization and, if unsuccessful, participate in labor negotiations. They often oversee organizational grievance procedures and serve as a resource to other managers about the provisions of the union contract. Implementing these responsibilities effectively requires both historical and current information about union members and contract provisions.

Administrative responsibilities involve monitoring and keeping records of the functions described so far. Human resource professionals track affirmative action plans and targets. They monitor the implementation and effectiveness of safety and health procedures. They also provide information requested by various government agencies to check compliance with local, state, and federal regulations.

Human resource management in a global environment adds additional information needs. Human resource managers must have cross-cultural information about the various human resource functions as well as detailed knowledge of practices in various countries or regions. They must understand the needs of diverse types of workers and translate this understanding into effective policies. Finally, they must effectively diagnose their specific information needs so that they can propose quality programs that respond to the requirements of a multinational and multicultural work force. Increasingly, human resource managers have required comprehensive, feature-rich information systems that allow information to be used for and support interfaces among multiple functions. Eventually human resource information systems may become an integral part of the administration of each part of the human resource function.[38]

Managers and Information Systems

Managers must determine the best way to acquire, monitor, and retain the information they need. They must find whether the information already exists in the organization and, if so, who controls it. If the organization does not have the information, the managers must determine who should collect it and identify reasonable sources. Finally, they must determine whether the information is or should be computerized. This section provides a brief overview of managers' use of the four-step process; subsequent chapters provide a more extensive discussion of managers' use of information systems.

Diagnosing Information Needs

Although managers are ultimately responsible for determining their own information needs, few are trained to specify their needs in a rigorous and comprehensive way. Information specialists trained in systems analysis and design (see Chapter 13) can help managers clarify their information needs. For example, a pricing manager at a company that manufactures industrial scales might ask for a report showing the number and dollar amount of sales of a particular model in a given period. An information specialist could help the manager clarify whether the term *sold in the period* means contracted for in that period, shipped in that period, received by the customer in that period, or paid for in that period. The specialist might alert the manager to the fact that sales could be gross, adjusted for anticipated returns, or adjusted to reflect actual returns, and that sales dollars might be before or after discount and before or after rebates (on promotional sales). He or she might also alert the manager to the possibility of accounting for foreign sales at the internal transfer price set for foreign subsidiaries, the price delivered to the customer converted to U.S. dollars at time of sale, or the price delivered to the customer converted to U.S. dollars at the time of payment. Because the manager probably receives other reports showing similar or related data, it might be important to present the information in such a way that it can properly be compared.

After the manager ascertains precisely what information is wanted, he or she will also need to decide how often, in what format, and in what medium the information should be delivered. If new information must be collected, the manager needs to determine whether or not the benefit of collecting such information outweighs its cost. It is difficult to make such an assessment in isolation. Managers tend to underestimate the cross-functional application of information that they generate or for which they are the primary user. As a result, they underestimate the value to the organization of information systems that would make their information available to the organization at large. Martin Marietta Aero and Naval Systems division assigns an IS specialist to all new project teams and requires the specialist to develop appropriate hardware and software immediately after winning a contract. The use of automated systems has contributed to Martin Marietta's ability to bid 20 to 30 percent lower because of less waste in manufacturing.[39]

MARTIN MARIETTA

At high levels in the organizational hierarchy, the information needs of managers cannot be defined according to content. Typically, information required by executives varies dramatically from day to day. As a result, executives often find that they must define their information needs broadly and in terms of process rather than content. For example, one information need might be the ability to observe a trend in the sales of any product by region over any period of time, to extract such data into a spreadsheet, and to extrapolate trends using one of several prespecified trend-analysis techniques. Another information need might be the ability to screen the news wire services for any information about competitors and/or suppliers. Needs such as these are difficult to communicate, in part because of their lack of specificity and in part because they are both limited and driven by technology. Chapter 11 addresses how executive information systems offer flexibility in meeting the needs of high-level managers.

Applying Information Technology

Dramatic improvements in technology during the past two decades have resulted in the computerization of much of the information managers require and use in their jobs. Still, some managers actively resist computerization. Managers may fear that computers will mechanize and standardize their activities and procedures, giving the managers less control and possibly a weaker understanding of the business processes they manage. They may believe that previously made decisions will become embedded in computer code, again reducing their control over them. When conditions change, the managers will expect to lose their ability to change the way decisions are made and perhaps even to recognize that change is needed.[40] Managers may also fear that computerization will change the content and skill requirements of their work. They may think that computerization of information will decrease their focus on the management of human resources. Chapter 11 dispels this myth in its discussion of management information systems.

Computers can effectively increase the coordination of group activities. Electronic communication systems reduce the effect of distance and permit one-way conversation when the intended recipient is not available. Computer-mediated communication has been shown to increase the number of links among organizational members and increase the number of messages exchanged among people who already communicated with one another.[41] Groupware (see Chapter 11) offers an effective technical solution to the problem of coordinating group activities. Project management systems (see Chapter 11) also provide such coordination as well as offer the capability to allocate resources at a project's inception. Some redundancy in information technology may be necessary in order to deal with legal and cultural differences encountered in different countries by multinational companies.[42]

Computers can promote effective leadership by opening channels for communication between managers and their subordinates. In particular, subordinates tend to feel less inhibited when corresponding with managers over a computer message system than they do when talking to managers in person.[43] The culture and protocol in many organizations tend to prohibit employees from entering a vice-president's office for an informal conversation but permit and even encourage speaking through electronic messages.[44] At Microsoft, CEO Bill Gates receives and responds to dozens of electronic messages every day from employees throughout the company.[45] Global managers find electronic messaging an important means of facilitating communication worldwide.

MICROSOFT

Interactions with Information Systems Professionals

Information systems (IS) professionals can help managers locate the information they require to do their jobs. Often IS professionals have access to or control of computerized information that can boost managerial job performance, but control over information and the systems that process it can create potential conflict between managers and IS professionals. They may disagree, for example, about the goals and time frames of systems development.[46] Multinational companies with centralized information systems development often experience this problem. Both distance and cultural differences may make it difficult for a programmer in New York to respond appropriately to a marketing manager in New Delhi, but improved electronic communication (see Chapter 8) has allowed such programmers and managers to work more closely.

The increasing presence of personal computers in the business environment has changed the relationship between the manager and the IS professional. More managers are becoming computer users and gaining appreciation of the degree to which computers can help meet their information needs. Also, more managers are taking control of their own information, either personally on their computers or with systems developed by IS professionals under the managers' direction and control. This decentralization of application development has made it more difficult to control and realize the organizational benefits of information sharing.

Summary

Managers at all levels in an organization have significant information needs. *Management* refers to the process of achieving organizational goals by planning, organizing, leading, and controlling organizational resources. Managers in a global setting face a dynamic and unpredictable environment that results in less-than-perfect information. They must learn to function effectively with less-than-optimal information and continually try to improve the quality of their information.

Top-, middle-, and first-line supervisors have special information concerns. Executives require information to help them focus on formulating the organization's overall direction. Middle managers use information in implementing the organization's strategies and policies. First-level supervisors use information to conduct their daily activities.

Managers at all levels engage in planning, organizing, leading, and controlling. These managers require information to conduct strategic, tactical, and operational planning as well as to make decisions. They also use information in implementing the formal reporting structure and system of accountability among workers as well as in coordinating the activities of a group. In their role as leaders, managers use information to help direct and motivate employees to accomplish personal and organizational goals. They require an array of information to serve as negotiators, problem solvers, disturbance handlers, and liaisons. Managers also use information to monitor the quality and impact of their actions. For example, they use information provided in budgets and financial reports to guide organizational activities.

Managers also require a broad range of information to perform their daily activities. Information needs exist in the areas of accounting, finance, marketing, engineering, operations, and human resource management. These needs apply at all levels of management.

Managers use information systems to help them acquire, monitor, and retain the information they need. They first diagnose their information needs and then evaluate existing systems to determine how well those systems meet these needs. Often working in a team with information systems professionals, managers help develop improved systems that provide them with the information they need. Dramatic advances in technology have resulted in the computerization of much of the information managers require to perform their jobs effectively and make effective decisions.

Key Terms

Accounting
Accounts payable system
Accounts receivable system
Budgeting
Capacity planning
Compensation design and administration
Controlling
Financial accounting
Fixed asset system
General ledger system
Human resource management
Human resource planning
Inventory control
Labor–management relations
Leading
Managerial accounting
Market research
Marketing
Operational planning
Operations management
Organizing
Performance management
Planning
Process design
Product and service planning and design
Project manager
Purchase order
Quality control
Receiving document
Recruiting
Scheduling
Selection
Staffing
Strategic plan
Strategic planning
Tactical objective
Tactical plan
Tactical planning
Training and development
Transaction
Transaction processing

Review Questions

1. Describe the use of information by global managers.
2. Compare and contrast the information needs of top-, middle-, and lower-level managers.
3. Describe the use of information in performing the classic management functions of planning, organizing, leading, and controlling.

4. Describe the differences among strategic, tactical, and operational planning. How do information needs differ among these three types of planning? How are they alike?
5. What are the unique information needs for managers planning in a global environment?
6. What types of information do managers need to lead effectively?
7. Describe the control process. What is the role of information in enabling managerial control?
8. What type of functional information is needed by managers responsible for accounting? What unique information needs are faced by accounting professionals in global organizations?
9. What type of functional information is needed by marketing managers?
10. What are the components of operations management? What type of functional information is needed for operations management?
11. What is a transaction? What is meant by *transaction processing?*
12. How should a manager be involved in diagnosing his or her information needs?
13. Describe the difference in the information needs of higher- versus lower-level managers in terms of content and process.
14. How can computers increase the coordination of group activities?
15. Describe the interactions of managers and information systems professionals.
16. How has the increasing presence of personal computers in the business environment changed the relationship between managers and IS professionals?

MINICASE

Ocean Spray Cranberries: Information Needs of the Marketer

If Jim Labelle could tear himself away from his spreadsheet, he might enjoy watching the cranberry harvest underway in a flooded bog just outside his office.

But Labelle, an assistant brand manager at Ocean Spray Cranberries, Inc.'s headquarters in Lakeville, Massachusetts, is occupied with a different kind of harvest. As the all-important holiday season draws near, he and his marketing colleagues must wade through a sea of data on sales, shipments and spending—and make snap decisions on the four P's of marketing: promotion, pricing, placement, and product mix.

While some marketers seldom even power-on their desktop PCs, a new breed of computer-savvy marketing managers like Labelle is sweeping into the consumer packaged-goods industry. These are quantitative jocks, mostly thirty-something MBA graduates, who are not afraid to test their marketing hypotheses rigorously with regression analysis.

"Some people think we spend all our time doing creative stuff like reviewing ad copy," Labelle says, "but I'm basically a number cruncher. My mind is on things like, 'What was our incremental lift from that promotion we ran in Buffalo last month?'"

To assist this important group of users, corporate information systems groups are busy building a new generation of marketing decision-support systems—along with databases that integrate [billions of bits] of syndicated scanner data with internal information on costs, shipments and consumers. According to Howard Dresner, a research director at Gartner Group, Inc., "business-intelligence systems for marketing are one of the hottest application areas today. They're the Holy Grail for marketing-driven companies."

Gordon Armstrong, a marketing scientist who serves as a liaison between marketing and IS at Ocean Spray helped to create such a system. Based on a prototype developed by Pro-

---

SOURCE: Brian McWilliams, Delighting the marketer? *Computerworld* (November 14, 1994): 129–133.

fessor John M. McCann at Duke University, a spreadsheet-based intelligent agent automates the repetitive task of assessing and reporting on the impact of promotions. McCann says, "The value of information comes from looking at very fine levels of detail and seeing what you can learn at the point of action to improve yourself. Then you have to do that every week for every retailer and for every brand item that you have."

Case Questions

1. What information do marketing managers at Ocean Spray need in order to perform their jobs?
2. How do computers at Ocean Spray help marketing managers analyze their data?

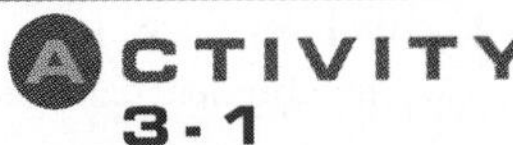

Managerial Activities Analysis

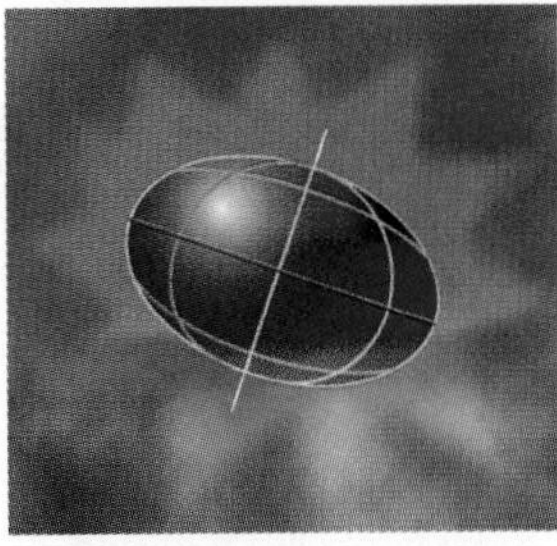

external contact

STEP 1: Review the excerpt of the daily work diary shown in Figure 3-11 of Joseph Michaelson's morning. Michaelson is the plant manager for one of five plants of a large manufacturer that produces and sells components for computers. The plant operates 24 hours, seven days a week.

STEP 2: For each activity performed, record the information the manager used during that activity as follows:

Activity	Information Used

STEP 3: Now select a manager to interview. Ask him or her to describe in detail two or three activities he or she performed during the previous workday. Then ask the manager to tell you what information was required to perform these activities. Ask the manager what additional information he or she needed to perform the activities more effectively.

STEP 4: Answer the following questions, in small groups or with the entire class:

1. Which activities did the managers perform?
2. What information did the managers use during those activities?
3. How did the managers secure the needed information?
4. What additional information did the managers require to perform the activities more effectively?
5. What recommendations would you offer for improving the acquisition and use of information by the managers? ●

FIGURE 3-11 Some Activities from Joseph Michaelson's Morning

8:00	Joseph meets the night supervisor for their daily meeting. They discuss the production runs during the previous night, problems with staffing, and plans for tonight's runs.
8:30	Joseph runs into the plant's human resource representative at the coffee machine. They discuss some new federal regulations that affect their plans for hiring temporary workers.
8:40	Joseph receives a telephone call from the corporate accounting department. He has been meeting regularly with a representative from accounting to discuss new ways of accounting for unused inventory. They chat for 20 minutes about the project as well as exchange some corporate gossip.
9:00	Joseph meets with the five people who report directly to him to review their plans for the week. They spend much of the meeting discussing their plans for increasing the number of self-managing work teams on the plant floor. They also spend some time talking about problems they are having with machining several key parts.
10:00	Joseph participates in a conference call with the four other plant managers to discuss the installation of some new assembly-line technology on the plant floor.
10:30	Joseph completes the paperwork for the performance evaluations of his subordinates that he performed over the past two weeks.
11:00	Joseph meets with two newly hired team leaders to welcome them to the plant.
11:15	Joseph speaks at length with a vendor who has been providing problem parts for use in one of the computer components. Together they discuss ways of solving the problem and schedule another telephone conversation for the next day.
11:30	Joseph takes his daily walk about the plant, speaking with about 30 workers on the floor.

ACTIVITY 3-2 Fine Leather Stores

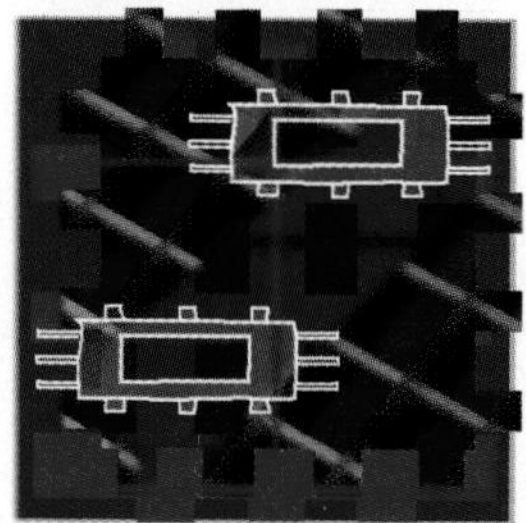

short case

STEP 1: Read the following scenario.

The owner of a chain of five leather goods stores has decided to install a computerized information system to support the accounting, sales, operations, and human resource functions for the stores. Located in small suburban shopping centers, these stores carry an assortment of luggage, briefcases, wallets, and other leather products as well as travel accessories and small electronic products. So far, each store in the chain has operated independently, with a single personal computer to support store functions at the manager's discretion. Some stores use it to record transactions; others maintain inventory records on it; still others use it for primitive payroll systems.

STEP 2: Individually or in small groups, diagnose the situation. List the types of information each store manager requires.

STEP 3: In small groups or with the entire class, share the lists you have developed. Then prepare a comprehensive list of information after answering the following questions:

1. What elements do these lists have in common?
2. What information has been omitted from the lists?
3. Which information can be part of a computerized information system? ●

ACTIVITY 3-3 What Information is Needed?

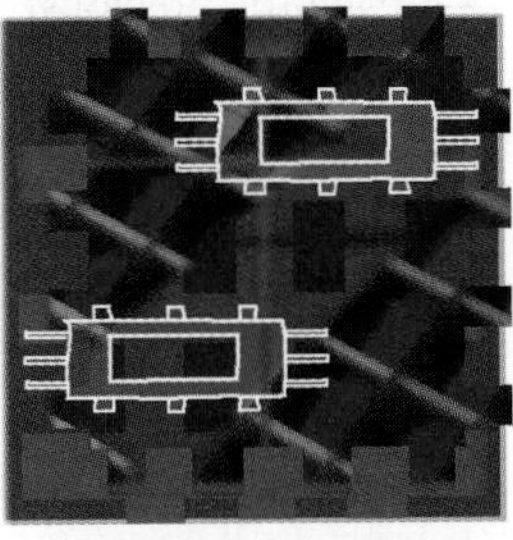

short case

STEP 1: Read each managerial problem below. For each situation, decide what information the manager needs to solve the problem.

Problem I: The manager of benefits in a moderate-size manufacturing company has just received four complaints from employees who state that their retirement accounts have not been properly credited for the third quarter in a row. What information does the manager need to ensure the correct assignment of monies?

Problem II: The owner of a chain of five ice cream stores has just spoken with one of his managers about an ongoing supply problem. The manager noted that a large number of comments in his customer suggestion box were complaints that the store was out of stock of the flavor of ice cream the customer wanted to purchase. Although such complaints do not seem to have affected sales yet, the manager is afraid that he will soon lose valuable customers to a competing chain. What information do the manager and the owner need to ensure the correct supply of ice cream to each store?

Problem III: As the project manager of a major audit, you are responsible for allocating the work to the various associates working on the project. You have heard one of the associates complaining that you play favorites in assigning tasks; she complained that the male associates get the more visible tasks that require fewer hours to complete. You do not believe that you discriminate in this way. What information do you need to refute this charge?

STEP 2: For each situation, describe two ways the manager could secure the information he or she requires.

STEP 3: Individually, in small groups, or with the entire class, answer the following questions:

1. What types of information needs do managers have?
2. How can they secure the information they require?
3. What role can information systems play in providing the needed information? ●

ACTIVITY 3-4 Middlebrook Hospital

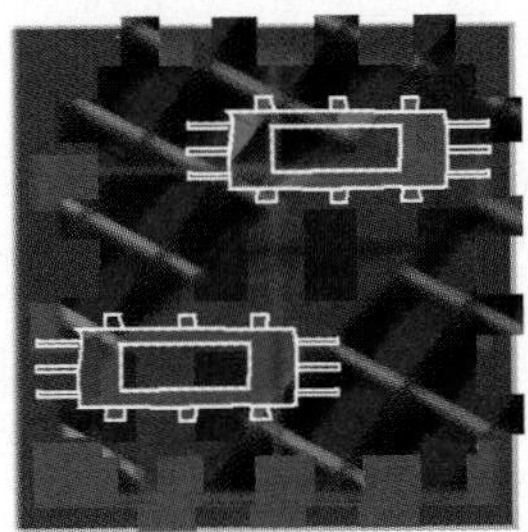

short case

STEP 1: Read the Middlebrook Hospital case.

Mrs. Scott, the Pediatric nursing unit head at Middlebrook Hospital in Hamilton, Ontario, noted a communication breakdown between her staff on one side and the physicians, particularly the residents, on the other. Mrs. Scott, having noticed frustration by both parties, decided in April 1984 to take action to resolve this conflict.

MIDDLEBROOK HOSPITAL

Middlebrook was a medium-sized teaching hospital. The patients of the hospital generally came from a large geographic area including Windsor, Thunder Bay, Buffalo, and Cleveland.

SOURCE: This case was written by Lori Haller during the 1984 Case Writing Workshop. Case material of the School of Business Administration is prepared as a basis for classroom discussion.

They came to the hospital because of its specialization in high-risk surgery, neurology, and medicine.

The formal lines of communication of the hospital are as most hospitals'. The nursing units were generally set up with a nursing unit head, responsible for one or two team leaders each with their own nursing teams.

THE PEDIATRIC UNIT

This unit comprised a ten-bed Pediatric unit organized under several services and an adult six-bed mixed services "overflow" area. The nursing organization consisted of the nursing unit head and her staff.

Mrs. Scott's major responsibilities included the coordination of all her staff's hiring, firing, disciplining, training, and evaluating. She also administered her unit's budget. She participated on nursing hospital committees and lectured occasionally in the Faculty of Nursing at the university.

The unit utilized the Primary Care Nursing System, where formally there was direct communication from the staff nurses to the physicians and vice versa. There were four nurses on days (0700–1900 hours), and two on nights (1900–0700 hours). There was one baccalaureate staff nurse and no registered nursing assistants. Mrs. Scott held a Master's degree in Nursing (Administration).

AWARENESS OF THE PROBLEM

Mrs. Scott felt that there were many factors leading up to the following and other similar situations.

On April 10, 1984, Mrs. Scott was told by one of her staff nurses that Susie, a patient, was being discharged in two days' time. Her parents had made arrangements to fly her home to Thunder Bay. Susie's X-rays, discharge letter, and prescription were to go with her. The nurses started preparing the necessary documents two days before the date of discharge. The patient's physicians were called several times during the two days with each physician replying that "someone will be there." X-rays were obtained. Physiotherapy had seen Susie and her parents about her home treatment plan. Until five minutes before leaving the hospital to catch their flight, Susie and her parents were not sure they could leave. The physician had not actually confirmed the discharge date and plans for follow-up care, nor had he written the discharge letter and prescriptions.

As the nursing staff viewed this situation, it was difficult to discuss the plans with the patient's specialist and those physicians under him. Nurses were unable to determine who bore the responsibility for the patient and the tasks involved. There was no written "rotation" of residents and interns of the various "teams," so nurses could not call the appropriate physician. "On call" lists were available monthly, but changes were often made without notification.

The staff nurses felt that the physicians did not respond to calls from the Pediatric unit. One reason may have been the relatively infrequent contact a particular medical service had with the nursing staff, leading to that service's not knowing the unit or nurses well. Residents came at their convenience, not at the nurse's or patient's. The residents would not sign requisitions for tests as they did on other floors. The difficulty for all nurses was that they were put in the frustrating position between the physician's behavior and the patient (family needs and requests).

Mrs. Scott felt that both the residents and the nurses perceived each other's roles differently. She felt that personalities also caused problems. The chief physician would avoid dealing with an issue and leave the responsibility to his residents. Mrs. Scott, however, felt that the residents were disorganized among themselves in assuming responsibility for patient care and follow-up.

Mrs. Scott felt that this was not a constant problem. It occurred in varying degrees of severity, becoming worse when the residents rotated (any time from each month up to every year). The new residents needed time to get acquainted with a new set of patients and a new "team." As a result, these residents expected more from the nurses than normal, and were angry.

CONCLUDING REMARKS

Mrs. Scott was wondering what potential actions she could pursue. She also wondered why the physicians had not approached her with the problem.

STEP 2: Prepare the case for class discussion.

STEP 3: Answer each of the following questions, individually or in small groups, as directed by your instructor.

Diagnosis

1. What management activities does Mrs. Scott perform?
2. What functional activities does she perform and supervise?
3. What information does Mrs. Scott need to perform her job effectively?

Evaluation

4. In what form does the current information exist?
5. How does Mrs. Scott secure the information she and her staff need?
6. What problems exist in securing the required information?

Design

7. What information required by Mrs. Scott and the department might be computerized?

Implementation

8. What are the probable costs and benefits of introducing a computerized information system?

STEP 4: In small groups, with the entire class, or in written form, share your answers to the questions above. Then answer the following questions:

1. What types of information does Mrs. Scott require?
2. What systems exist to supply this information?
3. How effective are these systems?
4. How might the systems be improved?
5. What are the likely costs and benefits of such changes? ●

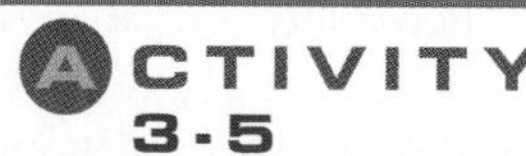

ACTIVITY 3-5 Managers Using Information Systems

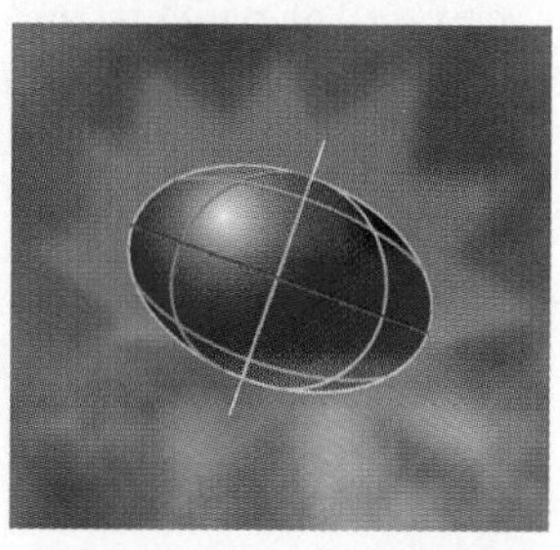

external contact

STEP 1: Locate a manager who uses a computerized information system.

STEP 2: Interview that manager about his or her use of the system and interaction with information systems professionals responsible for its design and implementation.

STEP 3: Answer the following questions.

1. What information needs does the system address?
2. How effectively does it address them?
3. What deficiencies exist in meeting the manager's needs?
4. How should the system be changed to address the manager's information needs better?

STEP 4: In small groups or with the entire class, compare your answers. Then answer the following questions:

1. What common needs do the systems address?
2. How effectively do they address the managers' information needs?
3. What role do information systems professionals play in the managers' use of the systems?
4. How could the information systems professionals interact more effectively with the managers their systems serve? ●

Notes

[1]William M. Bulkeley, Special systems make computing less traumatic for top executives, *The Wall Street Journal* (June 20, 1988): 17.

[2]Liselotte H. Davis, Business as (un)usual, *Computerworld* (December 21, 1992): 55–56.

[3]H. Mintzberg, *The Nature of Managerial Work,* 2d ed. (Englewood Cliffs, NJ: Prentice-Hall, 1979).

[4]Howard Dresner, For the data-hungry, *Computerworld* (July 26, 1993): 73–74.

[5]Bulkeley, op. cit.

[6]Diversity in a multitude of forms, *The New York Times* (December 1, 1991): 25.

[7]F. Bartoleme, Nobody trusts the boss completely—now what? *Harvard Business Review* 67(2) (March/April 1989): 135–142.

[8]See H. Mintzberg, *The Nature of Managerial Work;* G. A. Yukl, *Leadership in Organizations,* 2d ed. (Englewood Cliffs, NJ: Prentice-Hall, 1989); and F. Luthans and D. L. Lockwood, Toward an observation system for measuring leader behavior in natural settings. In J. G. Hunt, ed., *Leadership: A New Synthesis* (New York: Sage, 1984).

[9]See, for example, M. Kublin, The Japanese negotiating style: Cultural and historical roots, *Industrial Management* 29 (May-June 1987): 18–23; O. Shenkar and S. Ronen, The cultural context of negotiations: The implications of Chinese interpersonal norms, *Journal of Applied Behavioral Science* 23 (1987): 263–275; and E. S. Glenn, D. Witmeyer, and K. A. Stevenson, Cultural styles of persuasion, *International Journal of Intercultural Relations,* vol. 1 (New York: Pergamon, 1984).

[10]See B. M. Bass, *Bass & Stogdill's Handbook of Leadership: Theory, Research, and Managerial Applications,* 3d ed. (New York: Free Press, 1990) for discussion of this research.

[11]Carol Hildebrand, Financial affairs, *CIO* (March 15, 1994): 62–67.

[12]Hildebrand, op. cit.

[13]David J. Rachman and Michael H. Mescon, *Business Today,* 5th ed. (New York: Random House, 1987).

[14]Robert Crane, Accounting systems, *Computerworld* (February 24, 1992): 73–74.

[15]K. S. Nash, Johnson business units to get financial control, *Computerworld* (December 17, 1990): 67.

[16]Ellen Muraskin, Romance with finance, *Computer & Communication Decisions* (December 1987): 91.

[17]Hildebrand, op. cit.

[18]David C. Luman, PCs, financial industry: Growing up together, *Pension World* (March 1990): 10–14.

[19]Harper W. Boyd, Jr. and Orville C. Walker, Jr. *Marketing Management: A Strategic Approach* (Homewood,

IL: Richard D. Irwin, 1990).

[20]D. K. Goldstein, Information systems for sales and marketing: A study at a small grocery manufacturer, *Information & Management* 19(4) (November 1990): 257–268.

[21]M. A. Higby and B. N. Farah, The status of marketing information systems, decision support systems, and expert systems in the marketing function of U.S. firms, *Information & Management* 20(1) (January 1991): 29–35.

[22]H. K. Jain, E-R approach to distributed heterogeneous database systems for integrated manufacturing, *Information Resources Management Journal* 3(1) (Winter 1990): 29–40.

[23]Brian S. Moskal, GM's new-found religion, *Industry Week* (May 18, 1992): 46–52.

[24]Thomas M. Rohan, Designer/builder teamwork pays off, *Industry Week* (August 7, 1989): 45–46.

[25]Emily T. Smith and Peter Coy, Pumping up the Baby Bells' R&D arm, *Business Week* (August 5, 1991): 68–69.

[26]Mark Schlack, IS has a new job in manufacturing, *Datamation* (January 15, 1992): 38–39.

[27]Schlack, op. cit.

[28]Alan R. Earls, Keeping the customer ecstatic, *Computerworld* (February 21, 1994): 80.

[29]L. Z. Dix and J. Naze, Talk to your plants, *Computerworld* (December 28, 1992/January 4, 1993): 35.

[30]Richard B. Chase and David A. Garvin, The service factory, *Harvard Business Review* 67(4) (July/August 1989): 61–69.

[31]Otis Port, The responsive factor, *Business Week/Enterprise 1993* (1993): 48–56.

[32]Michael A. Palley, Hospital information systems and DRG reimbursement: The adaptation of large transaction processing systems to radical rule changes, *Information & Management* 20(3) (March 1991): 227–234.

[33]Bob Guise and John Lischefska, Finite scheduling software yields multiple benefits, *Controls & Systems* (March 1992).

[34]S. N. Chakravarty, Will toys "B" great? *Forbes* (February 22, 1988): 37–39.

[35]Thomas A. Butler, Your window to productivity: A close look at monitoring and control systems, *Controls & Systems* (March 1992): 27–29.

[36]Milan Moravec, Recruiting for tomorrow: High tech job posting—by computer, *Personnel Journal* (November 1991): 64–68.

[37]Larry Stevens, Recruiting for tomorrow: Automating the selection process, *Personnel Journal* (November 1991): 59–64.

[38]Bill Leonard, The myth of the integrated HRIS, *Personnel Journal* (September 1991): 113–115.

[39]Schlack, op. cit.

[40]H. A. Smith and J. D. McKeen, Computerization and management: A study of conflict and change, *Information & Management* 22(1) (January, 1992): 53–64.

[41]R. Rice and D. Case, Computer-based messaging in the university: A description of use and utility, *Journal of Communication* 33(1) (1983): 131–152; and S. R. Hiltz and M. Turoff, The evolution of user behavior in a computerized conferencing system, *Communications of the ACM* 28(7) (1985): 680–689.

[42]Elaine Waples and Daniel M. Norris, Information systems and transborder data flow, *Journal of Systems Management* 43(10) (January 1992): 28–30.

[43]Hiltz and Turoff, op. cit.

[44]L. Foster and D. M. Flynn, Management information technology: Its effects on organizational form and function, *MIS Quarterly* 8(4) (1984): 229–235.

[45]B. Schlender, How Bill Gates keeps the magic going, *Fortune* (June 18, 1990): 82–89.

[46]Smith and McKeen, op. cit.

Recommended Readings

Kotter, J. P. *The General Managers.* (New York: Free Press, 1982).

Luthans, F., Hodgetts, R. M., and Rosenkrantz, S. A. *Real Managers.* (Cambridge, MA: Ballinger, 1988).

Mintzberg, H. *The Nature of Managerial Work,* 2d ed. (Englewood Cliffs, NJ: Prentice-Hall, 1979).

Revolution in Real Time: Managing Information Technology in the 1990s. (Boston: Harvard Business School, 1991).

Steiglitz, H. *Chief Executives View Their Jobs: Today and Tomorrow.* (New York: Conference Board, 1985).

Wilkinson, Joseph W. *Accounting and Information Systems.* (New York: Wiley, 1991).

Chapter 4

The Organizational Perspective

OUTLINE

Quality Auto Rentals

Information and Organizational Strategy

Information and the Situational Analysis

Using Information For Strategic Advantage

- Reacting to Market Conditions
- Improving Customer Service
- Controlling Costs
- Improving Quality
- Expanding Globally
- Creating Strategic Alliances

Organization Structure and Information

International Strategy

Organizational Requirements of Information

- Cost
- Accessibility
- Reliability
- Security

The Strategic Use of Information Systems

LEARNING OBJECTIVES

After completing the reading and activities for Chapter 4, students will be able to

1. Illustrate the types of information required to make and implement strategic decisions in an organization.
2. Specify the steps in a strategic situational analysis and illustrate the use of information in each step.
3. Delineate six ways of using information for a competitive advantage and outline the information needs associated with each.
4. Comment about the relationship of information to the design and implementation of organization structures.
5. Cite four types of international strategies and the use of information in each.
6. Describe the four organizational requirements of information.
7. Identify two issues associated with the strategic use of information systems.

Quality Auto Rentals (QAR), one of the top ten automobile rental agencies in the United States, had started as a regional agency in the early 1970s. Following a strategy of low cost and wait-free service, Quality quickly established a significant presence in almost every major U.S. market. Quality's stock performed well for its investors, allowing Quality to fuel growth with periodic infusions of equity.

During the past three years, Quality's growth plateaued as it found fewer and fewer promising new markets to enter. Its growth in existing markets also proved to be slow. Profit margins, always narrow, remained perilously tight, especially in light of the projected downturn in the economy. CEO, Dwight Allen, recognized that the company had entered a new stage in its development and that it needed a new strategy to continue growing.

Allen was extremely positive about Quality's personnel and infrastructure. Quality had succeeded in part because experienced and knowledgeable people who worked well together held key management jobs. State-of-the-art information systems handled reservations and confirmations, optimized fleet purchasing and deployment, and supported key pricing and marketing decisions. Yet, Allen knew that Quality was not running as mean and lean as it had when it was small. Allen had expected overhead expenses to fall as a percentage of sales when the company grew. Instead, he found that he had been forced to add layers of management. Each new position was justified by a cost–benefit analysis, but Allen knew that management costs overall were squeezing the profit margin.

Allen's vision for the next five years, while still in its formative stage, centered around a strategy of continued growth. He wanted to make Quality a global competitor. Allen did not know whether the best approach was to buy foreign companies, to form looser marketing and sales alliances, or to create foreign subsidiaries from scratch. He did intend, however, to find new ways of marketing Quality's products and services in existing markets. He felt that Quality could do a better job of reaching customers to prevent them from renting from a competitor. He also felt that Quality could do a better job to assure that every customer would have the desire and incentive to use Quality for his or her next rental.

Dwight Allen looks within his organization to identify its strengths and weaknesses; he looks outside his organization for potential threats to its continued performance and opportunities for its further growth and expansion. What information does he need to make such assessments? How can Quality use the information it has about its customers and the knowledge it has about the auto rental business to make strategic decisions and further its organizational goals? What information could help Quality achieve a competitive advantage over other companies in the industry?

In this chapter we discuss the information an organization needs to make strategic decisions and the way it can use information to develop a strategic advantage over its competitors.

We begin by discussing the information required for strategy formulation and implementation. We then examine the use of information for creating a competitive advantage. We continue with a look at organizational structure, international strategy, and information. We then consider the organizational requirements of information. We conclude with an introduction to the strategic use of information systems, which is presented in Chapter 12 in greater detail.

Information and Organizational Strategy

HYATT HOTELS

WAL-MART

UNITED PARCEL SERVICE

MASTERCARD

UNIVERSITY OF IDAHO

Each organization must develop a **strategy**—its long-term direction or intended set of activities for attaining its goals. An organization needs extensive information to determine and then implement its strategy. Strategic-level decisions include plans for accomplishing long-term goals of market share, profitability, return on investment, service, and performance. They require determining the organization's distinctive competence by answering questions such as those shown in Figure 4-1. Answering these questions calls for obtaining information from both outside and inside the organization. Successful pharmaceutical companies, for example, must remain informed about changes within an array of scientific disciplines and integrate the knowledge throughout the organization to maintain innovation.[1] Hyatt Hotels needed information to help shorten check-in lines as a way of improving customer service and becoming more competitive; Wal-Mart needed information to assist in improving its purchasing and distribution systems so that it could compete more effectively against larger rivals; United Parcel Service realized that it needed to redesign its basic system for processing orders and information to obtain a competitive advantage; and MasterCard needed information to track transactions worldwide to reduce fraud.[2] The University of Idaho focused on improving its financial aid system as a way of gaining a competitive advantage in student recruitment.[3]

What strategy should Quality Auto Rentals pursue? More importantly for purposes of this book, what information do QAR and its top management need to determine its strategy? In the past, for example, Quality Auto Rentals concentrated its resources and management effort on the consumer auto rental business. After renting cars for one or two years, Quality sold most of its fleet at auction. Quality then leased the remaining cars to corporate clients. Taking a strategic view of the company, Dwight Allen now recognizes that other potential businesses Quality can pursue include corporate fleet leasing, leasing to the general public, and on-site, short-term rentals to automobile repair shop customers. The information

FIGURE 4-1 Questions That Help Identify an Organization's Distinctive Competence

What kind of business should we be in?

What should be the organization's markets?

What market niches exist in which the organization can compete?

What products or services should the organization offer?

What technological investment is required?

What human resources are available and required?

What financial, time, material, or other resources are available and required?

Where should the company allocate its resources and energies?

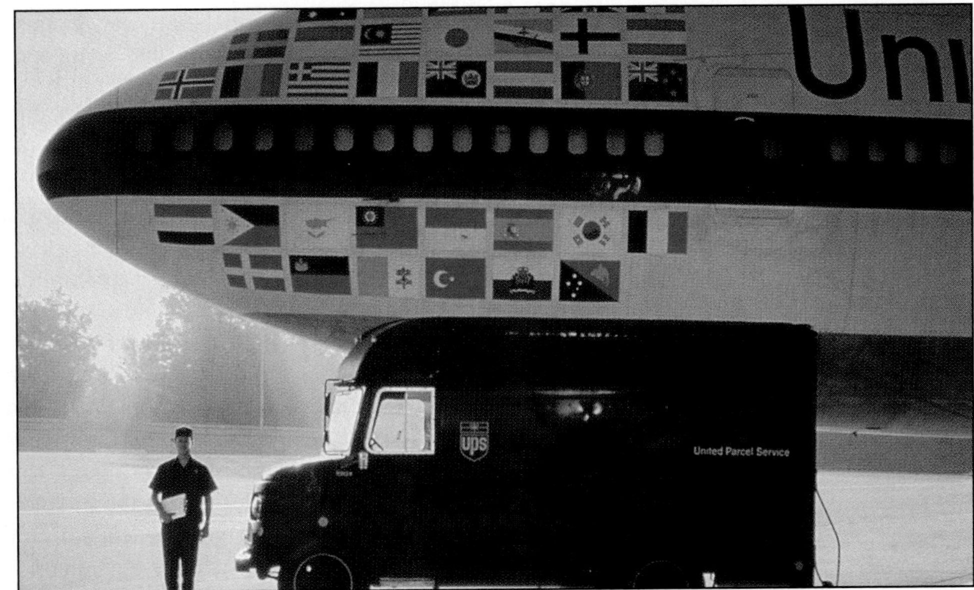

United Parcel Service (UPS) believes that information technology gives it a competitive edge. UPS's pioneering use of handheld computers to electronically capture customer's signatures is one of several technological innovations that helped it stem a loss of market share to competitor Federal Express.

Courtesy of United Parcel Service.

Allen needs to make such decisions differs from the information needed for the day-to-day running of the company. Allen must obtain significant environmental, industry, and marketplace information to make such decisions effectively.

Corporate-level strategy addresses which lines of business a company should pursue. It views an organization as a portfolio, agglomeration, federation, or amalgam of businesses or subunits. Strategic management at the corporate level focuses on decisions about acquiring new businesses, divesting old businesses, establishing joint ventures, and creating alliances with other organizations. For example, Dwight Allen might determine whether to purchase a small competitor, Rent-It Today, or whether to work with Asia Car to create a joint venture in Singapore.

Determining its corporate-level strategy requires top management to obtain information about business growth rate—the speed of industry growth—and market share—the portion of the industry market captured by the business unit, among other information. Information on industry growth and market share is often public, at least in the United States, due to the disclosures required of companies issuing stocks and bonds. Industry lobbyists, stock market researchers, trade magazine journalists, and other researchers also act as sources of this information. Information systems can regularly provide organizations with such information by tapping into commercially sold databases that offer extensive economic, technological, demographic, and even legal information. This ongoing availability of information allows organizations to determine their strategic position as well as the appropriate actions for maintaining or changing this position.

Information systems can provide the information for making resource allocation and other investment decisions. Information about market share, profit margins, patent ownership, technical capability, competitive strengths and weaknesses, quality of the management team, ability to compete on price and quality, customer requirements, and markets helps management determine its investment strategy. For example, business units with high ratings on both industry attractiveness and business strength make good financial investments; those low on both dimensions have no growth potential, and managers should consider divesting or liquidating them.[4]

Strategic management also involves business-level strategy, matching the strengths and weaknesses of each business unit or product line to the external environment to determine how each unit can best compete for customers. Strategic decisions include what products or services the company should offer, what customers it should service, and how it will deploy resources for advertising, research and development, customer service, equipment, and staffing. What specific strategic decisions must Quality Auto Rentals make? The company must determine which rental services to offer, whether to serve corporate or individual clients, which cars to purchase, how frequently to replace the existing fleet, where and how much to advertise, and the type of employees to hire to best accomplish the organization's goals, among other decisions. To make business-level strategic decisions, Quality Auto Rentals needs information about external conditions and opportunities, such as customer preferences, equipment availability and cost, the nature of the labor force, and even media options.

Firms can adopt five strategies to reap a competitive advantage: differentiation, cost leadership, focus, linkage, and information leadership.[5] Information systems can provide the information required to support one of these strategies (see Chapter 12 for a detailed discussion). A **differentiation** strategy seeks to distinguish the products and services of a business unit from those of its competitors through unique design, features, quality, or other characteristics and thereby enable the business to charge a premium for its product or service. Companies pursuing a differentiation strategy need current and accurate information about the market, including detailed information about competitors' products, customers' requirements, and changing environmental conditions.

A **cost leadership** strategy seeks to achieve competitive advantage by allowing the business unit to make more profit than its competitors when selling to customers at the same price. Complete information about costs makes costs easier to control and creates a competitive advantage. The company requires quality internal information to reduce costs by achieving efficiencies in production, distribution, and sales. Even hospitals can use information technology to reduce costs by eliminating paperwork and improving services: Bedside terminals can store patient records; electronic conferencing can bring the expertise of a team of physicians in remote locations to a single problem; home health terminals allow patients to consult with doctors on-line; and diagnostic systems can support physicians' diagnoses, identify preferred treatments, and specify their cost benefits.[6] Because The Travelers, Aetna Life & Casualty, Massachusetts Mutual, and Northwestern National Life insurance companies can reduce costs by obtaining quality information about fraudulent claims, each of these companies uses proprietary software to detect fraud.[7]

THE TRAVELERS

AETNA LIFE & CASUALTY

MASSACHUSETTS MUTUAL

NORTHWESTERN NATIONAL LIFE

A **focus** strategy achieves competitive advantage by concentrating on a single market segment. Companies following the focus strategy concentrate their resources to become big players in small markets rather than small players in larger markets. They require information about the nature of available markets and the characteristics of the players in them.

A **linkage** strategy obtains a competitive advantage by establishing special, exclusive relationships with customers, suppliers, and even competitors. Organizations require detailed information about customers' needs, special arrangements with suppliers, and potential synergies with competitors.

An **information leadership** strategy increases the value of a product or service by infusing it with expertise and information. Managers can also supplement products with summary and activity reports for an account or customer, product and market information relevant to the customer, or information about related products and services.[8] **Informationalizing** refers to this strategy of using information-based enhancements to revitalize mature businesses by enabling them to create or sell information as a core product.[9] For example, airlines can electronically track baggage in airports in ways that can correct problems before customers discover they have missing baggage; other examples of informationalizing include producing "smarter" cars and allowing customers to design desired features on computers in dealers' showrooms.[10]

Strategic management also addresses how functions such as finance, marketing, research and development, operations, and human resource management can best support the organization's strategies. **Functional strategies** direct the way individual departments perform their tasks to accomplish organizational objectives.[11] Marketing strategies focus on product development, promotion, sales, and pricing. Finance strategies focus on the acquisition, allocation, and management of capital. Operations strategies include decisions about plant size, plant location, equipment, inventory, and wages. Research and development strategies emphasize basic, applied, or developmental research. Human resource strategies revolve around the deployment of employees and the relations between labor and management. Chapter 3 discussed the information needs for these functional areas in great detail.

Information and the Situational Analysis

Strategic management includes **situational analysis**—the process of collecting and analyzing information about a company's strengths, weaknesses, opportunities, and threats. The acronym **SWOT** is often used for these four components of situational analysis. *Strengths* and *weaknesses* are internal characteristics of the organization that enhance and impede its ability to compete. A reputation for quality exemplifies a strength, while having costs above the industry average typifies a weakness. *Opportunities* and *threats* are external or environmental factors that may help or hinder an organization in meeting its strategic goals. Weak competitors illustrate an opportunity, while adverse regulatory rulings represent a threat. Figure 4-2 displays some major issues to consider in situational analysis.

Situational analysis requires extensive internal and external data. To evaluate internal strengths and weaknesses, for example, reputation for quality or above-average costs, a company must compare data on its internal condition with industry and competitor averages. Figure 4-3 illustrates some of the data sources that should typically be tapped in a situational analysis.[12] Some firms go to extensive lengths to obtain information about the market and their competitors, including hiring employees from competitors, suppliers, and customers, and even buying competitors' garbage.[13] Quality information systems can assist organizations in securing comprehensive information for the SWOT analysis. Organizations can use them to maintain, update, or access environmental and organizational data, such as demographic trends, potential customer lists, financial data, or staffing patterns.

Using Information for Strategic Advantage

In many, if not most, organizations, information management is a backroom operation intended to support the other functions of the business. As shown in Chapter 3, for example, information systems assist managers in communicating, planning, and monitoring; as shown in Chapter 2, information systems help individuals plan, schedule, and communicate. Information systems can also be used proactively and strategically as competitive weapons. In a recent survey of 200 CEOs and CFOs, 75 percent agreed with the statement "I believe that information systems hold the key to competitive advantage for my organization in the 1990s."[14]

Plains Cotton Cooperative Association

The Plains Cotton Cooperative Association (PCCA), for example, developed a computer-based system called TELCOT, which provides the associates with a competitive advantage in the cotton industry.[15] TELCOT helped PCCA become a major cotton broker, growing from a $50 million to a $500 million business in 15 years. The company handles between 115,000 and 240,000 transactions a day to provide 20,000 producers, 40 buyers, and 200 cotton gin operators with an electronic marketing service. In this section we explore six ways that information systems can help organizations such as Quality Auto Rentals and PCCA achieve a

Major Issues for Situational Analysis

Potential Internal Strengths	Potential Internal Weaknesses
A distinctive competence	No clear strategic direction
Adequate financial resources	Obsolete facilities
Good competitive skill	Lack of managerial depth and talent
Well thought of by buyers	Missing key skills or competence
An acknowledged market leader	Poor track record in implementing strategy
Well-conceived functional area strategies	Plagued with internal operating problems
Access to economies of scale	Falling behind in R&D
Insulated (at least somewhat) from strong competitive pressures	Too narrow a product line
Proprietary technology	Weak market image
Cost advantages	Weaker distribution network
Better advertising campaigns	Below-average marketing skills
Product innovation skills	Unable to finance needed changes in strategy
Proven management	Higher overall unit costs relative to key competitors
Ahead on experience curve	
Better manufacturing capability	
Superior technological skills	

Potential External Opportunities	Potential External Threats
Serve additional customer groups	Entry of lower-cost foreign competitors
Enter new markets or segments	Rising sales of substitute products
Expand product line to meet broader range of customer needs	Slower market growth
Diversify into related products	Adverse shifts in foreign exchange rates and trade policies of foreign governments
Vertical integration	Costly regulatory requirements
Falling trade barriers in attractive foreign markets	Vulnerability to recession and business cycle
Complacency among rival firms	Growing bargaining power of customers or suppliers
Faster market growth	Changing buyer needs and tastes
	Adverse demographic changes

SOURCE: Adapted from Arthur A. Thompson, Jr., and A. J. Strickland III, *Strategic Management: Concepts and Cases,* 5th ed. (Homewood, IL: BPI/Irwin, 1990): 91.

competitive advantage, as shown in Figure 4-4: 1) reacting to market conditions, 2) improving customer service, 3) controlling costs, 4) improving quality, 5) expanding globally, and 6) creating strategic alliances.

Reacting to Market Conditions

A firm that can respond quickly to market conditions has an advantage over its slower competitors in a number of ways. It can keep its costs lower by reducing excess inventory and eliminating mistakes in purchasing or manufacturing products that will not sell. It can tailor its prices more accurately to what the market will bear. It can react more quickly to lagging sales by adjusting advertising and price promotions. It can leverage its cash better, taking long or short positions and moving money quickly to where the opportunity for profit is the greatest. It can more quickly introduce products that the consumer wants; being first in the

FIGURE 4-3 Sources of External Data

Competitor and Trade Sources	Published and Government Sources	Third-Party Sources
Direct inquiry	Bibliographic works	Customers
Observation	Directories	Suppliers
Visits to facilities	Periodicals	Middlemen
Speeches	Clipping services	Other competitors
Company publications	Electronic databases	Journalists
Press releases	University case studies	Consultants
Investor information	Library of Congress	Unions
Advertisements and promotional material	Geological Survey	Advocacy groups
	Internal Revenue Service	Analysts and brokers
Help-wanted ads	Interstate Commerce Commission	Research services
Trade sources	Bureau of Labor Statistics	Credit agencies
Professional organizations	Patent and Trademark Office	Information specialists
Trade shows and exhibitions	State and local governments	
	Chamber of Commerce	

Adapted from Table of Contents of John M. Kelly, *How to Check Out Your Competition: A Complete Plan for Investigating Your Market* (New York: John Wiley & Sons, 1987).

market gives a company the opportunity to be a market share leader, with resulting scale efficiencies in manufacturing and marketing.

Companies can also use competitive pricing to give them a strategic advantage.[16] Information from computer systems can assist. Restaurants can assess the impact of various pricing and promotion strategies on their profit margins. A resort hotel can evaluate the success of special promotional packages by tracking an individual guest's expenditures by revenue center (e.g., golf course, restaurant, health club) and then adjusting the promotions offered to increase their effectiveness. Delta Airlines maintained a list of competitors' prices and could respond to changes within two hours.[17]

DELTA AIRLINES

What type of information does Quality Auto Rentals need to react to market conditions? The ability to react rapidly to the market depends on a firm's ability to monitor external conditions. The government, news providers, and many private enterprises collect leading indicators of economic and market trends that organizations can use to monitor external conditions. Most companies also collect information about external conditions in the normal course of business. For example, the record of customers' purchases can also become a weathervane of consumer opinion and product evaluation. Companies need to view such data not only from the context of operations management but also from the context of planning for competitive advantage. Information systems help companies such as QAR organize and use such data. Organizations with information systems that facilitate collecting and processing such data have a competitive advantage over those that do not. QAR can develop and implement a strategic information system to monitor market opportunities and changes, economic conditions, demographic shifts, and even competitors' behavior.

Improving Customer Service

Quality Auto Rentals knows that its customers will not tolerate a long wait to speak to its reservation agents; they will expect to be able to pick up the cars that they have reserved

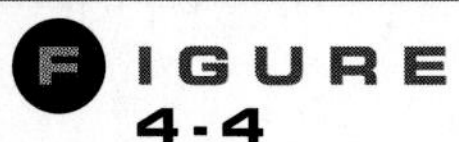

Ways Information Systems Help Achieve a Competitive Advantage

Company Gains a Competitive Advantage by:	IS Assists by Helping Organization to:
Reacting to market conditions	Reduce excess inventory Tailor prices to the market React quickly to lagging sales Leverage cash Introduce new products Set prices
Improving customer service	Maintain appropriate inventory Respond to customers' needs Monitor customer service
Controlling costs	Classify expenditures Monitor spending Control budgets
Improving quality	Provide feedback Give production workers immediate access to analyses
Expanding globally	Ease communication Support coordination
Creating strategic alliances	Share information with suppliers, customers, competitors Provide information links Create electronic markets

quickly, without a lot of paperwork, and without having to wait in a long line; they will want to drop off their cars without any wait if they are late for a flight; and they will expect their cars to work flawlessly while under rental. QAR strives to meet these expectations. To do so, and to diagnose and correct any failures, QAR needs to collect and monitor information about how well it succeeds in meeting the customer's objectives.

QAR constantly seeks information that would enable it to improve customer service. Assume, for example, that market research has indicated that automobile rental customers always want their preferred car available for rental. QAR then would benefit by being able to promise that "We have the car you want 95 percent of the time." Knowing how many times customers have not been able to reserve the car of their choice because of insufficient inventory would offer an advantage over competitors who do not have this information. Obtaining this knowledge requires collecting and maintaining information that would not otherwise be a part of QAR's transaction processing system. Let us assume that QAR's original reservation system did not log the failure to meet a customer's first choice of automobile type. QAR can likely increase the number of people who call Quality first by having such information available.

NEC Computers

Nabisco Foods

Managers need information not only to monitor customer service but also to improve it. NEC Computers gives information obtained from its customer service desk to its engineering and product development groups to refine its products in response to customer comments.[18] When Nabisco Foods introduced a new line of low-fat and fat-free snack foods, its consumer response line was soon ringing with complaints from 30,000 callers that the product was out of stock in their local stores. Operators noted the requests in an electronic data-

Rapid access to information improves customer service. Service agents can view a customer's history to anticipate customer needs and to respond appropriately and rapidly to requests.

Courtesy of International Business Machines Corporation.

base, which then triggered bakeries to increase production and sales managers to change their forecasts and delivery plans. Nabisco also placed commercials on national television to inform customers to "Be patient—more SnackWell's cookies are on the way!"[19]

Product and service innovations tend to increase an organization's competitive advantage.[20] For example, station managers at QAR recognized that they would be able to better satisfy customer reservation requests if their reservation clerks had access to data about fleet availability not only at their own station but also at nearby stations. When nearby stations shared fleet information, more first requests could be handled at only a marginal increase in cost (due to ferrying the cars between stations). A competitive advantage, however, can be short-lived. Enron Operating Company, a Houston-based petrochemical firm, introduced a new computer system and an interactive bulletin board that allowed clients to dispose of excess capacity more easily but found that its competitors quickly matched its technology, eliminating its competitive advantage.[21]

ENRON

The travel service industry in general has used technology extensively to meet customers' needs. Automatic call distributors, automatic ticket machines, satellite printers, travel management software, including databases, user-friendly terminals, programmable work stations, interfaces between personal computers and mainframes, and expert systems have together had a significant impact on the American travel industry.[22] United Services Automobile Association in San Antonio uses a single toll-free number accompanied by a voice processing system to direct customers to any of its businesses to meet customers' needs and create a one-company image.[23] Carolina Freight Company provides a variety of ways, including electronic mail and remote computer terminals, for different-sized customers to access the shipper's computer information.[24]

UNITED SERVICES AUTOMOBILE ASSOCIATION

CAROLINA FREIGHT

SCHNEIDER TRUCKING

Don Schneider, the CEO of Schneider Trucking, responded to the challenge posed by industry deregulation in the 1970s in part through the use of the latest information technology.[25] To increase responsiveness to customers, Schneider introduced a constantly updated information system that helps assign trucks and drivers and monitors their location; he put a computer and rotating antenna on each truck. Drivers no longer need to stop to report their location to dispatchers, and trucks can be rerouted quickly to deliver new orders more efficiently. A dispatcher can relay an order directly to the driver's onboard computer by satellite and include detailed directions about the delivery location, merchandise, and paperwork.

Controlling Costs

Recall that one of the competitive strategies is to become a low-cost producer. But how does a firm keep costs below its industry's average? Organizations can do so by achieving economies of scale in production, distribution, and sales. However, as volume increases, keeping track of and rationalizing business activities becomes more complex. The ability to handle, process, and summarize large amounts of information is, therefore, a prerequisite to achieving cost reduction through volume growth. Information systems can easily serve this function.

Systems to classify, monitor, and limit spending also facilitate cost control. To set budgets, managers need information about previous spending and about new plans and objectives. Budgetary information, in turn, permits managers to optimize their resources within prescribed limits.

Improving Quality

Having a reputation for quality offers a strategic advantage for any organization. Consumers will usually be willing to pay more for a product or service that they know will always meet their expectations than for one whose quality will vary. Improving quality has also been shown to decrease costs as it reduces waste, eliminates rework, and permits more orderly processing.

Achieving quality requires production workers to have constant feedback about the production process so that they can spot problems immediately and correct them. In the past systems were built so that production workers collected and entered data about production but did not have immediate access to analyses performed on the data that they had collected. Management information systems were built to provide summary and exception reports to the managers, who would then intervene in the process. Generally, managers would know about production problems before the production workers did. Companies operating in this fashion necessarily shipped inferior goods and provided inferior services. To improve quality, information about the goods and services being produced must be processed immediately, analyzed, and made available to production workers, who can intervene in a timely fashion to improve the process.

Florida Power & Light

Florida Power & Light (FPL) was the first U.S. company to win the annual Deming Prize, the most prestigious international award for quality. Part of FPL's strategy for improving quality was to develop a Trouble Call Management System (TCMS). Prior to the implementation of TCMS, it took 30 minutes from the time a customer called FPL with a problem until the time a repair order was issued. TCMS routed the information to the proper repair specialists in an average of six minutes. In addition, TCMS analyzes calls geographically to identify potential areas of difficulty. FPL then services these areas and improves them to eliminate problems before they occur.[26]

Expanding Globally

Prior to the 1980s, the inability of a company to obtain information about its foreign operations in time to compete with foreign companies operating in their own countries prevented organizations from operating globally. Most global corporations were holding companies that bought and sold regional companies in different parts of the world; each remote company, after acquisition, would continue to operate in its own realm with minimal management by the holding company.

Today's communication technology has reduced the barrier of distance. Now companies operating around the globe can exchange information with nearly the same ease as if they were in the same country. Toys "R" Us has expanded globally into Canada, England, Singapore, Hong Kong, and other locations since 1984. Its overseas stores are identical to American stores and rely on the same information processing systems as they do in the United States.[27]

Toys "R" Us

Although language differences, regulation of information flows, and lack of a communication infrastructure remain barriers to the exchange of information, in general, companies of all sizes now have the resources and information systems to allow them to operate globally. Information systems meet the need for coordination of diverse enterprises in distant locations.[28] At Imperial Chemical Industries, a $21.1 billion British manufacturer of pharmaceuticals, paints, agrochemicals, and polyurethanes, the rapid acquisition of firms outside Europe in the late 1980s posed major challenges for coordination.[29] The company has met this need by creating bridges between national and continental communication networks. Information technology meets information needs at Imperial Chemical with a worldwide net for document transfer, as well as with evolving common technical characteristics, systems, and databases, especially in office and financial systems.

Imperial Chemical Industries

Going global remains one of the easiest ways for a company to expand its market. A company pursuing the strategy of rapid growth and high market share increases its opportunities for success by considering the entire world as its market and using information systems to help it attain the information it requires to function internationally. Information technology helps multinational companies compete internationally by supporting foreign subsidiaries, better integrating worldwide operations, allowing greater flexibility in responding to local market needs, and serving clients more innovatively.[30] U.S. banks view information systems as a key ingredient in their ability to compete in the Pacific Rim in the next decade.[31] Creating a mature technological environment abroad helps meet customer needs for new products and management's needs for consistency and control in worldwide locations.

Information systems help companies such as Toys "R" Us to respond as rapidly to the market in foreign countries as they do in the United States.

Courtesy of Toys "R" Us.

Creating Strategic Alliances

The competitive advantage achieved by a company using information to react quickly to market conditions, improve customer service, control costs, improve quality, or expand globally will be short-lived if competitors can copy its strategy. Because the development of information systems typically takes several years, a company using information for strategic advantage needs time to establish its market share. Because its competitive advantage may be tenuous, an organization must be constantly vigilant for new strategic opportunities. Companies can also secure a competitive advantage by forming alliances with customers, suppliers, distributors, and producers of similar products, among others. If an alliance can be cemented by the exchange of information and information technology, the strategic advantages achieved will last longer.

Interorganizational information systems (IOSs) can meet information needs by serving as information links or electronic markets.[32] **Information links**—pathways for communication between two organizations—meet the need for coordination among an organization and its customers and suppliers. Information links enable or improve the collection and communication of information regarding inventory, sales, or other areas in which the two organizations interface. **Electronic market systems** are electronic, rather than physical, stores where products and services can be described, shown, sold, and purchased. They increase competition and efficiency in vertical markets by providing information about industry players and prices; buyers' ability to comparison shop reduces a seller's power in the market and creates lower prices. In Japan, used-car dealers buy and sell cars using their computers to participate in electronic auctions.[33] A seller of surgical gauze in New York City found a low-cost supplier in China through an electronic bulletin board and now sells to, rather than buys from, U.S. wholesalers.[34]

AMERICAN AIRLINES

American Airlines provides a well-known case of lasting competitive advantage achieved through sharing information and information services. In 1963 and the years immediately following, American Airlines provided travel agents with direct links to American's SABRE reservation system.[35] Because studies indicate that an airline that supplies a travel agency's computerized reservation system is as much as 30 percent more likely to have tickets on its flights sold to the agency's customers,[36] the basic marketing strategic of major airlines such as American, Delta, United, and TWA has emphasized these systems. By sharing access to its reservation information, American encouraged travel agents to book their clients on American flights. One developer of SABRE argues, for example, that agency use of computer reservation systems is the primary reason that passengers now book more than 80 percent of their tickets through agencies compared with less than 40 percent in 1976.

DELTA AIRLINES

UNITED AIRLINES

TWA

Allegations of favoritism in the presentation of flight information was a basis for several lawsuits that have been filed against American Airlines by other airlines seeking relief from such anticompetitive practices. American denies that flights are presented by SABRE in such a way as to favor the choice of American Airlines. In the 1990s SABRE has lost its ability to control alliances to some degree because the increasing standardization of microcomputer and network hardware makes it relatively easy for an agency to switch partners. In addition, federal regulations have attempted to limit the anticompetitive behavior encouraged by SABRE and similar air reservation systems.[37] At the same time, however, training, behavior, and business practices that apply to one system are not readily transferable, continuing SABRE's hold on its allies. Yet a similar attempt by American Airlines to create a new, technological state-of-the-art travel reservations system hooked into hotels and car rental agencies, called CON-FIRM, failed dramatically.[38]

What types of alliances might Quality Auto Rentals form to increase its strategic advantage? Creating partnerships with companies in Europe or Asia; joining with selected travel agencies or airlines; or linking with large automobile dealerships might offer such an advantage. Computer information systems and communications technology form the backbone of such alliances and allow the joint ventures to operate effectively. Of all information technologies, high-speed networking was rated in one survey of IS managers as the one most likely to have the greatest impact on their company's strategy over the next five years.[39]

Organization Structure and Information

An organization's **structure** refers to the division of labor, coordination of positions, and formal reporting relationships that exist in the organization. Effective organizations have a structure that is congruent with their strategy. The structure chosen may promote specific information needs for the organization.

We can characterize the organizations of the next century in two ways. First, increasing decentralization of decision making replaces centralization of this managerial function. A faster response to a dynamic and unpredictable environment requires that lower-level managers assume greater responsibility and accountability in an organization. Empowering of workers to make decisions calls for ensuring the ready availability of diverse types of information throughout the organization.

Second, organizations more frequently assume a more organic structure. In addition to pushing decision making down in the organization, this structure involves more flexible interactions among parts of the organization. A bank manager may serve on a task force to develop new products for the bank and several months later participate in a reorganization of the sales functions in the bank. Project and product management structures group workers according to the project or product on which they work; the matrix structure simultaneously groups workers functionally and by project or product. These structures create intense information needs for workers throughout the organization to ensure the coordination of activities. In more bureaucratic structures, in contrast, such coordination occurs through the hierarchy or by standard rules and procedures rather than through the widespread dissemination of information. The more organic structures also have a high information-processing capacity, which reduces barriers to lateral communication. Electronic media can further increase the information-processing capacity of such organizations.

These flatter, more decentralized organizations will become more information based, that is, "composed of specialists who direct and discipline their own performance through organized feedback from colleagues, customers, and headquarters."[40] Such a structure can replace managers, service staffs (e.g., legal, public relations), and central management with systems that make information readily available to workers at all levels in the organization. In information-based organizations individuals take responsibility for identifying their information needs and creating links to the sources of the required information. A recent study suggests that information technology will eventually result in more individuals acting as sources of information, fewer individuals formally included in an organizational subunit, fewer organizational levels involved in processing information, and more rapid decision making.[41]

International Strategy

In a global market, an organization may adopt a variety of strategies, including multinational, global, international, or transnational, to deal with its foreign subsidiaries.[42] A **multinational corporation** has built or acquired a portfolio of national companies that it operates and manages with sensitivity to its subsidiaries' local environments. The subsidiaries operate autonomously, often in different business areas. A company that follows a multinational strategy has little need to share data among its subsidiaries or between the parent and subsidiaries except to consolidate financial positions at year's end.

A **global corporation** has rationalized its international operations to achieve greater efficiencies through central control. Although its strategy and marketing are based on the concept of a *global market,* a headquarters organization makes all major decisions. A company pursuing a global strategy needs to transfer the operational and financial data of its foreign subsidiaries to headquarters in real time or on a frequent basis. A high level of information flows from subsidiary to parent, while limited data move from parent to subsidiary.

An **international corporation** exports the expertise and knowledge of the parent company to subsidiaries. Here subsidiaries operate more autonomously than in global corporations. Ideally, information flows from the parent to its subsidiaries. In practice, subsidiaries often rely on the parent to exercise its knowledge for the subsidiaries' benefit rather than simply to export it to the subsidiaries. For example, a subsidiary without a great deal of human resources expertise may "pay" its parent to operate its human resources function. Although the information theoretically should stay within the subsidiary, in this case it may flow back and forth between the parent's location and the subsidiary's location.

A **transnational corporation** incorporates and integrates multinational, global, and international strategies. By linking local operations to one another and to headquarters, a transnational company attempts to retain the flexibility to respond to local needs and opportunities while achieving global integration. Because transnationals operate on the premise of teamwork, they demand the ability to share both information and information services.

Organizational Requirements of Information

The information that an organization develops and retains should provide value to the company. *Diagnosing* the required information is the first step of the four-step approach to information management. Then collecting and maintaining the information in a cost-effective manner make up part of the subsequent steps of *evaluation* and *design*. We define **net value of information** as the difference between the value and the cost of information. Companies such as Quality Auto Rentals attempt to maximize the net value of information they collect organizationally. To do this, they consider four characteristics of information: cost, accessibility, reliability, and security.

Cost

The cost of acquiring, manipulating, and maintaining information can affect its net value. Reducing such costs allows information to add more value to the firm. Although the budget for information systems at most organizations falls between 1 and 3 percent of sales, the real cost of information is usually much higher. The budget for information systems at QAR, for example, does not include any part of the salary of its reservation agents, yet capturing and entering customer data into the company's reservation system demands a large portion of an agent's time.

The overall cost of information tends to be high, so small percentage reductions in the cost of information can have a large impact on its net value and on the profit of the firm. Information systems specialists need to focus on the tasks of collecting and maintaining information as well as on the value of the outputs of an information system when justifying its cost. Designers of information systems for QAR, for example, should minimize the time and effort required to collect or enter data. User-friendly touch screens offer one way to address this problem.

Accessibility

Designers of information systems seek to make the appropriate information available to users at the right time, in the right place, and in the right format. Nevertheless, designers cannot foresee every possible need for information. As a result, the value of information as an organizational asset can be maximized by making it as widely available as possible to all those who might need it and who have authority to see and use it. In Chapter 7 we explore how database technology strives to fill this need.

Reliability

The improper design and use of information systems can create unreliable data. A recent study of end-user data at 21 random Fortune 500 companies showed that **data pollution**—faulty, flawed, or unreliable data or data processing—existed in every company.[43] Users regularly generated reports and made decisions based on incomplete, inconsistent, or incorrect information. The problems in this study were caused by users who incorrectly entered data from reports generated by an MIS department into personal computers and then used these data as a source for further analysis.

Improper use of information systems can also motivate organizational conflict, which in turn results in the generation of unreliable data. One multidivisional company created a state-of-the-art information system to provide managers with real-time summaries of sales and distribution data at the touch of a button. Given the availability of these data, top management periodically confronted lower management with problems they had identified. Divisional managers considered this behavior to be meddling, and they quickly learned how to hide or delay the reporting of poor results. Not surprisingly, the data lost their accuracy and their value.[44]

The impact of "dirty data" on organizational performance can be immense. A 1992 *Computerworld* survey found that more than 60 percent of companies are aware of occasions when corrupted data negatively affected their operations.[45] For example, the U.S. General Accounting Office determined that data about student loan payments entered incorrectly into the U.S. Department of Education database had cost taxpayers $2 billion. The incorrect information was relayed to banks, which then allowed deadbeat students to continue to get loan renewals while deserving students were refused assistance. A New York securities firm missed a big trading opportunity that cost it more than $200 million. The firm eventually traced the problem to its employees' failure to enter key data into a new risk management system.

U.S. DEPARTMENT OF EDUCATION

Security

Security means protection against theft, manipulation, and loss of data. Theft of data should concern members of an organization because data theft is not as easily detected as theft of other corporate resources: Stealing data means taking only copies of data and leaving the original copy undisturbed. Burglars thus can continue to raid an organization's data, causing damage over an extended period. Despite the potential damage and difficulty of detection, most organizations assume that their information is relatively secure and take insufficient measures to protect against theft.[46]

The widespread use of personal computers has compounded the difficulty of security against corporate espionage. Competitors and foreign governments can pay employees to surreptitiously steal key information on diskettes or portable computers. Or, disgruntled employees may steal or modify essential information. For example, foreign intelligence agencies have used sophisticated technology to intercept data transmissions. Information such as proprietary technology, production methodologies, product data, and research and development breakthroughs may be sent directly to national laboratories or to competing organizations within the foreign country. Foreign and U.S. competitors can also use stolen information about production schedules, costs, margins, salaries, and performance reports as competitive tools.[47]

Many firms protect against the loss of data to fire or natural disaster by creating copies of the data, called **backups,** and keeping them at another location. Companies that fail to retain backups off site as well as provide for backup processing run the risk of suffering significant damage if they lose information about their customers, outstanding invoices, inventory, or financial status. Both technical and organizational measures can be used to promote data security. Federal agencies that oversee certain industries, such as banking, require detailed, written contingency plans. Technical measures are discussed throughout Part II of this text, and organizational measures are addressed in Part IV.

The Strategic Use of Information Systems

Computerized information systems can assist and improve strategic management in organizations. Information systems can be used strategically to support the strategic planning process and provide competitive advantage.[48] In the first case, a strategic decision support system addresses strategic problems, directly supports strategic decision making, recognizes the lack of structure in strategic decisions, and has the characteristics of a decision support system (see Chapter 11).[49] For example, some organizations use strategic decision support systems as tools that collate and analyze information to assist their strategic planning.

In the second case, information systems act as a resource similar to capital and labor in determining strategic plans. Information systems can change a business's or an industry's products and services, markets, and economics of production.[50] For example, airlines used their information systems as a resource in implementing their strategy of increasing market share by obtaining a greater percentage of ticket sales from ticket agents and quickly revising prices to respond to price changes by competitors. An organization can assess whether information systems or technology can be used strategically by answering questions such as the following: Can information systems technology build barriers to entry? Can it change the basis of competition? Can it generate new products? Can it build in switching costs? Can it change the balance of power between suppliers and customers?[51] Chapter 12 discusses strategic information systems in greater detail.

Summary

Organizations need information to make strategic decisions and can use it to develop an advantage over their competitors. They require information about such things as business growth rate and market share to make decisions about acquiring new businesses, divesting old businesses, establishing joint ventures, and creating alliances with other organizations. They also obtain information to help match the strengths and weaknesses of each business unit with its external environment. Firms can adopt the following strategies to obtain a competitive advantage: differentiation, cost leadership, focus, linkage, and information leadership.

Strategic management often includes a SWOT analysis. Top management requires information to determine an organization's strengths, weaknesses, opportunities, and threats. It secures data from competitor and trade sources, published and government sources, and third-party sources to use in a situational analysis.

Information can help organizations attain a strategic advantage by reacting to market conditions, improving customer service, controlling costs, improving quality, expanding globally, and creating strategic alliances. Effective organizations choose an organizational structure that promotes information needs and facilitates the securing of required information. An organization that functions in a global market can adopt a multinational, global, international, or transnational strategy to deal with its foreign subsidiaries.

Organizational requirements of information include low cost, accessibility, reliability, and security. Information systems can assist and improve strategic management in organizations.

Key Terms

Backup
Business-level strategy
Corporate-level strategy
Cost leadership
Data pollution
Differentiation
Electronic market system
Focus
Functional strategy
Global corporation
Information leadership
Information link
Informationalizing
International corporation
Interorganizational information system (IOS)
Linkage
Multinational corporation
Net value of information
Security
Situational analysis
Strategy
Structure
SWOT
Transnational corporation

Review Questions

1. What is the meaning of *strategy?*
2. Identify five strategies firms can use to obtain a competitive advantage.
3. Specify the steps in a strategic situational analysis and illustrate the use of information in each step.
4. Why is information important to a company that seeks a competitive advantage by reacting rapidly to market conditions?
5. Illustrate why information is important to improving customer service.
6. What type of information do companies need to control their costs?
7. What type of information is required by companies seeking a reputation for high quality?
8. What are the barriers to the exchange of information across national boundaries?
9. Give two examples of how information can help implement the creation of strategic alliances.
10. How can information systems help promote the decentralization of decision making in an organization? Why might that be desirable?
11. What is meant by an *organic structure,* and why is information processing important to establishing an organic structure?
12. Cite four types of international strategies and the use of information in each.
13. Describe the four organizational requirements of information.
14. Describe how information systems help support the strategic planning process.

MINICASE

Strategic Use of Information at Fingerhut

Fingerhut's revenue growth from continuing operations exceeded 17 percent in 1993, the 15th consecutive record year. "But we know that a good track record is not enough. Changes are occurring in [mail order] at an unprecedented pace. We must be innovators as the world moves more rapidly into the age of electronic media marketing," says Ted Deikel, Fingerhut's chairman and CEO, in the company's annual report.

Fingerhut is in the midst of redefining itself. Change seems to be the one constant at this preeminent mail order house. 1993 was quite a year: The company:

- Posted a record $1.8 billion in net revenues and $75.3 million in earnings;
- Completed a two-for-one stock split;
- Successfully tested its largest Fingerhut book ever at 440 pages;
- Expanded its participation in TV and announced a major investment in technology to redesign its mammoth database systems.

"Our strengths in database marketing—understanding consumers and their preferences—have positioned us for success in whatever media—cable, interactivity, direct broadcast, CD-ROMs or something else—ultimately become the standard," says Deikel. "While we will not chase technology, we will continually test opportunities within these media and will seek alliances that complement our strengths and enhance our visibility to customer groups. We were known for single product offerings [car seat covers] in the 1960s. Today, we are known for catalogs. We will be known for much more tomorrow."

The Minnetonka, Minnesota-based company has diversified beyond standard direct mail and catalogs, and is looking at new database structuring and media opportunities. Fingerhut's business units include:

1. **Fingerhut Corporation**—which uses various media (primarily direct mail and catalogs) to sell an array of general merchandise, including electronics, housewares, domestics, and apparel. All merchandise is sold on convenient, in-house credit plans. Also included in this group is the company's Financial Services Group which markets a variety of insurance products, service plans and other services to Fingerhut's customers.
2. **USA Direct Incorporated**—a television unit which provides the "first level in the company's multimedia marketing strategy using direct response TV infomercials to market proprietary products."
3. **Montgomery Ward Direct L.P.**—a joint venture that was established in 1991 with Montgomery Ward & Co., Inc. to market specialty catalog merchandise to a middle-income customer base.

Mining the Database

The database is central to all of Fingerhut's business units. "At Fingerhut, database marketing is our core competency. Over our 45-year history, we have developed and used proprietary databases to test new product concepts, target offers, and build the customer relationship through every contact," says Deikel. The company uses personalized mailings right down to children's birthdays.

Extracted from Millie Neal, Fingerhut movin' ahead, *Direct Marketing* (September 1994): 30–32, 72.

Other perks from today's database:

Control Credit Risk: The proprietary database gives Fingerhut detailed payment information on buyers, which has served the company well in focusing mailings and will become increasingly important as it moves into TV.

Predictibility. For example, when the company decided to reduce prices on some products, based on financial models, it was comfortable that response rates would increase, offsetting the drop in gross margins and leading to higher profits.

Enhanced targeting capabilities help Fingerhut identify the prospects with the highest propensity to buy certain services or merchandise. After a new system is up and running, the company plans to have more efficient database storage and retrieval and easier access to customer information—all at a desktop.

Since 80 percent of Fingerhut's customers are repeat buyers, it is necessary to be relentless about satisfaction and service. During 1993, the company implemented Phase One of its new Customer Contact System. For inbound callers, the system consolidates data from several databases into one format—putting more information at the phone reps' fingertips and facilitating order-taking for any of the 15,000+ products the company sells and assists its customer service. Phase II of the system will continue with the company's new on-line credit granting system, dubbed Frontier 2000.

The outbound telemarketing programs will also be expanded by phoning existing customers to let them know about products that complement recent purchases, new offerings or financial products that purchase history indicates would be relevant to them.

In September 1993, Fingerhut announced the development of a next-generation computer system that would reportedly create the "largest proprietary database marketing system in the world." The new system, called Profile 2000, should be on-line by year-end 1995.

Fingerhut's new Profile 2000, Frontier 2000 and Customer Contact Systems will combine 22 internal databases and nine external databases into three large integrated databases accessed by desktop workstations to provide better information faster to employees companywide. Fingerhut's investment in information systems was $39.8 million in 1990, and jumped to an average $75 million annually since 1991. The number has been upped again to $80 million for 1994, reflecting the first stage of the new database system's development.

Case Questions

1. Why does Fingerhut believe that the information it collects has strategic value?
2. What information does Fingerhut collect?
3. What competitive advantages does Fingerhut hope to obtain from the information it collects? Give an example.
4. How does Fingerhut make its strategic information available to the employees who can best make use of it?
5. What organizational requirements of information appear to be most important to Fingerhut?

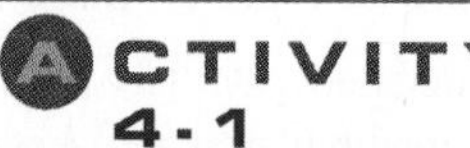

ACTIVITY 4-1 Recruiting at Community University

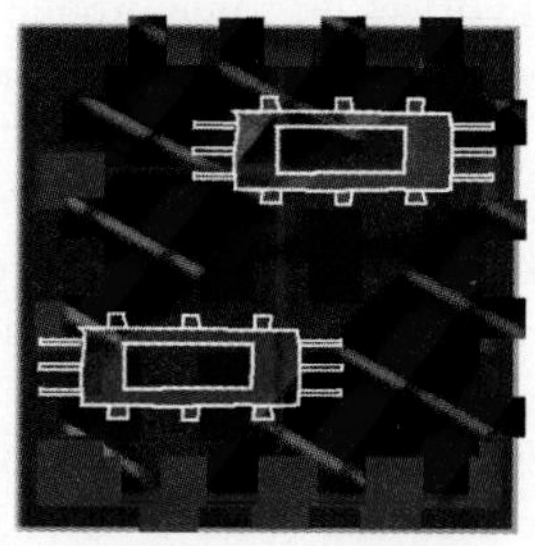
short case

STEP 1: Read the following scenario.

The graduate business school at Community University had recently experienced significant declines in the number of inquiries and applicants for both its full-time and part-time M.B.A. programs. The recently hired director of admissions, Susan Sellers, believed that the decline resulted in part from the decreasing interest in management education. Sellers also believed that the decline could be attributed to the lack of a clear strategy for selling the program. She intended to change the recruiting focus from students with business undergraduate degrees to recent graduates with a liberal arts background and significant work experience.

Sellers planned to use a large part of her budget to improve the information systems in the admissions office. Her initial step was to identify the particular information needs of the new strategic direction of the admissions process.

STEP 2: Individually or in small groups, develop a list of information Susan Sellers needs to support the new recruiting strategy.

STEP 3: In small groups or with the entire class, share the list you have developed. Then answer the following questions:

1. What are the information needs of the new recruiting strategy?
2. How can the organization satisfy these needs? ●

ACTIVITY 4-2 SWOT Analysis and Information

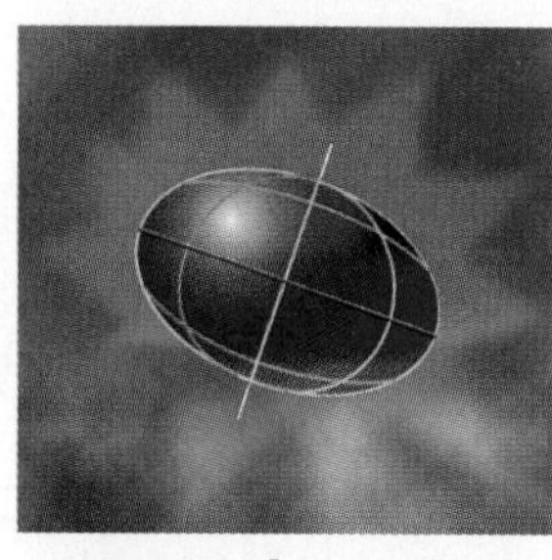
external contact

STEP 1: Individually, in twos, or in threes, choose a local business to analyze.

STEP 2: Locate four sources of information about the company.

STEP 3: Using this information, list three of each of the following:

Strengths:

Weaknesses:

Threats:

Opportunities:

STEP 4: In small groups, list the types and sources of data you used to perform the SWOT analysis.

STEP 5: With the entire class, formulate a comprehensive list of the sources and types of data used to perform a SWOT analysis. Then answer the following questions:

1. Which sources provided the most useful data? The least useful data?
2. What other information would be helpful in doing the SWOT analysis?
3. How could computerized information systems assist with the SWOT analysis? ●

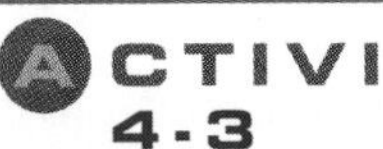

ACTIVITY 4.3 Increasing the Competitive Advantage

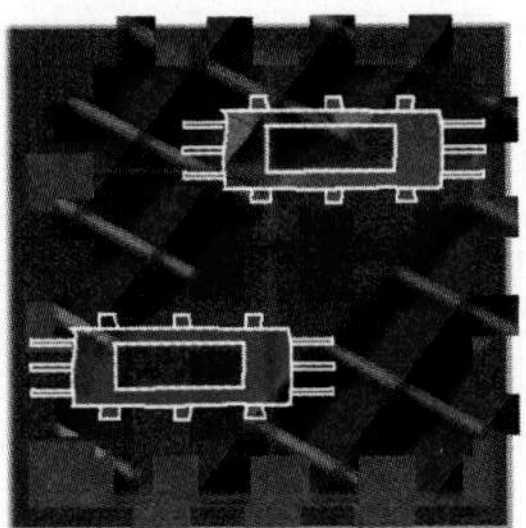

short case

STEP 1: Read the descriptions of the situations below. For each situation, offer two strategies for increasing the organization's competitive advantage over others in its industry. Then list three types of information required to implement each strategy.

Situation I: Stable pricing is difficult for restaurants like Red Lobster that specialize in such foods as crabmeat or shrimp, where costs are volatile. Customers react unfavorably to frequent changes in menu prices; therefore, the restaurant must protect itself against overpricing and losing customers or underpricing and losing margins.[52] How can Red Lobster use information to maintain a competitive advantage?

Situation II: The owner of a small manufacturer of digital scales has recently exhibited his product at a trade show in Germany. He has also begun to speak with representatives of the Chamber of Commerce in several small towns in Ireland about the issues associated with opening a manufacturing plant in their town. How can the company use information to increase its competitive advantage?

Situation III: A small real estate office that had specialized in residential properties recently began to list a small number of commercial properties. It also began a trial membership in a national network of real estate offices. The consortium provides national advertising and referrals as well as assists in human resource functions such as payroll, training, and recruiting. How can the small real estate office use information to further develop a competitive advantage over other real estate offices?

STEP 2: In small groups, compile the strategies that organizations can use to attain a competitive advantage. Then list the types of information required to implement these strategies.

STEP 3: Individually, in small groups, or with the entire class, answer the following questions:

1. In what ways can an organization increase its competitive advantage?
2. What types of information are required to do this?
3. How can the organizations secure this information?
4. What role can information systems play in providing the needed information? ●

ACTIVITY 4.4 Assessing the Quality of Information

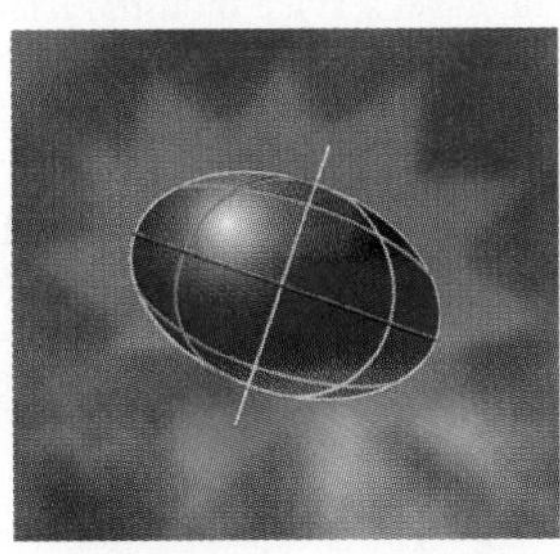

external contact

STEP 1: Individually or in small groups, design a questionnaire to assess how well an organization's information meets the criteria of low cost, accessibility, reliability, and security.

STEP 2: Select a department in your college or university or in an organization of your choice, and administer the questionnaire to two or three members of that organization.

STEP 3: Tabulate the results.

STEP 4: Individually, in small groups, or with the entire class, share your results. Next, list the conclusions you can draw from the data. Then answer the following questions: 1) How well does organizational information meet the criteria of low cost, accessibility, reliability, and security? and 2) What two recommendations would you offer for improving the quality of the organization's information? ●

Notes

[1]Rebecca Henderson, Managing innovation in the information age, *Harvard Business Review* (January/February 1994): 100–105.

[2]Peter Coy, The new realism in office systems, *Business Week* (June 15, 1992): 128–133.

[3]Joseph J. Geiger, Management implications of installing a modern financial aid system, *Journal of Systems Management* 43(3) (March 1992): 6–9.

[4]See J. H. Higgins and J. W. Vineze, *Strategic Management and Organizational Policy,* 3d ed. (Hinsdale, IL: Dryden, 1986).

[5]Michael Porter, *Competitive Strategy* (New York: Free Press, 1980); Michael E. Porter, From competitive advantage to corporate strategy, *Harvard Business Review* (May/June 1987): 43–59; S. Barrett and B. Konsynski, Inter-organizational information sharing systems, *MIS Quarterly,* Special Issue (December 1982): 92–105; H. R. Johnson and M. E. Vitale, Creating competitive advantage with interorganizational systems, *MIS Quarterly* 12(2) (June 1988): 153–165; J. F. Rockart and J. E. Short, IT in the 1990s: Managing organizational interdependence, *Sloan Management Review* (Winter 1989): 1–17; and Stan Davis and Bill Davidson, *2020 Vision* (New York: Simon & Schuster, 1991).

[6]Catherine Arnst and Wendy Zellner, Hospitals attack a crippler: Paper, *Business Week* (February 21, 1994): 104–106.

[7]Chris Roush, Call it bogus 1-2-3, *Business Week* (December 13, 1993): 97.

[8]Jae Hyon Song and Crumpton Farrell, An information age opportunity—providing information for customers, *Information & Management* 17(5) (December 1989): 285–292.

[9]Davis and Davidson, op. cit.

[10]Davis and Davidson, op. cit.

[11]This discussion is based on J. A. F. Stoner and R. E. Freeman, *Management,* 5th ed. (Englewood Cliffs, NJ: Prentice-Hall, 1992).

[12]John M. Kelly, *How to Check Out Your Competition: A Complete Plan for Investigating Your Market* (New York: John Wiley & Sons, 1987).

[13]Brian Dumaine, Corporate spies snoop to conquer, *Fortune* (November 7, 1988): 68–76.

[14]Joseph Maglitta, It's reality time, *Computerworld* (April 29, 1991): 81–83.

[15]D. Lindsey, P. H. Cheney, G. M. Kasper, and B. Ives, TELCOT: An application of information technology for competitive advantage in the cotton industry, *MIS Quarterly* 14(4) (December 1990): 347–357.

[16]Cynthia M. Breath and Blake Ives, Competitive information systems in support of pricing, *MIS Quarterly* (March 1986): 85–96.

[17]J. Koten, Fare game: In airline rate war daily skirmishes often decide winner, *Wall Street Journal* (August 24, 1984): 1.

[18]Jennifer DeJong, Smart marketing, *Computerworld* (February 7, 1994): 113, 117.

[19]DeJong, op. cit.

[20]P. B. Cragg and P. N. Finlay, IT: Running fast and standing still? *Information & Management* 21(4) (November 1991): 193–200.

[21]Melinda-Carol Ballou and Derek Slater, One-minute advantage, *Computerworld* (December 27, 1993/January 3, 1994): 52–53.

[22]W. J. Doll, Information technology's strategic impact on the American air travel service industry, *Information & Management* 16(5) (May 1989): 269–275.

[23]Mitch Betts, Serve or else, *Computerworld* (December 28, 1992): 29–30.

[24]Betts, op. cit.

[25]Myron Magnet, Meet the new revolutionaries, *Fortune* (February 24, 1992): 94–101.

[26]Adapted from Alan J. Ryan, IS strategies: Florida Power & Light: Where quality takes command, *Computerworld* (December 11, 1989): 1, 95, 96.

[27]Charles Wiseman, Strategic information systems: Trends and challenges over the next decade, *Information Management Review* 4(1) (1988): 9–16.

[28]J. Karimi and B. R. Konsynski, Globalization and information management strategies, *Journal of Management Information Systems* 7(4) (Spring 1991): 7–26.

[29]A. Pantages, The right IS chemistry, *Datamation* (August 15, 1989): 61–62.

[30]B. S. Neo, Information technology and global competition: A framework for analysis, *Information & Management* 20(3) (March 1991): 151–160.

[31]R. Poe, A U.S. banker in Singapore: Playing it safe with Big Blue, *Datamation* (October 15, 1987): 46–47.

[32]J. Y. Bakos, Information links and electronic marketplaces: The role of interorganizational information systems in vertical markets, *Journal of Management Information Systems* 8(2) (Fall 1991): 31–52.

[33]Thomas A. Stewart, Boom time on the new frontier, *Fortune* Special Report (Autumn 1993): 153–161.

[34]Stewart, op. cit.

[35]This discussion is based on M. D. Hopper, Rattling SABRE—New ways to compete on information, *Harvard Business Review* (May-June 1990): 118–125.

[36]Byron Belitsos, MIS pilots the air wars, *Computer Decisions* (March 1988): 36–41.

[37]Mitch Betts, House bill would restrict air reservation systems, *Computerworld* 26 (August 19, 1992): 1, 16.

[38]Wendy Zellner, Portrait of a project as a total disaster, *Business Week* (January 17, 1994): 36.

[39]Nell Margolis, Marching orders, *Computerworld* (October 19, 1992): 108.

[40]Peter F. Drucker, The coming of the new organization, *Harvard Business Review* (January-February 1988): 45–53.

[41]G. P. Huber, A theory of the effects of advanced information technologies on organizational design, intelligence, and decision-making, *Academy of Management Review* 15 (1990): 47–71.

[42]C. Bartlett and S. Ghoshal, *Managing Across Borders: The Transnational Solution* (Boston, MA: Harvard Business School Press, 1989).

[43]Donald L. Amoroso, Fred McFadden, and Kathy Brittain White, Disturbing realities concerning data policies in organizations, *Information Resources Management Journal* (Spring 1990): 18–26.

[44]Michael Schrage, When technology heightens office tensions, *The Wall Street Journal* (October 5, 1992): A12.

[45]The examples and statistics in this paragraph are all excerpted from Bob Knight, Executive report—data dilemmas: The data pollution problem, *Computerworld* (September 28, 1992): 81, 83.

[46]Detmar W. Straub, Jr., "Effective IS security: An empirical study," *Information Systems Research* 1(3) (1990): 255–272.

[47]Geoff Turner, In depth: I spy, *Computerworld* (October 26, 1992): 129–130.

[48]Ronald B. Wilkes, Draining the swamp: Defining strategic use of the information systems resource, *Information & Management* 20 (1991): 49–58.

[49]W. King, Strategic management decision support systems, Business Policy International symposium, University of Texas, Arlington, Texas, 1983. Cited in Wilkes, op. cit.

[50]G. Parsons, Information technology: A new competitive weapon, *Sloan Management Review* 25 (Fall 1983): 3–14; see also Michael E. Porter and Victor E. Millar, How information gives you competitive advantage, *Harvard Business Review* (July-August 1985): 149–160.

[51]F. McFarlan, Information technology changes the way you compete, *Harvard Business Review* 62 (May-June 1984): 98–103.

[52]Breath and Ives, op. cit.

Recommended Readings

Fird, G. R. *Strategic Information Systems: Forging the Business and Technology Alliance.* (New York: McGraw-Hill, 1991).

Primozic, K. I., Primozic, E. A., and Leben, J. *Strategic Choices: Supremacy, Survival, or Sayonara.* (New York: McGraw-Hill, 1991).

Roche, E. M. *Telecommunications and Business Strategy.* (Chicago: Dryden, 1991).

Starr, M. K. *Global Corporate Alliances and the Competitive Edge: Strategies and Tactics for Management.* (New York: Quorum, 1991).

Wiseman, C. *Strategic Information Systems.* (Homewood, IL: Irwin, 1988).

VIDEOCASE

Alamo Rent A Car, Inc.

Alamo Rent A Car, with annual revenues of more than $850 million, is the largest independently owned automobile rental agency in the United States. Starting with its first station in Fort Lauderdale, Florida, in 1974, Alamo grew rapidly as air travel became less costly and more commonplace following the deregulation of the airlines in 1978. Currently, Alamo serves more than 10 million customers per year, over half of whom are traveling on business. Alamo's station at Orlando International Airport is its largest, covering 74 acres, with 70 rental terminals and a capacity to rent as many as 500 cars per hour. Internationally, Alamo recently opened new stations in the United Kingdom, Switzerland, and the Netherlands.

Alamo's Marsha Wright, Executive Director of Computers and Communications, attributes Alamo's growth to business vision, people, and information technology. Alamo's reservation and customer service systems, in particular, have enabled Alamo to fulfill its vision of rapid, efficient, and hassle-free customer service.

The rental process starts with a customer or the customer's travel agent making a reservation. An Alamo reservation agent enters the customer's desired rental dates and car-type preferences into Alamo's database. When the customer arrives at the destination airport, the rental agent quickly retrieves this information along with information about any cars that are available. The agent can suggest an upgrade if appropriate. Alamo's information systems also show the agent a history of the customer's prior transactions with Alamo. This information allows the agent to address problems that the customer might have had with previous rentals and to suggest services or options similar to those the customer has requested in the past. Typically, this process takes less than three minutes. When the customer returns the car, Alamo uses a portable computer to retrieve the rental information, calculate costs, and provide a receipt. This car-side system generally handles the return in less than one minute.

From the customer's perspective, Alamo's information systems provide the benefits of rapid processing and personalized service. From Alamo's perspective, the systems provide the information its agents need to perform their services rapidly and efficiently. In addition, Alamo's managers use the reservation and fleet information to staff Alamo's stations and evaluate employee performance.

The designers of Alamo's information systems had to consider the worldwide nature of Alamo's operations. For example, according to Luis Arana, Senior Director of Data Processing, when Alamo entered the Swiss market, its systems had to be modified to reflect the lack of the equivalent of the penny in Swiss currency. Calculated amounts, such as tax and fuel charges, had to be rounded to the nearest 5 cents. Also, designers had to consider how cultural differences among countries affect the way the software presents upgrade alternatives to the rental agent. For example, the software needed to recognize that renters in Germany tend to select cars primarily on performance and features, whereas customers in the United States are most sensitive to price. Furthermore, Alamo's worldwide service requires its systems to appear to operate 24 hours per day, 7 days per week. For 16 hours of the day, the system usage peaks somewhere in the world. This pattern of usage limits the hours during which the system can be backed up and changes can be made to the hardware or software.

SOURCES: Cyndee Miller, U.S. marketers set sights south of Mexico, *Marketing News* (October 10, 1994): 9, 11; and Elaine Underwood, Alamo, HFS make synergy pact, *Brandweek* (June 27, 1994): 4.

Alamo can also use its customer information to strategic advantage. For example, in June 1994, Alamo entered into a four-year marketing agreement to share and cross-pollinate resources with Hospitality Franchise Systems, the parent of the Ramada, Days Inn, Howard Johnson, Super 8, and Park Inn International hotels. In September 1994, Alamo also teamed up with the Hyatt Corporation hotel chain and United Airlines to open service to Latin America. By supplying its rental agents with detailed and timely customer information, Alamo hopes to be the agency with which customers can book reservations most easily.

Case Questions

1. What information about a customer do Alamo's employees need, at a minimum, in order to process the customer's reservation?
2. What additional information would enable Alamo's agents to be more responsive to the customer? How well do Alamo's systems collect such information?
3. What information would Alamo's customers like to know at the time they make a reservation? What information and other needs do they have when they pick up the car? What are their needs when they return the rental? How well do Alamo's systems respond to all these needs?
4. What management decisions at Alamo depend on the information Alamo's systems maintain about reservations and the rental fleet?
5. How does Alamo's global presence affect the type of information it needs to collect from its customers?
6. How does Alamo's global presence affect the design of its information systems?
7. In what way(s) does Alamo use information for strategic advantage?

Part II

Information Technology

Information technology has enabled the information revolution. Advances in information technology have reduced the cost and increased the value of collecting, storing, manipulating, and disseminating information. Part II discusses the elements of information technology: software, hardware, database management, and data communications. Software provides instructions to control computers, specifying how they process information to meet individual and organizational needs. Hardware, consisting of computers and other devices, provides the equipment to carry out software instructions and to collect, store, and output information. Database management technology efficiently organizes and controls information storage retrieval. Data communication technology provides the means to move information rapidly. Managers who understand these technologies can make wise decisions about how to use information technology to satisfy their own information needs and the information needs of their organizations.

Chapter 5

Software Technology

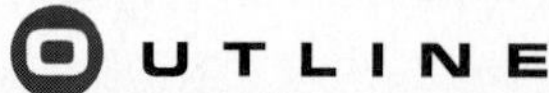

OUTLINE

Software Selection, Development, and Use in a Real Estate Development Company

What Is Software?

Horizontal Application Software

- Word Processing
- Desktop Publishing
- Presentation Graphics
- Spreadsheets
- Database Management
- Communications
- Accounting Packages

Vertical Application Software

- Off-the-Shelf Software
- Customized Software
- Home-Grown Software

Systems Software

- Operating Systems
- Systems Utilities
- Network Operating Systems

Software Development Tools

- Computer Languages
- CASE Tools

LEARNING OBJECTIVES

After completing the reading and activities for Chapter 5, students will be able to

1. Define *software.*
2. Compare and contrast horizontal application software and vertical application software.
3. Compare and contrast word processing, desktop publishing, and presentation graphics software.
4. List the major features a manager should seek in choosing particular word processing, desktop publishing, and presentation graphics software.
5. Briefly describe spreadsheet, database and file management, communications, and accounting software.
6. Cite the relative advantages of off-the-shelf, customized, and home-grown vertical applications software.
7. List the key features of operating systems and network operating systems that managers should consider in selecting such software.
8. Describe the use of systems utilities by managers and other software users.
9. Comment about the role of computer languages, data dictionaries, and CASE tools in software development.
10. Illustrate the way a particular type of software meets a manager's information needs.

Software Selection, Development, and Use in a Real Estate Development Company

Eighteen years ago, Tom Lynch and two partners founded the real estate development company of Lynch, Ryder, and McMillan (LR&M). Today, after surviving one of his partners and buying the other's share in the firm, Tom owns and manages the company.

LR&M had started as a general contracting company. A general contractor functions as a broker of construction services. The contractor bids on jobs and assembles a team of subcontractors to perform the actual work. A general contractor may also contract some of the material purchasing and construction work to itself.

As LR&M grew and Tom gained experience, Tom began to contract more and more of the construction work to LR&M. Currently, LR&M owns a large fleet of construction equipment and directly employs equipment operators, carpenters, and other skilled laborers. Increasingly, LR&M has involved itself in tract development. The company purchases a large tract of land, improves the land by adding roads, water lines, and sewers, divides the land into residential lots, sells the lots, and builds homes on them according to the designs selected by the buyers. Often, LR&M helps a buyer finance a house by offering below-market mortgages. LR&M repackages most of these mortgages and sells them to banks but continues to hold some in its own account. LR&M has also purchased several apartment buildings filled with rental units, converted the apartments to condominiums as renters left them, and then sold the condominiums. LR&M continues to collect rent from some long-term lease holders.

LR&M has accumulated an array of business computers and software over the years. Its marketing and sales people use Macintosh computers to prepare advertising and brochures and to track sales leads. Five years ago at the advice of a consultant, LR&M purchased Compaq computers, compatible with IBM-PCs, to support the construction side of the business. The consultant also recommended the quotation, contract management, billing, and general ledger software the company now uses.

The construction software, while adequate at first, did not meet the company's needs as it changed and grew. One year after purchasing the original software, Tom found that he could not easily add new software to manage and account for his growing fleet of construction equipment. The consultant who had selected and installed the software had gone out of business. The software company that developed the construction software was located three time zones away, was not interested in talking to end users, and had no plans to develop software that would meet LR&M's needs.

Tom also realized that he needed to computerize his manual system of tracking rent and mortgage collections. This task now overwhelmed his staff and had resulted in several recent incidents where he was not alerted in time to situations that required his intervention.

Tom realized that it was time to review and reevaluate LR&M's computer needs in an organized way. Although he expected to use a consultant to assist with the reassessment, he also vowed that this time he would be more knowledgeable about the software and would participate more actively in the process of evaluating and selecting software.

Tom Lynch must ensure that he has the appropriate software for his company to function effectively. He must *diagnose* his information needs, *evaluate* current software, *design* changes in the required software to meet the company's information needs, and then *implement* the new software system. Although he will likely need to secure expert assistance in identifying and procuring the appropriate software, Tom must play a significant role in assessing the company's needs and matching the software to these needs. In this chapter we provide an overview of the issues Tom must consider in evaluating and finding appropriate software, regardless of the type of hardware his company uses. We begin by defining software and identifying four basic types—horizontal application software, vertical application software, systems software, and software development tools. We then describe each of these categories in turn, focusing on the issues relevant to managers in the selection, development, and use of such software. The text in this chapter includes an overview of the major types of software in each of these categories.

What Is Software?

Software refers to commands that direct a computer to process information or data. Computers require software to perform the task the user wants to have executed. LR&M's computers, for example, need software to assist with word processing, financial analysis, contract management, and other functions. Computer software enables a user to type, edit, and print a document; to calculate and project financial ratios; or to schedule equipment usage. Tom Lynch uses software to support sales, marketing, accounting, and operations activities. Now he wants software to assist with tracking the collection of rent and mortgage payments.

Computer professionals commonly classify software by the type of task it instructs the computer to do. **Horizontal application software** performs generic tasks common to many types of problems and applications across and within industries. Word processing, desktop publishing, and presentation graphics software create letters, documents, and other publications and presentations. Spreadsheet software performs numerical calculations, financial projections, and transaction recording. Database software performs filing, sorting, and mass data storage. Communications software connects computers and users. Accounting packages help with the preparation of tax forms, cash flows, balance sheets, income statements, and other corporate financial statements. Tom Lynch, for example, might use generic word processing software such as Microsoft Word or WordPerfect or spreadsheet software such as Lotus 1-2-3 or Excel for the personal computers his business uses. Because of its wide appeal and mass market, manufacturers can produce horizontal application software for personal computers to sell at a relatively low price through retail outlets and mail-order houses. In the mainframe (large-scale computer) and minicomputer (mid-range computer) markets, horizontal software, such as Oracle, Ingres, and DB2 database management systems, typically offer additional and more sophisticated features but remain expensive despite competition because the size of the market is small compared with the size of the PC market and because software development costs are high.

Vertical application software performs tasks common to a specific industry. Programs to manage dog kennels, support hospital billing, or create architectural drawings illustrate vertical application software. Tom Lynch, for example, might find real estate vertical application software best meets his need to track his rental and mortgage income. Vertical software has more difficulty capturing a mass market because it addresses specialty needs. It is more often sold in relatively small quantities through such nonretail channels as software developers, consulting firms with expertise in an application area such as architectural planning or government contracting, and companies called **integrators,** who package hardware and software to meet a customer's specification. Vertical software tends to be expensive; for example, its price generally exceeds $5,000 for software running on personal computers. Although costs are higher for software running on minicomputers and mainframes, the cost per user is typically less.

Systems software provides the functions a computer needs to manage its various parts, such as its printers, keyboards, video screens, and data storage devices. It also provides functions that allow its users to control which application software they want to use. Every computer must be equipped with systems software simply to make it work. For example, each of LR&M's computers includes systems software that the computer vendor installed prior to LR&M's purchase. When buying new computers, Tom Lynch may have the opportunity to select among several brands of systems software that work with the computers he intends to buy. Afterwards, he may purchase additional systems software products to augment his ability to monitor and manage his computer, although most systems software is packaged and sold with its associated computer.

Software development tools, a fourth category of software, help people create new software. Computer professionals use software development tools such as programming languages, data dictionaries, and computer-aided software engineering (CASE) tools to create, maintain, customize, and apply software to specific tasks. Tom Lynch might hire computer programmers to modify vertical or horizontal software to better meet his firm's information needs. These programmers would need certain software development tools to perform their tasks. They might request additional tools to help them become more productive.

Horizontal Application Software

Managers such as Tom Lynch should be extensively involved in the choice of horizontal applications software. Evaluation of existing and possible software should occur after a complete diagnosis of a firm's information needs. In the next sections we discuss seven of the most popular types of horizontal applications software—1) word processing, 2) desktop publishing, 3) presentation graphics, 4) spreadsheets, 5) database management, 6) communications, and 7) accounting. Many additional categories exist. For example, electronic mail, addressed in Chapter 9, is heavily used on mainframes, minicomputers, and PC networks. Project management, scheduling, and group decision making, addressed in Chapter 11, are also popular horizontal applications.

Many vendors sell several types of horizontal aplication software in a single-package called a **suite.** Most software suites include word processing, spreadsheet, database, and presentation graphics software. Vendors usually sell their suites at a significant discount relative to the prices of the components they include. In addition to being less expensive, the components of a suite are also designed to work together. They present a common look and feel to the user and can easily exchange information. For example, someone working on a document in the word processor should be able to include tables and charts created with the spreadsheet and presentation graphics software. The disadvantage of using a suite is that it ties the user to a single vendor rather than providing a choice for each component. This disadvantage can be overcome by purchasing additional horizontal software from another vendor if its use can be justified.

Horizontal software is also sold as **integrated packages.** Microsoft Works, for example, is an integrated package consisting of software for word processing, communications, database management, spreadsheet work, charting, and drawing. The user of an integrated package does not have to switch between programs to use its different functions as he or she would with a suite. The integrated package appears to be a single program. Integrated packages are typically sold at a price well below the price of a suite. Their major disadvantage, however, is that they provide less functionality for each application, such as word processing, than that provided by software dedicated to that application or than that provided by a software suite.

Many organizations standardize on a single horizontal software package for a given application. For example, a company such as LR&M might standardize on the word processing package called WordPerfect, even though some users would prefer competitive packages such as Microsoft Word or Wordstar. In deciding to standardize, an organization must weigh the loss of flexibility and employee autonomy against gains in mass purchasing, common support, and common training.[1] When selecting a standard, an organization should survey all users for the features they require and compare these features with those provided by alternative candidates. Successful standardization requires that the product selected should have at least the features required by its users.

In evaluating a horizontal software package, potential buyers such as Tom Lynch should consider not only the quality of the software, but also the quality of the vendor or manufacturer, the quality of the documentation, and the availability of ancillary materials such as textbooks and training courses. The stability and market position of a software manufacturer affect the likelihood of continued development and support of its products and the continued availability of third-party auxiliary software and publications. For example, Microsoft and Lotus Development currently dominate the spreadsheet software market. The quality and responsiveness of a manufacturer's technical support staff is also important, even for organizations that have excellent internal support staffs. When software problems arise, often only the manufacturer can diagnose their causes, find ways to work around the difficulties, and fix them if necessary. Buyers can use trade magazines as primary sources of information about a vendor's market share and support quality.

Buyers of horizontal applications software should also assess a manufacturer's policies and pricing for support and upgrades. Vendors differ in the length of time for which they provide free technical support as well as in the price of technical support after this period. Some vendors offer a money-back guarantee to unhappy users. Some vendors provide free access to an electronic bulletin board for sharing information about known flaws or bugs, ways of working around problems, and upgrade release notices; other vendors provide bulletin boards on which users can talk with other users about their experiences with the product. In addition, a buyer should consider the hours of the vendor's technical support, particularly if the vendor is located in a distant time zone.

Managers of an organization that uses several types of hardware platforms (for example, IBM mainframe, IBM-PC, and Macintosh) or several types of systems software should assess whether or not the horizontal software can run on all these systems. The organization benefits from the portability of horizontal applications software because its users can use diverse computer hardware systems with minimal retraining. In addition, the computers' hardware and systems software can be changed without affecting the users' ability to perform their work.

Managers must recognize, however, that an organization that wants all or most of its computer users to have access to any horizontal software that it buys may incur a high cost in spite of the low price of a single copy. Software vendors generally offer **site licenses,** which give an organization the right to use a specified number of copies of the licensed software or the right to give a specified number of users access to a single copy of the software, at a discount relative to the price of an individual license. Sometimes, in exchange for this discount, the vendor requires that support be provided through a single contact at the organization's site and that the organization make sufficient copies of the documentation for all software users. Figure 5-1 summarizes the key criteria for selecting horizontal applications software.

Criteria for Selecting Horizontal Software

Quality and features of the product
Price of the product
Quality of documentation
Reputation of the vendor and manufacturer
Availability of textbooks, training, and other ancillaries
Price, availability, and terms of site license
Financial stability of manufacturer
Market share of product in software category
Quality and responsiveness of technical support staff
Time zone and hours of operation of phone support
Price and policies regarding support
Electronic bulletin board support
Satisfaction guarantees
Price and frequency of upgrades
Range of hardware platforms supported

Word Processing

Word processing software assists users in creating, editing, formatting, and printing documents, and is the most widely used type of software for personal computers.[2] LR&M likely has many employees who use word processing software to prepare letters, memos, reports, or other documents. Before selecting a word processing program, users should identify the types of documents they prepare and the features required to ease their preparation. They should also evaluate their own style and any other personal characteristics that will affect their use of word processing software. Diagnosis of personal and managerial information needs together with an evaluation of word processing software options should precede the design and implementation of a word processing system.

What are some of the basic features to consider in evaluating word processing software? Figure 5-2 offers a set of factors to consider when performing such an assessment. First, the user should evaluate the software's editing functions, that is, the process of inserting, moving, and deleting text. Editing features should include the ability to undo changes; search for and replace all occurrences of one word or phrase with another; mark a location in the text and then return to it after examining other parts of the document; show two or more parts of the document on the screen simultaneously; insert, move, or delete columns in a table; and perform high-quality automatic hyphenation.

Factors to Consider in Evaluating Word Processing Software

Basic editing features
Formatting and layout capabilities
Proofreading tools
Graphics handling and other multimedia support
Font and printer support
Indexing and cross-referencing tools
Document organization tools
Ease of importing and exporting files
Ease and power of document merging
Ease of creating macros and power of macro language
Network support
Linkage to spreadsheets
Linkage to other software using standard interfaces
Speed for editing and printing

Second, assessing word processing software involves evaluating the **formatting** options, or ways of changing the appearance of a document to make it more readable or attractive. Formatting includes functions to change the size or shape (font) of letters, numbers, or symbols in the text; show the text in bold, italicized, or underlined formats; and change the layout by altering the margins, paragraph spacing, line spacing, and indentations. Word processing packages differ in the variety and styles of the fonts they support. Some support a large range of fonts and font sizes upon printing but do not show text on the screen the way that it will appear when printed. Many users consider "What You See Is What You Get (WYSIWYG)" features to be highly important. Most word processors allow the user to switch between WYSIWYG and normal text format because the speed of entering and editing text in WYSIWYG format is slower. Most word processors include **style sheets,** which permit users to create a document that follows a template with variations in different parts of the document. Advanced features allow and support changes in the number of columns per page, allow text to flow around graphics, permit portrait and landscape orientations of the page within the same document, and ease the insertion of mathematical symbols and equations into a document.

Third, word processors include **proofreading tools,** such as a spell checker and grammar checker. The quality of these tools varies substantially among word processing products, and buyers should consult the trade review literature to ensure that the quality meets their needs.

Fourth, word processors differ in their ability to include and manipulate graphics and other nontextual data. Most software allows graphics developed elsewhere to be imported and inserted into the document. Advanced features include the ability to create simple graphics, rotate graphics, and include sound or motion pictures within a document.

Fifth, most word processing packages support the creation of an index and table of contents from the document. In addition, most support cross-referencing, a feature that automatically changes references to figure or table numbers within a document if the user adds or deletes figures or tables. Furthermore, many packages also support automatic references to page numbers at selected points in a document.

Desktop Publishing

Desktop publishing software (DTP) helps users lay out text and graphics in a form suitable for publication. Although both word processing and desktop publishing help users create highly presentable documents, word processors attempt to meet writers' needs, whereas desktop publishing software addresses publishers' needs. How might LR&M, for example, use desktop publishing? Employees might need it to prepare prospectuses for real estate offerings, draft advertising copy, or design sales brochures. They might use word processing software to prepare copy, which they then incorporate into the publication using desktop publishing. Users should consider layout, typographic control, text handling, graphics manipulation, and text importing and exporting features in evaluating desktop publishing software, as shown in Figure 5-3.

A DTP software user should first assess the features available to support the layout of a publication. At a minimum, the software should support the ability to have multiple columns on a page; to wrap text around graphics (ideally either in a rectangular fashion or at the user's option along the contours of a graphic object); to control the placement, size, style, and font of text material; to **snap** moved text or graphics onto some type of coordinate system, available for viewing on the screen; and to flow text across pages (as for a headline). Products differ in the ease with which graphics can be cropped and text can be sized; advanced DTP products also automate some features of layout, such as the balancing of columns on a page.

Factors to Consider in Evaluating Desktop Publishing Software

- Ease and sophistication of layout features
- Availability and quality of typographic controls
- Text and document handling features
- Strength of tools for creating and manipulating graphics
- Ability to import graphics and text from different packages
- Wide choice of output and export formats and features
- Linkage to other software using standard interfaces
- Speed of importing, formatting, saving, and printing
- Cross-platform similarity

Typographic controls include control over the justification, size, and font of text. DTP software should allow hanging indentations (where the indentation begins at the second line), block indentations (where an entire block of text is indented), control over kerning (dealing with the space used by a letter relative to its environment), and word spacing. Most DTP packages support mathematical and other symbols as well as colored type. Advanced features include the ability to rotate text, control the size and spacing of footnote marks and text, automatically set the vertical spacing of text placed in a box, and automatically hyphenate text properly (with optional override and a modifiable hyphen dictionary). DTP software differs in the smallest and largest font size supported and in the fineness with which font size, kerning, and horizontal or vertical alignment can be controlled.

Text handling features allow a DTP operator to compose or modify text as with a word processor. At a minimum, DTP software should include the ability to cut, paste, and copy text from one location to another. Less common features include the ability to search and replace text and check the spelling in a document. Advanced features include indexing, cross-referencing, table-of-contents generation, and chapter and section numbering. Table editing is particularly important: DTP software should facilitate the formatting of tables, sizing of columns, and drawing of column and row separators.

DTP software should also offer the ability to create and manipulate graphics. At a minimum, a product should provide the ability to draw lines, rectangles, ellipses, and circles, and to fill them with patterns or various shades of gray. It should also include the ability to crop and resize graphics with or without distorting the **aspect ratio**—the relationship between the length and width of a graphic. It should also have the ability to print text over graphics or vice versa. Advanced features include the ability to flip or rotate graphics, make square or round corners, fill regions with colors, and blend colors from one region to another. DTP products differ in the number of colors and patterns supported, the number of line types (arrowed, dotted, doubled, dashed, etc.) supported, and the fineness in control over the length or size of figures.

Importing text and graphics is a critical function of DTP software. Because DTP software lacks the full features of word processing software for the creation of text and the full features of presentation software for the creation of graphics, most users create text and graphics for publication using different horizontal software. Users may also buy pictures or **clip art** from graphics library vendors or use scanners to create a graphics file from a printed document. DTP software should be able to import text and graphics created elsewhere, preserving most or all of the formatting and graphics detail. Software reviews of DTP software normally include a section addressing which word processing software and graphics file formats each product supports.

The DTP software should also be able to export text to word processing files and graphics with text to presentation graphics programs after layout is completed. This feature allows a publisher to update files received from the composer to reflect changes made. Advanced packages support linking of such files through a commonly accepted interface (such as OLE for Windows and Publish and Subscribe for the Macintosh System 7). As a result, a DTP document automatically reflects changes a user makes to a word processing file and vice versa.

DTP packages differ dramatically in the speed with which they print a document, redraw a page on a screen after a major formatting change, save and retrieve a document, and convert text or graphics imported from other packages. Desktop publishing is an inherently complex process that requires a great deal of computer and printer time, so speed in DTP software may be considerably more important than in other software; for example, the time required to print a document may vary from 3 to 30 minutes. A purchaser such as Tom Lynch or one of his associates at LR&M can check reviews in trade magazines for information about DTP speed.

Many DTP packages operate on both IBM-compatible and Macintosh computers; some are compatible with several types of systems software such as DOS and Windows. Ideally, DTP software should appear similar when running on different systems. This cross-platform similarity eases the transition from one environment to another and reduces the amount of training needed at companies that support a multivendor environment.

Presentation Graphics

Presentation graphics software, such as Harvard Graphics and Powerpoint, enable users with little graphics training to produce professional-looking slides, overheads, or prints to support their presentations. Tom Lynch, for example, might use such software in preparing business presentations for possible lenders or clients. A 1993 study indicated that 64 percent of 962 respondents planned to purchase presentation software in the next year.[3] Reviewers evaluate presentation graphics products on the support they provide for text charting, numeric charting, and chart editing; the features they provide to coordinate the design among charts; and their support for delivering a presentation from the computer screen.[4] In addition, purchasers should consider compatibility with users' systems software, ease of interface to add-ons and peripherals, scalability for users with diverse expertise and experience, portability to different computers, ease of use, sophistication, and graphical user interface support.[5] Users such as Tom Lynch should also consider the software's ease of use and quality and speed of output.

Most presentations consist primarily of text charts, typically bulleted lists. Presentation graphics packages allow users to control the size, spacing, and centering of text; the choice of font and color; and the size and shape of bullets. Some also provide word processing features such as a spell checker, thesaurus, hanging indentations, text search and replace, and outlining. Most permit a user to import text from a word processing or ASCII file and assist in exporting text to a word processing package. Most packages ease data entry by providing templates for common types of charts such as title charts, bullet charts, multicolumn charts, and organizational charts. Advanced features include the ability to wrap text around objects; to present text on the screen in the same font in which it will be printed; and to have easy access to multinational, mathematical, and scientific symbols.

Numeric charts allow a user to easily convert tables of numbers into readable graphic displays. Almost all packages provide a large variety of chart types, including pie and exploded pie charts; bar and stacked bar charts; and area, line, and scatter charts. Most automatically determine the appropriate scale of the X and Y coordinates while giving a user the option to override. Most also offer three-dimensional perspectives of many chart types, along with optional shadows or shading to increase the 3-D effect. Most packages facilitate importing data from or exporting data to spreadsheet software; some provide direct links among packages so that the presentation graphic automatically reflects changes in spreadsheet data.

In addition to preparing text and numeric charts, presentation graphics packages allow the user to edit charts by adding lines, designs, and colors. Most packages allow the user to control the color and fill pattern of the chart background. Typically, users can add lines, rectangles, ellipses, circles, and polygons. Most packages allow the user to specify the border color and width, and interior color and fill pattern of such figures. Some permit drawing of figures via a mouse. Users may also select, place, and size on a chart predefined designs or symbols. Many packages also allow users to import clip art produced by other packages or sold by third-party vendors.

Presentation software should assist in preparing charts with a common, integrated design by providing overridable automatic or recommended colors, sizes, fonts, alignment, and background. It should create and support integrated presentations made directly from the computer, rather than from slides or transparencies, by providing a variety of visual effects when moving among charts, such as fading (one chart slowly disappears while the next chart slowly forms), wiping (one chart moves to the right while another replaces it from the left, or vice versa), and scrolling. A user preparing a computerized presentation should easily be able to preview his or her presentation and change the order of the charts. Users should also be able to enter presenter's notes that appear on charts used by the presenter but not on charts shown to the audience. In addition, the user should be able to adjust the level of detail or order of slides during the presentation in response, for example, to audience questions or time constraints. Advanced features allow the user to add multimedia effects such as voice or video to enliven a presentation.

Presentation graphics output is normally sent to a laser printer for high-quality copy. Almost all packages also support the use of dot-matrix printers, pen plotters, and standard graphics file formats. Many can also produce output for color thermal printers, color laser printers, Postscript devices (devices that support the Postscript standard for high-quality graphics output), and film recorders.

Spreadsheets

Spreadsheets are programs intended to facilitate calculation of tabular information containing interdependent values. The programs help automate the process of performing repeated calculations. Analysts at LR&M might use spreadsheets to calculate mortgage rates, project income, or track construction costs. After word processing, spreadsheets are used more widely than any other type of software for personal computers and are widely used on other types of systems as well.[6] Originally designed by Harvard MBA student Daniel Bricklin to quickly analyze alternative solutions to problems posed in the teaching cases used in his classes, spreadsheets incorporate a large number of repeated calculations.[7] Bricklin's software resembled an accountant's spreadsheet, a piece of paper having ruled rows and columns (see Figure 5-4). In addition to holding words and numbers in the cells of the spreadsheet, Bricklin's software could use formulas whose value was calculated and appeared on the screen. Using his automated spreadsheet, Bricklin could easily evaluate 10 or 20 scenarios in the same amount of time needed for other students to evaluate a single alternative.

Today the basic function and value of spreadsheet software remains the same. Two enhancements have influenced the use of spreadsheets: 1) Graphic functions allow data in a spreadsheet to be displayed as graphs or charts and motivate people to use spreadsheets to visualize data when few or no calculations are performed; and 2) basic database features allow a user to sort data by column or row, to identify and extract rows or columns meeting a specified set of criteria, or to compute statistics such as the minimum, maximum, mean, and standard deviation of data meeting specified criteria.

How do managers such as Tom Lynch or his associates evaluate and select the spreadsheet software that best meets their needs? Figure 5-5 lists factors users should consider in

IGURE 5-4 Illustration of a Spreadsheet

Microsoft Excel - TEMP2.XLS

File Edit View Insert Format Tools Data Window Help

	A	B	C	D	E	F	G	H	I	J
1	GRADE SHEET									
2										
3	Student	Paper	Paper	Quiz	Quiz	Midterm	Final	Final		Final
4	Name	#1	#2	#1	#2	Exam	Exam	Average		Grade
5	Adams	91	88	100	100	88	92	92.05		A
6	Aronson	65	70	60	80	55	75	67.75		D
7	Belson	78	70	70	68	75	75	73.50		C
8	Bronsky	83	88	71	88	85	87	84.65		B
9	Carlson	89	95	80	88	83	82	85.60		B+
10	Coleman	80	82	70	78	79	85	80.40		B-
11	Daley	85	85	65	70	65	70	73.00		C
12	Doran	95	85	95	73	91	78	85.40		B+
13	Edgars	70	90	82	82	80	81	80.70		B-
14	Freedman	78	74	74	92	82	96	84.60		B
15	Gregory	68	80	55	82	78	86	77.30		C+
16										
17	AVG	80.18	82.45	74.73	81.91	78.27	82.45	80.45		B-
18										

Sheet1 Sheet2 Sheet3 Sheet4 Sheet5 Sheet6

Ready NUM

evaluating spreadsheet software.[8] First, they should assess the ease of entering and manipulating data. A spreadsheet should recognize, for example, 4/5/92 as a date rather than as a division problem and "4th Quarter" as a label rather than as a value. Users should easily be able to identify regions of the spreadsheet, called **ranges;** the software should allow data entry into such ranges in a logical order without using the mouse or arrow keys, as well as easy combination and comparison of ranges. In addition, the user should determine how well the software meets his or her personal style, preferences, and experiences with data entry.

Speed of computation varies in importance, depending on the size of the spreadsheet and the speed of the user's computer. For users working on very large spreadsheets or for those using relatively slow computers, speed may become extremely important. The relative speed of different spreadsheet software varies for different tasks. One spreadsheet package may be faster in loading a large spreadsheet, while another may be faster for recomputing values, performing statistical calculations, or running small programs called macros. All spreadsheets should recalculate values almost instantaneously as a user enters new data. Purchasers can use benchmarks published in trade magazines to evaluate speed.

Users should also assess the software's ability to format data for presentation. Desirable features include the ability to use different print fonts on the screen and as output to the printer; ease in including graphics and text on the same page; simple pagination of multipage output; the ability to print wide spreadsheets sideways; the availability of predefined styles and a large number of colors and patterns for graphs; and automatic table formatting. Similarity of screen and printed output is particularly important when using graphics. The software should have the ability to manipulate graphics by scaling and moving, add graph-

Factors to Consider in Evaluating Spreadsheet Software

Ease of data entry and manipulation	Ease of importing text data
Speed of computation and printing	Statistical and optimization features
Ease and quality of data formatting and presentation	Support for building macros
Similarity of screen and printed output	Network support
Graph formatting and manipulation features	Linkage to database managers
File consolidation abilities	Linkage to other software using standard interfaces

ics by drawing, add text within graphics, and import or export graphics to and from other packages having different graphics formats.

Sophisticated users require that a spreadsheet support the development of statistical models using regression and other statistical techniques. In addition, the spreadsheet should allow the user to build **macros**—programs that automatically execute a series of spreadsheet commands. A user with little or no programming experience can develop such macros to manipulate the values in or formats of a spreadsheet.

Network support allows many people at once to use spreadsheet software stored on a network server (see Chapter 8). The software should let users identify those people authorized to use or modify the spreadsheets that they create and lock out unauthorized users. The software should also ensure that two or more users cannot simultaneously make inconsistent modifications to the same spreadsheet.

Spreadsheet software should allow standard interfaces to database management software (SQL, for example; see Chapter 7) in such a way that values in a spreadsheet can reflect the status of a database. Specifically, the spreadsheet should show only the most recent value of data in the database, and vice versa. Finally, spreadsheet software should provide links through systems software that enable other software to use or modify the values in a spreadsheet. For example, the Microsoft Windows systems software provides facilities known as **Dynamic Data Exchange (DDE)** and **Object Linking and Embedding (OLE)** that spreadsheet software can use to exchange data in a standard way with other programs using the same facilities.

Database Management

Database managers allow users to store, organize, and retrieve data of any type. Various managers at LR&M might use a database manager to store information about present and past customers and contracts, sales leaders, or the company's equipment. Most applications organize data into categories of **records,** for example, customers or employees. A database manager generates screens for data entry, cross-references data of different types (for example, which employee is the sales representative for a given customer), and retrieves data meeting a selected set of criteria and in a specified sorted order. Simple database managers that deal with only a single set of related records at a time are called **file managers.**

Database managers provide support not only for users needing to store data, but also for software developers who need to write programs that store and access data. A programmer who uses a database manager does not have to worry about designing or implementing efficient data storage or retrieval. He or she can pass data received from a user to the database manager, which in turn stores the data in an efficient manner. Similarly, the programmer does not need to write code to retrieve the data; instead, the programmer writes code to ask the database to retrieve the data in the desired order and format. The database manager sorts and indexes the data for retrieval. A database manager typically includes the following features: error checking upon data entry; guarantee of consistency among related data; management of simultaneous access and change to the same data by multiple users; ability to trigger an activity upon user-specified conditions (for example, to change a customer's credit status when the customer's payments are sufficiently late); automatic report generation; and recovery and backup from hardware or software failures.

Database management software is so important that some venders now incorporate it in their systems software (for example, in IBM's OS/2). We discuss database management systems in more detail in Chapter 7.

Communications

People use communications software along with communications hardware to move information among computers. LR&M may have a network of computers in its accounting, marketing, or operations departments that must share or exchange information. In addition, it may hook its in-house computers to computers in other locations or organizations to secure unique industry-related information. Chapter 8 addresses the technical and managerial issues involved in intercomputer communication. In this section, we briefly address the features that users should expect from communications software, as shown in Figure 5-6.

Terminal emulation makes a user's keyboard and screen appear to be connected to another computer (called the **remote computer**) rather than to the user's computer (called the **local computer**). If the remote computer is a minicomputer or a mainframe, its software will probably expect to receive input from a keyboard that differs from the user's and to display output on a different type of screen. Communications packages should allow your computer to emulate any common terminal (combination of keyboard and screen). With this capability, you can connect to different types of computers and run software that expects to interact with terminals different from your own.

Communications software must also work with a number of communications hardware devices—devices that translate characters typed at the keyboard into sounds or digital signals that can be sent over telephone lines, and then translate these sounds and signals at the receiving end into characters to be displayed on the screen. Most hardware communications devices also accept commands from the computer to perform such operations as dialing a telephone number, disconnecting a telephone line, or specifying the number of rings the

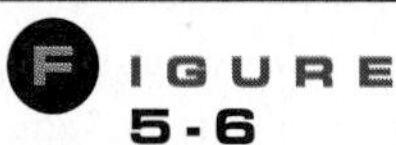
FIGURE 5-6 Features of Communications Software

- Large selection of terminal emulations
- Support of many types of modems
- Large selection of file transfer protocols
- Availability, power, and ease of use of script language
- Call-back feature
- Ability to poll a list of remote computers
- Ability to function as a host
- Security/password protection
- Storage of commonly used telephone numbers

device should wait for before answering a telephone call. Communications software should support all major standards for sending and receiving transmittal characters and for sending commands to a communications device.

Computers also exchange files, sending a large volume of data between two or more computers. Quality communications software ensures that noise on the communications channel does not affect the integrity of the data being transmitted. The computer software at the transmitting and receiving ends must use identical techniques, known as **protocols;** otherwise, they will not properly interpret each other's data. For example, the software may send messages back and forth to acknowledge receipt of data or to request retransmittal. Software receiving such messages must be able to distinguish between the control messages and the data being transmitted. Communications software should be capable of operating under any of the several existing standards for coordinating file transmittal. Most communications software allows file transmittal to take place without interfering with other activities that users may perform concurrently on their computers.

Most communications packages provide a language, called a **script,** in which a user having minimal training can write small programs to control the communications package. By using a script, a user might need only a single keystroke to dial a frequently called number, send identification and passwords to a remote computer, and issue a series of commands needed to start a session on that remote computer. Scripts for different communications packages vary in their power and ease of use.

Advanced features of communications software include the ability to send a file to a list of remote computers, poll a list of remote computers to receive data, and turn a personal computer into a **host computer**—one that other users can access from remote sites. Software that provides host services should also provide password protection so that only authorized users can access the host computer. In more secure environments, communications software should provide call-back features, which allow your computer to be accessed only from specified telephone numbers. When a user first accesses your computer, call-back software asks the user for a pass code. The software then breaks the connection and calls the user back at the number he or she has previously authorized. This feature keeps unauthorized users from accessing a computer even if they know the pass code.

Accounting Packages

Accounting software differs from the other horizontal application software because all accounting software must be customized to some degree to the user's application. In general, users perform this customization themselves as they install the software. For example, each company maintains its own list of ledger accounts whose titles and numbers are typically entered as data when a user sets up his or her system. Packages may differ in the number of digits allowed for an account number, whether or not alphanumeric characters are also allowed, and the number of characters allowed in account descriptions.

Users such as LR&M may purchase accounting packages in modules, such as general ledger, accounts receivable, accounts payable, inventory, payroll, order entry, purchasing, job cost estimation and invoicing, fixed asset management, bill of materials, material requirements planning (MRP), point of sale, shop floor control, professional invoicing, and retail invoicing. Buyers who purchase such modules generally obtain them from the same software manufacturer to ensure that data can easily transfer among modules without reentry. **Integrated accounting packages,** which combine all accounting functions into a single package with seamless interactions, maintain central files for all accounting functions, thereby eliminating reentry of data and data transfer problems. Integrated accounting packages generally contain software for at least general ledger, accounts payable, accounts receivable, and inventory. Two drawbacks of integrated accounting packages are that they reduce the buyer's ability to buy the best package for different accounting functions and that they often include unnecessary features or modules that add to their cost.

A buyer should evaluate accounting software on its ability to meet the buyer's functional needs, its match with the company's recordkeeping and operational practices, its adaptability to growth and expansion, its capacity to store the volume of records that the company anticipates, the quality and number of reports it provides, and the ease with which the user can create customized reports. Factors common to the evaluation of other horizontal software, such as the quality of documentation and the reputation of the manufacturer, are critical for accounting software because of the difficulty and expense of conversion to new software if the original decision is unsatisfactory or quickly outgrown.

Although many experts predicted that accounting would remain a horizontal application centralized on mainframe and minicomputers, a large percentage of small and medium companies now use accounting packages sold for desktop computers.[9] Vendors also report increasing sales of network-based accounting systems. Accounting, with its regular data collection and posting, fits well with the type of processing done efficiently on mainframes. Because so much of accounting work is data entry and its processes tend to be well defined and sequential, the graphical user interfaces that make desktop computers so attractive for other horizontal packages seem to be less important for accounting software. Only recently have networks that tie together data-entry workstations become sufficiently robust and microcomputer devices that store data became sufficiently developed to support typical accounting systems.[10]

Vertical Application Software

Vertical application software is designed for a particular industry, such as real estate development, or for a specific function within one or more industries, such as government contracting or accounting at advertising agencies. Developers of vertical application software possess expertise in the information needs and standard information processing activities within the industry they target. For example, companies with continuous manufacturing processes, such as chemical or oil manufacturers, have different information needs and require software different from those with discrete manufacturing processes, such as automobile or consumer goods manufacturers; a generic manufacturing package is unlikely to satisfy either group. Similarly, an airline and a railroad, both transportation companies, have unique information needs and require different software for tracking baggage or ticketing passengers.

In evaluating vertical software, managers should focus on whether or not the software supports the way their company conducts or wants to conduct its business. Unlike horizontal software, where the number and quality of advanced features is important because many people will be using it in different ways, vertical software must satisfy very specific requirements. For example, when Tom Lynch evaluates horizontal asset accounting software, he will find some packages that have all the features he needs to report the properties he owns correctly on his balance sheet and to calculate income properly for tax purposes. Some will have ten or more ways to calculate depreciation. However, horizontal asset accounting software is unlikely to satisfy LR&M's needs because it does not view these assets as the investments of a construction company. It does not provide the type of management information, such as property turnover rate, that Mr. Lynch needs to evaluate the company's performance. To find this type of information, Mr. Lynch will have to examine software written specifically for the construction industry. Furthermore, he will need to be sure that the software produces the specific reports he needs to perform his functions effectively.

Buyers of vertical software must also consider the quality and availability of support and customization. Vertical software vendors generally have a smaller customer support staff than horizontal software vendors. Buyers of vertical software must believe that the vendor can respond to the purchaser's unique needs and that the vendor has a sufficient base of installations to guarantee its existence for many years. LR&M, for example, purchased software to manage its equipment fleet from a consultant who went out of business soon after the purchase. Because companies rely on their vertical software for the daily operation of their business, failure of such software can have dramatic and disastrous consequences. Vendors must respond rapidly to both emergencies and requests for changes in the software's design. Because small companies often do not have the resources to purchase or develop customized software, they may instead customize their business practices to the available software, making the selection even more critical.

A company can acquire vertical software in three ways: (1) purchase off-the-shelf software from a software manufacturer and use it without modification; (2) customize the software; (3) develop the software from scratch, creating home-grown software.

Off-the-Shelf Software

Off-the-shelf software, also known as **packaged software,** refers to software that can be purchased from a retail outlet and installed without modification. Indeed, the license for off-the-shelf software generally prohibits its modification. Almost all horizontal software can be classified as off-the-shelf. Off-the-shelf software also exists for a wide range of vertical applications and industries.[11] For example, Tom Lynch might purchase software addressed to the requirements of government contractors for a minicomputer; he may also purchase accounting software specifically for the real estate development industry for use on a network of personal computers. Figure 5-7 offers examples of vertical software that can be purchased without customization. Good sources of listings of vertical software include the *Open Systems Software Referral Directory, Computer Associates International Catalog,* and *Data Sources,* as well as reviews of software in the trade and general press.

Advantages of Packaged Software. Packaged software offers two major advantages: price and a large base of users. Prices for vertical software for microcomputers typically range from $500 to $20,000, depending on the comprehensiveness and specialization of the software. Although these prices may seem high, computer programmers typically charge from $30 to $50 per hour and would require thousands of hours to write a program that has the same capabilities as even the most stripped-down off-the-shelf package.

Off-the-shelf software for minicomputers and mainframes is less common and more expensive. Minicomputer application software is typically priced between $10,000 and $50,000, with mainframe prices even higher. Often minicomputer and mainframe software vendors require an annual license fee as well as a fee for support and ongoing maintenance. Such costs may reduce the benefit of employing packaged software in such environments or motivate companies to replace mainframe and minicomputer systems with a network of desktop computers.

MOTOROLA

Packaged software benefits from the large number of users who have tested the software in a variety of environments. This wide use increases the likelihood that the software will not have major defects and will have desired features. Motorola, Inc.'s computer group recently migrated from a mainframe environment running home-grown software to an environment of workstations running mostly off-the-shelf software. This migration allowed the group to reduce its budget by 40 percent while shortening application development cycles. Use of off-the-shelf software reduced the amount of time that the in-house staff needed to spend modifying software for new versions of its systems software and new hardware

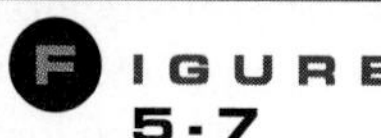
FIGURE 5-7 Examples of Off-the-Shelf Vertical Products

Banking—Loans and Mortgages
Loan Calculator, by Barr Software
Loan Plus, by Advanced Performance, Inc.
Loan Quality Assurance System, by Applied Micro Technology, Inc.
MORVAS Mortgage Administration System, by Formac Computer Systems, Ltd.

Civil Engineering/Architecture
ArchiCAD, by Graphisoft
AutoCAD Architectural Tablet Menus, by Applied Software Tech, Inc.
ISIS, by ISIS International, Inc.

Construction/Contractor Management
MacNeil Scheduling for Windows, by Turtle Creek Software
Job Cost System, by American Business Systems, Inc.

CPA Services
AccounTrax, by Information-Builders, Inc.
CPA Practice Management System, by Applied Computer Service, Inc.
Time & Billing, by Certified Systems, Inc.

Fuel Dealers/Distributors
Fuel Oil Management System, by Ashley McCormick Co., Inc.

Trucking/Freight/Warehousing
Fuel & Mileage Manager, by Compcar Services
Warehouse Services, by Ace Software

platforms. It also increased the group's ability to standardize on a single set of accounting and other operating packages that could be used across departments.[12]

Disadvantages of Packaged Software. Packaged software can create a dependency on the software manufacturer. Once a company installs one vendor's vertical software, it will incur heavy costs in licensing, training, and work redesign if it decides to change vendors. As a result, the vendor can charge high prices for upgrades and support. In addition, if a company wants an additional feature, it can only ask and wait for a future software release, somewhat losing the ability to control its own destiny.

Customized Software

OPEN SYSTEMS

Although most vertical software requires some degree of customization, **customized software** involves more than the user's customizing it upon installation. Instead, software manufacturers' representatives, known as **value added resellers (VARs),** customize the software to a customer's specification and hence add value to it. For example, about 700 of the 2,000 sales partners of Open Systems, Inc. are VARs, and approximately one-half of the accounting software these sales partners sell is customized.[13] Tom Lynch, for example, might consider customized software in areas related to the development of land tracts, where neither horizontal application software nor off-the-shelf vertical application software meets his company's information needs.

How to Buy Customized Software. A company may take a highly informal approach to purchasing customized software, selecting a package and a VAR because the company owner or CIO hears favorable comments about the VAR and software from a friend or relative in the same industry. Often this ad hoc approach to evaluation results in selecting software that does not meet the information needs of the purchaser. A more formal search process usually produces better results.

Experts suggest that a company prepare to purchase customized software by developing a **request for proposal (RFP)** that clearly identifies its information processing requirements and information needs.[14] The RFP should include details of how data should be collected and entered, the nature of all desired reports, and any other specifications. Next, the user identifies vendors and requests bids. Vendors should identify the requirements already met by their package and those that will need customization. The user then compares the responses, assessing the proposed features, costs, and vendor characteristics, and then selects two or three vendors for more detailed negotiation.

Each qualifying vendor should then perform an **operational capability demonstration (OCD)** that simulates the user's application as closely as possible. Such a simulation enables the user to judge how rapidly the system performs under the expected processing loads, gives a better indication of the system's operation, and helps identify the necessary changes in the software and the user's operations. Although users typically pay part of the cost of an OCD, the investment results in a more informed purchase decision. The final negotiations before selecting a vendor involve determining a payment schedule and agreeing on a test of the software's acceptability to the user.

Advantages of Customized Software. Customizing packaged software helps a company meet more of its information requirements. A company that customizes software also reduces its dependency on the software manufacturer to make needed changes: For example, the company can fix bugs without waiting for the manufacturer's next release. If the company uses a VAR to do the customization, it also buys influence with the manufacturer in the design of features in future releases. Because most software manufacturers who sell customizable software list many VARs who can provide support, the user does not depend on a single consultant, as Tom Lynch at LR&M did.

Disadvantages of Customized Software. Customized vertical software may suffer from a disproportionate number of software bugs. Although developers of packaged software spend a great deal of time and effort designing and testing their software, custom software developers do not because only one company will use the software. **Beta-testing,** in which software developers give potential users free copies of the software so that they can identify as many problems as possible before the software is released to paid users, is not feasible.

Second, a company that uses customized packaged software cannot readily use upgraded releases. As a result, the company does not benefit from the manufacturer's efforts at further development. Sometimes, for example, a company may spend many dollars to add a feature that the manufacturer might include in its next release for only a minimal upgrade fee.

Home-Grown Software

Organizations may develop their own **home-grown software** from scratch rather than use or customize packaged software for three reasons. First, no packaged software meets the required specifications, and modifying existing software is too difficult. Second, home-grown software may provide the company with a competitive advantage that the company wants no one else to access. Third, reselling the software may create a profit for the company.

Assigning the Responsibility for Software Development. Top management must decide whether to use internal company resources to develop software or to contract development to a third party for either home-grown or customized software. Generally, third parties, typically VARs, develop customized software because they have substantial expertise in the base software product. This advantage disappears for home-grown software because no preexisting packages are used.

Software development in small organizations is usually **outsourced**—given to a third party—because of a lack of internal resources for its development. Managers in large organizations either must use internal IS personnel or allow the IS staff to decide who will develop the software. Sometimes a company allows functional managers to seek development bids from both internal and external candidates. Chapter 14 examines the outsourcing decision in greater detail.

Advantages of Home-Grown Software. Home-grown software can offer a company a competitive advantage by providing services for customers and employees that the competition cannot reproduce. Thomas Cook U.S.A. a large travel agency that is now part of American Express, for example, developed state-of-the-art management information systems that allowed it to offer unique services and provide extensive cost information to its corporate customers. What type of software might LR&M develop to give it a competitive advantage?

AMERICAN EXPRESS

Disadvantages of Home-Grown Software. Home-grown software is expensive to produce, expensive to maintain, and subject to bugs. The competitive advantage gained by its use can be quickly diluted by third-party developers who take the opportunity to mimic the software's design and resell it to a company's competitors.

The Application Software Life Cycle. Customized and home-grown software progress through a life cycle of conception, development, birth, maturation, and decline. In the maturation phase, for example, a company makes minor modifications to enhance its software and to improve its functionality, usually in direct response to user requests. Software may then decline because the organization it serves changes and because the technologies that support it advance with time. A company should continually evaluate its software to ensure that it meets the organization's needs. At some point, the company must begin again to conceive of a software product that addresses the changed organizational requirements, incorporates modern software technology, and runs on the most cost-efficient hardware available.

Systems Software

Systems software, which includes operating systems, systems utilities, and network operating systems, performs background tasks that enable a computer to manage its devices and resources. An **operating system** consists of computer programs that perform the most basic housekeeping, resource allocation, and resource monitoring functions for a computer with a minimum of input or control by the user. It includes programs that start the computer when the user turns on the power switch, find and initiate application programs the user wants to run, and transfer the letters typed at the keyboard to the application program. **Systems utilities** programs also perform basic maintenance and resource control functions. They differ from operating systems in that the user controls their operations. For example, systems utilities would include a program that changes the name of a computer file. A **network operating system** consists of software that allows several connected computers to share common resources and communicate with one another.

Operating Systems

The way an operating system handles a computer's resources affects how users see those resources. Managers and other users should participate in selecting an operating system to ensure that it best fits with their needs, including their personal characteristics and their department's or organization's plans, objectives, and operating procedures. In particular, managers must recognize that operating systems differ in their user interface, their compatibility with different types of computers, and their ability to handle multiple users and tasks. After diagnosing his or her organization's information needs, the manager can then evaluate and choose the most appropriate operating system. Figure 5-8 compares and contrasts five common operating systems used in microcomputers along these three dimensions.

User Interface. Operating systems communicate with users. Tom Lynch at LR&M can choose among command-driven, menu-driven, and graphical user interfaces.

A **command-driven interface** requires users to direct a computer's next action by entering a command, typically by typing it at a keyboard. For example, in MS-DOS, an operating system with a command-driven interface for IBM-PC compatible computers, a C> prompt may appear on the computer screen; the user must then type a command, such as MODEM to start the modem functioning or DIR to display a listing of files. Most users and many professionals consider a command-driven interface relatively difficult to use because it requires the operator to know how to type and remember a large number of commands.

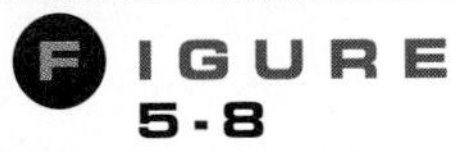

Characteristics of Five Popular Operating Systems for Microcomputers

Operating System	User Interface	Compatibility	Multiple Tasks	Multiple Users
MS-DOS	Command-driven	IBM-PC compatibles	No	No
Windows	GUI*	IBM-PC compatibles DEC Alpha	Yes	No
OS/2	GUI	IBM-PC compatibles	Yes	No
Macintosh Version 7	GUI	Apple Macintosh	Yes	No
UNIX	Command-driven**	Almost all computers	Yes	Yes

*Graphical user interface

**Most UNIX sites cover the standard UNIX command-driven interface with a GUI interface such as OSF/Motif.

Individuals who do not use a computer regularly may have difficulty remembering commands from one computer session to the next.

A **menu-driven interface** presents a list of possible commands. The user then chooses among them by typing the first letter of the preferred command or by highlighting the desired command using input devices such as a light pen or a mouse (see Chapter 6). Figure 5-9 illustrates a screen from a menu-driven interface. If the screen is too small to show all the possible commands at once, a menu-driven interface will organize menus hierarchically, allowing users to select a submenu from a main menu or return to a main menu from a submenu. Such a hierarchical structure increases the time needed to select a task or application, a drawback that may become excessive as the depth of the hierarchy increases to support a rich set of commands. Some systems utilities can create a menu-driven interface for most command-driven operating systems.

A **graphical user interface,** also known by its initials **GUI** and pronounced "goo-ey," uses both menus and **icons,** pictorial representations of operations or resources, to interface with a user, as shown in Figure 5-10. Typically, a user may use a pointing device such as a mouse to move an arrow to mark or highlight a preferred action. Microsoft Windows for IBM-PC compatibles and Version 7 for Apple Macintosh computers are among the most popular GUI operating systems. Most users prefer a graphical user interface to a command-driven or menu-driven interface because the graphical representation of objects and actions eliminates confusion and the mouse minimizes keyboard typing. Some users, particularly those who have used command-driven interfaces for many years, complain that the GUI

FIGURE 5-9 Screen from a Menu-Driven Interface

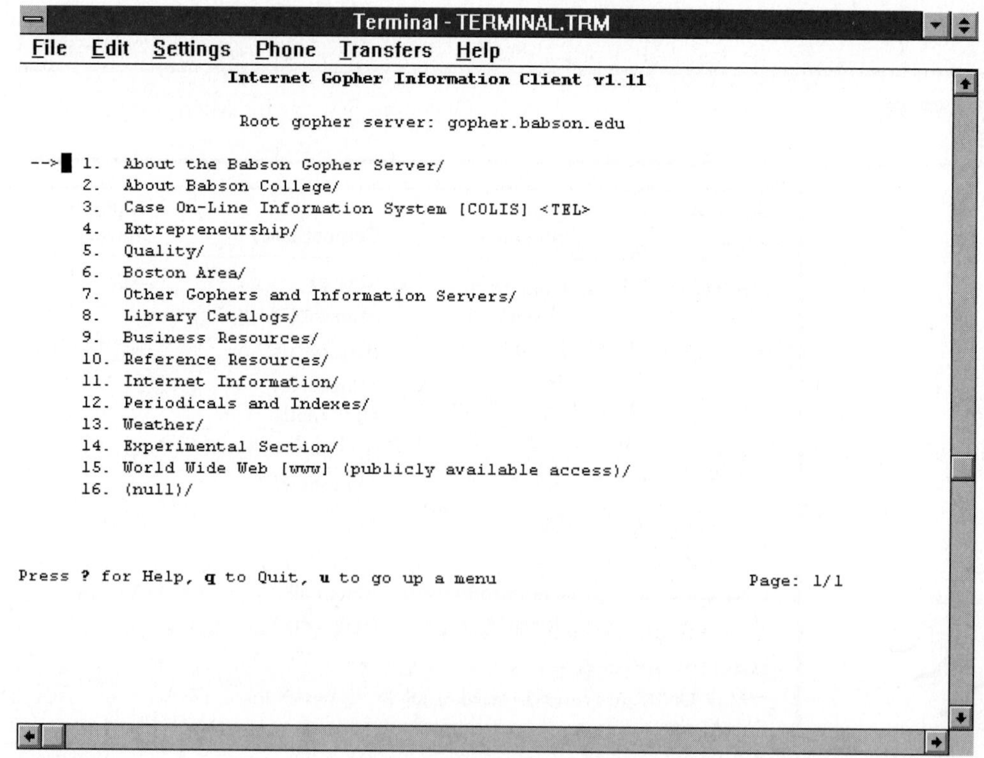

FIGURE 5-10 Graphical User Interface

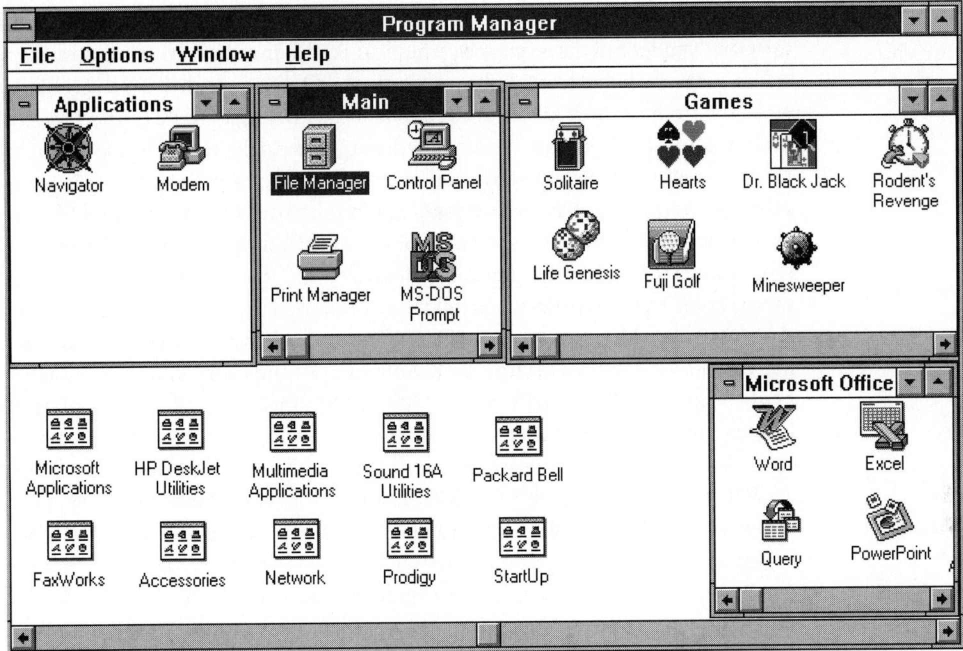

environment is relatively slow and tedious for performing simple repetitive operations that can be achieved in one or two keystrokes under a command-driven interface. Moving to a GUI may involve significant costs, including training/support and hardware/software upgrades.[15]

Portability and Openness. Because operating systems handle the most basic functions of a computer, they are usually customized for a specific type of computer hardware. The operating system for the Apple Macintosh, for example, lacks **portability**—the ability of other computers to use it; it cannot be purchased for the IBM-PC or for computers compatible with the IBM-PC. Because Apple believed that the design of its operating system provided Apple with a competitive advantage, the company did not offer its operating system to IBM users.[16] In addition, significant differences between the Macintosh and the IBM-PC, such as the relationship between the content of the computer's memory and what appears on the screen, seriously hinder portability. Although IBM and Apple have taken steps to provide a more common hardware through their joint development of the PowerPC chip, users of older, different systems must remain concerned about the portability of their operating systems.

Users increasingly want operating systems that will work on a range of computers to facilitate the migration of applications between computers. Users who employ a common operating system are not tied to a single type of hardware and can choose it according to price and performance. A common operating system also reduces users' training needs because the same knowledge applies to an array of computers.

UNIX was designed as such a common operating system. When introduced, UNIX was the proprietary software of AT&T, although it ran on several different types of computers.

AT&T provided licenses at relatively little cost to vendors who wanted to modify it for other computers. Versions of UNIX are now available for microcomputers such as IBM-PC compatibles and Apple Macintoshes; for minicomputers such as those of Digital (DEC), Data General, and Unisys; and for mainframes such as those of IBM and Hewlett-Packard. In spite of UNIX's portability, several problems arose. First, customers resisted being tied to a single software vendor in the same way they disliked being tied to a single hardware vendor. Second, users often found that the versions of UNIX provided by their hardware manufacturers lacked consistency with AT&T's standard. Finally, as AT&T updated UNIX, the versions provided by the hardware vendors did not necessarily reflect these changes.

As a way of addressing these concerns, users called for the development of an **open operating system**—namely, one whose operation would be specified and agreed to by a large group of vendors, whose specifications would not be owned by any one vendor, and for which a set of tests that check for conformance to a standard would be available. Versions of an open operating system could be developed by any company and made available for any computer. Users of such operating system software could, therefore, select from a number of software vendors. The Open Software Foundation (OSF) is a joint venture of several major software and hardware manufacturers, including IBM, Hewlett-Packard, and Sun Microsystems. The Foundation has created several open operating systems, "standards" that have been accepted by the members of OSF and others. Among these is a version of UNIX, a GUI for UNIX called OSF/Motif, and an environment for network operating systems called DCE (distributed computing environment). When Associated Grocers, a $1.2 billion supermarket cooperative, shifted to an open environment using products from a variety of vendors conforming to DCE and Open UNIX standards, it was able to increase computing flexibility, cut IS costs, allow the firm to adapt rapidly to changing business conditions, and boost productivity.[17]

OPEN SOFTWARE FOUNDATION

ASSOCIATED GROCERS

Performing Multiple Tasks and Serving Multiple Users. Many computers now have sufficient power to serve several users at once or support several tasks for a single user at one time. When multiple users or multiple tasks share a computer, the operating system must keep the data and commands of each task and user separate while it provides an opportunity for sharing information among them. Such multiuser and multitasking operating systems create special issues for the primary owner or operator of the computer because he or she must establish the rules and priorities for sharing the computer resources. A manager involved in selecting an operating system must weigh the efficiencies gained by sharing the computer against the effort required to manage a more complex system. When computer professionals make these decisions for managers such as Tom Lynch at LR&M, they set up the system and then alter the set-up parameters as needed.

Systems Utilities

Systems utilities are programs that operate primarily under user control and provide basic resource management functions, such as the ability to copy files or sort data, as shown in Figure 5-11. Most vendors of operating systems include many systems utilities as an integral part of their operating system software. As a result, the distinction between operating systems and systems utilities is often fuzzy. Computer scientists call the basic part of the operating system its **kernel** to distinguish it from the utilities packaged with the operating system. The kernel manages the parts and devices of the computer, and no computer can operate without it. A computer can operate without systems utilities, although users would find it extremely awkward and cumbersome.

Third-party vendors sell a variety of systems utilities to augment or improve the systems utilities included with an operating system. For example, utilities for a command-driven oper-

Examples of Systems Utilities

Archiving—Allows users to remove data to a permanent storage medium, such as a floppy or optical disk; may compress and/or encrypt the data for improved storage capacity and security. Advanced systems maintain histories of archives and can perform incremental as well as complete archiving.

Diagnostics—Allow users to diagnose problems with various parts of the computer.

Font extenders—Provide type fonts to change the way characters are displayed on the screen and at the printer. Advanced font extenders allow users to edit, rotate, shade, and manipulate fonts in many ways.

Keyboard modifiers—Allow keys on a keyboard to be reassigned or to be assigned a series of keystrokes so that one or two keystrokes can perform the role of many.

Menuing utilities—Allow users to write programs to create and edit menus for command-based operating systems or GUIs.

Miscellaneous—Includes programs to capture and recall screen displays; programs to recover data that have been erased; programs to allow the use of a mouse in place of arrow keys in programs that do not support a mouse; programs to manage several printers.

Screen savers—Display moving designs on the screen if the computer has not been used for a period of time. Prevents a pattern on the screen from permanently burning its image onto the screen's phosphor.

Security—Allows users to keep unauthorized users from using the computer or from accessing data; provides programs that encrypt data so that they cannot be read or profitably stolen; provides programs that check the integrity of data and/or programs to ensure that they have not been altered.

Sound—Provides advanced control of the speaker on a computer. Most operating systems provide little support in this area.

ating system might include programs to generate and use menus. They might also include programs that retain a history of commands that a user enters and allow the user to retrieve this history, select a past command, edit it, and then reissue it. Another type of systems utility, called a **screen saver,** blanks out a computer screen or shows a pattern on the screen if the computer has not been used for a certain period of time to prevent an image from "burning" onto the screen and reducing the quality of subsequent images. Although many operating systems include screen-saver software, separately packaged screen savers typically have a greater array of patterns and include more security devices, such as requiring a password in order to return to the original screen. Users must often decide whether the systems utilities included with the operating systems software are sufficient or whether separate, more full-featured utilities packages are required.

Network Operating Systems

A **network operating system (NOS)** manages and controls the joint or shared resources of a group of computers connected by a network. (See Chapter 8 for a detailed discussion of computer networks.) A NOS also provides functions that allow the connected computers to communicate with one another and with the resources they share, including the network itself, printers, other output devices, and data storage devices. A NOS also allows connections to other networks.

In addition to facilitating the sharing of information and devices, a network operating system has many other functions, as shown in Figure 5-12. First, it includes functions to add

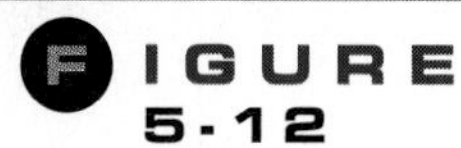

Functions of Network Operating Systems

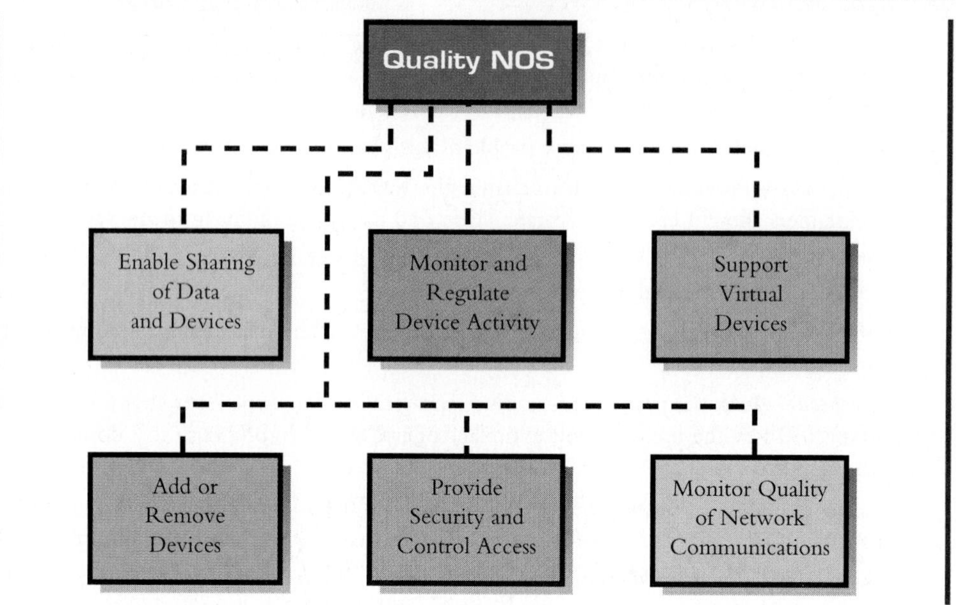

or delete devices, such as computers and printers, to or from the network. Second, it includes software to regulate the flow of information among these devices and monitor whether or not they are working properly. For example, if two users want to use a single printer at the same time, the NOS must decide which job should print first and then must ensure that the computer does not send data from the second job to the printer until the first job terminates. If a printer becomes jammed or runs out of paper, the NOS should advise the network supervisor.

Third, a NOS should support **virtual devices.** A virtual device, such as a virtual printer, is a feature of a NOS that simulates a real device. With a virtual printer, users will never have to wait for a busy printer. If the real printer is busy, the NOS holds the output data in a queue (virtual printer) until the printer becomes free. A NOS may provide other virtual resources for its users, such as those to send and receive fax transmissions or those to retrieve data from a large database.

Fourth, a NOS should provide security to control user access to software and data. Only authorized users should be able to connect to a network and access shared data or programs. In particular, a NOS must prevent users from copying or modifying licensed programs that the network's operators have purchased. A NOS should also include procedures to automatically and periodically create backup copies of data that users maintain on all shared storage devices.

Finally, a NOS should monitor the quality of network communications. Because interference from electromagnetic signals in the atmosphere or the failure of a communications medium, such as a cable, can cripple communications among computers, a NOS should identify communications errors when they exist and provide for the recovery from such errors.

Figure 5-13 lists some popular microcomputer network operating systems. The networking of corporate microcomputers during the early 1990s created an almost insatiable demand for NOS software and rapid growth for NOS vendors. Novell, Inc., for example, a company almost unknown in the mid-1980s, generated more than $1 billion in sales by 1993, largely due to its NetWare NOS.

FIGURE 5-13 Popular Microcomputer Network Operating Systems

Network Operating System	Vendor
NetWare	Novell
LANtastic	Artisoft
LAN Manager	Microsoft
Appleshare	Apple
Vines	Banyan
LAN Server	IBM

Software Development Tools

Software development tools, including computer languages, data dictionaries, and computer-aided software engineering (CASE) tools, facilitate the development of other software. Some operating systems include certain development tools, such as computer languages. Most software development tools, however, are purchased separately. Although managers such as Tom Lynch generally do not use such tools, they should recognize the possibilities for developing or modifying software for use in their organizations.

Computer Languages

Each type of computer recognizes and responds to a different set of instructions. Computer languages, such as C, FORTRAN, COBOL, Pascal, dBase, or SQL, among others, allow a software developer to create a single computer program that can be used to perform the same task on different computers. Programs written in such languages must be translated into the language of the target computer before they are run. In addition to making programs available to different types of computers, languages increase the efficiency of software development because programmers can use simple, understandable commands rather than instructions written in a format required by the target computer.

Computer languages differ in the way they are translated, in their level of abstraction, in whether they are procedural or nonprocedural, and in whether they are command/data oriented or object oriented. Figure 5-14 describes some common computer languages according to these parameters.

Language Translation. A **language translator** translates software from a language conducive to software development into the language of a computer. A translator permits software developers to use a common language for software destined for many types of computers. Each type of computer translates the same software into instructions that it alone can use.

Two types of language translators exist: compilers and interpreters. **Compilers,** such as C, COBOL, and FORTRAN, directly translate a program into computer code called an **object module.** Modules to perform related tasks are then linked to one another and to libraries of precompiled code that perform common functions to create a program that the computer can execute directly. This program, called an **executable module,** or a **load module,** can be loaded into a computer and run. A computer running executable code does not have to have a copy of the compiler because the program has already been translated.

FIGURE 5-14 Features of Some Common Computer Languages

Language	Primary Translation Method*	Level of Abstraction	Procedural	Object-Oriented
BASIC	Either	Moderate	Yes	No
C	Compiled	Low-Moderate	Yes	No
C++	Compiled	Low-Moderate	Yes	Somewhat+
COBOL	Compiled	Moderate	Yes	No
FORTRAN	Compiled	Moderate	Yes	No
Pascal	Interpreted	Moderate	Yes	No
Prolog	Interpreted	High	No	No
Smalltalk	Interpreted	Moderate–High	Yes	Yes
SQL	Either	High	No	No
xBASE	Either	High	Yes	No

*Compilers exist for most interpreted languages, and vice versa, often with some limitations. This table shows the most common translation method for the selected languages or "Either" if both methods are widely used.

+C++ supports most of the functions required to write object-oriented code; however, most purists do not consider it an object-oriented language.

An **interpreter,** such as most implementations of BASIC and Pascal, translates a software developer's language into computer code one instruction at a time and then executes each instruction before translating the next instruction. This approach catches errors as they arise; the software developer can interrogate the interpreter about the state of the program, reset values, and continue program execution. When using an interpreted language, the computer never actually runs the developer's software—it only runs the interpreter, which in turn treats the developer's software as data. Interpreters offer a friendly environment for the software developer.

Using an interpretive language poses several problems. First, an interpreted program runs slower than a similar compiled program because translation occurs during the run. Second, a user running an interpreted program must have a copy of the interpreter on his or her computer, while a user running a compiled program does not need a copy of the compiler. Finally, unlike users of compiled software, who have access only to the translated program, users of interpreted software must have a copy of the original, untranslated program in its easily understood form. As a result, protecting interpreted software from piracy is much harder than protecting compiled software.

Some languages, such as BASIC and xBase, exist in both interpretive and compiled forms. Developers can develop their software using the interpretive form of the language and distribute their software in the compiled form. This approach realizes the benefits of both a compiler and an interpreter. Other languages are compiled to an intermediate code, usually called **p-code,** that preserves much of the source language in a highly compact, incomprehensible form, yet still allows an interpreter to be run. The interpreter provides the support desired by software developers; the intermediate code can be translated more rapidly than the source code and provides protection from piracy.

Level of Abstraction. Computer languages differ in the amount of instruction provided by a single command. Second-generation languages are relatively low level: A single command provides very limited instructions. Third-generation languages are moderately abstract. Fourth-generation languages are relatively high level, and a single command includes an extensive amount of instruction. An analogy is useful for explaining this concept. Consider giving a robot instructions to brush its teeth. If the robot is sufficiently intelligent and trained, you might simply say, "Brush your teeth." If it has not performed this task before, you might instruct it as follows. "Take the toothbrush from its holder. Open the tube of toothpaste. Squeeze enough toothpaste onto the brush to cover the bristles. Turn on the cold water. Wet the toothpaste and toothbrush bristles. Brush the toothpaste onto your teeth. Rinse your mouth. . . ." If the robot is not sufficiently intelligent or trained, you might have to give it even more detailed instructions. For example, it might need to know how to take the toothbrush from its holder, or how to squeeze the tube.

The earlier general-use programming languages, known as **assembly languages** or second-generation languages, required programmers to specify in painstaking detail every step they wanted the computer to perform. Later languages, such as COBOL, FORTRAN, and Pascal, included single commands that were much more powerful. A single command in such a third-generation language might be translated into 10–50 second-generation commands. Later languages such as Progress and xBASE operate in conjunction with database management software (see Chapter 7) to convey even more meaning with each instruction. Such **fourth-generation languages (4GLs)** promote rapid, relatively bug-free software development. Because developers can convey a great deal of meaning with only a few instructions, they can be very productive. A single 4GL instruction is often equivalent to hundreds or even thousands of instructions written in a second-generation language. Software developers should select 4GL products that are comprehensive, provide user-friendly interfaces for end users, support linking personal computers with corporate computers, and facilitate rapid development of applications.

Low-level languages, such as 8086 Assembler or C, have two advantages over higher-level languages. First, they can provide more flexibility in how a job is performed. Using the robot analogy, a robot instructed at the highest level to brush its teeth will likely have a fixed way of doing it, perhaps brushing the top teeth before the bottom. If you wanted the robot to brush its bottom teeth before its top ones, you might have to resort to a lower-level language. Similarly, for some programming tasks, low-level languages allow a high degree of control over how the computer handles its data and instructions. Low-level languages also run faster. As instructions become more complex, they also are more general. As a rule, higher-level languages do more checking and allow for more contingencies than the same code written in a lower-level language.

Programmers can use both high- and low-level languages to develop a single software application. Where possible, they will want to use the highest-level language available to maximize their productivity and reduce development time. If parts of the program run too slowly or if the higher-level language is too inflexible to accomplish some tasks, the programmers can write some code in a lower-level language. The programmer will compile each part of the program using the appropriate language translator and link the compiled parts into one complete program with a software development tool called a **link loader.** Expert software developers can thus choose the level of language most appropriate for each task in a complex program.

Usually IS professionals rather than managers choose the language to use for a given application. However, managers should know that they can probably understand and use some high-level interpretive languages such as SQL well enough to meet some of their information needs.

Procedural versus Nonprocedural. **Procedural languages,** such as C, COBOL, or FORTRAN, force a software developer to give step-by-step instructions to the computer. The computer follows these steps the way a person follows an instruction manual. Procedural languages allow the computer to vary its steps depending on the data supplied. Extending the robot analogy, one instruction might read, "If the tube of toothpaste is empty, get a fresh tube from the closet." The steps performed by the robot following this command depend on the state of the toothpaste tube. Software written in a procedural language also allows the computer to determine its directions based on the data it finds.

There are two types of **nonprocedural languages.** The first, such as SQL, requires the software developer to state a desired outcome. The language processor rather than the programmer determines the instructions to give the computer to achieve this outcome. For example, a command in such a language might read, "Produce a report showing the name, address, and telephone numbers of all customers in the Northeast region owing over $3,000." How this output is achieved is the concern of the language translator, not of the software developer.

A second type of nonprocedural language is a language, such as Prolog, for stating facts and rules. Products called **expert systems shells** use an **inference engine** to process the language statements and data supplied by users to reach conclusions, answer questions, and give advice. The developer of expert systems software does not know and generally cannot specify the order or steps that the inference engine will use to reach its conclusions.

Following is a simple example of a short program (two facts and one rule) that might be expressed in the language of an expert systems shell (see Figure 5-15). Fact 1: Jane is Alan's

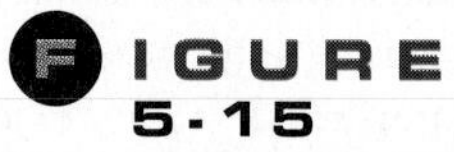

FIGURE 5-15 An Illustration of Rules and Facts for an Expert System

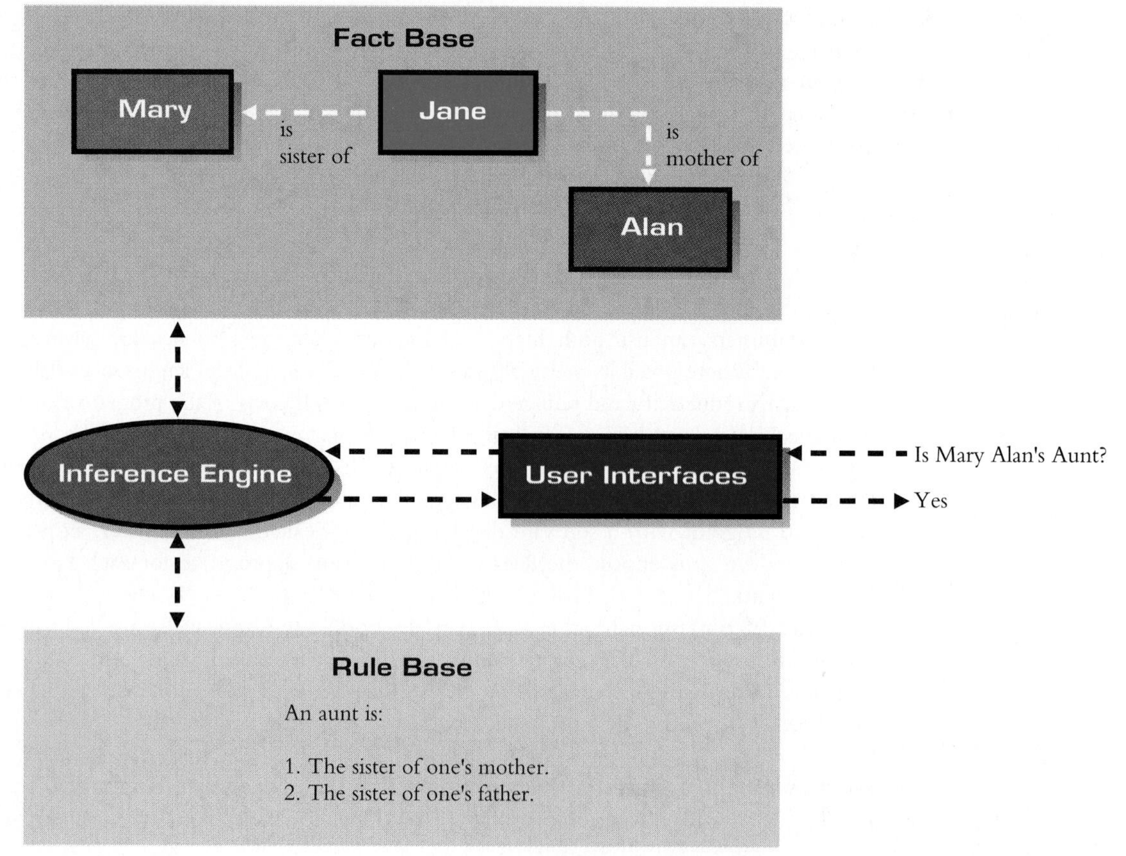

mother. Fact 2: Mary is Jane's sister. Rule 1: An aunt is the sister of one's mother or the sister of one's father. An inference engine would use this program to determine whether or not Mary is Alan's aunt. The order in which the facts and rules are processed in reaching this answer cannot be determined from the program. Expert systems and their applications are described in fuller detail in Chapter 9.

Command/Data-Oriented versus Object-Oriented. Command/data-oriented programming languages, such as FORTRAN, COBOL, or Pascal, separate data storage from procedural parts of a program. The procedural parts of a program operate on the data received.

Object-oriented languages, such as Smalltalk and C++, merge procedures and data into a structure called an **object.** A programmer uses an object-oriented language to build objects. He or she then builds a program by linking such objects to one another and to objects in a prewritten object library.[18]

The software developer who uses an object orientation specifies the relationships among objects in two ways. First, a hierarchical relationship is established in which instances or occurrences of objects create object classes, and object classes may belong to other classes. For example, Helen and Paul may be objects of the object class "employee," and the object class "employee" may be a member of the class "person" (see Figure 5-16). Second, the software developer specifies how objects communicate with one another through **messages.** For example, any person object should respond in an appropriate way to the message "What is your name?"

Using object orientation, a software developer models the objects and processes in an organization that are necessary to manage its information. Using such objects, the programmer can easily and relatively quickly create a limited prototype of a program to perform almost any information processing function required by the organization. Object-oriented concepts work for such diverse applications as a financial accounting system and a mail system. In the accounting system, each asset becomes an object;[19] in the mail system mail messages and mail boxes become objects.[20] Smalltalk, an object-oriented programming language developed in 1970 but beginning to attract significant interest in the 1990s, was used to

Hierarchy of Object Classes and Objects

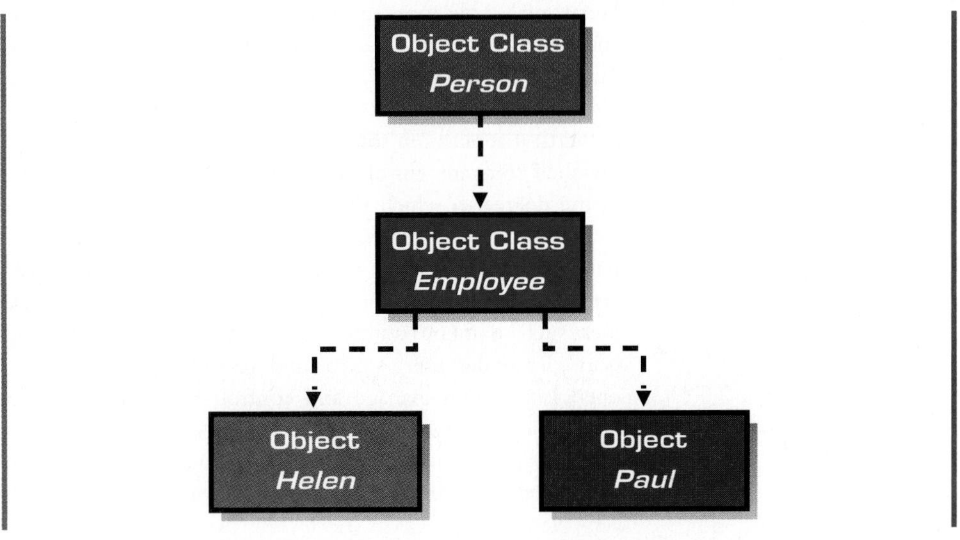

AMERICAN AIRLINES

write a system in record time with almost no errors to help American Airlines track and dispatch crew, meals, and other resources.[21] Object-oriented technology such as Smalltalk can reduce the development cycle time by more than 50 percent but requires three to six months of training for programmers accustomed to command/data-oriented languages.[22]

CASE Tools

Software developers, like the designers of physical products, think of software as a product to engineer. **Computer-assisted software engineering (CASE)** tools are software products that apply engineering principles to the design and maintenance of software products. They can form the basis for modeling, measurement, and management of software development and maintenance.[23] Excelerator from Index Technology Corporation, Structured Architect from Meta Systems, and Design/I from Arthur Andersen illustrate CASE tools that support the development of software systems. Products such as these include syntax verifiers, diagramming tools, and code generators to facilitate programming.[24]

A common CASE tool is a **data dictionary,** also known as a **data repository** or **data encyclopedia**—a database about all the data used within an organization. It defines the data precisely, clarifies differences among data that may appear to be alike but that are different, specifies the names that should be used for elements of data when they are referred to by programs, and identifies the programs that refer to or modify each data element. A data dictionary also maintains knowledge of the structure of data (for example, which data are kept about the company's employees) and relationships among data (for example, must every customer have a customer representative).

LINCOLN BENEFIT LIFE INSURANCE

CASE tools make modification of preliminary system designs easier, result in better standardization of systems, and allow easier documentation.[25] Lincoln Benefit Life Insurance Company used CASE to ease movement between company projects; Shadow, a CASE tool, allows a programmer to describe the differences in the new project and then translate the output into a C program, creating a complete application prototype.[26] Chapter 13 discusses CASE tools in greater detail.

Summary

The term *software* refers to commands that direct a computer to process information or data. Horizontal application software performs generic tasks common to many types of problems and applications within and across industries. It includes word processing, desktop publishing, presentation graphics, spreadsheet, database management, communications, and accounting software.

Vertical application software performs tasks common to a specific industry. It includes off-the-shelf software, customized software, and home-grown software. These three types differ in the degree to which they are customized before they are used.

Systems software provides the functions the computer needs to manage its various outputs. Operating systems include computer programs that perform the most basic housekeeping, resource allocation, and resource monitoring functions for a computer. Systems utilities, such as menu utilities, archiving, and keyboard modifiers, are programs that operate primarily under user control and provide basic resource management functions. Network operating systems manage and control the shared resources of a group of computers connected by a network.

Software development tools help people create new software. These tools include computer languages, data dictionaries, and computer-aided software engineering (CASE) tools.

Key Terms

Aspect ratio
Assembly language
Beta-testing
Clip art
Command/data-oriented programming language
Command-driven interface
Compiler
Computer-assisted software engineering (CASE)
Customized software
Data dictionary
Data encyclopedia
Data repository
Database manager (DBMS)
Desktop publishing software (DTP)
Dynamic Data Exchange (DDE)
Executable module
Expert systems shell
File manager
Formatting
Fourth-generation language (4GL)
Graphical user interface (GUI)
Home-grown software
Horizontal application software
Host computer
Icon
Inference engine
Integrated accounting package
Integrated package
Integrator
Interpreter
Kernel
Language translator
Link loader
Load module
Local computer
Macro
Menu-driven interface
Message
Network operating system
Nonprocedural language
Object
Object Linking and Embedding (OLE)
Object module
Object-oriented language object
Off-the-shelf software
Open operating system
Operating system
Operational capability demonstration (OCD)
Outsourcing
P-code
Packaged software
Portability
Presentation graphics software
Procedural language
Proofreading tool
Protocol
Range
Record
Remote computer
Request for proposal (RFP)
Screen saver
Script
Site license
Snapping
Software
Software development tool
Spreadsheet
Style sheet
Suite
Systems software
Systems utilities
Terminal emulation
Value added reseller (VAR)
Vertical application software
Virtual device
Word processing software

Review Questions

1. Define *software.*
2. Compare and contrast horizontal application software and vertical application software.
3. What is systems software, and why is it needed?
4. List seven types of horizontal application software.
5. What is a site license, and what is its advantage over individual licenses?
6. Compare and contrast word processing, desktop publishing, and presentation graphics software.
7. What is spreadsheet software?
8. What is a macro? Why is having a macro a desirable feature for horizontal application software?
9. What is a database manager?
10. What is terminal emulation? What other features might you look for in communications software?
11. What are the benefits and drawbacks of using integrated packages for accounting?
12. Cite the relative advantages of off-the-shelf, customized, and home-grown vertical application software.
13. Describe three types of user interfaces.

14. What is the meaning of *openness,* and why is it a desirable feature for an operating system?
15. Describe the use of systems utilities by managers and other software users.
16. What is the function of a network operating system?
17. Why is it important for a network operating system to support virtual devices?
18. In what ways do computer languages differ from one another?
19. What is the difference between a compiler and an interpreter?
20. Explain the difference between a high-level computer language and a low-level computer language. What are the advantages of each?
21. What advantages do CASE tools provide to software developers?

MINICASE

Customizing Sales Force Automation Software for Legent Corp.

The first generation of sales software products appeared in the early 1980s, but these products could not be modified to meet an organization's changing business requirements. As a result, many of the early users of sales force automation (SFA) software developed their solutions in-house.

Today, however, more and more organizations are buying off-the-shelf SFA packages. In 1991, 39 percent of those surveyed by the Sales Automation Association (SAA), a research consulting organization in Dearborn, Mich., developed their own sales automation software. By 1994, that figure had dropped to 27 percent.

The main reason for the decrease in the number of companies developing their own SFA software is cost. "For users to build [SFA systems] themselves, they have to have the vision of everything that's required and spend a lot of money," said Ken Dulaney, vice-president of sales leadership strategies for market research firm Gartner Group Inc., in Santa Clara.

Purchasing an SFA solution from one of the many vendors in the marketplace is much cheaper than developing one's own. Companies can spend up to $15,000 per salesperson to develop an SFA application, and then another $3,500 per year to maintain and support the application, according to Peter Perera, who heads The Perera Group, a consulting firm in Andover, Mass., that specializes in sales and marketing technology. But buying an off-the-shelf solution is not the bargain that some companies think. "Some companies see a notebook computer advertised for $2,000, run to Egghead [Software] to buy Act! [from Symantec Corp., Cupertino], and think that for $2,500 they have SFA," said Perera.

The cost of a true SFA solution is much higher, he said, when the customization required is factored in. "The big misconception is that there is something called sales and marketing software," he said. "Sales and marketing software really is an electronic toolbox that presents a suite of software applications." The main component is the prospect database, which is rarely designed from scratch. The other pieces are horizontal applications—word processing, E-mail, graphics—that are customized to some extent to fit a sales organization's needs.

Sales processes vary by industry, but even in the same industry, no two sales organizations are exactly alike, and neither are their selling cycles. But even for a sales department that operates like no other, a truly custom solution is often too expensive and time consuming

---

SOURCE: Extracted from Colleen Frye, Sales force automation? Not without customization, *Client/Server Computing* (December 1994): 34–38, 55. Reprinted with permission from *Client/Server Computing Magazine* (December 1994): 34–38, 55.

to develop. The "happy medium" is "to highly modify a great piece of application software," said Will Kenlaw, business unit executive of IBM Corp.'s Sales Force Transformation (SFT) team, a Bethesda, Md., unit of IBM that provides integration services to companies that want to implement SFA solutions.

One company that sought to custom-fit an existing package to its needs is Legent Corp. The Herndon, Va., software vendor needed an SFA system that could be standardized for its European sales offices, some of which already had sales force automation systems prior to becoming part of Legent. "To break down barriers between countries, we wanted a product we could customize," said international marketing director Don Imhoff.

Legent chose SPS from Saratoga Systems Inc., Campbell, Calif., and uses the package for account management, territory management, lead management, personal productivity, and pipeline/opportunity management. So far, nearly 300 Legent employees use SPS in offices in nine European countries, in five different languages. Legent will also soon install SPS in its offices in Italy and France, bringing those totals to 11 and seven. The North American sales organization is building its own system, according to Imhoff.

To Each Their Own Language

Imhoff's sales organization worked with Saratoga consultants from the U.K. and a translation agency to create screens in multiple languages so the salespeople could do queries in their own languages. Saratoga did the data importing and provided technical and systems administration training.

Each sales office has a 486/50-based server from Compaq Computer Corp. with a replicated SPS database updated nightly. A master database on the server in Frankfurt, Germany, serves the five German offices. In its international headquarters in England, Legent also has a "super copy" (master of everyone's master) of SPS, which is updated nightly with information from all the servers in each country. Laptop users dial in to send updates and receive changes from the server.

Legent's European operations had already standardized on Microsoft prior to the implementation of the SPS product. The European offices have 386- and 486-based PCs running Microsoft Office over a LAN Manager network. SPS has interfaces to Microsoft Word so salespeople can send out their own mailings, as well as to MS-Mail so sales reps can share notes about customers with anyone in the corporation.

Salespeople use SPS to search across the database for a customer environment that fits a customer's product line. Using contact information in the database, the rep can initiate a call with the customer and keep notes on the conversation. As the sales becomes more likely, the rep starts a pipeline record that shows what they propose selling, where they are in the cycle, the confidence factor, and tracks product trials.

It takes time for salespeople to get used to the system, Imhoff said. "In Germany, most people were already using a personal database, so it was difficult to get them to change and share with everybody else."

To address these issues, Legent familiarized users with Windows and trained staff in all the aspects of the sales process. Legent also created an SPS user group in each country, Imhoff said, "to keep SPS a living system"—meaning it can grow as the company's processes change.

Case Questions

1. Do you consider sales force automation software to be horizontal or vertical application software?
2. Why did Legent need to customize the SFA software it purchased?
3. Why do you think Legent did not develop its own SFA software?

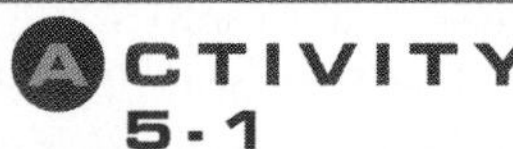

CTIVITY 5-1 Review of Software Packages

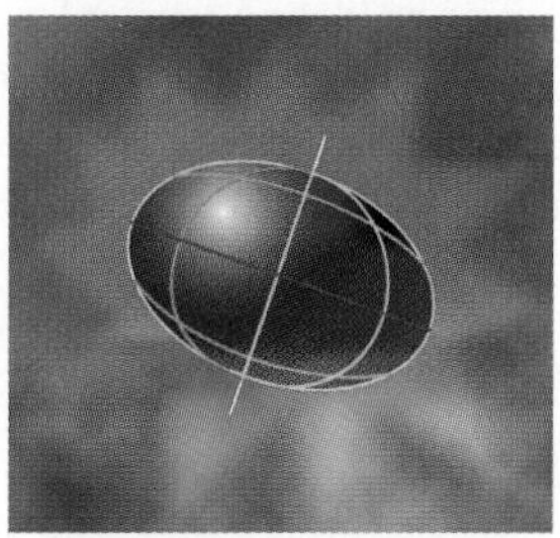

external contact

STEP 1: You are an intern assigned to the office manager of a medium-sized brokerage house. The company employs approximately 50 brokers and 100 staff to support the brokerage work, and there are 10 brokers and 10 staff people in the office in which you are working. Recently the vice-president of administration has asked your office manager to recommend a new word processing system for the office. Each employee has his or her own personal computer networked to the others in the office. Before the network, employees were allowed to select the word processing software they desired; hence, five or six packages are in use in the office.

Your office manager has given you the task of writing a brief review of three possible word processing programs the company might adopt as the standard for all computers on the network.

STEP 2: Individually or in small groups, prepare to write such a review. You should secure relevant information from the library, vendors, or other appropriate sources to assess the features of the software and provide the basis of your comparative analysis.

STEP 3: Write the review. Prepare enough copies to share with other members of the class.

STEP 4: In small groups or with the entire class, answer the following questions:

1. What are the basic features the word processing package should have?
2. How are the packages similar and different?
3. What factors should the office manager consider in choosing among the packages? ●

CTIVITY 5-2 Yarmouth Inc.

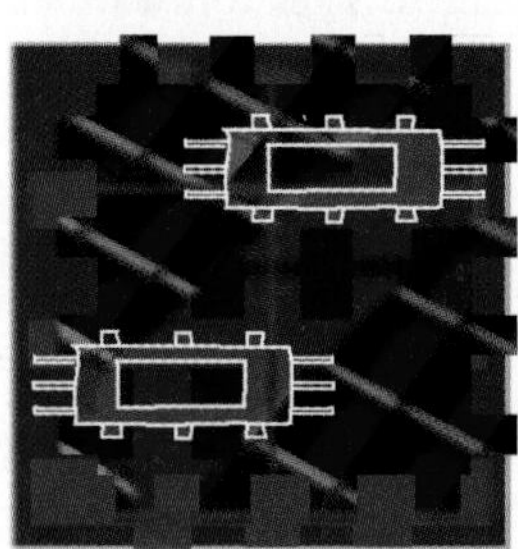

short case

STEP 1: Read the Yarmouth Inc. case.

The division manager, Lisa Harwood, had just told Dan Tobin, director of marketing, that the productivity of the sales staff had to increase. The statistics Harwood referred to came from a recent trade magazine. They suggested that the sales staff at Yarmouth was performing well below industry averages. Average order size per salesperson, for example, and the number of calls per day were about half those reported by other companies in the same business.

"Dan, we've got to act now or we'll never hit our profit goals for the quarter," Harwood said. "Can you get back to me tomorrow with some ideas on how we can show some fast improvement?"

Tobin had been with Yarmouth Inc. for six years. He was hired as a salesperson and last spring was promoted to director of marketing.

Yarmouth produces a line of industrial cleaning equipment including vacuum cleaners, waxers, and polishers, and maintains a staff of 142 salespeople who call on industrial accounts within a several hundred mile radius of their homes.

SOURCE: B. Shore and J. Ralya, *Cases in Computer Information Systems.* New York: Holt, Rinehart & Winston, 1988. Selections from CASES IN COMPUTER INFORMATION SYSTEMS by Barry Shore and Jerry Ralya,

Tobin went home that evening concerned about his ability to make the changes that were needed. On the ride home it occurred to him that he could give the staff a pep talk but it probably would have only a short-term effect. Without close supervision, they were on their own, and any effort to manage their performance from this distance was difficult. The only hard data he had were the monthly sales reports, which he received nearly a month after the reporting period closed. The January sales data, for example would be received at the end of February. Perhaps, he thought, he might get these data sooner. Then he could respond faster to those who weren't getting the job done.

CONSULTING THE MIS DEPARTMENT

Tobin's first stop the next morning was the MIS department. There he told Maurice Brown, director of MIS, about his problem.

"We're not your problem," Brown said. "You are. The data coming in from the field travel at a snail's pace. Your salespeople fill out order forms and then a few days later put them in the mail. Before the sales data show up here and are entered by data entry clerks into the sales order entry system, the data are sometimes several weeks old. Then, after the goods are shipped it takes another few weeks for the data to be entered by data entry clerks into the sales history database. The report we send you accesses the sales history file, and until that file is updated, we can't send you your monthly reports. If the past is an indication of the future, I'm afraid the best we can do is get you a report within a month of the end of the period, unless, of course, you get your orders in here quicker."

Although Tobin was not confident that Brown could help him obtain more timely data, he went on to explain some additional information he needed to maintain closer control over the sales staff.

NEW APPLICATIONS

"Maurice, last night I sketched a few reports that would help me maintain tigher control over the sales force. These reports would let me scrutinize their efforts much more closely. And I think the information the salespeople would get from these reports would help them to schedule their time more effectively and do a better job."

Tobin showed him two reports—sales diary, and sales productivity analysis.

Sales Diary

The sales diary would report the number of calls per day for each salesperson, the number of hours per day that the salesperson spent with prospects, the number of sales calls year-to-date, and the cost per call.

Sales Productivity Analysis

The order analysis report would include, for every salesperson, the cost per call, revenue per call, revenue to expense ratio, and the call to close ratio. The call to close ratio is the number of total calls made divided by the number of calls that resulted in a sale.

Tobin finished describing these reports. "Maurice," Tobin asked, "how long do you think it would take for you to begin producing these reports on a weekly basis?"

"Dan, I don't understand your logic. If I use the current sales history database to produce your reports, I might be able to get them to you a few weeks after the data are in that database, but you have just complained that a report like this would be too out-of-date to be useful."

STEP 2: Prepare the case for class discussion.

STEP 3: Answer each of the following questions, individually or in small groups, as directed by your instructor.

Diagnosis

1. What are the information needs of the sales staff and managers in the marketing department of Yarmouth Inc.?
2. Do they feel that these information needs are currently being met?

Evaluation

3. What software do they currently use to help meet these needs?
4. How well does this software meet their information needs?

Design

5. What characteristics should the department's software have?
6. What additional types of software do they require?

Implementation

7. What issues must the division consider in purchasing the new software?

STEP 4: In small groups, with the entire class, or in written form, share your answers to the questions above. Then answer the following questions:

1. What information does the marketing department need?
2. How well does the current software meet these needs?
3. What changes in the software are necessary to better meet these needs?
4. How can the required changes be implemented? ●

ACTIVITY 5-3 Software for Party Planners Plus

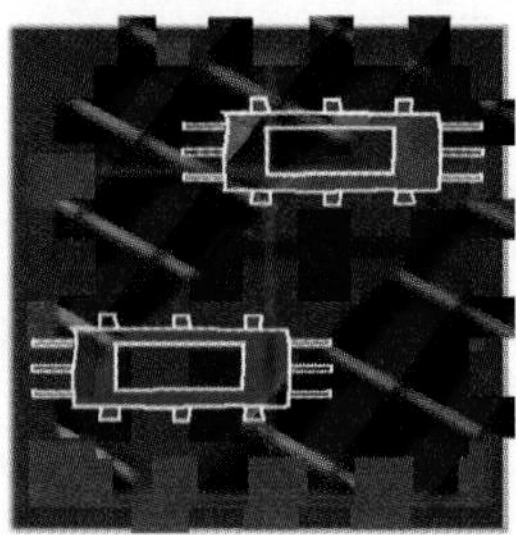

short case

Party Planners Plus is a six-person organization that provides party planning services. Jessica Tanner began the company in 1985 in the basement of her home. She offered planning services for a variety of social events, including weddings, anniversary parties, Bar and Bat Mitzvah celebrations, graduation parties, and major birthday parties. She advised her clients about the party's menu, decorations, and entertainment; ordered invitations, flowers, catering services, rental tables and chairs, party favors, tents, and tablecloths and napkins; set up the party location; and provided necessary staff, such as serving personnel, valets, coatroom attendants, and entertainers. As her business increased, Jessica added part-time and then full-time employees. She moved from merely ordering some supplies, such as unusual centerpieces, to actually hiring a craftsperson to make them on-site. When the company was seven years old, Jessica moved Party Planners Plus into a small storefront office.

In the early days of her business Jessica managed the flow of paperwork manually. Basically it involved making lists of orders, recording payments to vendors of the supplies, and tracking payments by her clients. Two years ago she bought an Apple Macintosh computer to assist with the paperwork. She purchased a good word processing package, which she used to replace much of the manual information recording. Still, the paperwork took a great deal of time and provided her with very little information about her costs and profits and minimal assistance in setting appropriate prices. She knows, however, that she should be able to use the computer for much more support in meeting her information needs.

STEP 1: You are Jessica Tanner. You want to hire a consultant to select and install software that will help you better meet your information needs. Individually or in small groups, prepare a list of your information needs.

STEP 2: Individually or in small groups, prepare a list of the types of software you believe you should purchase to meet these information needs. Also include a checklist of the features you think you will want for each type of software you expect to purchase.

STEP 3: In small groups or with the entire class, share your lists. Together, develop a comprehensive list of software and its characteristics.

STEP 4: In small groups or with the entire class, answer the following questions:

1. What issues did you consider in identifying the information needs of Party Planners Plus?
2. What types of software should receive the highest purchase priority? What types would be least beneficial?
3. What other issues should Jessica consider in purchasing software for her company? ●

Software in Use

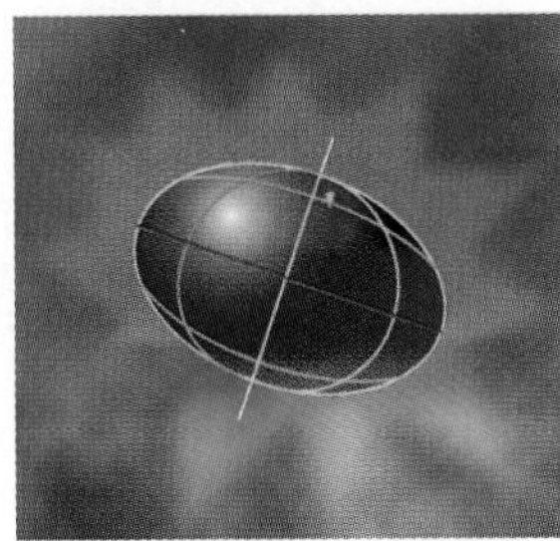

external contact

STEP 1: Select an organizational member who uses computer software to interview about the software he or she uses most frequently.

STEP 2: Prepare a set of interview questions that will help you understand the value of the software to the individual. You might include questions such as the following:

1. What software does the individual use most often?
2. What are the features of this software?
3. How well does the software meet the person's information needs?
4. What are the software's advantages and disadvantages?
5. What changes would make the software more useful?

STEP 3: Conduct the interview.

STEP 4: Share the results of your interviews in small groups or with the entire class. Identify the types of software used, their success in meeting the individual's needs, their advantages, their disadvantages, and proposed changes to make them more useful. ●

ACTIVITY 5-5 Programming Language Debate

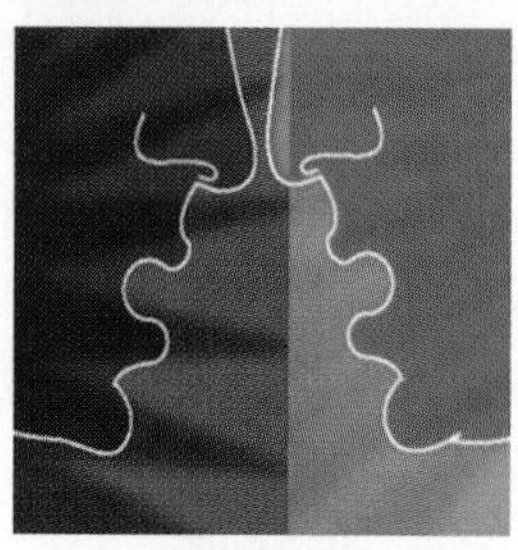
debate

Resolved. All managers should demonstrate competency in a programming language.

STEP 1: Your instructor will assign you to teams that will debate either the pro or con side of this issue.

STEP 2: Prepare your position.

STEP 3: Conduct the debate with the opposing team.

STEP 4: In small groups or with the entire class, answer the following questions:

1. Which side was more convincing?
2. Should all managers be required to demonstrate programming competency? ●

Notes

[1]David Rosenthal and Steven Gordon, Factors affecting the success of organizational software and hardware standards, *Proceedings of the 1993 Information Management Association International Conference: Challenges for Information Management in a World Economy* (Salt Lake City, Utah, May 1993): 450–455.

[2]InfoCorp, Applications in use, cited in *MacWeek* (January 11, 1993): 45. On the Apple Macintosh, use of graphics software exceeded that of word processing software.

[3]Linda Musthaler, What's behind the polished image, *Computerworld* (January 25, 1993): 65.

[4]See, for example, Derek Slater, Presentation tools: Buyers' scorecard, *Computerworld* (January 25, 1993): 66–67; and Alan J. Fridlund, Product comparison: Presentation graphics for DOS and Windows, *Infoworld* (September 16, 1991): 61–76.

[5]Musthaler, op. cit.

[6]InfoCorp, Applications in use, as cited in *MacWeek* (January 11, 1993): 45.

[7]Bill Laberis, Jean Bozman, Alan Ryan, Patricia Keefe, and Paul Gillin, Twenty-five people who changed the world: . . . , *Computerworld* (June 22, 1992): S20–S29.

[8]The following is based in large part on reviews of spreadsheet software found in John Walkenbach, Reviews: Excel for Windows 4.0 sets new standard, *Infoworld* (April 27, 1992): 78–80; and John Walkenbach, Reviews/product comparison: Opening the windows on spreadsheets, *Infoworld* (October 12, 1991): 104–128.

[9]Rob Kelly, In accounting software, less is more, *Information Week* (February 22, 1993): 78.

[10]Ned Snell, Mainframe accounting moves down, *Datamation* 38(22) (November 1, 1992): 112–115.

[11]Joseph D. Launi, A structured methodology for off-the-shelf software implementation, *Journal of Systems Management* 42(10) (October 1991): 6–9 offers a structured methodology for installing off-the-shelf software.

[12]Wayne Eckerson, User downsizes in an off-the-shelf way, *Network World* (July 13, 1992): 19, 21.

[13]Russell Letson, Install software off the shelf? FORGET IT!, *Systems Integration* 24(4) (April 1991): 55–58.

[14]This methodology is adapted from Joseph D. Launi, op cit.

[15]Christine Comaford, Assessing the real costs of GUI migration, *PC Week* (April 5, 1993): 65.

[16]Doug Bailey, Rebooting Apple, *The Boston Sunday Globe* (July 11, 1993): 65, 66.

[17]Jean S. Bozman, Grocer buys into open systems, *Computerworld* (March 22, 1993): 57, 59.

[18]Alan Deutschman, Writing software made easy, *Fortune* (March 8, 1993): 91.

[19]Pai-Cheng Chu, Applying object-oriented concepts to development financial systems, *Journal of Systems Management* 43(5) (May 1992): 28, 33–34.

[20]Feng-Yang Kuo, An object-oriented approach to the design of a mail system for a heterogeneous environment, *Information & Management* 15(3) (October 1988): 173–182.

[21]John W. Verity, Finally, the buzz is about Smalltalk, *Business Week* (April 19, 1993): 111–112.

[22]Garry Ray, Object orientation catching corporate eye, *Computerworld* (June 15, 1992): 77.

[23]Graham Tate, June Verner, and Ross Jeffery, CASE: A testbed for modeling, measurement and management, *Communications of the ACM* 35(4) (April 1992): 65–72.

[24]Donald L. Burkhard, Implementing CASE tools, *Journal of Systems Management* 40(5) (May 1989): 20–25.

[25]Richard E. Yellen, What do users really think about CASE? *Journal of Systems Management* 43(2) (February 1992): 16, 39.

[26]Cliff Chaney, Lincoln Benefit Life meets the market challenge with CASE, *Journal of Systems Management* 43(1) (January 1992): 10–12, 31.

Recommended Readings

Friedman, Daniel P., Wand, Mitchell, and Haynes, Christopher T. *Essentials of Programming Languages.* New York: McGraw-Hill, 1992.

Martin, Edward G. *Using Application Software.* Danvers, MA: Boyd & Fraser, 1993.

Nutt, Gary J. *Open Systems.* Englewood Cliffs, NJ: Prentice-Hall, 1992.

Tannenbaum, Andrew S. *Modern Operating Systems.* Englewood Cliffs, NJ: Prentice-Hall, 1992.

Winsten, Irwin. *Accounting Software and the Microcomputer.* New York: Wiley, 1990.

Chapter 6

Hardware Technology

OUTLINE

Outdated Hardware at Carter Manufacturing

Input Hardware
- Applications of Input Hardware
- Types of Input Hardware

Processing Hardware
- Measuring Processing Power
- Specialized Processors

Storage Hardware
- Measuring Storage
- Primary versus Secondary Storage
- Primary Storage Devices
- Secondary Storage Devices

Output Hardware
- Softcopy Devices
- Hardcopy Devices
- Other Output Hardware

Hardware Integration
- Constructing a Computer
- Micro/Mini/Mainframe Distinctions
- Scientific Processing
- Miniaturization of Hardware
- Virtual Reality

LEARNING OBJECTIVES

After completing the reading and activities for Chapter 6, students will be able to

1. Distinguish among four major types of hardware.
2. Comment about the types and uses of input hardware.
3. Discuss the role of hardware in processing information.
4. Differentiate among four major types of processing hardware.
5. Compare and contrast the uses and characteristics of primary and secondary storage devices.
6. Describe the types of primary and secondary storage devices.
7. Discuss ways of measuring the quality of graphics output.
8. Compare and contrast hardcopy and softcopy output.
9. Describe four softcopy and four hardcopy devices.
10. Comment about the issues involved in selecting hardware.

Outdated Hardware at Carter Manufacturing

Sarah Craig, a newly minted MBA, had recently been hired by Alexis Dufours, the president of Carter Manufacturing, a medium-size manufacturer of women's clothing accessories. Sarah's job responsibilities involved supporting the company's strategic planning effort and acting as an assistant to the president. Sarah was particularly excited about this job because she knew it was an excellent opportunity to apply the knowledge she had acquired in her graduate program.

Sarah met with each of Carter's top-level executives and middle managers to learn as much as she could about Carter's suppliers, customers, competitors, and operations. The managers impressed her with their knowledge, enthusiasm, and commitment to incorporating state-of-the-art procedures into their departments' activities. Repeatedly, however, the managers commented that the company's failure to buy appropriate computer technology had hindered their departments' performance. The marketing vice-president noted, for example, that his department wanted to control its own advertising program, but the software he desired would not run on Carter's computers. The human resource manager faced similar problems for the on-line data system she wanted for tracking employee performance, compensation, training, and recruiting. The warehouse manager wanted to introduce a state-of-the-art just-in-time inventory system but was warned that, although the software would run on Carter's computers, current systems already consumed so much of their processing power that the users of the inventory system would encounter unacceptably slow responses. Even the comptroller complained that the system was already too slow for processing the large amounts of data required for accounting and payroll.

Sarah noted that the chief financial officer was responsible for the company's information systems. He had limited knowledge about hardware options and had only low-level staff members to support the information function.

The company used an old IBM System 38 minicomputer for most of its information processing. Some of the managers and clerks also had stand-alone personal computers that they used for word processing and some spreadsheet analyses. Sarah Craig believed that the company needed to upgrade its computer equipment immediately. She had taken several advanced courses in information systems in her MBA program and knew she could identify a preliminary set of hardware options to discuss with Dufours. She needed to assess the company's information needs and associated software requirements and then consider what hardware would best meet these needs.

Computer hardware, or the physical equipment that handles information, can be classified into four categories, as shown in Figure 6-1 (1) **input hardware** captures information; (2) **processing hardware** manipulates information; (3) **storage hardware** saves information; and (4) **output hardware** presents and shares information. Computer manufacturers

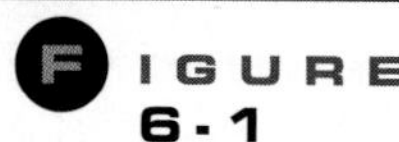
FIGURE 6-1 The Components of Computer Hardware

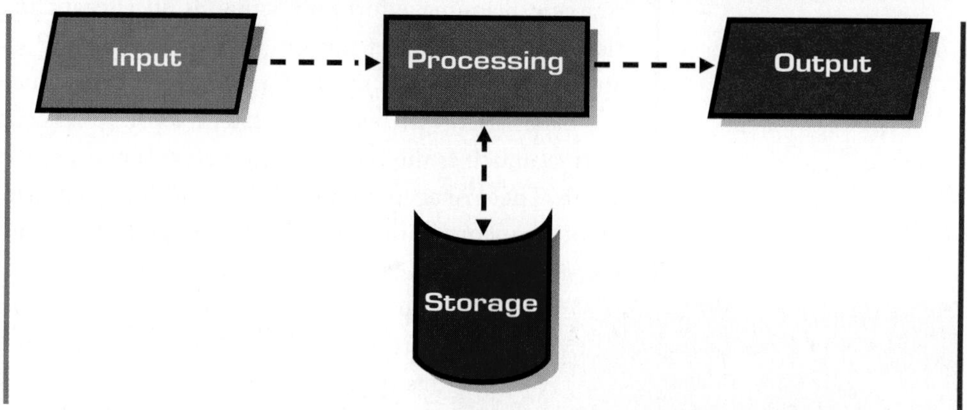

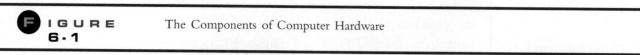

typically package all four elements into integrated hardware systems that require no additional assembly, although sophisticated users may assemble their own computers from various components. Input and output hardware include a class of devices known as **communication hardware** (see Chapter 8) that obtains data from and sends data to other computers.

A company's chief information officer (CIO) generally guides the organization in developing an **information technology architecture,** although other organizational managers (such as the chief financial officer at Carter Manufacturing) may be responsible for computer operations. The architecture specifies how much computing power and generally what types of computers should be applied to the various computing needs of the organization.

Managers participate in the design of an architecture by sharing their information processing needs and understanding the hardware options available. Evaluation and design of computer hardware configurations should follow the diagnosis of information needs. Designing an architecture involves technical judgments, an understanding of information needs and software used to meet them, and knowledge of organizational characteristics such as the employees' attitudes toward computers, the organization's culture, the responsibility for decision making, and the skills and size of the information systems staff. Designing an architecture becomes increasingly complicated in companies with multiple locations and/or international sites. A company's processing architecture should evolve with advances in technology to give the organization the most efficient and flexible hardware possible while providing a level of stability that ensures smooth technical and organizational transitions.

This chapter discusses each of the four hardware components—input, processing, storage, and output—that make up the information technology architecture. It emphasizes ways managers can assess the features, quality, and appropriateness of the different hardware devices available for performing these four functions. Although hardware can be discussed in any order, we have followed the typical flow of data through a computer: Input devices present data to the computer as electrical signals; the processor processes the data and places it in storage; and finally, the processor retrieves the data for output as requested by users.

Input Hardware

Input hardware consists of devices that send signals to a computer. These devices enable people to communicate with computers and allow computers to sense their environment. In this section, we examine the use and types of input devices.

Applications of Input Hardware

Input hardware functions to get information into the computer. The types of devices used to achieve this goal depend upon the applications being performed. We classify these applications into three categories—interactive dialogue, active data entry, and passive data entry.

Interactive Dialogue. **Interactive dialogue** refers to the discourse between a computer and its user. For example, when the computer presents a user with a menu of choices, the software expects the user to select one. In a GUI environment, when the computer is turned on, it presents the user with icons representing applications the user can select. As these examples show, input devices are used in interactive dialogue to send messages to the computer about actions the user wants to take.

Active Data Entry. **Active data entry** refers to ways that computers obtain data through the active involvement of a user, such as when the user types on a computer's keyboard. Consider, for example, the information needs of the human resource department at Carter Manufacturing—age, sex, employment history, wages, benefits, performance ratings, and so on, for each employee. Currently, these data exist in paper form. The human resource department might use a keyboard to enter these data so that they are available for computer analysis. Now consider how the facilities department at Carter Manufacturing might enter data about the design of their building. Clearly a keyboard is not appropriate for this application. Later in this chapter we discuss the devices that can capture the data in an electronic form so that architects planning a new addition to Carter's warehouse can manipulate the data.

Passive Data Entry. **Passive data entry** refers to ways that computers can obtain information without the active participation of a user. For example, Sarah Craig would like to use computers to inspect Carter's products as they emerge from the assembly line. Input devices could constantly monitor the output of the production line, without human participation, sending the computer information it could use to determine whether a particular item should be accepted, rejected, or passed to a human inspector.

Types of Input Hardware

In this chapter, we classify input hardware devices according to the technologies they use to recognize data. Figure 6-2 summarizes this classification scheme. This scheme may hide the fact that a number of technologies can accomplish similar input objectives. The performance of a device, rather than its technological design, is most important from the user's and manager's perspective.

FIGURE 6-2 Types of Input Devices

Keyboards	Video input devices
Pointing devices	Sound sensors
Readers of formatted text	Pressure sensors
Graphic scanners	Other sensors

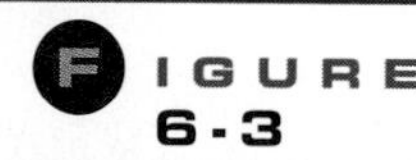

Keyboard Devices

Data Processing Keyboard
Courtesy of IBM.

Point-of-Sale Keyboard
Courtesy of IBM.

Keyboards. A **keyboard** input device consists of a plastic or metal housing containing keys that, when pressed, send a signal to the computer. Every key sends a different signal. Keyboards are the predominant device used for active data entry and, along with motion sensors, one of the most common devices for interactive dialogue. Only a small percentage of computers are sold without a keyboard. Figure 6-3 illustrates two common types of keyboards—data processing keyboards and point-of-sale keyboards.

Data processing keyboards are used for general-purpose computing. Most have three types of keys—code keys, hold keys, and toggle keys—that operate in different ways when pressed. (There is no standard terminology for the types of keys on a keyboard; the terms used here are purely descriptive.) A **code key,** such as the letter B, the Backspace key, or an arrow key, sends a specific code to the computer. Depending on the code sent, software may interpret the keystroke as a character of input, an instruction to move the **cursor** (the position marker on the computer screen), or an instruction to perform some function. A **hold key,** such as the Shift, Ctrl, or Alt key, affects the code sent by other keys pressed at the same time. For example, the code sent by the B key will differ, depending on whether or not the Shift key is simultaneously pressed. Hold keys allow a relatively small number of keys to send a fairly large number of possible signals. **Toggle keys,** such as Caps Lock or Scroll Lock, function in one of two states. Each time a toggle key is pressed, its state switches (toggles). For example, if the Caps Lock key is in an *off* state, it will change to an *on* state when pressed, and vice versa. The state of a toggle key affects the codes sent to the computer. For example, when Caps Lock is on, it reverses the effect of the Shift key (for letters only).

Many data processing keyboards arrange keys in four blocks, similar to the blocks shown on the keyboard in Figure 6-3. The keyboard has one area for letters, numbers, and special characters such as periods and dollar signs. Another area, called the **numeric keypad,** contains numbers and simple calculation signs (plus, minus, multiply, and divide). A user can easily manipulate the numeric keypad with a single hand to make high-volume numeric data entry more convenient. A third area contains **function keys,** special keys whose codes are interpreted by software as instructions to perform a particular function such as to check a document for spelling errors. The final area contains **arrow keys** and **positioning keys**. These keys send codes that most software interprets as instructions to move the cursor on the screen in the direction of the arrow pressed, to a particular location (e.g., the Home key may move the pointer to the top left corner of the screen), or through a specified range (e.g., up or down a page of the screen).

Point-of-sale keyboards such as that shown in Figure 6-3 are used with computers dedicated to a single application, usually sales order processing. These keyboards usually have only two areas, one for numeric data entry, and one for registering sales of different products. At Burger King, for example, one key may represent the sale of a chicken sandwich, while another key represents the sale of a fish sandwich. Hold keys may be used as modifiers, for example, to represent small or large when the key for a soft drink is pressed.

Pointing Devices. **Pointing devices,** used to identify a location on a computer screen, are commonly used for interactive dialogue. Two basic groups of pointing devices exist—motion sensing and position sensing. **Motion sensing devices** move a pointer across a screen in response to the way a user moves the input device; the final location of the pointer is relative to its initial position. **Position sensing devices** allow the user to identify a specific point on the screen by pointing to it with a device or touching it with a finger or stylus.

The two most popular motion sensors are the **mouse** and **trackball,** shown in Figure 6-4. A user operates a mouse by placing a hand on it and rolling it across a table top or other surface. As the mouse moves, it sends a signal about its speed and direction of movement to the computer. The computer processes this signal and moves an arrow or some other

FIGURE 6-4 Mouse and Trackball

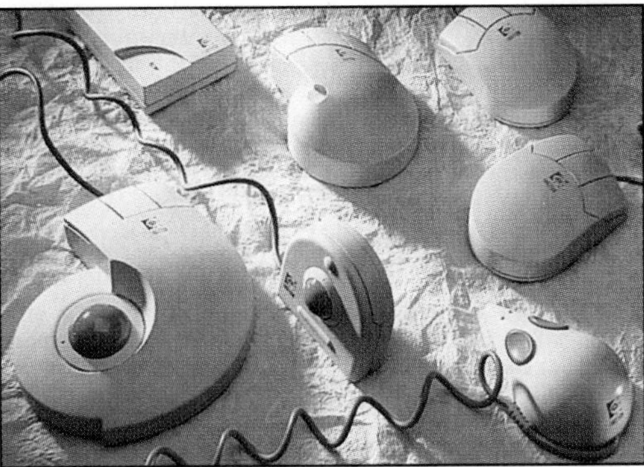

Courtesy of Logitech.

pointing symbol in parallel on the screen. A mouse also has two or three buttons that a user can "click" to send additional signals to the computer. A trackball differs from a mouse in that the user rotates rather than moves it.

The two most common position sensing devices are the **touch screen** and the **light pen,** illustrated in Figure 6-5. A touch screen is a transparent surface overlaying a computer screen that sends a signal to the computer indicating the location of contact when it is touched. A light pen consists of a stylus that transmits a narrow light beam and a transparent surface overlaying the computer screen. The device transmits a signal to the computer indicating where the light beam touches the screen.

Position sensing devices offer two major advantages over motion sensing devices: They are simpler to use and require little coordination or training. For this reason, information stands

FIGURE 6-5 Position-Sensing Devices

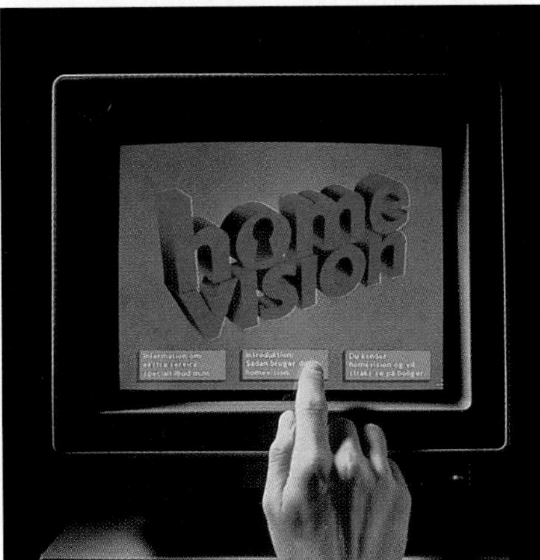

Touch Screen
Courtesy of IBM.

Light Pen
Courtesy of IBM.

INFO/CALIFORNIA

that attract the general public usually use position sensing devices. For example, Info/California operates a network of such stands at which the public can learn about and use government services.[1] Position sensing devices also offer greater convenience for portable and hand-held computer applications where there is no room to operate a mouse and where using a trackball is cumbersome. At the same time, position sensing devices cost more than motion sensing devices, particularly if a high degree of **resolution,** which expresses how precisely the device can differentiate between two closely placed points on the screen, is required.

Readers of Formatted Input. **Readers of formatted input** read text specially formatted for the device in use. They include bar code readers, mark sense readers, magnetic ink character readers, and optical character readers, as shown in Figure 6-6. Many of these devices support passive data input, allowing them to capture large amounts of data. Their major disadvantages include their applicability only to text input and their requirement for data in an appropriate format.

FLORIDA DEPARTMENT OF LAW ENFORCEMENT

ADOLPH COORS

GB ELECTRICAL

UNIVERSITY HOSPITAL OF CLEVELAND

Bar code readers have the broadest market acceptance of the readers of formatted input. The Florida Department of Law Enforcement uses bar codes to track forensic evidence; Adolph Coors Company uses bar codes to label pallet locations for securing and delivering beer; GB Electrical, Inc., a supplier of electrical hardware, uses bar codes in its on-line catalog to facilitate ordering; University Hospital of Cleveland uses bar codes to record patient diagnoses.[2] Bar code readers capture data quickly, cheaply, easily, and relatively accurately. Prices depend on a variety of factors such as size, reading speed, portability, how close the device has to be to a bar code to read it, and sensitivity to low light. Emerging standards for two-dimensional bar codes should increase the amount of information that a single bar code reading can enter.[3]

Carter Manufacturing might use bar code readers to input data about inventory. Carter could require its suppliers to provide bar code identification on all materials it orders. Carter's employees at the receiving dock would pass the goods received over a bar code reader to generate a record of Carter's receipts and update inventory. As the manufacturing division draws supplies from its bins or shelves, employees would again use a bar-code reader to record the change in inventory. Because these employees must move around the warehouse, they would use wireless portable readers that send their input to the computer using radio waves. Carter could inscribe its own bar codes onto the products it manufactures so that it can more easily create and retain a record of its inventory of finished goods.

Carter might use mark sense readers to tabulate customer preferences in a market research study. Carter employees can ask shoppers about the features they like or dislike about products like Carter's. Customers might respond more willingly because blacking out boxes that indicate their preferences takes only seconds. Carter could use a mark sense reader to input the hundreds of responses received daily.

Graphics Scanners. **Graphics scanners** input pictures and other graphics into a computer after first **digitizing** them, converting them into a numeric format that computers can process. The advertising department at Carter Manufacturing may choose to prepare drafts of advertisements using graphics scanners; the public relations department might use graphics scanners for preparing the annual report about the company. Scanners differ in their ability to capture detail, the number of colors or scales of gray they support, and the number of pages they can scan in a minute. Low-end scanners require the user to manually move the device over a page, as shown in Figure 6-7. More expensive scanners have a sheet feeder, read six pages per minute, and provide a resolution of 300 dots per inch or more. **Flat-bed scanners** scan books, magazines, and other media that cannot be fed through a sheet feeder.

FIGURE 6-6 Formatted Input Readers

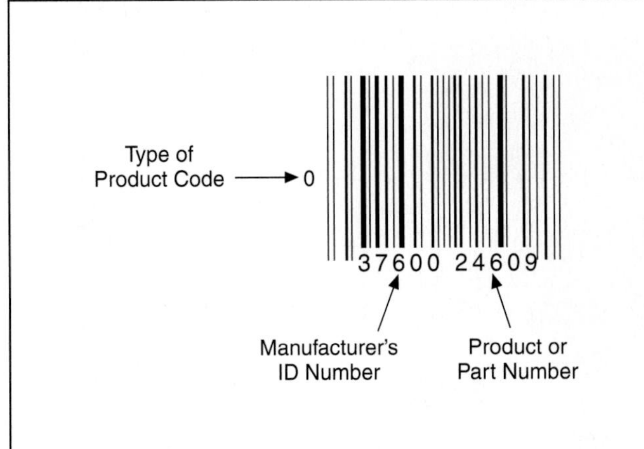

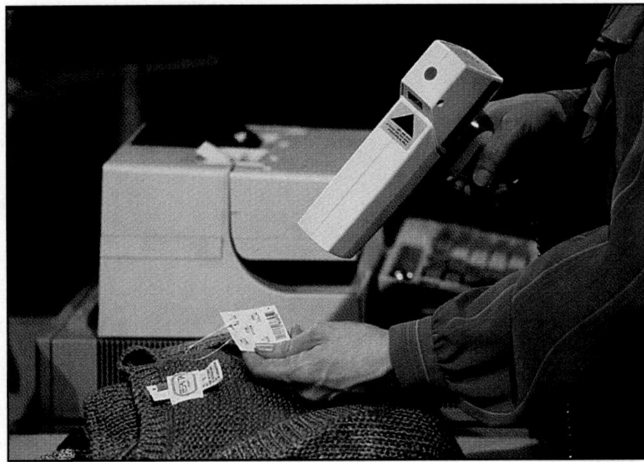

Bar Code Reader—Bar codes are a series of lines interpreted as numbers based on their width and spacing. Bar code readers include manually held devices such as wands that operators wave over bar codes and fixed devices that read bar codes that pass within their view.

Courtesy of IBM.

UNDERGRADUATE STUDENT OPINION SURVEY

U

INSTRUCTOR: ____________ DATE: ________

COURSE #: ____________ SECTION #: ______

COURSE NAME: ____________

For questions 1-19 blacken the appropriate letter if you:
A = strongly agree with the statement
B = agree with the statement
C = neither agree nor disagree with the statement
D = disagree with the statement
E = strongly disagree with the statement

############################

Instructor Performance:

1. The instructor set high standards of performance -1 [A] [B] [C] [D] [E]
2. The lectures and class discussions were of great value in understanding the subject matter -2 [A] [B] [C] [D] [E]
3. The instructor made excellent use of examples, illustrations, or personal experience to clarify the material -3 [A] [B] [C] [D] [E]
4. The instructor presented the material in a well-organized fashion -4 [A] [B] [C] [D] [E]
5. The instructor stimulated my desire to learn -5 [A] [B] [C] [D] [E]

Student/Instructor Relations:

6. I felt free to ask questions, express my own ideas, and disagree with the instructor's views -6 [A] [B] [C] [D] [E]
7. The instructor was available for office hours and appointments outside of class -7 [A] [B] [C] [D] [E]

Course Content and Workload:

8. The instructor assumed too much prior knowledge (Answer C for the right amount and E for too little) -8 [A] [B] [C] [D] [E]
9. Texts, handouts, etc. were useful for understanding course material -9 [A] [B] [C] [D] [E]
10. The instructor presented too much material (Answer C for the right amount and E for too little) -10 [A] [B] [C] [D] [E]

Testing and Evaluation:

11. The examinations were fair and reasonable -11 [A] [B] [C] [D] [E]
12. The examination(s)/paper(s) were valuable as a learning experience -12 [A] [B] [C] [D] [E]

Overall Questions:

13. The course achieved its objectives by the end of the semester -13 [A] [B] [C] [D] [E]
14. In comparison to other courses that I have taken, I would rate this course very difficult (Answer C for average difficulty and E for very easy) -14 [A] [B] [C] [D] [E]
15. This course contributed to my ability to think, reason, analyze, or solve problems -15 [A] [B] [C] [D] [E]
16. I learned a great deal from this course -16 [A] [B] [C] [D] [E]
17. Overall, the teaching ability of the instructor was high -17 [A] [B] [C] [D] [E]
18. I would recommend this instructor to other students who are going to take this course -18 [A] [B] [C] [D] [E]

Student Demographic Information:

19. Before the course started, I was interested in the subject -19 [A] [B] [C] [D] [E]
20. Class standing: (check only one) A = Freshman B = Sophomore C = Junior D = Senior -20 [A] [B] [C] [D]
21. Major(s): (check up to 4) -21 [A] [B] [C] [D] [E]
A = Acctng./Law B = Am.Studs. C = Communication
D = Economics E = Entreprshp. F = Finance - [F] [G] [H] [J] [K]
G = Investments H = Mgt./OB J = Marketing
K = MIS M = MIS/Acctng. N = QM - [M] [N] [O] [P] [Q]
O = Soc. & Tech. P = QM/Econ. Q = QM/Finance

Mark Sense Form—A mark sense reader identifies the location of dark marks on a page. Preprinted forms, such as the answer forms for the College Board Examinations, are marked by the data entry person and interpreted by software as data.

D. OR S. WEBSTER
LIC. 09882130 04044197
4302 YELLOWLEAF DR. PH. 370-2821
FORT WORTH, TEXAS 76133

1856

32-115/1110

6-1 19 94

Pay To The Order Of Security Partners $ 26 88/100

twenty six 88/100 Dollars

Texas Commerce Bank

TEXAS COMMERCE BANK, NATIONAL ASSOCIATION
FORT WORTH CITY CENTER OFFICE
201 MAIN ST
FORT WORTH, TEXAS 76102

Memo

⑆111001150⑆1856⑈3790450447 8⑈ ⑇0000002688⑇

Magnetic Ink Character Reader (MICR)—An MICR reads numbers and some special symbols shaped as shown above and printed in magnetic ink. Check-processing systems using MICR can handle over 2,000 checks per minute.

ABCDEFGHIJKLMN
OPQRSTUVWXYZ
1234567890

Optical Character Reader (OCR)—An OCR reads characters formed like those shown above. Some OCR readers can read handwriting if the form of the letters closely approximates the OCR standard.

FIGURE 6-7 Hand-Held Graphics Scanner

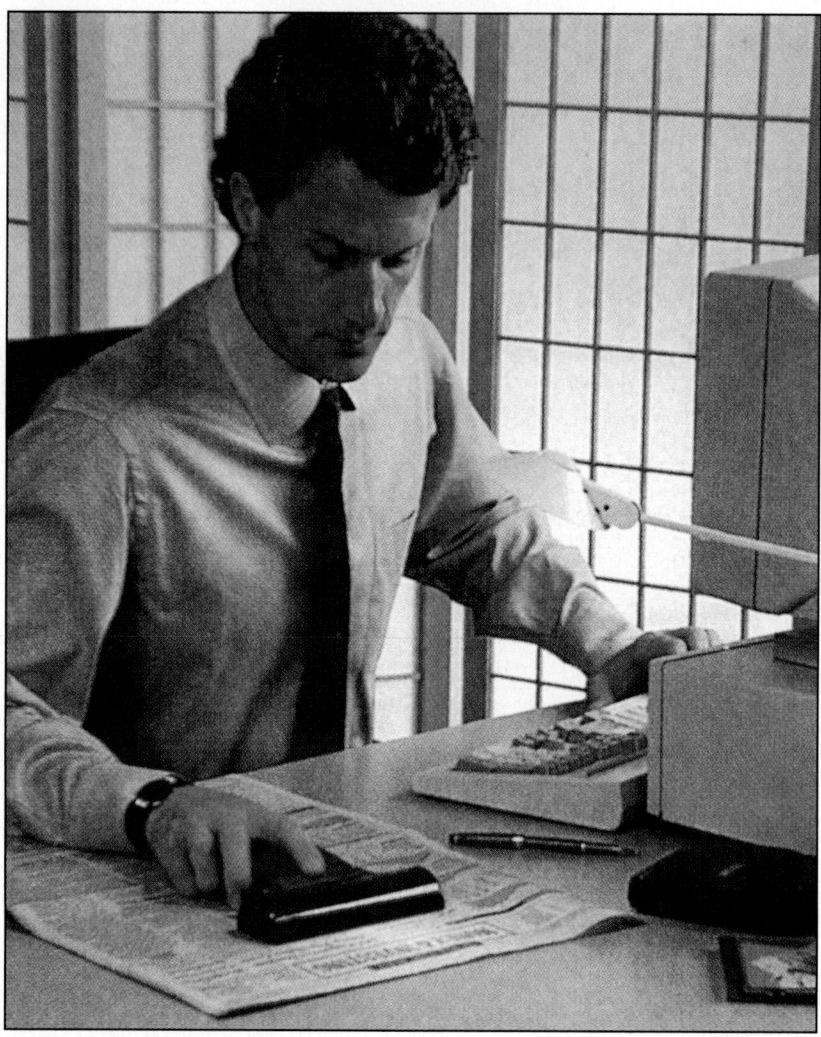

Courtesy of Caere Corporation.

The inability of software to mimic human abilities in processing graphical images limits the effectiveness of graphics scanners. To use scanners as an input device for text and numbers, the images received must be converted into data that can be processed by word processors and spreadsheets. Fortunately, low-priced software now typically achieves accuracies of more than 99 percent on clear typed or printed material input through a high-quality scanner. Scanning of faxed documents, second- and third-generation photocopies, and documents produced using a poor-quality printer generally achieve accuracies as high as 98 percent.[4] Although character recognition technology has improved and continues to improve rapidly, individuals use graphics scanners primarily to capture images (rather than text) and to archive documents that include both text and graphic material. The industry has adopted the term **OCR** to mean **optical character recognition software** even though it is also used to mean **optical character reader,** a device that recognizes specially formatted letters.

Video Input Devices. Images from video cameras can be digitized and input into a computer. The marketing department at Carter Manufacturing might use this technology for preparing product releases. The quality department might collect and input data about the manufacturing process using this technology. Video camera devices also allow computers to capture moving pictures. However, the technology and understanding necessary to extract meaningful information from moving pictures is even more immature than the technology to extract such information from still pictures. As a result, companies use video technology primarily to capture images for storage and output rather than for processing. Although data from moving images can be compressed, moving image storage still requires huge storage capacities.

Sound Sensors. The electronic signal from a microphone can be digitized for computer input. Potential applications of sound input include monitoring mechanical equipment, such as turbines, processing sonar data, saving and replaying voice messages or recorded concerts, and recognizing and responding to commands spoken by a human.

Pressure Sensors. Pressure-sensitive devices emit an electrical signal that indicates the amount of pressure placed upon them. This signal can be digitized for input into a computer. Applications of pressure sensors include touch-screen devices, pen-based input devices, intelligent scales, and control systems for aircraft and missiles.

Other Sensors. Sensors that measure moisture, temperature, chemical composition, and almost any form of sensory data can convert their readings into digital signals that can be passed to a computer. Manufacturing industries use sensor technologies extensively to collect data about and automate manufacturing processes. Carter Manufacturing might use such devices for monitoring the environmental conditions in its production area or for ensuring the correct functioning of its machinery. Sensors can even be used to detect brain wave patterns and intensity. Employing such sensors, computers can be programmed to respond to people's thoughts.[5] Figure 6-8 provides examples of other applications of sensor technologies.

FIGURE 6-8 Some Applications of Sensor Technology

Check the freshness of food—When you buy food at a grocery store, you may smell it to see whether it is fresh. Microsensors can "smell" it for you and alert clerks to pull spoiled food from the shelves.

Monitor vital signs—Microsensors can read a patient's blood pressure, blood oxygen content, pulse rate, etc. and input them continuously to a monitoring computer.

Detect gas leaks—Microsensors can "smell" gas leaks in mining or industrial settings or the leaks of other chemicals to monitor the safety of the work environment.

Detect need for auto maintenance—Sensors can detect engine oil viscosity, heat, whether or not water is mixed with oil, and other problems that demand automobile service.

Intelligent smoke detectors—Sensors can identify the chemical components of airborne particles, determining whether particles are related to smoke from fire, mist from a shower, or dust from other sources.

Humidity detectors—Microsensors that monitor humidity can save water by shutting off automatic lawn sprinkler systems after thay have delivered the right amount of moisture and keeping them from operating after rain showers.

SOURCE: Virginia Dudek, "Microsensors: devices that feel," *MIS Week* (September 1, 1989).

Processing Hardware

Processing hardware implements the instructions encoded into software. A special hardware device called an **instruction register** or **instruction counter** contains the **address** of a location in the computer's memory that holds the initial instruction a computer needs to start its operation. Turning on the computer activates this instruction. Thereafter, the processor executes instructions sequentially in the order in which they exist in memory unless it encounters an instruction that resets the instruction counter to a different memory address.

Figure 6-9 illustrates the steps needed for a computer processor to perform its work. First the processor retrieves, or **fetches,** the instruction stored at the location indicated by the instruction register. Next it **decodes** the instruction, that is, determines what the instruction tells it to do. Finally, it **executes** the instruction. The processor repeats the three steps of fetch, decode, and execute until someone turns off the power.

Measuring Processing Power

A manager who purchases a computer needs to understand how computer professionals talk about computer processing power so that he or she can evaluate and trade off price against performance. Sarah Craig, for example, should evaluate the current hardware and recommend changes after diagnosing the organization's information needs and making a preliminary assessment of the relative power of various processors. However, even experts cannot evaluate a processor on its specifications alone for several reasons. First, no single measure of

FIGURE 6-9 How a Processor Performs Its Work

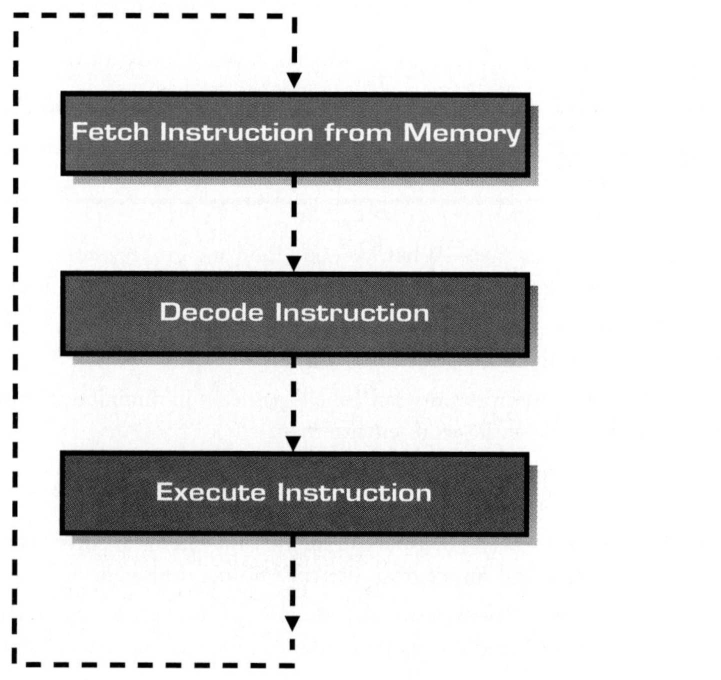

processor power exists; rather, several characteristics determine a processor's effective power. Second, processors differ in their speed and capability depending on the task they perform. Finally, the input, storage, and output devices that surround a processor will influence its power. Although the best way to evaluate a computer is to use it for a sample of tasks similar to those that it will perform, we can use six other characteristics to provide some assessment of a computer's power, as shown in Figure 6-10.

Speed is a key component of a processor's power. An electronic circuit called a **clock** emits a regular electronic beat or pulse that synchronizes the operation of the processor. With each pulse, the processor performs one operation, such as fetching or decoding. Some operations, particularly the execution of complex instructions, may take several pulses. Computer salespeople refer to the number of pulses per second, known as the **clock speed.** Most microcomputer processors operate at speeds of more than 20 **megahertz** (millions of hertz), where a **hertz** is one pulse per second.

A second measure of a processor's power is how fast it can perform arithmetic. Computers almost always use more than a single clock cycle to perform an arithmetic operation. **Floating point arithmetic**—calculations with numbers having a decimal point and stored in exponential format—consume the most time. The traditional measure of arithmetic prowess is the **megaflop** (millions of floating point operations per second). Some computers contain special fast-calculation devices called **floating point accelerators,** or **math coprocessors,** that boost a computer's speed by taking over from the main processor the performance of complex arithmetic computations.

A third component of a processor's performance is the average number of **instructions** it performs **per second.** This measure relates closely to clock speed but reflects actual experience rather than peak performance. Because a processor takes several clock cycles to execute many instructions, clock speed overestimates the number of instructions a processor performs per second. For example, a 25 megahertz processor may rate only 5 **million instructions per second (MIPS)** in practice. The speed measured in MIPS for a given

FIGURE 6-10 Characteristics for Assessing Processor Power

Clock speed—The maximum speed at which the processor can be regulated in clock cycles per second (Hertz).

Arithmetic power—The average number of floating point operations (FLOPs) the processor can perform in one second.

Instruction speed—The average number of instructions the processor performs in one second running a typical program (MIPS = million instructions per second.)

Instruction set complexity—The number of different instructions the processor understands. Typically, computers are classified simply as RISC (understands only a few simple instructions) or CISC (understands many complex instructions).

Word length—The number of bits the processor can handle at one time. Two numbers are often given, one for arithmetic data within the processor, and another for moving data of any type between the processor and storage, input, or output devices.

Pipelining—The ability of a processor to overlap the processing of two or more instructions.

processor type usually varies directly with the clock speed. For example, a 64 megahertz 80486 will have twice the MIPS of a 32 megahertz 80486. As a result, you can use MIPS and clock speed interchangeably when comparing similar processors. This relationship does not hold when comparing speeds of different types of processors because one processor may average one instruction every four cycles while another averages one instruction every eight cycles. MIPS is a better measure of speed in this case. However, speeds measured in MIPS must be interpreted carefully because the power of an instruction differs among processors. One processor may take eight instructions to do what can be done with only one instruction in another processor.

Until the late 1980s, experts often touted a fourth measure of a processor's power: the strength of its instruction set, as measured by the number of different instructions it could decode and execute. Experts began to question this measure, however, after they analyzed how commercial compilers translated computer programs into processor instructions. They found that a small number of instructions were used more than 90 percent of the time; less common instructions could be achieved through combinations of the simple instructions; and complex instructions required many more cycles to perform than simple instructions, reducing the computer's effective speed relative to its clock speed. To check whether a rich instruction set measured processor power, researchers created processors called **Reduced Instruction Set Computers,** or **RISC processors,** that understood only a few instructions, as opposed to **Complex Instruction Set Computers,** or **CISC processors,** as they described the commercial computers then available. By limiting the number of instructions understood by RISC processors, the researchers could design them more quickly, increase their clock speed, and dramatically increase their MIPS rating. Although manufacturers of RISC and CISC chips continue to make conflicting claims about the superiority of their technology, the marketplace is clearly moving toward RISC.[6] When comparing different processors, buyers should consider the processors' instruction sets in conjunction with their quoted MIPS or clock speeds. For example, a 50 MIPS RISC processor may perform tasks no faster than a 20 MIPS CISC processor.

A fifth component of a processor's power is its **word length,** the amount of data it can handle at one time. The smallest amount of data, called a **bit** (short for binary digit), is essentially a switch that may be set on or off, representing the digit 1 or 0. The earliest personal computers used processors that handled eight bits of data at a time. Most personal computers now handle 16 or 32 bits of data at a time, while most mainframes handle 32 or 64 bits of data at once. The number of bits a computer can move at one time from one area of memory to another, called its **bus width,** may differ from the number of bits that a computer can process at one time. Doubling the number of bits handled will more than double the speed of certain arithmetic operations, such as multiplying large numbers. Doubling the number of bits will have little effect on the processing of text or character data, although it will at least double the speed of moving characters from one area of memory to another.

Pipelining, a sixth aspect of power, refers to a processor's ability to overlap the fetching, decoding, and executing of different instructions. A processor with pipelining will operate faster than one without. While a pipelined processor decodes one instruction, it simultaneously fetches a second instruction. Then, while it executes the first instruction, it decodes the second and fetches a third.

Computer processing power, as measured by MIPS for newly introduced processors, has increased at a rate of about 20 percent a year for mainframes and 25 percent a year for microcomputers and minicomputers. At this rate, processing power doubles every three or four years and increases by a factor of ten every ten to twelve years. Because the price of state-of-the-art processors has not changed much within each category, the price of a MIPS has dropped about 20 percent per year. Experts believe these trends will continue unabated for the foreseeable future.

Specialized Processors

Specialized processors are those designed to do a specific job. Unlike the processors described earlier, which have a general capacity to manipulate data and change the order of their instruction execution, specialized processors respond to a limited set of commands, if any, to perform highly specialized tasks. Because their instructions have been "hard-wired" into their chips, and because their chips have been optimized for their designed tasks, they can perform these tasks more quickly than can general-purpose processors.

An **image compressor,** one example of a specialized processor, recognizes similarities among parts of a digitized image and among sequential frames of a moving image. By eliminating redundancies and using other "tricks," it can typically reduce the amount of data needed to represent an image to between 1/50 and 1/200 of the amount needed without compression.[7] As a result, computers can process and store the images more quickly. Inexpensive boards combining digitizers and image compressors, for example, can capture video in 320 × 240-dot resolution at 30 frames per second.[8] In addition, image compressors reduce the amount of storage needed to save images and permit images to be transmitted more rapidly over data communication networks.

Main processors can off-load work onto a variety of specialized processors, such as the floating point accelerator (discussed earlier), to increase their efficiency. Some specialized processors, such as those that handle input or output, can achieve further efficiencies by performing their tasks while the main processor independently acts on the next set of instructions.

Graphics processors rapidly manipulate images—rotate them, zoom in and out, present appropriate views of three-dimensional objects, color regions, and detect and draw edges. **Voice processors** can translate sound-wave inputs into sound-groups called phonemes and then into written words.

Digital signal processors or **DSPs** convert an electronic wave signal, such as one arising from sound or other sensory inputs, to a stream of digital bits, and vice versa. These processors, which cost about $500 in 1988, are now priced at under $5.[9] In addition, DSP manufacturers can easily customize their products to perform additional tasks such as data compression. Examples of DSP applications include digitally encoding cellular telephone transmissions to prevent eavesdropping and increase clarity, modifying recorded music to sound as if it were recorded in a specific concert hall, suppressing noise from vehicles and appliances by generating sounds that will cancel the offending sounds, recognizing phone numbers spoken aloud and automatically dialing them, recognizing military objects from their radar signals, and avoiding aircraft collisions by responding to radar and visual signals.[10]

Future computers likely will contain several specialized processors in addition to their general-purpose processor to perform diverse tasks quickly and efficiently. Sarah Craig will probably have to consider whether or not to purchase floating point accelerators, graphics processors, and other specialized processors for Carter Manufacturing's computer hardware.

Storage Hardware

Managers and other computer users rarely discard data immediately after collecting, processing, and printing them. They may save data to combine or average them with similar data, track or project sales, costs, or other information, and maintain archives of company records. They may keep data that relate to business transactions in progress, which take time to unfold and move forward. Companies typically retain transaction data as part of a permanent audit trail. Organizations may also need to store the software programs that perform office automation and other applications. Clearly, Sarah Craig must consider the types of storage devices appropriate for her organization's needs; she must evaluate the storage devices currently used and then identify the storage hardware that best meets the organization's information needs. Many individuals and most departments at Carter Manufacturing use computer storage for an array of purposes like those described above.

In this section we discuss what computer buyers, users, and managers need to know about storage devices. We begin by addressing the question they ask most often: "How much storage do I need?" Answering this question means understanding how manufacturers quote storage capacity and how computers use various types of storage for different computing activities.

Measuring Storage

A bit is the smallest amount of data that can be stored; it has one of two possible values—on or off—0 or 1. All information can be represented by sequences of bits. For example, a black and white picture can be portrayed, as in a newspaper or magazine print, by a series of inked dots separated by white space. If you lay a 1000 × 1000 line grid over a picture, you can observe the color, black or white, at each of the million points lying at the grid intersections. You can then represent the picture by 1 million bits set to 1 for black or 0 for white. If you require a finer resolution, you can increase the number of lines in the grid and the number of bits used to represent the picture.

Letters, numbers, and other characters can also be represented in this fashion, although such a scheme uses many more bits than necessary. A coding scheme, such as the Morse code with bits set to 1 for a dot and 0 for a dash, can represent a character with many fewer bits. Codes that use only seven bits, for example, can represent as many as 128 different characters. Two coding schemes that use eight bits have become industry standards. Most microcomputers use a code called **ASCII** to represent characters. IBM uses a code called **EBCDIC** for its mainframes and minicomputers; some other mainframe manufacturers also use EBCDIC.

Because of the use of standard eight-bit coding schemes, most manufacturers measure storage capacity in **bytes,** where one byte equals eight bits. Greek prefaces attached to the word *byte* indicate orders of magnitude: for example, a kilobyte is approximately a thousand bytes. Figure 6-11 presents a complete list of storage terminology.

Primary versus Secondary Storage

Primary and secondary storage differ in their speed in retrieving and storing data, their capacity, their durability, and their cost. We can view their differences as the differences between using a desk surface and a file cabinet for storage. An office worker or manager who wants

FIGURE 6-11 Terminology for Large Storage Amounts

Term	Approximate Number of Bytes	Abbreviation
Kilobyte	One thousand	KB
Megabyte	One million	MB
Gigabyte	One billion	GB
Terabyte	One trillion	TB

to work on a project moves documents and other items pertaining to the project from cabinet to desktop. After finishing the work, the employee returns the modified documents and any new material generated to the file cabinet for long-term storage. Similarly, when a computer needs to perform a task, it does not perform the task on data in secondary storage. Instead, it moves data from **secondary storage,** the file cabinet, to **primary storage,** the desk top. After manipulating the data in primary storage or creating new data (perhaps moving data collected by input devices into primary storage), the processor moves data back to secondary storage devices for the longer term.

Although primary storage is much faster in its ability to retrieve and store data than secondary storage, it costs much more. As a result, computers tend to have 10 to 100 times as much secondary storage as primary storage, and the ratio between secondary and primary storage may exceed 1,000 to 1. Continuing the analogy, the desktop always has much less room than the file cabinets, and desktop space is dear.

A manager should understand the distinction between primary and secondary memory when buying a computer. The computer needs only enough primary memory to support a single task or the tasks the user intends to perform simultaneously. The computer should have enough secondary storage to maintain all data and programs the user intends to collect. Sarah Craig must analyze her company's requirements for primary and secondary storage when formulating her recommendations for new computer hardware.

Primary Storage Devices

All primary storage occurs on **circuit boards** that include several **chips**—small wafers of silicon with millions of transistors, as shown in Figure 6-12. Because processors access primary storage directly, a computer equipped with primary storage that runs slower than its processor will operate more slowly than it should. Remember that a processor in a single machine cycle will want to retrieve its next instruction from memory. Processors operate at millions of cycles per second, so primary access devices must be able to retrieve and store whatever data the processor wants within a millionth of a second or less. This requirement precludes the use of mechanical devices for primary storage and suggests the use of chips that store electrical signals.

FIGURE 6-12 Computer Chip

Courtesy of Motorola.

Early memory devices used electrical currents to set or read the polarity of a magnet, which could represent one bit. But electromagnetic devices were relatively expensive and slow. Development of transistor technology improved the speed and lowered the expense of primary storage. A transistor can represent a bit because it can be set rapidly to either an on or off electrical state. An electrical signal can change the state of a transistor or determine its current state. Today's primary storage devices pack millions of transistors into a single chip. Tomorrow's primary storage devices may be opto-electrical, operating at or near the speed of light.

Cache memory describes a small amount of primary storage that is faster than the rest of the primary storage. In recent years, computer processor speeds have increased rapidly, and memory speeds have not kept pace, at least not inexpensively. To compensate for this problem and to keep processors from having to wait while retrieving data and instructions from memory, computer designers equip their fastest computers with a small amount of fast, expensive cache memory. When the processor requests data or instructions from an address not in cache memory, the computer moves that data along with a block of nearby addresses into the high-speed cache. Then, if the computer requests the instruction or data from nearby addresses, as it usually does, the data can be found rapidly in cache memory.

Volatile versus Nonvolatile Devices. Most chips cannot store data without power. This **volatile storage,** known as **RAM (random access memory),** loses whatever data it has if someone turns off the computer. Without any data or programs in its memory, the computer could not do anything when turned on. For computers to work when turned on, some portion of the computer's memory must retain instructions that the computer needs to start functioning and to copy **(load)** the operating system software from secondary storage into primary storage. Computer designers use a type of electronic storage device known as **read-only memory (ROM)** that retains its state in the absence of electrical power to hold the computer's initial instructions. The **non-volatile** ROM devices do not change their state in response to an electronic signal; data must be burned into ROM memory using special equipment. Because of the expense of ROM and because data on ROM cannot be changed, computers contain only a few kilobytes of ROM compared with megabytes of RAM.

Trends. The price, size, and power consumption of primary storage devices has been decreasing at a rapid rate, as shown in Figure 6-13; for example, 4 MB of RAM cost less in 1993 than 64 KB of RAM did when microcomputers first became popular. In 1982, most personal computers had only 64 KB of RAM. The amount of RAM had increased to 640 KB by 1986. Most personal computers were equipped with about 1 MB of RAM by 1990. Microsoft's Windows operating system, however, requires at least 2 MB of RAM to operate, and some software manufacturers recommend at least 8 MB for their programs that operate under Windows. As a result, microcomputer buyers now typically demand new computers with at least 8 to 16 MB of RAM.

Secondary Storage Devices

Computer users employ secondary storage devices, such as hard disks, diskettes, tapes, and compact disks, to retain data both temporarily and more permanently. Access to data in secondary storage occurs at speeds of 8 to 75 thousandths of a second, approximately a million times slower than access to data in primary storage. Still, secondary storage offers three advantages over primary storage. First, it is much less expensive. Second, it retains data without electrical power. Third, it can be removed from its computer, allowing the transfer of data

FIGURE 6-13 Trends in Primary Storage

Prices shown are the most common street prices based on advertisements in June issues of *Byte*.

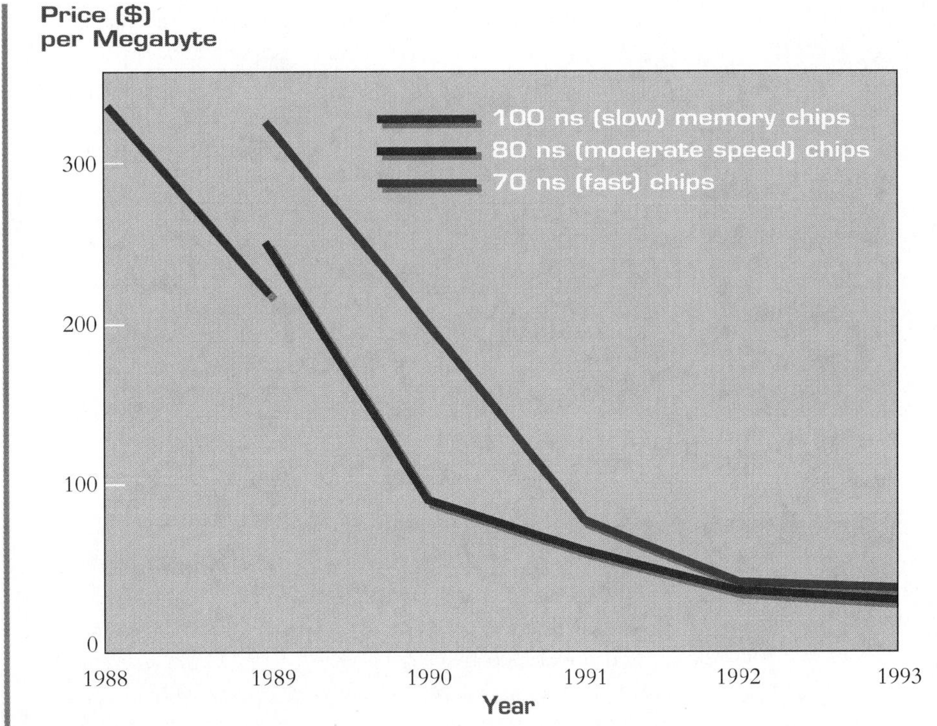

between computers or the shipping of data as products. Clearly, Carter Manufacturing will require secondary storage to meet information needs in most departments, including marketing, accounting, manufacturing, and human resources.

Unlike primary storage devices, secondary storage devices typically save data on a variety of nonelectrical media, such as magnetic or optical films covering tapes or disks. To retrieve data stored this way, electromechanical and other mechanical devices position the desired data under a sensing device that detects a magnetic flux or an optical property and interprets it as data. This mechanical positioning process is what makes retrieval of data from secondary storage so much slower than retrieval of data from primary storage.

Removable Media. Some storage devices write to and read from storage media that can be removed from the computer. Currently, four types of removable media are in common use—tapes, diskettes, disk packs, and read-only compact disks (CD-ROMs). Figure 6-14 illustrates these media and the drives that read them.

Tape storage devices use a thin mylar tape covered with a magnetic coating. **Cartridge tapes** resemble those used to record music, and **reel tapes** look like reels of movie film. Tape's primary advantage as a storage medium is its low cost per unit of capacity. Tape also provides an extremely compact medium for archiving large amounts of data (see Figure 6-15 for a picture of a tape library). But tape requires a relatively long time to retrieve data; positioning a tape to the desired data may take several seconds or even minutes unless the data are retrieved in the same order as stored. Organizations find tapes to be convenient for

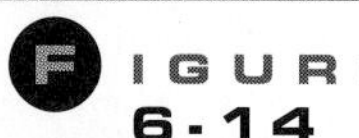

FIGURE 6-14 Common Removable Media

Reel Tapes
Courtesy of Hewlett-Packard.

Tape Drives
Courtesy of IBM.

Diskette Drive

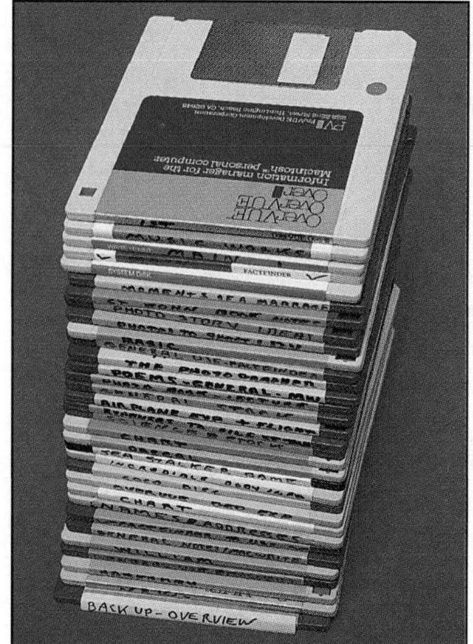

Diskettes
Dan McCoy/Rainbow.

Disk Packs and Drives
Donald Dietz/Stock, Boston.

CD-ROM
Gregory Heisler/Image Bank.

archiving or creating backup copies of data. The accounting department of Carter Manufacturing may choose tape to maintain its financial archives. Because Carter would rarely access archives and backups, its managers can tolerate tape's slow retrieval of data.

A **diskette** consists of a circle of mylar or similar material coated with a magnetic film and protected with a cardboard or hard plastic cover. Microcomputer users prefer diskettes for their removable storage needs. Individuals may also use diskettes for archiving and backup, although they hold much less data than tape. The primary advantage of diskettes relative to tape is their higher speed of data access. **Diskette drives** spin diskettes rapidly, exposing and reading any part of the storage surface within a few hundredths of a second.

A **disk pack** consists of a stack of magnetic-coated metal disks connected by a central spindle. A special disk drive creates a vacuum when the disk pack is inserted and then spins

Tape Library

Courtesy of IBM.

the pack rapidly. Minicomputer and mainframe users commonly employ disk packs for their secondary storage needs because of their speed and capacity. The cost of disk packs, the cost of disk drives, and the size and weight of the packs may limit their usefulness. Most users mount a disk pack associated with a particular application as they prepare to run that application and dismount the disk pack when processing of that application terminates. Because a typical disk pack is the size and weight of an automobile tire, some users never remove their disk packs from their drives. This characteristic makes disk packs less transportable and will influence their use in organizations such as Carter Manufacturing.

A **CD-ROM** refers to an optical disk similar to a compact disk used to play music. Software vendors and vendors of publications, abstracts, and indices for libraries commonly distribute their products on CD-ROM media. CD-ROM has a large storage capacity—equal to about 400 diskettes. Although access speeds are increasing, access to data stored on CD-ROM is about ten times slower than access to data stored on hard disk media. Nevertheless, users consider this speed acceptable for many applications. In particular, many companies use CD-ROM media to permanently archive their data because it is much more compact than tape. However, they do not use CD-ROM for temporary backup because they cannot reuse the media. The cost per megabyte of CD-ROM media compares favorably to that of floppy disk media. Devices to read CD-ROMs cost more than floppy diskette drives but their cost is dropping.

Another technology called **Write-Once Read-Many,** or **WORM** optical disks, operates by burning microscopic holes in a CD-ROM disk's surface coating. As a result, data stored on WORM disks, like CD-ROM, cannot be erased, and the disks cannot be reused. WORM disk drives generally have capacities of several gigabytes and cost several thousand dollars, with a price of under $5 per megabyte. They operate at approximately the same speed as most hard disk drives.

Attempts to develop and market low-cost, fast, reusable optical disks have been relatively unsuccessful. Fast, erasable optical disk drives generally have capacities of several gigabytes and cost several thousand dollars, with a price of about $10 per megabyte.

After diagnosing her organization's information needs, Sarah Craig must determine whether Carter should move more of its archived storage from microfiche to optical disk, where it can easily be indexed and stored. Although cost is her primary consideration, Sarah must also consider the ease with which employees can retrieve the archived data and the possibility that managerial decisions will improve when managers feel more free to access and analyze archived data. Sarah might also find that the marketing managers at Carter are eager to create a catalog, complete with pictures and prices, that can be distributed periodically on CD-ROM to key buyers.

Fixed Media. The most common type of fixed medium, a **hard disk** (see Figure 6-16), consists of magnetic-coated metal platters arranged on a spindle, encased in a vacuum chamber, and packaged with a device (motor, electronics, and magnetic sensors) that positions, reads, and writes data on the medium. Because of the small size and low power needs of microcomputers, their vendors usually package hard disks inside the computers' cabinet housings. This placement causes people who are unfamiliar with computer technology to confuse hard disk storage with RAM primary storage.

The price per megabyte of hard disk storage has declined rapidly in recent years, while disk speed has increased, as shown in Figure 6-17. This decline has helped fuel a growth in types of software that demand more disk storage. For example, in 1990, microcomputer users typically found that 40 MB of hard disk was sufficient for their text-based programs and data. Users of Windows, however, require at least 120 MB, and more typically at least 400 MB because the graphics images used in the Windows environment require more storage and the programs that process graphics images are more complex and larger, also demanding

IGURE 6-16

Hard Disk and Disk Controller

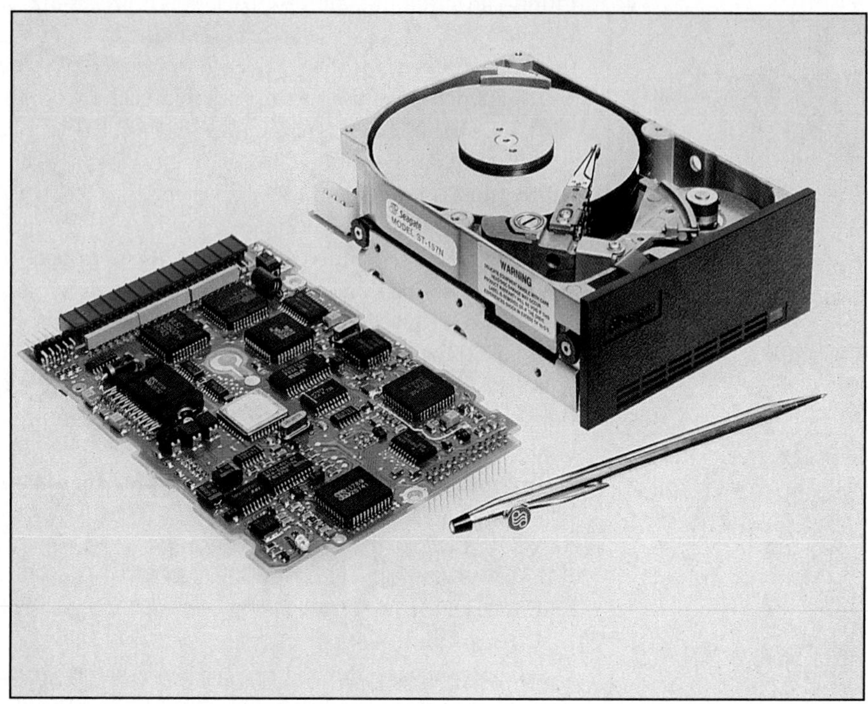

Courtesy of Seagate Technologies.

more storage. The growth of Windows would have been severely hampered had hard disk prices not declined significantly in the early 1990s.

The rapid decline in hard disk prices has also enabled the increased use of **file servers.** File servers—computers that provide programs and data to other computers through a network (see Chapter 8)—generally need capacities of several gigabytes because a single file server must satisfy the storage needs of many computer users. File servers allow organizations to centralize storage of data and take advantage of economies of scale in the price of disk capacity.

A third outgrowth of declining hard disk prices has been the increased use of **redundant arrays of inexpensive disks (RAID).** RAID storage devices use a large number of relatively small hard disks to create what appears to be a single storage device that can retain multiple copies of several gigabytes of data. If errors arise in any one of the hard disks, it can be disabled and replaced without a loss of data because of the redundancies in the system. Companies that depend upon their computer systems to transact business find this feature highly desirable.

Output Hardware

Computer systems use output devices to transfer information from computer storage into a form that individuals can see, hear, or feel. Output includes **hardcopy**—output on a medium such as paper that can be removed from the computer—and **softcopy**—output, such as that

FIGURE 6-17 Trends in Hard Disk Prices for Disks of Various Capacities

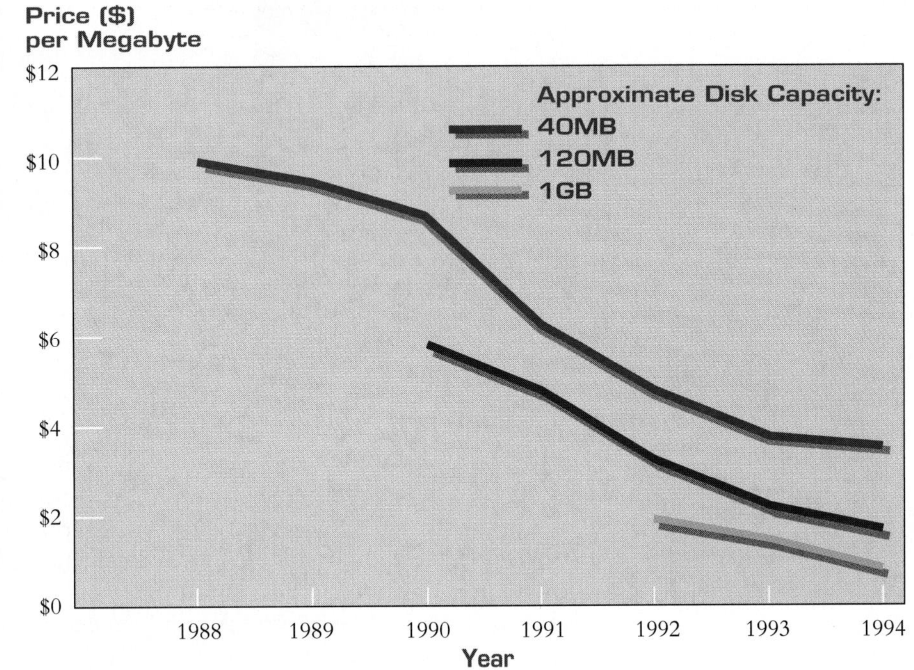

NOTE: For 1988 and 1989, prices are shown for drives requiring an average access time of over 35 milliseconds. For 1990 and 1991, the average access time decreased to approximately 25 milliseconds. For 1992 and afterward, 40MB drive prices are shown for 25ms access time, 120MB drives are shown for 18ms access time, and 1GB drives are shown for drives faster than 12ms. Prices shown are the most common street prices based on advertisements in June issues of *Byte.*

on a computer screen, that cannot be moved. Text devices produce letters and numbers such as those you would see on a typewritten page. Graphics devices generate pictures and diagrams. Graphics devices can also draw text by producing small dots in the design of characters, as shown in Figure 6-18. The text produced by this method may be hard to read if the output device cannot provide a sufficient density of dots and sufficient resolution in dot placement.

The purchaser of a graphics output device should consider the density or resolution of the output. **Density** refers to the number of dots a device produces per inch horizontally and vertically. The use of a single dot-per-inch (dpi) statistic in its specifications means that the vertical and horizontal directions have the same density (e.g., 300 dpi or 1,000 dpi). When horizontal and vertical dpi differ, manufacturers usually quote both numbers. Most users cannot tell the difference between output produced by text printers, graphics printers at 300 dpi, and professional typesetters at 1,200 dpi. The density for computer screens may be quoted differently—as the total number of dots (not per inch) in each direction. Alternatively, some manufacturers specify the space between adjacent dots, known as the **dot pitch.** Experts recommend a dot pitch of not more than .35 millimeters to minimize eye strain. Computer professionals often use the term **resolution** to describe the quality of output; they may say, for example, that a printer has a resolution of 300 dpi.

FIGURE 6-18 Characters Produced with a Graphics Output Device

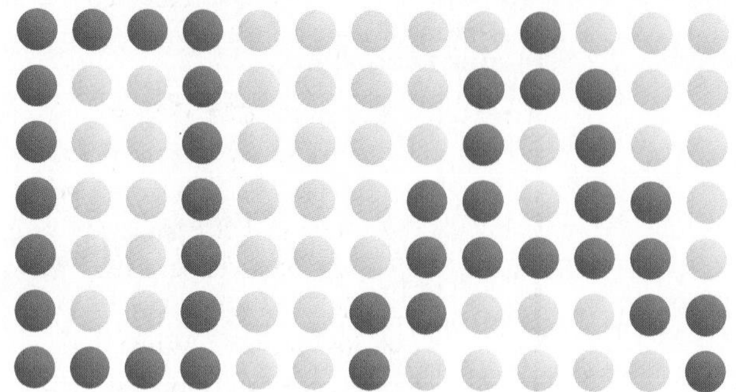

Softcopy Devices

Softcopy devices produce output that cannot be removed from the computer; users obtain softcopy output for temporary or intermediate time periods. The three most commonly used softcopy output devices are video monitors, video terminals, and sound output devices. Video monitors and video terminals are both called computer screens. Each of these devices consists of electronics that reside on a circuit board inside the computer and a physical device, such as a cathode ray tube or a speaker, that produces the output.

Video Monitors. **Monitors** are graphical devices. Each dot, or **pixel,** on the screen corresponds to a location or locations (for color monitors) in the computer's primary memory or in the memory of the **video adaptor**—a circuit board inside the computer that supports the monitor. A monitor receives an analog electrical signal from the video adaptor, a signal similar to that received by a television set, and then shows a display of text or graphics. Most microcomputers use video monitors as their primary display screens.

Video adaptor manufacturers have agreed on a small set of standards that specify how software should address video memory, how many pixels compose a video display, and how many colors each pixel may assume. Without such standards, software developers would have to provide different versions of their software for every type of video monitor. Video standards have evolved over time as electronics have improved. For example, an early standard known as CGA provided graphics with 200 rows of 320 pixels each. The later SVGA standard supplied 1,024 rows of 1,280 pixels each. Usually two or three standards are available in the market simultaneously, giving buyers a range of image qualities at a range of prices.

Video Terminals. A **terminal** differs from a monitor in that the terminal, rather than an adaptor board inside the computer, holds most of its intelligence. Video terminals receive a digital signal that consists of a series of codes. Some codes represent characters, which the terminal displays upon receipt at the next position on its screen. Some codes position a pointer (called the cursor) so that new characters will appear in a different place. Other codes may generate graphics, perhaps specifying the drawing of a line between two locations on the screen. Because minicomputers and mainframes that support tens or hundreds of users would require a tremendous amount of memory to store the screen pattern of each of its users, most multiuser computers employ terminals rather than monitors. On the other hand, sending a scanned picture to a video terminal is more cumbersome than sending a picture to a monitor. After scanning a picture, the computer stores the picture in its memory as a series of bits. The computer then sends these bits to a video monitor to output the picture. Sending the same picture to a terminal requires software that sends codes to sequentially position a pointer at each pixel and then turn that pixel on or off. A monitor paints a picture to the screen almost instantaneously; a terminal may take several minutes to laboriously draw the picture.

Sound Output Devices. Sound output devices produce an electrical signal that drives one or more speakers. This signal can produce music, special effects such as the sound of a passing train, or the sound of a voice.

Recent advances in DSP processors (see the section on specialized processors) have made voice output relatively inexpensive to produce. As a result, a number of new products take advantage of this technology. Voice mail illustrates a product that was unusual in 1990 but that is now quite common. When a person leaves a message on a voice mail system, a DSP digitizes the message and inputs it to a computer. The computer saves the data on a hard disk. When the message recipient signals the computer to play the message, the computer outputs the message to a device containing a DSP that reverses the digitizing process, converting the data back into a signal that sounds like the person who left the message.

Researchers are developing software that will produce the digital equivalent of voice from the digital representation of text.[11] When this technology becomes widely available commercially, programmers will be able to write programs that can give voice messages rather than display messages on the screen. Also, the blind will be able to order books in electronic form and then play them on their computers.

Hardcopy Devices

Hardcopy devices produce output on media that can be removed from a computer and retained for a long time. The most common hardcopy medium for computer output is paper, and a large variety of output devices produce paper output. In selecting a hardcopy device, the user must consider whether he or she requires character or graphics output as well as the density and resolution of output desired.

Printers. Printers, used by most individuals and businesses for the bulk of their output, produce text and graphics on paper without using a pen. Figure 6-19 shows the four most common types of printers: character impact, dot matrix impact, ink jet, and laser.

Character impact printers operate on the principle of a typewriter. The printer presses a metal or hard plastic image of a character into a ribbon, which leaves an ink impression on the paper. **Daisy-wheel** and **thimble printers** refer to character impact printers that have a single image of each character and produce one character at a time. These printers operate more slowly than other types of printers and tend to be more expensive. They leave a very solid and readable impression on the paper. Although these were once very popular printers, the new ink jet and laser technologies have virtually eliminated their use. Minicomputers and mainframes may use character impact printers called **band, chain,** or **line printers.** These printers contain many metal images of each character, so they can print much faster, appearing to print an entire line at a time.

Dot matrix impact printers use a print head that typically contains nine or 24 wires that can be fired individually at a print ribbon. Each wire hits the ribbon and then leaves a dot on the paper behind it. The more wires used, the higher the print density for a given print speed. Because dot matrix printers can operate in either text or graphics mode, they can produce graphics as well as text in different fonts and sizes. Dot matrix printers cost less than character impact printers and at low resolution typically print about 150 characters per second. Achieving a higher resolution may require a dramatic decrease in print speed,

FIGURE 6-19 Printers

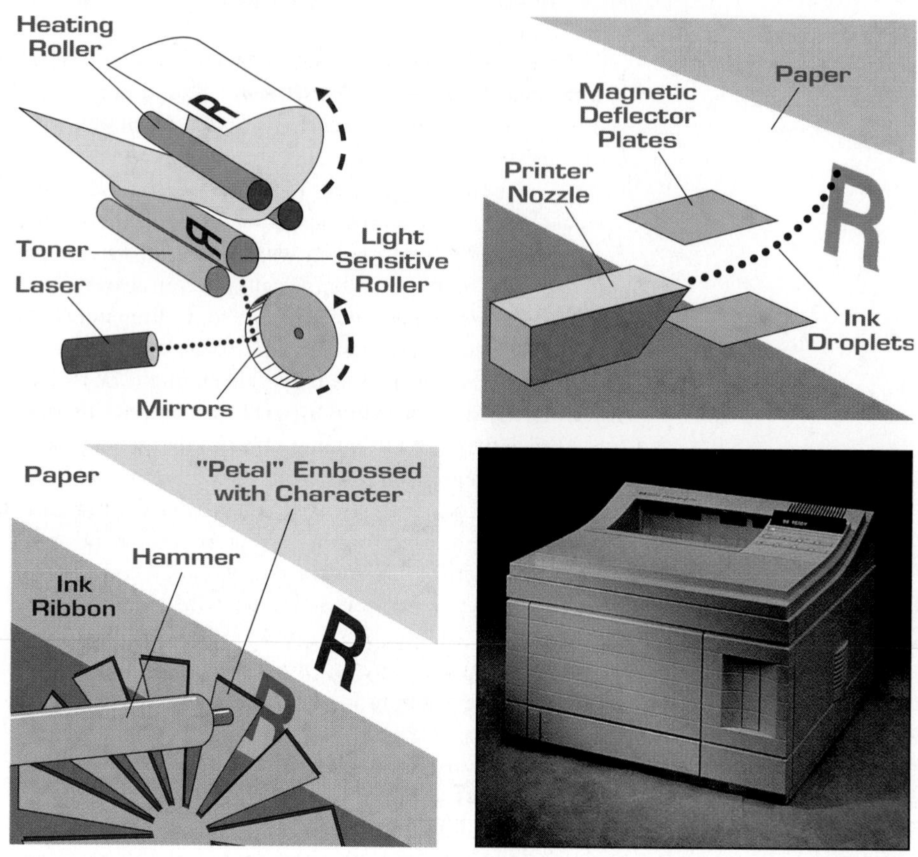

Courtesy of Hewlett-Packard.

approaching that of daisy-wheel or thimble printers. Even at high resolution, most dot matrix printers do not provide the character clarity of character impact printers.

Ink jet printers operate by spraying streams of ink at the paper. These streams produce dots, similar to those produced by dot matrix printers. The quality of output from ink jet printers approximates that of dot matrix printers, although some can achieve more solid-looking text. Their prices also resemble those of similar quality dot matrix printers. Unlike character or dot matrix impact printers, ink jet printers make little noise during operation. They also can produce fine color output by using multiple print heads holding colored inks. Ink jet printers cannot produce multiple copies of a page using carbon paper or pressure-sensitive multipart paper forms. Instead, users must print multiple copies of the desired output.

Laser printers produce high quality text and graphics output (typically 300 dpi or better) at a fast rate (typically four pages per minute or better). These printers use an internal laser to place dots of selective charge on a heated cylinder called a **drum** or **platen.** These charges attract particles of a dark powder called a **toner.** As paper rolls over the drum, the drum transfers the toner to the paper. The heat fuses the toner to the paper, permanently fixing the image. Laser printers are more expensive than ink jet printers having similar resolution.

Plotters. **Plotters** operate by moving a pen or pens over paper, much in the same way as a person writes. Architectural and engineering firms often use plotters rather than printers to produce drawings. The plotters produce high-resolution graphical output. They work on both oversized paper and long rolls of paper.

Other Hardcopy Output Media. Devices exist to produce output directly onto microfilm, microfiche, CD-ROM, overhead transparencies, and slides. These devices generally cost more than devices that produce output of similar quality on paper.

Other Output Hardware

Some **robotic output devices** physically move in response to signals from a computer. Usually the device interprets a digital code output by the computer as a signal to turn on, turn off, speed up, or slow down a motor. In more complicated devices, the output signal also addresses one of several motors. Advances in robotics depend less on the sophistication of such output devices than on the software needed to direct the output and processors that can rapidly run software to interpret input video and pressure signals. Only recently, for example, have scientists programmed computers to control a robot so that it avoids bumping into objects as it proceeds toward its goal. Such software must first synthesize the two two-dimensional signals produced by the robot's two eyes into a three-dimensional representation of its world. Then the software must logically plan and execute a route that safely negotiates this three-dimensional world.

A computer that communicates with other computers presents its output to a transmission medium. Chapter 8 discusses such output devices, devices that package and route computer transmissions over private and public networks, and devices that receive and prepare such transmissions for input at the receiving computer.

Hardware Integration

In the early 1980s and before, buyers used to purchase entire computer systems from a single vendor. For example, a company that purchased a large IBM processor would also buy its storage, input devices, and printers from IBM. Occasionally, buyers would substitute devices whose manufacturers claimed they were compatible with IBM systems. The first microcomputers were sold the same way. However, after one or two years, microcomputer vendors realized that they could benefit jointly from adopting standards about how the parts of a computer would interface with one another. For example, if the vendors agreed on how a processor would communicate with a disk drive, how much power a disk drive should use, and so on, a large number of disk drive manufacturers could make competing systems that would "plug into" the standard interfaces used by the computer manufacturers. They could standardize interfaces to input and output devices as well. Interface standards soon became common for all levels of computer systems and all types of devices.

Constructing a Computer

Figure 6-20 displays the parts of a typical personal computer. The processor is the single largest chip on the **motherboard.** The motherboard also contains connections to slots for circuit boards that act as interfaces to other parts of the computer. Already installed are a **memory board** that contains the circuitry to control RAM, a **disk controller** that provides the interfaces to both removable and permanent disk drives, a video adaptor that contains the interface to the computer's monitor, and standard interfaces known as **serial** and

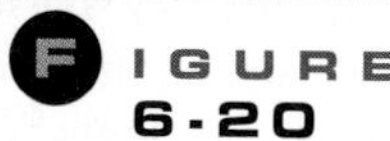

The Parts of a Personal Computer

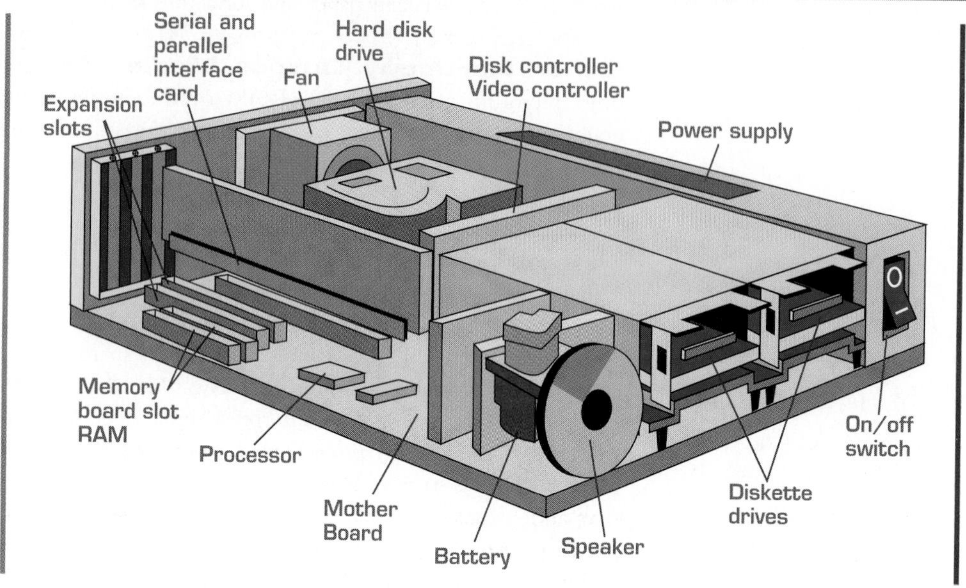

parallel interfaces for input and output devices. A single power supply provides power to the motherboard (and through it to the interface boards) and to the disk drives already installed in the computer. The monitor, keyboard, and other input and output devices will be connected to the computer with cables that connect through **ports** at the back of the computer to its interface cards (see Figure 6-21).

Larger computers, although built in a similar way, often do not have a motherboard. Instead, the main processor board fits into a slot just as the other interface boards do. Also, the disk systems of a larger computer usually do not reside inside the computer; they typically have their own power sources and are connected to the computer through cables attached to the interface boards.

Micro/Mini/Mainframe Distinctions

The terminology that computer manufacturers use to distinguish microcomputers, minicomputers, and mainframes confuses many computer buyers and users. A microcomputer is theoretically the least powerful and a mainframe the most powerful of the three types. Yet today's microcomputers possess far more power than the mainframes of 1980. These terms, then, are relative and subject to changing technology. Still, Sarah Craig must understand the differences before she offers recommendations for the design, selection, and purchase of hardware at Carter Manufacturing.

Traditionally, a **microcomputer,** commonly called a **personal computer** or **PC,** refers to a computer designed and marketed to be used by an individual or a small number of people and to be owned and managed by an individual. A **minicomputer,** often called a departmental computer, generally served a department, while a **mainframe** was designed and marketed to serve an entire organization, typically more than 100 people, simultaneously. Distinctions today are based more on differences in price, power, and physical size. A minicomputer typically costs more than $50,000 and requires one or two professionals to support its operation and service its users. A mainframe usually costs at least several hundred

FIGURE 6-21 Microcomputer Ports

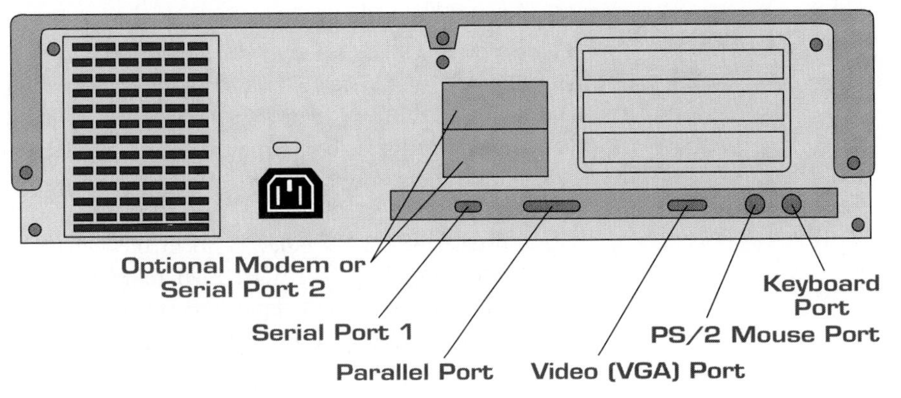

thousand dollars and requires a separate, air-conditioned room and a staff of trained professionals to support its use.

The distinctions among microcomputers, minicomputers, and mainframes involve more than processor power alone. For example, a processor capable of supporting the activities of more than 100 simultaneous users will probably have large and fast storage devices that support the multifaceted storage needs of so many users; it will be loaded with software that permits multiprocessing, interuser communication, and group activities. Because microcomputers support a single user, they are often built to be portable and rugged; some can tolerate temperatures higher than 135 degrees and lower than 32 degrees Fahrenheit as well as intensive shock and pressure.[12]

Workstations are powerful microcomputers used for engineering and for executive support systems. (See Chapter 11.) Engineering workstations will usually have not only a fast central processor but also graphics and floating point accelerators. In addition, many have 19- or 20-inch screens with very high resolution, and some even have two screens—one for selecting and showing commands and another for viewing the output. Some workstations have no disk drives, relying instead on a data communication network for their programs and data files.

TURNER CORPORATION

MOTOROLA

Companies that once relied on mainframes for processing have increasingly sought the flexibility provided by networks of personal computers.[13] In 1991, Turner Corporation, a 3,000-employee construction company located in New York City, cut its annual computer budget in half, to \$2.5 million, by shifting its processing from an IBM 4341 mainframe to a network of personal computers.[14] Starting in 1987, the corporate controller at Motorola, Ken Johnson, also oversaw a shift in his department's data processing from using two mainframes to using networks of personal computers; the shift saves millions of dollars yearly in corporate charges for his unit's computing requirements and allows a faster, more timely analysis of budget data.[15]

Some information systems professionals still maintain the cost-effectiveness and efficiency of mainframe computing. They argue that mainframes easily handle massive volumes of transactions; shield users from systems issues; keep information system costs down; ensure timely, secure, and accessible data; help attract more professional information systems staff; effectively support users' application needs; ease custom application development; preserve the investment in systems; ensure vendor support; and maintain clout with the systems vendor.[16] Still, analysts suggest that users will buy fewer, but larger, mainframes in the future.[17]

Scientific Processing

Computers that support scientific research, often called **supercomputers,** differ in basic ways from those that support business applications. Unlike business tasks such as data input and retrieval, scientific tasks generally involve massive calculations that require a great deal of processing power. Hence, scientific computers typically concentrate the processor's power on only one or two tasks at a time rather than spreading it widely over tens or hundreds of tasks and users. Carter Manufacturing most likely has no need for a supercomputer because the company performs limited research and development activities.

Scientific processors called **parallel processors** include hundreds of smaller processors connected to one another in complex and programmable ways; many supercomputers include several parallel processors. They perform the scientific processing tasks that can be divided into smaller tasks and then performed more efficiently in parallel. Scientists who forecast weather, for example, might model the atmosphere as thousands of atmospheric regions or cells, each 100 miles wide by 100 miles long and one-quarter mile high. They might also model temperature and pressure changes in each cell with a formula that incorporates the temperatures and pressures of the cells around it and other factors such as the amount of sun it gets and its distance from the earth. Because this formula would be the same for every cell, scientists can efficiently utilize a parallel processor computer. Each processor can devote itself to modeling a few cells of the atmosphere, simultaneously computing a new temperature and pressure while feeding the values it computes to the processors around it.

Miniaturization of Hardware

As scientists have put more and more transistors onto a 1-inch-square piece of silicon, the size, power consumption, and price of computers have fallen. As a result, portable systems now have the power of computers that previously required rooms full of hardware and dedicated cooling systems. This trend likely will continue.

Laptop Computers. **Laptop computers,** also known as **notebooks** and illustrated in Figure 6-22, refer to portable processing hardware that generally weighs less than 5 pounds and can be battery operated.[18] Laptops offer users the opportunity to retain their computing capability at remote locations. Particularly valued by travelers, laptops have become increasingly light, powerful, and inexpensive. Ensuring the connectability of laptops to other computers and hardware devices remains a major issue.[19] Making the physical connections, as well as transferring files between laptop and desktop, can pose significant challenges for the user. Experts predict that by the end of this century the laptop will become a personal information communications appliance, with characteristics such as those shown in Figure 6-23.

HYUNDAI MOTOR AMERICA

Currently, Hyundai Motor America has outfitted its 60 dealer representatives with laptop computers.[20] Their use has reduced the work load of central administrative staff, reduced telephone bills due to the use of electronic mail, allowed representatives to find key numbers on spreadsheets almost instantaneously, and improved relationships with dealers by giving sales representatives more discretion in decision making.

Palmtop Computers. Hand-held computers that fit comfortably into a person's palm, as shown in Figure 6-24, range from inexpensive schedulers and personal organizers to relatively high-powered computers.[21] Some personal organizers offer word processing and spreadsheet software as well as scheduling, memoing, and other organizing capabilities. **Palmtop computers** can use the same software as personal computers and typically interface

FIGURE 6-22 Laptop Computer

Courtesy of IBM.

with them. Although palmtops offer advantages of portability, relatively small keyboards and small screens have posed problems for some users. Advances in technology have made palmtops available with touch-sensitive screens and pen technologies.

Virtual Reality

An exciting outgrowth of recent advances in input and output technologies has been a marked increase in the ability of computer systems to simulate a "pretend" world. In the most powerful **virtual reality** systems, a user wears a helmet that provides pictures to each eye and sound to each ear. Computer software controls these outputs so that the user sees a three-dimensional image and hears sounds as if they had originated in a location within the image. As the user moves or changes his or her head position, sensors connected to the helmet detect these movements and adjust the user's perspective. To provide additional realism, the user can wear a glove or a suit connected to computer-controlled devices that sense the person's movement and adjust the environment accordingly. In addition, these movement sensors allow the user to control the environment, rather than being a passive spectator. For example, in a virtual reality game, a user can wound or slay a virtual dragon by "striking" it with a virtual dagger.

6-23

The Laptop Computer of the Future: A Personal Information Communications Assistant (PICA)

Resembles a paperback book in size, weight, and readability.

Has battery life measured in months.

Has chord keyboards, in which users press a few large buttons in combination for each letter and that could reduce keyboard size.

Has screen suitable for color motion video, perhaps initially, in the form of an inexpensive, small, separate LCD screen. Screen would be touch sensitive for selecting, sketching, and handwriting recognition.

Is multimedia capable.

Includes pager/receiver with file transfer capability and an optional wireless speakerphone and voice-mail facility.

Contains software for accessing and maintaining an internal database using built-in speaker.

Provides telecom access to users' private data as well as access to public data, integrated voice mail, and electronic mail.

Communicates over high-speed fiber and other networks.

Has detachable CD-ROM drive. User could load the text of a book into the PICA's memory and then remove the device while reading the book, without carrying or powering the drive.

Has partial-page scanner built into one edge and an optional, noncontact bar-code scanner.

Provides speech, audio, and music input and output as well as a built-in video camera for scanning text and recording scenery. By 1998, size will shrink to wallet size.

Reprinted with permission from Anne S. Kellerman and Palmer W. Agner, Plugged in, *Computerworld* (May 11, 1992): 113.

Advances in output devices and simulation software will soon enable virtual reality systems to simulate a sense of feel. As the player strikes the pretend dragon, the computer will change the pressure against the user's glove so that the user "feels" the resistance to the dagger provided by the dragon's skin. Ultimately, computer output devices will enable users to feel the edges, weight, and texture of imaginary items.

The first commercial applications of virtual reality were as training devices for pilots. Aircraft simulators would react to a pilot's manipulation of aircraft controls by altering the pilot's view out the window, the status of the aircraft instruments, the feel of the controls, and even the feel of the aircraft itself as it banked or rolled. In the early 1990s, virtual reality found an application as an expensive video game, where players played roles in a simulated adventure environment. Commercial applications of virtual reality include controlling robots, cranes, and other mechanical devices through hand movements; allowing scientists to walk around complex molecules such as those of drugs to observe their shape and functioning; allowing architects to walk through the corridors of a virtual building so that they can observe the visual impact of their designs from various perspectives; training doctors to use endoscopes without having to practice on real patients; designing cars by letting engineers experience the impact of such problems as inconveniently located knobs and controls; and reconstructing the progress of a crime for a jury.[22]

FIGURE 6-24 Palmtop Computer

Courtesy John Lund/Apple Computer.

Summary

Computer hardware can be classified into four categories: 1) input, 2) processing, 3) storage, and 4) output. Managers should diagnose their information needs, evaluate how well the existing hardware fits these needs, and then change or upgrade the hardware to better meet them.

Input hardware consists of devices responsible for capturing raw data and facilitating the interaction between the user and the computer. Most users are familiar with the keyboard, the mouse, and now the trackball. Other input devices include sight, sound, and sensor technologies that acquire data using the senses of sight, sound, and touch, respectively.

Processing hardware implements the instructions encoded into software. After an individual turns on the computer, the processor retrieves the instruction stored at the location indicated by the instruction register, decodes the instruction, and then executes it. Measures of the processor's power include its overall speed, its speed in performing arithmetic, the average number of instructions it performs in a second, the strength of its instruction set, the amount of data it can handle simultaneously, and its pipelining ability. Specialized processors, such as image compressors, floating point accelerators, graphics processors, and DSPs, are designed to do specific jobs.

Managers store data for both the short and long run. Bits and bytes measure the quantity of storage. Primary storage occurs on circuit boards. Volatile primary storage (RAM) loses data when the computer is turned off; nonvolatile storage (ROM) does not change its state in response to electronic signals. Secondary storage devices include removable media, such as tapes, diskettes, disk packs, and CD-ROMs, and fixed media, such as hard disks and RAID storage devices. Primary and secondary storage differ in their retrieval and storage speed, capacity, durability, and cost.

Output devices transfer information from computer storage into hardcopy or softcopy. Graphics output devices differ in the density, or resolution, of the output. Softcopy devices include video monitors, video terminals, and sound output devices. Hardcopy devices include printers, plotters, and devices that produce ouput on media other than paper.

Hardware integration refers to the interfaces among the various input, processing, output, and storage devices. Distinctions exist among microcomputers, minicomputers, mainframe computers, and supercomputers. Recently, the miniaturization of hardware has had a significant impact on the marketplace.

Key Terms

Active data entry
Address
Arrow key
ASCII
Band printer
Bit
Bus width
Byte
Cache memory
Cartridge tape
CD-ROM
Chain printer
Character impact printer
Chip
Circuit board
Clock
Clock speed
Code key
Communication hardware
Complex Instruction Set Computers (CISC)
Computer hardware
Cursor
Daisy-wheel printer
Decode
Density
Digital signal processor (DSP)
Digitize
Disk controller
Disk pack
Diskette
Diskette drive
Dot matrix impact printer
Dot pitch
Drum
EBCDIC
Execute
Fetch
File server
Flat-bed scanner
Floating point accelerator
Floating point arithmetic
Function key
Graphics processor
Graphics scanner
Hard disk
Hardcopy
Hertz
Hold key
Image compressor
Information technology architecture
Ink jet printer
Input hardware
Instruction counter
Instruction register
Instructions per second
Interactive dialogue
Keyboard
Laptop computer
Laser printer
Light pen
Line printer
Load
Mainframe
Math coprocessor
Megaflop
Megahertz
Memory board
Microcomputer
Million instructions per second (MIPS)
Minicomputer
Monitor
Motherboard
Motion sensing device
Mouse
Nonvolatile storage
Notebook computer
Numeric keypad
Optical character reader (OCR)
Optical character recognition (OCR) software
Output hardware
Palmtop computer
Parallel interface
Parallel processor
Passive data entry
Personal computer (PC)
Pipelining
Pixel
Platen
Plotter
Pointing device

Port
Position sensing device
Positioning key
Primary storage
Processing hardware
Random access memory (RAM)
Read-only memory (ROM)
Reader of formatted input
Reduced Instruction Set Computer (RISC)
Redundant arrays of inexpensive disks (RAID)
Reel tape
Resolution
Robotic output device
Secondary storage
Serial interface
Softcopy
Storage hardware
Supercomputer
Tape
Terminal
Thimble printer
Toggle key
Toner
Touch screen
Trackball
Video adaptor
Virtual reality
Voice processor
Volatile storage
Word length
Workstation
Write-Once Read-Many (WORM)

Review Questions

1. Into what four categories can computer hardware be classified?
2. Define active data entry and give an example. How does it differ from passive data entry and interactive dialogue?
3. How do point-of-sale keyboards differ from generic data processing keyboards?
4. Describe two types of pointing devices, and give two examples of each type.
5. What are the advantages and disadvantages of readers of formatted input as input devices?
6. What is the major limitation to the usefulness of graphics scanners?
7. Identify the steps that a computer processor goes through to perform its work.
8. Compare and contrast two measures of a computer processor's power.
9. Identify two types of specialized processors, and give an application of each.
10. Explain why computers typically have more secondary than primary storage.
11. What is ROM? Why do computers need ROM?
12. Identify four types of removable storage media.
13. What is RAID, and for what applications is it most desirable?
14. How is the quality of graphics output measured?
15. What is the difference between hardcopy and softcopy output devices?
16. Describe the difference between a video monitor and a video terminal, and explain why one is more often used with minicomputers and mainframes while the other is more often used with microcomputers.
17. Describe the difference between a printer and a plotter.
18. Describe how a mainframe, minicomputer, and microcomputer differ.
19. What is a parallel processor, and where is it most often used?
20. Identify some commercial applications for virtual reality other than entertainment.

MINICASE

Bar Coding at Bermans

Knowing the exact whereabouts of 5,000 client files once presented a daily challenge for one Manhattan law office. Personnel at the New York office of the international English firm Bermans often searched through stacks and shelves of paperwork before locating a badly needed file. To improve operations, the firm designed and installed an intricate bar code-based file management system. Now the office's 20 staff members need only consult a computerized database to determine a file's location.

"We're saving many thousands of dollars in clerical labor costs each month. And our database is always current, showing a listing of existing files and their immediate locations," said Keith Berman, founder and New York managing partner of the Liverpool, England-based corporate and commercial law firm.

After two years of system development, the firm installed a bar code printing network from Zebra Technologies to produce the labels that automated the New York office. Without bar coding, it took 45 minutes of keyboard data entry to inventory a trolley with 100 files. Now, one person can update 100 file locations within five minutes using the bar code scanning system. "Our attorneys use a multitude of paperwork to litigate cases in more than 100 countries each business day. At any given time, it's probable that each attorney in the office is working on about 150 files. These can change location five times every day. We need a sophisticated tracking system to be able to determine each file's precise location," said Mr. Berman.

The system produces three labels for every file. A 3¼- by 3-inch label adheres to each file tab and protrudes when a file is shelved for easy scanning during inventory. This label is bar coded with the file number and also includes the client's name plus alphanumeric codes for the file's contents and status. A more detailed 4- by 5-inch file label adheres to the front of each folder. This label includes bar codes for the file number and client profile number plus a brief synopsis concerning the case, the names of the partner and attorney who are handling the case, the jurisdiction where the case is being tried, the date the case was incepted, and the date the file was opened.

Finally, the Zebra system produces a 5- by 4-inch client profile label for each folder. This alphanumeric label includes all pertinent client background information such as names, phone numbers, and addresses. It adheres to the inner flap of each file for easy reference.

Custom Software Control

To drive the system, Mr. Berman and Jonathan Jenney, the firm's MIS director, created a program called Laser Forum. With the software, attorneys and staff use bar codes to enter time records, request files, record file locations, and manage client account ledgers and billing details. Although Laser Forum runs off the firm's minicomputer in New York, attorneys carry notebook computers and can access the database, create files, allocate file numbers, and issue "print label" commands from around the world by modem. Mr. Berman says that the system records thousands of transactions each day.

Bermans' attorneys use bar codes to record billable hours via computer. "All data entry is done by scanning bar codes from labels and preprinted menus. With this system, we've

---

SOURCE: Extracted from Elise M. Fleischaker, Rapid file retrieval, *ID Systems* (May 1993): 42–45.

eliminated the possibility that an attorney might transpose data," said Mr. Berman. To record progress on a case, an attorney using a wand scanner scans the bar code from the file folder to enter the file number, then scans codes from preprinted menus to record the billing reference for type of work completed—phone call, dictation, review of correspondence, etc.—and the amount of time spent on the file.

"The work-in-progress value is always instantly up to date and available on-line for billing purposes," said Mr. Berman. At any given time, an attorney can access the time recording screen to view all financial details pertaining to a case, including all time entries made on the file through the present, the bills that have been rendered for a client, the fee summary by attorney, and a breakdown of the work done to date.

The Laser Forum program also allows attorneys to "diary" files, or request them days in advance. To do this, the user simply scans the file number bar code and enters the number of days that he wishes to elapse before seeing the file again. The system generates a daily listing of files requested by each attorney for that day's preparation. Each morning, requested files are gathered, placed on a trolley, and moved into the attorney's office. "We have a complete database of files and their locations so we can request files and receive them quickly," said Martin S. Kenney, one of the four attorneys who practices in the firm's New York office. "It has made me much more productive. I can concentrate on my cases because I don't spend time searching for files."

System Expansions

Mr. Berman and Mr. Jenney are currently adding new capabilities to the system. Soon the firm will print bar coded labels to identify and track closed files, which are stored in bankers' boxes. The labels will include a bar code to indicate box contents, the date a file was closed, and the date a file may be destroyed. When the system prints a label, it will automatically assign a storage bin location for the box. If an attorney needs to know what files are in a box, he will simply scan the box label to produce a detailed index. "When the system is installed, we will be able to inventory every box, upload the data, and get an instant exception report within a couple of hours. We'll be able to locate missing files before they are needed," said Mr. Berman.

Plans also are underway to install the system in the firm's rapidly expanding London, Liverpool, and Manchester offices, which in aggregate have approximately 150,000 active files in circulation. "I've always maintained the philosophy that to attain the highest level of success, you have to make use of the most advanced technologies. Automation can certainly help other companies in the law, insurance, and financial industries," said Mr. Berman, who currently is talking with several firms in the software industry that are interested in marketing the Laser Forum system. "We never would be able to control operations as we do without bar codes. The technology is invaluable."

Case Questions

1. What savings did Bermans expect to achieve by modernizing its data input?
2. Describe the tasks involved in legal billing and filing. For each of these tasks, identify the data input requirements.
3. What alternatives to bar coding exist for recording billable work at Bermans? What are the advantages and disadvantages of each?
4. What alternatives to bar coding exist for managing the files at Bermans? What are the advantages and disadvantages of each?

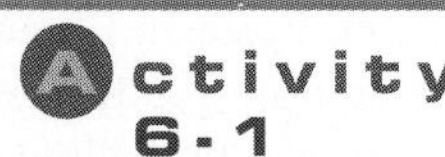

Activity 6-1 Shopping for Hardware

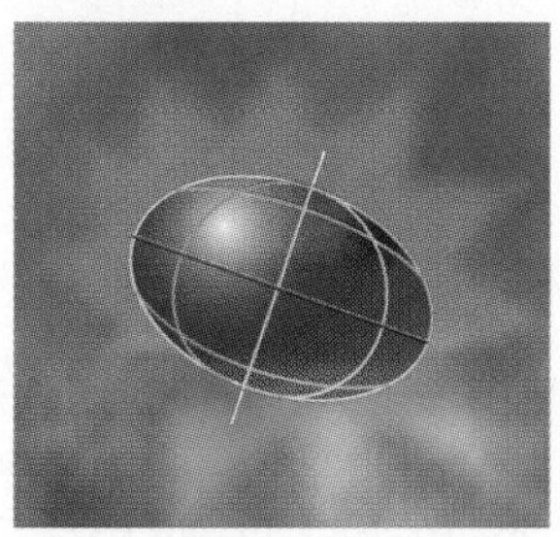

external contact

STEP 1: You have a friend who recently started a small home business selling customized baskets filled with food, toys, and other products. Your friend has told you that she wishes to purchase a personal computer to help keep track of her purchases, sales, customers, and finances. Your friend knows that you are taking a course in information systems and wants your advice about which computer she should buy. Before offering your recommendation, you feel that you need to learn more about the available hardware. You plan to give her a brief review of three possible computers she could buy—two desktop computers and one laptop.

STEP 2: Individually or in small groups, select three computers to review. Then collect the following information on each one: 1) input, storage, processing, and output specifications; 2) relative speed; 3) features and options; 4) price; and 5) ease of use. Secure information from vendors of the product, literature about the product, articles in computer magazines and journals, interviews with users, and your own tests of the computers.

STEP 3: Write the reviews. Include the specifications, advantages, disadvantages, and potential uses of each computer. Prepare sufficient copies to share with other members of the class.

STEP 4: In small groups or with the entire class, answer the following questions:

1. What are the basic features of the computers you reviewed?
2. How do the computers differ?
3. What tradeoffs does a computer buyer make when selecting a computer?
4. What criteria should a buyer use when purchasing a computer? ●

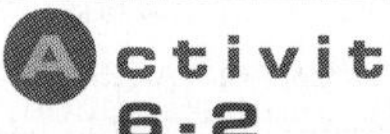

Activity 6-2 Childlife Centers, Inc.'s Purchasing Problem

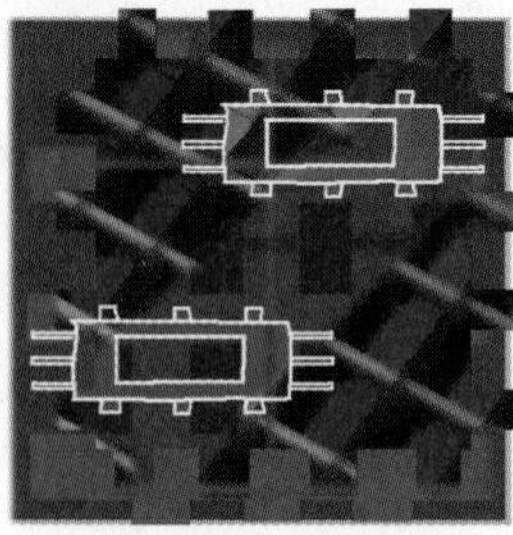

short case

STEP 1: You have just been hired as the first business manager for Childlife Centers, a chain of ten day-care centers for infants, toddlers, and preschool age children. Jane Stewart began the company ten years ago when she expanded a small preschool in her home into Childlife's first full-service center. Since that time Ms. Stewart has added nine additional centers to the company. During the next five years she expects to double the size of the company by opening ten additional centers. Each center services approximately 60 children and has 12–15 staff members. Until recently Jane used a combination of part-time clerical employees and outside services to meet the administrative needs of the company. Jane's secretary has the only computer owned by the company; she uses it solely for preparing correspondence.

You have been given a budget of $25,000 during this fiscal year to begin computerizing the company's administration. You and your small staff will eventually be responsible for handling personnel data, student information, accounts payable, accounts receivable, payroll, and purchasing. You have hired a consultant to assist you in making the final decisions about appropriate computer hardware and software, but you want to use her time as effectively as possible. Therefore, you want to list the general types of hardware you expect to purchase.

STEP 2: Individually or in small groups, identify Childlife Centers, Inc.'s information needs in the areas for which you are responsible.

STEP 3: Individually or in small groups, outline the types of input, processing, storage, and output devices that you think will best meet these needs.

STEP 4: In small groups or with the entire class, share your diagnoses of information needs and lists of potential hardware purchases. Identify the similarities and differences among the needs identified and hardware options proposed. What types of hardware would most effectively meet the needs of Childlife Centers, Inc.? ●

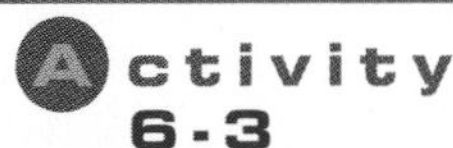

Baker & Young

short case

STEP 1: Read the following scenario.

Baker & Young is a national distributor of industrial machinery and accessories. The firm carries a range of manufacturing equipment and supplies including drill presses, electric motors, workbenches, precision measuring equipment, and fasteners.

Twice each year Baker & Young mails 5,000 catalogs to its customers. The current catalog is over 300 pages long and includes some 20,000 items.

THE ORDER ENTRY PROCESS

Orders are placed in one of three ways. Most customers call through an 800 number; others send an order through the mail; and some place orders through independent sales reps that carry the line.

When an order is received, it is written on an order entry form and sent to central data processing, where data entry clerks enter the data using machines that transfer what is typed at the keyboard directly to computer diskettes. After the data are entered and verified they are later used to update the central order file.

Although this order entry system has proven satisfactory in the past, Peter Barbera, vice-president of marketing, feels that technological developments in the computer industry offer the firm the opportunity to upgrade the order entry process and obtain several benefits. These would include a strategic edge over their competitors, lower error rates in the order entry process, a reduction in the cost to process an order, and quicker shipments of customer orders.

At the present time it takes about four working days for an order to get through the system. Since shipping by UPS—the carrier used to ship most small orders—takes on the average another three days, customers must wait at least a week for a shipment to arrive. In many situations this is simply too long.

Errors in the data entry process have always been a problem. In the worst case a customer places an order with a rep, the rep calls the order into headquarters, the order taker writes the order on an order form, and the order is entered by data entry clerks in the data entry department. With four people involved, there are many opportunities for order numbers, quantities, and shipping instructions to be relayed incorrectly.

STEP 2: Individually or in small groups, prepare a plan for improving the order entry process. Be sure to identify the information needs and specify the computer hardware that will best meet these needs. Where possible, include estimates of costs of the equipment you recommend.

STEP 3: In small groups or with the entire class, share the proposals you have developed. Then answer the following questions:

1. What problems exist with the order entry process?
2. What recommendations did you offer for improving the process?
3. How effective are these recommendations likely to be? ●

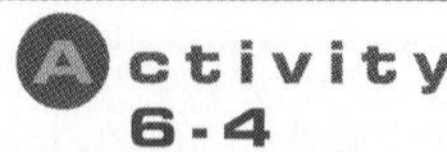

Activity 6-4 State of Kansas Imaging System

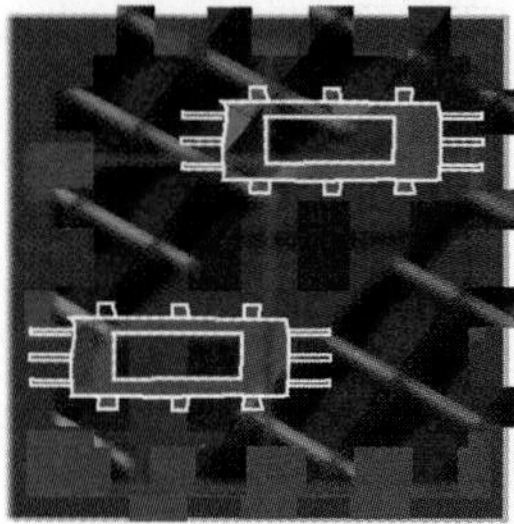

short case

STEP 1: Read the State of Kansas Imaging System case.

Topeka, Kan.—Birth and death go on pretty much as they always have here. But now the state does a far better job keeping track of life's starts and finishes.

A document imaging system deployed by the State of Kansas' Office of Vital Statistics has dramatically decreased the time it takes to process citizens' requests for records, while using fewer staff members.

"At our low point, in 1987, we were taking four to six weeks to process a request," State Registrar Lorne A. Philips acknowledged.

Even so, the manual system was turning a profit for the state.

"But we were providing lousy service," said Philips, who is also director of the Division of Information Systems at the Kansas Department of Health and Environment.

SPEEDIER DOCUMENT TURNAROUND

Nowdays the office, which issues 250,000 to 300,000 certified documents annually, claims a turnaround time for requested documents of less than a day, down from four to six weeks with the manual system. Turnaround time on the imaging system is a mere 12 seconds.

This process involves a mainframe query to find a match on the mainframe document index, the retrieval of the correct optical disc from the optical disc juke box and, finally, the sending of the image record to a high-speed laser printer. In addition, a number of security checks are undertaken during this process.

The system currently contains about 2.5 million document images.

With the new system, the office was able to reduce its work force by six, to 32 employees. So successful was the imaging deployment, in fact, that the Office of Vital Statistics received the 1991 Recognition Award for Outstanding Achievement in the field of information technology from the National Association of State Information Resource Executives.

The major impetus for the imaging system was a number of changes in the late 1980s in state and federal legislation.

The Internal Revenue Service began to demand Social Security numbers for children, and the Departments of Labor and Housing and Urban Development began requiring birth certificates for citizens seeking jobs and housing.

"And nationally," Philips said, "there was a push to do something about missing children—such as requiring the use of a birth certificate for entry into and transfer between schools."

Costa Mesa, Calif.-based Filenet Corp. won out over a pack of several document imaging vendors, including finalists Eastman Kodak Co. and Wang Laboratories, Inc.

Philips said Filenet won the job because it "learned what vital statistics were all about and didn't say, 'Oh, your [application is] just like this bank's or this trucking company's.'"

At a cost of $1.5 million—including the cost to convert the backlog of paper documents—the imaging system features Filenet's largest optical jukebox, the OSAR 288; a dedicated jukebox server and a dedicated image index server (both with backups); 11 image terminals; two high-capacity print stations; and two document-entry stations.

The jukebox has a maximum storage capacity of 288G bytes, or roughly 300 years' worth of Kansas birth and death certificates.

Within a year, a fax server will be added to the configuration, allowing the central office in Topeka to send certificates by a fax to the six regional offices.

STEP 2: Prepare the case for class discussion.

STEP 3: Answer each of the following questions, individually or in small groups, as directed by your instructor.

Diagnosis

1. What information needs did the State of Kansas's Office of Vital Statistics have?

Evaluation

2. How effectively did the 1987 system process requests for records?
3. What changes in the system were necessary?

Design

3. What new features does the image processing system contain?
4. How effectively does it process records?
5. Do any limitations exist to the new system?

Implementation

6. What issues did the Office of Vital Statistics consider in implementing the new system?
7. How effectively did it handle these issues?

STEP 4: In small groups, with the entire class, or in written form, share your answers to the questions above. Then answer the following questions:

1. What information needs did the Office of Vital Statistics have?
2. What type of system did they originally use to meet these needs?
3. What were the features of the image processing system they introduced to replace the original system?
4. How effectively does the image processing system work? ●

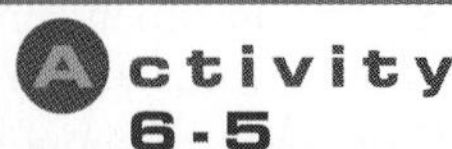

Activity 6-5 Evaluating Computer Hardware

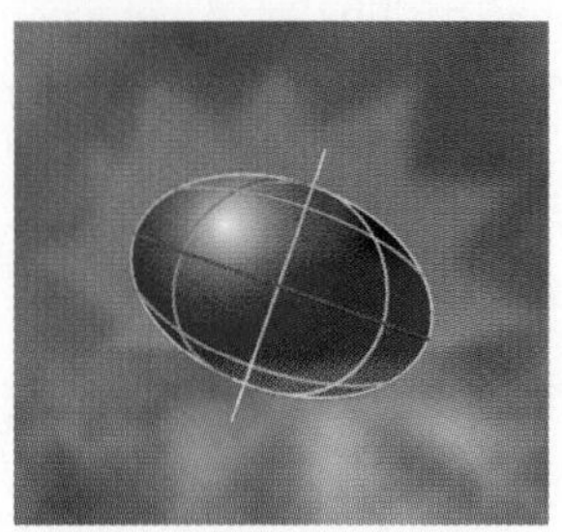

external contact

STEP 1: Select a department in your college or university or in an organization of your choice.

STEP 2: Individually or in small groups, design a checklist or questionnaire for describing the computer hardware used by the department you selected. The checklist or questionnaire should allow you to specify the types and characteristics of the input, storage, processing, and output devices the department uses.

STEP 3: Visit the department and administer the checklist or questionnaire to obtain an inventory and description of the hardware used in that department. Briefly interview one or two department members about their experiences using the equipment.

STEP 4: Individually, in small groups, or with the entire class, share your results. Compare and contrast the types of equipment available for various users. How well do you think the equipment meets the departments' needs? What changes in hardware might improve information processing in the department? ●

NOTES

[1]Mitch Betts, States redefining public service, *Computerworld* (April 19, 1993): C20.

[2]Mitch Betts, IS must get a handle on bar coding, *Computerworld* (September 9, 1991): 57, 60–61; Ned Snell, Bar codes break out, *Datamation* (April 1, 1992): 71–73.

[3]Kevin R. Sharp, Big bad bar code, *Computerworld* (May 25, 1992): 81–83.

[4]Mike Heck and Ann Marcus, Optical character recognition software for Windows, *InfoWorld* (April 26, 1993): 70–86.

[5]Jerry Zeidenberg, Multimedia computing: A virtual reality by 2001, *Computing Canada* (November 9, 1992): 17.

[6]Neal Nelson, The Reality of RISC, *Computerworld* (March 22, 1993): 72.

[7]Nick Lippis, Putting the squeeze on video data, *Data Communications 22* (February 1993): 67.

[8]Kelley Damore, 'Captain Crunch' plays back video at 30 frames per second, *InfoWorld* (April 5, 1993): 29.

[9]Gary McWilliams, Putting a concert hall on a chip, *Business Week* (April 13, 1992): 90–91.

[10]*Ibid.;* Alicia Hills Moore, A U.S. comeback in electronics, *Fortune* (April 20, 1992): 77–86; Stephan Ohr, Hot DSP market tantalizes analog and digital IC makers, *Electronic Business* (July 1992): 106–109.

[11]Mark Fischetti, Pursuing the universal translator, *Technology Review 95* (November/December 1992): 16–17; Ned Snell, Making IS accessible, *Datamation 38* (May 15, 1992): 79–82.

[12]Alan Radding, Sturdy PCs built to take beating, *Computerworld* (June 8, 1991): 105.

[13]John W. Verity, Rethinking the computer, *Business Week* (November 26, 1990): 116–124.

[14]Evan I. Schwartz, Finally, software that slays giants, *Business Week* (March 15, 1993): 96–98.

[15]Ibid.

[16]Ten reasons to stand by your mainframe, *Computerworld* (November 19, 1991): 75.

[17]Johanna Ambrosio, Mainframe metamorphosis: Not a disappearing act (Part 1), *Computerworld* (August 17, 1992): 1, 62–64.

[18]Cheryl Goldberg, Notebook computers, *Computerworld* (June 22, 1992): 111–117.

[19]Anne S. Kellerman and Palmer W. Agnew, Plugged in, *Computerworld* (May 11, 1992): 111–114.

[20]Michael Fitzgerald, Hyundai hits road with laptops; shifts to second part of project, *Computerworld* (January 6, 1992): 37, 44.

[21]Paul Eng, Power in your palm, *Business Week* (March 15, 1993): 128–130.

[22]David Churbuck, Applied reality, *Forbes* (September 14, 1992): 486–490; Joan Hamilton, Emily Smith, Gary McWilliams, Evan Schwartz, and John Carey, Tools to amplify the mind, *Business Week* (October 5, 1992): 97–105; Virtual reality gets real, *The Economist* (February 20, 1993): 61–62.

Recommended Readings

The following publications provide regular features about computer hardware:

Byte
Computer Equipment Review
Computerworld
InfoWorld
Mac World
PC Week

Chapter 7

Database Management Systems

OUTLINE

Database Management at Insureco
Defining Database and Database Management System
Functions of Database Management Systems
- Storage and Retrieval of Data
- Storage and Retrieval of Metadata
- Limit and Control of Redundancy
- Support of Simultaneous Data Sharing
- Provision of Backup and Recovery Services
- Provision of Authorization and Security Services
- Enforcement of Business Rules and Data Integrity
- Increasing Programmer Productivity

Distribution Architectures
- Decentralized Architecture
- Centralized Architecture
- Client/Server Architecture
- Distributed Architecture

Data Models
- Relational Model
- Network Model
- Hierarchical Model
- Object Model

Data Design
- The Entity-Relationship Model
- Normalization

Specialized Database Management Systems
Global Issues in Database Management
Selecting a Database Management System
Database and Data Administration
- Database Administration
- Data Administration

LEARNING OBJECTIVES

After completing the reading and activities for Chapter 7, students will be able to

1. Define a database management system and discuss its use in organizations.
2. Describe eight functions of a database management system.
3. Describe four distribution architectures and their uses.
4. Cite the advantages and disadvantages of the four distribution architectures.
5. Describe the relational, network, hierarchical, and object models and their uses.
6. Cite the advantages and disadvantages of the four database models.
7. Describe the need for and process of data design.
8. Identify three types of specialized database management systems.
9. Show how the globalization of management has affected database management in organizations.
10. Offer a protocol for selecting a database management system.
11. List the responsibilities of a database administrator and data administrator.

Jim Allen was frustrated. Although the information he needed was already stored in Insureco's computers, he was told it would take at least a month to retrieve it.

For the past three years, Insureco's Statewise Profit and Loss Report had shown that Insureco, a national firm, was losing money on automobile policies written in New York. Jim and other senior managers had attributed this to an unfavorable regulatory climate and a high rate of theft and accidents, a set of conditions that seemed unlikely to change in the near future. Jim was ultimately responsible for deciding whether or not Insureco would continue to sell auto insurance in New York.

Jim recalled that when Insureco had discontinued auto insurance in California under similar conditions, losses had increased even further. Apparently, a large percentage of Insureco's auto clients who had also purchased homeowner's insurance (which was quite profitable for Insureco) had decided to switch their homeowner's policies to another company when Insureco dropped their automobile coverage.

Based on the California experience, Jim felt reasonably confident that he could estimate the impact on the bottom line if he only knew how many Insureco customers in New York held both homeowner's and auto policies. Unfortunately, these products were managed by different divisions. When their systems were computerized many years ago, there was no anticipated need to share data. The divisions used two different and incompatible software packages to track their policyholder information.

What information does Jim need? Can he secure it easily and cheaply? How does Insureco track the profitability of its products? What changes are necessary to ensure that Jim Allen obtains the information he needs in a timely and cost-effective way? This chapter examines the use of a database management system with a computerized database as a solution to problems such as the one Jim Allen faces.

Defining Database and Database Management System

A **database** is an organized collection of related data. The key terms here are *organized* and *related*. A collection of data is not *per se* a database. By organized, we mean that you can easily find the data you want. For example, a file cabinet, with folders sorted alphabetically, is a database; a bunch of papers stuffed into a drawer is not a database. By related, we mean that the data have significance when viewed together. A collection of data about the books you own and about your friends' telephone numbers is not a database because the data are not related. Instead, they form two separate collections, or two databases. Relationships among data, however, can change unexpectedly. For example, if you decide to keep track of which friends have borrowed your books, then the data about books, friends, and borrowings may form a database. Many organizations consider all their organized data to be part of a database because they are potentially related.

What databases does Insureco have? Each division might have a list of all customers and their account balances organized by geographical area. The human resource department might have a list of each employee, together with his or her wages, deductions, and benefits, organized by division of employment. Insureco maintains a great deal of additional data about its customers and employees. Whether these data form a database or databases depends on the extent to which they are organized in a meaningful and systematic way and the degree to which they are related.

Computerized databases are those stored on computer-readable media such as tape, disk, or CD-ROM. Computerization of data does not necessarily ensure that they form a database. For example, many companies use word processors to computerize their correspondence; however, these data are usually organized in a haphazard fashion and cannot be considered a database. Many companies keep both computerized and noncomputerized, or manual, databases. For example, Insureco may maintain a computerized database of payroll information and a manual database of training seminars available to its employees.

When magnetic media first became available, programmers wrote instructions in each of their application programs to store and access data. For example, an accounts receivable program might include code to call up customer invoice and customer payment records. Quickly programmers noticed that the data storage and retrieval portions of different programs were quite similar. This recognition motivated the development of special programs whose sole function was to store and retrieve data in response to a request. Then, instead of including code to retrieve a customer invoice in an accounts receivable program, a programmer would pass the request for such data to one of these special programs.

The immediate advantage of this approach was to remove from every programmer the need to write data storage and retrieval code. As you will see, the centralization of data management in a few specialized programs also provides users and programmers the ability to perform much more sophisticated data management than would otherwise be possible. A **database management system** or **DBMS** comprises programs to store, retrieve, and otherwise manage a computerized database as well as to provide interfaces to application programs and to nonprogramming users. Today a company developing serious application software should use one or more DBMSs for its data management functions. DBMSs are a pervasive and central component of almost all vertical application software.

Functions of Database Management Systems

The centralization of data management functions and their separation from application programming permitted data management to evolve in highly sophisticated ways. Modern DBMSs perform a large number of data management functions, as shown in Figure 7-1. Which of these functions address Jim Allen's needs at Insureco? The following sections examine these objectives individually.

Storage and Retrieval of Data

COLD SPRING HARBOR LABORATORY

A database management system simplifies the storage and retrieval of data. People using a DBMS can permanently store and retrieve data by striking a few keys on the computer keyboard. Users can create data-entry forms, such as the one illustrated in Figure 7-2, that automatically check the format of entered data before the DBMS stores it on a permanent medium such as a diskette or a hard disk. Users can retrieve data sorted in a prespecified way or according to criteria that they specify at the time of retrieval. Scientists at the Cold Spring Harbor Laboratory in New York, for example, use the GenBank database to secure

FIGURE 7-1 Functions of DBMS

- Simplify data storage and retrieval
- Maintain metadata about the stored data
- Reduce, limit, and control redundancy of data
- Support simultaneous data sharing to ensure consistency
- Provide backup and recovery services for data integrity after computer failures
- Provide authorization and security services to control access to sensitive data
- Enforce business rules and data integrity to guarantee consistency among related data
- Increase programmer productivity

information about the structure of DNA; such information helps them determine the causes of disease.[1]

If Insureco had a comprehensive database and had used a DBMS, it is likely that Jim Allen could have secured the information he wanted in five or ten minutes without the aid of a programmer. He could have requested and obtained by using a few keystrokes a list of all clients whose automobile and homeowner's insurance were both provided by Insureco. With a few more keystrokes, he could have instructed the DBMS to calculate and present the total amount of all premiums for the policies of clients that were selected.

Programmers may also use a DBMS to quickly modify programs that use data. Before DBMSs existed, programmers typically wrote code to compress and store different types of data, such as dollar amounts, customer codes, or invoice numbers in different ways to minimize the amount of computer storage needed and maximize the speed of retrieving the

FIGURE 7-2 A Data Entry Form Automatically Generated by a DBMS

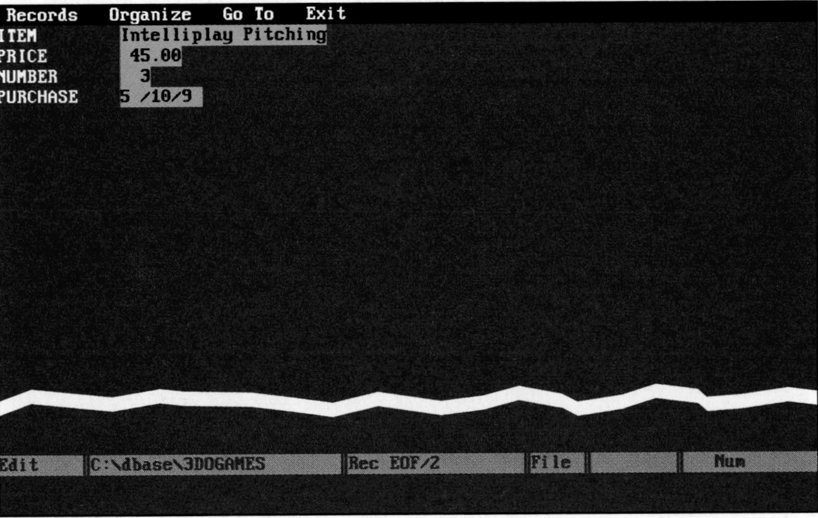

data. Other programmers writing code to access the same data had to know how they were originally stored. This caused many errors, especially in large, complex systems. Furthermore, an efficient storage scheme for one application might not be efficient for others. If it was determined that a storage scheme needed to be changed, all programs addressing that data would have had to be changed. This was true as well if the nature of the data changed. For example, if the space required for the customer zip code increased from five to nine digits, programmers likely would have had to modify any programs that accessed customer information whether or not those programs used the zip code.

Using a DBMS, the programmer specifies only the data to be stored or retrieved. The DBMS concerns itself with how the data are physically organized and represented on the storage medium. Database experts refer to **logical views** and **physical views** of the data. The database sees the physical view of the data but presents a logical view to the user. As a result, if the data organization changes, programs usually do not have to be rewritten.

As we approach the year 2000, many companies are realizing that software written many years ago stored only the last two digits of the year. As they sort data by these digits, the year 2000 appears before 1999. Even worse, the software may indicate that May of 00 comes before December of 99, causing such problems as mistaken classification of bills as overdue and miscalculated interest. DBMSs help solve this limitation by allowing data administrators to increase the space for data fields to four digits and by adding 1900 to all two-digit dates.

Storage and Retrieval of Metadata

Metadata are data about data. For example, the fact that a company's invoice numbers are six digits long, with the first digit either a 1 or 3, is metadata. Another example of metadata is the fact that zip codes are nine digits, the last four digits are optional, zeroes are always shown, and a dash occurs between the fifth and sixth digits. Also, metadata might indicate that zip codes shown in a report should be titled "Zip," while zip codes that appear in a data entry screen should be titled "Zip Code:".

A DBMS stores metadata in a formal way so that programs that access an invoice number or a zip code know enough about them to store and display them properly. Metadata also allow the DBMS to check for errors when the data are entered. Many DBMSs also allow the user to access metadata in the same way as they access data. As a result, users can request formal reports about the data stored in the database. Furthermore, they can search the metadata. For example, they can identify all data titles that include the word *zip.*

Limit and Control of Redundancy

Companies often collect and store the same data in two or more different computer systems, a condition called **data redundancy.** For example, a company that manufactures and sells office equipment may maintain information about its customers in three places: a service system that tracks customer service requests and mails service bulletins; an accounts receivable system that tracks the amount customers owe the company; and a sales system that assists sales agents in identifying customers who may need additional equipment. Not only does this waste computer storage, but it also wastes time and may cause inconsistencies in data entry. For example, if a customer moves to a new location, the customer's new address must be entered in all three systems. Furthermore, if the customer tells the sales agent about the address change, the agent might not relate the change to those who have authority to revise the address in the service or accounts receivable systems. Two or more inaccurate addresses would be stored for the customer.

A DBMS reduces the need to store redundant data because it easily joins information

FIGURE 7-3 Illustration of How a DBMS Combines Information about Different Business Entities

Automobile Policies			Homeowner's Policies		
Policy #	Customer #	# of Autos	Policy #	Customer #	Property Location
3N-4658	16340	3	157231A	16340	341 Woodward Rd.
4X-3215	37126	1	168232C	16340	12 Mozart Ave.
2Y-1919	21371	2	395274X	31319	191 Robin Way
.			.		
.			.		
.			.		

Customer Contacts

Customer #	Name	Phone
16340	Arlington Software	512-347-1234
37126	Hanson Widgets	512-190-3190
21371	Marion Assocs.	613-858-1650
31319	Generic Products	912-827-1680
.		
.		
.		

Combined Policy Data Sorted by Customer

Policy #	Type	Customer #	Customer Name	Customer Phone
3N-4658	Auto	16340	Arlington Software	512-347-1234
157231A	Home	16340	Arlington Software	512-347-1234
168232C	Home	16340	Arlington Software	512-347-1234
2Y-1919	Auto	21371	Marion Assocs.	613-858-1650
395274X	Home	31319	Generic Products	912-827-1680
4X-3215	Auto	37126	Hanson Widgets	512-190-3190
.				
.				
.				

about different business components. As illustrated in Figure 7-3, Insureco needs to store only a customer number in the data it retains about each automobile and homeowner's policy. If a manager requested a list of policies sorted by customer name, a DBMS would look up the customer number in the customer contact list to retrieve the detailed customer data, such as name and telephone, associated with each policy. In the example shown, use of a customer number saves repeating the customer name (Arlington Software), its telephone number, and possibly other information such as its address in the records for policies 3N-4658, 157231A, and 168232C. Similarly, a DBMS makes it easy to combine this general customer information with information unique to other systems. For example, the customer address could be combined with the customer's unpaid invoices for accounts receivable, the customer's list of hardware for the sales agent, and the customer's calling record for the service agent. The customer information, while related to many records, is stored only once, reducing redundancy and eliminating the possibility of inconsistent records.

Of course, errors can occur in data entry and manipulation. One airline installed some defective software that created false passenger reservations. The airline corrected the software problem but failed to correct the data in the database, resulting in partially empty planes due to the booking errors.[2]

Support of Simultaneous Data Sharing

Unless sophisticated control procedures are used, errors will arise when two people or programs attempt to access and update the same data at the same time. Consider the following example. John and Mary call the same national mail-order company to order two sweaters in style #1037. The clerk handling John's order determines that there is an inventory of three such sweaters. Simultaneously, the clerk handling Mary's order obtains the same information. John and Mary, both assured that the two sweaters they want are in stock, request immediate shipment. As John's clerk registers the sale, the computer completes the transaction by changing the available stock to one. At the same time, Mary's clerk registers the sale, also changing the available stock to one. Although the available stock is insufficient to fill both orders, such processing allows both clerks and customers to think that the orders have been fulfilled.

L. L. BEAN

Concurrency control describes the proper management of simultaneous data updates. L. L. Bean, for example, a leading mail-order retailer, prides itself on its quality of service. Its order entry systems, therefore, require concurrency control. This concurrency control is likely provided by the DBMSs that the order entry systems use to manage their data. DBMSs employ a variety of techniques to ensure concurrency control.[3] In critical applications, such as the disbursing of cash or reservation of inventory, a DBMS will allow only one user to update the specific data at a given time. For example, it would show both John's and Mary's clerks the inventory of three sweaters. However, when both clerks decide to reserve two of the sweaters, the computer would only allow one update to proceed. Then, before processing the second update, it would again read the inventory data and would find that the request

An employee at L. L. Bean's Casco Street facility consults the company's catalog and its order-entry system to assist a customer.

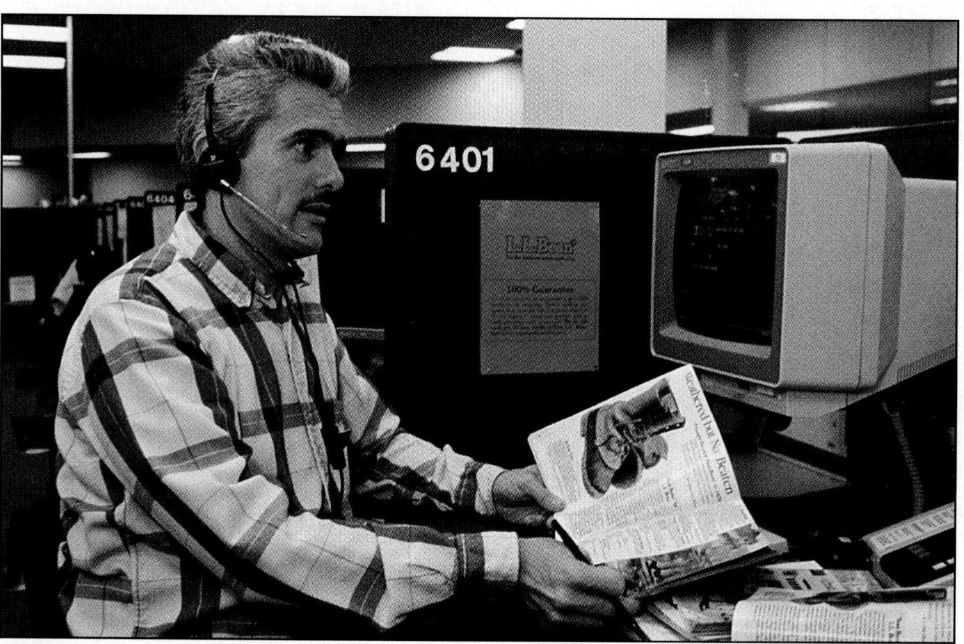

Courtesy of L. L. Bean.

for two sweaters exceeded the inventory of one and inform the clerk. Although programs other than a DBMS can implement concurrency control, they tend to be less rigorously tested.

Provision of Backup and Recovery Services

Backup and recovery services prevent errors when processing a transaction that affects several data elements or requires multiple steps. For example, a computer program to transfer $100 from a savings to a checking account must reduce the checking account balance *and* increase the savings account balance. If the checking balance is reduced and the computer crashes before the savings balance is changed, or if the savings balance is increased and the computer crashes before the checking balance is changed, then the balances will be inconsistent, resulting in an unwarranted and undesired loss for either the bank or the customer.

Most DBMSs provide tools to identify and correct incomplete transactions before they can cause any damage.[4] They do this by automatically creating a temporary record of the beginning and ending of each transaction and each successful update. The DBMS uses this record, known as a **log,** to trace the transaction process and hence handle all partially completed transactions when the computer recovers. Thus, applications supported by a DBMS tend to be more robust than others. Incorporating tools to provide such security into every program that processes multiple-update transactions, rather than using a DBMS, is exceedingly complex and difficult.

Provision of Authorization and Security Services

Although information is meant to be shared, not everyone in an organization should always have access to it. For example, managers consider salary data and personnel evaluations to be confidential information. They also treat some financial information as confidential. In addition, managers must protect accounting information against tampering and fraud.

Most DBMSs allow a database manager to provide controls, limiting who has access to specific data.[5] A DBMS may provide access control through a prescribed **view**—a subset of the database that can be made available to certain classes of users or certain applications. For example, most users may see a view of employee data that contains job title, length of service, and name of health-care insurance but not salary information. Views can also be created for metadata; the availability of such views, for example, may prevent certain users from knowing whether the database contains salary information.

In addition to views that hide data, most DBMSs allow views of aggregated data or joined data. For example, a user may be authorized to view average salary by department without being given access to individual salary data.[6] Care must be provided in allowing statistical views of data, as sophisticated users can often infer detailed data by asking dividing and overlapping queries. Joined views are useful for combining data that are often viewed together. For example, a view that combines customer name with data relating to the customer's sales representative will allow users to see the name, telephone number, and address of each customer's sales representative as if they were all stored with the customer.

Before the existence of DBMSs, each program needed to store information about who was allowed to use that program and for what purposes. Systems usually included many programs written by different programmers, so it was difficult to coordinate systems to avoid allowing users to see unauthorized data and to ensure that users could see all data to which they were privileged. In fact, non-DBMS systems generally cannot hide data from all users because users have access to an entire record. DBMSs centralize this function, dramatically simplifying software development and providing additional power to a data administrator.

If Insureco had used a DBMS, Jim Allen would probably have been granted permission to retrieve, but not store, customer information. He may not have had access to customer names, but this limitation would not have hindered his analysis. Should he have needed the customers' names, he could request that the data administrator, as described later in this chapter, change the database permissions.

Enforcement of Business Rules and Data Integrity

A DBMS enforces rules ensuring that related data are logically consistent, a condition known as **data integrity.** For example, assigning a sales representative to every customer expresses a relationship between two types of data: customer and sales representative. Without a DBMS, each program that modifies information about either sales representatives or customers would have to check that the assignment of sales representative to customer occurred. For example, the program deleting a sales representative would have to check that all his or her customers had first been reassigned; deleting a sales representative and then leaving some customers without a representative breaks the assignment rule. When a DBMS modifies data, it can enforce such rules, simplifying the programs and ensuring that business rules cannot be violated due to the ignorance of a programmer or program designer.

Increasing Programmer Productivity

Because a DBMS provides many of the functions that programmers would otherwise have to develop on their own, a DBMS increases programmer productivity. Furthermore, a DBMS can access metadata to automatically "write" the descriptions of data that are required by some computer languages such as COBOL. Some DBMSs can even write programs that display data entry screens, accept data into those screens, and create standard reports. This facility of a DBMS simplifies software maintenance because metadata automatically document the meaning and use of data elements. The DBMS also reduces the number of functions that need to be implemented by programs.

Distribution Architectures

Distribution architecture refers to how data and database processing are physically distributed among the computers in an organization. Because modern computer networks allow data stored on one computer to be shared with others, data may be stored at one site or distributed among several sites on a computer network. DBMSs differ in the way they handle data stored at multiple sites and in the way that they distribute the processing associated with the DBMS functions discussed in the preceding section. In this section we first describe decentralized and centralized architectures and then present two common architectures for databases in a networked environment: client/server and distributed.

Decentralized Architecture

A **decentralized architecture** is one in which databases are developed as separate entities as required by individual applications, without central planning, without central control, and without thought on sharing the data. A decentralized architecture has no central planning hurdle for new applications to overcome. Thus, users have more freedom to develop applications that meet their needs and maintain more control over the applications they develop. But this architecture generally prevents users from easily combining or comparing data in various databases, as Jim Allen discovered when he tried to find Insureco customers having both homeowner's and automobile policies. Another disadvantage is that data may be duplicated, requiring dual entry and dual storage and possibly leading to inconsistencies. Decentralized architectures often arise in companies having a decentralized management approach and in companies that have been built through acquisitions.

Centralized Architecture

A **centralized architecture** refers to running a DBMS on a single computer. Its primary advantage is that it is easy to control and manage, at least for relatively small databases. One disadvantage is that as a database and its usage grows, more powerful equipment must often replace the existing hardware to respond to greater processing and data storage needs. The integration of new with existing applications also becomes increasingly complex and time consuming as the centralized database grows. Nevertheless, having a centralized storage capability makes it easier to consolidate corporate-wide data and to determine whether or not a data item a user desires currently exists within the database.

NORTHWEST POWER PLANNING COUNCIL

Engineers at the Northwest Power Planning Council introduced a centralized DBMS to consolidate massive amounts of data about fish movement along the Columbia River and its drainage system in the northwest United States. For example, they needed data about salmon according to river, hatchery, and dam. They use the data about these and other fish to site hydroelectric dams appropriately.[7]

Client/Server Architecture

U.S. HOUSE OF REPRESENTATIVES

A **client/server architecture** divides the functions of a DBMS among connected computers on a network while centralizing permanent storage for all data on one or more computers known as the **database servers.** The computers connected to server(s) are called **clients.** The clients run the parts of the DBMS that process user requests and display results. The server runs the parts of the DBMS that store and retrieve data. A number of models have been implemented to divide the functions of the DBMS between the client and the server.[8] The U.S. House of Representatives, for example, moved from the Member Information Network, consisting of 80 independent databases on an IBM mainframe where combining or linking databases for queries was extremely difficult, to a client/server model, called Integrated Systems and Information Services. In the new network, local office systems act as clients to mainframe servers that contain the databases.[9]

To illustrate the application and benefits of the client/server architecture, consider an accounts receivable program running on one client and a customer service application running on another client. At the accounts receivable station, the data entry clerk processes a customer's check, first entering the customer ID. The accounts receivable program sends a request to the client DBMS to determine whether or not the customer ID is a valid one. The client DBMS passes this request to the server DBMS, which accesses the database to determine that the ID is valid. The server responds to the client DBMS, and the client DBMS responds to the application program, which then proceeds to accept data about the check. When all the payment data are entered, they are processed and compressed by the client DBMS and forwarded to the server DBMS for storage. At the customer service station, the clerk also accesses client data, such as a list of payments outstanding, through a program running on his or her computer. If the server receives two requests to update the same data at the same time, it mediates the conflict. The server may also keep a log to help in recovering from system crashes.

The primary advantage of the client/server architecture is that it off-loads the application programs and many of the functions of the DBMS from the server. In the example above, the accounts receivable station operates almost autonomously, barely affected by the number of other programs running on the network. With a centralized architecture, the accounts receivable and customer service applications would run on the same computer. As other applications were added, accounts receivable processing would slow down unless the computer were upgraded to provide more processing power.

One disadvantage of the client/server architecture is that it encourages the movement of a large amount of data over the network. Because processing occurs at many client locations and the client and server interact frequently and extensively, data must flow rapidly between server and clients for adequate DBMS performance. The client/server DBMS thereby places a heavy load on the network capacity.

Another disadvantage of the client/server architecture is the difficulty of controlling data. Client computers equipped with diskettes may be used to remove data that are meant to be kept confidential within the organization. As a result, some organizations insist that no client computers be equipped with removable media. This policy, however, limits the usefulness of such computers for other functions.

Distributed Architecture

The **distributed DBMS architecture** allows data to reside anywhere on the network (or at least on some subset of computers).[10] Any computer on the network, not only the server, can handle requests for data. If the data requested can be obtained locally, the request is executed locally. If the data are not local, then the local DBMS determines where the data are stored, issues a request to obtain the data from the appropriate computer, and processes the data that are received.

The major benefit of a distributed architecture is the reduction in network traffic that arises when data are kept near where they are needed. For example, the West Coast sales office of a national company can keep information about its customers on the West Coast computer, while the East Coast office keeps similar data on the East Coast computer. Data can be retrieved from either computer or stored on either computer, but most processing can be done locally. If an East Coast firm calls the West Coast sales office, the DBMS will try to find the customer's data locally; failing to do that, it will send a message to the remote (East Coast) computer to retrieve the data. The West Coast computer user will not need to know where the data are stored. In addition to reducing network traffic, the distributed architecture allows most transactions to occur rapidly because the data affecting these transactions are stored on the local computer.

In addition to its technical benefits, the distributed architecture provides a managerial advantage to companies, such as Insureco, who value distributed management control. The distributed architecture allows a greater degree of local control over the design of databases than would be possible in a centralized architecture. Local data managers can add or delete elements of data in their databases without compromising the integrity of the combined database. To support the distributed architecture, however, DBMS software must be in place or obtainable at all computers that intend to store data. If Insureco had used distributed DBMSs for both its automobile and homeowner's policies, data about both policies could have been accessed as if they existed on a single, centralized system.

Distributed DBMSs are more complex than single-computer DBMSs for several reasons. First, the distributed DBMS must be able to determine where specific data are stored. Second, it must be more sophisticated in determining the optimal way to request data. The order in which a request is processed can make a significant difference in the amount of data sent over the network. Finally, anticipating computer failures and prioritizing requests for data are extremely complex.[11] Sometimes it is difficult to determine whether or not a request for data has been implemented before the failure of either a remote computer or the network itself. In addition, when two requests to access the same data occur at about the same time, it is not easy to determine which request came first or what other requests are part of the same transaction if one of the requests must be blocked.

Besides the technical difficulties, organizational issues sometimes impede the acceptance of distributed DBMSs.[12] Database systems have traditionally been tightly designed and controlled by a single administrator or administrative office. One of the reasons that DBMSs were developed was to reduce redundancy in data entry and processing by centralizing control of data in an organization. Distributing authority and control over the data resource negates this reason for using DBMSs. Many managers believe that isolated and potentially conflicting islands of data will arise as local managers add their favorite modifications to the enterprise's data model. Of course, an organization can use a distributed architecture purely for its technical advantages, such as reducing network flow and increasing response time, while refusing to relinquish control to local managers. Still, many managers view distributed architecture as the first step toward distributed control and potential loss of personal information and power.

Data Models

DBMSs do not completely eliminate an organization's need to be concerned with how its data are organized. Although users and programmers need to worry less about the way that their data are physically stored, they must still pay attention to the logical relationships among the data. For example, a student and the courses he or she takes are logically related. Also, a student is logically related to his or her phone number. But these two relationships are quite different. A student takes many courses at a given time, and the history of courses that a student takes is of interest. By contrast, a student usually has only one or two phone numbers, and old phone numbers are of no interest. A phone number might be considered to be an **attribute,** or characteristic of the student, as might his or her hair color, height, and weight. Courses, on the other hand, exist independently of students and have attributes of their own, such as prerequisites, time of day, and professors. In addition, the relationship between a student and the course he or she takes may have attributes, such as the grade received. To organize their data properly, organizations should be concerned with the relationships among the data elements.

Different DBMSs treat relationships among data elements differently; however, their approaches fall into a few broad categories known as **data models.** In this section, we review the four most common data models—the relational model, the network model, the hierarchical model, and the object model. Historically, the hierarchical model was the first to be developed; it was followed by the network model, the relational model, and then the object model. We begin with the most widely accepted—the relational model. Then we describe the network model and the hierarchical model, which have historical importance and which continue to be used for large transaction-based systems. We present the object model last because it has only recently attracted significant attention. Figure 7-4 compares the data models and lists some representative products for each.

Relational Model

The **relational model** was first proposed as a theoretical model in 1970.[13] In the early 1980s products based on the model became commercially available. IBM's relational product for mainframe computers, DB2, first announced in 1983, legitimized the relational model in the eyes of many database specialists, even though it was not widely used until the late 1980s. Other than DB2, the most popular relational products for the mainframe and minicomputer markets include Adabas (Software AG), CA-Datacom (Computer Associates), Ingres (Ask),

Comparison of Data Models

	Relational	Network	Hierarchical	Object
Standards exist	Yes	Yes	No	Yes*
Relative speed	Low	Moderate	High	Moderate
Ease of query	High	Low	Low	High
Ease of software development	Moderate	Low	Low	High
Primary target application	Decision support/ ad hoc query	Transaction processing	Transaction processing	GUI environments/ complex objects
Ease of data distribution	Moderate	Low	Low	Moderate
Representative products	Access DB2 Oracle Sybase	IDS IDMS	IMS	Gemstone Ontos Versant

*The ODMG-93 standard is relatively new with few implementations.

Informix, Oracle, RDB (DEC), SQL/DS (IBM), Supra (Cincom), and Sybase. A number of these products were not designed as relational products but have recently incorporated relational features and now compete as relational products. In the microcomputer market, Clipper (Nantucket), dBASE (Borland), FoxPro (Microsoft), Access (Microsoft), Oracle, Paradox (Borland), and R:Base (Microrim) are among the major competitors.

In the relational model, a type of data object (called an **entity**), which is a person, event, or thing about which data are collected, is described by a table (called a **relation**) of rows (called **tuples**) and columns (called **attributes**). For example, look at the data in Figure 7-5. This table of data describes various customers—an entity in this database. A customer might have characteristics of a customer number, name, address, and credit limit. As shown in Figure 7-5, data about a company's customers (the data object or entity) would be conceived as a table. A row, or tuple, describes each customer, giving its number, name, address, and credit limit. Each column presents a specific attribute for all customers—the left-most column shows all customer numbers, the right-most column all credit limits.

Illustration of a Relational Table

CUST#	CUSTOMER-NAME	ADDRESS	CREDIT-LIMIT
16340	Arlington Software	341 Woodward Rd.	5,000
37126	Hanson Widgets	21 Park Dr.	10,000
21371	Marion Assoc.	19 Avalon Ave.	5,000
31319	Generic Products	113-51 71st St.	25,000
87615	Electric Co.	1 Electric Plaza	25,000

How does this model link two entities, for example, customer and sales representative? The relational model provides for logical connections among entities by including certain data in its tables. For example, the fact that each customer has a sales representative would be implemented by including in the customer table a column or columns that uniquely identify the customer's sales representative, perhaps a sales-rep number or sales-rep name. The DBMS can then link the customer table to the sales-rep table to obtain more detailed information about the sales representative for a particular customer. The DBMS would answer any questions about a customer's sales representative by first looking in the customer table, then finding the row for that customer and identifying its sales representative from the sales-rep column. Next the DBMS would look in the sales-rep table and find the row of information about the specific sales representative. The DBMS can also identify all customers of a particular sales representative by scanning the customer table and selecting only those who have the specified sales-rep identifier (name or number, for example) in the appropriate column. Most relational DBMSs internally organize the data in a way that makes such retrievals quick and efficient.

Because all relationships among data in the relational model are specified through data, a user can retrieve the data he or she wants simply by identifying the data in prescribed ways. An easy-to-use language called **SQL** has been adopted as the standard for the relational model.[14] Unlike most other programming languages, SQL is nonprocedural; the user specifies only the characteristics of the data desired, not the steps the DBMS must take to retrieve the data. For example, to find all customers with a credit limit of over $5,000, the command might be

```
SELECT CUSTOMER_NAME FROM CUSTOMER_TABLE WHERE
CREDIT_LIMIT > 5000.
```

Joining data from two or more tables is only slightly more complex. For example, to answer Jim Allen's question about how many of Insureco's New York automobile customers also hold homeowner's policies, the SQL command would be

```
SELECT COUNT (DISTINCT AUTO.CUSTNUMB) WHERE
AUTO.CUSTNUMB = HOME.CUSTNUMB AND
AUTO.CUSTNUMB = CUSTOMER.CUSTNUMB AND
CUSTOMER.STATE = 'NY'
```

Jim Allen might encourage Insureco to install a relational database because nonprogramming users such as himself could easily access the data to answer managerial questions and to perform analyses not anticipated at the time the database was created. He might encounter resistance among MIS managers who fear that Insureco's hardware resources lack the capacity to handle the level of processing implied by hundreds of people like Jim who might want to perform similar analyses.

Network Model

The **network model** builds a tighter linkage (called a **set**) between elements of data, such as between customer and sales representative. The fact that each customer has a sales representative would be implemented by creating a customer/sales-rep set. Customers would be part of the set of a particular sales representative (see Figure 7-6). The network model does not store the sales-rep identifier with the customer's data; rather, it stores the customer's data as parts of the set belonging to its representative. Similarly, a set of vendors might include

FIGURE 7-6 Sets

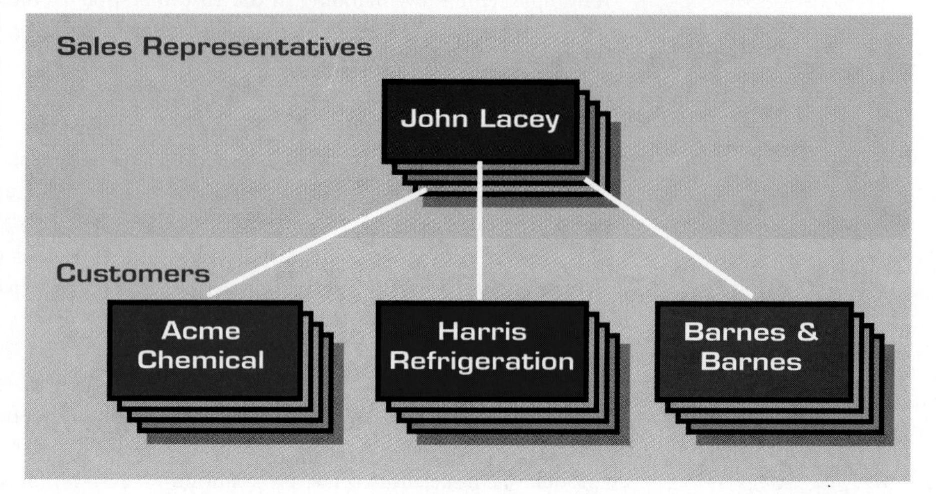

data about the product the vendor sells; the network model would store product data as part of the vendor set.

The network model derives its name from diagrams, such as the one in Figure 7-7, that show sets (indicated by arrows) connecting **data elements,** similar to entities in the relational model (indicated by boxes). The set of customer–sales-rep is reflected by arrow 1, which connects the sales representative and customer boxes of data. The set of customer contacts, reflected by arrow 2, connects the boxes of customer data and contact data. Figure 7-8 shows all sets in Figure 7-7. Combining all sets and elements gives the overall impression of a network connecting the elements of the database.

In the network model, one data element may belong to several sets. For example, each customer may be part of a sales-rep–customer set and a discount-class–customer set (arrows 1 and 3), as shown in Figure 7-7. Furthermore, an item may be a **member** of one kind of a set and an **owner** of another. For example, as shown in Figure 7-7, a customer may be a member of a sales-rep–customer set (arrow 1) but an owner of a customer–invoice set (arrow 4). Products belong to a vendor–product set (arrow 6) and own both product–order-line (arrow 8) and product–inventory (arrow 9) sets.

A set represents a **one-to-many relationship:** a sales representative may have many customers, but a customer can have only one sales representative. To represent a **many-to-many relationship,** such as when a product may exist in several warehouses and a warehouse may hold many products, network model users must create an additional data element and two sets. For the product/warehouse example, as shown in Figure 7-7, users must create the inventory data element and the sets shown by arrows 9 and 10. The set shown by arrow 9 for a given warehouse then contains one inventory element for each product held by that warehouse. Similarly, the set shown by arrow 10 for a given product contains one inventory element for each warehouse holding that product.

The use of sets makes the retrieval of related information quicker and more efficient than with the relational model. In most network DBMS implementations, the database administrator may specify that members of a set should be stored near one another so that the storage medium will easily retrieve them in a single access. For example, one disk access might retrieve a customer and all its invoices.

FIGURE 7-7 The Network Model

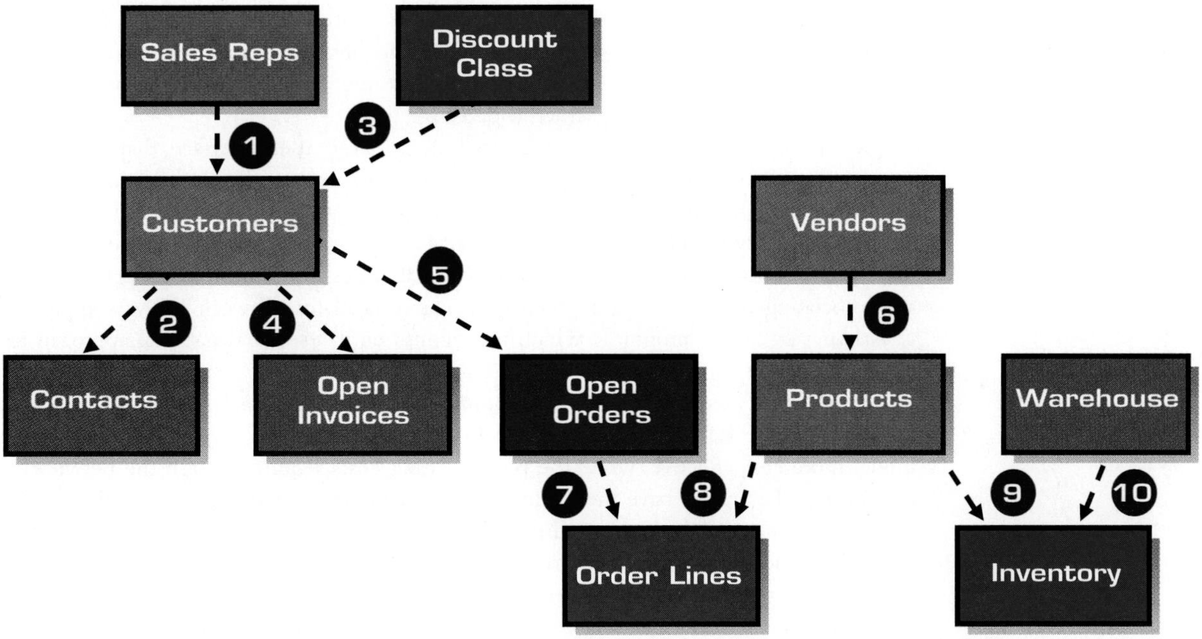

From the user perspective, however, sets complicate rather than simplify data access. The user cannot access data simply by its title or characteristics. Instead, the user must prescribe procedures to get the data. For example, how would a customer services manager determine which customers must be contacted about delays in processing their order due to a product recall? First, the database user must find all order lines in which the defective product appeared. Then, for each of these lines, the user would find the appropriate order. Finally, the user must identify the customer based on the order. Or, as shown in Figure 7-7, the user directs the DBMS to move from the set shown by arrow 8 of products and order lines to

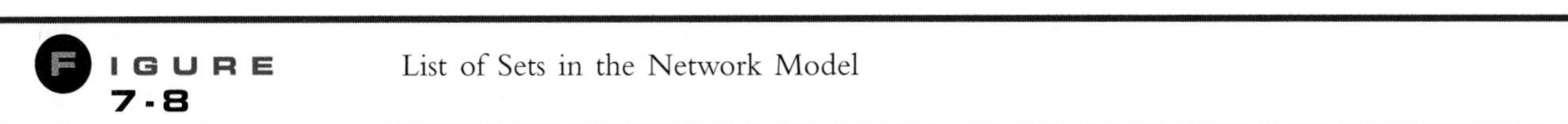

FIGURE 7-8 List of Sets in the Network Model

Set	Owner	Members
1	sales rep	customers
2	customer	contacts
3	discount class	customer
4	customer	open invoices
5	customer	open orders
6	vendor	products
7	open order	order lines
8	product	order lines
9	product	inventory
10	warehouse	inventory

the set shown by arrow 7 of order lines and open orders to the set shown by arrow 5 of open orders and customers. This process of specifying a path through the network, called **navigating,** is procedural. Usually a program written in a procedural language such as COBOL implements the path specifications. To answer the same request with the relational model, the user would instead simply specify the relationships among the data requested. Loosely speaking, the user would ask the DBMS to obtain the names of all customers having an identification number the same as the customer identification number in the order table and an order line that specified a defective part.

Modern network DBMSs generally include an SQL user interface that translates SQL requests into programs that navigate the databases to extract the desired data. In practice, similar interfaces are more difficult to use, have slower performance, and are more limited in their functionality than SQL or relational DBMS products. In addition, they require the database administrator to prepare the database for SQL access by creating appropriate data names and associating them with paths. Finally, SQL interfaces for network DBMSs apply only to *ad hoc* queries, not to programs, which must continue to use a navigational approach to data retrieval.

Several factors explain the growing popularity of the relational model over the network model. First, the decreasing cost of faster computer processing makes using the relational model more cost effective, while the programming costs required to use the network model remain high. Few users have the ability to use more complicated languages such as COBOL, whereas they can quickly learn and use SQL or other languages for accessing relational databases. Thus, more powerful hardware compensates for the reduced efficiency of the relational model, whereas the difficulty in accessing data in the network model remains critical.

Second, the increasing availability of personal computers has caused users who are not computer professionals to insist on the ability to access data without programming. PC users are used to doing their own analysis and resist applications such as those surrounding a network model, where they must enlist the aid of a computer professional.

Finally, the relational model is more flexible than the network model. For the relational model, changes in the relationships among data can be expressed simply by adding and deleting columns; rarely must programs be changed. In contrast, when relationships change among data in the network model, sets must be redefined, and the entire method of access to data might have to be changed, resulting in the costly reprogramming of applications.

General Electric released the first widely used commercial network DBMS, IDS, in the late 1960's.[15] Subsequently, CODASYL, a voluntary organization consisting of computer users and vendors (and the organization responsible for the definition of COBOL), created a task group to standardize network DBMSs. The task group published a report of its findings in 1971 and updated them in 1984; these findings established *de facto* standards among network DBMS vendors.[16]

Hierarchical Model

The **hierarchical model** is a precursor to the network model and can be viewed as a network model with additional restrictions. The hierarchical (sometimes called **hierarchial**) model views data as organized logically into a hierarchy. This hierarchy can be viewed as an inverted tree (see Figure 7-9), with a trunk (known as a **root**), nodes (called **segments**), and **branches** extending from these nodes. The resulting diagram is like a network, except that (in the terminology of the network model) an entity may be a member of no more than one type of set—for example, customers can belong only to sales-rep, not to discount-class or any other data set.

The hierarchical restriction makes it extremely difficult to represent many interrelationships among data. For example, an order may consist of several lines, each for a different

FIGURE 7-9 The Hierarchical Model

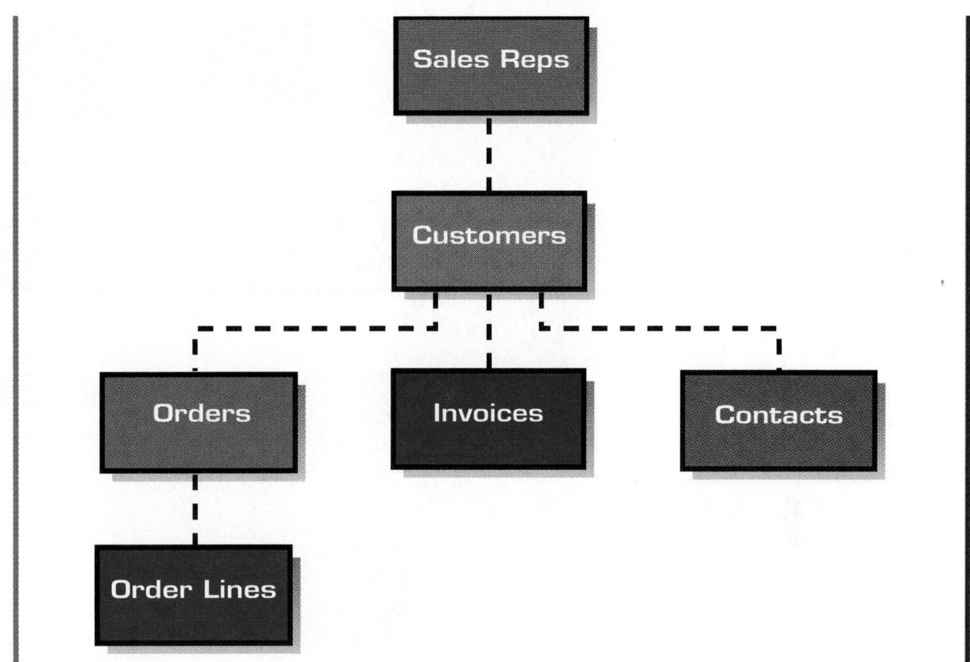

product. As shown in Figure 7-10, the relationship among orders and the vendors that sell the products cannot be easily represented, as they could in the network model. The problem is that the order line logically deserves to be part of both the order set and the product set. This is prohibited by the hierarchical model because it violates the hierarchical view of data. Instead, the data must be represented by two hierarchies, resulting in the order lines being stored twice.

Most implementations of the hierarchical model have technical ways to loosen the hierarchical restriction to some degree, thereby eliminating data duplication. Still, the model remains cumbersome for data modelers. Although the speed of access is intrinsically faster for the hierarchical model than for the network model, current computer technology has removed this advantage.

Despite its drawbacks, the hierarchical model remains one of the most widely used models because of the large installed base of a product called IMS.[17] Developed by IBM in 1968, millions of applications have used IMS. In many cases, and particularly for transaction-based systems, the costs of reprogramming these applications outweighs the benefits of converting them to a network or relational form.

Object Model

The **object model,** the most recent of the widely accepted data models, derives from object-oriented programming (see Chapter 5).[18] Recall that this type of programming views an object as a combination of attributes (or data) and programs (called **methods**) that are **encapsulated**—tightly bundled and closed from the view of users and other programs. For example, a customer might be an object with attributes such as name, sales-rep, credit-limit,

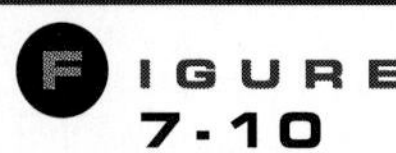

FIGURE 7-10 Difficulty of Representing Multiple Hierarchies with the Hierarchical Model

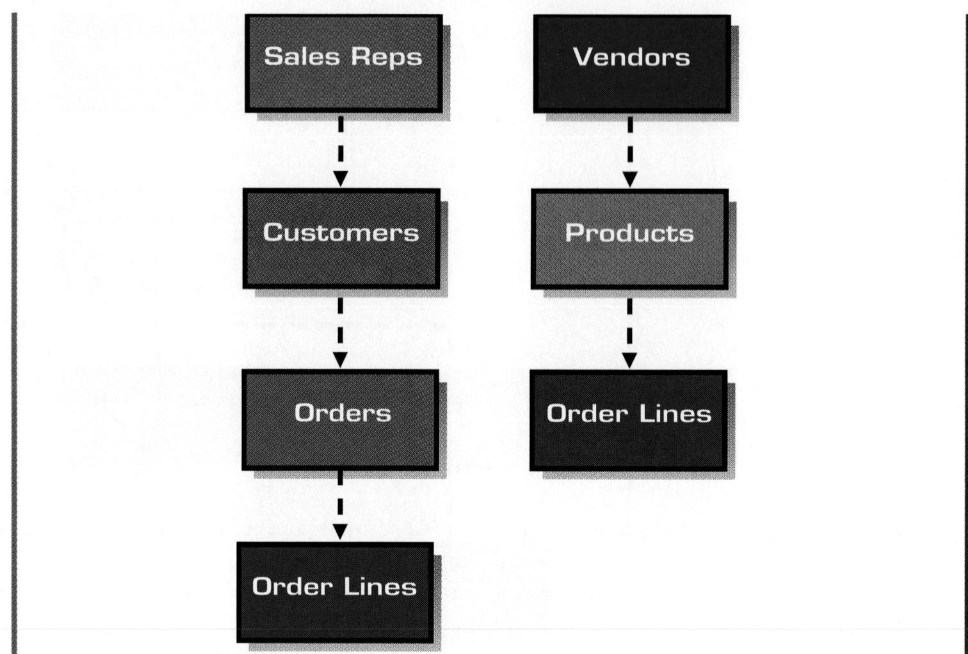

and invoices along with methods such as change-credit-limit and pay-invoice. Some attributes, such as invoice, may themselves be other objects.

Because of encapsulation, the only interface between the user and an object or between objects is a **message** directed at an object. The customer object might react to the message "tell me your name" by sending its name in a reply message; it might react to the message "change credit limit to 3000" by changing its internal representation of the customer's credit limit and replying with the message "done." An object is built so that it reacts to messages by either changing its state (attributes or programs), such as its internal coding of its credit limit, or sending out messages in response, such as "done." The advantage of encapsulation is that it allows programmers to change the way attributes of an object are represented or its methods are implemented without affecting any other objects.

Objects may belong to an **object type,** also called an **object class,** of which there may be a hierarchy. For example, one object type may be company, with attributes of name, phone-numbers, and contact, and the method add-phone, which accepts and processes messages about additional phone numbers. Two possible subtypes of the company object type are the object types customer and vendor. Object types inherit the characteristics of their supertype. As a result, customer would implicitly have attributes of name, phone-numbers, and contact, and method add-phone. In addition, it could have other attributes, such as products-sold, and other methods, such as add-product-sold. Object-oriented DBMSs store particular individual objects for which object types have been defined.

The major advantages of the object model are the ease with which it integrates with object-oriented programs and its ability to more easily represent complex data types such as images, sound, and objects embedded within other objects. For example, organizational charts and engineering drawings, which are hard to represent using the traditional data models, are relatively easy to represent using object-oriented models.

Current implementations of object DBMSs have evolved in two ways.[19] First, they have been built as extensions to an object-oriented language to allow an object to have permanence. Object DBMSs that have evolved in this fashion tend to have less robust data management facilities (such as data sharing and backup and recovery features) than are available from traditional DBMS vendors. Second, object DBMSs have evolved from relational DBMS vendors who have added object features. These tend not to support the full object paradigm. Industry experts expect these paths to converge by the mid-1990s as relational vendors and early developers of the object technology form partnerships.[20]

Jim Allen would endorse a decision to adopt an object-oriented DBMS because he, like most nonprogrammers, finds it easy to relate to data as objects.[21] Automobile policies and homeowner's policies are easily viewed as subtypes of the object type policy. Although standards have not yet been adopted for database queries, most object-oriented DBMSs use a graphic interface that pictures objects as icons on a screen. When clicked on by a mouse-directed pointer, these icons open to reveal the indicated data. Relationships among objects are also usually illustrated on the screen with lines, arrows, and buttons that can be clicked on to move between object types.

Data Design

Data design is the process of identifying and formalizing the relationships among the elements of data that will form an organization's database. For example, must a customer have a sales representative? If so, how should the database store a customer, if at all, before its sales representative has been assigned? How many customers can be assigned to a sales representative? What happens to a sales representative's customers when the sales representative leaves the company? Should the database contain the same information for walk-in customers as for repetitive customers? If the customer's shipping address is the same as its billing address, how should this be indicated?

Decisions such as these are not simple and tend to evolve over the life of a database application. DBMSs, however, make it possible to consider an organization's data design independently of its application programs. As a result, it is often possible to change the design without a massive reprogramming effort. Nevertheless, software developers, database managers, and functional managers must understand the interrelationships among an organization's data elements so that they can be properly reflected in the database.

The Entity-Relationship Model

Although a number of models have been developed to express the relationship among an organization's data elements, the **entity-relationship (E/R) model** is one of the most widely used. The E/R model, introduced in 1976, offers a pictorial way of showing the interrelationships among various types of data.[22] The model has been modified and refined numerous times since its introduction. In this section, we give only a brief overview of its most salient features.

Figure 7-11 illustrates a portion of an E/R model for a hypothetical wholesaler. Entities about which the organization collects data, corresponding to tables of the relational model or object types of the object-oriented model, are illustrated with rectangles, as shown for customers and sales reps in Figure 7-11. Relationships between entities are named and enclosed in diamonds; in the figure, the fact that sales reps represent customers is indicated by the *represents* relationship. The lines connecting entities to the diamond representing the relationships among them also shows whether or not the relationship is exclusive. In this example, each sales rep represents many (M) customers, but every customer is represented exclusively by one (1) sales rep. This illustrates a **one-to-many** relationship. Relationships

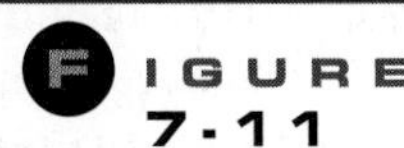

Illustrative Portion of an Entity-Relationship Diagram

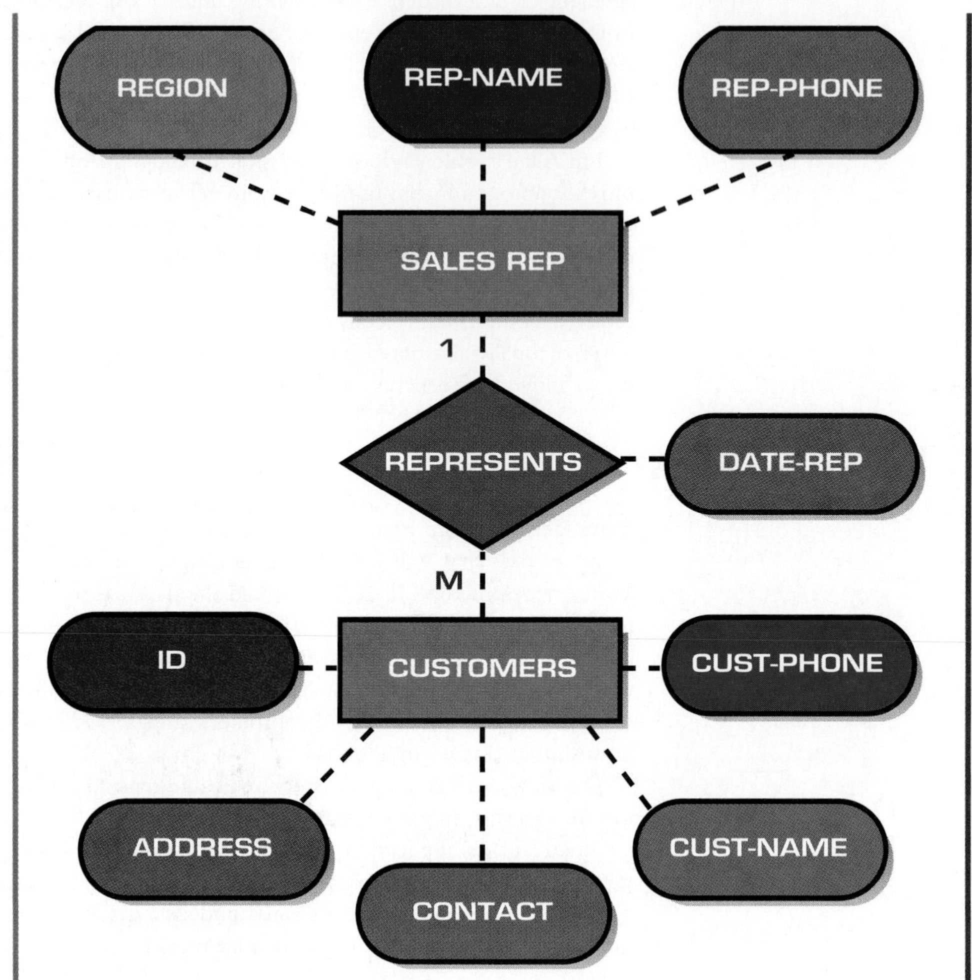

can also be **one to one,** as when each employee has a company car and each car is assigned to one employee, or many to many, as when each student is enrolled in multiple courses and each course enrolls multiple students. Finally, attributes of entities and relationships are illustrated with ovals. For example, cust-phone is the phone number of customer, and date-rep indicates how long sales-rep has represented customer.

The entity-relationship model can be translated directly and almost automatically into either relational, network, or hierarchical data models. Commercial products currently exist to generate an entity-relationship model by eliciting information from the user about the relationship among data elements.

Normalization

Although the relational model of data is conceptually the simplest to use, its benefits can be negated by poorly designed data tables. **Normalization** is a formal procedure that relational designers can use to assure that the data elements of a database are grouped into tables in a way that simplifies retrieval, reduces data entry and storage, and minimizes the likelihood of data inconsistencies.

To illustrate the problem associated with a poor design, consider a single table having a row for each customer containing the customer's name, phone, and credit limit as well as his or her sales representative's name, telephone number, and address. With this unnormalized design, the database could hold two different and conflicting telephone numbers for a single sales rep. Also, to change the telephone number of a given sales representative, the user or DBMS would have to adjust many rows of the database because a sales representative services many customers. Finally, if a sales representative's customers are all deleted, important information about the sales representative, such as his or her telephone number, will also be lost. Experienced relational designers know how to group data into a **normalized form** that will prevent such errors.

Specialized Database Management Systems

So far we have examined DBMSs used for traditional business functions. Some applications, such as text processing, engineering (particularly CAD/CAM), and archiving, use DBMSs designed specifically to support the unique requirements of these applications. This section briefly reviews the features of some of these specialized DBMSs.

Document DBMSs include intradocument and interdocument DBMSs. **Intradocument DBMSs** decompose a document into a database of words, images, and so on. This decomposition allows the user to search for information of interest within a document. Among the most popular of these are **hypertext** systems, which allow database designers to build cross-references, or linkages within a document. Users traverse a hypertext database typically by selecting from among the linkages by positioning an arrow on the appropriate button, or location on the screen, and clicking a mouse (see Figure 7-12).

Interdocument DBMSs apply to groups of related documents. They are used by library and research systems to identify documents or articles about a particular subject. Such DBMSs may also be linked electronically to image or text retrieval systems that allow selected documents to be retrieved, read, and edited. Office automation also uses interdocument DBMSs to allow managers and secretaries to store and retrieve documents in an organized fashion.[23] Applications include systems for storing electronic mail or for storing and retrieving documents related to a particular project or client. Companies that sell information often use interdocument DBMSs to allow buyers to preview and select the information they want. For

REUTER'S

example, Reuter's Textline includes data of general and business news from more than 2,000 sources around the globe.[24]

Temporal DBMSs are designed to store and retrieve historical changes to information.[25] As information is updated, temporal databases retain the old as well as the new. As a result, it is possible to query the database as to its state at any time in the past. Such DBMSs are often used to store such things as engineering drawings and computer programs, where users are interested in addressing changes that have been made since a prior date, or where users may want to return to an older version to make new changes. If Jim Allen had a temporal DBMS, he could not only perform his analysis at the current date, but he could also see how much the company could have saved had the decision been made a year earlier.

Spatial DBMSs enable users to analyze and change the spatial relationship among objects stored in a database.[26] Computer-aided design (CAD) and computer-aided manufacturing (CAM) use spatial DBMSs extensively. They are also used to model geographical systems, such as roadways, electrical lines, and water/sewer systems. Emergency services, such as fire and police, use such geographical DBMSs to locate addresses in large cities and to identify

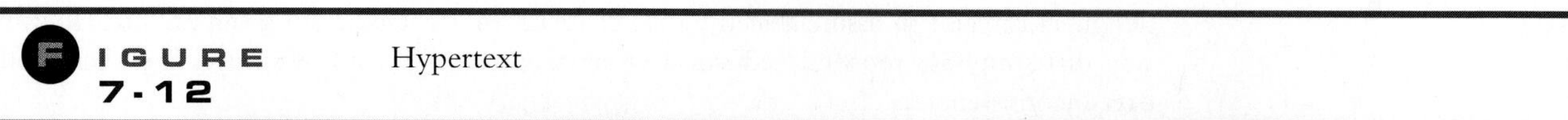

FIGURE 7-12 Hypertext

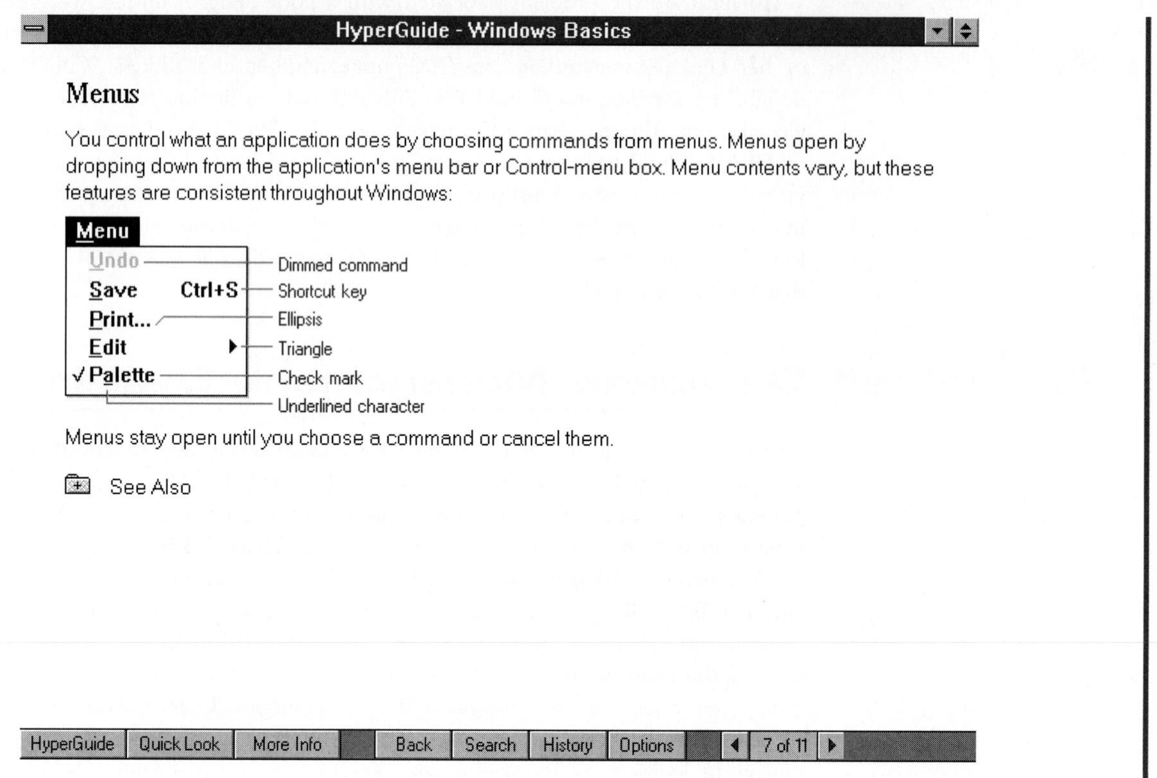

the units that can respond most quickly. In traditional databases, the relationships among data elements are specified at the time of data design and are not expected to change much once the database is used. By contrast, the relationships among data elements in spatial databases are expected to change.

Global Issues in Database Management

Companies that operate globally often find that there is no convenient time to halt their processing and allow their databases to be backed up. Twenty-four hours a day, business is being conducted in some part of the world. A number of approaches address this problem. One solution uses DBMS systems that operate in parallel on two storage devices. Periodically, one of the storage devices is detached from the database application so that it can be backed up. The database is then updated using the log of the database that continued to run. Another approach writes all database updates to a temporary log during the backup process. The database itself thus remains constant during the backup. The DBMS may use both the database and the temporary log to answer queries so that the user always "sees" current versions of the data. After the backup is complete, the database is brought up to date using the log.

For global companies, the data architecture is often more critical than for domestic companies. Transferring data internationally is often difficult because of the poor data communication infrastructure in some countries. In addition, some countries impose regulations on the export of data. As a result, it may be better, if possible, to keep local data at local sites using a distributed architecture.

Selecting a Database Management System

A DBMS is one of the most important software investments a company can make. Figure 7-13 offers a set of factors to consider when choosing among alternatives. As a user or manager, you will probably want to delegate DBMS selection to an IS professional who has the expertise to evaluate individual products on the criteria you specify. You will need to understand how products differ so that you can specify the criteria that are most important to you.

Among the most important factors to consider are which data model and architecture best suit your environment. For example, if you intend to use the DBMS primarily for decision support, you should select a relational DBMS; if you intend to do transaction processing, either a relational DBMS or a network DBMS with a relational front end would be satisfactory. Also, if the organization currently uses a DBMS, it is important to determine whether the new DBMS will interface with the existing one or replace the old one.

The remaining issues deal with flexibility, performance, vendor quality, and DBMS features. Conformance to standards gives an organization the freedom and flexibility to change vendors without requiring applications to be reprogrammed. This protects the organization against financial failure of the DBMS vendor, poor service from the DBMS vendor, and price inflexibility from the vendor.

FIGURE 7-13 Factors to Consider in Selecting a DBMS

Integration
- Match with existing systems
- Match with data model needs
- Match to architectural requirements
- Match to hardware and operating system platform(s)
- Conversion difficulty for existing data, if relevant
- Interfaces with other DBMSs
- Conformance to standards

Performance
- Reputation for system availability
- Ease of recovery upon crashes
- Quality of performance monitors
- Performance on transaction benchmarks
- Theoretical and practical number of concurrent users

Vendor issues
- Price
- Vendor's track record and financial stability
- Price of updates and revisions
- Frequency of updates and revisions
- Quality of documentation
- Quality and price of training
- Historical vendor response to customer problems and reported bugs
- Availability of site licenses

Features
- Size limitations
- Integration of CASE tools
- Multilevel security features
- Support for concurrent update
- Support for distributed and client/server architectures
- Quality of screen and report generators
- Ease of use of query languages
- Integration with data dictionaries
- Support for image and voice storage

Performance is a serious issue that should be viewed from at least two perspectives. First and most importantly, the DBMS should be robust: System availability should be high, the system performance should be easy to monitor, and recovery from crashes should be automatic and smooth. Mainframe users consider this to be the most important factor in measuring satisfaction with their DBMSs.[27]

The second performance issue is the DBMS's response time in performing queries and executing transactions. DBMSs that execute too slowly may result in poor performance unless run on more powerful computers. **Benchmarks** are measurements of the speed of the DBMS as controlled for the hardware platform.[28] DBMS vendors often report their performance on standard benchmarks in their sales literature, especially if they perform well. Occasionally, trade journals also report the performance of selected DBMSs on a suite of benchmarks. Unfortunately, every benchmark test assumes a type of usage that might not correspond to that planned by the company.[29] A benchmark suite that emphasizes transaction processing would not be appropriate for a DSS application, for example, because transactions primarily update the database while DSSs primarily are used for queries.

Database and Data Administration

Database and data administration involves overseeing the design or selection, implementation, and use of database applications in the organization. Administrators oversee both the technical functions of maintaining the DBMS and the management functions relating to the control of data. In small organizations, the functions of data and database administration generally reside in the same individual, often called the **database administrator,** computer information manager, or manager of database applications. Often people in the data and database administration roles also have programming and systems analysis responsibilities. Larger organizations may separate the technical and management functions and have staffs of experts for each.

Database Administration

Typically, the more technical functions are called **database administration.** The database administrator monitors the performance of the DBMS on a particular database, perhaps modifying the data design if necessary to correct performance problems. The administrator regularly backs up the database and recovers the database when the system crashes. He or she supervises or monitors the development of software that uses or affects the database. He or she creates separate development databases for testing new software and approves the transfer of such software to the production database after the software is fully tested. The administrator also installs updates to the DBMS software when its vendors issue new releases. The database administrator should have strong technical skills, extensive experience with the DBMS in use, and excellent communication skills.[30]

Data Administration

When the database administration and **data administration** functions are separate, the **data administrator** is primarily responsible for ensuring the integrity of the data resource. The data administrator at Depository Trust Company, which provides post-trade services to the securities industry, takes a corporate view of the data rather than acting as an analyst for individual systems.[31] The data administrator must know what data are collected by the organization, where they are stored, and how they are named. He or she is responsible for establishing data security and setting up appropriate access controls. The data administrator

DEPOSITORY TRUST

attempts to minimize data redundancy by keeping centralized documentation of all data elements and may impose naming standards on the data throughout the organization to facilitate nonredundancy and easy access to data. In addition, the data administrator may use a **data dictionary** (also known as a **data encyclopedia** or **repository**) to keep track of the data resource. The data dictionary, a database itself, holds information about data stored in each of a company's databases, as shown by the sample dictionary entry in Figure 7-14. Most data dictionaries, in addition to describing each data element in great detail, contain information about the programs in which each data element is used, in which reports it appears, in which screens it is input, and so on. This information makes it relatively easy to analyze the impact of changing the characteristics of any data.

IGURE 7-14 Illustration of Data Stored in a Data Dictionary

CUSTOMER-PAYMENT-AMOUNT

Attribute of: CUSTOMER-PAYMENT

Data input screen:

Prompt:	Amount of payment:
Edit(s):	>0
	<100,000
Type:	Currency
Display:	$99,999.99

Report heading:
Payment
Amount

Aliases: CUST-PAYMENT, CHECK-AMOUNT, CPAMT

Appears in the following views: ACCTS-PAYBLE, CUST-RECRD, PAYMNT-RECRD

Appears in the following programs: ARP-84X, ARP-84Y, ARP-85Z, CUS-RECPT-PROC
I54X3T22, I23X4T23, P94.XX.2;2

Security level (without view): 12

Owner(s): John Marshall

Help prompt: Enter payment amount without dollar signs or commas.

Integrity:
On creation of CUSTOMER-PAYMENT:
Update TOTAL-PAYMENTS = TOTAL-PAYMENTS + CUSTOMER-PAYMENT-AMOUNT
On update:
Update TOTAL-PAYMENTS = TOTAL-PAYMENTS + change

Summary

A database is an organized collection of related data. Database management systems perform numerous functions in organizations, including the storage and retrieval of data and metadata, the limit and control of redundancy, the support of simultaneous data sharing, the provision for recovery and security services, the enforcement of business rules and data integrity, and the improvement of programming productivity.

Distribution architecture refers to how data and database processing are physically distributed among many computers in a typical organization. A decentralized architecture is one in which databases are developed on an *ad hoc* basis as required by individual applications, without central planning or central control. A centralized architecture refers to running a DBMS on a single computer. A client/server architecture divides the functions of a DBMS among connected computers on a network while centralizing permanent storage for all data on one or more computers known as the database servers. The distributed architecture allows data to reside anywhere on the network of computers.

Four types of data models reflect the logical relationships among data in a DBMS. The relational model describes a data object by a table of rows and columns. The network model builds a tighter linkage, called a set, between elements of data. The hierarchical model can be viewed as a network model with additional restrictions; it views data as organized logically into a hierarchy. The object model derives from object-oriented programming, which views an object as a combination of attributes and programs.

Data design is the process of identifying and formalizing the relationships among the elements of data that will form an organization's database. The entity-relationship model is widely used. Normalization of data is a formal procedure that relational designers use to assure that the data elements of a database are grouped effectively.

Specialized DBMSs include document DBMSs, interdocument DBMSs, temporal DBMSs, and spatial DBMSs. Global issues in database management include timing backups and choosing flexible data architectures. Those selecting a DBMS should consider issues related to integration, performance, vendor, and features. Implementation involves both database and data administration.

Key Terms

Attribute
Benchmark
Branch
Centralized architecture
Client
Client/server architecture
Computerized database
Concurrency control
Data administration
Data administrator
Data design
Data dictionary
Data element
Data encyclopedia
Data integrity
Data model
Data redundancy
Database
Database administration
Database administrator
Database management system (DBMS)
Database server
Decentralized architecture
Distributed DBMS architecture
Distribution architecture
Document DBMS
Encapsulation
Entity
Entity-relationship model (E/R model)
Hierarchial model
Hierarchical model
Hypertext
Interdocument DBMS
Intradocument DBMS
Log
Logical view
Many-to-many relationship
Member
Message
Metadata
Method
Navigating
Network model
Normalization

Normalized form
Object class
Object model
Object type
One-to-many relationship
One-to-one relationship
Owner
Physical view
Relation
Relational model
Repository
Root
Segment
Set
Spatial DBMS
SQL
Temporal DBMS
Tuple
View

Review Questions

1. Define database. Must data be computerized to form a database? Justify your answer.
2. Identify six functions of a database management system.
3. What are metadata? Why do DBMSs store metadata?
4. What is data redundancy? Explain why reducing data redundancy is advantageous.
5. What is meant by concurrency control? Why is it necessary?
6. How do database management systems increase programmer productivity?
7. What is meant by distribution architecture? List four distribution architectures.
8. Identify the advantages and disadvantages of a client/server architecture relative to a centralized architecture.
9. What is a data model? List four data models.
10. What is meant by a set in the network model? What advantages and disadvantages do sets give the network model relative to the relational model?
11. What are the advantages of the object model relative to the other data models?
12. Give an example of a problem that might arise from using a data model that has not been normalized.
13. List three types of specialized DBMSs.
14. How do global companies back up their data while doing business 24 hours a day?
15. What factors should you consider in selecting a DBMS?
16. Explain the difference between a data administrator and a database administrator.

MINICASE

A Database for the William Morris Agency

Every up-and-coming actor and actress in Hollywood depends on an agent to get them auditions. If they don't get auditions, they pump gas and wait on tables. And their agents get axed. In short, "It's a very competitive business," said Alex Henry, MIS director at the William Morris Agency (WMA), based in Beverly Hills, California.

Founded in 1898, the talent agency is the world's oldest and, with more than 150 agents, the largest, according to Henry. There are offices in London, New York City and Nashville, Tennessee.

To place a client, an agent must know the industry. If a studio wants an actor to play someone 20 to 30 years old, in a film being shot from July to October, an agent prepares a short list of which clients meet these requirements and would have their careers advanced by the role. Developing the mental database agents need is labor-intensive (it calls for lots

Reprinted with permission from *Client/Server Computing Magazine,* August 1994, pp. 22–24.

of schmoozing) and personal (it requires listening to lots of gossip). That database isn't stored on a PC. It's stored in the agent's head and, if the agent takes another job (and it's a high turnover industry), that knowledge leaves the agency.

Last year WMA realized it needed a custom application to solve this problem. But knowing it lacked the staff to perform the development itself, the agency turned to its computer supplier, NeXT Computer Inc., and systems integrator, SHL Systemhouse. SHL was already doing development work on NeXT computers and had managed projects of about the same size as the planned WMA application. "We decided it was more appropriate to get someone who specialized in custom software," Henry said.

The first decision WMA and SHL made was the database for the talent management application. The choice came down to SQL Server from Sybase Inc. and Oracle from Oracle Corp. They picked SQL Server because of its high-volume transaction processing capabilities, because it ran on NeXT, and because they felt it offered better price/performance, Henry said.

The result of all this will be the Talent Management System (TMS), a custom application that will let agents access all the necessary information on clients and their schedules, while ensuring that the information stays with WMA should an agent switch jobs.

The entry point into TMS will be the Directory, a read-only module that gives summary information on clients, people, companies and projects. From there, users will be able to go to the next level of four more modules: Details, Authorization, Projects, and Phone Sheet. "Most times, users go to the directory for queries, and it's faster for them to search the summary information," Henry said.

In Details, users will be able to get and update information about people or companies. The Authorization module will maintain client-specific information aside from their addresses and telephone numbers. Projects will contain details about projects such as an upcoming movie, which production company is handling it, whether the production company is looking for a cast and whether it needs a director. Telephone numbers and call log information will be maintained in Phone Sheet.

The Directory, Detail, and Phone Sheet modules are already in use by more than 100 agents using NeXT front ends. The Projects module is in final testing. WMA expects to have TMS fully implemented by mid-1995, Henry said.

Currently, agents keep information about bookings and quotes in filing cabinets. But another module, Quotes, will computerize this information. Named for a reference to the show biz phrase for the amount an entertainer was paid for a previous job, Quotes will let agents, using a GUI front end, look up their client's availability, how much they were paid for their last movie, and what kinds of roles they want. The Quotes module will be rolled out for the motion picture division in August or September.

For calendaring, Quotes will be integrated with PencilMeIn, the scheduling program from Sarrus Software Inc., Foster City, California.

Like other TMS modules, Quotes will be used by agents in both the Beverly Hills and New York City offices. Agents in New York access it over the Internet. There is no timetable for rolling TMS out to the London office.

WMA agents don't have to worry about being replaced by computers. "The system will never replace the agent," Henry said. "You need the in-depth knowledge of clients and the industry that only an agent can provide."

Case Questions

1. Why did WMA feel that it needed a database application?
2. What data will WMA's database contain?
3. How did WMA select a DBMS for its application? Do you agree with its approach?
4. Do you believe that WMA's database objectives will be achieved? Why or why not?

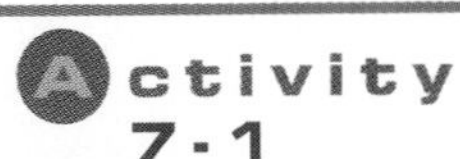

Activity 7-1 The Human Resources Database Problem

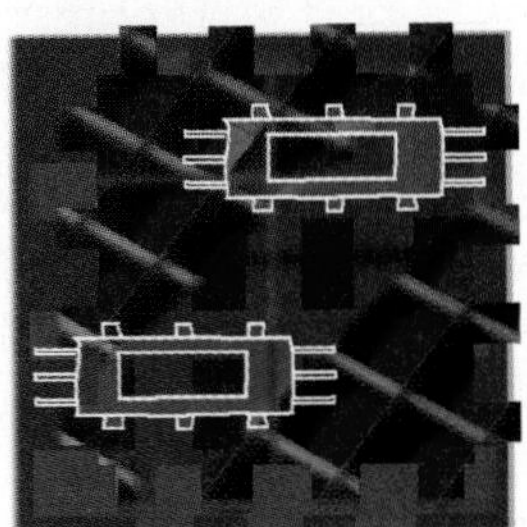

short case

STEP 1: Read the following scenario.

Westin Hotels & Resorts, a corporate hotel management company, has the responsibility for centralized payroll, benefits administration, and a variety of other human resources services. Westin's corporate payroll and human resource departments have historically relied on multiple systems. An outside service bureau processed payroll for its 4,000 salaried employees, and individual, hotel-based stand-alone computers processed the payroll for its 6,000 hourly employees. The service bureau collected general personnel data, such as performance evaluations and employment histories, for the analysis of trends across all member hotels. It also tracked data for use in government reporting for tax purposes and other regulatory requirements. The benefits department used several in-house PC databases to administer group benefits, including group medical and life insurance benefits for management and hourly, nonunion employees at all hotels. This department negotiated with local health maintenance organizations, paid insurance premiums, and acted as a central office for claim and eligibility inquiries, among other functions.

The compensation department used an in-house PC database to process statistical information, such as employee salaries, in order to analyze it for competitive purposes. The human resources department used a manual filing system to maintain and update employee personnel records. Making a single personnel change, such as a hiring, termination, salary adjustment, or position transfer required significant negotiations among the various departments and complicated procedures to interface the various reports and information. Each department in turn would then process the information using its individual system. This resulted in very high costs, a perpetually backlogged work load, inconsistent data, and inconsistently timed data changes. The individual hotels also were dissatisfied with this approach because when they received their benefits and payroll registers, they had to spend time reviewing them and cross-referencing the two, checking that all changes were accurate and consistent.

STEP 2: Individually or in small groups, offer a plan for integrating the multiple systems into a single database management system. Discuss the objectives of the database, the appropriate data model and data architecture for the new system, the nature of the data it would include, and plans for administering it.

STEP 3: In small groups or with the entire class, share the plans you have developed. Then answer the following questions:

1. What elements do these plans have in common?
2. How well do the plans respond to the information needs at Westin?
3. What are the strengths and weaknesses of each plan?
4. What should be the components of an effective and responsive database management system for the hotels? ●

SOURCE: Based on information presented in J. E. Santora, Data base integrates HR functions, *Personnel Journal* (January 1992): p. 92 with permission.

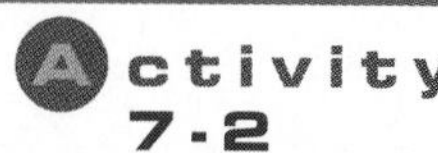

Activity 7-2 Using a Micro DBMS

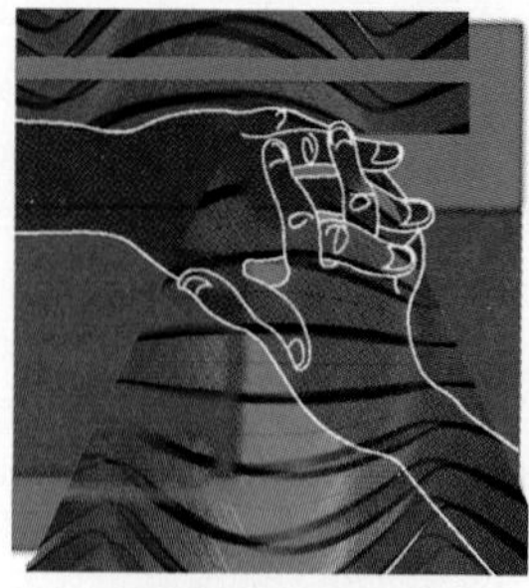

hands on

STEP 1: Your instructor will give you instructions for accessing a DBMS on your computer system. Then follow the directions presented below.

STEP 2: Create the structure for the STUDENTS table with seven fields of the lengths shown: SID (3), LAST (20), FIRST (20), MIDDLE (1), SEX (1), MAJOR (3), GPA (3 with one decimal place).

STEP 3: Add the data for the 10 student records shown below.

SID	LAST	FIRST	MIDDLE	SEX	MAJOR	GPA
987	Peters	Steve	K	M	Mgt	3.2
763	Parker	Charles		M		2.7
218	Richard	Sally		F	Fin	3.6
359	Pelnick	Alan	R	M	Fin	2.4
862	Fagin	Emma		F	Mgt	2.2
748	Meglin	Susan	B	F	MIS	3.8
506	Lee	Bill		M	Fin	2.7
581	Gambrell	Ted		M	Mkt	2.8
372	Quigley	Sarah		F		3.5
126	Anderson	Robert	F	M	Acc	3.7

STEP 4: Sort the records to appear in descending GPA.

STEP 5: Modify the structure of the table to reflect the possibility of a student last name of 25 characters.

STEP 6: Create a form named STUFORM that forces the user when inputting data to limit GPA values to be between 0.0 and 4.0.

STEP 7: Create a query that finds all female students who have a GPA greater than 2.5.

STEP 8: Create a printed report of the information about each student that allows the dean of students to identify only those who qualify for Latin honors (top 5 percent of their class). ●

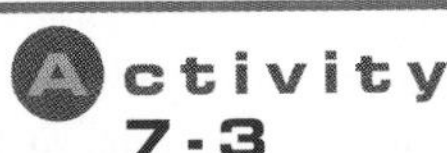

Using Database Systems to Improve Customer Service

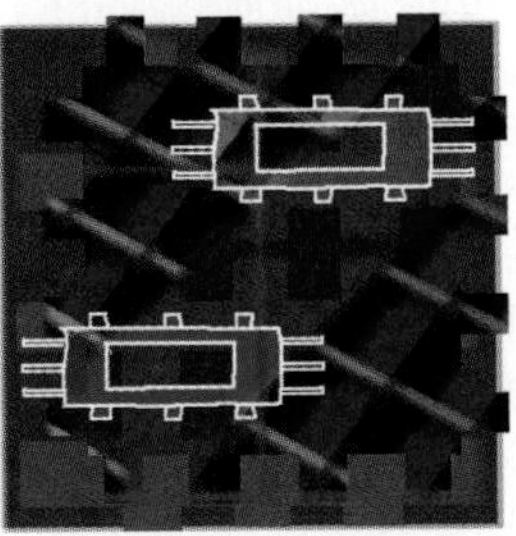

short case

STEP 1: You are the new regional sales manager for Akron Industrials, a medium-size company that distributes household supplies to pharmacies and hardware stores. You have been reading about the use of databases as a sales tool and believe that the salespeople in your regions would significantly improve their performance if they had access to a database. Top management has agreed that introducing such a database system is feasible and has asked you to develop a proposal for such an introduction.

STEP 2: Individually or in small groups, develop such a proposal. Briefly describe the nature of the hardware and software required. Discuss the likely costs as well as the financial benefits of such a system. Where possible, cite specific examples.

STEP 3: In small groups or with the entire class, share your proposals. Then answer the following questions:

1. What elements do these plans have in common?
2. How well do the plans respond to the information needs for salespeople at Akron Industrials?
3. What other options exist for improving their performance?
4. What justification exists for purchasing the hardware and software required for a salesperson database system?
5. What should be the components of an effective and responsive database management system for the salespeople? ●

Problems in Database Administration

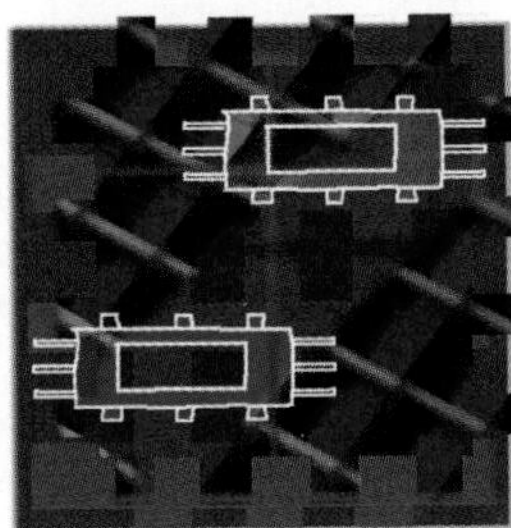

short case

STEP 1: Read the following problems with administering a centralized database system. For each problem, decide what you would do, and then offer a way of preventing the situation from occurring again.

Problem 1: Since its installation the centralized database at Watson Manufacturing has had duplicate records. When customer service converted to its new system it did not want any duplicate records transferred from the centralized database to the new system. Therefore, the department personnel carefully reviewed all records, identified duplicates, and purged them from the system. Several months after this occurred, the director of market research attempted to analyze the potential customer base for a new product the company was considering. The director was distressed to find that some customers were labeled "duplicate record" and that no further information about them existed. The director was further outraged that anyone could erase information about customers from the database.

Problem 2: Human resources (HR) is responsible for capturing and maintaining personnel data. HR quit the centralized system because of concerns over system security. However, certain personnel data, which had been maintained by HR, were also used by a number of other offices. When HR abandoned the system, it informed administrative systems that it would not pass new or changed information to other offices. Maintaining employee addresses, locating employees in emergencies, generating mailing labels, verifying employment, and countless other functions now all had to be routed through HR because data on the central system became unreliable. Management reports or analyses requiring the merging of HR data with other system data (e.g., employee workload analysis) became impossible. Multiple, alternative, and disparate personnel files began to be maintained by various offices, each for its own office's use. The advantages of a common database were lost, and people could not understand why administrative systems, which maintained the database, couldn't just "fix" this.[32]

Problem 3: Jennifer Smith recently joined the Hartley Engine Company as its first database administrator. Hartley Engine had a sophisticated distributed database management system that encompassed all basic business functions. The system had grown from a multitude of individually designed applications to a coherent system that an external consultant had designed and implemented. Managers at Hartley were used to making their own decisions about what data would be included in the database, who would have access to the data, and what applications should be included. Making changes in the system had been as easy as writing a request for the IS department to make the adjustment. After her first month on the job, Jennifer discovered that the system was not working as efficiently as it should be: Managers often had to use convoluted ways to access data held in remote locations; the security for data access was ineffective, and anyone could read confidential information; no rationale existed for placing data on the corporate database as opposed to retaining it on local microcomputers. The system was overloaded, processing was slow, and it was costing the company at least three times the money that was reasonable for a firm the size of Hartley.

STEP 2: In groups of four to six students, reach a consensus about how to handle each situation.

STEP 3: In small groups, with the entire class, or in written form, as directed by your instructor, offer a set of five guidelines for developing an effective way of administering a centralized database system. How would these guidelines change if the database system were distributed? ●

Notes

[1]Gary H. Anthes, In depth: High-tech heroes, *Computerworld* (June 15, 1992): 97.

[2]William M. Bulkeley, Databases are plagued by reign of error, *Wall Street Journal* (May 26, 1992): B6.

[3]See P. A. Bernstein, V. Hadzilacos, and N. Goodman, *Concurrency Control and Recovery in Database Systems* (Reading, MA: Addison-Wesley, 1987). For a discussion of concurrency control in less traditional applications, see N. S. Barghouti and G. E. Kaiser, Concurrency control in advanced database applications, *ACM Computing Surveys* 23(3) (September 1991): 269–317.

[4]A survey is presented in T. Haerder and A. Reuter, Principles of transaction oriented database recovery—A taxonomy, *ACM Computing Surveys* 15(4) (December 1983): 287–317. See also Bernstein et al., op. cit.

[5]For a discussion of security issues and techniques, see T. F. Lunt and E. B. Fernandez, Database security, *Sigmod Record* 19(4) (December 1990): 90–97.

[6]For a full discussion, see A. Shoshani, Statistical databases: Characteristics, problems, and some solutions, *Proceedings of 8th International Conference on Very Large Data Bases,* Mexico City, Mexico, September 1982.

[7]Melinda-Carol Ballon, CompuServe database simplifies fish-tracking task, *Computerworld* (December 28, 1992): 103, 108.

[8]See N. Roussopoulos and A. Delis, Modern client-server DBMS architectures, *Sigmod Record* 20(3) (September 1991): 52–61.

[9]Gary H. Anthes, U.S. House awaits relief from old IS technology, *Computerworld* (December 3, 1990): 25, 29.

[10]See M. T. Ozsu and P. Valduriez, *Principles of Distributed Database Systems* (Englewood Cliffs, NJ: Prentice-Hall, 1991).

[11]W. Cellary, E. Gelenbe, and T. Morzy, *Concurrency Control in Distributed Database Systems* (Amsterdam: North-Holland, 1988).

[12]S. R. Gordon and J. R. Gordon, Organizational hurdles to distributed database management systems (DDBMS) adoption, *Information & Management* 22 (1992): 333–345.

[13]E. F. Codd, A relational model of data for large shared databanks, *Communications of the ACM* 13(6) (June 1970).

[14]American National Standards Institute, *Database Language SQL, ANSI X3.168-1992,* 1992. (See International Organization for Standardization, *Database Language SQL, ISO DIS 9075:1991,* 1991.)

[15]For a detailed description, see CODASYL Systems Committee, *A Survey of Generalized Data Base Management Systems,* Technical Report, May 1991. Available from ACM.

[16]Data Base Task Group of CODASYL Programming Language Committee, *Report,* 1971. Available from ACM.

[17]For a detailed description, see CODASYL Systems Committee, *Feature Analysis of Generalized Data Base Management Systems,* Technical Report, May 1971. Available from ACM.

[18]W. Kim, Object-oriented databases: Definition and research directions, *IEEE Transactions of Knowledge and Data Engineering* 2(3) (September 1990): 327–341; D. Livingston, Here come object-oriented databases!, *Systems Integration* (July 1990): 50–58.

[19]An interview with Paul Butterworth, *Database Programming & Design* (July 1991): 55–62.

[20]J. S. Bozman, First links between object, relational databases forged, *Computerworld* (July 27, 1992): 12.

[21]P. Palvia, On end-user computing productivity: Results of controlled experiments, *Information & Management* 21(4) (November 1991): 217–224.

[22]P. Chen, The entity-relationship model—Toward a unified view of data, *ACM Transactions on Database Systems* 1(1) (1976); Robert W. Blanning, An entity-relationship framework for information resource management, *Information & Management* 15(2) (September 1988): 113–119.

[23]D. C. Blair and M. D. Gordon, The management and control of written information: Growing concern amid the failure of traditional methods, *Information & Management* 20(4) (April 1991): 239–246.

[24]M. O'Leary, Reuter's Textline specializes in covering the foreign scene, *Link-Up* 9(3) (May/June, 1992): 24–25.

[25]R. Snodgrass, Temporal databases: Status and research directions, *Sigmod Record* 19(4) (December 1990): 83–89; M. D. Soo, Bibliography on temporal databases, *Sigmod Record* 20(1) (March 1991): 14–23.

[26]O. Guenther and A. Buchmann, Research issues in spatial databases, *Sigmod Record* 19(4) (December 1990): 90–97.

[27]D. Slater, Adabas stays one step ahead, *Computerworld* (August 17, 1992): 66.

[28]See, for example, R. Finkelstein, Benchmark wars, *DBMS* (February 1990): 14.

[29]P. O'Neil, Revisiting DBMS benchmarks, *Datamation* 3(15) (September 15, 1989): 47–54.

[30]Julia King, Demand for database managers intensifies, *Computerworld* (September 23, 1991): 81.

[31]Lisa Levinson, Tales of migration, *Database Programming & Design* (February 1992): 26–34.

[32]Reprinted from P. T. Farago, J. Whitmore-First, and E. A. Kallman, Managing data standards and policies in an integrated environment, *Journal of Systems Management* (March 1992): 33.

Recommended Readings

Cattell, R. G. G. *Object Data Management: Object-Oriented and Extended Relational Database Systems* (Reading, MA: Addison-Wesley, 1991).

Chen, P. "The Entity-Relationship Model—Toward a Unified View of Data," *ACM Transactions on Database Systems,* 1:1, 1976.

Codd, E. F. "A Relational Model of Data for Large Shared Databanks," *Communications of the ACM,* 13:6, June 1970.

Date, C. J. *An Introduction to Database Systems,* 5th ed. (Reading, MA: Addison-Wesley, 1990).

Hawryszkiewycz, I. T. *Database Analysis and Design,* 2nd ed. (New York: Macmillan, 1991).

Ozsu, M. T. and Valduriez, P. *Principles of Distributed Database Systems* (Englewood Cliffs, NJ: Prentice-Hall, 1991).

Shepherd, J. C. *Database Management: Theory and Application,* 3rd ed. (Homewood, IL: Irwin, 1990).

Chapter 8

Data Communication

OUTLINE

LEARNING OBJECTIVES

After completing the reading and activities for Chapter 8, students will be able to

1. Describe ways of measuring the capacity of communication lines.
2. Cite the uses, advantages, and disadvantages of five telecommunications media.
3. Discuss the function of interface devices in communication.
4. Illustrate the nature and use of communication standards and protocols.
5. Compare and contrast local area networks and wide area networks.
6. Distinguish between client/server, peer-to-peer, and unstructured architectures.
7. Define downsizing and discuss its role in improving organizational performance.
8. Distinguish among routers, gateways, and switches, and comment about the role of each in effective communication.
9. Briefly describe five applications of communication technology.
10. Discuss the issues that affect international data communication.

Electra Lighting sells lamps, lighting fixtures, and other electrical components through both wholesale and retail channels. The company also assembles special-order products from components it stocks in its warehouse. A $20 million company, Electra employs approximately 100 employees in various aspects of administration, sales, service, warehousing, and assembly.

Electra recently hired a consultant to evaluate its information systems and assess how well they were meeting the company's information needs. This study was prompted by Electra's top management's feeling that it lacked easily accessible, high-quality information for making important tactical and strategic decisions. Too often top management used incomplete or inaccurate information, and it had no effective system for making solid pricing, inventory, and distribution decisions. The sales department, too, felt that it operated in a vacuum. Too often a sales employee would promise customers next-day delivery only to discover that the required inventory was not available. Limited information sharing between departments occurred, which resulted in a cumbersome system for updating data about customers, suppliers, and products. No flagging of overdue accounts occurred for the sales staff, who in some cases continued to sell to long delinquent customers. Pricing of special-order items was often inaccurate because the sales staff could not readily access data about the costs of various components, particularly those obtained by rush orders or in special bulk purchases.

After extensively analyzing all parts of the business, the consultant recommended that Electra replace the single minicomputer it used for all data processing activities with a network of microcomputers to improve its data communication. The consultant believed that implementing this recommendation would result in improved information sharing within the company. Improving data communication should also speed the updating of data in the various departments and ensure the availability of accurate information for pricing, inventory, and purchasing decisions. Improving data communication between the company and its customers and suppliers could speed the distribution of products and reduce the administrative overhead involved in purchasing and sales.

Top management agreed to the consultant's recommendation and assigned Tom Hurley, the newly hired company comptroller, to oversee the change. Tom formed a committee of managers and staff employees from the major departments to work with the computer consultants who would be developing and installing the new system to ensure it would meet the employee's needs.

In this chapter we examine some of the issues Tom Hurley and his committee should consider in working with the computer consultant. The consultant has diagnosed Electra's information needs, evaluated the existing computer systems, and determined that data communications should be redesigned. Tom and his committee should assist the consultant in revisiting Electra's information needs and ensuring that the redesigned communications system meets them.

We first discuss the basic issues associated with data communication. Next we examine various types and components of networks. The chapter concludes with a consideration of international data communication.

Data Communication Basics

Data communication refers to the transfer of data between two or more computers. The new computer system at Electra Lighting is intended to improve interaction among departments by enabling data communication among computers in sales, service, assembly, warehouse, and administration. For example, computers in the sales department and the warehouse department might communicate to give users in both areas information about current inventory levels. Computers in the accounting and sales departments might communicate to ensure that both groups have current information about customer accounts and outstanding accounts receivable. In addition, data communication might occur between computers at Electra Lighting and computers at customers' and suppliers' sites; the companies might establish direct links for entering and filling sales orders and purchase orders.

Data communication requires at least the following five steps, as shown in Figure 8-1. First, one computer outputs its data to a communications device. Second, the device creates a signal on the transmission medium. Third, the medium transports the data from source to destination. Fourth, another device at the destination converts the signal to computer input. Finally, the receiving computer accepts the input data.

Although computer professionals use complex equipment and software for data communication, managers and other users do not need a highly technical background to make reasoned decisions about connecting computers or transmitting information between them. Organizational members should act as intelligent consumers of communication equipment and services. This section focuses on five basic concepts that help users evaluate the effectiveness of the data communication system for meeting their information needs: 1) the capacity of data communication hardware, 2) the transmission media, 3) types of data communication devices, 4) terminal software, and 5) the role of standards and protocols in effective communication.

FIGURE 8-1 Steps in Data Communication

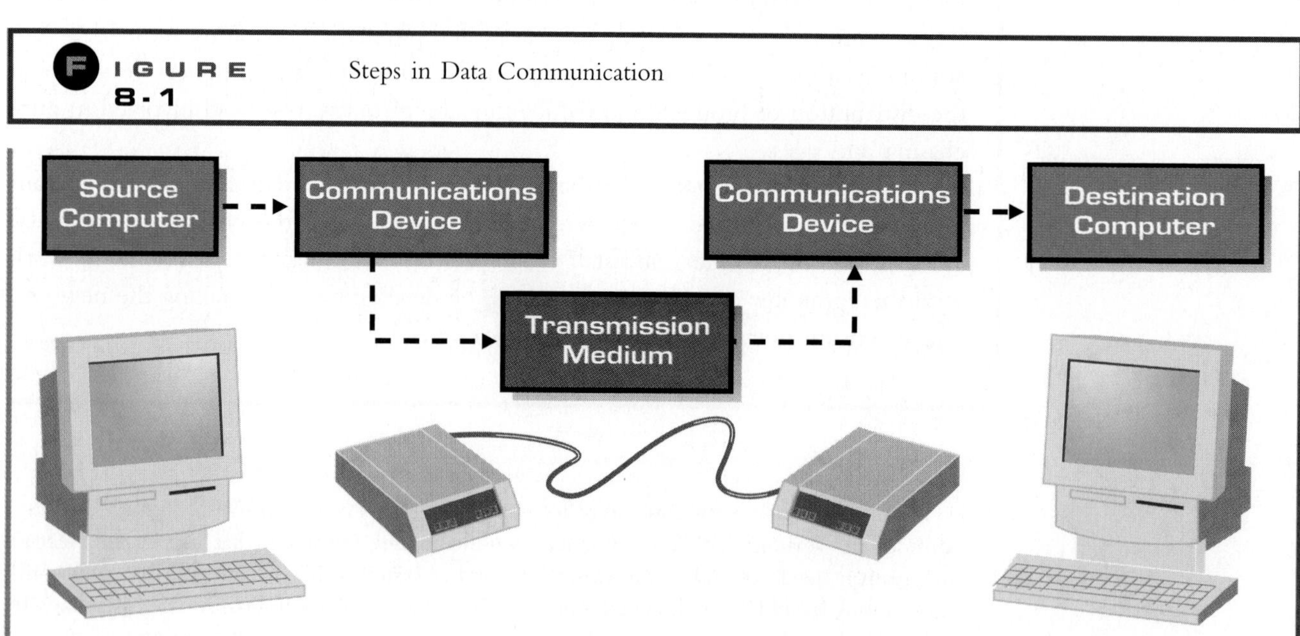

Hardware Capacity

A **communication channel** is a path that data follow as they move from their source to their destination computer. Electra Lighting's new system might have communication channels between one or more microcomputers in the sales department and warehouse; it might also have channels between the computers in the accounting department and selected customers' purchasing departments. The computer channel resembles a water channel such as a river or stream. A river can carry only a fixed volume of water in a specified period; if more water streams into the river, it will overflow its banks. Similarly, a computer user who attempts to send more data through a communication channel than it can carry will lose information.

The capacity of a communication channel is usually measured using either bits per second or bandwidth. **Bits per second (bps)** specifies the maximum number of bits of data that a channel can accept in one second without losing information. This measure is a very practical one that users can apply to determine whether the capacity of a channel meets their needs for communicating data; they should purchase equipment and media that can move bits of data between their computers at a rate that satisfies their current and moderate-term needs.

Bandwidth is a more theoretical concept that data communication professionals use to measure the information-carrying capacity of a communication channel. The unit of bandwidth is a **hertz,** the number of times a signal (normally in the form of a wave) can be repeated in a second. As a generality, doubling the bandwidth will double the bps data capacity. However, the relationship between bandwidth and bps is complicated by such factors as the strength of the information-carrying signal compared with the amount of electrical interference (noise) and the efficiency with which the data communication devices use all the available bandwidth.

Each device or medium in the communication chain has a capacity that can also be measured in bps or bandwidth. The device or medium with the smallest capacity sets the limit on the capacity of the communication channel. For example, Builders' Outlet, a large chain of building supply superstores, electronically orders fixtures from Electra Lighting. Builders' Outlet uses a communication device that can send data over the phone line at up to 9,600 bps. The phone company can transmit data over its network at 9,600 bps. But Electra's communication device can receive data at no more than 2,400 bps. As a result, the channel between Builders' Outlet and Electra Lighting is limited to 2,400 bps. The volume of transactions between Electra and Builders' Outlet is sufficiently low that Electra has not considered upgrading the capacity of its communication device.

Control messages that sending and receiving computers transmit to each other to ensure the integrity of transmitted data reduce the effective capacity of a communication channel. For example, many data communication software packages send data in **packets** of a fixed number of bytes. A packet may contain a special code to mark its beginning and another to mark its end. Packets may also include information, such as the address of the intended recipient and a count of bits in the message set to 1 (as opposed to 0) so that the receiving computer can verify that the packet received is identical to the packet sent. Each ancillary code and message takes up some of the channel capacity and reduces the capacity available for data.

Compression software can be used to shorten a message at the sending computer so that it requires less capacity for data communication. Similar software at the receiving computer restores the message to its original form without loss of data. Data representing pictures with a high percentage of white space can often be compressed by a factor of 100, or even more. Vendors of data communication hardware generally ignore control messages and compression when specifying communication capacity for their devices or media unless these techniques are built into their hardware.

Telecommunications Media

The **medium of transmission** refers to the carrier of a data signal between two or more computers. The most common media include twisted-pair wire, coaxial cable, fiber optic cable, microwave signals, infrared signals, and radio frequencies. Figure 8-2 highlights the most relevant characteristics of the most commonly used media. Tom Hurley and his committee likely will discuss with the consultant the most appropriate media for Electra's data communication. Obviously they must consider the price, capacity, durability, and flexibility of any media they choose for meeting their needs in the short and long run.

Twisted-pair wire connects a telephone to its jack in most homes. It offers the advantage of low cost and high availability. Many buildings have excessive amounts of this wire that can be used for telecommunications purposes. In the mid-1980s, data communication over voice-grade, twisted-pair wire typically could not exceed 10K bits per second. However, by the early 1990s, the technology for sending data over this medium had developed significantly, allowing transmission speeds of up to 10M bits per second. Twisted-pair wire is also available in higher grades, supporting data transmission rates of up to 100M bits per second at a modest premium in cost. Despite the promise of higher-capacity media, twisted-pair cabling continues to be the primary medium for telecommunications (see Figure 8-3).

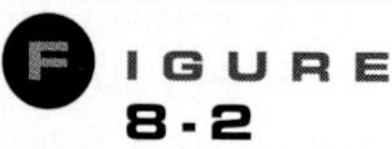

FIGURE 8-2 Characteristics of Data Communication Media

Twisted-pair wire	Least expensive Widely available Moderate capacity Easy to install
Coaxial cable	Moderately expensive Moderate to high capacity Cumbersome and thick wires Entry into homes through cable TV
Fiber optic cable	Relatively expensive Very high capacity Very high security Difficult to bend or manipulate
Microwave signals	Expensive Requires no cabling Can use satellite Best for high volume, long distance Limited to line of sight
Infrared and radio signals	Inexpensive Low to moderate capacity Short-distance limitation Requires no cabling Limited to line of sight

NOTE: Expense is calculated for the lowest capacity connection between two points and does not include the cost of signal boosting devices for long-distance connections.

FIGURE 8-3 Twisted-Pair Remains the Most Popular Cabling Medium

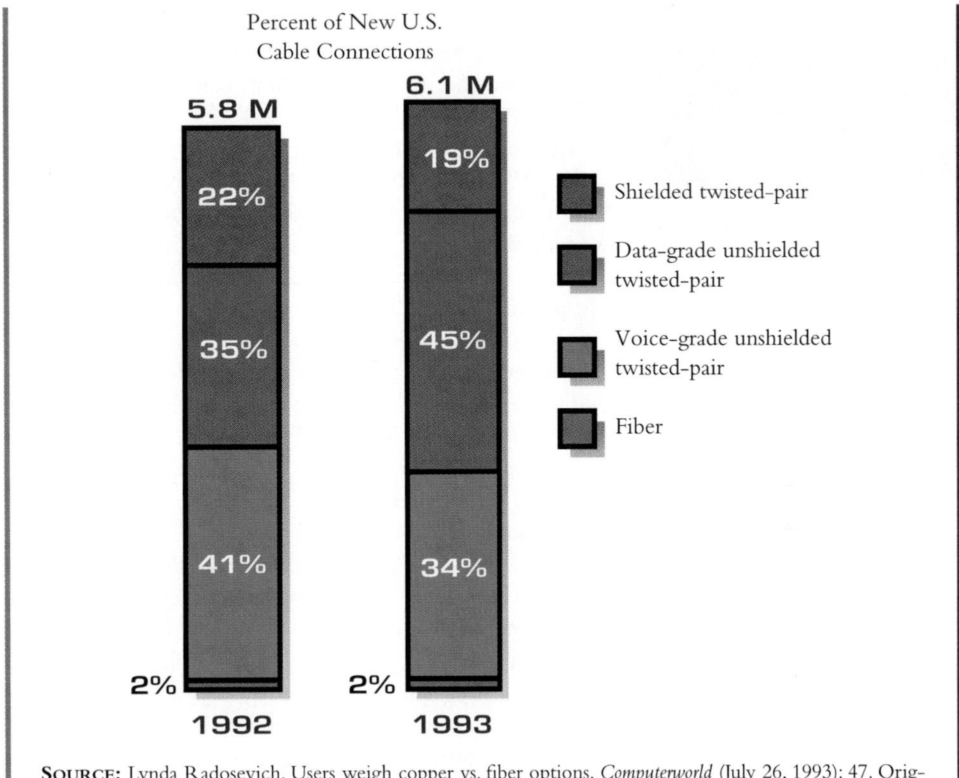

SOURCE: Lynda Radosevich, Users weigh copper vs. fiber options, *Computerworld* (July 26, 1993): 47. Original source: Forrester Research, Inc., Cambridge, MA.

Cable television companies use **coaxial cable** to bring television signals into the home. It is more bulky, more expensive, and less common in the conduits of existing buildings than twisted-pair wire. Theoretically, it has a higher bandwidth, but communication device manufacturers, responding to consumer demand for twisted-pair capacity, have developed devices and standards for twisted-pair wire that provide bit-per-second throughput roughly equivalent to that achieved with standard coaxial cable devices.

Fiber optic cable carries messages on a beam of light rather than using an electrical signal and has the greatest capacity of the telecommunications media. Many long-distance telephone companies use fiber optic cable to carry thousands of telephone calls simultaneously between major switching stations. Private companies also use fiber optic cable to carry data within their buildings and between closely spaced sites. This medium offers great security because of its low resistance to tapping. It also provides greater immunity to electrical interference than does electrical cable. But fiber optic cable is the most expensive cable medium; it is also fragile and difficult to install. Companies are increasingly using fiber distributed data interface (FDDI), a technology that uses fiber optic cables in networking, particularly to link buildings inside a 6-mile radius.[1] The use of FDDI should increase even more with recent improvements in the technology that mates it with twisted-pair wire, thus reducing the cost of replacing copper cable with fiber.

The price of fiber optic cable has been dropping rapidly, but as of 1994 it remained at least 20 times more expensive than the cheapest twisted-pair wire when purchased in bulk.

Cables are a popular transmission medium.

Courtesy of International Business Machines Corporation.

However, its capacity is more than 1,000 times that of twisted-pair wire, so it is far cheaper when measured in dollars per bps. In addition, fiber optic cable can transmit a signal over 100 miles without the assistance of any intermediate electronic devices. Copper, in contrast, requires electronic devices called **repeaters** to boost the signal because it weakens, or attenuates, as it travels through the cable. Depending on its grade and intended capacity, copper cable requires repeaters spaced between 1,000 feet to 5 miles from one another. These repeaters and the maintenance they require add to the effective cost of copper cabling over extended distances.

Microwave signals also carry data. Microwaves can be transmitted through the air among stations located within view of one another. Relay towers can be used for long-distance transmission; they receive an incoming signal and retransmit it to another station. Companies may also buy capacity on a communications satellite that orbits the earth to receive and retransmit their microwave signals. Microwave equipment is expensive, but microwave is the only practical medium that a company can use to transmit data over long distances without employing the services of a telephone company.

HAWKEYE BANK & TRUST

WRIGHT-PATTERSON AIR FORCE BASE

LEHMAN BROTHERS

Infrared signals and **radio frequencies** carry data for short distances, such as within a building; infrared signals function only within a line of sight, whereas radio waves can penetrate walls. A large number of vendors now supply wireless hardware for intercomputer communication. Hawkeye Bank & Trust Company recently used radio-frequency technology to add several small, nearby branches to its local communication network and used directional antennas to connect several remote branches to its headquarters.[2] Wireless links can penetrate walls, although they must generally reside on the same floor.[3] Wright-Patterson Air Force Base uses wireless systems to supplement cable; using some radio frequencies helps speed changes in communication systems by reducing the time required to install cable.[4] Lehman Brothers has pilot tested wireless electronic mail on its trading floors to increase the number of daily trades; the company uses a pen-computing/wireless combination to replace telephone calls and written documentation.[5] Although capacity varies, the high-end systems can provide nearly the same capacity as most coaxial cable systems. The lack of standards about capacity and speed may hamper the development and acceptance of wireless systems.[6]

Many organizations use telephone companies or other private carriers to transmit their long-distance data communications, relieving them of the need to worry about the communication media used. Telephone companies use a variety and often a combination of media to carry a signal from its source to its destination.

Interface Devices

Interface devices output data from a computer onto a communications medium or process signals from a communications medium for input into a computer. As explained in Chapter 6, a computer represents data internally as a series of bits. Recall that a bit can take on one of two possible values or states. To present a bit on a transmission medium, a computer can output a high- or low-voltage signal for a period of time. As bits are output from the computer, these high and low voltages form a signal known as a **digital signal** (see Figure 8-4). In contrast, a telephone handset produces a smooth electrical wave that corresponds to .the pressure wave produced in the air by the sound of your voice. This smooth wave is known as an **analog signal** (see Figure 8-5). One of the earliest interface devices, known as an **acoustic coupler,** consisted of a cradle in which the telephone handset could be placed along with electronics to produce an analog tone from a digital signal. A similar acoustic coupler at the receiving end converted the transmitted sound into a series of bits.

A device, such as an acoustic coupler, that converts a digital to an analog and an analog to a digital signal is called a **modem.** Today's modems bypass the telephone handset and send a signal directly to the telephone's wall connector, known as an **RJ-11 jack.** An **inter-**

FIGURE 8-4 A Digital Signal

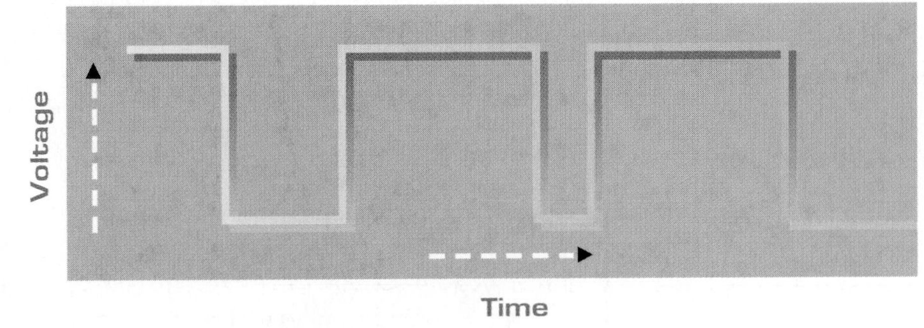

nal modem** is a circuit board that resides inside a computer and has a connector, extending through the back of the computer, for a telephone cord. Communications software can use this device directly to convert data to and from signals suitable for transmission over phone lines. An **external modem** is a stand-alone device that has one connection for a telephone cord and one connection for a cable to the computer's serial port. Communications software dealing with an external modem sends digital signals through the serial port to the modem, which converts them to analog signals for output to the telephone line.

Modems differ significantly in the speed with which they transmit data, ranging from 1,200 bps to 28,800 bps for typical microcomputer uses. Most computer applications now require at least a 2,400-bps modem, and increasingly 14,400-bps, for effective data transmission. Modems also differ in the technologies they use to encode and decode their signals and to coordinate the timing between the sender and receiver of information. The two most common technologies are called **synchronous** and **asynchronous communication.** Asynchronous modems have captured the microcomputer markets, while synchronous modems are more common among minicomputers (particularly IBMs) and mainframes. The two types of modems are not compatible with each other.

Minicomputers and mainframes often employ devices that can simultaneously send and receive signals over multiple phone lines. These devices typically include a circuit board inside the computer with a thick cable to a computerized switchboard or to a separate device that has sockets for many phone lines. Such devices tend to be proprietary to the minicomputer or mainframe vendor.

Another data communication device employed by minicomputer and mainframe users is a **multiplexor,** a device that combines the signals from multiple computers into a single phone line for long-distance transmission to another multiplexor that separates the signals at the receiving end. More complex and intelligent devices, usually called **controllers,** are needed to combine and route messages over an organized multicomputer network; other devices to route messages between networks are discussed later in this chapter in the section "Connecting Networks."

Terminal Software

Terminal software supports a temporary connection, typically a telephone connection, between two computers, and it resides at two locations. Software at the **remote computer,** the computer originating the connection, sends signals to the communication device, typically a modem. These signals call the destination computer, also known as the **host.** The host, typically a multiuser computer, accepts the call. The host does not distinguish between

FIGURE 8-5 An Analog Signal

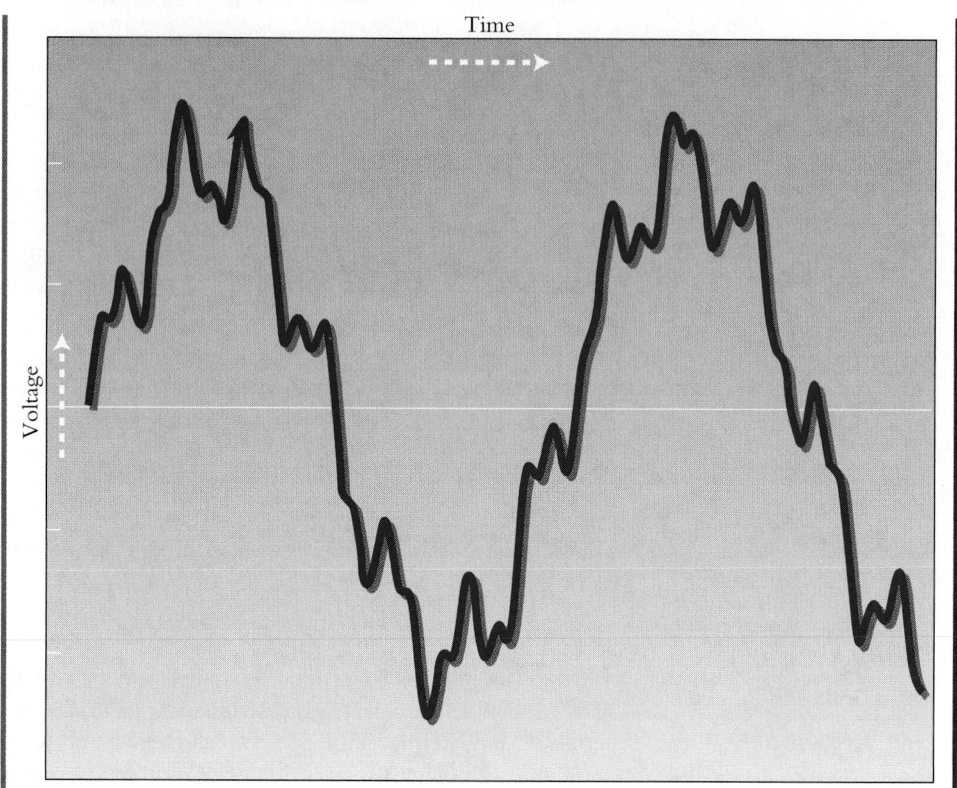

a terminal as a caller or a computer running terminal software as the caller. When the connection is completed, the terminal software passes keystrokes typed at the remote keyboard to the host computer and displays characters sent by the host on the screen of the remote computer.

Installing terminal software at the host computer that matches software at the remote computer allows the remote computer operator to initiate a transfer of files between the two computers. The terminal software on the remote computer communicates with similar software on the host to ensure the successful transfer of files. Chapter 5 discusses other desirable features of terminal software.

Communication Standards and Protocols

The computer and communications industries have developed standards—specific characteristics of telecommunications equipment—that make it possible to mix computer and communications equipment from different vendors. Such data communication standards exist at a variety of levels, along dimensions that range from the shape and size of connectors between computers and communication devices to the logical interface between applications and network operating systems. Typically, several standards at each level exist to provide multiple combinations of price and power. Data communication professionals who understand these standards can choose equipment from competing vendors to assemble working data communication channels between computers that meet users' needs. We describe some of these standards in more detail later in this chapter.

Data communication software and devices follow standard procedures called **protocols** that establish acceptable connections between devices, ensure the integrity of data transmission, and protect against the simultaneous transmission of data by two or more computers sharing the same transmission medium. When one computer initiates communication with another, as part of a protocol the first computer ensures that the other computer is ready to receive its transmission. The communication devices associated with each computer send a prescribed series of messages back and forth at the beginning of a conversation to verify their readiness to transmit and accept data, agree upon a transmission speed, and agree upon a format for transferring the data.

Once transmission begins, again as part of the protocol, data communication devices may send signals to each other to verify the integrity of the transferred data. The devices compare the data received with the data sent because transmission media do not operate reliably. Other electronic signals sent through the same medium, sunspot activity, cable breaks, and random electronic interference can corrupt a data signal. If a receiving computer detects data corruption, it returns a message to the sending computer to retransmit the data. The sending computer must send data in one of several special formats to allow the receiving computer to detect errors in the data stream. These formats permit the receiving device or software on the receiving computer to assess the quality of the data and, upon detecting an error, to tell the sending computer which data it should retransmit. Some formats permit a computer to correct the received information so long as only a small percentage of the data has been corrupted.[7] Obviously, the data communication system at Electra Lighting will include protocols for detecting errors and retransmitting corrupted data.

Networks

Most data communication occurs in networks of people and computers. A **network** refers to a collection of individuals, work groups, departments, divisions, or organizations that agree to communicate with one another, together with the computers, communication devices, and media that enable such communication. Electra Lighting might develop a network that includes all users and computers in the accounting, purchasing, and warehousing departments. They might develop a second network that includes all users and computers in the sales and service departments as well as a prescribed group of suppliers and customers.

Users form a network to share data, programs, and output devices. The sales staff at Electra, for example, might require seven computers but only two printers; they may also wish to share information about clients and products. Microcomputer users find a network particularly helpful for sharing data because exchanging diskettes to share information is slow and cumbersome. Also, storing multiple copies of the same programs on each computer wastes precious storage. Creating copies of data makes it difficult to ensure their consistency, particularly if the data are modified regularly. Finally, giving each user a dedicated printer, such as a laser printer, is wasteful because individual users can rarely keep printers busy all the time.

Most networks that extend beyond a single organization, such as a telephone network, are formalized among the participants by contract and may employ third parties to provide and administer the network hardware. Many individuals, organizations, or other parties belong to several networks. For example, a sales manager may belong to four independent networks: a telephone voice-mail network; a network of computer users in the sales department; a network of sales specialists who share technical information on an electronic bulletin board; and a corporate electronic mail network.

The term **network** also describes the hardware connections among computers that coordinate operations and share data with one another. Such networks, called **clusters,** increase the processing power of minicomputers and mainframes. When furnished with the proper hardware, the operating systems of two or more connected computers can determine which among them has the most spare capacity to perform tasks. The cluster then acts as a single computer, sharing secondary storage, printers, and even jointly providing output to a single screen. The networked computers appear to be a single computer from the user's perspective. Typically, computer professionals decide whether to use networks to integrate computers so tightly. The communication channels in such networks require high megabyte-per-second or gigabyte-per-second capacity to support their integration. IBM, for example, plans to cluster its RS/6000 RISC workstations using a 1G bit-per-second fiber channel.[8]

Network software supports the creation and continued operation of a network. A network operating system includes software that enables network participants to share common resources and communicate with one another. Portions of the network operating system must reside on the computers of each network participant. Other parts of the network operating system reside at a single station, typically the network server that initiates communication among the parties to the network. Chapter 5 discusses the features of a network operating system in more detail.

Evaluating the appropriateness of networks for data communication involves understanding the available network types and architectures. It means knowing the options for connecting networks as well as standards for forming and operating networks. Finally, such an assessment calls for understanding situations in which networks should replace mainframes and minicomputers.

Local Area Networks

Metropolitan Life Insurance

Miller Mason & Dickenson

Local area networks (LANs) connect parties in the same building or in clusters of buildings within a few miles of one another. A LAN uses media, typically cable, dedicated especially to it. Universities, for example, may use LANs to connect computers in faculty and administrative offices, and even in student residence halls.[9] Metropolitan Life Insurance Company replaced 100 minicomputers in the field with LANs of personal computers.[10] Miller Mason & Dickenson, a benefits consulting firm, switched from centralized computing to a series of LANs in most of its nine offices as a way of becoming more responsive to its clients; the largest networks have 150 and 200 users on them.[11]

Due to the widespread acceptance of standards, the decreasing cost of hardware, and the increasing sophistication and power of network operating systems, organizations are implementing LANs at a remarkable pace; the number of personal computers connected to LANs, estimated at only 3 million in 1987, had grown to an estimated 33 to 37 million by 1992.[12]

LANs have been blamed for the drop in mainframe and minicomputer usage. As discussed in Chapter 5, PC monitors provide a graphics capability that mainframes and minicomputers cannot easily replicate. Furthermore, they have lower costs per MIP, are easily scalable, and usually have lower software costs. However, without LANs, data collected and processed at individual workstations could not easily be shared, limiting the PC to isolated applications. The development of LAN equipment eliminated this limitation, allowing PCs to compete with mainframes and minicomputers for companywide applications. LANs can also be used to connect PCs to larger computers for **cooperative processing,** using each type of equipment for what it does best.

LAN Technology

Although designing and implementing a LAN is a complex task best performed by network specialists, nontechnical managers should understand the terminology surrounding LAN technology. This section defines some of the key terms and concepts of LAN design. Discussion of the advantages and disadvantages of alternative designs is beyond the scope of this text.

IBM's OS/2 LAN Server software helps network specialists manage the resources of a local area network.

Courtesy of International Business Machines Corporation.

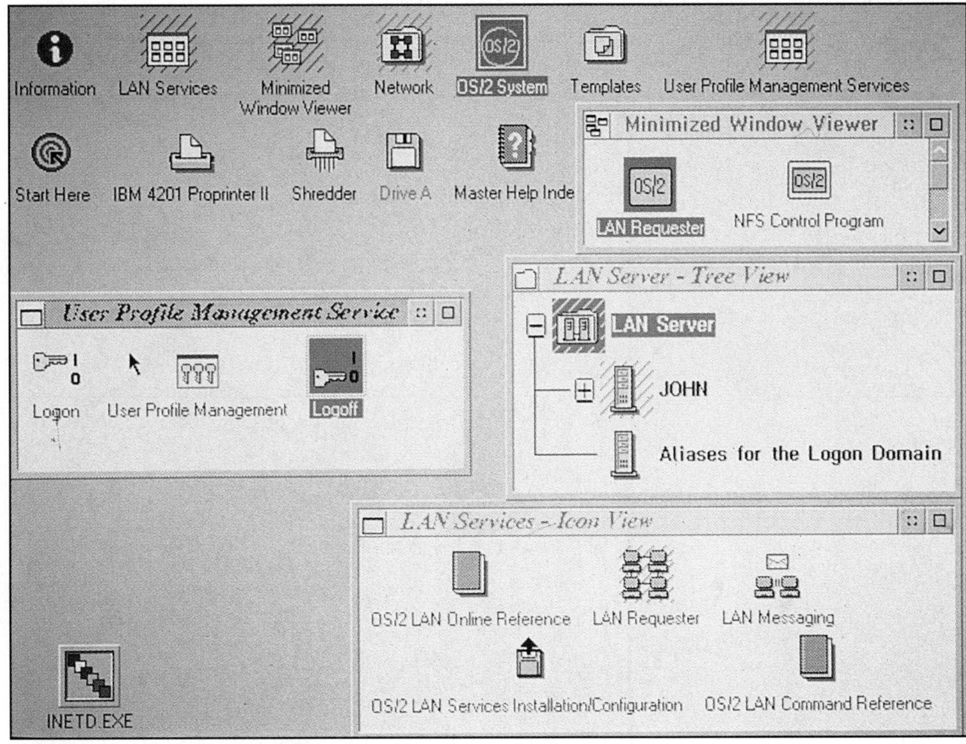

Topology refers to the structure of interconnections among the workstations and devices attached to the network. The most common topologies are ring, bus, and star. A **ring topology** consists of a series of repeaters joined point to point into a closed loop (see Figure 8-6). A workstation or device is connected to each repeater. To transmit data from one device to another, the originating device sends its message, enveloped in a packet identifying the intended recipient, to its repeater. This repeater sends the packet directly to the next repeater, which, in turn, examines the packet address to determine its destination. In most cases, the repeater simply passes the packet to the next repeater in sequence. When the repeater recognizes packets destined for its device, it sends the packet to the device rather than forwarding it to the next repeater. Often a ring topology uses a pair of loops to provide redundancy and to reduce delays by passing messages in opposite directions.

A **bus topology** exists when all workstations and devices are connected to a single communication medium without any repeaters (see Figure 8-7). Messages are enveloped in a packet, as with the ring technology, and placed on the medium to be read by all the devices. Each device accepts signals intended for it and ignores all other signals. A device at the end of the bus, called a **terminator,** absorbs all signals to remove them from the network.

A **star topology** exists when all workstations and devices are connected to a single central repeater/switch (see Figure 8-8). The switch reads the address of any message it receives and forwards it directly to the intended recipient.

Layout refers to the physical shape of a network. Layouts may be linear, tree, star, or some combination of these options. A **linear layout** seeks to minimize the amount of cable used by connecting nearby devices to one another so that they all line up along the cable. Either a bus or ring topology can be used with a linear layout.

A **tree layout** can reduce the amount of cable even further by allowing branches in the cable medium. For example, a single cable can run among the floors of a building, with sev-

FIGURE 8-6 Ring Topology

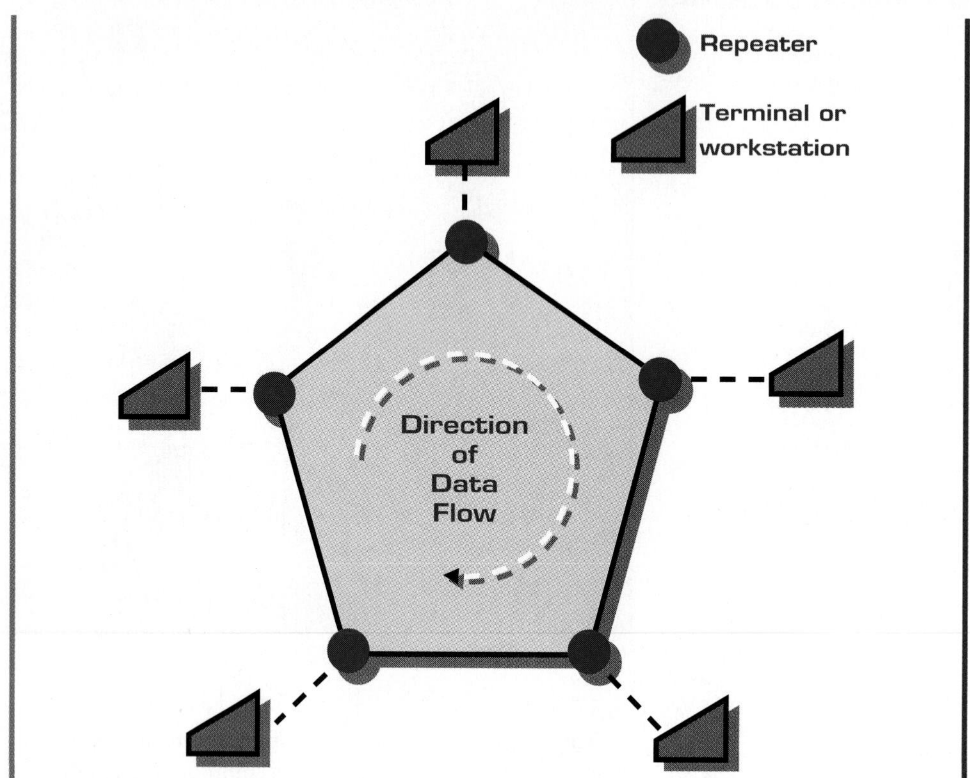

eral branches heading in different directions on each floor. A tree is best implemented with a bus topology.

A **star layout** uses an individual cable from a central point to each device on the network. This layout requires the most cable but reduces the impact of cable breakage and allows ring, bus, or star topologies. If ring or bus topologies are used, a very short ring or bus is "hidden" at the central point, and long "taps" are used to reach the network devices.

Signaling technologies can be **baseband** or **broadband.** Baseband uses a digital signal, while broadband uses an analog signal. The choice of signaling technology has implications for the type of medium used and even for the network topology and layout. Several standards exist within each technology for different transmission capacity requirements.

Access control techniques refer to methods used to determine which device or devices can put a signal on the network. The primary techniques are collision detection **(CSMA/CD)** and collision avoidance **(token passing).** With CSMA/CD technology, a transmitting device must first "listen" to the transmission medium to determine whether another device is transmitting. If it senses that the network is idle, it may transmit. If two devices simultaneously sense an idle network and transmit at the same time, the devices must sense the **collision** and wait before attempting to transmit again. With collision avoidance, a special signal called a **token** is passed around the network. Each device knows where to pass the token next. No device can send a message unless it is in possession of the token. When a device receives the token, it can either pass it to the next device, or it can send a message. When a message is sent, the device receiving the message immediately launches a new token to start the cycle again.

FIGURE 8-7 Bus Topology

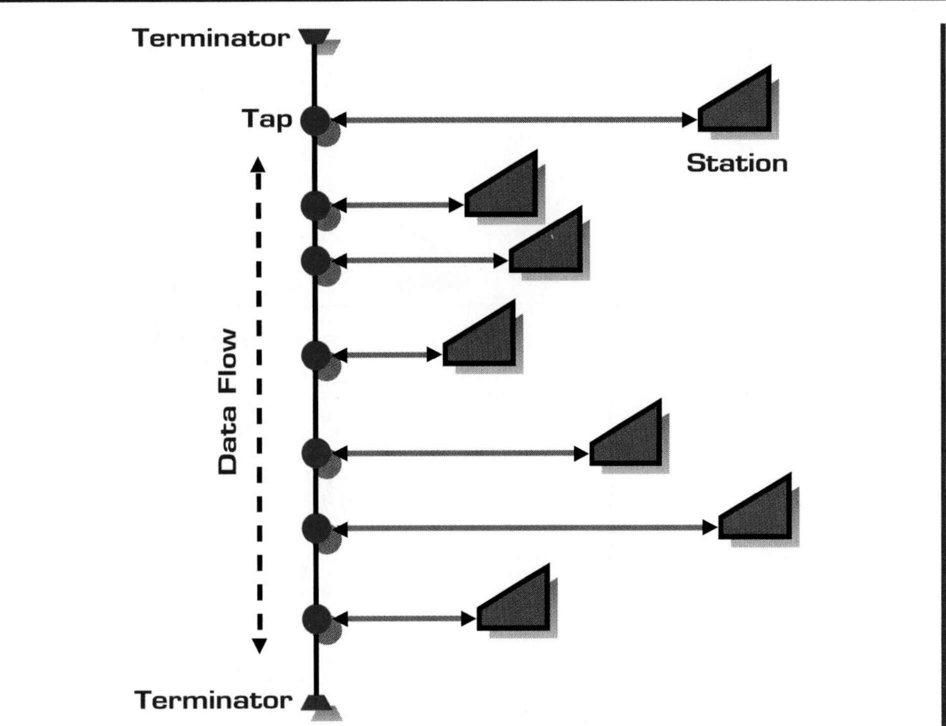

Wide Area Networks

An organization with offices in different parts of the city or in different cities around the world cannot connect its offices directly using dedicated media, such as cable. Instead, the company will rely on a variety of third-party services to connect its sites. Networks that span one or more cities and require the use of third-party media are commonly called **wide area networks (WANs).** The term **metropolitan area network (MAN)** is sometimes used for networks spanning a metropolitan region.

CB COMMERCIAL REAL ESTATE GROUP

TEXAS UTILITIES SERVICES

AMERICAN AIRLINES

As local area networks take over computing functions previously provided by central minicomputers and mainframes, companies need wide area networks to tie together and provide access to the massive volumes of data disbursed across these LAN sites. The CB Commercial Real Estate Group, Inc., for example, is replacing its corporate data center with locally run LANs in each of its 80 offices in 35 cities across the United States. A WAN will connect these LANs, providing a means for sharing information among offices and retaining central management control.[13] Texas Utilities Services Inc. of Dallas began with a 40-node WAN; in two years the network doubled in size to include more than 800 channels and 10 additional nodes each year.[14]

Companies can also use WANs to electronically forge alliances with vendors, customers, and distributors. For example, American Airlines provides travel agents using its Sabre System with WAN access so that these agents can centrally register and confirm reservations made on behalf of their customers. Electra Lighting might consider allowing its larger customers to place orders directly into its computers through a wide area network. This service would reduce paperwork for the customer, reduce the order/delivery cycle time, and should lead to improved customer satisfaction and a sense of partnership.

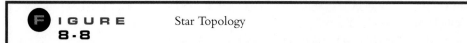

FIGURE 8-8 Star Topology

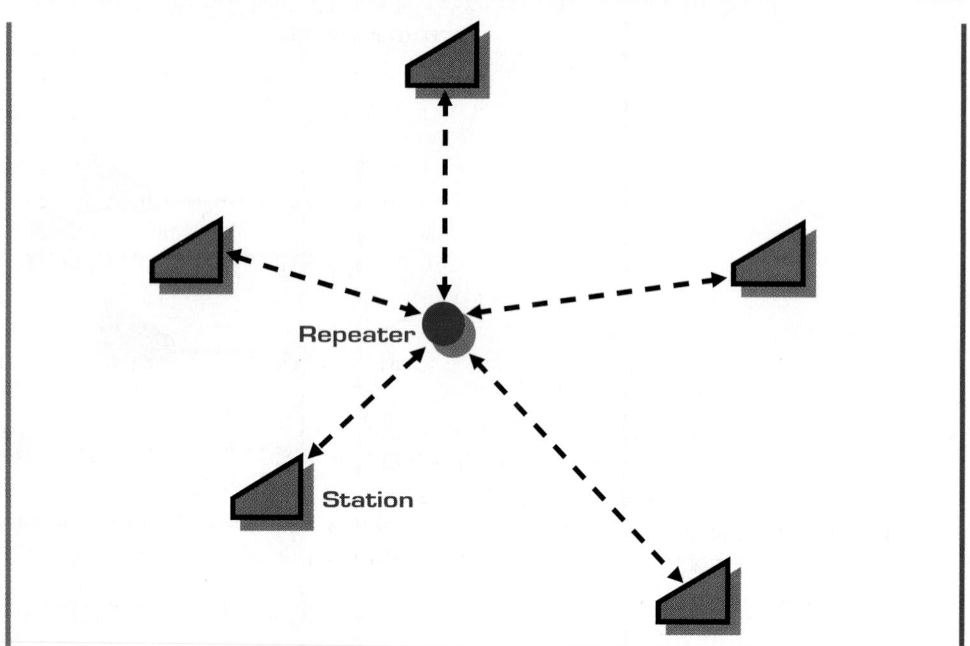

Options for Connection in WANs. Organizations use three major approaches to connect the sites of a WAN. They can purchase transmission capacity from telephone companies, satellite operators, or cable television operators to connect the sites. As the amount of communication increases, the company must purchase increasing amounts of capacity, and communications costs can become prohibitive.

Alternatively, a company can lease capacity for extended or regular periods. A **leased line** is transmission capacity that telephone companies allocate between two points to a single customer. The cost of a leased line depends on its transmission capacity and the distance between the ends of the line, not on the number of calls or the amount of data transmitted. Electra Lighting might purchase a leased line to connect its sales department to a major customer.

Organizations can also purchase transmission capacity from resellers of telephone and satellite capacity, commonly called **value-added networks.** By bundling the messages of many companies and individuals, resellers achieve scale economies that allow them to purchase long-distance communication capacity at a cost below what most companies would otherwise pay. In addition, to attract customers, such resellers also supply additional services, such as electronic mail, access to electronic databases, and electronic banking.

UNITED STATES DEPARTMENT OF DEFENSE

Supernetworks. **Supernetworks,** or networks of networks, are typically established in two ways. A consortium of organizations may want to share information. A group of manufacturing companies, for example, may want to share their success stories in involving workers in decision making. A group of scientists may want to share information about their current research. Alternatively, a government may wish to promote communication among its citizens or enable the exchange of information by military researchers to improve logistics. In 1969, the United States Department of Defense established a supernetwork called ARPANET that defense contractors and military agencies used to share information. In 1990, the entire scientific community gained access to an expanded ARPANET, established as

NSFNET. (NSF refers to the National Science Foundation.) Meanwhile, research universities that did not participate heavily in military research had created their own supernetwork, called **BITNET,** to establish communications among researchers throughout the world.

The **Internet,** a supernetwork that includes supernetworks such as NSFNET and BITNET, consists of thousands of networks (over 10,000 in early 1993) worldwide linking over 4 million individual users.[15] The Internet began as a research and engineering supernetwork. It includes the National Science Foundation's NSFNET, which links together regional networks supported by connection fees from colleges and other nonprofit organizations and NSF subsidies.[16] Users pay a low monthly cost, typically for a leased line or dial-up service. They can then access commercial and noncommercial services in more than 40 countries.[17]

UNOCAL

The Internet offers low-cost global communications and includes useful on-line software and unique databases.[18] It provides global bulletin boards, electronic mail capabilities, and support for collaborative work. Users can also secure free, public domain software through the Internet. For example, Unocal Corporation, an energy company, obtains free state-of-the-art software for modeling seismic data from the California Institute of Technology over the Internet.[19]

Although Internet policy prohibited commercial activity, that prohibition has now been lifted. Many companies, for example, use the Internet to offer databases about their products and services to the general public. A purchasing agent, for example, can view an electronic catalog on the Internet and then purchase selected items electronically. Recently developed technology can support concurrent engineering and manufacturing processes using the Internet.[20]

Network Architectures

Network architecture refers to the relationship that network designers intend to establish among a network's participants. A **client/server architecture** refers to a network in which one or more computers exist solely to perform specialized services for the others. A **peer-to-peer architecture** refers to a network in which no hierarchical relationships exist among the network participants. **Unstructured architectures** place few, if any, restrictions upon the participants. Combinations and variants of these three types of architectures may exist. Tom Hurley and his committee at Electra Lighting can assist their consultant in selecting the most appropriate architecture for their new system based on the users' information needs.

Client/Server Architecture. A client/server architecture dedicates one or more computers, called **servers,** to perform special services for the other parties in the network, known as **clients.** Clients and servers cooperate in performing tasks, with the servers performing duties that are best centralized and clients performing tasks that are best distributed. For example, a client/server architecture might use a **print server** to allocate and control printing devices. Clients send their output to the print server, which then assigns it to an appropriate printer or other output device. In this way, a network's users can share expensive output devices. Client/server architectures generally use a **file server** to store and retrieve data and programs for the clients.

When a user starts a program, the client first determines whether it has a copy of the program to run. If not, it requests a copy from the server, which centralizes storage of shared programs. Similarly, as a client needs data files, these are requested from the server. A client may also ask the file server to store new or modified files. The user may not be aware that the files and programs are not stored at his or her computer.

Servers can exist for almost any application. Examples include a **database server,** which generally handles data storage and retrieval but leaves data manipulation, query processing, and screen or print formatting to the client (see Chapter 7); a **mail server,** which acts as the postmaster and sometimes as a post office in electronic mail applications; and a **network**

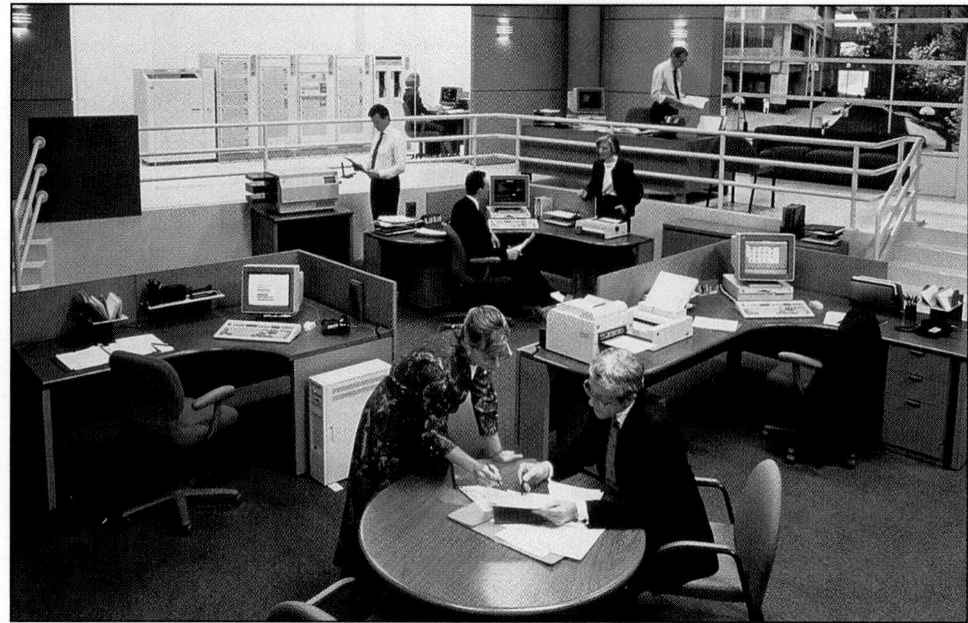

The computers and printers in this office are connected to one another and to the mainframe in the background via a local area network.

Courtesy of International Business Machines Corporation.

management server, which might handle such tasks as adding new clients to a network and providing authorization for users upon login.

Mainframe and minicomputers often act as servers for applications that were written before PCs became popular. PC clients can provide a graphical interface to such an application, translating a user's mouse clicks into commands for the larger system, passing entered data to the system for processing, and displaying data output by the server in formats more readily used at the desktop, including spreadsheet formats. The term **middleware** describes software that operates between the PC client and the mainframe and minicomputer servers to translate client requests into traditional or standard minicomputer and mainframe packages.[21]

Port of Seattle

One 1993 survey of more than 1,000 information system professionals reported that 22 percent of their companies had implemented client/server systems, and an additional 12 percent planned to implement one.[22] The Port of Seattle, having moved from a mainframe to minicomputers, now is moving into a client/server network of microcomputers.[23] The new system, which will have four to seven servers, is intended to benefit from lower costs, including an anticipated savings of $500,000 annually, economies of scale from newer technologies, availability of development tools that speed the introduction of effective systems, and the ability to communicate worldwide with business partners. The IS director for the Port sees the new system as offering his organization flexibility and stability and a fit with the highly distributed business environment of the Port.

CSX Technology

CSX Technology, which tracks 150,000 locomotives and freight cars in 21 transportation centers for its parent CSX Corporation, moved to a client/server architecture from a decentralized Macintosh desktop environment in which each transportation site had been acting independently. This change attempted to rationalize the location of information and make it more quickly accessible to all users.[24]

1992 Olympic Games

The 1992 Olympic Games in Barcelona used a client/server system to produce scoring results. Figure 8-9 illustrates the scoring process. A LAN at each site was linked to a central database that acted as the server for clients at each location.[25]

The client/server architecture works only if data storage can reasonably be centralized on a few common servers. Technically, this limitation rarely poses a problem. Some companies, however, have organizational reasons for decentralizing data storage. They may fear that the person or department holding and controlling centralized data will have too much power. They may find the installation of high-capacity media (for example, fiber optic cable) required for this architecture too costly or too disruptive. Organizations with nonlocal networks may have an insufficient media capacity to guarantee the timely transmission of data among computers at reasonable costs. In such situations, users may prefer to maintain data at many different computers across the network.

Client/server networks can hinder corporate performance if the networks lack sufficient capacity. One furniture company lost almost $2 million in business because slow data transmission stalled its operation.[26] Updating databases on a distributed network, ensuring sufficient security, and distributing computers physically to diverse locations can strain a network with inadequate capacity. Other problems include the need for retraining of IS professionals and end users, the difficulties in supporting hardware and software from multiple vendors, inadequate development tools, and technical failures.[27]

Peer-to-peer Architecture. A peer-to-peer architecture recognizes and accepts the dispersion of data across the network while treating data and program elements as sharable resources for authorized network participants. This architecture requires the network operating system to know where data are maintained so that parties in the network can retrieve the data as needed. We can view a peer-to-peer architecture as an extension of the client/server architecture in which each network party can act as a server according to the

Scoring the Barcelona Games

1. Competition data are collected at 34 locations

Timing and Measuring Systems	Manual Data Entry	Automatic Data Entry
In 17 sports, data are collected from touch panels, video finish, infrared beam, and meteorological devices.	In 22 sports, EDS-trained volunteers enter scores directly into the Results Information System.	In nine sports, judges input scores on individual keypads.

2. Stand-alone networks tabulate, verify, and report results on site to scoreboard, broadcast commentators, judges, and media.
3. Within seconds, results information is distributed via client/server systems to 3.5 billion viewers worldwide and to 3.5 million spectators, media, athletes, and coaches at 2,200 locations throughout Barcelona, Spain.

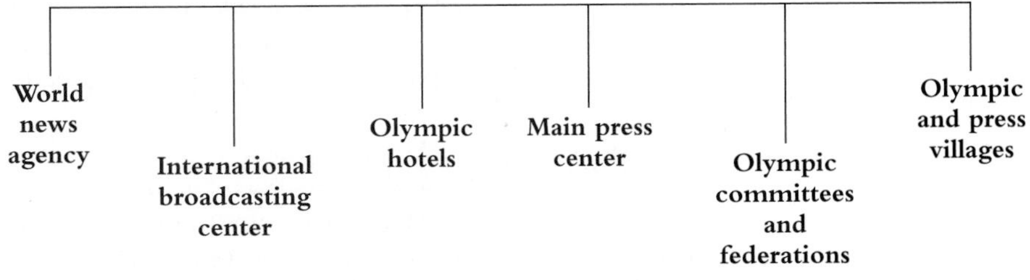

Alan Radding, Network to score perfect 10 at Olympic Games, *Computerworld* (December 9, 1991): 66.

application. Peer-to-peer architecture also supports the redundant storage of data and programs at two or more locations on the network. Redundancy allows a network to operate even if one of its servers should fail. However, redundancy imposes additional problems in ensuring the consistency of data at the redundant storage locations.

Unstructured Architectures. Most supernetworks operate in an unstructured way. Network participants establish their terms, within broad parameters set by the network designers, when they join the network. Some participants may operate as servers for some applications, as peer-to-peer participants for others, and as strict observers for others.

Connecting Networks

Suppose an organization has two networks, one for order entry and the other for purchasing and inventory control. You, as the manager responsible for managing information systems in the organization, are considering acquiring software that would integrate the two applications. The software would allow the order takers to view the availability of items in inventory and the purchasers to access information about demand so that they could accurately time purchase decisions. Each application must access and sometimes update data that currently reside on different networks. Building a new network that combines all of these uses would address the limitation of two separate networks. But this solution would probably be expensive, especially if the two networks used different types of cables, operated at different speeds, and used different protocols. Employing a router or gateway between the two networks provides an alternate solution.

Gateways and routers move data between networks. A gateway connects two or more networks that are so dissimilar that data on one cannot be understood by the other. Typically, this is because the networks run different types of software. A **gateway** is a computer that accepts data from one network, processes it into a format for another network, and retransmits it. Depending on the priority that the gateway assigns to the task, internetwork communication through a gateway may take either a fraction of a second or several hours.

A **router** connects two or more like networks. A router may modify the packet surrounding the data it transmits, but it never changes the data within the packet. Routers pass their data between networks almost instantaneously and without apparent delay. A **bridge** is like a router except that it connects only two networks. Because it does not have to read addresses in the data packet, a bridge operates even faster than a router.

A LAN switch, also called a **smart hub,** is a router residing on several networks that accepts and responds to commands to connect two or more of these networks. This powerful device allows the construction of networks from among a number of small network modules or even individual workstations. Using such devices, for example, network administrators can move a printer from one work group's network to another's network without having to rewire the printer. They can also program the switch to automatically reconfigure a network at fixed times of the day when needed for particular applications or when capacity requirements normally change.[28] LAN switching products first became available in 1993 but lacked capacities sufficient for high-speed networks. Telephone switches have performed similar functions for many years; however, the technology has not been configured and sold commercially for network administration until recently.

Networking Standards

Standards allow equipment and software manufacturers to develop products that guarantee to work with other equipment and software. The early and widespread acceptance of standards for data communication on LANs explains the widespread adoption of local area networks. Figure 8-10 lists and explains a number of the most widely accepted industry standards.

The International Standards Organization (ISO) is an international agency with voluntary participation that was formed to encourage standardization in a variety of areas. The ISO created a model of data communication, known as the **Open System Interconnection (OSI) model,** which divides the communication process into seven layers (see Figure 8-11) for which standards can be independently created. Standards organizations often use this model to set boundaries on the scope of new standards. Although many standards cross one or two larger boundaries, the existence of the OSI model is often credited for the extent and quality of standards in the data communications field.

Some Standards for Data Communication

ATM—Asynchronous Transfer Mode. A standard that packages all types of data, including voice, video, fax, and electronic mail into packets of 53 bytes, which are routed over a network using a switching technique known as "cell relay."

Ethernet—A suite of standards for local area networks, primarily at the hardware level, initially developed by Xerox and jointly specified by Xerox, DEC, and Intel in 1980. Ethernet can achieve 10M bit/second speeds on unshielded twisted-pair cable. Hardware devices are required to sense when two or more devices attempt to send data at the same time and to resolve these "collisions" according to the Ethernet protocols. Proposals for "Fast Ethernet" standards, with speeds of up to 100M bits/second on unshielded twisted-pair, are currently being debated.

FDDI—Fiber Distributed Data Interface. A standard for local area networks using two rings of fiber. The dual rings ensure continuous communication even if one of the rings is cut or broken. They also improve speed by carrying messages in opposite directions so that bottlenecks at any one node can be bypassed.

Frame Relay—A standard similar to X.25 (see below) except at speeds between 56K bits/second and 2.048M bits/second. Frame relay also supports a broader range of device protocols by including information about these protocols in the packet that surrounds the data.

SNA—Systems Network Architecture. A suite of standards designed by IBM to provide a framework within which IBM computers of all sizes could communicate with one another.

TCP/IP—An early protocol for intercomputer communication that became part of early versions of the UNIX operating system and then an accepted standard for Internet communication.

X.25—A standard promulgated by the American National Standards Institute (ANSI) that specifies how data are grouped into variable-length packets containing source and destination addresses. Once data are placed on a conforming network, X.25 switching devices read the addresses and forward the data to their destination. X.25 protocols allow speeds as low as 1.2K bits/second and as high as 56K bits/second. X.25 service is available from a large number of public carriers.

X.400—An ANSI software standard for packaging documents for data transmission, originally intended for electronic mail but expanded to deal with fax, sound, color photos, and video.

FIGURE 8-11 The OSI Layers

Layer	Definition
1. Physical	Concerned with transmission of unstructured bit stream over physical link; involves such parameters as signal voltage swing and bit duration; deals with the mechanical, electrical, and procedural characteristics to establish, maintain, and deactivate the physical link.
2. Data link	Provides for the reliable transfer of data across the physical link; sends blocks of data (frames) with the necessary synchronization, error control, and flow control.
3. Network	Provides upper layers with independence from the data transmission and switching technologies used to connect systems; responsible for establishing, maintaining, and terminating connections.
4. Transport	Provides reliable, transparent transfer of data between end points; provides end-to-end error recovery and flow control.
5. Session	Provides the control structure for communication between applications; establishes, manages, and terminates connections (sessions) between cooperating applications.
6. Presentation	Performs generally useful transformations on data to provide a standardized application interface and to provide common communications services; examples: encryption, text compression, reformatting.
7. Application	Provides services to the users of the OSI environment; examples: transaction server, file transfer protocol, network management.

Reprinted with permission from William Stallings and Richard Van Slyke, *Business Data Communications,* 2nd ed. (New York: Macmillan, 1994).

Integrated Services Digital Network (ISDN). **Integrated Services Digital Network (ISDN)** describes a set of standards for integrating voice, computer data, and video transmission on the same telephone line. Its ultimate goal is the creation of an all-digital, seamless, global network.[29] ISDN lines increase transmission capacity by a factor of 10 over the capacity of non-ISDN lines. After excluding the portion of ISDN bandwidth used for voice, the remaining capacity available for data communications increases dramatically. This capacity allows users to jointly edit a word-processing document or examine a spreadsheet while conversing.

Telephone companies have adopted ISDN in many regions of the United States, but ISDN service remains unavailable from some local telephone companies.[30] ISDN is less common outside the United States, although in some countries, such as Germany, ISDN is widespread and heavily used.[31]

Downsizing

UNITED AIRLINES

SPALDING SPORTS WORLDWIDE

A network of microcomputers with a high-capacity, high-speed server may provide many of the functions of minicomputers and mainframes at a lower cost. **Downsizing** describes the process of replacing minicomputers and mainframes with microcomputer networks. United Airlines shifted a crew scheduling application from a mainframe to a client/server system and saved between $3.5 and $4.5 million immediately.[32] Spalding Sports Worldwide shifted from a mainframe to a client/server network of personal computers to improve the use of inventory data and hence speed product shipping.[33] Most companies that have downsized have reported cost savings of between 30 percent and 50 percent. At UPS, which now has more than 1,000 LANs, one $8 million downsizing project paid for itself after only six months by reducing costs for hardware and labor and increasing productivity.[34]

UPS

Many companies consider a LAN for the first time when faced with the prospect of upgrading their mainframe hardware to run a new application or to accommodate increased computing volume. Justifying the installation of a LAN on the basis of cost is more difficult if its purpose is simply to move one application from the mainframe to personal computers; the company may still require the mainframe for other applications and hence potentially increase rather than decrease the cost of computing.

In addition to reducing costs, the movement from mainframe to client/server networks can increase user productivity, increase developer productivity, improve customer service, and provide competitive advantage for the company using it, as summarized in Figure 8-12. These benefits come primarily from the more friendly interfaces and the advanced software development tools available on microcomputers.

Downsizing does not work well for every application, and it may pose a variety of operational problems. One consultant at the Boston Systems Group cautions companies with the following types of applications to avoid downsizing: those with large databases that cannot

FIGURE 8-12 Benefits of Downsizing

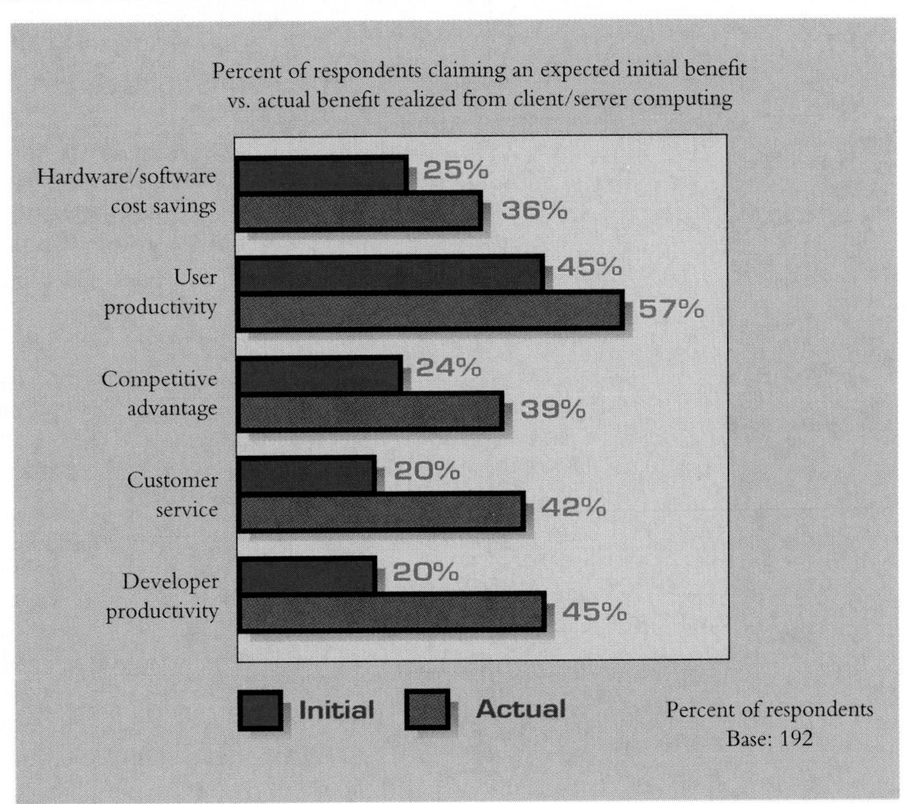

SOURCE: International Data Corporation in Rosemary Cafasso, Client/server strategies pervasive, *Computerworld* (January 25, 1993): 47.

be easily distributed or otherwise partitioned; high-transaction-rate systems that provide real-time response to thousands of users; those that require centralized security or administration; and those that require around-the-clock availability.[35] Other potential problems include the cost and difficulty of reprogramming existing systems, the need to retrain software developers and systems operators, and the limited availability of "mainframe-quality" software that operates on microcomputer hardware.[36]

Network Management

Networks connecting more than 100 users typically require a full-time professional to manage network services. Network services include planning, upgrading, and maintaining the physical network; monitoring network traffic and message delays; adjusting the physical or logical network layout and number of servers to respond to transmission delays; procuring third-party services for wide-area communication; adding new workstations, printers, and other devices to the network; adding and deleting users and user passwords and modifying user authorizations; installing shared software and controlling the number of simultaneous users if limited by license; and providing appropriate backup of shared data and files. Even small networks require a part-time network manager to provide these services.

Security (discussed more fully in Chapter 14) is one of the most important concerns for network managers. Data are most vulnerable to theft, sabotage, and accidental corruption when being transmitted. For applications where security is critical, data can be encrypted before transmission and decrypted when received. Information systems are particularly vulnerable when they permit access from physically remote facilities. This problem is acute for wide area networks, where network managers may not be fully able to control who connects to their networks.

Applications of Communication Technology

Advances in data communication have had a profound impact on the way organizations function. In particular, organizations' increased reliance on facsimile machines to transmit documents electronically has influenced the pace of business. The increased use of digital telephone services for joint transmission of voice and data and increased data bandwidth have allowed the more rapid transmission of greater quantities of data of various types. Organizations worldwide increasingly rely on a set of standards called EDI to transact business electronically with their trading partners. Electronic mail, too, has become more accessible and important with the increased span of LAN and WAN networks. The ability to store voice data digitally has spawned the creation of the voice mail industry. Finally, advances in communication technology, particularly the development of groupware, have made feasible the operation of geographically distributed work groups.

Facsimile

Facsimile machines (faxes) electronically transmit documents (also called **faxes**) almost instantaneously over normal telephone lines. One fax at the originating end digitizes a source document into a series of bits, which are then transmitted over telephone lines. Another fax at the receiving end reverses the process, recreating a copy of the original document. **Computer faxes,** facsimile machines installed in computers, transmit a computer file or image on a computer screen like a paper document. When computer faxes receive a transmission, they translate it into a bitmapped image they can then display on the screen or printed medium. Graphics software can manipulate the image or import it into a word-processing document.

The transmission speed of fax versus that of mail or other physical delivery systems allows the rapid delivery of important data, hence speeding response time or action. It also gives individuals facing a deadline extra time to produce required documents. Many companies have even begun to deliver news services by fax.

A facsimile machine's ability to transmit pictures provides an option telephone conversations lack. For example, engineering drawings cannot be transmitted by voice telephone without a fax. Fax also produces a permanent record, which voice conversation does not: The sender and receiver of a fax both save time because the receiver does not have to take notes. Recognizing this benefit, take-out restaurants increasingly use fax to accept orders.

Although fax technology has been available since the early 1980s, pre-1980 faxes used analog rather than digital technology, resulting in poor images and slow transmission. Recent advances in scanning, printing, and transmitting have improved the quality of faxed documents, increased the speed of transmission, and reduced the price of fax machines. As a result, businesses and individuals are using fax with increasing frequency. Eventually E-mail may replace fax because of E-mail's quality, speed, and ease of use.

Electronic Data Interchange (EDI)

NIBCO

Electronic data interchange (EDI) refers to the exchange of data (usually transactions) between two business organizations using a standard electronic format. Companies routinely exchange purchase orders, invoices, shipping notices, and checks using EDI. NIBCO, a $250 million-a-year manufacturer of flow-control products, installed a customer-oriented purchasing system that allowed manufacturers' representatives and wholesalers to check the status of their accounts and orders and place new orders. The system also supported inventory tracking and communication between headquarters and the company's warehouses/sales offices.[37]

SAFELITE GLASS

US AUTOMOBILE ASSOCIATION

Safelite Glass Corporation and the US Automobile Association used EDI to implement an electronic billing system for handling automobile insurance claims.[38]

EDI should reduce the cost of data entry, printing, and mailing. For example, when sending an invoice to a customer using paper documentation, a company will print a copy of the invoice, stuff it into an envelope with a window (or even print an envelope and match it to the invoice), and mail it. The customer at the receiving end enters the invoice data into its accounts payable database. EDI produces an electronic version of the document and delivers it over telephone lines in a form immediately understood by the accounts payable program of the customer. EDI saves paper, mailing, and data entry work at the customer's end. In addition, the company automatically receives an electronic acknowledgment of receipt of the data and knows the time its invoice was received. EDI should also reduce costs associated with mail delivery time and check clearing time.[39]

Two recent studies suggested that most companies implement EDI to improve customer service, reduce errors, lower inventory levels, and form tighter strategic alliances with suppliers and customers.[40] EDI improves customer service because the lack of human involvement in order taking reduces error, speeds the shipping of products, and eases the processing of invoices. In addition, some EDI implementations allow a company's customers to query whether an item is in stock, obtain pricing of products, or secure information from a selected set of databases that pertain to a customer's orders. EDI lowers inventory levels because a company can reduce the amount of safety stock required to handle uncertainty in order time. EDI tightens relationships between customers and suppliers because they spend a significant amount of time at the outset of an EDI relationship negotiating the specifics of the relationship (for example, the types of documents to exchange). This investment of time and effort strengthens an existing relationship and discourages both the customer and supplier from forming a relationship with another partner.

EDI standards exist at three levels. The highest level specifies a general EDI format, specific formats for various types of documents, and parameters within which industry standards must comply. The American National Standards Institute (ANSI) set EDI standards for the United States known as ANSI-X12. Canada observes the same standards, but European companies and many Asian companies have embraced a different standard called EDIfact. The divergence of these standards poses difficulties for companies that do business both domestically and internationally.[41] Standards for a particular industry modify the universal standards within the allowable parameters to reflect the unique ways that industry does business. These standards not only add detail to the universal document types but also introduce additional documents that are common to the industry. For example, the insurance industry may have several claim formats that brokers can use to send claim requests to an insurance provider. The automobile repair industry recently formed a standards consortium called the Collisions Industry Electronic Data Interchange Standards Group to determine communication needs, foster standards, encourage integration of different repair functions, and encourage vendors to create systems that work on diverse types of hardware.[42] Industry standards allow individual trading partners to customize standards for their own needs.

A company's applications software packages must produce and accept EDI documents for this system to achieve the greatest benefits. Interfacing EDI with applications software poses a major problem for companies with systems developed before EDI became popular or systems that do not support EDI.[43] Such companies can modify or replace all applications software incompatible with EDI. A less expensive alternative involves building or buying **mapping software** that translates the company software's output into an acceptable EDI format and translates standard EDI formats into the input format the company's software requires. Most value-added-network suppliers provide utilities that perform this translation at the time that the document is transmitted across their network.

MELLON BANK, N.A.

PPG INDUSTRIES

GENERAL MOTORS

WESTINGHOUSE ELECTRICAL SUPPLY

Early resistance to EDI's growth derives in part from the fact that it takes two companies to transact business using EDI; in the late 1980s companies did not want to invest in EDI because few suppliers or customers transacted business using EDI. Now most large companies can transact business using EDI, and some will transact business only with other companies that use EDI. For example, Mellon Bank, N.A. lost PPG Industries, Inc. as a client when it could not process the EDI payments PPG received from General Motors, PPG's largest customer.[44] In 1989, Westinghouse Electrical Supply Company began cutting suppliers not using EDI and advertising for suppliers who did use EDI.[45] Following this pattern, EDI has moved slowly from industry to industry. The number of companies using EDI has increased from about 2,000 in 1987 to approximately 37,000 in 1992.[46] The growth potential of EDI remains high: Experts estimate that fewer than 5 percent of all intercompany documents moved by EDI in 1992.[47]

Electronic Mail

STATE OF INDIANA

Electronic mail involves the use of computers to deliver written messages among users. A user writes and mails a letter, memorandum, or other message to one or more individuals using data communication technology. Each user has his or her own electronic mailbox with a unique address and a special password for security. Communication hardware and software have supported the widespread use of electronic mail, both within and among organizations. The number of new products has increased the ease and availability of large-scale and global electronic mail systems.[48] The State of Indiana has connected 27 state agencies through an electronic mail system.[49]

People use LAN-based, mainframe, minicomputer, or public electronic mail. LAN-based systems alone are expected to grow at a rate of 70 percent per year, suggesting that by 1995 its number of users alone will exceed 50 million.[50] Tom Hurley at Electra Lighting, for example, might send his committee members the dates and agenda for meetings about the new computer system using electronic mail. He would type a message onto his computer and enter the appropriate instructions for its destinations, and then the computer would transmit the message using the available transmission media. Chapter 9 discusses the role of electronic mail in automating intra- and interoffice correspondence.

Voice Mail

Voice mail also uses computers to deliver messages but typically requires a touchtone telephone and uses telephone lines or cables to deliver voice messages. A caller dials the voice mailbox of the person to whom he or she wishes to speak. After receiving a signal to begin, the caller leaves a voice message. The recipient can access the message either locally at his or her telephone or remotely by dialing into the voice mailbox. Communication technology records the voice data in the appropriate location and retrieves it for replay. Current development efforts are focusing on integrating voice mail with electronic mail to produce a single listing of messages and to enable users to route voice messages using the electronic mail network.[51] Chapter 9 discusses the role of voice mail in automating the office.

Groupware

Groupware describes computer hardware and software that support a group's interactions in performing a task or accomplishing its goals. Group members use groupware to support information sharing among group members and hence to improve group coordination, meetings, and problem solving. Some futurists believe that improvements in communication and networking technologies will fundamentally change the way people work, deriving productivity not from the individual but from the group.[52] Chapter 11 discusses groupware in more detail, focusing on the way it facilitates group decision making and group project activities.

International Data Communication

Foreign countries generally have a less well-developed communications infrastructure than that of the United States. The quality and capacity of telecommunication lines may be poor. Organizations requesting new service may have to wait several months or even years to obtain them. Government monopolies often regulate and control telecommunications outside the United States. European companies, for example, cannot choose an inexpensive private network, although some telecommunication carriers have formed partnerships with private networks: British Telecommunications PLC offers global private networks through Syncordia, its United States subsidiary.[53]

BRITISH TELECOMMUNICATIONS

SYNCORDIA

The European Community (EC) (now known as the European Union, or EU) published a telecommunications plan in 1987 called the Green Paper that identified ten principles agreed to by each EC country.[54] These principles included continuation of monopolies over network infrastructure, continuation of monopolies over basic voice services, increased competition in all other services and in the manufacture and sale of terminal equipment, and provisions for reviewing monopolies to avoid abuse. The Green Paper did not specify deadlines for implementing these principles, and the EC countries have progressed at different rates.[55]

NIPPON TELEPHONE AND TELEGRAPH

KOKUSAI DENSHIN DENWA

Japan is somewhat more deregulated by law; however, Nippon Telephone and Telegraph has a *de facto* monopoly for national telecommunications, and Kokusai Denshin Denwa maintains a similar monopoly in international telecommunications.[56]

Many industrialized and developing countries have rules that restrict the flow of data across their boundaries or restrict or license the data that companies can collect. Some of these restrictions derive from local privacy laws that cannot be enforced once the data have been exported. For example, Sweden does not allow transnational companies to export payroll or personnel data to the United States because U.S. law does not provide the same level of privacy protection as does Swedish law.[57] Most European countries, and many non-European countries, have similar rules to protect the privacy of their citizens.[58] Some countries, such as Denmark, extend privacy protection to any legal person, including companies, associations, and trade unions.[59]

Other countries, such as Germany and Canada, limit data export by requiring companies operating there to locally process a certain percentage of the data they collect in these countries. The purpose of such restrictions is to improve economic development by increasing the amount of local data processing business.[60] Less-developed countries often view the loss of local data processing caused by data export as colonial exploitation; just as raw materials had been exported to return as finished goods in colonial times, developing countries now export raw data for processing abroad; vendors then resell the information to the exporting country. Continuing this pattern of data flow would reduce or eliminate the need for information processing within the developing countries. The export of raw data for processing thereby limits the diffusion of information technology, continues the unequal distribution of skilled labor internationally, and impairs the developing countries' ability to become economically self-sufficient.[61]

Summary

Data communication refers to the transfer of data among two or more computers. Transmission occurs along a communication channel, measured using bits per second or bandwidth. Media of transmission differ in their cost, capacity, and availability and include twisted-pair wire, coaxial cable, fiber optic cable, microwave signals, infrared frequencies, and radio frequencies. Interface devices, such as a modem, output data from a computer onto these media or process signals from the media for computer input. Several standards address the quality and capacity of the transmission devices.

Networks of users and computers structure data communications in most organizations. Local area networks involve parties in the same or proximate buildings; wide area networks involve users and computers in distant locations. Both types of networks can have client/server, peer-to-peer, or unstructured architectures. A network of microcomputers with a high-capacity, high-speed server can replace the functions of minicomputers and mainframes at a lower cost. Gateways, routers, and switches connect networks to create larger networks.

Communications technology is evident in organizations' use of facsimile machines, EDI, electronic mail, voice mail, and groupware. Data communication internationally poses special problems due to limitations in the quality and capacity of telecommunications media. Governments frequently control the allocation of communication media. They may also limit the export of raw data to prevent exploitation by more industrialized countries.

Key Terms

Access control technique
Acoustic coupler
Analog signal
Asynchronous communication
Bandwidth
Baseband
BITNET
Bits per second (bps)
Bridge
Broadband
Bus topology
Client
Client/server architecture
Cluster
Coaxial cable
Collision
Communication channel
Compression software
Computer fax
Controller
Cooperative processing
CSMA/CD
Data communication
Database server
Digital signal
Downsizing
Electronic data interchange (EDI)
Electronic mail
External modem
Facsimile machine (fax)
Fiber optic cable
File server
Gateway
Groupware
Hertz
Host
Infrared signal
Integrated Services Digital Network (ISDN)
Interface device
Internal modem
Internet
Layout
Leased line
Linear layout
Local area network (LAN)
Mail server
Mapping software
Medium of transmission
Metropolitan area network (MAN)
Microwave signal
Middleware
Modem
Multiplexor
Network
Network architecture
Network management server
Open System Interconnection (OSI) model
Packet
Peer-to-peer architecture
Print server
Protocol
Radio frequency
Remote computer
Repeater
Ring topology
RJ-11 jack
Router
Server
Smart hub
Star layout
Star topology
Supernetwork
Synchronous communication
Terminator
Token
Token passing
Topology
Tree layout
Twisted-pair wire
Unstructured architecture
Value-added network
Voice mail
Wide area network (WAN)

Review Questions

1. Identify the five steps required for data communication.
2. Describe ways of measuring the capacity of communication lines.
3. List five types of telecommunications media.
4. Describe the advantages and disadvantages of twisted-pair wire relative to the other telecommunications media.
5. What is the function of interface devices in communication?
6. Describe the difference between a digital signal and an analog signal.
7. Why are communication protocols necessary?
8. What is a local area network?
9. What is meant by network topology? List and illustrate the three most popular network topologies.

10. What is the objective of a linear layout? How is it implemented? Can it be used for a ring topology? Explain why or why not.
11. What is a token? What access control technique uses one? Why?
12. List three options for connecting sites in a wide area network.
13. What is a supernetwork? Give an example of one.
14. List three network architectures.
15. Identify one advantage and one disadvantage of a peer-to-peer architecture relative to a client/server architecture.
16. Describe three options for connecting separate networks.
17. What is meant by downsizing in the context of networking? Identify the advantages and disadvantages of downsizing.
18. What network services need to be managed by a full-time professional in a large network?
19. What are the advantages of facsimile transmission relative to mail or other physical delivery systems?
20. What are the advantages of EDI relative to the traditional means of exchanging transaction data between two businesses?
21. Describe and explain the hierarchical approach to standards for EDI.
22. What are the primary impediments to the widespread adoption of EDI?
23. Identify three issues affecting the communication of data across national boundaries.

MINICASE

The Local Area Network at the Gulf Coast Hazardous Substance Research Center

The Gulf Coast Hazardous Substance Research Center (GCHSRC) is a consortium of Gulf Coast universities headquartered at Lamar University–Beaumont, Texas. It is funded by federal, state and private industry grants, has an annual budget of more than $3 million, and is in a growth mode.

Research done through the Center is concentrated in the areas of Waste Minimization and Treatment Technology development. Research is done by the faculties of the member universities on their campuses. Proposals for research projects within the framework of the Center's program are submitted for review by the Science and Industrial Advisory Committees. These committees advise the Center Director on the technical and scientific quality of the proposals and assist him in selecting the projects which will make up the program.

The Research Center was originally established in a single office with a director and a secretary. Later, when the Center had grown to a size requiring larger quarters, the move to a new site was thought an ideal time to set up a local area network. Communication and sharing of large amounts of data have played important roles in the Center since its beginning. Additionally, the traditional advantages of a LAN such as sharing of peripherals were deemed beneficial.

At present, the Research Center's LAN consists of seven user workstations (PCs), a network server and three printers. The network server serves primarily as a data store, with some data available to all, and other data stored in individual subdirectories. Most of the software used in the network is installed on the individual workstations rather than on the network server.

Each of the workstations can be used in a stand-alone manner but is also able to access shared storage and output devices. There are some programs common to all the workstations

---

Extracted from Carolyn R. Harris, Donald L. Jordan, and Thomas J. Pinson III, Small-sized LAN support for a research center, *Journal of Systems Management* (January, 1994): 14–17, 41.

(for example, those provided by the electronic messaging system). Other software may be on some PCs but not on others. Each user has the freedom to structure his or her menu in the way which is individually preferred.

Personnel

The original Director of the Center has assumed a semi-retired status and has moved out of the state. His duties include establishing broad guidelines for focus and operation of the Center, but he is not overly involved with day-to-day operation. He communicates with the Center via the network, logging on through a modem. A dialogue screen allows online "conversation" with the Assistant Director. Other options include accessing his electronic calendar and E-mail. Frequently, he may find an E-mail message regarding a document (file) requiring his attention. This file can be transferred via modem, reviewed/revised, and transmitted back to the Center. Generally, the Director communicates daily with the Center. The capabilities of the network allow him to still be involved with the operation of the Center even though he is geographically removed.

The Assistant Director tends to day-to-day management tasks and also serves as the Network Systems Administrator. He is in charge of data/files, training and network users. He uses the E-mail facility extensively to communicate with staff members regarding assignments. For example, he may type a draft of a letter, save it in a particular subdirectory on the network server, and send a message to the secretary telling her where/how to retrieve the letter for editing and printing.

Additional personnel include:

1. An **Administrative Technician** who tracks payroll, purchasing, and other accounts of the Center with the help of the network. She uses Form Filler (from BLOC Corporation) to generate such items as purchase requisitions, travel vouchers, employee forms, and personnel reports. Additionally, she uses a spreadsheet program, the custom-built Project Management Information System (PMIS), and some word processing. All of her programs are on the network because she shares input/output extensively with the Assistant Director. A strong advantage of using the LAN for her work is that she is charged with making changes to the PMIS, which is accessed frequently by others. By having the file only on the network (other than the backup copy), changes can be made to that copy with the assurance that all users have access to current rather than outdated information.
2. An **Administrative Secretary** who uses the network programs to keep track of the Center's clients and to manage mailouts. She uses the electronic calendar extensively to schedule and maintain awareness of appointments for the Director and Assistant Director. In addition, she has a variety of office automation software (some off the shelf and some developed in-house) to suit her individual needs. She also supervises other clerical personnel working with mailing lists for the extensive collection of clients, researchers, and other contracts.
3. A **Special Assistant to the Director** who uses the network to organize all the publications resulting from research conducted with funds from the Center and to keep track of all researchers and their work. All publications resulting from research sponsored by the Center are sent to the GCHSRC, where they are cataloged and installed into a database. Thereafter anyone desiring the publications can access them through the network, via modem if needed.
4. Other **Clerical Personnel,** full-time and part-time.

Network Users and Information Protection

To use the files on the network, or access the network, a person must have the appropriate hardware and software and be designated as a network user. Users can be assigned three levels of responsibility on the network—

- regular network users,
- operators, and
- network supervisors.

Regular network users can run applications and work with files according to the rights assigned to them. Operators are regular network users who have been assigned additional privileges. Network supervisors are responsible for the smooth operation of the network, restructuring, and updating when needed.

All data files on the network are stored at a central location—the network server's hard disk. However, all users are not given access to all the data. Users also cannot access a data file simultaneously while in the update mode, to prevent overwriting of each other's work. They can simultaneously access a data file while in the query mode.

There is an extensive security system to protect the data on the network. It consists of a combination of passwords and trustee rights assigned to the user and the attributes assigned to the directories and files. It is also possible to restrict when and how users can work on the network.

Messaging Software

GCHSRC uses WordPerfect Office LAN as its electronic messaging system. This provides certain communication capabilities to all network users, including electronic mail, electronic calendaring, and a notebook. There are six levels of security, and messages can be encrypted. Users access the various functions via menu.

Electronic Mail

The electronic mail feature allows users to communicate individually with each other via computer over the network. Through the use of E-mail, much of the work a secretary would do in a more traditional office is eliminated or simplified.

Electronic Calendaring

The electronic calendar provides an easy way to determine who is available when. The calendar has space for schedules, memos, and personal reminders.

All users in the Research Center have access to the electronic calendar as part of WordPerfect Office. The administrative secretary has the schedules of the Director and Assistant Director and makes appointments for them. They log in daily to the calendar to check for appointments. The Director's Special Assistant uses the calendar to schedule staff meetings. Other users check their electronic calendars daily to find out about these meetings. When it is necessary to reschedule, this can be accomplished silently via computer instead of interrupting the users as they go about their normal tasks.

Notebook

The Notebook is a free-form database that can be used for various functions. At GCHSRC, one of the secretaries uses the notebook as an electronic index for the Center's filing systems. The software enables a search to locate files. Notebook can also be used to store addresses in appropriate files.

Other Software

Personnel of the Center use other software for individual or group purposes, some of which is off-the-shelf and some of which has been custom-developed in-house or by consultants. These programs assist in file and database management, hardware and software optimization, and generation of frequently used forms (legal documents, for example). In-house personnel have created macros in several of the software packages for commonly used tasks. One of the major customized programs is the Project Management Information System. This keeps track of the different projects that the center is conducting for various organizations. It is used by the Assistant Director, his secretary, and the administrative technician who keeps track of the finances. This system is discussed in more detail below.

Project Management Information System

The work of the Research Center involves considerable interlinking of funds, projects, advisors, universities, and users. There is a tremendous amount of data/information coming in and going out.

PMIS is a menu-driven system designed to support the Director in collecting, storing, processing, and manipulating information on research proposals and projects pertinent to the research center. It consists of the main PMIS system and two subsystems: the Financial Package and the Technology Interchange System. Each of these is described in subsequent paragraphs. The software was written using the Clipper 5.01 compiler. Installation of PMIS and its associated data on the network allows more than one person to work with it.

In the main PMIS system, new proposals are entered, monitored, and tracked until they are approved or rejected. Once a project is approved and funded, it is monitored until it is completed/canceled and archived. Some projects are modified after approval, and these changes must be incorporated into the database. When questions arise concerning the status of a given project/proposal, status of a given project/proposal at a specific university, or status of projects/proposals of a certain type, the director of the research center can quickly query the database and display the appropriate information. Also, an efficient reporting system must be maintained to satisfy reporting requirements of various governing agencies. Reports are generated easily and are routed to a line printer.

In the Financial Planning System, the Director is given an opportunity to manipulate federal, state, and other funds at the university level. Options for a given university are set to facilitate the computation of fringe benefits and indirect costs. The package will then pull all proposed projects from the database and allow the Director to manipulate the available funds among the proposals. When the resources have been arranged in a satisfactory manner, the approved proposals can be flagged and moved into the PMIS system as funded projects.

The Technology Interchange System is designed to track one or more technical papers that are associated with a particular project, as well as any number of presentations or publications that can be associated with each paper. Any number of authors can also be credited for each paper.

Implementation Problems

We chose a standard twisted-pair Ethernet wiring scheme for our network, The three main cabling schemes for Ethernet that we studied included thick Ethernet, thin Ethernet, and twisted pair. We found that twisted-pair wiring typically is used when you want a central network-control area with all systems independently wired from that point. An important criteria in this choice was that we felt that we might frequently add or remove single computers from the network and the integrity of the network would not be disturbed.

This caused some problems in that our LAN was only the second such network installed on our campus. The Telecommunications Department was still learning. We also learned the hard way that shielding our cables was important as the cleaning crew caused our network to crash while cleaning the building. Our original installation plan required a bridge between our LAN and the university fiber optic network for communication with Internet. Only one bridge was available for this purpose on our campus but was in use in another building. We had to wait several months to install it.

Most of the staff employed at the Center had no experience with networks and had to be trained before they could use it. This caused a delay of several days. Our network manager was also a novice to networks and eventually went to a management training seminar.

Costs

The initial hardware cost of our LAN was approximately $4,300 and included the purchase and installation of an i80386/SX processor as file-server, Ethernet cards for each PC, and a laser printer. We already owned the six PCs that formed the original network. Cabling was not a factor because our Telecommunications Department furnished and installed it. Software costs amounted to $1,500 for an ELS-II system. We have since upgraded this to the Novell Netware 3.1.1 system. Training costs for the network manager were $800. Most of our PCs, including the server, have been upgraded to the i80486/DX class.

Case Questions

1. Why did the GCHSRC network its computers?
2. What are the advantages and the disadvantages of the LAN relative to independent workstations?
3. What are the advantages and disadvantages of the LAN-workstation solution relative to a minicomputer solution?
4. What topology did the GCHSRC use for its network? How did it justify its choice?

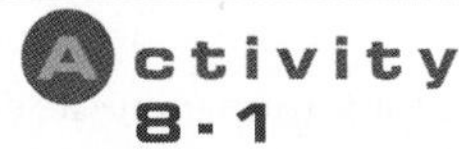

Activity 8-1 American Sterilizer Company

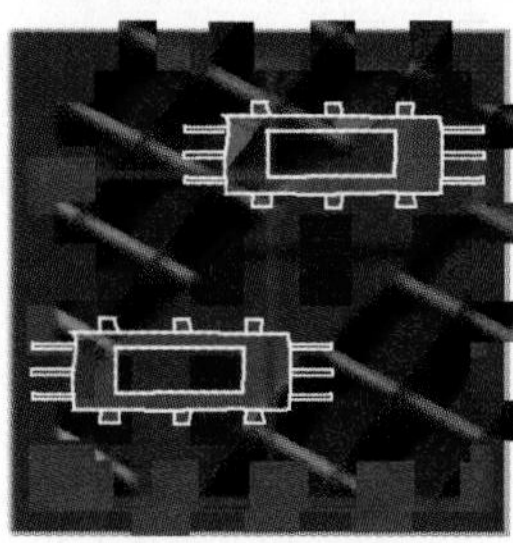

short case

STEP 1: Read the American Sterilizer Company case.

Almost three years ago, hospital equipment manufacturer American Sterilizer Co. took the knife to its mainframe operation and grafted on a personal computer network that has become the lifeblood of its business. The technology transplant was originally intended to improve response times and reliability. As an added bonus, the measure has also saved money and boosted productivity at the Erie, Pa., company.

Those cost savings and productivity strides were very welcome at American Sterilizer. The $270 million company has had sluggish sales in recent years due to economic pressures on the health care industry and increased use of disposable medical supplies. The medium-sized manufacturer's primary product line includes sterilizers, surgical tables and lights, scrub sinks, and electronic cleaners. Disposable testing supplies are made by its American Sterilizer Scientific Division in Apex, N.C.

American Sterilizer's commitment to PC networks grew gradually over the last five years. That commitment started to take shape as the company gained experience with PCs and with PC local area networks (LANs). The PCs were initially brought in in 1986 to take some of the work load off the company's mainframes—an IBM 4341/model 2 and an IBM

SOURCE: Mark W. Doll and William J. Doll, A productive PC operation, *Datamation* (October 15, 1989): 77–78.

4381/model P14, both running under the VM operating system. The telecommunications system in place before the networks were installed consisted of leased lines that connected 3174 cluster controllers via bisynchronous modems to front-end processors.

By 1984, after an information center had been established, mainframe use exploded. At the end of that year, some 700 IBM 3178 terminals at 14 locations were running more than 500 on-line programs. The growth in end-user computing put a serious drain on mainframe resources. Response times deteriorated, significantly reducing the productivity of user departments that relied on on-line applications. In addition, the flood of on-line applications made system reliability problems even more serious.

Computing costs escalated rapidly, as the company endeavored to keep up with end-user demand. In a futile attempt to control these costs, American Sterilizer's IS department launched a chargeback scheme. User departments, facing a choice between lower productivity or increased computer charges, were forced to increase their computer budgets.

In November 1984, then IS director John J. Prehoda began assessing the capabilities of an IBM PC as a platform for end-user computing.

Two years later, the IS team was asked to develop a stand-alone manufacturing and accounting system for the North Carolina division.

The resulting system was based on customized 286 PCs from Fortron/Source Corp. in Livermore, Calif.

The PC networking scheme was a hit with the development staff in Erie because debugging was easier and compiling was faster. It was also a hit with Prehoda, who quickly became convinced that PC networks could be used for many of American Sterilizer's on-line and database-intensive applications.

So, in July of 1986, to reduce mainframe load, American Sterilizer's IS staff began converting the on-line accounts-receivable system from the 4381 to a network of Fortron/Source PCs at the company headquarters in Pennsylvania. During this two-month conversion, the system was enhanced to provide better access to customer accounts. Response time became faster and the productivity of the accounts-receivable staff picked up as a result of the new system.

By this time, the IS group at American Sterilizer was sold on PC networks for nonmanufacturing on-line applications. At the end of 1986, the company devised an enterprisewide systems integration strategy in which PCs and LANs would play the primary role in meeting the company's information processing, office automation, and connectivity needs. In addition, a three-year plan to convert all mainframe applications to PC networks was approved by American Sterilizer's top management.

PLANS UNDER REVIEW

However, a recent change of top IS management has prompted a review of the final leg of that plan. Prehoda had hoped to transfer all applications off the mainframes, but his departure this year has thrown into question the transfer of the remaining applications. Production planning, factory floor, computer-aided design (CAD) and computer-integrated manufacturing (CIM) applications all remain on the 4381. A review of the company's direction was under way in 1989.

In 1986, the improvements in response time and reliability made the PC network very attractive to American Sterilizer. Reliance on PC networks increased as response times on the 4381 lengthened with each additional user.

American Sterilizer had been running CICS applications on a mainframe. Even though such applications looked like a lot of separate programs to users, they were in fact one big program. If it crashed, the whole system came down for everyone.

COST CONCERNS

Cost avoidance was another issue that came into play. For example, if applications were not offloaded to the PC networks, the company would have to shell out more than $500,000 a year for upgrades to improve mainframe response time and reliability.

Some of those mainframe costs are no longer relevant because the company got rid of its 4341 and downgraded its 4381 to a Model P3 in the summer of 1987. The smaller mainframe was replaced by 600 Fortron PCs along with a mixture of 286 and 386 file servers also supplied by Fortron/Source. The company configured these PCs on 27 networks using the NetWare network operating system from Novell Inc. and ARCnet adapters from Datapoint Corp. of San Antonio. Fortron/Source configured both the network nodes and the servers to American Sterilizer's specifications.

Now, under the company's existing network architecture, 13 servers are bridged together to form a backbone structure. Remote vendor dial-in capability is provided through an asynchronous gateway. An electronic mail system enables American Sterilizer's suppliers to receive purchase orders and messages from the offices and manufacturing plants in Erie.

So far, systems for payroll and personnel, accounts payable and receivable, service order entry, sales quoting and forecasting, general ledger, sales commissions, preventive maintenance, and some manufacturing applications have been transferred to the PC network.

Transferring these applications improved interaction between IS professionals and the user community at American Sterilizer. This, in turn, has facilitated meaningful system changes that have increased productivity. American Sterilizer's managers using the network have become more knowledgeable about their applications and have felt an increased sense of ownership.

THE WIDER LESSONS

Lessons learned at American Sterilizer can have general applications in other companies. One conclusion illustrated by American Sterilizer's experience is that, to achieve effective integration, users must have a sense of ownership of their data and effective avenues for interpersonal communication with other users and systems personnel. By reducing the differentiation between the user and analyst roles, PC networking technology may help create this type of environment.

Firms that have a big investment in custom programs may choose to convert their software to run on a network. American Sterilizer's experience indicates that COBOL applications can be converted without unusual difficulty. It's also worth noting that although conversion costs can be high, they are only one-time charges. And, furthermore, the hardware and software savings are usually large enough to justify these expenses.

Today, PC networking is rapidly taking off. Many companies will soon be able to use this technology for the majority of their on-line applications. By subdividing applications into simpler, loosely coupled systems or sets of applications, this technology can enable companies to reap the rewards of enhanced productivity through better reliability and response times.

STEP 2: Prepare the case for class discussion.

STEP 3: Answer each of the following questions, individually or in small groups, as directed by your instructor.

Diagnosis

1. What were American Sterilizer Co.'s information needs in the early 1980s?
2. How did these needs change during the 1980s?

Evaluation

3. What were the components of the original mainframe system?
4. How effective was the mainframe in meeting the organization's needs?
5. What problems did using the mainframe system create?
6. What advantages did the personal computer network offer?

Design

7. How effective has the computer network been since it replaced the mainframe at American Sterilizer?
8. How has the computer network changed since its installation?
9. Should American Sterilizer totally eliminate mainframe computers?

Implementation

10. What implementation issues did American Sterilizer face in its downsizing efforts?
11. How effectively did it handle these issues?
12. What problems still exist with the computer system?

STEP 4: In small groups, with the entire class, or in written form, share your answers to the questions above. Then answer the following questions:

1. How have the information needs at American Sterilizer changed since 1980?
2. What computer hardware has the company used to meet these needs?
3. How effective has the change to personal computers been?
4. How did the company ensure a smooth transition? ●

Downsizing Debate

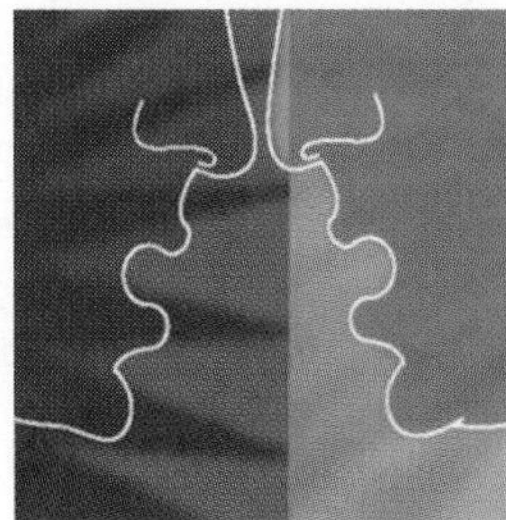

debate

Resolved. Downsizing is the wave of the future; most organizations should plan to downsize their computer systems within the next five years.

STEP 1: Your instructor will assign you to teams that will debate either the pro or con side of this issue.

STEP 2: Prepare your position.

STEP 3: Conduct the debate with the opposing team.

STEP 4: In small groups or with the entire class, answer the following questions:

1. Which side was more convincing?
2. Should all organizations with multiple users plan on downsizing their systems within the next five years? If not, which organizations should plan to downsize, and which should not? ●

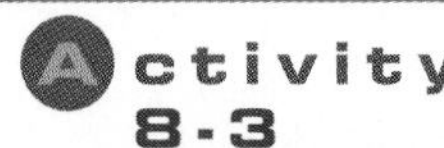

Activity 8-3 An Internet Hunt

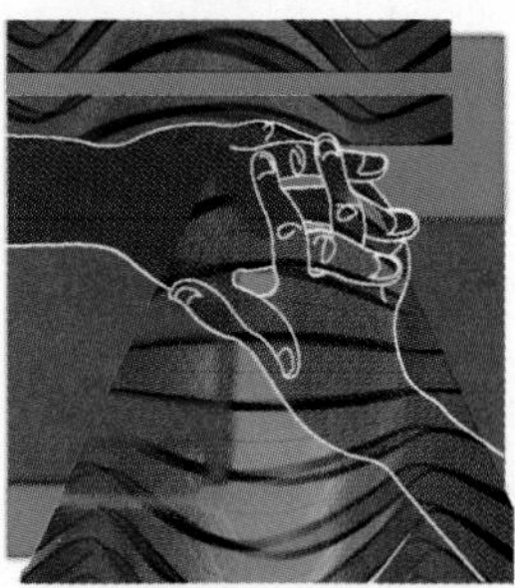

hands on

STEP 1: Your instructor will provide you with instructions on how to access the Internet on your computer system and how to use various Internet tools. Read these instructions carefully before performing the following steps.

STEP 2: Read the "Internet Hunt Questions." The answers to these questions can be found on the Internet. The number of points associated with each question (indicated in parentheses) reflects the difficulty of finding the answer on the Internet.

STEP 3: Assume that you are helping a friend who understands how to use the basic Internet tools (World Wide Web, Gopher, Telnet, ftp, Finger, etc.) find the answers to the "Hunt" questions. For each question, write down instructions for your friend so that he or she can find the answer. Be as specific as possible. For example, answers like:

ftp to host.university.edu

will not score as high as:

anonymous ftp to host.university.edu
cd /pub/documents
file is called important.txt.Z

Internet Hunt Questions

1. I'm leaving for France tomorrow. Approximately how many French francs can I get for my dollar? (3)
2. I'm writing a paper on the politics of international trade. I am looking for the full text of position papers of the candidates for the U.S. Presidency in 1992 (Bill Clinton, George Bush, and Ross Perot) on the subject of the North American Free Trade Agreement (NAFTA). (6)
3. What are the latitude and longitude of Wellesley, Massachusetts? (4)
4. What's happening with the U.S. stock market? The more up to date, the better. (5)
5. I'd like a summary of the budget for NASA (the U.S. National Aeronautics and Space Administration) for the current year. (5)
6. I want to send an electronic mail message to the President of the United States. What's the President's Internet address? (3)
7. I'm traveling to Los Angeles next weekend. Are any of the area's professional or college sports teams playing at home on Saturday or Saturday night? If so, against whom? (5)
8. I'd like to settle an argument with my mother about which has more calories: an ounce of salmon or an ounce of swordfish. (6)
9. What line follows the line "The Lord is my shepherd, I shall not want," in the King James version of the Bible? (5)
10. I'd like to use Judith R. Gordon's *Organizational Behavior: A Diagnostic Approach* as the text for my organizational behavior class. What is the most recent edition in print, and what is the year of its copyright? (5) ●

These questions were adapted or extracted verbatim with permission from several Internet hunts proposed and organized by Rick Gates of the University of California, Santa Barbara.

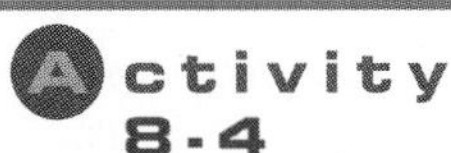

Activity 8-4 — The Airport Problem

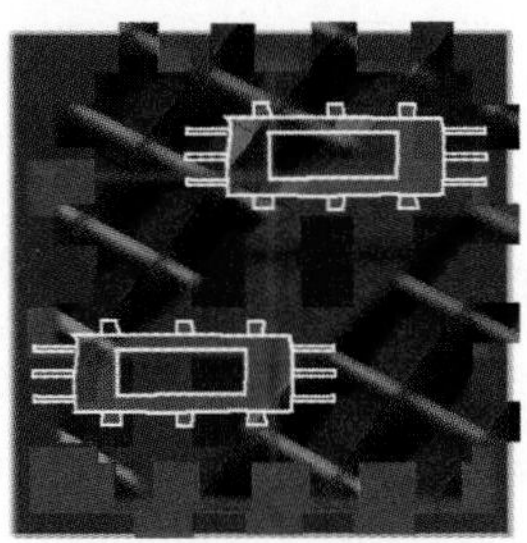

short case

STEP 1: Read the following scenario:

Ryan Daly is the operations manager for Central Airlines at O'Hare International Airport in Chicago. Central leases 12 gates at O'Hare handling roughly 150 flights per day and 15,000 passengers per day. In addition, Central has a significant cargo operation; it shares a cargo hangar/warehouse with a major international shipper.

Ryan supervises a staff of 32 ticketing/baggage agents, 18 gate agents, 30 baggage handlers, a small maintenance crew, and a variety of lower-level managers such as shift supervisors at the ticketing counters, a cargo manager, and a manager of customer service. He is responsible for the operation of all Central's passenger and flight services at the airport. Examples of his responsibilities include arranging the overnight accommodations for flight crews, ensuring that the food that caterers load on the aircraft for in-flight meals meets Central's quality standards, and negotiating leases for space with the airport authorities. Ryan reports to the vice-president of operations at Central's headquarters office in Kansas City.

For the most part, Ryan relies on the information systems services provided by Central Airlines's MIS group. This group has a staff of almost 200 people worldwide with an acquisition and operating budget that exceeds $3 million per year. Ryan's office is equipped with a personal computer that is connected, over a value-added network, to Central's mainframes in Kansas City. Ryan obtains information about reservations, flight schedules, and other centrally collected or centrally produced data from the mainframe. Ryan has also developed a few spreadsheets he uses to keep track of his local operations and to help him evaluate decision alternatives.

Currently, Ryan communicates with his employees and with his peers at other airports by phone and in person. Electronic mail systems were once available on the mainframe but were discontinued for all employees except those at headquarters when a budget crunch forced cutbacks in communication expenses. Ryan has proposed a local area network for O'Hare in order to improve communications among his managers and employees and to help them share data with one another. Ryan has estimated the price to network his key employees to be $25,000. The twisted-pair wire needed for the network is already in place at O'Hare.

STEP 2: Individually or in small groups, identify the pros and cons of the proposal from the perspective of Ryan's boss. Be sure to consider all alternatives.

STEP 3: Acting as Ryan's boss, write him a memo communicating your decision and the reasoning behind it. Be prepared to support your decision before the entire class. ●

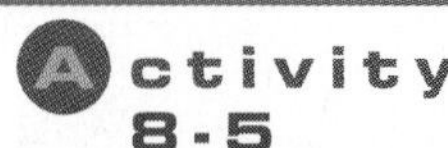

Introducing EDI at the Harkness Hardware Company

role play

STEP 1: Read the following scenario.

Harkness Hardware Company, a $60 million distributor of hardware supplies to steel companies, building contractors, and major retail outlets, was recently approached by an EDI vendor about introducing an electronic data interchange system into the workplace. The EDI vendor suggested that Harkness Hardware establish computer links with all its major suppliers and customers to allow them to check inventory, place orders, and send payments electronically. Harkness Hardware stocks approximately 10,000 items of various sizes. The company publishes a catalog that lists the items, and it also regularly sends sales representatives to meet with customers and identify their needs. Increasingly its customers have been complaining about the difficulty of reaching order clerks. They also say that they frequently order items that are out of stock but that could easily be replaced with other items if they were informed quickly about the problem. The executives of Harkness Hardware understand their customers' frustration because they have experienced the same problems with Harkness's suppliers.

The EDI vendor argued that installing this system should reduce the cost of data entry, printing, and mailing, as well as costs associated with mail delivery time and check clearing time. For example, the company would automatically receive an electronic acknowledgment that specifies the time the invoice was received. EDI should also improve customer service because the lack of human involvement in order taking reduces errors, speeds the shipping of products, and eases the processing of invoices. It should also improve the speed of processing purchase orders and delivering supplies.

STEP 2: Your instructor will assign you to one of three groups: 1) top management of Harkness Hardware Company, 2) a major supplier to Harkness Hardware, or 3) the largest customer of Harkness Hardware.

STEP 3: In your groups, prepare a response to the vendor's recommendation from your perspective as management, customer, or supplier. Be sure to consider the pros and cons of using EDI.

STEP 4: The instructor will convene representatives for each of the groups. Each representative must decide whether his or her group will participate in an EDI system at Harkness Hardware.

STEP 5: The instructor may repeat the role play with different representatives of the parties involved.

STEP 6: What are the advantages and disadvantages of EDI from the perspective of the company, the customer, and the supplier? Under what conditions should Harkness Hardware introduce EDI.? ●

Notes

[1]Warren Childs and Kathryn A. Tito, Networks fly with FDDI, *Datamation* (January 15, 1992): 70.
[2]Ellis Booker, Wireless LANs, WANs draw new attention, *Computerworld* (May 18, 1992): 80.
[3]Susan Kerr, Wireless works, within limits, *Datamation* 7 (February 1, 1992): 38, 40.
[4]Ibid.
[5]Joanie M. Wexler, Wireless intrigues IS executives, but technical obstacles stunt use, *Computerworld* (March 22, 1993): 1, 8.
[6]Kerr, op. cit.
[7]For additional information about error detection and correction formats and algorithms, see V. Cappellini (Ed.), *Data Compression and Error Control Techniques with Applications* (London: Academic Press, 1985); and Djimitri Wiggert, *Codes for Error Control and Synchronization* (Norwood MA: Artech House, 1988).
[8]Mary Fran Johnson, Clustering to turbocharge RS/6000, *Computerworld* (May 4, 1992): 1, 16.
[9]Ronald L. Lancaster and Dennis D. Strouble, One university's approach to the requirements of academic computing, *Journal of Systems Management* 43(3) (March 1992): 19–20, 31.
[10]Sally Cusack, Insuring success with patience, *Computerworld* (August 5, 1991): 45, 48.
[11]Michael Fitzgerald, Switch to LAN the right plan, *Computerworld* (June 15, 1992): 51.
[12]Based on data reported in the fourth-quarter issues of the 1993 and 1988 *Computer Industry Forecast.* The original sources of the 1992 data include: Ethernet seen leading network growth, *Infoworld* (June 12, 1993): 37; and *Infoworld* (August 16, 1993): 41. The original source of the 1987 data is *Network World* (June 25, 1988): 17.
[13]Howard Baldwin, Realtor tracks client needs via client/server net, *Network World* (September 13, 1993): S21–S23.
[14]Tom McCusker, Now you can plan your network, *Datamation* (October 15, 1991): 66–68.
[15]Networks in FOCUS, *Focus* (June 1993): 21–24.
[16]Thomas J. DeLoughry, NSF released long-awaited plan to reduce U.S. role in Internet, *The Chronicle of Higher Education* (May 26, 1993): A17.
[17]Gary H. Anthes, Internet commercial uses blossom: Service could offer small businesses access to 11,000 networks worldwide, *Computerworld* (June 28, 1993): 71, 73.
[18]John H. Quarterman, The Internet, *Computerworld* (February 22, 1993): 81–83.
[19]Ibid.
[20]Anthes, op. cit.
[21]Johanna Ambrosio, Somewhere in the middle, *Computerworld* (March 15, 1993): 65.
[22]Garry Ray, Bumpy road to client/server, *Computerworld* (April 26, 1993): 63, 65.
[23]Nell Margolis, Client/server ship docks in Seattle, *Computerworld* (July 12, 1993): 6.
[24]James Daly, Client/server setup targets tracking maze, *Computerworld* (June 24, 1991): 47.
[25]Alan Radding, Network to score perfect 10 at Olympic Games, *Computerworld* (December 9, 1991): 65–66.
[26]James A. Hepler, Network jam, *Computerworld* (April 26, 1993): 89–90.
[27]Ellis Booker, Users step carefully to client/server, *Computerworld* (December 14, 1992): 10.
[28]Joanie M. Wexler, Smart hub vendors flock to switching, *Computerworld* (March 1, 1993): 51.
[29]Andrew J. Kennedy and David Yen, The coming of ISDN, *Information & Management* 17(5) (December 1989): 267–275.
[30]Michael Gawdun, ISDN: A view from the trenches, *Business Communications Review* (June 1993): 39–42.
[31]Primary-rate ISDN speeds German networks, *Data Communications* (April 1993): 63–64.
[32]Ellis Booker, United shift to Unix heats up, *Computerworld* (November 18, 1991): 6.
[33]Rosemary Cafasso, Spalding tees up client/server, *Computerworld* (March 22, 1993): 51.
[34]Jean S. Bozman, Mainframe-to-PC LAN shift taking hold, *Computerworld* (August 31, 1992): 4.
[35]Dirk Faegre, Lessons from a seasoned downsizer, *Computerworld* (August 10, 1992): 68.
[36]Alan Radding, Dirty downsizing, *Computerworld* (August 10, 1992): 65–67; and Johanna Ambrosio, Client/server DBMS: Walk, don't run, with it, *Computerworld* (March 15, 1993): 65.
[37]John H. Sheridan, Making customers 'more efficient,' *Industry Week* (June 6, 1988): 75.

[38]Frank Vedock and Bob Wheeless, EDI revolutionizes the auto insurance industry, *Journal of Systems Management* 41(10) (October 1990): 17–19, 30.

[39]Daniel M. Norris and Elaine Waples, Control of electronic data interchange systems, *Journal of Systems Management* 40(3) (March 1989): 21–25.

[40]Joanne Cummings, Cost savings not a factor for firms moving to EDI, *Network World* (February 1, 1993): 37.

[41]For a review of the culture and history behind the divergence in EDI standards and a review of recent attempts to achieve a global EDI policy, see Eileen M. Trauth and Ronald S. Thomas, Electronic data interchange: A new frontier for global standards policy, *Journal of Global Information Management* 1(4) (Fall 1993): 6–16.

[42]Joanie M. Wexler, Auto repair needs EDI standards fix, *Computerworld* (June 28, 1993): 73.

[43]Ruth Andersen and D. J. Masson, EDI everywhere, *Computerworld* (October 5, 1992): 75–79.

[44]Jim Brown, Banks increase use of EDI, *Network World* (January 25, 1988): 1, 82; and James Johnston, EDI implementation at PPG industries, *Journal of Systems Management* 43(2) (February 1992): 32–34.

[45]Jeanne Iida, Companies that lack EDI may lose trading partners, *Management Information Systems Week* (April 17, 1989): 17.

[46]William C. Symonds, Getting rid of paper is just the beginning, *Business Week* (December 21, 1992): 88–89.

[47]Ruth Andersen and D. J. Masson, op. cit.

[48]Lynda Radosevich, E-mail products, services multiply, *Computerworld* (June 28, 1993): 76.

[49]Joa S. Heldman, The State of Indiana solves a connectivity problem, *Journal of Systems Management* 43(4) (April 1992): 18, 40.

[50]Nina Burns, E-mail software, *Computerworld* (February 10, 1992): 83–84.

[51]Ellis Booker, E-mail meets voice mail, *Computerworld* (April 26, 1993): 28.

[52]Margie Wylie, Will networks kill the corporation? *Network World* (January 11, 1993): SS9–SS12. The author quotes Paul Saffo of the Institute for the Future.

[53]Frederick V. Guterl, Telcos offer private networks, *Datamation* (December 1, 1991): 64–1.

[54]P. Heywood and L. Mantelman, Untying Europe's tangled web of communications, *Data Communications* (March 1989): 171–182.

[55]Jerry McCreary, William Boulton, and Chetan Sankar, Global telecommunications services: Strategies of major carriers, *Journal of Global Information Management* (Spring 1993): 6–18.

[56]Ibid.

[57]P. Candace Deans and Michael J. Kane, *International Dimensions of Information Systems and Technology* (Boston, MA: PWS-Kent, 1993).

[58]Sid R. Ewer, Whose borders are barriers to financial data communications? *Financial & Accounting Systems* (Winter 1992): 5–10.

[59]Deans and Kane, op. cit.

[60]Eli Cohen, Metanational information technology, national sovereignty, and social responsibility, *Emerging Information Technologies for Competitive Advantage and Economic Development*, Mehdi Khosrowpour, ed. (Harrisburg, PA: Idea Group Publishing, 1992).

[61]Edward M. Roche, International computing and the international regime, *Journal of Global Information Management* (Spring 1993): 20–28.

Recommended Readings

Berson, Alex. *Client/Server Architecture.* New York: McGraw-Hill, 1992.

Kehoe, Brendan P. *Zen and the Art of the Internet: A Beginner's Guide.* Englewood Cliffs, NJ: Prentice-Hall, 1993.

Leinwand, Allan and Fang, Karen. *Network Management: A Practical Perspective.* Reading, MA: Addison-Wesley, 1993.

Potts, William F. *McGraw-Hill Data Communication Dictionary.* New York: McGraw-Hill, 1993.

Sproull, Lee and Kiesler, Sara. *Connections: New Ways of Working on the Networked Organization.* Cambridge, MA.: MIT Press, 1992.

Stallings, William. *Computer Communications: Architectures, Protocols, and Standards.* Los Alamitos, CA.: IEEE Computer Society, 1992.

VIDEOCASE

Dell Computer Corporation

Dell Computer Corporation, with annual sales of more than $2 billion, is one of the largest manufacturers and direct marketers of personal computer equipment in the world. Dell believes that the personal computer has become a commodity product. The components that make up a computer are essentially identical from one computer to another, and few customers buy on brand name alone. So how does Dell succeed in building sales?

Michael Dell, the company's founder, believes that the route to success is a customer-oriented approach. Dell seeks to know and service its customers better than the competition does. Every service representative has a personal computer on his or her desk. These computers have access to a number of different databases. The customer database is a critical component of Dell's customer-oriented strategy. In addition to information such as name and address that are normally contained in a customer database, Dell maintains a complete customer history from the time the customer first contacts the company. This history includes information about every order, every service dispatch, and every call to customer service or technical support that the customer has made. This historical information remains a part of the customer record indefinitely. Customer service representatives rely upon this information to react rapidly and efficiently to customer orders, questions, and requests. They can also decide whether or not to make concessions outside their normal guidelines to a customer, based on information in the database such as the amount of business the customer does with Dell or the frequency or nature of the problems the customer reported.

Dell builds approximately 3,000 computer systems per day at its Austin, Texas plant. Each system is built to an individual customer's specification. Dell believes that this customization strategy is unique and an integral part of its customer-oriented approach. When a customer representative takes a new order, Dell's information systems transfer the order, via a network, to the assembly plant, and create a work order called a *traveler.* The traveler follows the computer through the assembly process. Assembly begins with a motherboard. Chips such as the CPU and memory and video upgrade chips are added. Assemblers place the completed motherboard into the chassis, along with other components such as hard and floppy disk drives and possibly a CD-ROM unit. Every component bears a bar code that is scanned and automatically checked against the traveler. After running diagnostic tests on the completed unit, assemblers connect it to a local area network for loading of software. An automated process downloads the appropriate software for each system, according to the customer order, from server workstations. Assembling a computer takes only ten minutes, but loading it with software and testing it takes about five hours. The final step in the manufacturing process is to pack the computer and prepare it for shipment.

Dell handles about 24,000 customer-service calls per day. Customer-service calls are taken by a technically qualified customer-service agent who is the single point of contact for the customer. Although the agents have a large technical staff they can call with questions, they also have a great degree of autonomy and are empowered to send replacement parts or authorize return or repair of faulty equipment.

According to John Varol, Director of Production, Manufacturing, and Engineering, Dell purchases the parts and software for its computers from 200 to 300 different vendors. Of

SOURCES: Jay Palmer, Goodbye, buzzards, *Barron's* (October 17, 1994): 22–24; and Brian Gillooly, Dell to expand its services, *Information Week* (March 13, 1995): 80.

these, 20 to 25 are "key" vendors, those that Dell considers the primary suppliers for the components they use most often. To keep costs low, these key vendors participate in Dell's "just-in-time" inventory system, which limits the quantity of their parts on hand to a one- or two-day supply.

Despite efforts to keep costs low and customer service high, Dell's profit margins and profitability slipped markedly in 1993 after nearly a decade of spectacular, uninterrupted growth. However, in 1994, after Dell refocused its marketing on its superior technical support and introduced a strong laptop product, its sales and profits rebounded. Fiscal year 1995 revenues exceeded $3.4 billion.

Case Questions

1. From what components do Dell's assemblers build computers?
2. Why do Dell's strategists consider the personal computer to be a commodity product?
3. Do you believe that Dell's order-entry, customer-service, and assembly-monitoring software were purchased off the shelf, customized, or developed in-house? Why?
4. In what way(s) has Dell simplified data input for its assemblers?
5. How does Dell use databases? What data does Dell retain that its competitors do not?
6. Where in the order-entry and assembly processes are data communications necessary? Do you believe that Dell uses local area networks, wide area networks, or both? Explain your reasoning.
7. What information do Dell's customer-service representatives need to handle technical questions from Dell's customers?
8. What information do Dell's managers need to support a just-in-time inventory system? What information do Dell's suppliers need?
9. In what way(s) does Dell use information for strategic advantage?

Part III

Information Systems

Information systems apply information technology to satisfy information needs. Part III examines four types of information systems: automation systems, transaction processing systems, management information systems, and strategic information systems. Automation systems use information technology to increase the accuracy and speed and reduce the cost of work that might otherwise be performed manually. Transaction processing systems collect and disseminate information associated with the day-to-day operation of an organization. Management information systems combine the internal information that transaction processing systems collect with external information to support and enable management decisions. Strategic information systems apply information systems to help an organization define its direction and achieve an advantage over its competition.

Chapter 9

Automation Systems

OUTLINE

Automation at Monarch Beer

Automation of Manufacturing and Design

- Computer-Aided Manufacturing (CAM)
- Computer-Aided Design (CAD)
- Computer-Integrated Manufacturing (CIM)

Office Automation

- Office Automation Functions
- Electronic Mail
- Electronic Imaging
- Integrating Office Automation with Information Systems

Automation of Education and Training

- Advantages and Disadvantages of Automating Education and Training
- Tools for Automating Training

Expert Systems

- Components of an Expert System
- Developing Expert Systems
- Neural Networks

LEARNING OBJECTIVES

After completing the reading and activities for Chapter 9, students will be able to

1. Define computer-aided manufacturing and offer two advantages and two disadvantages it poses compared with the monitoring and control of machinery by humans alone.
2. Offer two examples each of the use of flexible manufacturing, robotics, and automated guided vehicles in manufacturing.
3. Describe the use of computer-aided design in automating design processes in organizations.
4. Describe the role of computer-aided manufacturing and computer-aided design automation systems in computer-integrated manufacturing.
5. List five functions office automation can support.
6. Describe the uses of electronic mail and electronic imaging in office automation.
7. Cite the advantages and disadvantages of automating education and training.
8. Describe three major tools used to automate training.
9. Cite five potential applications for expert systems.
10. Describe the components of an expert system.
11. Describe the major characteristics and uses of neural networks.

Janice DeMarco is vice-president of production at Monarch Beer, a regional manufacturing company. The production of beer is a complex process that starts with acceptance of the raw ingredients and ends with the packaging of the cans and bottles. The taste of the finished product is highly sensitive to minute variations in a large number of factors including recipe and process; sugar and mineral contents of raw ingredients; temperature and humidity during various stages of production; the time spent in various stages of production; the materials used to make the brewing vessels; and even the process for cleaning brewing vessels between batches. DeMarco views her primary responsibility as ensuring a consistent taste for Monarch Beer while keeping costs as low as possible and output as high as possible.

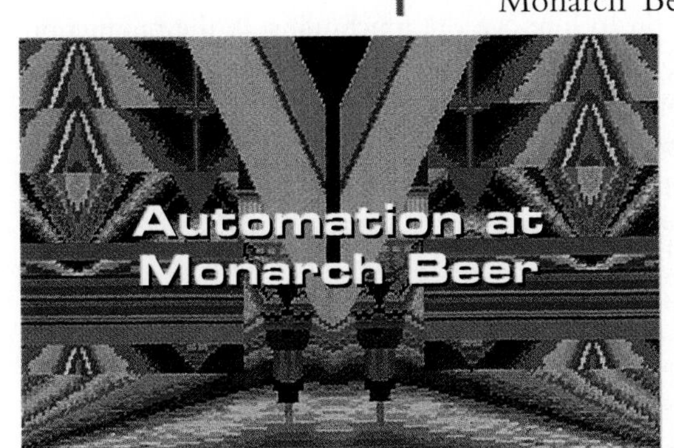

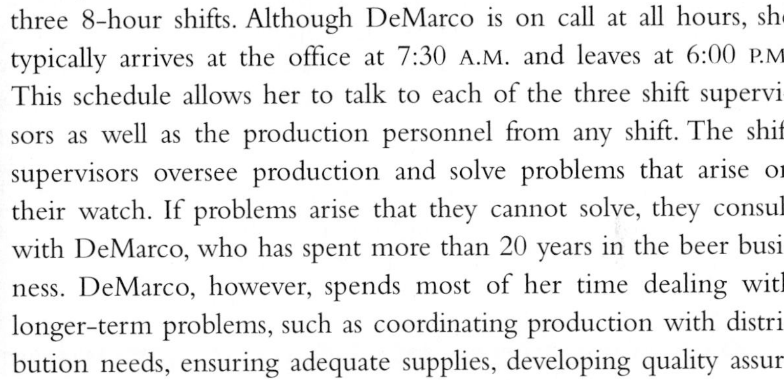

Monarch Beer is produced at a single plant that operates 24 hours a day on three 8-hour shifts. Although DeMarco is on call at all hours, she typically arrives at the office at 7:30 A.M. and leaves at 6:00 P.M. This schedule allows her to talk to each of the three shift supervisors as well as the production personnel from any shift. The shift supervisors oversee production and solve problems that arise on their watch. If problems arise that they cannot solve, they consult with DeMarco, who has spent more than 20 years in the beer business. DeMarco, however, spends most of her time dealing with longer-term problems, such as coordinating production with distribution needs, ensuring adequate supplies, developing quality assurance systems, and planning for equipment maintenance.

Monarch has automated most of the production process. Quality assurance remains the most labor-intensive part. The company monitors quality at every step of the production process, from the acceptance of the raw ingredients to approval of the brewed product. Although the chemical and physical characteristics of the ingredients and product can be monitored electronically, taste and appearance are the ultimate arbiters of acceptance.

Janice DeMarco spends a significant part of each day reviewing production schedules, checking output statistics, and informing her superiors and subordinates about adjustments in the production process. She has a small office staff that supports the production area. DeMarco and her clerical staff use word-processing and spreadsheet software on their personal computers to produce all correspondence, schedules, and reports. The office staff then makes a sufficient number of photocopies for distribution. Janice knows that the organization can use computers in other ways to improve the production process, office management, and even worker training. She needs to diagnose the needs in the production area more completely and then evaluate the appropriate computer systems to meet these needs. In particular, she believes that increased automation could increase the efficiency and effectiveness of her area.

Automation describes the use of computers to perform tasks previously performed by people. The traditional definition is more inclusive, allowing any machinery to replace human or animal work. Automation should free workers from performing tedious, precise, or dangerous tasks, thereby increasing their productivity and theoretically improving their efficiency. It should also allow the increasingly educated work force in the United States and other developed countries to better use its skills. Automation should improve the reliability and even uniformity of some products and services.

Automation can have negative side effects as well. In some cases, workers displaced by automation may lack the skills to perform other, more demanding work and ultimately have their employment terminated. Automation may decrease the amount of available work, creating a need for fewer employees and resulting in layoffs. It may disrupt the social environment in an organization and result in alienation among workers.

How can Janice DeMarco use automation to improve the functioning of the production department? In this chapter we examine four facets of automation: 1) automation of manufacturing and design, 2) office automation, 3) automation of education and training, and 4) the use of expert systems. In our discussion of automation we acknowledge that individuals and organizations can use computers for purposes other than processing information, such as controlling a robot or acting as a teacher. The process of automation may only incidentally involve manipulating information, or it may actively and more efficiently use and generate information. In this chapter we specifically highlight the interface between automation and information systems.

Automation of Manufacturing and Design

Design includes the creation and development of products and processes. **Product design** refers to the creation of a concept and specifications for a finished good. **Process design** describes the creation and specification of equipment and procedures for manufacturing the finished good. Computers can automate the process by which designers translate their mental images into physical drawings and specifications. **Manufacturing** transforms raw materials into finished products: Monarch Beer, for example, transforms raw ingredients such as sugar, hops, and yeast into an array of beers. Electronic machinery, including computers, can control, monitor, and generally support this physical process.

Computer-Aided Manufacturing (CAM)

TIMKEN

Producing an ingot-ton of steel at most steel mills requires seven person-hours of labor. The automation of manufacturing at the Timken Company's Faircrest plant has reduced labor requirements to only two person-hours.[1] In addition to decreasing the amount of labor required to produce a product, automation can reduce production time, increase quality, and improve reporting. Automation also increases the flexibility of the manufacturing process.

The Industrial Revolution saw machines replace human and animal power in the production and manufacture of many products. People assumed the more complex role of monitoring and controlling the machines that performed the labor. Now computers can undertake many of these monitoring and controlling functions. **Computer-aided manufacturing (CAM)** systems designate such automated or partially automated manufacturing systems.

Computers provide many advantages over people in monitoring and controlling machines. First, they are more reliable—they do not make as many mistakes, forget to act as expected, get sick as often, or tire. Second, a single computer can control more machines and can monitor them more frequently and precisely than a person can. Third, automation eliminates costly employee training programs. Companies typically do not experience the same loss in efficiency when they bring new computers on-line as when new employees gain their initial experience.

Managers such as Janice DeMarco at Monarch Beer must weigh the advantages of automating machine monitoring and control against its disadvantages. Companies must assess the feasibility, cost, and appropriateness of automation. Although a single computer may replace several people, it can still be more expensive to procure, operate, and maintain. Companies must also consider the implications of automation system failure. A computer malfunction may affect many machines and reduce production for several days; a pool of operators in a manual production environment, in contrast, can generally compensate for the loss of a single machine operator.

Managers must also decide to what extent automation can replace human judgment in machine monitoring and control. They attempt to implement an optimal combination of computers and humans, each performing what they do best. Computer automation systems vary in their ability to determine when to shut production lines for maintenance, evaluate which machinery or machinery parts may cause quality problems in a finished product, and schedule the order and length of production runs of multiple products sharing production equipment. Janice DeMarco has begun to automate these aspects of beer manufacturing but can extend the automation even further. Expert systems software, discussed later in this chapter, gives a computer the ability to "think" and act as an expert in the field and to learn from its experience. In some environments, such systems even outperform experts and typically make better judgmental decisions than the average employee.

Some activities, such as the repair of some equipment, remain too complex for automation. Increasingly, however, **robots,** described later in this chapter, can perform such activities. Rapid technical advancements continue to extend this capability.

Flexible Manufacturing. During most of the twentieth century, automobile, steel, and other large manufacturers invested millions of dollars in factories designed to produce a single product, such as one car model or one type of steel. Because changes in the product design generally required significant changes in the manufacturing machinery and plant layout, manufacturers could not rapidly respond to changes in consumer demand. By the late 1980s these manufacturers began to face competition from and lose market share to companies that had adopted a flexible manufacturing strategy.

NISSAN

Flexible manufacturing requires that machinery be adaptable and potentially have multiple uses. Computers have made flexible manufacturing possible. Nissan's factories in Zama, Japan and Smyrna, Tennessee employ a flexible manufacturing system called the Intelligent Body Assembly System (IBAS).[2] IBAS is a system of computerized machines that position parts and perform the initial welds. Changing the robotic software can accomplish many of the changes required by a new model. Because assembling an automobile body requires precisely positioning over 300 stamped parts and welding them together at over 3,500 different spots, prior to installing IBAS Nissan required approximately a full year to retool for a new model. IBAS has reduced assembly time to about three months, saving the company nearly 80 percent on changeover costs of several billion yen. It has also increased welding accuracy, resulting in tighter-fitting body panels. IBAS can support the manufacture of as many as four different models, including eight body types on a single assembly line.

TIMKEN

ALLEN-BRADLEY

The flexible manufacturing system at the Timken Company, a company cited earlier in this chapter that manufactures specialty steel and steel parts such as bearings, allows it to rapidly customize the mixture of materials used in creating steel to satisfy each customer's specifications. The system can also quickly change the design of products and packages.[3] The Allen-Bradley Company, a manufacturer of automation controls and systems, built a flexible manufacturing facility that allows the company to produce smaller lot sizes while maintaining at most one day of work in process in the facility.[4] Could Janice DeMarco use flexible manufacturing at Monarch Beer? She might, for example, introduce a system that offers the ability to rapidly adjust the mix of ingredients, packaging, or labeling of different types of beer to meet specific customers' demands.

Robotics. A **robot** is a computer-controlled machine that has humanlike characteristics, such as intelligence, movement, and limbs or appendages. The trade literature sometimes calls any computer-controlled machine a robot. Figure 9-1 shows modern robots used in manufacturing. General Motors purchased the first commercial robot, called Unimate, in 1961. Robots of the 1960s and 1970s were expensive and unreliable. The second generation of robots evolved in the mid-1980s and benefited from technical advances in both mechanics and electronics. Today's robots have further gained from advances in computing technology. Three-quarters of the cost of the Unimate robot was attributed to the cost of its electronics; today most robots have superior control capabilities, but their electronics account for less than one-quarter of their cost.[5]

GENERAL MOTORS

Advances in robotics allow machines to perform tasks that were previously too complex for automation. Small, precise motors allow robots to position items more accurately than people can. Video cameras and pressure-sensitive sensors give robots sight and a sense of touch, enabling them to align one item with another even if the first item is imperfectly placed or formed. Software allows a computer to identify and classify different types of objects, select those required for a given task, and move around obstacles to their tasks. The robot has become a flexible machine—one that can perform a wide array of tasks and whose skills increase with advances in software technology.

SOUTHWEST MOBILE SYSTEMS

Companies use robots to monitor and control almost every type of equipment. For example, Southwest Mobile Systems Corporation uses robotic welders for a variety of welding

FIGURE 9-1 Robots on an Automobile Production Line

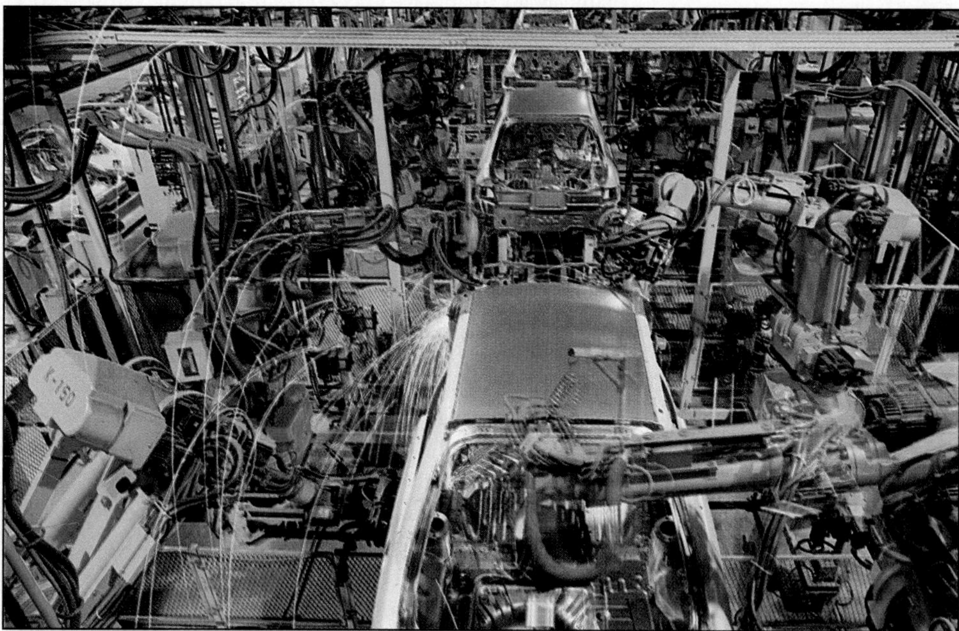

Courtesy of Ford Motor Company.

INCO

PUBLIC SERVICE ELECTRIC & GAS

KAWASAKI ROBOTICS

FORD

GENERAL MOTORS

K&M

operations to produce its M100 Heavy Equipment Transport semitrailer.[6] INCO Limited's Port Colborne plant uses drum-filling robots to increase employee productivity and improve safety.[7] Robots fill two types of drums with approximately 35 million pounds of five nickel products annually. The Public Service Electric & Gas Company uses a submersible robot called MiniRover for inspecting parts at its nuclear plant. The robot can perform work in one hour that takes manual inspectors approximately eight hours. Not only does the MiniRover reduce the time that the plant must be shut down, saving the company over $600,000 per inspection, but it also reduces the costs of providing radiation shielding for human inspectors.[8] Kawasaki Robotics designed a system for automotive assembly that uses two robots: The first robot picks up the required battery from its storage pallet and places it on the conveyor; the second robot puts the battery inside the engine compartment.[9] Ford's Utica, Michigan trim plant uses electric finishing robots in the basecoat, clearcoat, and primer paint booths.[10] General Motors' Opel division in Antwerp, Belgium installed a flexible robotic welding system that uses robots to grip, position, and weld stamped automobile parts for the Astra.[11] The K&M Company, a manufacturer of office stationery products, introduced robots to support the packaging and shipping of its annual volume of 60 million units. The robotic installation supported just-in-time packaging, reduced the potential for worker injuries, and significantly reduced costs.[12]

NEW ENGLAND BAPTIST HOSPITAL

Companies have also found applications for robots in the service sector. For example, ScrubMate is designed to clean restrooms. A janitor merely wheels it into a restroom and turns it on. The robot cleans the toilets, washes the floor, and even wipes mirrors. It knows to bypass locked toilet stalls and revisit them later or notifies the janitor if he or she returns before the stalls become unlocked. A similar type of robot now carries food, medicines, and other supplies at more than a dozen hospitals.[13] The New England Baptist Hospital in Boston has joined with five other medical centers to use Robodoc, a surgical robot, to perform a key step during hip replacement surgery; Robodoc is especially skilled in drilling the long hole in a patient's hipbone into which the metal hip joint slides, in hope of reducing the number of subsequent replacements required.[14]

Experts believe that robots will have taken the place of more than 3 million factory jobs in the United States by the year 2000. They believe that by the year 2025 robots will have replaced most machine operators, a job class that currently accounts for approximately 8 percent of the work force.[15] Could robots play a greater role at Monarch Beer? Such equipment might assist with packaging and shipping, replacing workers in the warehouse or distribution center.

Automated Guided Vehicles (AGVs). **Automated guided vehicles (AGVs),** as illustrated in Figure 9-2, are computer-controlled vehicles that move along a guidance system built into a factory or warehouse floor. Primarily used for material handling, AGVs can be programmed by managers or workers to retrieve parts for constructing an assembled unit. Computer guidance even allows modern AGVs to depart from the guidance system for short distances as long as no obstacles block their paths.

DELTA AIRLINES

MORTON INTERNATIONAL

SEARS ROEBUCK

Delta Airlines uses a 24-vehicle AGV system to handle warehousing at its 247,000-square-foot international cargo facility in Atlanta. The AGVs can pick up cargo from and deliver it to loading docks, departure areas, or space within the warehouse. Computers control where the AGVs place cargo in the warehouse so that they can automatically retrieve the required freight. The AGVs can place cargo at its destination with an accuracy of one-quarter of an inch.[16] Morton International, a manufacturer of automotive airbags, uses AGVs for its entire materials handling operation. Twenty-eight sideloading vehicles transport materials as well as handle pallets and containers in the plant.[17] Sears Roebuck & Company's Logistics Services' distribution center in Jacksonville, Florida uses AGVs to move loaded trailers and replace them with unloaded ones.[18]

FIGURE 9-2 Automated Guided Vehicles at Denver International Airport

© Chris Sorensen.

AGVs can also create a flexible manufacturing environment. If a manufacturer mounts assembly-line conveyors on AGVs, it can reconfigure its assembly lines simply by moving the AGVs. Workers and machines in such an environment then assemble the finished goods directly on the vehicles.[19] Monarch Beer might use AGVs in its packaging and distribution center for adjusting product lines.

Computer-Aided Design (CAD)

Design is a creative process. Although computers recently have had some success emulating human creativity,[20] by far their greatest contribution to design has been to remove much of the drudgery from the process. Before computers, for example, composers had to laboriously transcribe their ideas onto music scoresheets. Today, computers automatically transcribe the music that composers play on a piano-like keyboard input device. This automation can significantly increase the time available for a musician's creative work. Word processors have similarly automated and removed the tedium from creative writing.

Manufacturing designers can use computers to transcribe their ideas into engineering drawings, redraw designs from different angles, and evaluate the technical characteristics of alternative designs. **Computer-aided design (CAD)** software automates these processes and removes other noncreative tasks associated with manufacturing design.

CAD software allows engineers, architects, graphics designers, and others to compose their designs on a computer rather than on paper. The designers can then view their designs from various angles, analyze them from an engineering perspective, edit them, document them, and output them in a format suitable for those doing the manufacturing. In addition, they can save designs for subcomponents and insert them into other designs. CAD software for networked computers allows several designers to work together on complicated products. In selecting CAD software, users should consider its ability to handle the processes of composition, viewing, modeling, editing, documentation, and output and storage.

Composition. The design process begins with sketching or drawing. Individuals generally find sketching on a computer more difficult than sketching on paper. CAD products should allow the user to scan in a hand-drawn sketch; use a pen interface to draw directly on the screen; import sketches from business graphics packages; or compose directly using a mouse, trackball, or keyboard. The software should support the drawing of a three-dimensional design from either a single perspective, as two-dimensional slices at selected intervals, or as projections of the design from each of three dimensions. CAD software should offer a large number of tools for sketching within a CAD package. Users can evaluate the composition functions of a CAD package by asking the questions shown in Figure 9-3.

Viewing. CAD software products provide a wealth of tools for viewing a draft or completed design. Users should be able to rotate an object, view it from any angle, zoom into or out from a particular point on the object, render it in three dimensions as it would appear with light coming from one or more lamps placed at the user's direction, render it as a wireframe diagram (see Figure 9-4), or display slices. In addition, some CAD systems can provide a physical model of the design. We address the creation of such a model, called rapid prototyping, when we discuss CAD output features.

Modeling. Modeling allows users to determine not only how a design looks, but also how well it likely will perform. Engineers might like to know how a design stands up to heat or pressure, changes when placed under various stresses, affects air flowing around it (creating drag and/or noise), conducts heat flowing through it, or resists fluid flowing through or around it. For example, CAD software can help design dies that stamp out parts from sheet metal. It can predict the thickness of material in different locations as well as the distribution, wrinkles, tears, and deformation that occur after pressing. This predictive ability avoids designing dies by trial and error because when software predicts flaws, the designer can change the shape or material of the die.[21]

Questions for Evaluating the Composition Function of a CAD Package

1. Is there a library of common shapes, such as ellipses, spheres, cones, rectangles, and boxes that can be positioned anywhere on the screen, sized (typically by placing the shape within a box whose corners are pointed to by the user), and deformed?
2. Does a user have options for selecting various styles, widths, and colors of lines?
3. Does the package support a wide variety of curve-drawing tools, including the ability to automatically fit curves to points, tangents, or polylines (connected short, straight lines)?
4. Is a wide variety of shading patterns and/or textures to fill areas available?
5. Can the user stretch or shrink lines, surfaces, or even an entire picture, along any dimension or radially?
6. Can the user draw lines or curves parallel or perpendicular to other lines or curves?
7. Can the user generate a grid of any size and automatically "snap" the design to the grid, that is, position selected corners of the design to the closest grid point?

FIGURE 9-4 CAD Wireframe Diagram

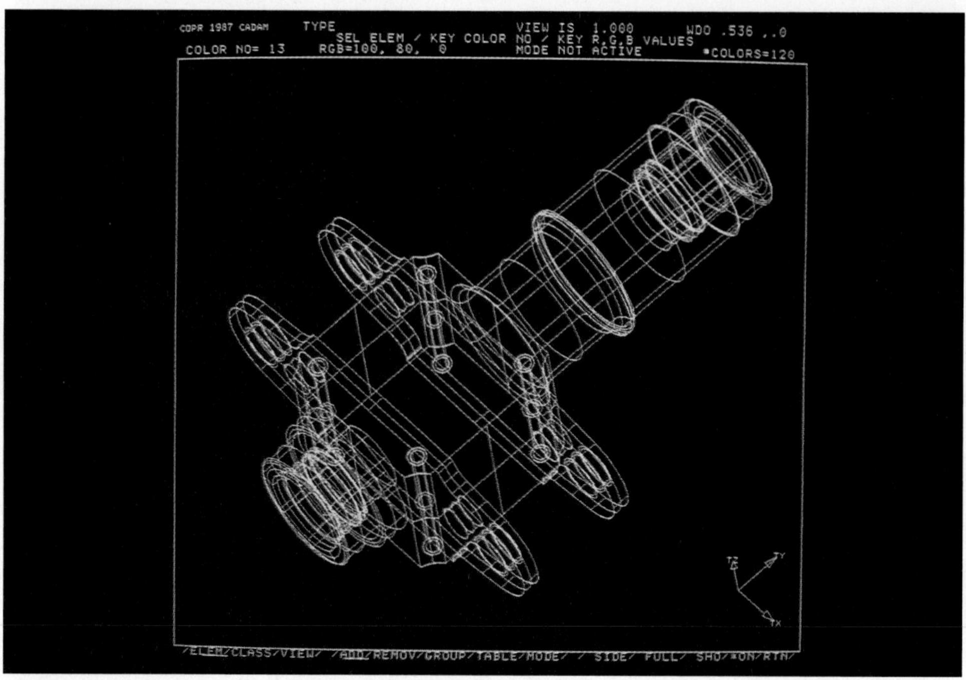

Courtesy of International Business Machines Corporation.

Off-the-shelf CAD software cannot incorporate the array of models required to address the needs of all designers because models tend to be highly specific to a particular type of design. Third-party vendors fill this need by developing and selling modeling software that works with specific CAD packages and focuses on niche markets, such as structural analysis or heat transfer.[22] A company with modeling needs should select its modeling package before purchasing CAD software to ensure that the modeling software supports the CAD package selected.

Editing. Editing functions allow a CAD user to modify a design simply and easily. As a word processor allows its user to move sentences or paragraphs, CAD software allows users to move, rotate, size, color, shade, and apply new textures to previously defined objects. CAD software should also allow a user to simultaneously place several views or parts of the design on the screen, thereby showing the complete implications of the editing. The package should allow undoing the last edit or any previous edits so that a designer can work back and forth in a design—erasing and building repeatedly. Some modeling software assists the editing process by suggesting design changes to meet a given objective.

Documentation. Documentation consists of putting labels, measurements, and symbols on a design. Most CAD packages provide standard tools to perform such documentation. Generally, they include functions to rotate, size, and color text and symbols. In addition, most CAD software allows users to attach nonprinting attributes, such as a part number, vendor, price, or other descriptive information, to parts or subparts of the design. The software should allow a designer who creates a part to attach attributes, such as material type, function, color, and so on, for storage in a database that other designers retrieve as needed.

Some CAD packages include their own database functions, while others interface with commercial database packages.

Output and Storage. CAD software should support a wide choice of printers and plotters. Software should allow the user to zoom, position, and crop the picture when printing it. The software should also support standard graphic storage formats, such as GIF (Graphics Interchange Format) and TIFF (Tagged Image File Format), as well as the DXF (Drawing Exchange Format) and IGES (Initial Graphical Exchange Standard) formats used for exchanging designs between different CAD packages. **Product information managers** control large volumes of engineering information; they store such metadata about drawings and documents as part numbers, date of last revision, storage location, and acceptable viewers.[23]

BLACK & DECKER

FORD

JOHNSON & JOHNSON

3M

TEXAS INSTRUMENTS

Rapid prototyping describes the production of three-dimensional output from CAD designs. Imagine designing a product, pressing a key, and having a plastic, wax, metal, or ceramic model of the product produced in your office. Several technologies now support rapid prototyping at relatively low cost.[24] For example, a product called Sculptor, by Visual Impact, creates a physical model of a design by building it in slices. It uses one material to correspond to solid parts of the design and another material to correspond to the void or empty areas. The process ends with heating the cube; the material corresponding to the void or empty areas melts and drains away, leaving a model of the design. Alternatively, the solid part can be made to melt away, leaving a mold that can be used to cast the product. Black & Decker's Household Products division used computers to assist in two- and three-dimensional modeling during the design of its "retro"-style Metropolitan toaster, which won the silver IDEA92 Award for industrial design excellence.[25] Companies such as Ford, Johnson & Johnson, 3M, and Texas Instruments use rapid prototyping to save between 50 and 95 percent in time and labor in their product design.[26]

Computer-Integrated Manufacturing (CIM)

Companies should design products that they can manufacture easily and efficiently. A failure to integrate their design and manufacturing automation systems can cause design engineers to spend a great deal of effort to produce a prototype that either cannot be manufactured or costs too much to make.[27] Integrated systems permit design engineers to participate in the solution of manufacturing problems. Advanced computer automation systems can even create a manufacturing plan from the design produced by design engineers.[28]

VOLKSWAGEN AG

HARLEY-DAVIDSON

CARNATION

Computer-integrated manufacturing (CIM) refers to the coordination of CAD and CAM automation systems with each other and with information systems that depend on or relate to design and manufacturing. CIM attempts to improve business processes by sharing information across departments through automating the flow of data among design, manufacturing, and the other functional areas. Volkswagen AG has committed to developing a system that automates tooling, manufacturing, cost checking, and quality processes.[29] Harley-Davidson, Inc., the motorcycle manufacturer, recently gave engineers information technology tools that allow them to access the company's warranty database and assess the performance of their designs.[30] The Carnation Company, a division of Nestlé, at its ice cream plant in Bakersfield, California; integrated automation in production and storage with business systems used in planning and control; the automation resulted in improved product consistency, waste reduction, more accurate reporting, improved quality, and increased manufacturing flexibility.[31]

Product designs should benefit from a review by marketing people who have a customer orientation, production engineers who can anticipate manufacturing difficulties, financial planners and controllers who can pass judgment on the implications of the design for cost

Carnation Company's ice cream plant in Bakersfield, California, where CIM improved quality.

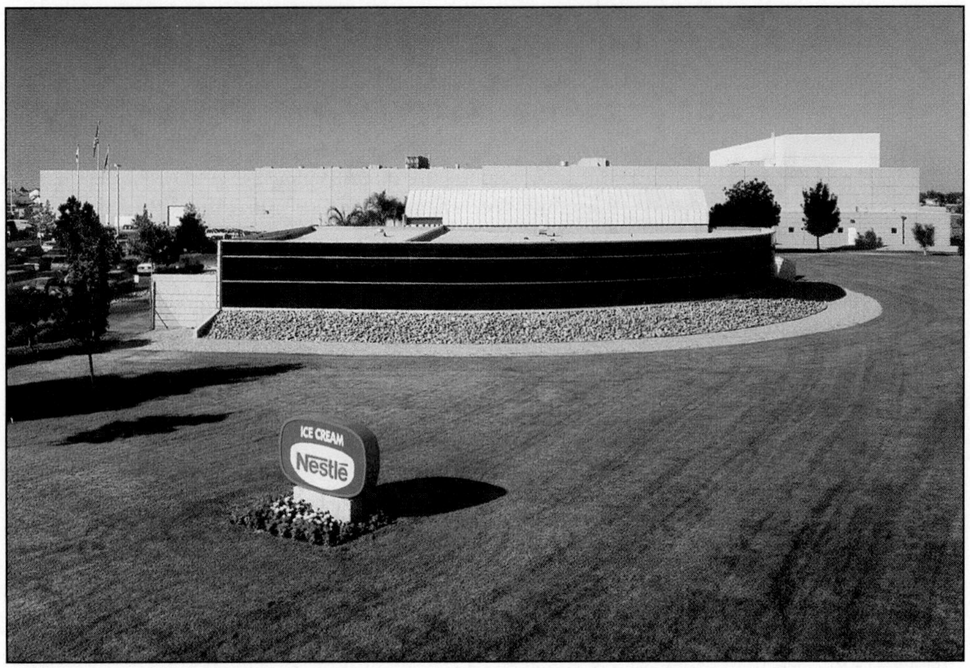

Courtesy of Nestlé Ice Cream.

and financing, and senior management who can assess how well the designs reflect the company's strategic focus. Also, production managers can better schedule their manufacturing equipment if they have access to product orders; in fact, the scheduling of production runs and reconfiguration of equipment could be automated. Organizations can also integrate production schedules with inventory and purchasing systems to ensure the availability of materials for production. Because production requirements affect staffing, human resource information systems would benefit from integration with manufacturing systems.

Should Janice DeMarco introduce computer-integrated manufacturing at Monarch Beer? What are the costs and benefits of introducing such a system? Clearly Janice must diagnose her department's and even the organization's needs and then evaluate and select systems that best fit these needs.

Office Automation

Office automation poses different issues from the automation of manufacturing and design processes. It attempts to improve communication and record keeping by more effectively acquiring, organizing, manipulating, and exchanging information. Office automation refers to computerizing nontransaction-oriented activities, including communication, decision making, desktop publishing, scheduling, document creation, and graphics production.[32] Traditionally, most offices have used paper for maintaining and storing information. But paper has many flaws as an information medium—it is hard to share, easily lost or misplaced, and requires extensive storage space. Automating an office eliminates these problems by using the computer as the primary medium for information generation, storage, retrieval, and exchange.

Computerized information is easily shared; it can be sorted, organized, cross-referenced, and filed in ways that make it difficult or impossible to misplace; and its storage is compact.

SOUTHTRUST BANK OF ALABAMA

SouthTrust Bank of Alabama discovered that its retail sales incentive program could not and did not become successful until it was augmented with branch automation software that allowed the bank's platform personnel to become more productive.[33] The Office of the Audi-

OFFICE OF THE AUDITOR GENERAL OF CANADA

ONTARIO MINISTRY OF CONSUMER AND COMMERCIAL RELATIONS

tor General of Canada, for example, developed an easy-to-use electronic briefcase that allows the auditor to access, analyze, and report an array of data quickly and effectively.[34]

Computers can also improve interpersonal communication. Automating the office allows communication to occur when the parties involved are not present at the same time and place. For example, when Janice DeMarco needs to solve problems jointly with her three shift supervisors, she can bring them together in an electronic forum where they can raise issues, discuss options, and obtain feedback even though they are never at the plant at the same time. The Consumer Information Centre in the Ontario Ministry of Consumer and Commercial Relations introduced a voice-processing system that allowed staff members to answer callers in a timely fashion who previously might have waited as long as 45 minutes.[35] Although the automation of interpersonal communication opens communication paths that might not otherwise exist, it also can decrease accuracy by reducing the amount of information exchanged through body language and other physical signals, and it can slow the rate of information exchange.

Office Automation Functions

Most office activities can be automated to some degree. This section briefly examines the automation of filing, calculating, preparing documents, managing time, and communicating. Janice DeMarco might diagnose needs in these and other areas of the production department and then specify potential candidates for automation at Monarch Beer.

Filing. Filing and retrieving paper documents wastes time and space and creates opportunities for loss of information. Information created electronically can be automatically stored in a database as it is created, eliminating the filing function entirely. For example, when a salesperson records a sale on an electronic terminal rather than on a paper sales receipt, database management software can automatically file this information. Not only does electronic filing eliminate the need for a filing clerk, but it also increases efficiency in retrieving the information: A customer service representative, for example, may retrieve the sale by customer, date, sales clerk, or type of item; in contrast, the customer service representative could retrieve a paper receipt only according to the single characteristic by which it was filed (for example, date of sale).

Calculations. Office workers in a paper-based office spend a great deal of time calculating summaries of data for accounting and management. Office clerks at Monarch Beer might summarize logs of production runs, tallying output by beer type, date of production, or machines used. Computers can calculate such summaries automatically and produce them periodically. Spreadsheet software (see Chapter 5) allows office workers to perform calculations that otherwise would be too costly or would take so long that results would not be available in a timely fashion. It can also display the results of such calculations graphically so that managers can understand them more readily.

Document Preparation. Software for word processing, desktop publishing, presentation graphics, and electronic mail has automated the process of document production at many offices. Office workers using these products can write, edit, and package almost any type of document with minimal professional assistance and without retyping or reentry of information by other means. Chapter 5 presents an extensive discussion of software used for document preparation.

Time Management. Time management includes preparing schedules and making appointments. Project management software and calendar software can achieve some efficiencies by automating these tasks. For example, an office worker can enter a standing weekly meeting onto an electronic calendar without having to manually pencil it onto 52 dates. Also, calendar software that accesses and compares the calendars of intended meeting participants can determine possible appointment dates and times for meetings. Manually arranging such meetings might otherwise take several hours of clerical time.

Communication. Electronic mail, voice mail, bulletin boards, electronic notes, and a host of other software can facilitate interpersonal communication, both for information exchange and for decision making (see Chapter 8 and later in this chapter for additional discussion). Groupware typically includes communication software that supports group decision making (see Chapter 11).

The Desktop Paradigm. A person who can organize electronic work in the same way as he or she organizes papers on a desk can increase job efficiency. GUI operating systems (see Chapter 5) support this function by presenting an **electronic desk** that shows all office automation functions, such as electronic mail, word processing, and spreadsheets, as options (see Figure 9-5). GUI operating systems allow a user to shift among functions at will, keeping several open at one time and facilitating the movement of information from one function to another.

Electronic Mail

Electronic mail software permits users of a multiuser computer to communicate electronically with one another. When electronic mail is installed on a network, users on any of the connected computers can communicate. In addition, individuals can use public networks such

FIGURE 9-5 The Electronic Desk

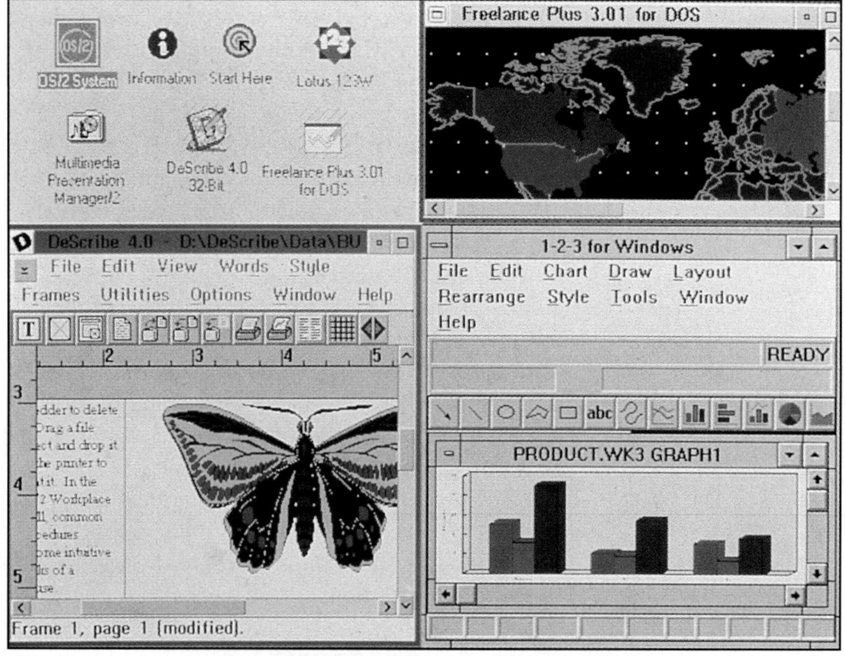

Courtesy of International Business Machines Corporation.

as Compuserve and supernetworks such as the Internet to send messages to users outside their organization.

Electronic mail systems have varying features but generally operate as follows. Assume you want to send a message. You begin by identifying the intended recipient or recipients by their **electronic address(es),** also known as their **electronic mailbox(es).** Your electronic mail system should provide a directory to help you find the electronic address of intended recipients if you know their names, titles, or locations. After you find these addresses, you can compose a message using either your word processor or an editor provided by the electronic mail program. Most electronic mail software will allow you to attach graphics, spreadsheets, or other office automation material to the document to be mailed. After you have composed a message, edited it, and attached material to it, you may give the order to deliver it. The software then puts copies of your message into the electronic mailboxes of the specified recipients. When the recipients next use their computers, they will be notified that they have received mail. They can then use their electronic mail software to read the message, extract any attached data, forward the message to other parties, or reply to it.

Figure 9-6 identifies additional features common to many electronic mail packages. Managers responsible for selecting electronic mail systems should evaluate how well the available features meet their information needs. A **distribution list** or **mailing list** is a list of mailboxes that you can create, name, and use to identify recipients of your messages. Janice DeMarco might create three distribution lists for workers on each of the three shifts so that she can send a message to all workers on a given shift. Managers must ensure that workers can access E-mail from both compatible and incompatible systems. Synchronizing incompatible electronic mail directories poses a major challenge.[36] **Carbon copying** refers to sending a message to someone other than the intended recipient. The carbon copy recipient, identified as such in the message header, understands that the message was intended for another person. Many packages also allow the sending of **blind carbon copies:** The software does not tell the intended recipient who has received blind carbon copies.

Delivery control includes priority delivery, receipt verification, failure notification, and delayed delivery. **Priority delivery** allows the message sender to attach a priority—for example, urgent, regular, or low—to each message. Knowing a message's priority helps the recipient respond to it in a timely fashion. **Receipt verification** notifies the sender when the receiver reads the message. **Failure notification** alerts the sender to a message that could not be delivered: Most often, the sender specified an incorrect mailbox. However, the sender might also request failure notification if the recipient has not read the message before a specified date. **Delayed delivery** allows the user to specify that the message should not be delivered until a specified date in the future. Some people use delayed delivery to send reminders

Features of Electronic Mail Software

Distribution lists	Flexible ordering of unread messages
"Carbon" copying	Flexible message searching
Priority delivery	Message encryption
Receipt verification	Mail logging for administration
Failure notification	Automatic forwarding
Delayed delivery	Forms
Orderly archiving of read messages	Macro language

to themselves. **Automatic forwarding** allows all messages (or all messages that meet certain criteria) to be forwarded to another mailbox. If a person plans to be away from the office on vacation, he or she can use automatic forwarding to allow another person to receive and respond to the messages.

People who receive a great deal of mail appreciate the archiving and searching features available with most electronic mail packages. Most packages allow users to group messages into folders: Some mail packages allow folders to contain other folders, creating a hierarchical structure. Janice DeMarco might, for example, create a folder for all mail she receives about problems with temperature control and a subfolder for those problems she has handled. Electronic mail systems should allow organizing messages by date, sender, subject, or priority. Sophisticated packages allow users to identify and read all messages containing a specified word or phrase. Forms for different types of mail messages, such as memos or press releases, can facilitate the composition of messages and be used as a criterion for message sorting or searching. Macro languages, or scripts, allow sophisticated mail users to automate series of keystrokes for performing repetitive tasks, such as deleting all messages in a folder meeting certain criteria.

Security is a critical issue for electronic mail. Some electronic mail packages automatically encrypt mail messages so that systems administrators or others who have access to mailbox files cannot read the messages. When the recipient wants to read a message, the software decodes and displays it. This feature does not protect against others reading a person's mail at that person's unattended computer terminal. Some mail packages provide additional security by requiring the recipient to know a password in order to decode a message you send.

Electronic Imaging

Electronic imaging management (EIM) systems store documents on computers instead of in filing cabinets. An EIM system can store all types of documents, from photographs to invoices, retrieve and show them on a screen in seconds, and even reproduce them on paper. An EIM system requires a high-speed, high-resolution scanner to capture documents in digital form. Usually, to store the massive amount of data generated requires an optical disk system. An EIM system should include software that applies special data compression techniques to reduce the amount of storage needed to save a picture. Finally, it demands a high-speed laser printer to produce quality images on output.

U.S. Patent Office

U.S. Internal Revenue Service

J.C. Penney

Image Engineering

Chubb Services

D. B. Kelly

Christensen & Jones

EIM systems offer particular advantages to organizations that otherwise retain a large amount of paper. An organization that can keep all its files in a few office cabinets probably does not need an EIM system. The U.S. Patent Office, U.S. Internal Revenue Service, local registries of deeds, and insurance companies exemplify organizations that require entire buildings to store their documents. Paper processing in such environments becomes difficult because several hours or days may be required to find and retrieve filed documents. The Internal Revenue Service, for example, is now moving to EIM to automate its paper processing.[37] J.C. Penney Company uses EIM to improve customer service and claims processing in its insurance applications.[38] Image Engineering, Inc. developed an imaging system that tracks blood donations.[39]

Smaller organizations can also benefit from EIM systems. For example, Chubb Services Corporation has used EIM systems since 1992 to make claims data and document images available on demand to claims-processing service representatives. Chubb Services believes that EIM gives it a competitive advantage because it can handle claims faster and at a lower cost.[40] The D. B. Kelly Company, which operates a network of automobile inspection locations, uses EIM to store color photographs as well as records about vehicles inspected.[41] Christensen & Jones, Inc. creates and monitors employee benefit plans; it uses EIM for paper-free storage—files scanned into the system can be called onto the screen almost instantaneously.[42]

Integrating Office Automation with Information Systems

Information systems professionals should anticipate how office workers will generate new information as well as use the information their organization maintains. They can then integrate office automation into the formal information systems used in the organization. For example, a worker who tracks overdue accounts should have access to information about the state of each account and should be able to modify account files upon renegotiating a payment agreement. The formal accounts payable system should automate these capabilities for the office worker.

Because information systems professionals cannot anticipate all information needs, information systems should have an ability to interface with office automation systems. Using a database management system to implement the functional information systems and then providing interfaces between the selected database management system and all software products used for office automation can accomplish this objective. For example, Janice DeMarco should be able to load production data from her information systems into a spreadsheet for analyzing trends and into a graphics presentation package for presenting key information to Monarch Beer's board of directors.

Automation of Education and Training

Computers cannot yet totally replace teachers and trainers in a classroom. However, they can automate many functions that teachers traditionally perform, such as giving lectures, administering and grading multiple-choice examinations, showing slides or movies, and answering some student questions. **Courseware** refers to software that automates education and training; **computer-based training (CBT)** describes training programs that use courseware. Many banks use computer-based training to allow workers to learn information at their own pace.[43] CBT has been used to teach auditors basic computer processing and how to audit accounts payable operations.[44] Major domestic and international airlines use CBT to prepare pilots to participate in simulations about flying and maintaining glass-cockpit airplanes; CBT reduces the amount of simulator time required and, thereby, the cost of pilot training.[45] Those responsible for training and development in organizations must first assess the training needs of workers and then determine whether automation of training and education meets these needs.

Advantages and Disadvantages of Automating Education and Training

Automating education allows students to receive a customized experience at a relatively low cost. For example, computer software can mimic the role of a tutor, and training software can provide more explanation more slowly than otherwise possible. Monarch Beer might use automated training software to help educate office staff or even production workers. Computer software can also offer as much practice and testing as a student needs. It allows a student to spend as much time as necessary on a subject without substantially increasing the costs of training the individual. Finally, CBT can standardize the delivery of material and assessment of outcomes across trainers: Organizations using CBT can ensure that students are exposed to all relevant material and that all students who pass the course have a common set of skills and knowledge.

The disadvantages of automating training include the high cost of developing courseware, the lack of personal contact during training, the inability of computer software to anticipate every question a student might ask, and difficulty in giving qualitative feedback. The value in developing courseware depends largely on the number of people who need training because the fixed cost of courseware must be amortized over the number of people trained. As the number of people trained increases, the cost per person declines. The relatively small size of Monarch Beer's work force may limit the cost effectiveness of automating its training. Sales of courseware outside the organization can defray the expense of developing it. Alternatively, courseware developed by third parties can be purchased at a cost well below an internal development cost.

Although some individuals prefer to work alone, most people find the lack of personal contact in CBT to be a psychological disadvantage. Combining computer-based training and instructor-led training can reduce such limitations. Such a mixture also alleviates the problem of responding to questions that the courseware developer did not anticipate. Some students require more qualitative feedback than CBT can provide. For example, history teachers provide such feedback by responding to written work such as essays or research papers. Also, trainers should provide qualitative feedback when teaching interpersonal skills; little software currently exists that evaluates the student's application of interpersonal skills and that provides appropriate activities and feedback. Most job training, however, seeks a different type of outcome, one that can be readily evaluated quantitatively. Such training includes acquiring a base of knowledge or a specific set of skills, and the success of such training can be assessed by how well the student demonstrates application of the knowledge or skills in response to computer exercises. The most effective CBT combines appropriate self-pacing, interactivity between the user and the program, and the use of multimedia.[46]

Tools for Automating Training

Currently, the automation of training comprises three major tools: 1) authorware, 2) multimedia and virtual reality technologies, and 3) distance education. Users can evaluate the quality of available tools and determine which technology best fits their needs.

Authorware. **Authorware** refers to software used by trainers to develop courseware.[47] For example, trainers can use computer software to assist in scripting or developing text materials. Authorware includes tools that enable developers to incorporate audio, graphics, text, and animation into course materials. Recent advances have included the ability to incorporate peripheral presentation devices, such as interactive videos, CD-ROM, and other multimedia. Authorware can also keep track of lesson parameters, such as the amount of time students spend on various questions or sections, the number of questions answered correctly, and whether students finish the course in the time allotted.[48]

Multimedia and Virtual Reality. A computer that stores and displays pictures, movies, and sound can present materials in a more interesting fashion than can a book or even some teachers. A virtual reality environment, which allows the student to act upon and affect the computer images and other output in a realistic fashion (see Chapter 6), provides an even more stimulating and effective opportunity for training. A student of human anatomy, for example, can view a three-dimensional image of a brain, rotate it, zoom in and out, and even dissect it. A training program for servicing copy machines can show students the parts in detail, illustrate their interconnections, and allow students to take the machine apart and put it back together without needing a copy machine for each student in the class.

HOLIDAY INN WORLDWIDE

Holiday Inn Worldwide uses multimedia technology for training employees at some of its hotels. Front-desk clerks, for example, can use a mouse to click on an icon for "customer," and the computer responds with pictures and sound to lead them through the training they need to deal with customers on a routine basis. In addition, the computer presents employees with alternative picture and voice problem scenarios that they must address.[49] This type of experience, in an environment where trainees can make mistakes without causing damage and where their actions can be evaluated and corrected, gives trainees the competence they will need when they assume the full responsibilities of their jobs.

Distance Education. **Distance education** describes the application of data communication technology to bring educational resources to students at distant locations. An instructor in New York City can use computers to simultaneously provide training to a company's employees in multiple sites around the world. Not only can employees seated at terminals connected to the communication system see and hear the instructor, but they can also enter questions or answers addressed to the instructor or other trainees at their terminals. For example, the Canadian Progressive Conservative Party used distance education to broadcast a five-hour meeting to 300 participants across the country. Individuals at various sites used individually activated keypads to participate in the meeting.[50] Distance education also allows instructors to call upon remote resources. For example, the instructor in New York can take the trainees on a live tour through a manufacturing plant in Ireland guided by an employee at the Irish plant.

CANADIAN PROGRESSIVE CONSERVATIVE PARTY

Expert Systems

An **expert system (ES)** describes computer software that automates the role of an expert in a given field. The software acts like an expert by providing advice to employees, helping them solve problems and make decisions (and even making decisions itself), and explaining the reasoning behind its recommendations. Expert systems incorporate the findings of **artificial intelligence,** the branch of computer science that emulates human behavior and thought in computer hardware and software.[51]

Because expert systems can help people make decisions, many texts classify them as a tool for decision support (see Chapter 11). In practice, however, companies apply ESs most often to technical rather than managerial decision making. For example, repair technicians often use ESs to help them diagnose and solve problems with machinery.[52] Human resource professionals might use expert systems to support staffing, training and development, and control activities.[53]

Figure 9-7 lists an array of application areas in which expert systems can be useful. Production engineers at Monarch Beer might use expert systems to assist with equipment maintenance. Paper mills use vibration analysis expert systems to diagnose and eliminate machine problems.[54] DuPont uses an ES called Transportation Emergency Response Planner to guide field technicians through the proper procedures for controlling and cleaning up chemical spills when accidents occur during transport of the chemicals.[55] Digital Equipment Corporation uses an ES called XCON to ascertain the correctness of customer orders. The minicomputers made by Digital are assembled by mixing and matching different input, output, storage, and processing parts to best meet specific customer requirements. Although orders are written up by trained salespeople, the number of possible parts is so large and the constraints that determine which parts work together are so complex that experts or expert systems are needed in most cases to put together a final assembly plan.[56]

DUPONT

DIGITAL EQUIPMENT

Pacific Bell uses expert systems to identify, track, and bill more than 1.5 million previously unbillable calls per month.[57] Federal Express uses the Ramp Management Advisory System to help schedule and direct aircraft on the approximately 400 acres it manages at its Memphis hub so that aircraft wait a minimal amount of time for free ramp space and so that their traffic patterns do not cross.[58] Ford Motor Company uses an expert system that translates structured English descriptions into detailed plant-floor assembly instructions and labor standards.[59] Planners who develop process plans at Northrop can work as much as 18 times faster using an expert system.[60] Managers must diagnose their information needs and then determine whether expert systems can meet these needs.

PACIFIC BELL

FEDERAL EXPRESS

FORD

NORTHROP

FIGURE 9-7 Potential Applications for Expert Systems

Configuration
- Selection and arrangement of components of systems or facilities
- Selection of quality assurance methods

Diagnosis
- Computer hardware
- Computer networks
- Mechanical equipment
- Mechanical parts
- Electronic instruments
- Circuits
- Data exchange troubleshooting
- Preventive maintenance of machines

Assembly
- Robotic assembly
- Visual verification of assembly techniques
- Process or materials selection

Interpretation and analysis
- Interpretation of SPC data
- Circuit analysis
- Interpretation of diagnostic instrument output
- Recommendation for disposition of rejected components and assemblies
- Part master set-up
- Incoming material inspection
- Voice input of product faults
- Identification of parts with vision systems
- Automated visual inspection
- Self-configuring production lines

Monitoring
- Equipment
- Factory monitoring/crisis management
- Industrial reports
- Product design for design for manufacturing
- Open work on shop floor for dynamic reassignment of work due to down machines or material shortages

Planning
- Asset and liability management
- System specification and selection
- Intelligent object-oriented material requirements planning
- Contracts
- Shop scheduling
- Project management
- Planning experiments
- New product introduction
- Computer-assisted process planning (routing and standards generation)
- Object-oriented MRP
- Natural language planner advisors

Design systems
- Object-oriented mechanical CAD
- Manufacturability testing
- VLSI
- Circuit synthesis
- Design of manufacturing facilities
- Design of automated storage and retrieval systems
- Process development (IDEF input and evaluation)

Software development
- Automated programming

Management
- Preparation of first article delivery schedule
- Return on investment planning
- Intelligent policies and procedures

Education
- Qualification of employees for technical jobs
- Tutoring systems based on complete work (i.e., the development of a test evaluation program that suggests changes for optimization to the test engineer)

Reprinted with permission from Dan Rasmus, AI in the '90s: Its impact on manufacturing, Part 2, *Manufacturing Systems* (January 1991): 36.

HALLIBURTON SYSTEMS

Expert systems may also automate training. They can provide instructions to trainees who do not know how to accomplish a particular task or solve a particular problem, and they can identify, correct, and explain errors that trainees might make in addressing the problem. Halliburton Systems uses expert systems as a training tool for operators and engineers engaged in the cementing of oil wells.[61] Some organizations have used ESs to automate their

help desk, the office that employees or customers call to receive help in using their computers or other technical products.[62] Some researchers have argued that unlike other automation systems, expert systems have no dysfunctional effects such as lower job satisfaction.[63] A recent survey of 500 systems analysts, directors of information centers, and data processing managers indicated that 70 percent of their companies had expert systems.[64] These systems offered the benefits of improved decision making by nonexperts, greater consistency in decision making, faster response time in making decisions, savings in operational costs, and more available information for decision makers. Reported drawbacks include the lack of qualified knowledge engineers and expert system designers as well as the high development cost.

Components of an Expert System

An ES consists of four components: 1) a knowledge base, 2) an inference engine, 3) an explanation module, and 4) a user interface. Each expert system has a unique knowledge base; the other parts of the ES function in any expert system and are sold off-the-shelf as **expert systems shell** software.

The **knowledge base** consists of specific facts, rules-of-thumb, relationships, historical scenarios (known as **frames**), and other information that an expert knows and might use to solve problems in a particular area or domain. Development of such a base of knowledge is the primary problem in creating an ES. Some expert systems software treats facts and rules differently. It draws its facts from databases whose information may change continuously. The rules it uses, however, are placed in a special **rule base** by the expert systems developer, who changes them rarely. Other expert systems software simply treats rules and/or relationships as one of several types of facts and makes no distinction between the fact and rule parts of the knowledge base.

The **inference engine** applies the knowledge base to a particular problem. For example, suppose the knowledge base states the following: A and B are brothers; C is A's daughter; and a niece is defined as the daughter of one's brother or sister. If a user asks the ES to identify B's nieces, the inference engine applies the rules and data to determine that C is B's niece. The **explanation module** then tells the user how the inference engine applied the rules and facts to reach its conclusion. In this case it would say that C is B's niece because C is the daughter of B's brother A.

Inference engines work not only upon known facts but also upon suspected facts, or facts that are probably true. Most inference engines can understand and process facts expressed in terms of likelihood—in terms of probability, or in ordinal terms—just as human experts would. For example, if a medical ES knows that John is old and that old people are likely to suffer from heart disease, its inference engine will conclude that John likely suffers from heart disease as it performs its other diagnoses.

The **user interface** acquires and modifies the rules and knowledge in the knowledge base, accepts a description of the user's problem, asks the user for additional information if necessary or desirable to address the problem, and presents its conclusions, recommendations, and explanations in an understandable fashion. User interfaces can be textual or graphic, depending on the nature of the problem to be solved. The user interface may also directly control machines and provide input into information systems that use the output of the ES decision.

Developing Expert Systems

Given the quality and sophistication of today's ES shells, the critical and most difficult component of expert system development is translating the knowledge of experts into the knowledge base that the shell software requires. A **knowledge engineer,** a professional trained to probe experts on how they know, understand, or suspect their diagnoses to be true, often performs this task. Recent advances in expert systems shells have improved their ability to obtain an expert's knowledge by directly asking the expert questions without the assistance or interference of a knowledge engineer. Recent research has found that experts can generally acquire the computer skills necessary to generate and test a knowledge base more easily and successfully than knowledge engineers can acquire knowledge about a particular problem domain.[65]

AMERICAN EXPRESS

Developing an expert system, even to automate what appears to be a simple task, often takes a great deal of time. American Express, for example, required almost six months to develop a 520-rule prototype of an expert system called Authorizer's Assistant, which automates the authorization of credit-card purchases. The final product took more time to develop and included more than 1,000 rules. Was it worth the investment? American Express claims that Authorizer's Assistant now saves tens of millions of dollars per year and does the work of 700 authorization employees.[66] Coopers & Lybrand estimates that it spent almost $1 million on the development of ExperTax, an expert system to assist auditors performing corporate audits. The development effort occupied more than 1,000 hours of some of Coopers & Lybrand's most expensive talent, but now that talent is available to each of its 96 offices through the ExperTax system.[67] Although examples like these are common, expert systems do not have to be complex to help address well-defined problems. Reportedly, the majority of corporate expert systems use fewer than 100 rules and are built in a six-week to six-month time frame.[68]

COOPERS & LYBRAND

Neural Networks

Neural networks are a class of self-teaching expert system that operate by mimicking the human brain. Rather than using built-in or programmed rules and an inference engine, a neural network is built to identify and recognize patterns. Like the neurons (nerves) in the brain, a neural network expert system connects, combines, and weighs inputs (signals) through several layers of connectivity to produce outputs. A neural network "learns" (or more correctly, is trained) by having an expert evaluate its output. When it performs correctly, the software reinforces the connections that produced the valid response. When it performs incorrectly, it reduces the weights or connections responsible for the bad response. To properly train a neural network, experts must provide a large number of examples over as broad a spectrum of inputs as possible. But the trainers do no programming; the neural network programs itself as the trainers evaluate its responses.

One of the primary advantages of neural networks over traditional expert systems is their ability to recognize a pattern or predict a result using data that are incomplete or not entirely accurate.[69] Although this ability, sometimes called **fuzzy logic,** can be incorporated into traditional expert systems rule evaluation,[70] traditional systems incorporating fuzzy logic do not have a memory, cannot learn from experience, and are much harder to train to recognize patterns. Neural networks, therefore, are particularly useful for activities such as forecasting, where inputs are often unknown or inexact. For example, using neural networks, a professional bettor picked the winning horse 17 out of 22 times using past performance data; a courthouse in Pennsylvania used data on juror utilization to determine the precise number of jurors required to service the next day's trial schedule.[71] Neural networks have helped the manager of Fidelity's Stock Selector fund to return an average of 30 percent per year, more than 50 percent above the market average.[72] Because written or typed characters are often not well formed, neural networks are incorporated in some commercial optical character recognition software.[73] They are also useful for speech recognition applications.[74]

FIDELITY

Another advantage of neural networks over traditional expert systems is their ability to dynamically adjust to changing conditions. This characteristic allows them to learn on the job and to modify their work as the job changes. Ravenswood Aluminum Corporation uses

RAVENSWOOD ALUMINUM

neural network software at its West Virginia mill to monitor the quality of aluminum milled for its can-making customers. Engineers train the software, as it works, by identifying and classifying flaws they observe in the mill's aluminum sheets.

NOISE CANCELLATION TECHNOLOGIES

NEUROMEDICAL SYSTEMS

RICOH

Neural networks are incorporated in a variety of consumer, scientific, and medical products. For example, in a Noise Cancellation Technologies' headphone product called the NoiseBuster, neural networks help cancel external noise; in Neuromedical Systems, Inc.'s product called Papnet, they help identify cancerous cells in pap smears; they control the voltage in copiers made by Ricoh Corporation; in fax machines, they help cancel echoes created by telephone lines; and in automobiles they can control antilock brakes, active-suspension systems, and idle speed.[75]

Summary

Automation describes the use of computers to perform tasks previously performed by people. It attempts to increase the efficiency and reduce the cost of performing various tasks in the workplace. Three common applications for automation include 1) manufacturing and design, 2) the office environment, and 3) education and training. Expert systems is a software technology that automates the consultation of an expert.

Computer-aided manufacturing, computer-aided design, and computer-integrated manufacturing describe three ways of automating manufacturing and design. Computer-aided manufacturing (CAM) automates machine monitoring and control through the use of flexible manufacturing, robotics, and automated guided vehicles. Computer-aided design (CAD) allows engineers, architects, graphics designers, and others to compose their designs on a computer rather than on paper. Computer-integrated manufacturing (CIM) coordinates CAM and CAD systems into an integrated information system that automates data sharing among departments.

Office automation systems perform filing, mathematical calculation, document preparation, time management, and communication using computer hardware and software. They also can include electronic mail and electronic imaging systems. IS professionals can integrate office automation into formal information systems in the organization.

Automating education and training occurs through the use of authorware, multimedia capabilities of computers, and distance education. Automation allows students to receive customized learning experiences at a relatively low cost, although it virtually eliminates personal contact with experts during the training.

Expert systems can support manufacturing, design, training, and an array of other functional activities in organizations. Composed of a knowledge or rule base, an inference engine, an explanation module, and a user interface, an expert system automates the role of an expert in a given field. Neural networks are a class of self-teaching expert system that operate by mimicking the human brain. Developing expert systems can pose significant challenges to organizations.

Key Terms

Artificial intelligence
Authorware
Automated guided vehicle (AGV)
Automatic forwarding
Automation
Blind carbon copy
Carbon copying
Computer-aided design (CAD)
Computer-aided manufacturing (CAM)
Computer-based training (CBT)
Computer-integrated manufacturing (CIM)
Courseware
Delayed delivery
Delivery control
Design
Distance education

Distribution list
Electronic address
Electronic desk
Electronic imaging management (EIM)
Electronic mail
Electronic mailbox
Expert system (ES)
Expert systems shell
Explanation module
Failure notification
Flexible manufacturing
Frame
Fuzzy logic
Help desk
Inference engine
Knowledge base
Knowledge engineer
Mailing list
Manufacturing
Neural network
Priority delivery
Process design
Product design
Product information manager
Rapid prototyping
Receipt verification
Robot
Rule base
User interface

Review Questions

1. Define computer-aided manufacturing and offer two advantages and two disadvantages it poses over the monitoring and control of machinery by humans alone.
2. Offer two examples each of the use of flexible manufacturing, robotics, and automated guided vehicles in manufacturing.
3. List five features you would want in a computer-aided design software package.
4. What is rapid prototyping? How does it help designers?
5. What is the purpose of computer-integrated manufacturing? What problems might manufacturing companies face without CIM?
6. List five functions office automation can support.
7. What are the benefits of automating filing?
8. What are the two primary functions of time management software?
9. What features would you expect to find in electronic mail software?
10. What advantages can small organizations find in electronic imaging?
11. What are the advantages and disadvantages of automating education and training?
12. What is authorware? What features and functions should it provide?
13. How can virtual reality be used for training?
14. How can expert systems be used for training?
15. What advantages and disadvantages can companies expect in developing and using expert systems?
16. What are the four components of an expert system?
17. Describe the major characteristics and uses of neural networks.
18. Cite two advantages of neural networks over traditional expert systems.

MINICASE

Kaiser Foundation Health Plan: Expert System Modernizes Membership Qualification

An expert system-based application has helped Kaiser Foundation Health Plan, Inc. journey "from the 19th century to the 21st century," said Ila Sullivan, manager of special enrollments.

Sullivan's group, based in Oakland, Calif., evaluates individual Kaiser applicants to determine whether they medically qualify for membership. Prior to the development of an expert system application to help manage this process, the group handled all information manually.

For example, Sullivan wrote information on scratch pads, and other employees transferred that data onto index cards. All told, there were "something like 15 handoffs from start to finish" during the process of putting together applicant data, according to Sullivan. Every application had to be reviewed by medical staffers. Processing applications could take four to six weeks.

Enter Joe Yuson, a project manager at Kaiser Permanente Northern California based in Walnut Creek. Because Kaiser was already a shop that used Texas Instruments, Inc.'s Information Engineering Facility, Yuson and his staff evaluated the Oakland site's requirements and did a business area analysis a year ago.

"There were two primary issues: customer satisfaction and improving turnaround time, and redeploying and redeveloping insurance applications to meet the needs for the next decade or two," Yuson said. "This particular area had zero automation."

His group redesigned some of the business processes to reduce the number of handoffs, and it purchased a rules-based expert systems shell that lets the developers codify the rules the medical staffers use when they review client applications.

Dubbed System for Individual Marketing and Review (SIMR), the system has cut in half the amount of time a doctor needs to review applications, Yuson said. The expert systems shell also allows users to maintain their own rules so that, for example, if they want to change the number of cigarette packs allowed in one year or if they feel a rule relating height to weight is too restrictive for prospective members, they can change it, according to Yuson.

SIMR now handles about 80 percent of individual applications to Kaiser, with approximately 28 percent immediate acceptances and 12 percent immediate rejections that do not require medical review. Applications with immediate responses are turned around in two days; those requiring medical review take two to three weeks.

Case Questions

1. What problems did Kaiser Health Plan, Inc. face in its process of medically qualifying individuals for membership?
2. What tool did Kaiser choose to automate this process?
3. How does Kaiser measure the quality of its process? How does the SIMR system compare to the pre-automated system?

SOURCE: Melinda-Carol Ballou, Expert system modernizes Kaiser, *Computerworld* (November 14, 1994): 121.

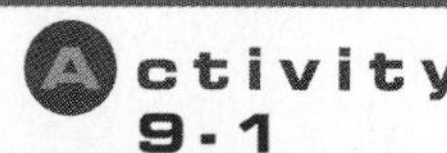

Activity 9-1 Will Automation Help?

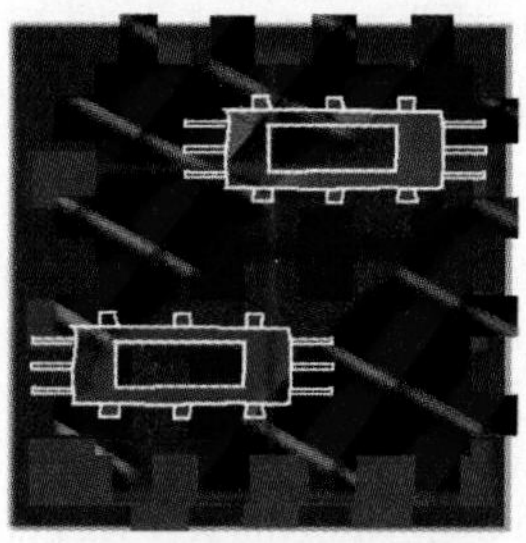

short case

STEP 1: Read each case below. Then determine for each situation whether automation could improve it.

Case 1: Fabulous Candy Company began in the owner's kitchen in 1970. The company soon opened a larger plant with ten employees who guided the manufacturing process. All candy was made by hand until the late 1970s, when the owner installed some assembly-line equipment to speed up the processing. In the 1980s, the company introduced a number of new products that sent sales skyrocketing. The company had difficulty keeping up with demand for chocolates in the original plant and soon opened several additional plants that produced more standard chocolate bars and other novelties. Company performance remained strong through most of the 1980s. Recently, some of the original employees, who had a strong sense of taste, color, and aesthetics, which was key for the chocolate production, retired. The owner of Fabulous Candy, which has become a major national candy manufacturer, feels that product quality and output are suffering.

Case 2: Taco City is a national chain of fast-food franchises that sells Mexican-style food in the United States. Taco City recently made a public offering of stock and plans to expand from 150 outlets to 400 outlets in the next two years. Currently, individual franchise owners use a basic menu in their stores but can make any adjustments in the product they wish. For example, one store owner recently introduced a special hot sauce based on an old family recipe. The executives of Taco City believe that there may be some benefits to standardizing the product across all franchises and are considering automating purchasing, cooking, and sales.

Case 3: Secretaries, Inc. is a ten-person firm that provides secretarial and graphics design services to approximately 50 clients. A client calls Secretaries, Inc. with job specifications, and the firm's office manager records the relevant information and then gives the client a price for the job. Assuming that the price is acceptable, the office manager then assigns the job to either the most qualified employee or a qualified employee with the lowest work load. Employees log in the job and then maintain a work log until it is finished. Currently, all record keeping is done manually.

Case 4: Greybolt University, a moderate-sized private university, is experiencing significant financial problems. Increases in faculty salaries and benefits plus major capital improvements have had a tremendous impact on the university's budget. The school has introduced new technology to support classroom learning but has not used technology to increase class size or replace faculty in the classroom. The provost of Greybolt University has read extensively about industry's experiences in automating training and is considering automating the classroom experience at Greybolt.

STEP 2: For those situations in which automation would help the situation, 1) identify the elements of the situation that should be automated, and 2) offer an approach for automating those elements.

STEP 3: Individually, in small groups, or with the entire class, review your answers to step 2. Then answer the following questions:

1. What elements do the cases described in step 2 have in common?
2. What factors influence whether a system should be automated?
3. What options for automation exist? ●

Activity 9-2 Automating a Physician's Office

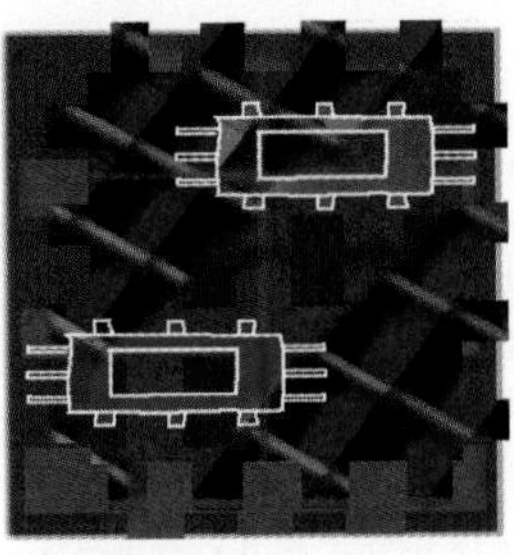

short case

STEP 1: You have recently been hired by Drs. Janice Johnson and Jeffrey Johnson to automate their medical office. They have a pediatrics practice that has grown dramatically since they completed their medical training ten years ago. They have recently moved into a new office building. They have already added two nurse practitioners to their practice and plan to add two more physicians within the next year. The doctors know that they must have an administrative system that can support this growth.

Currently, the office has one secretary/receptionist, Mary McGuire, who schedules patients, does patient billings, updates medical records after patient visits, and generally performs the clerical and administrative functions in the office. She uses a personal computer for word processing but has not computerized any other aspects of her job. The physicians have periodically hired temporary employees to assist Mary McGuire with the administrative work but now know that they must invest in automating the office. They are prepared to acquire the hardware and software necessary to support their busy practice as well as hire any additional staff required within reasonable limits.

STEP 2: In groups of two to four students, diagnose the information needs in this practice. Then propose a plan for automating the office. Be as specific as possible in proposing specific hardware and software. Design how the information will flow in the office and who will input and have access to the data. You may find it helpful to visit a physician's office and interview the office staff to obtain a better understanding of how it functions.

STEP 3: Share your plans with the rest of the class. Compare the information needs you identified. Compare and contrast the various approaches for meeting these needs.

STEP 4: In small groups or with the entire class, answer the following:

1. What types of processes should be automated?
2. What options for automating these processes exist?
3. What tradeoffs must one make in selecting the hardware and software for automating the office?
4. What can the physicians expect to be a reasonable cost for automating the administration of their practice? ●

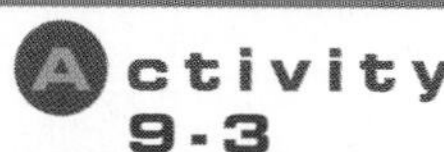

Activity 9-3 The Automated Guest-History Program

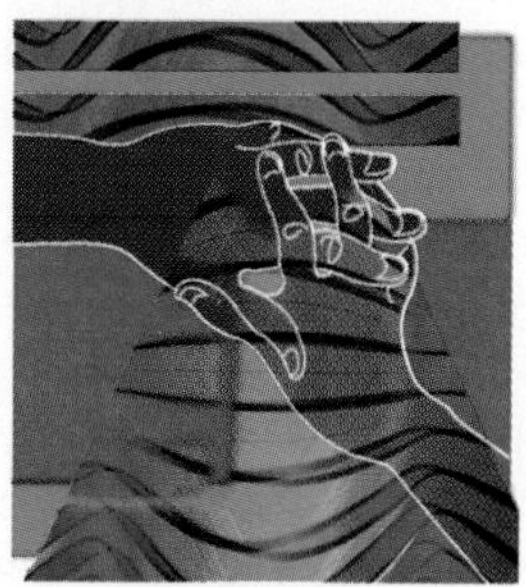

STEP 1: Read the following scenario.

Business traveler Chris Talioferro has just picked up luggage at the airport baggage claim area. As Chris steps out to the ground transportation stop, the hotel courtesy van is waiting to meet the flight. In the van is Talioferro's favorite caffeine-free soft drink. Arriving at the front desk, the clerk greets Chris by name and asks for a quick signature on the hotel's registration card. All relevant guest information is already on the card, including the method of payment. Just to be sure Talioferro hasn't changed plans, the clerk confirms that payment will be by Gold Card. Chris can see that his assigned room is the same as he had during his last stay at this hotel. During that visit Chris mentioned that the room's glass-topped dinette-style table was useful. Entering the room, the bellhop turns the television to the recently merged Disney-CNN network, which the housekeeper noticed was always on when Talioferro occupied the room before. In the closet are much-needed hangers plus a personally monogrammed robe. On the table is the *International Herald Tribune,* the newspaper Chris requested during the last visit. Opening the minibar, Talioferro finds plenty of macadamia nuts (the minibar attendant noticed that five packages disappeared during Chris's last stay) and Famous Amos chocolate chip cookies. Chris also notices a bottle of 1964 Chateau Latour, a preferred wine. Finally, Chris notes a message from the concierge telling about tickets to tonight's performance at the theater.

STEP 2: Individually or in small groups, identify the components of the automated guest-history program described here.

STEP 3: Write a computer program that incorporates three of these components into a mini guest-history program.

STEP 4: Propose at least two additional components for the guest-history program. ●

Reprinted from Carl R. Ruthstrom and Charlene A. Dykman, *Information Systems for Managers Casebook* (St. Paul: West, 1992): 67–68; adapted from Chekitan S. Dev and Bernard D. Ellis, Cornell University, Guest histories: An untapped resource, *The Cornell H.R.A. Quarterly* (August 1991): 29–37.

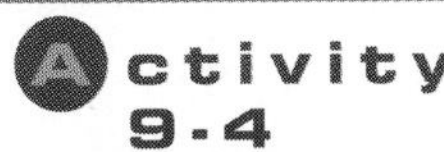

The Training Problem

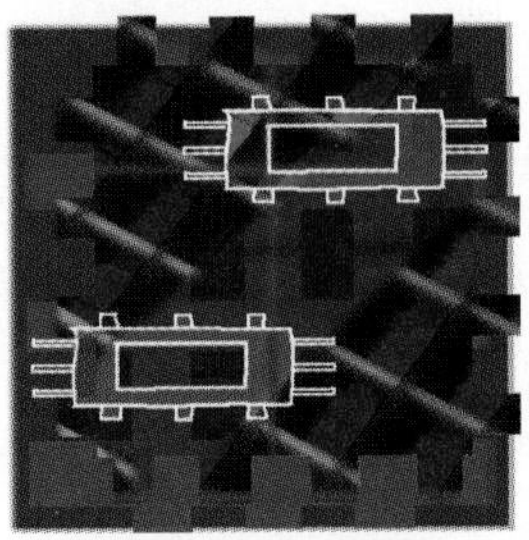

short case

STEP 1: You are the director of training for a Fortune 500 insurance company. Your company conducts more than 1,000 seminars worldwide in both technical and managerial subjects; these range in length from a few hours to several weeks. Your training budget for next year has been slashed by 25 percent, although you are expected to continue the same level of training worldwide.

STEP 2: Individually or in small groups, offer a plan for automating some aspects of training to allow you to meet your budget constraints while maintaining your training target.

STEP 3: In small groups or with the entire class, share your plans. Identify the advantages and disadvantages of each plan. Specify any additional options for automating aspects of the training. ●

Notes

[1]Michael L. Sullivan-Trainor, A gamble and a long-term view pay off at Timken, *Computerworld* (September 11, 1989): 66, 68.

[2]John Teresko, Japan's best plants: Lean, efficient, flexible, and worker-friendly, *Industry Week* (September 7, 1992): 33–58.

[3]Michael L. Sullivan-Trainor, op. cit.

[4]Kim Blass, World-class strategies help create a world-class CIM facility, *Industrial Engineering* 24(11) (1992): 26–29.

[5]The history and statistics quoted in this paragraph were adapted from John Teresko, Robots: Poised for new arms race, *Industry Week* (December 7, 1992): 48–58.

[6]Cutting costs through welding, *Production* 105(4) (April 1993): 55.

[7]*PEM: Plant Engineering & Maintenance* 16(1) (February 1993): 19.

[8]Harry T. Roman, Robots cut maintenance costs at PSE&G, *Power Engineering* 96(10) (October 1992): 66–69.

[9]Robots load automotive batteries at assembly plant, *Robotics World* 11(1) (March 1993): 453–456.

[10]Electric finishing robots at Ford's Utica trim plant produce top-quality parts, *Robotics World* 10(4) (December 1992): 30–31.

[11]Leo O'Connor, Flexible welder used for GM's Opel Astra in Europe, *Mechanical Engineering* 114(6) (June 1992): 20.

[12]Mark Spaulding, Robotic palletizers tie 10 lines together, *Packaging* 38(1) (January 1993): 28–31.

[13]John Teresko, Robots move out of the factory, *Industry Week* (December 7, 1992): 58.

[14]Richard Saltus, N.E. Baptist to try out robot for hip surgery, *The Boston Globe* (September 29, 1993): 29.

[15]Robert K. Robinson, Ross L. Fink, and William B. Rose, Jr., *Robotics Today* 5 (Third Quarter 1992): 5–6.

[16]Douglas W. Nelms, Delta's automated cargo, *Air Transport World* 29 (August 1992): 57–58.

[17]Les Gould, Multi-function AGVs takes on spiraling growth, *Modern Materials Handling* 47(50) (April 1992): 32–35.

[18]Les Gould, How Sears moves six pallets at a time, *Modern Materials Handling* 46(5) (April 1991): 55–57.

[19]Guy Castleberry, *Robotics World* 10 (September 1992): 10, 12.

[20]See, for example, Kyle Heger, Whiz . . . bang . . . eureka! The automation of creativity, *Communication World* 8(11) (November 1991): 18–21; and Patricia D. Prince, A showcase for computer art, *Personal Computing* 13(10) (October 1989): 132–134.

[21]Paul Dvorak, FEA software shapes manufacturing's future, *Machine Design* (May 28, 1993): 102–114.

[22]Lisa Kempfer, Fine-tune your CAD engine, *Computer-Aided Engineering* (March 1993): 20–28.

[23]Seth B. Hunter, PIM systems manage the information morass, *Machine Design* (May 28, 1993): 114–124.

[24]See Dan Rasmus, Conceptually speaking, *Manufacturing Systems* (March 1993): 14–18 for examples of rapid prototyping.

[25]Barbara Dutton, Focus on: Quality by design—engineering the aesthetic, *Manufacturing Systems* 11(3) (1993): 20–22.

[26]Tim Stevens, Rapid prototyping moves to desktop, *Industry Week* (February 1, 1993): 38–44.

[27]Julia King, Life in the slow lane, *Computerworld* (February 3, 1992): 67, 71.

[28]Jerry R. Robertson, How to accelerate manufacturing, *Machine Design* 65 (April 9, 1993): 79–82.

[29]VW's drive for manufacturing advantage, *Manufacturing Engineering* 110(4) (1993): 89–91.

[30]Julia King, Harley-Davidson revs up IS teamwork, *Computerworld* (February 3, 1992): 71.

[31]Moshen Attaran and Carl E. Upthegrove, Integrating automation in an ice cream processing plant, *Journal of Systems Management* 42(5) (1991): 6–8, 30.

[32]Veronia M. Cooper, Office automation: Myth or reality?, *Journal of Systems Management* 40(2) (1989): 35–36.

[33]Dave Seaman, Branch automation and productivity at SouthTrust Corporation, *Journal of Systems Management* 43(5) (1992): 10–12.

[34]Janine Strom, Creating an "electronic briefcase," *I.T. Magazine* 25(2) (1993): 27–28.

[35]Brenda Darby and Helena Taylor, New voice technology improves Ontario Ministry's service, *Journal of Systems Management* 43(4) (1992): 13–16.

[36]See, for example, Lynda Radosevich, Users want unified mail directories, *Computerworld* (August 30, 1993): 12.

[37]Ellis Booker, The paper chase, *Computerworld* (April 12, 1993): 20.

[38]Ellis Booker, Imaging, work flow expand at JC Penney, *Computerworld* (April 12, 1993): 52.

[39]Reality check: Tracking blood donations, *Computerworld* (April 5, 1993): 85.

[40]Gordon E. J. Hoke, Imaging streamlines operations at Chubb unit, *National Underwriter* 97 (April 12, 1993): 5, 25.

[41]Eileen Feretic, At last the paperless office (no kidding), *Success* 39(7) (1992): 34–35.

[42]Ibid.

[43]Camilla Cornell, Trendy training, *Canadian Banker* 100(2) (1993): 39–41; and Turning to multimedia, *Banking World* 10(8) (1992): 26, 28.

[44]Morton T. Siegel and Timothy R. Manholm, Computer-based training—The payoff, *Internal Auditing* 7(4) (1992): 84–88.

[45]Danna K. Henderson, On the CBT bandwagon, *Air Transport World* 29(8) (1992): 55–75.

[46]Bob Filipczak and Michele Picard, Put SPIMM in your CBT, *Training* 30(2) (1993): 12–14.

[47]Nick Rushby, The expanding market in authoring systems, *Personnel Management* 22(4) (April 1990): 89; and Nico Krone, Third parties embrace windows for multimedia, *InfoWorld* 13(8) (February 25, 1991): S15.

[48]See, for example, Gary P. Maul and David S. Spotts, A comparison of computer-based training and classroom instruction, *Industrial Engineering* 25(2) (February 1993): 25–27.

[49]Michael Fitzgerald, Multimedia to save hotel time, money, *Computerworld* (May 3, 1993): 94.

[50]Carolyn Van Brussel, End-user training: If it's in-house and interactive, it's hot, *Computing Canada* 18(19) (1992): 47.

[51]Dan Rasmus, AI in the '90s: Its impact on manufacturing, Part 1, *Manufacturing Systems* (December 1990): 30–34 discusses the relationship of artificial intelligence to robotics and expert systems.

[52]Marc H. Meyer and Kathleen Foley Curley, Putting expert systems technology to work, *Sloan Management Review* (Winter 1991): 21–31.

[53]Marian M. Extejt and Marc P. Lynn, Expert systems as human resource management decision tools, *Journal of Systems Management* 39(11) (1988): 10–15.

[54]Ian Liddle and Steve Reilly, Expert systems offer precise analysis, diagnosis of mill rotating machinery, *Pulp & Paper* 67(2) (1993): 53–55.

[55]Lawrence Meador and Ed G. Mahler, Choosing an expert systems game plan, *Datamation* (August 1, 1990): 64–69.

[56]Ibid.

[57]Willie Schatz, Who's calling, please?, *Computerworld* (November 23, 1992): 69, 73.

[58]Maryfran Johnson, Expert systems put Fedex in flight, *Computerworld* (November 18, 1991): 45.

[59]Dan Rasmus, AI in the '90s: Its impact on manufacturing, Part 2, *Manufacturing Systems* (January 1991): 32–39.

[60]Ibid.

[61]D. D. Onan, D. Kulakofsky, M. S. Van Domelen, and W. G. F. Ford, Expert systems help design cementing and acidizing jobs, *Oil & Gas Journal* (April 19, 1993): 59–61.

[62]Bob Francis, Help for the help desk, *Datamation* 39(7) (April 1993): 59–60.

[63]Terry Anthony Byrd, Implementation and use of expert systems in organizations: Perceptions of knowledge engineers, *Journal of Management Information Systems* 8 (Spring 1992): 97–116.

[64]A. Ansari and Batoul Modarress, Commercial use of expert systems in the U.S., *Journal of Systems Management* 41(12) (1990): 10–13, 32.

[65]Meyer and Curley, op. cit.

[66]H. P. Newquist, It actually works! *Computerworld* (April 18, 1994): 133, 135.

[67]Ibid.

[68]Harvey Newquist, Nearly everything you want to know about AI, *Computerworld* (July 29, 1991): 64–65.

[69]Harlan L. Ethridge and Richard C. Brooks, Neural networks: A new technology, *CPA Journal* (March 1994): 36–39.

[70]Lotfi A. Zadeh, Fuzzy logic, neural networks, and soft computing, *Communications of the ACM* (March 1994): 77–84.

[71]Gene Bylinsky, Computers that learn by doing, *Fortune* (September 6, 1993): 96–102.

[72]Susan Kuh, The new perilous stock market, *Fortune* (December 27, 1993): 48–62.

[73]Darryl K. Taft, OCR packages debut, *Computer Reseller News* (February 21, 1994): 139; E. I. Schwartz and J. B. Treece, Smart programs go to work: How applied-intelligence software makes decisions for the real world, *Business Week* (March 2, 1992): 97–105.

[74]David E. Rumelhart, Bernard Widrow, and Michael A. Lehr, The basic ideas in neural networks, *Communications of the ACM* (March 1994): 87–92.

[75]Bernard Widrow, David E. Rumelhart, and Michael A. Lehr, Neural networks: Applications in industry, business, and science, *Communications of the ACM* (March 1994): 93–105.

Recommended Readings

Asfahl, C. *Robots and Manufacturing Automation.* New York: Wiley, 1992.

Gallant, Stephen I. *Neural Network Learning and Expert Systems.* Cambridge, MA: MIT Press, 1993.

Irving, Richard H. and Higgins, Christopher, C. *Office Information Systems: Management, Issues, and Methods.* New York: Wiley, 1991.

McKerrow, Phillip. *Introduction to Robotics.* Reading, MA: Addison-Wesley, 1991.

Rose, Marshall T. *The Internet Message: Closing the Book with Electronic Mail.* Englewood Cliffs, NJ: Prentice-Hall, 1993.

Sproull, Lee and Kiesler, Sara. *Connections: New Ways of Working in the Networked Organization.* Cambridge, MA: MIT Press, 1991.

Watkins, Paul R. and Eliot, Lance B. (Eds.) *Expert Systems in Business and Finance: Issues and Applications.* New York: Wiley, 1993.

Chapter 10

Transaction Processing Systems

OUTLINE

Inventory Management at Jordan's Furniture

Reasons for Recording Transactions
- Information for Employees
- Information for Management
- Records for External Parties
- Audit Trails

Capturing and Processing Transactions
- Paper Data Capture
- Electronic Data Capture
- Transcribing from Paper into Electronic Form
- Batch versus Real-Time Processing

Requirements of Real-Time Transaction Processing Systems
- Speed
- Reliability
- Accessibility

Examples of Transaction Processing Systems
- Point-of-Sale (POS) Systems
- Order Entry Systems
- Reservation Systems
- Purchasing/Receiving Systems
- General Accounting Systems

Developing and Modifying Transaction Processing Systems
- Development, Testing, and Production Environments
- Database Management Systems as the Heart of TPS

LEARNING OBJECTIVES

After completing the readings and activities for Chapter 10, students will be able to

1. Define and give examples of a transaction and a transaction processing system.
2. List four reasons that companies record transactions.
3. Describe four ways of capturing and processing transactions.
4. Describe three requirements of real-time transaction processing systems.
5. Illustrate the use of a TPS to record point-of-sale transactions.
6. Cite the key components of order entry systems.
7. Illustrate the use of reservation systems for processing transactions.
8. Give two examples of purchasing/receiving systems.
9. Show why a general accounting system is a TPS.
10. Describe two key issues for developing and modifying transaction processing systems.

Jordan's Furniture has succeeded where others have failed. In the midst of a recessionary economy that has dealt heavy blows to the furniture industry—1,500 furniture retailers have gone out of business in the United States during the past year alone—Jordan's has grown, in part because of its innovative use of new technology.

"Our computer system has allowed us to expand and grow in a controlled way. It has given us a real competitive advantage over other furniture stores," said Eliot Jordan, co-owner of the $70 million company.

Ready Fast

For example, a computerized receiving system allows Jordan's three stores to make inventory available to customers only 20 minutes after it has been unloaded from delivery trucks. The system has reduced inventory errors by 90 percent, according to Patrick Malloy, Jordan's computer systems manager. In addition, Jordan's has gained an edge in customer service by maintaining five years of customer data on-line, Malloy said.

The center of Jordan's computing strategy is a Data General Corporation Aviion 6240 running Unix System V Release 4. About 200 DG terminals are sprinkled throughout Jordan's main store and warehouse and at its two sister stores in Waltham, Massachusetts and Nashua, New Hampshire. The three stores are connected by Codex Corporation multiplexers and 56K-bit dedicated lines with a backup line. Each department has a direct line to the computer, which minimizes the risk of companywide problems.

The company's major software package is an Oracle Corporation-based furniture retail system from GE Retail in San Diego. Jordan's has been using the software since 1977.

With more than 14 trucks and 1,200 pieces of furniture coming in each day, Jordan's needs a heavy-duty tracking system. Bar coding the receiving system has enabled Jordan's to reduce human error dramatically and make inventory available more quickly.

Ready to Move

The night before a truck comes in, the receiving staff prints out bar codes for the incoming merchandise. When the truck arrives, bar code stickers are immediately placed on furniture.

The codes are then scanned as furniture is received, stacked, and stored in the warehouse, and the scanned information is uploaded to the DG host.

Salespeople can check the availability of stock by using terminals throughout the store. "We can tell [customers] exactly what we have in stock or when an item is coming in, and they can also see the price," Malloy said. "It gives them more confidence in us."

Using the new computer system, Jordan's can count inventory about 30 times a year. The process of counting and verifying inventory used to take a month and could shut down the warehouse for as long as five days. Now it is done in a week, with no downtime.

While he could not chalk up a specific cost-saving figure to Jordan's computer investment, Chief Executive Officer Steven J. Gaskins said the company's early leap into high technology gave it a crucial edge. "When we put in computers in 1977, none of our competitors knew what a computer was."

Jordan's plans more changes for the coming years. By mid-1993 it hoped to install new radio frequency scanners to cut response time and mistakes, Malloy said.[1]

A **transaction** is an event that affects an organization's conducting its business. Although transactions historically refer primarily to events in which money changes hands, we have adopted a broader, more current definition. Examples of transactions include ordering a part, receiving an ordered part, manufacturing a product, moving a product into a warehouse, moving a product from a warehouse to a retail area, selling a product, checking a customer's credit rating, transferring cash from a savings to a checking account, and hiring an employee. A large company such as an airline or a bank may perform hundreds of transactions every minute of the business day. **Transaction processing** describes either the manual or computerized recording of the transactions of a business. Jordan's Furniture, for example, maintains records of current inventory. The company also likely maintains information about sales, special orders, and deliveries. A **transaction processing system** (or **TPS**), either manual or computerized, formulates, maintains, and updates such records for the business. Companies vary considerably in the sophistication of their transaction processing systems. Jordan's Furniture, for example, developed a fairly sophisticated and well-integrated TPS both to support transactions and to provide an advantage over its competitors.

In this chapter we focus primarily on computerized transaction processing systems. We first explain why organizations record transactions. Next we discuss capturing and processing data. We continue with a discussion of the requirements of a real-time transaction processing system. Then we present some examples of transaction processing systems. The chapter concludes with a discussion of issues for developing and modifying transaction processing systems.

Reasons for Recording Transactions

Companies record transactions for four primary reasons: 1) to provide information needed by employees to transact business and perform their job functions; 2) to collect information that managers need in order to make informed decisions; 3) to provide receipts, purchase orders, and other transaction records to external parties, such as customers and vendors, who participate in the transactions; and 4) to create records called **audit trails** that auditors use to verify corporate information reported by the company. Executives can diagnose whether these needs for recording transactions exist and then design a suitable transaction processing system to meet them.

Information for Employees

Most business activities, even fairly simple transactions, involve many employees. A salesperson at Jordan's Furniture, for example, requires information about a product's availability when processing a sale. Prior to the sale, in a separate transaction, a receiving clerk may have accepted the item into stock and recorded its receipt. The receiving clerk and the salesperson should not have to talk with each other to communicate that information. Whether Jordan's uses paper-based or computer-based transaction systems, the recording of a transaction by one employee can provide information needed by another.

Consider, for example, what happens when an airline agent sells a ticket, as illustrated in Figure 10-1. First, the agent verifies the price and availability of the seat requested. Because other agents transacting sales affect seat availability, agents log these transactions so that they do not sell the same seat twice. The sales agent can quote the prices of a seat to the customer because another employee had previously logged a transaction that set the prices. If the customer wants to reserve a seat, the agent consummates the sale, perhaps with a credit-card transaction. This transaction provides information to parties outside the company, such as notification of the credit-card company. The transaction also creates information that airline employees will use internally: a record of cash due from the credit-card company and data for the ticket and boarding pass. Later, another employee may use the sales information to generate and mail the ticket and boarding pass. Still later, if the customer does not take the trip, another agent will use the transaction information to process a refund. Other transactions, such as aircraft and crew scheduling, must have already occurred for the sale to succeed. Many employees, each relying on the record of transactions to handle their own part of the job, perform the transactions that lead to and include the ticket sale and supply of the service.

FIGURE 10-1 The Transaction of Selling an Airline Seat

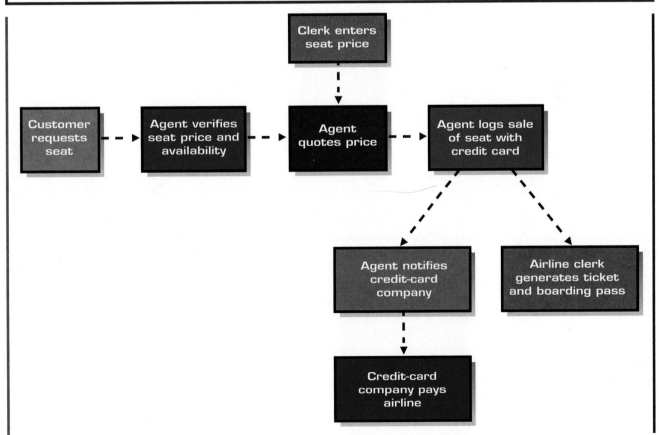

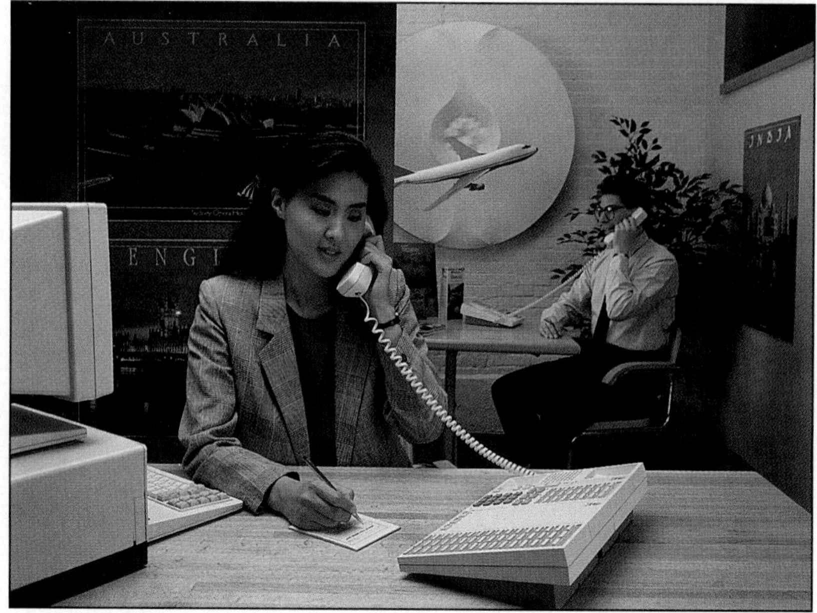

Travel agents rely on transaction processing features of reservation systems to ensure that two agents cannot book the same seat for two different customers at the same time.

Tony Stone Worldwide © John Riley

As this example illustrates, businesses record transactions so that employees executing related activities can coordinate their work. However, even companies that have a single employee need to record transactions to track business activities over time. Consider, for example, an attorney who bills clients for the number of hours she works for them. The attorney records the time spent and the content of the work for each client so that she can accurately bill her clients. When a client has questions about a bill a month or two later, the attorney can then explain her charges by telling the client precisely what work she did and how much time she spent doing it. In this case, recording the transaction preserves information needed to generate revenue.

Information for Management

Managers use summarized and detailed records of business to make decisions. They need to follow trends, identify problems, and verify that their decisions have the impact they expect. A distribution manager, for example, might view all data about product delivery to assess whether workers choose the most effective routes. A sales manager might analyze the impact of special promotions on the sales of new products after a comprehensive review of orders processed during a specified day, week, or month. A purchasing manager at Jordan's Furniture might, for example, identify problems with specific suppliers by checking the lead time required to secure products from them. At Nordstrom, a clothing retailer, buyers frequently scrutinize a database of sales transactions and transaction summaries to identify trends and predict what their customers will want.[2]

NORDSTROM

Decision makers at all organizational levels use transaction data to make decisions. At Duracell, the world's largest alkaline battery maker, CEO C. Robert Kidder cut his German sales staff and replaced them by local distributors after he determined that too many salespeople in Germany wasted time calling on too many small stores. He had zeroed in on Germany after first comparing the sales of salaried and hourly employees in the United States and abroad. These sales data were compiled from detailed sales transactions recorded by the company's TPS.[3] Chapter 11 further addresses how transaction processing systems feed data into managerial decision-making processes.

DURACELL

Records for External Parties

Transaction processing systems provide records of transactions between two companies and those between a company and an individual. For example, when you purchase an item at a department store, the sales clerk will likely hand you a receipt that describes the merchandise and shows the amount and the way you paid for it. While the internal record of the transaction recorded by the store's TPS may be the only record that the store needs, your physical receipt provides many benefits to you, and some to the store. You might, for example, use the receipt to reconcile your charge-account statement at the end of the month or to prove that you purchased the item if you wish to return it. The receipt also establishes the price you paid, which might be important if the item has since gone on sale. Your receipt, in this case, also helps the store identify the purchase transaction. You might need the receipt if a security clerk questioned you about shoplifting on your way out of the store.

In transactions between two companies, receipts and other documents, such as purchase orders, produced by one company's TPS enable the other company to verify and record the transactions into its own TPS. For example, when Jordan's buys furniture from a supplier located in another city, its purchasing agent probably sends the supplier a purchase order communicating the items ordered, the expected price, the quantity, and the terms of sale. Upon receipt of the purchase order, the supplier's sales department may log the order into its TPS. When the supplier ships the order, its TPS will probably produce copies of the shipping documentation for the shipper and for Jordan's, plus an invoice for Jordan's. Jordan's TPS needs this information to prepare for and verify the receipt of new inventory and to prepare to pay the supplier.

Many companies exchange transaction data electronically using EDI (see Chapter 8) to avoid manual data entry, to speed communication between customer and supplier, to reduce transcription errors, and to avoid loss of data through bad paper filing or postal errors. Using EDI, transaction processing systems effectively communicate with one another over telecommunication media with little or no human intervention, using forms that have been standardized and accepted by both parties.

Audit Trails

Most countries have laws that require businesses to record transactions in order to substantiate the calculation of tax due to the government. In addition, the United States government and most state and foreign governments require every company doing business with them to verify periodically that the company charges fairly for the goods and services it sells. When government agencies audit a business, they use transaction records to trace and verify the company's reporting of its revenues and expenses.

Public corporations, those that sell stock to the public, have a fiduciary responsibility to accurately report their financial state. Most countries codify this responsibility into law and regulate it via government agencies such as the Securities and Exchange Commission in the United States. Companies in the United States must employ independent auditors to corroborate their financial reporting. These auditors rely on the transaction records of the company to verify that its financial statements accurately summarize and reflect its activities.

Companies also use audit trails internally to trace problems, as shown in Figure 10-2. For example, suppose a customer at Jordan's Furniture complains that he failed to receive an item he had ordered and paid for. Consider the trail of information the company might use to address this complaint: First the company would verify that it received the order and payment. Next the company would certify that it filled the order. Finally, the company would access the records that register the shipment of the order. The company identifies the shipping company, shipping date, and waybill number from these records. This information now allows the company to contact the shipper to verify delivery.

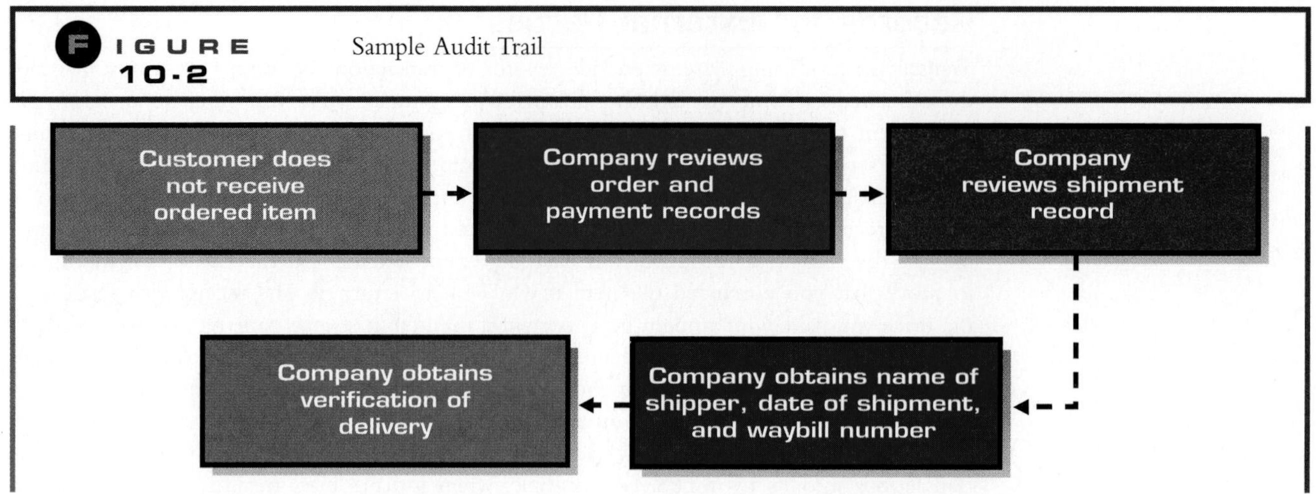

FIGURE 10-2 Sample Audit Trail

Capturing and Processing Transactions

As Figure 10-3 illustrates, companies can capture data in either a paper or an electronic form. Data captured on paper must be processed manually or converted into an electronic form to be processed by computer. Data captured electronically generally undergo some simple verification and storage processing as they are captured. Many systems, however, do not fully process data at the time they are captured. For example, a system that collects data electronically about shipments as they arrive may not update its inventory data until the end of the day. This delayed processing is called batch processing.

Paper Data Capture

Companies typically use predesigned forms, called **source documents,** to capture transactions on paper. Examples of source documents include purchase orders, sales receipts, invoices, and check registers. Typically, clerks or employees performing transactions complete these source documents. In some cases, such as with order forms, the customer, supplier, or out-

FIGURE 10-3 Methods of Capturing and Processing Data

Data Processing Method	Data Capture Method: Paper	Data Capture Method: Electronic
Manual	Paper-based TPS	—
Deferred Computer	Transcribed	On-line Batch
Immediate Computer	—	Real-time

side party may complete the source document without the assistance of company employees. Source documents provide a secure, hard-copy record of transactions. Many companies, even those having computer-based TPSs, use source documents to record transactions containing information that cannot be input by keyboard, such as a customer signature or a drawing.

Electronic Data Capture

Computers can capture transactions directly, eliminating the need for source documents. This process is called **on-line data entry.** Companies using on-line data entry may use predesigned forms similar to source documents, except that these forms are pictured on a computer screen, as shown in Figure 10-4. As an employee performs a transaction, he or she records transaction data in the appropriate place on the screen.

Computerizing the recording of transactions offers many advantages. First, employees can use input hardware such as bar code scanners to reduce the amount of work and time required to record transactions, particularly when compared with employees recording transactions by hand. Jordan's Furniture uses bar code scanners as the furniture enters storage; salespeople can then access these data and quickly check the availability of specific items. Second, computers can perform calculations, find prices, and automate other tasks for an employee performing a transaction. Third, computerization reduces the amount of paper that needs to be stored. Finally, computers handle information more effectively; they minimize information loss, provide more flexible access to information, promote and enable sharing of transaction data among employees, allow the summarizing of data for management planning and control, and allow the data entry person to immediately verify data and catch errors at their source.

FIGURE 10-4 A Screen Form for Real-Time Data Entry

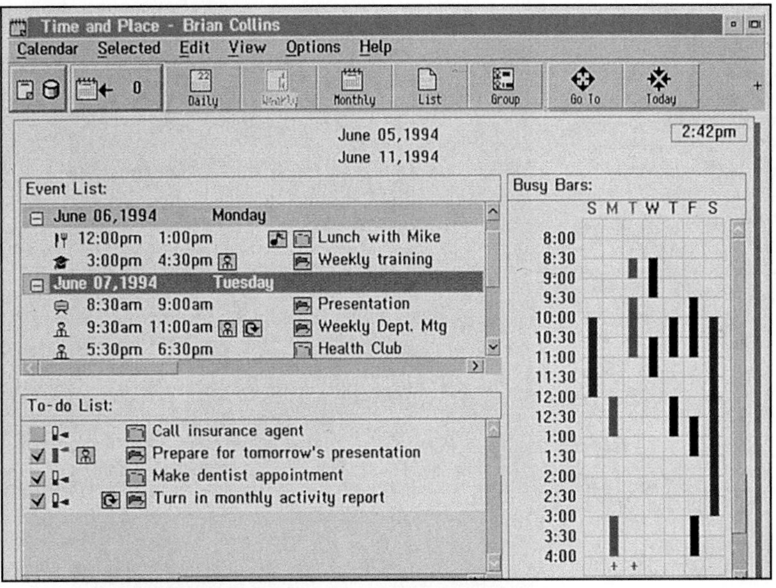

Courtesy of International Business Machines Corporation.

On-line data entry also has disadvantages. It requires a computer or a computer terminal at each location at which a transaction may occur: The number of terminals used and the computer hardware and software to support their use can be expensive. Also, a company that uses computers to record its transactions may experience significant problems if the computers fail. Consider, for example, the difficulties an airline passenger encounters when an airline's computer reservation system fails to operate. Although most companies rely on paper transaction systems in case of computer failure, business slows dramatically and often inconveniences customers.

Transcribing from Paper into Electronic Form

Organizations that capture data on paper can realize many of the benefits of on-line data entry by transcribing their paper records into an electronic form. **Data entry clerks** perform such transcription. Using source documents rather than entering transaction data directly into a computer can realize cost savings by reducing the number of data entry terminals required. In addition, computer failures become less problematic. However, the transcription process invariably introduces errors, duplicates work, and increases the time between the transaction's occurrence and the information's availability. The absence of advanced input devices and a computer to make calculations and perform table lookups at the time at which the transaction occurs increases the time and effort needed to process transactions.

Batch versus Real-time Processing

Companies use two substantially different methods to process transaction data. **Batch processing** stores electronic records or transcribed paper records in a stand-alone computer file that other parts of the company's information system cannot use or access. Periodically, typically at night, the computer processes the entire batch of records, thereby updating the company's information system. **Real-time processing,** in contrast, attends to data upon their entry, immediately updating the information system and making the data available to all users.

The primary advantage of batch processing over real-time processing is that it uses fewer

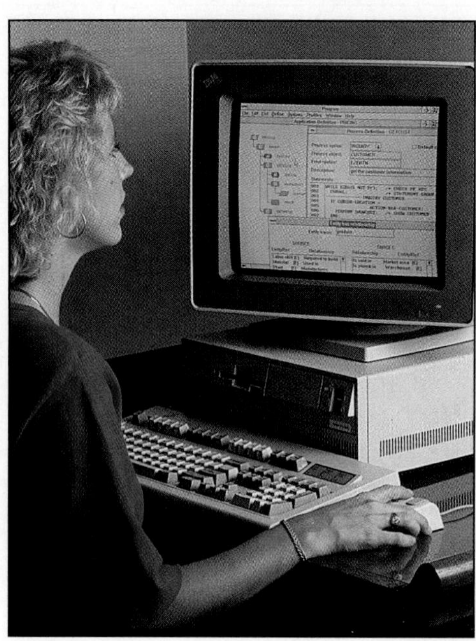

Customer service agents using on-line data entry can look up prices and respond to other customer information requests. When the transaction is complete, the information that the agent enters is immediately available for recall and analysis.

Courtesy of International Business Machines Corporation.

and less costly computer resources. Real-time processing must handle transactions as they occur, requiring the computer to simultaneously run programs to handle every type of active transaction. When the computer operator instead batches transactions by transaction type, the computer can run one program at a time. Reducing the number of programs running simultaneously decreases the amount of memory the computer requires and also reduces the amount of time the computer spends loading and unloading the programs from disk. Batching transactions allows a company to evenly spread the load on its computers over the entire day, reducing the peaks and thereby reducing the need for processor power during peak periods. This increase in efficiency can dramatically reduce the cost of the computers necessary to handle the TPS. Batch processing also allows the use of microcomputers and other low-cost devices to create the electronic batch. A diskette or network connection then transfers the batch to the computer that integrates the data into the information system. This division of labor reduces the load on the computer or computers that run the information system.

The primary advantage of real-time processing is that it makes transaction information immediately available to anyone who might need it. At Jordan's Furniture, for example, inventory is available to customers only 20 minutes after it has been unloaded from delivery trucks. With batch processing, information about inventory would probably be unavailable until the next day.

Another advantage of real-time processing is that it simplifies error processing and may reduce the amount of data being entered. Consider, for example, the processing of customer orders at a store such as Jordan's Furniture. The order form contains the customer's name and address. Using real-time processing, when the data entry clerk enters the name of an existing customer, the computer can retrieve the address; the clerk simply verifies it, making entries only upon observing an error. Using batch processing, the data entry clerk must always enter the customer address because he or she does not know whether the file already contains information about the customer. If a company used customer codes on the order form, the real-time processing would check the codes upon entry for validity. Using batch processing, no data checking would occur until the computer processed the batch. Errors would be logged to an error file for correction and entry in another batch.

Requirements of Real-Time Transaction Processing Systems

Increasingly, organizations prefer real-time transaction processing systems over those that involve any manual recording or entry of data or batching of data processing. Regardless of their applications and functions, all real-time transaction processing systems should be fast, reliable, and accessible. Managers should evaluate existing systems using these criteria; they should also ensure that any new systems have sufficient speed, reliability, and accessibility.

Speed

Employees and others who use a real-time TPS expect it to respond immediately to their input. TPS developers typically apply the following rule of thumb to ensure such performance: A user should have to wait no longer than three seconds for a TPS response. Lack of a rapid response delays the activity of business, possibly increasing costs or resulting in lost revenue.

Consider again a sale at Jordan's Furniture. What will happen if the salesperson cannot instantly check the availability of particular furniture? The customer may choose to purchase from another store. What will happen if the salesperson must wait five to ten minutes for credit authorization for the customer? Again, the customer might consider leaving the store without completing the purchase. Now consider a travel agent who cannot almost instantaneously confirm a desired flight for a customer because the transaction processing system responds too slowly. The seat at the desired fare may no longer be available when the transaction finally occurs. In each of these cases, the inability to process transactions quickly may impact customers' behaviors, employee performance, and the organization's bottom line.

Reliability

Because an electronic record might be the only record of a transaction for companies using a real-time TPS, the failure of a TPS to record a transaction properly might have significant consequences. At Jordan's Furniture, for example, such a failure might result in furniture not being delivered to a customer as promised or payment for furniture not being collected. TPS failures fall into two categories: 1) incorrect (including missing) recording of a transaction and 2) system inoperability. System inoperability causes less damage than incorrect recording because the person executing the transaction can abort it or record it manually for later computer entry. Incorrect or missing transactions leave no record of failure and can result in a company's making poor decisions, losing revenue, and failing to abide by promises made to customers or suppliers. Systems designers can create fault-tolerant systems and recoverability procedures to address these problems.

Fault-Tolerant Systems. Users of systems that record the transfer of money, such as banking TPSs, have an especially low tolerance for hardware or software failures. They require systems, known as **fault-tolerant systems** and **nonstop systems,** that achieve high reliability by using hardware incorporating redundancy and software designed to take advantage of this redundancy.

Fault-tolerant systems use redundant hardware and power supplies to minimize the likelihood of a computer failure. Systems designed for maximum reliability use dual or triple processors, RAM, and disk storage. The amount of redundancy depends on the extent of reliability desired. Additional hardware identifies component failures, which causes the system to automatically shut down the failing parts so that operators can replace circuit boards and other hardware components while the redundant parts of the system continue to operate. An **uninterrupted power supply** provides secondary sources of power, such as a battery or electric generator, along with circuitry that can recognize and react to a loss of power from the primary supply before it can affect the computer. Fault-tolerant systems generally include remote diagnostic capabilities so vendors can troubleshoot a system in operation.

Systems that have a higher tolerance for failure may limit redundancy to disk storage. They may use operating systems software called **disk mirroring** to simultaneously send data to two or more disk devices whenever data are written to disk.[4] Upon retrieving the data from disk, the system compares the copies and corrects or flags any discrepancies. If one of the redundant disks should fail, the operating system continues to use the remaining disk(s) until the problem is corrected. The second method, known as **disk duplexing,** is a hardware solution that passes data destined for storage to two separate controllers with two separate disks;[5] this approach relies on RAID technology, described in Chapter 6. When the operating system sends data to the RAID controller, it automatically creates multiple copies of the data for storage on redundant devices.

Recoverability. When failures occur—even in fault-tolerant systems—the TPS, along with users and computer professionals, should be able to reconstruct incorrectly processed or partially processed transactions. Because database management systems provide a variety of tools and services to help achieve these objectives (see Chapter 7), TPS developers generally build a TPS onto a database management system.

Accessibility

Accessibility enables employees to record transactions whenever and wherever they occur. Employees who perform their transactions away from a desk may require innovative solutions and advanced communication technologies. Consider, for example, the way a delivery agent of a parcel delivery service might record a package delivery. The delivery agent could place a cellular phone call to a central computer as the delivery is made, enter his or her employee identification code on the touch-tone pad, and then enter the waybill number of the delivered package. United Parcel Service uses a similar on-line interactive electronic system for tracking packages: Drivers use a hand-held computer to record delivery, pickup, time, and customer signature information.[6] Alternatively, the employee can use the less-expensive option of making entries onto a laptop computer as packages are delivered; when the employee returns from his or her round of deliveries, the entries are off-loaded to the central computer.

UNITED PARCEL SERVICE

Most companies stop their real-time TPS for an hour or more each day to back up their systems in a stable environment, that is, when data are not changing. Changing data during system backup may preclude operators from reconstructing the state of the system upon a hardware or software failure. Companies that operate globally experience the problem of keeping real-time transaction processing systems operating 24 hours a day. Real-time TPSs may deal with this problem in either of two ways. First, they may partition the transaction data by area of the world, backing up independent partitions when they are inactive. Second, they may keep multiple transaction logs, starting new ones when old ones are ready for backup.

Examples of Transaction Processing Systems

Transaction processing systems include components to 1) collect or capture transaction data, 2) retrieve and report transaction data, and 3) make transaction data available for processing other transactions. Information systems used for management purposes (see Chapter 11) often include transaction processing systems. A well-designed TPS that interfaces with customers or suppliers can also offer a strategic advantage to an organization (see Chapter 12).

In this section, we examine five typical applications of TPS: point-of-sale systems, order entry systems, reservation systems, purchasing/receiving systems, and general accounting systems. Although we discuss them as stand-alone applications, most companies include these TPS applications as components of a more comprehensive system.

Point-of-Sale (POS) Systems

A **point-of-sale (POS) system** records the sale of a product or service and updates company records related to or affected by the sale. Jordan's Furniture and other retailers generally install such transaction processing systems. A typical POS transaction occurs as shown in Figure 10-5. When a customer brings an item to the sales counter or register, the sales clerk scans the product code with a bar code reader, manually enters the code for the product into the POS terminal, or presses the appropriate button for that product on the POS terminal. The POS system retrieves the price for the item and uses it to create a receipt for the customer and the company.

Simultaneously, the TPS records the type of item, sale price, method of payment, and often the time and date of purchase into the corporate database. If the customer pays by check, the POS system may interrogate a database of bad checks to verify that the person is not a known "deadbeat." In addition, it will receipt the check for processing at the bank. If the

FIGURE 10-5 A Point-of-Sale Transaction

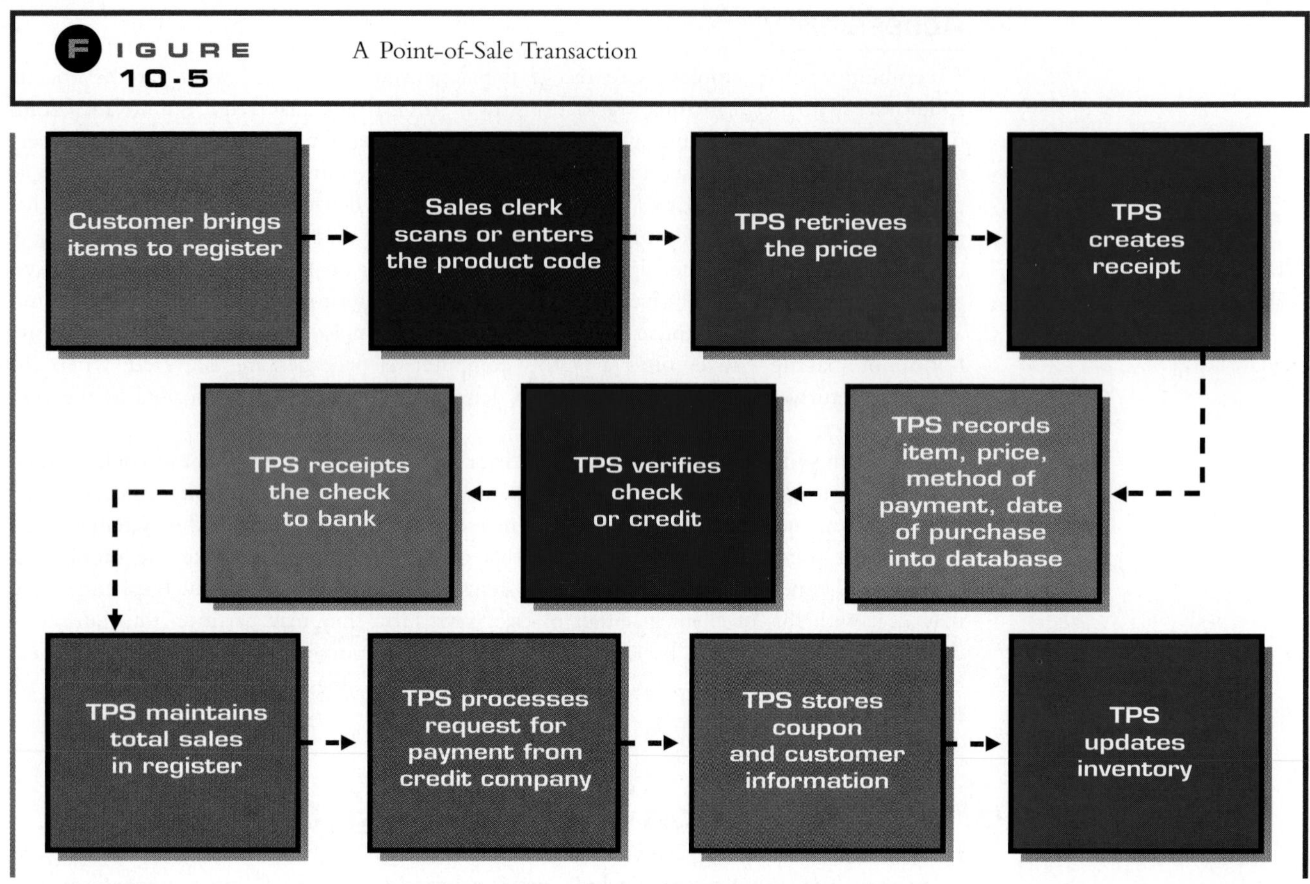

customer pays by credit card, the POS system may access an internal or external (available by telephone) database to verify the customer's credit and to process the request for payment by the credit-card company. If a customer uses a discount coupon, the TPS will also store information relating to the coupon. The POS system will store key elements of the payment, such as the credit-card or check number, along with the other transaction data.

The TPS may also store ancillary data, such as the ZIP code of the customer, entered by the sales clerk and subsequently used for marketing research. The POS system can track the amount of cash and checks in the register. Some systems also update inventory, either at the time of sale or in a batch process after the sales registers are closed.

STATE OF MARYLAND

INFO/CALIFORNIA

Point-of-sale systems can record service as well as sales transactions. State of Maryland residents eligible for welfare can draw their benefits from point-of-sale terminals in 3,000 grocery stores.[7] Info/California, a network of touch-screen kiosks, helps individuals order birth certificates and locate a variety of government services.[8]

LECHMERE

Point-of-sale systems often use special input hardware to improve the speed, ease, and convenience of transacting a sale. Lechmere, Inc. installed sales kiosks in more than half its stores to allow customers to purchase merchandise without waiting for an available cash register; the kiosk includes a touch screen, credit-card reader, speaker, and printer.[9] In addition to POS terminals (see Chapter 6), POS systems often include magnetic card readers to assist in processing credit-card and bank cash-card transactions and scanning devices to process bar codes attached to products and discount coupons.

POS terminals may be networked to a central computer or may operate independently. Independent terminals usually have more limited functionality because they have self-contained databases. For example, they often do not contain pricing information or customer credit information. Diskettes can transfer transaction logs from independent POS stations located at a single site to a central computer for consolidation and batch processing to update sales and inventory databases. POS systems with stations at several sites poll the POS terminals by telephone to collect the transaction records and provide an alternative to the real-time updating of inventory.[10]

Networked POS stations provide the benefit of centralized database management, greater storage, and increased computing power. If the central processor or the network fails, however, the failure affects all POS stations, which may significantly slow the selling process and reduce the number of sales. Installing a network may also be difficult and expensive and result in less flexibility for the organization. Wireless LANs (see Chapter 8) have increasingly emerged as a solution to this problem.[11] Younkers, Inc., for example, leases more than $1 million of wireless LAN equipment to connect its POS terminals in its stores.[12]

YOUNKERS

Small companies often lack the expertise to select, purchase, install, and run a POS system. This problem has spawned the creation of a number of businesses that support the POS needs of small companies. For example, AT&T provides a service that links the POS terminals of a client company to computers at designated companies that perform the transaction processing for their clients.[13] Third-party vendors also perform credit checking. SPS Transaction Services of Riverwoods, Illinois processed more than 240 million POS transactions from around the country in 1992; its system checked customer credit in as little as seven seconds.[14]

AT&T

SPS TRANSACTION SERVICES

Companies that want to run their POS systems in-house can purchase **turnkey systems** (hardware and software bundled as a single product) from POS vendors. Vendors in the early 1980s sold specialized systems, highly customized by industry, such as restaurant, fast food, retail, and hardware. The increasing power and standardization of personal computers in the late 1980s has changed the industry. PCs and their peripherals now act as the central components of POS systems.[15] Buyers can select from a broad range of customized input devices, monitors, and keyboards, all of which interface with standard PCs running any of a number of customized POS vertical packages.

Order Entry Systems

Order entry systems record and process the taking of an order. Used in such diverse businesses as pizza stores, mail-order distributors, insurance companies, newspaper advertising departments, and steel manufacturers, the primary objective of an order entry system is recording an order so that it can be properly filled. Such systems must also support prompt and rapid customer service. In addition, order entry systems should capture customer information for expediting and obtaining future orders. American Hospital Supply Corporation, for example, has a computerized system for ordering, tracking, and managing hospital supplies that performs both transaction processing and strategic functions.[16] Pizza Hut in Puerto Rico uses a single telephone number to receive all orders in the greater San Juan area. The company receives orders at a centralized location and then automatically dispatches them to the Pizza Hut store closest to the customer. Order time has declined from three or four minutes to 30 to 45 seconds as a result of using this system; sales volume has increased by 6 to 7 percent.[17] Banks can link to a check-printing vendor's communications system for ordering checks; they can place the order from a terminal in the bank by entering a customer's account and order information into a database at the vendor's site.[18] Hitachi Metals America Ltd. has an integrated order management system that encompasses all processes from the receipt of the order to its administration, scheduling, allocation, production configuration, distribution, installation, invoicing, and collection.[19]

AMERICAN HOSPITAL SUPPLY

PIZZA HUT

HITACHI METALS AMERICA

An order entry system typically functions as follows: When a customer calls to place an order, a clerk requests identifying information. The customer identifier requested by a mail-order company might appear as a number on the catalog received by the customer. Other companies use the customer's telephone number, birthdate, corporate federal identification number, individual social security number, club membership number, or name. If the order entry system determines that the company database includes the customer, the system displays additional identifying information, such as the customer's telephone number and address, for verification. The order entry system may require the clerk to register an unregistered or incorrectly registered customer. This transaction updates the company's customer database. Occasionally order entry systems, such as in the restaurant industry, do not require or store specific customer information.

The system next takes the order. An order entry system should include many features of a POS system, such as identifying and recording the price and quantity of specific items purchased, as well as the method of payment. Unlike POS systems, however, order entry systems may also require a shipping address, a billing address, and the ability to deal with back orders. Order entry systems must verify the inventory of ordered goods so that the sales clerk can inform the customer about shipping delays and so that the system can generate orders to replenish depleted stock.

Order entry systems differ markedly among industries and often need customization for companies within an industry. Consider, for example, the differences between the types of data necessary to describe products in several industries: A mail-order distributor uses a product number, which displays a product description; a fast-food chain uses a food name and size; a clothing distributor uses a product code, size, and color; a lumber distributor uses a lumber type, quality, and three dimensions (e.g., 1″ × 8″ × 20′); and a newspaper's advertising department accepts advertising text, its size, and its date of publication. These differences illustrate the difficulties of designing order entry software that crosses industry boundaries.

Reservation Systems

A **computerized reservation system (CRS)** describes a special type of order entry system used by airlines, hotels, car rental agencies, and other companies that sell, rent, or otherwise allocate a limited capacity to provide a service or the use of an asset. Because they sell from a limited capacity, reservation data entry stations must have access to a common database that tracks the capacity sold. If they lacked a common set of information, two stations could inadvertently sell the same unit of capacity because neither would know the capacity sold by the other.

CRSs typically use large mainframe computers. As the transaction volume (the number of reservations) in a CRS increases, the computer that accesses the common database will eventually become overloaded, resulting in slow and unacceptable performance. Computer systems can divide the capacity in a logical fashion and partition the database to reflect this division. In practice, however, companies have instead purchased more powerful computers to handle high loads.

CHOICE HOTELS INTERNATIONAL

ITT SHERATON

Choice Hotels International has introduced the Choice 2001 system, which offers direct, 24-hour access to customers about the availability of various rooms at various rates. Front-desk managers in Choice Hotels can adjust the available rooms, rates, and other amenities virtually instantaneously.[20] ITT Sheraton Corporation currently is integrating its reservation system with a property management system that handles all guest-related operations such as registration, check-out, and room expense tabs.[21]

QANTAS AIRWAYS

Qantas Airways developed its own subsidiary to develop and implement computer reservation systems. Its design allowed ticket agents worldwide to reserve seats on Qantas Airways. The airline linked its reservation service with reservation systems of other airlines, tour operators, hotels, and rental car agencies, among others, as a way of improving customer service.[22] Because of their open accessibility, airline reservation systems such as these can pose

BRITISH AIRWAYS

VIRGIN ATLANTIC AIRWAYS

significant security problems. For example, in 1993, after the filing of lawsuits and countersuits, British Airways acknowledged that members of its staff had tapped into Virgin Atlantic Airway's reservations data to obtain the home telephone numbers and flight information of first-class passengers booked on Virgin's flights. The staff members had then called these passengers to persuade them to change their tickets to British Airways.[23]

Purchasing/Receiving Systems

Purchasing systems and **receiving systems** document transactions between a company and its suppliers. Jordan's Furniture likely incorporates a purchasing/receiving system into its transaction processing system. These transactions have both internal and external implications, as suggested by the following scenario.

When a company orders goods, it either pays for the goods at the time of the order or commits to paying for them at a later date. In either case, the order reduces the budget available for further orders of a similar type. The purchasing TPS records the encumbrance on the budget so that other people who use the same budget can determine whether additional funds remain.

An order may produce an inventory notice to advise clerks and managers that inventory is being replenished. This notice reduces the likelihood that other employees will attempt to place duplicate orders. Also, the notice allows order entry clerks to advise customers that the items they need will shortly be in stock.

LEVI STRAUSS

FORD

An order also produces and records a purchase order. A **purchase order** is a form sent to a supplier to document an order. The purchasing staff can refer to the purchase order record when suppliers call with questions about the order. In some cases, the TPS may use EDI (see Chapter 8) to transfer the order electronically to the supplier. The purchase order record in this case is an electronic copy of the EDI order sent to the supplier. Levi Strauss & Company, for example, ties its retailers into an EDI to allow rapid adjustment of orders to match customer demands.[24] Ford Motor Company opened its internal inventory systems to suppliers so that they could check the stock levels of parts for Ford's North American assembly plants and rapidly ship any parts that were in short supply.[25]

When the supplier ships the items ordered, it may send an EDI or paper record of the shipment that usually arrives prior to the shipment itself. The TPS logs this record to alert receiving and inventory clerks and managers to the impending delivery. If the delivery does not arrive when expected, clerks can contact the shipping company to address the difficulty.

The arrival of the shipment generates additional transaction records: A record of the shipment's contents notes any discrepancy between the contents and the order; the customer can then accept or return the order. In addition, the customer may perform quality tests on the received goods. The TPS logs the results of these tests so that managers responsible for deciding which suppliers to use for future orders can base their decisions on concrete data. The TPS then updates the inventory with goods passing the quality tests. It may also generate an order return record, packing slips, and quality documentation for items not passing quality inspection. Finally, if the customer has not prepaid the order, the TPS makes a record of the amount owed to the supplier and enters it as an account payable. Companies that generate an account payable record at the time of order may need to modify that record to reflect differences between the goods accepted and received and those ordered.

General Accounting Systems

Every financial transaction affects the income statement and the balance sheet of the company. **General ledger systems** maintain records of the company's accounts; they incorporate payroll, accounts receivable, accounts payable, and cash management systems. **Payroll systems** track employee hours, wages, and other benefits; they automatically generate paychecks and records of additional benefits or payments to employees on a prescribed schedule. **Accounts receivable systems** track monies and other debts owed to the company as payment for goods and services provided; the TPS may generate reports used for checking credit, monitoring bad debts, pursuing overdue accounts, and reducing payment lags. **Accounts payable systems** may generate purchase orders and produce checks for paying the organization's bills. The accounts payable system may automatically review the discounts received by the company for early payment of bills, select the optimal time for paying the bills, and automatically generate the checks. **Cash management systems** maintain information about the receipt and distribution of cash. **Billing systems** generate account statements and bills to customers.

A general accounting TPS records all financial transactions and classifies them into specific accounts. Periodically, the TPS summarizes and consolidates these accounts so that managers and investors can assess the financial health of the company. Nevertheless, the TPS retains the transaction detail for some period so that auditors can verify the accuracy of the accounting system.

Developing and Modifying Transaction Processing Systems

Transaction processing systems pose unique challenges to their developers. Although Chapter 13 explores the general issues of systems and software development, we discuss issues important to TPS in this section.

Development, Testing, and Production Environments

The reliability requirements of TPSs oppose modification because TPSs often consist of more than 100,000 lines of code that have withstood the test of long-term use. Even small changes in one line of a TPS program can produce unanticipated errors that occur rarely and remain undetected for days or weeks and cause significant damage when they occur. For this reason TPSs are often called **legacy systems,** passed on by their developers to generations of successive support staffs, with little opportunity for change or replacement. Nevertheless, as a business changes, situations will arise that demand changes to its TPS.

How can a business ensure that its TPS remains reliable as developers change the TPS software? The most common solution creates three parallel environments—production, development, and testing. The **production environment** contains the current software and all transaction data and emphasizes high system reliability. The **development environment** contains copies of the TPS software and data for software developers to use in checking their new programs. When software developers believe that the changes work properly, they move a copy of the software to a **testing environment,** which also contains a complete copy of all transaction data. Subsequently, the system records all transactions in both the testing and production environments. Periodic tests verify the compatibility of the data in both environments. Typically, the developers correct any errors found in the development environment and retest the software in the testing environment. When users believe they have a sufficiently robust testing environment, they move the modified software to the production environment.

Database Management Systems as the Heart of TPS

Database management systems provide a variety of services needed by a TPS. For example, a DBMS simplifies the storage and retrieval of data, supports the control of simultaneous access to and update of data by two or more users, maintains transaction integrity when hardware or software failures terminate processing in the middle of a transaction, and facilitates the development of screens to automate data entry. In addition, a DBMS reduces the dependence of the TPS on a particular hardware environment, allowing systems to grow and evolve without major redesign. For these reasons, TPS software usually uses a DBMS to record its transactions.

Summary

Transaction processing describes either the manual or computerized record keeping in a business. Transaction processing systems refer to systems that perform such collection, maintenance, and updating of business data.

Companies record transactions to provide information needed by other employees in order to transact business and perform their jobs, collect information that managers use in making decisions, and create audit trails for verifying corporate financial information. Businesses may capture transaction data using predesigned paper forms called source documents or directly in electronic form. Companies that use electronic capture can process the data via batch or real-time processing. Real-time systems must demonstrate speed, reliability, and accessibility.

Point-of-sale systems record the sale of a product and update company records related to or affected by the sale. Order entry systems record and process the taking of an order. Computerized reservation systems are specialized order entry systems used by companies such as airlines or automobile rental agencies. Purchasing/receiving systems document transactions between a company and its suppliers. General accounting systems track financial transactions and translate them into income statements, balance sheets, and other accounting records in an organization.

Transaction processing systems pose special development challenges. The large amount of computer code and reliability requirements of such systems constrain their subsequent revision.

Key Terms

Accounts payable system
Accounts receivable system
Audit trail
Batch processing
Billing system
Cash management system
Computerized reservation system (CRS)
Data entry clerk
Development environment
Disk duplexing
Disk mirroring
Fault-tolerant system
General ledger system
Legacy system
Nonstop system
On-line data entry
Order entry system
Payroll system
Point-of-sale system (POS)
Production environment
Purchase order
Purchasing system
Real-time processing
Receiving system
Source document
Testing environment
Transaction
Transaction processing
Transaction processing system (TPS)
Turnkey system
Uninterrupted power supply

Review Questions

1. What is a transaction? Give an example of one.
2. List four reasons that companies record transactions.
3. Why do companies retain and maintain audit trails?

4. What is a source document? What are the advantages and disadvantages of using source documents rather than capturing data electronically?
5. What are the advantages and disadvantages of batch processing as opposed to real-time processing?
6. Identify three requirements of real-time transaction processing systems.
7. What are the two major causes of TPS failure? Which causes the most damage? Why?
8. How can companies protect against the inoperability of their TPS?
9. Identify two ways that a point-of-sale system can be designed so that information (such as reduction of inventory) can be shared among the POS terminals.
10. Identify two ways that companies lacking the resources to develop a POS system can process their POS transactions.
11. Illustrate by an example why order entry systems differ markedly from one industry to another.
12. What functions does EDI serve in purchasing/receiving systems?
13. Why is a general accounting system a TPS?
14. What characteristic of a TPS makes it resistant to change?
15. How can a business ensure that its TPS remains stable as developers change the TPS software?
16. Explain the problems that would arise when developing a TPS without a DBMS.

MINICASE

Processing Inventory Transactions at GTE's Standish Plant

The problem at GTE's Standish, ME plant was paper. "We had paper everywhere," explains logistics manager David Michaud. "From receiving, from scheduling, and from manufacturing—and most of it ending up at the warehouse. We were a paper-heavy operation, and in any heavily paper-based inventory control system, data entry errors are absolutely inevitable."

How does Michaud define "paper heavy"? Here's one illustration: Under the old system, employees had to make some 4,000 data input transactions per month. Each transaction could contain 40 keystrokes, so processing data was a major effort. No matter how carefully the entries were made, errors crept in. With every error, the integrity of the inventory data was degraded further. The data entry errors had a ripple effect throughout the facility, like leaves dropping into a mill pond.

Managers at the plant not only wanted to tackle the paper problem, they also wanted their newly implemented MRP II (manufacturing resources planning) program to be class A certified. This required inventory accuracy to be 95 percent or better, consistently.

The GTE Control Devices plant manufactures and assembles electromechanical protective devices for the automotive and AC electric motor markets. Because most of the devices and their component parts tend to be quite small, manual handling is used throughout most of the manufacturing operation.

Materials are moved on hand carts or pulled from cartons on pallets. Finished products are bulk packaged in cartons and manually stacked on pallets. Without conveyors or other stationary handling equipment, a data collection system based on fixed scanners was not a workable option.

Finding the Right Solution

The project team hired a consulting firm to help design and implement a new system that would satisfy the needs of the Standish plant.

After studying several approaches to automatic data collection, the project team and its consultants chose a spread-spectrum RF-based system that uses hand-held portable terminals and bar code scanners (Intermec Corp.) to provide plant employees with on-line real-time inventory data.

Dock to Stock

Let's take a look at the plant's newly designed system at work.

As incoming materials arrive at the plant, employees in the receiving department divide them according to two classifications: "Certified" materials that do not require inspection are transported directly to the warehouse and "preferred" materials, which go to the warehouse after specific inspection requirements are documented or satisfied.

Because vendors are not credited until materials pass inspection, one of the goals was to speed up the process by having the new system software perform the necessary administrative steps that slowed the "preferred" product.

Now, instead of a receiver doing a time-consuming combination of hand-written data entries on paper forms and on a CRT screen, the computer does the tracking. It will even inform the receiver which of the lots must be inspected, and it selects the appropriate transaction command to use. If labels are required, as many as necessary can be generated from this system by user request. All of this can be determined remotely through use of the portable terminals. From this point scanning is possible on all future product moves.

The system also calculates overage. If an amount exceeds a permissible level, the receiver is alerted and even told who the appropriate scheduler is to contact so that a determination can be made on what to do with the extra material. And if the scheduler instructs that extra material be applied to other open line items on the purchase order, the receiver can do so automatically and remotely, of course.

To store and retrieve pallet loads from the racks in the warehouse, the company uses two reach trucks and an order-picker truck. The scanners and portable terminals accompany the truck operators on board their vehicles. All warehouse materials are stored in racks, which have bar coded address labels.

ADC on the Production Floor

According to Michaud, requisitioning materials had to be improved because it generated most of the paper—all handwritten and much of it not easily understood.

The new system provides the production employee with a method to research available inventory levels and then to electronically transmit those needs to a bar code printer located in the warehouse. This printer then prints a card that contains the quantity of the request, the description of the material requested, the rack address where the material can be found (FIFO order), and the work cell to be charged. The appropriate bar codes are included on this request so that the warehouse employees can complete the issuing process by scanning the data necessary to update the inventory system.

Prior to implementing the new system, production employees had to manually write and tally their production figures at the end of the day.

Now, all of this data collection work is performed using an electronic production turn-in system. Using a personal access code, an employee enters data at a terminal on the work cell to credit the part number; the computer then displays a description of the product for confirmation. The employee then enters the package quantity and the number of cases that are produced. The computer calculates the total and automatically assigns a bar coded identification number to the work transaction.

Next, the computer instructs a printer to generate one or more labels, which the employee affixes to the carton(s). The employee then stacks the carton on a pallet.

Once a full pallet load of cartons has been produced, a worker uses a pallet truck to move the load to the warehouse for storage or shipping. In the warehouse, an employee scans the identification number, the quantity turned in, and the rack address to which the pallet load will be assigned. These actions verify the quantity of the product with what was requested and credit the work cell all at the same time.

Adding Up the Benefits

"Our inventory accuracy rate used to hover in the 85 to 90 percent range, and this was with hard work," says Michaud. "Now we're consistently in the 98 to 99 percent plus range and it's much easier. This improvement in inventory accuracy has not only met the class A MRP II requirement, but it has also exempted us from conducting annual physical inventory audits, which were an extremely costly and nightmarish event for this operation."

At Standish, a number of paper-intensive and time-consuming steps have almost disappeared. Included are data input labor, the verification process, excessive rack address and inventory level lookups, cycle count problems, looking for lost paper, looking for someone to interpret his or her handwriting, and off-line bar code label printing. The annual labor savings adds up to over 6,000 hours. Paperless data collection also has contributed to other goals such as improved cycle time, increased first pass yields, just-in-time operation, and inventory reduction.

As the design of these systems includes prompts that warn or advise the user and/or have informational screens built in for reference purposes, the systems also are tools that can be used to resolve problems quickly. David Michaud explains: "In the past, problems had a tendency to mushroom as more and more people became involved. What our objective has been is to combine automated data collection with a tool that can provide information as well, giving our employees the ability to resolve problems on their own and remotely if necessary."

Case Questions

1. What activities do GTE employees perform to move material into and out of inventory?
2. How does GTE's transaction processing system ease the task of recording the arrival of incoming materials?
3. How does GTE's transaction processing system ease the tracking of materials through the warehouse and onto the production floor? Describe both inputs and outputs of the computerized system.

Activity 10-1 The Catalog Problem

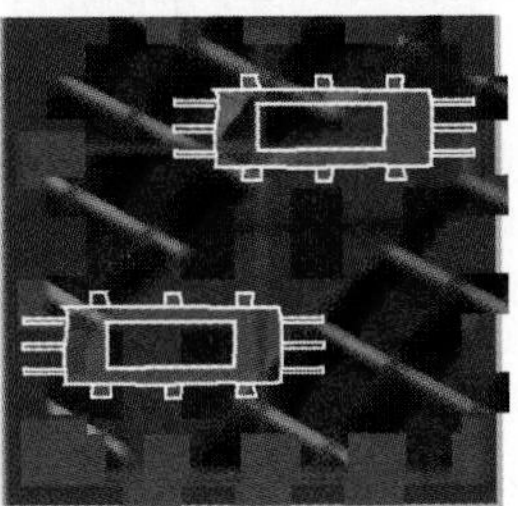

short case

STEP 1: You run a small business that sells children's toys through a catalog distributed by mail to 10,000 families. You publish four catalogs a year. Each catalog includes about 200 items, with about 30 percent overlap in items between catalogs. Many of the items are specially crafted and require some lead time to bring into inventory. You have developed a selective customer group, and most of your customers order significant numbers of toys from you each quarter.

You use a personal computer with a DOS/Windows system and off-the-shelf database software to maintain inventory and customer records. Recently, however, you have experienced significant problems with this system. The system has failed to flag out-of-stock items in time to reorder them; customer billings have lagged, and receivables have increased dramatically. Each quarter the number of items with very few sales and those with huge sales have increased, but you have not been able to explain which products sell well and which do not so that you can adjust future catalogs. You have an 800-number for telephone sales, but the number of errors in recording product numbers has increased. You believe that the system needs some adjustments.

STEP 2: Individually or in small groups, propose five changes for the existing system.

STEP 3: In small groups or with the entire class, share your list of changes. Together, compile a comprehensive list of changes and develop a plan for upgrading the system. ●

Activity 10-2 Automating Airline Sales

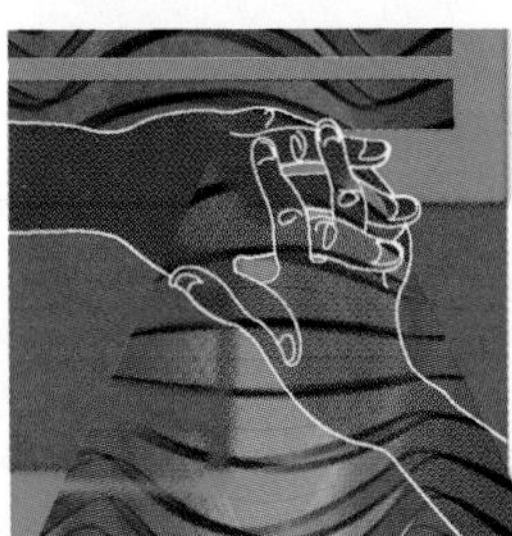

hands on

STEP 1: Read the following scenario.

Air America operated subsidiary sales offices in various parts of the world. The airline company was experiencing severe financial problems due to competition from newer, low-cost carriers. The company operated nine subsidiaries in Latin America, each located in a city on the airline's route system. Passenger flight coupons were collected by each subsidiary and mailed to the corporate accounting office in the United States to be entered into a centralized accounting system. Reports on the performance of each office were routed back through the international division and on to the subsidiary's management. The airline experienced several problems with this approach. First, the corporation wanted to integrate the accounting functions of its newly acquired international operations with the established corporate accounting practices. Reporting methods of the South American subsidiaries lacked consistency; no common data or reporting formats were used. Second, the company wanted to reduce the cost of data entry; it believed that shifting data entry to the South American locations would reduce the high labor costs incurred when data entry occurred solely in the

SOURCE: This case is adapted from Daniel Robey and Andres Rodriguez-Diaz, The organizational and cultural context of systems implementation: Case experience from Latin America, *Information & Management* 17 (1989): 229–239.

United States. Third, local management needed to receive more timely information for making decisions.

STEP 2: Individually or in small groups, offer a plan for automating the recording and reporting of sales information. Diagram the relationship of the sales transactions to the other transaction processing systems used in such an organization.

STEP 3: In small groups or with the entire class, share your plans. Identify the advantages and disadvantages of each plan. What alternatives are available for this type of transaction processing?

STEP 4: Your instructor will provide you with instructions for accessing a database management system on your computer. Using this database management system, design and implement a data entry screen and database to capture the following transaction sales information from a customer:

Customer last name

Customer first name

Customer phone number

Cost of ticket

Method of payment (check, cash, or credit card)

Payment reference number (Check number or credit card number)

Credit authorization number (if paid by credit card)

Number of ticket stubs

For each ticket stub:
- Date of travel
- Airline code
- Flight number
- Class of travel
- Origin airport code (three letters)
- Destination airport code (three letters)
- Departure time
- Arrival time

Test your database by making up and entering some sales information.

STEP 5: A real transaction processing system would assist the data entry clerk by checking the validity of some data entry items (for example, a check of the airport code to see that it represents the code of an airport served by the airline booked) and automatically calculating some of the information that your database cannot calculate. Identify which data items should be checked for validity and which should be automatically calculated. What other information is needed to perform these calculations and validity checks? Do you believe that it is reasonable to provide each subsidiary with local copies of such data, or will the subsidiaries require data communication capabilities? ●

Activity 10-3 Kids Limousine Service

hands on

STEP 1: Read the following scenario.

John Cardy began an after-school limousine service for children in 1987 using a single van. He transported local children from school to after-school activities, lessons, friends' houses, or home. Parents paid an annual fee to enroll their child in the service plus an additional toll for each trip. During the first two years, business boomed, and John bought two additional vans and hired additional drivers. During the next three years he expanded the service throughout the eastern part of the state. He bought 15 more vans and hired additional drivers. John relinquished his role as a van driver and part-time manager and devoted all his time to managing the business. He soon discovered that the manual system of recording clients' requests, scheduling drivers, and billing customers was not working. Although John's reputation was based on the reliability and safety of his service, he had several near-misses: Drivers almost failed to pick up several children from school because of scheduling mistakes. In addition, many vans criss-crossed their towns several times because John did not have time to determine the best routes and schedules for them and their drivers. Bills were mailed late, and John did not have time to track tardy accounts.

John knew that the business could operate more effectively if he computerized the entire system. He believed that improved cash flow and the savings obtained from a more efficient scheduling of vans and drivers would offset the costs of computerization.

STEP 2: Individually or in small groups, identify what transactions John Cardy and Kids Limousine Company need to record in order for John to operate the business more effectively. Specifically, consider the order entry, scheduling, and billing processes as well as any other processes you feel might generate transactions.

STEP 3: Select one of the transactions you identified in step 2 and determine exactly what data items need to be recorded as the transaction takes place. Identify how the transaction you selected uses data from other transactions or creates data that is needed for efficiently processing other transactions.

STEP 4: Your instructor will provide you with instructions for accessing a database management system on your computer. Using this database management system, design and implement a data entry screen and database to capture the transaction you have selected in step 3. Create some hypothetical transactions and enter them into your database using the data entry screen you created. ●

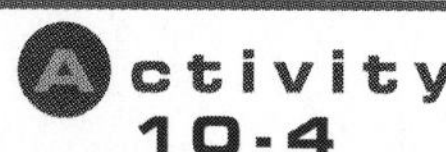

Flight, Inc.

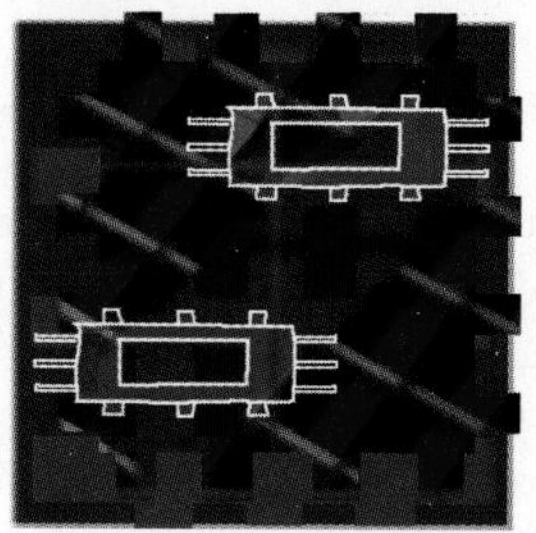
short case

You have recently joined the family business, an aircraft repair service that provides maintenance services for corporate aircraft. Your father began the service in 1962 at a single location. Since its founding, Flight, Inc. has expanded to five sites across the United States and 50 technicians. The company has developed a reputation for offering impeccable, highly personalized customer service. Company representatives meet charter customers at the airport, quickly complete a service order, and then arrange for accommodations for the pilot during servicing of the aircraft. The company attempts to minimize the time the aircraft is out of service and prides itself on solving mechanical problems quickly and accurately.

Although your father has built a successful business, you know that its future success will rely on increasing its efficiency while continuing to ensure personalized service. In addition, you hope to expand the business and know that the manual system for recording customer requests, repair schedules, regular aircraft maintenance, and even customer billing is antiquated and will hinder your expansion plans.

STEP 1: Individually or in small groups, design a transaction processing system for this company. Your instructor will provide you with the specifications for the system.

STEP 2: Exchange your systems with a partner group. Individually or in small groups, critique your partner group's plan. Offer suggestions for improving its system.

STEP 3: Revise your system based on suggestions received from your partner group. What components would an effective transaction processing system for Flight, Inc. include? ●

Notes

[1]Reprinted with permission from David A. Kelly, From truck to customer in 20 minutes, *Computerworld* (January 11, 1993): 48.

[2]Stuart J. Johnston, A good deal for Nordstrom's buyers, *Computerworld* (May 23, 1994): 61, 65.

[3]Patricia A. Langan, At last, software CEOs can use, *Fortune* (March 13, 1989): 77–83.

[4]See Alan Radding, What, me worry? *Computerworld* (March 22, 1993): 76; Roderick Chapin, Automatic workstation mirroring, *InfoWorld* 15(10) (March 8, 1993): 77; and Sheldon Lowenthal and Barbara Robidoux, Disk mirroring under AIX protects against critical data loss, *Computer Technology Review* 12(4) (Fall 1992): 49–52.

[5]Bruce Strom, Prevent double trouble with double backup, *Computers in Accounting* 8(5) (July 1992): 61–63.

[6]Dennis Livingston, United Parcel Service gets a special delivery, *Systems Integration* 24(11) (November 1991): 54–58.

[7]Mitch Betts, States redefining public service, *Computerworld* (April 19, 1993): C20.

[8]Ibid.

[9]Derek Slater, Lechmere offers kiosk system worth checkin' out, *Computerworld* (March 2, 1992): 64.

[10]For example, Mrs. Fields Cookies operates in this fashion; see Jack Schember, Mrs. Fields' secret weapon, *Personnel Journal* 70(9) (September 1991): 56–58.

[11]Judy Murrah, Service maximized in the wireless store, *Chain Store Age Executive* 69(4) (April 1993): 76.

[12]Paul Fredric, Wireless LANs fit the bill for retailer's net, *Network World* (February 8, 1993): 11–12.

[13]Bob Wallace, AT&T rolls out new transaction service, *Network World* (March 29, 1993): 25–26.

[14]Sally Solo, SPS Transaction Services, *Fortune* (March 22, 1993): 91.

[15]Gary Robins, PCs as POS devices, *Stores* 75 (February 1993): 31–32.

[16]James E. Short and N. Venkatraman, Beyond business process redesign: Redefining Baxter's business network, *Sloan Management Review* 34(1) (Fall 1992): 7–20.

[17]Pizza Hut slashes order time, boosts sales with computerized order handling, *Systems 3x/400* 20(1) (January 1992): 1044–1239.

[18]Charles Korbell, High-tech checks, *Texas Banking* 80(10) (October 1991): 5, 34.

[19]Emily Kay, Relief for your order entry headaches, *Datamation* (July 1, 1991): 51–52.

[20]Gerald W. Petitt, CRS tech: Focus on the basics, *Lodging Hospitality* 49(2) (February 1993): 28.

[21]Mark Halper, Hotel chain integrates systems via Unix, *Computerworld* (April 19, 1993): 66.

[22]Novak Niketic and Glen R. J. Mules, How Qantas Airways uses EDI for travel reservation processing, *Journal of Systems Management* 44(1) (January 1993): 9–13.

[23]Elizabeth Heichler, Airline hacking case reveals CRS' security shortcomings, *Computerworld* (January 18, 1993): 2.

[24]Barbara Sehr, Levi Strauss strengthens customer ties with electronic data interchange, *Computerworld* (January 30, 1993): 12.

[25]Wayne Eckerson, Ford profits by letting suppliers tap into systems, *Network World* (July 1, 1991): 1, 49.

Recommended Readings

Siewiorek, Daniel P. and Swarz, Robert S. *Reliable Computer Systems: Design and Evaluation.* Burlington, MA: Digital Press, 1992.

Vytopil, Jan (Ed.). *Formal Techniques in Real-time and Fault-tolerant Systems.* Boston: Kluwer, 1993.

Wilkinson, Joseph W. *Accounting and Information Systems,* 3d ed. New York: Wiley, 1991.

Chapter 11

Management Systems

OUTLINE

Information Systems at PizzaCo

Review of the Information Needs of Managers

Management Reporting Systems (MRSs)

- Types of Reports
- Report Schedules
- Relationship to Transaction Processing Systems

Decision Support Systems (DSSs)

- Components of a DSS
- Answering Unforeseen Questions
- Relationship to Transaction Processing Systems
- External Data Interface
- Analytical Elements of a DSS

Groupware

- Elements of Groupware
- Problems in Managing Groupware

Executive Information Systems (EISs)

- Typical Features of an EIS

LEARNING OBJECTIVES

After completing the reading and activities for Chapter 11, students will be able to

1. List three types of management reports and describe the types of information they provide to managers.
2. Describe alternative schedules for producing reports.
3. Show how information systems support decision making and meet managers' needs for information.
4. Offer two ways information systems can answer unforeseen managerial questions.
5. Identify the components of a decision support system and present the types of information the system offers managers.
6. Describe the analytical elements of a decision support system.
7. Describe the elements and use of groupware.
8. Identify three problems in managing groupware.
9. Describe the typical features and uses of an executive information system.
10. Compare and contrast management reporting systems, decision support systems, groupware, and executive information systems.

Jerry Tatum owns and serves as the chief executive officer of PizzaCo, a chain of pizza restaurants. He inherited the first store in the chain from his parents and soon expanded it into a modest, family-style restaurant with an emphasis on good food, value, and casual atmosphere. The next year he opened a second restaurant. Both restaurants were highly profitable, and Jerry began to expand the chain. Jerry and his partners have since opened five more restaurants. They plan to open at least 30 more within the next three years and have a major national presence within the next five to seven years.

Jerry retains tight control over the chain's performance, ensuring consistent service and quality throughout the restaurants. Each restaurant has the same menu items offered at the same price. Jerry has developed a small but effective headquarters staff who controls purchasing and product development. The restaurant managers are responsible for ordering, staffing, and local advertising; they must meet both cost and revenue objectives set by top management.

Jerry has begun to install computer systems in each restaurant and in corporate headquarters to aid him and his staff in obtaining the information they need to make effective decisions about the company's performance and future direction. He wants to ensure that these systems can help him and other managers in the company perform effectively and support the company's growth.

What types of information do Jerry Tatum and his managers need in order to perform their jobs effectively? What types of information systems provide the information Jerry needs? In Chapter 3 we answered the first question; we *diagnosed* the information needs of managers. In this chapter we focus on the second question. We answer it by examining four types of management information systems—1) management reporting systems, 2) decision support systems, 3) groupware, and 4) executive information systems—and showing how they provide the information required for managers to perform effectively.

Review of the Information Needs of Managers

Managers at all levels of an organization require extensive and diverse types of information to perform effectively. Top-level managers provide for the overall direction of an organization and hence need information that assists in formulating strategy and policies. Middle-level managers focus on implementing these long-range plans; they emphasize internal issues and need information that helps increase employee performance, product quality, and customer service. First-line supervisors require information to help them ensure the effective conduct of the organization's daily activities. The management processes of planning, organizing, leading, and controlling call for information about the organization's mission, strategies, structure, products, staff, standards, and performance. Performing the managerial roles of information sharing, decision making, and motivating, influencing, and building relationships also requires information about various organizational constituencies, including employees, customers, suppliers, and competitors, as well as data about the organization and its environment.

Managers in the functional areas of accounting, finance, marketing, engineering, manufacturing, and human resource management have unique needs. The controller and lower-level accounting managers need information for recording, classifying, and summarizing the financial activities of the organization. Financial managers focus on the acquisition and use of money and require information about the flow and use of funds in the organization, the availability of capital, and potential investment alternatives. Marketing managers seek information about consumers' needs and preferences, product characteristics, and other qualities of the marketplace. Engineering managers need information such as product specifications, engineering designs, and characteristics of materials to contribute to product design and execution.

Operations managers seek information that helps them plan, organize, direct, and control the physical operations of an organization; they acquire information related to product, process, service planning and design, capacity planning, scheduling, and inventory control. Human resource managers need information that assists with the design and implementation of human resource planning, staffing, training and development, performance appraisal, compensation, and labor–management relations. Considered together, managers' information needs include data about transactions, financial and operational control, team and project management, forecasts, competition, and communication.

Managers who function in a global economy face complex, unpredictable events and problems that call for an effective managerial response. They must first diagnose the information required to deal with these situations. These global managers must have information systems that ensure they can both access current comprehensive information and analyze it. In the next sections we describe management information systems intended to assist in meeting managers' needs for information.

Managers seek information from their subordinates, peers, and superiors. Information technology can help ease and coordinate the flow of information.

Courtesy of International Business Machines Corporation.

Management Reporting Systems (MRSs)

Management reporting systems (MRSs) help managers monitor the operations and resources of an organization and the environment in which the organization operates. PizzaCo, for example, might have an MRS that lists the daily sales of every product in each restaurant, summarizes these sales for the entire chain, and marks products in a restaurant that sell below the chain's average sales. The company's MRS might also include the hours and wages of each member of the wait and cook staff as well as a summary of the labor costs for each restaurant. An MRS should produce three types of reports, scheduled to provide the needed information at the appropriate time without overloading the manager with information.

Types of Reports

Jerry Tatum revises the menu in his restaurants twice a year; he needs to know which products sell well and which sell poorly to make appropriate menu changes. What types of reports would provide Jerry with this information? Managers generally use detail reports, summary reports, and exception reports to monitor organizational performance and identify problems. An MRS should provide all three types.

Detail Reports. **Detail reports,** as shown in Figure 11-1, provide managers information useful in overseeing the day-to-day operations of a department or working group. For example, a desk manager at a hotel might use a detail report of reservations to resolve conflicts between what the desk clerk sees on his or her computer screen and the reservation confirmation form brought by a customer. Used primarily by low-level managers, detail reports provide data about individual transactions, such as payments made by customers, parts manufactured, and debits and credits to the general ledger. Detail reports can also offer managers information from outside the organization, such as consumer purchasing power by ZIP code. Management systems should provide detail reports frequently enough that managers can readily use the information they contain.

Different detail reports contain information from the same transaction data arranged in different orders or showing different parts of the transaction. For example, one report of customer payments, showing only the customer name and amount of payment, might be sorted by customer. Another report referring to the same transactions might be sorted by open invoice number and might show the prior balance, the customer code, the amount of payment, the check number (or a cash indicator), and the final balance.

Higher-level managers may refer to detail reports when summary data do not help them resolve a particular problem. For example, a manager responsible for quality control in a manufacturing process might notice that product defects arise more frequently after a certain part has been fixed or replaced. He or she may review the detail reports for the previous several months to confirm or reject that hypothesis. Then the manager can recommend appropriate corrective actions. Or, a national sales manager noticing an overall sales decline in a particular region may refer to the detail reports on sales of particular items in that region to identify more specific causes of the decline.

What types of detail reports would the managers at PizzaCo find useful? Restaurant managers might want a report of the items sold by time of day, as shown in Figure 11-2, so that they can adjust their cooking or serving schedules. Jerry Tatum might want a listing of items sold by store to determine whether the company should change the menu, offer daily specials in certain locations, or use coupon incentives to attract more interest in certain items. He might also want data about customers' dining-out preferences in various towns to help in locating future restaurants.

FIGURE 11-1 Example of a Detail Report

Employee Service Report for Sales/Marketing Department 7/31/95 14:33

Service	May Hours	May Payroll	May $%	Year to Date Hours	Year to Date Payroll	Year to Date $%	Projected Year Hours	Projected Year Payroll	Projected Year $%
01 Larry Chessam									
051 /Client contact	0.00	0.00	0.0	44.00	440.00	100.0	106.36	1,063.58	100.0
$$$$$ EMPLOYEE TOTALS $$$$$	0.00	0.00		44.00	440.00		106.36	1,063.58	
BILLABLE	0.00	0.00	0.0	44.00	440.00	100.0	106.36	1,063.58	100.0
NON BILLABLE	0.00	0.00	0.0	0.00	0.00	0.0	0.00	0.00	0.0
Jerry Marshall									
051 Client contact	8.25	165.00	48.5	63.25	609.00	72.6	152.89	1,472.09	72.6
057 Production supervision	8.75	175.00	51.5	14.75	230.00	27.4	35.65	555.96	27.4
$$$$$ EMPLOYEE TOTALS $$$$$	17.00	340.00		78.00	839.00		188.54	2,028.05	
BILLABLE	17.00	340.00	100.0	78.00	839.00	100.0	188.54	2,028.05	100.0
NON BILLABLE	0.00	0.00	0.0	0.00	0.00	0.0	0.00	0.00	0.0
Cheryl Hall									
051 Client contact	0.25	5.00	0.6	0.25	5.00	0.6	0.60	12.09	0.6
053 Creative Development	2.25	45.00	5.1	2.25	45.00	5.1	5.44	108.77	5.1
055 Layout and design	2.50	50.00	5.7	2.50	50.00	5.7	6.04	120.86	5.7
057 Production supervision	14.75	295.00	33.5	14.75	295.00	33.5	35.65	713.08	33.5
060 Paste-up	22.25	445.00	50.6	22.25	445.00	50.6	53.78	1,075.66	50.6
06 1Illustrations	2.00	40.00	4.5	2.00	40.00	4.5	4.83	96.69	4.5
$$$$$ EMPLOYEE TOTALS $$$$$	44.00	880.00		44.00	880.00		106.36	2,127.15	
BILLABLE	44.00	880.00	100.0	44.00	880.00	100.0	106.36	2,127.15	100.0
NON BILLABLE	0.00	0.00	0.0	0.00	0.00	0.0	0.00	0.00	0.0

SOURCE: Microbase Software, Inc., Promotional Material for *Adman_System,* circa 1984.

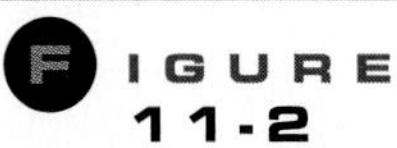

Excerpt from the Detail Report of Menu Items by Time of Day

```
          Prod #                Description                Qty
         --------   ------------------------------------  -----
            .
            .
            .
   11:31-12:00
              101    House salad                              6
              102    Caesar salad                             4
              103    Guacamole salad                          5
              201    Pizza, cheese                           15
              202    Pizza, pepperoni                         6
              203    Pizza, veggie delight                    3
              204    Pizza, eggplant and artichoke            3
              301    Chicken fajita                           4
              302    Beef fajita                              4
              321    Manicotti, baked                         1
              322    Eggplant parmesan                        2
              351    Spaghetti, marinara                      5
              352    Spaghetti, meat                          2
              353    Spaghetti, special                       4

   12:01-12:30
              101    House salad                              8
              102    Caesar salad                             6
            .
            .
            .
```

Summary Reports. **Summary reports** or **statistical reports** show totals, averages, maximums, minimums, or other statistical data aggregated over time, personnel, products, or some other quantity. Each line of a statistical report summarizes large amounts of transaction data that can be examined in a detail report. Because data can be aggregated at many levels, each detail report may give rise to several statistical reports. Typically, as managers move up the organizational ladder, they deal with reports that have data aggregated to increasing degrees.

Figure 11-3 illustrates a summary report a manager at each of the PizzaCo restaurants might receive. The manager can compare his or her customers' average bill, sales of specific items, and staffing expenditures to other restaurants in the chain. The manager can use these data to adjust advertising and labor budgets.

Exception Reports. **Exception reports** alert managers to potential problems by showing only data that fall outside an accepted or expected range. For example, an accounts receivable exception report might show only seriously overdue accounts or those accounts whose payments are later than usual based on a historical account history. A manufacturing exception report might cite all parts whose rate of defects exceeds company standards or the historical rate of defects for those parts.

Exception reports show data at either a transaction or a summary level. They differ from transaction and summary reports in that they do not show all data. As a result, they should enable managers to quickly target problems without wading through a morass of data. Figure 11-4 shows an excerpt from a sales exception report that Jerry Tatum might receive; it

IGURE 11-3 Excerpt from the Summary Report for PizzaCo Managers

Summary Operating Statistics
Store # 32
Week of 3/15/93

	Your store	Avg. PizzaCo
Seats	92	105.3
Customers	3,216	3,532.6
Customers/seat/day	4.99	4.79
Restaurant Sales	45,703	50,129
Sales/customer	14.21	14.19
Sales/seat/day	70.97	68.01
Take-out sales	.	.
Total sales	.	.
Take-out/total sales	.	.
Returns	.	.
Returns/total sales	.	.
Employee-hours	.	.
Average labor rate	.	.
Emp-hrs/customer	.	.
Emp-hrs/sales	.	.
Emp-cost/customer	.	.
Emp-cost/sales	.	.
.	.	.
.	.	.
.	.	.

FIGURE 11-4 Excerpt from the Sales Exception Report at PizzaCo

Sales Exception Report
Month Ending 3/31/93
Store #35

Prod #	Description	Code
202	Pizza, pepperoni	A,M
321	Manicotti, baked	M

Codes:
A: Sales of this product are at least 10% below that of the average PizzaCo store's sales as adjusted for total sales volume.
M: Sales of this product are at least 5% below that of last month as adjusted for total sales volume.

highlights menu items that sold less than they did in the previous month or relatively less than they do at other stores. Jerry can use this information to refocus management's efforts in selling the product, alter the price, or delete the item from the menu. He might also receive a report that lists suppliers who do not offer discounts for early payment so that he can attempt to renegotiate contracts with them or replace them with different suppliers.

Report Schedules

Most organizations produce a large proportion of their reports on a scheduled basis and distribute them to a predetermined list of recipients. Management systems may also produce reports on demand or generate them in response to a prespecified event. Figure 11-5 compares the three schedules.

Periodic Reports. Management reporting systems produce most reports as **periodic reports,** generating them on a periodic basis and delivering them to a prespecified list of employees. For example, one company produces a report of sales by region every weekend so that all senior managers receive the report on Monday morning prior to their weekly planning meeting. Each day an airline produces a report of reservations by rate class for each flight so that managers can adjust the number of seats open for special fares. Most companies produce financial statements every month or every quarter. What types of reports might PizzaCo generate daily? Weekly? Monthly? Periodic reports should provide information essential for managerial decision making and action without overloading the manager with detail.

Event-Initiated Reports. MRSs may also generate **event-initiated reports** on the occurrence of a prespecified event, typically either a milestone or an expected problem. For example, a government contractor produces a contract status report each time the contractor completes part of its contract and each time a deadline passes without completion of the contracted work. A catalog company produces a back order report when a customer orders a product that is out of stock and again when it replenishes the stock. Event-initiated reports are also usually distributed to a prespecified list of recipients.

On-Demand Reports. Most management reporting systems provide **on-demand reports** for authorized managers when they request the information. In most cases, the system already includes programs to generate the reports, and managers can activate them when

FIGURE 11-5

Report Preparation Schedules

Report	Frequency	Delivery	Example
Periodic	Periodically—daily, weekly, monthly	To prespecified list of recipients	Financial report
Event-initiated	After occurrence of prespecified event	To prespecified list of recipients	Contract progress report
On-demand	Upon manager's request	To requested list of recipients	New customer report

desired. In some cases, technically skilled managers are authorized to use a high-level report-generating language to prepare reports in a variety of formats as desired. The restaurant managers at PizzaCo, for example, might want a one-time report of their recent advertising expenditures, employee hires, or customer complaints.

Relationship to Transaction Processing Systems

Management reporting systems in many organizations comprise the reporting components of a transaction processing system. Sometimes, MRSs combine data from two or more TPSs to provide data that managers could not otherwise obtain from the individual systems. For example, MRSs might combine reports about the types of defective items with those about the sales of those items. PizzaCo might combine reports about the restaurants' sales of various types of pizzas and the cost of ingredients for those same pizzas or reports about sales and payroll costs for making and selling the pizzas.

The use of both management reporting systems and transaction processing systems can strain computer resources. MRSs require significant computer resources for accessing, sorting, and otherwise manipulating data. When an MRS runs concurrently with a TPS, the requirements for computer resources may slow the TPS, resulting in unacceptable or unreliable response times for important business transactions.

Organizations have two options for dealing with this overload. First, they may run MRSs only on weekends, overnight, or at hours when transaction activity is likely to be low. While this is an acceptable solution for most reporting purposes, it may not be feasible for organizations whose transaction processing occurs all day, every day. A second solution involves downloading selected detail and summary data from a transaction processing system into a separate database called a **data warehouse,** an **information warehouse,** or simply a **warehouse,** which usually resides on a different computer. This solution frees the TPS from performing the time-consuming data sorts typically required by management reports and allows it to run more smoothly and with a more regular and predictable response time. The downloading also gives managers broader access to data because they cannot delete, modify, or corrupt the transaction data. The warehouse's database interface allows more flexible access to data than does a typical TPS; therefore, managers can more easily generate on-demand reports.

Decision Support Systems (DSSs)

Should two pieces of equipment be replaced by a newer, more powerful machine? Should the company sell directly to the retail market, continue to sell through distributors, or both? Should the company order parts more frequently and in smaller lots? Will lower marketing and sales expenses offset the revenue loss of a price decrease? **Decision support systems (DSSs)** help managers make more effective decisions by answering complex questions such as these; they provide information required for effective planning and organizing.

Middle- and upper-level managers use DSSs to reach decisions in ambiguous and complex environments. Unlike management reporting systems, which provide managers primarily with current data to use in problem analysis, DSSs also offer forecasts of future conditions. More distinctively, they give managers the ability to quantitatively analyze alternative choices. Essentially, they model a complex set of circumstances; the decision maker can manipulate various parameters of the model to assess the impact of diverse conditions. Jerry Tatum of PizzaCo might use a DSS to help him evaluate alternate sites for new restaurants or select the best time frame for corporate expansion.

EGYPT

ISRAEL

Teams of computer experts, for example, assigned and implemented decision support systems to help top policy makers in Egypt and Israel prioritize and address key governmental

Decision support systems help middle- and upper-level managers analyze alternative decisions in complex and ambiguous situations.

Courtesy of International Business Machines Corporation.

issues. The systems included a DSS for the formulation of customs tariff policy and collation of information about all industrial companies in each country.[1] Decision support systems might also ease facilities management by helping to answer questions such as the following: What space is unoccupied? What impact does reducing space standards have? What should be the preventative maintenance schedule for specific equipment? What is the best sequence of moves for relocating a department?[2]

The benefits of DSSs include improved decision making through better understanding of the business, an increased number of decision alternatives examined, the ability to implement *ad hoc* analysis, and faster response to expected situations. DSSs also result in improved communication, more effective teamwork, better control, and time and cost savings.[3] The Arab National Bank in Saudi Arabia, for example, developed an on-line retail banking DSS that let managers directly control and monitor branch operations and that reduced customer service transactions from 30 minutes to one minute.[4] A survey of 146 organizations in Singapore showed that the benefits of their DSSs included a better quality of information use in decision making, increased managerial productivity, and increased competitive advantage.[5]

ARAB NATIONAL BANK

Most studies confirm that information systems can increase decision effectiveness.[6] The extent to which they help, however, depends to a large degree on the user's familiarity and expertise with the decision support tool, the user's knowledge about the problem to be solved, and the interaction of the cognitive style of the user with the DSS.[7]

Components of a DSS

A full-featured decision support system consists of four major components: 1) a database, 2) a knowledge base, 3) a model base, and 4) a user interface. A database (see Chapter 7) provides access to internal or external data that may influence or be affected by decisions under consideration. DSSs also use data from a database to form a baseline that mathematical models use in extrapolating from past to present to future conditions. The DSS may also use these data to calibrate and validate parameters of models used for forecasting. For example, in evaluating a proposed price cut, the DSS should have the capability of analyzing how past price changes have affected sales. Historical data allow the modeler to estimate the price elasticity of demand.

A **knowledge base,** like that in an expert system (see Chapter 9), provides information about the relationships among data that are too complex for a database to represent. It consists of rules that can constrain possible solutions as well as alternative solutions and methods for evaluating them. For example, in analyzing the impact of a price reduction, a DSS should signal if the forecasted volume of activity exceeds the volume that the projected staff can service. Such signaling requires the DSS to incorporate some rules-of-thumb about an appropriate ratio of staff to sales volume. Such rules-of-thumb, also known as heuristics, make up the knowledge base.

A **model base** includes an array of spreadsheets, simulation packages, forecasting tools, and statistical packages. The user can access the appropriate tools without developing a new model each time. The user should also have access to models that have been developed previously and that can be reused. Managers should understand the assumptions and limitations of the models to effectively use the DSS.[8] For example, a DSS that helps managers of portfolios of income-producing properties evaluate properties for purchase, expansion, renovation, conversion, or sale includes a variety of mathematical models that perform the analysis.[9]

Finally, a DSS must include a sophisticated **user interface,** which allows users to control which data and models to include in their analyses. The design of user interfaces is an MIS specialty that combines information and technology concepts with the rich realms of human factors and psychology.[10] With transaction processing systems and management reporting systems, in contrast, the user is more passive, receiving data in limited formats or entering data into carefully crafted screens or forms. A DSS must be designed to support the greater freedom users experience in manipulating data and processing information. A state-of-the-art DSS should ease data and knowledge assembly from a variety of sources as well as their use as inputs to previously developed models or models currently under development. Because DSSs support complex decision making, users typically analyze many alternatives and extensive data about each alternative; a high-quality DSS should support facilities to compare, contrast, and aggregate data in a wide range of graphical and tabular formats.

U.S. DEPARTMENT OF HOUSING AND URBAN DEVELOPMENT

The U.S. Department of Housing and Urban Development developed in the late 1980s a decision support system that serves headquarters and field offices for the Urban Development Action Grant Program. The DSS supports the operations and work processes of the program office as well as managerial decision making regarding grant applications. It includes the following: "quantitative analysis techniques and tools, management decision-making support, 'what if' capability, direct and intermediary control by decision maker, support to nonprogrammable decisions, real-time analysis capability, and contingency planning features."[11]

Answering Unforeseen Questions

Planned systems can handle unforeseen questions by providing access to internal and external data and models to manipulate the data. A decision support system provides such access in two ways: 1) supporting *ad hoc* queries and 2) offering analytical capabilities.

Support of *Ad Hoc* Queries. Management reporting systems provide access to data in a predefined format. In most cases, these formats do not address unforeseen questions. Suppose, for example, a manufacturer receives a bad set of circuit boards from a supplier and has unwittingly used the boards in its own product, which has been shipped to customers. When the problem is discovered, the manager responsible for recalling the finished goods from customers could begin to solve it by looking at receiving reports that identify the serial numbers of the bad boards. Then, the manager could scan the manufacturing reports to identify which products were assembled with the boards having the identified serial numbers. Then, the manager could trace these products to shipping orders to identify

FIGURE 11-6 An Object-Oriented User Interface

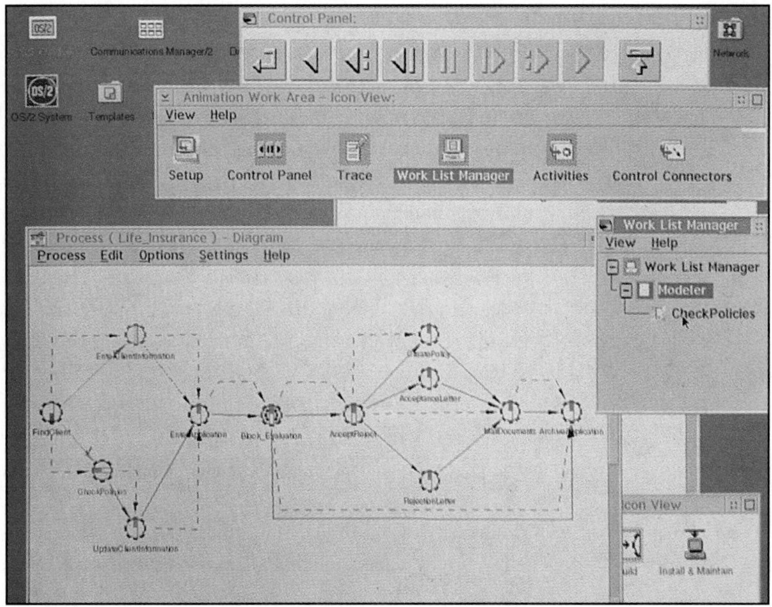

Sources: Bob Zuick, The good, the bad, and the ugly, *DBMS* (February 1993):26; Advertisement for Quadbase-SQL for Windows, Quadbase, Inc., 1993.

where they had been sent. Finally, a perusal of detail customer reports could provide the telephone numbers and contact names of customers identified from the shipping records. This laborious process could be circumvented if the manager could perform an ***ad hoc*** **query** on the database of information. In such a query, the manager would request the names and phone numbers of all customers who were shipped any product that included any board that was received in a specified shipment from the supplier.

An *ad hoc* query calls upon the computer system to perform the comparison and linkages among the elements of a database, combining them in ways that were not previously expected. Because managers are usually not computer programmers, it is important that a decision support system provide a language for queries that managers can understand. Originally, SQL was expected to be such a language (see Chapter 7), and indeed, some managers have been able to master SQL. Most managers, however, require a more intuitive query language.[12]

Object-oriented user interfaces, as illustrated in Figure 11-6, are beginning to become widely used for this purpose. In the example above, the manager might perform the query as follows: Initially, a screen showing icons for suppliers, shippers, parts, and other information would appear. The manager would click on the supplier icon. A list of suppliers would appear. The manager would then click on the company that supplied the bad board. Attributes of the company, such as its address and phone number would appear, along with a number of buttons for more detailed information, such as shipments from the company. The manager would click on the shipments button and identify the bad shipment. The list of circuit boards in the bad shipment would appear. Proceeding in this manner, the manager would cross-reference the circuit boards with the company's finished product and then with the customers receiving the product. This process would take only a few seconds. Then, the manager would click on a report button, identify the information that the report should include by clicking on the list of available fields, and select which field or fields should be used to sort the report. Finally, a copy of the report would be printed.

Provision of Analytical Capabilities. A decision support system should give managers the opportunity to evaluate the impact of alternative decisions, such as whether to locate a new restaurant in a city or in a suburb of a large metropolitan area. Because a decision's impact will not be felt for a period of time, a DSS must include an ability to forecast the effect. In addition, the impact of decisions often depends on numerous factors outside the manager's control, such as general economic conditions, introduction of new technology, or changing customer requirements. Accordingly, the DSS must provide opportunities for the manager to vary the assumptions inherent in the forecasting process to account for such factors. Finally, the DSS must support the manager in comparing, contrasting, summarizing, and evaluating the alternative scenarios that arise from the forecasting effort. Jerry Tatum can use a DSS to help him decide whether to open a 100-seat, 200-seat, or 300-seat restaurant in suburban St. Louis.

Relationship to Transaction Processing Systems

A DSS usually obtains its database from an organization's TPS. The DSS, like a management reporting system, usually requires significant computer resources that would interfere with a company's TPS if run on the same computer. As a result, DSS databases are usually downloaded from selected, and sometimes aggregated, TPS data. Because managers use DSSs primarily for medium- to long-term decisions, the fact that the DSS data are not completely current is usually not a concern.

Systems administrators must determine which data to download from the TPS and how frequently to download the data. Managers' data needs cannot always be anticipated, so some companies download their entire transaction database. This strategy wastes valuable computer storage space. In addition, a transaction processing system usually keeps only current records and maintains extremely limited historical data on-line. DSS users, in contrast, often need access to extensive historical data to develop trends and test hypotheses about the impact of past behaviors and actions.

Most companies use a combination of two strategies. The first strategy requires the design of the DSS database to include data that decision makers will use frequently. The second strategy calls for the retrieval of specific data for the DSS from the TPS or data archives when the user requires the data. Regardless of the solution, the DSS data dictionary must report to DSS users the data currently on-line as well as the data available or retrievable from other sources.

External Data Interface

Companies tend not to store data from external sources on-line. These data include macroeconomic data about foreign countries, financial data about publicly traded companies, demographic data about potential customers, information about patents, and a wide range of other data. Some of these data can be purchased on CD-ROM by subscription from market research firms, the government, the press, and other suppliers of electronic information. Time-critical data can be purchased, usually at a much higher price, from firms that collect and distribute these data daily and even hourly by electronic mail and in other data communication formats. While most decision support systems currently support neither directories of external data nor automatic access to it, any full-featured, state-of-the-art DSS must allow the user to import data from external sources and incorporate such data into the analysis. Demographic information about customers would assist Jerry Tatum in making his expansion decisions.

Analytical Elements of a DSS

The analytical elements of a DSS vary dramatically among organizations depending on the industry, the sophistication of the DSS users, and the computing resources available in the organization. Selecting a DSS product should include evaluating, first, the general characteristics of an acceptable product, and second, the technical capabilities of the specific product.[13] In the following paragraphs we discuss the most common analytical tools available in state-of-the-art DSSs—simulation languages, goal-seeking (optimization) software, statistical packages, geographical systems, and expert systems. Figure 11-7 lists additional elements that DSSs incorporate less frequently.

Simulation Languages. **Simulation** is the process of representing real processes with analytic models. In effect, all DSS involves simulation. Most DSSs provide several languages to assist a user in developing a simulation. Spreadsheets, the most common simulation language, provide a simple one-, two-, or occasionally multidimensional way of interrelating data using formulas. Most simulation languages, including spreadsheets, contain a means of representing random occurrences in nature or business, such as unexpected changes in the Gross Domestic Product, the rate of inflation, or the unemployment rate. Some simulation languages such as SIMSCRIPT and GPSS are particularly well suited to performing random processes many times and automatically calculating and storing statistical information about the outcomes. Such languages effectively represent processes where operations are performed in sequence or in a variety of sequences over a period of time, such as occurs on the floor of a manufacturing shop.

Goal-Seeking Software. Simulation languages excel in analyzing the impact of a few decision choices. When the number of choices becomes large or infinite, goal-seeking software can quickly narrow the choices to one or a few. **Goal-seeking software** requires that the user specify in advance the criteria—cost, speed, or revenues, for example—for evaluating the outcomes of different decisions. After the user supplies such a formula, the software applies a variety of tools to quickly determine the best or optimal solution. Such an approach has been shown to be useful for locating branch banks.[14] A food products com-

FIGURE 11-7 Analytical Components of a Decision Support System

Simulation languages	Forecasting models	Risk assessment and evaluation models
Optimization model support	Database support	Stochastic modeling support
Statistical software	Graphical analysis tools	Multi-criteria decision models
Geographical systems	Word-processing integration	Capital finance models
Expert system shells	Markov process models	Pert/CPM and other project management models
Accounting modeling support	Decision tree models	

pany could use a least-cost linear programming model to set the percentage of ingredients in soups, weiners, or even baked goods.

Unfortunately, most goal-seeking software puts fairly severe constraints on the nature of the problems that can be solved in such a fashion. The most popular goal-seeking software includes packages for linear programming, integer programming, goal programming, quadratic programming, and unconstrained optimization.

Statistical Packages. Statistical packages assist managers in drawing inferences about the relationships among data elements. Building effective models calls for developing such relationships and having confidence that they reflect underlying processes rather than random occurrences. For example, assume that historical analyses show that in general, an 8-percent increase in sales accompanies every 10-percent decrease in price. But this relationship would not describe perfectly the relationship between price and sales. Sometimes sales increases by a larger amount, and sometimes by a smaller amount, given the same price change, reflecting perhaps differences in economic conditions, type of product, or time of year. Statistical packages would determine the degree of confidence a manager can have in the 10/8 formula and its likelihood of applying to future price cuts or increases.

Geographical Information Systems (GISs). Certain decisions require the ability to examine and manipulate geographical information.[15] To meet these needs, a **geographical information system (GIS)** includes mapping software, databases that hold geographic and demographic data, and a user interface that facilitates simultaneously changing data on a map and its associated databases. A GIS often incorporates dedicated hardware such as oversized screens, light pens, digitizers, and plotters (see Chapter 5) to make graphical input and output easier. Johanna Dairies, based in Union, New Jersey, identifies more efficient delivery routes by using a GIS to examine the database of current routes. Chemical Bank evaluates its compliance with antidiscrimination laws by using a GIS to compare its mortgages (available on a database) with census tract boundaries and ensure that no bias in lending occurs. AT&T uses a GIS along with a demographic database to create territories for its sales representatives. The Federal Emergency Management Agency (FEMA) with help from Digital Matrix Services, Inc. relied on a GIS to coordinate the cleanup of Florida's South Dade County area after it was devastated by Hurricane Andrew in 1992.[16]

JOHANNA DAIRIES

CHEMICAL BANK

AT&T

FEDERAL EMERGENCY MANAGEMENT AGENCY

DIGITAL MATRIX SERVICES

Expert Systems. Expert systems, as discussed in Chapter 9, may assist a manager in making decisions when the analysis requires expertise that the manager does not possess in a limited domain.[17] Jerry Tatum may use expert system components of a DSS to assist with pricing, staffing, advertising, or expansion decisions. Expert systems add power to DSSs by improving analyses when data are unreliable, contradictory, or of limited validity.[18]

Groupware

Groupware, also known as **computer-supported cooperative work (CSCW),** describes information technology designed to support a group's interactions in performing a common task and accomplishing its goals. Groupware also provides information about the group members, the project status, and even the social atmosphere.[19] A relatively young and rapidly growing application of information technology, groupware sales are expected to grow at an annual rate of 50 percent through 1997.[20] While other information technologies, such as database management systems, may also support group performance, groupware distinguishes itself by its primary objective of facilitating the effective functioning of a group. Because managers participate in groups both as supervisors and as members working on common tasks, groupware assists them in exchanging information, coordinating activities, and managing work flow.

Groupware provides an electronic mechanism for exchanging information among group members and, hence, improving group coordination, discussions, problem solving, and meetings. In global organizations, assembling team members from around the world into a single meeting room is both time consuming and costly. Groupware can be used to simulate such a meeting electronically. PizzaCo, with managers in many locations, may also benefit from groupware for conferencing. Marriott, Inc. used Vision Quest, a product of Collaborative Technologies Corporation, to generate and organize ideas; in a computerized meeting room during a two-month period, 1,000 people generated and organized 10,000 ideas, a task that would have taken nine to twelve times longer if done in a conventional meeting format.[21] Groupware also helps managers and other group members resolve problems and answer questions as they occur, rather than waiting until a meeting is convened.

MARRIOTT

Although meetings help managers coordinate groups, exchange ideas, and reach consensus on difficult problems, managers continuously seek ways to reduce the time spent in meetings or make that time more productive. Most managers agree that meetings do not relay information in the most efficient or effective way. Groupware assists managers in improving the efficiency of meetings. Boeing Aircraft Company, for example, found that the use of groupware reduced the total time involved in meetings for 64 work groups by 71 percent and the time required for team projects that involved meetings by 91 percent; a group of machinists, engineers, designers, and manufacturing managers in designing a standardized control system for machine tools used groupware to conduct 15 electronic meetings, which reduced development time from a year to 35 days.[22]

BOEING

Elements of Groupware

How does groupware work? What technologies are necessary to support it? Groupware is not a single technology, and no product on the market packages the entire spectrum of groupware functions. Currently, groupware technologies include message systems, multiuser editors, group decision support systems, intelligent agents, computer conferencing, and coordination systems.[23]

Message Systems. Electronic mail, lists, notes, and bulletin boards enhance group work through improved communication. **Electronic mail** enables members of an organization to send messages to one another and to others outside the organization. Individuals may send text or, in some cases, multimedia information to a precreated or *ad hoc* list of users. These messages are transmitted over a computer network to the recipient's **electronic mailbox,** a storage area on the network reserved for electronic mail users. The electronic mail program routes the message to the appropriate box, even if it must send it through several gateways that connect different networks. Many companies use public mailboxes on value-added networks such as Compuserve (see Chapter 8) so that they can receive messages worldwide. When the electronic mail recipient uses his or her computer, a signal indicates that a message has arrived; the recipient can then reply, edit, or forward it.

HARVARD MEDICAL SCHOOL

Implementing an E-mail system at the Harvard Medical School, for example, reduced response time from several days to a few hours.[24] It even allowed people who had questions in the middle of the night to get responses. A network linking Harvard to 18 other medical sites created a virtual university, as shown in Figure 11-8, greatly enhancing the benefit of the electronic mail system.

FIGURE 11-8 The Virtual University

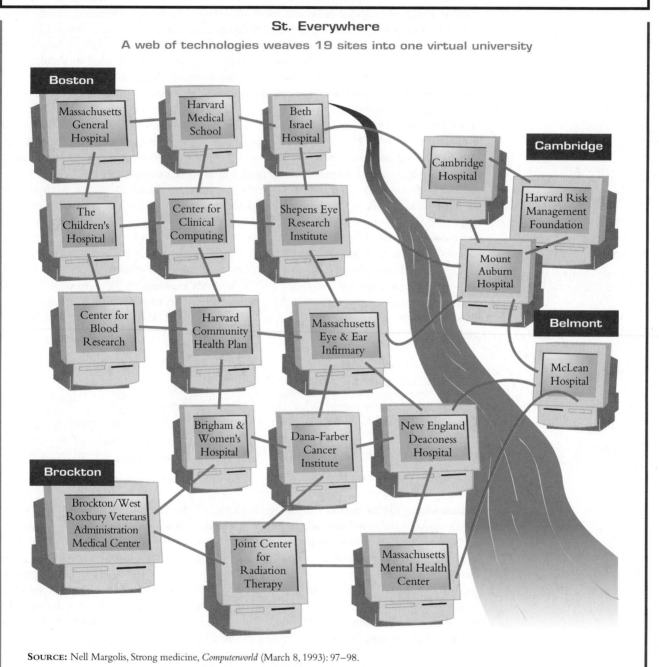

St. Everywhere

A web of technologies weaves 19 sites into one virtual university

Boston

Massachusetts General Hospital

Harvard Medical School

Beth Israel Hospital

The Children's Hospital

Center for Clinical Computing

Shepens Eye Research Institute

Center for Blood Research

Harvard Community Health Plan

Massachusetts Eye & Ear Infirmary

Brigham & Women's Hospital

Dana-Farber Cancer Institute

New England Deaconess Hospital

Cambridge

Cambridge Hospital

Harvard Risk Management Foundation

Mount Auburn Hospital

Belmont

McLean Hospital

Brockton

Brockton/West Roxbury Veterans Administration Medical Center

Joint Center for Radiation Therapy

Massachusetts Mental Health Center

SOURCE: Nell Margolis, Strong medicine, *Computerworld* (March 8, 1993): 97–98.

Electronic lists, a feature of some electronic mail systems, allow people interested in a particular topic to share electronic mail. Individuals interested in a particular topic, such as those working in a group, agree to share information by subscribing to the list. Messages sent to the list mailbox are automatically forwarded to every member of the list. Individuals can also subscribe to public electronic lists, such as the list on the topic of doing business in Eastern Europe. Electronic lists have the drawback of creating large and potentially unmanageable volumes of mail as the number of subscribers increases. A list of ten members who each generates one message a day results in 100 mail messages per day, but adding 40 members results in 2,500 messages per day sent over the network.

Electronic mail typically provides poor archiving and auditing; therefore, electronic mail and lists do not effectively support cooperative work on documents. Electronic notes address this limitation. **Electronic notes** resemble electronic mail except that a **group** or **topic mailbox** rather than a **user mailbox** holds messages. All authorized members of a group may send messages to the common mailbox or read messages from it. Although electronic notes software normally creates mailboxes for each topic of interest, it may create boxes with more specific topics. For example, if a group member posts a message asking a question, replies to the question could be organized so that users could read the responses to select questions or review all messages associated with the general topic. Some electronic-notes software allows any authorized party to modify existing notes; this facility offers groups the ability to jointly develop a document. The notes software tracks who made changes and the nature of those changes; it also allows changes to be undone. As a result, electronic notes both enhance communication and help automate an office. Figure 11-9 illustrates the use of Lotus Notes, an electronic notes product.

Electronic bulletin boards resemble electronic notes because they use a central repository for storing messages. Unlike notes, bulletin boards have a central manager, called a **sysop,** who controls (or abdicates control over) all topics of conversation on the board. Although users with access to the board may read messages on all topics, users wishing to post a message may first have to clear the message with the sysop.

Multiuser Editors. Groupware technology includes **multiuser editors,** software that allows multiple users to access and modify a common document. Each user has a copy of a master document available to view on the computer screen. As each user edits this copy, the program alters the master to reflect the changes made by group members. Individual users then have two options for viewing the update: They may see changes made by other members on their screen as they are working on their own changes, or they may receive a copy of the updated document only after they have saved their own copy.[25]

Despite the increased use of computer-assisted collaboration in writing, research on its effectiveness is limited. One study found that computer assistance in collaborative writing fails to alter product quality or reduce the time needed to draft a document, although it seems to increase the ability of writers to assume the perspective of a reader.[26] The study also suggested that computer assistance affects the process of writing, reducing the amount of group planning, increasing the amount of individual work, and increasing the amount of revising.

NETWORK WORLD

Groups whose members maintain different portions of documentation can benefit greatly from multiuser editing. At *Network World,* for example, multiuser editing significantly improved the real-time development of a presentation by a group consisting of technical experts, editors, and publicists, as shown in Figure 11-10.

Group Decision Support Systems. Just as decision support systems increase the effectiveness of managerial decision making, **group decision support systems (GDSSs)** have evolved to support group decision making. GDSSs attempt to accelerate the decision-making process and to produce better decisions.[27] GDSSs typically support *ad hoc* queries and analytical capabilities; they also include a database, knowledge base, model base, and user interface. They may address any or all of the following aspects of joint decision making: idea generation, alternative analysis, alternative evaluation, and consensus building.[28]

FIGURE 11-9 Use of Lotus Notes

GROUPWARE CAN GET EVERYBODY IN A COMPANY INTO THE ACT

While groupware generally aims to help established teams work more efficiently, Lotus's Notes helps create ad hoc teams. It provides interlinked electronic bulletin boards that allow people in a company who have insights or expertise on a particular problem to find one another. At Price Waterhouse a Notes user logs on and sees a screen with lists of different databases (large screen at left). Need to know who in the firm is an expert on nonferrous mining? The box called FSIP Resumes will tell you. (The initials, which also appear in the Hot Topics box, stand for Financial Service Industry Practice, an internal PW designation.)

The Notes program differs significantly from electronic mail, where senders must select the recipients of a message. With Notes, anyone with an interest in a subject can read the information. It's not uncommon for a Notes conversation to include people from five or six cities around the world. A query from London may be answered by someone in Toronto, who may be challenged in turn by someone else in Los Angeles. Before Notes, only four members of Price Waterhouse's 15-person senior executive committee used PCs at all. Now they all do.

Price Waterhouse auditors in offices all over the world can keep up to date by selecting the Hot Topics database . . .

. . . on the Financial Accounting Standards Board (FASB) . . .

. . . as summarized by Diane Altneu in New York.

Techies in any company love to talk shop, in their own esoteric shorthand. At PW, they can hit this window and shoptalk away . . .

. . . in this case about a new type of software . . .

. . . as described by Tina Tierney in the Hartford office . . .

. . . and commented on by Anthony Todd in San Francisco.

SOURCE: David Kirkpatrick, Here comes the payoff from PCs, *Fortune* (March 23, 1992): 94–95.

Dell Computer

In addition, GDSSs may address planning, administrative, and data analysis tasks.[29] Dell Computer uses groupware for strategic planning, product planning, and developing marketing strategies.[30]

Many GDSSs require electronic meeting rooms. Participants work at their own computers on a U-shaped table facing a common computer at the front of the room, which can be seen by all participants, as shown in Figure 11-11. Any participant can control the common computer. Alternatively, the computer can merely assimilate the entries of the participants onto a single, large screen; this approach allows participants to contribute anonymously to the problem-solving effort. Such anonymity allows GDSSs to improve conflict management and foster group cohesiveness.[31] Groups focusing on a public screen tend to perceive all ideas as "our" ideas rather than as "my" idea or "your" idea. This perspective tends to reduce the emotional ownership of ideas and allows decisions to be made with less conflict.

Intelligent Agents. GDSSs may include the computer as an active participant, or **intelligent agent,** in the group decision making process. The intelligent agent, driven by an expert system, may contribute to both the content and process of decision making by the other participants.[32] The PizzaCo managers, for example, may use a GDSS that includes an expert advertising system to discuss advertising expenditures.

Computer Conferencing. Telecommunication technology has created three new ways to hold conferences: real-time computer conferencing, teleconferencing, and desktop conferencing.[33] **Real-time conferencing** allows people at the same or different locations to hold meetings electronically. The participants' computers must be networked or remotely connected through a conference call. Instead of speaking, participants type their contributions into their computers. The text of their speech appears simultaneously on all the conferenced computers. Protocols exist to allow participants to interrupt and take the floor, as with normal meetings.

Teleconferencing, which includes audio and video conferencing, overcomes the slow speed of typing versus talking and the absence of video to capture body language that limit the effectiveness of real-time computer conferencing. Teleconferencing, still a relatively expensive technology, allows people in different locations to hold a conference as if they were in one room. It requires special rooms to hold the hardware necessary to capture and forward the video and voice, as well as technical operators to work the equipment effectively.

Desktop conferencing offers a compromise between real-time computer conferencing and teleconferencing. Sophisticated workstations that include a video camera connected over a network or high-capacity conference line can transmit text, graphics, voice, and video. Participants see others in windows on their screens and hear them in voice output played through the computer. Desktop conferencing provides a poorer quality of video and voice than teleconferencing. It also can display only one or two video images if text sharing occurs. Although adequate for small conferences, desktop conferencing is quite awkward for more than four people. It also costs more than real-time computer conferencing but less than teleconferencing.

Coordination Systems. **Coordination systems** improve project management by giving managers information required to coordinate the scheduling of project activities and team member participation. Coordination systems assist with all phases of project management. In the planning stage, project management software can determine the order of the tasks, estimate each task's time to completion, and identify the most time-constrained tasks. It can schedule employees efficiently so that they have an appropriate work load and work on tasks to which they are most suited. Coordination systems can also evaluate tradeoffs in labor overtime and cost. The group features of project management software particularly aid

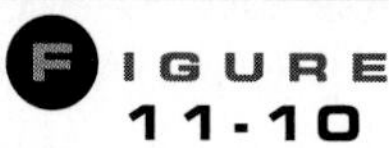

How *Network World* Used Groupware to Create This Figure

At the front line with groupware

Often, the only way to understand how well something works is to use it yourself. That's just what we did when we used groupware to put together one of the graphics to illustrate this article.

In publishing, when the author developing a graphic idea isn't working on the premises of the magazine or newspaper, a sketch is faxed to the publication for review and comment. The publication makes changes and returns the graphic to the author for similar review.

This process continues until each party is satisfied with the changes made by the other. It can be a long and tiresome process, especially if there are misunderstandings between the two parties.

Such misunderstandings usually occur because no two people describe the same thing the same way. So even when each party is looking at identical hard copies of the graphic, there is too much room for misinterpretation.

To get first-hand experience with groupware and to determine whether it really is possible to save time and money using such products, we used document conferencing software — a product called Aspects, made by Group Technologies, Inc., of Arlington, VA — to prepare the graphic on page 36.

Network World and TeleChoice, Inc. were joined by Group Technologies in a conference call. Group Technologies was included to assist us in our first-time use of their product.

We at TeleChoice in Montclair, N.J., initiated the conference call with all three parties. We dialed into the local-area network at Group Technologies' headquarters in Arlington and also into the Macintosh-based graphics system at *Network World* in Farmingham, Mass., using 2,400-bit/sec modems over standard telephone lines.

The conference was supplemented with a three-way audio conference, also over standard dial-up lines. (If we were using an Integrated Services Digital Network Basic Rate Interface circuit, we could have combined voice and data on the same facility.)

Using Aspects, TeleChoice and *Network World* designers were able to jointly develop the graphic. Each party was able to see in real time what the other created as it was created. Changes made by each party appeared nearly instantaneously on everyone's screen.

Moreover, the input of each interested party was instantly available and usable. *Network World's* designers and editors were able to direct the size and style of the graphic and ensure that it would be clearly presented. TeleChoice was able to add or delete information as directed and to redesign the graphic "on the fly." And Group Technologies was able to verify the accuracy of the technological information.

Overall, the entire process took about an hour — quite a savings in time over the standard two to five days and multiple facsimiles and telephone calls such a process previously required. And the end project was satisfactory to all concerned, and — most important — correct the first time through.

While we cannot extrapolate our experience with one product to all products across the groupware spectrum, we did convince ourselves — and our editors — that groupware can work well when applied correctly.

—Daniel Briere and Bruce Guprill

continued

planning when the project spans diverse departments. Although functional managers can plan independently, the groupware features of project management software help them identify and resolve potential conflicts in interdepartmental interactions, such as the timing of tasks or the use of labor resources. During project performance, project management software can compare actual to planned performance. Groupware facilitates joint evaluation of alternative approaches for handling unplanned problems.

Coordination systems may also support the creation and manipulation of joint calendars and schedules. Public on-line calendars help managers schedule meetings; if, for example, the vice-president of human resources wants to schedule a meeting with the training manager,

FIGURE 11-10 Continued

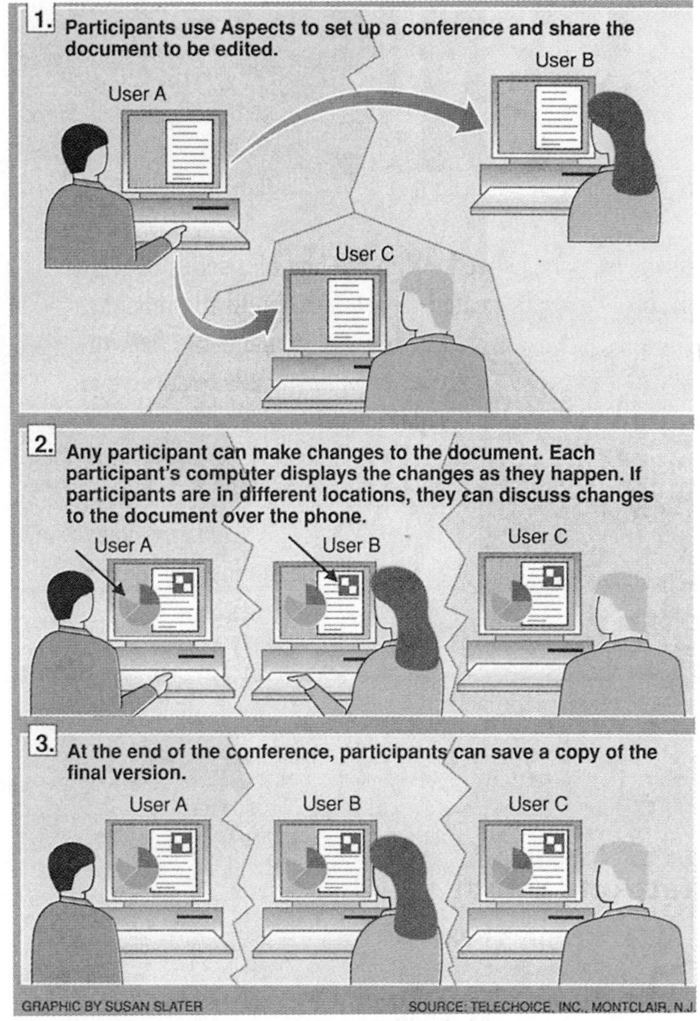
1. Participants use Aspects to set up a conference and share the document to be edited.
User A
User B
User C
2. Any participant can make changes to the document. Each participant's computer displays the changes as they happen. If participants are in different locations, they can discuss changes to the document over the phone.
User A
User B
User C
3. At the end of the conference, participants can save a copy of the final version.
User A
User B
User C
GRAPHIC BY SUSAN SLATER
SOURCE: TELECHOICE, INC., MONTCLAIR, N.J.

SOURCE: Box on p. 34 and figure on p. 36, *Network World,* September 16, 1991.

the vice-president can request a list of the manager's unscheduled times and select one time to meet. This calendar software also eases scheduling of meetings of larger groups; it can, for example, identify free times for all members of a six-person team as well as for various team subgroups.

Problems in Managing Groupware

Groupware does not solve all group performance problems. As shown in Figure 11-12, the implementation of groupware may create problems such as information overload.[34] In general, the belief that increasing the amount of information people share will increase their

A computerized meeting room.
Courtesy of International Business Machines Corporation.

FIGURE 11-11 A Meeting Room for GDSS

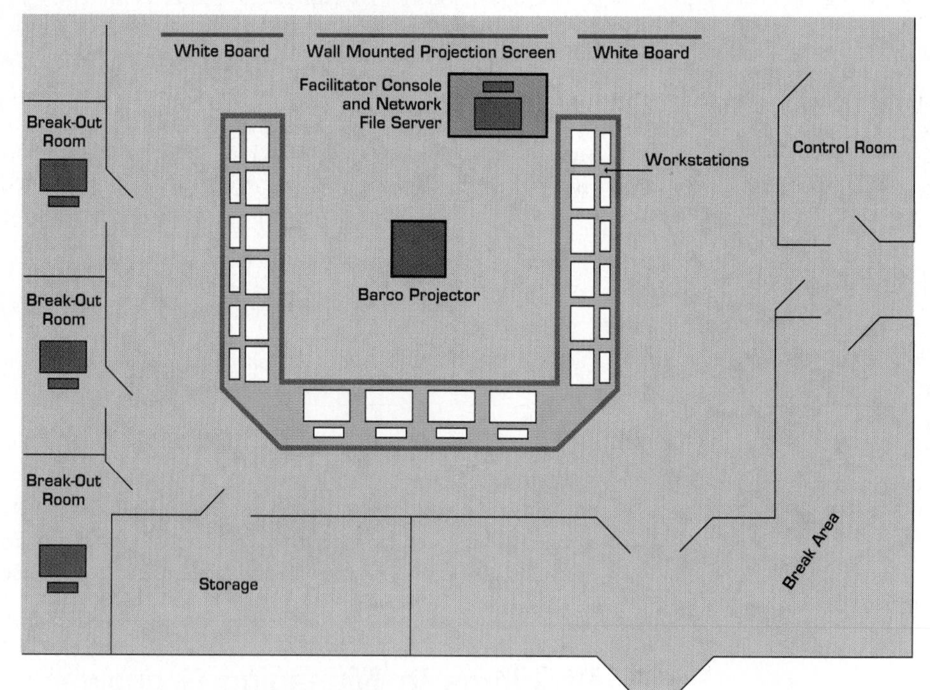

SOURCE: Doug Vogel and Jay Nunamaker, "Group decision support system impact: Multi-methodological exploration," *Information & Management,* 18 (1990): 20; Rosemary Hamilton, Electronic meetings: No more ZZZ's, *Computerworld* (December 14, 1992): 109.

Problems Associated with Groupware

Too many messages cause information overload.

Network requirements increase.

Common carrier communication costs increase.

People easily schedule unnecessary meetings.

On-line meetings are ineffective for some types of communication.

Some people feel reduced responsibility.

Some people will not share information despite the technological capability.

People can easily share irrelevant or unnecessary information, making it difficult to stay focused.

Integrating groupware into existing communication systems is difficult.

People may need to check too many mailboxes.

The corporate culture may be averse to sharing information electronically.

Groupware encourages socializing, and social conversations are difficult to monitor.

SOURCE: Alice LaPlante, Group(ware) therapy, *Computerworld* (July 27, 1992): 71–73.

productivity is unfounded. When faced with a flood of information, managers often cannot differentiate important from unimportant information.[35] **Workgroup editors** that screen, edit, and consolidate messages, especially with electronic lists and notes, offer one solution to the overload problem.[36]

Groupware may also have the unintended consequence of increasing the number of meetings because it reduces the time needed to arrange meetings and videoconferences from hours or days to seconds or minutes. At the same time, groupware devotees may ignore the value of conducting meetings in person rather than electronically. Although interpersonal interaction may have less value in technical work, such managerial activities as negotiations or staff evaluations benefit from face-to-face communication. Users who fail to diagnose the precise information required as well as the best context for its delivery may use electronic meetings inappropriately or find that the meetings take longer and are less effective.

Executive Information Systems (EISs)

METROPOLITAN LIFE INSURANCE

Executives require somewhat different information from middle- and lower-level managers. Although they resemble decision support systems, **executive information systems (EISs)** respond to the particular requirements of top-level managers. Executive computer users differ from others in their need to look at and evaluate information rather than create it.[37] Metropolitan Life Insurance Company's pension division has an EIS that regularly updates databases of sales information, staffing figures, corporate budgets, and financial information. Top division executives have access to information available to department heads and often use it for business forecasting, to signal missed sales targets, or to examine salespeople's progress reports.[38]

Most EISs include mainly *hard* information such as financial data, sales, shipments, and other historical information. Increasingly they include *soft* data such as predictions, opinions, explanations, forecasts, and even hearsay; for example, state senators in one state use an EIS

FIGURE 11-13 Comparison of Hard and Soft Data for EIS

Characteristics	Hard	Soft
Perceived accuracy	High	Depends on source
Source	Machine-resident; often internal	Human; often external
Subject to interpretation	Generally accepted	Individually assessed
Timeliness	Historical	Current
Perceived value	Low	High
Availability	Regular	Ad hoc
Standardization	High	Low
Richness	Low	High
Existence	Generally known	Often unknown
Ownership	Generally available	Often tightly held
Lifetime	Long	Short
Communication channel	Formal	Informal

SOURCE: L. Z. Dix, A bunch of softies, *Computerworld* (October 19, 1992): 105.

that includes constituents' opinions on pending legislation.[39] Figure 11-13 compares these two types of information.

XEROX

External and internal pressures, shown in Figure 11-14, lead to the development of an EIS. Usually an organization's chief executive officer or president sponsors development of an EIS, but over time its use spreads to lower-level employees as subordinates become aware that they can access unique information available to the organizational leaders.[40] Xerox, for example, expanded its EIS from 15 to 100 managers and may expand it to 500.[41]

Typical Features of an EIS

Because most executives use an executive information system without the benefit of technical intermediaries, an EIS must have a friendly user interface. In addition, an EIS must provide the capabilities shown in Figure 11-15.

User Interface. Most executives cannot type well and so dislike using a keyboard to request information. EISs provide a variety of techniques to limit the required keyboard use. An EIS generally includes a graphical user interface; an executive can access the desired reports and screens using a mouse or touch screen to select from alternatives listed in a menu, represented by icons, or shown by example. Again, the design of such interfaces melds information and technology concepts with human factors and psychology concepts.

Most systems allow presentation of numeric data in a variety of tabular and graphical formats. The user can select among the formats using a mouse or touch screen. The systems use color and graphics consistently to cue the user to the information. For example, red might highlight any number outside an expected range, and blinking red might highlight an item that requires immediate attention. Often the screen shows the names and telephone numbers of individuals responsible for acting on the data presented on the screen.

External and Internal Pressures to Develop an EIS

	Relative Weight
External Pressures	
Increasingly competitive environment	113
Rapidly changing external environment	59
Need to be more proactive in dealing with external environment	46
Need to access external databases	25
Increasing government regulations	15
Internal Pressures	
Need for timeline information	61
Need for improved communication	39
Need for access to operational data	35
Need for rapid status updates on different business units	34
Need for increased effectiveness	27
Need to be able to identify historical trends	27
Need for increased efficiency	25
Need for access to corporate database	25
Need for more accurate information	15

SOURCE: Hugh Watson, R. K. Rainer, Jr., and Chang Koh, Executive information systems: A framework for development and a survey of current practices, *MIS Quarterly* 15(1) (1991): 23.

Most EISs also provide a **drill down** capability, as illustrated in Figure 11-16. They first present data at their most aggregated levels. The executive can then select a line and request the detail behind it (**explode** the line). The executive can drill down through greater and greater levels of detail or return to higher levels of aggregation as desired.

Communication with Employees. Most EISs contain a variety of groupware features, including calendaring systems, electronic mail, electronic notes, and electronic bulletin boards. Top executives who travel frequently use electronic mail to contact key employees, suppliers, and customers. Once or twice a day, the executive may use a portable

Capabilities Available on an EIS

Capability	Percent of Firms
Access to company data	88
Electronic mail	65
Other external database	57
External news access	56
Word processing	34
Spreadsheet	37
Automated filing	22

SOURCE: Hugh Watson, R. K. Rainer, Jr., and Chang Koh, Executive information systems: A framework for development and a survey of current practices, *MIS Quarterly* 15(1) (1991): 26.

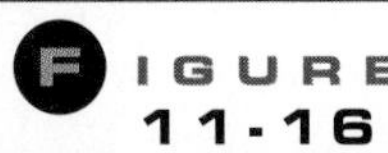

FIGURE 11-16 Drill-Down Screens

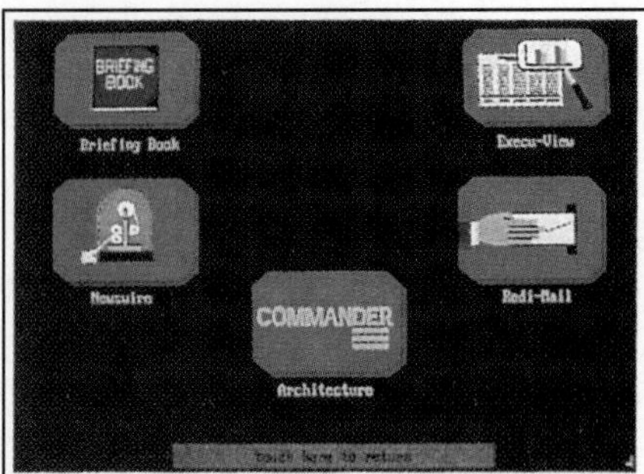

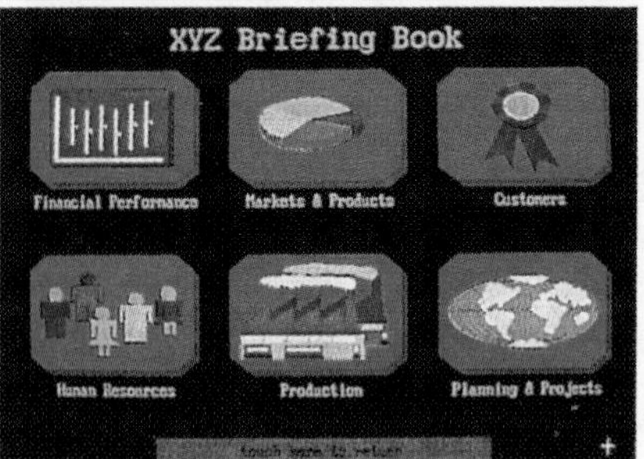

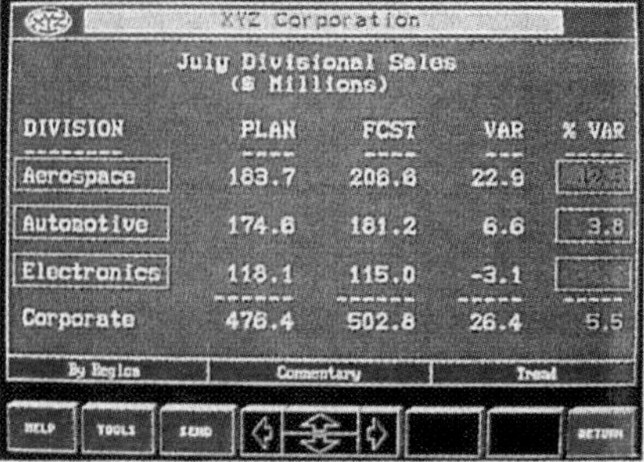

Comshare's Commander lets the CEO "drill down" for detail. Here, the executive touches "briefing book" (first screen), then chooses "financial performance" (second screen), which highlights in red the slip in electronics sales in July (third screen). Then . . .

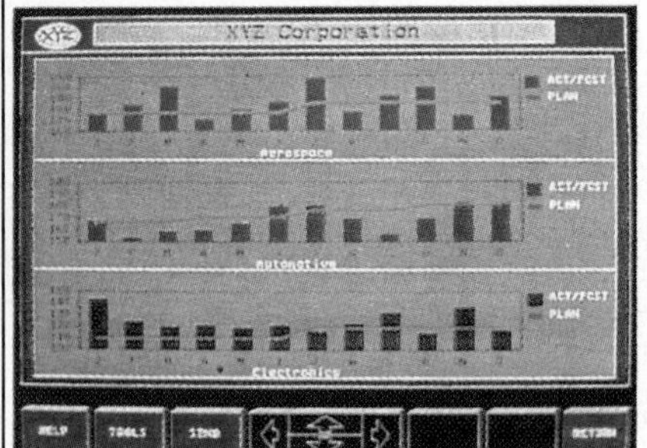

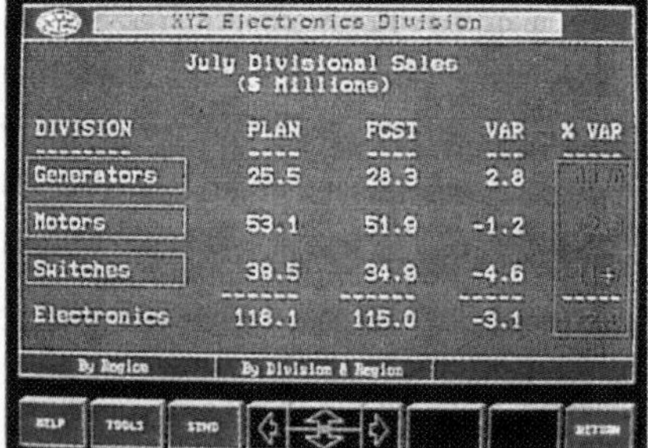

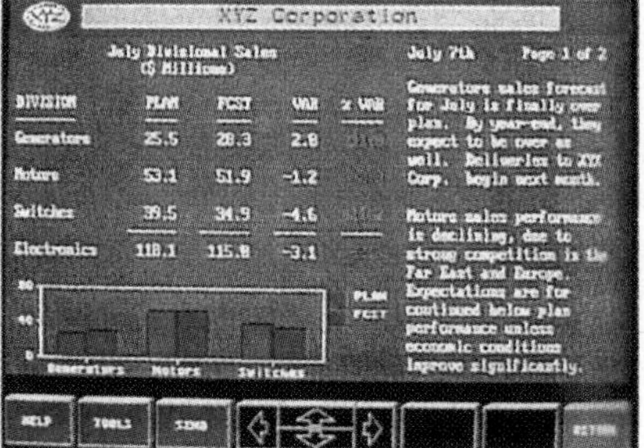

. . . after checking trends for the year (first screen), the executive gets more detail on the troubled electronics division (second and third screens). Switch sales have slumped badly. By touching the −11.7% figure, he can call more screens to probe more deeply.

SOURCE: Patricia A. Langan, At last, software CEOs can use, *Fortune* (March 13, 1989): 78.

computer and modem to deliver messages to employees in the office and to receive news and data that may be important in meetings outside the office. In addition, many executives encourage all employees to communicate with them over electronic mail as a way of empowering workers. This practice allows a large number of employees to communicate directly with the president or CEO without feeling intimidated and without wasting too much of the executive's time. Executives can either respond directly or forward the received messages to the employees responsible for particular areas of concern.

Scanned News Updates. Although executives read newspapers and magazines to learn about events that might have an impact on their organization's operations, searching through news sources for relevant articles is time consuming and relatively unproductive. Many organizations have an executive staff member who scans news sources for relevant items. Recent improvements in expert systems have made them at least as accurate as staff members in identifying important articles. Executives specify in advance the types of articles they find relevant, and computerized expert systems with on-line access to news services and article abstracts scan for them. Such systems improve their searches over time. During the first few weeks of scanning, the executives rank the articles that they receive and send the ranking back to the expert system. The expert system learns more precisely the executive's needs and improves its article selection. As the expert system becomes fine tuned, it begins to rate the value of various articles to the executive; feedback from the executive, in turn, improves the ratings.

Summary

Top-, middle-, and lower-level managers require extensive and diverse types of information to perform their jobs. Managers in a global environment need information systems that help them access and analyze current comprehensive information. They can use four types of management information systems—1) management reporting systems, 2) decision support systems, 3) groupware, and 4) executive information systems—to assist in performing their jobs.

Management reporting systems (MRSs) include detail, summary, and exception reports. Reports can be produced periodically, initiated by a particular event, or published on demand. MRSs in many organizations comprise the reporting components of a transaction processing system.

Decision support systems (DSSs) include a database, knowledge base, model base, and user interface. DSSs can answer unforeseen questions by supporting *ad hoc* queries and providing analytical abilities. A DSS usually obtains its database from an organization's transaction processing system and has an external interface. The analytical elements of a DSS can include simulation languages, goal-seeking software, statistical packages, geographical information systems, and expert systems.

Groupware supports a group's interaction in performing a task or reaching a goal. Groupware can include message systems, multiuser editors, group decision support systems, computer conferencing, intelligent agents, and coordination systems. Organizations can face new challenges in managing groupware.

Executive information systems (EISs) are used primarily by top-level executives to help them look at and evaluate already-analyzed information. Typical EISs include a user-friendly user interface, facilities for communicating with employees, and options for scanning news updates.

Key Terms

Ad hoc query
Computer-supported cooperative work (CSCW)
Coordination system
Data warehouse
Decision support system (DSS)
Desktop conferencing
Detail report
Drill down
Electronic bulletin board
Electronic list
Electronic mail
Electronic mailbox
Electronic notes
Event-initiated report
Exception report
Executive information system (EIS)
Explode
Geographical information system (GIS)
Goal-seeking software
Group decision support system (GDSS)
Group mailbox
Groupware
Information warehouse
Intelligent agent
Knowledge base
Management reporting system (MRS)
Model base
Multiuser editor
Object-oriented user interface
On-demand report
Periodic report
Real-time conferencing
Simulation
Statistical report
Summary report
Sysop
Teleconferencing
Topic mailbox
User interface
User mailbox
Warehouse
Workgroup editor

Review Questions

1. List four types of management information systems.
2. List three types of management reports. Describe the types of information each provides to managers.
3. Identify three types of scheduling for generating management reports. Give an example for each of a report that is best produced under that scheduling practice.
4. What two options do companies have for coping with the resource constraints they encounter while simultaneously running their TPS and MRS systems?
5. What is the function of a decision support system? What are its benefits? What affects its effectiveness?
6. What are the components of a decision support system?
7. Describe the difference in the way that users interact with decision support systems as compared with management reporting systems or transaction processing systems.
8. What two features of a decision support system enable managers to use it to address questions that were unforeseen when it was designed?
9. Identify five analytical elements common to decision support systems.
10. What types of inputs do users typically have to provide in order to use goal-seeking software?
11. Identify and describe six elements of groupware.
12. Identify and describe four types of message systems.
13. Identify and describe three ways to hold electronic conferences. List the advantages and disadvantages of each.
14. Identify three problems in managing groupware.
15. How do the information needs of executives differ from those of middle- and lower-level managers?
16. Describe the typical features and use of an executive information system.
17. Describe the typical user interface of an executive information system.

MINICASE

Groupware at KPMG Peat Marwick

Like many of its Big Six consulting and accounting firm brethren, KPMG Peat Marwick is rolling out a corporation-wide groupware system meant to help its 17,000 employees more efficiently share their expertise. The system, dubbed Knowledge Manager, is built on a groupware product called FirstClass from SoftArc, Inc. KPMG personnel using Knowledge Manager on their Macintosh or PC workstations can click on icons to access information, such as examples of successful proposals for floor space utilization, stored in various databases at local or remote locations. Knowledge Manager provides a unified front end, making the data appear to come from a single, local source.

According to Michael Donahue, a management consulting partner, an early version of Knowledge Manager helped KPMG bid successfully on a project to plan a major technology overhaul for a northeastern insurance company. The insurance company had called KPMG at 3 P.M. on a Friday in August 1994. Over the weekend, four KPMG partners working in different cities collaborated on a proposal that they delivered by noon on the following Monday. Their work required them to assemble background information from

---

Adapted from Lynda Radosevich, KPMG turns to FirstClass groupware, *Computerworld* (November 21, 1994): 56.

KPMG's data libraries, to communicate with one another as they planned their individual tasks, and to comment on and modify drafts on each others' work, including graphics and diagrams. Without Knowledge Manager, Donahue estimates, the partners would have had to work at full steam for three to five business days to complete the proposal. The outcome of KPMG's effort using Knowledge Manager was that it won the contract.

Before Knowledge Manager existed, professionals working on a proposal often had to call offices around the world to find in-house expertise in the areas they needed for completing their work. Allan Frank, managing partner at the advanced technologies division in Radnor, Pennsylvania, sees the objective of Knowledge Manager as ". . . deliver[ing] in every individual in the firm the combined intellectual global assets of the firm." This task, however, was not easy, as much of KPMG's information is contained in Microsoft Word documents, Excel spreadsheets, and PowerPoint presentation files, not in formal databases. FirstClass allowed KPMG to build software that provides directories to the information and the ability for users to access it in its native form simply by clicking on icons. Because the data did not have to be converted, KPMG furthermore retains the ability to migrate Knowledge Manager to another groupware product such as Microsoft Exchange when it becomes available.

KPMG found that its greatest technological challenge in implementing Knowledge Manager was to build the network to support groupware activities. The company uses both Macintosh and IBM/PC-compatible equipment, and its LANs at different locales operate under different network operating systems. KPMG's chief information officer, Tony Ottavio, observed that integrating different equipment and protocols created problems that were difficult to diagnose and fix.

Case Questions

1. What was KPMG's objective in developing Knowledge Manager? How well do you think that Knowledge Manager satisfies that objective?
2. What difficulties did KPMG have to overcome to develop and implement its groupware product?
3. What are the benefits to KPMG managers and partners of the use of groupware?
4. What was the benefit of using FirstClass to develop Knowledge Manager?

Designing a Management Reporting System

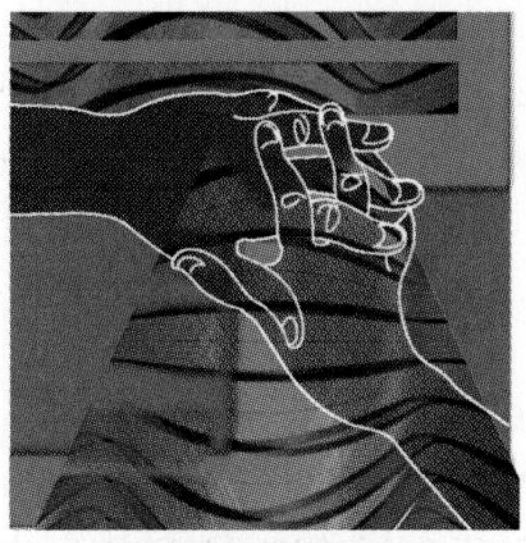

hands on

STEP 1: Read the Specialty Engineering Company case.

Specialty Engineering Company is a designer and manufacturer of a full line of special scientific and engineering instruments. In addition to its instruments, the company sells its services in the research, design, and development of new electronic products, builds prototypes of products based on new technology, and tests new manufacturing processes.

Your supervisor, Chris Yelton, the chief information officer at Specialty, is responsible for the company's information and communication systems. She reports directly to the president and is included in the company's monthly "cabinet meetings."

At the most recent cabinet meeting, James Morgan, the vice-president for finance, announced that phone costs had become excessive. Mr. Morgan had complained about phone

SOURCE: Reprinted with the permission of Simon & Schuster, Inc., from the Macmillan College text *Casebook for Data Processing,* third edition, by John C. Windsor and J. Wayne Spence (Chicago: Science Research Associates, Inc.). Copyright © 1989.

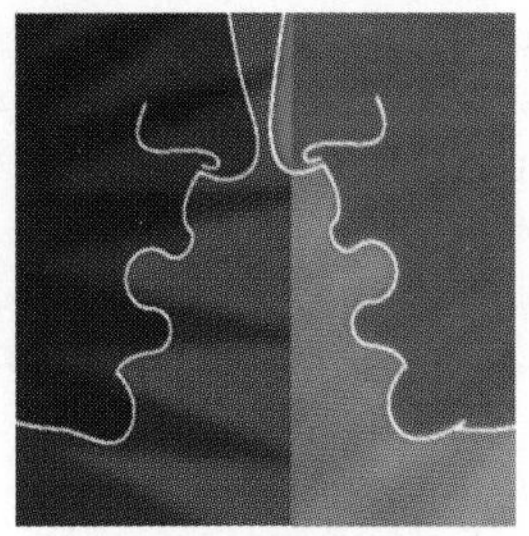

charges only a couple of years ago. At that time, Ms. Yelton had recommended that the company subscribe to the Wide Area Telephone System (WATS) and that it install its own switching system. Both recommendations had been accepted, and phone costs had decreased substantially. But, as Mr. Morgan noted, "The drop in expenses was short-lived. We must now either reduce our telephone expenses again or start billing our clients for actual telephone costs. In addition, we are finding more and more errors in our bills from the telephone company. Looking for these errors is simply too costly to continue. We wouldn't have found the ones we have if we hadn't been trying to make some sense of the daily reports from the switching system."

Bert Cortney, the vice-president for operations, asked for a description of the data that Specialty receives from its switching system. Ms. Yelton showed him the sample below and explained, "The current switching system prints a report every time its status changes. What is printed is the date at the top of each page and a list of activities. For example, when a phone call is made, the phone number at which the call originated is reported along with the time the call was made, the phone number called, and whether it went out on a WATS line or a trunk line. When the call ends, the same information is printed again, along with the time the call ended. The report can sometimes be hard to read, but all the information is there."

Date: May 10, 19xx

		Telephone Number		
Time-In	**Time-Out**	**From**	**To**	**Line**
0730		565-4147	(404)386-6867	WATS
0735		565-3161	(512)762-4014	WATS
0736		565-1162	(613)986-4132	WATS
0736		565-4149	(212)326-7854	WATS
0737		565-3116	(215)475-2316	TRUNK
0730	0740	565-4147	(404)386-6867	WATS
0740		565-1000	49-228-942-6321	WATS
0736	0741	565-4149	(212)326-7854	WATS
.	.	.	.	.
.	.	.	.	.
.	.	.	.	.

Jan Keres, the vice-president for engineering, then jumped into the discussion. "You're talking about cutting the phone expenses, but I've got a real problem. My people are constantly on the phone to our clients, and we can't always get the outside lines we need. It's almost impossible for us to get the WATS lines. We already have difficulty doing our job. If you cut the phone budget, we will have serious problems."

After further discussion, the president, Lee Samuals, finally called a halt and said, "As I understand the discussion, telephone expenses are out of control. In addition, as evidenced by Jan's comments, the service isn't what it should be, and we don't have the data in usable form to make an informed decision. Is that about the size of it?"

When everyone agreed, Mr. Samuals asked Chris Yelton to "get your people on this right away. Set up a system to get us the information we need to make a decision. Find out from Jim exactly what we need. Also, I want this system to last. I don't want to come back next year with the same problem and have no information to base a decision on."

After she left the cabinet meeting, Jan called you into her office and turned the problem over to you. The next day, you visited Jim Morgan to get a handle on the task. Mr. Morgan spent nearly two hours describing the types of analysis he needed to be able to evaluate telephone expenses. Mr. Morgan wanted to know the daily telephone expenses for a month broken down by the name of the employee, an aggregate by job title, and an aggregate by department. He also wanted to know the number of phone calls made and their duration. As he pointed out, one long call is less expensive than two or three short calls. "Maybe our solution is to teach people how to use the telephone more efficiently."

Finally, Mr. Morgan said, "I also need to know who is being called. I don't really need a person's name, although that might become necessary. What I need is the name of the company. When calls are made to client companies that are buying our research services, we should be able to bill them for the telephone expense."

After leaving Mr. Morgan's office, you explored the sources and availability of data. You quickly learned that the switching system can download its report to your mainframe. Then, Allen Trainor, the company's data administrator, discussed the corporate information maintained about employees and customers. Portions of the schema are reproduced below. Some employees have several phones, so employee phone data are kept in a record separate from the rest of the employee data. Also, because most companies have several contact people, contacts are kept in a record separate from the other customer data.

Employee Data	
Employee Code	6-character, alphanumeric
Employee Last Name	15-character, alphabetic
Employee First Name	10-character, alphabetic
Employee Middle Initial	1-character, alphabetic
Employee Office Number	4-character, alphanumeric
Employee Social Security #	9-character, numeric
Employee Department	10-character, alphabetic
Employee Job Title	15-character, alphabetic

Employee Phone	
Phone Extension	4-character, numeric
Employee Code	6-character, alphanumeric
Customer Code	7-character, alphanumeric
Company Name	25-character, alphanumeric
Billing Address, First Line	25-character, alphanumeric
Billing Address, Second Line	25-character, alphanumeric
Billing City	10-character, alphanumeric
Billing State	2-character, alphabetic
Billing Zip Code	10-character, alphanumeric

Customer Contact Data	
Contact Phone	10-character, numeric
Contact Extension	4-character, alphanumeric
Contact Name	25-character, alphanumeric
Specialty Account Exec Code	6-character, alphanumeric

STEP 2: Individually or in small groups, as directed by your instructor, design a set of reports that provide the information needed by Mr. Morgan. Your design should indicate what information is included in each column of the report, how the report should be sorted, what totals, if any, should appear, and on what schedule (periodic, on demand, etc.) the report should be produced.

STEP 3: Exchange your report designs with another student or group as directed by your instructor. Compare the designs you receive with your own designs. Then answer the following questions:

1. How many reports do you think are necessary to give Mr. Morgan enough information to control telephone costs?
2. Are exception reports useful for this application? If so, in what way? If not, why?
3. Are detail reports useful for this application? If so, in what way? If not, why?

STEP 4: Your instructor will divide you into groups and assign you the affirmative or negative position on the issue, "A decision support system would be more appropriate for this application than a management reporting system." You will have ten minutes to prepare your case. Select one member to present your case and another member to rebut the case of your opponents. Your instructor will select two teams to debate before the class. The order of presentation will be 1) affirmative case; 2) negative case; 3) affirmative rebuttal; 4) negative rebuttal. ●

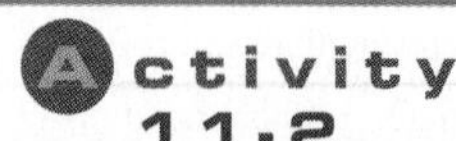

Activity 11-2 Using a Decision Support System

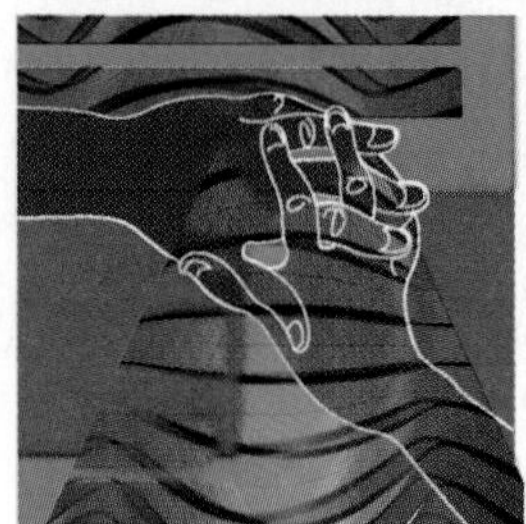

hands on

STEP 1: Read the Schips, Inc. case.

Schips, Inc. is a large department store chain that has six branch stores located throughout the city. The company's Western Hills store, which was built some years ago, has recently been experiencing some problems in its receiving and shipping department because of the substantial growth in the branch's sales volume. Unfortunately, the store's truck dock was designed to handle only one truck at a time, and the branch's increased business volume has led to a bottleneck in the truck dock area. At times the branch manager has observed as many as five Schips trucks waiting to be loaded or unloaded. As a result, the manager would like to consider various alternatives to improve the operation of the truck dock and reduce the truck waiting times.

One alternative the manager is considering is to speed up the loading/unloading operation by installing a conveyor system at the dock. As a second alternative, the manager is considering adding a second dock area and dock crew so that two trucks could be loaded and/or unloaded simultaneously.

What should the manager do in order to improve the operation of the truck dock? Obviously more information is needed before a course of action can be taken. While the alternatives being considered should reduce the truck waiting times, they will also increase the cost of operating the dock. Thus the manager will want to know how each alternative will affect the waiting times before making a final decision.

STEP 2: As directed by your instructor, start up the MINI-DSS software provided on the disk accompanying this text. Because this software was developed expressly for this case, it does

SOURCE: Adapted from D. R. Anderson, D. J. Sweeney, and T. A. Williams, *Quantitative Methods for Business,* 3rd ed. (St. Paul, MN: West Publishing Co., 1986).

not have the features of a full DSS system; however, the two classes of models it has in its model base will allow you to analyze the Schips, Inc. dock problem in several ways, just as you might with a full-featured DSS.

STEP 3: Using MINI-DSS, explore alternative solutions to the Schips, Inc. dock problem. Historical data show that typically 24 trucks arrive per eight-hour day and that their arrival times appear to be "random." Furthermore, assume that with the current dock setup, Schips can unload about four trucks per hour under normal conditions, but that the unloading speed depends somewhat upon the truck contents.

STEP 4: In small groups, as directed by your instructor, answer the following questions.

1. What did you learn by using the simulation model?
2. What did you learn by using the queueing model?
3. Explain why a DSS should have several models that can be used for addressing the same problem.
4. What additional models and data might you need to make a logical decision about how to solve the dock problem? ●

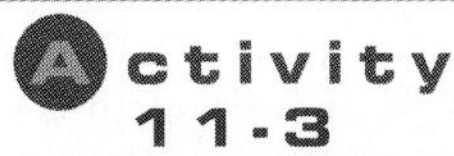

Decision Making Using Groupware

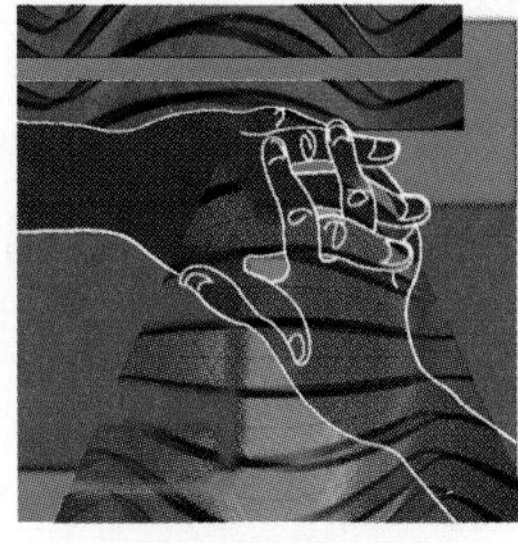

hands on

STEP 1: Your instructor will organize you into small groups and provide you with a decision problem to solve.

STEP 2: Now your instructor will arrange for you to use groupware to solve a similar decision problem.

STEP 3: Individually, in small groups, or with the entire class, compare and contrast your experiences. Then answer the following questions.

1. What are the advantages of using groupware for making decisions?
2. What are the drawbacks of using groupware for making decisions?
3. What types of decision making would groupware help?
4. What types of decision making would groupware hinder?
5. How does the groupware product you are using affect the ability of a group leader to emerge in the decision-making process?
6. How does the groupware product you are using affect your ability to make your views known?
7. How does the groupware product affect your opinion of the views of the other members of the group? ●

Notes

[1]O. A. El Sawy and H. El Sherif, Issue-based decision support systems for the Egyptian Cabinet, *MIS Quarterly* 12 (December 1988): 551–569; and Dov Te'eni, Support systems for high level policy making: What makes them special, *Information & Management* 19(1) (August 1990): 41–50.

[2]Mohammad Dadashzadeh, Microcomputer-based decision support for facilities planning and management, *Journal of Microcomputer Systems Management* (Fall 1991): 22–31.

[3]P. G. W. Keen, Value analysis: Justifying decision support systems, *MIS Quarterly* 5 (March 1981): 1–14.

[4]M. H. Omar, A DSS approach for implementing an online retail banking system: A case study, *Information & Management* 21(2) (September 1991): 89–98.

[5]K. S. Raman and C. K. Phoon, Decision support systems in Singapore: Issues in their management and their beneficial contributions, *Information & Management* 18(3) (April 1990): 153–165.

[6]R. Sharda, S. H. Barr, and J. C. McDonnell, Decision support systems effectiveness: A review and an empirical test, *Management Science* 34(2) (1988): 139–159.

[7]Jane Mackay, Steve Barr, and Marilyn Kletke, An empirical investigation of the effects of decision aids on problem-solving processes, *Decision Sciences* 23 (1992): 648–672.

[8]A. K. Aggarwal, Simulations as a DSS modeling technique, *Information & Management* 19(5) (December 1990): 295–305.

[9]Robert R. Trippi, A decision support system for real estate investment portfolio management, *Information & Management* 16(1) (January 1989): 47–54.

[10]Ben Schneiderman, *Designing the User Interface,* 2d ed. (Reading, MA: Addison-Wesley, 1992).

[11]Christopher K. Carlson, Information management approach and support to decision-making, *Information & Management* 15(3) (October 1988): 135–149.

[12]Lamont Wood, Paving the way for end-user SQL tools, *Datamation* (November 15, 1992): 53–55.

[13]H. Bidgoli, DSS products evaluation: An integrated framework, *Journal of Systems Management* 40(11) (1989): 27–34.

[14]Hokey Min, A model-based decision support system for locating banks, *Information & Management* 17(4) (November 1989): 207–215.

[15]David Forrest, Seeing data in new ways, *Computerworld* (June 29, 1992): 85–86.

[16]Maryfran Johnson, GIS helps clean up in Andrew's wake, *Computerworld* (September 28, 1992): 49.

[17]Michael C. Kettelhut, Using a DSS to incorporate expert opinion in strategic product development funding decisions, *Information & Management* 20(5) (May 1991): 363–371.

[18]Alfs T. Berztiss, Software methodologies for decision support, *Information & Management* 18(5) (May 1990): 221–229.

[19]C. A. Ellis, S. J. Gibbs, and G. L. Rein, Groupware: Some issues and experiences, *Communications of the ACM* 34(1) (January 1991): 38—58.

[20]Jim Nash, Lack of standards inhibits groupware, *Computerworld* (December 16, 1991): 68.

[21]W. M. Bulkeley, 'Computerizing' dull meetings is touted as an antidote to the mouth that bored, *Wall Street Journal* (January 28, 1992): B1, B2.

[22]David Kirkpatrick, Here comes the payoff from PCs, *Fortune* (March 23, 1992): 93–102; and Bulkeley, op. cit.

[23]This discussion is based on Ellis et al., op. cit.

[24]Nell Margolis, Strong medicine, *Computerworld* (March 8, 1993): 97–98.

[25]Daniel Briere, Groupware: A spectrum of productivity boosters, *Network World* (September 16, 1991): 1, 33, 34, 36, 46.

[26]Marjorie Horton, Priscilla Rogers, Laurel Austin, and Michael McCormick, Exploring the impact of face-to-face collaborative technology on group writing, *Journal of Management Information Systems* 8(3) (Winter 1991–92): 27–48.

[27]K. L. Kraemer and J. L. King, Computer-based systems for cooperative work and group decision making, *ACM Computer Surveys* 20(2) (June 1988): 115–146.

[28]Kenneth R. MacCrimmon and Christian Wagner, The architecture of an information system for the support of alternative generation, *Journal of Management Information Systems* 8(3) (Winter 1991–92): 49–67.

[29]Renee A. Beauclair and Detmar W. Straub, Utilizing GDSS technology: Final report on a recent empirical study, *Information & Management* 18(5) (June 1990): 213–220.

[30]Kirkpatrick, op. cit.

[31]Laku Chidambaram, Robert P. Bostrom, and Bayard E. Wynne, A longitudinal study of the impact of group decision support systems on group development, *Journal of Management Information Systems* 7(3) (1991): 7–25.

[32]S. J. Gibbs, LIZA: An extensible groupware toolkit, in *Proceedings of the ACM SIGCHI Conference on Human Factors in Computing Systems,* Austin, Texas, April–May, 1989.

[33]Ellis et al., op. cit.

[34]S. R. Hiltz and M. Turoff, Structuring computer-mediated communication systems to avoid information overload, *Communications of the ACM* 28(7) (July 1985): 680–689.

[35]Bruce D. Sanders of Workgroup Associates, Vacaville, CA, quoted in Alice LaPlante, Group(ware) therapy, *Computerworld* (July 27, 1992): 71–73.

[36]Michael Mandelbaum, Vice-President of Systems Development, Chase Manhattan Bank NA, quoted in LaPlante, op. cit.

[37]W. M. Bulkeley, Special systems make computing less traumatic for top executives, *Wall Street Journal* (June 20, 1988): 17.

[38]Kim S. Nash, An EIS turnaround at Met Life, *Computerworld* (September 9, 1991): 29.

[39]Hugh Watson, Candice Harp, Gigi Kelly, and Margaret O'Hara, Soften up! *Computerworld* (October 19, 1992): 103–104; and L. Z. Dix, A bunch of softies, *Computerworld* (October 19, 1992): 105.

[40]Hugh Watson, R. K. Rainer, Jr., and Chang Koh, Executive information systems: A framework for development and a survey of current practices, *MIS Quarterly* 15(1) (1991): 13–30; and C. Barrow, Implementing an executive information system: Seven steps for success, *Journal of Information Systems Management* 7(2) (1990): 41–46.

[41]Jeremy Main, At last, software CEOs can use, *Fortune* (March 13, 1989): 77–83.

Recommended Readings

Burkan, Wayne C. *Executive Information Systems: From Proposal Through Implementation.* New York: Van Nostrand Reinhold, 1991.

Greif, I., (ed.). *Computer-Supported Cooperative Work: A Book of Readings.* San Mateo, CA: Morgan Kaufmann, 1988.

Huseman, Richard C. and Miles, Edward W., "Organizational communication in the information age: Implications of computer-based systems," *Journal of Management* 14(2) (1988): 181–204.

Johansen, Robert. *Groupware: Computer Support for Business Teams.* New York: Macmillan, 1988.

Keen, Peter G. W., *Decision Support Systems: Effective Decision Making for Managers.* New York: Wiley, 1991.

Rhodes, Paul C. *Decision Support Systems: Theory and Practice.* Oxford: Blackwell Scientific, 1993.

Watson, Hugh J., Rainer, R. Kelly, and Houdeshel, George (eds.). *Executive Information Systems: Emergence, Development, Impact.* New York: Wiley, 1992.

Chapter 12

Strategic Systems

OUTLINE

LEARNING OBJECTIVES

After completing the reading and activities for Chapter 12, students will be able to

1. Describe the three levels of strategy.
2. Differentiate between strategy and tactics.
3. Identify the five strategies companies use to derive a competitive advantage and the objectives of each strategy.
4. Illustrate four major ways companies can use information systems to reduce costs.
5. Illustrate how a company can use information systems to differentiate products and services on quality and customer service.
6. Compare the use of information systems for identifying opportunities in existing market segments and in creating new market segments.
7. Discuss the use of information systems for customer, supplier, and logistical linkages.
8. Offer examples of infusing products with information and selling proprietary information.
9. Identify the best approaches for creating a sustainable competitive advantage.

Electronics Superstores is a national chain of 100 retail stores that sell a wide variety of computer hardware and software, video and audio equipment, and other electronics products. Each store resembles a large supermarket in which shelves are continuously restocked with inventory and individuals make all purchases at a check-out counter. As one of the first chains specializing in consumer electronics, Electronics Superstores had a significant competitive advantage for several years. Recently, however, numerous competitors have adopted the supermarket-like approach to consumer sales and cut into the chain's profits and market share.

The top management team at Electronics Superstores, led by Suzanne Brown, is currently reevaluating the company's strategy. Ms. Brown believes that her company has successfully integrated the use of automation, transaction processing systems, and management information systems into the company's operation. Now she is particularly interested in identifying ways her company can use information systems more strategically—in ways that will provide her company with a stronger competitive advantage.

What strategic options are available to the top management of Electronics Superstores? How does the development and use of information systems fit with each option? What types of strategic information systems should Brown institute? Brown and her executives should first diagnose the situation faced by Electronics Superstores and determine what strategic information needs exist. (See Chapter 4 for discussion of this step.) Then they should evaluate any existing strategic information systems used at Electronics Superstores. They can then design or redesign information systems to meet the strategic needs. They must also consider the issues associated with implementing the new systems.

In this chapter we answer the questions facing Suzanne Brown and her managerial colleagues by focusing on five corporate strategies—low-cost leadership, differentiation, focus, linkage, and information leadership. In particular, we discuss the role of information systems in instituting each strategy. We also consider the issues involved in implementing strategic information systems more generally in an organization.

What Is Strategy?

Strategy refers to the long-term direction or intended set of activities that an organization uses to achieve its goals (see Chapter 4). Strategies occur at three levels, as shown in Figure 12-1: corporate, business, and functional. Corporate-level strategy addresses which lines of business a company should pursue as well as which business units it should buy, sell, merge, divide, grow, or eliminate. Business-level strategy focuses on the way each business unit can earn the greatest profit or the highest return on investment to the corporation and its shareholders. Business-level strategy involves determining which products or services the business should offer, which customers it should serve, and how it will deploy resources for advertising, research and development, customer service, equipment, and staffing. Functional-level

Levels of Strategy

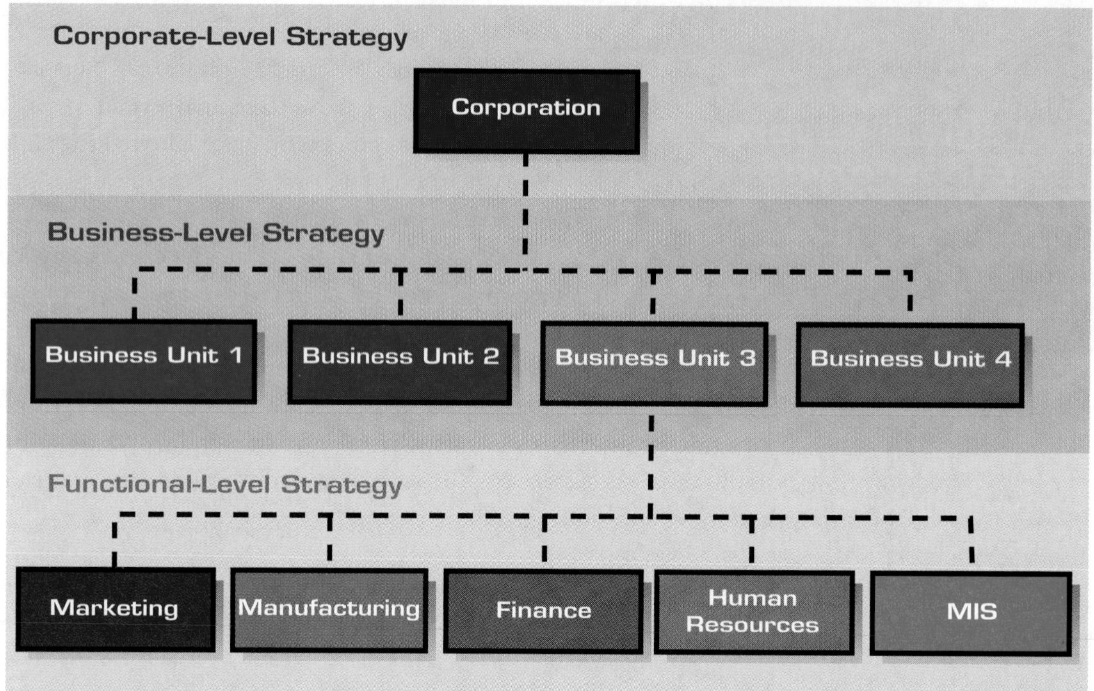

strategy concentrates on the way business functions, such as finance, marketing, operations, and human resource management, can best support business-level strategies. Information systems can support strategic objectives at all levels. In addition, they can create strategic opportunities, particularly at the business level. The executive team at Electronics Superstores must identify the company's strategic information needs and then determine the best systems to meet those needs.

Strategy versus Tactics

Organizational leaders often make decisions in response to changes in the environment, such as the introduction of a new product by a competitor, an unexpected decline in the prime rate, or the availability of new technology. **Tactical decisions,** or **tactics,** such as reducing a product's price or increasing its advertising budget for a specified amount of time, describe decisions that help organizations achieve their strategic objectives. Electronics Superstores might reduce the price on a laser printer for one week to attract new customers into the store; or the company might introduce a special sales promotion for music CDs. Assume, for a moment, that Electronics Superstores has a marketing strategy that emphasizes price over service. Tactical decisions to implement this strategy might include setting a maximum employee-to-sales ratio that no outlet may exceed, identifying products or product classes that the company guarantees to sell to the public at the lowest price, or guaranteeing customers that the company will match any competitor's lower price. Organizations increasingly use management information systems, such as those discussed in Chapter 11, to implement such tactical decisions and consequently achieve strategic goals. Organizations must evaluate how effectively their current information systems support such decision making and redesign them as necessary.

The line between tactical and strategic decisions may blur. For example, most business analysts would label a grocery or department store's decision to be a medium-cost, service-oriented provider of goods or services as a strategic decision. In contrast, they would likely label the same company's decision to offer a single new product at a low introductory price as a tactical decision. For companies that sell only a few products and introduce new ones rarely, such as automobile manufacturers, the decision to offer a low introductory price may be both strategic and tactical. Although we focus on systems designed to implement corporate and business strategy, we note that sometimes these systems also have tactical applications.

Types of Business Strategies

Companies like Electronics Superstores typically use one of five strategies to derive a competitive advantage: 1) low-cost leadership, 2) differentiation, 3) focus, 4) linkage, and 5) information leadership[1] (see Chapter 4). A **low-cost leadership** strategy attains an advantage through high profit margins and carefully controlled, typically low costs. **Differentiation** is a strategy for obtaining a competitive advantage by distinguishing a company's products and services from those of its competitors through unique design, features, quality, or other characteristics. A **focus** strategy secures an advantage by dominating a market segment. **Linkage** describes the strategy of meeting competitive threats and gaining competitive advantage by establishing special, exclusive relationships with suppliers, customers, and even competitors. The **information leadership** strategy increases the value of a product or service by infusing it with expertise and information. In contrast to low-cost leadership, which maximizes margins by minimizing cost, information leadership maximizes margins by maximizing the value of a product or service and thereby allowing a company to charge higher prices for its goods. In the remainder of this chapter we examine these strategies in turn and discuss the role information systems play in each.

Low-Cost Leadership

A company with a low-cost leadership strategy tries to achieve high profits by maintaining lower costs than its competitors. With prices set by the marketplace, the lowest-cost producer will have the highest margins and highest profits in the industry. A company can return these profits to investors to attract more capital, reinvest the profits in the company to foster growth and expansion, or sacrifice the profits to eliminate competition and increase market share. If Electronics Superstores chooses this strategy, the company will rely on achieving economies of scale in marketing and purchasing to keep cost and prices low and maximize sales volume. Such economies enhance the low-cost position of the low-cost leader and extend its competitive advantage over time. Electronics Superstores will need to determine the information it requires to support this strategy and ensure that its information systems provide it.

Using Information Systems to Reduce Costs

Early users of computer systems achieved cost reductions primarily by automating highly labor-intensive processes. Today, automation is only one of a large number of ways information systems help managers reduce costs and implement a low-cost leadership strategy. Automation can decrease costs by reducing the amount of labor, the time required for some processes, and the rework and waste. Automation's savings are partially reduced by the cost of purchasing and maintaining automation equipment and the cost of the skilled labor necessary to operate automation equipment. Chapter 9 presents a detailed discussion of automation systems. In this section we examine other ways of implementing a low-cost strategy; these include business process redesign, quality purchasing and manufacturing, employing just-in-time inventory, and flattening the organizational hierarchy.

Business Process Redesign (BPR)

Companies that blindly automate existing systems rarely eliminate their inefficiencies. Manual processes at most companies evolved to accommodate human limitations. Automated processes that accomplish the same work without such constraints may often be designed quite differently. **Business process redesign,** also known as **business process reengineering (BPR),** takes maximum advantage of information technology to break traditional notions of how an organization accomplishes its work. As Michael Hammer, one of the early proponents of redesign, urges managers, "Don't automate, obliterate."[2]

FORD

Ford Motor Company's redesign of its accounts payable processes offers a vivid example of the difference between automation and reengineering.[3] Before reengineering, Ford relied on a detailed paper audit trail to ensure that it paid only for supplies it had ordered and received. Its accounts payable staff of more than 500 people had to reconcile purchase orders cut by the purchasing department, receiving documents that arrived with the supplies, and invoices sent by suppliers before it could issue a check. When discrepancies arose, the accounts payable department would hold the check until staff members could resolve the discrepancies. Resolution of differences among these source documents was a tedious task, accounting for most of the time spent by the accounts payable staff. Automating this process would save only a small amount of time and money because very few changes in the discrepancy resolution process would occur. Ford decided instead to eliminate the discrepancy checking by disregarding invoices and rejecting shipments that did not match purchase orders. An electronic purchase order entered by a purchasing clerk into the purchasing database now acts as the controlling document. When Ford receives a shipment, the recipient enters it into the database, where the computer automatically matches it against open purchase orders. If the computer fails to make a match, Ford rejects the shipment. Otherwise, the computer automatically creates a check, which the accounts payable department prints and sends to the supplier. Ford has reduced its accounts payable staff by 75 percent as a result of this reengineering. In addition, Ford's elimination of discrepancies between its financial and physical records has made both financial accounting and material control simpler and more accurate.

TIMBERLAND

Timberland Company, a New Hampshire shoemaker, reengineered order delivery by introducing scanners that track inventory and create bills. Before reengineering, Timberland had measured productivity by the size of its deliveries. This bias had forced it to focus on department store orders despite its knowledge that the boutique market was expanding rapidly. The new system allows the company to serve the boutique market as it can now handle both small and large orders with equal ease. The reengineered order-entry process also saves costs, as stores can now send orders directly to the company's computers, decreasing the number of employees required to increase sales.[4] Wishard Memorial Hospital in Indianapolis has introduced information technology that has reduced costs by $900 per patient.[5] The hospital requires doctors to order all treatments and drugs by computer; the system then indicates any potential problems, including duplicated tests. Electronics Superstores could potentially reengineer processes in its accounting, customer service, manufacturing, and human resource departments if it chooses a low-cost leadership strategy. Evaluating the ability of existing information systems to support business process redesign would follow the diagnosis of information needs associated with such a reengineering. Design of information systems plays a key role in this process.

WISHARD MEMORIAL HOSPITAL

Because BPR implies discontinuous rather than incremental change, a successful BPR can instantly propel a company into a position of cost leadership. But companies can also apply

Timberland Company, the Hampton, New Hampshire, manufacturer of shoes and boots, reengineered its inventory management and order processing so that it could better compete in new markets.

Courtesy of Timberland.

BPR to implement strategies other than low-cost leadership. Later in this chapter we examine how organizations can use information technology to support the redesign of processes for other strategic objectives.

Quality Purchasing and Manufacturing

Poor quality not only affects customers' perceptions of a company's products and services, but it also increases a company's costs. For example, a company incurs unnecessary costs when it manufactures a defective unit that it cannot sell. A failure to identify defective products before shipping may cause customers to refuse delivery or return products after quality inspections or when the product malfunctions. Such returns not only reduce revenues but also affect the reputation of the firm, which in turn influences future sales. Even unreturned defective products can significantly affect a firm's reputation and subsequent sales. Quality-oriented organizations first diagnose their information needs and then design the strategic information systems to meet these needs.

GENERAL TIRE & RUBBER

General Tire & Rubber Company reduces costs by using computers and information systems to monitor the quality of its raw materials.[6] Employees on the floor of a tire production plant provide data about the quality of raw materials as they enter the factory and the quality of produced tires as they leave the production line. The plant operators use this information to shut down production before they manufacture too many bad tires. Prior to the introduction of this system, plant operators sampled quality information periodically, producing graphs and charts that lagged production and resulted in costly defective products.

CARRIER

Carrier Corporation, a manufacturer of air-conditioning equipment, reduced costs by installing an expert system (see Chapter 9) to improve the quality of its order entry and manufacturing.[7] Carrier had found that the complexity of matching its products to its commercial customers' orders had resulted in error rates as high as 70 percent. The expert system coordinates the flow of information from the customer, to the sales agent, to the factory floor; it ensures that the products and manufacturing steps meet the customer's specifications.

Just-in-Time Inventory

Excess inventory increases costs by tying up capital, increasing requirements for warehouse space, increasing the costs of maintaining, insuring, and servicing inventory, and increasing the costs of searching for and retrieving inventory. Insufficient inventory may also increase costs by forcing a company to shut down, reschedule production, or generate costly rush orders and back orders. **Just-in-time inventory (JIT)** reduces costs by obtaining inventory precisely as needed—neither too early nor too late. JIT requires computers and information systems to monitor complex and interrelated inventory and to plan and monitor the logistics required to replenish inventory.

CATERPILLAR

Caterpillar's factory in Aurora, Illinois provides an example of the strategic use of information systems to reduce inventory costs.[8] Caterpillar manufactures large earth-moving and construction vehicles. Employees use single-keystroke codes at terminals on the factory floor to keep Caterpillar's information systems informed about the vehicles' progress through the assembly stages. The computer terminals monitor the use of parts and automatically transmit orders to suppliers when inventory drops below a level required for the planned production; reordering considers the history of delivery times for the specific parts. The system uses automated guided vehicles (see Chapter 9) to deliver parts directly to locations where they are needed on the factory floor. The system has cut inventory at the plant by nearly 40 percent. Production time for a wheel-loader, one of the plant's products, has been cut to five days from 16.

Flattening Organizational Structures

Advances in telecommunications and improvements in networking hardware and software in the early 1990s spurred companies to use information technology to reorganize. Technology allowed the flattening of organizational hierarchies and a reduction in the number of managers motivated by the movement to team-based management.[9] Electronics Superstores, for example, could follow this trend of instituting team-based management and use information systems to distribute its management functions, ultimately flattening the organizational structure.

Improvements in communication technology have also supported the management of geographically separate business units from a central corporate headquarters. For example, in 1994 the management of New England Telephone and New York Telephone, two independent subsidiaries, was consolidated in NYNEX's corporate headquarters in New York. As a result, companies such as NYNEX could lower their costs by achieving economies of scale in labor.

NYNEX

Differentiation

The differentiation strategy seeks a competitive advantage by distinguishing a company's products and services from those of its competitors. When a company and its competitors produce a product or provide a service that the market perceives as indistinguishable, such as toothpaste, shampoo, blank video tapes, or blank audio cassettes, that product or service becomes a commodity whose price is determined by its marginal cost. A company must differentiate its products from those of its competitors to increase profits or market share. The degree of differentiation determines whether or not the market will perceive a competitor's products to be substitutes for the company's products: Can Crest toothpaste substitute for Colgate toothpaste, for example. The availability of bonafide substitutes diminishes a company's latitude in setting prices and makes market share hard to retain.

Companies can differentiate on both a product's physical characteristics, such as size, shape, style, and packaging, and its nonphysical characteristics, such as quality, features, options, and embedded services. A company can also apply differentiation strategies to the way it distributes and promotes its products or services. The Fuller Brush Company, for example, sells cleaning products "door to door" rather than through more traditional retail outlets. Electronics Superstores might decide to offer extensive, high-quality customer service to distinguish itself from its competitors. The company must diagnose the information it requires to provide such service and then ensure that its information systems satisfy the information needs.

FULLER BRUSH

Using Information Systems to Differentiate Products and Services

Information systems have only a limited ability to differentiate the physical characteristics of a product (except as affected by computer-aided design). They can, however, achieve a strategic advantage in addressing nonphysical attributes such as product distribution and logistics, quality, and pre- and post-sale customer service. In this section we focus specifically on quality and customer service.

Using Information Systems to Differentiate on Quality

If two competitors sell similar products with the same features at the same price, customers typically will choose the product that they judge to be most reliable, least likely to have defects, and most likely to perform as advertised. If two companies offer similar services of equal value at the same price, customers will typically select the one that delivers the most accurate and timely information about the services being provided. A company can differentiate between its own and its competitors' offerings by establishing a reputation for quality. Information systems can help assure quality by monitoring the raw materials used in production, the manufacturing process, and service both before and after the sale. Information systems also help identify and correct quality defects at the earliest possible stage.

THE STANLEY WORKS

The Stanley Works, a $2 billion manufacturer of tools and hardware, uses information systems to differentiate itself on quality.[10] Stanley's sales force uses hand-held terminals tied into a sales automation system to improve the speed and accuracy of answers to customers' questions about their orders. It uses an integrated manufacturing planning system to match its production capacity to customer's needs. It also uses a warehouse management system with bar code readers, weight-verification equipment, and other information technology to assure that products are shipped to customers exactly as ordered. The information systems reduce errors from order taking through manufacturing and order fulfillment.

Using Information Systems to Differentiate on Customer Service

UNITED SERVICES AUTOMOBILE ASSOCIATION

Information systems can help companies differentiate on customer service by improving ease of ordering, reliability of delivery, accuracy and timeliness of product support and servicing, and flexibility in response to changing customer needs. United Services Automobile Association (USAA) uses document imaging to improve the service it provides to customers making claims.[11] All USAA's customer service representatives have electronic access to images of claim forms, related documents such as damage photographs, and claim status information for each of USAA's 2.2 million customers. If it used paper-based systems, the company would be unable to process customer information requests in a timely fashion.

NORFOLK SOUTHERN

Norfolk Southern Corporation (NSC) is a transportation holding company that runs a railroad with more than 100,000 cars and the North American Van Lines trucking firm. NSC wanted to differentiate itself on customer service by providing one "800" phone number operating 24 hours a day, 7 days a week, providing customers with information about shipping, billing, tracking, and schedules. In 1993, it implemented a system that in most cases identifies the callers' phone number (using the Automatic Number Identification features provided by AT&T's ISDN service) and matches it with the caller's file within two phone rings. The file and call are automatically routed to an agent who specializes in the commodity being shipped. This system allows NSC's agents to answer more than 80 percent of inquiries on the first call and to make a commitment for a call-back time when they cannot answer questions immediately.[12]

Information systems can speed a company's response to a customer's request for product maintenance through the use of product monitoring systems and computerized dispatch systems. An oil company can use its IS to identify when the home heating oil reserves in an individual household drop too low—considering weather and other usage factors—and automatically send an oil truck to fill the tank. Otis Elevator Company builds its elevators with digital equipment that can be queried over phone lines. This feature allows its repair technicians to arrive at the scene of a malfunction promptly with the right replacement parts and the right repair equipment so that customers do not have to be bothered to diagnose the malfunction. ISs can offer high-quality technical advice through the use of expert systems. An automobile repair center, for example, can use information systems to facilitate troubleshooting and support its claim as an excellent diagnostic center. Electronics Superstores might use in-store expert systems to help customers identify computers that best meet their needs.

OTIS ELEVATOR

Focus

Focus, the third competitive strategy, seeks an advantage through attaining dominance in a focused market segment. A company may segment a market on the basis of geography, customer demographics, distribution channels, price, product characteristics, and other attributes of the customer, the product, or the product's distribution. A company can use combinations of these characteristics to further segment a market: For example, a company may choose to focus on the West Coast luxury market for a particular product. A company choosing a focus strategy believes that it can attain a high market share more easily in a focused market than in a broad market, and that this high market share provides an effective barrier to competitors.

Companies often use a focus strategy in concert with a low-cost or differentiation strategy to further cement their competitive advantage.[13] For example, a regional company might not be secure against market penetration by a low-cost national chain unless it can profitably offer competitive pricing. Frito Lay, a division of PepsiCo, used a strategic marketing information system to ward off competition from regional snack brands. It equipped its 10,000 field salespeople with hand-held computers that they used to update inventory, place orders, and even change prices as they examined market conditions at the local stores. The hand-held computers transmitted their data instantly to headquarters via satellite, where they were added to the corporate database. The ability to react so quickly and track sales at such a detailed level has allowed Frito Lay to increase its market share by about 1 percent per year since the system's adoption.[14]

FRITO LAY/PEPSICO

Companies pursuing a focus strategy can use information systems effectively to identify promising market segments and create new markets. Such companies must evaluate how well their existing systems meet these strategic needs and then redesign them accordingly.

Identifying Opportunities in Existing Market Segments

The on-line availability of demographic information from the U.S. Census Bureau and private sources has made electronic searching one avenue for identifying market opportunities. Market research companies, coupon-processing companies, and mailing-list purveyors also offer sales data electronically by region, product, and buyer demographic characteristics. Geographic information systems can display such data as density of disposable income, the location of pizza parlors, and the average rental price of commercial real estate. Such indicators can help companies implement a geographically based focus strategy by identifying underserved markets.

Creating New Market Segments

Businesses can use information systems to create market segments by customizing or personalizing products and delivering products or services electronically. Electronics Superstores might create a new market by selling its products through an electronic catalog in Prodigy, America Online, or some other network service. Companies can also create market segments by altering their existing products to increase the amount of information that they contain; the information leadership strategy discussed later in this chapter includes this aspect of a focus strategy.

CHRIS-CRAFT

Chris-Craft sells pleasure boats in an essentially flat market. It tries to gain market share by creating new products that will address unfilled market niches. The use of sophisticated computer-aided design systems allows Chris-Craft to design new products quickly and cheaply enough to fill these niches. After installing its CAD systems, Chris-Craft tripled the number of new designs it could produce in a year and halved the cost of developing those designs.[15]

Some real-estate companies have used information technology to offer videos of homes for sale to prospective buyers. These companies store their videos on CD-ROM disks accessed through a friendly user interface. Buyers select a geographical region and price range and specify any other requirements. Software identifies homes on the CD-ROM disks that meet these criteria and displays outdoor pictures of those selected. Buyers can then decide which houses they want to inspect in more detail. The software allows the user to see rooms, views through windows, outdoor views from other angles, and other scenes from the selected homes. This product focuses on a segment of buyers who would rather screen houses in an office or kiosk than in person. The companies that first used these products created a new market segment. Other companies created a different new market: They sold the video display as a service (videotaping, transferring pictures to CD-ROM, and providing hardware and software) to interested real-estate agents.

Linkage

Linkage describes the strategy of forming interorganizational alliances. Although always a strategic option, linkage was previously a highly risky strategy because of the ease with which alliances could shift. A competitor could woo a company's ally and achieve a competitive advantage, first by breaking the alliance, and second by stealing the knowledge and expertise the company had invested in the ally.

Advances in computer and telecommunications technology, however, have increased companies' ability to link their operations more tightly to one another. New technologies have strengthened the bond between allies, making it harder and more costly to break ties, and thereby changing a risky strategic tool into a mainstream strategic practice. Diagnosing opportunities for such linkages and the information needs associated with them has become a strategic priority in many organizations.

Two models of industry competition motivate the linkage strategy. In the first model, Michael Porter identified five forces that govern industrial competition, as shown in Figure 12-2: 1) the threat of new entrants; 2) the threat of substitute products or services; 3) the bargaining power of suppliers; 4) the bargaining power of customers; and 5) competition within an industry.[16] Consider, for example, the impact of the bargaining power of suppliers. If only a few suppliers manufacture a product needed by an industry (for example, memory chips needed by the computer industry), then these suppliers can exert their power by giving manufacturing or delivery priority to the customer who offers the best price. By forming tight alliances with suppliers and customers, and occasionally even with producers of substitute products and/or competitors, an organization hopes to lessen the impact of Porter's forces upon itself relative to other organizations in the industry. This linkage strategy controls the external industrial forces by internalizing them in a new, linkage-based organization. In extreme cases, companies can make external forces internal through mergers. In strategic mergers, the line between corporate-level strategy and business-level strategy fades,

FIGURE 12-2 Porter's Model of Forces Governing Industrial Competition

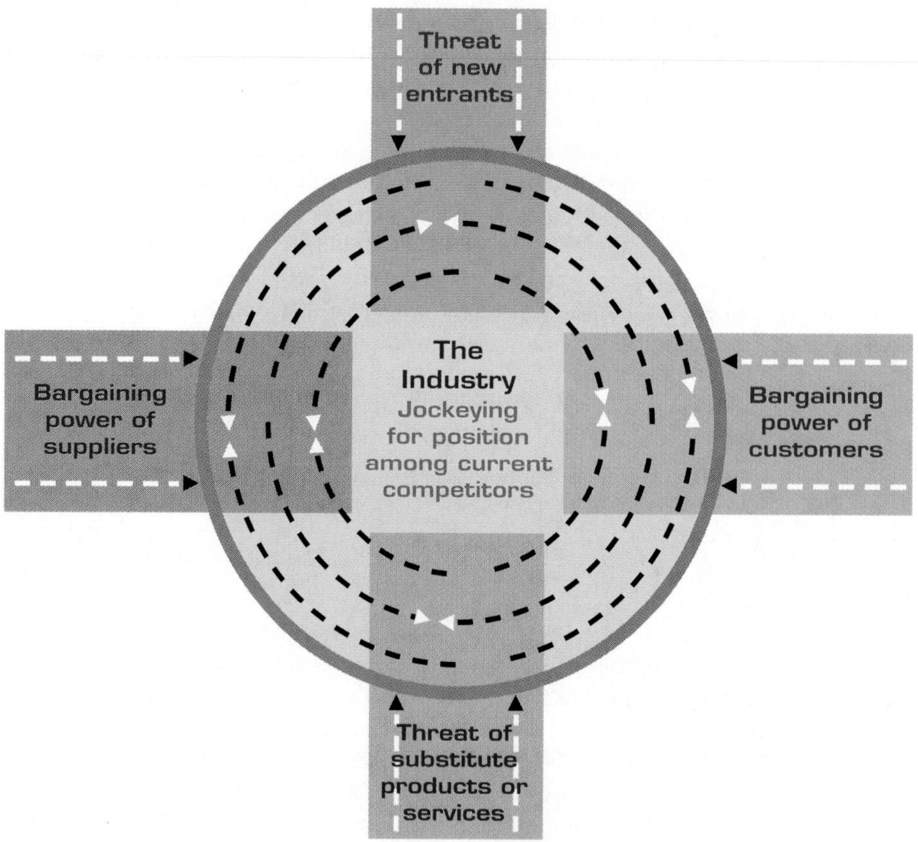

SOURCE: Michael E. Porter, How competitive forces shape strategy, *Harvard Business Review* 57(2) (March–April 1979): 141.

and the role of information systems declines. Nevertheless, some IS strategists consider mergers part of a linkage or alliance strategy.[17]

IBM

APPLE

MOTOROLA

The relationship among IBM, Apple, and Motorola to create the PowerPC chip illustrates an alliance whose formation can be explained by Porter's model. IBM likely participated to break its reliance on Intel as the sole supplier of its PC processor technology. Motorola's participation was likely due to its desire to reduce its dependence on Apple as its major customer. Apple's participation was likely forced by fear that its major competitor (IBM) would achieve the upper hand in market positioning if Apple did not have an equivalent technology.

The second model motivating the linkage strategy is the concept of a **value system,** illustrated in Figure 12-3.[18] The value system evolved from the concept of a **value chain**—a system of generic interconnected activities, such as design, engineering, manufacturing, distribution, and sales, that a company performs to add value to its products or services.[19] The value system extends the value chain beyond the firm to **upstream companies,** such as suppliers, who add value to materials and services that the firm uses, and **downstream companies,** such as customers, who add value by distributing, repackaging, and reselling the product or service or incorporating it into other products and services. The linkage strategy seeks to capture internally with alliances that part of the value added by upstream and downstream companies.

MITSUBISHI

MOBIL OIL

NATIONAL BROADCASTING

WESTINGHOUSE GROUP

Mitsubishi, for example, has a family of companies joined under various financial agreements known as **keiretsu** that includes suppliers, such as Mitsubishi Oil and Mitsubishi Plastic Industries, core companies, such as the Mitsubishi Bank and Mitsubishi Heavy Industries, and customers, such as Mitsubishi Motors.[20] In the United States, companies such as Mobil Oil maintain less-controlling relationships with service-station owners who sell their products. The value chain ties producers of television and radio programming, such as the National Broadcasting Company, to television and radio station owners, such as the Westinghouse Group.

Recent advances in information technology, particularly in communication technology and communication standards, have eased the integration of steps in the value system.[21]

FIGURE 12-3 The Value System

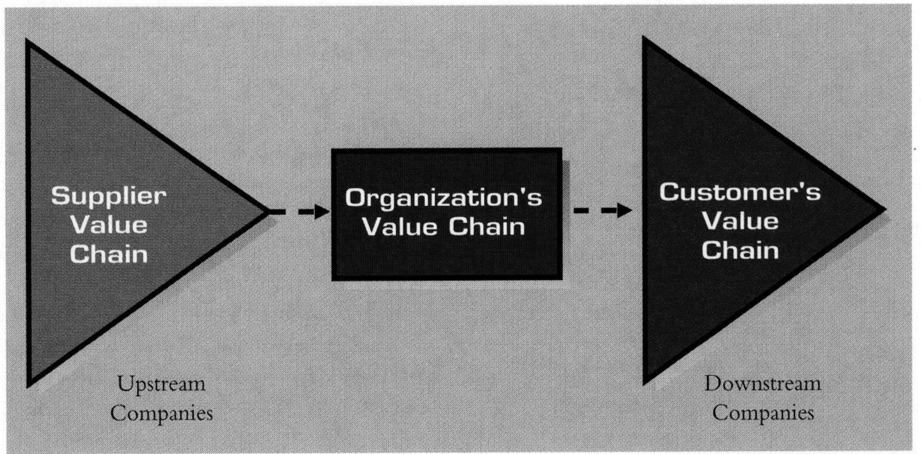

SOURCE: Based on Michael E. Porter and Victor E. Miller, How information gives you competitive advantage, *Harvard Business Review* (July–August 1985): 151.

Value-adding partnerships (VAPs) refer to the linkage of companies that view the whole value system, not just the value chain, as their competitive unit and who share information freely with others in the value system so that they can compete successfully in this environment.[22] Companies in the value system generally rely on an **interorganizational system (IOS)**—an automated information system that two or more companies share—to support their linkages.[23] In this section we explore how an IOS benefits and provides a strategic advantage for its participants.

Customer Linkage

A customer-focused IOS attempts to forge a linkage between a company and its customers by providing or hosting information services that mutually benefit the customer and the host. Electronics Superstores might decide that strengthening the linkages with its customers offers a strategic advantage. It might then identify a number of major corporate customers and use an IOS to forge a stronger linkage with them. Such an IOS might allow selected customers to order electronically, query Electronics Superstores' database on its inventory and pricing, and use Electronics Superstores' electronic mail to log complaints and suggestions, request product specifications and service information, and even simply communicate among their own employees. Figure 12-4 lists the benefits of a customer-focused IOS for both the customer and the host company.

The benefits of an IOS to the host company arise from increased sales, lower costs, better management information, and greater bargaining power. Sales generally increase because the IOS provides additional services and benefits to customers. Customers should find it easier and more efficient to order from the host company than from the company's competitors. An IOS can increase sales by displaying higher-margin products favorably on order-entry screens, cross-selling them in place of products customers may have originally intended to buy. An IOS may also increase sales by removing or reducing the role of distributors; a company that sells directly to the customer can expect to receive a higher price than if it sold the same product through a distributor, even if the customer pays a lower price in a direct sale. An IOS can extend the market to distant or small customers who a conventional field sales force cannot easily reach.

IOS customer linkages lower costs in several ways. For example, an IOS reduces the need for customer service agents because customers do their own shopping. Also, an IOS reduces the data entry and editing normally associated with order-entry processing. Instead, customers do their own order entry directly on the IOS system. Cost savings generally arise from better coordination of operations among production, distribution, and sales. For example, a customer IOS can capture precise and timely sales data, improving production scheduling and reducing required inventory.

The management information derived from a customer IOS can be used in other ways. An IOS provides data that enable management to quickly and economically evaluate the effects of advertising, rebates, and other marketing programs. This knowledge allows marketing managers to increase the efficiency and reduce the cost of promotional programs. Savvy marketing managers can also observe customers' shopping habits and tailor promotions, products, and services to these habits. They can customize sales messages, including prices and other terms, to a buyer's previous experience with a particular product.

The bargaining power of the host company over its customers increases with the use of an IOS because the IOS raises the cost to the customer of ordering from a different supplier. The importance of an IOS as a bargaining tool grows when products are extremely complicated to specify or order. The customer has little choice but to use a company's IOS, as switching to another purveyor would require the customer to retrain employees, modify operating procedures, and invest in new hardware and/or software.

FIGURE 12-4 Benefits of a Customer-Focused IOS

Benefits to the Host Company

Increases sales of products and services due to ease and efficiency of ordering and to favorable display on order-entry screens.
Reduces the need for customer service agents, as customers do their own shopping.
May increase profits by removing or reducing the role of distributors.
Captures more precise and timely sales data, improving production scheduling and reducing required inventory.
Facilitates cross-selling of additional or higher-margin products.
Raises the cost to the customer of ordering from a different supplier due to the need to retrain employees, modify operating procedures, and invest in new hardware and/or software.
Provides data enabling management to quickly and economically evaluate the effects of advertising, rebates, and other marketing programs.
Extends the market to reach customers who could not be economically served by conventional field sales calls.
Makes it possible to observe customers' shopping habits and to tailor promotions, products, and services to these habits.
Can customize sales message, including prices and other terms, to previous experience with buyer by product.
Reduces data entry and editing work by placing it in hands of customers.

Benefits to the Customer

Improves service; response is immediate and customized to company's needs.
Provides immediate feedback on product availability and price.
Reduces cost and paperwork involved in placing an order.
May improve price by eliminating distributor.
Improves communication for problem resolution.
May identify opportunities to obtain volume discounts by altering order patterns slightly.
For companies in out-of-the-way locations, provides information about products and services that is otherwise distributed by travelling sales agents.
Makes the product or service purchased easier or less expensive to select, to order, and to account for.
Improves access to information about product shipment.

A company's customers would not use its IOS unless they received benefit from its use. Generally, an IOS makes it easier and less expensive for the customer to select, order, and account for the products and services it buys. In particular, the IOS provides immediate feedback on product availability and price. It also reduces the cost and paperwork involved in placing an order. If orders do not arrive when expected, the customer can interrogate the IOS to determine when the product was shipped. The customer can then communicate problems with shipping, product quality, or other areas directly to the host company through the IOS.

A well-designed IOS accounts for a customer's previous orders, makes it easy for the customer to place similar orders, and allows the customer to take advantage of special offers or discounts associated with the merchandise the customer normally buys. An IOS can even ease a customer's operations, reducing its costs substantially. McKesson Drug Company, for

McKesson Drug

example, arranges the contents of the shipping cartons for its pharmacy customers in the order in which the products will appear on the customer's shelf; optionally, McKesson even includes the customer's pricing on the product.[24] This level of integration between a company and its customers may be unusual, but today's technology makes it feasible.

Supplier Linkage

A supplier-focused IOS attempts to forge a linkage between a company and its suppliers by providing information services that mutually benefit the suppliers and the host. A company that uses a supplier-focused IOS might allow selected suppliers to monitor its inventory and sales database and assume responsibility for keeping the inventory of identified products within specified bounds. Electronics Superstores could create such an IOS with vendors of various audio and video components, computer hardware or software, and other electronic products as a way of ensuring efficient delivery of supplies.

CALYX AND COROLLA

Calyx and Corolla (C&C), a mail-order flower business based in San Francisco, uses a supplier-focused IOS to support its promise to deliver fresh flowers nationwide the day after cutting. The flowers are fresher than flowers bought at the local flower shop because they are shipped directly from the grower. C&C's suppliers are 25 flower growers who are electronically tied into C&C's order and delivery system. When a customer places an order with C&C, the IOS transmits the order to a PC at one of C&C's suppliers. The PC automatically prints the order, including type, vase, card, and message, along with a C&C shipping label containing a bar coded Fed Ex airbill. Growers are attracted to C&C's system because they have no paperwork to handle. In addition, if a grower has a surplus of one type of flower, it can reduce its inventory by selling it at a lower price; the special price will be highlighted on the screens of C&C's customer service representatives.[25]

In most cases, the benefits to the host far outweigh the benefits to the suppliers, as shown in Figure 12-5. Unlike customers responding to customer-focused IOSs, suppliers have little incentive to participate in supplier-focused IOSs other than the threat of lost business. As a result, supplier-focused IOSs are most common in industries such as the automotive indus-

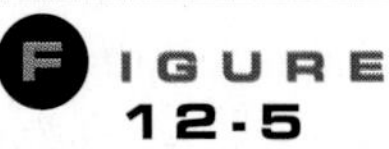
FIGURE 12-5 Benefits of a Supplier-Focused IOS

Benefits to the Host Company

Lowers inventory costs by allowing "just-in-time" delivery.

Encourages standardization of data representation, improving internal handling of data.

Improves preparation for incoming goods by communicating with transport companies.

Improves pricing and problem resolution by dealing directly with suppliers rather than through a distributor.

Lowers the costs of shopping for best price/product combination.

Reduces data entry and editing work by automating ordering and making supplier responsible.

Benefits to the Supplier

Increases likelihood of getting orders from the host company.

Improves supplier's ability to schedule production and inventory most efficiently by improving knowledge of demand.

try, where many suppliers vie for the attention of a few major purchasers. Here, the purchasers can force acceptance of their IOS by virtue of their superior market power.

While supplier-focused IOSs improve a company's ability to shop well for the products and services it buys, the greatest benefit of such an IOS is its ability to increase the efficiency of the company's operations. For example, an IOS might lower inventory costs by allowing just-in-time delivery. It might also improve the shipment receiving process by allowing a company to anticipate receipts and schedule its operations accordingly.

Logistics Linkage

Logistics refers to the transport of goods and its associated activities, such as warehousing. **Inbound logistics** describes the transport of raw goods to a company from its suppliers. **Outbound logistics** refers to the transport of finished products from a company to its customers. Both inbound and outbound logistics are critical components of the value chain; they add value by moving product from where it is created to where it is needed. Poor logistics results in damage or lateness of the product. Superior logistics can give a company a reputation for excellent service and reduce its inventory requirements and those of its suppliers and customers.

Most companies do not provide their own logistics services, relying instead on outside contractors or public carriers. Nevertheless, the importance of logistics to the relationship between supplier and customer and to the quality of product and service demands that companies pay close attention to logistics. In many cases, companies forge alliances with logistics providers to improve control over service.

FORD

AMERICAN PRESIDENT COMPANIES

Ford Motor Company (FMC) and American President Companies (APC), for example, have forged an alliance to transport automobile parts to FMC's assembly plant in Hermosillo, Mexico. APC bears the responsibility for coordinating all the information and activities associated with picking up the components from the auto-parts vendors, delivering them just in time to the Hermosillo plant, unloading them at the plant, and returning the containers to the United States carrying the specialized racks for specific parts and products from the Hermosillo region for sale in the United States. APC deals with FMC, four different railroad

Ford Motor Company's assembly plant in Hermosillo, Mexico, participates in the company's logistics alliance with American President Companies. Interrorganizational information systems support this relationship.
Courtesy of Ford Motor Company.

companies, and Mexican customs officials in performing this service.[26] APC's information needs include access to FMC's internal production schedules to perform just-in-time delivery; APC also needs to influence the production schedules of the parts suppliers. APC does not drive the railroad's scheduling but must rely on the information systems of its railroad partners to monitor service, make adjustments when necessary, and prompt changes to FMC's production schedule dictated by logistics requirements. Information integration plays a critical role in this logistics alliance. Alliance members must share production information and request information to make the alliance work. IOSs help make this sharing smoother and more efficient.

Information Leadership

Information leadership is the strategy of increasing the value of a product or service by infusing it with expertise and information. Most products and services incorporate some degree of information in their design and sales. A refrigerator might come with a user's manual that explains how to set the temperature, operate the appliance safely and efficiently, and obtain parts and service. The refrigerator may also process information; for example, its control systems read the temperature and humidity to decide when to turn on and off its cooling systems, operate its fans, and put the freezer through its defrost cycle. Some furniture stores include detailed information about the care of each product on special labels. Electronics Superstores could create a competitive advantage by offering more detailed and accurate information than its competitors do about the specifications of its products, their performance compared to comparable products, and their servicing requirements.

Advances in technology have made it possible to improve products by increasing a product's ability to collect and process information and use it to improve the product's functioning. Specialized computers in automobiles can sense a tire beginning to slip and adjust the thrust or braking applied to the tire to keep the car from skidding. They can sense engine performance and adjust the flow of gas and air so as to most efficiently react to the operator's demands or to environmental conditions. They can measure gas usage and storage to predict and advise the driver when to refuel. They can even sense bumps in a road and adjust the ride so quickly that the passenger does not notice them.

Information leadership creates additional value in one of two ways: 1) infusing an existing product with information and 2) selling information as a product in its own right. These two information strategies either use proprietary information or techniques to incorporate copyrighted or patented information in the product.

Infusing Products with Information

AMERICAN EXPRESS

Appropriate information adds value to almost any product or service. Information systems supporting or embedded in a product can provide features that customers want, differentiate the product or service, and provide competitive advantage. American Express, for example, recognized that corporate credit-card customers had to organize their expenses into categories for accounting purposes. American Express introduced a categorized breakdown of each customer's expenses with the monthly bill to help customers do this accounting. Diagnosing the need to provide this information to customers, which American Express could do at relatively little marginal cost, differentiated American Express's service from that of its competitors and added value that drew customers to use its card rather than others. American Express then needed to ensure that its information systems supported the provision of this information. As additional companies adopted this practice, however, American Express's competitive advantage decreased.

FEDERAL EXPRESS

UNITED PARCEL SERVICE

Shipping companies can provide information about the status of shipments to give themselves a competitive advantage. Federal Express was one of the first companies to recognize the value of shipping status information to customers and one of the first to use it as a competitive weapon.[27] United Parcel Service of America, which offered a competing delivery system, found in 1986 that it earned approximately 25 percent of what Federal Express earned on approximately eight times the volume; UPS attributed its inferior position to its inability to provide the same information services.[28] Although UPS invested billions of dollars to offer such services, Federal Express took the lead again in 1992 when it launched its Powership program, giving qualified customers the means to directly access the Federal Express internal computers to obtain package-tracking information.[29]

Selling Proprietary Information

Some businesses own proprietary information as a by-product of their normal business activities. Grocers that use bar code scanners have information about the products consumers buy. A grocer can create a new business or earn additional profits from its existing business by selling information about consumers' purchases and preferences to market research firms or food processing companies. Vendors of durable goods such as automobiles, televisions, and audio equipment can sell the customer names to companies that provide third-party service contracts or extended warranties.

SEARS

AMERICAN AIRLINES

In many cases, a company can build on its experience with processing a certain type of information to form a new business providing similar processing for others. For example, Sears's experience with processing credit-card transactions on a large scale enabled it to sell credit-card transaction processing to other companies.[30] Small banks frequently subcontract their back-room check-processing operations to a larger financial institution, creating a subsidiary business for the larger banks. American Airlines' SABRE reservations system illustrates the formation of a new business around a specialized information system.

Issues in Strategic Information Systems Implementation

Implementation of information systems for strategic purposes, which follows the diagnosis, evaluation, and redesign of systems, poses three main issues for top-level managers and information systems executives. First, they must ensure that strategic information systems create a sustainable competitive advantage for the organization. Second, they must recognize the key role of IS in business process redesign. Finally, they must ensure a fit between the organization's strategic goals and its information systems.

Creating a Sustainable Advantage

The design and introduction of strategic information systems create a sustainable competitive advantage when barriers to duplicating the technology exist, when the original systems innovator can almost totally control the market, and when the innovation alters key industry characteristics, such as standard business activities, among other factors.[31] Generally, externally focused strategic initiatives—those that customers, clients, or suppliers use—offer a more sustainable advantage than internally focused initiatives—those used within the firm to reduce costs, increase profits, or improve quality.[32] Customer linkage IOSs, for example, an externally focused initiative, provide a sustainable advantage because they create barriers to a customer's switching suppliers. Any customer who switches to a new supplier must spend time and money to investigate the price, quality, reliability, and economic stability of the alternative supplier. After selecting a new vendor, the company must spend more time retraining people to follow the ordering procedures required by the new supplier and must adjust to its shipping, delivery, and invoicing practices. A customer-focused IOS increases the costs of switching. The customer may lose investments in computer terminals that interfaced with the IOS. The customer will also need to transfer historical information to systems provided by the new supplier. The more rapidly a customer-focused IOS enables a company to capture market share in its initial years, the more sustainable the advantage becomes. Early entrants in the airline reservations business, for example, established a market presence among travel agencies that competitors have not penetrated.

Strategic programs that have focus as an objective can also offer a sustainable advantage because the focus strategy defines a limited market that is typically too small to sustain competition. Companies cannot easily displace a competitor's large initial penetration in such a market. In addition to facilitating the search for niches, information systems help a company maintain and manage information about the characteristics of the niche markets in which it competes. Customers who feel that the company from which they buy understands their needs are likely to be loyal and difficult for competitors to attract.

Although internal strategic systems are less sustainable, they may confer some advantages on the initiator. For example, companies that implement a low-cost strategy often rely on economies of scale. Systems that cost a lot to develop can earn a return for a company supporting a large sales volume, while smaller companies simply cannot afford the investment to copy the initiator. Factory automation systems illustrate this situation. Large companies can reduce their costs by implementing such systems, while smaller competitors, spreading the cost over a smaller volume, will increase their unit costs by adopting factory automation. As a result, the low-cost strategy becomes even more effective for the low-cost leader, and the strategic advantage endures.

Patents may also sustain the advantages achieved by the initiator of internal strategic systems. However, the initiator must design a system that somehow depends on or augments the advantages gained by the patent to retain this advantage. Although automated teller machines (ATMs) and the banking systems built around them are often cited as examples of nonsustainable strategic systems, their competitive benefits might have endured had one bank held the patents for the hardware.

An internal (or external) strategic system that uniquely reflects the culture of the organization that developed it may also be sustainable.[33] Other organizations will not be able to imitate such systems without modifying their own cultures. Organizations that developed information systems to support a total quality management effort may sustain the benefits until their competitors also adopt a culture that supports total quality. Organizations resist changing their cultures, and even if they succeed in changing in response to a need, such a culture shift takes time.

Strategic thrusts that do not raise barriers to competitive entry and do not provide the initiator with other long-lasting advantages may not be worth implementing immediately. Implementation of an unprotectable strategic initiative changes the basis of competition, forcing competitors to imitate the initiative and perhaps raising the costs for all parties.[34] The initiative then becomes a **competitive necessity** rather than a competitive advantage. In such cases, the follower, or **second-mover,** may benefit more than the initiator.[35] For example, the second-mover can examine the technology and improve it, forcing the initiator to upgrade its systems. The second-mover may also benefit by the groundwork the initiator laid (and paid for) in educating the market to accept the new systems.

GIRARD BANK

Even where a sustainable advantage appears certain, achieving it may be difficult. When the Girard Bank, the largest bank in Philadelphia, introduced George, its proprietary ATM network, it recognized that other banks might follow with their own ATMs. The fixed overhead of the ATM networks of these smaller banks likely would result in higher transaction

PHILADELPHIA NATIONAL BANK

costs. Philadelphia National Bank, however, recognized that it could not compete in this environment and instead created an ATM network called MAC that all banks could access. Other banks, realizing that they could not compete alone against George, installed MAC terminals in their banks. After a series of mergers that included the successor to George, MAC became the only ATM network in Philadelphia.[36]

Companies that are contemplating the development of strategic information systems must consider the nature of the likely competitive response and the risk associated with failure to sustain a competitive advantage. Sustainable strategic systems can catapult a company into a position of leadership for many years. Nonsustainable systems, in contrast, may evoke competitive responses that raise the costs to all competitors and compromise the position of the initiator.

Information Technology and Business Process Redesign

Information technology plays an important role in the redesign of business processes critical to successful strategic change and focus. Nevertheless, managers of change often fail to involve information technology experts early enough in their redesign effort. The conventional wisdom that information systems should respond to the business requirements of a function or an organization, rather than be a partner or leader, helps foster this mode of operation. Because the individuals who set the business requirements generally have neither the time nor the expertise to keep informed about the state of the art in information technology, they miss strategic opportunities for redesign. Information technology specialists also miss opportunities for redesign because they have insufficient knowledge of the business processes. A solution that can pay great dividends is for business leaders in partnership with IS specialists to make identifying potential organizational impacts of information technology one of the early steps in any BPR effort.[37] Figure 12-6 illustrates how business managers can scan their companies' IT capabilities to identify potential strategic impacts in the early stages of a reengineering project. IT can transform unstructured processes into routine transactions; for example, the Massachusetts Registry of Motor Vehicles plans to introduce kiosks in shopping malls, where individuals can renew a driver's license without interacting with a service representative. This use of IT allows the Registry to change job descriptions of its employees and thereby allocate its personnel resources more effectively to tasks that better accomplish organizational goals.

MASSACHUSETTS REGISTRY OF MOTOR VEHICLES

Information technology tools, particularly those used for computer-aided software engineering (see Chapter 5), can assist a BPR effort because they can help automate the redesign process. Although CASE tools were originally designed to help automate the development of application software, they have evolved to support generic process redesign. In particular, they provide tools to draw and analyze process models. Simulation tools can analyze the impact of process changes, identify bottlenecks in work flow, and estimate the cost implications of alternative designs.

Strategic Alignment

Strategic alignment refers to a congruence and synergy between an organization's strategic goals and objectives and its information systems. Traditionally, organizations developed information systems to automate manual processes and back-office functions. Information systems departments operated in a reactive mode, developing software and procuring hardware to meet the operational needs of functional departments. Rarely did companies use information systems to lead the strategic initiatives of the organization. Recently, however, organizations have begun to view information technology as a potential strategic weapon.

IT Capabilities for Strategic BPR

Capability	Organizational Impact/Benefit	Strategic Direction
Transactional	IT can transform unstructured processes into routinized transactions	Low-cost
Geographical	IT can transfer information with ease and across large distances, making processes independent of geography	Linkage focus
Automational	IT can reduce human labor in a process	Low-cost
Analytical	IT can bring complex analytical methods to bear on a process	All
Informational	IT can bring vast amounts of detailed information into a process	Information Leadership Differentiation
Sequential	IT can enable changes in the sequence of tasks in a process, often allowing multiple tasks to be worked on simultaneously	Low-cost
Knowledge Management	IT allows the capture and dissemination of knowledge and expertise to improve the process	Information Leadership Low-cost
Tracking	IT allows the detailed tracking of task status, inputs, and outputs	All
Disintermediation	IT can be used to connect two parties within a process that would otherwise communicate through an intermediary (internal or external)	Low-cost Linkage

SOURCE: Adapted from Davenport and Short, The new industrial engineering: Information technology and business process redesign, *Sloan Management Review* (Summer 1990): 17.

They are now developing information systems more externally focused, with a view toward creating new market opportunities and enhancing relationships with customers and suppliers.

As information systems become more important to the strategic focus of an organization, the alignment between systems and strategy increases in importance.[38] Numerous surveys indicate that senior managers outside the IS function are most concerned about the alignment of information systems with business strategy rather than their cost or performance.[39] IS executives, too, have set the alignment of IS and corporate goals as a critical priority for the 1990s.[40] American Express, for example, lists strategic alignment as one of its criteria for evaluating proposals for transferring technology within its organization.[41] Recent research suggests that a firm's financial performance depends on the extent to which its information systems and technology align with its business strategy.[42] Securing the commitment of top management to the introduction of strategic information systems is key and may require the IS department to help top management recognize strategic information systems' potential.

AMERICAN EXPRESS

Summary

Strategy refers to the long-term direction or intended activities an organization uses to achieve its goals. Organizations can have corporate-level, business-level, or functional-level strategies. Companies might use low-cost leadership, differentiation, focus, linkage, and information leadership strategies to attain an advantage over their competitors.

Companies with a low-cost strategy attempt to attain high profits by maintaining lower costs than competitors. Information systems can help these organizations reduce costs. Information systems play a particularly important role in business process redesign, quality efforts in purchasing and manufacturing, creating a just-in-time inventory system, and flattening the organizational structure.

A differentiation strategy seeks a competitive advantage by a company's distinguishing its products and services from those of its competitors. Such companies can use information systems to help distinguish products and services on quality and customer service.

A focus strategy seeks to attain a competitive advantage through dominance in a specific market niche. Some companies use a focus strategy together with a low-cost or differentiation strategy to strengthen their competitive advantage. The role of information systems in companies that use this strategy is to monitor and analyze the marketplace, identifying new opportunities in existing markets and new market segments.

A company with a linkage strategy forms interorganizational alliances to achieve a competitive advantage. These companies may use interorganizational information systems (IOSs) to help them create customer, supplier, or logistic linkages.

Finally, organizations can use an information leadership strategy; this strategy increases the value of a product or service by infusing it with expertise and information. Information technology creates additional value either by infusing an existing product with information or by selling information as a product in its own right.

Implementation of strategic information systems focuses on creating a sustainable advantage. Externally oriented initiatives typically offer a more sustainable advantage than do internally oriented strategies. In addition, information technology accompanies business process redesign and hence is critical to successful strategic change. A strategic alignment, or congruence between the organization's strategic goals and its information systems, is critical for effective organizational performance.

Key Terms

Business process redesign (BPR)
Business process reengineering (BPR)
Competitive necessity
Differentiation
Downstream company
Focus
Inbound logistics
Information leadership
Interorganizational system (IOS)
Just-in-time inventory (JIT)
Keiretsu
Linkage
Logistics
Low-cost leadership
Outbound logistics
Second-mover
Strategic alignment
Strategy
Tactical decisions
Tactics
Upstream company
Value chain
Value system
Value-adding partnership (VAP)

Review Questions

1. Contrast the objectives of corporate-level, business-level, and functional-level strategies.
2. Contrast strategy and tactics. Give an example to illustrate how the line between tactical and strategic decisions may blur.
3. Identify the five strategies companies use to derive a competitive advantage. Identify the objectives of each strategy.
4. Identify four major ways companies can use information systems to reduce costs.
5. Describe the difference between automation and business process redesign.
6. How does JIT reduce a company's costs?
7. Identify two ways that a company can use information systems to differentiate its products and services.
8. Identify two ways that information systems can help a company pursue a focus strategy.

9. From the perspective of Porter's model of competitive forces, how does a linkage strategy help a company succeed?
10. From the perspective of Porter and Millar's value system, how does a linkage strategy help a company succeed?
11. Identify the benefits of a customer-focused IOS to the host company and to its customers.
12. Identify the benefits of a supplier-focused IOS to the host company and to its suppliers.
13. Identify two ways that companies can achieve information leadership.
14. Give an example of infusing a product with information.
15. What is the difference between a competitive advantage and a competitive necessity?
16. Identify the best approaches for creating a sustainable competitive advantage.
17. Why is it important for business managers involved in business process redesign to work with IS specialists?
18. Why is strategic alignment important, and how can it be achieved?

MINICASE

Royal Ahold Achieves Competitive Advantage through Customer Service

Reen van Marion makes it clear from the outset: The point of Royal Ahold's much-heralded self-scanning system is not to save on labor costs. The point is to provide a service to the customer that translates into a competitive advantage for the store.

Whether that kind of return-on-investment will be enough to bring the system into the mainstream in the United States, or in Europe for that matter, is far from clear.

But Van Marion, vice-president of corporate information systems and technology for Ahold, based in Zaandam, the Netherlands, believes tests to date have shown the system to be promising enough to warrant upcoming pilots in two additional Dutch stores, plus possibly one store in the United States.

Ahold's self-scanning experiment began in April 1993, in a 10,000-square-foot Albert Heijn supermarket located in Geldermalsen, the Netherlands. Albert Heijn is the flagship banner of the Dutch company, which owns five supermarket chains in the United States and recently agreed to acquire a sixth.

Upon entering the store, shoppers who have signed up to participate in the program may use their magnetic stripe identification card to unlock a handheld laser scanner from a dispensing unit, which holds a maximum of 96 scanners.

They then use their scanner to record and tabulate product purchases as they walk through the store and remove items from the shelves.

To make it seem less forbidding, the scanner is shaped more like a telephone than like the usual gun, says Van Marion. Three keys are on the scanner: a plus sign, a minus sign, and an equals sign.

A shopper scans an item by pressing the plus sign when the item is to be purchased, or with the minus sign to cancel the purchase. Pressing the equals sign displays a running total of the purchase price, plus the number of items bought.

There is no radio frequency communication involved with the scanner. Instead, the store's price-lookup file is downloaded to each scanner's internal random access memory each day through a PC wired to the dispensing unit. That PC communicates to the in-store proces-

---

SOURCE: Bruce Fox, The self-scanning Dutchmen, *Chain Store Age Executive* (May 1994): 101–102.

sor, an NCR series 3000 UNIX machine, which in turn communicates with an IBM mainframe at Albert Heijn headquarters.

At the end of the shopping trip, the scanner is returned to the dispensing unit, which prints an itemized receipt with a bar code on it. The shopper then brings that receipt to a special checkout lane, separate from the lanes used by shoppers who do not participate in the system.

If it's the first time the shopper has used the system, the cashier rescans the items and then scans the bar coded receipt to confirm that the shopper scanned the items accurately. Then payment is tendered as usual.

On subsequent trips, the shopper's accuracy will be checked depending on their past performance, about 17 percent of the time on average. The rest of the time the shopper will pay for the items with no checking of accuracy.

"Accuracy" is the operative term here. For Ahold, the shopper's "honesty" is never outwardly questioned. And indeed, Van Marion says he honestly believes that most shopper errors are unintentional.

"A dishonest customer doesn't need this system to be dishonest," he says. "In fact, we've found that mistakes balance themselves out, with the majority of them in our favor."

As further evidence, Van Marion points out that the shrink percentage within the store is no greater than when the test began. He adds that shrink in the store is average for Holland, where shrink tends to be minimal, even in communities with high unemployment.

Nor have any scanners themselves been stolen, since the identity of the shoppers who use them is tracked by the system.

Van Marion concedes, however, that a U.S. inner city would not be a "first choice" for a U.S. test of the system, although a nearby suburb would be plausible if standards for shoppers accepted as system participants were made more selective (a name, address, and phone number are about all that's asked for in Holland).

The culmination of two years of work, the self-scanning system was co-developed by Symbol Technologies, Bohemia, NY; TNO Product Centre, a leading Dutch engineering firm based in Delft, the Netherlands; and the Albert Heijn chain.

It is being marketed to other retailers by Symbol. Recently, Safeway in the United Kingdom (unrelated to Safeway in the United States) became the first non-Ahold retailer to announce a test of the system.

Faster checkout: The system is a departure, Van Marion says, from other self-scanning systems now being tested involving stationary units in separate checkout lanes, in which consumers are required to unload their carts and then scan and bag items themselves.

For all the labor they contribute to this process, Van Marion argues, customers who use such systems receive no time savings or any other measurable advantage in return.

Shoppers who use the Albert Heijn system, on the other hand, get out of the store much more quickly than shoppers who don't, especially when the store is busiest. Dutch supermarkets are required by law to close Sundays, plus by 6:30 P.M. on weekdays (except one evening a week by 9 P.M.), so Saturdays and the few evening hours tend to be extremely busy.

Case Questions

1. Using the value chain, explain how Royal Ahold hopes to achieve a competitive advantage.
2. How does information technology support Royal Ahold's attempt to achieve a competitive advantage? What other changes is Royal Ahold counting on to make its experiment a success?
3. If Royal Ahold succeeds in obtaining a competitive advantage through self-scanning, do you believe that it will be a sustainable competitive advantage? Why or why not?
4. How might information technology be used to counteract some of the problems anticipated by the critics of self-checkout?

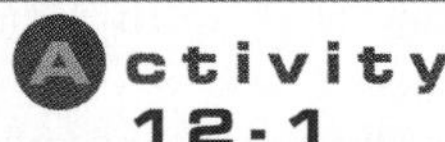

Activity 12-1 Strategic Information Systems for Fitness, Inc.

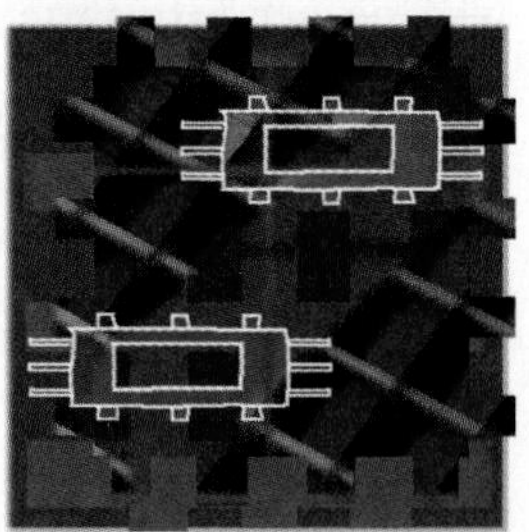
short case

STEP 1: Read the following scenario.

Fitness, Inc. was founded by Jim McCarthy in 1990 in a suburban office park as a health club for professionals who wanted high-quality, personalized service and convenience in meeting their fitness needs. The initial membership fee was quite steep, $700; monthly fees of $75 also made this club one of the more expensive to join. Jim's original strategy was to offer state-of-the-art equipment and services in a top-notch physical setting and bundle all services and fees into a single price. He believed that Fitness, Inc. could attract a sufficiently large number of members from the workers in the office park who could afford such fees and would join only a club that pampered them.

Club facilities included extensive weight equipment, 60 pieces of cardiovascular equipment, including treadmills, rowing machines, and stair climbers, and an olympic-sized swimming pool. A club cafe served meals and snacks throughout the day. The club offered an initial fitness screening and regular reevaluations at no cost to the member. Aerobics and other fitness classes occurred at intervals throughout the day for no charge. Members could secure a prespecified number of hours of personal training, nutrition counseling, and swimming instruction each month for no fee; additional services were available for a small fee.

Jim projected that a club membership of 1,500 would return a minimal profit; 2,000–2,500 members was more desirable. After the initial year, 800 members had joined the club, but most of those joined during the first six months after the club's opening, and membership had been relatively stagnant for the past six months. Jim wondered whether his initial vision for Fitness, Inc. still made sense. He considered adjusting the type of services the club provided and trying to attract a different type of member, perhaps suburban housewives or more senior citizens. Jim had installed a relatively sophisticated computer system that provided detailed purchasing, accounting, and sales data. He wanted to develop a computer system that would help him reassess his strategy and develop a new one.

Jim has asked you to help him analyze his existing strategy and determine which alternative strategies are available. He knows that he should be able to use his computer system to help in determining the most appropriate strategy.

STEP 2: In groups of two to four students, analyze Fitness, Inc.'s current strategy and identify a range of strategic alternatives Fitness, Inc. might pursue. For each alternative, sketch a general plan for using information systems to support the strategy.

STEP 3: Share your plans with the rest of the class. List the alternatives identified. Then identify the types of strategic information systems that would support each alternative. Cite the advantages and disadvantages of pursuing each strategy and developing the required strategic information systems. ●

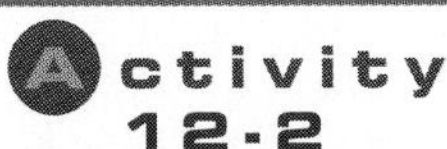

Activity 12-2 Can This Job Be Reengineered?

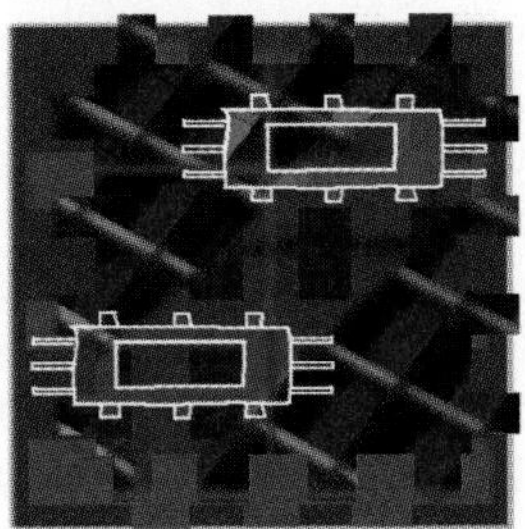

short case

STEP 1: Read each case below. Then determine for each situation whether business process reengineering could improve it.

Case 1: At Plantland, a medium-sized retail distributor of houseplants and other gardening supplies, workers spend hours each day recording the status of thousands of plants and other items. The company buys small plants from wholesalers and grows them to the requirements of their customers in on-site greenhouses. Four times a year, the company opens late to allow the managers to hire temporary employees to validate their counts of inventory. In both their daily and quarterly inventory checking, the workers record their updated information in large ledger books, indicating changes in the size, quality, and availability of certain plants. By analyzing these records, the managers can determine how they should alter their orders.

Case 2: At Builders' Supplies, Inc., contractors place orders for lumber, hardware, and other supplies at any one of 400 stores nationwide. These stores then individually submit the orders to the appropriate mill, plant, or warehouse to fill. Often the stores order from and bill one another to meet a customer's requirements. These processes result in a significant paper flow among the company's stores, warehouses, and suppliers.

Case 3: The River City Library orders approximately 2,000 new books each year. Because all orders in the city originate from the city purchasing department, a librarian sends the order to the purchasing department for authorization. When the library receives the book, the librarian sends a copy of the shipping slip and invoice to the city purchasing department for payment. After the purchasing department checks that the order received by the library matches the one ordered by the department, the clerk authorizes the library to catalog the book.

STEP 2: For those situations in which business process reengineering would help, offer a proposal for reengineering the job.

STEP 3: In small groups or with the entire class, review your answers to step 2. Then answer the following questions:

1. What elements do the cases described in step 2 have in common?
2. What factors influence whether a situation should be reengineered?
3. What options exist for reengineering a job?
4. Which options does information technology make possible, and in what ways does it allow these options? ●

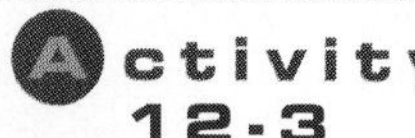

Activity 12-3 Planning a Strategic Information System for Nashville Barbecue

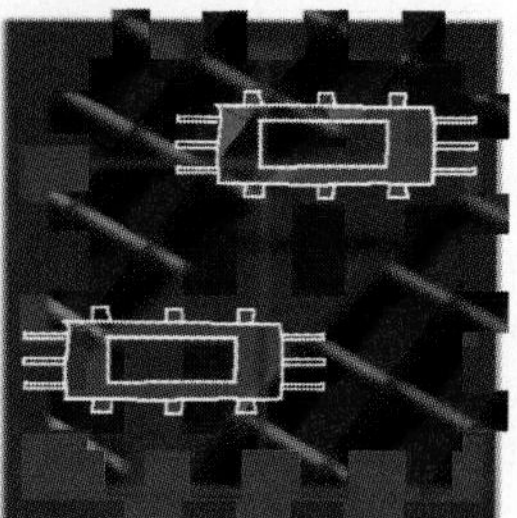

short case

STEP 1: You have just been hired as a consultant to Nashville Barbecue, a chain of 40 stores that sells barbecued ribs, brisket, and chicken nationwide. The chain began as a single store in Nashville and has grown to its current size in the past three years. Stores included in the early expansion of the chain operated somewhat autonomously; the owner could introduce some unique products and even slightly adjust the recipe for the standard products. Owners of the last 20 stores added to the chain have been required to use only chain-authorized recipes and purchase the bulk of their ingredients from a central commissary. The chain has just had a successful public offering of stock. Top management has told you that they plan to double the number of outlets each year. Your job is to design a strategic information system to support this expansion.

STEP 2: Individually or in small groups, design the specifications of such a strategic information system. Specify the information needs of top management. Then indicate the types of hardware and software necessary to provide this information.

STEP 3: In small groups or with the entire class, share your plans. Identify the common elements in each plan. Then answer the following questions:

1. What information needs does Nashville Barbecue have?
2. How can strategic information systems meet these needs?
3. What would be the specifications for such a strategic information system? ●

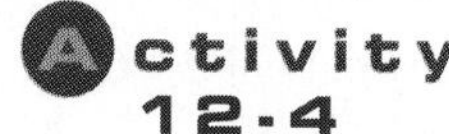

Activity 12-4 Frontier Mortgage Role Play

role play

STEP 1: Read the following scenario.

The chief executive officer of Frontier Bank believes that Frontier should implement a strategy that calls for expanding its mortgage business substantially through the use of expert systems. The CEO is proposing that the IS department develop expert computer systems that can authorize mortgages remotely by telephone or in kiosks in shopping malls. The chief information officer believes that Frontier should implement a strategy that calls for using information systems to support transaction processing. The CIO believes that the bank should continue to use mortgage officers to authorize mortgages but that the IS department can make computer systems available that ease the paperwork required in the authorization.

STEP 2: Your instructor will divide the class into pairs—one person will play the CEO, and one will play the CIO. Your instructor will then distribute more detailed information about each role to the group. After choosing one role for each group member, read the role descriptions. Then spend five minutes "getting into your role."

STEP 3: After you have read about your roles, meet with your partner and determine an appropriate strategy for Frontier Bank.

STEP 4: The instructor will ask each pair to report its agreement.

STEP 5: In small groups or with the entire class, answer the following questions:

1. What strategic options were available to Frontier?
2. How did the IS department influence the choice of strategy?
3. What type of information systems does Frontier need to support its strategy? ●

Notes

[1]Michael Porter, *Competitive Strategy* (New York: Free Press, 1980); Michael E. Porter, From competitive advantage to corporate strategy, *Harvard Business Review* (May/June 1987): 43–59 identifies and discusses low-cost leadership, differentiation, and focus. Linkage as a valid and successful corporate strategy and the role of information systems in implementing linkage are discussed in S. Barrett and B. Konsynski, Inter-organizational information sharing systems, *MIS Quarterly, Special Issue* (December 1982): 92–105; H. R. Johnston and M. E. Vitale, Creating competitive advantage with interorganizational systems, *MIS Quarterly* 12(2) (June 1988): 153–165; J. F. Rockart and J. E. Short, IT in the 1990s: Managing organizational interdependence, *Sloan Management Review* (Winter 1989); Charles Wiseman, *Strategic Information Systems* (Homewood, IL: Irwin, 1988); B. R. Konsynski and F. W. McFarlan, Information partnership: Shared data, shared scale, *Harvard Business Review* (September/October 1990): 114–120; and D. J. Bowersox, The strategic benefits of logistic alliances, *Harvard Business Review* (July/August 1990): 37–45.

[2]Michael Hammer, Reengineering work: Don't automate, obliterate, *Harvard Business Review* (July/August 1990): 104–112.

[3]Ibid.

[4]Gary McWilliams, Putting a shine on shoe operations, *Business Week* (June 14, 1993): 59.

[5]John Carey, Physician, reengineer thyself, *Business Week* (June 14, 1993): 60.

[6]Alice LaPlante, For IS, quality is "job none," *Computerworld* (January 6, 1992): 57–59.

[7]Ibid.

[8]Stratford Sherman, Information technology special report: How to bolster the bottom line, *Fortune* (Autumn 1993): 15–28.

[9]For a discussion of team-based management and its implications for organizational structure, see P. F. Drucker, The coming of the new organization, *Harvard Business Review* (January/February 1988): 45–53.

[10]Catherine Marenghi, Stanley hammers on quality, *Computerworld* (January 6, 1992): 63.

[11]Kathleen Melymuka, The CIO high performance 100: Banking on the basics, *CIO* (August 1992): 68–72.

[12]Joseph E. Maglitta, Reengineering the workplace: Customer service, *Computerworld* (May 16, 1994): 102.

[13]G. G. Dess and P. S. Davis, Porter's (1980) generic strategies as determinants of strategic group membership and organizational performance, *Academy of Management Journal* 27(3) (1984): 467–488.

[14]Ronald Fink, Data processing: PepsiCo, *Financial World* (September 29, 1992): 52.

[15]Sherman, op. cit.

[16]Michael E. Porter, How competitive forces shape strategy, *Harvard Business Review* (March/April 1979): 137–145.

[17]Wiseman, op. cit.

[18]Michael E. Porter and Victor E. Millar, How information gives you competitive advantage, *Harvard Business Review* (July/August 1985): 149–160.

[19]Michael E. Porter, *Competitive Advantage* (New York: Free Press, 1985).

[20]The mighty *keiretsu*, *Industry Week* (January 20, 1992): 52–54.

[21]T. W. Malone, J. Yates, and R. I. Benjamin, Electronic markets and electronic hierarchies, *Communications of the ACM* 30 (1987): 484–497.

[22]R. Johnston and P. R. Lawrence, Beyond vertical integration—The rise of the value-adding partnership, *Harvard Business Review* (July/August 1988): 94–104.

[23]J. I. Cash, Jr., and B. R. Konsynski, IS redraws competitive boundaries, *Harvard Business Review* (March/April 1985): 134–142.

[24]H. Russell Johnston and Michael R. Vitale, Creating competitive advantage with interorganizational information systems, *MIS Quarterly* (June 1988): 152–165.

[25]Joe Panepinto, Special delivery, *Computerworld* (March 7, 1994): 79–81.

[26]Bowersox, op. cit.

[27]Jeffrey Carr and Gene Tyndall, Planes, trains . . . And trucks, *Chief Information Officer Journal* 5(7) (September/October 1993): 58–61.

[28]Sharen Kindel, When elephants dance, *Financial World* (June 9, 1992): 76–78.

[29]Alice LaPlante, Federal Express gives clients on-line access to tracking system, *InfoWorld* 14 (November 16, 1992): 108.

[30]Porter and Millar, op. cit.

[31]Eric K. Clemons and Michael C. Row, Sustaining IT advantage: The role of structural differences, *MIS Quarterly* 15 (September 1991): 275–292.

[32]Eric K. Clemons, Information systems for sustainable competitive advantage, *Information & Management* 11 (October 1986): 131–136.

[33]Claudio Cibbora, From thinking to tinkering: The grassroots of strategic information systems, *Information Society* 8(4) (October–December 1992): 297–309.

[34]Michael R. Vitale, The growing risks of information systems success, *MIS Quarterly* 10 (December 1986): 327–334.

[35]Anitesh Barua and Charles H. Kriebel, An economic analysis of strategic information technology investments, *MIS Quarterly* 15 (September 1991): 313–327.

[36]Eric K. Clemons, Evaluation of strategic investments in information technology, *Communications of the ACM* 34 (January 1991): 22–36.

[37]Thomas H. Davenport and James E. Short, The new industrial engineering: Information technology and business process redesign, *Sloan Management Review* (Summer 1990): 11–27. The authors also cite J. C. Henderson and N. Venkatraman, Strategic alignment: A process model for integrating information technology and business strategies (Cambridge, MA: MIT Sloan School of Management, Center for Information Systems Research, Working Paper No. 196, October, 1989).

[38]Jerry N. Luftman, Paul R. Lewis, and Scott H. Oldach, Transforming the enterprise: The alignment of business and information technology strategies, *IBM Systems Journal* 32(1) (1993): 198–221; and Henry Pankratz, Strategic alignment: Managing for synergy, *Business Quarterly* 55(3) (Winter 1991): 66–71.

[39]Yolande E. Chan and Sid L. Huff, Strategic information systems alignment, *Business Quarterly* (Autumn 1993): 51–55; and Pankratz, op. cit.

[40]Roger Woolfe, The path to strategic alignment, *Information Strategy: The Executive's Journal* 9(2) (Winter 1993): 13–23.

[41]Steve Ditlea, How AMEX leverages technology assets, *Datamation* (December 1, 1992): 95–96.

[42]Chan and Huff, op. cit.

Recommended Readings

Firdman, G. R. *Strategic Information Systems: Forging the Business and Technology Alliance.* New York: McGraw-Hill, 1991.

Hammer, Michael and Champy, James. *Reengineering the Corporation: A Manifesto for Business Resolution.* New York: Harper Business, 1993.

Laudon, K. C. and Turner, J. A. (Eds.). *Information Technology and Management Strategy.* New York: Prentice-Hall, 1989.

Wiseman, Charles. *Strategic Information Systems.* Homewood, IL: Irwin, 1988.

VIDEOCASE

McKesson Corporation's ACUMAX System

McKesson Corporation is a major distributor of pharmaceutical drugs, supplies, and systems. It franchises the Valu-Rite chain of independent pharmacies and in 1994 sold its pharmacy benefit management subsidiary, PCS Health Systems, to Eli Lilly & Company for $4 billion. Earnings for 1993 exceeded $130 million.

McKesson has made customer satisfaction its number one objective. To achieve this goal, McKesson hired Electronic Data Systems (EDS) to design and develop a state-of-the-art system that would eliminate errors in order fulfillment. The system, dubbed ACUMAX, works as follows: Warehouse workers called pickers (because they pick items off the shelf to fill an order) wear portable computers strapped to their waist. Each computer includes a two-way radio that communicates with a computer at the distribution center through antennae wired into the warehouse. Each picker also wears a device on his or her hand and forearm that incorporates a laser scanner and small screen, looks like a plaster cast, and connects to the picker's portable computer. When a customer places an order, ACUMAX plans the most efficient route through the warehouse to pick all the items on the order. It then prints a customer shipping label at the warehouse. A picker in the warehouse scans the label and receives instructions on his or her screen about where to find the first item on the pick-list. The picker then locates the shelf and scans the bar code on the shelf for verification. If the picker identifies the wrong shelf, the computer responds with an error message and repeats instructions about where to find the item. If the picker locates the correct shelf, the computer displays the number of items to be placed into the customer's tote bag. The picker scans each item as he or she puts it into the tote bag and scans the bar code on the tote bag for verification. Filling an order incorrectly is virtually impossible because the computer will not allow the picker to proceed to the next item until the correct item is placed into the tote. When the tote is finally filled and delivered to the customer, the delivery driver scans the tote bag to verify that the correct order has been delivered.

McKesson's attention to quality order fulfillment actually begins before any orders are taken. When the distribution center receives items from drug manufacturers, workers scan these items and follow a procedure similar to that described above to ensure that the items are placed on the correct warehouse shelves. Scanning takes place during item return, replenishment, shipping, and any other time materials are handled.

McKesson initially installed the ACUMAX system at its 22,000-item warehouse in Spokane, Washington. Just three weeks after this installation, McKesson reported that the system reduced item-handling time by 10 percent while reducing incorrect picks by 72 percent. Currently, McKesson operates the warehouse with only 12 pickers who pick as many as 600,000 items each month. Shortly after ACUMAX's installation at the Spokane distribution center, McKesson repeated its success by installing ACUMAX at its Delran, New Jersey distribution center.

More important than saving time and labor is the fact that ACUMAX helped McKesson meet its goal of customer satisfaction. When the system was first installed, customers could

SOURCES: Third annual productivity achievement award winner distribution, *Modern Materials Handling* (February 1993: 71; Myron Magnet, Who's winning the information revolution, *Fortune* (November 30, 1992): 110–117; Iris Rosendahl, McKesson looking brighter after period of adjustment, *Drug Topics* (June 13, 1994): 122; and Greg Muirhead, Behind the PCS-Eli Lilly merger, *Drug Topics* (July 24, 1994): 16.

hardly believe that their orders were filled perfectly. McKesson was able to tell them, "100 percent accuracy is what you can expect from McKesson."

Questions

1. Identify the activities that take place at McKesson from the time a clerk takes a customer order until the order is delivered to the pharmacy.
2. What are the information needs of the picker? What are the information needs of the driver who delivers the pharmaceuticals?
3. What hardware does McKesson use for data input? Why did the designers of ACUMAX choose this input technique? What special needs does McKesson have for processing and output hardware?
4. Why do you think McKesson hired EDS to develop the software behind ACUMAX? Why doesn't McKesson use off-the-shelf software?
5. What information is contained in ACUMAX's databases? Do you think these databases are managed by a DBMS? Why or why not?
6. Does a local area network connect the computers in McKesson's warehouse? Justify your answer.
7. Is ACUMAX a transaction processing system? Support your reasoning.
8. How might managers at McKesson use the data in ACUMAX's database?
9. Can ACUMAX be considered a strategic information system? Why or why not?

Part IV

Managing the Information Resource

Information systems, like other corporate assets, have a limited life. Organizations must constantly renew their systems to support their changing information needs and to keep pace with evolving information technology. Sometimes organizations must develop or purchase new systems to address novel information needs or to automate manual activities that have failed to keep pace with organizational growth or competitive pressures. The process of renewing or developing information systems is well structured in most organizations. Part IV looks at the methods used and the organizational infrastructure necessary to assure quality in building, rebuilding, or purchasing information systems.

Chapter 13

Systems Planning, Development, and Implementation

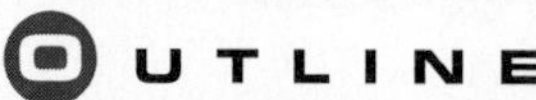

Systems Planning and Development at Midwest Family Services

The Systems Development Life Cycle
- Why Systems Have a Limited Life
- Stages in the Life Cycle
- Prototyping to Condense the SDLC

Analyzing Current Systems and Needs
- Information Collection for Requirements Analysis
- The Role of the Systems Analyst
- Needs Analysis Methodologies and Tools

Assessing and Defining Alternatives
- Cost/Benefit Analysis
- Risk Analysis

Designing New Systems
- Interface Design
- Data Design
- Process Design
- Physical Design
- Design Tools
- Design Specification

Developing New Systems
- The Develop-or-Purchase Decision
- Hardware Selection and Procurement
- Database Management System Selection
- Language Selection
- Quality Control

Implementing New Systems
- Implementation Strategies
- Managing Risk

Maintenance and Postimplementation Review
- Maintenance
- Postimplementation Review

Why Systems Fail

Methodologies and CASE Workbenches

Learning Objectives

After completing the reading and activities for Chapter 13, students will be able to

1. Identify and describe the stages in the systems development life cycle.
2. Discuss the reasons why systems have a limited life.
3. Show how prototyping shortens the systems development life cycle.
4. Specify four ways of collecting information for a requirements analysis.
5. Compare and contrast the techniques of cost/benefit analysis and risk analysis for assessing systems alternatives.
6. Describe the key elements of interface design, data design, process design, and physical design and illustrate the use of design tools in each of these design components.
7. Specify the key decisions in the development stage of the systems development life cycle.
8. Cite the advantages and disadvantages of four implementation strategies.
9. Distinguish between implementation and maintenance.
10. Discuss the role of methodologies and CASE workbenches in the systems development life cycle.

Systems Planning and Development at Midwest Family Services

Midwest Family Services provides a variety of social services for individuals and families in Milwaukee, Wisconsin. Founded by five social-work school classmates as a counseling center, the agency has grown significantly during the 20 years since its founding. The staff now includes 75 full-time and part-time professional and nonprofessional staff and a client base of almost 1,000 individuals and families. Social workers still offer individual counseling, but the center also offers programs for adolescents, children at risk, divorced men and women, and widows and widowers, among others. The agency administers a number of state and federal grants that assist clients with job training, dealing with alcoholism, and recognizing mental health needs.

The agency relied on manual systems for information processing until about five years ago. The administrative director at that time hired an information systems consultant who convinced the agency's board of directors that purchasing 15 personal computers with word-processing and spreadsheet software would meet the agency's needs, which the staff identified as document preparation, client billing, and scheduling. Midwest Family Services has since purchased an additional 15 computers, which staff members use for preparing team reports about clients, preparing budgets for workshops, and tracking use of various services. As staff members have become more comfortable using their computers, they have expressed increasing dissatisfaction with the availability of information about clients and services. For example, when two or more staff members provide services to the same family, they cannot easily enter information about the family into a single record; rather, each staff member maintains a separate set of information about the family. A recent audit of the agency by its federal contracts officer also called for improving the agency's computer information systems.

In response to these criticisms, Sharon Sinclair, the present administrative director, prepared a proposal for developing a high-quality computerized information system for Midwest Family Services. She also secured partial funding for the system from a special federal grants program that encourages the development of model computer systems in nonprofit organizations. After much haggling about the likely cost of such a system, the agency's board of directors authorized additional funds and asked Sinclair to oversee the system's development. She is currently preparing a memorandum for the agency's staff that describes what they can expect as part of the systems development process.

What should the Midwest Family Services staff expect to occur as part of systems development? What role will they play? What role will Sharon Sinclair play? Will Sinclair need to hire a consultant or any additional staff to help with the system's development and use? This chapter focuses on the fourth step of the management approach to information management: implementation. Implementation occurs after organizations have diagnosed their information needs, evaluated the ability of existing systems to meet these needs, and completed the preliminary recommendations for ways of redesigning information systems to better meet these needs or address deficiencies in the existing systems. The chapter describes the systems development process as a structured approach to the implementation step. We discuss each stage in the systems development life cycle as well as some ways systems developers and their managers can respond to a dynamic business environment by shortening cycle times. This chapter focuses on computerized systems, although the development of manual systems can follow a similar cycle.

The Systems Development Life Cycle

The **systems development life cycle (SDLC)** refers to the analysis of user needs and the selection, design, development, implementation, and maintenance of application systems, such as the system for Midwest Family Services, to meet these needs. Information systems appear to pass through stages as if they had lives of their own. They are developed or born, often in a primitive state. They grow and change rapidly for some time after their development in response to user needs and objectives. Eventually they reach a mature stage, where they remain stable or evolve slowly. Finally, as systems become too old or too complex to change, or as the applications they had addressed change, their use declines, and newer systems replace them. The term **cycle** reflects the emergence of newer systems from the older ones, as illustrated in Figure 13-1, to solve problems in improved ways and to address new problems.

Why Systems Have a Limited Life

Business managers often believe that they can describe and specify application systems to meet business needs for an indefinite future. Seasoned IS managers know that this expectation is usually an illusion. Although users may describe their needs well, their descriptions can rarely provide sufficient detail and precision to drive the development of satisfactory sys-

FIGURE 13-1 The Life Cycle Concept

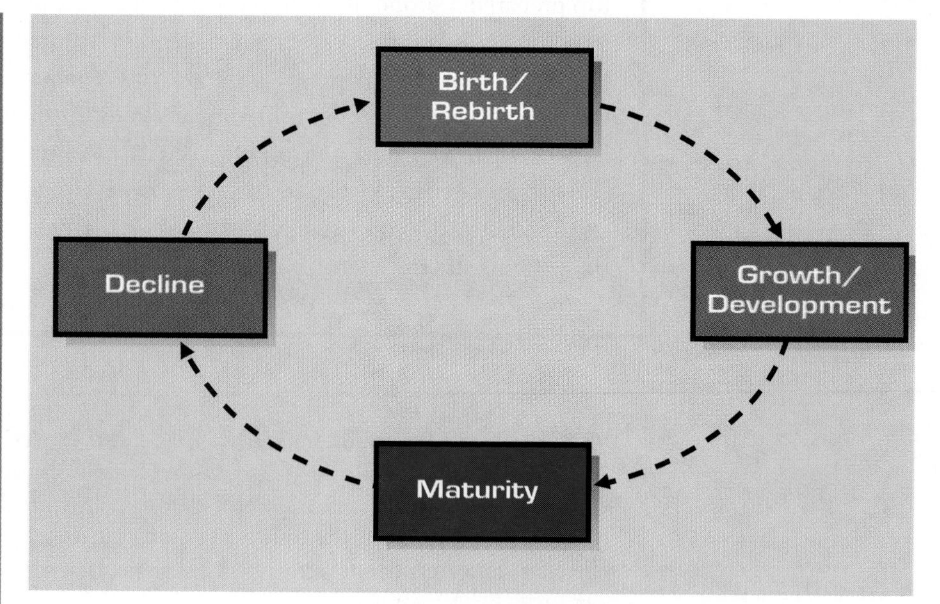

tems. Also, because users cannot easily or completely envision the way they will use information, the resulting systems often disappoint them. Not only do the users' needs change over time, but users typically fail to recognize the way the designers could have modified the systems to incorporate newer technology. Consider the situation faced by Midwest Family Services. Originally, their needs encompassed basic document preparation, billing, and scheduling; subsequently, these needs expanded to include better tracking of client services and budgeting, among others. Now they can anticipate using their computer systems for maintaining detailed information about each client that different staff members can readily access. The original system did not consider the possibility of networking computers, a common technology in the 1990s.

Large systems usually require several years to reach stability and maturity. During that period the organization may grow or shrink, move into new markets, or acquire new businesses. Technology will also change: Hardware that met the initial needs may remain adequate, but incorporating more recent, more advanced technology into their systems may provide other organizations a competitive advantage. For example, a company that developed its inventory systems before bar code scanners became widely available would have used inferior technologies to those used in more recently developed systems. Similarly, systems that incorporate voice input and multimedia devices will surpass the capabilities of earlier systems that lack these technologies. Software technology also improves and becomes more efficient with time. Systems developers who maintain existing applications must rely on older, less efficient technology and cannot modify their applications to meet new demands as rapidly as competitors who use newer technology.

The decision to replace rather than modify an old system is a difficult one for managers to make. The old system may represent an investment of many years and thousands, or even millions, of dollars. Managers, users, and the information systems staff feel comfortable and secure in using the system; they know that despite its limitations, it works. A new system poses potential risks. It should work better than the old system but may fail in unexpected ways. The organization must retrain its systems development staff in the new technologies and then train end users in the new system. Management typically has no reliable way to quantify the benefits of a new system and faces some uncertainty in estimating the system's development costs and time. The board of directors of Midwest Family Services, for example, hesitates before approving expenditures for a new system. The typical manager who faces these concerns will often try to keep current systems operating instead. As maintenance costs mount and competitors' new products display more advanced, sleeker features, managers consider replacing older systems. One rule of thumb calls for renovation rather than replacement of the existing system if the functional match between it and user requirements is at least 65 percent to 85 percent.[1] We begin our discussion of the systems development life cycle at the time of the replacement decision.

Stages in the Life Cycle

Figure 13-2 presents the stages of the SDLC: 1) needs analysis, 2) alternative analysis, 3) design, 4) development, 5) implementation, and 6) maintenance. Systems development at organizations such as Midwest Family Services begins with an analysis of how well the current system meets user needs. Under normal circumstances, business managers, such as those at Midwest, examine new opportunities, assess information needs, and address weaknesses in the existing systems in an ongoing fashion. IS/IT managers respond to these needs by continuously improving existing systems. **Needs analysis** differs from this ongoing process in that it is a formal, integrated, and usually time-limited process of 1) gathering data about the needs and opportunities of end-users and their managers; 2) evaluating and ranking the importance of these needs; and 3) addressing the possibility that they cannot be satisfied by continuous improvement of the existing systems. The needs analysis must effectively address

FIGURE 13-2 Stages of the Systems Development Life Cycle

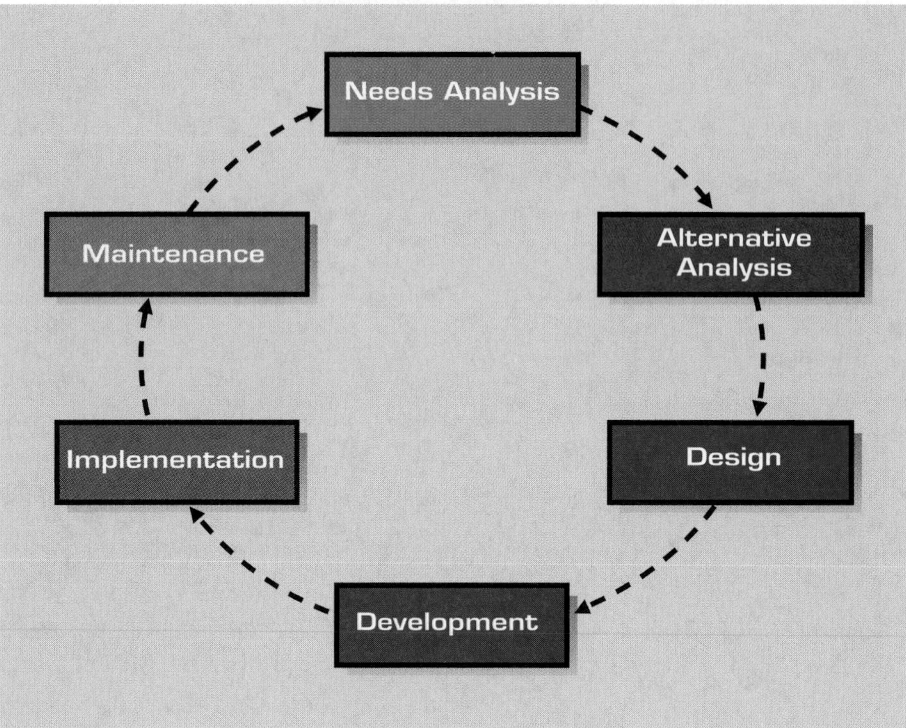

both technical issues and user concerns.[2] It may result in managers' deciding either to continue maintaining the current system or to replace it. Managers who decide to replace the system and move to the next stage of the SDLC do not eliminate the option of retaining the current system. They may halt the development of the new information system at any stage except maintenance, although the cost of abandonment after the second stage, alternative analysis, is usually steep.

The second stage of the SDLC, **alternative analysis,** focuses on assessing the feasibility of alternative systems. In this stage, developers propose one or more alternative designs and analyze their advantages and disadvantages. One of the alternatives may be to modify the existing system. At the end of the second stage, the developers select a preliminary design for further analysis.

The third stage is the **design,** or detailed specification, of the proposed system. Software developers require detailed specifications in order to begin their work. Just as a contractor would not begin to build a house without knowing the size and placement of its rooms and the location of plumbing and electrical fixtures, systems developers prefer to work with detailed specifications and usually produce better results this way. If the organization plans to contract the development of the system to a third party, it must develop a detailed specification to enable contractors to estimate costs and submit bids.

The fourth stage of the SDLC comprises **development** of the new system. Systems developers procure hardware and develop or purchase software. They also test the new system during this stage to ensure that it meets the specifications formulated in the design phase. Combining the design and development phases may improve the design and reduce the overall time required to design, develop, and implement new systems.

Implementation, the fifth stage of the SDLC, includes deactivating the old system and activating the new one. Implementation may proceed in steps that include training, pilot testing, and phasing in new systems.

The final stage of the SDLC, **maintenance,** includes not only correcting errors, or **bugs,** in the way that the system operates, but constantly seeking ways to provide new features or improve the system. As the system ages and maintenance demands become more frequent and difficult to implement, the organization will likely want to undertake a formal needs assessment, starting the cycle anew. After discussing ways to shorten the SDLC in the next section, we examine each phase in the systems development life cycle in greater detail.

Prototyping to Condense the SDLC

As organizations face an increasingly dynamic environment, where businesses evolve rapidly and technology changes rapidly, management no longer can afford to spend the time required to implement new systems following the formal systems development life cycle. Users of information systems in this environment, who think of themselves as customers of the information systems providers, demand more rapid responses from IS staff than previously offered. To meet these demands, information systems managers now can speed the development of information systems by using approaches such as **rapid prototyping** or **rapid application development (RAD)** to shorten the systems development life cycle.[3] Systems development for Midwest Family Services might use RAD if the projected system development time is unacceptably lengthy.

Most variations of rapid prototyping work essentially as illustrated in Figure 13-3. Users of various parts of an information system meet with systems developers for one or two hours each day for three to six weeks. During the initial meetings, the users describe their needs. Software developers use special rapid-prototyping tools between sessions to quickly develop a

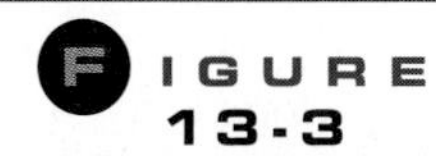
FIGURE 13-3 Steps in Rapid Prototyping

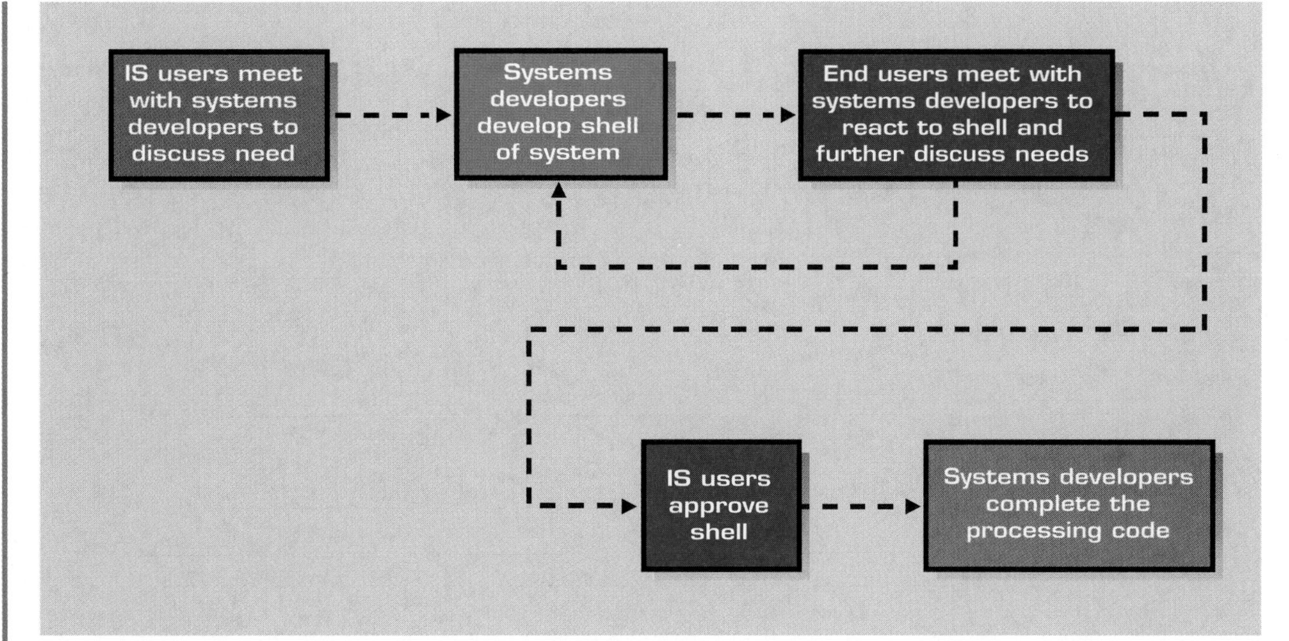

shell of a system that appears to meet these needs. This shell typically includes data entry screens, reports, query screens, and other parts of the interface between the users and the system, but the shell usually performs only a small portion of the processing of a fully implemented system. Developers sometimes create dummy data to present an illusion of a working system. After completing the initial needs identification, the developers present the shell they are developing to the users at their working sessions, and the users suggest modifications.

Discussion meetings alternate with development time for the systems developers. These ongoing discussions between users and developers enable users to communicate their needs more accurately to developers than would occur by building a formal specification statement during the design phase of the SDLC. As the system develops and unmet needs diminish, the frequency of meetings between users and developers decreases. Developers then spend more time on implementation issues, optimizing the use of system resources, such as storage and computing, and completing the code for processing.

Rapid prototyping calls for an incremental delivery of the system, typically at intervals of three to six months.[4] This ongoing and frequent delivery serves three major functions: 1) assuring end users that information systems developers accurately understand their needs; 2) rapidly identifying potential problems for the developers; and 3) providing positive feedback to the end users who participate in the systems design. Delivering a system incrementally also may pose conceptual design problems. Sometimes breaking the system into easily linkable stand-alone components is difficult. Such linking can waste effort by requiring frequent recoding of the interfaces between systems components.

Rapid prototyping offers several advantages over the conventional software development process. First, rapid prototyping significantly decreases the amount of time between analysis and implementation. Second, rapid prototyping more accurately ensures that the new system addresses users' needs. Third, rapid prototyping reveals the benefits of developing a new system before the effort and cost invested in the new system become excessive. Experts estimate, for example, that as many as 65 percent of very large IS projects (those with more than 1 million lines of code) are cancelled before they are completed.[5] Although the cancellation rate falls as the project's size and complexity decrease, to less than 10 percent overall,[6] rapid prototyping decreases the risk associated with new systems development.

The major disadvantage of rapid prototyping compared with the conventional approach is that rapid prototyping tends to raise the expectations of users to levels that developers cannot achieve. When users see how rapidly developers can produce the shell of a new system, they tend to believe that the entire systems development effort will be equally fast and easy. The cost of the rapid-prototyping tools poses a second disadvantage of rapid prototyping. The software programs that enable software developers to quickly develop the shell of a new system and rapidly customize it to user demands currently command high prices. Although the code that many of them produce may reduce the final cost of development by more than the cost of the tool, such savings are not guaranteed. A third disadvantage is that prototyping delays the demonstration of system functionality: As much as one-half of the functionality may not appear until the final 10 percent of the development schedule.[7] Finally, the benefits of prototyping are reduced if the company decides to buy existing software rather than develop its own. If Midwest Family Services, for example, expects that third-party software exists to meet a large portion of its needs, prototyping will not benefit the agency greatly.

Analyzing Current Systems and Needs

The needs analysis stage, also called the **requirements analysis** stage, identifies an organization's information needs. As part of this effort, analysts compare the identified needs with the specifications and performance of the current information system to determine which needs remain unmet. In later stages of the SDLC, managers evaluate the costs and benefits of developing new systems to satisfy these unmet needs.

Business managers analyze current systems and needs periodically. Some organizations, such as Midwest Family Services, have no formal review process; they have users who rarely complain or who constantly demand changes that force IS managers to conduct such a review. Other organizations have formal systems for examining current systems and prioritizing and scheduling changes.

What distinguishes the activities that take place in the needs analysis phase of the SDLC from those in the maintenance phase? The activities in the needs analysis phase resemble those of the maintenance phase, but the needs analysis is more rigorous, formal, comprehensive, and proactive. Furthermore, while maintenance implies continuous improvement to existing information systems, needs analysis addresses the possibility of completely redesigning and rebuilding these systems.

Documenting all the information needs of an organization is a daunting task, especially because these needs constantly change. Nevertheless, research shows that when systems developers identify needs early in the development cycle, the likelihood of development success increases, and the cost of corrections in later stages declines.[8] In this section, we identify the types of information collected during a requirements analysis, explore the role of the systems analyst in eliciting this information, and characterize the methodologies used to collect the information.

Information Collection for Requirements Analysis

Analysts determining an organization's or users' information needs typically focus on three types of needs: 1) outputs—the data the organization can or should use; 2) inputs—the data the organization collects or should collect; and 3) processing—the relationship of inputs to outputs.

Output Analysis. **Output analysis** describes the process of systematically identifying ways people in an organization use information: What types of reports do people receive? How frequently do they obtain the reports? What information do they retrieve from manual files? What information do they gain from on-line queries? What information would they like to obtain, and in what form?

Analysts can identify fairly easily the formal uses of information by looking at reports and query screens that existing information systems generate and by asking employees how they use hard-copy files stored in cabinets. Analysts can also help users to compose wish-lists of information that would help them perform their jobs better. Without analysts' help, end users often include on these wish-lists only information they believe they can obtain; they often do not know the breadth of information that the organization can secure.

Business managers, along with IS professionals, can expand a traditional output analysis by benchmarking similar applications developed at other companies, even in other industries. For example, Sharon Sinclair and other employees of Midwest Family Services might canvas other social work agencies to find a state-of-the-art accounting system to emulate; and they might seek an executive recruiter whose system for maintaining personnel records is similar to one the agency would use for its client records.

Input Analysis. **Input analysis** refers to a formal cataloging and review of the information an organization collects, stores, and uses. It also includes an analysis of the data collection process. Typically, input analysis follows output analysis so that analysts can identify missing or duplicate sources of information needed to produce the desired output. Input analysis also addresses the potential input of information that an organization collects but currently does not input into its information systems. Most organizations informally collect large amounts of data, such as word-of-mouth opinions or nonstatistical projects, that do not reside on formal information systems. For example, sales agents rarely enter into manual or computerized information systems more than a small percentage of the data they obtain when conversing with prospective or existing customers. Because informal data can provide useful information, product designers, executive strategists, and marketing managers would highly value a system that captures them. Educating users to identify the information they collect can be difficult because most users lack an awareness of how they and others use and collect information.

Procedure Analysis. **Procedure analysis** is the step during which developers attempt to determine whether or not the organization collects the information it needs, uses the information it collects effectively, and has efficient processes to address its information needs. Procedure analysis should examine all computerized and manual systems. A data-flow diagram, as shown in Figure 13-4, provides a complete picture of the relationship between inputs and outputs. Note that the data-flow diagram shows the steps in creating various outputs from specified inputs. For example, the employee submits a time card, which the system uses as an input to calculate gross pay; gross pay together with benefits information then becomes the input for calculating nontaxable income. Developers working in the design stage of the SDLC use data-flow diagrams extensively, and we discuss them in greater detail later in this chapter.

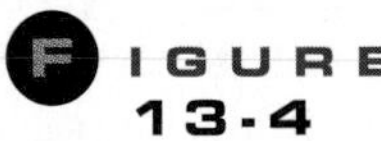
FIGURE 13-4 A Data-Flow Diagram

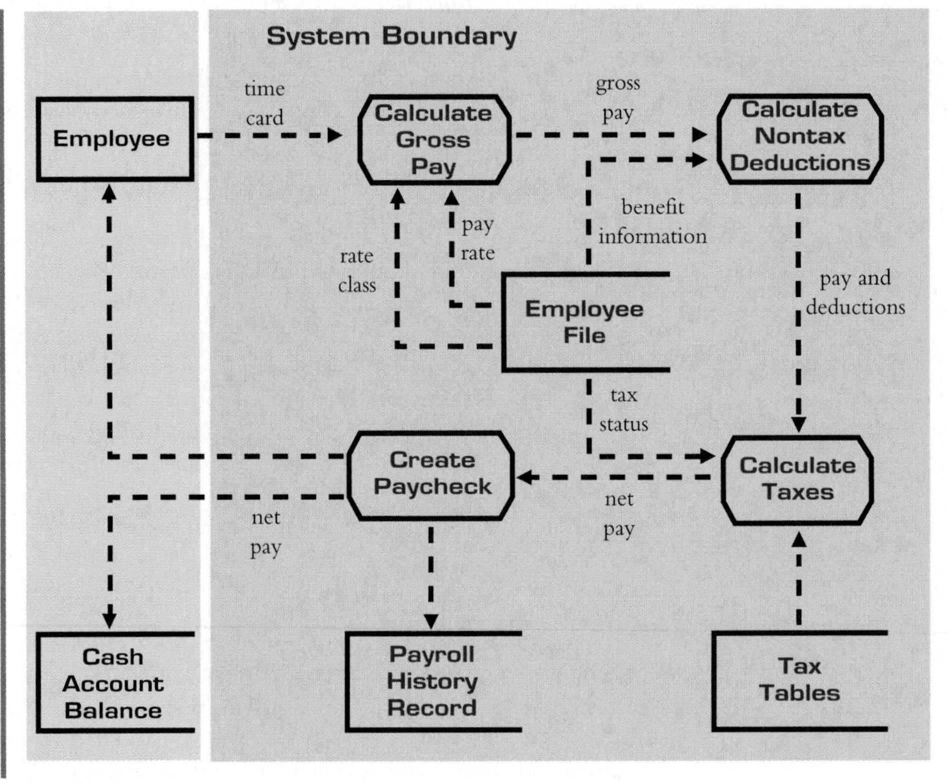

The Role of the Systems Analyst

Users of information systems often cannot understand the jargon that computer professionals use, and computer professionals often do not know enough about specific business processes to understand the needs and language of its users. This communication gap could reduce the quality of a company's requirements analysis. A **systems analyst,** a person who provides the interface between the information systems user and the information systems developer, can bridge this gap. A successful systems analyst understands the technical aspects of the system and can assess their implications for the users.[9]

Sharon Sinclair, for example, might hire a systems analyst to participate in developing the computer system at Midwest Family Services. The analyst should understand the organization's business needs as well as have expertise in software and systems development. Systems analysts should also have strong interpersonal skills: They should listen well and ask probing questions in an unthreatening manner. The complexity of business processes often motivates systems analysts to work in a single applications area for several years to maximize their knowledge of the business specialty and its requirements. Line managers rely on such specialists to interface with IS managers. In many large organizations, systems analysts report directly to a line manager rather than to an IS manager.

Needs Analysis Methodologies and Tools

Systems analysts use a large and varied set of techniques and data sources to perform needs analysis. These include interviews, on-site observation, questionnaires, structured analysis, a data dictionary, and reverse engineering.[10]

Interviews. Systems analysts typically obtain information about existing systems and needs by interviewing users and their managers. Users and managers know the most about the systems they use, although they perform many activities almost subconsciously. One problem with relying on interviews is that users often report only standard operating practices, forgetting the exceptions that occur infrequently. Analysts must ferret out these exceptions if the new system is to operate effectively and efficiently. Another problem is that users are often reluctant to report how they bypass the formal or standard systems to perform their work more efficiently. They may fear being fired or demoted if they tell what they actually do rather than what they are supposed to do. An analyst may need several interviews with the same people to verify the analyst's understanding of the processes performed, provide feedback on how the collected information will be used, and build the trust necessary to reveal exceptional and nonstandard processes. An analyst working on the Midwest Family Services system may interview numerous secretaries and case workers to determine how they schedule clients. The analyst may also interview top management and the accounting staff to understand how the agency's budgeting is done.

On-Site Observation. Another way of collecting information about how users perform their work is to watch them working or to work alongside them.[11] This approach, also called **contextual inquiry,** lacks efficiency because it often requires several days or weeks to obtain information that an analyst could obtain in an hour's interview. The major advantage of on-site observation relative to interviews is that it reveals exceptional and nonstandard processes more often and more completely.

Questionnaires. Systems analysts may use questionnaires to collect information when many people or geographically disbursed workers need to provide information about the processes affected by the new system. Analysts may also use confidential questionnaires to obtain information about hidden processes. Questionnaires may not yield quality data, however, because employees often fail to complete them, and those who do often offer incomplete answers. Midwest Family Services may have too few employees in each area to merit the use of questionnaires for data collection. In addition, analysts prefer techniques that involve users and build a sense of user ownership in the proposed system; questionnaires may fail to develop such a stake.

Structured Analysis. **Structured analysis** involves diagramming existing and proposed systems so that users can understand and critique an analyst's perception of information relationships. Structured analysis breaks down a complex system into smaller, understandable components and illustrates the connections between these components. It focuses on what a system does or should do rather than on the way individuals complete their work. Development of the system for Midwest Family Services may include a structured analysis to identify the specific functions and interrelationships that the system must represent.

Data Dictionary. A **data dictionary,** also known as a data encyclopedia or repository, is a database that contains descriptions of all the computerized data items maintained by the organization (see Chapter 7). Users can access the data dictionary to 1) validate their perceptions of the data an organization collects and uses; 2) identify gaps in any data they require for their business functions; and 3) specify and clarify terms used by end users to describe their business activities. For example, when a user refers to *revenue from sales,* the analyst working with that user can refer to the data dictionary to learn whether the term refers to the undiscounted price of items sold, the money that changes hands at the time of the sale, or the revenue adjusted by any returns that occur after the sale.

Reverse Engineering. Large systems often consist of thousands of programs written and modified over an extended period. These programs and the processes they implement may have such complex interrelationships that no one in the organization knows exactly how they work. For example, programmers no longer employed by the organization may have made significant changes in the programming code years ago. Even if these programmers documented the changes that they made, they may not have documented why they made the changes. The large size of current systems compounds the problem of identifying what those systems do. Unless the development of existing systems included excellent documentation, analyzing them manually is likely to be an expensive and time-consuming task.

Reverse engineering describes the process of analyzing the software that implements an existing system. Special software packages automate much of this process by performing at least the following functions: 1) identifying and organizing the names of variables used by the code to represent data; 2) identifying where the code performs input and output; 3) identifying, organizing, and diagramming the sequence of operations performed; 4) determining under what circumstances the operations are performed; 5) monitoring the frequency of use of various parts of the software; and 6) translating the software into languages that provide clearer or more terse code or conform to current software standards. Reverse engineering often requires specialists to interpret the output of these programs and make decisions about the way the current system operates when the software cannot determine the system's functioning. Although improvements in artificial intelligence allow reverse engineering software to make many decisions about the code, reverse engineering remains more of an art than a science.

Assessing and Defining Alternatives

The second stage of the SDLC includes identifying and evaluating alternative systems and ultimately focusing on a single design more extensively. Often the chief IS manager or senior executives will establish a committee consisting of managers from the user departments and IS specialists to make the decisions required at this stage. Sharon Sinclair might form a committee primarily composed of top management, with a few representatives from the rest of the professional and nonprofessional staff. Decisions about the nature of the system made at this stage often encumber sufficient funds to warrant review by senior executives. Afterwards, a project can no longer be abandoned without a substantial loss of effort and money.

Selecting an alternative for further design involves making tradeoffs between designs that meet few user needs but have low costs and designs that meet many needs but have high costs. In addition, some designs are more likely than others to be successfully completed, installed, and used. Executives often use cost/benefit analysis or risk analysis to help them assess the relative costs, benefits, and risks of alternative solutions. A key decision focuses on whether to renovate an old system or build a new one. Renovating a system requires significant energy spent on assessing and improving the quality of the code, checking and augmenting the documentation, and making other functional and technical improvements.[12]

Cost/Benefit Analysis

Selecting among alternative projects involves more than simply counting the number of needs met and estimating the cost of meeting them. First, different systems may meet a given need with varying effectiveness. Consider, for example, a shipper who wants to trace the location of a package in route without waiting for the daily transport report. One solution might locate the package within an hour, another within five minutes, and a third within seconds. Each solution meets the need with a different relative benefit and at a different cost. A cost/benefit analysis weighs the benefits against the costs.

Second, costs and benefits often arise in different time periods. Although some costs are ongoing, most costs for a new system occur during its development and when procuring hardware. Benefits, in contrast, accrue over time; they may even decline as competitors develop similar systems. Cost/benefit analyses can use economic, analytic, portfolio, or strategic methods[13] that include such techniques as discounted cash flow, internal rate of return, and payback period to translate costs and benefits accruing over time into numbers that can be compared on a current basis.

Third, estimating the cost of a project may be difficult at this early design stage.[14] Various techniques exist to estimate software development costs based on the number of application functions the software will provide.[15] However, counting such functions is complex, even for a fully specified design, and estimates at this stage may err by 50 percent or more.

Fourth, executives may be unable to estimate a system's benefits accurately. They can assess some benefits, such as savings in the cost of processing transactions or lower inventory holding costs, reasonably correctly. Estimating the value of other benefits, such as those that derive from better operations, including the ability to respond to customers more rapidly or with less lead time, can pose difficulties. Although these improvements should lead to increased sales, calculations of the impact on sales and profits may contain significant errors. Finally, intangible benefits, such as improving morale by changing the nature of an employee's work, may be almost impossible to quantify accurately. Typical cost-justification errors include exaggerating cost savings, underestimating costs, failing to identify hidden costs, and relying on false numbers.[16]

Risk Analysis

Every IS project involves risks as well as benefits. One systems solution may provide more benefit than another solution at the same or lower cost, but it might require the use of unproven technology or the mastery of the new technology by the IS staff. Risks exist with both technology and people. Some designs might, for example, automate a job previously performed manually; as a result, the company may lay off some staff. While benefits accrue from reduced labor costs, risks arise from possible labor unrest or loss of morale. **Risk analysis** requires managers to identify where risks might arise and trade them against costs and benefits. Managers can use a variety of tools to quantify their risk aversion and help them make decisions in this environment.[17]

Designing New Systems

The third stage of the SDLC focuses on providing the detailed specifications of the selected design. System design includes determining the user interface with input and output; the database; the processes and procedures; and the physical characteristics of the system, such as the number, types, and locations of workstations, processing hardware, and network cabling and devices. No programming occurs. Instead, systems analysts specify the design in enough detail for programmers to subsequently write programs that meet the specifications and for third parties to bid to develop or modify programs to meet the specifications. Some practitioners overlap the design and alternative selection stages. For example, they may select two or three alternatives for additional design, partially proceed through the design stage, and then return to the alternative selection stage to make a final decision.

Many practitioners overlap the design and development stages of the SDLC. Certain elements of design, such as the design of the user interface, lend themselves to prototyping, as discussed earlier in this chapter. After designers specify a preliminary user interface and programmers implement the design, users can test the interface and suggest improvements. Then designers, in consultation with the programming staff, can alter the design to reflect the feedback. System designers at Midwest Family Services might regularly provide the agency's staff with designs to test and critique. Data design and development may also be iterative because the data design affects system performance. For example, preliminary tests may show that response time for common queries is too slow, requiring a modification in the data design after development has begun.

U.S. PATENT OFFICE

In some cases, design and development may occur in parallel, although this is a highly risky approach. For example, after attempts to exhaustively and accurately state requirements for automating manual search and retrieval processes in the U.S. Patent Office contributed to significant delays in the project, project managers allowed the project to proceed while uncertainties in requirements still existed and were being resolved.[18] After four years of effort and hundreds of millions of dollars in contractual and internal expenses, the system was not working, and the project was in danger of being canceled. A new project manager hired to rescue the project imposed rules to prohibit implementation of functions that were not in the design. Within a short period of time the project was back on track and on budget.

MERIDETH

When the Merideth Corporation, an Iowa-based publishing, real estate, and broadcasting company, attempted development of a project to fulfill subscriptions before the design was frozen, the company found that it was continually playing a game of catch up in matching systems to requirements. The project was eventually scrapped after nearly ten years and a budget that had tripled.[19]

Interface Design

Interface design refers to the specification of the form and methods of data output and entry. Outputs flow from the needs assessment and drive the design of the project; in the design stage, designers focus on the media, content, and form of the output. They determine which information is best displayed on various media, such as a computer screen, paper report, microfiche, or microfilm. They also provide for the transfer of some output directly into a spreadsheet or database on a user's personal computer.

The designers also specify the **content,** the elements of data that appear on an output report or screen. Ideally, a design specifies only the needed information; extraneous information clutters a screen or report, making the required information more difficult to find. The designer might also provide options to obtain related information, such as clicking a button on a screen to select a more detailed report about certain aspects of the output.

During interface design, designers determine the **form** of output—the way information is presented. They determine, for example, whether certain data should appear in tabular form or graphically. Designing the display of tabular data includes determining the layout, the amount of white space, page margins, page length, the frequency of breaks, and the location of subtotals in the data, among other features. Designing graphical displays involves deciding these issues as well as the graphical form to use (pie, bar, or line chart) and options for switching among forms. Form also considers the choice of color. Some systems give every color a different meaning; for example, red may always show data outside the usual range, or it might identify items that demand user attention.

On the input side, designers must determine whether users will enter data in batch or on-line modes, the characteristics of input screens, the nature of error checking during data entry, and the standards that apply among data entry screens. For example, they might decide that the F1 function key on the keyboard will always elicit help about the function that the data entry clerk performs and the F2 key or a mouse click on a scroll button will display a list of options.

Interface designers also determine the type of hardware used for input. For example, they may decide that users should enter inventory data with a bar code reader rather than use a keyboard or OCR device. Although designers have made some of these decisions in the previous stage of the SDLC, they can revisit their decisions and return to the second stage for a review of major changes.

Data Design

Data design refers to the design of the database underlying the system. Users, business managers, and data design specialists start with a list of data elements that act as inputs to or outputs of the system. They may need to resolve **synonyms** in this list. For example, different employees at Midwest Family Systems may have used the terms *client* and *case* to refer to the same thing. In addition, data design participants may need to identify **homonyms,** different items that have the same name. For example, some employees use the term *agent* to mean a social worker, while others use *agent* to refer to any employee of the agency. They then need to identify relationships among the data items. Does every case have one case worker in charge, or can several workers team up on a case? Database specialists help data users and managers formalize relationships such as these to create the logical design. Ultimately, the data users and managers are responsible for the design's accuracy.

Database specialists generate a physical design to structure the data for ease and speed of retrieval, to keep storage requirements as low as possible, and to promote data integrity (see Chapter 7). Along with process designers, they should specify the data model (hierarchical, network, relational, or object-oriented) used by the DBMS. The model selected constrains the physical data design and forms the basis for the way the designers view and process the data. Designers may also select the DBMS vendor at this time, although this selection more typically occurs in the development stage.

Data designers work with the organization's data administrator to coordinate the storage and use of data that independently designed information systems might share. Data designers should develop a data dictionary for an application before any programming occurs. Programmers can then use this specification of the data dictionary to automatically generate the parts of the code that relate to the data their programs will use.

Process Design

Process design refers to the design of both the computational and logical processes underlying the system. The calculation of pay for hourly employees illustrates a computational process. The employees receive overtime pay for hours that exceed 40 and for work on Sundays and holidays. Process designers for a payroll system will identify the procedure for calculating the payroll of these employees. As users and business managers are most familiar with the business processes, they form the core part of the process design team.

The removal of an item from inventory illustrates a logical process. The system should check whether an item has fallen below a prespecified or computable restock level. When the stock of certain types of items reaches the prespecified level, the system should alert affected managers by producing a report, sending an electronic mail message, or even initiating an EDI transaction to automatically reorder the item. This example demonstrates the computer taking one or more procedural steps in response to a transaction. Process designers must specify the precise steps the system should take in response to any transaction that might occur. They must also specify the steps the computer must take to process inputs and outputs. Although the computer code may be generated by IS specialists, the process specifications are written from the perspective of the business manager.

Physical Design

Physical design refers to decisions about the hardware used to deliver the system. Physical design usually follows data and process designs because they determine the required amount of data storage, the volume of transaction processing, the amount of data communication activity, and the complexity of processing. Designers use such information to determine whether existing hardware will accommodate the new system or whether the organization must procure new hardware. For example, designers recommending new hardware purchases should determine whether centralized or decentralized development and delivery of the system should occur. Although analysts may address these issues during the alternative selection phase of the SDLC, they cannot develop accurate estimates of cost and response time until they have complete data and process designs. Costs and response times that fall outside the ranges forecast during alternative analysis may call for revisiting the second stage of the SDLC.

Design Tools

Several formal tools exist for designing systems, most of which have been incorporated into software to help automate the design process. The most widely used design tools include data-flow diagrams, structure charts, screen generators, report generators, and code generators.

Data-Flow Diagrams. A **data-flow diagram (DFD)** graphically illustrates the use of data and their creation by system processes. Figure 13-4 illustrates a data-flow diagram for a simplified payroll system. Following the most common notation, arrows indicate data flows; open-sided rectangles represent stored data; round-edged rectangles indicate processes; and squares represent sources of input or users of output. This example shows the employee as both a source of input (time card) and a user of output (paycheck). An employee file maintains stored data about the employee's pay class, pay rate, and deductions; processes to determine gross pay and calculate net pay use these stored data. Analysts also use data flow diagrams for structured analysis during the needs analysis phase of the SDLC.

Structure Charts. A **structure chart** shows the relationship among the programs and subprograms that will make up the finished system. Figure 13-5 illustrates a structure chart for a payroll system. Note that it emphasizes the modular design of the payroll system. To perform a given task, such as calculating net pay, all tasks below—calculating taxes and calculating deductions—must be performed.

FIGURE 13-5 A Structure Chart

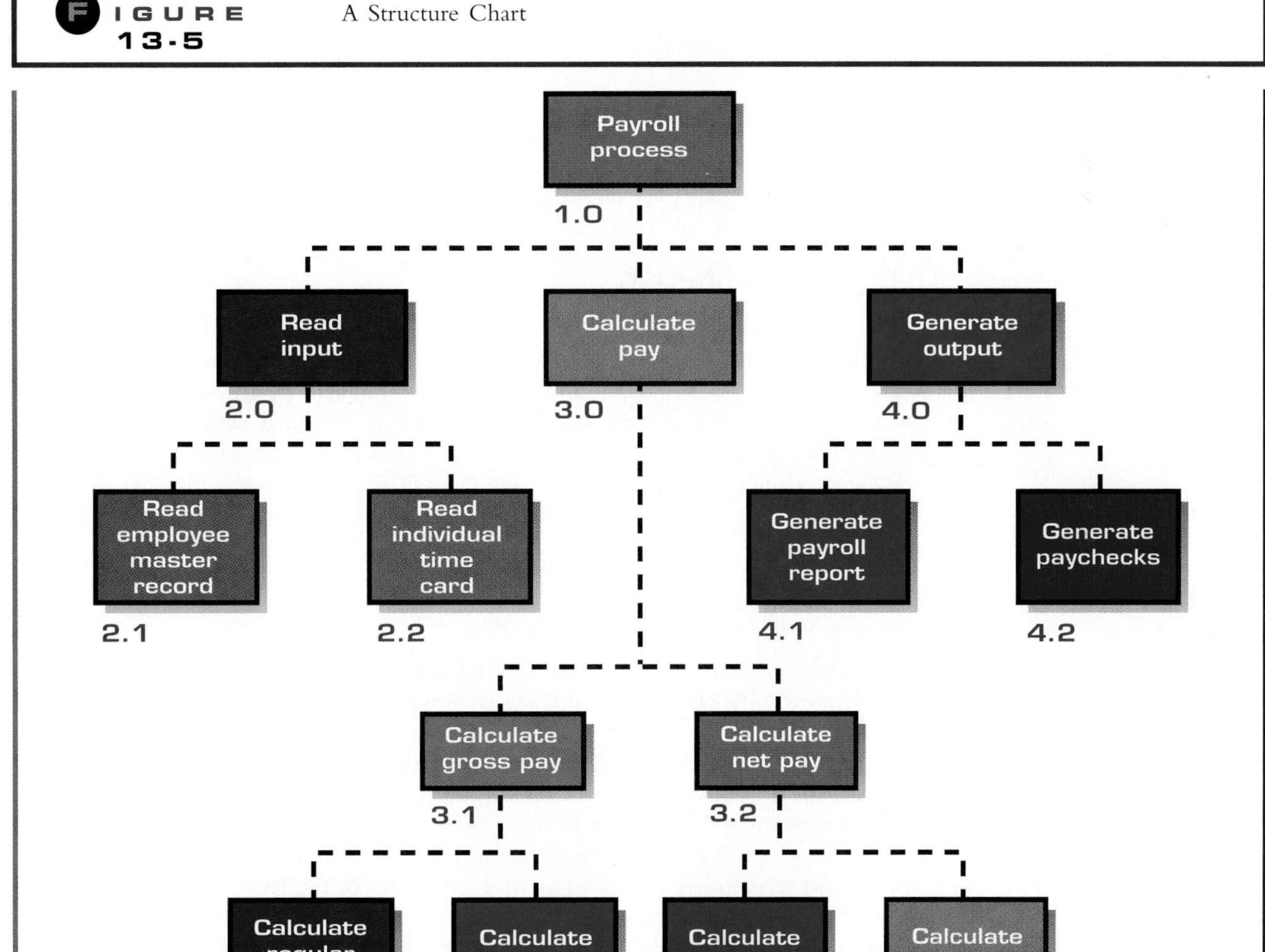

SOURCE: Reprinted with permission from Sarah E. Hutchinson and Stacey C. Sawyer, *Computers and Information Systems* 1994–1995 edition (Burr Ridge, IL: Irwin, 1994): 8, 21.

Screen Generators. **Screen generators** help designers generate programs for screen-based data entry or screen-based queries. The designer can lay out the text and data portion using standard text and drawing tools; specify where the data will appear or be entered; specify ways to check the entered data for validity; position mouse buttons, pull-down menus, and scroll bars; cross-reference the data layout with data names from the data dictionary or DBMS; and specify many other features of a data-entry or query screen. Modern screen generators lead the designer through the process of creating, testing, and editing a screen, as well as generating the screen program.

Report Generators. **Report generators** allow a designer to lay out a report using standard text and drawing tools; identify the placement of headings; determine what triggers breaks or subtotals; identify the sources of data for columns; specify the order for sorting rows; identify the criteria that determine whether to display a given row; and establish other features of a standard report. Report generators also guide the developer through the design process, identifying available options, testing the report, and then generating a computer program that will create the report.

Code Generators. A **code generator** refers to sophisticated software that can generate complete and working programs based on designer specifications. It may use a combination of specification and design tools, such as data-flow diagrams, data dictionaries, structure charts, and the outputs of screen and report generators, as its input.

Design Specification

Design specification refers to means for communicating the design to the programmers who will implement it. Prototyping most readily communicates the interface design. The tools available for designing input and output screens, sample reports, and GUI interfaces facilitate the prototyping of these interfaces and, consequently, their design. Common interface standards can be specified in hard copy as an interface standard guide. A data dictionary or an entity-relationship diagram (see Chapter 7) can also communicate the data design. In addition, software can help automate data design as well as store and print the result.

Developing New Systems

The development stage includes procuring hardware, developing or procuring software, and testing the system. IS professionals assemble a working system that meets the specifications formulated in the design stage. Users should test the new system during the development phase but will not use it until the implementation stage of the SDLC. Unless development is by prototype, IS professionals work more independently of end users and their managers during the development stage than at any other stage of the SDLC.

Systems developers face three pressing issues: 1) whether to entrust all or part of the development effort to outside contractors; 2) which databases to use to store the data generated by the system; and 3) which language(s) to use for development of the code. In this section, we explore how managers and IS professionals address these issues as well as how they ensure the quality of the developed system.

The Develop-or-Purchase Decision

The choice of whether to develop or purchase a new system is one of the most difficult decisions senior information systems managers and other top executives must make. Medium

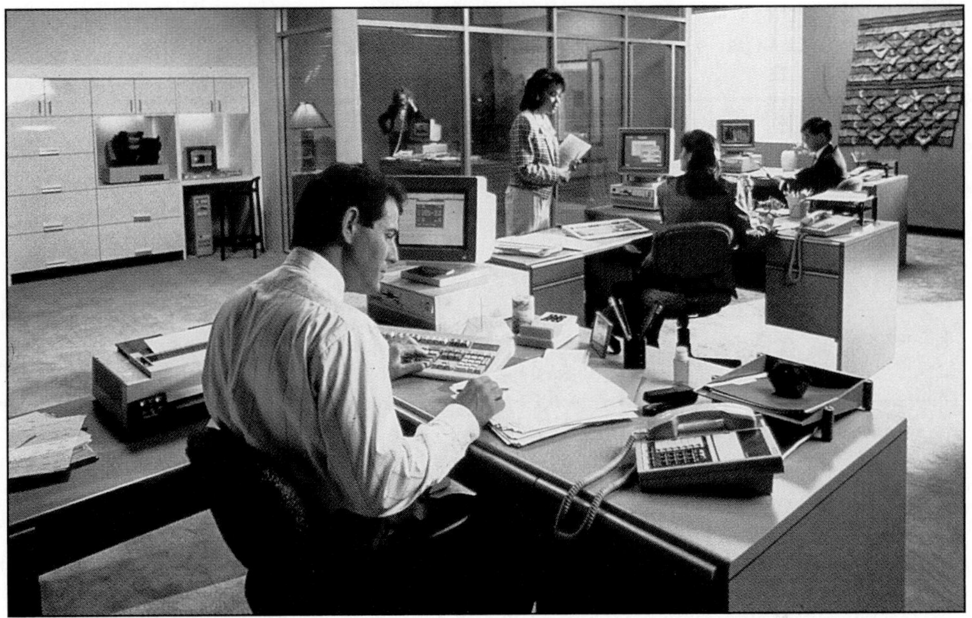

A programmer creates software to design specifications.
Courtesy of International Business Machines Corporation.

to large organizations usually find that off-the-shelf vertical application software does not entirely satisfy their complex information needs, although third-party software may satisfy a substantial portion of them. The unique needs of organizations such as Midwest Family Services may also preclude their buying only third-party software for their system. Such organizations can purchase modules for the system and then add or modify features as necessary. A company's ability to modify third-party software depends on the vendor's licensing agreements. Some prohibit any modification of the software except by the vendor itself; some authorize value-added resellers (VARs) to modify their software; and some provide all or portions of their computer code to the purchasing company so that its staff can modify the software. Companies that do not have the resources and skills to develop their own software but that need functionality not provided by off-the-shelf products may hire another company to develop software for them. Meritor Savings Bank of Philadelphia chose this approach: It decided to outsource all its systems development and maintenance. Working with Electronic Data Systems as its systems integrator, the bank saved almost $9 million in two years.[20]

MERITOR SAVINGS BANK OF PHILADELPHIA

ELECTRONIC DATA SYSTEMS

Chapter 5 discusses the advantages and disadvantages of customizing vertical application software versus developing it in-house or using off-the-shelf software. To review briefly, companies that customize software lose the ability to easily integrate the manufacturer's updates and increase the likelihood of introducing bugs, but they gain more flexibility to provide the functionality they need. They also gain some freedom by reducing their reliance on a single party for their information systems needs. By developing systems entirely in-house, companies likely spend more both in initially developing and then in maintaining the system, but they can more likely use the system strategically and meet their needs more precisely. Most large companies use software that is developed entirely or partially in-house (see Figure 13-6).[21]

VIRGINIA DEPARTMENT OF TAXATION

The Virginia Department of Taxation faced a develop-or-purchase decision in its overhaul of the commonwealth's tax processing systems. The scope of the project included 1,500 programs, 40 databases, and 25 application systems, affecting 1,800 users. The system design established deadlines for the installation of major software components every three to six months over a nine-year period. Despite having a staff of only six people, the director of IS at the department strongly felt that the project should be developed in-house because the

FIGURE 13-6 Who Develops Systems

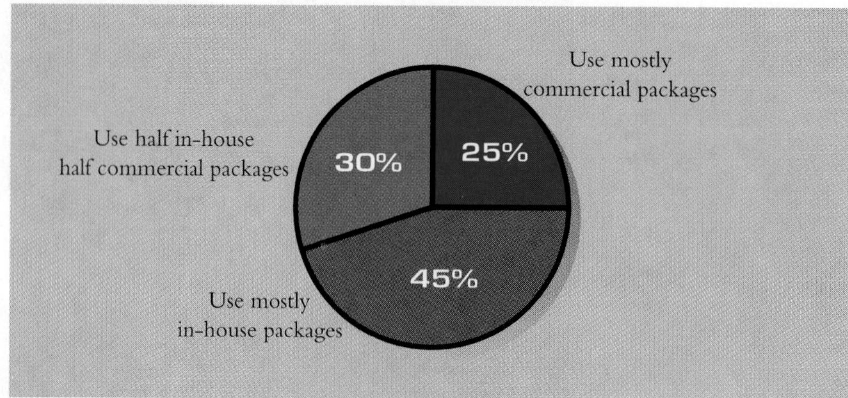

SOURCE: David Baum, Brain strain, *Computerworld (Premier 100)* (September 13, 1993): 34.

department would need to maintain the system in order to respond quickly to changes in the tax laws. Although this decision required her to increase the IS staff to 45 people, including the full-time assignment of six managers from user areas, the system was delivered on time and saved the commonwealth an estimated $80 million.[22]

Hardware Selection and Procurement

The design stage of the SDLC requires many hardware decisions, particularly those related to selecting input and output devices and deciding whether to use centralized, distributed, or decentralized equipment. The development stage, too, includes some hardware decisions, such as evaluating and selecting alternative vendors for equipment purchases. IS professionals might decide during the design stage, for example, to use laser printers to provide certain system outputs. During the development stage, the IS professionals would evaluate the laser printer products of several vendors, seek bids from manufacturers and distributors, and select, order, and install the equipment to use in testing the system in its real-life environment.

If a company chooses to buy rather than develop its software, it may deal with software manufacturers who sell **turn-key systems.** Organizations that purchase a turn-key system can plug it in and turn it on (presumably, with a key), and it will run. The software will already be loaded onto the computer, and the vendor optimizes the hardware/software combination for the buyer's needs.

Database Management System Selection

System developers should select the DBMS for storing the new system's data before programming begins. Although relational DBMSs provide relatively standard interfaces, companies should restrict their systems to standard relational features if they want to retain the flexibility of changing their DBMS during or after systems development without incurring too great a penalty in cost or time. Most companies use the productivity software (typically fourth-generation language, or 4GL) bundled with the DBMS that they employ. Unfortunately, such software can use nonstandard features of the DBMS selected. Even productivity software that works with a number of DBMSs customizes its code to the specific DBMS. Nonrelational DBMS models rely even more extensively on unique coding. Although standards exist for network models and are emerging for object-oriented models, these standards provide only limited common features; most implementations differ considerably.

A company's information architecture (see Chapter 14) may constrain the developers' choice of DBMS for a given system. Companies often standardize on a database manager because the choice of DBMS is so central to the development and implementation of their systems. Standardization provides a number of benefits, including easing the transfer of information between systems and reducing the training needed for the information systems development staff. Companies may also standardize on a particular DBMS to allow them flexibility in hardware selection or to optimize performance on a standard hardware platform. For example, General Cinema Corporation, now a division of Harcourt General, Inc., chose Sybase as its relational DBMS when it converted from a mainframe to a client/server environment. Now, every application package it writes or purchases must work with Sybase.[23] As most third-party vertical application software packages interface with a single DBMS, Harcourt General's DBMS standard limits its choices of products to support its financial and accounting needs.

GENERAL CINEMA/ HARCOURT GENERAL

Language Selection

The choice of languages for systems development depends on several factors. First, the company may have standards that limit the choice of programming language. At small companies, even without formal standards, staff expertise is often limited to at most one or two languages. Second, the DBMS selected may restrict the languages to a small number that it supports. Third, customization of third-party software may require a language that interfaces with that used by the third-party vendor.

Chapter 5 discusses some common issues in language selection, including the choice of interpretive versus compiled, procedural versus nonprocedural, and command/data-oriented versus object-oriented language. Although selecting computer languages for software development is a technical decision in most organizations, business managers should address the impact that language choice has on their functions, including their ability, for example, to make changes or to have IS professionals make changes in a timely fashion. Standard Oil rebuilt its system for ship scheduling and operations, known as its Marine Operating System (MOS), with essentially the same functionality as the system it replaced, but written in a 4GL instead of a combination of COBOL and a 4GL. The language change enabled users to modify the software without support, to achieve better ad-hoc reporting, and to reduce the delay between their request for changes and implementation of those changes by IS professionals. After five months, the change reportedly saved the company 6,000 employee hours.[24]

STANDARD OIL

Quality Control

Quality control describes the process of ensuring that the system developed works as designed. Successful quality assurance includes defining and measuring IS quality in useful and meaningful ways as well as identifying the responsibilities of managers and developers in ensuring quality.[25] Florida Power & Light, for example, introduced a set of statistical quality-control procedures for all departments that resulted in improved software code and more satisfied internal users.[26] Costs of poor quality include additional user training and support, more frequent calls to the help desk, and loss of productivity. Quality control includes implementing a **testing plan,** typically introduced during the design stage of the SDLC. The testing plan states precisely how users will recognize whether a delivered system meets their needs and expectations. The development phase of the SDLC includes four levels of test-ing to ensure quality: 1) unit testing, 2) string testing, 3) integration testing, and 4) system testing.[27]

FLORIDA POWER & LIGHT

Unit testing refers to testing each small component of the system to guarantee its proper operation. A single programmer writes the code for a unit, such as a data entry program for one type of data, over a relatively short period.

String testing examines the interaction of a series of programs within the system that likely will be used in concert, such as those that process a transaction. One transaction, such as placing an order, might use programs for data entry, customer verification, credit checking, inventory reduction, billing, and so on. String testing involves creating and processing a large number of different transactions to ensure that the linkages among the various program components that deal with the transaction work properly.

Integration testing addresses the interaction between large, independently developed components of the new system that were internally checked at the unit- and string-testing levels. For example, developers can test the order entry and inventory parts of a system to verify that the order function has access to the current inventory and that orders properly trigger the appropriate changes in inventory.

System testing, also known as **alpha testing,** refers to testing the entire system under realistic conditions. System testing simulates the production system in a laboratory environment. System testing should expose the system, to the extent possible, to the same level of activity as would occur under normal circumstances and with a realistic set of data. Although simulating this degree of activity directly, especially for systems intended for use by an entire organization or a large subset, may be difficult, software products help testers simulate such high levels of activity. These products can generate transactions from a transaction profile, provide statistical data about the speed with which the system responds, and compare outputs and the final value of data elements to the outcomes.[28]

In the first stage of system testing, **performance testing,** developers identify and correct problems that might cause the system to become inoperative or result in creating and saving erroneous information. Once they know that the system works properly in a well-controlled environment, they subject it to usability testing.[29] **Usability testing** compares the developed system to users' expectations and needs. Users ideally test the system in a **usability lab,** a place where developers can observe and record their reactions to the system for later analysis. Most companies employ usability labs only for large and complex projects. Midwest Family Services, because of its relatively small size and the expense of setting up a usability lab, would probably perform usability testing by observing users in action after the new system is installed.

A typical usability lab costs from $60,000 to $200,000 and includes two rooms connected by a one-way mirror, as shown in Figure 13-7. Video cameras record and store users' reactions to the system; computer equipment, including software to log the user's keystrokes, tests the application; and an audio system allows users to communicate with application developers and usability professionals. Professionals look for the time required to complete specific tasks, the types of errors made, the ways errors are corrected, whether errors are repeated, the speed of learning, the frustrations users experience, and so on. Testing should occur on a variety of subjects, from experts in the application to new employees. Experts suggest that eight to ten users should identify 95 percent of the usability problems and that a single test in a usability lab will identify 70 to 100 possible improvements for a typical system. Organizations too small to have their own usability labs can hire the services of a usability consultant and use the consultant's labs to test their software.[30]

Implementing New Systems

Moving the new system into the production environment follows obtaining satisfactory testing results. IS professionals or other organizational members must manage the transition from the old system to the new. Sharon Sinclair likely will manage such a transition at Midwest

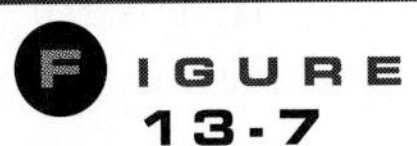
FIGURE 13-7 A Usability Lab

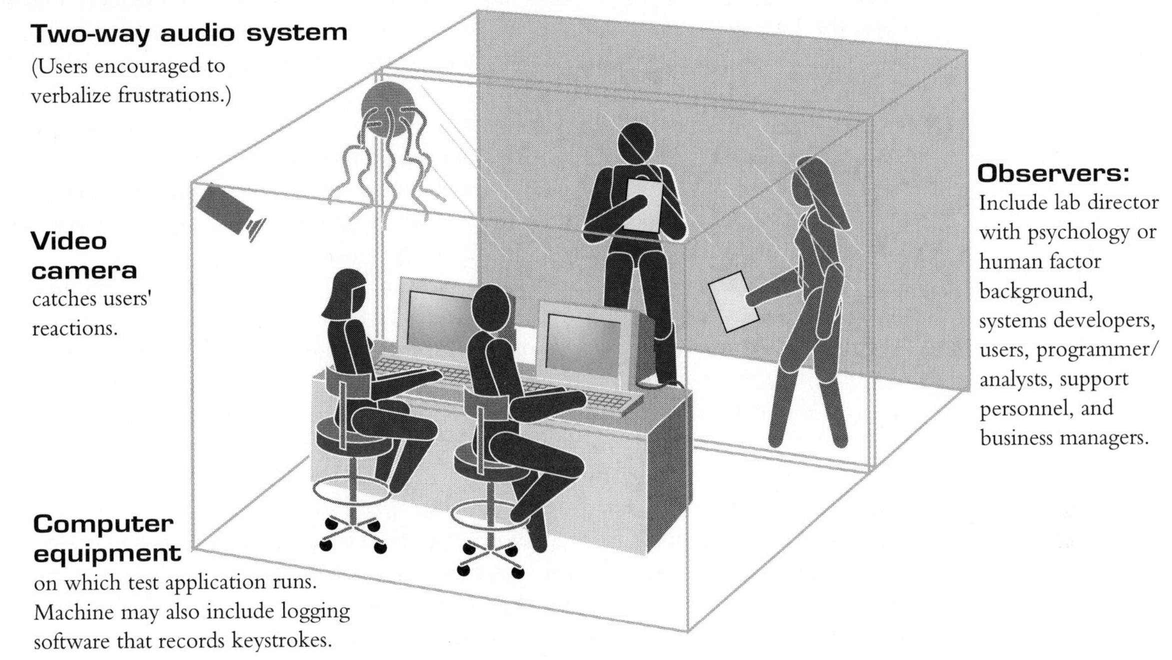
Two-way audio system
(Users encouraged to verbalize frustrations.)
Video camera
catches users' reactions.
Computer equipment
on which test application runs. Machine may also include logging software that records keystrokes.
Observers:
Include lab director with psychology or human factor background, systems developers, users, programmer/analysts, support personnel, and business managers.

Family Services; alternatively, she can hire a consultant or special employee to oversee the transition and implementation. Organizations use a variety of strategies to move new systems into the production environment. They simultaneously act to reduce the risk of incurring serious business problems during transition and implementation.

Implementation Strategies

Companies generally use some combination of four implementation strategies: 1) direct cut-over—the overnight replacement of one system by another; 2) pilot implementation—system replacement for a targeted population in the organization, increasing the target size over time; 3) phased implementation—introduction of the system component by component; and 4) parallel implementation—introduction of the new system without disabling the old system.[31] Each of these strategies creates certain difficulties for achieving complete implementation. The proper strategy or combination of strategies for a given organization depends on the project, the amount of risk the organization can tolerate, the budget, characteristics of the target users, and the culture of the organization.

Direct Cut-over. The **direct cut-over** strategy describes the replacement of the old with the new system overnight, over a weekend, or over some other period when the company does not operate. Theoretically, a direct cut-over from one system to another can be performed almost instantaneously. A direct cut-over requires that the new system has the data that it needs to run. Transferring data from the old to the new system poses one of the major challenges of the direct cut-over approach. Programmers should write utility programs during the development stage to transfer data from the old system to the new. They should test these programs well in advance of implementation to ensure that the programs work properly. The cut-over period, when neither system is in use, involves the automatic transfer of data from the old to the new system. Performing such a data transfer on a large system and confirming that the data are properly transferred usually take many hours but can generally be completed over a weekend.

Companies that operate continuously or almost continuously experience difficulties in using the direct cut-over approach. One or two days before implementation, data transfer from a backup of the old system to the new system occurs. Then transaction logs from the old system are fed into the new system. The new system should process these transaction logs as fast as or faster than the old system originally processed the transactions. When the new system has processed these logs, the almost instantaneous switch of processing from the old to the new system can occur. Another approach is to keep old files on line and access them as needed.[32] This approach, however, requires development of code for the new system that will not be used shortly after the cut-over is complete.

The direct cut-over approach has the lowest cost but the highest risks of the four implementation strategies. Organizations such as Midwest Family Services might use this approach if they willingly trade reduced cost for high risk. No amount of alpha testing can negate the risk that the system might operate improperly or fail completely. Having the new system maintain a transaction log that can update the old system and return it to action if necessary can reduce this risk. Using such a backup does not eliminate the risk completely because improper processing might not appear until it has affected business transactions in a way that harms the business. For example, if the new system fails to generate invoices for certain products or services, the company might not notice this defect until its cash flow deteriorates.

The direct cut-over strategy may also result in employees who lack sufficient training to use the new system properly. Although employees receive training in the new system before the cut-over date, no employee will have used the system for an extended period, and no one can act as an expert to assist users who have trouble with the new system. In addition, user dissatisfaction may not surface immediately; experiencing difficulty in retrieving information for customers may affect the business only after longer-term use of the system; returning to the old system then may be difficult or impossible.

Pilot Implementation. A **pilot implementation** strategy, often called **beta testing,** requires one or more segments of the company to use the new system before the entire company uses it. For example, the Los Angeles office of a company with 20 regional offices may beta test the system. Such a pilot implementation reduces risk by limiting exposure to a small fraction of the business. This limited implementation does not eliminate risk because even a few costly mistakes in a small branch of an organization can harm the organization's overall performance. Also, even if a new system works properly in one part of the organization, it may not function properly when the entire organization uses it. The increased load on the system, for example, might slow response time to an unacceptable level.

Implementing a pilot system increases the cost of a cut-over. Particular difficulties arise in dealing with transactions that cross the boundary between the old and new systems. For example, what happens to an order placed in Los Angeles using the new system for a customer in New York using the old system? What happens if the Los Angeles office wants to serve its customer by pulling from New York's inventory? Systems developers must address questions such as these before implementation by building potentially costly programs that allow the old system to access the new system's data and vice versa.

Phased Implementation. A **phased implementation** introduces components of the new system one at a time. For example, the organization implements the accounts payable portion of an accounting system before it implements the rest of the system. Midwest Family Services could easily introduce its new system using this strategy. Phased implementation reduces risk by limiting exposure to the new system—users can slowly become accustomed to it. However, the cost of building interfaces to deal with transactions that cross the boundary between the new and old systems becomes a problem, particularly as the number of phases increases. Practitioners can reduce the cost of the phased strategy by combining it with parallel implementation.

Parallel Implementation. A **parallel implementation** strategy refers to the use of both the new and the old system for a period of time. The parallel implementation essentially eliminates the risk of failure because ongoing comparisons of the results of the two systems identify inaccuracies. Parallel implementation remains infeasible where employees lack the time to use both systems or when the cost in employee time of using two systems becomes excessive. Midwest Family Services could use this approach, although doing so may require too much employee time.

Managing Risk

Employing quality measures throughout previous stages of the SDLC and paying particular attention to training can reduce the major risks of implementation. To achieve high quality, users and their managers must involve themselves in system design from the outset, demand that designs meet their needs, and ensure that they have a forum to communicate their expertise regarding the processes they perform. High quality also requires a rigorous testing program that detects design or development errors early, thereby preventing a defective system from reaching the implementation stage.

Training ensures that employees have the proper skills to make the new system work. Even the best system can fail if employees cannot use it properly and efficiently. Training should occur both before and after implementation. Preimplementation training prepares users to use the features they need and deal with exceptional conditions. Postimplementation training focuses on using the system efficiently.

Maintenance and Postimplementation Review

Maintenance refers to making corrections to software that does not operate properly and adding features to systems in response to user demands. **Postimplementation review** refers to evaluating how well the system meets user needs, setting priorities for new development, and determining when to reinitiate a needs analysis. Maintenance and postimplementation activities typically occupy between 80 and 90 percent of IS professionals' time.[33]

Maintenance

Maintenance is a continuous-improvement activity that initially consists of correcting bugs in the system. Bugs almost always exist and may even appear after a system has operated for several years because testers cannot foresee all possible contingencies that might arise in using the system. Bugs may result from improper development or improper specification during the design phase of the SDLC. Recently developed automated testing software has successfully reduced the number of bugs.[34] Increasingly, programmers attempt to create maintenance-free software.[35]

Users also tend to discover new needs after a system has been in use for several months. These needs may arise from changes in the nature of the business or changes in the environment. For example, the company may develop a new product having sales data or post-sales data needs that differ from those for other products. Or, a competitor may launch a new program, such as a frequent-buyer discount or extended warranty program, that the company must emulate but that requires data not captured by the existing system, reports not currently generated, or even new operating procedures. Ensuring that the information system responds to such needs generally does not require completely redesigning or rebuilding the system.

Once users assimilate the process improvements supported by the new system, they begin to realize that the wishes they expressed in the needs-analysis phase were too limited. They now propose changes to make the system more usable; allow managers to make better, faster, and more informed decisions; or improve the workflow of employees using the system. These users, together with IS professionals, must evaluate each change on the basis of its costs and benefits. Those changes judged worthwhile will require redesigning and reprogramming as part of maintaining the system.

Modifying the system and not introducing new bugs poses a significant challenge. Any changes in complex systems are likely to produce side effects. Following the SDLC should minimize and document the interactions among different parts of the system, thereby reducing the likelihood and scope of side effects. Maintenance remains problematic because some interactions are unavoidable and because documentation may not always be complete. As more maintenance is performed on a system, the likelihood of new bugs increases, and the accuracy of the system's documentation decreases.

Business managers should be aware of the political pressures facing the IS staff during the maintenance phase as they vie among themselves to have their needs addressed. Because IS managers view end users as their customers, they often find refusing end-user requests difficult. Limits on IS resources mean that accepting too many projects places too few resources on each, resulting in delivery delays, an overworked and demoralized staff, and poor product quality. Forming steering committees composed of end-user managers and IS professionals who rank projects and allocate additional resources to the IS staff can help overcome the dilemmas of choosing among projects.[36] In the absence of such committees, managers should internally justify their maintenance requests before acting on them. One study of 500 companies in the United States reported that approximately one-half of all software maintenance projects requested by users and managers had no business value.[37]

Postimplementation Review

The first postimplementation review should occur several months after a new system's release. This first review should audit the SDLC process: The IS staff and the users who were involved in the needs analysis and design stages should reconvene to examine any flaws in the final product, determine their causes, and modify the systems development process to prevent such mistakes in the future.[38] This committee should also identify any remaining changes necessary to rectify the most major problems.

Subsequent system reviews should focus on establishing priorities for maintenance and determining whether the cycle should be restarted with a complete needs analysis. An effective redesign strategy is proactive and attempts to implement changes before the system reaches capacity or experiences other major problems.[39] Post-implementation review, like system maintenance, is an ongoing process involving both IS professionals and end users.

Why Systems Fail

Extensive research has attempted to explain the abandonment of some systems before completion and the late or over-budget completion of others. Large-scale systems development poses a major challenge to organizations, even those with extensive IS experience. For example, Citicorp, a sophisticated technology leader that spends an estimated $1.5 billion a year on its computer systems, was forced to abandon its MortgagePower Plus project for techni-

CITICORP

cal and business reasons after three years and a significant investment in time and money. The project was intended to approve and grant a mortgage loan in 15 minutes. In practice, mortgage brokers and real-estate agents struggled to even connect to the system, and once connected usually had to wait several hours for a reply. Furthermore, the system rejected loans it should have approved and approved loans it should have rejected.[40] The London Stock Exchange spent an estimated 400 million pounds ($575 million) to develop a product called Taurus that was to have been a paperless system for settling security trades within three days. The project was scrapped on March 11, 1993, after six years in development and numerous delays and missed deadlines, when market participants and outside experts testing the software concluded that the project would take at least two more years, require much more funding, and not meet many of the original specifications.[41]

London Stock Exchange

A recent survey of IS problems in federal projects by the U.S. General Accounting Office indicated ten problem areas shown in Figure 13-8. Too often IS professionals or other managers involved in systems development do not recognize systems development as a bona fide organizational change.[42] Lack of user involvement can lead to systems that do not fully meet user needs, resulting in multiple redesigns and even user antipathy and sabotage.[43] Lack of top management involvement and support can result in the development of systems that fail to anticipate the long-term needs of the organization and that conflict with strategic organizational goals.[44] Lack of congruence between the system development methodology and the culture of the organization can result in political problems, false risk assessment, and a lack of congruence between the system developed and the organization's needs.[45] Incorrect estimation or inadequate tracking of time or budget can lead to IS staff fatigue, late and over-budget delivery, quality problems, and the development of unnecessary or overly costly features.[46]

Another common problem is that requirements change after development has begun. Sometimes these changes arise from alterations in the business environment, but more commonly they are caused by a poor initial needs analysis, poor communication among developers and users, and the failure of users to become involved at the earliest stages of the SDLC. Unless management denies new user requests during the development phase or delays

After spending more than 400 million British pounds on development of a paperless system to settle trades, the London Stock Exchange, shown here, scrapped the project. Cost overruns and inadequate performance are common problems for projects that are not carefully managed.

Wide World Photos, Inc.

Problems in U.S. Government IS Projects

In a recent summary of its findings during a 32-month period, the GAO said federal IS problems stem from the following 10 problem areas:

Inadequate management of IS life cycle (66 citations). In 1990, the GAO cited poor capacity planning as the reason it believed the Federal Aviation Administration's new computers planned for the Los Angeles area might not be able to handle the work load there.

Ineffective oversight of information resources management (29 citations). Because of poor system procedures, the U.S. Department of Education gave $109 million in new student loans to students who had defaulted on earlier loans.

Security, integrity, and reliability flaws (16 citations). Because access control at a sensitive data center was inadequate, and software that could bypass security safeguards was easily available, the U.S. Department of Justice could not ensure the security of highly classified information, such as names of informants and undercover agents.

Inability of systems to work together (14 citations). Because key systems at the VA could not exchange data, clients faced lengthy delays having claims processed.

Inadequate resources to accomplish goals (9 citations). The U.S. Navy put together an ambitious schedule for developing software for a submarine target detection system. The schedule assumed the use of experienced Ada programmers, but the contractor doing the work had an inadequate Ada training program.

Cost overruns (22 citations). The GAO unearthed $7 billion in cost overruns, including an $800 million increase in the IRS's estimated cost to automate the examination of tax returns.

Schedule delays (20 citations). By 1994, the Navy will have spent 17 years developing a system to automate the preparation and editing of payroll and personnel documents. The system was originally due for completion in 1982.

Systems not performing as intended (7 citations). Problems in the 1988 tax filing season stemmed from an imaging subsystem that did not work, forcing IRS workers to use stopgap measures with paper copies of returns.

Inaccurate or incomplete data (18 citations). NASA had incomplete or missing data from many important space missions. No data from one Apollo mission could be found.

Difficult access to data (8 citations). The U.S. Coast Guard's major law enforcement system was so difficult to use that it was essentially ignored.

Source: Reprinted with permission from Gary H. Anthes, Why Uncle Sam can't compute, *Computerworld* (May 18, 1992): 20.

action on them until the maintenance phase, projects are likely to run significantly over budget and behind schedule.[47]

Methodologies and CASE Workbenches

In this chapter we have focused on a single **systems development methodology,** the SDLC. Most IS professionals use variants of the traditional SDLC or rapid application development prototyping for developing new information systems. Others, however, use substantially different methodologies, such as the Yourdon Structured Method, Structured Systems Analysis and Design Methodology, Effective Technical and Human Implementation of Computer Systems, Advanced Systems Development Methodology, and Object-Oriented Systems Design.[48] Proponents of different methodologies usually develop software tools and training materials so that others can easily apply the methodologies they support. As of 1992, more than 100 commercial methodologies existed.[49] In addition, many companies have created their own methodologies for internal use. Often other companies adopt such internal

ISRAELI MINISTRY OF FINANCE

methodologies even without supporting software or materials. For example, the Israeli Ministry of Finance developed the System Engineering Framework (SEFR) methodology when it found that traditional methodologies put so much focus on software-development processes that the end product suffered. Other businesses in Israel, including a major bank, a power company, and a construction company, subsequently adopted the SEFR methodology, which focuses on the system to be produced rather than the process for producing it.[50]

Usually a company selects a single systems development methodology to use for all its information systems projects. Through the late 1980s, organizations made choices based on their past experiences, the recommendation of consultants, and the availability of tools to assist in the process. As the number of methodologies has grown, companies increasingly devote time and effort to evaluating alternative methodologies. Current thinking suggests that the choice of methodology should depend upon the characteristics of the project or the phases of the systems development life cycle.[51]

Computer-aided software engineering, CASE, describes the use of software tools that apply either a given methodology or support multiple methodologies (see Chapter 5). A **CASE workbench** is a single software package that provides a set of CASE tools for addressing a significant part of or an entire systems development methodology. Figure 13-9 identifies the primary application areas of commercial CASE workbenches. CASE workbenches provide a consistent interface among the various CASE tools in the package, a smooth transition for moving among tools as they follow one or more methodologies, and a common database of information about the project under development. In addition, they provide consistent and cross-referenced documentation of user needs, application processes, data flow and structure, and software design. Shell Oil Company found that the documentation features of KnowledgeWare's CASE workbench allowed Shell to keep its documentation current with rapidly changing software code. In addition, once the programs were complete, preliminary documentation was also complete.[52] System methodologies and CASE tools facilitate the development of systems that respond to users' needs in a cost-effective, timely, and technologically current fashion.

SHELL OIL

Summary

The systems development life cycle (SDLC) refers to the analysis of user needs and the selection, design, development, implementation, and maintenance of application systems to meet these needs. It provides a systematic way for managing the development of computer systems, although other methodologies exist. Experienced managers know that applications

Primary Application Areas of Case Workbenches

Business planning and modeling	Verification and validation
Analysis and design	Maintenance and reverse engineering
User interface development	Configuration management
Programming	Project management

SOURCE: Alfonso Fuggetta, A classification of CASE technology, *IEEE Computer* (December 1993): 25–38. Excerpted from Figure 2, p. 32.

systems undergo regular transformation and updating to meet the changing needs of users. Rapid prototyping can condense the SDLC to allow replacement or modification of existing systems to proceed more quickly.

Needs analysis begins the SDLC. End users, their managers, and IS professionals analyze current systems and document users' needs as completely and accurately as possible. IS professionals and other organizational members involved with development collect information about inputs, outputs, and procedures as part of the needs analysis. Systems analysts often serve as liaisons between the IS department and the users to facilitate the complete identification of needs. Needs analysts use interviews, on-site observation, questionnaires, structured analysis, data dictionaries, and reverse engineering to assist with their data collection.

The second stage of the SDLC, assessing and defining alternatives, focuses on specifying and evaluating various options for the system and tentatively selecting a single system. Such selection involves both cost/benefit analyses and risk analyses.

Designing the new system follows. This stage provides detailed specification for the selected system design. Components include the interface design, data design, process design, and physical design of the system. Tools that support such design include data-flow diagrams, structure charts, screen generators, report generators, and code generators. Design specification includes the tools for communicating the design to the programmers who will write the required computer code.

Development, the fourth stage of the SDLC, focuses on procuring hardware, procuring or developing software, and testing the system. IS professionals and system users must determine whether to purchase or develop the new system; this decision has implications for the purchase of hardware and software. IS professionals also select the database management system, as well as the languages for systems development, as part of the development stage. Development also includes quality control, that is, implementing a plan for testing the new system. Such testing involves unit testing, string testing, integration testing, and/or system testing.

Organizations then implement the new system using one or a combination of four strategies. Direct cut-over involves the overnight replacement of one system by another. Pilot implementation means replacing the system for a targeted population in the organization and increasing that target over time. Phased implementation means introducing each component of the system individually and sequentially. Parallel implementation refers to the introduction of the new system without disabling the old system.

Maintenance and postimplementation review conclude the SDLC. These activities involve finding and correcting bugs in the system and introducing required process improvements. CASE workbenches support the application of the SDLC or other methodologies used in systems development.

Key Terms

Alpha testing
Alternative analysis
Beta testing
Bug
Computer-aided software engineering (CASE)
CASE workbench
Code generator
Content
Contextual inquiry
Cycle
Data design
Data dictionary
Data-flow diagram (DFD)
Design
Design specification
Development
Direct cut-over
Form
Homonym
Implementation
Input analysis
Integration testing
Interface design
Maintenance

Needs analysis
Output analysis
Parallel implementation
Performance testing
Phased implementation
Physical design
Pilot implementation
Postimplementation review
Procedure analysis
Process design
Quality control
Rapid application development (RAD)
Rapid prototyping
Report generator
Requirements analysis
Reverse engineering
Risk analysis
Screen generator
String testing
Structure chart
Structured analysis
Synonym
System testing
Systems analyst
Systems development life cycle (SDLC)
Systems development methodology
Testing plan
Turn-key system
Unit testing
Usability lab
Usability testing

Review Questions

1. Identify and describe the stages in the systems development life cycle.
2. Why do systems have a limited life?
3. What is rapid prototyping, and why does it shorten the systems development life cycle?
4. Identify the advantages and disadvantages of rapid prototyping relative to the conventional software development process.
5. What distinguishes the activities that take place in the needs analysis phase of the SDLC from those in the maintenance phase?
6. What is output analysis? How do systems analysts and business managers perform an output analysis?
7. Specify four ways of collecting information for a requirements analysis.
8. What are the advantages and disadvantages of on-site observation relative to interviews as a technique for collecting information about how users perform their work?
9. Describe the techniques analysts can use to evaluate alternative designs.
10. What characteristics of a system do analysts define during the interface design?
11. What characteristics of a system do analysts define during the data design?
12. What is the role of the business manager in the process design of a new system?
13. Identify and describe five tools used during the design phase of the SDLC.
14. Identify four key decisions in the development stage of the systems development life cycle.
15. Identify and describe four types of testing for the quality of newly developed systems.
16. Describe a typical usability lab.
17. What are the advantages and disadvantages of a phased implementation relative to a direct cut-over approach?
18. Which implementation approach carries the least risk? Which carries the most?
19. What measures can managers take to reduce risk in implementing new systems?
20. Why do information systems need to be maintained?
21. Identify two challenges that exist in managing maintenance, and describe how these challenges may be addressed.
22. Identify four reasons why systems fail.
23. What advantages do CASE workbenches provide to software developers and managers during the phases of the SDLC?

MINICASE

Systems Development at Lend Lease Trucks, Inc.

There's a mystique about the trucking business. The open road calls independent men and women who drive America's highways fueled with coffee to keep going day after day, hour after hour.

But that image may not be accurate. In reality, a good part of the trucking business is technology-intensive. At Lend Lease Trucks, Inc., a $200 million national truck leasing company based in Minneapolis, the wheels could have ground to a halt this spring.

In 1992, when Lend Lease found out it had just six months to go off a mainframe system, install a new computer system customized for their business and convert all data—including thousands of contracts and vehicle records—they were more than worried. They thought they might be gearing up for one of the most deflated years in their history.

Lend Lease had been caught in a complicated web of business deals. First, they had been spun off from their parent company, National Car Rental (NCR) a few years before and NCR had agreed to honor their information processing contract. Second, NCR outsourced its processing including that for Lend Lease to another company which wasn't interested in handling Lend Lease's processing beyond the next six months.

This unfortunate chain of events placed Lend Lease, and its information services consultant, Information Solutions Group (ISG) of Minneapolis, under the gun to transfer all processing to their own system. They had a challenge they thought might be insurmountable.

"The conversion window was so short, the odds of success were stacked against us, but we felt we had to try. We couldn't stand by and watch a client in trouble and not try," says ISG President Wayne Carlson.

Billing Makes the Wheels Go Round

To understand the crucial place of IS in truck leasing, you need to know a little about how the business runs. Trucking is somewhat of a commodity business. Lend Lease Trucks competes with the biggest trucking lessors in business: Ryder, Ruan, and Penske to name a few. For dedicated trucking services, like moving and storage companies which frequently lease trucks, a truck is a truck, with a few minor exceptions. So price is a primary consideration for lessors.

Then how do trucking services like Lend Lease break the tie with other companies? The answer is servicing their customers' needs through flexible pricing, including special extras like diesel fuel, which Lend Lease sells at a discount to customers, and individualized contracts for mileage, usage, and maintenance. The ability to offer individualized extras and flexible billing to meet a company's particular needs is tantamount to success.

Choosing to Right-size

Though they were facing a very real deadline, Lend Lease simply didn't want to transfer data to another system like the one they had. They wanted to install a new system that would meet their primary business goal: improved customer service. The old mainframe hadn't been

---

Extracted from Elizabeth Child, High-speed teams get Lend Lease trucks rolling, *Journal of Systems Management* (January 1994): 18–21.

efficient. First, there had been little flexibility in the billing system. Second, outsourcing their processing was financially draining: it had cost $120,000 a month. Third, the information Lend Lease needed to run its business was inaccessible on a timely basis. If customers wanted to look at their contractual arrangements on-line, they couldn't. If Lend Lease wanted to find their clients' financial position—for example, the value of leased vehicles, how much was owed and how much had been paid to date—they couldn't. At least not right away, because there was always a backlog of requests for information in the centralized IS department.

In addition, the Lend Lease mainframe system had been transaction-based. It emphasized data storage over data retrieval and analysis. All on-line data was entered by a group of data processors in South Bend, Indiana. So, 60 Lend Lease offices around the country reported their data to the center daily and it was batch-processed overnight. Most account information was available only at month-end when billing was done.

There were other problems with the system, too. Lack of editing and processing integrity resulted in hundreds of erroneous bills generated each month. This meant that payments to Lend Lease were delayed and customers were often frustrated with the errors. Billing errors can cause cash flow problems within truck leasing companies, because vehicles leased are paid for in advance by a truck leasing company.

The Lend Lease Challenge

Based on the new goals established for the system, ISG was to select and install a new processing platform, develop and or purchase application software, document, test, train, and install the applications. The process was complicated by the fact that no billing software packages on the market even closely resembled Lend Lease's requirements.

On the Fast-Tracks

After determining requirements for the system, the most crucial decision made early on was to use "parallel tracks," trusted teams working simultaneously to downsize areas while fitting them into a model that was being created at the same time.

ISG pioneered the use of track management as a part of an IS methodology, borrowing "parallel tasking" from the scientific community. Parallel tasking was employed for the Manhattan Project to create the first nuclear bomb during World War II, for the Moon Shot in the late 1960s and many more major projects with seemingly impossible deadlines. It tends to produce synergistic, focused teams partly because they are working toward a goal, and partly because they are working against a common enemy: Time.

The tracks designated for Lend Lease were:

- Technology
- Billing Applications
- Financial Applications
- Data Conversion
- Support Services

The Core Team

Developing effective teams for each track was the next key factor for Lend Lease. "I know of no activity in the course of a project's life, which is so important and done so haphazardly as putting together the project team," says Carlson. "Our basic belief is that 'smaller is better.' A small team of skilled, knowledgeable motivated persons will out-perform a larger team of lesser qualified persons by a geometric factor."

The majority of the project teams were made up of management and operational users from Lend Lease. They were people who would be using the system once it was installed.

And they were creative thinkers with a really clear idea of what needed to be done in their work environment, as well. They didn't necessarily know all of the details about how the old systems operated, but they knew what they could and couldn't do, and they knew what information they needed to improve their job performance.

"In"-sourcing

Aside from important in-house team members, project teams were composed of analysts and programmers from outside the company. Naturally, the number of outside consultants and contractors used in any project depends on the availability of required skills, experience and objectivity in-house. Given that technologies and development processes planned for Lend Lease's downsizing were new to the company—and to most IS people—outside resources were brought in until in-house IS staff could be trained.

In fact, ISG's development methodology uses the project as a technology transfer mechanism to build in-house resource capabilities.

Selecting Track Managers

The Track Manager is the engineer on the train, making sure that a full head of steam is maintained at all times and that each destination is reached at the right time. Track Managers can be from the consulting organization or the client organization but need to possess leadership and problem solving skills and be strong communicators.

The Technology Track

Track number one, the technology track, was responsible for assisting in selecting the 20 components of the processing platform, installing and testing of the hardware, systems software, and network components, technical training and backup and recovery procedures, and general technical support.

To create an effective technology track, Lend Lease needed an expert in new technologies—someone who had installed, managed and maintained the processing platform components that were under consideration. In this case, an entire company was chosen: Connect Computer Company from Minneapolis. Connect Computer interfaced components from a dozen or more different vendors which comprised the new Lend Lease platform. To save time and disruption from other activities, one set of all hardware and network components was installed and tested at Connect Computer before installing any components at Lend Lease.

Billing and Financial Tracks

The billing and financial applications are the cornerstone of Lend Lease's system. A customized application for billing was developed because of Lend Lease's unique billing requirements. But financial applications were purchased packages. Barbara Hoganson was the financial track manager. Besides being a CPA, Barbara was knowledgeable in existing financial software and helped the financial team select and install the Concepts Dynamics Inc. financial software package.

The billing and financial applications had to be separate, but in constant communication. The billing system was to describe vehicles and customers and their individualized contracts for leasing vehicles. All financial transactions had to be communicated to the new system. As changes in accounts payable and accounts receivable occur, they must be communicated to the billing function so records are up-to-date.

Systems Migration, Inc., a Twin Cities-based company that specializes in development of distributed and downsized platforms, was brought in to help customize the billing system because of their skills in developing systems using the Informix 4GL programming language and relational database management system. They produced the billing system programs more than 10 times faster than the original programs had been developed.

Conversion Track

Conversion meant taking all of Lend Lease's data off of the NCR systems where it had been stored in batch-processing format (hierarchical organizations) and putting it into relational tables on the new system where it could be accessed by users on a real-time basis.

An inability to make the conversion work the first time around, with no glitches, would have created extreme financial pressures on Lend Lease. It all had to work like clockwork. And in the old system there had been no data models and no up-to-date system documentation. Meanwhile, thousands of data elements had been stored redundantly.

Target tables on the new system were defined simultaneously, so, even though the extract programs were defined, the output format for numerous extracts had to wait until the upload programs were constructed before the conversion could be completed. As a result of the severity of the tight time table the initial billing had to go out the same day the new programs were uploaded.

Support Track

There's a time in every project when the consultants should go home. At least most of them. ISG vice-president Gary Eads was to stay on for a period of time after the conversion to smooth any bumps out of the new system, but the goal for Lend Lease was to have a system it could run itself. So a support track was created to train a group of Lend Lease staff members to troubleshoot and help other users support the new systems. This track was composed of staff members from billing, finance and other operating departments. Early on, the team also established the "help desk" concept, along with local and remote maintenance procedures, and problem identification, tracking and solution procedures. They also established procedures for microfilming and microfiching system transactions and data.

Accelerating a High-Speed Chase

Several additional decisions helped speed the process of development over six months, including a "RAD" Rapid Application Development approach. A textbook approach wouldn't have worked in the time allotted. That would have required the following steps: 1) requirements definition, 2) process flows, 3) data table layouts, 4) screen layouts, 5) creation of programming specifications, 6) program construction, 7) testing and 8) writing user documentation. In addition, a data model for application construction would have usually been constructed at the outset.

Instead, while steps one to four above were carried out sequentially, user documentation and processing specifications were developed simultaneously. The user documentation was written extremely thoroughly so it could replace the processing documentation. As applications were developed, they were also tested. Eads calculates that application development time was reduced by about 50 percent by merging tasks, and by having users sit down with the developers and jointly create those screens which would best help the users to do their daily work. "We were able to hold down development costs, reduce opportunities for failure by reducing processing time and remaining fully focused on the task at hand," says Eads.

Other time-frame accelerators included the availability of electronic and voice mail systems, ensuring that project team members had access to home computers which were also linked to the process or, at work, readily available secretarial support and any other support that could reduce administrative activity by project personnel. Making notebook computers available to some team members so they could perform processing activities at the same speed at work, home, or often times in transit, also provided significant benefits.

Case Questions

1. Why did Lend Lease Trucks have to build new systems rapidly?
2. What is the meaning of "parallel tasking"? How, if at all, does the parallel tasking approach used by Lend Lease Trucks differ from the conventional SDLC?
3. In what ways might Lend Lease's tight deadline have hurt the development effort? In what ways might it have helped?
4. How did Lend Lease determine which tasks were best outsourced and which were best done in-house?
5. What do you think are the risks and potential rewards to Lend Lease's development methodology?

Requirements Analysis for the Ridgeway Company

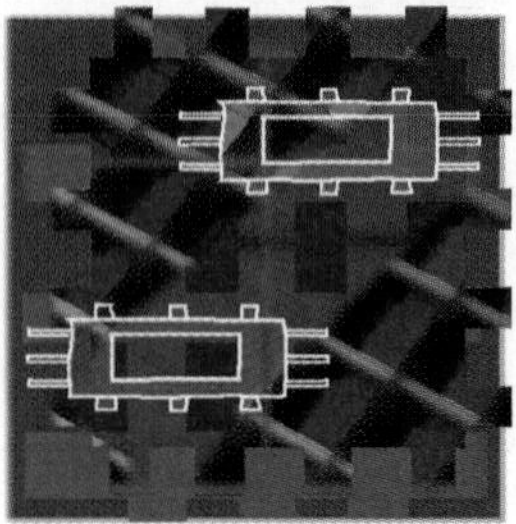

short case

STEP 1: Read the following scenario.

Ridgeway Company, whose main business is the purchase and development of recreational land, has successfully managed the Ridgeway Country Club for the past three years. When they originally acquired the club, it had 20 lighted tennis courts, an 18-hole golf course, a swimming pool, a pro shop selling tennis and golfing supplies and related items, and a clubhouse containing a restaurant, bar, and exercise room.

Over the past two years Ridgeway Company has expanded the facility by adding a second 18-hole golf course, a second swimming pool, and 20 more lighted tennis courts. Ridgeway Company has completed the construction of the first ten condominiums as part of a ten-year plan to build a total of 60 on the property. The facility sits on the shores of a lake, so Ridgeway recently changed the name of the club to the Blue Waters Country Club.

Memberships at the facility are limited to 2,000 full members with unlimited privileges and 1,000 social members who are permitted use of the clubhouse and swimming pools only. There is a waiting list for both types of memberships. A full member buys a share in the club. Each member pays monthly dues: $150 for a full member, and $50 for a social member. Thomas McGee, vice-president of operations, manages the club's operations.

Ridgeway management has funded a project to develop a new membership billing system for the Blue Waters Country Club.

STEP 2: Individually or in small groups, prepare a requirements analysis for the new membership billing system.

STEP 3: In small groups or with the entire class, share your requirements analyses. What elements do the analyses share? How do they differ?

SOURCE: Reproduced from Gary B. Shelly, Thomas J. Cashman, Judy Adamski, and Joseph J. Adamski, *Systems Analysis and Design* Copyright 1991 by boyd & fraser publishing company. All rights reserved.

STEP 4: In small groups or with the entire class, answer the following questions:

1. What are the key components of the requirements analysis?
2. What is the best way to determine the requirements of the Ridgeway Company?
3. What are the major requirements of the new membership billing system? ●

Activity 13-2 Systems Analyst Hiring at Vailton College

role play

STEP 1: Your instructor will divide you into five groups; one group will represent the Registration Redesign Committee (RRC) at Vailton College and the others, competing systems analyst candidates.

STEP 2: Read the following scenario.

Vailton College is a small but well-respected business school located in the southeastern United States. Six years ago, the college computerized its class registration process. Nevertheless, much of the process remains manual and cumbersome. Students have complained, year after year, about waiting in line to register, having to re-register after being closed out of their selected classes, and having to make frequent trips to the registrar's office during the drop–add period. Faculty have complained about the length of time it takes before they receive final class rosters. The computer system also allows students to register for classes for which they do not have the necessary prerequisites; although students are supposed to have their registration plans approved by their faculty advisor in advance of registration, and faculty are supposed to check prerequisites, this process has not eliminated the problem and other similar ones associated with students not completing their requirements. The president of the college has commissioned a committee of faculty members, staff from the registrar's office, and staff from the information systems division (the technical group that runs the college's computer systems) to redesign the registration process and the information systems that support it. The committee has developed a broad outline of a new telephone-based registration system and must now design the information systems to support it. Their current task is to hire a systems analyst to coordinate the project. After an initial screening, the committee has narrowed the search to the following four candidates:

Gene/Jean Smith: A 54-year-old systems manager who has recently been laid off from Digital Equipment Corporation (DEC) when the division he/she worked for was closed. Smith's background includes more than 30 years of systems development work at DEC, exclusively in the DEC environment. Smith has dealt with many different DEC products, customers, and their needs. Although Smith has never previously been at Vailton, he/she is thoroughly familiar with Vailton's current DEC computer equipment.

Bobbie/Bobby Jones: A 23-year-old Vailton graduate with a recent MBA, an undergraduate major in MIS at Vailton, and limited work experience. Jones is currently self-employed as an IS consultant but is looking for more permanent employment in a small company. Having gone through the registration process at Vailton, Jones is familiar with it and agrees strongly with the need to revise it.

Pat McDonald: A 32-year-old former employee of Pacific Bell who has relocated near Vailton. At Pacific Bell, McDonald worked in the customer relations department and has experience dealing with customers and using computer systems. He/she enrolled in the part-time MBA program at Vailton upon returning to the area and was one of the people affected by problems with the current registration system. He/she has some wonderful ideas for improving the system.

Terry Wilson: A 38-year-old programmer for the Shawton Bank, the largest bank in the state. He/she learned programming at Georgia Tech in the late 1970s and has been a very reliable, well-liked, easy-to-get-along-with employee of Shawton ever since. The bank has recently undergone some restructuring and appears headed for further restructuring as the recession runs its course; Wilson is looking for a more stable environment. His/her programming skills are excellent in four languages: Fortran, COBOL, BASIC, and C. He/she feels that a college community would permit further enhancement of his/her skills and valuable opportunity for additional education.

STEP 3: If your group is assigned the role of one of the candidates, select one of your group members to represent your candidate in an interview. Prepare a short presentation for your candidate to explain why he/she is the best person for the job. Also anticipate the questions that the committee will ask and prepare your candidate to answer them in the most favorable light.

STEP 4: If your group is assigned the role of the RRC, prepare a job description for the systems analyst and a set of questions to ask each candidate.

STEP 5: The instructor will call each team's representative to present its case. Members of the RRC will sit at the front of the class and ask the prepared questions and any additional questions they may have after each candidate has presented his/her case. Please be advised that it is illegal to ask candidates about their personal lives and families.

STEP 6: The RRC will discuss the merits of the candidates in open executive session. The RRC will then vote on the four candidates.

STEP 7: With the entire class, answer the following questions:

1. What are the most desirable attributes of a candidate for the job of systems analyst?
2. In selecting an analyst for a project, which is more important: familiarity with the business process, or familiarity with the role of systems analyst? What are the pros and cons of each?
3. Did the RRC use appropriate criteria in selecting the candidate? ●

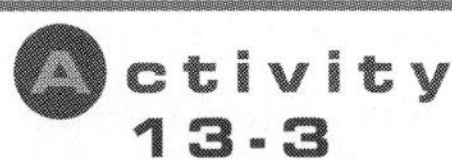

What Went Wrong?

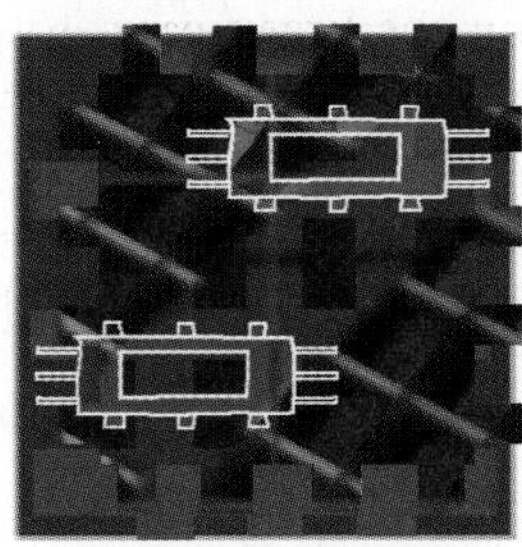

short case

STEP 1: Read the two cases below.

CASE 1: A SYSTEM FOR COMPUTER-ASSISTED DISPATCHING

A police car dispatching sequence typically begins with a call from a citizen for police assistance. The call is answered by a complaint evaluator, who selects one of four courses of action:

1. No need exists for a police response (e.g., caller requests the local town hall's address),
2. No need exists for a police response, but a police report is required (e.g., caller reports his car stolen),
3. A police response and a police report are required (e.g., crime is in progress), and
4. A police response but no police report is required (e.g., police involvement is limited to directing traffic in an emergency situation).

Only in the last two situations is a police car required, and the complaint evaluator places the request for assistance in a queue, where it awaits processing by the next available dispatcher.

Computer-assisted car dispatching (CAD) systems have been operating successfully for nearly 20 years. Thus, when the St. Louis Police Department required such a system, it was natural to look for standard off-the-shelf software that could operate on the department's mainframe. However, police departments differ in how they perform this day-to-day task. Additionally, police information systems, rather than being isolated entities, communicate and exchange data with regional and national information systems.

With these issues in mind, the department's database administrator, accompanied by several members of the police force, visited four cities with CAD systems similar in specifications to those needed in St. Louis. They selected a system in use in Kansas City because it used dispatching procedures in close agreement with those followed by St. Louis dispatching personnel. The only obstacles to implementing an exact duplicate of the Kansas City system in St. Louis were the dissimilar database systems of the two applications. The database administrator planned to bridge these differences by a partial rewrite of the software, which was not thought to affect the success of system implementation.

To ensure a smooth implementation, police personnel initially operated the modified system at approximately 20 percent of its intended capacity alongside the existing manual dispatching system. The entire cycle of dispatching a car requires information displayed on four different screens. In the modified system the dispatcher had to look at two screens at a time; thus, the completion of a dispatching task required alternating between screens. The time needed to alternate between screens was only a few seconds, but the St. Louis dispatchers considered this time to be much too long because it had the potential of placing police officers in undue jeopardy during crisis situations. Displaying all four screens simultaneously on one video display terminal, however, required significant changes in hardware and software.

SOURCES: Case 1—Reprinted with permission from Carl R. Ruthstrom and Charlene A. Dykman, *Information Systems for Managers Casebook* (St. Paul: West, 1992). Case 2—Reproduced from Gary B. Shelly, Thomas J. Cashman, Judy Adamski, and Joseph J. Adamski, *Systems Analysis and Design* Copyright 1991 by boyd & fraser publishing company.

CASE 2: GREEN PASTURES LIMITED

Kirby Ellington graduated with a two-year degree in microcomputer programming and worked as a programmer for three years at a large insurance company in Hartford, Connecticut. Kirby was responsible for maintenance programming on the company's credit insurance information system. He was competent in carrying out his duties, but he wanted to advance to a systems analyst position and did not feel this opportunity was forthcoming at the insurance company.

Kirby answered an ad that he saw in a computer periodical for a systems analyst position at Green Pastures Limited, located in Plattsburgh, New York. Kirby decided to add to his resume that he had a four-year degree in computer information systems and over two years experience as a systems analyst. When Green Pastures reviewed Kirby's resume, they were impressed with his bachelor's degree and systems analyst experience and flew him in for an interview.

During the interview Kirby communicated well and appeared to be knowledgeable about programming, microcomputer packages such as spreadsheets and word processors, and all the latest microcomputers on the market. This fit in well with Green Pastures' needs because they had only just started using computers in their business six months ago when three microcomputers were installed in their office headquarters. Because Green Pastures had no one with computer experience on their staff, they felt a systems analyst would be able to develop the specialized information systems they needed. Green Pastures offered Kirby a job as a systems analyst, and he accepted the offer.

Kirby initially did a great job at Green Pastures. He was able to help everyone with their spreadsheet and word processing problems and advised Green Pastures on the purchase of a data management package. Kirby next started to develop a billing information system. He had really enjoyed the C programming language when he was in school and decided to use this language for the billing system.

After four months of work, Kirby finished the billing system. The clerks at Green Pastures began using the system and encountered immediate problems. The clerks had difficulty understanding what they should do and when they should do it. Although there was no documentation or written directions for the system, Kirby was always available to help them out. The clerks spent one week entering data and making corrections to the data until all the input was correctly entered, and the time came to print the billing statements. The printing went well, and the statements were mailed out to customers.

Two days later Green Pastures began receiving calls from irate customers complaining about the errors in the billing statements they had just received. After a thorough review, they discovered that all the billing statements were wrong and would have to be redone manually.

STEP 2: Individually or in small groups, for each case, diagnose what went wrong in the systems development.

STEP 3: Individually or in small groups, propose a way of correcting the problems that occurred in the systems' development. ●

Notes

[1]Connie McCandless, Systems renovation, *Computerworld* (December 2, 1987): Focus 19–20.

[2]Ben Pitman, Technical and people sides of systems project start-up, *Journal of Systems Management* 42(4) (April 1991): 6–8.

[3]Lowell Jay Arthur, Quick & dirty, *Computerworld* (December 14, 1992): 109–110; Stuart L. Gavurin, Where does prototyping fit in IS development?, *Journal of Systems Management* 42(2) (February 1991): 13–17; David Baum, Go totally RAD and build apps faster, *Datamation* 38(19) (September 15, 1992): 79–81; and Alison Eastwood, RAD: Not an instant fix, *Computing Canada* 17(7) (August 15, 1991): 17–18.

[4]W. Burry Foss, Fast, faster, fastest, *Computerworld* (May 31, 1993): 81–83.

[5]Capers Jones, Sick software, *Computerworld* (December 13, 1993): 115–116.

[6]Susan Nykamp and Joseph Maglitta, Software speeder-uppers, *Computerworld* (August 26, 1991): 51–53, original data attributed to CSC Index, Inc.

[7]John G. Voltmer, Selling management on the prototyping approach, *Journal of Systems Management* 40(7) (July 1989): 24–25.

[8]See, for example, M. Telem, Information requirements specification I: Brainstorming collective decision-making approach, *Information Processing and Management* (1988): 549–557.

[9]Kenneth T. Fougere, The future role of the systems analyst as a change agent, *Journal of Systems Management* 42(11) (November 1991): 6–9.

[10]For a more complete list and description, see Terry A. Byrd, Kathy L. Cossick, and Robert W. Zmud, A synthesis of research on requirements analysis and knowledge acquisition techniques, *MIS Quarterly* (March 1992): 117–138.

[11]See K. Holtzblatt and S. Jones, Contextual inquiry: A participatory technique for system design, *Participatory Design: Principles and Practice*, A. Namioka and D. Schuler, Eds. (Hillsdale, NJ: Erlbaum, 1993).

[12]McCandless, op. cit.

[13]A sampling of justification methods, *Computerworld* (November 11, 1991): 85.

[14]Michiel Van Genuchten and Hans Koolen, On the use of software cost models, *Information & Management* 21 (August 1991): 37–44.

[15]See, for example, Capers Jones, *Applied Software Measurement* (New York: McGraw-Hill, 1991).

[16]Tom Koulopoulos, Getting technology you want and need, *Computerworld* (November 11, 1991): 83–84.

[17]See, for example, *Management and Design Division Colloquiums on Risk Analysis Methods and Tools* (London: Institution of Electrical Engineers, 1992).

[18]Gary H. Anthes, Slashing away at sacred cows, *Computerworld* (April 6, 1992): 115–116.

[19]Gary H. Anthes, No more creeps!, *Computerworld* (May 2, 1994): 107–110.

[20]Katie Crane, Meritor opens the integration door, *Computerworld* (February 4, 1991): 57, 64.

[21]David Baum, Brain strain, *Computerworld (Premier 100)* (September 13, 1993): 29–35.

[22]Gary H. Anthes, Triumph over a taxing project, *Computerworld* (November 4, 1991): 65, 69.

[23]Colleen Frye, With financial apps, DBMS support often drives the sale, *Software Magazine* (June 1994): 55–71.

[24]Jan Snyders, Make it quick, make it easy, *Infosystems* (February 1988): 36–45.

[25]Robin F. Goldsmith, Quality time, *Computerworld* (October 21, 1991): 119–121.

[26]Ellis Booker, Quality in IS: Managing with facts, not intuition, *Computerworld* (December 11, 1989): 97.

[27]Dennis H. O'Brien, Software quality starts with the customer, *Quality* (June 1991): 22–24.

[28]See, for example, Ned Snell, Quality tools for quality software, *Datamation* (January 1, 1992): 53–54.

[29]See Michael J. Prasse, Achieving better systems development through usability testing, *Journal of Systems Management* 42 (September 1991): 10–13.

[30]Alice Laplante, Put to the test, *Computerworld* (July 27, 1992): 75–80.

[31]Shailendra C. Palvia, Efrem G. Mallach, and Prashant C. Palvia, Strategies for converting from one IT environment to another, *Journal of Systems Management* 42(10) (October 1991): 23–27 discusses the relationship of these strategies to system size, timing, and target organization size.

[32]Merle P. Martin, The day-one systems changeover tactic, *Journal of Systems Management* 40 (October 1989): 12–14.

[33]Nykamp and Maglitta, op. cit.

[34]James Daly, Bug-free code: The competitive edge, *Computerworld* (February 17, 1992): 55.

[35]Steve Hearn, Zero! Zippo! Zilch! *Computerworld* (February 24, 1992): 87–88.

[36]John F. Barlow, Group decision making in computer project justification, *Journal of Systems Management* 42, (June 1991): 13–16, 37.

[37]Nykamp and Maglitta, op. cit.

[38]For postmortem analysis methodologies, see Tarek K. Abdel-Hamid and Stuart E. Madnick, The elusive silver lining: How we fail to learn from software development failures, *Sloan Management Review* (Fall 1990): 39–48; Ben Pitman, A systems analysis approach to reviewing completed projects, *Journal of Systems Management* 42 (December 1991): 6–9, 37; and John M. Nicholas, Successful project management: A force-field analysis, *Journal of Systems Management* 40 (January 1989): 24–30, 36.

[39]Ralph M. Stair, Jr., Using application redesign to maintain continuity and profitability, *Journal of Systems Management* 42(8) (August 1991): 32–35.

[40]When machines screw up, *Forbes* (June 7, 1993): 110–111.

[41]When the bull turned, *The Economist* (March 20, 1993): 81–82; and What is a stock exchange for? *The Economist* (March 13, 1993): 93.

[42]Albert L. Lederer and Raghu Nath, Managing organizational issues in information systems development, *Journal of Systems Management* 42(11) (November 1991): 23–27, 39.

[43]Robert S. Tripp, Managing the political and cultural aspects of large-scale MIS projects: A case study of participative systems development, *Information Resources Management Journal* (Fall 1991): 2–13.

[44]W. J. Doll, Avenues for top management involvement in successful MIS development, *MIS Quarterly* (Spring 1985): 17–35; M. L. Markus, Power, politics, and MIS implementation, *Communications of the ACM 26* (June 1983): 430–444; K. B. White and R. Leifer, Information systems development success: Perspectives from project team participants, *MIS Quarterly* (1986): 214–223; and Robert A. Rademacher, Critical factors for systems success, *Journal of Systems Management* 40 (June 1989): 15–17.

[45]Mo Adam Mahmood, Information systems implementation success: A causal analysis using the linear structural relations model, *Information Resources Management Journal* (Fall 1990): 2–14; Louise H. Jones and Christine T. Kydd, An information processing framework for understanding success and failure of MIS development methodologies, *Information & Management* 15 (December 1988): 263–271; and Terry Peterson, Death, taxes, and systems implementation problems, *Journal of Systems Management* 42 (October 1991): 18, 34.

[46]Jones, op. cit.

[47]Anthes, op. cit.

[48]E. Yourdon, *Modern Structured Analysis* (Englewood Cliffs, NJ: Prentice-Hall, 1989); G. Longworth, *Getting the System You Want: A Users Guide to SSADM* (Manchester, England: NCC Blackwell, 1988); E. Mumford, *Using Computers for Business Success: The ETHICS Method* (Manchester, England: Manchester Business School, 1986); John E. Jaakkola and Kalvin B. Drake, ASDM: The universal systems development methodology, *Journal of Systems Management* (February 1991): 6–11; and Ronald J. Norman, Object-oriented systems design: A progressive expansion of OOA, *Journal of Systems Management* (August 1991): 13–16.

[49]P. Hornby, C. W. Clegg, J. I. Robson, C. R. R. Maclaren, S. C. S. Richardson, and P. O'Brien, Human and organizational issues in information systems development, *Behavior & Information Technology* 11 (1992): 160–174.

[50]Asher Yuval and Dror Chevion, Build me a system, *Computerworld* (February 10, 1992): 93–95.

[51]Prashant Palvia and John T. Nosek, An empirical evaluation of system development methodologies, *Information Resources Management* (Summer 1990): 23–32; Timo Saarinen, System development methodology and project success: An assessment of situational approaches, *Information & Management* 19 (October 1990): 183–193; M. E. Louadi, Y. A. Pollalis, and J. T. C. Teng, Selecting a systems development methodology: A contingency framework, *Information Resources Management Journal* (Winter 1991): 11–19; and Hornby et al., op. cit.

[52]David Baum, Publishing tools easing chore of documentation development, *Client/Server Computing* (January 1994): 58–65.

Recommended Readings

Arthur, L. J. *Improving Software Quality: An Insider's Guide to TQM* (New York: Wiley and Sons, 1993).

Keller, M. and Shumate, K. *Software Specification and Design* (New York: Wiley and Sons, 1992).

Martin, J. and Odell, J. *Object-Oriented Analysis and Design* (Englewood Cliffs, NJ: Prentice-Hall, 1992).

Namioka, A. and Schuler, D., Eds. *Participatory Design: Principles and Practice* (Hillsdale, NJ: Erlbaum, 1993).

Sommerville, I. *Software Engineering* (Reading, MA: Addison-Wesley, 1992).

Wood, J. and Silver, D. *Joint Application Design* (New York: Wiley and Sons, 1989).

Chapter 14

The Information Systems Infrastructure

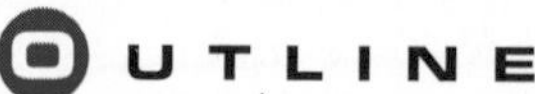

UTLINE

Information Systems at Brookstone

What Is the Information Systems Infrastructure?

Information Technology Architecture

- Standardization
- Right-sizing
- Architecture for the Global Organization

The Human Infrastructure

- Jobs in Information Systems
- Education and Training
- End-User Computing

Organization and Procedures

- Centralization versus Decentralization
- Outsourcing
- Accounting Issues
- Steering Committees
- Security

National and Global Infrastructures

- The Legal Environment
- Communication Infrastructure

LEARNING OBJECTIVES

After completing the reading and activities for Chapter 14, students will be able to

1. Define an organization's information systems infrastructure and identify its components.
2. Define an organization's information technology (IT) architecture and discuss the advantages and disadvantages of having an architecture.
3. Discuss the advantages and disadvantages of standardization in the IT architecture.
4. Illustrate the use of right-sizing for information systems.
5. Identify four issues that should be considered in selecting an architecture for a global organization.
6. Offer six examples of information systems jobs.
7. Describe the role of the help desk.
8. Cite the advantages and disadvantages of outsourcing of information systems services.
9. Discuss three options for accounting for information systems services.
10. Identify steps managers may take to provide security for their information and information systems.
11. Identify the major legal issues related to the use of information and information systems.

Brookstone (a specialty mail-order and retail firm) followed a somewhat unusual path to computerization—a cow path, to be exact. The company rented its first computer time from a local organization, the Guernsey Cattle Club, more than a decade ago.

But computer systems designed to track bovine life histories are not necessarily well suited to tracking product inventory, and finding ways to make such a system function has long been the work of Edward Stanley.

When Stanley started at Brookstone 11 years ago, the company was primarily oriented toward mail order. It took in $20 million in annual sales from the catalog and $4 million from retail sales.

That situation has reversed itself in recent years, however. Currently, only $15 million of the company's $100 million in sales is derived from the catalog. The rest comes from 97 stores nationwide.

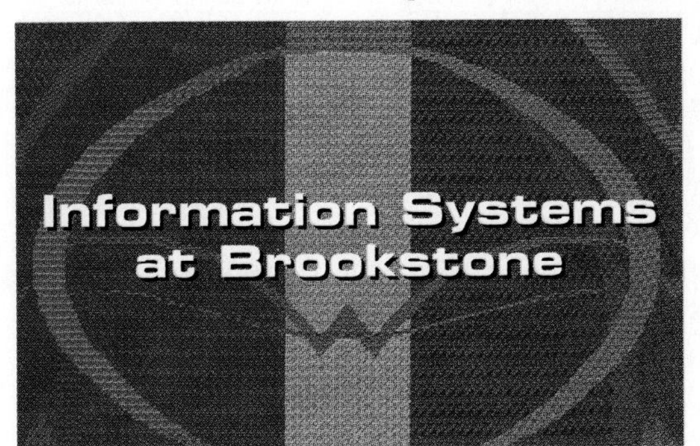

However, Brookstone's computer systems have long been pushing their limits. When the company moved from renting time from the Cattle Club to running its own system, the decision was made to hire away one of the club's programmers and buy an IBM 4381 rather than design a system from the ground up for sales.

"It was the easiest and quickest way," Stanley says. "the company was growing, and they didn't want to slow things down."

Brookstone paid a long-term price for the decision, however. Two years ago, the company decided to take serious action to head off what appeared to be an imminent systems collapse.

"We knew we were in tough times," Stanley says. "We knew we had to make some changes. We knew we had to survive a couple of Christmases." Those changes, including a "right-sizing" from the mainframe to an AS/400 (a minicomputer) for retail operations, will be taking place over the next year.[1]

Edward Stanley and other executives at Brookstone have determined that the current information systems do not meet the company's information needs. For example, inventory control associated with the mail-order business was not appropriate for inventory control at retail outlets. As Brookstone's software developers scrambled to meet changing needs, they had installed "four or five years of Band-Aids on top of [their mail-order systems]." To reduce spending from 1.2 percent of sales to an industry average 0.8 percent of sales, and to bring their merchandise systems to a state that could support their intended level of sales, Brookstone's executives decided to move their computer operations from a mainframe to a minicomputer and to eliminate custom software development, relying instead on off-the-shelf packages.[2]

The changes targeted for Brookstone's information systems are changes in infrastructure, the underlying structure or features of its systems. In this chapter we focus on four aspects of the IS infrastructure that are a key part of the implementation stage of the four-step managerial approach presented in this book. First, we explore the ways organizations develop a long-term plan, known as an architecture, for the technology components of their IS infrastructure. Second, we discuss ways companies utilize the human component of the infrastructure. Third, we focus on how the organizational and procedural infrastructure affects information systems, their use, and security. Finally, we examine how the systems and technology infrastructure of the country or countries in which an organization operates can affect its internal information systems and infrastructure.

What Is the Information Systems Infrastructure?

The IS **infrastructure** of an organization consists of 1) its hardware, software, and communication equipment; 2) its IS staff and related personnel; and 3) its organization and procedures that affect the use and processing of information. The IS infrastructure provides the foundation for an organization to manage its information and information systems.

One key feature of the infrastructure is that it is typically unwieldy and resistant to change. It represents an accumulation of investments in labor, equipment, software, and experience. These investments are organizational assets that need to be managed rather than discarded. As an organization grows or responds to a changing environment, elements of the infrastructure should change, but the infrastructure as a whole forms the base upon which change is anchored.

Information Technology Architecture

Information technology **architecture** describes the long-term structural plan for investing in and organizing information technology; it acts as the blueprint for the technology portion of an organization's information systems infrastructure. For example, the architecture for an advertising firm of 30 employees might involve networked PCs, each loaded with at least word-processing, presentation, and electronic mail software; future plans might include the addition of groupware and some CAD software. Brookstone, in contrast, has used a mainframe architecture with custom software and will switch to a minicomputer architecture with packaged software.

The architecture determines the types of equipment the organization should acquire, the types of software it should use, and the telecommunications technology it should buy. Decisions about the architecture also involve decisions about standardization, right-sizing, and global performance. The architecture may specify both the current and future state for the infrastructure as well as a transition plan for reaching the desired state.

Not all organizations develop an information technology architecture. Companies may instead make their investment decisions on an ad hoc rather than a planned basis, as Brookstone initially did. An architecture offers the advantage of increasing the likelihood that an organization will make coordinated investment decisions that reflect the organization's long-term strategy.

The major disadvantage of developing an architecture is that, as with any planning, it takes time, effort, and money. Also, an architecture may reduce an organization's flexibility to respond to technological change. Once an organization implements architectural plans and purchases the technology that the architecture prescribes, technology managers and others resist investing in nonconforming technology. Such resistance may be counterproductive in periods of rapid technological change. Some companies with an architecture retain flexibility by seeking less rigid technologies and formalizing a structured approach for trying, evaluating, and eventually adopting appropriate technological advances.

The IS infrastructure includes equipment, personnel, and the organization and procedures for handling and processing information.

Courtesy of International Business Machines Corporation.

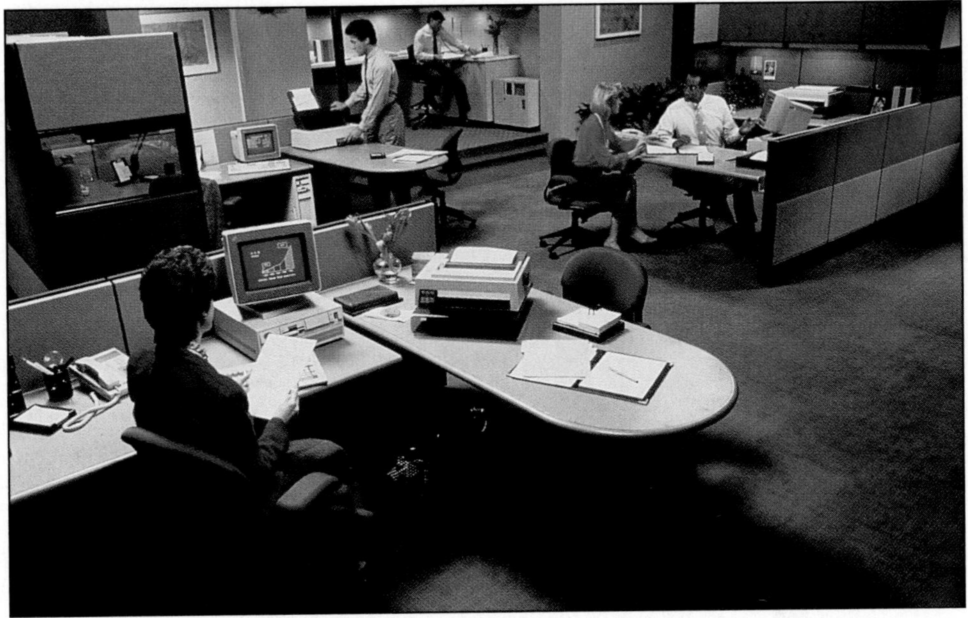

Standardization

A **standard** is a set of rules governing the types of investments the organization may make in information technology. The IT architecture reflects decisions about whether and at what level to set standards for hardware, software, and communication equipment acquisition. Figure 14-1 identifies some types of products for which a company might set standards. Many companies, for example, standardize on IBM-compatible equipment for personal computers. An employee who wants to use an Apple Macintosh may have difficulty obtaining one in such an environment. Depending upon how rigorously the standard is enforced, the company may prohibit the employee from using a Macintosh at work, allow the employee to use one if he or she pays for it, purchase one for the employee with the understanding that he or she will receive no support in dealing with hardware or software problems, or refuse to connect the Macintosh to the office computer network. Hardware and software manufacturers themselves often now standardize on **ISO 9000**, a set of five related quality management standards that ensure complete documentation and rigorous business practices in manufacturing.[3]

Figure 14-2 identifies some benefits and drawbacks of standardization policies. Many of the benefits illustrate how standards can help reduce costs, sometimes substantially. For example, standardization can reduce costs by minimizing the duplication of software development. If each division of a company develops its own inventory system, the company will probably spend a great deal more money in development than if the company standardized on a single inventory system that could handle the needs of all divisions. Brookstone, for example, has decided to use only packaged software as a way of reducing costs. Other examples of cost saving include economies of scale in purchasing and improving the company's negotiating position for better pricing. A company that buys 1,000 PCs can expect to pay less if it orders them from a single supplier than if it buys 100 of ten different kinds of computers from ten or more suppliers.

Many of the benefits shown in Figure 14-2 relate to efficiency rather than cost. For example, standards improve managerial and operating efficiency by increasing the integration of

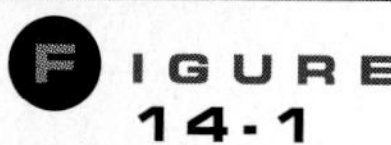

Key Technologies Amenable to Standardization

Computers
- Specific vendors (e.g., DEC)
- Level of compatibility (e.g., runs Windows 95, has 8MB RAM)

Communications equipment
- Network interface cards
- Network protocol compatibility
- LAN media
- Routers and hubs

Operating systems

Network operating systems

Office automation software
- Word processors
- Spreadsheets
- Presentation graphics packages
- Personal DBMS

Software development tools
- Languages
- Methodologies
- CASE products
- Data dictionary software

Database management systems

Vertical application software
- Order entry
- Inventory
- Accounting

systems and easing the interchange of information among systems. A work team that writes a proposal under tight time constraints will fare better if each staff member prepares his or her component of the proposal using the same word processor. Standardizing on a word processor guarantees that the company's staff can easily integrate the parts of the proposal into one document. The absence of such integration would prevent cross-referencing, and changes to one part of the document, such as deleting a figure, would require reworking other parts of the document to achieve a coherent product. First Union National Bank of North Carolina, the ninth largest bank in the United States in 1994, standardized, for example, on Lotus Development's SmartSuite, not only to improve integration, but also to reduce support costs and gain the efficiencies of working with a single vendor.[4]

FIRST UNION NATIONAL BANK OF NORTH CAROLINA

Standards can increase efficiency by increasing flexibility in the use of IS personnel. If a company standardizes on a single DBMS, its managers can assign programmers to different projects as needed. Managers in a less standardized environment could assign only programmers who were familiar with the DBMS in use for the project. Most organizations also find that they must provide some control over the variety of computers that their employees purchase; otherwise, they cannot effectively achieve a critical body of experience to provide the know-how and support that users need.

Standardization also increases managerial effectiveness. Managers who can easily obtain data related to their decisions more likely refer to the data and make better-informed decisions than do managers who find access to the data difficult. Standards, particularly in the user interface, database management systems, and data dictionary systems, increase the likelihood that managers can find the data they want quickly and easily.

Standards do not automatically increase the ease of systems integration and data exchange. For example, in the 1970s and 1980s, exchanging information among a wide variety of personal computers and minicomputers was easier than exchanging information among different types of IBM computers. Companies that standardized on IBM found that data exchange was difficult because IBM's mainframes, minicomputers, and PCs used incompatible operat-

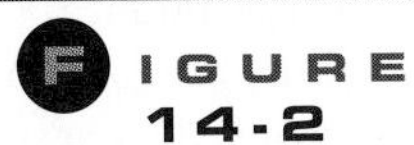
FIGURE 14-2 Benefits and Drawbacks of Standardization

Benefits	Drawbacks
Minimizes duplication of software development	Reduces flexibility in applications
Increases the quality of developed software	Stifles innovation and creativity
Increases integration of systems for improved efficiency	Interferes with other requirements of applications
Increases ability to exchange data among systems	Reduces ability to go with lowest cost solution in each case
Achieves economies of scale in purchasing and maintenance	Consumes political good will
Improves negotiating position for better pricing	Increases frequency of revision and upgrade installation
Promotes and facilitates coherent mission and strategy	Decreases users' comfort about opportunities to meet their direct needs
Reduces applications development time and cost	Increases impact of any major changes
Reduces outside projects with runaway costs	Decreases ability to make major changes
Increases flexibility in use of IS personnel	Requires more review and consensus for software/hardware selection
Reduces the cost and increases the quality of support	Increases impact of poor decisions
Reduces training costs and time	Increases costs of purchasing due to reduced supplier options
Lifts burden of product research from the user	Impedes the acquisition of new technology
Reduces number of specially built interfaces	

SOURCE: Steven R. Gordon, Standardization of information systems and technology at multinational companies, *Journal of Global Information Management* (Summer 1993): 6.

ing systems and supported different database managers. These companies might instead have standardized on a DBMS such as Oracle that ran on mainframes, minicomputers, and personal computers, and easily exchanged information among its databases on different systems.

The major disadvantage of standardization is that it may conflict with the objective of letting business needs determine systems development and acquisition priorities. In particular, standards reduce a company's flexibility in selecting its application software and decrease users' comfort about whether new systems can meet their needs. For example, one type of computer might work best for accounting applications, whereas a different type might work best for laboratory applications. One inventory system might function better for discrete items, such as chairs, that exist in whole quantities, whereas another might function better for continuous items, such as chemicals, that can be stored in any volume. Brookstone's standard of using only packaged software may result in such inflexibility. Most organizations respond to the inflexibility of standards by specifying a standard that accepts several alternatives. For example, a company may specify one type of computer for its personal computer needs, a second for business applications, a third for network servers, a fourth for scientific or laboratory work, and a fifth for computers on its manufacturing floor. A company should also review its standards frequently so that it can be responsive to its changing needs in a dynamic business environment.

Standardization can also require a significant organizational effort to support its implementation. IS executives and other top managers must acknowledge that employees resent having limited choices. An employee who uses a Macintosh at home, for example, might resent having to learn to use a new system at work, especially one he or she does not like as well. The political significance of standardization increases when it affects a division or business unit. Managers of a subsidiary may object to changing its inventory system for the sake of standardization when its employees are already trained to use an existing system that works perfectly well. In particular, managers may object if the standard system does not provide features of the old system they used and valued.

THE TRIBUNE

The Tribune Company is a Chicago-based conglomerate consisting of 28 business units that include newspapers, radio and television stations, and the Chicago Cubs baseball team. The Tribune's business units operate independently, and many have their own IS staffs. For reasons of efficiency, however, the Tribune has centralized equipment procurement and maintenance and standardized certain business applications such as general ledger, accounts payable, and credit and billing. The Tribune counters the resistance of subsidiaries by justifying each standardized application with a cost/benefit analysis done at the subsidiary's site, by including users and IS staff of the subsidiary on the project team, and by encouraging line managers at the subsidiary to talk with their peers at other subsidiaries that have gone through the change.[5]

The organizational cost of standards includes the time and effort required to establish and review them. Setting a standard that affects the entire organization involves gathering input from many people to properly assess the standard's impact. High-level managers who have a stake in the outcome should, and usually will, lobby extensively for their choice. Standard setting thus uses time that might better be spent on more pressing business issues.

Ironically, standards may increase costs if poor decisions result. For example, many companies that standardized on Digital Equipment Corporation's DEC-Mate personal computer in the early 1980s discarded their entire investment in PCs when the IBM PC and compatibles became the industry standard. While software vendors produced numerous products for the compatibles, users of the DEC-Mate had little or no choice of word-processing, spreadsheet, and other productivity software. Eventually, even Digital abandoned its PC product. Similar stories abound for terminal equipment, network products, and software.

Standards may also increase costs by requiring more frequent hardware and software updates. Companies that require a common configuration for their personal computers for easier maintenance and exchange must upgrade all computers when one user needs more capability. Similarly, many organizations require that all workstations use the same version of word-processing software. When one or two people need the features of a new release, the organization must purchase the new release for everyone. If the company lacked or did not enforce such standards, it would pay to upgrade only for those demanding the new release. These users, however, might then be unable to share their documents easily with others retaining the older software.

Right-sizing

The hardware architecture specifies the type of computers and communication equipment an organization will use. Prior to the mid-1970s, almost all computing was centralized on a single computer, making the hardware architecture easy to design. IT architects likely believed that economies of scale in computing made the use of more than one computer uneconomical. The major issue was how large to size the computer to avoid having to replace it with a larger, incompatible model. The spread of minicomputers in the mid-1970s complicated architectural decisions. Should a company invest in a large, single mainframe, or should it instead invest in minicomputers, which individually had less power but were more easily scalable? Today architects choose among mainframes, minicomputers, networks of microcomputers, stand-alone workstations, and combinations of these options. The absence of economies of scale and the ability to link dissimilar hardware into workable systems makes choosing an IT architecture more complex.

New companies and those with minimal IT investments can choose from an array of computer technologies. Large companies, in contrast, may have mainframe systems that are legacies from a time when personal computer networks were not available. These companies must make decisions for both new IS development and their legacy systems. **Right-sizing** is the process of determining the overall architecture to employ for individual systems or for the company as a whole.

Downsizing is the decision to move some or all of a company's computing to a larger number of less powerful computers, generally to PCs connected by a network. Brookstone downsized from a mainframe to a minicomputer architecture; although not currently planned, they might ultimately downsize some functions to a PC network. Spalding Sports Worldwide downsized from a mainframe with thousands of terminals to an architecture having dedicated servers and thousands of PC clients; they write applications for desktop computers that use corporate data.[6] Sometimes the mainframe continues to play a role in the downsizing effort. For example, instead of upgrading a mainframe to meet requirements for additional capacity, a company may implement a client/server architecture to off-load some of the mainframe's processing to connected PCs.

SPALDING SPORTS WORLDWIDE

Figure 14-3 lists some of the advantages and disadvantages of downsizing. Although companies should reap tremendous savings by downsizing because hardware and systems software cost significantly less (even when calculated per user), some questions exist about the actual cost savings that result.[7] The hidden costs of client/server systems have become more apparent. The cost of PC software for each workstation is usually quite low, but the costs become significant when multiplied by the large number of workstations in an organization. The costs of network and end-user support and training can exceed those for mainframe systems. Converting legacy systems to the downsized environment also may have a significant cost. Finally, end users may waste time developing their own programs and assisting others in using PC software on downsized systems: One study suggests that this time adds between $6,000 and $15,000 to the cost of each PC.[8]

PC users used to a GUI environment exert a primary force for downsizing: They demand a GUI environment for all applications. Graphics processing requires too much memory per workstation for efficient implementation on mainframe systems, and few GUI tools for the mainframe environment exist. These limitations often force systems developers to choose a client/server architecture to meet user demands. Although the mainframe can remain a central part of the architecture, with the PC providing only the GUI processing, many organizations, including the Port of Seattle; Calspan, Inc., a diversified manufacturer headquartered in Buffalo, New York; and the G. Heileman Brewing Company of La Crosse, Wisconsin, have seized the opportunity to eliminate the mainframe entirely.[9] Many organizations retain their

PORT OF SEATTLE

CALSPAN

G. HEILEMAN BREWING

FIGURE 14-3 Advantages and Disadvantages of Downsizing

Advantages	Disadvantages
Lower cost for hardware	High cost to convert legacy systems
Easier development for GUI environment	Higher cost for user support
Wider availability of object-oriented tools	Increased cost of providing physical and data security
Better utilization of PC investment	Greater difficulty managing performance problems
Easier integration with PC office automation tools	Need to retrain IS staff and end users
An opportunity for reengineering	Decreased ability to control data
Increased end-user involvement and empowerment	Difficulty of managing multiple platforms
Better scalability	Fewer software development methodology tools
	Greater difficulty in providing support

mainframes as servers and archivers, to handle high-volume transaction processing, and to avoid having to reprogram existing systems, even as managers downsize other applications.

Downsizing also offers an increased ability to use object-oriented languages and databases for development (see Chapter 5). Object-oriented software first became widely available on PC systems, in large part because of its synergy with the graphical user environment. However, many companies now see object orientation as a way to reduce maintenance and increase software development productivity.[10] Because the large majority of object-oriented tools are available only in the PC environment, systems developers who want to use object-oriented technology find a client/server architecture advantageous.

Some organizations move to a client/server architecture to better utilize their personal computers. If employees must have personal computers for office automation applications, it appears inefficient to waste their power by using them only as terminals to the mainframe. Instead, PCs can perform much of the computing, relieving the mainframe to perform other processing or allowing the company to reduce its mainframe investment.

Downsizing increases the cost and complexity of managing the security of information.[11] The multiple entry points into the system make security more challenging; for example, viruses can infect client PCs, the network, or the server. Failure of the network or server can result in a loss of activities or transactions on client computers, making restoration of data integrity more complex. System backups and recoveries after failures are more manageable in a centralized architecture. Finally, system administrators cannot easily monitor the security precautions users take for data they store only on their own systems.

Performance problems in the client/server environment are also more common and more difficult to deal with than in the mainframe environment. Performance problems may arise from inadequate server capacity, inadequate network capacity, or underpowered PC clients; such situations make the sizing of systems difficult. Rapid application prototyping, more common in client/server applications than in mainframe applications, compounds the difficulty of system sizing. For example, developers may successfully test an application with a few screens and a few users but find that the application does not provide the appropriate response time when 200 or more users are entering data and searching the database.[12] Database updates cause particularly heavy traffic flow if coordination is required among different clients accessing the same database. Experts estimate that the overhead required to coordinate transaction processing increases network traffic by as much as 40 percent.[13]

The cost of retraining or replacing developers, end users, and the IS support staff may create a major hurdle in moving to a client/server architecture. IS developers not only must learn to use different products but also must think differently. Experienced programmers may find moving from a traditional to an object-oriented language or from a procedural to a nonprocedural language more difficult than do new programmers. Developers who formerly wrote batch-based code must now respond to meet the needs of users in a GUI environment.

The advantages of downsizing appear to outweigh the disadvantages for an increasing number of applications. The marketplace clearly reflects the movement from mainframe computing. In 1991, only 14 percent of Fortune 500 companies said that the number of terminals connecting people to their IBM mainframes was decreasing; that percentage had increased to 64 percent by 1993.[14] An estimated 55 percent of all employees in large corporations in 1993 used personal computers, and about 70 percent of those were connected to local area networks.[15] Still, in 1993, 45 percent of IS executives had no client/server plans or were unsure about them.[16] As industry gains experience with client/server architectures, the trend toward downsizing likely will accelerate.

Companies that migrate to a client/server environment generally pursue one of the following four strategies: 1) They convert all existing systems as rapidly as possible; 2) they pilot a few systems, taking a wait-and-see approach to determine whether further conversion is necessary; 3) they do no conversion but phase in the client/server architecture for all new development; or 4) they phase in old systems by first converting to a GUI interface and then converting to a client/server environment as necessary.[17] The first strategy is the fastest and most risky, and the last is the slowest and least risky. In addition to reducing risks, the slower strategies also give users time to adjust to the client/server architecture and developers time to acquire and perfect their skills and tools for dealing with client/server development.

MOTOROLA

Business users or senior executives can demand more rapid change. For example, at Motorola's computer group, top management, in a drive to cut costs, instructed IS managers to reduce the cost of MIS from 3.7 percent of sales to 1 percent of sales. Because the group's mainframes were costing $60,000 per month to maintain and program, they simply became too expensive to retain under the cost-reduction mandate. In two years, the IS staff converted the mainframe applications so they could run on a client/server network and removed the mainframes, reducing MIS costs to 1.2 percent of sales.[18] In contrast, Spiegel, Inc. moved more deliberately, beginning with a client/server application used by 50 people in one department for decision support and inquiry only. For its second project, Spiegel plans an application that collects information, will be used by as many as 400 people, and taps into the mainframe database.[19]

SPIEGEL

Architecture for the Global Organization

Companies that operate internationally have unique problems in designing an architecture and building a coordinated infrastructure. Although Brookstone currently operates both its mail-order and retail divisions only in the United States, executives may anticipate future overseas stores as they develop the company's information systems infrastructure. Standardization and networking have eased global differences in some organizations, although they may impede the local sensitivity companies should retain in meeting global needs.[20]

FEDERAL EXPRESS

MARRIOTT

Federal Express developed a five-year worldwide IS plan in the late 1980s that described projected hardware, software, communications, and applications; and Marriott viewed standardization and support as the pillars of its global IS strategy.[21]

Language poses the most obvious barrier to coordinating the global software infrastructure. Software tools exist to help developers simultaneously create software to be run in multiple languages. These tools work by separating textual screen prompts and textual report headings from the rest of the software, allowing easier customization. Nevertheless, difficulties still remain because some languages are much more compact than others. Programmers often lay out screens differently, adjust report columns, and change the display of dates and currency for each country. Displaying and printing characters for languages such as Japanese, Chinese, Korean, and Arabic may require special hardware.

Global architecture designers must also consider the international support provided by hardware and software vendors. Companies may have difficulty standardizing on either hardware or software if vendors do not support the product selected in all countries in which the company does business. Some companies provide multiple standards to deal with this problem so that each foreign office can find local support for at least one standard. Other companies select standards only from products that receive support worldwide. Accepting multiple standards increases the cost of support and integration. Limiting selection of products reduces a company's flexibility in meeting its needs and generally increases the cost of its investments.

The laws and regulations of foreign countries may also confound a company's attempt to implement a consistent architecture. Countries differ in their laws regarding accounting practices, documentation of business transactions, and reporting requirements. Although some vendors provide packaged software that deals with the laws in many countries, such software is expensive and requires frequent updates. Most companies either customize their systems for the countries in which they do business or allow the organization in each country to make its own IS decisions. Some countries even insist that companies purchase all or a percentage of IT investments from local companies.

The organization of a global company affects whether it can implement a global architecture. Centrally organized companies, typically domestic companies doing international business, usually have the easiest job of designing and controlling the infrastructure. Such organizations have a central IS department that can make and implement plans. Most companies organized along geographical lines, even if not centrally controlled, often rely on a central IS staff to coordinate their infrastructure. Individual geographical divisions rarely have the required resources for developing their own IS planning expertise. Global companies organized along product lines more likely will establish their own IS planning capabilities.[22] They are typically able to do so because different product divisions have very different business needs. Also, such organizations often evolve from mergers between companies that had already developed their own IS capability. Coordinating the infrastructure in such an environment poses political challenges unless strong business needs can overcome the parochial perspectives of local managers.

The Human Infrastructure

Human resources provide an equally or even more important component of the information infrastructure than do physical resources. Brookstone's human infrastructure includes IS staff members and end users, as well as training and support for them.

Jobs in Information Systems

The array of available IS jobs increases as information technology becomes more complex and more highly diffused throughout an organization. The positions described here, and shown relative to their usual skill and pay in Figure 14-4, present a sample of the positions found in many organizations.

Data Entry. **Data entry clerks** hold a relatively low-skill, low-paying position in the IS hierarchy and work for companies that process large numbers of paper transactions. An insurance company, for example, often employs data entry clerks to process its customers' paper claims. Organizations that use on-line data input generally do not have data entry positions; for example, department stores or fast-food companies may use employees trained for another function, such as sales, to perform data entry as part of their job.

Operations and Technical Support. Operations and technical support personnel install, maintain, and operate computers and communications equipment. In a mainframe environment, these employees are usually responsible for such tasks as mounting tapes and disk packs, changing the paper and print elements in the printers, running periodic system backups, restarting jobs after a system failure, and installing upgrades and new releases of system software and horizontal software such as database management systems. In a client/server environment, the operations and technical support staff retains responsibility for such tasks as backup and recovery, refilling paper and toner in laser printers, and installing software upgrades. The staff may also be responsible for performing some hardware upgrades, such as installing new network cards in users' computers, increasing the amount of RAM or disk storage capacity in users' workstations, and configuring or reconfiguring communication equipment such as routers.

FIGURE 14-4 A Sample of Information Systems Jobs

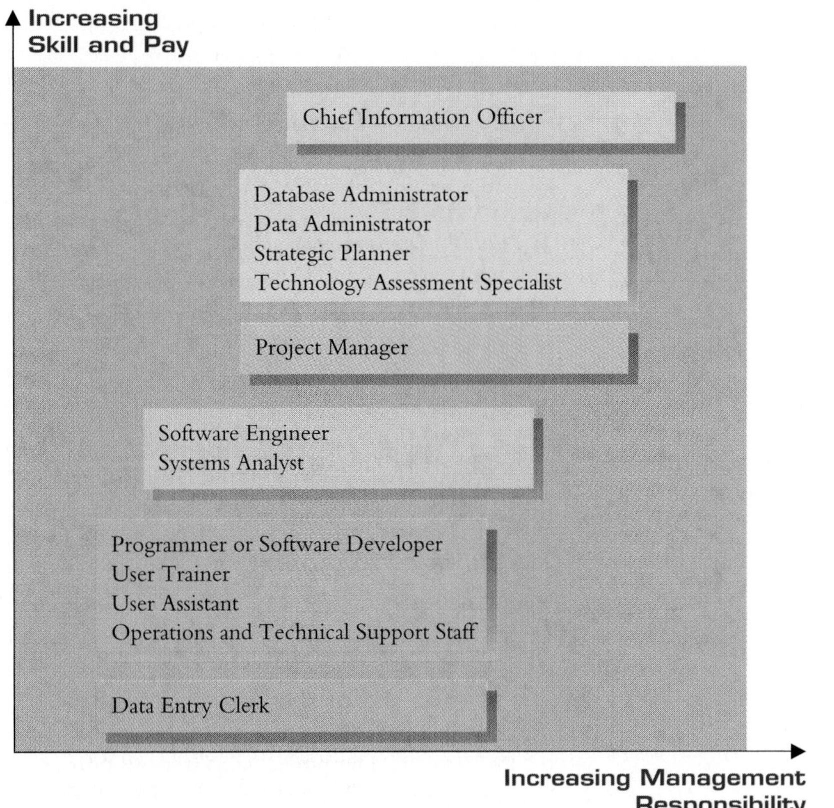

Although operations and technical support employees must have a general technical background, typically they still require in-house or outside training shortly after hiring because they rarely have extensive experience with the specific hardware or communications equipment their employer uses. In addition, they must receive additional training as the IT infrastructure changes.

User Training and User Assistance. Employees who train computer hardware and software users and help them diagnose and solve problems with their equipment and software require both technical and interpersonal skills. Some companies hire full-time trainers, although many organizations prefer to use consultants as trainers or send their employees to intensive training courses provided by third parties. Almost all medium to large companies employ individuals whose job involves only assisting the end users of information technology. These employees often work from a help desk, which is discussed later in this chapter.

Programming and Software Development. **Programmer** describes a highly technical position associated with the production of custom software. Companies expect applicants for this position to have a two-year or four-year college degree with a computer-related major or a certificate from a technical training school, plus working knowledge of at least one programming language. Programmers need not have a business education or background. As software development tools (see Chapter 13) become more powerful, many companies are replacing their programmers with or retraining them to be **software developers,** specialists in one or more software development tools. Typically, software developers also have programming skills.

Systems Analysis and Software Engineering. **Systems analyst** is a technical position associated with all aspects of the systems development life cycle (see Chapter 13) focusing most directly on needs analysis. Companies often recruit systems analysts from the graduating classes of four-year colleges, especially those offering degrees in business and/or information systems. Although, technically, systems analysis involves no programming, companies typically require analysts to be proficient in one or more programming languages, and many combine the analyst and programmer positions into a single job. As CASE tools become more powerful, companies are requiring or training systems analysts to be proficient in one or more CASE workbenches and are using the title of **software engineer** to reflect these skills. Some systems analysts and software engineers who work on one application or in one application area for several years acquire expertise in that application through the process of designing and implementing software. Because of their expertise, they may be assimilated into the line function, where they may assume project management responsibilities.

Project Manager. A **project manager** directs a software development project and must ensure that the project meets user requirements within a specified budget and time frame. He or she has significant supervisory responsibilities for technical and personnel decisions and therefore typically has both technical expertise and strong management skills. Project managers may have prior experience as analysts or programmers. Alternatively, project managers are business specialists who report to line managers rather than to (or in addition to) IS managers. The project manager position may be temporary, lasting only for the duration of a project. In some organizations, however, project manager is a permanent position whose holders move from project to project and may supervise several projects concurrently.

Data Administrator and Database Administrator. The **data administrator** and **database administrator** organize, manage, and guarantee the integrity of an organization's data (see Chapter 7). Most organizations combine the data and database administrator position into a single job. Otherwise, the data administrator maintains the data dictionary, assists project managers in defining and coordinating data needs associated with their projects, develops an enterprise-wide data model, sets and implements company policies regarding data security and data access, and specifies data integrity rules. The database administrator has more technical responsibilities, setting and fine-tuning database parameters that affect performance, performing database backups, managing database recovery upon system crashes, and installing DBMS updates and software tools.

Strategic Planner and Technology Assessment Specialist. Most large companies have at least one full-time employee who monitors advances in information technology, educates the key managers about these advances, and plans how the company can take advantage of these advances. Often these specialists have a staff and budget to pilot new technologies on real or hypothetical applications. Separate job holders in specific areas of technical specialty, such as communications, expert systems, and object-oriented technology, may have these responsibilities in sufficiently large organizations. Such specialists tend to be highly technical, although those who supervise a staff and have long-term planning responsibilities should have both a technical and managerial education.

The Chief Information Officer (CIO). An organization's **chief information officer (CIO)** manages its information-related resources and activities. The CIO may also be called manager, director, or vice-president of data processing, information services, or management information systems. Organizations that do not have a full-time CIO position generally delegate the CIO functions and responsibilities to the chief financial officer. The CIO usually reports to either the chief financial officer, the chief operations officer, or the president of the company. Companies that have a distributed information architecture may have several managers of information systems and technology who report to their own divisions or business units rather than to a single CIO.[23] Most chief information officers have had significant technical experience, although increasingly their background has a more managerial focus.[24] In this position they should act as a leader, have a vision for the IS architecture, and have the managerial savvy and political clout to implement that vision. Increasingly, the CIO must act as the technology adviser for major organizational restructuring and reengineering.[25] The CIO must successfully educate upper management about the application and value of information technology for securing a strategic advantage and then secure the financial resources to appropriately shape the infrastructure.

Education and Training

Many people outside the IS community believe that a technical education is necessary and desirable for people working in IS. Programming skills can provide a good background for entry-level jobs.[26] Most IS positions actually require good communication and problem-solving skills; some also require strong management skills; and technical skills generally have a lower priority. One recruitment firm that analyzed the background of the IS professionals it represented determined that 36 percent majored in liberal arts subjects such as history or literature and had no intention of pursuing a technological career when they entered college.[27] Although most IS managers and other IS professionals believe that nontechnical skills are more important than technical skills for advancing in IS professions,[28] most IS jobs require some technical skills. Applicants for an entry-level IS position should be computer literate and should know how to program in at least one computer language or have experience with GUI software development tools. Although some companies look for those who have experience with certain equipment, computer languages, or software development tools when hiring, others will train applicants on the equipment and software they will use on the job.

End-User Computing

End user describes a consumer of IS services; he or she uses a computer to accomplish such tasks as word processing, electronic mail, statistical analysis, and report generation.[29] End users at Brookstone include sales clerks, store managers, customer-assistance clerks, and warehouse workers, among others. As end users become more computer literate, they increasingly perform their own systems development. While not officially part of the human IS infrastructure, they contribute to building the technical infrastructure through the development of systems and the creation and storage of data; the distinction between end users and the IS staff often becomes fuzzy.[30] More and more often, end users play a more formal role in systems development by serving on development task forces, participating in rapid prototyping efforts, or engaging in sophisticated needs assessments. IS staff can support end users informally or through the use of a help desk.

The Help Desk. The **help desk,** also known as the **information center,** comprises the IS staff and associated systems that help end users solve immediate problems with their equipment or software.[31] The staff of the help desk addresses problems as diverse as how to turn on the computer, replace the cartridge in a laser printer, handle an exception in an otherwise routine data-entry application, and produce a customized report from the corporate database. In some organizations, the user training staff also reports to the help desk. The typical help desk has four full-time professionals, serves 500 to 1,000 internal users, and solves 64 percent of the problems reported to it on the first call (as seen in Figure 14-5).[32] In small organizations, typically one or two individuals recognized for their technical expertise informally perform the function of the help desk.

Originally, large organizations had several specialized help desks scattered geographically or organized by expertise; now the centralized help desk has become a standard way of addressing end-user needs rapidly and efficiently. The organization of the help desk varies by company. Some companies have help desk operators with extensive expertise in the hardware and software the company uses and who, with the help of expert systems software, can handle most problems independently. Other companies have help desk operators who identify the problem and route it to the appropriate technical person or function in the company. This approach in effect distributes the help desk function throughout the organization. Still other companies use third-party help desk services. For example, Electronic Data Systems Corp. handles all of the help desk operations for Continental Airlines.[33]

ELECTRONIC DATA SYSTEMS

CONTINENTAL AIRLINES

A help desk can identify system flaws or user training needs through monitoring problems that arise and tabulating the speed of their solution. Recently, many help desks have

FIGURE 14-5 The Typical Help Desk

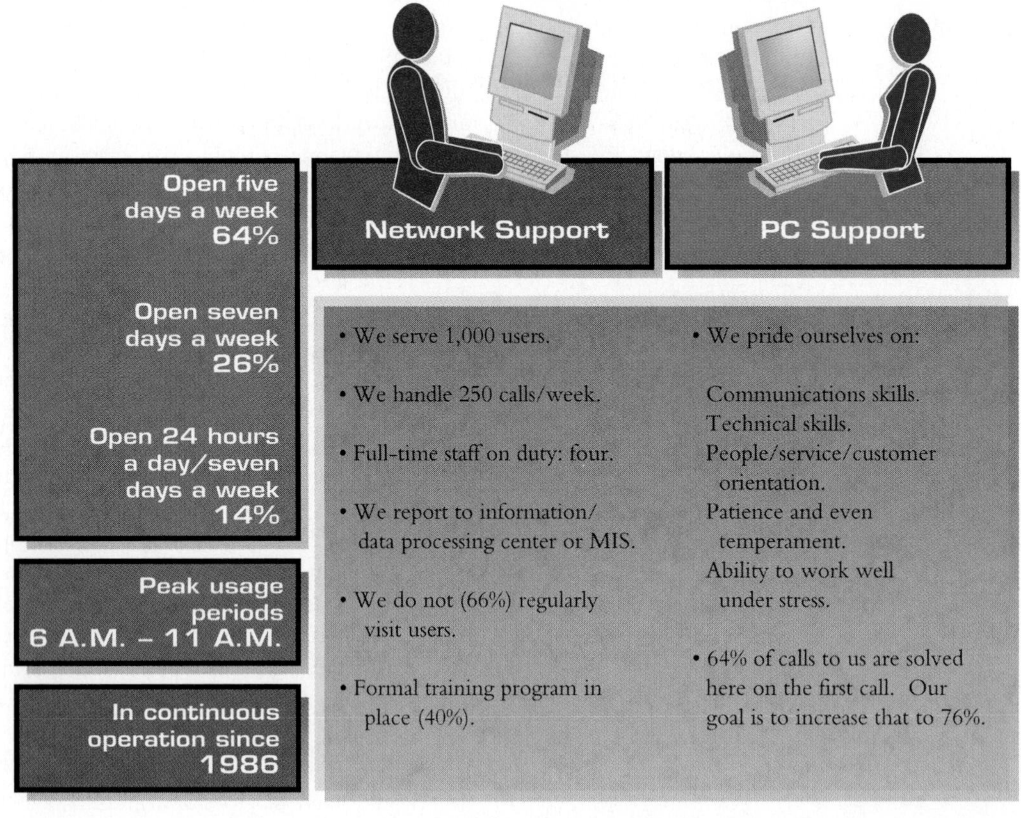

Open five
days a week
64%
Open seven
days a week
26%
Open 24 hours
a day/seven
days a week
14%
Peak usage
periods
6 A.M. – 11 A.M.
In continuous
operation since
1986
Network Support
PC Support
• We serve 1,000 users.
• We handle 250 calls/week.
• Full-time staff on duty: four.
• We report to information/ data processing center or MIS.
• We do not (66%) regularly visit users.
• Formal training program in place (40%).
• We pride ourselves on:
Communications skills.
Technical skills.
People/service/customer orientation.
Patience and even temperament.
Ability to work well under stress.
• 64% of calls to us are solved here on the first call. Our goal is to increase that to 76%.

SOURCE: Julia King, Hello, help desk? HELP!, *Computerworld* (November 11, 1991): 74.

AIR FORCE MATERIEL COMMAND

focused extensively on their role as problem logger rather than problem solver. This change in role typically results in end-user dissatisfaction because it motivates end users to solve their own problems rather than use the help desk. For example, some users at the Air Force Materiel Command found that their computers displayed no availability for parts that actually were in the warehouse; these users did not call the help desk to report the problem because the help desk would log the problem but not solve it.[34] The type and quality of services provided, users' expectations about the information center, the technological environment in which the information center functions, and the organization's commitment to the information center influence its success.[35] In addition, the information center must have a competent staff and deliver effective end-user training.[36]

Organization and Procedures

The information systems infrastructure includes the organizational structure that affects control of information, control of information processing, and the policies and procedures surrounding information processing and use. These factors may be more easily changed than the equipment, software, and human infrastructure, but they are no less important in shaping an organization's use of information and information systems. Among the organizational and procedural concerns are whether to control information and information systems in a centralized or decentralized fashion; whether to use outside contractors to perform some or all of an organization's information systems services; how to budget and account for the use of information services; whether and how to use steering committees to oversee and advise information service providers; and how to address security issues.

Centralization Versus Decentralization

AMOCO CORPORATION

MOBILE CHEMICAL

The IS function typically either forms into a single corporate department with separate areas for individual IS functions or operates as support staff to business units. Organizing the IS function involves deciding how much control to centralize in a corporate IS staff and how much to distribute throughout the organization. Some organizations, such as Brookstone, have structures in which all IS activities emanate from a corporate IS department. Other organizations place most IS activity under the control of separate business units and have only two or three employees in a corporate IS department. Amoco Corporation, for example, reassigned about one-fourth of its corporate IS staff to end-user divisions; without changing physical location it switched its reporting relations from solid line to IS and dotted line to the operating companies to the exact opposite.[37] The trend toward IS downsizing and the proliferation of client/server architectures have eased this movement of information systems functions into the business units. Mobile Chemical's Petrol Chemical Division uses ad hoc coordinators, formerly PC technical experts in engineering or financial analysis groups, to administer its local area networks at the coordinators' business sites.[38] Business units now hire IS professionals with titles such as business systems analyst or marketing systems coordinator.[39]

PRINCIPAL FINANCIAL GROUP

Other companies have taken a slow approach to decentralizing the IS function. For example, Principal Financial Group (PFG), an insurance company that has operated nearly 30 years under centralized computing, remains committed to centralized IS for key corporate applications but is slowly pushing some applications to the business units. As a first step, the company has relocated some software developers to one of its three business units—personal insurance, employee benefits, and pension group. This relocation allows users to talk directly and spontaneously with the developers rather than limit their interactions to formal meetings, resulting in IS's better meeting their needs. The second step will involve a slow rollout of client/server applications that PFG calls cooperative processing. The mainframe will manage the corporate database, but workstations will initiate applications and provide the user interface and error checking upon data entry.[40]

Many IS professionals believe that increases in client/server computing may force companies to recentralize IS control despite the decentralization of IS activities.[41] The central IS staff in such a distributed environment would coordinate IS use and provide long-term planning functions. IS professionals argue that without central control, the duplication of effort that occurs as end users build systems in a vacuum will waste too much time and money.[42] Pacific Gas and Electric, a California utility company, has a decentralized architecture for computing and application development. However, many of its divisions found that their applications could not communicate with one another over the corporate network, and their developers were having trouble building software that ran on the broad range of workstations and platforms that the company had acquired without central control. To respond to these problems, Pacific Gas and Electric assigned to its centralized IS group the task and responsibility of policy making, standard setting, and data administration.[43]

PACIFIC GAS AND ELECTRIC

Outsourcing

Outsourcing refers to the contracting of a service, such as information processing and applications development, to a party outside the organization. A company that outsources its information systems services reduces or eliminates its own information infrastructure. Brookstone, for example, could outsource the processing of accounting and payroll data. Outsourcing moves both capital and human investments to a company that specializes in the outsourced service. The outsourcing company obtains better service at the same price or similar service at a lower price. Presumably, the service provider leverages its expertise and investments over many companies to provide economies of scale that an individual company could not secure. Companies often consider outsourcing their mainframe operations after downsizing several applications to a PC network. As the mainframe becomes underutilized, costs can be lessened by outsourcing operations to a company that can combine the remaining services with those of another company to fully utilize the mainframe.

Before 1989, few large companies considered outsourcing significant portions of their information services to be a viable option. They viewed information systems and technology as strategic resources and their information too proprietary to risk loss of control. In 1989, Eastman Kodak stunned the business world by selling its mainframes to IBM and hiring IBM to process its data for the next ten years.[44] Although experts disagree on whether Kodak made a wise deal or a terrible mistake, its deal with IBM legitimized the outsourcing of information services. Outsourcing has since become a popular alternative to internalization of the information infrastructure, as illustrated in Figure 14-6. National Car Rental, for example, contracted with Electronic Data Systems (EDS) in the early 1990s to operate its reservation system, corporate data center, programming staff, and even terminals at its service counters. National relinquished direct control in part because the company could not hire or retain well-qualified programmers to develop its systems.[45]

EASTMAN KODAK

IBM

NATIONAL CAR RENTAL

ELECTRONIC DATA SYSTEMS

General Dynamics gave Computer Sciences Corporation a $3 billion ten-year contract for computer services in 1991; CSC bought General Dynamics's data centers for $200 million and now provides data services (worth approximately $350 million in the first year alone) to General Dynamics.[46] The brokerage industry has outsourced significant parts of the computer operations since 1990: For example, Salomon Brothers outsourced its software maintenance on IBM mainframes to Andersen Consulting, Inc.[47] Blue Cross/Blue Shield of Massachusetts has given EDS an $800 million outsourcing contract to provide data processing and develop future applications: Blue Cross and EDS will share the office of the CIO; Blue Cross will transfer almost 600 Blue Cross IS employees and all facilities to EDS; and Blue Cross will retain a small staff of IS workers to develop strategic applications.[48]

GENERAL DYNAMICS

COMPUTER SCIENCES

SALOMON BROTHERS

ANDERSEN CONSULTING

BLUE CROSS/BLUE SHIELD OF MASSACHUSETTS

FIGURE 14-6 A Sample of Large Outsourcing Contracts

Company	Value	Contract Under
General Dynamics Corp.	$3,000M	CSC*
Continental Airlines	$2,100M	EDS**
Enrol Corp.	$750M	EDS
Continental Bank	$700M	EDS
First City Bancorp	$600M	IBM
Eastman Kodak Co.	$500M	IBM
National Car Rental System, Inc.	$500M	EDS
First Fidelity Bancorp	$450M	EDS
First American Bankshares, Inc.	$400M	Perot Systems

* Computer Sciences Corporation

** Electronic Data Systems

SOURCE: Clinton Wilder, Giant firms join outsourcing parade, *Computerworld* (September 30, 1991): 1, 91. Data is attributed to Merrill Lynch Capital Markets.

EASTMAN KODAK

Figure 14-7 lists some of the advantages and disadvantages of outsourcing information services and technology. Questions exist about whether outsourcing significantly reduces costs. Outsourcing at least makes costs more explicit, leading to better decisions about where to spend company money. For example, the CIO at Eastman Kodak noted that users considered the costs of implementing systems before outsourcing "just Kodabucks." Outsourcing the services to IBM made people pay closer attention to the costs.[49] In addition, service providers such as IBM and EDS can realize economies of scale that they can share with their customers.

Outsourcing can also ease staffing and other resource problems encountered in software development efforts. Consider a company that needs to develop a large application rapidly. Such an organization often cannot add staff simply for that effort because it would have excess staff at the end of the project. Instead, the company can contract to a third party for a fixed quantity of software development concentrated into chunks or spread over a long period. The service provider can more easily move its staff from one company's project to another's. This same flexibility applies to all IS resources, not only staffing.

ULTRAMAR

POWER COMPUTING

MERITOR SAVINGS BANK

Outsourcing creates a major disadvantage by locking the outsourcing company into a long-term contract. A company may have difficulty firing a provider that misses deadlines, develops poor-quality programs, delivers insufficient processing capacity, or generally acts unresponsively. Ultramar, Inc., an oil refiner and marketer, addressed this problem by limiting its contract with Power Computing Corporation to three years.[50] Other companies, such as Meritor Savings Bank, which in 1989 shrunk to two-thirds of its original size, included a contract clause that addressed such extraordinary events.[51] Although the contract may specify performance penalties and divorce clauses, an unsatisfied outsourcer may have to sue its service provider to terminate the contract. Long-term contracts also do not reflect rapid changes in the cost of technology, which may penalize either party; what seems like a good contract at the outset can become very costly over time.[52]

Outsourcing also requires organizations to relinquish control in an area of potential strategic advantage. Although a company still directs its contractor, it retains no expertise in IT and might experience difficulty in ever returning the outsourced functions into the

FIGURE 14-7 Advantages and Disadvantages of Outsourcing

Advantages

- Saves money/increases value
- Reduces cost of fluctuations in size of systems development staff
- Takes advantage of scale economies in hardware where they exist
- Makes cost/service tradeoffs explicit; improves decisions
- Allows more rapid or timely development
- Consolidates operations
- Frees management to focus on business
- Offers improved reliability and stability
- Provides opportunity to learn from the contractor

Disadvantages

- Costs more
- Locks company into a provider
- Fails to guarantee responsiveness
- Reduces control
- Removes knowledge of processes from the company
- Decreases ability to use information technology strategically

organization. For this reason organizations generally outsource only selected functions. Figure 14-8 illustrates the IS functions that a representative sample of 19 companies outsourced.

Even within the functions shown in the figure, outsourcing is not necessarily exhaustive. For example, a contract for PC maintenance may cover only IBM compatibles, excluding Macintosh computers. Similarly, organizations may limit outsourcing of systems development to major projects and handle minor projects in-house. Successful outsourcing occurs when companies can divide the IS activities into meaningful segments for outsourcing, identify appropriate segments to outsource based on sound business analysis, and treat the outsource provider as a partner.[53] A company should consider outsourcing if it cannot easily create a competitive advantage with its information technology processing operations or the quality of its applications, if it can accept interrupted information technology service, if it can retain critical technical competencies for future use, and if it has limited information technology capabilities.[54]

Accounting Issues

The method by which an organization accounts for its information systems has implications for acquiring and applying information technology and information systems resources and for the structure of the IS function. A company such as Brookstone must determine whether its information systems department should exist as 1) an unallocated cost center, 2) an allocated cost center, or 3) a profit center.

Unallocated Cost Center. End users and their managers who view information services and technology as a free resource from an information systems department estab-

FIGURE 14-8 What Companies Outsource

IS Function	Number of Companies*
Training	18
Systems planning and development	14
Data center operations	13
Technical support	10
Wide-area communication	9
PC maintenance	9
Voice communication	8
Disaster recovery	8
LAN support	7
Others	14

* Based on 19 companies

SOURCE: Tor Guimaraes and Stuart Wells, Outsourcing for novices, *Computerworld* (June 8, 1992): 89–91.

lish an **unallocated cost center.** This setup considers all costs of operating the IS department and related IS services as an organizational expense rather than as costs attributable to particular budgets. Brookstone, for example, might charge all IS costs to the central IS department rather than attribute them separately to the retail stores' or mail order business's budgets. Viewing the IS department as an unallocated cost center benefits organizations just developing their information architecture because it encourages users to experiment with and learn about the technology and subsequently build the infrastructure. It also encourages users to request the development of new systems.

The unallocated cost center approach allows the development of systems without regard to their economic return. As a result, the costs of information technology can quickly rise out of control. Companies then tighten their budgets for systems development and resource acquisition to control costs. Because no economic basis for choosing any particular budget level exists, financial officers usually determine the budget for information systems and technology as a percentage of sales, according to the experience of similar companies in similar markets. This measure fails to reflect the company's current status, whether it needs to build its infrastructure to catch its competition, or whether it can coast and wait for its competition to catch it. This approach to budgeting can stifle creative and strategic uses of information technology that would yield significant benefits because other companies do not have such uses for comparison.

The unallocated cost center approach also does not give information systems professionals a way of allocating a fixed budget among conflicting requests for resources. When the IS staff or other executives decide not to fund or to delay certain projects, the user community may become angry at the lack of response and long lead times for their projects. The information systems department then becomes an antagonist rather than a partner in systems development. Having IS staff determine the cost of requested services and the user department identify and quantify the expected benefits of its request can alleviate some problems with an unallocated cost center. This approach helps the IS department determine those projects likely to have the greatest net benefit and justify its decisions to end users.

Allocated Cost Center. As an **allocated cost center,** the IS department allocates and charges its costs to the departments that use its services. Brookstone, for example, could allocate the costs of IS usage to its accounting, operations, and human resources departments, among others. Unlike the unallocated cost center approach, the allocated cost center approach avoids the use of and request for services that do not provide an ample benefit. This approach works particularly well in environments in which departments charge other services to their internal customers. Such charge-back systems should clearly specify their objectives and emphasize simplicity, equity, minimal overhead, and consistency.[55]

Using the allocated cost center can create problems in determining the appropriate allocation. Ideally, the cost center should charge user departments for resources in proportion to both the costs of those resources and their usage. In addition, the charges levied should fully reimburse the cost center for its expenses. Calculating costs in this way uses information about technical factors such as units of computer use, internal memory use, input–output use, and data storage requirements, which users may find unintelligible and which likely change between periods. For example, the per-unit charge for computer time is low in a period of high usage, whereas the per-unit charge must be higher in a period of low usage to recover the fixed costs of owning and running the computer system; this variation in charges motivates additional usage during the peak periods of the year.

Another problem in the allocated cost center approach is that the average cost does not reflect the marginal cost—the economic way of allocating resources. For example, a company that upgrades its equipment for a new application distributes the cost of the new equipment among all applications. The purchasers of the application see their own unit costs: They do not experience changes in unit costs for other applications that, although likely to be small, when added together might have made their application uneconomical. In addition, other users see fluctuations in their costs without any changes in their activity. This costing behavior can lead to friction among user departments and between user departments and IS.

Finally, an allocated cost center has no incentive to operate efficiently. Because it receives reimbursement for all costs, it has little incentive to keep these costs low. If some users attempt to bypass high charges by outsourcing, the cost center simply charges each of the remaining users more. This leads to overinvestment in IS and IT resources and results in dissatisfied users.

Profit Center. An IS department that operates as a **profit center** becomes an internal option to the outsourcing of IS services. It bids for the work of internal users, charges internal users the price it would charge external users, and often actively seeks external users.

KIMBERLY-CLARK

Kimberly-Clark created a wholly owned subsidiary, Kimberly-Clark Computer Services, for its IS department, making it a separate business venture. The company began by selling a software engineering tool that helps companies convert any of their current systems to a different IBM systems architecture.[56]

Internal users do not have to use the services of their IS department. The company may limit the fees the profit center can charge internal users to avoid monopoly prices for those projects that share data with other applications and for which the users have no other choice of IS supplier.

The profit center approach offers the primary advantage of providing the IS department incentives to operate efficiently. It motivates users to request only economically viable services; however, it also encourages outsourcing because internal prices and service likely resemble those of outsource providers. Also, IS as a profit center attempts to earn a return on its investments, so it generally charges users more than it would as either an unallocated or an allocated cost center (assuming that such centers operated with equal efficiency). These higher costs tend to discourage the use of information systems and technology for solving business problems.

Steering Committees

An **IS steering committee** includes top business managers, selected users, MIS managers, and technical specialists who provide direction and vision about the use and development of the IS infrastructure. Such a steering committee increases the likelihood that IS investments and activities will align with organizational goals, and it increases the participation and buy-in of key managers in the development of the IS architecture. A steering committee, however, may take too long to make decisions; steering committee meetings may take valuable time of high-level managers; arguments in committee may divide rather than unify the approach toward IS; and committee participants may lack the expertise to help make sound decisions. Steering committees work best when IS is significant for accomplishing organizational goals and the organizational culture supports a participative management style.[57] The MIS manager in less participative cultures may resent a committee that infringes on his or her managerial prerogatives.

The organization and composition of a steering committee influence its effectiveness. The committee should include current and potential user managers who have some exposure to information technology, but a user manager should chair the committee.[58] Companies in which IS has strategic value (see Chapter 12) should include top-level managers, such as the executive vice-president, president, or CEO, on the committee. Companies in which IS plays a less strategic role should include only middle-level managers if top-level managers feel that the committee requires too much of their time.[59]

Security

Information users and IS professionals should jointly develop procedures to ensure the security of their systems and data. Security risks include the deliberate theft or sabotage of data and systems by individuals or organizations and the inadvertent loss of data and systems through the use of damaging programs called viruses or through major hardware or software failures.

Fraud and Unauthorized Use. Information systems that hold confidential or competitive data should employ a scheme to keep people from seeing or changing data unless authorized. Companies such as Brookstone, for example, may want to limit access to their payroll database, ensure that only selected users have access to their customer list, or maintain the confidentiality of their pricing schemes. Experts argue that companies remain unprepared for the security challenges of the next century and should take a proactive approach to integrating security precautions into their infrastructure: Illegal access to computer dial-up lines remains high, and disgruntled workers may disrupt business by retaining access to corporate records.[60] For example, the General Accounting Office of the U.S. government found major security and control problems in five of six stock exchanges in the United States.[61] The U.S. Department of Defense computers experienced several break-ins and tampering by **hackers**—individuals who access computer systems without authorization, often for the challenge of doing so—during the Gulf War.[62]

U.S. Department of Defense

The simplest and least secure schemes require authorized users to know one or more secret passwords. The major problem with password protection is that unauthorized users with enough skill and opportunity can usually obtain a password surreptitiously from one or more of the authorized users. The techniques that a security cracker can use to break password schemes include searching desk space for written passwords, guessing the password that a user might select (often names or nicknames of family members), watching an authorized user as he or she types the password, reading and decoding the files in which the computer stores encrypted versions of valid passwords, and even replacing the keyboard with one that transmits a radio signal as each key is pressed. A system's vulnerability to a security breach increases as the number of people authorized to access a system increases.

A more secure approach to protecting against unauthorized access requires the computer to recognize the physical appearance of its users. Devices can screen users based on their voices, finger or palm prints, or the shape and color of their eyes. Combining such systems with password protection provides a much higher level of security but a greater likelihood of malfunction. For example, a person's voice may change if he or she has a cold; his or her finger or hand print may be unrecognizable if the print contains dirt or oil. Finally, physical recognition may not be appropriate in a mobile environment where authorized users employ telecommunication equipment to address the system.

No system can prevent authorized users from using it in unauthorized ways. Computer fraud in commercial banks, for example, has increased with the use of electronic funds transfer and averages $400,000 per occurrence.[63] Managers can divide tasks among two or more employees or have two or more employees perform the same tasks to guard against such unauthorized use. These countermeasures increase security but reduce productivity and can still fail if the parties can collude. Restricting some users, especially those who maintain databases, develop software and systems, or provide security, from accessing a broad range of programs and data and potentially inflicting serious harm is almost impossible.

Virus Infection. A **computer virus** is a program that inserts a copy of itself into other programs. A computer virus, like its biological namesake, spreads from one host to another, but unlike a biological virus, it hides inside programs rather than in the cells of its host. Running **infected programs** causes the virus to instruct them to infect other programs. A virus can spread from one computer to another by diskettes being used legitimately to move data from between computers or by messages on networks that electronically connect several computers.

A virus, in addition to infecting other programs, can perform other undesirable or destructive acts, such as erasing data or programs, blanking or printing unwanted messages on the screen, or dispatching electronic mail messages. Most viruses are not set up to actually damage information systems until a certain amount of time has passed or until they have infected several other programs. During this latent stage, unsuspecting users spread the virus during the normal course of business. The delay between the initial viral infection and its discovery considerably complicates the process of finding and prosecuting the parties responsible for the infection.

The challenge of bypassing the security protection schemes of commercial systems apparently motivates some people to develop new viruses. Other viruses, however, appear to result from innocent pranks or experiments gone awry. For example, in 1988, Robert Morris, Jr., introduced a virus into the Cornell University computer system (technically, Morris unleashed a worm, not a virus, because the program did not infect other programs, only other computer systems). Morris's program used electronic mail programs to infect certain types of computers connected to Cornell through the Internet and through other networks.[64] Infected computers, in turn, infected other computers with which they exchanged mail. Although not designed to damage data or disable computer systems, and, although designed to recognize and avoid already-infected systems, Morris's virus did not work properly in all cases. The virus infected many systems numerous times and halted them as a result of the computing demands of multiple copies of the virus running at the same time. System administrators who recognized the virus disconnected their computers from the Internet to limit the spread of the infection. This reduction in Internet connections, along with the exponentially growing volume of communication generated by the virus, caused the Internet to become clogged. Researchers around the world could not use their own computers or the Internet for almost three days while virus specialists developed antidotes to bring the infections under control. Morris was quickly caught, convicted under the 1986 Computer Fraud and Abuse Act (discussed later in this chapter), fined $10,000, given a three-year suspended jail term, and sentenced to 400 hours of community service; his attorney fees were estimated to exceed $150,000.[65]

Governments may employ viruses in times of war to disable or gain access to enemy systems. For example, in the 1991 war against Iraq, U.S. agents reportedly programmed a virus onto a computer chip on a printer destined for Iraq. The virus successfully infected the mainframe to which the printer was attached, making it impossible for Iraqi technicians to access data on the computer.[66] Viruses similar to the Morris program have been used to identify passwords on foreign computers and to create new accounts with known passwords for the purpose of espionage.

The IS infrastructure should include software and procedures to protect against viral infection. Commercial antiviral software should be installed on all systems and used regularly. In addition, computer users should, to the extent possible, avoid transferring software from unprotected sources, such as their home computers or public bulletin boards, to the systems they use at work. If a user brings in a diskette from outside the organization, he or she should check it with antiviral software before using it.

Major Crashes and Natural Disasters. The information systems infrastructure at organizations that are heavily dependent on computerized information systems should also include equipment, contracts, and procedures for recovering from major systems crashes, especially those caused by natural disasters. A standard practice to protect against most hardware or software failures is to back up data periodically. Transaction processing systems (see Chapter 10) are normally designed to maintain a transaction log, often on a separate disk or tape, that describes all transactions that have occurred since the previous backup. If the failure does not destroy the transaction log, the backup and log together can reconstruct the data to a time just prior to the failure.

Many organizations periodically move backup copies to off-site locations where they can be recovered if a fire, flood, earthquake, or other natural disaster damages the building where

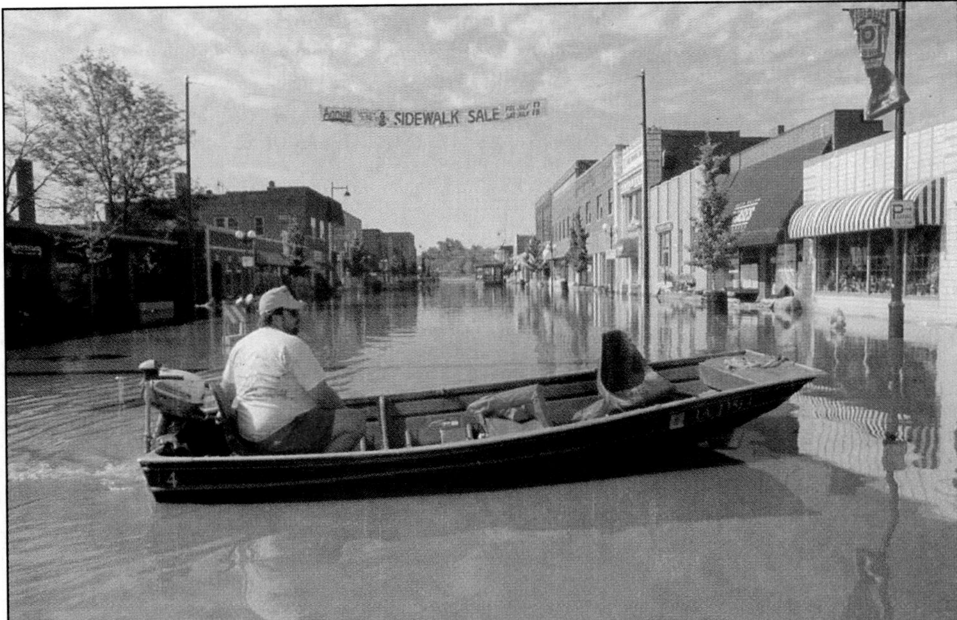

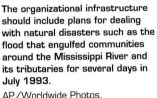

The organizational infrastructure should include plans for dealing with natural disasters such as the flood that engulfed communities around the Mississippi River and its tributaries for several days in July 1993.

AP/Worldwide Photos.

the data and its immediate backup are normally stored. If damage is sufficiently severe to require recovery from off-site backups, some data will invariably be lost. However, the level of recovery will usually be complete enough to enable the company to continue to operate if computers can be found to run its software and access its data. Companies that house their computer equipment at multiple locations can simply transfer the backed-up data to another company site. Those that house their computer equipment at a single location should contract with third parties to ensure their ability to operate in the face of natural disasters.

DES MOINES, IOWA

The major flooding of the midwest United States in 1993 caused the computers at two main administrative centers of the city of Des Moines, Iowa, to cease functioning. The city's lack of a disaster recovery plan kept its computers useless for more than a week. Meanwhile, several other Des Moines companies, including a bank, a wheel and tire manufacturer, an insurance company, and a financial services company, used disaster recovery services purchased from Comdisco, Inc. in Rosemont, Illinois, SunGard Recovery Services, Inc. in Atlanta and Chicago, and IBM Business Recovery Services in Minneapolis to continue running their transaction processing systems at normal capacity.[67] A recent survey of companies operating mainframe computer systems found that 56 percent have a stand-by site in case of disaster, that 68 percent have a disaster recovery plan in place, and that recovery plans were tested on average more than once per year.[68]

National and Global Infrastructures

Organizations are affected by external infrastructures that provide a framework for their internal and external operations. Among the most important of these is the legal infrastructure that regulates the use, potential abuse, transportation, and communication of information. In addition, the physical infrastructure for communication among organizations affects how an organization operates. In the United States, many companies take the communication infrastructure for granted, but organizations operating globally need to carefully assess the communication infrastructures in the countries where they plan to do business.

The Legal Environment

Laws pertaining to computers, information processing, and software liability and theft exist in almost every country. These laws protect companies and individuals from the misuse of information about them and from the theft of information and property rights.

Information Systems and Privacy. The computerization of information has limited the ability of individuals to maintain their privacy. Computers in business organizations, government, and even religious organizations hold extensive, marketable personal information.[69] When a person applies for credit, for example, the bank likely will place information about his or her employer, salary, current and past residences, and names of previous creditors into a database. A person who purchases goods through mail order or television order likely will have information about products purchased and even personal preferences entered into a database. Your travel agency's database may hold historical information about where and what times of the year you most often travel. Computers can now easily summarize and retrieve data about individuals from an array of such databases, and computer networks have eased the task of connecting, searching, and matching data from diverse databases. Almost any person can obtain a profile about another individual that includes that person's age, hobbies, income, number of children, number of credit cards, and annual spending on travel and entertainment for less than $500. Leaks in medical and insurance data have resulted in individuals losing or being denied jobs, and false or misleading data have resulted in worthy consumers being denied credit for houses and cars. Electronic mail poses special problems because 1) users may not realize that a recipient of a message has forwarded it to another party, 2) individuals other than the addressee may read the mail, 3) the message does not necessarily disappear upon receipt, and 4) confusion about the impact of various commands, such as "reply," may result in broader dissemination of the message than intended.[70]

In the United States and in many other countries, the legal system provides some measure of protection against the unwanted and abusive use of personal information. The United States Constitution itself provides no explicit right to privacy, although the Fourth Amendment, which protects against "unreasonable searches and seizures," can be broadly construed as granting a person physical privacy on his or her own property and person. The Supreme Court has prohibited the disclosure of personal information contained in company or government databases only when it infringes upon other guaranteed liberties.[71] To protect the public against possible abuses of computerized information, the U.S. Congress has enacted a number of laws since 1970 increasing individual privacy; Figure 14-9 shows the most important ones. Many states have also enacted laws to protect against the abusive use of information contained in their own databases.

Many foreign governments provide more privacy protection for their citizens, and IS systems may incorporate these provisions into their infrastructures. For example, France requires the registration of all governmental and private databases with the National Commission on Informatics and Freedom; prohibits the use of fraudulent, dishonest, or illegal means in collecting the data; and insists that data so collected be used only for the purposes declared at the time of collection. The Commission must also give prior approval for any person, company, or agency to match data from two or more databases to provide a combined profile of any person.[72] Most European governments provide similar guarantees of privacy.

Unauthorized Use and Computer Fraud. The Computer Fraud and Abuse Act of 1986 protects government computers and government data from unauthorized access. U.S. law currently does not punish anyone for accessing a private computer so long as that person did not use the access for espionage and did not examine or alter another user's files. Of course, if individuals or organizations obtain access to private computers by fraudulent means, they may be prosecuted under the general laws regarding fraud. Earlier in this chapter we discussed measures that companies can take to protect their data and systems against unauthorized access.

Software Liability. Software, like any other product, can contain flaws that cause it to operate in unintended ways. As software plays a role in many critical products such as x-ray and air traffic control equipment, its malfunction can have damaging consequences. IS professionals should understand the nature of their own or other vendors' software liability. Software sold as part of a product carries an implied guarantee that it will work properly. If the software fails to work properly, users can sue the developer for breach of warranty or negligent design.

Courts need to determine whether software not sold as part of a product should be judged as a product because only manufacturers are subject to breach of warranty. Publishers and authors are judged under different standards; they are not subject to breach of warranty because it is assumed that the buyer has the knowledge to interpret the information in a book and use it wisely. There is insufficient case law at this time to determine whether software and electronic information will be treated more as a product or as a service.[73] Similarly, how courts will deal with software that works properly but whose instructions are sufficiently vague that the user suffers harm is not clear.

Computer Viruses and Related Sabotage. Although U.S. law does not provide direct penalties for development and use of a computer virus, the Computer Fraud and Abuse Act of 1986 can be applied if the virus affects computers or databases funded in

Major U.S. Privacy Laws

Fair Credit Reporting Act of 1970

This law regulates the usage of data contained in credit bureau files. Data owners are prohibited from selling credit information to or sharing credit information with anyone who does not have a "legitimate" business need. Also, consumers have the right to examine and challenge credit bureau files and must be notified of certain credit investigations. The law limits the amount of time certain derogatory information, such as bankruptcy or arrest, can be kept on file.

Freedom of Information Act of 1970

This law gives U.S. citizens the right to examine information that the U.S. government retains about them.

Privacy Act of 1974

With some fairly broad exceptions, this law prohibits federal government offices from sharing information about an individual with other government offices without the individual's consent. This law also increases an individual's power, granted by the Freedom of Information Act of 1970, to examine records that the government maintains about that individual and provides a process for correcting errors in such records.

Family Educational Rights and Privacy Act of 1974

With some exceptions, this act prohibits educational institutions that receive federal funds from releasing personal information about students without their consent except to their parents and to school officials with a "need to know."

Equal Credit Opportunity Act of 1974

This act prohibits creditors from requesting information about a person's sex, race, color, religion, or national origin.

Right to Financial Privacy Act of 1978

This act limits federal government access to data maintained by financial institutions such as banks. Access is permitted only by subpoena, court order, or search warrant, and the individual must be notified.

Electronic Funds Transfer Act of 1978

This act requires that customers be told in advance if any data kept about them in an EFT system might be provided to third parties.

Cable Communications Policy Act of 1984

This act requires that cable operators notify their customers about any information that the company collects about them or their cable use. Companies must have customer permission to release this data to third parties.

Electronic Communications Privacy Act of 1986

This act regulates the personal information that the government can obtain from records collected by communications providers, such as telephone companies. It also protects the privacy of electronic mail carried exclusively by and stored on public networks.

continued

FIGURE 14-9 Continued

Computer Fraud and Abuse Act of 1986
This act makes it illegal for anyone to access without authorization any computer or databases funded in whole or in part by the federal government.

Video Privacy Protection Act of 1988
This act prohibits companies from disclosing a customer's video rental records without his or her permission or a court order.

Computer Matching and Privacy Protection Act of 1988
This act regulates, but does not prohibit, the use of computer data to determine a person's eligibility for federal benefits or for recovering debts. It specifies that a person has a right to dispute the data before they can be used against him or her.

whole or in part by the federal government, even though the virus's creator has little or no control over it once it is unleashed. As discussed earlier in this chapter, Robert Morris was effectively prosecuted under this act for the worm program he unleashed on the Internet.

Copyright Protection of Software and Information. Organizations face the challenge of developing policies for disseminating software to users that abide by U.S. copyright laws. A **copyright** refers to the right of an author of an original work to receive payment from those who copy it. A copyright, which is valid throughout the life of the author and for 50 years after his or her death, extends only to the expression of the work fixed in a tangible medium, not to the idea or concept of the work. A **patent** protects an idea from being copied. Patents have been applied to software, but the case law in this area is still evolving. Software users and internal developers rarely need to concern themselves with patent law in performing their work.

The **fair use doctrine,** which permits the legal production of copies in a variety of circumstances that either encourage the progress of arts and science or cause no substantial diminution of the author's market, limits the scope of a copyright. The fair use doctrine, for example, applies to news reporting, criticism and commentary, research and teaching, and relatively small portions of a larger work.[74] Users often do not understand the fine points of software licenses and other contracts with software vendors, which contributes to copyright violations.[75]

The Copyright Act of 1976 explicitly extends copyright protection to software. As amended, however, the act permits the rightful owner of a copy to make an additional copy if the new copy is an essential step in using the computer program or if the copy is only for archival purposes. Both source and executable code are protected on any media, including ROM. An individual cannot rent software without violating copyright law. Congress specifically prohibited this because of the ease of making copies. Violating copyright laws may be a misdemeanor or felony punishable by jail, depending on the number of copies made and their value.[76] Software pirating occurs commonly in some countries outside the United States. Taiwan, South Korea, Italy, and Poland led the list in flagrant violation of copyright laws in 1992.[77]

Publishing of information in electronic formats, such as searchable databases, has increased significantly in the last decade, and copyright law typically protects such published information. For example, publishers distribute encyclopedias, stock price histories, legal databases, clip art, and electronic journals on media such as diskette, CD-ROM, and the Internet. Copyright protection does not easily extend to searchable databases. An individual could copy data in the database and sell it. Prosecuting individuals who illegally use such products has posed significant dilemmas[78] because theft involves the *removal* of an item from its owner, while stealing information involves *copying* rather than removing the information. The owner of the original copy suffers a loss due to the reduction in the value of his or her copy. Most often, these types of crimes have been prosecuted on the basis of unauthorized use rather than theft.

Communication Infrastructure

The communications infrastructure consists of terminal equipment (telephones, for example), local lines, long-distance lines, switching equipment, satellite services, and other equipment owned by telecommunications providers, as well as the regulations affecting the design, sale, ownership, and operation of such equipment. Most countries regulate various aspects of the communication industry. Many governments treat telephone service at the local level and even at the national level as a monopoly. Many countries have state-owned telephone equipment and telephone service companies. Their governments often participate in rate setting and may specify minimum service levels and service alternatives. Almost all countries regulate wireless communication, including radio, television, and cellular telephone, more tightly because of the limited capacity of the electromagnetic spectrum and the potentially unlimited demand for its use. Governments determine the wavelengths available for particular media and typically reserve some of the wavelength spectrum for police and military use.

Companies require telecommunications services to exchange information internally among different sites and externally with customers and suppliers. Managers need to be aware that they cannot be assured of obtaining adequate telecommunication services in many places, especially in third-world countries. Even where they can obtain such services, the cost may be prohibitive. For example, in 1993, the cost of a data link from New York to Los Angeles was about $1,200 per month. A data link with similar capacity between Hong Kong and Tokyo cost about $11,500 per month.[79]

Summary

An organization's information systems infrastructure consists of its hardware and communications equipment, its software and systems, and its staff. Information technology architecture describes the long-term structural plan for investing in and organizing information technology. The architecture includes the specification of standards for hardware, software, and communication equipment. Standards refer to the rules that govern the types of investments the organization makes in information technology. Increasingly companies have downsized their computer operations, often selecting a client/server architecture for information processing. Selecting an architecture for a global organization presents a unique set of problems and issues.

The human infrastructure includes the IS jobs individuals hold. These include the positions of data entry clerk, operations and technical support staff, user trainer, user assistant, programmer, systems analyst, project manager, data administrator, database administrator, strategic planner, technology assessment specialist, and chief information officer. These positions require a combination of technical, managerial, and interpersonal skills for successful job performance. End-user computing focuses on the consumers of the IS services. Increasingly end users contribute to systems development. Most organizations establish a help desk to help end users solve their information systems problems.

The information systems infrastructure includes the organizational structure that affects control of information and information processing and the policies and procedures surrounding the processing and use of information. Organizing the IS function involves determining whether to centralize or decentralize the IS staff. The IS function can operate as an unallocated cost center, an allocated cost center, or a profit center. In addition, organizations must decide to what extent to outsource IS services. Often steering committees composed of top executives, IS professionals, and other users guide the IS effort in organizations. Information users and IS professionals should jointly develop the infrastructure to assure the security of their systems and data against malfunction, theft, viruses, and natural disasters.

Organizations operate under an external infrastructure of laws affecting information and its exchange as well as an external telecommunications infrastructure. Managers should recognize that information systems can infringe on the privacy of individuals and introduce protections to safeguard information. They should also protect their systems from unauthorized use and computer fraud. Furthermore, they should recognize and obey copyright law in their use of computer software and use copyright law to protect the interest of their company in software it has developed. Finally, managers of global organizations should be aware that the telecommunication infrastructure differs markedly from country to country and that the free transfer of information within or between many countries may be difficult, costly, and/or illegal.

Key Terms

Allocated cost center
Architecture
Chief information officer (CIO)
Computer virus
Copyright
Data administrator
Data entry clerk
Database administrator
Downsizing
End user
Fair use doctrine
Hacker
Help desk
Infected program
Information center
Infrastructure
IS steering committee
ISO 9000
Outsourcing
Patent
Profit center
Programmer
Project manager
Right-sizing
Software developer
Software engineer
Standard
Systems analyst
Unallocated cost center

Review Questions

1. Define and identify the components of an information systems infrastructure.
2. Describe the difference between infrastructure and architecture.
3. What are the advantages and disadvantages of having an architecture?
4. Discuss the advantages and disadvantages of standardization in the IT architecture.
5. Identify several advantages and disadvantages to downsizing.
6. Why are performance problems more common and more difficult to deal with in the client/server environment than in a mainframe environment?
7. Identify four strategies companies use to migrate to a client/server environment.
8. Identify four issues that should be considered in designing an architecture for a global organization.
9. List and describe six information systems jobs.
10. Contrast the roles of data administrator and database administrator.
11. Describe the typical help desk.
12. Describe three options for organizing the help-desk function.
13. What are the advantages to centralizing control of IS services even as a company migrates from a mainframe to a client/server environment?
14. Identify the advantages and disadvantages of outsourcing information systems services.
15. Identify three options for accounting for information systems services. Discuss advantages and disadvantages of each.

16. What benefits can be provided by an IS steering committee? What problems can such a committee present?
17. Identify three types of security problems that IS professionals and information users should guard against.
18. What are the problems with password systems as a protection against fraud and unauthorized use of a company's computer systems?
19. How can companies protect against loss of data and the inability to operate during and after natural disasters?
20. Explain why the computerization of information has limited the ability of individuals to maintain their privacy.
21. Describe how the fair use doctrine limits the scope of a copyright.
22. What problems do global companies face in dealing with the communication infrastructure in countries throughout the world?

MINICASE

United Airlines: Downsizing a 25-Year-Old Aircraft Maintenance System

United Airlines is putting its 25-year-old aircraft maintenance information systems in the repair bay for a re-engineering overhaul.

By so doing, the $14.5 billion airline said it is continuing its three-year drive toward client/server systems by rolling out Unix-based servers. The airline has previously tested its client/server wings at its primary hub center at O'Hare International Airport in Chicago as well as in food-service operations.

By 1998, the fully deployed Engineering and Maintenance System (EMSys) wil run on about 350 Unix servers and 10,000 client machines. The clients, including IBM-compatible PCs, Macintoshes, and Unix workstations, will be used by mechanics from San Francisco to Tokyo to London to access on-line databases of technical information.

United plans to save $175 million to $200 million over five years and to reduce airplane stays in repair hangars by 10 percent, said Wayne Anderson, director of MIS systems at United's maintenance division. United estimates it will save enough to buy five jets, while expanding its overall fleet from 550 jets to 600 by 1998.

First, an on-line database called the Technical Information Management System (TIMS) will put paper-based repair data on-line, using federal Computer-aided Acquisition and Logistics Support standards to exchange data with airplane manufacturers. In 1996, after the Material Management System for warehousing engine parts and a new Planning & Control scheduling system ship, some mainframe applications will be taken off-line at United's Chicago headquarters.

Mainframe Inspired

To write all the EMSys applications, United and IBM's Integrated Systems Solutions Corp. (ISSC) consulting unit fielded a team of more than 200 developers. The revamp of maintenance systems is part of an IS effort that will change business processes as it replaces mainframe applications.

The arrival of the new Boeing 777 jet was a strong reason for replacing outdated paper-based maintenance systems, said Joe Mihalik, business development manager at ISSC in Boul-

---

SOURCE: Jean S. Bozman, United's maintenance flies client/server skies: Worldwide mechanics to gain access to on-line manuals, *Computerworld* (November 7, 1994): 79.

der, Colorado. Mechanics will soon be able to log on to many different Unix servers to access more than 80,000 pages of technical manuals on Boeing 777 parts.

Distributed databases are expected to prevent system downtime as they bring TIMS's on-line technical manuals closer to end users. Replicated Sybase, Inc. System 10 databases will prevent work outages if one or more of the distributed Unix servers fail, Anderson said.

Although United did not disclose the full cost of the system, EMSys architecture creator Qadrant International PLC in Sydney, Australia, said a complete EMSys would cost from $10 million to more than $50 million, depending on airline size. Qadrant is affiliated with the Australian airline Qantas Airways Ltd.

Stephan Regulinski, vice-president of base maintenance for United's worldwide maintenance operations, said United had budgeted less than $100 million for the EMSys project because it is developing much of the EMSys application code in-house.

Substantial Benefit

Airline industry experts said United's up-front investment will be well worth the cost, particularly if it creates more efficient operations. "They're in it for the long run," said Alan R. Youngberg, national director at Ernst & Young's aviation consulting practice in Washington. "They're willing to expend capital to improve their competitiveness."

By running a more effiicient repair shop on five continents, United plans to save both time and money. "The fundamental change in the business process is that about 60 percent of the work we do is nonroutine," said John Curphey, manager of project development engineering at United's operations division here. "We want to reduce that nonroutine work from over 50 percent to under 20 percent."

Case Questions

1. What technical changes does United Airlines intend to make in its aircraft maintenance information systems?
2. What advantages does United expect to gain when it replaces its mainframe architecture with a client/server architecture?
3. How does United plan to phase in the changes it foresees?

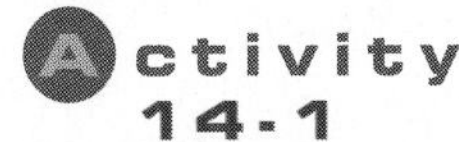

IS Job Interview

external contact

STEP 1: Interview three information systems job holders about their job responsibilities, past and anticipated career path, and interactions with other IS professionals and non-IS job holders in the organization. (Your instructor may direct you to conduct your interviews outside class or may convene a panel of IS job holders for you to interview.)

STEP 2: Prepare a job description for each position.

STEP 3: In small groups or with the entire class, share the job descriptions.

STEP 4: In small groups or with the entire class, answer the following questions:

1. What types of jobs exist in information systems?
2. What types of career paths exist in information systems?
3. How do IS job holders relate to other organizational members? ●

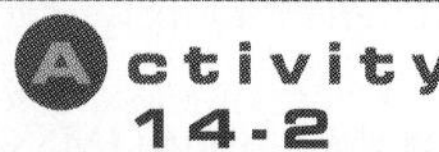

Activity 14-2 End-User Quiz

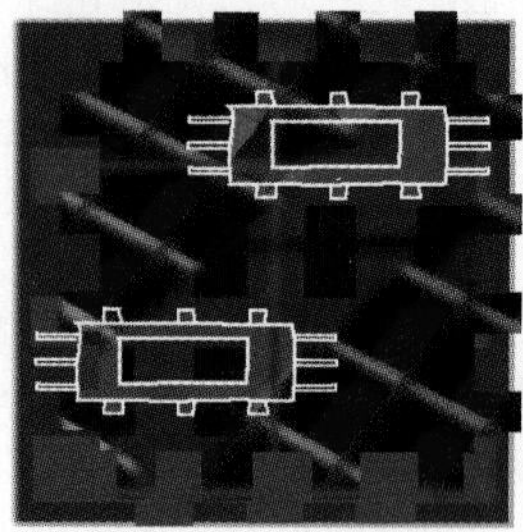

short case

STEP 1: Complete the following quiz. Interpret each statement as a stand-alone situation; there is no relationship among the various scenarios. Answer each question according to this scale: I sympathize . . .

A. with the user. B. with IS. C. with both. D. with neither.

Then indicate the major problem that exists in each situation.

SCENARIO 1

User manager: Our charge-back expenses are astronomical. Sky-high salaries on the IS side don't help the situation.

IS manager: I'm sorry you feel that way, but our salaries are market driven. We pay the salaries we have to pay to attract good people—as your department does. We should sit down and discuss your charge-back expenses. They are based on the time that our people and hardware devote to your priorities.

SCENARIO 2

User manager: System development time is always quite a bit more than you estimate. Why? Why can't we ever get a system on time? What are we doing wrong?

IS manager: It's simple—you are constantly changing requirements. The system we are developing today is not the same as the system we began developing last month. You have to be more careful at the front end in gathering systems requirements. The more time you spend gathering requirements for the system, the less time it will take to code, test, and maintain the system.

SCENARIO 3

User manager: Instead of waiting for the new system, we've purchased a personal computer package and are going ahead with implementation plans. The package meets our needs perfectly. We won't have to bother you at all.

IS manager: That's fine with us as long as you don't need any help from us.

SCENARIO 4

User manager: The CEO tells me IS will not approve the purchase of any equipment other than IBMs. What is the reason for this? We want to buy Hewlett-Packard printers because they are much quieter than IBMs.

IS manager: In the interest of uniformity and standardization, we want all the computer equipment in the company to come from one vendor. The uniformity simplifies billing, maintenance, and support. Besides, IBM is the largest computer company in the world. IBM is a "safe" purchase.

SCENARIO 5

User manager: We need your staff to perform a small modification to the open purchase order inquiry display.

IS manager: It's going to take a long time. The programmer who wrote that particular program left the company, and no one else understands it very well.

STEP 2: Your instructor will provide directions for scoring your responses.

STEP 3: In small groups or with the class as a whole, answer the following questions:

1. What issue does each scenario describe?
2. Which party presents a better analysis and perspective on the situation?
3. What actions would improve the situation described? ●

Legal Dilemmas

short case

STEP 1: Read cases 1–4. For each case, first decide what you would do and why. In doing so, consider the information you would use to investigate the question, the alternatives you would consider, and the criteria you would use in making your decision.

CASE 1

You manage a group of ten financial analysts who determine the feasibility of loans to large corporate customers. One of the analysts started using a new financial software package three weeks ago. The analyst said that the package really improved the accuracy and speed of assessing risk in potential loans. He convinced you that the new package would help all the analysts. When you requested that the IS department purchase copies for your analysts, they refused, stating that your department had already spent its software budget. What do you do?

CASE 2

You own a small real-estate agency. You recently purchased new accounting software from a small, newly incorporated vendor. You purchased the software because it has features that work especially well for the mix of properties your agency sells. After installing and using the software for approximately three months, you discover that the software has created major errors in your accounting of commissions for your salespeople. You try to speak to the vendor but discover that it is no longer in business. What do you do?

CASE 3

You manage the clerical staff responsible for accounts payable in a moderate-size university. You have heard on local newscasts that a computer virus has affected all Macintosh computers that had any interaction with the Internet in the past month. The virus will erase all data from the system in exactly one week at midnight. Your department uses only Macintosh computers, and you know that some of the clerks spend their free time "surfing" the Internet. What should you do?

CASE 4

You manage the mail-order business of a firm that specializes in home furnishings. You have developed a substantial database about the preferences and purchases of your customers over the past five years. A political candidate has recently approached you about selling information from your database to him. What do you do?

STEP 2: In groups of four to six students, reach a consensus about how to handle each situation.

STEP 3: In small groups, with the entire class, or in written form, as directed by your instructor, answer the following questions:

1. What issue did each case raise?
2. What alternatives are available in dealing with the issues raised?
3. What would you recommend that the manager in each case do next? ●

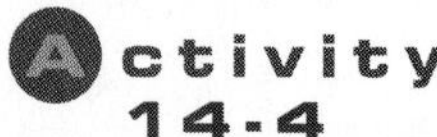

Activity 14-4 IS Structure in a Full-Service Bank

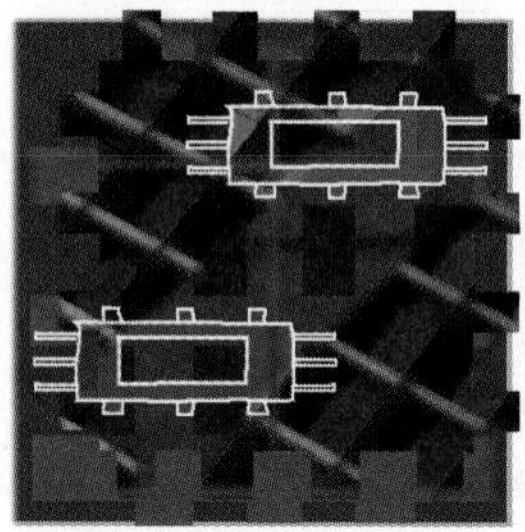

short case

Delta Bank offers a full range of financial services, including commercial, personal, and trust accounts through a statewide network of branches. The bank has approximately 150 branches and 6,000 employees organization-wide; the operations department has approximately 1,000 employees, 700 of whom belong to information systems groups. The bank has four major functional areas with the overall responsibility of managing IT centralized in the operations group. IS services include the following: technical services, systems services, quality assurance, planning, data security, training, data center, voice networks, data networks, and word processing,

STEP 1: Review the two organizational charts shown in Figure 14-10. What are the advantages and disadvantages for Delta Bank of organizing its IT function in each of these ways?

STEP 2: Design a third alternative for structuring the IT function at Delta Bank.

STEP 3: Share your design with the entire class. Evaluate the relative advantages and disadvantages of each group's proposed design. Which structure is likely to be most effective? ●

FIGURE 14-10 Two Organizational Charts for Delta Bank

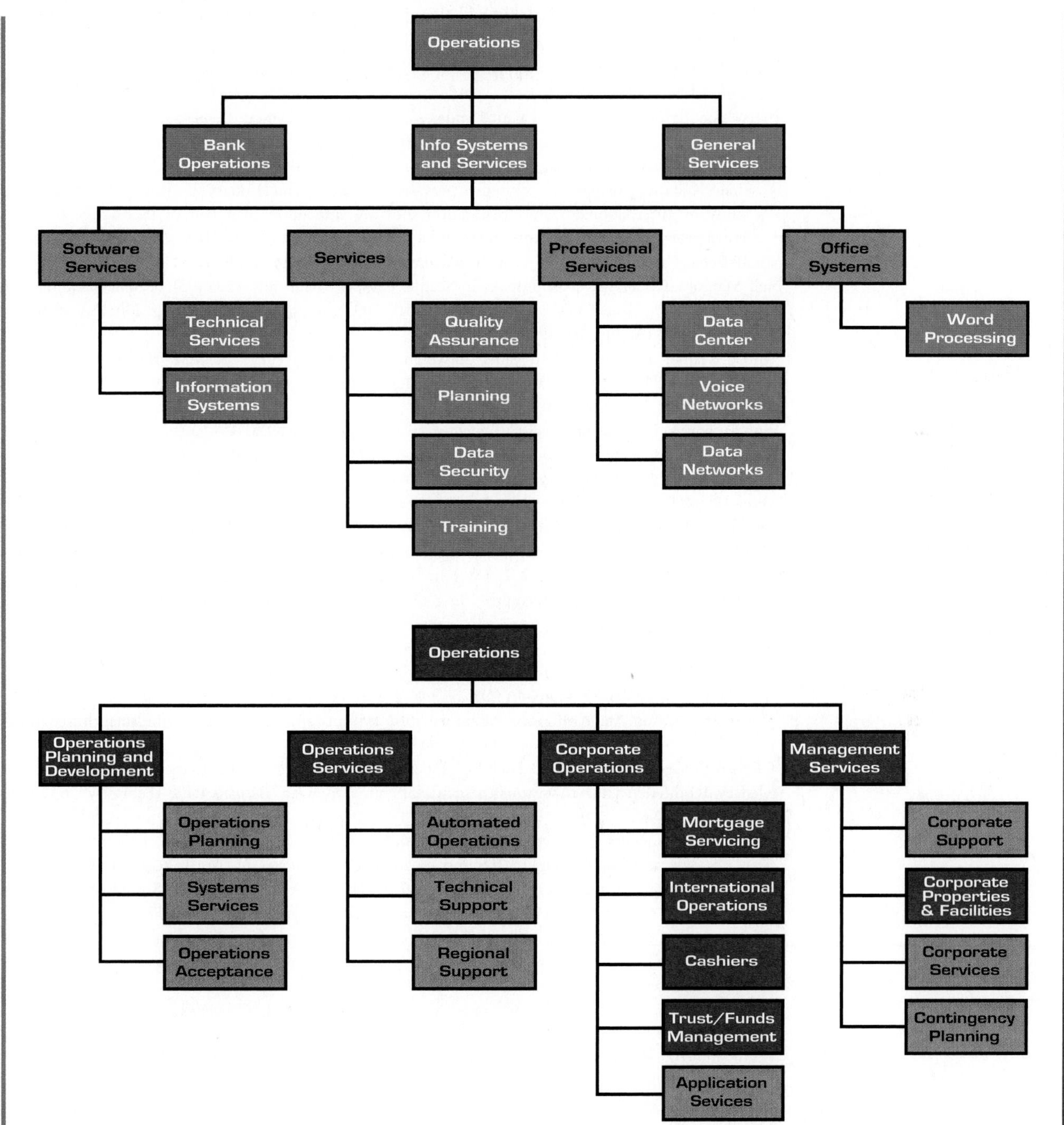

Reprinted with permission from J. Ellis Blanton, Hugh J. Watson, and Janette Moody, Toward a better understanding of information technology organization: A comparative case study, *MIS Quarterly* (December 1992): 531–551.

Notes

[1]Reprinted with permission from Christopher Lindquist, Round 'em up, *Computerworld* (July 27, 1992): 89.

[2]Christopher Lindquist, Changing the game at Brookstone, *Computerworld* (July 26, 1992): 77, 89.

[3]Gary H. Anthes, ISO standard attracts U.S. interest, *Computerworld* (April 26, 1993): 109

[4]Richard A. Danca, One bank's approach to IT: Standard—but not stodgy, *Client/Server Computing* (August 1994): 34–36, 95.

[5]Sheryl Kay, Tribune strives to balance independence and efficiency, *Computerworld* (December 10, 1990): 91.

[6]Rosemary Cafasso, Spalding tees up client/server, *Computerworld* (March 22, 1993): 51.

[7]Rosemary Cafasso, Client/server strategies pervasive, *Computerworld* (January 25, 1993): 47. Cafasso cites a study by International Data Corporation showing that more than half of IS managers believe client/server applications increase costs, while only 34 percent believe they reduce costs.

[8]Mitch Betts, The bite of hidden costs, *Computerworld* (July 26, 1993): 66.

[9]Nell Margolis, Client/server ship docks in Seattle, *Computerworld* (July 12, 1993): 6; Alan Radding, The accidental downsizer, *Computerworld* (August 10, 1992): 66; and Alan Radding, Dirty downsizing, *Computerworld* (August 10, 1992): 65–67.

[10]Mitch Kramer, Developers find gains outweigh OO learning curve, *Software Magazine* (November 1993): 23–33; and Mitch Kramer, Large app development a job for OO A&D tools, *Software Magazine* (January 1994): 39–49.

[11]Bob Janusaitis, LAN management, *Computerworld* (January 27, 1992): 91–100.

[12]Joe Panepinto, Client/server breakdown, *Computerworld* (October 4, 1993): 107–111.

[13]James A. Hepler, Network jam, *Computerworld* (April 26, 1993): 89–90.

[14]Peter Nulty, When to murder your mainframe, *Fortune* (November 1, 1993): 109–120.

[15]Joseph Maglitta and Carol Hildebrand, A bridge too late, *Computerworld* (May 31, 1993): 69–74.

[16]Joe Panepinto, op. cit. Source: An Interactive Data Corporation 1993 survey of 858 information systems executives.

[17]Adapted from Jean S. Bozman, Approaching migration, *Computerworld* (March 22, 1993): 51–52.

[18]Peter Nulty, op. cit.: 114.

[19]Johanna Ambrosio, Walk, don't run, with it, *Computerworld* (March 15, 1993): 65.

[20]Thomas Hoffman, Here and there, *Computerworld* (April 12, 1993): 81–82.

[21]Linda Runyan, Global IS strategies, *Datamation* (December 1, 1989): 71–78.

[22]Steven R. Gordon, Standardization of information systems and technology at multinational companies, *Journal of Global Information Management* (Summer 1993): 5–14.

[23]Clinton Wilder, When the CIO becomes expendable, *Computerworld* (February 17, 1992): 1, 16; and Jeffrey Rothfeder, CIO is starting to stand for 'career is over,' *Business Week* (February 26, 1990): 78–80.

[24]Joseph Maglitta, Meet the new boss: A new tradition, *Computerworld* (March 14, 1994): 80–82.

[25]Alan Radding and Joseph Maglitta, Techno renaissance, *Computerworld* (April 26, 1993): 67–68.

[26]Thomas C. Padgett, Catherine M. Beise, and Fred J. Ganoe, Job preparation of IS graduates: Are they ready for the real world? *Journal of Systems Management* 42(8) (August 1991): 17.

[27]Emily Leinfuss, Remember English Lit 101? *Computerworld* (June 15, 1992): 104.

[28]M. B. Khan and Sal Kukalis, MIS professionals: Education and performance, *Information & Management* 19 (November 1990): 249–255.

[29]S. Rivard and S. L. Huff, Factors of success for end-user computing, *Communications of the ACM* 31(5) (May 1988): 522–561.

[30]Carol Hildebrand, FirstLine blurs IS and users, *Computerworld* (May 31, 1993): 74.

[31]See, for example, R. K. Rainer, Jr., and H. H. Carr, Are information centers responsive to end user needs?, *Information & Management* 22(2) (February 1992): 113–121; and Efraim Turban and Joseph Walls, Usage of and support for information centers: An exploratory survey, *Information Resources Management Journal* (Spring 1990): 2–15.

[32]Julia King, Hello, help desk? HELP! *Computerworld* (November 11, 1991): 73–75.

[33]Bob Francis, Downsize the help desk, *Datamation* (February 15, 1992): 49–51.

[34]Elisabeth Horwitt, Basic instinct: Air Force Materiel Command puts the 'user' into user support—one logical step at a time, *Computerworld* (January 11, 1993): 75, 77.

[35]Simha R. Magal and Dennis D. Strouble, A user's perspective of the critical success factors applicable to information centers, *Information Resources Management Journal* (Spring 1991): 22–34.

[36]Robert L. Leitheiser and James C. Wetherbe, A comparison of perceptions about information center success, *Information & Management* 21(1) (August 1991): 7–17.

[37]Johanna Ambrosio, Amoco brings IS closer to end users, *Computerworld* (December 17, 1990): 12.

[38]Leslie Goff, Remote LAN administration requires different approach, *Management Information Systems Week* (March 20, 1989): 20.

[39]Shirin Saks, Career opportunities broaden as MIS moves out to departments, *MIS Week* (September 4, 1989): 30.

[40]Rosemary Hamilton, Insurer keeps the old with the new, *Computerworld* (November 11, 1991): 67, 70.

[41]Ernest M. Von Simson, The "centrally decentralized" IS organization, *Harvard Business Review* 68(4) (July/August 1990): 158–162.

[42]Nell Margolis, Need for central IS grows, *Computerworld* (June 7, 1993): 1, 16.

[43]Joseph Maglitta and Mark Mehler, The new centralization, *Computerworld* (April 27, 1992): 85–86.

[44]David Kirkpatrick, Why not farm out your computing? *Fortune* (September 23, 1991): 103–112.

[45]Ibid.

[46]Clinton Wilder, Giant firms join outsourcing parade, *Computerworld* (September 30, 1991): 1, 91.

[47]Ivy Schmerken, Outsourcing holds the line on technology costs, *Wall Street Computer Review* (January 1991): 13–24.

[48]Michael Fitzgerald, System odyssey leads to outsourcing, *Computerworld* (February 17, 1992): 73, 76.

[49]Kirkpatrick, op. cit.

[50]Nell Margolis and Clinton Wilder, Early adopters give qualified approval, but urge IS to keep its hands on the reins, *Computerworld* (May 4, 1992): 1, 20.

[51]Willie Schatz, Bailoutsourcing, *Computerworld* (January 25, 1993): 57–58.

[52]John Teresko, Outsourcing: Tie it to the right objectives, *Industry Week* (June 1, 1992): 42–44; and Ivy Schmerken, Outsourcing holds the line on technology costs, *Wall Street Computer Review* (January 1991): 13–24.

[53]Paul Clermont, Outsourcing without guilt, *Computerworld* (September 9, 1991): 67–68.

[54]Ibid.

[55]Daniel Sommer, Information centers debate billing for services, *InfoWorld* (January 11, 1988): 38.

[56]Bob Francis, Kimberly-Clark sees profits in IS, *Datamation* (May 15, 1990): 53–54.

[57]Harish C. Bahl and Mohammad Dadashzadeh, A framework for improving effectiveness of MIS steering committees, *Information Resources Management Journal* (Summer 1992): 33–44.

[58]D. H. Drury, An evaluation of data processing steering committees, *MIS Quarterly* 8 (1984): 257–265.

[59]J. I. Cash, Jr., F. Warren McFarlan, J. L. McKenney, and L. M. Applegate, *Corporate Information Systems and Management: Text and Cases* (Homewood, IL: Irwin, 3d ed., 1992): 634; and Bahl and Dadashzadeh, op. cit.

[60]James Daly, Out to get you, *Computerworld* (March 22, 1993): 77–79.

[61]Wayne Eckerson, Network security lacking at major stock exchanges, *Network World* (September 16, 1991): 23.

[62]Hackers at war, *Datamation* (January 1, 1992): 21.

[63]R. Leon Price, John S. Cotner, and Warren L. Dickson, Computer fraud in commercial banks: Management's perception of risk, *Journal of Systems Management* 40(10) (October 1989): 28–33.

[64]This is a simplification. For full details, see Eugene H. Spafford, Crisis and aftermath (The Internet worm), *Communications of the ACM* (June 1989): 678–687.

[65]Peter J. Denning, Sending a signal, *Communications of the ACM* (August 1990): 11–12.

[66]Bacterial warfare, *Datamation* (February 15, 1992): 21.

[67]Ellis Booker, Data dowsed in Midwest floods, *Computerworld* (July 19, 1993): 6.

[68]Trends handling system outages, *Computerworld* (February 8, 1993): 86. Source: Xephon/WPWS, Oviedo, FL.

[69]David F. Linowes, "Changing customer concerns in the 1990s: The privacy issue," *Vital Speeches* 58(7) (January 15, 1992): 198–200; and Mitch Betts, Personal data more public than you think, *Computerworld* (March 9, 1992): 1, 14.

[70]Ernest A. Kallman and Sanford Sherizen, Private matters, *Computerworld* (November 23, 1992): 85–87.

[71]Michael D. Rostoker and Robert H. Rines, *Computer Jurisprudence: Legal Responses to the Information Revolution* (New York: Oceana Publications, Inc., 1986): 235.

[72]Michael R. Rubin, *Private Rights, Public Wrongs: The Computer and Personal Privacy* (Norwood, NJ: Ablex Publishing Corporation, 1988).

[73]Pamela Samuelson, Liability for defective electronic information, *Communications of the ACM* (January 1993): 21–26.

[74]Pamela Samuelson, Computer programs and copyright's fair use doctrine, *Communications of the ACM* (September 1993): 19–25.

[75]Nell Margolis, War between EDS and CA sparks debate, *Computerworld* (March 2, 1992): 51.

[76]Samuelson, op. cit.

[77]Gary H. Anthes, S. Korea, Spain cited as software pirates, *Computerworld* (February 22, 1993): 101.

[78]Rostoker and Rines, op. cit.: 342.

[79]The expert's opinion: An interview with Jack M. Sparn, vice president of data center operations and technical services, Time, Inc., *Journal of Global Information Management* (Summer 1993): 45–48.

Recommended Readings

Deans, Candace and Kane, Michael J. *International Dimensions of Information Systems.* Boston: PWS-Kent, 1992.

Information Technology and Organizations: Challenges of New Technologies. Mehdi Khosrowpour, ed. Harrisburg, PA: Idea Grove Publishing, 1994.

Lacity, Mary Cecilia. *Information Systems Outsourcing.* New York: Wiley, 1993.

Raymond, Patrick. *IT Infrastructure: An Introduction.* Manchester: Blackwell, 1994.

Regan, Elizabeth A. *End-User Information Systems: Perspectives for Managers and Information Systems Professionals.* New York: Macmillan, 1993.

Revolution in Real Time: Measuring Information Technology in the 1990s. Boston: HBS Press, 1991.

The Information Infrastructure. Boston: HBS Press, 1991.

VIDEOCASE

United Parcel Service's International Distribution System

United Parcel Service (UPS) was founded in 1907 by two Seattle teenagers to run errands and deliver packages. By 1930, it had grown throughout the West Coast and had expanded to New York and other large East Coast markets. UPS became international in 1975 when it added Canada to its service district. Germany was added as the first European location in 1976. Now, UPS handles 11 million packages a year in 186 countries and territories around the globe. Approximately 10 percent of its $20 billion in annual revenues comes from foreign operations.

According to Ken Lacey, Vice-President for Information Services, moving information about packages has now become as important to UPS, from a competitive standpoint, as moving the packages themselves. In 1986, UPS committed $1.5 billion to build its information technology infrastructure because the old infrastructure could not respond to customers' demands for information and could not offer the types of information and services that UPS's competitors were providing.

The International Shipments Processing System (ISPS) is one of several systems that were built as part of UPS's infrastructure upgrade. The ISPS transmits data about a package as it is shipped. This information arrives at the destination and intermediate points, such as international custom-clearing checkpoints, hours, or even days, before the package arrives. Because of this advance notice, customs agents can process the paperwork in advance of the package receipt, significantly reducing delays at international borders.

The ISPS works as follows. When a package is received, it is labeled with a bar code. At each point during its shipment, the bar code is rescanned, updating the location of the package in UPS's database. Customers and waiting recipients can check on the progress of a package by calling UPS or by accessing the database from their own computers using a UPS product called MaxiTrack. At most locations, when the package reaches its destination, the customer signs for it on a special computer that includes a pressure-sensitive pad. The image of this signature is then sent to the database, where it can be viewed by the sending party or by UPS customer service agents.

The ISPS took several years to build. During design, analysts had to address differences among countries in date, time, currency, and measurement units, as well as technical differences such as in the layout of keyboards. Accounting for cultural differences among countries was also important, for example, ensuring that icons or language appropriate in one country were not offensive to people in another country. The volume of transactions that the ISPS was designed to handle also makes it unique. Furthermore, designers had to account for differences in the communications infrastructure across national boundaries. For example, the telecommunications systems in many Latin American, Far Eastern, and some Eastern European countries cannot support the instant transfer of information from the UPS truck to the central database.

UPS has aggressive plans to build its telecommunications infrastructure around the world. In North America, it has teamed with 75 cellular carriers to create a massive cellular network to support its information systems. More than 50,000 UPS vehicles in the United

SOURCES: Andrew Tausz, UPS: Tracking parcel over the airwaves, *Computing Canada* (September 14, 1994): 1, 7; and Neal McGrath, United Parcel Service: Steady as she goes, *Asian Business* (September, 1994): 14.

States and some 4,000 in Canada are linked to the network. To support a direct satellite link between the United States and Germany, UPS recently installed a satellite earth station in New Jersey. UPS plans to build a $3.8 million logistics center in Singapore to help support development in Asia. The company expects foreign operations to account for one-third of its revenues by the year 2000.

In 1991, *Computerworld* presented UPS with the Smithsonian Award for transportation in recognition of its excellence in information technology achievements. UPS intends to continue to build on these achievements to remain a leader in the international package shipping industry.

Questions

1. What information does UPS need to properly handle and deliver a package?
2. What information about the status of the package shipment do customers want or need to know? What information do customs inspectors need to know?
3. How does UPS's choice of hardware for the ISPS system reflect its needs?
4. Why do you think that the ISPS could not be purchased off the shelf or customized from other vertical systems?
5. What are the components of UPS's wide-area network?
6. Is ISPS a transaction processing system? Explain your reasoning.
7. How might managers use the information generated and maintained by the ISPS?
8. Using Porter's theories, explain how the ISPS can be considered a strategic use of information technology.
9. What were the unique problems that developers of the ISPS faced? How did UPS's global operations affect the design of the system?
10. Identify the components of UPS's infrastructure necessary to support the development and continued operation of the ISPS.
11. How is UPS affected by the communications infrastructures of the countries in which it operates?

Activities and Readings in Information Systems

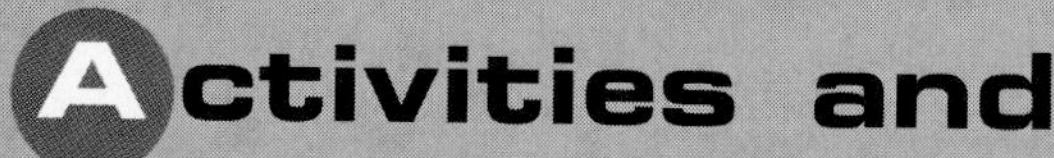

Activities and Readings in Information Systems

Steven R. Gordon | *Babson College*
Judith R. Gordon | *Boston College*

THE DRYDEN PRESS
Harcourt Brace College Publishers

Fort Worth Philadelphia San Diego New York Orlando Austin San Antonio
Toronto Montreal London Sydney Tokyo

Activities Contents

Readings Contents

Activities

Activity 1 Durley Hall Hotel

STEP 1: Read the Durley Hall Hotel case. (This activity is especially suited for use in conjunction with Chapter 2 of *Information Systems.)*

DURLEY HALL HOTEL

"Value for Money" is the motto of the Durley Hall Hotel. Originally, the hotel had 100 bedrooms—it now has 82 as the number of rooms with private facilities has been increased to 54 and the restaurant enlarged, which all helped to convince the AA and the RAC that the hotel deserved its recent three-star rating. The hotel is situated on the beautiful Westcliff of Bournemouth and is within easy walking distance of both the sea and the main shopping and entertainment area of the town. There is color TV, including a video receiver in each bedroom, a games room, and two bars and dancing featured in the Salisbury Bar every evening in the summer season (a different style of music each evening), and this coming winter will see off-season entertainment increased to include Thursday nights as well as the usual Friday and Saturday nights. There are "Mid-Week Bargain Breaks" and "Mini-Weekend Breaks" tariffs that put the accent on "Value for Money" during the winter, but conference business is taking on increasing importance during the off-season.

The hotel has two conference suites, the Canford Suite and the Forum Suite, both purpose-built and equipped with up-to-date audiovisual equipment. Both have two adjoining syndicate rooms. The Canford Suite has double doors so that large exhibits can be brought in for promotional events, air conditioning, recessed track lighting and plenty of power points. For training management courses, a capacity of 35 is appropriate, but 120 delegates can be accommodated theater-style and, as this suite has a portable dance floor, cocktail parties, dinner/dances, and discos can readily be held as well. The Forum Suite, which is situated in the Malborough Annex (adjacent to the main hotel), is very suitable for smaller, more intense meetings/courses, as it is set in quiet and peaceful surroundings overlooking the putting green and is completely self-contained.

Conference arrangements are made by the hotel, and it attracts a variety of clients—from carpet trade shows to training courses for major commercial and industrial organizations. "Getting the balance" right between individual guests and conference delegates is sometimes difficult, so bookings have to be carefully allocated. However, the main conference period is November to May, which does not conflict with the high-volume "holiday-maker" traffic prevalent in the summer season.

Increasingly, more municipal conferences are being held in Bournemouth during the summer months, and this type of delegate is seeking accommodation only in Bournemouth hotels. With training courses and "in-house" conferences, delegates require single occupancy of rooms, and all must have private facilities en suite. This is not always the case with municipal conference delegates as, in many cases, they are willing to share twin-bedded rooms. Within the last two years, quite a few larger Bournemouth hotels have tended toward the conference business—building conference suites and changing their facilities accordingly—but many more specialize in tourist business. There are also other specializations; for exam-

This case was made possible with the cooperation of the proprietor of the Durley Hall Hotel, Mr. M. J. Murray. It was prepared by Barbara Duchesne (B.A. Hons), Conference Officer of the Durley Hall Hotel as a basis for discussion and practical exercise rather than to demonstrate effective or ineffective handling of a particular situation.

ple, the Broughty Ferry Hotel in Boscombe caters exclusively to families with small children, and there are Orthodox Jewish hotels, Christian hotels, and indeed, "dry" hotels, that is, hotels that have no bar facilities whatsoever but rather encourage their clients to bring in their own drinks!

Although the conference facilities at the Durley Hall Hotel are not the largest in the area, they do rate among the very best in Bournemouth, especially in the "three-star" category, and the rates charged are extremely competitive. Generally speaking, the aim of the management team is for profitability rather than turnover and, apart from the revenue gained on its conference facilities, bars, restaurant, and accommodation, the hotel is constantly looking at ways to increase its sales while, at the same time, ensuring that it offers its clientele the best "value for money." At present, bar food has been introduced over the lunch-time period, which is proving extremely popular as the "traditional" lunch now seems to be fast losing its attraction except, of course, to conference delegates, where it is offered as part of the "all-inclusive" conference package. The new system seeks to attract nonresidents by providing a much needed facility—many of the smaller hotels on the Westcliff offer their guests dinner, room, and breakfast only. Similarly, traditional Sunday lunches are also on offer to residents and nonresidents alike at the Durely Hall Hotel with two choices of menu—regular and economy. In the winter months, candlelight dinner dances are held on Saturday nights, and the banqueting season brings into the hotel groups from local industry and commerce for annual celebrations such as office parties, dinner dances, and so on.

A four-night Christmas package is offered, which includes entertainment throughout for all tastes and age groups, and this has proved to be extremely popular, attracting regular guests year after year.

The hotel accommodation is sold in a variety of ways: from entries in the "Bournemouth Guide" produced by the Bournemouth Department of Tourism & Publicity, advertisements in the national press, mail shots, and so on, but much of it is now taken up by "repeat" business, that is, satisfied clients returning again to stay at the Durley Hall Hotel. Some accommodation is also sold via referrals from other hotels in the town full at the time, and vice versa. Of course, there is strong competition from other hotels, but it is of the friendliest kind and, as yet, there is little threat from the large "chains." Crest owns what used to be the Round House Hotel, Ladbroke has taken over the Savoy Hotel, and the De Vere group controls the five-star Royal Bath, the four-star Dormy Hotel, and others, but, generally, the buildings in Bournemouth that are available for purchase for hotel operation are too small to attract the interest of the major "chains." Similarly, planning applications for large purpose-built hotels seem unlikely to succeed, although this situation may change with the advent of the new municipal conference Center, which was under construction on the Westcliff and due for completion in 1984.

The Murray family, who own the Durley Hall Hotel, also own the Sun Court Hotel, a two-star family hotel also situated on the Westcliff and well known for its good food and friendly atmosphere. Mr. M. J. Murray operates from an office in the Durley Hall Hotel, whose Chief Executive is Mr. P. E. J. Williams. A new manager, Mr. S. J. Badger, has recently been appointed and is due to take up his duties shortly. Mrs. M. A. Murray works from the Sun Court, and the Murray's eldest son, Jon, is manager of the Sun Court Hotel.

Marketing is carried out on a "group" basis, and the two hotels are moving toward a "group" identity with the standardization within each hotel of literature/logos, and so on, used in brochures and correspondence and, to some extent, to staff uniforms, but styles do have to differ to reflect the unique image of each hotel. All the staff are aware of the role they play in the marketing of the hotel, and their interest in this respect is thoroughly encouraged by the management team. This generally results in a very high standard of customer service and promotion of the facilities while maintaining staff morale to equally enviable standards.

The Durley Hall Hotel was occupied by the Atomic Energy Commission as a training establishment for many years up to 1970. It was then taken over by the municipality to prevent its conversion into flats and leased to the Murray family in 1972. At the time it was in a fairly derelict condition and since then has needed a large injection of capital to bring it up to its present three-star standard. Capital expenditure is still necessary to constantly maintain and upgrade, where possible, both accommodation and facilities. Indeed, the hotel is presently involved in converting its small cocktail bar and "dry" lounge into a large but still intimate bar with a lounge that will also be licensed but that will still cater to the needs of clients who require soft drinks, coffee, and so on. Also, more and more, bathrooms en suite are being demanded by clients as expectations have been raised via foreign holidays and, of course, for business occupancy, they are essential. It has, therefore, become increasingly difficult to sell rooms without private facilities. Special offers attractively discount rooms without bath, but there is still a wish by the management to steadily increase the number of rooms with bath. Plans are now also being made to modernize the reception area and thereby use the space more efficiently while, at the same time, offering a better and faster service to customers. Tourism is a vital "sterling earner," and Mr. Murray feels that aid should be available, perhaps in the form of government grants or cheap loans, to improve Britain's accommodation stock. At the present time, however, assistance is only available for these types of projects in so-called "development" areas of the country.

As far as the home tourist market is concerned, the Bournemouth season, which used to stretch from Whitsuntide right through to the end of October, is now curtailed to the five or six weeks of the school summer holidays, and there is a strong attraction for tourists without families to go abroad on holiday. Therefore, the Durley Hall Hotel management team are constantly seeking conference business for a considerably longer period each year; but, in the main, the emphasis still lies on the winter months.

After a poor 1980–81 winter conference season, due to the cancellation at a very late stage of prebooked regular weekly training courses by a large motor company, October and November 1981 were looking extremely healthy as far as conference bookings were concerned, and the hotel was awaiting confirmation of further regular weekly training courses from two major British companies. Conference advertising expenditure, as such, was pared down to the bone during 1981 because of economic necessity, but regular attendance at the now biannual "Meet Bournemouth" exhibitions (arranged by the Bournemouth Department of Tourism & Publicity in conjunction with Bournemouth's "Conference" hoteliers and held usually in the major centers like London over a two-day period) helped to secure new business as well as cement existing client relationships, and the Durley Hall Hotel entered 1982 confident in the knowledge that it had both a firm and wide base on which to build further conference business.

General tourist advertising is done via the national press and various specialist publications such as "Let's Go," the "Michelin Guide," the "Bournemouth Guide," and "Bargain Breaks," the latter being published by the Bournemouth Department of Tourism & Publicity and specifically geared to the promotion of off-season business. Moreover, in 1981, in view of the particularly difficult situation in which hotels were finding themselves, the English Tourist Board sponsored part of the cost of specific advertisements carried in the national press to promote Bournemouth and her hotels. These advertisements were produced by the hoteliers and coordinated by the Bournemouth Department of Tourism & Publicity. Analysis of the bookings received carried out by the Durley Hall Hotel as a result of these advertisements showed them to have been most effective, and it is therefore their policy to continue to take part in all such future advertising. No advertising agency is employed by the hotel, but the services of a professional layout artist are called upon to advise on the more ambitious promotions and advertisements.

In addition to the information gleaned from the hotel register, client feedback is also obtained by means of questionnaires left in rooms for completion. These give a constant appraisal of the standards and service of the hotel along with information on the effectiveness of advertising by requesting the clients to say how this particular hotel came to their notice, why they made their booking, and so on. The questionnaires also form the basis of a "Mail Shot Club" by which clients are regularly mailed with details of special offers, new tariffs, and so on, and from this Mail Shot, it is encouraging to see that the hotel is attracting more and more "repeat" business. At the same time, it also helps in the judgment and assessment of how special offers do appeal to a mass clientele.

Plans to expand "in-house" sales, as mentioned above, are tempered by experience in that, in the past, guests have traditionally been alienated by the idea of a large number of separate charges. "Simplicity is the key," as Mr. Murray puts it—"the client generally wants a package tied up in a single charge and it is always our policy to give the client what he wants." Interestingly enough, however, a change in client thinking is becoming apparent in that full-board terms no longer seem to be the requisite of holiday visitors—dinner, bed, and breakfast or bed and breakfast terms are very popular so the hotel, as well as offering bar food at lunch-time, is now looking into ways of changing its traditional lunch service in the restaurant. Of course, capital investment is always worthwhile if it means a cut in labor requirements, but dramatic changes would not be acceptable to regular clients.

The management team of the Durley Hall Hotel feels that the hotel industry is undergoing a major change, a tendency toward "business" custom and away from traditional "holiday-maker" business, and this is duly reflected in their actions regarding tariff structuring and pricing, advertising, and so on, but certainly, caution still remains the byword. One must try to foresee changes and adjust to them accordingly, but sweeping changes cannot be made until the market research has been thoroughly carried out. Customer satisfaction has to go hand in hand with profitability.

STEP 2: Prepare the case for class discussion.

STEP 3: Answer each of the following questions, individually or in small groups, as directed by your instructor:

Diagnosis

1. What are the information needs of the Durley Hall Hotel management team?

Evaluation

2. What market research has the team already done?
3. What market information does the team still need?
4. What other information does the team need to adjust for anticipated changes?
5. What needs could computer systems meet?

STEP 4: In small groups, with the entire class, or in written form, share your answers to the questions above. Then answer the following questions:

1. What information needs exist in this situation?
2. What types of information management are required?
3. What aspect of these information management requirements might be computerized?
4. What issues would be associated with computerizing the systems? ●

Activity 2 The Mike O'Chip Maintenance Company

STEP 1: Read the Mike O'Chip Maintenance company case.* (This activity is especially suited for use in conjunction with Chapter 2 of *Information Systems.*)

Bits and Pieces is a retail supplier of microcomputer systems and associated products with four outlets, all situated in Sheffield area. They used to market the products of four manufacturers of international repute together with ancillary equipment and software products. Most of their buyers are local small businesses.

However, the business microcomputer market has become more sophisticated. Distributors of the market-leading products expect higher standards from authorized dealers, and will not supply nonauthorized dealers any longer. Authorized dealers are expected, among other things

to stock an extensive minimal product range;

offer consultancy;

offer a range of introductory and advanced training courses;

offer an implementation service;

offer hotline support.

Only dealer staff who have attended courses run by the distributor are allowed to operate these services.

Accordingly, B & P have taken the strategic decision to become an authorized dealer for one main hardware distributor only, and to discontinue the arrangements with the other three as the contracts expire.

Among the problems created by this major decision is the question of honoring maintenance contracts, especially to customers of the discontinued ranges.

At present, maintenance as a function is treated as a necessary after-sales service, administered by the sales department. Even without the impetus of the new policy, it was becoming clear that the existing arrangements have become too inflexible for the maturing market base. There is evidence that sales have been lost because of this.

Since their establishment seven years ago, B & P have offered all new customers the benefits of a hardware maintenance contract administered by B & P. For an annual outlay of 10 percent of the purchase price, paid in advance, all servicing and repair work is carried out promptly and subject to no additional charges. The customer brings the item to any of the outlets and collects it again on notification of completion of the job, usually within 48 hours. Each day items for attention are collected and taken to the repair center on site at one of the outlets, whose serviced products are delivered back to the appropriate outlet.

A small number of products are not subject to maintenance contract, for example, those where it is known that replacement parts are in irregular supply and the terms of the contract would be difficult to honor.

This case was compiled from generalized experience. It was prepared by the author specifically for class discussion on the "IT in Management" option of the University of Sheffield MBA.

*All names in this case study are fictitious. Any similarities with real names are purely coincidental.

Once a contract has been entered into, B & P are obliged to renew it on demand for three more years on the same terms. After this time, B & P reserve the right to cancel the whole contract or remove selected items from it following an inspection. In addition, or as an alternative, the annual charge may be increased, often by as much as 50 percent per annum.

Where new equipment is added to the system (such as extra storage or a printer), the customer is offered a separate maintenance contract on this equipment. This happens quite often. In effect, a separate contract is issued for each self-contained piece of computer hardware such as visual display screen (monitor), keyboard, system unit, and so on. In practice this is complicated by the fact that suppliers may integrate some separate components into a single cabinet (e.g., hard disk and system unit, keyboard and system unit).

During the past 12 months problems of increasing severity have afflicted the maintenance function. A significant number of customers are complaining of matters such as undue delays in repair work, damage to cabinets of goods undergoing maintenance, and being offered the wrong goods for collection.

On inspection, it is discovered that most of the delays are being caused by increased workload plus a scarcity of parts for the older products. It appears that long-standing maintenance contracts are being automatically renewed on existing terms without the stipulated conditional inspection because of poor communications between sales and the maintenance section. Again, there is a suspicion that repeat sales are being lost because of this.

B & P management believe that the long-term solution lies in setting up a separate maintenance function which is better organized to anticipate and serve the needs of the customer base. In the short term, however, they are more concerned with the plans to reorganize the business.

Matters are brought to a head when B & P's maintenance engineer, Mike O'Chip, announces his intention to quit and set up on his own. He is tired of suffering avoidable customer complaints, has recognized the long-term opportunities in computer maintenance, and wishes to start his own business.

B & P Management immediately enter into negotiations and do a deal with Mike which they hope will ensure a friendly parting and the creation of a new long-standing and mutually beneficial relationship.

The essence of the deal is as follows:

1. For an agreed nominal amount, B & P will transfer all of its maintenance contracts to a company set up by Mike and cease all maintenance work of its own.
2. Mike will honor all existing maintenance contracts although he may alter the terms of fresh ones. In addition, Mike will have the option of purchasing at cost price all maintenance spares and equipment he wants.
3. B & P will provide Mike with a list of all customers not presently covered by maintenance contracts.
4. In the future, B & P will attempt to sell maintenance contracts on behalf of Mike's company to all purchasers of new equipment. For each successful sale, B & P will take a once-only introduction fee of 20 percent of the value of the contract in its first year. B & P will also provide Mike with the names and addresses of other purchasers who do not take out maintenance contracts.

By means of this agreement, B & P seek to offload their maintenance problems permanently and present customers with a better service at a stroke.

For his part, Mike O'Chip is acquiring an ongoing business at minimal cost with development potential in a number of directions.

He has several ideas for improving customer service. He intends to innovate an on-site contract at once. Repairs and servicing will be carried out at the place of use of the computer. If a case proves too difficult, the offending part will be removed to his workshop and, whenever possible, a substitute part fitted to leave the customer with a working machine. There will be a premium charge for this service.

Mike believes that this change will also smooth his workload and enable him to run the business single-handedly for a year or so, with the aid of an efficient administration, his wife. Peaks can be coped with by evening and weekend work, or so he hopes.

Most of his other ideas will be shelved until he decides which way to develop the business.

For example, he would like to break away from the rigid charging structure. Given sufficiently detailed information he would like to offer a 'No-claims' bonus to customers as an incentive not to call him out for trivialities. Likewise he would like to offer preferential terms for customers owning products with a proven reliability record.

At the moment he sees 3 broad alternatives, but others may present themselves in time, and anyway nos. 2 & 3 are not mutually exclusive.

The alternatives he sees are as follows:

1. Expand passively—that is, employ staff in response to additional work generated by B & P.
2. Expand aggressively—that is, generate new business by such methods as advertising his improved services to current users without maintenance contracts or by attempting B & P-type deals with other computer system suppliers.
3. Expand selectively—offer a superservice (at super-charges) to the larger business machine sector operating Local Area Networks.

Mike made his original decision to start the business through "back-of-an-envelope" figuring and personal frustration. However, he resolves to base future development decisions on sound information about the industry and his own operations.

He believes there are 3 essential ingredients of a good internal information system.

1. Determination in advance of what information he will need.
2. Carefully designed records and an easy way to use the system to provide such information from these records.
3. A simple, effective system for updating the records.

B & P had never bothered much about maintenance records. Being sales oriented, each shop kept a file for each customer, and following a maintenance operation a note would be entered containing the date, the nature of the maintenance, labor time and total parts cost. Parts were ordered centrally by telephone from the original equipment suppliers, following a telephone call from Mike. Purchase orders seldom got recorded on paper.

No attempt had ever been made to reconcile the total cost of the maintenance function against income. The original policy had been to set the annual maintenance charges at the level which would ensure that income would comfortably cover the operational costs, and everyone assumed, probably correctly, that this was still the case. Maintenance had never been seen as a profit-generating function.

Because his overall aim is growth, Mike decides to be ready and computerize his information system from the start using a relational database package. Hardware will, of course, be no problem and there are sufficient software writers around who owe him favors to enable him to get a system off the ground in the three months he has before the new business commences. In the longer term, the customer records system should be integrated with the accountancy system (i.e., items such as cost of parts employed on a callout should be picked up directly from the inventory control system). However, to keep things manageable in the short term, some such items will be input from data transcribed onto the callout form from manual records. In other words, he sees the customer records system primarily as a sales aid and information system.

Information on which Mike based his decision to start the business:

Number of customers of B & P to date = 2,100

Number of maintenance contracts to be transferred to Mike O'Chip's company = 500

Average value of each complete business hardware system sold = £2,760

Estimated number of new customers next year = 1,000

Estimated proportion of customers taking out hardware maintenance contracts = 5%

Estimated number of callouts/customer/year = 2

Estimated number of callouts dealt with per day = 5

Estimated average cost of parts/callout = £80

STEP 2: Prepare the case for class discussion.

STEP 3: Answer each of the following questions, individually or in small groups, as directed by your instructor:

Diagnosis

1. What are Mike's information needs?
2. How, if at all, have they changed since his split with Bits and Pieces?

Evaluation

3. What were the deficiencies in Bits and Pieces's information systems regarding maintenance services?
4. How could Mike use a computer to help with information management?

STEP 4: In small groups, with the entire class, or in written form, share your answers to the questions above. Then answer the following questions:

1. What information needs exist in this situation?
2. What types of information management are required?
3. What computer systems could be introduced to help manage information?
4. What are likely to be the issues associated with computerizing the management of information? ●

Activity 3 Lewis Foods Fleet Management

STEP 1: Read the Lewis Foods Fleet Management case. (This activity is especially suited for use in conjunction with Chapter 3 of *Information Systems.*)

LEWIS FOODS FLEET MANAGEMENT

On June 1, Lee Foods, an Omaha-based distributor of cheese and other foodstuffs, acquired Wisconsin Food Distributors, a similar company also based in Omaha, Nebraska, to form Lewis Foods. Lee Foods distributed cheese and other foodstuffs to fast food restaurants, pizzerias and Mexican restaurants throughout the states west of the Mississippi River. Lee Foods owned a fleet of 160 tractors and 230 refrigerated trailers. Wisconsin Foods was a distributor of perishables to retail grocery stores in a nine-state area centered in Omaha. Wisconsin Food Distributors had 90 tractors and 160 refrigerated trailers. A total of 26.5 million miles was driven by the two fleets in 1988 and that figure is remaining constant this year. Management anticipated that a total of 31.5 million miles, an additional 5 million miles, will be driven next year to support new customers.

At Lee Foods, John Richards, the chief mechanic, had also been serving as the dispatcher/fleet supervisor for the past year. At Wisconsin Foods, Al Lopez was the chief dispatcher with responsibilities similar to John's. After talking to both Al and John, Harlan Highsmith, the President of Lewis Foods, had the uneasy feeling that in the excitement generated by the potential savings in overhead costs, the increased productivity and efficiency due to economies of scale, and the larger market area, upper management may have overlooked some major issues in the merger of the two fleets.

As a result, he created the position of fleet manager to oversee the entire fleet. John Richards was to be named chief mechanic for Lewis Foods, the newly formed company and Al Lopez was to take the position of chief dispatcher when the merger of the two fleets was completed. Harlan Highsmith knew whom he wanted as fleet manager. He contacted Bill Carnes and offered him the job. He voiced his uneasy feelings and emphasized that he wanted a smooth changeover.

On July 15th, Bill Carnes became the Fleet Manager for Lewis Foods, the newly formed company. His first concern was to merge the operation and management of the two groups of trucks into a single fleet rather than continue to operate two separate fleets. The warehouse division of the company had completed their plans and expected to close the Wisconsin Foods facility in about 90 days. At that time all route planning and dispatching of loads would be out of the main warehouse.

Bill began his job of integrating the two groups into a single unit by evaluating the past performance of the two fleets. The major expenditures in fleet operations are for fuel, engine maintenance and tires. The staff anticipated Bill's information needs and prepared a report on fuel economy, maintenance and tire life for the trucking industry as shown in Table I and a comparison of the two fleets as shown in Table II. This report failed to identify the strengths and weaknesses of the operations of the two fleets. Bill Carnes visited both terminals and obtained the following additional information.

At Lee Foods, John Richards, the chief mechanic, provided much of the information Bill wanted. The Lee fleet consists of tandem Kenworth and Peterbilt tractors. Eighty percent of

This case was written by Carl R. Ruthstrom, University of Houston–Downtown, David Cross, Robert Bosch Power Tool Corp., and Arthur Nelson, Lufkin Industries. Published with the permission of the North American Case Research Association.

Table I Operating Performance-Industry Averages

Fuel Economy	5.7 mpg
Engine Overhauls	Every 450,000 miles to 475,000 miles
Tire Life	Recapped at every 150,000 miles, replaced at 500,000 miles

Table II Lee/Wisconsin Performance Comparisons

	Lee Averages	Wisconsin Averages
Fuel Economy	5.0 mpg	5.8 mpg
Engine Overhauls	330,000 miles	450,000 miles
Tire Life	Recapped at every 100,000 miles, replaced at 345,000 miles	Recapped at every 150,000 miles, replaced at 500,00 miles

the tractors are powered by the Cummins 350 Big Cam III governed at 1800 RPM. The phrase "governed at 1800 RPM" means that a governor or speed control device is installed on the engine to limit the maximum engine speed to 1800 revolutions per minute. This extends the operating life of the engines. The other twenty percent of the fleet's engines are Caterpillar 3406Bs governed at 1600 RPM.

The Lee fleet uses eight Goodyear 167 radial tires, four on each of the two drive axles, and two Goodyear Unisteel IIs on the single steering axle of each tractor. The trailers have another eight tires, four on each of the two axles. Tires removed from the steering axles are recapped and used on trailers. At the third recap, drive axle tires are moved back to the trailers. Only recapped tires are used on the trailers.

Two years ago, Lee had improved the fuel economy to 5 miles per gallon (MPG) by using fuel saving devices such as Paccar's Varashield air deflectors, Rudkin Wiley cab extenders, Rockford viscous fans, and lower horsepower engines. "But, somehow we seem to have hit a plateau and cannot get above 5 MPG," said John Richards.

Driver comfort and safety have always been important considerations at Lee Foods as shown by the cabs with their deluxe carpeted interiors, AM/FM radio-tape players, air conditioning and seats with air-ride suspensions. The estimated cost of upgrading the interiors is $2000 per tractor. In addition, Lee has awarded drivers completing one million miles of safe driving with a $1000 bonus check. Every month, each driver attends a half-day driver safety and improvement class conducted by company instructors. As a result, Lee, with a turnover rate of three percent, has one of the lowest driver turnover rates in the trucking industry.

John Richards said, "There are not any labor problems at Lee. The only new drivers we have hired replaced those lost to retirement or physical disability."

At the Wisconsin Foods terminal, Al Lopez, the chief dispatcher, provided similar information. The Wisconsin fleet is entirely Kenworth tractors powered by the Cummins 350 Big Cam III engines governed at 1800 RPM. Fuel saving devices similar to those used by Lee are installed on all the tractors. Drivers are allowed to customize their tractors at their own expense resulting in interiors similar to the Lee tractors.

Two and one-half years ago, Wisconsin implemented a transportation improvement (TRIM) program. The program includes Stemco's on-board computer monitoring system (trip recorder) and Stemco's vehicle management system (VMS) software package. The recorders are installed in all Wisconsin's tractors. The hardware for this system averages $2200 per tractor. The memory cartridges are in the tractors when drivers are dispatched. At the end of a trip, the last thing a driver does is to remove the cartridge and turn it into dispatch. There he is given a blank cartridge, which he installs before leaving for the day. The driver enters his identification, the vehicle number and the route number at the start of each trip. In addition, he enters the number of gallons of fuel purchased for the trip. The computerized recorder stores times, engine RPM, speed in MPH, foot brake applications, and stops.

The data for each trip is downloaded from the memory cartridge to an IBM PC and subsequently stored on a floppy disc. The VMS program analyzes the data and prints out a Basic Trip Summary. Included in this summary are the statistics of various performance criteria management selected to evaluate driver performance, such as engine on time, idle time, road time, speed RPM, and fuel consumption plus a grade (from 0 to 100) of the driver's performance.

The drivers were introduced to the TRIM program in meetings of 10 to 15 drivers. In these meetings, the emphasis was on improving fleet performance by identifying the problem areas in each driver's performance. Initially, the computer trip summaries showed 50% to 60% of the drivers were speeding (running above 58 MPH).

Al Lopez said, "We knew that the greatest savings for large tractors can be achieved through improved gas mileage and reduced wear on the vehicle. Better efficiency in either area would make a very visible difference in costs. We started informally counseling the drivers with emphasis on driver awareness of economical driving habits. The non-threatening approach produced dramatic results in reducing our fleet costs. Our fuel economy rose rapidly to 5.8 MPG where it remains today. Tire wear and engine maintenance costs have declined noticeably."

The single most noteworthy incident occurred when one of the drivers blew a Cummins engine in Texas. Cummins claimed it was attributable to over-revving and speed. The driver brought the memory cartridge with him when he flew back to Omaha. The VMS program analyzed the data and showed no speeding or over-revving, saving the company a $17,000 engine repair bill.

"The most disappointing thing about the TRIM program is that we have never reached the anticipated 6-7 MPG that the Stemco salesmen assured us could be attained. In addition, we seem to be continually training new drivers on the system. Over 40% of our drivers have less than one year with the company," volunteered Al Lopez.

Further discussion with Al Lopez revealed that while 20 to 25% turnover of drivers was not unusual in the trucking industry, other underlying problems did exist. Both the chief dispatcher and the drivers feel that all the benefits of the computerized vehicle management system are reserved for the company.

The drivers are of the opinion that having "a cop" in the cab limits their potential earnings and does not allow the driver much freedom in terms of length of driving day, breaks, and sleeping time. Therefore, most of the turnover of drivers is generated by the lure of higher incomes and more individual freedom in other trucking companies.

Upon his return to his office, Bill Carnes decided to review that data in Tables I and II to compare the performance differences in fuel consumption, maintenance and tire wear. After reviewing the data in Table II, he decided to visit accounting and acquire cost data comparisons for the two fleets. Since the two fleets had continued operating separately, accounting had maintained separate books. The data Bill needed was readily available and Bill constructed Table III.

Before leaving, he questioned the accounting supervisor, Shirley Williams, about the differences in operating costs per mile between the two fleets. Shirley confirmed his finding that the Lee trucks were reporting higher fuel, tire and engine repair costs per truck than the Wisconsin fleet. Shirley Williams had begun investigating the differences in operating costs and found that both fleets were reporting approximately the same unit costs for fuel, tires,

Table III Lee/Wisconsin Cost Comparisons

	Lee Averages	Wisconsin Averages
Cost per mile		
Equipment	$0.82	$0.65
Drivers	$0.61	$0.58
Miles per year		
Per tractor	112,708	94,075
Per driver	77,420	73,127

Table IV Unit Costs

Item	Unit Price
Engine Overhauls	$7000 per engine
Diesel fuel	$1.15 per gallon
New tires	
Steering Axles	$175 per tire
Drive Axles	$195 per tire
Recapping	$65 per tire

and engine overhauls as listed in Table IV. Shirley also found that the company policies for both fleets included the replacement of 15 percent of the fleet with new tractor-trailer rigs each year.

At first she was puzzled by the difference in the drivers' cost per mile. "Both groups of drivers are paid union scale. I'll have to look into this for you," Shirley said. As Shirley reviewed the records used to calculate the drivers' cost per mile for the two fleets, the only differences she could find were the safe driving bonuses paid to Lee drivers and lower pay to Wisconsin drivers during their initial probationary period. Shirley did find that the total pay and benefits package was larger for the Lee drivers because of the greater number of miles driven annually.

As Bill Carnes walked back to his office, he remembered Al Lopez's final remark, "Over 40% of our drivers have less than one year with the company." He made a mental note to confirm this with Shirley Williams in the morning.

When Bill Carnes returned to his office at 4:00 p.m., his secretary handed him a message to call Harlan Highsmith, President of Lewis Foods, immediately. Bill was surprised when Harlan Highsmith answered the phone without the assistance of a secretary.

After preliminary salutations, Harlan Highsmith said, "Bill, you have been with the company long enough to evaluate our current fleet operations. I've scheduled you to present your plans for integrating the Lee and Wisconsin fleet operations into a single fleet for 3:00 p.m., tomorrow. Have a good evening."

Bill Carnes realized that his recommended program must address both fleet operating costs and employee relations. He realized that capital investments may be needed in both fleets to achieve improvements in these areas.

At 6:00 p.m., before leaving the office, he called both John Richards and Al Lopez at home. He explained why he was calling and solicited their help in preparing for the 3:00 p.m. meeting. Both men agreed to be in Bill Carnes' office at 9:00 a.m. the next morning to assist in developing the plans for integrating the two fleets.

At 9:00 a.m., the next morning John Richards and Al Lopez report to Bill Carnes' office. By this time, Bill Carnes has begun to feel the same uneasiness that Harlan Highsmith, the President, had expressed when he hired Bill.

Bill Carnes begins, "After tossing and turning all night, I finally got dressed and prepared this list of questions that need to be answered."

1. What problems do you anticipate from the employees related to the merging of the two fleets if we do not make any changes in the treatment of the two groups of drivers?
2. What issues do you anticipate will cause the most concern among the drivers and what approach should we use to integrate the two fleets without alienating drivers?
3. Some of the drivers already qualify for the safe driving bonus. Could we continue this and add a bonus of $.03 per mile for every mile driven under 58 MPH?
4. Since any changes or improvements will cost money, where will we get the money to implement our plans?
5. Assuming that we decide to upgrade the tractors, would your first action be to install the Stemco trip recorders in all the Lee tractors or upgrade the driver comfort items in the Wisconsin tractors? Why?

"I have been listening to all of the drivers' comments at Lee and can give you a long list of answers for those first two questions," exclaimed John Richards.

"I'll bet my list of gripes is longer," said Al Lopez.

"Great! John, if you and Al will work on the first two questions, I'll get to work on the last three. Remember that we need more than just a list of gripes. We need a plan detailing how we are going to integrate the two groups of drivers without creating more problems. Let's meet back here at 11:00 a.m. and see what progress we have made."

STEP 2: Prepare the case for class discussion.

STEP 3: Answer each of the following questions, individually or in small groups, as directed by your instructor.

Diagnosis

1. What management processes and roles does Bill perform?
2. What information does he need to manage the fleet merger?

Evaluation

3. What systems exist for collecting, analyzing, and reporting the information?
4. Are these systems computerized?
5. What problems exist in securing the necessary information?

STEP 4: In small groups, with the entire class, or in written form, share your answers to the questions above. Then answer the following questions:

1. What types of information do managers at Lewis Foods Fleet Management require?
2. What systems exist to supply this information?
3. How effective are these systems?
4. What changes should be made in the information systems? ●

Activity 4 Connor Spring

STEP 1: Read the Connor Spring case. (This activity is especially suited for use in conjunction with Chapter 4 of *Information Systems.*)

THE KNOWLEDGE FACTORY

By the mid-1980s Joe and Henry Sloss, the twin brothers who had built up the family business, were getting on in years and were thinking about retirement. Joe's son Bob, the only member of the next generation on the payroll, was ready to take over.

Ready. OK, that might be an understatement. More like chomping at the bit. Pounding at the door. Because Robert Sloss, then in his thirties, had discovered not just a job but a mission.

The company he was inheriting was a small metal-spring manufacturer, successful in its day but exactly the kind of old-line, low-tech business likely to be eaten alive by aggressive and innovative Far Eastern competitors. Young Bob—an alumnus of Stanford's summertime executive-education program and a fan of Tom Peters—set out to search for excellence right in his own backyard. American industry, he decided, could be revived, its loyal employees rewarded and reinspired. The Japanese and Taiwanese and Singaporeans could be repulsed. Spearheading the attack would be the Sloss family business, Connor Spring.

Once in charge, Sloss made all the right moves. He bought state-of-the-art machinery. He decentralized the company, ceding day-to-day authority to the managers of its four plants. He set up an employee stock ownership plan (ESOP) and instituted a quarterly cash bonus based on each plant's profits. He plunged into statistical process control and the other accoutrements of modern quality assurance. And he made sure—through stylish videos, glossy brochures, slick sales presentations—that customers heard about the all-new, world-class Connor.

The blitz almost worked. Connor's shipments rose from $12.4 million in 1985 to $16.4 million in 1989. The company landed new jobs from big customers such as Aerojet; it became a certified vendor to the likes of Hewlett-Packard and Xerox. Japanese transplants searching for U.S. suppliers began sniffing around Connor. Employees seemed more content and more committed. What else could Sloss want? Really, just one little thing. He would have been happier if the company were making decent money.

He knew that Connor's loses in 1989, the first year in at least two decades the company actually wound up in the red, could be chalked up to the closing of a plant in Phoenix and the transfer of many employees to Connor's Dallas facility. But he also knew the financial problems ran deep and that they weren't being solved by all his fancy footwork. The Dallas operation, established in 1984, hadn't yet seen a profitable year. The flagship plant in Los Angeles, Connor's biggest, was barely squeaking by. Only the little shops in Portland, Ore., and San Jose, Calif., were solidly in the black, and at best they pulled the company a few percentage points above break-even. Something had to be done.

It was then that Sloss, almost unwittingly, found himself presiding over a change that would leave Connor Spring looking remarkably different, not only from its most recent incarnation but from most other companies in the United States. The change didn't involve yet another hotshot management philosophy, only a new tool for making the company run better. Or so it seemed at the time: today, midway through the process, the tool seems to be transforming Connor's whole culture.

The tool—the driving force behind this ongoing metamorphosis—is information. Now, the astute use of information is one hot topic among management gurus these days. Gather more data about your customers! Communicate more with your employees! Analyze those critical financial indicators! Such injunctions never hurt. But they may not help much either, because they address maybe 10% of a business's information flow.

The other 90%, the part that never shows up in market-research studies or employee newsletters or monthly P&Ls, is the mundane, nuts-and-bolts information that permeates a company every minute of every day, determining how managers allocate resources and how employees spend their time. Why Customer X is complaining. Which jobs absolutely, positively have to be done by Friday. How much money we stand to make this month on the National Widgets account, why Bill in sales has been spending so much time in Chicago, what's causing the bottleneck in shipping. Small companies' chief executives typically know or learn the answers to those and a hundred similar questions: that's why they feel—and frequently are—indispensable to smooth operations and why they intuitively understand bigger-picture issues such as cost ratios or market trends. Most CEOs, however, never think about sharing what they know with any but a few top managers.

But ask yourself—suppose all employees in the company had easy access to everyday knowledge of this sort? And suppose they could not only receive but exchange information, adding what they know to the pool and thereby enabling everyone to work just a little more intelligently? As Harvard Business School professor Shoshana Zuboff argues in her book *In the Age of the Smart Machine,* modern computer and communications systems allow knowledge that once resided "in people's heads, in face-to-face conversations, in metal file drawers, and in widely dispersed pieces of paper" to be disseminated throughout an organization, moving upward and sideways as well as downward. People with access to all that information work differently—work smarter—because they suddenly know a whole lot more about what they and everyone else in the business are doing.

Bob Sloss hadn't read Zuboff. But he did want to boost his bottom line, and he figured Connor's information systems were a good place to start tightening things up.

Connor Formed Metal Products, as the company has recently been rechristened, is a job-shop manufacturer, making springs and other components to a customer's specifications. In some ways it's a prototypical business enterprise. Like a professional-services firm, it has hundreds of customers, each one with unique, complex, and usually urgent needs. Like a retailer, it has to manage a sizable and varied mix of products, and like a high-tech manufacturer, it has to guarantee near-flawless quality.

And like many, many small American companies, Connor was, less than two years ago, processing information much as information was processed in 1950. In the Los Angeles plant, engineers cranked out cost estimates by hand, penciling in figures for raw materials and machine speeds and labor hours, then erasing and starting over when the bottom line seemed too high or too low. Salespeople kept handwritten trip reports and copies of letters in cumbersome loose-leaf notebooks. In the office, clerical workers typed out highly detailed shop orders, 10 carbons deep, using Wite-Out on errors. Out in the shop, supervisors did their best to read specs off a finger-smudged copy of the order.

Even managers were often flying blind. Once a job was out the door, for example, no one could be sure whether it had been profitable. For a while, Connor kept labor-time records for each job by hand. But the data were never collated or analyzed, in part because their accuracy was suspect. Ironically, Sloss had spent nearly $300,000 on computers a few years earlier, installing several IBM System 36 minicomputers. But the big machines and their canned software proved too clumsy for daily plant-level chores such as estimating or job costing, and managers mostly ignored them.

By 1989 Sloss had begun thinking about using personal computers, which were getting more powerful by the day, and about custom software. His San Jose plant manager had already begun experimenting with PCs, albeit with packaged programs. And now here was this young man named Michael Quarrey looking for a job.

Quarrey had some unusual credentials. He had worked for the National Center for Employee Ownership and was an ESOP expert. He was also an experienced programmer and was just leaving a position with another job shop. After a moment's hesitation—"the idea of a little company like ours hiring a computer programmer was mind-boggling"—Sloss hired him and installed him in Los Angeles with instructions to develop an effective job-tracking and job-costing system. On Quarrey's recommendation he immediately began buying PCs and networking software.

Before long Quarrey was writing programs to computerize the L.A. operation's information flow. Before long, too, the two men realized they shared an agenda going well beyond computerization.

Ever since he took over, Sloss had been chipping away at Connor's old-fashioned, secretive style of management. Employees had become part owners of Connor through the ESOP, he argued; they should be treated like owners. So he explained the company's financial statistics to them, and he made a point of walking around the plant, answering questions. Now, he figured, the new computer system gave him a chance to disseminate day-to-day operating data, exactly what owners ought to see. Quarrey, similarly inclined toward employee involvement, designed his system to ensure broad access. He also designed a two-way flow of information: each electronic shop order would contain "notes" areas, so that engineering or quality control, for example, could enter comments about a particular job.

But it was Roy Gallucci, a blunt-spoken machinist in Connor's coiling department, who may have had the biggest impact on the new system.

"Gallucci stopped me one day in the shop," remembers Sloss, "and pretty soon we were talking in the plant manager's office behind closed doors." The machinist's message to the boss was simple. At least one computer should be out in the shop. Blue-collar employees should have the ability not only to enter comments about a job but to somehow force the office to pay attention. He didn't know exactly how it might work, but if the company was going to put in a whole new system, it had better do it right.

Bingo, thought Sloss: Gallucci was touching on a perennial complaint, namely, that the office never listened to the shop. Here was a chance to deal with it.

Quarrey agreed—not that he had much choice. "There was no discussion," he remembers. "Bob said, 'do it.'" By May of 1990 Quarrey had his unusual new system up and running.

Pull up to Connor's L.A. plant—it's actually in Monterey Park, on the outskirts of the city—and you won't be immediately impressed. It's housed in a standard-issue industrial building. Inventory spills out from the shipping door into the weed-rimmed, California-size parking lot. Inside, Connor looks like a company on a bare-bones budget. There's no receptionist: visitors are invited to use the phone in the lobby. The office staff—which, it turns out, handles customer service, invoicing, purchasing, bookkeeping, personnel, production scheduling, and all related paperwork—numbers exactly six.

But don't be misled by the seeming austerity: this is not a company done in by the recession. In the last two years the plant's head count has dropped (through attrition) by 15—yet its sales have *risen* 28%, to an annual level of $10 million. In 1990 Connor's L.A. division turned a 5% pretax profit. It's maintaining that pace this year, despite the downturn in the economy.

On the face of things, the difference between today's Connor and 1989's is purely technological. Customer-service reps now prepare shop orders on a quietly humming PC—no more carbons and Wite-Out. Engineers use an estimating program to calculate trial quotes in minutes, not hours.

But dig a little deeper—talk to people throughout the company about what's different now—and the magnitude of Connor's ongoing transformation becomes apparent. Plenty of companies computerize their information systems. Not many disseminate information to every nook and cranny of the organization—let alone share the power all that knowledge carries with it.

At Connor, that's pretty much what is happening.

Thanks to Roy Gallucci, for example, every employee has full and instant access to data about the jobs he or she is working on. Not just the customer's name and the specs, but a full history of the job to date, special notes or instructions from engineering or customer service, and management information once thought of as sensitive, such as the price and the margin. An employee who spots (or develops) a problem with a job can go to the computer and put a "shop hold" on it. Until the engineering department investigates—and makes a formal written disposition of the problem—the software won't allow Connor to take any new orders for the same part.

In one recent six-week period, Quarrey counted 117 holds emanating from machine operators and their supervisors. "This grinding can only be done by A-1 Surface Grinding," read one, adding the address, a contact name, and the price per part that the preferred outside vendor would charge. "OK, will change the master," responded engineering. "Change run speed from 850 pcs/hr to 700 pcs/hr," answered the not-totally-compliant engineer. Gallucci himself admits to using the feature regularly—for example, to propose sending a three-part order out for heat treating all together rather than one batch at a time. And Quarrey points out that similar holds can be put on a shop order by quality control, by engineering ("Don't allow this estimate to become an order until we have a clean blueprint"), or by customer service ("Don't ship without clearance from us").

A direct effect of sharing information and power is that problems get nipped in the bud and jobs that cause difficulties the first time around rarely cause the same difficulties the second time. Closing the loop, Quarrey calls it: the people who need feedback get feedback. That effect shows up most graphically in a number calculated monthly by Armando Lopez, Connor's head of quality control, and posted on the bulletin board outside the lunchroom. In 1989 Connor's "cost of discrepant material"—rejects, rework time, and so on—came to 4.28% of sales. A year later the figure was just over 1%; through May of this year it was .5%.

But the indirect effect of Connor's unusual system may be even more dramatic: just as Harvard's Zuboff might have predicted, it is altering the way the company operates. Information is now both widely available and easily accessible, so employees all over the organization have begun to ask questions and to learn more about matters affecting their own jobs. Then too, the company evidently welcomes initiative—so plenty of employees have begun to propose new ways of doing things. Consider four examples:

- Javier Castro, a setup man working the second shift, has begun making it a practice to consult the computer about upcoming jobs. Noticing that a part for Hughes Aircraft was being done in two steps, he checked the price, then calculated that he could do it more cheaply in one step on his computer-numerical-control machine. So he proposed the change to his supervisor, Ron Washburn. "Within three days I had the job, with no secondary operations," says Castro. "We saved probably 200 hours of secondary operations per order."
- Judy Quinn and Jan Morgan, who handle most of Connor's customer service, always knew they were spending a sizable chunk of their time handling change orders on jobs, but couldn't figure out where all those changes were coming from. Earlier this year they asked Quarrey if the new system would allow them to track the orders. It would. Pulling up the

reports, the two women found that roughly one out of every five change orders was internally generated—and that a significant fraction of those were caused by initial errors in entering an order. "So we developed a purchase-order checklist," says Quinn, "a list of items to be checked to make sure we didn't miss anything. That's cut down on the internal change orders significantly."

- Karla Penalba, in charge of purchasing, was hearing from top management that raw-material quality was key to Connor's manufacturing quality. Yet she realized she had no systematic information on individual vendors' performance in such areas as on-time delivery. So last February she and Quarrey set up a spreadsheet-based program to track every shipment; since then she has produced reports rating Connor's suppliers. Later this year new purchasing software will be integrated with the shop-order system, making it possible for anyone in the building to learn the status of raw-material deliveries.
- Jeff Applegate, an outside sales manager, asked for and got a laptop computer last January. Until then he had relied on phone calls and occasional handwritten reports to keep the shop up to date about his customers' needs; since then he has been generating a flood of neatly printed memos, which are circulated to the appropriate people and posted on the bulletin board. "The more information people get from me, the more they understand the customer's needs," says Applegate. "Pretty soon the toolmaker and the production foreman and engineering are anticipating, not just reacting." Later this year Applegate and Connor's other salespeople will get high-speed modems allowing them, too, to tie into the shop-order-system—and to check a job's progress or enter comments from remote sites.

Sloss and Quarrey themselves have plenty of ideas for the future. The "quality alert" notices issued for troublesome jobs by Lopez's quality-control department will soon pop up automatically on shop orders. Late deliveries will automatically be flagged for later analysis. Most ambitious, each step in every job will soon be coded, so the corporate office can then calculate and produce a P&L statement not only by plant but also by department. That information, too, will be shared. The rationale? "We're taking the knowledge necessary for business decision making and giving it to people in the shop," says Quarrey. "That has been the philosophical objective—to give people enough information to change their roles."

Introducing the new system in the Los Angeles plant cost close to $100,000 in computer hardware, plus maybe half of Quarrey's time over two years. Spreading the system to the other plants, a process that will be completed by the end of 1991, won't be so expensive, but some plants will have to buy PCs, and employees will have to learn the system. Connor's information mania is not coming cheap.

The payoff, however, is already plain, at least for the L.A. division. Late jobs have declined over the past two years, from 10% of backlog to less than 1%. Connor's scores in the annual quality ratings provided by many of its customers have climbed to near perfection. The company's service and quality record commands a premium in the marketplace. An Indiana customer hired Connor as the sole source for several items, even though Connor's price was considerably higher than the other bids. A Los Angeles County customer invented the acronym CDBWGDCS, for Cost of Doing Business with Goddamn Connor Spring. "That was my purchasing manager," chuckles Al Wentzell, materials manager for Anthony Industrial Products. "Every time I wondered why we were paying this much for a part, he'd put those letters on the board. But the quality and service they give us are phenomenal."

The information systems also reduce Connor's costs. In 1989, 14% of defective jobs had similar problems the second time around. By 1990 that figure was down to 4%. Credits issued to customers fell from almost 4% of sales, in 1989, to slightly over .5%, in 1990. The company's overall sales per employee have risen about 20% in the past two years.

There are other payoffs as well.

For the employees and managers of Connor, there's the knowledge that they own 42% of a company whose stock value rose 35% last year—and that increased earnings will be reflected in fat bonus checks. Arguably, it's that financial interest in the company that makes the information system work. There's a tangible reward for making the kind of improvements the new system encourages.

For Bob Sloss, the payoffs are both tangible and intangible. His family's 55% interest in Connor is worth as much as its 100% interest was worth when the ESOP was started, in 1985. His company is once again profitable and seems to be weathering the national recession well.

Maybe more important, he has the satisfaction of accomplishing at least part of that original mission to revive American industry. Spring making as a whole hasn't done too well in recent years. But Connor has taken on all comers and won its share of victories.

"We're competing with the best house in Japan, and the best in Germany, and the best in Korea," says Sloss. "And we're still in the game."

STEP 2: Prepare the case for class discussion.

STEP 3: Answer each of the following questions, individually or in small groups, as directed by your instructor:

Diagnosis

1. What business problems was Connor Spring experiencing?
2. What strategy did the top executives at Connor Spring develop?
3. How did they plan to secure a competitive advantage over other companies in the industry?
4. What information did the management and employees of Connor Spring require to obtain this advantage?

Evaluation

5. Did Connor Spring have any information systems for meeting these needs?
6. How effective were these systems?
7. What types of information systems did Connor Spring introduce?
8. How well did they provide the information the company required to compete effectively?

Implementation

9. What costs were incurred in implementing these information systems?

STEP 4: In small groups, with the entire class, or in written form, share your answers to the questions above. Then answer the following questions:

1. What information needs existed in this situation?
2. How would meeting these needs give the company a competitive advantage?
3. What computer systems were introduced to meet these needs?
4. What have been the costs and benefits of these systems? ●

St. Thomas Psychiatric Hospital—A Strategic Planning Framework

STEP 1: Read the St. Thomas Psychiatric Hospital case. (This activity is especially suited for use in conjunction with Chapter 4 of *Information Systems.*)

Chris Bailey, Coordinator of Planning and Management Services at the St. Thomas Psychiatric Hospital in St. Thomas, Ontario, met with Bob Cunningham, the hospital administrator, late July 1989. "You mentioned that we should get together to discuss my proposal for a hospital strategic planning process," she said. "What do you think of it so far?"

THE HOSPITAL

St. Thomas Psychiatric Hospital (STPH) was one of ten provincial psychiatric hospitals operated by the Ontario Ministry of Health, the government body responsible for overseeing personal, community, and institutional health care in Ontario. It was a 500-bed hospital with 2000 registered outpatients and 800 staff. Its mandate was to serve people aged 16 and over living in St. Thomas and five nearby southwestern Ontario counties. The psychiatric services offered to patients included assessment, diagnosis, treatment, rehabilitation, consultation, and education. STPH provided out-patient and crisis services, and acted as a resource for general hospitals in the counties served. Patient treatment at times involved individual, group, and family therapy, occupational therapy, physiotherapy, rehabilitation for community living, as well as vocational and recreational services.

STPH Computing Resources

The hospital had a Data General MV4000 minicomputer with five Megabytes main memory, and a 354 Megabyte disk drive. Installed on the Data General were ADT (admission, discharge, transfer), pharmacy, and business application software, and a query language, Forthwriter.

Several STPH departments had also installed PC-based information systems, as depicted in Exhibit 1. These systems utilized Epson Equity II+ personal computers and IBM-compatible software. Department heads and program directors used the PC-based information to supplement the data available from the minicomputer when analyzing departmental and program efficiency and effectiveness. This information was especially valuable to them at this time because of increasing government cost control requirements.

MOTIVATION FOR STRATEGIC PLANNING

In recent years, government cutbacks had resulted in annual hospital budget increases below the inflation rate. It had thus become important for hospitals to allocate scarce funds optimally, in a manner consistent with their overall objectives. Government hospitals, STPH included, were now placing greater emphasis on proactively managing the services provided. At STPH, Bob Cunningham had asked Chris Bailey a few weeks earlier to recommend a

This case was prepared by Yolande Chan, under the direction of Professor Sid L. Huff, as the basis for classroom discussion.

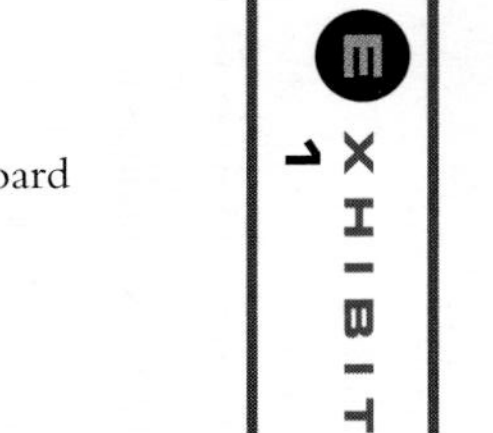

EXHIBIT 1 Organizational Overview—St. Thomas Psychiatric Hospital

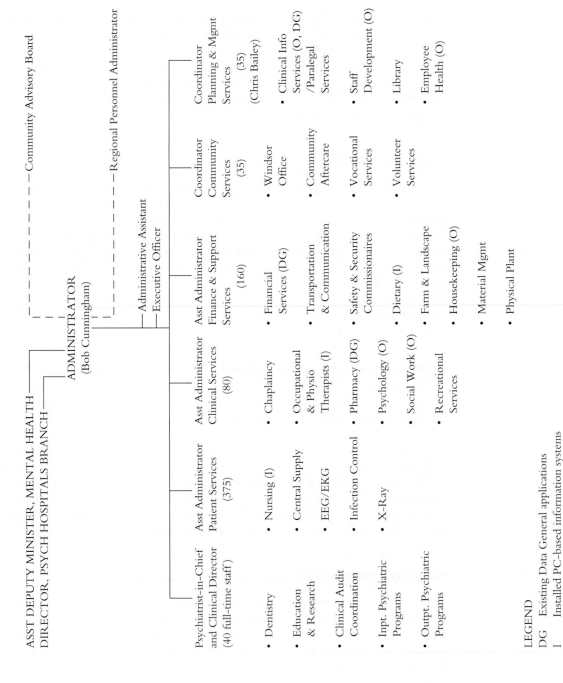

ASST DEPUTY MINISTER, MENTAL HEALTH
DIRECTOR, PSYCH HOSPITALS BRANCH

ADMINISTRATOR
(Bob Cunningham)

- - - Community Advisory Board
- - - Regional Personnel Administrator

— Administrative Assistant
— Executive Officer

Psychiatrist-in-Chief and Clinical Director (40 full-time staff)	Asst Administrator Patient Services (375)	Asst Administrator Clinical Services (80)	Asst Administrator Finance & Support Services (160)	Coordinator Community Services (35)	Coordinator Planning & Mgmt Services (35) (Chris Bailey)
• Dentistry	• Nursing (I)	• Chaplaincy	• Financial Services (DG)	• Windsor Office	• Clinical Info Services (O, DG) /Paralegal Services
• Education & Research	• Central Supply	• Occupational & Physio Therapists (I)	• Transportation & Communication	• Community Aftercare	• Staff Development (O)
• Clinical Audit Coordination	• EEG/EKG	• Pharmacy (DG)	• Safety & Security Commissionaires	• Vocational Services	• Library
• Inpt. Psychiatric Programs	• Infection Control	• Psychology (O)	• Dietary (I)	• Volunteer Services	• Employee Health (O)
• Outpt. Psychiatric Programs	• X-Ray	• Social Work (O)	• Farm & Landscape		
		• Recreational Services	• Housekeeping (O)		
			• Material Mgmt		
			• Physical Plant		

LEGEND
DG Existing Data General applications
I Installed PC-based information systems
O PC systems on order or under development

planning strategy that might serve as a basis for future hospital resource and program planning. A 32-year-old with an MBA from York University, she had been with the hospital for just over three years and was keen to make her contribution.

THE VISION FOR STRATEGIC PLANNING AT STPH

Chris envisioned that strategic planning at STPH would involve the formalized ongoing process of developing, evaluating, and implementing STPH goals, and guiding hospital decision-making processes. Information collected could be used to determine departmental and program strengths, weaknesses, and utilization. In this way, strategic planning could assist the hospital in optimizing its service levels.

Chris had recommended that a corporate database be created to support the STPH strategic planning effort. Her goal was to have enough departmental, program, and environmental information available so that management could track past, present, and expected required hospital services and performance. It would be necessary to quantify what the hospital was already doing, analyze departmental and program effectiveness, and identify possible cost savings through, for example, resource sharing.

Chris had recently recommended to Bob Cunningham the strategic planning framework depicted in Exhibit 2. She believed that strategic analysis should begin with an environmental assessment which could be used to refine the STPH mandate. Hospital operations could then be evaluated relative to the mandate in terms of effectiveness, efficiency, technological change and possible risk. The results of these ongoing evaluations could be used also to further refine the hospital mandate. The process would be iterative.

The *environmental assessment* that Chris was considering for STPH included monitoring:

1. Demographics, i.e. population trends and socio-economic statistics
2. Canadian and provincial disease incidence statistics
3. Designated service area psychiatric diagnosis statistics
4. STPH admission statistics
5. Socio-political conditions
6. Local hospital profile and image
7. Financial conditions including funding trends and forecasts
8. Competitive analysis including:
   - Substitute services and technologies provided by other facilities such as nursing homes and psychiatric wards of general hospitals
   - Suppliers of professional and technical resources, i.e. staff
   - Buyers of services, i.e. the agencies, facilities, and individuals who referred patients to STPH
   - Potential entrants and providers of similar services

This environmental analysis might highlight factors which could influence specific services or even the entire hospital.

Chris expected *STPH's mandate,* encompassing its stated mission, goals and objectives, to change over time to meet future requirements. The mandate could be formally stated and updated annually to reflect changes in:

1. Key problems faced by the hospital
2. A prediction of how these problems would change and what new challenges would be faced
3. A statement of the services to be provided and to whom
4. A description of the ongoing relationship the hospital had with the local community, other institutions, and agencies

EXHIBIT 2 A Proposed Framework for Strategic Planning at STPH

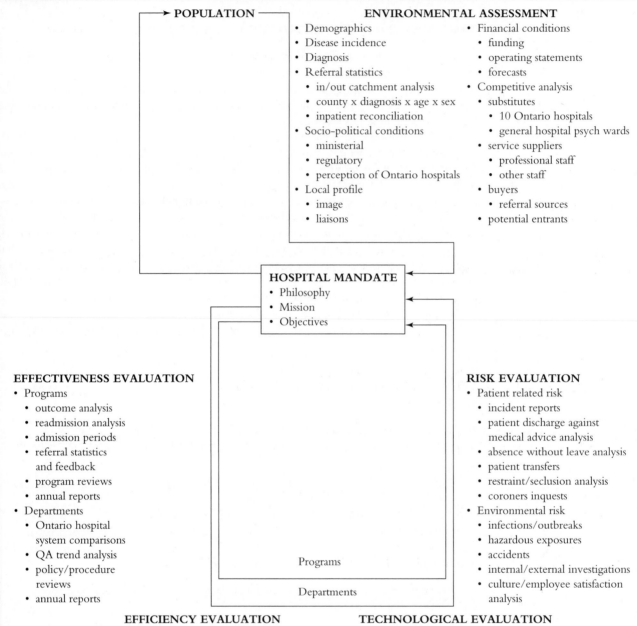

POPULATION

ENVIRONMENTAL ASSESSMENT

- Demographics
- Disease incidence
- Diagnosis
- Referral statistics
  - in/out catchment analysis
  - county x diagnosis x age x sex
  - inpatient reconciliation
- Socio-political conditions
  - ministerial
  - regulatory
  - perception of Ontario hospitals
- Local profile
  - image
  - liaisons
- Financial conditions
  - funding
  - operating statements
  - forecasts
- Competitive analysis
  - substitutes
    - 10 Ontario hospitals
    - general hospital psych wards
  - service suppliers
    - professional staff
    - other staff
  - buyers
    - referral sources
  - potential entrants

HOSPITAL MANDATE

- Philosophy
- Mission
- Objectives

Programs

Departments

EFFECTIVENESS EVALUATION

- Programs
  - outcome analysis
  - readmission analysis
  - admission periods
  - referral statistics and feedback
  - program reviews
  - annual reports
- Departments
  - Ontario hospital system comparisons
  - QA trend analysis
  - policy/procedure reviews
  - annual reports

RISK EVALUATION

- Patient related risk
  - incident reports
  - patient discharge against medical advice analysis
  - absence without leave analysis
  - patient transfers
  - restraint/seclusion analysis
  - coroners inquests
- Environmental risk
  - infections/outbreaks
  - hazardous exposures
  - accidents
  - internal/external investigations
  - culture/employee satisfaction analysis

EFFICIENCY EVALUATION

- Programs
  - outcome analysis
    - patient days
    - bed utilization
    - occupancy
    - outpatient contacts
  - resource input analysis
    - human (direct/indirect)
    - supplies
    - equipment
- Departments
  - output analysis
    - QA statistics
  - input analysis
    - human FTEs
    - supplies
    - equipment
  - operational review analysis

TECHNOLOGICAL EVALUATION

- Technological changes
  - techniques
  - organizational structuring
  - equipment
  - drugs
  - therapeutic treatments

5. A description of the hospital's commitment to education and research
6. A description of the hospital's culture and a summary of its history

Chris felt sure that a *service effectiveness evaluation* would be key to any successful strategic planning effort. The important questions to be asked here included:

1. What is the business of this department or departmental program?
2. How effectively are these services being provided?
3. Are these services appropriate for the department or program?

Information on individuals, programs, and departments could be collected on a monthly basis and then spreadsheet and trend analyses carried out. On an annual basis, the following information also could be analyzed and reviewed:

1. Departmental quality assurance statistics
2. Comparisons with other departments in the Ontario hospital system
3. Feedback from patients who had used departmental services

Chris thought that *efficiency evaluation* might involve quantifying both departmental and program inputs and outputs. These inputs would include people (both direct and indirect staff involved in patient care), equipment, supplies, etc. Program outputs could be reflected in statistics on patient days, staff/patient ratios, and so on. Departments might also be asked to specify more detailed breakdowns of their services and to conduct more frequent operational reviews.

Technological evaluations could be carried out at the department or program level. It would be difficult to do technological planning centrally because of the large volume of information and the specific technical expertise required. Ongoing monitoring of the following could take place:

1. Changes in state-of-the-art techniques for patient care
2. Changing availability of equipment
3. Changes in drug usage

Risk evaluation would involve capturing information to assist with identifying and preventing action that might lead to patient, employee, or visitor injury, or damage to hospital property. Patient incident reports, disturbances, accidents, etc. could be monitored. Trend analyses also could be carried out.

The STPH strategic planning process would be followed by strategy implementation. This would involve determining specific action plans, resource allocation and budgetary processes, as well as monitoring newly acquired hospital resources.

THE ADMINISTRATOR'S RESPONSE

Chris Bailey had recommended a strategic planning process to be followed and the information to be gathered. It was now up to Bob Cunningham, the Administrator, to give Chris his feedback.

STEP 2: Prepare the case for class discussion.

STEP 3: Answer each of the following questions, individually or in small groups, as directed by your instructor:

Diagnosis

1. Why did the hospital engage in strategic planning?
2. What information did it require as part of its strategic planning effort?
3. How could the hospital secure a competitive advantage?
4. What information did the hospital need to obtain this advantage?

Evaluation

5. What information systems does the hospital have to meet these needs?

Design

6. What changes would help the hospital obtain the needed information more cost effectively?

Implementation

7. What costs might the hospital incur in implementing its strategic planning effort?

STEP 4: In small groups, with the entire class, or in written form, share your answers to the questions above. Then answer the following questions:

1. What information needs existed in this situation?
2. How would meeting these needs give the hospital a competitive advantage?
3. What computer systems exist to meet these needs?
4. Do the existing systems appear to be adequate? ●

Activity 6 Three Minicases

STEP 1: Read each of the minicases. (This activity is especially suited for use in conjunction with Chapter 5 of *Information Systems.*)

MINICASE 1: AN INTERORGANIZATIONAL SYSTEM

Certain lines of insurance such as personal property, health, and travel, involve large numbers of customers who each take out relatively small dollar amounts of coverage. Processing insurance claims requires a great deal of information, usually supplied in written form by the insured party, which is then manually entered into the company's database. Often information on a single claim comes from multiple sources as a car accident may involve claims for auto repair, hospitalization, and personal liability.

Filing claims is frequently complicated because many insurance accounts originate at independent insurance agents. Much of this information is transferred by public mail, which is slow and is becoming increasingly more expensive. Reducing the paperwork flow between the insurance company, its customers, and its independent agents is an important cost-cutting strategy for the insurance firm: it simplifies the reporting tasks for the independent agents and customers, and it provides the customer with a speedier claims settlement.

Because of these advantages, linking independent agents to the insurance company's information system support functions will induce independent insurance agents to favor that company when signing up new customers for insurance. This benefits the company because it obtains a strategic advantage over its competitors.

With this in mind the Finnish insurance firm SAMPO started a pilot project to link its mainframe-based information system with the PC-based information systems of car dealers and trucking firms. The car dealers provided insurance to new car buyers, and the trucking firms purchased insurance for their trucking fleets. The software required in these interorganizational information systems was designed by the insurance firm with the cooperation of, but at no cost to, the participating organizations.

This business operates in a highly competitive environment and its information system is considered to be essential to achieving its corporate totals. Management would be averse to buying off-the-shelf software if this software would negate the company's advantage over its competitors. Furthermore, the application requires the exchange of large quantities of data between the insurance company's information system and the information systems of its independent agents.

MINICASE 2: A SYSTEM FOR COMPUTER-ASSISTED DISPATCHING

A police car dispatching sequence typically begins with a call from a citizen for police assistance. The call is answered by a complaint evaluator who selects one of four courses of action:

1. no need exists for a police response (e.g., caller requests the local town hall's address);
2. no need exists for a police response, but a police report is required (e.g., caller reports his car stolen);

Minicase 1 is reprinted from Carl R. Ruthstrom and Charlene A. Dykman, *Information Systems for Managers; Casebook* (St. Paul: West, 1992). Minicase 2 is adapted from Marius A. Janson, University of Missouri, St. Louis, Evidence to support the continuing role of the information systems department in organizations, *Journal of Management Information Systems* (Fall 1989): 22–31. Minicase 3 is reprinted by permission of M. E. Sharpe, Inc., Armonk, NY 10504.

3. a police response and a police report are required (e.g., crime is in progress), and
4. a police response but no police report is required (e.g., police involvement is limited to directing traffic in an emergency situation).

Only in the last two situations is a police car required and the complaint evaluator places the request for assistance in a queue, where it awaits processing by the next available dispatcher.

Computer-assisted car dispatching (CAD) systems have been operating successfully for nearly 20 years. Thus, when the St. Louis Police Department required such a system, it was natural to look for standard off-the-shelf software that could operate on the department's mainframe. However, police departments differ in how they perform this day-to-day task. Additionally, police information systems, rather than being isolated entities, communicate and exchange data with regional and national information systems.

With these issues in mind, the department's database administrator, accompanied by several members of the police force, visited four cities with CAD systems similar in specifications to those needed in St. Louis. They selected a system in use in Kansas City because it used dispatching procedures in close agreement with those followed by St. Louis dispatching personnel. The only obstacles to implementing an exact duplicate of the Kansas City system in St. Louis were the dissimilar database systems of the two applications. The database administrator planned to bridge these differences by a partial rewrite of the software, which was not thought to affect the success of system implementation.

To ensure a smooth implementation, police personnel initially operated the modified system at approximately 20% of its intended capacity alongside the existing manual dispatching system. The entire cycle of dispatching a car requires information displayed on four different screens. In the modified system the dispatcher had to look at two screens at a time; thus, the completion of a dispatching task required alternating between screens. The time needed to alternate between screens was only a few seconds, but the St. Louis dispatchers considered this time to be much too long because it had the potential of placing police officers in undue jeopardy during crisis situations. Displaying all four screens simultaneously on one video display terminal, however, required significant changes in hardware and software.

MINICASE 3: AN INFORMATION SYSTEM FOR ENERGY CONSERVATION

Adequate information about energy consumption by end-use type is crucial in any effective energy conservation program. This case relates the failure of an energy information system installed to support the energy conservation effort for a midwestern state's publicly owned buildings. The energy agency purchased standard off-the-shelf software that had already been extensively used in other states to target buildings for energy consumption measures. The software was part of a system consisting of data collection, system operating manuals, and instruction manuals for staff members at individual buildings to help them complete the self-administered data collection forms. The agency collected data on approximately 300 variables for several thousand buildings and prepared reports indicating whether energy conservation measures were desirable. Subsequent analysis of these results by agency personnel revealed that the recommendations contained in the reports were erroneous and the system was abandoned.

This application seems a fitting candidate for commercial software because demand for similar information existed at other state energy agencies. Thus the availability of standard off-the-shelf software was likely, and no data exchange with other systems was required. Then what were the causes of its failure?

First, the energy agency was unaware that its objectives differed from those of the software house. The software house wanted a database for its own future use that contained as much information as possible on the energy consumption of publicly owned buildings. Thus, the amount of data collected was far in excess of what was needed for the energy agency's limited goal of targeting buildings for energy conservation measures. The data collection and data entry processes became unnecessarily complex and were sources of many data errors. The resulting poor quality data demonstrates that end-user computing without adequate attention to data integrity can place an organization at considerable risk.

Second, the software contained an engineering model for identifying buildings that consumed excessive amounts of energy compared to buildings with similar structural and operational characteristics. Because the model was incorrectly calibrated for climatic conditions and building characteristics unlike those found in the midwestern state, grossly inaccurate predictions resulted. The problems with the model and the data were uncovered after an in-depth study that required expertise on energy conservation, information technology, and statistical techniques for improving data quality.

STEP 2: Prepare the cases for class discussion.

STEP 3: Answer each of the following questions for each minicase, individually or in small groups, as directed by your instructor:

Diagnosis

1. What are the information needs in this situation?

Evaluation

2. What type of software is currently used?
3. How well does it meet the information needs?

Design

4. What are the relative advantages and disadvantages of horizontal applications software, off-the-shelf software, customized software, and home-grown software in the situation?
5. What type of software should be used to meet the information needs in the situation?

Implementation

6. What issues exist in purchasing, installing, and using the new software?

STEP 4: In small groups, with the entire class, or in written form, share your answers to the questions above. Then answer the following questions:

1. What are the information needs in each situation?
2. What types of software best meet these needs?
3. What are the assets and liabilities of each type of horizontal and vertical applications software?
4. How can the required changes in software be implemented? ●

Activity 7 Lufkin-Conroe Telephone Exchange, Inc.

STEP 1: Read the Lufkin-Conroe Telephone Exchange, Inc. case. (This activity is especially suited for use in conjunction with Chapter 6 of *Information Systems.*)

LUFKIN-CONROE TELEPHONE EXCHANGE, INC.

The Lufkin-Conroe Telephone Exchange, Inc. (LCTX), incorporated in 1986, is an independent local telephone exchange operating as a privately held public utility with administrative and operating offices located in Lufkin, Texas. Customers are located in Lufkin and its surrounding areas, in Alto (30 miles away), and in Conroe (approximately 85 miles south of Lufkin). The company serves approximately 66,000 access lines and is located in the Houston Local Access Transport Area (LATA). The service area extends over 1400 square miles and includes a network of nearly 4,000 miles of telephone cable.

The company employs over 400 people with 28 working in the Information Systems Department. The department has 19 programmers, three operators, and six people in administration and technical support. The computers and Information Systems staff are located in Lufkin. The computers discussed in this paper are used for company operations and commercial business. These are not the computers used by LCTX to record telephone call data. The latter, Northern Telecom digital switches, are located separately from the application computers with the only communication being via magnetic tape.

LCTX provides operator services for the Lufkin area and Southwestern Bell provides operator services for the Conroe customers. Typical user applications include billing inquiries from customers who call LCTX with billing questions and the accounting department staff making inquiries regarding accounts payable issues. One of the major systems supported by the Information Systems Department is the Toll Processing System which records and processes the billable telephone traffic traveling throughout the Lufkin-Conroe Telephone Exchange network.

THE TOLL PROCESSING SYSTEM

The Toll Processing System processes records entering the system from three different points. The first is LCTX (Northern Telecom switches) recorded calls that are long distance, mobile traffic, or directory assistance calls. The second entry point is calls recorded outside of the LCTX service area yet billable by LCTX. Included are credit card, collect, and third-party billing calls. The third point of entry is conference calls originating in the Lufkin area. These are recorded manually and entered through a CRT. Also included here are Centralized Ticket Investigation (CTI) rebills following customer initiated inquiries regarding billing irregularities.

The information comes into this system in hexadecimal and is converted to character format. Calls not billed individually are separated out as are Access Usage Records. The latter are used to apportion out the monies to various companies whose facilities may have been used for the calls. The information goes through a rating process that involves a search of tables for the correct rate given the start time of the call, the call date, etc. Service charges

This case was written by Charlene A. Dykman and Carl R. Ruthstrom, University of Houston–Downtown, and Chris B. Copenhaver, Lufkin-Conroe Telephone Exchange, Inc. Reprinted with permission from C. R. Ruthstrom and C. A. Dykman, *Information Systems for Managers: A Casebook* (St. Paul, Minn.: West, 1992).

for activities such as operator assistance are added at that time. The system then goes through a settlement process using industry guidelines and the Access Usage Records to set the actual value of the money to be shared between the phone companies.

Following this processing, a sampling process is conducted resulting in 5% of LCTX's traffic being sent by tape to Southwestern Bell each week. This is then sent to AT&T where the information is used for trend analysis. A third process divides out LCTX, Southwestern Bell, and Contel traffic. LCTX records some of Contel's traffic in one area. A tape containing this information is sent to Southwestern Bell and Contel each week.

LCTX uses different billing cycles to spread out the printing and mailing work load. Customers' billing cycles are determined by the first three digits of the phone number. There are two cycles for the Conroe area and three for the Lufkin area. This printing and mailing process occupies one full-time person. It is easy to see the heavy processing requirements that result from the complexity of today's telecommunication networks.

THE TECHNOLOGY

LCTX processed all applications and development work on a single IBM System 38 until 1986. The Conroe and Alto areas were connected to the computer via modems and Lufkin was direct wired. Conroe users began to experience unacceptable response time as business grew dramatically during the 1980s. This was accompanied by growth in the size of the programming staff and the amount of development work being performed. A second System 38 was installed in October, 1986 and was dedicated to the Conroe users. Lufkin and Alto users, as well as the programming staff, used the larger of the two System 38s.

In July, 1988, IBM announced the introduction of the AS/400 line of computers. This line was to replace the System 38 in the IBM midrange family line and was to be much faster, more reliable, and have more memory than the System 38. The System 38 would no longer be manufactured by IBM and at some point in the future IBM would no longer offer service for the System 38. The 38 model would become what is known as "orphaned" and users would need to rely on private vendors for support and service.

IBM's long range plans for the AS/400 include increasing the potential of the computer over the next decade. This will be accomplished by new operating systems with minor changes to the hardware. When IBM announced the phase-out of the System 38, LCTX had to make several critical decisions about the future of the computer hardware they were using. LCTX was totally dependent on these computers and the enormous amounts of code, written in RPG3, which resides on these computers.

ALTERNATIVES

LCTX Information Systems personnel were now faced with alternatives to consider. What about making no changes? This would not require any capital investments or hardware or software changes. However, over time, support for the 38s would become a major issue and this prevented serious consideration of the "do nothing" alternative.

The second option was to purchase two AS/400 computers and configure them in the same manner as the 38s with a small one dedicated to Conroe users and a larger one for Lufkin and Alto users and developmental activities. This offered possibilities for one computer serving as a backup for the other, avoided problems with user competition for batch processing resources, assured good response time for Conroe users, gave flexibility to the operations staff for scheduling the nightly production jobs, and gave the programming staff easy access to test data on the same machine. This configuration had some disadvantages also. Production jobs requiring data from both machines meant operator intervention and tape handling. Program changes had to be installed on two machines and complex interfaces were needed for access to common applications that shared data because these applications resided on one machine. Redundant programs and data existed and this required more memory. With programmers doing testing on a production machine, there was always vulnerability to erroneous updates of production data.

The third alternative considered was to purchase two AS/400s and configure one as a developmental platform and the larger one to serve the entire user population. This would eliminate complex hardware interfaces, separate development work from the production data, reduce memory requirements caused by program and data redundancy, and eliminate the competition for resources between the users and the programming staff. There were disadvantages associated with this configuration also. Program testing now would require the importing of live data to the development machine. Nightly production scheduling would become much more difficult and the volume of production jobs on one machine would nearly double. Jobs that shared data could no longer be run at the same time. Response time for the users in Lufkin, who access the system through modems, might degrade during peak periods.

The manager of Information Systems at LCTX has to make a decision that will have a long-term impact on the department, the entire company, and its users. Neither of the viable alternatives is without risks. The manager contemplates the future, weighing the various advantages and disadvantages, and finally develops a proposal and recommendation for the acquisition and implementation of the AS/400 computers.

STEP 2: Prepare the case for class discussion.

STEP 3: Answer each of the following questions, individually or in small groups, as directed by your instructor.

Diagnosis

1. What information needs did the Toll Processing System meet?

Evaluation

2. How effective were the System 38 minicomputers in meeting the company's needs?
3. How well would they meet those needs in the future?
4. What limitations exist to the continued use of System 38 computers?

Design

5. What alternatives were available to the LCTX Information Systems Department in dealing with IBM's phase-out of the System 38 computers?
6. What are the advantages and disadvantages of each alternative?

Implementation

7. What issues should the LCTX Information Systems Department consider in choosing among the alternatives?

STEP 4: In small groups, with the entire class, or in written form, share your answers to the questions above. Then answer the following questions:

1. What information needs does the Toll Processing System meet?
2. How effectively do the System 38 computers meet these needs?
3. What options for replacing the System 38 computers exist?
4. What implementation issues must be considered in replacing this hardware? ●

Activity 8 The United States Postal Service

STEP 1: Read the United States Postal Service's Address Management System case. (This activity is especially suited for use in conjunction with Chapter 7 of *Information Systems.*)

Every day, Americans mail over ½ billion letters, parcels and magazines. Each piece of mail then begins a processing journey during which it is collected, postmarked, sorted and delivered to one of over 120 million final destinations throughout the country. Mail processing is a labor-intensive operation which is occurring around the clock in every town and city across the country.

Mail volume, which grew over 300 percent in the past two decades, exploded in the 1980s. In 1992, the United States Postal Service (USPS) processed over 170 billion pieces of mail. In contrast, twelve years earlier, 97 billion pieces of mail were processed. Although alternative forms of communication are rapidly becoming available, mail volume is projected to continue to grow into the foreseeable future. Along with this increasing demand for service, millions of business and residential addresses are created or changed every year.

Although this demand from today's rapidly changing environment suggests an ominous growth in personnel and infrastructure support, the unacceptable cost implications of such growth, which would ultimately be passed on to the public via price increases, necessitates a dynamic approach to mail processing. Postal managers realized the strategic importance of automating mail sortation processes and, thus, initiated an aggressive automation plan which seeks to continuously maximize emerging information technology. As part of this plan, the USPS undertook a major corporate effort to design, develop, and implement an information system with a consistent and current address database. This paper discusses the innovative information system developed to meet this challenge—the Address Management System (AMS). AMS is the official record of all addresses in the U.S. and its territories; its database contains the critical information resource of the U.S. Postal Service.

BACKGROUND

The initial implementation of the Address Management System (AMS) involved consolidating three independently-supported, concurrent address files into a single database. Prior to consolidation, these three distinct files—the Five Digit ZIP Code file, the Carrier Route Information System file, and the ZIP+4 file—reported common information inconsistently (such as duplicate address data) and required users to update each file using independent system methods. Since a more accurate and centralized address management system was needed, a network-based software database management system was proposed to create an on-line, real-time data entry and query system.

The AMS project team faced an array of start-up challenges. The size and functional requirements of the new database pushed the limits of what was technically achievable at the time AMS was conceptualized. There were no similar-sized existing models on which the proposed system could be based. Numerous physical design options were possible. Technical expertise in a new system development technology did not exist and needed to be developed. A national structure of over 300 AMS support personnel had to be positioned, trained, and equipped to handle address information and maintenance functions. A compressed development and implementation schedule, which was dictated by business needs, generated skepticism from peers and experts outside the organization.

Extracted from Joseph M. Feliu and Harry Aldstadt, The address management system: Improving customer information flow, *Journal of End User Computing* (Winter 1994): 26–32.

THE FUNCTION OF AMS

The true power of AMS lies in its role as the source database for all address information products necessary for the essential business processes involved in moving America's mail. AMS' primary function is maintaining, extracting, and distributing the data used by 1) all automated mail sorting machines, 2) other internal systems, and 3) mailing customers via products needed to create 'automation ready' mail (Figure 1). AMS is critical to effectively managing the USPS' huge capital investment in automation technology and to realizing the intended benefits.

A new generation of highly sophisticated automated mail processing equipment sorts mail using information extracted from the AMS database. This equipment constitutes the backbone of the Postal Service's automation strategy. It scans the address on a mail piece, matches it against the AMS directory, and then sprays a bar code representing that address on the envelope. In a manner similar to the way price scanners are used in supermarkets, the mail can then be sorted by bar code at a rate of nine letters per second into the exact sequence that letter carriers walk their routes. The efficiency of the automated equipment is dependent on the accuracy of address data which AMS provides. Automation reduces the volume of mail that must be sorted by manual or mechanized processes and provides greater accuracy of delivery.

AMS also provides data for other internal systems such as the Computerized Delivery Sequence File, the Computerized Mail Forwarding System, and ZIP+4 Encoding Services. These subsidiary systems all utilize the AMS database for accurate address information. By directly supporting these systems, AMS further unifies and advances the automation of mail processing and delivery functions. Additionally, significant cost savings are realized. For example, the National Change of Address and the Address Change Service systems realize a savings of $9,000,000 a week by utilizing AMS data.

Business mailers, mailing houses, list management firms and service bureaus depend on AMS products to maintain and improve the accuracy of their address records, to target specific customer areas, and to qualify for presort discounts. USPS customers use AMS products in conjunction with commercially available ZIP+4 conversion and bar coding software to increase the quality and efficiency of their internal business mailing operations and to realize immediate cost savings. Customers using 4-digit add-on codes or a unique Five-Digit ZIP Code, can direct mail to specific departments within their company. Payments and time sensitive replies can be separated from other correspondence as incoming mail is sorted. When AMS products are used by businesses to prepare their mailings, the Postal Service is then able to process their mail faster and with greater accuracy.

AMS products are available on paper, microfiche, magnetic tape, cartridge, and CD-ROM. The Postal Service also provides monthly and quarterly address subscription services to over 8,600 mailers. These products currently generate more than $1.3 million in annual revenue for the USPS. The demand for them has increased every year since these services began.

The following high-level AMS process flow chart illustrates the flow of data through the primary address information functions (Figure 2).

CONTINUAL SYSTEMS DEVELOPMENT

Currently, the on-line AMS database contains 28 million address block records representing areas serviced by over 40,000 Postal Service facilities. Weekly directory updates ensure the most current information is available. Direct file maintenance is performed on-line by 200 postal facilities where analysts report new building and housing starts, demolitions, letter carrier route changes and other delivery information. AMS provides consistent up-to-date data and, on a daily basis, averages 500 users who generate over 500,000 transactions.

IGURE 1 Address Management System-Primary Address Data Source

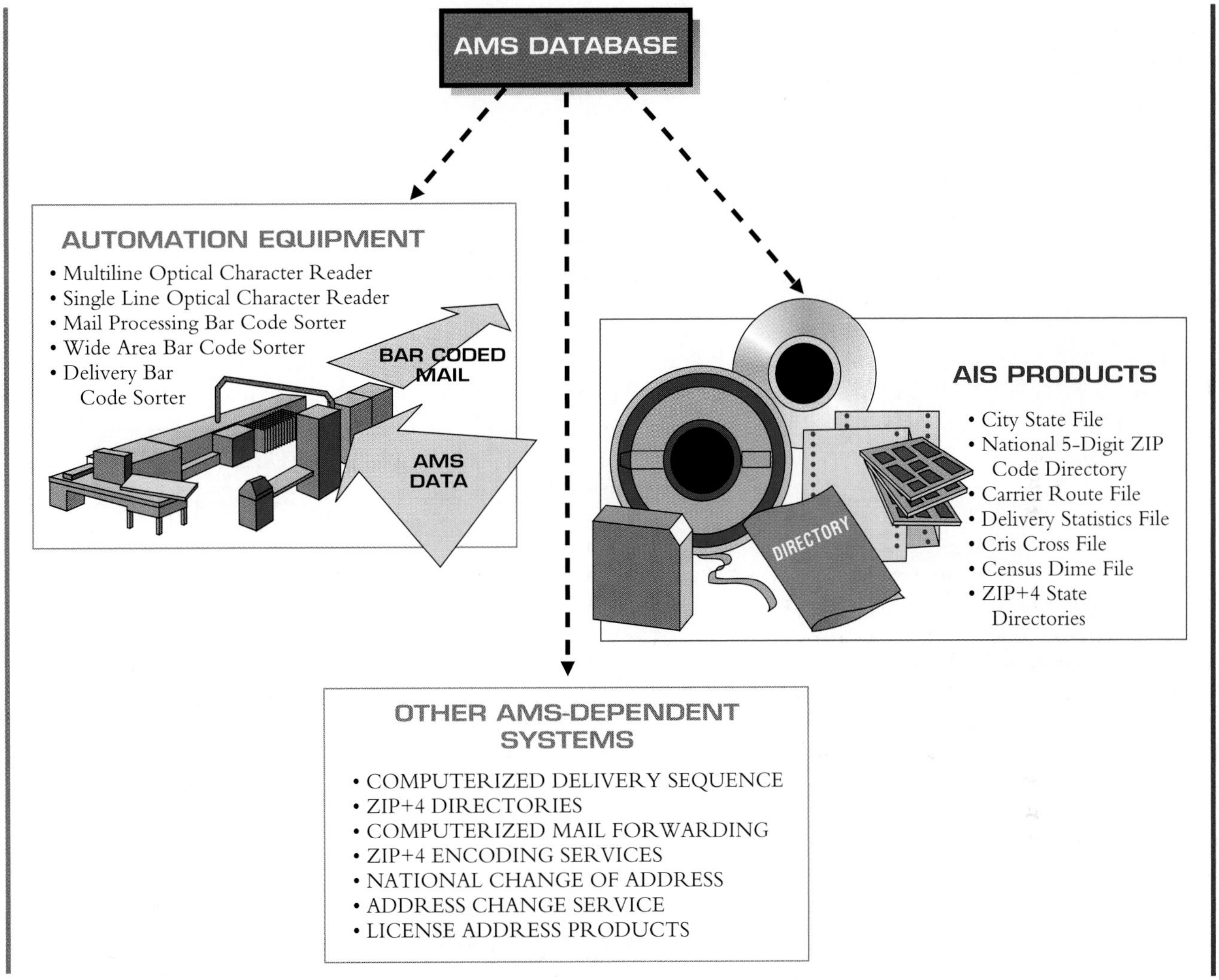

AMS DATABASE

AUTOMATION EQUIPMENT

- Multiline Optical Character Reader
- Single Line Optical Character Reader
- Mail Processing Bar Code Sorter
- Wide Area Bar Code Sorter
- Delivery Bar Code Sorter

BAR CODED MAIL

AMS DATA

AIS PRODUCTS

- City State File
- National 5-Digit ZIP Code Directory
- Carrier Route File
- Delivery Statistics File
- Cris Cross File
- Census Dime File
- ZIP+4 State Directories

DIRECTORY

OTHER AMS-DEPENDENT SYSTEMS

- COMPUTERIZED DELIVERY SEQUENCE
- ZIP+4 DIRECTORIES
- COMPUTERIZED MAIL FORWARDING
- ZIP+4 ENCODING SERVICES
- NATIONAL CHANGE OF ADDRESS
- ADDRESS CHANGE SERVICE
- LICENSE ADDRESS PRODUCTS

The Address Management System is continuously evolving as both technology and business needs change. By late 1993, AMS will be expanded from 28 million address block records to 125 million delivery point addresses. The 242 billion character database will soon have the capacity to store over 150 million records. These enhancements will further support sorting mail in letter carrier walk sequence and will consolidate additional existing address information support systems. A client/server-based front-end system for AMS is also under development. This system promises revolutionary change in internal business practices because it allows distribution of the centralized data store to local processing and distribution sites.

Employing emerging technologies as they become available has further enhanced AMS applicability. For example, the increased availability of CD-ROMs provides the USPS with an additional medium on which to provide the entire ZIP+4 database to AMS products

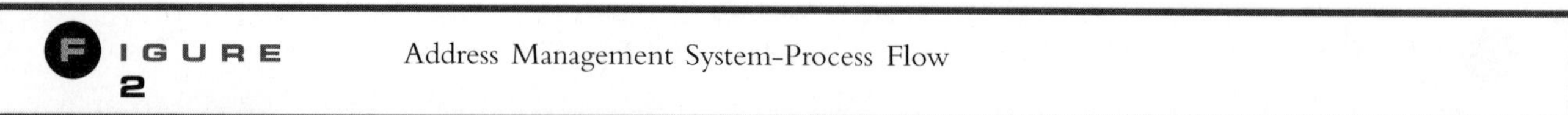

FIGURE 2 Address Management System-Process Flow

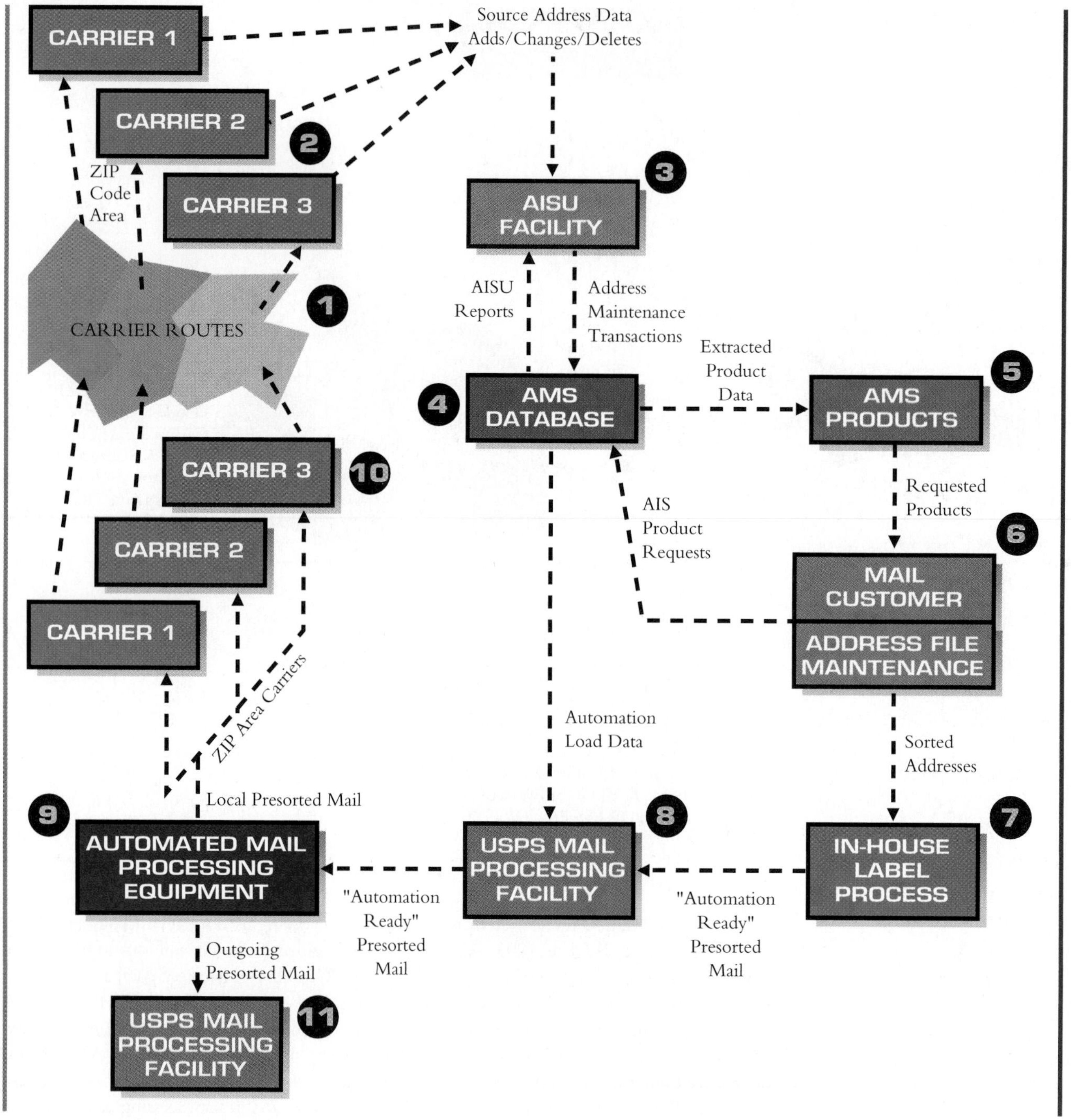

Continued

Address Management System Process Flow

Flow #

1. **ZIP Code Area**
   - Basic defined delivery area
   - Served by multiple letter carriers having route identifiers
   - Can contain other "unique" ZIP codes for businesses, hospitals, government buildings, etc.
   - Defined to AMS database via data elements
   - 43,274 ZIP codes in database
2. **Carrier Routes**
   - Streets and delivery points within ZIP code area assigned to a single carrier
   - Initial source of address change data via letter carrier
   - 501,046 carrier routes in database
3. **Address Information Support Unit**
   - Update AMS database using on-line terminals from address change information received from carriers
   - 167 screens provide required database update capability
   - Receive updated listings/reports for updated ZIP codes
   - 200 facilities serve all USPS delivery areas
4. **AMS Database**
   - Hierarchical database containing USPS organizational address and product fulfillment/customer data
   - 45 million records - 106 billion characters
   - 200 data elements define AMS data
   - Update, extract, report, audit, and fulfillment processes via 850 programs/utilities that comprise the Address Management System
5. **Address Management System Products**
   - Products provided to mailers and USPS operational facilities to enable and support the creation and processing of "automation ready" mail
   - Carrier Route Information System file
   - ZIP +4 file
   - 5-digit ZIP file
   - Additional products are produced in a variety of formats and media
6. **Mailing Customer**
   - User of AMS Product(s) to update in-house address lists and pre-sort outgoing mail to receive rate discounts and improved delivery window
7. **In-House Label/Address Process**
   - System/process used by AMS customer to generate "automation ready" mail for delivery to USPS mail processing facility
8. **USPS Mail Processing Facility**
   - Presorted mail positioned for appropriate automation process
   - Automation equipment on site
   - AMS products provide automation equipment update data
9. **Automated Mail Processing Equipment**
   - Multi-Line Optical Character Readers
   - Bar Code Sorters
   - Bar Code Readers
   - Delivery Point Bar Code Sorters
10. **Letter Carriers**
    - Receive deliverable mail for individual route sorted in delivery sequence
    - Manual sorting hours reduced

customers. Similarly, electronic imaging has permitted the use of Remote Barcode Sorting for letter mail that can not be read by the optical character scanners.

RESULTS

Developing and implementing AMS has produced dramatic improvements for the information systems function, the Postal Service's mail processing capability, and for external customers' mailing operations.

The AMS database, products, and operational support structure are now essential components of the Postal Service's operations capability. Currently, 90% of business letter mail volume is processed on mechanized or automated equipment using sort programs developed from the AMS database. This mail accounts for 70% of letter mail volume and requires less handling because it bypasses manual processing. A single piece of automated equipment using two operators can sort 30,000 letters per hour, a rate thought impossible just a few years ago. In contrast, 40 people would be required to accomplish the same task manually.

Without this critical database of addresses, the Postal Service's new state-of-the-art automation equipment could not be successfully exploited. For example, compressed AMS address directories for the Multi-Line Optical Character Reader (MLOCR) provide each MLOCR site access to all ZIP+4 national files. Use of compressed directories has reduced nonbarcoded mail by 2.5%, realizing a $50-$75 million annual savings.

Businesses benefit directly from the availability of AMS products. Timeliness of delivery is dependent on the quality of a company's mailing list, the addressing format of their mail piece, and the ability to get the mail piece to the mail carrier in the most expedient manner. Incorrect, incomplete, and "Undeliverable As Addressed" mail can drain a company's budget and impair their public image. Mailers currently spend an estimated $2 billion annually on material, preparation, and postage for mail that cannot be delivered as addressed. The USPS spends an additional $1 billion annually handling "problem" mail. Matching customers' address files to the AMS database allows identification and correction of incomplete or inaccurate addresses before they enter the mail stream.

Customers using AMS products have realized considerable postage discounts and savings. For example, Alabama Gas Company saves a quarter of a million dollars annually on postage, labor, and supplies by using AMS products to convert to delivery point barcoding. After realizing increased operational effectiveness, their President, Wm. Michael Warren, Jr., stated, "If this is a partnership that makes sense for Alabama Gas, it's the kind of partnership that makes sense for many companies...It's not just something that's valuable to the mega-company..."

Many businesses have also learned that other aspects of their business improve as a result of more efficient mailing operations. For example, Texaco, which processes over four million credit card statements a month, now realizes an annual savings of $2.4 million from postal rate discounts. As a result of improving their mail operations, they also reduced the payment and billing cycle and thereby improved the availability of funds generated from customer payments.

STEP 2: Prepare the case for class discussion.

STEP 3: Answer each of the following questions, individually or in small groups, as directed by your instructor:

Diagnosis

1. What information does the United States Postal Service (USPS) need to support its automation of mail sorting? Why is the automation of mail sorting important to the USPS?

2. What information can the USPS supply to its customers to reduce the costs of handling their mail?
3. Before the development of the Address Management System (AMS), how did the Postal Service handle its address-sorting information needs?

Evaluation

4. Was the pre-AMS system effective?
5. What systems could meet the USPS's information needs?

Design

6. Was the development of a database an appropriate solution?
7. Was the choice of a hierarchical database an appropriate choice for this application?
8. What roles should the following parties have played during the design of the AMS database: the address-management staff; the engineering staff who were responsible for the automated equipment; and the information systems staff?

Implementation

9. Has the AMS database been effective in meeting the USPS's information needs?
10. What additional benefit does the AMS provide for the USPS and its customers?

STEP 4: In small groups, with the entire class, or in written form, share your answers to the questions above. Then answer the following questions:

1. What information needs exist in this situation?
2. What systems existed to meet the needs prior to development of the AMS?
3. What deficiencies existed in these systems?
4. Was a hierarchical database an appropriate solution?
5. Was the AMS effective in meeting the USPS's needs? ●

Activity 9 Hisuesa (Hidroelectrica del Sur de Espana, S.A.)

STEP 1: Read the Hisuesa case. (This activity is especially suited for use in conjunction with Chapter 7 of *Information Systems.*)

Mr. Alfredo Málaga, Director of Distribution and Sales for the utility Hidroeléctrica del Sur de España, was very annoyed with the company's Data Processing Service (DPS). He let it be known to Samuel Balmes, head of Planning and Control, who was the highest-ranking manager with responsibility over the DPS in the firm. Málaga declared: "In order to resolve the problems posed by your Service in terms of writing different customer database access programs which I need to develop on a routine basis, I've had to create my own data processing center. Now, the company urgently needs a support system for its marketing activities, and the answer I get from the Data Processing Service is that they'll start analyzing the problem in 1991! This is ridiculous! Data Processing has become a giant which feeds on itself to survive. Maybe we should just leave it at Data Processing and omit the "Service" part."

HISTORY

The utility Hidroeléctrica del Sur de España is one Andalucías' foremost generators and suppliers of electrical power. The company, based in Algarinejo (Granada) has a production capacity of 1,060 mega watts (Mw) from hydroelectrical sources, 1,564 thermal Mw from coal and gas, and 820 Mw from its joint operations in three nuclear power plants. Its supply network reaches 1,450,000 customers throughout the whole "Autonomous Community" of Andalucía and has a total length of approximately 15,000 miles. In 1988, HISUESA invoiced over 120 billion pesetas. The utility has 40 branches spread out over its area of influence; personnel assigned to the branches are in charge of sales and collection activities, systems maintenance and expansion work and consumption read-out monitoring.

The utility's organization structure is shown in Exhibit 1. The Board of Directors is made up of shareholders' representatives, and an important bank is the majority owner of the utility company, and therefore designates HISUESA's president. At present, as all the country's utilities, the company is planning a restructuring which will strengthen the commercial side as opposed to the classical areas of emphasis of production and engineering.

During the 60's and—to a lesser extent—the 70's, Spanish utilities underwent tremendous expansion because of the need to provide the country with the necessary production infrastructure in order to maintain the enormous economic development during this period. However, according to the Energy Plans of recent years, no productive capacity expansion has been necessary. As a result, the industry—and HISUESA along with it—has moved to dismantle its engineering and construction departments, which have been packed with engineers specialized in the design and construction of power facilities, and instead focus on commercial and quality of service aspects. But now there are signs that indicate a future need for additional production capacity as of 1994, which may require new construction activity beginning in 1991. At any rate, due to its location in Andalucía and its fuel mix, it is highly unlikely that the government will single out HISUESA to build the new power plant.

This case was prepared by Professors Rafael Andreu, Joan E. Ricart, and Josep Valor. June 1989. The names and figures given in this case have been altered to maintain confidentiality.

EXHIBIT 1 Organization Structure

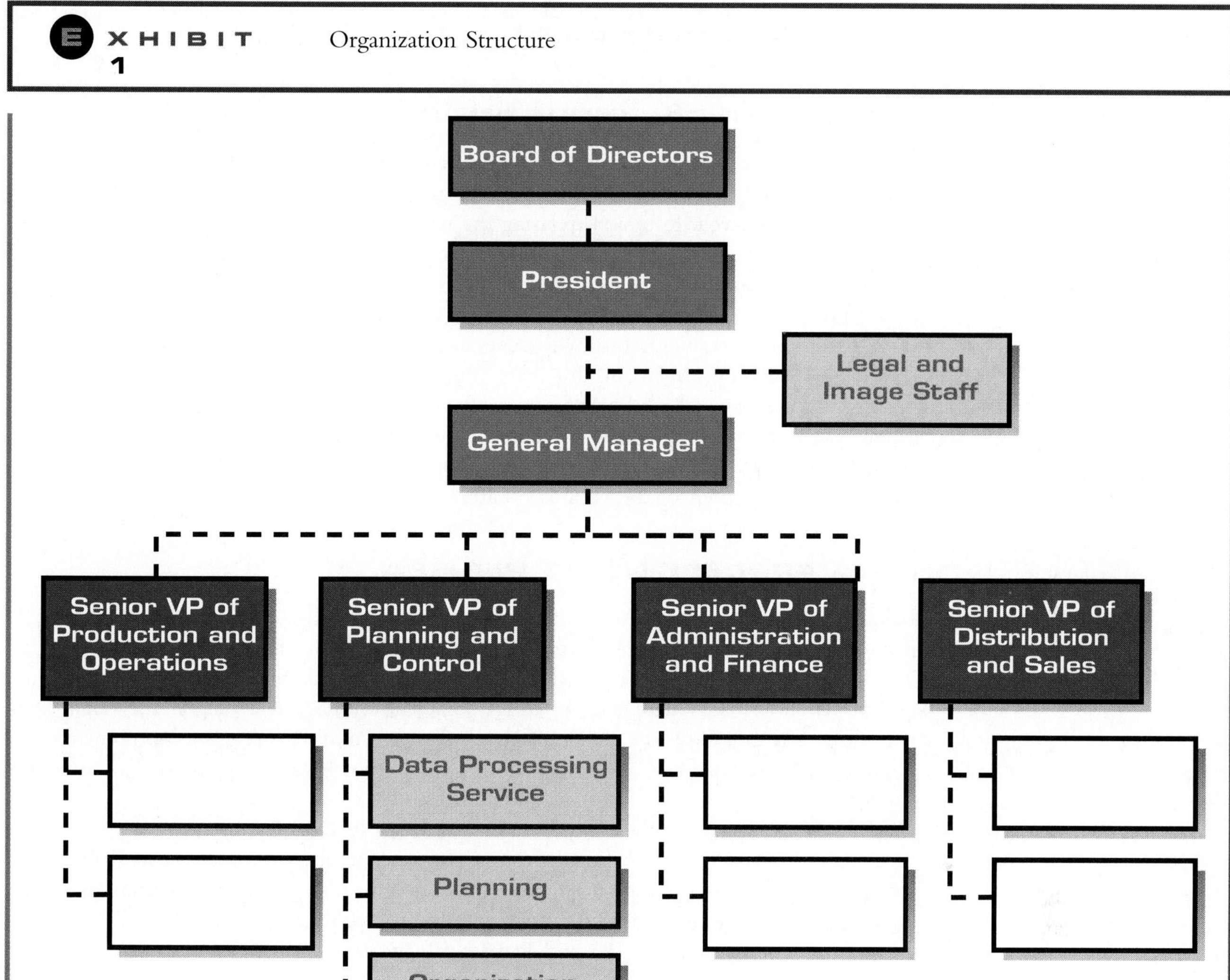

Operating a utility the size of HISUESA is no easy task. For example, each year there are some 230,000 jobs of maintenance, upgrading and extension of the medium- and low-voltage supply networks (new customer service connections, repair work, power line replacement, etc.) which involve some 2,000 utility and subcontracted workers.

A recent study by a prestigious American consulting firm established the two following basic strategic objectives for HISUESA:

1. Reduce costs, especially through (i) improving efficiency in existing power plants, (ii) reducing loss of power in medium- and low-voltage lines, and (iii) reducing the level of customer fraud.
2. Increase sales per customer, promoting the replacement of other energy forms, such as natural gas or diesel fuel, in favor of electrical power. Good sales pitches would be convenience, safety and savings in the case of installing double-rate meters and storing heat overnight in special accumulators. These sales pitches are valid for both domestic and industrial users.

However, it is obvious that in order to fulfill these objectives, it is necessary to upgrade the service quality, reducing power outages and instabilities to a minimum.

THE ELECTRICAL INDUSTRY IN SPAIN

The Spanish electrical industry is very highly regulated, both in terms of price (set by the Government) and production. In Spain, power is transported from the power plants to the transformers (high-voltage transport) using the national system owned by REDESA[1] which, in cooperation with the utilities themselves, sets production figures which must be adhered to by each of them. It is assumed that REDESA, which knows the cost variables of each power plant in Spain, as well as each water and coal supply point, makes the optimum decisions taking into account the national scene, so that any number of utilities could have several power plants shut down and distribute energy produced by other utility's plants. This is, in fact, the most general case, because one of the state-owned companies ENDESA, has no supply system and sells all of its production to the utilities, including HISUESA. There is a complicated system of economic compensation in order to offset the different cost structures and consumption levels of the various utilities.

DATA PROCESSING AT HISUESA

Exhibit 2 shows the organization structure established by HISUESA for Data Processing. It is classified as a "Service" and reports to the Senior Vice-President of Planning and Control. The head of the DP Service is Mr. Pablo Mateu, an industrial engineer specializing in computer science since graduating in 1973. He joined HISUESA as a programmer right after graduating and moved up the ladder within the Service until reaching the top post in 1981. Nobody in HISUESA would ever question Mateu's knowledge and expertise in computer science.

The organization is divided into functional areas, in such a way that maintenance is separate from new systems development. There is a group in charge of user-oriented PC-based computer applications, maintaining the utilities 126 compatible personal computers and training the users in the operating system and in the basic tools adopted by the utility, specifically DOS, Word-Star, Lotus 123 and D-Base III. In 1988, 311 HISUESA employees successfully completed the training program set up by the Data Processing Service's user support group.

At present, the Service had 104 employees, of whom 56 were technical personnel, most of them college graduates. The other 48 made up the support group: operators, administrative staff and support personnel. The Service operates 24 hours a day, 365 days a year.

The basic technology used by HISUESA's systems is IBM or compatible. The Service has three main frames: two IBM and 1 IBM-compatible, each with 16 Mb of memory and a processing capacity of 4 MIPS. Throughout the utility there are 468 terminals, in addition to the 126 PC's which have already been mentioned.

The utility has a proprietary communications network, totally independent from the national telephone company. Utilities are allowed to set up their own communications system, as they must provide a public service that depends heavily on communications and cannot be subject to the ups and downs of the state-owned telephone system.

The Data Processing Service's expenses for 1988 were approximately 1,234 million pesetas, which included hardware maintenance costs. Communications costs, however, were not included in this figure, as they are considered an expense attributable to Production and Operations.

---

[1] Red Eléctrica S.A., partially owned in conjunction by all of the utility companies, although majority ownership is in the hands of the public sector.

Industry experts in Spain considered HISUESA's computer department as fairly high-quality, although internally the service provided to the company is considered deficient.

Applications in operation are grouped into 12 large systems, which are all interconnected in some way or another. Some of them, such as Payroll or Customers, are derived from the first "programs" developed by HISUESA on punchcards in the late 60's and later put on tape in the 70's. This has lead to the coexistence in the same computers of systems whose basic technology is very outdated (assembly language and flat files), and very advanced (relational data bases and fourth-generation languages).

The situation of HISUESA's information systems is typified by the Management Control System. This System, developed in the late 70's using sequential flat file technology,[2] provides relevant information of company operations to HISUESA's top-level management. All of the utility's systems, such as Invoicing and Payroll, generate a specific communications file for the management control system every time they are executed. Once a month, the management control system reads all of the "summarized" files generated by the other systems and prints reports accordingly.

The last important system developed was the distribution support system. This system includes the control of all the resources employed: personnel, materials, equipment, etc. It was implemented in early 1988, and due to its implementation, each branch had to install a new terminal connected to the HISUESA mainframe. 45 man-years were invested in this system, developed in conjunction with an independent firm which supplied the analysts, programmers, work methods and management of large computer projects.

OPINIONS OF SEVERAL USERS

HISUESA users are dissatisfied with the service provided by Data Processing. Complaints are abundant, and the company is permeated by the sense that "Data Processing is dictatorial and inoperative," to the extent that general management and the Senior VP of Planning (who

[2]Sequential flat files are those which have no other logical structure than that all of the records follow the order in which they were entered into the computer; in order to access a certain record, it is necessary to read all the previous records.

Data Processing Service Organization Structure

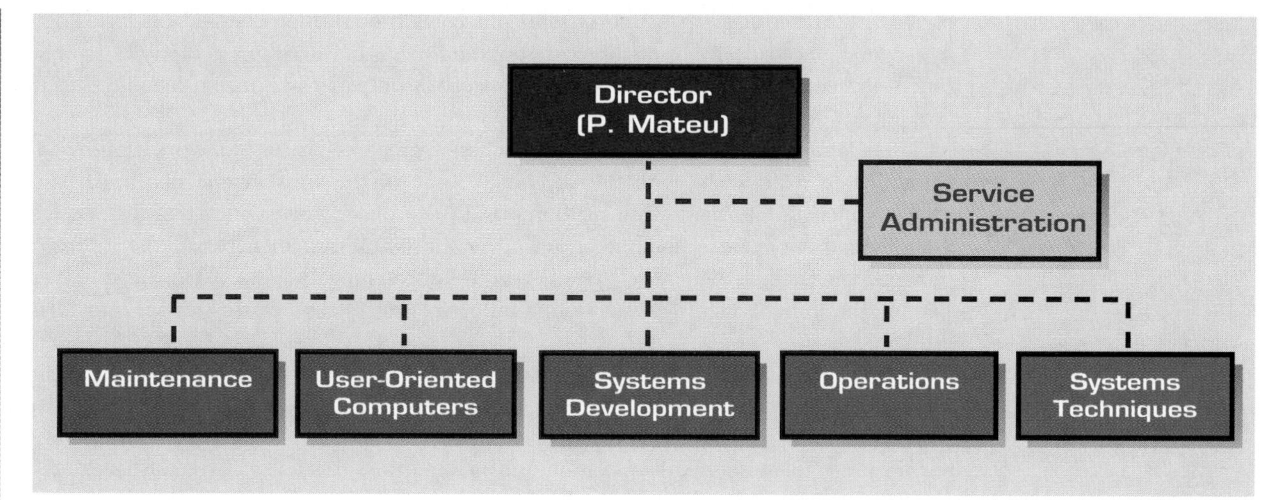

was assigned Data Processing responsibility one month before writing this case study—before that DP reported to Administration and Finance) have seriously questioned the continuity of the Data Processing management team. In following is a summary of situations of several users.

Distribution and Sales (D & S): The largest internal user. According to calculations, some 60% of the systems transactions done by Data Processing are for D & S. D & S's systems are centered on customer-based applications in which all of the information HISUESA has on its customers is collected. The application was designed to run on magnetic tape and was transferred to magnetic discs exactly in the same form. With this customer data base two basic groups of operations are carried out: routine operations and special operations.

The routine operations include meter readouts, opening and closing of accounts, invoicing, power changes in service connections, etc. For several reasons, the most common being the need to adapt to legislation in force, the systems in charge of handling the customer data base are continually modified. At present there are 5 Data Processing Service employees dedicated full-time to "customer maintenance." There are approximately 350 programs which use this database on a more or less regular basis.

Special operations, also called "non-routine operations," are those that are performed only occasionally and usually following unpredictable patterns. A typical example would be: "to make a list of customers in Jaén who have reduced energy consumption 30% or more in the past month." Every time this type of customer database access is required, a specific program (in RPG II) has to be written. Until 1987, these requests were made directly to Data Processing, which in turn put them in a maintenance "queue" until it could assign the necessary resources to fulfill the request. In some cases, this process had taken over a year to complete. In 1987, Distribution and Sales created a "Computer Operations Group (COG)," placing at the head of this new office one of the computer technicians who had an intimate knowledge of the customer system. The COG's mission was to provide specific support to D & S's management in computer-related matters. By the end of 1988, the group employed 35 people who were dedicated to fulfilling non-routine information needs. Of course, it goes without saying that the relationship between the Data Processing Service and the Computer Operations Group was not especially cordial.

A completely different problem occurs with the low voltage distribution network management group. HISUESA's distribution network is generally run down and needs a large quantity of repair work and upgrading operations. In this context, D & S had decided to replace the more than 4,000 maps and diagrams depicting the power system which had to be modified every time a small repair job was done, with a graphics-processing system which would allow quick access to any network point in the supply system, visualize both the map of the area and a diagram of the system, and enter modifications desired on-line. The system would automatically print the corresponding maps and diagrams and would emit work orders. Presently, the whole process is done manually on paper by some 10 people, 5 of them professional draftsmen.

The Computer Operations Group brought a graphics-processing work station and is beginning to experiment with the coding of some of the areas in one of the Andalucian capitals, entering information on medium- and low-voltage power lines, transformers, etc. It is thought that once the computers can cover the whole system network, the information provided on facilities will allow, together with "dispatching," a more adequate monitorization of the same, which will no doubt influence the quality of the service provided by HISUESA.

The Data Processing Service doesn't agree at all with the development of a system as important as that proposed by D & S in graphic information without them having a say in the matter, because in the future it will be important to be able to connect with this system in order to use network operation and maintenance data on a corporate level.

Administration and Finance: HISUESA's accounting system is traditional. The accounting operations are entered into the computer and each month an accounting budget is prepared, in which any deviations are calculated, etc. Its connection to the utility's other systems is not sufficiently developed. For example, there is an application of Bond and Debenture Management that control the sale of these instruments, coupon payment, etc. This application was designed so that each week it could generate a printout which was then sent to the accounting department for its further translation into accounting operations and incorporation into the accounting method. This procedure is still carried out in the same fashion, even though both applications are computerized and in the exact same computer, that is, the bond management application prints a routinely recoded summary which is re-entered into the computer, but this time within the Accounting application.

Commenting on the situation with the heads of the Data Processing Service, P. Mateu affirmed that, "it had been blown out of proportion, because it only represents a secretary's dedication of two hours a week of work."

Production and Operations: This department has practically no interaction with the Data Processing Service. This department is responsible for operating the power plants and transporting the energy to the transformer substations ("dispatching") and has large computers which work in real time to (1) follow REDESA's production orders, (2) transport the energy in the least costly fashion to places of consumption, and (3) confront multiple "incidences" that occur during the normal operation of any utility company.

The present dispatching computers are relatively old, and change is foreseen in the near future. The new equipment will be compatible with that of REDESA and will generate automatic reports on breakdowns and incidences and, consequently, help to improve service quality.

The purchases of these new dispatching computers, leaving the Data Processing Service completely out of the matter, was seen by Mateu as another potential source of problems, as when information on breakdowns and incidences was generated it had to be processed by his service's computers and consolidated with other reports on service quality. Mateu believes that the Data Processing Service should be involved in the equipment-purchasing decision in order to guarantee future compatibility.

STEP 2: Prepare the case for class discussion.

STEP 3: Answer each of the following questions, individually or in small groups, as directed by your instructor:

Diagnosis

1. What problems is Hisuesa experiencing in managing its information?
2. What systems does it currently use for data management?

Evaluation

3. How effective are the current systems?
4. What deficiencies exist in coordination of databases?
5. Does the Data Processing Service play an appropriate and useful role?
6. What systems could meet the utility's information needs?

Design

7. How should the current information systems be changed?
8. What changes should occur in the role of the Data Processing Service?

Implementation

9. What costs will result from the proposed changes?
10. Who should be involved in implementing the changes?

Step 4: In small groups, with the entire class, or in written form, share your answers to the questions above. Then answer the following questions:

1. What information needs exist in this situation?
2. What systems exist to meet the needs?
3. What deficiencies exist in these systems?
4. How should the systems be redesigned to meet the needs?
5. What issues should be considered in implementing the redesigned systems?

Activity 10 Bank Consolidates Data Processing Operations

STEP 1: Read the Bank Consolidates Data Processing Operations case. (This activity is especially suited for use in conjunction with Chapter 8 of *Information Systems.*)

The Bank of Boston, a super-regional bank holding company, has acquired banks in Rhode Island, Maine, Vermont, Connecticut, and Massachusetts. "When you attempt to merge five fairly large banks, the technology infrastructure is duplicated across all entities," says Kevin Roden, Bank of Boston's director of data processing technology. To reduce expenses and eliminate needless duplication, the bank recently launched an extensive consolidation program for its data processing operations.

"Consolidation saves systems, software, programmers, and operations personnel," Roden says. "For example, in the systems technology department, we had to make the technology meet the needs of our 'business partners'—the various business units we serve throughout the holding company—while reducing the cost of providing that service."

During the first stage of consolidation, Bank of Boston assembled teams to define corporate-wide requirements. The overall objective was to place all of the affiliate banks on a common technology platform, including common systems and similar product offerings. Using this approach, a new financial product would be applicable in all five states. Although the same products could be marketed under different names to suit local market conditions, only one development effort, instead of five, was required.

BUILDING A COMMUNICATIONS HIGHWAY

Once the bank established its equipment needs and existing product lines, the next step was to consolidate five different computer centers to provide a high-speed, reliable file-transfer network with a central data-archiving capability.

This step began with the data communications equivalent of an interstate highway system—a HYPERchannel network from Network Systems Corp. of Minneapolis, Minn. This network connects five computer centers and, within each center, links other networks as well. The result is analogous to "state highways" and "county roads" connecting the computers and peripherals.

High speed and reliability were the deciding factors in selecting HYPERchannel. According to John Osterman, Bank of Boston senior systems consultant, "There are hundreds of products that will move data. However, determining how many can do it quickly, while fitting within our existing operations and scheduling systems, was a key issue. Automation was the answer. Also, data needs to be independent of location and needs to move freely across the entire network."

Once the high-speed network was in place, Bank of Boston began removing mainframes from its data centers in Maine and Connecticut. The bank converted those sites to distribution centers that house peripherals, including laser and impact printers, tape drives, terminals, and fiche machines.

With HYPERchannel providing fast and reliable file transfer, the Bank of Boston installed USER-Access with Central Archiving, a software package from Network Systems that runs on HYPERchannel and TCP/IP networks. "USER-Access gives us a lot of flexibility," Osterman says. "For example, we can provide contingency backup for data on Tandem systems using IBM jobstreams. It solves the problem of having disparate computer systems, since we already have procedures and processes in place to manage backup and recovery in the IBM mainframe environment."

SOURCE: Bank consolidates data processing operations, *Network Management,* August 1991: 73, 74.

The Bank of Boston now has two IBM mainframes—one in the Boston location and one in Providence, R.I. The Boston mainframe supports most of the production workload for the bank, and the Providence mainframe serves as a development and contingency operation.

In addition to these systems, Tandem systems handle automated teller machine and teller transactions, and DEC VAXes handle money wire transfers, commercial loan services, treasury, trade services, purchasing and procurement, protective services, and coin room operations. The bank also has three Stratus systems and three IBM AS/400 midrange systems that handle other applications. All these systems are now part of the bank's HYPERchannel network (see Figure 1).

"Because [they] have data that is critical to the operation of the bank, these systems must be able to feed into other systems," says Roden. For example, before installing USER-Access, several manual transfers were required. "Now, USER-Access eliminates these manual transfers with its any-to-any file transfer network. Moving data can now be accomplished without risks and delays and, most importantly, we are able to retain existing operating procedures and schedules," Roden says.

AUTOMATIC ARCHIVING

Because every system holds critical information, the ability to archive computer data is a top priority in the consolidation plan. USER-Access with Central Archiving gives the bank an automated, centrally controlled backup capability to assure that all the bank's data is protected and that all information is available in the event of a disaster.

After a day's work is done, the backup of the system begins. Using the Central Archiving system, one of the IBM mainframes automatically polls the minicomputers on the network and initiates each system's backup utility to perform that day's backup. This process is completed every evening. The IBM tape drives are much faster, and the backup system is automatic. When all the data has been backed up by the system, the tapes are transferred to the Rhode Island center, where they are held for transfer to a remote archive vault.

Because archiving is controlled by the automated job scheduling system, human assistance is not required, reducing the opportunity for human error. Using Central Archiving, the IBM can back up 610 MB of Digital Equipment Corp. data in 47 minutes, while simultaneously backing up Tandem data and processing thousands of interactive transactions.

In addition to being efficient, the new system has reduced the bank's operating expenses. The system has also helped the bank's redeployment process, which ensures that employees are working on priority tasks.

"Our business partners charge us with the responsibility of providing data movement, computer power, and data security," Roden says. "We seek to meet those requirements while staying as clean and simple as possible. We employ technology that meets the needs of our business partners in the hope that it will help create a competitive advantage for Bank of Boston. USER-Access with Central Archiving is helping us to achieve this objective."

STEP 2: Prepare the case for class discussion.

STEP 3: Answer each of the following questions, individually or in small groups, as directed by your instructor.

Diagnosis

1. How did the information needs of Bank of Boston change as a result of its bank acquisitions?

Evaluation

2. What types of systems existed before the consolidation?
3. How effectively did these systems meet Bank of Boston's needs?

 Bank of Boston Central Archiving Network

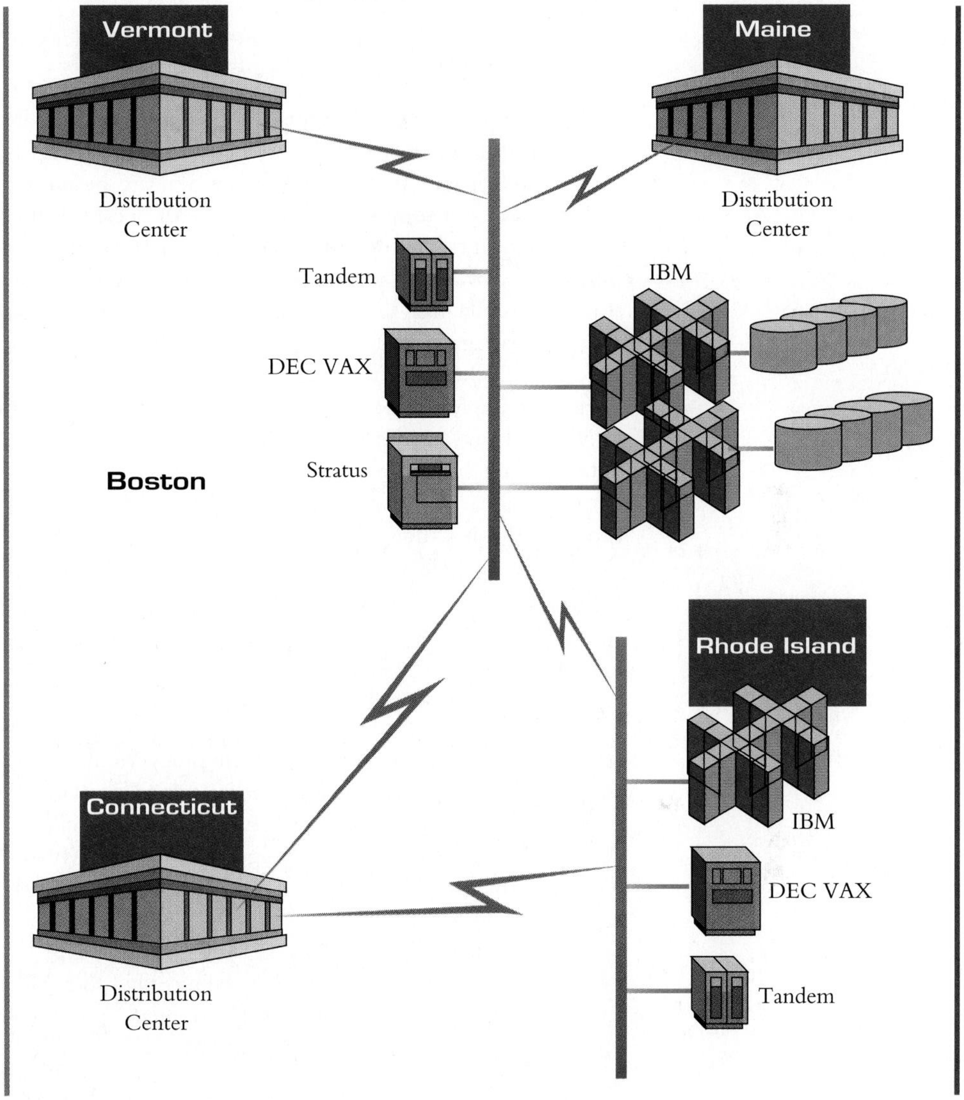

Design

4. How did Bank of Boston consolidate its communications operations?

5. Did the communications highway selected by Bank of Boston meet its needs?

Implementation

6. What issues did Bank of Boston face in implementing the new system?

7. How effectively did it handle these issues?

STEP 4: In small groups, with the entire class, or in written form, share your answers to the questions above. Then answer the following questions:

1. What impact did the acquisition of new banks have on Bank of Boston's information needs?

2. What types of hardware did Bank of Boston select to meet these needs?

3. How well does the new system meet the bank's needs?

4. How effectively did Bank of Boston handle the implementation issues it faced? ●

Activity 11 Airtour Vacaciones

STEP 1: Read the Airtour Vacaciones case. (This activity is especially suited for use in conjunction with Chapter 9 of *Information Systems.*)

"I think that we should start *now* to think how we are going to use information technology in this business, even before deciding our business strategy. It occurs to me that they are not two separate matters. If we really want to be innovative in this industry—if we really want to carry out those ideas which made us decide in the first place to leave those bogged-down companies because they were devoured by the day-to-day inertia, then I think we should do it by taking information technology into account from the onset. I am convinced that if we do it like this, we will find better ways of approaching the business itself. As a matter of fact, my nephew was telling me the other day about a database system...."

José Mª Echegoyen was impatient. He believed, as did his associates, that it was possible to "greatly improve" the tour-operating industry, so he was determined to establish an innovative company—AirTour Vacaciones. There was no doubt in his mind that, in time, computers would be an indispensable part of the business. His associates Alfonso Ruiz and Ricardo Palma, who were both as experienced as José M^{a} in the tour-operating industry, agreed with him, though less enthusiastically.

Ricardo plunged in: "Cut the sermon, José M^{a}. Here we go again with your love affair with technology! I am not arguing about the fact that we were going to need the computers' support, nor that when we do use it, we will use it better than what they did in our old companies (it won't be all that difficult), but I refuse to put computers before business. I want us to become outstanding tour operators who use computers creatively whenever we need them, not outstanding computer specialists who sell packaged tours because they think the business is well-adapted to the technology. We'll get to the computers, but only once we are perfectly clear about what we are going to do with the business."

The discussion wasn't new. Alfonso, always the conciliatory type, timidly stepped in. "Actually, Ricardo, I think you are exaggerating a little. My impression is that José M^{a} was just proposing thinking about the business and computers at the same time... I don't think it is a matter of subordinating one thing for the other. In fact, I think we should seriously consider this. . . after all it might not be such a silly thing."

"Thanks a lot, especially about it being silly," José M^{a} couldn't help showing his irritation. Slamming the door as he left, he shouted, "See you on Monday! I hope that you rest up this weekend and come back a little more reasonable on Monday morning!"

HISTORY

According to the founding partners, AirTour Vacaciones was to be a tour-operating firm that was "small, for now, but with a lot of ideas." "We are going to make some people in the industry look pretty bad. We are sick of obsolete procedures that impose constraints on business opportunities. AirTour will be different. We will give more service and be more efficient than the rest. It is going to be very hard for our future competitors to react; they are too big, and the years they have been following the old procedures have made them sluggish."

This case was prepared by Professor Rafael Andreu. It is intended to be used as a basis for class discussion rather than to illustrate either effective or ineffective handling of an administrative situation.

The 80's were just underway. José M^{a}, Alfonso and Ricardo had worked almost 20 years each in different tour-operating concerns and combined, their experience was tremendous in several important facets of the business: purchasing, product design, sales, reservations, management, finance, etc. Above all, they were convinced that, "the paperwork involved in this business borders on sheer lunacy; if we start from scratch, it will be relatively easy to be a lot more efficient than what is normal for this industry."

Besides being experienced professionals, the three partners were close personal friends. Despite never having worked for the same company in the past, they had often exchanged ideas and had finally decided to set up shop on their own. The main reason for doing this was to implement these ideas without having to adhere to pre-established structures that were simply out of place in the context of the 80's. For this reason, they did not want the control of the new company to get out-of-hand. Given the rather reduced availability of capital, they decided to start up with a small-scale operation.

Without the necessary resources to start up activities with a powerful infrastructure, they had decided to focus their initial activities in the Barcelona Metropolitan area, offering their products exclusively to travel agencies in this area. They thought that this could be achieved with a very small staff, starting with 6–8 people including the three partners. In addition, the initial intent was to structure their products around stays in typical tourist spots, both on a national level, especially the Balearic and Canary Islands, and some traditional international destinations, such as Greece, Egypt and Italy.

Another desired characteristic of the new company related vaguely to the concept of "quality service" towards their direct customers (travel agencies) in addition to the end-consumers of the products (tourists who bought packaged tours designed by a tour operator through one of the travel agencies). They had decided upon the name AirTour Vacaciones in an attempt to convey the idea that the supply consisted basically of packaged tours in which transport would be mainly by air (during the early 80's, this usually meant by means of charter flights, which had to be specifically contracted in advance).

THE BUSINESS

Basically, the tour-operating business consisted of combining attractive travel and lodging arrangements, describing them in a brochure with information related to dates, seasons, rates, special features of the hotels (location, services, etc.), and supplied these combinations to travel agencies, which in turn would offer them to their customers. When the travel agency's customer chooses a package from a specific operator (typically travel agencies have a selection of brochures from different tour operators), the agency contacts the tour operator in order to confirm space availability, both in transportation and in lodging arrangements. In case the specific arrangements chosen by the customer are unavailable, the tour operator offers alternatives until the travel agency finally reaches agreement with the end-customer (the traveler). Thus, the travel agencies play the role of middleman between the tour operators and the end-customers, offering a wider choice of arrangements to the latter and a sales-distribution channel to the former.

One of the most important activities in the tour operator's business process is purchasing, both of travel and lodging arrangements.

The job of designing a package on the basis of transportation and lodging pre-arrangements is also one of the basic activities in the tour-operating business. Experience played a predominant role (combining different hotels with transportation on certain dates and different lengths of stay which had proven successful in the past), as well as the ability to offer attractive prices which wouldn't dismay the customer right from the start. The process was complicated by the fact that one hotel could offer a myriad of pricing alternatives: depending on the size of the hotel room, its location (view of the sea, of the parking area, etc.), different plans (half-board, full-board), and different possibilities (additional cots for children, maximum specified and associated extras, etc.).

Although a considerable percentage of the price for the package indicated in the brochure was attributed to transportation and lodging costs, there were other important costs incurred: administrative procedures associated with reservation management and control, confection of lists for controlling aircraft boarding and room allotment procedures (for the latter, it was necessary to send a telex to each hotel with information on who was going to arrive, on what day and for how long), and the retail sales activity, i.e., the commission accorded to the travel agencies. Some of the product cost components were not completely independent: for example, providing hoteliers with precise and reliable information created an image which could lead to improved contracting arrangements over the successive seasons; similarly, a rapid and reliable reservations system could affect travel agencies' inclination to "push" a specific operator's products.

THE INDUSTRY

In the early 1980's, the relationship between travelers and travel agencies in Spain, and the relationship between the travel agencies and the tour operators as well, suffered from several inefficiencies that, in certain cases, rendered them virtually ineffective. For example, most tour operators (at least most of them with a national presence, that is, which sold vacations through travel agencies throughout the whole country) used a manual process for controlling the reservations and confirming them for the travel agents. Delays were commonplace when an agent telephoned a tour operator in order to reserve accommodations for one of its customers. The operator's response time was even lower when they had to offer alternatives due to a lack of availability of the chosen accommodations; in many cases, these delays forced the end-customer to visit the travel agency on two—and sometimes even more—occasions in order to confirm his reservations and obtain the necessary travel vouchers.

In addition to this time-consuming process, the relationship between the tour operator and the travel agency suffered from other incidences which caused inconveniences to all concerned. One of these was the common industry practice of letting the travel agencies themselves prepare the travel vouchers for their customers once the reservation was confirmed by the tour operator. This procedure, which would probably be justified in the case of travel agencies located in different cities than the tour operator, was a generally applied practice, but in fact it gave final control of the reservation to the travel agency, opening the way for possible errors in issuing a document in the tour operator's name. If, for example, one of these mistakes lead to over-booking of a hotel or of a flight, the traveler would blame the tour operator, whose name appeared in the travel documents along with—on occasion—the travel agency's name. Despite the fact that the end-customers were more customers of the travel agency than of the tour operator (by virtue of the fact that the customer usually did not specify the tour operator which would be arranging his accommodations; rather, the determining purchase factors were convenience of dates, destinations, accommodations and price), it was considered that a negative experience could, in fact, affect the customer's perception of a certain tour operator, who would thus lose the possibility of repeat purchase from that customer.

Tour operators normally invoiced travel agencies after take-off of each flight as, on many occasions, the documents needed to issue these invoices weren't freed by the manual reservations process until after the departure of the flight in question. Therefore, the invoicing was variable, because two reservations that were made a month or more apart could be invoiced at the same exact time if the same flight was used. This didn't represent a major problem for the travel agent, who usually charged cash for this type of activity; but a slight inconvenience did arise in the process of checking invoices, which was done according to flight departures, while in his file they were usually filed according to the date of the reservation. Travel agency personnel would check the tour operator's invoices during low periods of sales activity. For the tour operator, this process often meant delays in payment and made cash discounts almost impossible. Exhibit 1 shows a schematic summary of the process structure followed by the industry in the relationship among tour operators, travel agencies, and end customers.

The manual process of reservations control, which was highly labor-intensive, had several other inconveniences apart from the slowness of confirmations and invoicing. In effect, maintaining an ongoing control of sales per flight was very complicated because it interfered with the sales and reservations process. However, this control was very important for the tour operator, who had contracted a charter flight and would lose any forthcoming revenues by unoccupied seats. The possibility of offering package discounts, which increased as the departure date neared, was seriously hindered by this circumstance. The same problem, although with less ill-fated circumstances, occurred in hotel sales control because of the number of hotel rooms secured before the season, a certain proportion of which could be cancelled with sufficient advance notice; at any rate, these cancellations brought on complications with the hotel trade.

As already mentioned, during the period we are referring to, a great majority of air transportation contracted by tour operators was in the form of chartered flights, which had to be contracted in full and in advance. There was a very limited supply of charter flights and very little price difference among the suppliers. It was possible to secure part of a passenger capacity from other tour operators that had previously contracted the whole flight, but that obviously lead to more costly flight arrangements and the possibility of not having guaranteed availability of seats.

Hotel rooms also had to be secured in advance, usually at the beginning of each season and specifying the days and numbers of rooms. Obviously, the supply was much more abundant, although the system by which rooms were contracted was virtually standard for the whole industry. This system consisted of contracting beforehand a certain number of rooms which could be "released" for a set date; the period in which the pre-reservation could be cancelled was called the "release period," which had to be negotiated on an individual basis with each hotel for each season. Practically none of the industry participants negotiated hotel reservations without this release clause, due to the risk involved in making a firm reservation before the beginning of the season. Although this could feasibly mean reducing costs, very few tour operators considered the extra risks worthwhile. However, it often occurred that after cancelling pre-reserved rooms within the period established by the release conditions, many tour operators were forced to contract rooms on an as-needs basis as a result of requests for reservations in certain hotels which, for one reason or another, were successful or popular among the clientele. It was very difficult to predict the hotels for which this would be necessary, so the tour operators would forego firm reservations and would accept the price increase which would surely accompany a last-minute reservation. Besides, this could give a sense of improvising which, as almost always happened, would soon enough be known by travel agencies and even by the end-customers.

In the early 80's, there were very few tour operators in Spain which operated on a national level; most of them had local operations, mainly within the larger cities' spheres of influence.

THE FUTURE

The next Monday, the three partners were once again trying to figure out the most appropriate business profile for AirTour Vacaciones. Over the weekend, Ricardo had decided to make a few treasury and balance sheet forecasts which encompassed the next three years and were based on fairly conservative sales and purchasing estimates. The results were not brilliant, but they weren't completely discouraging either.

Basic Structure of Industry Procedures

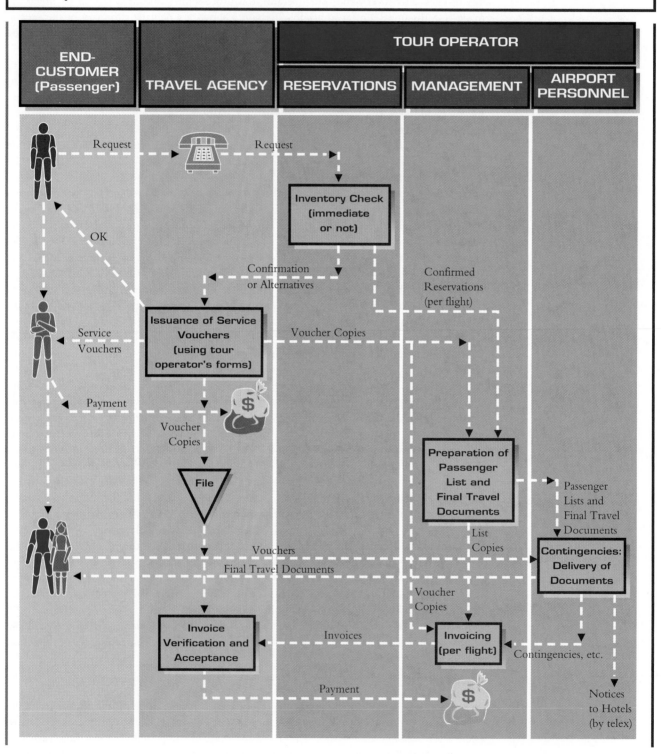

END-CUSTOMER (Passenger)

TRAVEL AGENCY

TOUR OPERATOR

RESERVATIONS

MANAGEMENT

AIRPORT PERSONNEL

Request

Request

Inventory Check (immediate or not)

OK

Confirmation or Alternatives

Confirmed Reservations (per flight)

Issuance of Service Vouchers (using tour operator's forms)

Service Vouchers

Voucher Copies

Payment

Voucher Copies

File

Preparation of Passenger List and Final Travel Documents

Passenger Lists and Final Travel Documents

List Copies

Vouchers

Contingencies: Delivery of Documents

Final Travel Documents

Voucher Copies

Invoice Verification and Acceptance

Invoices

Invoicing (per flight)

Contingencies, etc.

Payment

Notices to Hotels (by telex)

"One thing is for sure, we are going to have cash problems at the beginning. The bad thing is that I haven't been able to isolate one sole cause for it. It looks like there are a bunch of little problems that have gotten together to ruin our predictions. I spent all Sunday testing different scenarios with the help of this damned spreadsheet and I always come up with one financial black-hole or another. Do we really want to be independent? We could fix it all up with a venture capitalist."

José M^a and Alfonso reacted almost simultaneously. "Of course we want to be independent! We have talked about this over and over, Ricardo. We don't want anyone telling us what we have to do just because they are the ones that have the money. If we are convinced of our approach, we have to take the chance all by ourselves. If not, it isn't worth the hassle. I understand that after one weekend of working alone, the situation might begin to lose its perspective . . . Let's focus on this again."

"Alright. Let me tell you both about a little of what I've done and why I'm so worried. The first difficulty I have come up against is the problem of securing aircraft space. Either way, whether we buy whole flights or just a few seats from another tour operator, the problem is that you have to pay up front. And this is even before we start generating sales, which in this industry comes later. On top of that, if we purchase seats from a competitor, it will come out more expensive. It is a different story, though, with the hotels. You can pay late; hotels invoice you late for real occupation, because in the middle of high season, when they are up to the rafters in tourists, they don't have time to take care of administrative matters until the season is almost over. I'd still like to know what would happen if we could negotiate other payment conditions . . . although, how are we going to pay if we get paid so late?"

Alfonso joined in the discussion: "Well, couldn't we discuss ways of changing all that? If we are going to innovate, this is as good a place as any to start. Couldn't we get the travel agents to pay us earlier?"

Ricardo didn't think matters were so clear. "How are you going to make the travel agents pay earlier? Nobody likes doing that! Unless you offer something in exchange . . . The first thing that comes to mind is that we could offer cash discounts, something that nobody has ever offered in this industry . . . But how credible will that be, coming from the newest and youngest members on the scene? Besides, in order to do that, you have to invoice earlier too. The invoicing is done after the flight because, if not, it could create a big mess in the reservations activity. And don't forget, reservations are our sales activity! If we mess up the reservations side of the business, we'll find ourselves pushing up the daisies."

José M^a couldn't hold back any longer. "And what about the computer aspect? Are computers going to help us or not? This is exactly what I wanted to say last Friday! After all, maybe starting out small could give us some kind of advantage. I think a good reservations system wouldn't be that difficult to set up if we are just going to operate in Barcelona. As I was telling you the other day, they are coming out with database systems even for small computers . . . And with a good database, developing a satisfactory reservations system can be relatively easy."

"Don't start up with that again, José M^a," Ricardo said in a less belligerent tone than the Friday before. "You are getting me nervous with all this computer business. Maybe you are right, but I don't understand the first thing about computers! What the hell is a database system? Is it a fast reservations system? Or is it just something which will let us have a reservations system if we use it correctly? If it all boils down to that, I don't trust it. The truth of the matter is that I have seen too many of these schemes fail utterly."

Once again, Alfonso intervened to avoid what looked like a possible outbreak of hostilities. "Well, as long as we are supposed to be creative, I have some other ideas. For example, why don't we do something in the line of welcoming arrangements? We could charge cash on the spot for that and maybe that way, cover up some of the holes in Ricardo's estimates."

"Hey, that's not such a bad idea. I'm sure we can't just start off doing that, but I suppose that we could take it into account in the future. At any rate, I still think that we need something a little more radical. For instance, we need to grow very quickly. We need to be able to contract full flights as soon as possible. I know it is risky, but at least we can save ourselves the extra charge if we have to go to our competitors for seats. Besides, I really don't think they would respect their contracts with us if they suddenly got more demand for a certain flight. If we could contract whole flights, we wouldn't have to face that risk."

"I'm sorry to have to insist, but I think it is my duty. If we can set up a reasonable reservations system, I think we could probably consider opening up in Madrid pretty soon. We could even do it initially by 'postal express' or something of the sort, simultaneously centralizing reservations management in Barcelona."

"I think we should deal with all this a lot more in depth and do it from a cohesive and global standpoint. Maybe you are right after all. Maybe it is true that this damned computer business can open up ways out of this impasse that we're up against. If we are able to break the vicious circle of 'small—high cost—unattractive pricing—growth problems—small,' which is really what is behind our difficulties, maybe we can finally take off and do what we've always said we wanted to do."

"Well, Ricardo. You really flatter me! I never thought I would be able to convince you. Let's get to work! Look, I think that a quick and efficient reservations system is just the beginning. The efficiency itself will help us in terms of cost, but we'll also be able to do more. This morning we haven't spoken about hotel contracts. I'm sure that we could do something interesting in that field if we have computer capacity. After all, our sales are part of their reservations! And what about the end-customers? Don't you think that the image of a young, technologically advanced firm with computerized documentation, etc., would help us to attract more customers? And what about the travel agents? A good reservations system is almost as important for them as it is for us. Maybe by doing this we could convince them to work with us before going to the others. Ricardo, let's see that spreadsheet! We have to take a look at your forecasts! With computers, we'll sell more, we'll be more efficient and instead of having 'black-holes' we'll have . . . What do you call them? Buffers? Yeah, that's right, a financial buffer!"

Ricardo, desperate, sunk back down into his chair.

STEP 2: Prepare the case for class discussion.

STEP 3: Answer each of the following questions, individually or in small groups, as directed by your instructor.

Diagnosis

1. What information needs does AirTour Vacaciones demonstrate?
2. What types of problems does such a company typically encounter?

Evaluation

3. How can the company use information technology to address these problems?
4. How can AirTour Vacaciones use information technology to support its business strategy and make the business more competitive?
5. What aspects of the business should be automated?

Design

6. What would be the components of an automated system for this company?
7. What types of hardware and software would support such automation?

Implementation

8. What issues must the owners consider in automating their company?

STEP 4: In small groups, with the entire class, or in written form, share your answers to the questions above. Then answer the following questions:

1. What information needs does AirTour Vacaciones have?
2. How can automation address these needs?
3. How would an automated system look?
4. What issues should be considered in implementing the system? ●

Activity 12 Shorko Films SA[1]

STEP 1: Read the Shorko Films SA case[1] (This activity is especially suited for use in conjunction with Chapter 9 of *Information Systems.*)

"Computerized process control was all upside down for us, with no downside. It was an investment which gave us a chance—it meant change but it was a symbol of the future." Christian de Pierrefeu, General Manager of Shorko Films SA, was reviewing the last two years' experience of introducing a distributed process control system to his packaging film factory. "We had our backs to the wall in 1987 and there was no alternative—it was a marvelous opportunity. The plant is now profitable. But this is only part of the achievement. Process Control is a starting point; it changes your thinking—you look at quality, consider customer service, change your methods . . . rethink competitive strategy." Bernard Delannoy, Information Technology Manager, reflected on Process Control a little differently. "When you've tasted it, just like wine, you realize it is rather good."

COMPANY HISTORY AND BACKGROUND

Shorko Films SA is located at Mantes-la-Ville, northwest of Paris, by the River Seine. It is the second European manufacturing plant of Shorko Films, one of 30 "Full Reporting Businesses" which make up the UK chemicals and textiles corporation, Courtaulds Plc. The sister production site and Shorko headquarters is at Swindon, England, which also provides common services such as financial management, gross production scheduling, marketing and information technology support. Within Courtaulds and Shorko, the two sites are usually referred to as Swindon and Mantes.

Mantes, prior to 1984, belonged to Rhone Poulenc. The plant had been losing money steadily since 1974 and annual losses had increased in 1982. Shorko Films, in contrast, had shown consistent profits over the same period in spite of operational problems. Through the acquisition in 1984, Shorko gained European market share in its sole product, OPP (oriented polypropylene) coextruded film, and prevented capacity falling into competitors' hands in a growth market.

Principal rivals included Mobil, ICI, Kalle, Wolff and Moplefan. Courtaulds paid nothing for the fixed assets, but provided, £1.9 million of working capital. They paid a somewhat larger sum for goodwill, for both the OPP and cellophane product lines, the latter being increasingly substituted by the former in the packaging industry. There also was an understanding that Mantes would be kept at least until the end of 1986 and that Shorko would assume responsibility for any redundancy costs.

By 1988 the Shorko division's total sales were £65 million, yielding a return on sales of roughly 13% (Appendix 1). Mantes contributed profits of £2 million. Shorko occupied second position in the European OPP market behind Mobil.

OPP film resembles cellophane in many ways and is used primarily in the food packaging industry. By the mid 1980s OPP had overtaken cellophane in terms of market tonnage. OPP is cheaper by between 25% and 35%, not least because it is not so dense, producing 30% more

[1]This case was prepared as a basis for class discussion rather than to illustrate either effective or ineffective handling of an administrative situation.

film for an equivalent weight of cellophane. Other comparative advantages include appearance, machinability, heatsealing properties, gauge thinness, finishes and printing capabilities.

During the early 1980s, the OPP market grew at 15% per annum, slowing down to about 7% in the latter half of the decade. Finished rolls of OPP are either taken by end-users or further processed by "converters"—usually involving printing or meeting other special customer requirements—before delivery to the end customer. Courtaulds owns some converter businesses.

MANUFACTURING PROCESS

All OPP film is based on the homopolymer of propylene. Polypropylene is a thermoplastic resin supplied to film manufacturers as granules. The resin is melted, stirred to ensure homogeneity and filtered for purity before extrusion through a horizontal slit to form a thick band about 0.5–2 cm thick and up to 1 metre wide. Plain film is then formed by stretching the thick band both lengthways and sideways under carefully controlled conditions (biaxial orientation). Orientation gives the film its stiffness and clarity. For heatseal applications, each side of the film has to be given a thin layer of material, with a lower melting point so that seal can be formed without distortion of the base. As well as imparting heatseal properties, the outer layers can be formulated to give optical properties such as sparkle, and handling properties such as slip and crackle.

Manufacturers have a choice of technical methods both for adding the outer layers to the base film and for the orientation process. Heatsealable layers can be added to the film by either coating or coextrusion. Orientation is achieved by either a stenter or a tubular method. Shorko pioneered the coextrusion method, against early industry skepticism, and uses the stenter process. Coextruded films are, in effect, three-ply laminates comprising a central layer of homopolymer and two outer layers of copolymer. By varying the thickness of each layer and the type of copolymers used in the outer layers, the properties of the finished product can be extensively varied to suit specific customer or market requirements.

A schematic of the Mantes manufacturing process is shown in Appendix 3. Raw materials in the form of polymer chips and special additives (plus scrap) are fed into hoppers which feed three extruders. The main extruder produces the central homopolymer layer of film and two satellite extruders each produce a melt which passes through a filter and then a slot die to form a single three-ply web of film. This web is then chilled and drawn through a system of rollers which reheats and stretches it to a specified ratio. The stretched web is then fed into a stenter which stretches the web in the transverse direction to yield a film up to 4.5 metres wide.

Passing through the stenter, the web is thermo-fixed to enable it to withstand normal conversion and end-use temperatures. It then cools and passes through an electrostatic treatment process which allows the film to accept print or additional coating by third party converters. The treated film web is then wound onto a mill roll which is removed, stored as work-in-progress and eventually moved to the rewinding machine. Coating has turned out to be the costlier process. It requires an extra operation, the prices of coating materials have risen faster than for copolymers, and coated film scrap cannot be recycled.

Three basic film types are produced by Shorko: transparent, pearlized and metalized. Film rolls finally undergo a slitting process to provide the sizes the converters require. Typical users of OPP are wrappings and seal packaging of biscuits, confectionery, potato crisps and cigarettes by companies such as United Biscuits, Nabisco, and Rowntree Mackintosh.

At Mantes, there are two film production lines. Line 1 can produce 4600 tons per annum of 4 m wide film while Line 2 produces 6500 tons per annum of 4.4m width. The main film processing variables which can be controlled are line tension, speed, pressure and film gauge. The lines at Swindon are newer and faster than those at Mantes. Swindon had three lines in early 1989, with a fourth being installed. Their existing three lines could produce 25,000 gross tonnes per annum. Shorko's strategy has been to become the lowest cost producer of OPP, to build market share, and to extend the product range (thereby reducing the reliance on commodity product-markets). This strategy often has led to high volume, easy to make product types being scheduled on Swindon's bigger, faster lines. One consequence was recent investment in an automated warehouse at Swindon in order to stock the output of longer runs and be able to offer more immediate response to commodity film customers.

TURNAROUND

Since 1984, Shorko's strategy assumed that Mantes would be closed down at some point. Retention of the two sites was seen to prejudice the low cost manufacturing strategy and it had been planned that Mantes would cease to operate in 1988. However, considerations of avoiding single plant exposures, maximizing continental market share, and smoothly managing expansion at Swindon persuaded Shorko's management to retain the Mantes capability until market growth declined—despite its inherited higher labour, energy and tax costs.

"When I arrived in 1985, the future of Mantes was limited," explained Christian de Pierrefeu, "unless we made drastic changes. The factory capacity was 6000 tons per annum, employing 210 people. There were too many Chiefs and not enough Indians. The management system was loose. Under Rhone Poulenc, the decline of cellophane put Mantes into the red. There had been strikes and general discontent. Given Shorko's declared strategy, I had to persuade the management team to take its own action to survive." A rationalization plan resulted including a first reduction of fixed costs, shedding labour, introducing more flexible working, finding more volume and specializing in certain qualities of film in agreement with Swindon, in order to create longer runs. The outcome was a profit of £1.1 million in 1985 on 7000 tonnes.

"Early on we reduced the workforce by 10%. We had to perform to get any investment whereas Swindon, because of the strategy, was getting, almost automatically, new lines," explained de Pierrefeu. "Then at the same time that the go-ahead was given for the fourth line at Swindon, the Board approved our investment in Process Control. It was probably a psychological move that some investment went to Mantes to show faith in the future."

De Pierrefeu attributes the idea to the former Managing Director of Shorko, Chris Matthews. The IT Executive for all Courtaulds Films and Packaging businesses, Bill Hedley, confirmed this. "When Chris first looked at Swindon lines, he said they were ten years behind in electronics. He concluded that the existing engineering and research experience in Courtaulds was very limited in this area. He then visited Mantes and reckoned the management team had the motivation and capability to implement state of the art Process Control." The Mantes General Manager agreed. "I saw Process Control as a good opportunity to expand. Nobody else would have helped us bring in new technology except Chris Matthews. He understood Process Control and he knew the supplier we chose, Valmet. Introduction of new technology gave us the chance to change the organization, tackle problems, look at jobs—it was a tool for new systems and a new organization. I had no better alternative."

Shorko Films SA signed a contract to supply a Valmet "dramatic classic" distributed process control system, with ACV, using local Valmet agents, at the end of March 1987. The system was to be installed on both lines. The following benefits were identified:

- Labour reduction and optimization.
- Reduction of mechanical and electrical failures.

- Speed optimization leading to increased production.
- Faster start up times.

The system was successfully commissioned in August 1987 and was in full use for day and night working two months later.

"From an IT perspective," commented Bill Hedley, "the project has several interesting aspects. First, leading edge technology was introduced into Mantes without the drive or assistance of the group's Research, Engineering or IT functions. What do we learn from this? Second, the General Manager took Mantes' new IT Manager away from the division's programme of implementing a package-based set of integrated basic business systems in order to concentrate on the Valmet system. Fortunately, Bernard Delannoy is an electrical engineer by background with both computing and engineering experience. It has been helpful to have one person responsible for both factory systems and commercial data processing. Then before long we have to decide how to interface the process control data and computing with the Trifid package of business systems running on the McDonnell Douglas computer. This will be essential for both process improvement work and management information."

DISTRIBUTED PROCESS CONTROL

"Basically," explained Jean-Claude Caillaud, the Production Director, "the Valmet system comprises hundreds of sensors or nodes reading or acting on all the variables in the process. There are 1000 nodes on each line and 500 in the reclaim area. The sensors record temperature, pressure, speed, air velocity, time, length, gauge, tension, voltage and similar parameters all wired up to the HP computers in the control room."

The distributed process network acquires and processes measurement data, monitors processes, controls valves and motors, generates alarms, executes mathematical expressions and conducts logic operations. In the control room are two screens for each line. The operators can see synoptics, change control parameters, examine recent process histories and analyse trends on speed, temperature, recipes and other key variables. Alarms on key parameters and parts of the line also show up on the screens and ring bells.

Many of the benefits are those which come from any automation. Jean-Claude Caillaud graphically described one impact. "A change of recipe takes 20 minutes now instead of 2 hours to 2 days previously. This is possible because all the parameters are in the system memory and the computer does all the necessary changes. When it was manual, we always forgot one parameter."

In the Mantes system, the control room (Appendix 4) was made the centrepiece of the factory. The VDU screens replaced three large control panels on the shop floor which previously had partially controlled separate sections of the lines. The Mantes management team decided to have the control room as big as possible to create enough space for the technology, provide an organized atmosphere, and provide a conducive environment for the operators. The intention was to reinforce the notion that the process control system was integral with the factory—the two were interdependent. Thus, everything electronic is connected to it and all control activities are directed from it. Plant meetings are held there, the shift manager's office is in the rear and the quality control laboratory is to one side. Finally, all the processing, switching and memory units are housed in the control room. In late 1988, a new HP 9000 computer was ordered to add 800 Mb of memory in order to store one year's data for analysis. Without this, only 32 hours' process data could be stored.

Valmet, the system supplier, is a Finnish corporation. The Damatic Processing Automation System was the first system ever to integrate logic, motor and sequence controls into one single system with regulatory control functions.[2] Major adopters have been pulp and paper mills and subsequently chemical and petrochemical plants.

SYSTEM INSTALLATION

"It was important that we used our own team for specifying the system and defining the parameters, rather than relying on external advisers," explained François Gaillard, the Management Accountant. "For our part, we knew nothing about process control and for their part, Valmet knew nothing about our process." A team of four Mantes personnel and four Valmet specialists jointly built the software, customizing the Damatic system to fit the Mantes process, lines and practice. This took three months. The Mantes members comprised the Information Technology Manager, an electrician and two foremen. In addition, shop floor representatives were appointed to help communicate the system to the shop floor, to contribute their process knowledge and line experience, and to specify screen contents and formats.

Simultaneously, Valmet built the control hardware. The whole team was then transferred to Finland to progress the hardware and software integration. The technical room was built in May and June, the hardware installed in July, and the control room built in the first three weeks of August. Total commissioning time was four months. Line 1 started up under the new system on 21 August.

"Back in March I explained the project to the workforce and emphasized it meant organizational change," recalled Jean Claude Caillaud. "We took key people to a small factory in Paris who had installed a process control system. The aim was to demystify the project." In May, 24 operators had two days' on-site training on process control, cabling and computing provided by the local Valmet agency, ACV. "Employees had to learn to control the process from a keyboard instead of by hand," commented de Pierrefeu. "They had to define parameters on-line rather than apply screwdrivers and turn valves. Now everything is visualized. They get a view of what is happening from graphics and synoptics. They see all the automatic adjustments happen in the right order, compared with the old days of going to all the sensors and controls and forgetting one." In July the head of each line was able to see the screens and work the test system. In August the wiring was done during the factory shutdown, helped by 15 operators who took no holiday.

"Between August and November," commented Caillaud, "we did automatic start ups and then gradually improved start ups, closures and restarts. We worked to improve everything we could on the line—downtime, manning, changes. We set targets for the operators with bonus payments if the process control system achieved previous performance. It did."

Throughout this period and for six months after installation, Valmet supplied a Project Manager. His task was to analyse and understand the plant, create a document and drawings and oversee the software development back in Finland. He worked on site and according to Caillaud was "key to our success and a very good technologist."

Christian de Pierrefeu was clear about the scale of change being demanded. "I explained to everybody what the challenge was. I spent a lot of time on this. I spent week after week explaining what we were doing and why. I stressed that we were fighting for survival. Process Control changes everything. I discussed the project with the trade unions and explained that everything would change. Process Control imposes a different approach to manufacturing. Before, your management of the process was as good as the best foreman's experience. Afterwards, it is a question of what is the best way, because you specify the parameters from the best knowledge of everybody and codify it into the software. So people must act as a team and follow the system. Mantes employees didn't like it at first but now they are convinced

---

[2]As claimed in the Valmet product brochure.

it is better. They see the system as a summation of all the best people's knowledge and experience. Now our people could not work, and would not work, without the Valmet system."

"The biggest change," de Pierrefeu observed, "is we now have employees not workers. This change of status is the crunch. We have given the operators responsibility. If they are not on the line, they are working somewhere else, perhaps in packaging, or on the grinder. Once the system is running correctly, people must accept flexibility. Their jobs are automated and in previous terms there is nothing for them to do. But now with Process Control you need flexible working. If something goes wrong on one line, you move people from another. If the screen tells you a motor is heating up, you send a commando team to sort it out wherever they are. Before, if one line performed better due to its engineering, or because of the grade it was making, the line workers would say 'we are better than the others.' They all have to work together now."

Jean Claude Caillaud confirmed this experience. "We used to have three operators per line and five shifts. Now we have five operators, often only four, on both lines and they can all work the system. Their flexibility agreement includes checking, feeding the masher, grinding, attending to problems and doing lab tests. The shift foreman runs the plant but now he is operating the system, looking at system problems. The foremen have become 'managers'."

EVALUATION

The initial capital cost for the Valmet system was £700,000 and the predicted payback was two years. Payback was seen as the key financial criterion for two reasons. The lines were old and the future of Mantes was uncertain. Valmet said the system would perform better than the expectations built into the capital proposal. A novel agreement was made. The turnkey contract was priced at a 20% discount. However, if results exceeded expectations the full cost of FF1 117,920 would be paid by Mantes in the last term of payment in 1989. This agreement is reproduced in Appendix 5.

When asked why Valmet was chosen as the supplier the General Manager replied, "Chris Matthews said Valmet was best from day one and he was proved right."

In early 1989, a post audit suggested that most of the operational goals were being met. Operators had been reduced by five. Mechanical and electrical failures had not really reduced, because maintenance had increased as the lines aged. Speed optimization exceeded expectations on both lines. Downtime had reduced on Line 1 from 6.9% to 5.8% and on Line 2 from 6.3% to 5.8%. Likewise start up time after filter changes had improved by approximately 30%. Job changes on average had been reduced from 100 minutes to 57 minutes on Line 1, and from 100 minutes to 64 minutes on Line 2.

These operational gains translated into financial benefits in excess of the original payback calculations. Christian de Pierrefeu believed the Process Control investment had been a major contributor to increased profitability at Mantes. In three years return on sales had risen from 2.24% to 9.53% and return on investment from 19.56% to 34.1%. Tonnage had increased by 3000 tons, of which 1000 tons was attributed to the impact of the new system in 1988. De Pierrefeu added, "We really invested because our back was to the wall. We were not afraid to change organization, practices and philosophy. It has been a very deep change."

"Yes, the big change from the production viewpoint," commented Caillaud, "was not technological but human. You can't invest in technologies if you don't invest in people, especially in training. Otherwise you get problems very quickly. We had two motivation factors which helped though. First, it was a matter of survival. Second the fact that we had an investment project was a plus."

"We also managed the project as a team," noted de Pierrefeu. "I spent about one-third of my time on it because it was a key project with big issues. I went to Finland and took the team to get them to believe in it. I had to be convinced to get them convinced." Caillaud commented that gaining belief and commitment is easier when the management team is small. "The intensive timeframe also provided a good challenge. And maybe it helps to be a foreign subsidiary." François Gaillard agreed. "If performance is bad, it is no problem for a foreign parent to close the factory. Therefore we just had to improve our profitability."

NEXT STEPS

"The Valmet system soon showed us we didn't know enough about the process. Process control raises questions and you must improve knowledge of the system." Christian de Pierrefeu went on, "The next change is to drive the system and not be driven by it. Having got people to work the system, the next stage is to change the direction of dominance. It has taken one year to learn how to work the system. Now we must close the loop."

The General Manager described three investment phases. Computer process control of the two lines was the first phase. "Next we started to say how can we improve quality? Valmet had a Canadian subsidiary who had developed a gauge control system for paper mills which guaranteed a constant gauge overall. We asked them to apply the same idea to film to link the extrusion die to the film end to achieve autocorrection." This was installed in Mantes in September 1988 and quality improvements of 20% had been recorded. The slit yield on Line 2 was reaching nearly 90%. This was due to producing more flat film and losing less edge trim. Improved yield and fewer customer complaints had resulted in a paycheck of less than three months.

Phase three is investment in a process management system (PMS). This is seen as the means of learning how to drive Process Control rather than be driven by it. PMS allows analysis of historical data and process simulation to learn more about the process. "We are not necessarily sure what is, say, the correct temperature for a grade or what are the tolerances," explained de Pierrefeu. "We need PMS to help us improve the whole line and understand and optimize all the parameters. In two weeks' time I am taking the team to a paper mill to see PMS in operation."

The Mantes team were planning for PMS. In October 1988 operators had begun four weeks of post-implementation training. Each operator had to attend a local technical college to acquire new knowledge and skills before they installed PMS. The course required mathematics, physics, polymer science, extrusion technology, laboratory measurement and microcomputing. The aim was to get everybody to a best and common level before the PMS arrived.

"Our next problem," noted Bernard Delannoy, "is not only developing PMS on top of the Valmet system but how to link it to the McDonnell Douglas computer for storage, analysis and management information reporting." It had been made a requirement by Chris Matthews and Bill Hedley early on that Valmet's technology would be compatible with plans for developing basic business systems and MIS.

Christian de Pierrefeu, however, was considering the next opportunity. "After PMS," he commented, "and with our experience of running an automatic plant, Mantes would like to have Shorko's next new line. I want to make Mantes the specialty films plant for Shorko. We can't beat the 300 metres per minute and 8 metres per width line at Swindon. We realized all along that we couldn't match them for speed or width on any of their lines. Thus we have decided to go for specialty films which attract higher prices and earn more profit. Process Control has given us the capability—we can produce smaller quantities and more product lines and still achieve a good slit to sale efficiency. We can change from grade to grade now because of Process Control. So we don't want a faster or wider line but one designed for reliability and flexibility. With computerization we now have a systems approach not a 'fix it' mentality and we can get the specialized film business."

PPENDIX 1 Courtaulds Films and Packaging, Shorko SA, Mantes. Profit and Loss Account (1988)

1. Volume	
Production:	
Standard	10,404 tonnes
Sub-standard	418 tonnes
Total:	10,822 tonnes
Sales:	
Standard	11,727 tonnes
Sub-standard	529 tonnes
Total	12,256 tonnes

2. Financial	**£000s**
Sales	21,303
Raw materials and variable production costs	12,869
Gross margin	8,434
Fixed costs:	
Production	4,828
Selling and marketing	947
Finance and administration	679
Total:	6,454
Trading profit	1,980

APPENDIX 2 Shorko Films SA—Management Organization Chart

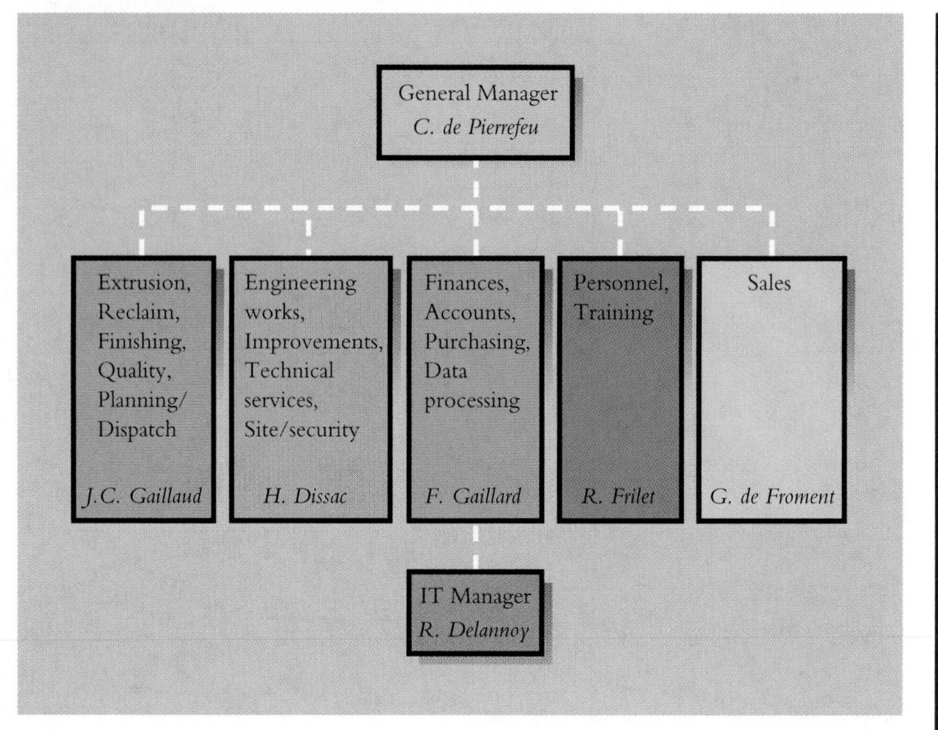

APPENDIX 3 Schematic of OPP Process

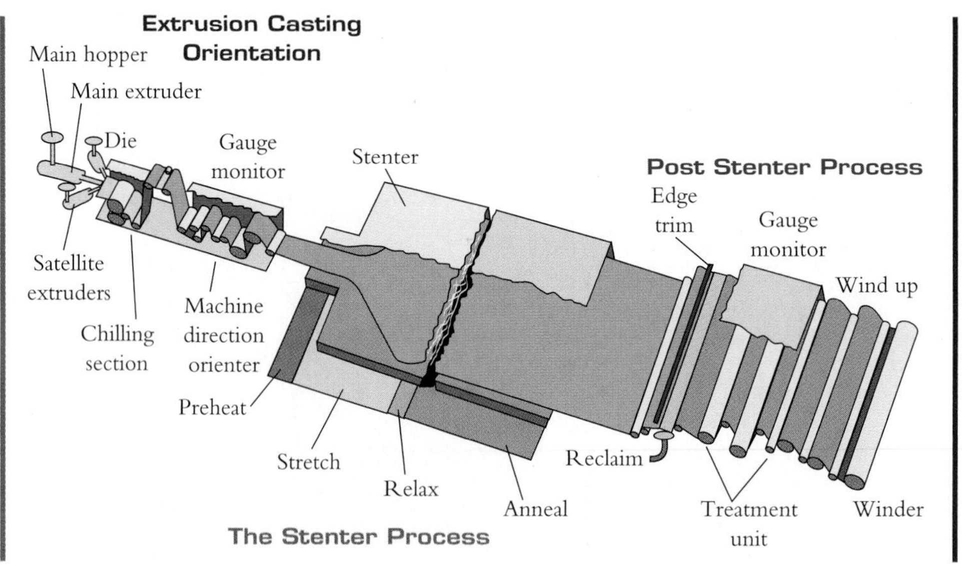

Appendix 4 Process Control Room

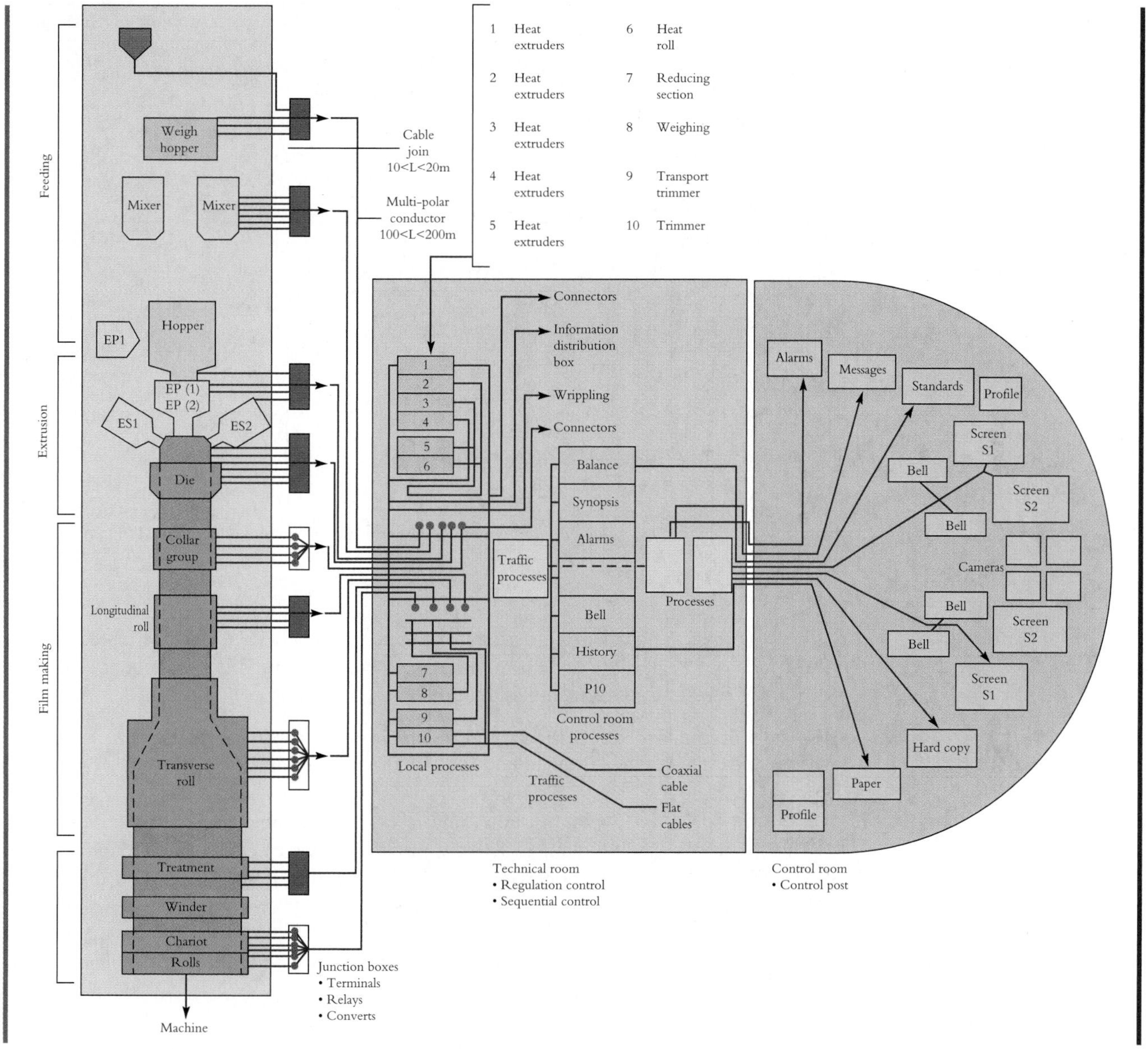

1	Heat extruders	6	Heat roll
2	Heat extruders	7	Reducing section
3	Heat extruders	8	Weighing
4	Heat extruders	9	Transport trimmer
5	Heat extruders	10	Trimmer

Feeding
Extrusion
Film making
Weigh hopper
Mixer
Mixer
EP1
Hopper
EP (1)
EP (2)
ES1
ES2
Die
Collar group
Longitudinal roll
Transverse roll
Treatment
Winder
Chariot
Rolls
Machine
Cable join 10<L<20m
Multi-polar conductor 100<L<200m
Junction boxes
• Terminals
• Relays
• Converts

Connectors
Information distribution box
Wrippling
Connectors
1
2
3
4
5
6
7
8
9
10
Local processes
Traffic processes
Balance
Synopsis
Alarms
Bell
History
P10
Control room processes
Processes
Traffic processes
Coaxial cable
Flat cables

Technical room
• Regulation control
• Sequential control

Alarms
Messages
Standards
Profile
Screen S1
Bell
Screen S2
Bell
Cameras
Bell
Screen S2
Bell
Screen S1
Hard copy
Paper
Profile

Control room
• Control post

APPENDIX 5 Agreement with ACV

		Amount of Savings	
1	Labour reduction: 5 operators less	PDS	75,000.00
2	Reduction of mechanical/electrical failures 1.30 h production/month	PDS	25,000.00
3	Speed optimisation +0.5% on S1 +2% on S2 increase production: 130 t	PDS	90,000.00
4	Production downtime/film break 5.3% to 3.8% on S1 and S2: 140 t	PDS	100,000.00
5	Improved start-up time after filters change and reduction of lost time after shut down: 45 t	PDS	30,000.00
6	Job changes for S1 and S2 4 h reduced to 2 h on basis 3 per month on S1 7 per month on S2 i.e.: 185 t production increase 500 t	PDS	130,000.00
		TOTAL SAVINGS PDS 450,000.00	

"After analysis of the goals to be reached in Mantes with a DAMATIC distributed control system, we have the pleasure to inform you that we accept to bind the settlement of the last term of payment to a performance guarantee on the following basis:

- Principle of bonus for AVC is accepted if the guarantee results are better than expected.
- Maximum value of penalty of bonus: 20% of the total value of our turn-key offer, i.e. : FF 1,117,920.00
- Period of evaluation: 12 months: from January 88 to December 88.
- Saving objectives are based on a 500 t/y production increase. This production increase together with labour reduction will cause a GBP 450,000 savings (rate of exchange and film cost price: Jan. 87).
- Savings costs are as follows:
- Variations on the several saving points will be accepted as long as the total amounts remain unchanged
- Penalty or bonus calculation:
  At the end of the evaluation period, SHORKO or ACV will have 4 week time to prove respectively that:
  - the objective has not been reached. SHORKO will bring elements to prove its claim,
  - the objective has been exceeded: ACV will bring elements to prove its claim.

  Then, the companies will have 4 weeks to settle the matter. If SHORKO makes no claim, the last term will be settled as agreed.

STEP 2: Prepare the case for class discussion.

STEP 3: Answer each of the following questions, individually or in small groups, as directed by your instructor.

Diagnosis

1. Why, when he arrived in 1985, did Christian de Pierrefeu feel that the future of Shorko's Mantes plant was limited?

Evaluation

2. Why did Chris Matthews suggest the idea of automated process control?
3. What benefits did de Pierrefeu expect to achieve from automation?
4. What was the attitude of the machine operators to the proposal for process automation? How did de Pierrefeu and Jean-Claude Caillaud manage their expectations?

Design

5. What types of information does the automated system need to collect in order to properly control the machinery at Mantes?
6. What was the role of the managers at Mantes in the design of the automated systems?
7. What was the role of the machine operators in the design of the automated system?
8. How effectively did the management team and its contractors address the opportunity to design the system to collect information that could be used to further improve process management?

Implementation

9. How effective was the automation system in achieving its design objectives?
10. What was the impact of automation on the machine operators? What was its impact on the managers?
11. What should de Pierrefeu do next?

STEP 4: In small groups, with the entire class, or in written form, share your answers to the questions above. Then answer the following questions:

1. What were the objectives of automation at the Mantes plant?
2. How well did the Valmet system meet these objectives?
3. What additional changes are possible to increase the value of the automated system?
4. How did implementation of the system change the roles and perspectives of operators and managers? ●

Activity 13

Benetton SpA

STEP 1: Read the "Fashion Success Story of the 1980s: Benetton SpA" case. (This activity is especially suited for use in conjunction with Chapter 10 of *Information Systems.*)

> One reason why the Roman Empire grew so large and survived so long—a prodigious feat of management—is that there was no railway, car, airplane, radio, paper, or telephone. Above all, no telephone. And therefore you could not maintain any illusion of direct control over a general or provincial governor, you could not feel at the back of your mind that you could ring him up, or that he could ring you, if a situation cropped up which was too much for him, or that he could fly over and sort things out if they started to get in a mess. You appointed him, you watched his baggage train disappear over the hill in a cloud of dust and that was that. There was, therefore, no question of appointing a man that was not fully trained, or not quite up to the job; you knew that everything depended upon his being the best man for the job before he set off. And so you took great care in selecting him; but more than that you made sure that he knew all about Roman government and the Roman army before he went out.
>
> Antony Jay[1]

THE WORLDWIDE TRANSACTION SYSTEM

"We want to provide our agents with the information they need to control their own sales and account receivables," said Bruno Zuccaro, Director of Information Systems at Benetton SpA in Treviso, Italy, as he explained the Worldwide Transaction System (WTS). At Benetton, the WTS represented the latest effort to formalize the company's unusual business system, developed over several years and highly dependent on informal and implicit policies. Although the WTS was not out of character for a company which prided itself on the use of information technology (IT), Bruno worried that its introduction would not preserve Benetton's culture based on informality and trust.

"To work for Benetton, Luciano says, you have to be a little crazy. Let me explain," Bruno said, as he proceeded to describe some of Benetton's informal business policies:

- Being crazy is having originality in solving problems, imagination in design, creativity in management, vision of the business, no fear of making mistakes, because there are very few guidelines.
- Second, the important things are few; in whatever you do, start by making things simple. Don't complicate matters, reduce them to their essentials. There are no complicated rules in the Benetton system. For example, we never intended to install our Point of Sale (POS)[2] system to control our agents, quite the contrary, we wanted to give maximum support to the company's agents, our *Centurioni*.
- Third, it is important to be ready. Try to anticipate what is happening, and use your imagination to identify and adapt to the new situation. For example, we have two fashion seasons a year and by the time you get feedback from the market, you are already working

[1] *Management and Machiavelli,* Hutchinson Business, London 1987.

[2] Luciano Benetton wanted a system which could register information at the point of sale (POS) and transmit that information at the end of the day during the first two weeks of the season.

for the next season. In 1989 this meant 2,000 items every six months. The problem here is to anticipate the market, not to follow the market.

Giovanni Cantagalli, Vice President of Operations, underscored Bruno's comments regarding the flexible atmosphere at Benetton.

> This company is a miracle: there is no organization chart; it isn't clear who does what. It was created on a non-industrial framework. Compared to the experiences that I've had in other more structured companies, it seems everything holds together by chance, and yet we turn over more than L 1,600 billion a year.

In referring to POS, Bruno was hinting at a previous problem created by the careless introduction of information technology to the Benetton culture.

> There were a number of managers who saw POS as an opportunity to control and monitor our agents and shopowners. Where Luciano emphasized maximum support to the agent, one can understand why he was opposed to installing POS in a way that might undermine the relationship between himself and his Centurioni. In fact, the reason we wanted to install POS was to monitor the market, not to monitor the agents or control the shops. It supported the reassortment process which had become a whole new business—a task which had become increasingly complex with the growth of Benetton in recent years. POS was simply a tool to keep the company from becoming too complicated.

Unlike POS, however, the WTS was a far more sophisticated tool for information management and formalizing company rules. That is, where POS served as a "market thermometer" providing the latest sales information on fashion trends, WTS would go one step further and enable agents to manage their accounts more closely without having to resolve problems through Treviso. Nonetheless, what was intended to serve as a decentralizing tool, to move the responsibility of shop coordination from Benetton headquarters in Treviso to the agents in their respective areas, could be viewed by some agents as a supervisory tool, thus threatening to undermine the company's implicit policies and working procedures. "Based on the POS experience, is it possible to introduce the more complex WTS without damaging the entrepreneurial flare and informal atmosphere so fundamental to our success?" asked Bruno.

THE BENETTON SYSTEM IN 1989

Under the leadership of Luciano Benetton, he and his three siblings—Guiliana, Carlo, and Gilberto—had, in the course of 25 years, created the classic American rags to riches story, albeit in remote Northeast Italy. By 1989, the world-renowned industrial fashion company had an annual turnover of $1 billion generated by over 5,000 shops worldwide, supplied primarily by Italian manufacturing facilities.[3] The company, however, had not attained this position without growing pains and, by the end of the 1980s, the management of Benetton looked back on several growth phases. Toward the end of each phase, management had been inclined to review the company's business system and consider the best way to introduce information technology while preserving the company's success.

Design

Though outside designers had been used since the company's beginning, by 1988 their length of stay was limited to a maximum of six seasons (three years) to guarantee a regular supply of innovative ideas. In addition to outsiders, Benetton had a series of design teams for each of its clothing themes. Aside from the company's main theme—*The United Colors of Benet-*

---

[3]For a more thorough discussion of the company's history, see IMD case *Building the Benetton System*.

ton—some of the more recent themes included: "Anthology" which featured United States clothing styles of the 1950s; "Marina" with a nautical emphasis; and "Type de Nimes" dedicated to denim garments. For each of these themes, design teams completed or adapted product ideas within given cost boundaries. Given this variety of themes, the company's designers rarely set a fashion trend but, given the conservative styling policy, they rarely missed one either. "Benetton is not fashion. Ralph Lauren, Yves St. Laurent, and Chanel are fashion and we respect them, but we're a whole other world," said one Benetton executive in charge of corporate communications. "We don't challenge people to buy our latest ideas, we find out their ideas and desires, and provide them," he added.

Cut, Make and Trim (CMT)

In the apparel industry, raw material sourcing and manufacturing were highly dependent upon the fashion cycle. Aldo Palmeri, Chief Executive Officer (CEO) of Benetton Group SpA, described his company's fashion cycle.

> We show two major fashion collections a year, 12 months in advance of the sales season. For example, for Autumn/Winter 1989, we began to show our collection in November 1988, and we started to order raw materials at the same time. We go long, according to prices and ranges, but we buy less than half our total needs at this stage. We complete our purchases only when we have firm orders from our store owners at the beginning of January (refer to Exhibit 1).
>
> The production cycle, starting between November and January, is divided between functions undertaken at Benetton and those subcontracted out. We start to deliver the products at the end of April, but the starting point for credit to shopowners is September 1; that's when the clock starts ticking. Payments are due at 30-, 60-, and 90-day intervals. In other words, the first payment is due at the end of September, the second at the end of October and the third at the end of November. This means that the peak of indebtedness at Benetton is when we've completed production and delivered the goods, but haven't yet been paid by our customers. That's between May and the end of September for the Autumn/Winter collection.

Specifically, Benetton took 90–120 days to pay its suppliers, whereas it took only 30 days to pay its subcontractors. "The subcontractors can't handle the strain of extended credit, but the raw material suppliers can," added Palmeri. Furthermore, since raw material suppliers benefitted from guaranteed volumes, they were asked in return to take charge of the inventories, and be flexible and responsive to Benetton's needs.

By the end of the 1980s, the production process at Benetton had evolved towards internal and external locations. Internal production concentrated on capital intensive steps of the business system such as raw material sourcing, cutting, dyeing and distribution. External production, on the other hand, focused on labor intensive steps in the business system, including sewing and 99% of the wool knitting (refer to Exhibit 2). Knitting facilities, or laboratories as they were called within Benetton, invested in their own equipment and owned 12 machines on average, of up to six different types. Also, Benetton kept track of which laboratories owned what equipment, in order to send each laboratory the appropriate type and amount of work. Specifically, subcontractors' resources were optimized by limiting their involvement to one or two production stages while guaranteeing them a 10% profit margin on cost. In addition, company policy kept investment costs down by adapting old machinery to new tasks instead of replacing it.

Benetton Group SpA was sensitive to the needs of its external subcontractors and attempted to keep them busy year round—except during Benetton's August vacation. In addition, Benetton assisted these laboratories financially. That is, in arm's length competition, one typically paid subcontractors as little as possible. Benetton, on the other hand, tried to pay the right price, defined as the time for operations, the cost of manpower and a plant

Collections Timing

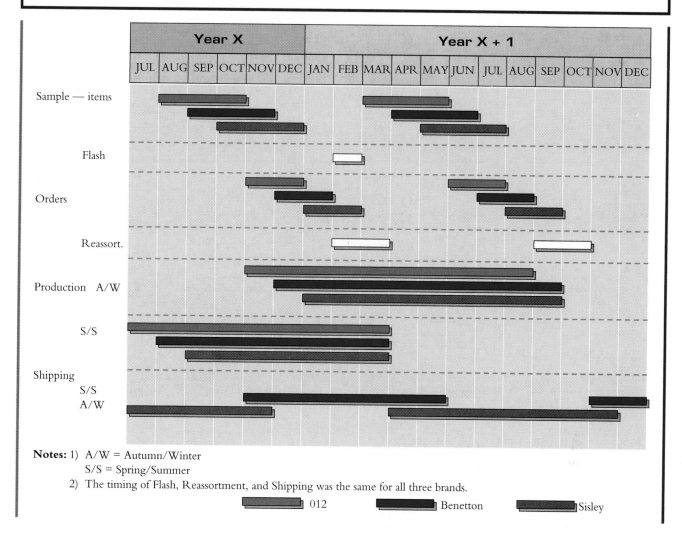

Notes: 1) A/W = Autumn/Winter
S/S = Spring/Summer
2) The timing of Flash, Reassortment, and Shipping was the same for all three brands.

fee. Moreover, Benetton sometimes helped subcontractors upgrade their machinery in line with fashion trends by buying the old equipment. As a second alternative, the company allowed subcontractors wide margins on some orders, thereby freeing up the capital to invest in new machinery. Still, where subcontractors had difficulties in purchasing their equipment, Benetton provided lease arrangements.

In addition to the financial support and guaranteed work at full capacity, subcontractors lowered social costs[4] and corporate overhead yet, as owners, closely supervised operations. Moreover, subcontractors benefitted from small sales, marketing, and accounting departments and thus concentrated on manufacturing and making one invoice per month. This system,

[4]In Italy, companies with more than 15 employees were subject to union and state control, and paid 49% of workers' salaries in social costs. Thus, subcontractors lowered their social costs by limiting employees in their family enterprises to fewer than 15 people.

Flow of Materials

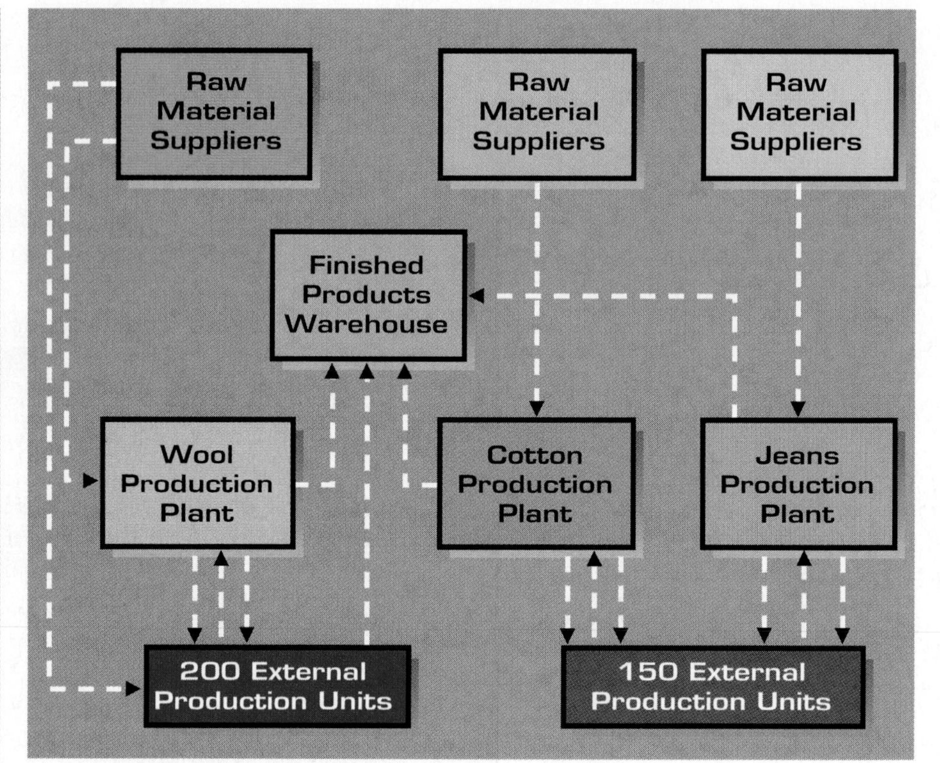

Luciano believed, encouraged people to work exclusively for Benetton—even on weekends if necessary—and reinvest their profits in the business.

The CMT cycle, therefore, particularly the eight months between order taking and delivery, provided Benetton time to adjust the level of its external resources. To summarize, Benetton purchased raw materials and, after inspection at Benetton plants, sent them to subcontractors before bringing the semi-finished products back to its own plants for completion. Knitting or non-knitted materials requiring cutting with the latest computerized technology, for example, were performed at Benetton with capital intensive equipment.

Once knitted, sweater parts were sent out and assembled in laboratories. Thereafter, some assembled garments were returned to Benetton for the capital intensive dyeing phase, a process which some executives believed accounted for 90% of the perceived quality image in Benetton's distinctly colored sweaters. In the finishing stage, which included inspection, pressing, folding, bagging and packing, garments were again sent to subcontractors, before being shipped to warehouses.

As a rule, Luciano tried to reproduce this system when moving into new markets and did not manufacture outside Italy unless required by local conditions. Two examples were Brazil, which was closed to imports, and Spain, where cotton imports were controlled. Local conditions aside, the internationalization of manufacturing provided a degree of protection from exchange rate fluctuations. In the early 1980s, Benetton established production facilities in France and Scotland; Spain in 1985, and Rocky Mount, North Carolina, in the US in 1986. Though small in volume, these foreign facilities complemented Benetton's Italian manufacturing capabilities. For example, high value added cashmere garments were produced in Scotland, woolen garments in France, and cotton articles in the US.

Excluding the US articles, the French and Scottish products represented less than 5% of Benetton's total sales. Moreover, products manufactured at these sites had limited distribution. Specifically, in France, only woolen garments were produced and distributed to a portion of the French retail stores. The cashmere garments produced in Scotland, on the other hand, were distributed primarily in Japan, France and Belgium through normal department stores that had no association with the Benetton name.

Distribution

By the late 1980s, distribution became the most automated function at Benetton. Aside from distributing goods automatically, the system reduced the average delivery time and improved the level of service. For example, all merchandise was bar-coded in local currencies and could be processed electronically at the point of sale. Furthermore, the company tried to get 60% of a season's order to each shop at the start of the season. As Giancarlo Chiodini, Director of Logistics, said, "We have succeeded in linking the shop and the factory floor, eliminating everything in between. Our physical distribution and manufacturing system is completely in phase with commercial realities in the store." (Refer to Exhibit 3.)

Informally, Carlo Benetton oversaw production, subcontracting, and distribution. Generally speaking, the role of manufacturing had changed substantially in recent years and, by 1989, a strong emphasis was placed on innovation and cost reduction. As part of their responsibilities, plant managers had to coordinate the manufacturing details of all production facilities, and plan and control quality. Moreover, a plant manager's success depended on securing the trust of Carlo, who maintained informal relations with long time and trusted subcontractor-employees. In other words, to become a Benetton partner-subcontractor, good relationships with Carlo were a necessity. Then, too, if an employee left the company, he could continue to subcontract or, alternatively, lose his guaranteed business with Benetton—it all depended on Carlo. As a result of this uncertainty, there was a great incentive to stay in the company and continue earning money as a subcontractor.

Distribution Network

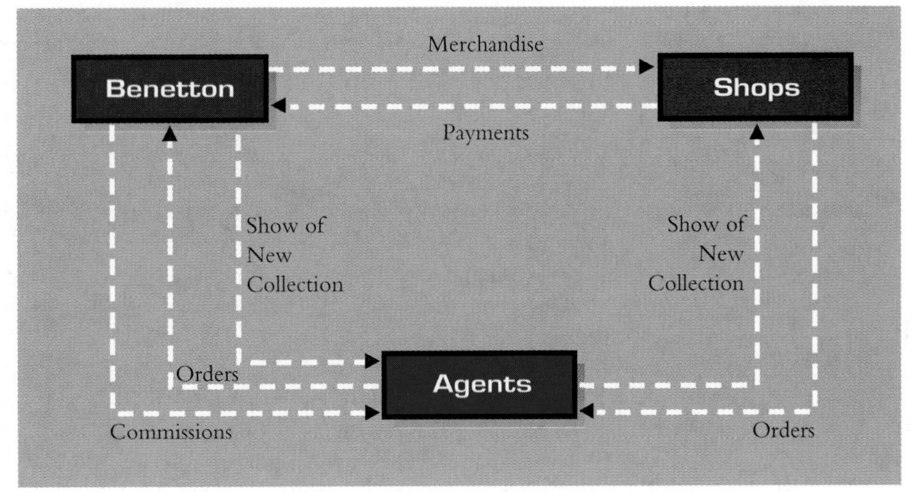

Agents

Mainly through verbal agreements, company agents were assigned large territories which they sought to populate with Benetton shops. These verbal agreements were managed primarily on the basis of trust, and it was not until the early 1980s that formal contracts began to be written between Benetton SpA and the agents. Shopowners themselves kept a close eye on the market, constantly passing on information and suggestions. "We are one with the commercial department of Benetton," asserted Paolo Panizzo, Benetton's agent in London and owner of five shops. When each new collection was ready, agents took about 30 days to present the sample collection to each shopowner and helped the owner in selecting his order; at the end of the day the order was sent to Benetton. As no inventory was to be left in the shops at the end of a season, the agents, who were ultimately responsible for inventory, shifted it to other stores to minimize inventory losses. At the end of a season, any remaining inventory was turned over to a specialized organization which distributed it in third world countries, outside Benetton markets.

By using self-employed agents who promoted and supervised their territories with the rigor of actual owners, Luciano encouraged entrepreneurial energy in the business and fast expansion in the number of shops. The agents' major incentive and source of income came from the high risk, high reward opportunity to invest in the prime-sited shops they oversaw. Thus, agents could move items between stores if the owners agreed; they also monitored markdowns and were expected to maintain contacts with the final consumer. Manlio Tonolo, agent for Northeast Italy, who owned 40 of the 200 shops he supervised, said, "It's important to be able to read the culture of young people; an agent who has nothing to say about customer trends is of no further use to the company. My clients can learn from my shops and vice versa. The company's basic needs have not changed, it still needs a certain level of craziness." Normally, agents had a small organization to perform their multiple activities; they hired young assistants who controlled the shops' overall image and problems on a weekly basis. In addition, assistants helped the agent to monitor new trends in young people's culture by visiting bars, discotheques, etc. to observe behavior and fashion trends.

Agents were formally coordinated by eight area managers, most of whom had been hired since 1984, to choose new agents, open new markets, monitor sales and payments, and follow item movements. In other words, the area managers' job was operational in that they supported the agents in the merchandising task; a service aimed at maintaining clean, well managed shops—essential for a quality image. Furthermore, area managers collected the Basic and Reassortment orders from the agents, checked windows, and conducted market research by opening up a shop. As a norm, however, area managers did not own shops themselves, which built a potential motivational problem into Benetton's formal structure. For example, Ricardo Weiss, who was the area manager for the US, Canada, Japan and some other countries, supervised 25 agents and was responsible for 1,000 shops. In other words, area managers were employees of the corporation and were paid employee salaries. Agents, on the other hand, were impresarios in nature and earned a lot more money than area managers—sometimes creating a difficult relationship.

Under Luciano, the commercial director and the area managers were the marketing department. Nearly all the members of the commercial department were Italian, had been hired by Luciano, and were accustomed to working directly for him. Franco Furno, Head of Organization and Development, commented on the informal versus formal reporting relationships at Benetton.

> Informally, the real marketing manager at Benetton is Luciano. He has three people reporting to him: Venturato, mainly for Europe; Weiss, for the Far East; and Martinuzzo, for Africa and the Middle East. Formally, however, these three persons report to Cantagalli.

Although the commercial directors acted as staff for Luciano, they were not told what had to be done, as Luciano expected employees to understand what was needed. Aldo Palmeri explained in an interview in February 1989:

> Luciano Benetton has created a breed of new entrepreneurs among our agents and shopkeepers. The most important agents now fly their own private aircraft. They're people who were not necessarily in the commercial field before Benetton came into their lives. Luciano wanted people without the pre-fixed ideas of conventional agents in the fashion field. He wanted young, enterprising energetic people who, with proper motivation, would be sympathetic to Benetton's way of doing business and would give their maximum.

Luciano had rarely replaced an agent for failure to meet expectations. Similar to Europe, the marketing organization for America was split into regions, each of which was supervised by an agent.

Retailing

Though Luciano selected shop locations at first, by 1989 locations were also chosen by agents. Each store had standard fixtures such as open shelves and could accommodate about one-third of a season's sales. Also, the shops' window displays, developed by Tobia Scarpa, changed each week and started new trends. Displays, which reinforced ongoing advertising campaigns, were set up by store managers trained by Benetton agents. Typically, the clothes were placed near the window to create a cumulative attraction.

Shopowners were obliged to buy only Benetton clothes, achieve minimum sales levels, follow guidelines for price mark-ups, adopt the standard shop layouts designed by Tobia Scarpa,[5] pay on schedule, and allow for agent-partners. Generally, a shopowner had five shops and did not have to accept returned goods sold by another outlet. Likewise, they could not return merchandise and had to pay for whatever they ordered. Prices, which were set by Benetton, tried to provide 50% gross margins.

Affiliates invested about $70,000 per shop, providing Benetton with a captive distribution network without financial commitments, expensive staff or the need to oversee day-to-day performance. Furthermore, Benetton controlled markdowns, stockouts, and inventory risk while enjoying a costless source for financing retail growth. "The classic shopkeeper had to be killed and we killed him. The real strength of our company is that a whole group has accepted the same policies for production and sales," declared Luciano. In 1989, fewer than 10 Benetton stores were owned and operated by the company, and turnover among shopowners was low. For example, of the 200 stores supervised by Manlio Tonolo, only five shopowners had been replaced during the last 10 years.

Promotion

At Benetton, approximately 4% of sales was spent on direct advertising. Television campaigns concentrated on Benetton's young and sporty image, while magazine advertisements depicted color and lifestyle images. In addition, the company sponsored sports events reflecting the interests of the family. Since the early 1980s, the switch away from country campaigns stressed Benetton's image as a worldwide company with a single theme and position—an infinite variety of color possibilities. In 1983, Benetton launched a global advertising campaign showing interracial crowds of children wearing Benetton clothes and the flags of various countries. Using slogans such as "Benetton—All the Colors of the World" and "United Colors

---

[5]Tobia and Afra Scarpa were both natives of the Veneto area where the Benetton story began. After designing the first Benetton factory in 1965, the Scarpas became close friends of the Benettons. Therafter, Tobia Scarpa designed all Benetton shops, starting with the first shop in Belluno in 1967.

of Benetton," the campaign sought to convey the message that Benetton products had no frontiers. The latter slogan proved so successful that, at the end of 1989, the management agreed to make it the new logo.

THE INCREASING ROLE OF INFORMATION TECHNOLOGY

With the advent of computer-aided design (CAD) at the Ponzano factory, Benetton used computers capable of developing complex stitching in 256 basic colors, or 17 million shades. And, five kilometers away at Villorba, CMT underwent a revolution with the introduction of computer-aided manufacturing (CAM). Thus, from the early 1980s on, raw materials were fed into preprogrammed machines which cut 15,000 garments every eight hours. The combined impact of CAD/CAM on CMT shortened the time span between design approval and manufacture, significantly reducing material waste.

In 1986, Benetton completed its famous automated warehouse in Treviso with the expectation that it would suffice for 20 years. However, within a year and a half after completion, the company's turnover began to test the 300,000 box per day limit of the facility. In 1989, the facility was run by a handful of technicians and had a top operating capacity of 18,000 packages per day. Among its automated features were robots that slid silently between storage racks, programmed to handle cartons of garments. In turn, cartons were moved along by a series of belts, chutes, and cranes under the guidance of a sophisticated computer system.

Aside from revolutionizing a number of tasks within each step of the business system, the information age also brought those steps closer together. For example, CAD and CAM together made it economically feasible to design and manufacture 2,000 products each season, appealing to a host of narrow market segments. In other words, Benetton's integrated distribution, sales and communication systems had effectively removed much of the inventory risk from its business system. (Refer to Exhibit 4 for Benetton's information systems organization.)

Using advanced telecommunications, Benetton received data on sales trends around the world 24 hours a day, every day of the year. Daily updates on sales and inventory were transmitted to Ponzano, where they were analyzed and passed on to the relevant departments. "This technology has brought us closer to the consumer, to eliminate all the filters between the factory and the man who buys," said Giancarlo Chiodini, Director of Logistics, in 1987. "In this way, we have been able to become a global operation with a global vision," he added.

Benetton committed itself to using the best information systems available and, because of the company's fast growth, systems were constantly being restructured. On average, Benetton spent about 1.2% of its annual turnover on hardware, software and computer personnel. In 1985, for example, as part of its ongoing commitment to IT, the company bought a 5% participation in the Italian subsidiary of Nolan Norton, a leading United States information systems consulting firm. In summary, information technology served as the bridge between the manufacturing companies and the market, provided the programming and control of all the external production units, managed centralized distribution around the world, and supported the centralized management of financial flows.

At Benetton, the most important information system was that which connected agents to the firm. Originally, Benetton used a network system consisting of dedicated minicomputers, in seven European cities, connected to mainframes in Italy. With growth, this network became too expensive and, by the end of 1987, agents were connected to the Mark III General Electric Information System's value added network. Available round the clock in 750 cities in 25 countries, Mark III provided network access to customer data such as order-entry, confirmations, color instructions, which orders were sent to which plants, and which orders were transferred among plants. Furthermore, Mark III used General Electric's telecommunications satellite, thus eliminating long distance, transcontinental telephone charges for

EXHIBIT 4 Information Systems Organization

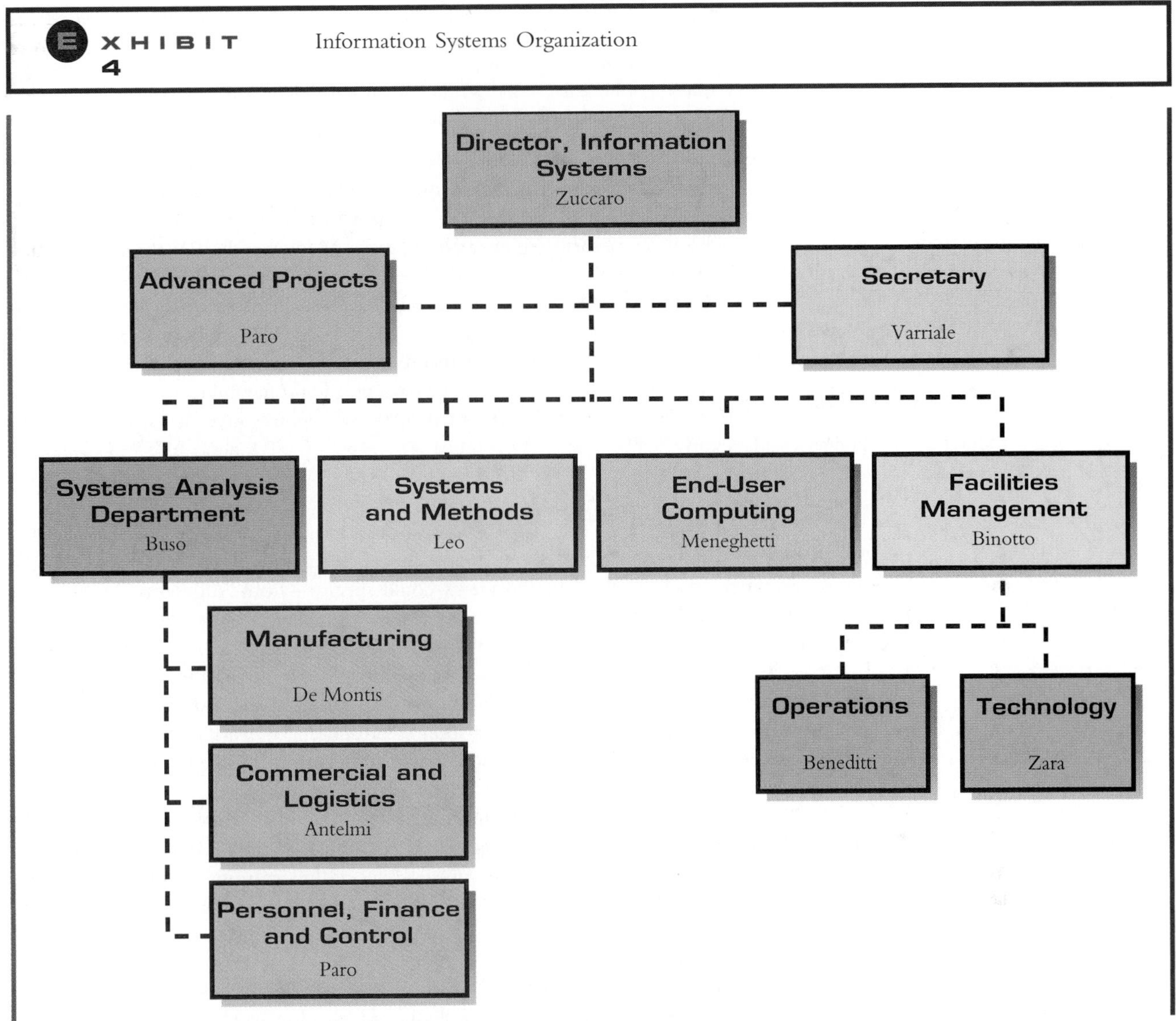

data transmissions as well as for the company's 24-hour Information System Center at headquarters.

Mark III proved to be indispensable for managing Benetton's large database from one computer and at a low cost. During reassortment, for example, shop orders forwarded by agents were collected twice a day through the Mark III network and stored in a central order portfolio. Thereafter, agents were informed on the status of their orders; the plants and the forwarding department were informed of orders as soon as they were collected; plants received finishing and packing instructions each morning; and the forwarding department was informed about the estimated arrival times from plants. "All this," explained Bruno, "would not be possible without a sophisticated information system."

EVALUATING THE BUSINESS SYSTEM

Aldo Palmeri attributed Benetton's success to its entrepreneurial culture in distribution; its philosophy of laying off risk in production, and its highly developed customer-led marketing.

> Setting up a classic direct sales network is often weakened by people being paid to be bureaucrats. Intermediaries tend to dominate such a structure and take the benefits from people at the sharp end. What we've done at Benetton is strip down the distribution network to the essentials; we've cut out the middlemen—the wholesalers in our fashion business and the intermediaries in the financial services field—and created dynamic sales forces in each business.

In 1989, Benetton SpA was run by only 30 executives; the company itself employed about 1,500 people, but provided employment for some 10,000 people altogether.

In the past, the system succeeded because all the partners in the chain—the Benetton family, agents, and subcontractors—enjoyed good profits. Moreover, the Benetton family took a lead role in reinvesting those profits and, thus, set an example for their agent and subcontractor partners. In brief, profits provided the financial muscle for growth and were reinvested into shops, laboratories and the high technology needed to support a growing business. In the early 1980s, analysts estimated that Benetton's productivity was on a par with that of producers from Asia. "It's not difficult to have speed and flexibility when you're small. It's harder when you're big. Having more than 5,000 sales points gives us that dimension," Luciano said in early 1989.

POS FOR REASSORTMENT

At Benetton, shopowners had three opportunities to adjust their orders. Using the Spring/Summer season as an example, agents could specify—from August to December—the color of up to 30% of previously ordered woven items held *in greggio.*[6] Later, a "Flash" collection, based on early customer requests, added about 50 new items to the basic product line. Thirdly, the reassortment process allowed shopowners to reorder the 30–50 items they expected to be the most successful in the ongoing season. It was then Benetton's responsibility to produce and ship those items as soon as possible.

For a given product portfolio in a season, prices at Benetton declined over time. That is, Benetton products were sold at their full price for three months, then at 70% for 30 days, and finally at 50% of full price. In volume terms, shops sold 70% of their offering at full price. Thus, missing a popular selling item at the beginning of the season strongly affected the profitability of the shops, because of missed sales at full margins. With this in mind, Luciano saw an opportunity to get early feedback on the style and colors that would be popular in the season. With that information, the 50 bestselling items could be identified and included in production at the start of the season.

However, in obtaining that feedback, Luciano sought objective information which avoided the bias of shopowners' opinions. Furthermore, that information had to be provided quickly and far enough in advance to meet Production's five weeks' lead time. Most importantly, that information had to provide a service to the agents. To perform the task, a $5,000 POS system was chosen, consisting of a cash register and microcomputer. Typically, each installed system captured and processed the price, style, color and size of about 30 items per day.

At the time of its introduction, there was no intention to install POS in all 4,000 shops; only a selected sample of 100 shops would use POS to determine early trends in the marketplace. Specifically, POS served as a market thermometer by providing advance planning notice for the reassortment business by identifying the 12 bestselling items, colors and styles at the beginning of the season. Thereafter, orders were put into production under the constraints of available lab capacity, types of machines that could be reprogrammed, and availability of raw materials. The season's production schedule was adapted as much as possible, without creating bigger costs by disrupting the manufacturing plan. However, if an agent

---

[6] "Greggio" was the Italian word for unbleached. At Benetton, holding items "in greggio" meant leaving them undyed.

demanded a big enough order, and the capacity was there, Benetton SpA would also put it into production, consulting other agents on the same items.

POS created the reassortment business by telling the stores what they should reassort—shopowners did not get a chance to order what they thought the market wanted. Quite the contrary—agents told them what POS's sample said the market wanted. That is, the whole technique was essentially a statistical polling problem. Over time, reassortment changed significantly and grew to become 10% of the business. In other words, POS was a tremendous success and, by 1989, every agent in the world had information on what would be available at Benetton factories. Agents then proceeded to sell these products to their shops. In summary, POS supported the Benetton belief that information about customer needs was inherent in the marketplace; it was only a matter of keeping in touch with the market to translate these needs into garments.

FORMALIZING ENTREPRENEURIAL POLICIES

Benetton Group SpA, which in 1989 included over 5,000 stores around the world, needed to create as homogeneous a behavior as possible among its 80 agents. Yet, because of the company's growth, the standardization of procedures had become increasingly dependent on information technology like POS, designed to support the agents. For example, from 1982 to 1989, the average number of shops coordinated by an agent had increased from 25 to 60, respectively.

About 2,000 administrative clients owning more than one shop were having problems with blocked shipments because of their credit rating. In fact, by the late 1980s, area managers were spending up to 35% of their time following up on payment problems. Bruno explained:

> The following situation often happens. The shop calls the agent complaining, "I'm not receiving the items." The agent calls the warehouse saying, "Why don't you send the items?" Then, the warehouse calls the commercial people asking, "Why do you block his credit?" and so on. So the agents call Luciano and complain about bureaucracy! "My clients will not pay until they receive their merchandise!"

One executive added a bit more insight on the scenario by describing the sequence of shipping activities. Once finished, goods were shipped directly from the central warehouse to the shop; there were no warehouses in foreign countries. In turn, the company billed clients with no billing to companies in between. In other words, customers received bills from Benetton, Atlanta, Columbia, etc. Thus, to receive quick payments, with no costs attached, information on customer payments was needed. Otherwise, shipments could not be made if payment of previous shipments had not been received. This scenario, he added, was why the company needed a Worldwide Transaction System (WTS)—purely for business reasons.

By the same token, Luciano Benetton believed in providing the agents with easier access to shop information; agents should decide the shipment priority of the stores within their territories. Bruno explained:

> The agents should see the situation at the customer level (shops). What was ordered, what was in possession, what was in the warehouse, and what was shipped. Then, they should also get information on credit maturity so that in the future, the agents will make the decisions (directly through computers) on what is shipped to whom, and when. If part of the items are blocked, it will be the agents' decision and responsibility, not Benetton's.

Bruno went on:

> The WTS was meant to help the agents, but these people are supermen, fantastic promoters and salesmen, and you cannot believe everything they say. Objective information and service to the

EXHIBIT 5 Commercial Organization Benetton Group as of January 1990

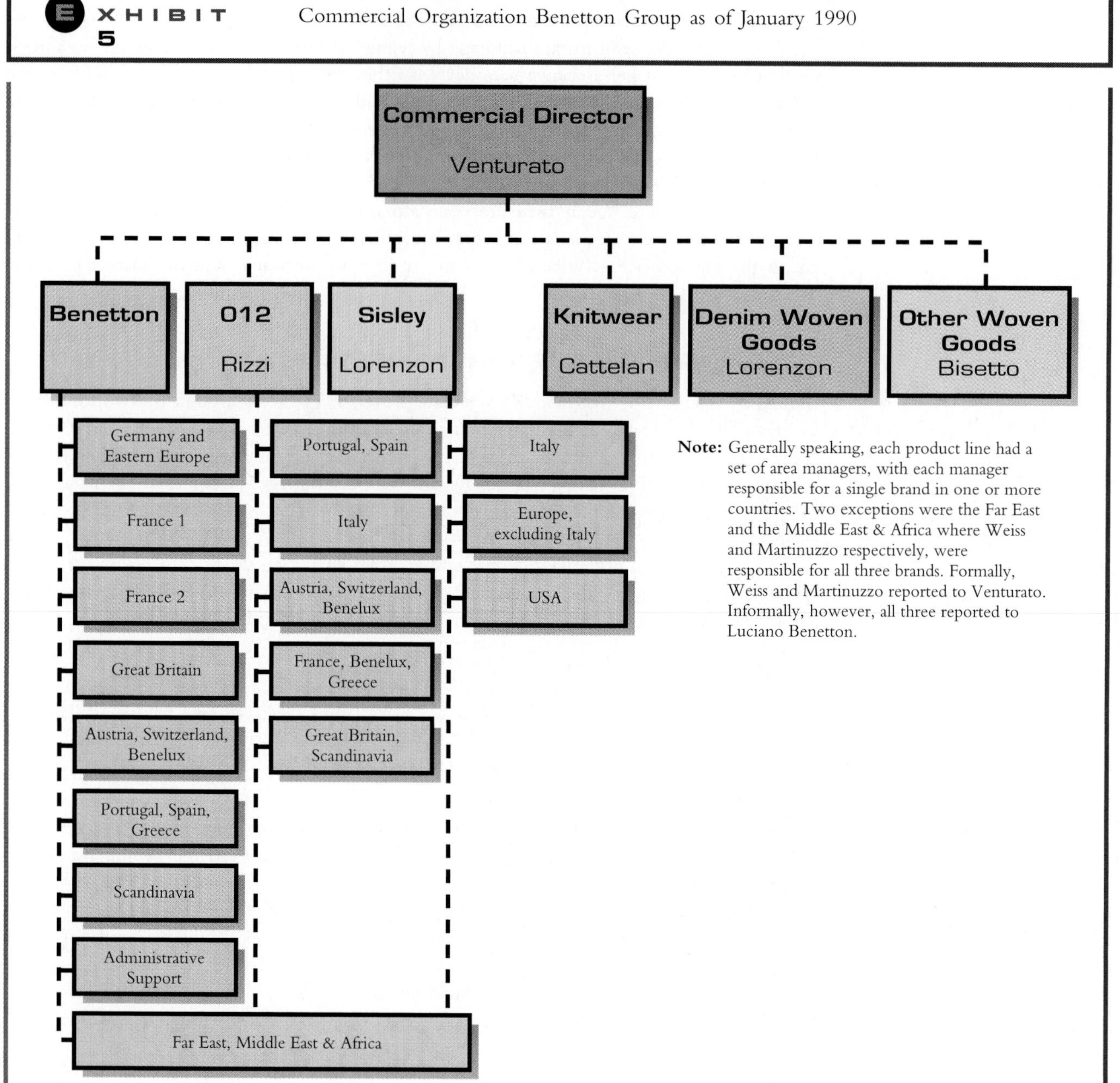

Note: Generally speaking, each product line had a set of area managers, with each manager responsible for a single brand in one or more countries. Two exceptions were the Far East and the Middle East & Africa where Weiss and Martinuzzo respectively, were responsible for all three brands. Formally, Weiss and Martinuzzo reported to Venturato. Informally, however, all three reported to Luciano Benetton.

business is the main objective of our computer systems. Luciano says, maximum support to the agents, our Centurioni. When I arrived in 1985, my predecessors were fired because they tried to develop POS as a system to control the shops and agents; the would have destroyed the Benetton system. Luciano does not give precise instructions, only vague guidelines. If you interpret them well, you are OK. It is not enough to simply say "I understand." Also, Luciano is a promoter, salesman, and entrepreneur. You cannot believe everything Luciano says either, you have to interpret what he needs.

A number of agents were concerned that the Worldwide Transaction System might be used to monitor their performance. In that case, what guarantee was there that agents would use the system or the information it would provide? "Creativity is born of the people around you, and we have many who contribute to our success," said Luciano Benetton. "We are only one part of a large clan," he added. Bruno was concerned that, in the process of installing the new system, there could be a repeat of the "POS experience" on a far greater scale. In an organization where some of the most important policies were implicit, Bruno wondered if he could introduce the new system without disrupting the company's proven strategy.

Bibliography

Signorelli, Sergio and Heskett, James L., Benetton (A) & (B), ISTUD and Harvard Business School, 1984/85.

Lee, Andrea, "Profiles: Being Everywhere," *The New Yorker,* November 10, 1986.

Vitale, Michael, Benetton SpA: Industrial Fashion (A), Harvard Business School, 1987.

Bruce, Leigh, "The Bright New Worlds of Benetton," *International Management,* November 1987.

Finnerty, Anne, "The Internationalization of Benetton," *Textile Outlook International,* November 1987.

Ketelhohn, Werner, The European Women's Outerwear Industry in 1987, IMEDE, 1988.

Jarillo, Carlos and Martinez, Jon I., Benetton SpA, Harvard Business School, 1988.

Lorenyoni, Gianni, Benetton, London Business School, 1988.

Barry, Mary E. and Warfield, Carol L., "The Gloabalization of Retailing," *Textile Outlook International,* January 1988.

"Benetton Learns to Darn," *Forbes,* October 3, 1988.

"From Fabrics to Finance," *The Banker,* February 1989.

STEP 2: Prepare the case for class discussion.

STEP 3: Answer each of the following questions, individually or in small groups, as directed by your instructor.

Diagnosis

1. Why did Luciano Benetton want a POS system?
2. What types of information does Benetton's POS system collect?
3. What types of information do shopowners and agents require?

Evaluation

4. What benefits does the POS system provide for Benetton's shopowners, agents, area managers, and headquarter managers?
5. What evidence exists to indicate that the system has improved productivity at Benetton?
6. What problems does the existing POS system fail to address?

Design

7. What changes should be made in the transaction processing system to address the shipment-blocking problems at Benetton?
8. What types of hardware and software are needed to support such changes?

Implementation

9. What problems did Benetton experience during the initial roll-out of the POS system?
10. What problems do Bruno and some of the agents anticipate if a new system were to be built to address the deficiencies in the existing POS system?
11. What benefits would such a system provide?
12. How should Benetton proceed?

STEP 4: In small groups, with the entire class, or in written form, share your answers to the questions above. Then answer the following questions:

1. What information needs do Benetton, its agents, and its shopowners have?
2. How effectively does the current POS system address these needs?
3. What changes would allow the company to have its information needs met more effectively?
4. What issues should be considered in upgrading the system? ●

Activity 14 Acme Engineering

STEP 1: Read the Acme Engineering case. (This activity is especially suited for use in conjunction with Chapter 10 of *Information Systems.*)

COMPANY BACKGROUND

Mr. John D. Smith is the chief accountant at the Acme Engineering Co. in Christchurch, New Zealand. Mr. Smith reports to the company CEO, Mr. J.F. Acme (as do all other top departmental managers). The company manufactures large metal fabrication equipment on special order from customers. The industry of which it is a part is highly competitive and this has put increasing strain upon corporate finances through depressed profit levels. Since the company is family owned change has come slowly. The company has yet to adopt many of the newer methods for controlling:

- costs
- project tracking
- inventory level management
- cash flow control

Unfortunately the competitors have not been standing still and as a result of their implementing innovative control procedures they have seriously eroded Acme market share. Over the past 5 years Acme's share of this market has slipped from 23% to 14% of total industry sales. However the market has been growing and as a result sales over this period have increased from 3.2 million dollars to 4.7 million dollars per year.

The company currently has 120 employees in total.

ABOUT ACME OPERATIONS

The machines that are used in manufacturing are high precision multi-process metal forming and handling equipment. There are typically 50 orders or so in the shop at one time with average manufacturing duration of 3 to 4 months. The typical machine requires 120 unique operations (with an average duration of 1 to 3 hours per operation) to be performed in its manufacture at different points along the production schedule.

An additional indication of the complexity of the products that are produced is the inventory of parts that must be maintained for making Acme's product range. Currently held in stock are 8200 unique parts with an average item turnover of 6 months. Unfortunately there is no formal reporting system to determine turnover or demand for particular items in the existing inventory system.

Purchasing is generally notified by the inventory control department using a purchase requisition when a part is out-of-stock, but there is no specific system for determining when a part is low in stock. A card file is maintained which records when an item was last purchased, purchase price, description, part number and quantity purchased.

This case was made possible by the co-operation of an organisation which wishes to remain anonymous so the names of people have been disguised. It was written by John Vargo, Department of Accountancy, University of Canterbury, Christchurch, New Zealand. This material should be useful for class discussion or as an outside project.

The Problem

Low profitability has triggered much concern on the part of the family members, who are the primary shareholders. This brought about the employment of a number of new top level managers. These were hired for the express purpose of straightening out the existing information systems and management procedures, and implementing, if feasible, changes to the existing systems.

In discussions with the current management team a number of problems have been discovered. It has been reported that many employees are dissatisfied with current working conditions and this has affected productivity. There are also customer complaints that delivery of their ordered machines are usually overdue, often by as much as 30 to 60 days. Industry averages and statistics also show the following anomalies:

	Industry Average	Company Average
Inventory Turnover per year	4.1	2.5
Rate of Return on Total Assets	12.3%	4.6%
Avg. time to deliver an order	102.0 days	143.0 days
Average staff seniority	14.8 years	15.4 years

Other key company figures for the most recent year include:

Total Assets	$5,000,000
Total Inventory	$1,540,000
Total Sales	$4,750,000
Total Cost of Sales	$3,980,000

At the current rate of decline the profitability of the company is likely to go negative during the next twelve months and the owners have decreed that there shall be a solution preventing such an occurrence. Given the current technological changes in Acme's industry it also is becoming imperative that investment be made in a number of new and rather expensive manufacturing machines. Unfortunately at this point there is insufficient information available from the current information systems to do any sort of Return On Investment (ROI) calculations for current machines or new acquisitions. As a result the owners are understandably hesitant to invest more funds in new equipment until this lack of information is rectified.

ORDER ENTRY

Interviews have been conducted with a number of management staff; the responses to these interviews are presented in the following pages. One of the first interviews was with Lou Ming, order entry supervisor (reporting to the Marketing manager). Lou was asked about which areas he felt needed improvement.

> **Lou:** "The starting point for all activity here is at the point of order entry. When a firm order is received it starts the ball rolling for everyone else. Upon receipt of an order, purchasing must buy any special items required to manufacture the machine. Naturally this means the stock control clerk must determine if the necessary parts are already in stock and notify the purchasing department of out-of-stock items. In parallel with this the production control department schedules the new order into the production area, queuing behind all previously entered jobs, unless of course it is a priority job, and which ones aren't? There are a lot of politics played by the sales reps trying to fulfill promises they have made to customers regarding prompt delivery dates."

Interviewer: "Does this encompass the full chain of events as you see it?"

Lou: He paused, and then replied, "No, a number of other factors come into the picture as well. For example the customer credit status must be checked by Customer Service and the order approved. This is supposed to be done before the order is entered for scheduling, but more often than not we discover after the fact that this has not been done. This usually occurs because the salesperson was under pressure from marketing to meet the monthly quota, which has become harder and harder to achieve over the last year or two."

INVENTORY CONTROL AND PURCHASING

Interviews were next conducted with Maxwell Lu (inventory control manager) and Rita Nair (purchasing manager) both of whom report to the manufacturing manager.

Interviewer: "Maxwell, what is the condition of the inventory control system?"

Maxwell: "We run reasonably smooth most of the time, but there is the occasional hiccup when a new order enters the system since each machine we make is specially manufactured. As a result we often do not have in stock all of the parts needed to manufacture the entire machine. The order entry department sends to us a copy of the engineering specification which includes a parts list for the order. It is on the basis of this list that we determine if all parts and materials are in stock. For the parts we are missing a purchase requisition is prepared, which is given to the purchasing department."

Rita: "The only problem is that the purchase requisition doesn't usually include all of the items that are needed, and later on when the delivery date for the job has become critical, we usually receive an urgent request for the missing parts. Naturally we try to honour these requests, but inevitably it takes longer than we would like to procure the needed parts. Often we end up paying a premium for the parts due to the "rush order" nature of the request."

Maxwell: "This does happen occasionally, but it is just part of the complexity of the business environment and level of technological innovation in which we work."

Interviewer: "How often would you estimate this occurs?"

Maxwell: "Oh, perhaps two or three times a month, and we send through four purchase requisitions for each job that comes in."

Rita: "Bunk!! We must receive at least 10 or 12 such special requests per month which would be concerned with half of Acme's total active job orders at any given time!"

Interviewer: "Do either of you have any records dealing with this question of urgent requests?"

Rita: "I thought you would never ask! I maintain a log of all purchase requisitions coming through Acme's office and I annotate the log with the nature of the request. I go through and tabulate the categories monthly and I have the results of that tabulation with me. As you can see here, over the last six months the range of urgent requests has varied from eight in November to 14 in January."

Maxwell: "Well it isn't my fault, I just send on requests coming from production control. They are the ones who are supposed to get the list right in the first place."

PROJECT CONTROL

The next interview was with Jo Napp, the manager of production control, (responsible to the Manufacturing Manager).

Things in production control were pretty tense at the time; the following interview reveals a great deal of that tension.

Interviewer: "Well Jo how are you today? Got everything under control?" (making a little pun to put Jo at ease which he obviously was not when the interview began. Unfortunately he did not take it very well).

Jo: "What is that supposed to mean? Do you think you could do a better job controlling such high technology manufacturing? I want you to know I have been on the job here at Acme for over twenty years and every year we have turned a profit! Could you do better?"

Interviewer: "I was only making a small pun, not commenting on your competency. Now relax, I didn't come down to argue with you, just to have an open talk about how we can work together to overcome the problems the firm is facing. Now honestly Jo, what do you see as the primary problems in your department?"

Jo: "That is what I keep saying, the problem is not in this department, it is the bloody incompetents in engineering who keep messing up our schedules, and giving us incomplete data!"

Interviewer: "Easy now, instead of pointing the finger at engineering, let's just work together to solve our mutual problems. Now what exactly is the trouble, without hammering engineering please, just tell me your point of view."

Jo: "Nearly every new contract that comes in initially looks fine. The project file appears complete and suggested manufacturing operation duration times and parts lists look reasonable. But no sooner do we get a detailed schedule for the project worked out, printed and in the file, then the salesman and engineer come in with some changes. The next week there are more bloody changes, and on she goes ad infinitum! How on earth are we supposed to keep to schedule if they keep changing the requirements? To compound the problem purchasing offers us a bundle of useless excuses about suppliers being on strike, material shortages and out-of-stock conditions. To top it off the INVENTORY control department doesn't know the meaning of the word control! They have tons of parts for machines we manufacture rarely, and are constantly out of stock on the materials we use most."

Interviewer: "But we do live in a rapidly changing environment, surely we can expect some changes and have to learn to live with them?"

Jo: "Well I suppose some changes are reasonable, but every week? Besides it takes days to set up a decent schedule for these projects given the ten manufacturing stations we are trying to control with up to 50 projects being in the shop at one time. We cannot possibly maintain accurate schedules for all those projects with constant changes. We don't have enough clerks, and they cannot write up and coordinate the changes quickly enough to provide useful information. Besides that inventory control tells us one thing and does another. Max Lu often claims that we have parts in stock. Then later on when the parts are actually required in Manufacturing we discover that his records were wrong and the parts are not actually there. Naturally then we have to issue a rush request for parts. So don't blame me if things are all fouled up, what do you expect me to do, smart guy?"

Interviewer: "Well thank you for giving me your point of view, you have certainly given me much to think about, I'll be in contact in the near future."

RESOURCE SCHEDULING

The manufacturing department was next on the list, in order to discover their view regarding schedules and optimum equipment usage. Frank Tate was the manufacturing manager and known for being very competent.

Interviewer: "Everything running smoothly today Frank?"

Frank: "Yes, things seem to be going well, aside from the usual hiccups due to lack of parts, or Marketing climbing on our backs to shorten delivery times. But all in all we run as smoothly as can be expected."

Interviewer: "What do you attribute the smooth running of the manufacturing area to?"

Frank: "The team of workmen under me are all well trained and enjoy their work. Generally speaking, we have the latest in equipment and a good maintenance crew. This all keeps the jobs flowing through as well as possible given the difficulties with scheduling."

Interviewer: "Excuse me, but could you tell me more about the difficulties with scheduling, exactly what problems have you noticed?"

Frank: "Well, there seem to be a number of perspectives to be considered. From our point of view we work most efficiently when the jobs are scheduled into our ten workstations in such a way as to avoid long queues of jobs. But we often have times when one machine workstation will have five or six jobs waiting and other stations will be standing idle. This creates obvious inefficiencies both in terms of equipment usage and manpower utilization. The problem seems to be that the original scheduling of jobs is done by Production Control based on what they believe is the availability of time on the workstations and the delivery time promised by Marketing. Unfortunately their information is rarely up-to-date. In addition the parts required to manufacture the machine are not always in stock, and any delays in one job can affect other jobs that are in the queue behind it. To compound the problem the Marketing department together with Engineering often put pressure on us through Production Control to change the schedule of a particular job, because the customer is screaming."

"Naturally we try to accommodate Production Control's subsequent changes, but it does throw off the other scheduled jobs. Although we may get that particular job out in record time, it just passes the problem down the line so that the next week there may be one or two other jobs on the "critical" list with necessary queue jumping changes in the schedule."

Interviewer: "Overall how does that affect your productivity?"

Frank: "It certainly doesn't help. The owners want increased efficiency, but given the constraints from Marketing and Engineering it has been very difficult to make much improvement. We have 10 basic resources (workstations) to schedule, at present our average utilization is about 52%. And Marketing keeps bringing in more jobs on the over-utilized machines while some of our best equipment stands idle. To be honest with you this really irritates me! Why can't they sell some products which would soak up a bit of our excess capacity?"

Interviewer: "Do they know which workstations have excess capacity at particular times so they could concentrate on selling related products?"

Frank: "Well … in all fairness the idle workstations do vary a bit. Because of the fluctuations in the scheduling of jobs I'm not always sure where our idle capacity is located in terms of workstations and time periods. This problem of resource scheduling is a tough one and I'm not really sure how to solve it."

Interviewer: "Do you know what sort of information you would like to get out of a resource scheduling system if there were such a thing?"

Frank: "If someone wanted to design a resource scheduling system I could certainly tell them what I would need in terms of reports for myself, and I also have a few ideas as to what Production Control and Marketing could use in the way of information!!"

MARKETING

Steve Thompson (Marketing Manager) had worked hard trying to maintain the company's market share, but the market pressures and his reaction to them had painted him as the villain in a number of earlier interviews.

Interviewer: "Have a seat Steve."

Steve: "I do not have a lot of time to spare, I'm a busy man you know."

Interviewer: "The reason I rang you Steve was to discuss your information needs as marketing manager and look at some potential solutions to the problems that are facing the company. What are the biggest problems facing you and your department?"

Steve: "Primarily we face a very competitive market where price and timely delivery are the main factors. Both of these seem to be a problem here at Acme."

Interviewer: "I understand that you very often rush through "priority jobs" for key customers?"

Steve: "Yes that is right, and all Acme customers are 'key customers.'"

Interviewer: "What information would be most useful to you to avoid the need for 'rush orders' and allow you timely delivery?"

Steve: "If I knew what Acme manufacturing resource availability was, projected over the coming 2-3 months I would know what equipment to promote through our sales force. This factor together with up-to-date projected delivery times for jobs that are in the manufacturing process currently would allow me a much more accurate projection of delivery times. Naturally this would increase our esteem and integrity in the eyes of Acme customers. Cost is also a factor that has plagued us. To compete we have to keep our prices in line, but with our cost structure some sales actually lose us money. At least if we knew what our costs were going to be for a particular job we could decide whether to take the contract or not. As it stands however it is usually weeks after the tenders are due that we finally discover what cost on the job will be, and even that is usually a bit of a wild guess!"

MEETING OF POTENTIAL USERS

After interviews with department heads it was decided to call a meeting of potential users and top management to discuss the prospective information system. Included in the group which met were managers from:

Marketing
Order Entry
Manufacturing
Purchasing
Production Control
Inventory Control
Engineering
Customer Service

This group decided to form a Steering Committee for this Systems Development project. It was agreed that the first task was to discuss and enumerate the problems and develop a list of users needs and requirements for such a potential system. Some of the basic facts that came out in these early discussions including advice from consultants are included in the following information.

BASIC SYSTEM REQUIREMENTS

It is estimated that initially six VDU's will be required if a computerized installation were used, with possibilities for adding another 6 to 8 VDU's over the next five years. Only one new employee would be required, an experienced computer operator who could also do some light programming. All data entry operators would be retrained from current clerical positions and remain attached to their current user departments. Each user department would require their own dual purpose (draft quality and letter quality) high speed (200+ cps) dot matrix printer for producing reports, invoices, purchase orders etc.

Given the probable complexity of the software for the applications being considered and the need for on-line access at all times by purchasing, inventory control, marketing, and manufacturing, it is estimated that at least 6 megabytes of RAM will be required initially in any computer that might be considered. Hard disc storage capacity has yet to be estimated.

ADDITIONAL INFORMATION

The following additional points arose in these early discussions and are based on the assumption that satisfactory systems can be installed on a timely basis to overcome the basic information systems problems.

- The expected useful life of the new system is five years with salvage value estimated at 20% of initial hardware cost at the end of that period.
- Estimated cost of data conversion is based on 120 characters per minute (verified) being keyed into the database.
- Insurance is estimated to be 1.3% per year of the estimated replacement cost.
- Estimated cost of hiring a new employee is 50% of first year salary, and cost of retraining existing clericals to become data entry operators is two months salary each.
- "Off the shelf" software could be found to handle most applications but some applications would require extensive modification.
- It is believed that utilization of manufacturing equipment could be increased from the current level of 52% to 68%.
- 5% of the current cost of sales is due to the "rush" nature of many orders.
- Turnover rates could be brought into line with industry averages.
- Data Information:
    - Individual order = Prox. 400 char.
    - Engineering Specs for indiv. order = Prox. 80 char. per operation per order.
    - Individual Item of stock = Prox. 240 char.
    - Scheduling record = Prox. 160 char. per operation per order.
    - Purchase requisition = Prox. 320 char.
    - Master workstation record = 240 char. (1 for each workstation)
- Only information for the current year's orders need be "on-line" at a given time, since all data for completed orders from prior years could be loaded on to tape for storage.

STEP 2: Prepare the case for class discussion.

STEP 3: Answer each of the following questions, individually or in small groups, as directed by your instructor.

Diagnosis

1. What concerns did low profitability trigger?
2. How effective are the company's control procedures?
3. What types of information does Acme Engineering require?

Evaluation

4. What types of transaction processing systems does Acme Engineering currently use?
5. How effective are the order entry, inventory control, purchasing, project control, and resource scheduling systems?
6. How effectively do these systems interface?

Design

7. What changes should be made in the transactions processing systems at Acme Engineering?
8. What types of hardware and software would support such systems?

Implementation

9. What issues must the owners consider in upgrading the transaction processing systems?
10. What are the likely costs and benefits of such improvements?

STEP 4: In small groups, with the entire class, or in written form, share your answers to the questions above. Then answer the following questions:

1. What information need does Acme Engineering have?
2. How effectively do current systems address these needs?
3. What changes would allow the company to have its information needs met more effectively?
4. What issues should be considered in upgrading the system? ●

Activity 15 Norman Furniture Generation Ltd.

STEP 1: Read the Norman Furniture Generation Ltd. case. (This activity is especially suited for use in conjunction with Chapter 11 of *Information Systems.*)

1.0 A Depressing Meeting

Brian Robertson was far from happy and was in the process of telling the directors of Norman Furniture Generation Limited the reason for his current state of depression.

Mr. Robertson had in front of him the half-yearly financial report for NFG Ltd. (Appendix 1) and it was the contents of this which was the main contributor to his feelings.

Addressing the Financial Director, Mr. O'Connor, he said, "Peter, these are the worst figures I've ever seen. O.K. I know all about the recession but these figures reek of disaster. We're really missing the boat somewhere. If these figures don't improve by the next shareholders meeting then heads are going to roll."

Peter O'Connor had expected just such a reaction when he had prepared the interim financial report but then, as now, he felt very much at a loss as to the prime cause.

"I've been over the report Brian and hate to say it, but they all point to the recession as the reasons for our poor performance, maybe we could tighten up on costs but other than that . . . ." "That's just a poor excuse for a poor performance," replied Brian Robertson, "We have everything on our side, new factory, new machinery, good industrial relations and a damn good product range, if we can't make this work then there's no hope for any of us. As for costs that new computer of yours should be able to keep a tight enough rein on those!"

The other board members were Jim Allyn, Production Manager, Otto Gustaf, Chief Designer, Liam Murphy, Marketing, and John Butler, Personnel. Liam Murphy spoke next, "The product might be a good one but it's becoming near impossible to get retailers interested. It's not that our prices aren't competitive but that our competitors' products are simply more popular."

"Then it is to me that you place the blame!" snapped Otto Gustaf, "I design a superb product range; your salesmen just can't sell."

"Let's not start blaming each other, that's a sure road to bankruptcy. I know that in Production I have reported inability to complete some specialised orders in order to maintain capacity on our standard product range. That's been a policy adopted from our parent but maybe we need to change our thinking."

Brian Robertson had cooled off somewhat but listening to his directors he didn't like what he was hearing.

"Gentlemen," interceded Brian Robertson, "I am getting the impression that none of you know what the rest are doing. Two years ago we spent a small fortune introducing an information system and you Peter (Finance) were placed in charge of the computer. It seems to me that the one thing we don't have is an information system. If that piece of electronic junk can't do its job then we'd better get a system that can! I want an appraisal of your individual information needs by the next meeting in one month's time."

The rest of the meeting was uneventful but the directors all left with a gloomy feeling and some reservations about their own future with NFG Ltd.

This case study was compiled by T.J. Young of Sligo R.T.C. based on general experience in the problems of M.I.S. development and computerisation. All personnel are fictitious.

2.0 COMPANY BACKGROUND

Norman Furniture Generation Ltd. had been set up in Ireland three years ago as a result of pioneering work by the Industrial Development Authority (IDA) to attract wood processing companies to the West of Ireland. The parent company is Norman Wood Products Limited, a hugh establishment with its head office and main processing plant in Cleveland, Ohio. The Great Lakes provided a ready made shipping outlet as did the railway to New York. The vast forest of both hard- and softwoods to the west of the Appalachian Mountains provided an almost endless supply of raw material.

The "sell" to Norman Wood Products had been relatively easy. Along with the tax incentives, the IDA was able to offer an advanced factory, large areas of maturing forest and an attractive set of demographic statistics regarding population growth. Norman Wood Products were also committed to a move establishing manufacturing in Europe, and Ireland became a natural choice.

Norman Wood Products is an old established company set up from an amalgamation of lumbering companies of the late 19th century. It became a public concern in 1910 and was one of the largest existing wood processing concerns. Initially the work undertaken was straight lumbering and sawing but during the late twenties expanded into the area of furniture manufacture. This was achieved by the setting up of a subsidiary company, Prime Furniture Limited, of which the parent held 51% of all shares. The policy was to leave the subsidiary company to its own devices. Basically, Norman Wood Products acted simply as supplier of the wood for the furniture making company. The post war boom years of the 1950s and 1960s saw a vast expansion of Norman Wood Products with the establishment of furniture manufacturing, paper making and wood processing companies throughout North America. The policy of ownership and noninterference became a matter of course.

These policies were taken to Ireland, although Norman Furniture Generation Ltd. not only designed and manufactured its own products, but also sawed its own wood supplied by the Forestry Commission. In addition, wood not available locally was imported from Europe rather than the United States. It was up to Norman Furniture Generation to design its own products, primarily with a view to supplying the Irish market but with plans for expansion to export into Britain and the European mainland. These longer term objectives would involve expansion in size and further investment by the parent company.

2.1 Setting Up NFG Ltd.

Brian Robertson was given full autonomy for this and was moved from the board of the parent company to become Managing Director of NFG Ltd. Much of the initial planning took place in the States and consequently the advance factory at Shannon became operational within six months of Brian Robertson stepping off the plane. Local labour was readily available and only one member of the board, Otto Gustaf, had to be consulted.

The initial work involved sawing and planing timber and manufacturing chipboard and hardboard sheets. A year after this work began the first furniture products rolled off the production lines.

The current operations may be summarised as follows:

a) Sawing and planing softwood timber supplied locally.
b) Manufacturing chipboard and hardboard from "sawing waste."
c) Domestic furniture production. (See Appendix 2 for product range and description.)

2.2 Data Processing

The parent company had computerised its data processing in 1962 with a relative degree of success and Brian Robertson, a graduate of M.I.T., was familiar with the advantages of computerisation although he had not been directly involved with either the design or running of an information system. An enthusiasm for M.I.S. was brought to Ireland by Brian Robertson and consequently he had felt ready to commit NFG Ltd. to computerisation at a very early stage.

The initial production and operations of NFG had not involved a heavy D.P. burden and all functions had been manual for the first year of operation. The functions in the early days had involved payroll, purchasing, budgeting and stock control. Since the early operation did not involve customer supply but simply to stock-pile seasoning timber and chipboard, no order processing departments had been necessary. Liam Murphy had dealt with early inquiries and as furniture products became available for sale an assistant to Liam Murphy, dealing with order processing, was recruited. Effectively no order processing had been carried out on a manual basis, since the computer had been installed ready for this function.

Six months prior to the commencement of furniture manufacture, Brian Robertson had introduced the concepts of computerisation to the board. His enthusiasm influenced the other board members and generated a high level of commitment from the functional heads to EDP. The tender for the computer was won by IBM. Peter O'Connor, a qualified Chartered Accountant, was sent to England for an intensive two week course provided by IBM. Upon his return the "computer project" was handed to him by Brian Robertson, who then himself took little interest. The traditional accountancy view of Peter O'Connor, with an emphasis on budgeting and cost control, was built into the D.P. system. The administrative functions were computerised in rapid succession by the use of standard software packages. The computer, an IBM System 38 has now been installed for two years. Details of the computer system are given in Appendix 3.

3.0 PRESENT COMPANY OPERATIONS

3.1 Finance and Accounting

Peter O'Connor is the Finance Director. He is a fully qualified chartered accountant of fifteen years standing and is now forty years of age. Prior to his appointment to NFG Ltd., he had worked for an accountancy and auditing company in Galway.

He had extensive knowledge of auditing and had learnt from his dealings as an external auditor that if the costs are controlled then "the rest of the company will look after itself." Consequently, he kept tight control over budgeting and insisted on weekly expenditure breakdowns from the other departments. The ability of the computer to analyse these reports and produce a mass of financial control information had impressed him. He confessed, however, that he rarely has time to read all of the reports he receives but is confident that his Budget Controller, Frank Henry, utilises these reports within his department. A typical Department Performance Summary Report is shown in Figure 1.

3.1.1 Budgeting and Costing

Working primarily from computer reports the department is concerned with appraising the performance on a weekly basis of the individual departments and the company as a whole.

Frank Henry explains, "We are primarily concerned with negative variances. I produce a report outlining these from the computer printouts and feed the figures to Peter. In this way we can react quickly to large variances or continuing negative trends. It seems that the discrepancies in some areas are getting larger, especially those for Marketing and Sales while Production's variances are improving, if anything. I'm not sure that the budgets are in line any more but Peter is not the sort of bloke you could tell that to. You see the budgets for next year are based on an increase based on the previous year's average lending rate, plus a proportional increase, which is pretty conservative to allow for increased turnover."

1

NORMAN FURNITURE GENERATION LTD.

DEPARTMENT PERFORMANCE SUMMARY

Date . . . .

Department . . . .

Current Week				Year to Date		
Budget	Actual	Variance	Cost Category	Budget	Actual	Variance
			Materials			
			Direct Labour			
			Supplies			
			Indirect Labour			
			Taxes			
			Insurance			
			Depreciation			
			Equipment			
			Building			
			Department Total			

3.1.2 Purchasing

A daily computer produced stock for re-order report is simply matched to a preferred vendor file and orders placed accordingly. A weekly stock ledger is received and, providing there is available time, a member of the purchasing staff carries out a physical walk through and spot check. This occurs maybe 25% of the time. Twice yearly, a full inventory check takes place in order to identify discrepancies. Where they occur, the book value is adjusted manually and the EDP department notified. These adjustments are typically of the order of +/−5% of average stock held.

3.2 Production

The three main departments of sawing, chipboard manufacture and furniture manufacture are essentially independent. Where possible the timber sawing and chipboard manufacturing act as suppliers for furniture production but all of the furniture departments' needs are not met in this way, nor are all of the other departments' products totally absorbed by NFG Ltd.

The surplus sawn timber and manufactured chipboard is sold at a relatively high profit.

The policy of Norman Wood Products was always one of "push the standard lines" and this was pretty well adhered to by NFG Ltd. It was felt that this helped Marketing. In the entire operational life of NFG only a dozen or so complaints had been received regarding faulty products. In general, the products were regarded as being well designed and of high quality.

APPENDIX 1 Half-Yearly Interim Reports

(A) Trading and Profit and Loss Account

June of Current Year—6 Month Report

		Sales	
Opening Stock	200,000		
Add Purchases	622,000		
Closing Stock	244,000	Sawn Timber	100,000
Cost of Sales	578,000	Chipboard & Hardboard	300,000
Gross Profit	522,000	Furniture —	
Salaries	400,000	Bedroom	400,000
Rates	5,000	Other	300,000
Insurance	10,000	TOTAL	1,100,000
Computer-			
Rent	14,000		
Main	8,000		
Media	10,000		
Marketing	80,000		
Other Expenses	60,000		
Profit	(65,000)		
Tax	—		
Net Profit	(65,000)		

Balance Sheet

June of Current Year

Owner's Capital		**Fixed Assets**	
Owner Equity	1,000.000	Building	400,000
Retained Profit	20,000	Other	300,000
		Depreciation	(28,000)
			672,000
Current Liability	**Current Assets**	**Inventory**	
Tax	—		
Creditors	120,000		
		Timber	100,000
		Sawn Trees	50,000
		Chipboard	50,000
		Other	44,000
			244,000
		Debtors	200,000
		Cash	24,000
	1,140,000		1,140,000

The only complaint from Jim Allyn was regarding special orders, "I'd like to be able to tout for jobbing orders, say a specialist product range to equip an hotel, but we're so wrapped up in standard products that there's no chance of that. Mind you, with all the paperwork for budgeting control and inventory, there isn't much time either. Still, I've got faith in the marketing guys; there are some damn good area reps employed here."

3.3 Marketing

Liam Murphy had a reputation as a task master who expected results and usually said exactly how he felt about matters. As a Manager, he was pretty well-liked, or at least respected, and the sales team was well-organised and coordinated. In Liam Murphy's own words, the Marketing Department . . . "is there to sell products. We make or break a company and if we can't sell, then we all go under. I've negotiated good rates of commission for the salesmen and as long as they reach their quotas I'm happy. Things have been difficult with the recession, almost as hard to sell as to fill out Peter's quota and budget forms! It just means we'll have to push a bit harder."

Liam also insisted on professionally produced product brochures and good advertising campaigns. These were carried out by the Marketing Services Department who also handled customer enquiries.

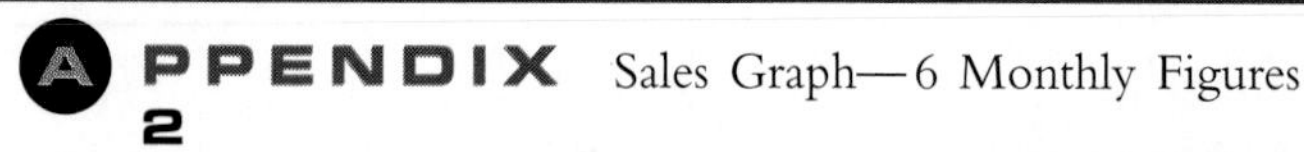

APPENDIX 2 Sales Graph—6 Monthly Figures

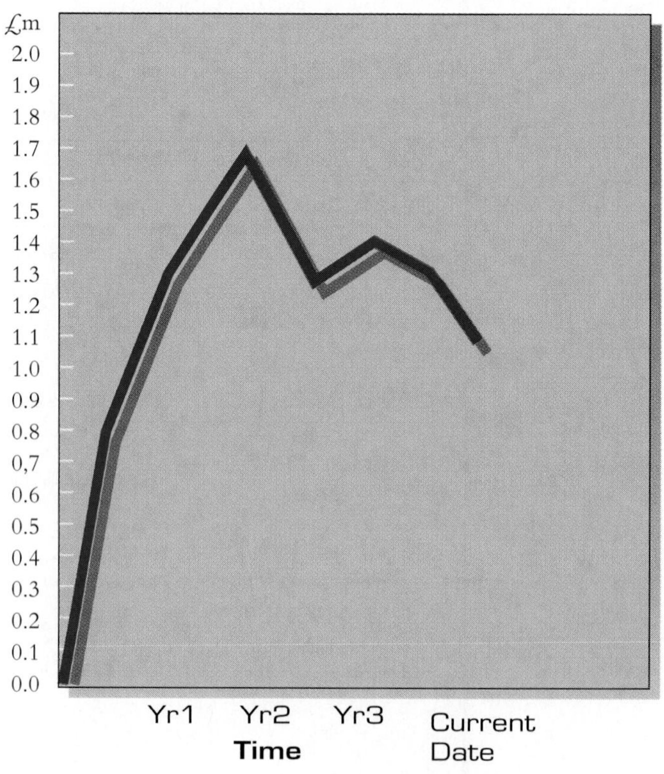

APPENDIX 3 Computer System

C.P.U.:	IBM System 38, 2MBytes Memory
Disks:	Fixed Disks with 258MBytes
Tape Drives:	4 Units; 60 I.P.S. Read
V.D.U.:	6 Units
Lineprinter:	1 Unit: 300 L.P.M.
Software:	RFG II, COBOL
Database:	Facility Part of CPU Architecture

APPENDIX 4 Report Analysis

Report	Frequency	For	Inputs	Files
Budget Variance	Weekly	Costing	–Actual Costs	–Dept. Costs File
Payroll Suite	Weekly	Wages	–Clock Cards –Overtime Slips	–Wages Master
Stock Ledger	Weekly	Production	–GRN Issues Returns	–Stock Master
Stock for Reorder	Weekly	Purchasing/Supplier	–Issues Returns GRN	–Stock Master –Vendor File –Open Order File
Invoices	Weekly	Finance/Customer	Orders	–Cust. M.F. –Finished Goods
Delivery Report	Weekly	Distribution/Customer	–Orders	–Cust. M.F. –Finished Goods
Statements	Monthly	Finance/Customer	–Orders –Cheques –Returns	–Cust. M.F.
Back Order Analysis	Monthly	Production	–Stock for Reorder –Delivery Report	–Stock Master
Bad Debts	6 Monthly	Finance	–Statements –Invoices –Cheques	–Cust. MF.
Production Schedule	Monthly	Production	–Finished Goods –Delivery Report Summary	–Finished Goods
Sales Performance	Weekly	Finance	–Sales	–Cust. M.F.
Sales/Area	Monthly	Marketing	–Sales	–Cust. M.F.

STEP 2: Prepare the case for class discussion.

STEP 3: Answer each of the following questions, individually or in small groups, as directed by your instructor.

Diagnosis

1. What information needs do the managers of finance and accounting, production, and marketing have in this company?
2. What computer systems exist to meet these needs?

Evalaution

3. What objectives should the computer system have for each functional area?
4. How well do the existing systems meet the managers' and the organization's needs?
5. Does the existing system have the characteristics of a state-of-the-art decision support system?

Design

6. What changes should be made in the existing system?
7. What reports should the new system provide?

Implementation

8. What are the likely costs and benefits of these changes?
9. Offer a schedule for implementing the changes.

STEP 4: In small groups, with the entire class, or in written form, share your answers to the questions above. Then answer the following questions:

1. What information needs exist at Norman Furniture?
2. What types of systems exist to meet these needs?
3. What changes would you propose in the system to better meet these needs?
4. What are the costs and benefits of implementing these changes? ●

Activity 16 Pinsos Galofré, S.A.

STEP 1: Read the Pinsos Galofré, S.A. case. (This activity is especially suited for use in conjunction with Chapter 11 of *Information Systems.*)

THE USE OF A DECISION SUPPORT SYSTEM IN A NEW FIELD

The chief financial officer of Pinsos Galofré S.A., Josep Cortada, was sitting behind his desk reflecting over what Fernando Vallvé, product manager in the industrial division, had just told him on the phone. They had been talking about the success their recent decision support system for animal feeding was having in the field. The latest release had now been used in the field for some time and seemd to be working well. The dealer network, althought initially very skeptical, was now using the system more and more and was even suggesting modifications to be made to the system.

Josep Cortada could still remember the day when he first became involved in the project. It had been while he was temporarily responsible for the Formulation group, which formed part of the Research and Development Department. (See Exhibit 1 for an outline of the organization.)

Quite by chance while walking about the offices one day, the general manager and himself ran across a student from the local university who was working at the company during his summer job. The student explained that he was in the finishing stages of writing a decision support program for the Sales Department. He went further to explain that some people from that Department had expressed a need for a tool to help them calculate the "ideal" food rationing for animals in farms where there was already animal food available, resulting, as byproduct, of normal farm operation.

The request had been for a program that would take into consideration the nutritional value of the products that the farmers already had, and compute the best product mix of Pinsos Galofré products to supplement those. The idea behind the request was very much in line with the overall business focus of the company, which emphasized trying to provide a total service to customers, not just selling animal food products.

It took the general manager and himself about 10 minutes to understand the problem, then he told the student: "Isn't this problem a rationing problem? In that case, why don't you use linear programming, which is what we use in the formulation processes that we run here every day?"

BACKGROUND INFORMATION

Pinsos Galofré S.A. has existed for 21 years, and has grown continuously over this period. Sales in 1985 exceeded 20,000 million pesetas.

The company consists of two operative divisions as shown in Exhibit 1. The Consumer Goods division produces and sells pet foods, while the Chow division produces and sells animal food to farmers. There are two corporate staff functions; Finance and Administration, and Research and Development.

EXHIBIT 1 Organizational Outline

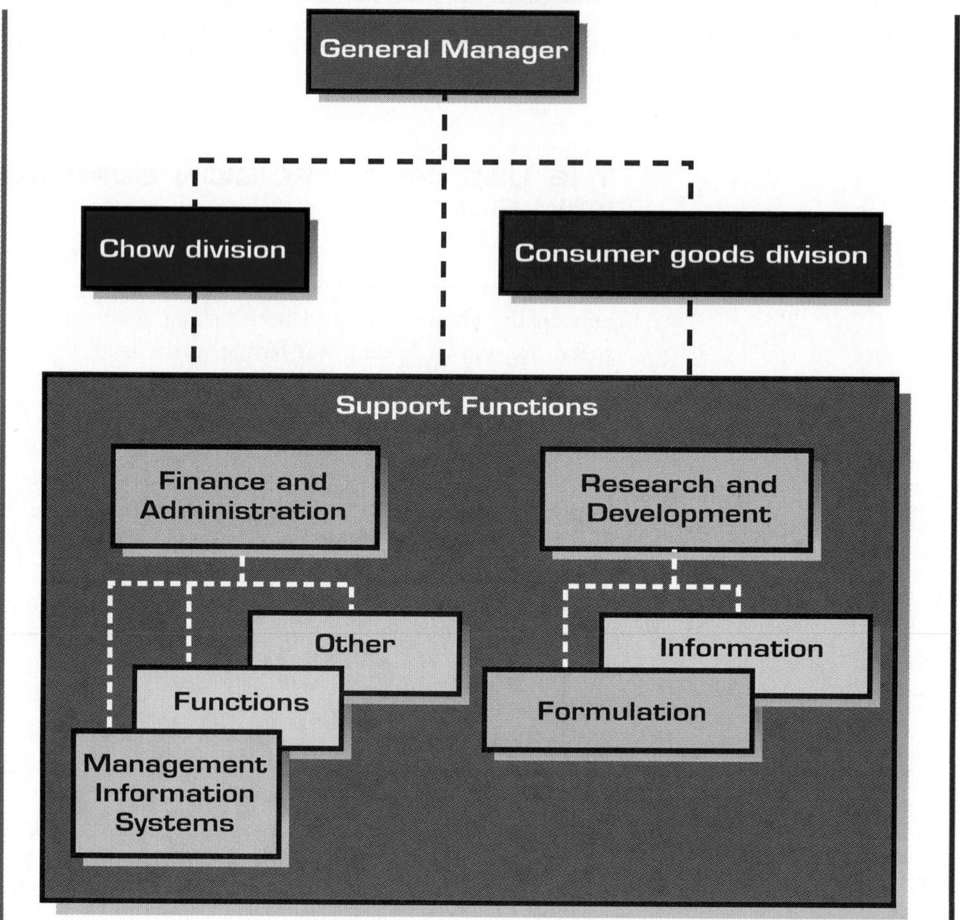

The main customers in the milk production sector of the Chow division are small to medium size farmers, although not many of them have less than 10 cows. (For an estimate of the structure of Spanish dairy farms, see Exhibit 2.) These farmers are generally too small to be able to support by themselves the services and technology that Pinsos Galofré can.

Pinsos Galofré's products are manufactured in seven factories located throughout Spain, and they are sold through a network of 500 independent dealers. The dealers can sell other products in the agricultural sector but, in virtue of an explicit agreement, not any product competing directly with those of Pinsos Galofré. This dealer network gives the company practically 100% market coverage in Spain.

From a very general standpoint, the chow or animal food business involves the following activities: buying/importing raw materials, mixing them, adding some other components, pelleting, and finally sending the products to the dealers for selling. One of the key steps in the process is the so-called "formulating" step, in which the mixings to be performed are designed. In this step, linear programming is used to a very great extent.

EXHIBIT 2 Estimated Structure of Spanish Dairy Farms in 1984

No. of cows/farm		No. of farms	Mean no. of cows	Total no.of cows
1 to	2	50,000	1.5	75,000
3 to	4	60,000	3.5	210,000
5 to	9	100,000	7	700,000
10 to	25	40,000	15	600,000
25 to	50	18,000	30	240,000
50 to	100	1,700	70	120,000
More than	100	300	133	40,000
Total		260,000	7.6	1,985,000

THE DEVELOPMENT PROCESS

In fact, the idea for the tool that the Sales Department was requesting had originated as a consequence of the good working relationship existing between the Marketing department and the Research and Development department within the Chow Products division. This was in turn due to the fact that there was a lot of interaction between the two groups. It was well understood that Marketing being directly in touch with the market, it could sense the needs there and ask for support from Research and Development, which then would come up with proposals for solutions to whatever problems were identified.

Josep Cortada explained how they had gone about developing the program package:

> The first attempt to give an answer to the problem was done back in 1984 by a student working here during the summer. He used some kind of a "rule of thumb"—heuristic—approach, which produced reasonable but unequal results. The problem with such an approach was that it could not assure an optimal solution. This led to a search for better procedures, which in turn resulted in a process of continuously adding new heuristic rules to the algorithms employed. As a consequence, the corresponding computer program was growing and growing and nobody seemed able to anticipate "how near" it was from definitive.
>
> When I first heard about the project, it struck my mind that this would be a perfect application for Linear Programming (L.P.), which is a nice tool for solving exactly these kind of problems. I had spent several years of my earlier career working in an Operations Research group in an oil company, where I was heavily involved in the development of L.P. models. Besides being a nice tool for solving the problem, linear programming would also identify an optimal solution. It was my personal opinion that a solution which was good, but not optimal—so that the farmer might be able to come up with a better one himself—would be a somewhat dangerous solution. It would never get much credibility.

He continued:

> The first thing we did after we decided to try a linear programming approach, was to experiment with an old package that I had in one of my files. Since it seemed to work, we then spent some 5 to 6 months, a few hours during the day, some evenings, and some weekends, trying to develop a prototype tool using linear programming. The most challenging aspect of this work was working out and testing the appropriate L.P. constraints. We worked with Fernando Vallvé, a product manager who used to do the hand calculations, coherently with his theoretical knowledge of nutritional constraints and the needs of the animals. Converting these rules into valid formulas that could be used in the linear programming model did not turn out to be all that easy, however. I suppose that his lack of knowledge about programming and modelling, and our lack of

> knowledge about his field made it difficult for us to communicate effectively. Eventually, however, we did manage to come up with some 10–12 valid constraints that worked well.
>
> Some of those constraints were not at all obvious. For example we had to introduce the concept of the animals' stomach, which is affected by both food weight and volume. Although these can be linked by taking into consideration the concept of food density, and this seemed to introduce non-linearities in the model. Eventually we were able to remove them, after some algebraic manipulations. This process shows, in my opinion, the importance of being able to combine biological and modelling expertise in order to be successful in this kind of work.
>
> The next step in the development was to "commercialize" the product. To make it suited for the field, a user interface had to be added, as well as reporting and recovery facilities, etc. This work took about another year to be completed, and the program was introduced in the field late in 1985.

The introduction into the field was not totally without problems. Most farmers, as well as many of the dealers, had never touched a computer before. When they were told that a "hi-tech" product like this computer package was going to be used as a tool to solve their day to day practical problems, their response was only: "You can't be serious!" It took some time to sell the idea to the people in the field, and a lot of effort had to be put into training both salespeople and the dealers.

The second version of the program, which was released about half a year later, included a post optimal analysis facility, which allowed users to perform sensitivity analyses. More specifically, it would show by how much some characteristics of a critical component would have to change in order to trigger its inclusion (or exclusion) from the optimal blend, and it could also provide answers to the question of why a specific component was not included in the optimal blend. The program package used two data files, one specifying the different Pinsos Galofré products, and the other defining the different by-products that the farmers might have. In the latest version of the package, each different customer could be represented in this second file with his own products.

Regarding the experience after having completed the project, Josep Cortada commented:

> In order to succeed in a development process like this, certain conditions need to be fulfilled. You normally need to have experts in different fields who are able to communicate and work well together. In addition, you also need to have some "generalist" who can see the project as a whole, and be able to lead it in the right direction. We were lucky to have all these criteria reasonably fulfilled.

There have been requests to extend the package so that it can better fulfill its users' needs. For example, somebody who has different types of cattle, for milk and meat production, wanted the program extended so that it would be capable of taking both categories into consideration. However, these types of requests turn out to require integer programming, and thus have not been attended yet.

WHY A DECISION SUPPORT SYSTEM?

Fernando Vallvé, product manager, commented on why the decision support system was introduced:

> First of all it was the natural thing to do, given our business approach. Our dealers are trained to give the farmers a good service. The farmers have different products and by-products on their farms which combined with our products can give complete nutrition for their animals. We wanted to introduce the concept of total cost for the farmer. To obtain this, we needed to identify a balanced diet. An unbalanced diet contains a surplus of certain components, which are thus wasted. What our dealers needed was a powerful tool to analyze what would be the cheapest and best way to combine the different nutritional components available. Since we had the appropriate tool within the company, namely linear programming, and also had the technical

> skills required in form of the vets and technicians, the whole thing seemed only natural. Combining these factors with the aid of a PC, we could provide the powerful tool required. Chow or animal food is to a very great extent a commodity business. By introducing this decision support system, we differentiated ourselves from our competitors, introducing higher efficiency and quality. It improved our image and built confidence amongst our customers.

Josep Cortada added:

> You might say that the introduction of this decision support system in a field where this technology until then had been very little used, was a strategic one. Strategic in the sense that we wanted to use this technology to provide better service, and by this we believed that we would gain competitive advantage. Personally, I believe that computer systems today should be used as much as possible to move the decision support systems closer to the field.

After the start-up difficulties—train people in the use of the package, etc.—were circumvented, the system was an immediate success. Dealers and customers were very pleased with the service it provided. There were several "success stories" and the program turned out to be quite "creative" in the sense that it came up with feasible solutions that nobody had thought of before. Like one farmer put it: "I'd never thought that a cow could eat this much of this by-product and still produce the normal amount of milk!"

In some cases, the Pinsos Galofré representative believed that the genetic capacity of the animals had been underestimated. By providing a better balanced feeding plan using the package, the production of these animals had indeed been improved. The program was used a lot and the dealers said that they were able to sell more because of this improved service. Specific sales increases were difficult to measure though, since sales were very dependent on what the farmers were growing themselves, which in turn depended, amongst other things, on the weather.

Overall, however, customers were very pleased, since they could now go to the dealer, run the program in less than ten minutes, try several options, etc., and thus use the package as a tool for themselves to arrange the optimal feeding plan for their animals. They were also in this way able to include their by-products in their feeding plans. In addition, if the nutritional contents of a farm by-product is unknown, Pinsos Galofré can also offer analysis services to establish this with accuracy.

About advantages of the decision support package the Chief Financial Officer comments:

> One PC can easily handle many products, which means that we can become more flexible, and be able to supply more "customized" products. The package can also be used to indicate what kind of products we should sell in different regions, and thus it can help us in this context to make product decisions which eventually will make us more competitive. By designing products "customized" for a specific region, we will be able to sell a blend that together with the farmers' components will make a very cheap total package for the farmers. In this way we will be able to adapt our product offer to the characteristics of different regions. Eventually, both the farmers and ourselves will be better off by this; the farmer getting cheap feeding and we getting competitive advantage. There is also another important factor in the feeding of cows in which the program can be of help. The production of the cows may, to a certain degree, vary between a maximum and a minimum depending on how they are fed. This fact can be used by the program to suggest different feeding programs for different market situations.

THE SITUATION IN JUNE 1986

On the question of how we viewed the situation in June 1986, Josep Cortada answered:

> We're quite content with the situation as it is right now. We have improved our customer service, and we are now ahead of our competitors in the use of this kind of new technology in our field. However, we cannot expect this situation to last forever. There are already some soft-

> ware companies delivering similar, although not comparable, packages, and we must of course expect some kind of reaction from the competition. There are limitations to what we can do to stay ahead of the competition, since we don't feel we have the resources to keep a person working full time on the use of information technology in this area. Today some 200 of our 500 dealers have installed a PC and are using this package regularly.

After his very optimistic conversation with the product manager, Josep Cortada was wondering what the future would bring in relation to the advantages they could gain from the use of this software package. . . .

Some three years had passed since the introduction of the last version of the decision support system for feeding of animals. Thinking back on what had happened over those years, Josep Cortada thought that most of it had been inevitable.

First of all, their major competitors had come up with similar packages. There were several software packages in the market which could do similar things, although they were not as complete as Pinsos Galofré's system. In addition, some local public institutions in Catalonia and Navarra had started projects to develop similar tools for the farmers, which would be offered for free, as a means to support growth in the farming sector. In this respect it seemed that the kind of computer tool that Purina had developed some years earlier was turning into an almost commonplace product. However, the "Galofré System" still had some advantages. Josep Cortada explained:

> In our system we have a file including all our products, and we can run the program and test against all these specific products to find the optimum solution. Other programs will be a lot more difficult to use in this respect. For instance, the programs provided so far are very general, and try to take all possibilities into consideration. There is also the problem related to the constraints that have to be specified in the program. We spent a lot of time and effort working out the different constraints, and I know that we have some constraints included in our program which are not present in some of the other similar packages. These constraints are of prime importance to the "goodness" of the program. Our program is also very user friendly and oriented towards the specific task it is supposed to solve. Take for example the way we solved the rounding problem. In the field you cannot operate with 10.0035 kilograms of grass. Therefore our program rounds these numbers off and tells how this affects the constraints given. Some other software packages just leave the decimals in, leaving the farmer with an impossible mixing and measuring job, without saying anything about what will happen if the blend doesn't come out exactly as prescribed.

In addition to the advantages of a good software package, Pinsos Galofré had an advantage of having a good dealer network. In the chow business the most important measure of quality is the "guaranteed quality" offered at any time. The customers know they can rely on Purina to support all their needs; they have tried the package and know that it works. As a consequence, the customers will be reluctant to change to somebody else's software packages and products.

Purina is currently the market leader in its field in Spain. Fernando Vallvé, the product manager of Pinsos Galofré, was wondering what, if anything, he should do to keep the competitive edge the company had in the market. Should he look into new ways to get competitive advantage? If so, how? Would an extended use of information systems be a proper way to go to try and achieve this competitive advantage?

STEP 2: Prepare the case for class discussion.

STEP 3: Answer each of the following questions, individually or in small groups, as directed by your instructor.

Diagnosis

1. What information needs was the decision support system designed to meet?

Evaluation

2. How well does the existing system meet the managers' and the organization's needs?
3. What factors influenced the components of the decision support system?
4. Does the existing system have the characteristics of a state-of-the-art decision support system?
5. What has been the impact of the existing system?

Design

6. Should any changes be made in the existing system?

Implementation

7. How should changes be made?

STEP 4: In small groups, with the entire class, or in written form, share your answers to the questions above. Then answer the following questions:

1. What information needs exist at Pinsos Galofré?
2. What types of systems exist to meet these needs?
3. What changes would you propose in the systems to better meet these needs?
4. What are the costs and benefits of implementing these changes? ●

Activity 17 Executive Information System Design for Frito Lay

STEP 1: Read the following scenario. (This activity is especially suited for use in conjunction with Chapter 11 of *Information Systems.*)

Back in 1930, our founder, Herman Lay, did everything. He bought and cooked the potatoes, packaged the chips and put them in his truck, brought them to the stores, and sold them. He did his own quality control: if people yelled at him when he went back the next day, he knew his chips didn't taste good. He had his accounts payable in one pocket and his accounts receivable in the other, and he could tell just by patting his pockets if he could afford to buy a few more potatoes or maybe a newer, bigger truck.

Herman was in constant touch with the marketplace. And so the company grew, took in partners, and built a group of strong regional companies, each of which put out products different from all of the others.

And then, in the 1960s, things began to change. Frito Lay merged with PepsiCo and, like other large companies at the time, emphasized its size and scale. It entered the era of national products, TV commercials, and professional management.

Built on functional excellence and high productivity, supported by national consumer polls, the company prospered. But, in the early 1980s, the competitive environment changed again. Small, regional companies geared to local tastes began to emerge, and large companies, especially those that could not move quickly, began to have problems. Because their frame of reference was national, the large companies were not focused on regional marketplaces and on the delivery outlets, or channels, for their products.

But advances in technology now make it possible for large companies like Frito Lay to return to the regional approach, to be in close touch with their customers, and to let people at every level of their organizations understand the dynamics of what they do and how what they do affects their companies' balance sheets. And they are able to do this while maintaining consistency in the quality of their products and the marketing leverage of well-known brand names.

Here's how we're doing it at Frito Lay.

BUSINESS VOLUME AND VELOCITY

One of the two most critical aspects of Frito Lay's business is volume. We sell four to five billion bags of our various products each year and move them from 40 plants through 10,000 salespeople into 400,000 stores. We had to master volume early on.

The second element critical to our business is velocity. Since we sell impulse items, we need very high service levels and penetration. If you walk by a shelf and our product is there, you'll buy it. But if it's not there, you won't go elsewhere and look for it. Furthermore, our product has a shelf life of 35 days, so we build very small warehouses. We invented "just-in-time" manufacturing because, if nothing left the warehouses for three days, our storage facilities would be full. At the other extreme, if production were to stop, the entire system would be empty in 10 days.

Excerpted and reprinted with permission from Charles S. Feld, Directed decentralization: The Frito Lay story, *Financial Executive,* November/December, 1990, pp. 22–25.

COMPLEXITY

Up to the early 1980s, our business wasn't very complex. We had national patterns. We were predictable. A bag of Doritos bought in New York tasted exactly the same as a bag of Doritos in California. We had an orderly process of building and implementing our annual plan, measuring its results, analyzing what worked and what didn't, and making the requisite changes. We had 10,000 employees in 40 plants who did their jobs very well.

Then the world changed, and, as our regional competitors got stronger, we kept introducing new marketing programs in the belief that we had to become less predictable if we were to be competitive. The problem was, as we became less predictable to our competitors, we also became less predictable to our own plants and sales force. So we had lots of short runs, shipped product by air quite often, and ran promotions on Thursday for a product that didn't arrive until the following Monday. As we shrank our cycle time, our business system became increasingly dysfunctional.

SYSTEMATIC CHANGES

To become flexible and sensitive to the local marketplaces while continuing to maintain national standards of quality and service meant we had to make changes to our business culture, organization, and infrastructure. We had to get off all paper systems, off the functional orientation, off the annual planning cycle. We needed to be a "short-cycle" company, and so we embarked on a seven-year program to completely rewire our information system. And, because our budget was essentially flat, we had to fund this project largely through the greater efficiency it produced.

We decided to build our new information system around three major frameworks: a planning and analysis system, an operational transactional system, and an executive decision support system.

THE PLANNING AND ANALYSIS SYSTEM

The planning system is really a system for measurement. These measurements give us the chance to think about our company as sales, the same way small regional companies think about their businesses.

The planning system contains detailed data from each locality: its P&L, products, and promotion and pricing proposals. We also buy sales records from supermarket scanners, which contain information about our own products as well as those of our competitors. With this information, we can spot trends; we can begin to plan.

These data can be recalled by locality, by brand, or by distribution channel. All our field, brand, and channel managers have instant access to these data; if the competition appears to be gaining ground, our managers can immediately plan the appropriate promotion or pricing strategies. And, because the system tells everyone what is going on, our people in purchasing, manufacturing, and logistics can speedily implement any such plan.

In order to facilitate all this interaction, we built a lot of different technologies into the system so that users don't have to hunt for product codes or location numbers; nor do they need more than basic computer skills.

THE TRANSACTIONAL SYSTEM

With our regional products, specialty brands, and the promotions we run at different times in different cities, our business has become very complex. If sales and operations are not in sync with each other, the plants will overship or undership products because they have to guess about demand, and then they end up airshipping or sending trucks out half empty. But because every one of our 10,000 salespeople has a hand-held computer through which he or she processes orders, we are able to coordinate sales and production effectively.

The goal of the transactional system is a constantly updated database that covers every inventory point. It will show what shipments left the plants yesterday and that today's shipments will be delivered tomorrow. Everyone who needs to, knows exactly where every bag of Doritos is. In due course, we will try to tie our suppliers into this network also.

Despite our short cycle time, this network of databases will allow us to anticipate sales and to meet our sales orders 99.5 percent of the time without having to do short runs at the plants. An additional benefit of the system is that all the actuals get posted into each region, channel, and brand where they belong—every bag, every check request, every gallon of gas that comes through the operational systems. Having these data in one place, rather than scattered throughout the company, gives us an immediate readout, allowing us to build forecasts.

THE EXECUTIVE DECISION SUPPORT SYSTEM

It's not unusual these days for a large company to install an executive support system. Usually, such a system is available only to the 20 or so top executives. What is unusual about our system is its pervasiveness throughout the company.

In this, the fourth year of our systems project, 120 people are linked through PCs, but we expect to reach our intended total of 600 in a year or so—our senior staff and field managers at all levels nationwide. We call it directed decentralization, where decisions at every level can be made quickly and from a well-informed perspective. Everybody sees immediately where he or she stands.

Much of the project so far has been involved in getting our measurement system in place, which we have done. With our old system, we used to spend our time measuring things, but we didn't have time to analyze our findings. Now our measurement is done in a day and we have the time to find out what all this information means. Why are we losing market share? Where did our plans go off, by how much, and why?

The system has also shown us how to eliminate unproductive effort. We haven't been forced to lay off people; rather, we have converted unproductivity into value-added activity.

We are also building analytical capability into the system, such as the set of rules that watches the competitive data. Our system software can, for example, examine the data loaded into our system from the supermarket scanners and send off an alarm when it picks up a new product. If the system picks up a new product in, for instance, St. Louis, it alerts our division manager in St. Louis, the brand manager of our competing product, and our senior staff. We track the success of the new product, and we can begin to develop our own new product if we feel it's necessary.

And so we're back to Herman Lay again. He knew about a change in his market as soon as it happened. With our new system, so do we. Information quickly moves up in the organization, and just as quickly down. Clear and immediate information is available at every level, and communication is constant and continuous. The world will never be simple again. Nor will it be predictable.

STEP 2: Individually or in small groups, develop a proposal for the contents of an executive information system for Frito Lay. The proposal should identify the needs of the president and CEO at Frito Lay, the objectives of the EIS, its components, and its outputs.

Directed Decentralization: How It Works

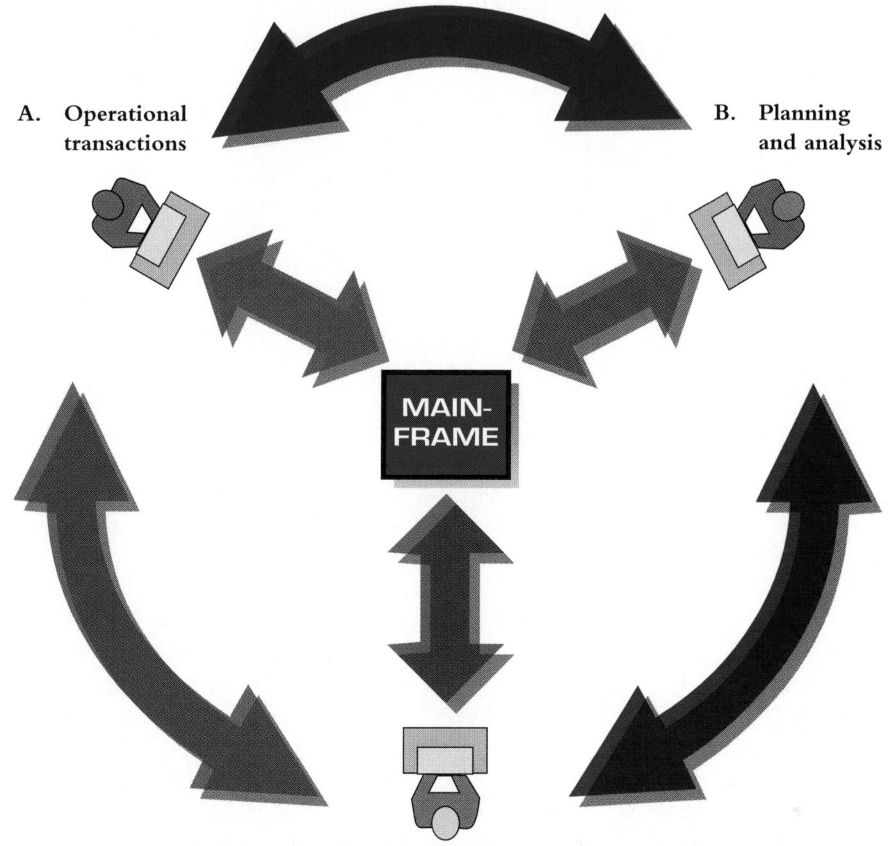

Frito Lay's system is built on a relational database. Any information entered into the system is immediately accessible to all users:

A. *A salesman processes an order on his hand-held computer. The purchasing, manufacturing, and logistics facilities are notified immediately and begin processing the order. Each successive transaction is entered as it occurs; that is, the company can track where the order is in manufacturing, when it left the plant, and when it will be delivered.*

B. *At the same time, this information is available to the planning and analysis system. This allows the brand manager, the channel manager and the area manager to spot trends in consumption. Competitive information from supermarket scanners is also fed into the mix, enabling managers to see their markets in wider perspective and to develop appropriate strategies to respond to market needs.*

C. *This information, broader and more general in scope, becomes instantly available to top management. This allows managers to understand what is going on throughout the company, where the firm is losing market share, and why. This in turn allows the executive process to enter the picture sooner and with greater impact.*

STEP 3: In small groups or with the entire class, share your proposals. Then answer the following questions:

1. What are the top executives' needs at Frito Lay?
2. What elements should be included in the EIS?
3. What issues should be considered in designing an EIS? ●

Activity 18 Implementing Business Process Reengineering: A Case Study

STEP 1: Read "Implementing Business Process Reengineering: A Case Study." (This activity is especially suited for use in conjunction with Chapter 12 of *Information Systems.*)

PAYOFF IDEA. A business process reengineering project at Blue Cross and Blue Shield of Massachusetts illustrates the fundamental precept of empowering employees to act on their own. Information technology, including a departmental LAN and client-server enabled the business change. This article describes both the organizational and IT shift needed to support the new business concepts. The IS department's role (and its failings) offers lessons for IS managers seeking greater involvement in line management–directed business reengineering.

INTRODUCTION

Health care and health care costs have become a national priority. The current economic environment, an aging population, and the advances in extensive and expensive medical treatment are having a revolutionary impact on companies in the health insurance field. There are many more options, choices, and combination packages as well as ever-changing government and state regulations and programs. Like many industries, the health insurance field is going through a volatile deregulation phase.

The 1990 annual report of Massachusetts Blue Cross and Blue Shield set the stage for a business process reengineering effort to create a new company, one that is open to change, able to react quickly and aggressively, able to offer an integrated line of health plans in a coordinated manner, and competitive in both benefit costs and administrative costs. This case study describes how information technology was used in the company's effort to reengineer its organization and, in particular, its approach to marketing. The experience draws lessons for the IS department and its involvement in business process reengineering programs initiated by business management.

COMPANY BACKGROUND

Massachusetts Blue Cross and Blue Shield is an old-line company in the health care field. It offers health maintenance organization (HMO) plans, preferred provider organization (PPO) plans, and traditional health plans. Premiums earned in 1990, when the reengineering program began, were in excess of $3 billion. The company employs some 6,000 people.

Starting out in a highly regulated portion of the industry, the company operates in a rapidly changing environment with new competitors, new products and services, and ever-increasing demands from its customers. In addition to such broad-based competitors as Aetna, John Hancock, Prudential, and various HMOs, there are niche players, including organizations that assume benefit management for a company and provide other services. The companies they service expect a reduced rate from their insurers.

Massachusetts Blue Cross was experiencing an eroding market, declining sales, and strained service levels. It had a high cost structure and an organization that reflected a traditional

Source: Written by Fay Donohue-Rolfe, Vice-President, Plan Initiatives, Massachusetts Blue Cross and Blue Shield, Boston, MA; Jerome Kanter, Director, Center for Information Management Studies, Babson College, Babson Park, MA; Mark C. Kelley, Vice-President, Small Business and Select Markets Division, Massachusetts Blue Cross and Blue Shield, Boston, MA. Auerbach Publications,

hierarchical business with multiple layers of management. The combination of a heightened competitive structure and reduced sales effectiveness because of an inability to reach new markets was having a marked business impact. The company was losing members within its accounts as well as entire accounts.

The Marketing Organization

The marketing organization was based on geographical territory within Massachusetts. A salesperson might have 300 accounts ranging from companies having 1 to 4 members, to small businesses with 5 to 24 members, to larger accounts. The salespeople had complete cognizance over their territories, servicing accounts, acquiring new business, and retaining existing business. Customer contact has traditionally been through the salespeople, who make frequent calls and handle all questions and matters of their clients either in person, over the phone, or in writing.

At the start of 1990, there were 140 salespeople and a support staff of more than 300. The marketing organization was organized into seven regional sales offices ranging from 15 to 60 employees, with several levels of management. A sales office handled multibillion-dollar high-technology companies as well as local business that fell into its territory. The seven regional offices were organized strictly by geographic territory. The other groups with direct sales responsibilities were the national accounts sales office, which sold to certain large and designated Massachusetts corporations, and separate offices for two extremely large accounts, General Electric and NYNEX. Four other groups—marketing communications, advertising, sales and service training, and marketing information systems—provided support to the sales offices.

The IT Support Infrastructure

The technical computer infrastructure that supported the sales offices was a carryforward from the traditional centralized mainframe environment (see Exhibit 1a). In the case of Massachusetts Blue Cross Blue Shield (BC/BS), there were two incompatible mainframes and two incompatible minicomputers. One mainframe housed the master data base for companies, institutions, and individual members. This system was used to calculate rates, enroll and bill new and current customers, and process renewals of existing customers. The other mainframe processed claims from groups, individuals, doctors, and hospitals. One of the minicomputers was installed to handle the new HMO and PPO insurance while the other was used for accessing marketing data bases and prospect information (a system known as Marketrieve).

These systems progressed over the years from primarily a batch COBOL orientation to an online mode with terminals (not personal computers) installed in the sales offices. The terminals connected to the claims mainframe were on each desk, but there were only one or two terminals per office connected to the group data mainframe. There were even fewer terminals for the HMO processor. The different security access codes and protocols for the mainframes and minicomputers resulted in a specialization among the office staff.

Questions concerning claims, membership, enrollments, and rates were routed to the sales office handling the account. As might be expected, in this technical environment, few, if any, calls can be answered on the spot if access to one or more mainframes is required. If a particular salesperson or administrator is not available, the call must be returned later. Processing a service call can require multiple hand-offs to different administrators. In essence, although the systems have online terminals, the process is still essentially batch oriented. A major effort has been under way by the central IS department to replace the two mainframes with a single unit that would handle both group data and claims processing, but this has proved difficult and costly to implement.

IT Support Infrastructure Before and After Reengineering

Desk Terminals

Group Data Mainframe (IBM)

Claims Processing Mainframe (Bull)

HMO Processor (DEC)

Marketrieve (DEC)

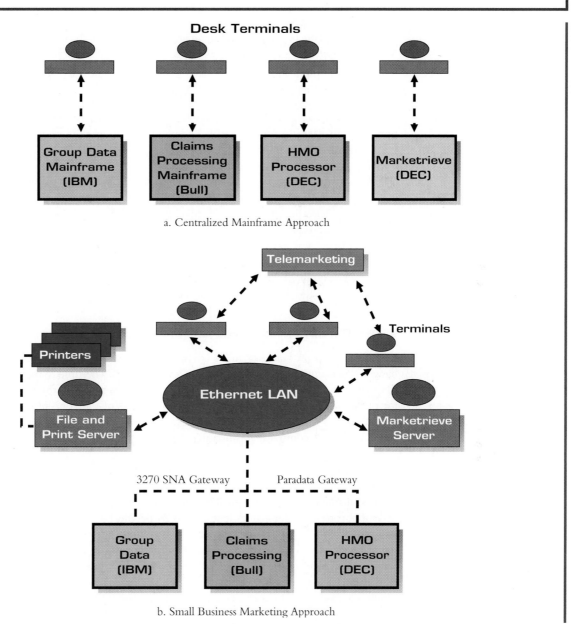

a. Centralized Mainframe Approach

Telemarketing

Terminals

Printers

File and Print Server

Ethernet LAN

Marketrieve Server

3270 SNA Gateway

Paradata Gateway

Group Data (IBM)

Claims Processing (Bull)

HMO Processor (DEC)

b. Small Business Marketing Approach

The Small Business Marketing Group

An initial study area in the change initiative was the small business market segment, defined as companies with 5 to 24 employees. Small account losses had been averaging 14% a year. Senior management realized that new business practices were a necessity for survival. The need was compelling and changes had to be made quickly, according to the findings of an in-depth consultant study done at the end of the previous year.

THE DECISION TO REENGINEER

External pressures drove the small business marketing project. First, the consultants had senior management attention. By mid-1990, the marketing vice-president knew that January 1991 would be a high renewal month and crucial period for sales. Presentations of 1990 results were scheduled to be made to senior management and the board of directors at year's end. Marketing wanted a success story to tell by that time. The marketing VP evaluated options and decided to spin off small business accounts to a separate sales force that would use telemarketing techniques.

This change involved breaking several deep-seated corporate tenets. Telemarketing and teleservicing were culturally unacceptable to Massachusetts Blue Cross. The strong assumptions were that health insurance is too complex to sell over the phone and relationship selling is essential. A key ingredient was a sales force dedicated to a specific market segment, breaking down the long-standing geographic territory concept for new business sales. A crucial part of the new strategy was a customer focus; indeed "customer driven" became the battle cry throughout the project.

From the start, the project was business driven. Marketing took the initiative, conducting customer and prospect surveys that showed that a direct sales force was not needed if policy information was available on an accurate and timely basis by telephone. The marketers knew enough about telemarketing to realize it could be the technological enabler; however, the change required a major organizational shift as well as a major information technology shift to support the new business concepts.

REENGINEERING THE ORGANIZATION

The decision to proceed was made by July 1990 and was quickly followed by a $2 million budget (indicating the project had senior-level support). The time frame was seven weeks for the new department to become operational. The marketing director was appointed director for the project. The project director had a solid grasp of the conceptual, strategic, and practical elements of the program and the ability to implement plans. The seven-week time period was a significant constraint in initiating the project.

The Self-Managed Work Team Model

Exhibit 2 represents the new sales department organization with the spin off of the small business marketing office. The small business office was originally given responsibility for sales and support to small companies having 5 to 24 people, but this was later expanded to include companies with 1 to 4 people and extended to companies with 25 employees. The remaining accounts were organized into five regional offices; national accounts were combined in a single unit, as were the four support units. Not only were the direct reports to the VP of marketing reduced to four, but the organization levels within the units were reduced and simplified. Five levels of management were truncated into two.

By September, 20 people were hired for the new department. Four team leaders were designated. The project director delegated the recruitment and hiring of the people so that the project director only reviewed finalists after they had been screened. The people were chosen on the basis of their sales abilities (not necessarily insurance) and their experience with telemarketing. The stated objective was to hire and train leaders, not managers, who could facilitate self-managed work teams. The goals were to reengineer people, systems, and attitudes to empower people to act, and to provide the technology base they needed. The 20 people started a six-week training program, focusing on product, process, and the information systems that would play a vital role in the new marketing approach.

Senior management made a substantial investment to accommodate the major cultural change by providing an extensive education program, both up front and continuing. Cur-

EXHIBIT 2 The Reengineered Marketing Organization

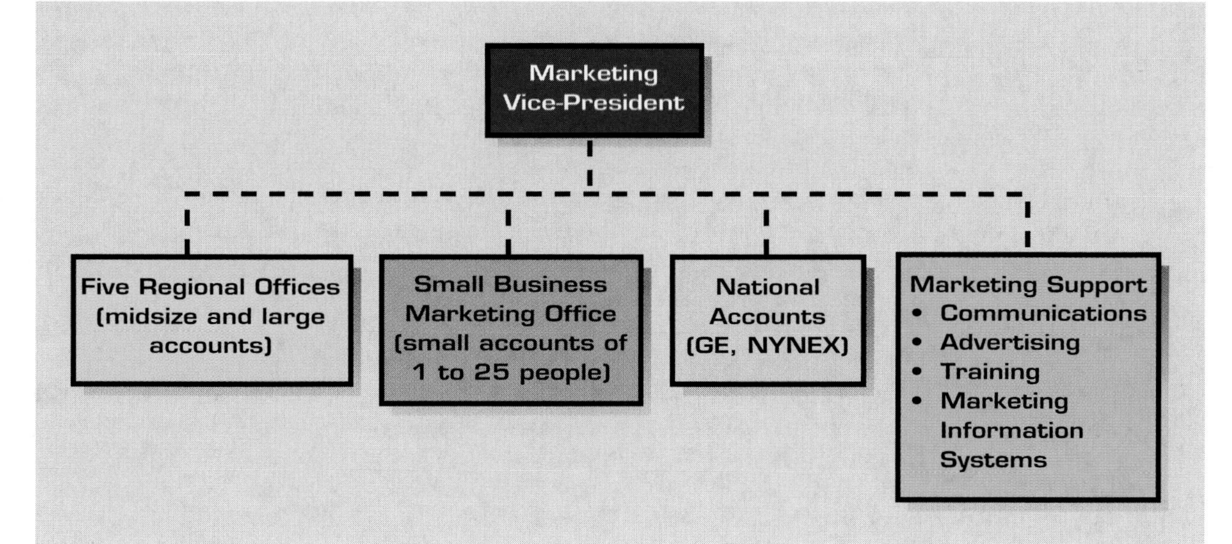

rently, the department allocates one day a week after-hours time for a training session. Team communication and team building, which promotes the individual review of one another's work while suggesting alternate ways of accomplishing work, are important elements of the new organization. Work and results are shared. On the sales floor, for example, graphs of performance versus quota and other key indicators of group performance are displayed. In addition, the first-ever incentive system has been established.

REENGINEERING THE TECHNOLOGY

In concert with the staff, the project director, who before the program started had never used a personal computer, created the systems requirements. The project director assigned an internal IS specialist who had been a member of an experimental four-person telemarketing unit that was eventually disbanded. However, the IS specialist's experience was limited to spreadsheet and word processing software.

The small business marketing group gave its requirements to several outside vendors who were hands-on implementers, rather than to the traditional planners and consultants. The official in-house IS response was to develop an RFP, but this would take too long. The IS department worked with the project director on the evaluation and selection of the vendor; from that point on, it was a team proposition.

Line Management Leadership

The project director relied on IS because of the complex interconnections that the new system would have with the existing data bases. The real challenge was to have a single IBM-compatible terminal with a Windows interface capable of tapping into the available information from the two disparate mainframes and the two minicomputer systems. In addition, the 20 telemarketers needed to be linked by a local area network (LAN) to share current information on a client-server type architecture. The project director selected the graphical interface Windows as the common interface (at the consultant's recommendation) rather than opening up the decision on interface selection, because that would potentially jeopardize the deadline. The new system was scheduled to be in operation by the end of October 1990.

The systems designer assigned to assist and provide the central IS resources needed by the small business group expressed concern at the beginning and skepticism that the project could be carried out. At first, the support from the IS group was limited because it already had a sizable work backlog. The central IS group had been working on a multiyear, $50 million project to combine the two mainframe systems onto a single integrated platform, and to completely realign IT to the business. Five years later and many million dollars over budget, the project was still far from completion. With this history, it was difficult for the system designer to believe that a project directed by department people with scant computer background and involving several technologies new to the company could meet successful completion within seven weeks.

IS acknowledged, however, the benefits of the system, both from what the application could do from a business standpoint and also from a pure IS cost perspective. Replacing four terminals with one would have a significant impact on hardware and software costs, training, and support. However, numerous problems occurred during the course of the implementation.

The Reengineered Systems

An Ethernet LAN was installed that allowed direct linkage using Windows 3.0 into both the group data mainframe and claims mainframe (See Exhibit 1b) and the HMO minicomputer (implemented subsequent to the October 1990 start-up). In addition, the Marketrieve system, which was acquired from a software company, was modified from its previous use and was connected to the LAN. The files are tailored for Massachusetts businesses. All sales representatives use this file and add their notes on individual prospects to afford continuity for themselves and their colleagues as the sales campaign unfolds. These files are accessible by anyone on the LAN and have been instrumental in the highly successful new business sales produced by the small business marketing group.

In addition to accessing the two mainframes and the minicomputer, the group has its own client-server that allows the sharing of five laser printers and other resources, including E-mail, word processing, spreadsheets, and data bases. Because of the instant access from the desk workstation to the various remote data bases and to notes that have been appended to the individual account file from previous calls and contacts, any of the sales and support people can handle an inquiry. If everyone is on the phone at a particular time, the caller has the option of waiting or leaving a voice message.

Exhibit 1b appears more complex than the original architecture (Exhibit 1a), but to the user, a transformation has occurred in simplicity and ease of use. The complex interconnectivity is transparent to the user.

PROJECT OUTCOME: GREATER EFFECTIVENESS AT LOWER COST

The results of the new dedicated telemarketing sales team with rapid access to account information have been impressive. Previously, an inquiry may have gone through six people before a response was made. Now one person handles the inquiry and in a far more expeditious manner.

By the end of 1990, according to the annual report, the small business group made almost 13,000 prospect calls. Sales totaled 73 new medical groups and 13 new dental groups, representing a total of 1,001 members. The unit established itself as an important contributor to the company's future success.

Results continue to be impressive, both on the qualitative side and the quantitative side. A year later, in the small business market there was a cost saving of $4.7 million (costs of running the old process less cost of the reengineered process), or 62%, a sales increase of 24%, a sales-retention increase of 6%, with total additional revenue of $22 million. The group made 86,000 prospect calls in 1991, a figure equal to the previous five years. Quality of service has also improved. Calls are recorded and timed. No caller waits longer than 45 seconds and 90% of the inquiries are resolved in one call of five to eight minutes. Those calls that require correspondence are handled in less than five days.

Organizational and Operational Results

A walk through the 15th floor of the Massachusetts BC/BS building, where the small business marketing group operates, reveals an open office environment with individual cubicles for managers, team leaders, and customer service representatives. There is little to distinguish who is who, based on office size or location. There are no technicians or IT professionals on site, although the LAN network is quite complex. One of the team leaders acts as the IT liaison and local network manager. All network or technical questions go to this individual, who now handles about 80% of the problems. Other problems are routed to another IT liaison in the personal computer applications area, situated on another floor.

The horizon of the small business marketing group keeps expanding and the entrepreneurial spirit has become more pervasive. The group continually searches for opportunities to improve its existing business and for new areas to apply telemarketing/teleservicing skills. It is a classic case of what can happen when the individual is empowered.

Technically, the group is in the process of installing fax capability at the workstation to reduce the time away from the phone. Another development is to enhance the client-server to have more of the customer data available locally instead of having to access the mainframe. However, the accomplishments made in such a short period are a strong motivator to the small business marketing group that these extensions will materialize.

LESSONS LEARNED FOR THE INFORMATION SYSTEMS ORGANIZATION

It is interesting to review the role of IS (or its lack of a role) in this example of business process reengineering. Although there is a large central IS organization at Massachusetts Blue Cross/Blue Shield, there was scant participation by IS professionals in the implementation. The central IS group was preoccupied with a major conversion of its old legacy systems into a new hardware/software platform. The impetus for reengineering was initiated and led by the functional department, in this case, the small business marketing group.

Business Goals Drive IS Development

The first lesson learned is that the leadership for reengineering must come from those closest to the business process affected. The marketing group dealt directly with outside consultants and software developers; there was only one central IS participant in the project. In retrospect, greater IS involvement would have alleviated problems that later arose in connecting to the central system. In this case, IS missed the opportunity to recognize the scope and importance of the new approach and to become more actively involved.

The driving force in this example, as it is in most cases, is the need to become business competitive. Information technology is the enabler, not the driver. The technology used need not be the most advanced technology on the market; many successful users of IT apply common technology uncommonly well. This is not a case study about technology: it is about business change in the way a company markets its product. Information technology has enabled the company to tap into systems that were 20 years old and to use telemarketing, which, though common in the overall industry, represented a major cultural business change to Massachusetts Blue Cross.

Timely Delivery

Another lesson learned is that line departments often set goals that seem impossible to meet, yet somehow the job gets done. Often this means arranging alliances with third parties using rapid application development approaches. Business and competitive pressures require that product cycle times be reduced. If American businesses have learned anything from the Japanese business model and from total quality management (TQM), it is that the design-to-delivery cycle of products must be compressed. This holds for IS products, particularly as information technology becomes more embedded in the business.

Redefining the IS Role

Though applications can be implemented by line departments quickly and often effectively, there is still a valuable role that IS must play. Rapidly produced programs often lack the industrial-strength qualities needed when the application moves into mainstream operation. Security, backup, documentation to incorporate the inevitable changes that occur, linkage with other systems, and error controls are just a few of these elements. Massachusetts Blue Cross/Blue Shield found that many of these problems did arise and could have been avoided with IS involvement.

Another important lesson is for IS to build an architecture that can respond to changing business needs, exemplified by the small business marketing group. The original system could not incorporate the changes necessitated by the switch to telemarketing. It was built on separate and disparate data bases. A major outside effort was required, and even then the user interface was not a completely smooth or transparent one. A future architecture must have the flexibility to easily adapt to changing business conditions and demands.

The key to success is increasingly built around alliances: alliances with outsourcers, software developers, and consultants outside the company, and alliances with operating departments and business units within the company. IS can no longer be a back-office superstructure.

The small business marketing group typifies business departments that are accomplishing work that sometimes IS claims is impossible. Technologies such as client-servers, graphical user interfaces, and a plethora of improving application software packages have become the enablers. Business managers want to see immediate response to their problems and they seek control of the resources necessary to see it happen. Whereas the central IS group may experience a priority problem, a line department does not.

CONCLUSION

This article gives an example of a company taking a high-risk course of action that it thought the business environment and the changing competitive dynamics warranted. The company proceeded to break with tradition and to reengineer the organization and its approach to marketing. One of the most important changes was the fundamental precept of empowering people to act on their own.

Information technology enabled the change. The implementation involved the installation of a department client-server, which together with a department LAN and the use of telemarketing and teleservicing, gave salespeople shared access to relevant and current information about their customers and prospects. Included in the rapid formation of a new department and a new approach to doing business was a time frame and schedule that demanded action and decision. It is a classic example of a line department–led transformation that was supported and enabled by a transformation in the use of technology. This case study illustrates that a solid business technology partnership can reengineer a company to improve its competitive position.

STEP 2: Prepare the case for class discussion.

STEP 3: Answer each of the following questions, individually or in small groups, as directed by your instructor.

Diagnosis

1. Why did Massachusetts Blue Cross and Blue Shield believe that it needed to reengineer the activities of its small business marketing group?
2. What did the new sales department organization look like?
3. What were the information needs of the new sales department?

Evaluation

4. What information technology infrastructure existed before the reengineering?
5. How well did the IT infrastructure meet the needs of the new sales department?

Design

6. What changes were proposed for the IT infrastructure?
7. How well did the new infrastructure meet the information needs of the new sales department?
8. What, if any, changes are still required?

Implementation

9. What steps were included in the implementation of the new systems?
10. What role did the IS organization play in the implementation?
11. What role did the line management play in the implementation?
12. How effective was the implementation?

STEP 4: In small groups, with the entire class, or in written form, share your answers to the questions above. Then answer the following questions:

1. What prompted the reengineering at Massachusetts Blue Cross and Blue Shield?
2. What information needs did the business process redesign create?
3. How effectively did existing information systems meet these needs?
4. How effectively did the new information systems meet these needs?
5. Was the implementation of the new information systems effective? ●

Staying at the Top with Otis Elevator

INTRODUCTION

Otis has been the leader in the elevator industry in France for more than a century. In fall 1991, about six months before the scheduled implementation of SAFRAN-O, the last of five information technology (IT) applications resulting from the new Master Plan launched in 1986, Bruno Grob, CEO of Otis France, wondered how and to what extent IT had contributed to sustain this unique market position, as well as if and how it could do so in the future.

> "The competitive advantage doesn't come from the tool [the computer system]. The tool is a tool, and the tool will remain a tool. . . . The tool should be served by a strategy, by a human resource, training, motivation, and anything else."

OTIS WORLDWIDE (OVERVIEW)

Otis Elevator was founded by Elisha Otis in 1853. Over the last 150 years, it has been one of the world leaders in the manufacture, sales, and service of elevators and related products. It is renowned for its long standing tradition of quality products and dependable customer service. Since Otis Elevator is perceived to be the best, its products and services are sold for a premium price. Otis especially dominates the markets for the sales and maintenance of elevators for large projects. It specializes in customized elevators. During the last five years it has increasingly turned into a service company, whose main business is "to transport people, not to manufacture lifts." (Pierre Istace—Quality, Marketing, and Communication Manager at Otis France).[1]

In 1975, Otis Elevator became a subsidiary of United Technologies Corporation (UTC), one of the fifty largest industrial companies in the world. UTC owned 100% of the stock of Otis New Jersey (ONJ), which is the parent company of Otis. (For the legal structure of Otis see Exhibit 1.) This affiliation opened the door to massive research resources for Otis. Through collaboration with the United Technologies Research Center, Otis developed electronic elevators and increased its efficiency in installing elevators.

> "Being part of a $19.8 billion corporation gives us a stature in global markets we would not enjoy standing alone."
>
> Karl Krapek
> Former President of Otis

Otis Elevator with its four geographical divisions, North American Operations, Latin American Operations, Pacific Area Operations, and European Transcontinental Operations (ETO) was the only elevator company with a strong presence in every continent.[2] It maintains offices in 45 countries. About 46,000 Otis employees work out of approximately 570 headquarters and district and branch offices around the globe. Otis world headquarters are located

[1]Every nine days, Otis moves the equivalent of the world population.

[2]ETO includes Africa and the Middle East.

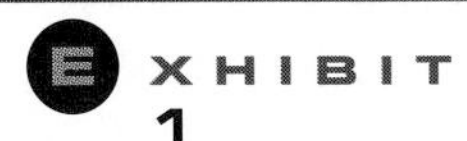

The Legal Structure of Otis Elevator, Worldwide

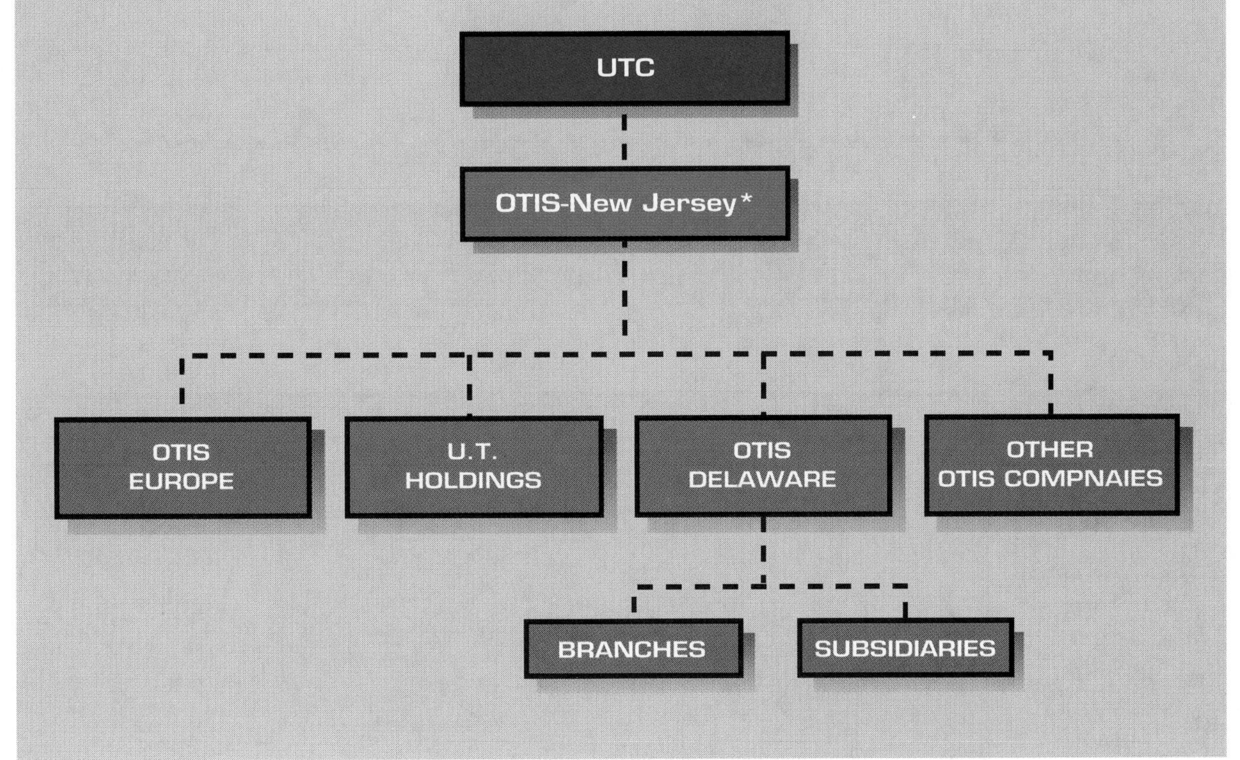

*Includes Otis HQ, Otis Engineering Center, and the U.S. part of North American Operations (NAO).

SOURCE: Company Document.

in Farmington, Connecticut, USA. For an overview of the management organization see Exhibit 2. The structure of Otis Europe, a holding company domiciled in France, is shown in Exhibit 3.

Otis worldwide revenues are almost twice that of its nearest competitor. Otis's rivals range from elevator divisions of multi-billion dollar conglomerates to small local firms with a handful of employees and no manufacturing capabilities of their own. Otis's worldwide competition comes mainly from six major companies: Schindler (Switzerland), Mitsubishi Electric Corp. and Hitachi Ltd. (Japan), Kone (Finland), Dover Elevator International (U.S.), and Thyssen (Germany).

THE ELEVATOR INDUSTRY

The two main business sectors of the elevator industry are "New Equipment" and "Service." Due to the direct correlation with the building cycle, elevator sales represent a cyclical business sector, while the elevator service market is characterized by strong stability. Of the two business sectors, service accounts for a significantly higher portion of profits. Elevator manufacturers therefore often accept a low margin on the sale of new equipment in order to obtain the service contract and sustain the company growth.

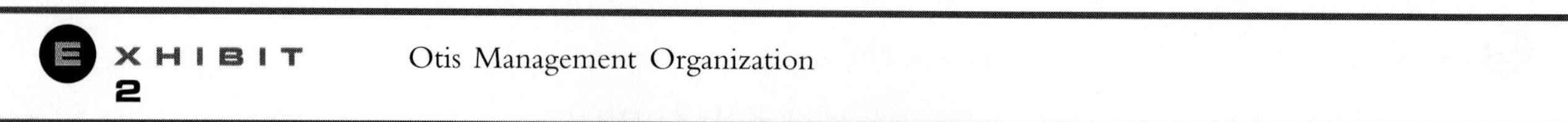

EXHIBIT 2 Otis Management Organization

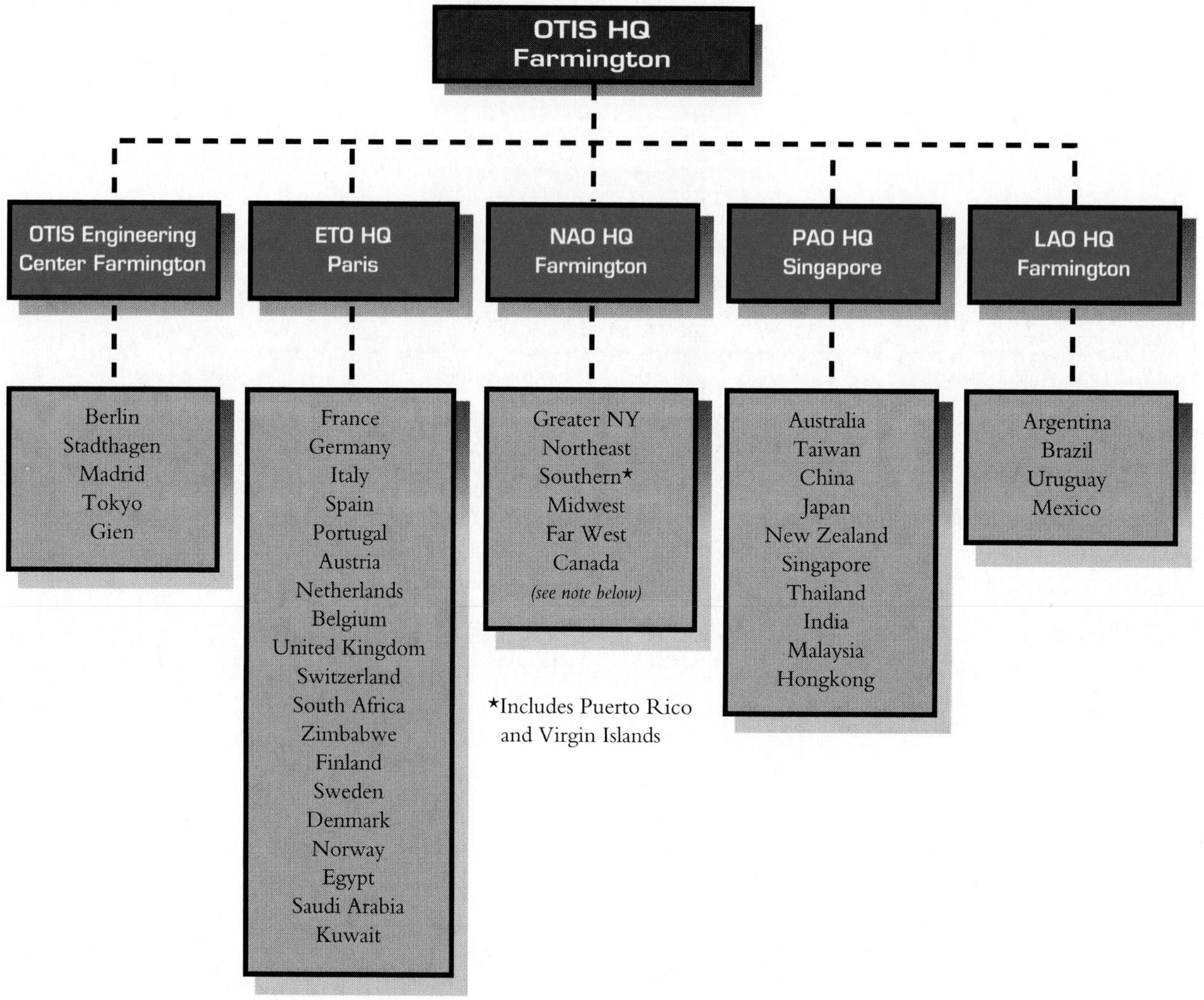

- **OTIS HQ Farmington**
  - **OTIS Engineering Center Farmington**: Berlin, Stadthagen, Madrid, Tokyo, Gien
  - **ETO HQ Paris**: France, Germany, Italy, Spain, Portugal, Austria, Netherlands, Belgium, United Kingdom, Switzerland, South Africa, Zimbabwe, Finland, Sweden, Denmark, Norway, Egypt, Saudi Arabia, Kuwait
  - **NAO HQ Farmington**: Greater NY, Northeast, Southern*, Midwest, Far West, Canada *(see note below)*
  - **PAO HQ Singapore**: Australia, Taiwan, China, Japan, New Zealand, Singapore, Thailand, India, Malaysia, Hongkong
  - **LAO HQ Farmington**: Argentina, Brazil, Uruguay, Mexico

*Includes Puerto Rico and Virgin Islands

Note: The NAO organization is currently being restructured.

ETO = European Transcontinental Operations

PAO = Pacific Asian Operations

LAO = Latin American Operations

SOURCE: Company Document.

The service market has attracted many small companies that did not produce elevators themselves. As long as elevators operated on the basis of electromechanical devices, these companies could compete successfully, since the interior design of almost all lifts on the market was very similar. With the introduction of microchips in the manufacture of elevators, some small companies had to reduce their service offers; they had neither the equipment nor the appropriately trained personnel to cope with these new developments in the elevator market.

EXHIBIT 3 Legal Structure of Otis Europe

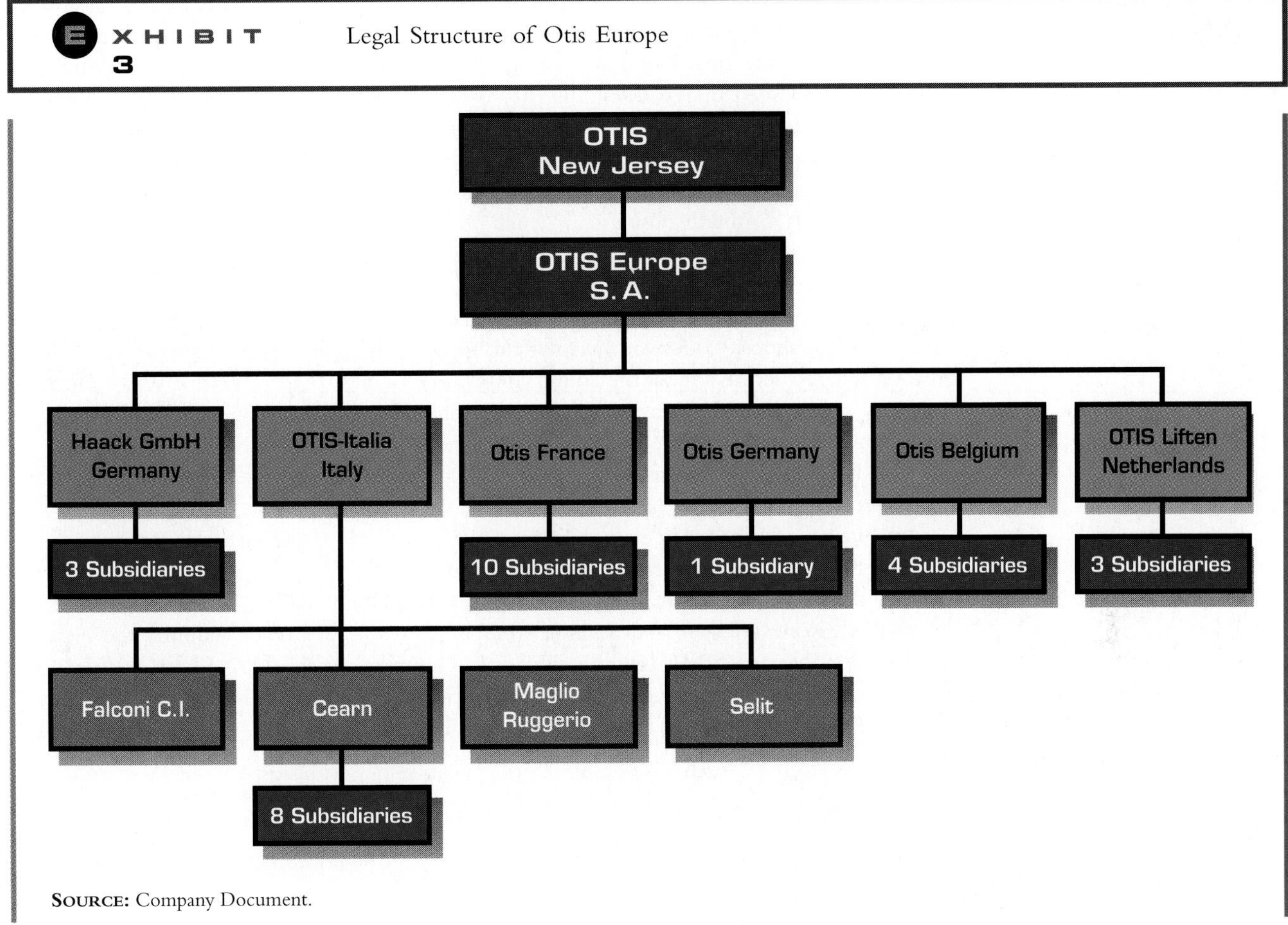

SOURCE: Company Document.

Thus the use of new technologies increasingly "regulates" the oligopolistic elevator market, providing additional benefits to the big players who are also producers of equipment: An elevator manufacturer typically receives service contracts for 60% to 80% of its newly installed equipment. Furthermore, for elevators with microprocessor-based control systems, the manufacturer is likely to keep the service contracts since small, local companies cannot provide appropriate maintenance. To support this trend, many elevator manufacturers offer discounts for long-term service contracts to attract and maintain customers.

OTIS FRANCE

While Otis has only one family of products—elevators/escalators—it nevertheless has two very different activities dealing with this product: New Equipment and Service. The New Equipment business is in turn made up of sales, manufacturing, and construction. There are three common types of elevators: gearless traction, geared traction, and hydraulic. Escalators and travolators can be viewed as complementary products.

The Service business is made up of some sales (spare parts), a small amount of manufacturing, and a large field labor force engaged in four types of services: contractual maintenance, repair, modernization, and replacement.

Contractual maintenance is about 70% of total service sales. Usually, the contractual maintenance customer is not the same as the new equipment customer (the construction contractor is seldom the final building owner). Therefore, the selling price of the maintenance contract is established once the building is completed and separately from the new equipment contract. Repair service consists of putting the elevator back in order, while modernization improves its operational condition. Repair margins are generally less than the margins for contractual maintenance, but higher than the modernization ones. However, modernization is a growth business in which—by definition—the market increases by age.

Otis France with about 6,400 employees serves approximately 40,000 customers. While about 1,400 people are employed in staff, management, sales, R&D, and administrative jobs, another 1,100 persons work in one of the two company factories in Gien (800) and Argenteuil (340), and almost 4,000 work in the field.[3] Due to the scope of its business, Otis France's organizational structure divides the country into three "zones" (East of France, West of France, and Paris with suburbs), 28 branches, and 180 commercial agencies. (The organizational structure of top management [the Executive Committee] is shown in Exhibit 4.) This organization also includes 10 subsidiaries (100% owned) grouped under the name of CFA and covering the whole country.

Otis France is the leader in elevator sales and service in the French market. With a turnover of more than $0.7 billion it has a market share of 39.6% of the elevator market in France. Its three main competitors in the French market are Schindler (18.3% of total turnover in the market), Kone (12.4%), and Soretex[4] (8.5%). (In 1988, Schindler acquired the elevator and escalator interests of Westinghouse Electric Company in the US.) About 60% of Otis turnover originates in service, while 40% results from new equipment sales or intercompany exports of equipment to Otis sister companies in Europe or agents in the third-world countries.

[3]The remaining people were employed in commercial positions in the branches.

[4]Soretex is a subsidiary of Thyssen (Germany).

EXHIBIT 4 Otis France Executive Committee (Top Management's Organizational Structure)

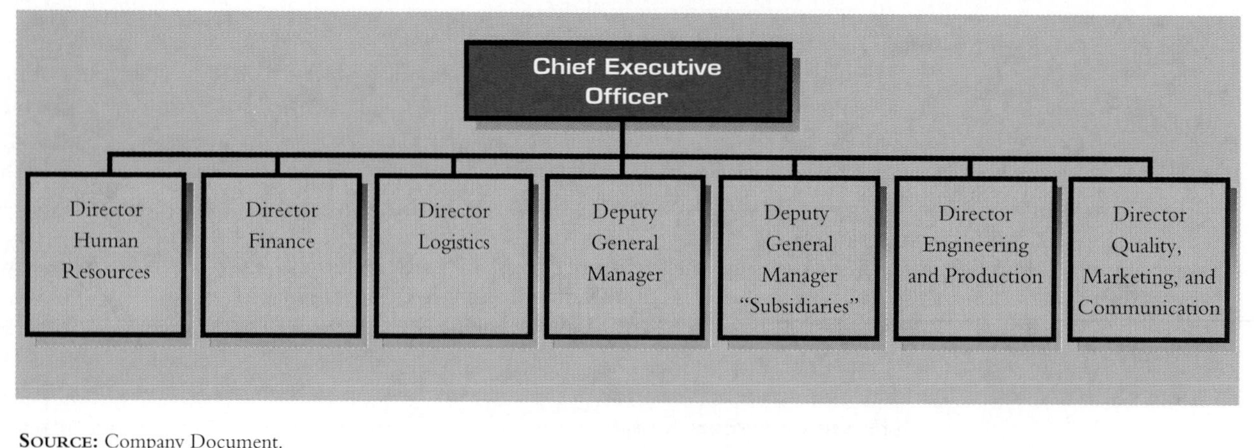

SOURCE: Company Document.

INFORMATION TECHNOLOGY AT OTIS FRANCE

In early 1986, Otis France used three main IT applications to support its elevator business: OTISLINE, the Customer Database, and REM (Remote Elevator Monitoring). OTISLINE was adapted from a successful implementation at Otis North America. REM was introduced to the French market after it had been developed and tested as a prototype in the United States.

OTISLINE

In late 1981, Otis North America (one of Otis's four regional divisions) began exploring the opportunities for enhancing their customer service operations through the use of information technology. This resulted in the development of OTISLINE, a centralized customer service center. Underlying OTISLINE was the concept of enhancing responsiveness to customer service requests. This necessitated the creation of a centralized dispatching unit with complete access to all customers and their associated product and maintenance data.

With these new capabilities Otis North America experienced dramatic improvements in their responsiveness to call backs. OTISLINE translated into not only a complete redesign of their customer information systems, but also into the creation of a new industry standard for service. Due to its success in North America, the OTISLINE concept was adopted and installed by other divisions within the company, including Otis France.

In France OTISLINE was also developed into a national communication center for the Otis maintenance activity. However, due to some local features (e.g., a different ZIP code and address structure and a telephone network that was much less accessible for technicians than in the United States) the installed OTISLINE was different from its U.S. counterpart.

OTISLINE in France, as in North America, operates 24 hours a day, seven days a week, receiving customer phone calls from building management and users and dispatching Otis service teams as necessary with the shortest possible delay. The French concept for this new use of IT led to offering OTISLINE as a service and charging the customer for it. This additional payment increased expectations on the customers' side, and thus in the beginning, led to hardly any increase in Otis benefits. Over time, Otis customers started to consider a service like OTISLINE more as a new industry standard than as a special offer. By dialing 05-24-24-07 (toll-free number) they communicate with Otis. 2,400 phone calls are received daily from customers and 800 from Otis technicians.

OTISLINE keeps a record on each lift; every event (e.g., an elevator inspection, repair, etc.) is stored in the computer database system. The Otis Maintenance Service as well as any other authorized employee within the company can access this database and use the relevant information for his/her activities.

Customer Database

With more than 40,000 customers stored, the customer database can be used by sales people, marketing, and communication. For each customer a variety of information is available. Address, phone number, name of people involved with elevator activity, annual turnover with Otis, pending negotiation, direct marketing campaigns, and results of customer satisfaction surveys can be launched from this database.

Remote Elevator Monitoring (REM)

Otis North America successfully introduced the prototype of a "Remote Elevator Monitoring" (REM) system which utilizes microchip technology to monitor an elevator and automatically notify Otis if it is malfunctioning. Through a master unit installed in the machine room, REM monitors lift performance. If performance deviates from predetermined standards, the REM Master Unit sends a message over a dedicated telephone line to Otis.

Functions with abnormal performance readings are corrected during regular maintenance. If a shutdown occurs, the REM system allows Otis to determine whether passengers are trapped (bidirectional automatic voice link between the cab and OTISLINE).

The major market for REM is France, where more than 7,000 units are implemented. In other European countries, only a few hundred REM systems are installed, while in the United States Otis North America has not sold any.

REM is characterized by the dual focus on external and internal business aspects. Introduced as an additional service to the customers (external focus), it is an excellent tool for the communication between the cab (trapped passengers) and the Otis Service division. From the internal perspective, it serves as a diagnostic tool which automatically feeds the shared company database. It leads to pre-emptive maintenance (striving for the goal of zero call backs) and thus to reduced maintenance/service costs and customer satisfaction improvement.

> With REM we should have no breakdowns anymore because we should be able to be on the job site before they occur.
>
> Pierre Amar
> Logistics Manager

THE BIRTH OF THE MASTER PLAN

In the summer of 1986, top management at Otis France contemplated the use of IT within the company. They were aware of the competitive advantage resulting from OTISLINE and REM, from both an external (customer) viewpoint and an internal (organizational) perspective. They thought that additional benefits could be gained from the development of new IT applications that improve efficiency and facilitate the flow of information across the company.

For internal processes, Otis was still using a system that was developed in the early 1960s, based on the technology that was available at that time. This system suffered mainly from a lack of providing business estimates and processing customer information. Every time during the last twenty years that a change was made in the organizational structure or in the business conduct, there was an attempt to adjust the computer system to the introduced changes.

> We realized that the system, the technology, and the organization were the three dimensions of the problem. So we felt that we'd try to understand where we go from now and we decided to set up the 'schema directeur' [the Master Plan] of our project.
>
> Pierre Amar

The idea of an IT system that could contribute to a redesigned retail system was introduced. However, top management was convinced that the development of further IT applications had to be based on an organizational redesign. They agreed that any new system could only serve as a tool for a predeveloped new strategy.

> The tool itself won't create the strategy, the motivation, the teamwork. The tool itself will create nothing. If it comes within a strategy, then it's outstanding; but it has to be prepared far in advance.
>
> Bruno Grob

THE "MASTER PLAN" PROJECT

The Concept

Otis France's goal was to design and implement a simplified version of the managerial and operational procedures surrounding the processing of a customer order. Central to the project was the interrelationship between the development of the procedures and the organizational structure, with decentralization of responsibility driving the design. The entire process, from the initial contact with the customer through the installation of the elevator, was reviewed and redesigned.

> Simplify processes and make them clearer, that was the main point. Once that was done, even imperfectly, we could design systems to respond to them. Obviously we had the computer in mind, but it was not the purpose of our exercise.
>
> Bruno Grob

The People Involved

The decision of top management to launch the Master Plan was the starting point for involving in the project a number of employees in different positions within the company. Pierre Amar noted that "the first step was not to leave that to the EDP people." Three committees (the Steering Committee, the Project Team, and the Users' Council) were officially formed to participate in a variety of tasks.

Otis started putting in place a Steering Committee. It consisted of the managing director (CEO) and all the directors in his first line. This committee was "in charge of talking to each other and trying to understand where they would like Otis to go in terms of systems to support the company strategies" (Pierre Amar).

The Steering Committee monitored the progress of the entire project, validated the results, and gave general guidelines. Bruno Grob, who started as Deputy General Manager in this committee, was later promoted to the position of CEO. From that point on, he became the key driving force of the project, even more than before.

The project itself was assigned to a newly set up dedicated team, what they called "La Direction de l'Organisation." Its composition was intended to cover a broad range of experience and knowledge about the company. It had five members from the Organization Department, including the Corporate Organization Manager.

The Users' Council, consisting of thirty individuals coming from the various areas of the company, examined and ratified the work and recommendations of the Project Team. It ensured the coherence and completeness of the project and carried out the management decisions. Furthermore, the User's Council submitted its own proposals to the Project Team and set up determined priorities among the Steering Committee's actions.

The Beginning of the Project

> Our approach was not to look at the problem from the system point of view, but to audit the existing situation, the organization itself.
>
> Pierre Amar

Otis started with investigating the characteristics of its business. The goals of that process were twofold. The first was to analyze the current business situation and to improve the understanding of what the company was actually doing in order to generate profits. The second goal was to increase awareness for the "Master Plan" project. The Users' Council became enthusiastic about the subject because its members were able to talk about what they knew. Thus the Project Team had successfully created broad commitment for the subsequent steps.

Pierre Amar described these steps as follows:

> We started explaining what we were doing: designing, manufacturing, selling, and maintaining elevators, managing people, etc. We tried to match the major business areas with the organizational units as they were at that time. This resulted in a matrix reflecting who did what. Afterwards we attached ratios to the matrix fields showing each person's resource allocation.
>
> We had two industrial locations: Did we need both of them or would one suffice? We were organized in branches which were providing two main services: modernization and maintenance

of elevators. Was that the right way to handle our business? People started looking differently at the way the company behaved.

During that process we discovered that one aspect was missing in our approach: the customers. We had never had the customer as a driving factor in what we were doing. In the branches we were driven by geography rather than by market segments, or even by the customer himself. We found that our whole business was contract-oriented: We were handling contracts rather than dealing with customers. That was the very big start.

Then we started thinking of what should be a) the processes and b) the system to support these processes. We described each process and analyzed who our customers were. Afterwards we investigated the communication: Who dealt with whom and what kind of information was exchanged?

We ended up with the target architecture of our processes rather than of our systems (which did not exist). We described the processes and determined the amount of the information we wanted to handle in the future.

The Development Methodology Applied

In defining their information systems requirements, Otis—with the help of an external consulting company—developed and applied a methodology which used the company's strategic goals to drive the system design process. This methodology divided the whole process into four main phases, which were implemented in a step-by-step manner. The four phases were: a) assessment of the current organizational structure and analysis of management areas, including a functional breakdown of its business as depicted in the strategic plan, b) assessment of the existing information systems, including the conceptual and data systems as well as resource feasibility studies, c) planning of the new organizational structure, and d) planning of the new information systems (including the systems' architecture and implementation). The outcome of these four phases was the "Master Plan" which detailed the functional and technical design of the new retail system. The development sequence of the Master Plan's phases and their associated time frames are shown in Exhibits 5 and 6.

The development phases determined three levels of investigation (conceptual, organizational, and physical) as well as two main tasks in the process (evaluation of the present situation and generation of solutions). The conceptual level, "What has to be done," provided the link with the strategic dimension and resulted in the redefinition of the business domains. The organizational level, "The way to do it," investigated alternative choices for the com-

EXHIBIT 5 Development Sequence of the Master Plan's Phases

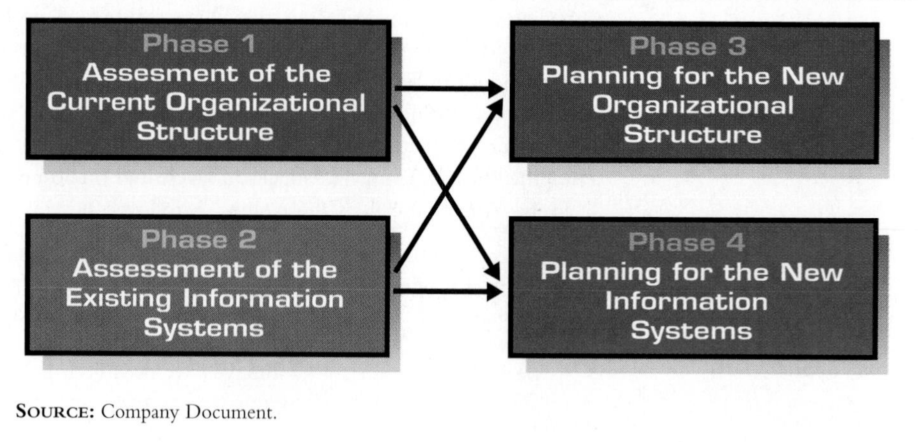

SOURCE: Company Document.

EXHIBIT 6 Time Frame for the Development Phases

	Feb. '86	March '86	April '86	May '86	June '86	July '86
Phase 1	21 X, 24 Y					
Phase 2			7 X, 24 Y			
Phase 3				5 X, 14 Y		
Phase 4					6 X, 18 Y	3 Y

X = Meeting of the Steering Committee
Y = Meeting of the User's Council

The meetings always mark the end of a phase.
Source: Company Document.

pany; its findings suggested a new organizational structure and a set of information systems. The physical level, "The means of doing it," determined the resources needed for the implementation of the project.

RESULTS OF THE MASTER PLAN

The results of the Master Plan can be categorized into two main areas: organizational changes and new IT applications. The interdependence between these two areas is obviously very important.

As far as information systems are concerned, the Master Plan includes a conceptual description of five new IT applications [SAGA, SALVE, STAR, SAFRAN-N,S,K, and SAFRAN-O] to be implemented between 1986 and 1992. These applications support negotiation, sales and contract management, invoicing and accounts receivable, purchasing management, and accounting. Their design is based on the concept that each type of sales activity (be it sales to a new customer or to an existing one, maintenance, repair, or modernization) follows the same basic procedure.

The New IT Applications

The five new IT applications include SALVE, a support system used by sales representatives in their negotiations with the customer from the initial contact to the booking stage. Once the order has been booked (order received by the factory), it is passed to SAGA, a contract management system, which creates and maintains the sales order. SAGA can be viewed as a special contract control system. The information gained from SALVE and SAGA serves as input for STAR, the purchasing and supplier management system. SAFRAN-N,S,K handles invoicing and other accounting functions regarding modernization as well as sales of new equipment for new or existing buildings. SAFRAN-O, planned to be implemented by May 1992, will handle the billing of maintenance services. Otis expects a high productivity increase from the introduction of SAFRAN-O, since the company has currently 60,000 maintenance contracts covering 130,000 elevators for which bills have to be prepared on a regular basis (quarterly). A short description of the functions and users of each of these systems is provided in Exhibits 7 to 11.

7

SALVE
(Systéme d'Aide à la Vente)
Negotiation Support System

Main Functions:

- Negotiation Support and Price Simulation
- Configuration of Products and Services Offered
- Price Calculations
- Preparation of Final Offers
- Real-Time Booking of Contracts
- Amendment to Existing Contracts
- Transfer of Orders to the Factories

Key Objectives:

- To Improve the Quality of Offers
    - Reliability (Feasibility, Zero Defects)
    - Speed (Reduced Delay)
    - Quality of Presentation
    - To Provide Sales Representatives with a User-Friendly and Flexible Negotiation Support Tool

Primary Users:

- Sales Representatives
- Secretaries/Assistants
- Field Superintendent
- Field Supervisor
- Sales Directors/Marketing
- Branch Managers

Source: Company Document.

The new IT architecture (see Exhibit 12) implies the development of systems for business functions (e.g., negotiation), compared to the previous systems, which were targeted toward specific activities such as repairs or sales. "SALVE, for instance," explains Jean-Claude Casari,[5] "is a system that offers capabilities for negotiation management up to the booking stage. It is the same system for new equipment or service sales. That was a big change compared to the old system where we managed operations by activity. For new sales, we had one type, and for repairs, we had another type of management. So we never had a global view of what we did per unit [elevator]." Pierre Amar goes on, "This choice was driven by our objective to get systems independent from organization. The previous architecture required a specialized sales organization for New Equipment and Modernization or Maintenance. The new one allows a high level of flexibility. A salesman can receive a mixed portfolio of whatever activity. Access to the related system functions is achieved through workstation customization."

For 1992, three additional accounting systems are planned to allow the full integration of the systems developed based on the Master Plan. These IT applications include SYGECO, a system handling accounts receivable, an accounting system managing accounts payable as well as an accounting and cost analysis system. Finally, a service management system, counterpart of SAGA for maintenance activity, will be developed.

---

[5]At Otis France until June 1991; now Strategic Planning Manager at Otis ETO headquarters.

EXHIBIT 8

SAGA
(Systéme d'Aide à la Gestion des Affaires)
Contract Management System

Main Functions:

- Support for Contract Management with Regard to
  - Relations with the Factories
  - Planning and Scheduling
  - Costs per Contract
  - Contract Financial Completion

Key Objectives:

- To Realize Contract Confirmations in Response to Customer Inquiries with Concern for
  - Planning
  - Efficient Contract Handling (Goal: Margin Completed versus Margin Booked)
  - Efficiency and Productivity (Number of Hours Used to Complete the Contract)

Primary Users:

- Field Superintendent
- Field Supervisor
- Control Department
- Audits

Source: Company Document.

EXHIBIT 9

STAR
(Système de Traitement des Achats en Région)
Purchasing and Supplier Management System

Main Functions:

- Management of Suppliers
- Purchase Orders Processing
- Invoice Validation and Processing
- Cash Management of the Local Branches

Key Objectives:

- Initiate (Regularly) Payments
- Manage all Contracts in Coordination with SAGA
- Ascertain Flexibility, Decentralization, and Control of Administrative Tasks

Primary Users:

- Purchasers in Local Districts
- Secretaries/Assistants

Source: Company Document.

EXHIBIT 10

SAFRAN N,S,K,*
(Système d'Aide à la Facturation en Région)
Invoice and Billing System for New Equipment in New and Existing Buildings as Well as Modernization

Main Functions:

- Invoicing Data
- Calculation and Printing of Invoices
- Credit Notes
- Bonds Management

Key Objectives:

- To Optimize Cost in Process Coverage
- To propose a Flexible Organization of Invoicing Procedures (Standardize Billing Rules)
- To Customize Invoices to Customer Needs

Primary Users:

- Accountants
- Employees in Charge of Invoicing
- Assistants/Secretaries
- Financial Director (Validation)

Source: Company Document.

*N = New Equipment in New Buildings
K = New Equipment in Existing Buildings
S = Modernization

EXHIBIT 11

SAFRAN O*
(Système d'Aide à la Facturation en Région)
Invoice and Billing System for Maintenance

Main Functions:

- Invoicing Data
- Automatic Quarterly Preparation of Maintenance Invoices
- Support Correction of Wrong Invoices
- Price Increases

Key Objectives:

- Increase Productivity
- Correct Invoice for the Maintenance

Primary Users:

- Accountants
- Employees in Charge of Invoicing
- Financial Director (Validation)
- Branch Manager Assistants

Source: Company Document.

*O = Maintenance

Otis France Information Systems 1991

MARKETING & SALES

FACTORIES SYSTEMS

Customers Database

Standard Products Database

Units Technical Data

Portfolio Contracts Database

SALVE
Negotiation Mgt
Configuration/Pricing
Proposals

Requirements

Factories Orders

Gien Systems

Argenteuil Systems

CONTRACT MGT

Contract Shedules

Costs

SAGA
Contract Mgt
System

Hours

FMO
Time Sheets
Entry System

"O" Contracts & Units

Maintenance Operations Management

Hours

BILLING

PURCHASING

HUMAN RESOURCES

Otis Line Data

Otis Line

OTIS LINE

SAFRAN
Billing System
N.S.K.&O

STAR
Purchasing
& Suppliers Mgt.

Human Resources Mgt

Payroll

Human Resources Mgt

SYGECO
Accounts
Receivable

GAP/GAP III
Accounts
Payable

GALLION General Ledger

ACCOUNTING & COSTS ANLAYSIS

New Applications Developed within Master Plan

Other Applications

Major Databases

Contract Accounting & Analysis

Efficiencies

FHR
Field Hourly
Rate

Costs Analysis

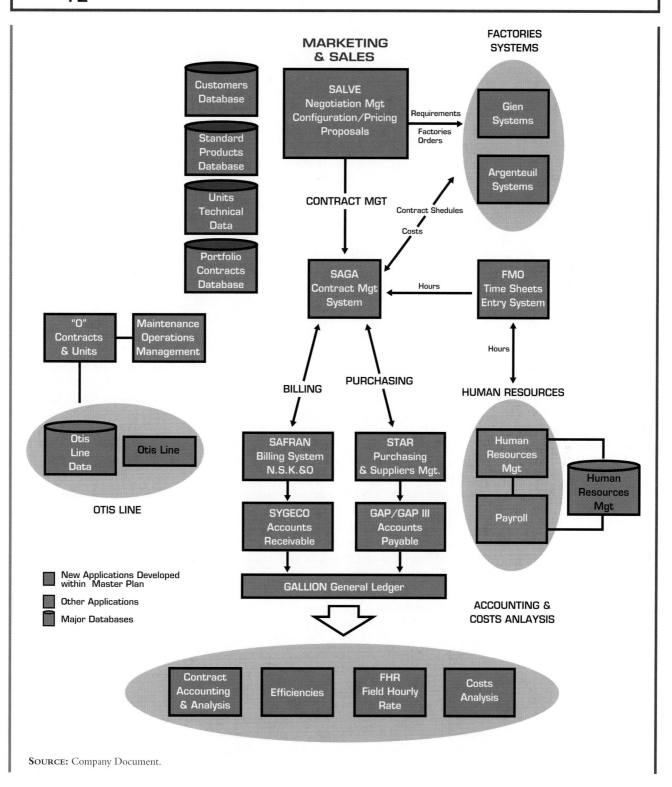

Source: Company Document.

SALVE is the first system that was implemented; it served as a basis for the other applications that were developed later on. Giving the salesperson the authority and responsibility to set a price required implementing some control mechanisms.

The first consists of having built in the system a "plus/minus x percent" margin within which a price can be set. The second mechanism is basing the salesperson's premium on his/her sales performance (incentive).

From the salesforce's perspective, the major benefit of SALVE is the drastic reduction of lead time. The processing time from having a signed customer order to forwarding the material form to the factory was reduced from one month to 48 hours. In addition, the salesperson is in a stronger bargaining position with the customers since he/she has, through SALVE, a complete record of previous negotiations/contracts with each customer.

From a management perspective, SALVE offers two main advantages. First, orders get to the factory faster. Second, unlike in the past, when too many customized units were sold, there are now more sales of standard products because the salesperson could "bring" the customer to the product line.

At the beginning, the implementation of SALVE caused significant problems. There was major resistance to change by the salesforce, which had never been exposed to computers before. This necessitated a strong educational commitment and the need "not to change the tool and the process at the same time." In spite of the misfit caused by this situation, the company did not want to implement both changes simultaneously; "Otherwise," as Pierre Amar put it, "people [would have been] completely lost. We [Otis] found that adapting to a computer terminal is always a burden for people."

Before the introduction of SALVE, salespeople played the role of a "mail box," letting staff members in the corporate headquarters execute most tasks (e.g., determining prices for units, contract processing, etc.) for them. With SALVE they are able to, and they are also responsible for processing all such tasks themselves in the field. Of course, in the beginning, that appeared to them to mean a significant increase in their workload.

Management had expected that, once SALVE was in place, the salesforce would have more time to spend in the field meeting customers. However, experience proved the opposite: salespeople spent a lot of time in front of the computer screen. This turned out to be a major concern for customers as well, who did not want to pay somebody for operating a computer. (After one year SALVE became much more user friendly and salesmen reduced time spent on the keyboard.)

In spite of the Master Plan's goal of developing a common database throughout the company for the new IT applications, it was never intended to integrate the OTISLINE database with those of the internally oriented applications. Christian Madrus de Mingrelie, Organization Manager, explains the situation: "The two databases have to be meaningfully connected, but there will always be two databases."

Organizational Changes

The step-by-step implementation of the Master Plan's applications also resulted in a number of organizational changes in the company headquarters as well as in the field. Dominique André, Manager of the "West France" Zone, thinks that "the organizational changes were expected in advance, but not formally planned."

The main goal and the actual achievement of the Master Plan was "decentralization through centralization." The main areas of decentralization were data entry, invoicing, pricing, and booking. Consequently, the introduction of each new application was followed by changes in the human resources allocation. Although nobody was laid off, as the company proudly states, the number of headquarters employees has been reduced by about 20% since the launch of the project in 1986.

> For me as an outsider within the company,[6] the main idea of the Master Plan was decentralization. Once we had decided to give more responsibility to the people working in the region, we had to give them the tools to cope with that. And then, after they had more responsibility, we [in the headquarters] wanted to know what the salespeople did every day. Therefore, we needed to introduce control mechanisms.
>
> Tibor Gyoengyoesi
> Marketing Studies Manager

Control as an inevitable consequence of increased autonomy and responsibility is also crucial from the financial department's point of view.

> You see that we give more autonomy to the salesman and thus dramatically improve our response time. On the other hand, we have also a dramatic control problem. Salesmen can cheat, purposefully violate the control rules. We realized that we had to be tougher regarding the control issue and created a new Audit Department.
>
> Charles Vo
> Financial Manager

THE MASTER PLAN IN RETROSPECTIVE

The systems resulting from the Master Plan enable Otis to benefit from:

1. A major decentralization of responsibility resulting in reduced administrative overheads. Previously, all orders had to be verified at corporate headquarters in Paris (to assure that the requested elevator configuration is viable and the price is within the defined limits) prior to making an offer to the customer. With the new systems in place, because the computer system can perform all the necessary checks, the routing through Paris is no longer needed. Furthermore, the company benefits from the improved accuracy.
2. A drastic reduction of the order processing time (i.e., from the time a customer places an order until it is forwarded to the factory) from 1 month to 48 hours. This has significantly improved responsiveness and customer service.
3. Better management reports containing information on elevators sold or maintained, contracts finalized, or troublesome units. "For example," says Dominique André, "we now receive the bookings per branch every day; it used to be once a month with two weeks delay."
4. A complete flexibility enabling salesmen to prepare all types of affairs with an unlimited number of options and alternatives.

Dominique goes on listing decentralization, quality, and productivity as the major benefits of the Master Plan. He added: "Our situation is easy to understand: We are number one in the French market, both in New Equipment and Service, with more than 35% market share. All our competitors try to reduce our part of the elevator cake. It is a daily challenge to keep our maintenance contracts. For a strong market leader with a service that can be easily imitated the first strategic objective is to keep the number one position and market share. The Master Plan helped to reach this objective. As a next step we will try to improve it."[7]

Dominique goes on reflecting on the SALVE system, "Although, in the beginning, we had huge problems with the new applications, especially with SALVE, we would definitely do it again like that. Immediately after the introduction of SALVE, there was some resistance, but now [in 1991] even the sales representatives would not want to live without the system. They ask for more." "In any case," says Bruno Grob, "we feel comfortable with what we have done, since we know that our competitors now are trying to do the same thing as we did."

---

[6]Tibor Gyoengyoesi has been working for Otis France since, but was not directly involved in, the project.

[7]In this context, Dominique agreed that the results of the Master Plan were more a competitive necessity than a competitive advantage.

Regarding the other Otis subsidiaries in Europe, Bruno Grob adds:

> Yes, they all want to come to France and even though our Master Plan is not perfect, everyone wants to use it.

Nevertheless, the Master Plan is by no means viewed as perfect. Drawbacks and future threats are also recognized at different management levels. They include the lack of training, the time-consuming data input, and the reduced time that sales representatives have to be in the field.

Dominique elaborates on the latter point: "The biggest problem is the time that productive people have to spend in front of the computer. We want our sales representatives to be face to face with our customers, and SALVE is one obstacle to that."

Moreover, management is aware of the risk that a sales representative can leave the company and start his/her own business.

Management realizes the threat that competitors can easily imitate Otis products or service. There is the example of Servitel, a service offered by Schindler with similar capabilities as OTISLINE. Or, as reported in a business article, ". . . one competitor in the elevator industry copied the other's move to centralize service records. But the copycat company went a step further: it identified elevators that chronically failed, then approached the clients with proposals to rebuild those units. The innovator had [in 1987], at least temporarily, a whole new market to itself."[8]

In November 1991, four months after joining Otis, Christian Madrus de Mingrelie thinks that "user-friendliness, simplicity, and flexibility" are the three main areas needing further improvement. Bruno Grob took a different perspective when he commented on the future success of the systems and of the company as a whole by saying: "The major threat in the future comes from the Japanese companies. They have the ultimate in management, they all have the same goal, and that will finally outweigh the strengths of any information system."

SOME PERSPECTIVES FOR THE FUTURE

Zero callbacks as a new slogan for Otis—A new USP (Unique Selling Point) or just an empty promise? Pierre Istace thinks that "zero callbacks are not yet expected by the customer. Would such a slogan raise expectations to a level that could not be guaranteed? Or would it be the best pre-emptive measure against the threat of Japanese companies entering the French market? Japanese companies, most likely, would base their marketing on such a slogan."

More flexible systems to fulfill the needs of different units within the company—Such a development could also serve as a basis for a Pan-European system, which requires a high degree of flexibility. "We have to become more flexible," says Christian Madrus de Mingrelie. "We need subsystems for the different requirements of the regions where we have similar functional, but different physical, processes. Just look at the Paris area and the small local branches in the field. . . . And then we need to work on the interfaces between the different subsystems."

Shortened Cycle Time—The optimal goal for the internal procedures is to shorten the "flow" path of a contract through the different business processes. "Two main steps are to be accomplished in order to pursue that goal," says Charles Vo. "Strict benchmarks will have to be introduced with the intention to save time in each process separately. Secondly, the integration of the different processes and systems within the headquarters and between the headquarters and the regions will have to be optimized."

---

[8]Burns, W. J. and McFarlan, F. W. "Information Technology puts power into control systems," in *Harvard Business Review,* September–October 1987, pp. 89–94.

European Integration—The goal is a common, standardized maintenance contract. One of the obstacles of this difficult project, which is "not yet very advanced," as Pierre Istace put it, is the variety of technical environments which are in place in different countries and the resulting problem of portability. "So far, a first agreement has been achieved on the programming language (NATURAL) and the database system (ADABASE) to be used," says Christian Madrus de Mingrelie. Other problems regarding standardizing the European maintenance contract stem from the diversity of legal frameworks (e.g., accounting procedures) and the different ways of doing business in various European countries.

THE END . . .

In the fall of 1991, about six months before the launch of the last system that resulted from the Master Plan, Bruno Grob, sitting in his office at the top floor of the new headquarters, was assessing the current corporate situation. He was not only pleased that the company was still market leader, but also that the investment in IT seemed to have paid off. He recognized that the use of IT had certainly played an important role in gaining and keeping Otis's position in the market. But had the investment in IT resulted in a sustainable competitive advantage? When pondering this critical question, he remembered a comment made previously by one of his subordinates:

> I think we have to look again, now that we have finished implementing the IT applications, how to simplify the organization. Of course, we have changed, but in my mind we have not changed enough. When you implement systems step by step, for instance in some applications we are still using the old system because we have not replaced it with a new application, we are obliged to design an organization that is not completely ideal. So the next step is to look again at the processes in the branches, to see again how to simplify, then to take advantage of our good on-line system. I have just (in 1990) hired some people to work on that. It's a never-ending process.
>
> Jean-Claude Casari

STEP 1: Read the Otis Elevator case. (This activity is especially suited for use in conjunction with Chapter 12 of *Information Systems.*)

STEP 2: Prepare the case for class discussion.

STEP 3: Answer each of the following questions, individually or in small groups, as directed by your instructor.

Diagnosis

1. What information needs did Otis's salespeople have? What information needs did Otis's customers have?
2. Why did Otis France develop an Information Technology master plan?
3. What strategy or strategies did Otis pursue?

Evaluation

4. How well did the OTISLINE, Customer Database, and REM systems meet Otis's strategic needs?
5. What deficiencies existed in Otis's information systems?

Design

6. What advantages did SALVE offer?
7. How did SALVE fit with Otis's strategy?
8. How did the other new IT applications (SAGA, STAR, and SAFRAN-N,S,K) fit with SALVE and with Otis's strategy?

Implementation

9. What problems did Otis's managers have to overcome to implement SALVE?
10. How effective was the implementation of SALVE?
11. What, if any, changes are still necessary?
12. Has the implementation of Otis's IT master plan provided a sustainable competitive advantage?

STEP 4: In small groups, with the entire class, or in written form, share your answers to the questions above. Then answer the following questions:

1. What strategy or strategies did Otis pursue?
2. What information needs did Otis have? How do these needs relate to Otis's strategy?
3. How well did Otis's information systems reflect its strategy and meet its information needs?
4. What factors influenced the implementation of Otis's information systems?
5. What changes are still necessary for Otis to accomplish its strategic objectives? ●

DMV

STEP 1: Read the DMV case. (This activity is especially suited for use in conjunction with Chapter 13 of *Information Systems.*)

"Why can't we go back to our old system? At least we know it works! Maybe it can get us out of this mess." Bill Maloney, the state's attorney general, was on the phone with Mark Bridger. Bridger, the director of the Department of Motor Vehicles (DMV), was doing his best to cope with a crisis that was becoming worse by the hour.

Two months earlier, the state began using a new data processing system designed to streamline operations at the DMV. Although the cutover—direct conversion—to the new system was without incident, problems began to mount soon after the system was placed in operation.

Now the system was unable to cope with the workload. More than a million drivers had been unable to register their cars. To make the situation even worse, many of those who registered their cars after the system went into operation were incorrectly listed in the database as operating unregistered vehicles. And renewal notices—issued automatically by the new computer system—had been sent to the wrong drivers. In fact, so many drivers had been forced to drive without a registration that the attorney general, Bill Maloney, had ordered the state police to cease citing drivers for this offense. No one, it seemed, had been spared: Even some of the vehicles operated by public works departments and local police forces throughout the state were registered to the wrong municipalities!

BACKGROUND

When the system was first conceived, a little over three years ago, the DMV expressed a need for a more up-to-date information-processing system than the ten-year-old system it was using. The DMV especially needed a system with a strong DBMS, to have more flexibility in accessing data and in making changes in the application software. Its current system used a conventional file-management approach.

In addition to performing all of the routine record-keeping functions such as maintaining automobile registration data, the DMV wanted the new system to automatically notify the state's five million drivers of license and registration renewals. It also wanted the system to be capable of allowing updates of the state's rating surcharge database to be made on a daily basis. This surcharge database keeps track of violation points against individual drivers and is used to penalize bad drivers by making them pay higher insurance rates. Under the old system, this database was updated periodically, but it was not unusual—due to inefficient update procedures—for the driver's record to be updated as much as three or four months after the conviction took place.

POLITICAL FACTORS

When the idea for a new computer system was originally suggested to the governor, he agreed that an effort such as this was long overdue. But he was not pleased to hear that it would take five years to develop and bring the project into full operation. It is alleged that

SOURCE: Selection from *Cases in Computer Information Systems* 'Yarmouth Inc.,' pp. 175–176 by B. Shore and J. Ralya, copyright © 1988 by Holt, Rinehart Winston, Inc., reprinted by permission of the publisher.

he then asked DMV director Bridger to find a consulting firm to develop the system in two years so that the completed system would be finished in time to be used during his reelection campaign as an example of his administration's accomplishments.

THE CONSULTANTS

Shortly after the governor's alleged request to expedite the development of the system, Bridger met with the information services division of Driscol and Russell, one of the country's leading public accounting firms. After studying the project's objectives, the manager of this division, Mike Price, suggested that the only way it could be completed in two years would be to use a fourth-generation language.

"We will still use a structured approach and build the system in modules," explained Price, "but the 4GL will save us a lot of time in programming, debugging, and testing the project."

Bridger was impressed with Price's confidence in his firm's ability to deliver the needed software and, above all, to deliver it on time. Within three months a $6.5 million contract was signed with Driscol and Russell.

The software development process went smoothly for the DMV. The senior systems analyst for Driscol and Russell spent six weeks at the DMV, during which time he learned about the current system and the characteristics of the new one. Once the systems analysis was complete and a preliminary plan approved, Driscol and Russell had few interactions with the DMV. According to the senior systems analyst at Driscol and Russell, the DMV preferred it this way, as the DMV was already overburdened with day-to-day problems.

THE SYSTEM FAILS

The system was delivered right on schedule, and during the first few weeks, as the workload on the new system increased, it seemed to perform well. Data entry was made from on-line terminals, and users found the system efficient. As might be expected at the start, those who used the system complained a little about the new procedures, but no serious problems emerged.

But as more and more new tasks were added to the system, the operators began to report an increase in response time. When the system was finally in full operation, the response time became intolerable. At best, response times were in the five-to-eight second range and frequently took as long as one to two minutes. The original contract specified that response times were to be no longer than three to five seconds.

An increase in response time, however, was just the tip of the iceberg. First, it was not possible to process all of the jobs on the new system. Even an increase to a 24-hour operation was insufficient to update the database. Within a few months, the backlog grew to such proportions that 1.4 million automobile registrations had not been processed. Meanwhile, when police stopped cars that did not have valid registrations, the drivers were arrested. As the protest from drivers began to mount, the attorney general's office stepped in and ordered the police to stop making arrests for invalid registrations.

Then an even more dramatic problem surfaced. It slowly became apparent that the database was contaminated with bad data, that the automobile registrations listed the wrong owners.

STATE DEPARTMENT OF DATA PROCESSING

With the system in total chaos, the DMV director and the attorney general decided to call in Gail Hendrix, the director of the state department of data processing. Hendrix had known about this project since its inception, when she had been appalled not only that her department had been frozen out of the development process but that the bid had apparently gone to a company without the usual competitive bidding process.

Hendrix was not surprised at the DMV's problems. During her first meeting with Bridger and Maloney, she shed some light on the sources of the problem. "I can't understand why Driscol and Russell used PROWRITE. Everyone knew it was a new 4GL, that it had lots of bugs to be worked out, and that no one had really tested it on a large project yet. Not only that, but PROWRITE was developed to run smaller MIS jobs. I don't think it was even meant to run transaction jobs where the system must handle several transactions per second."

Bridger asked, "How would you have developed the system?"

Hendrix replied, "I think COBOL should have been used for those modules that did the heavy processing. Then a 4GL, but not PROWRITE, could have been used for some of the other modules, especially the report-writing ones."

FINDING A SOLUTION

At the meeting with Hendrix and Bridger, Maloney insisted that they come up with a solution. "We've got our motor vehicle system in a shambles. To solve the problem tomorrow is even too late. What are we going to do?"

Bridger was in favor of holding a meeting with Driscol and Russell to determine what they could do to straighten out the situation. "Perhaps they could rewrite some of the transaction modules in COBOL, as Hendrix suggested."

Hendrix felt differently. "They've lost their credibility with me. I think we should write this software off as a complete loss and begin the development of a new system here in our own DP organization."

Maloney, however, was certainly not satisfied. "Look, why can't we bring our old system back into operation? At least we'll get the public and the politicians off our back."

"Bill, you asked me that on the phone last week, and I told you that it would take months to get the old software running again," replied Bridger. "And besides, we developed this new system to solve problems that our old software couldn't. I don't think yours is a reasonable solution."

STEP 2: Prepare the case for class discussion.

STEP 3: Answer each of the following questions, individually or in small groups, as directed by your instructor.

Diagnosis

1. What information needs did the DMV have?

Evaluation

2. How well did the old system meet these needs?

Design

3. What advantages did the new system offer?
4. What problems existed with the new system?

Implementation

5. Why did the system fail?
6. Can the DMV return to the old system?
7. How effectively did system development occur?
8. What should happen now?

STEP 4: In small groups, with the entire class, or in written form, share your answers to the questions above. Then answer the following questions:

1. What information needs did the DMV have?
2. How did it attempt to meet this need?
3. How effective was the resulting system?
4. How did the development of the system affect its performance?
5. What should the DMV do now? ●

Activity 21 A Case Study of Participative Systems Development

STEP 1: Read the following case. (This activity is especially suited for use in conjunction with Chapter 13 of *Information Systems.*)

BACKGROUND: THE REQUIREMENTS DATA BANK (RDB)

The Air Force Logistics Command's (AFLC) primary mission is to ensure that materiel resources are available to support Air Force weapons systems. This mission greatly depends on the AFLC Materiel Requirements Planning (MRP) process, which involves forecasting the acquisition and repair requirements of approximately 900,000 spares, repair parts, and equipment items worth nearly $28 billion (BDM 1986). This forecasting process involves predicting approximately $15–17 billion annually for acquiring and maintaining these items (Air Force 1982).

Beginning in the mid-1970s, the Air Force MRP process was criticized as inefficient. Specifically, in managing MRP tasks, the AFLC used 22 different data systems, and because these systems were developed in the 1950s and 1960s, they were antiquated. To meet logistics objectives, AFLC realized it had to improve the existing MRP process. To develop and implement these improvements, the Air Force undertook the Requirements Data Bank (RDB) (Air Force 1982)—a major MIS development project (which is still in progress).

A cadre of top functional people were identified and removed from day-to-day management activities to identify the requirements for the RDB. The result was a seven-year planning effort that culminated in the publication of a master functional description (MFD) for the RDB. The MFD was a general document that contained RDB goals and broke down development into several modules that could be developed relatively independently.

After thoroughly staffing the MFD, AFLC to management decided to develop a statement of work to solicit bids from professional services contractors to develop the RDB rather than attempt to develop it in-house. The statement called for each bidder to propose the best computer and functional architecture to meet MFD needs and for the selected contractor to submit specific functional descriptions for each MFD module. A later section of this paper discusses the practicality of this provision and the actual process of developing the specific module functional descriptions (FDs).

Bids were received from several contractors and a "fly-off" between the to two contractors was called for to verify that the contractors could deliver their proposed designs. aS a result, a contractor was selected to develop the RDB, AFLC funded the ten-year development, and development begain in January 1985 (BDM 1986).

The RDB has involved an enormous development effort. When completed, it will handle both the automated and manual areas involved in the AFLC MRP, developing nearly 3.7 million lines of code to replace the primarily batch-oriented 22 main data systems. It will involve over 5,600 users throughout the United States and will cost nearly $300 million to develop and operate over the next ten years (Air Force 1982).

SOURCE: Robert S. Tripp, "Managing the political and cultural aspects of large-scale MIS projects. A Case Study of Participative Systems Development." *Information Resources Management Journal* (Fall 1991): 2–13.

THE RDB PROJECT MANAGEMENT ORGANIZATION

The main problem in managing the contractual development of such a large MIS involved bringing together three diverse cultures—users, in-house systems analysts, and contractor systems developers. Because users know little about MIS technology and in-house and contractor MIS professionals know little about functional processes, the project called for some means of coordinating these groups. To meet this challenge, AFLC established an RDB project management organization (PMO).

As indicated in the organizational chart shown in Figure 1, AFLC acknowledged the importance of information as a management resource by creating a headquarters organization to manage it—AFLC Director of Information Systems and Communications—and by placing this activity on the same level as the functional staff. The AFLC Chief Information Officer (CIO) holds the same rank and follows the same reporting channel to the AFLC Command Section as his functional counterparts.

As shown in Figure 1, the CIO has both line and staff functions reporting to him. To manage both functions, the CIO is "dual hatted"—he holds a headquarters staff position and controls a line organization simultaneously.

The CIO's staff functions include planning for future MIS directions and developments; obtaining the resources necessary to design, develop, operate, and maintain all AFLCMIS; establishing software and hardware architectural standards; developing database, application software, and hardware integration policies to coordinate major MIS developments; and producing contracts for MIS developments and hardware acquisitions. Because AFLC has several large, geographically dispersed operating sites, CIO staff responsibilities included providing MIS operating policy and guidance to each of the Chief Information Managers (CIMs), who report to the decentralized site commander and not to the CIO.

The CIO's line functions include managing and controlling the design, development, operations, and maintenance of all MIS to be used at each site. To accomplish these functions, the CIO has a separate organization that reports to him, as indicated in Figure 1. The line organization consists of several divisions that have a number of PMOs reporting to these divisions. The PMOs are responsible for major MIS developments. Another major part of the line organization is the unit responsible for current MIS operations at the AFLC's headquarters site.

The RDB is one of several MIS being developed for the Director of Materiel Management. This division is appropriately called the Materiel Management Systems Division. Five of these major divisions report to the CIO, which is responsible for developing the five major systems, with a total development cost of more than $800 million. Of these, the RDB is the largest and most important to AFLC.

The Project Manager and the User Representative

The RDB PMO, a variant of the "shared responsibilities" project team suggested by Synnott and Gruber (1981), was structured primarily to promote user participation in the project. The primary difference between the RDB PMO and "shared responsibilities" model is that the senior user representative reports directly to his functional line manager instead of to the project manager. The chief user representative is a senior functional manager with the same corporate rank as the RDB project manager. This arrangement is intended to foster strong user commitment and support during the development. The functional specialists, who work directly for the chief user representative, are assigned from the headquarters, but have the authority to "order" functional specialists in each area from AFLC operational sites to development sites when necessary.

Under this arrangement, the project manager is responsible for all aspects of the project, including costs and schedules, while the user representative is responsible for making sure

RDB Project Management Organization (PMO)

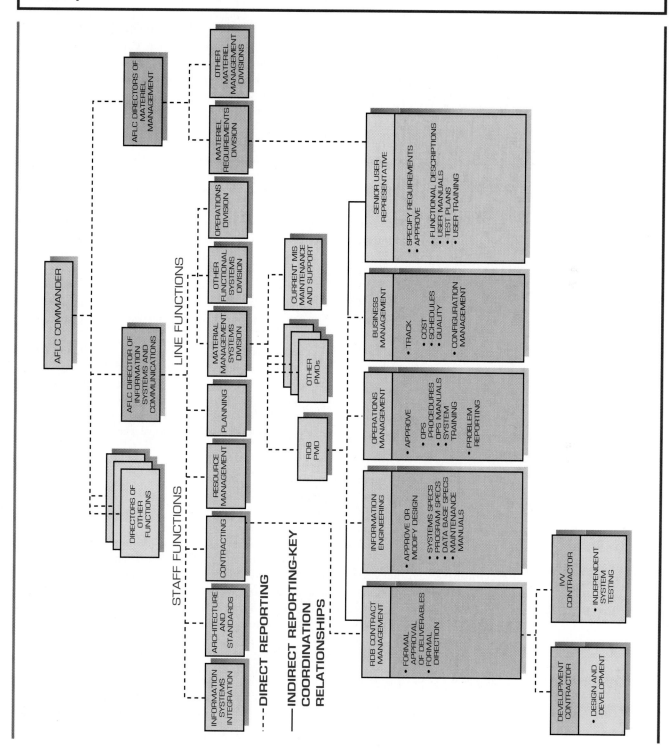

AFLC COMMANDER

AFLC DIRECTORS OF MATERIEL MANAGEMENT

AFLC DIRECTOR OF INFORMATION SYSTEMS AND COMMUNICATIONS

DIRECTORS OF OTHER FUNCTIONS

OTHER MATERIEL MANAGEMENT DIVISIONS

MATERIEL REQUIREMENTS DIVISION

LINE FUNCTIONS

OPERATIONS DIVISION

OTHER FUNCTIONAL SYSTEMS DIVISION

MATERIAL MANAGEMENT SYSTEMS DIVISION

STAFF FUNCTIONS

PLANNING

RESOURCE MANAGEMENT

CONTRACTING

ARCHITECTURE AND STANDARDS

INFORMATION SYSTEMS INTEGRATION

CURRENT MIS MAINTENANCE AND SUPPORT

OTHER PMOs

RDB PMO

SENIOR USER REPRESENTATIVE
- SPECIFY REQUIREMENTS
- APPROVE
- FUNCTIONAL DESCRIPTIONS
- USER MANUALS
- TEST PLANS
- USER TRAINING

BUSINESS MANAGEMENT
- TRACK
- COST
- SCHEDULES
- QUALITY
- CONFIGURATION MANAGEMENT

OPERATIONS MANAGEMENT
- APPROVE
- OPS PROCEDURES
- OPS MANUALS
- SYSTEM TRAINING
- PROBLEM REPORTING

INFORMATION ENGINEERING
- APPROVE OR MODIFY DESIGN
- SYSTEMS SPECS
- PROGRAM SPECS
- DATA BASE SPECS
- MAINTENANCE MANUALS

RDB CONTRACT MANAGEMENT
- FORMAL APPROVAL OF DELIVERABLES
- FORMAL DIRECTION

IVV CONTRACTOR
- INDEPENDENT SYSTEM TESTING

DEVELOPMENT CONTRACTOR
- DESIGN AND DEVELOPMENT

--- DIRECT REPORTING

— INDIRECT REPORTING-KEY COORDINATION RELATIONSHIPS

the system meets user needs. This organization demands that the project manager and user representative agree on costs, schedules, and capabilities. Under the Synnott and Gruber arrangement, the senior user would report directly to the project manager and have his effectiveness rating reviewed by the functional line manager. This approach aims to increase the user's cost and schedule commitment. The primary strength of the RDB approach is to make sure user views are considered in all aspects of project development. Control of the requirements baseline under the RDB approach must be given priority attention by the project manager. The senior user must also support stability of requirements specification.

As indicated in Figure 1, the RDB Project Manager reports to the Materiel Management Systems Division manager, while the senior user representative reports directly to a functional line manager with a rank and organizational level equal to the Materiel Management Systems Division manager. This arrangement allowed the RDB Project Manager to report to the same level of corporate management as the senior user representative, ensuring that user needs were balanced with cost and schedule considerations.

The selection of the project manager, senior user representative, and key members of their staffs in this organizational structure was very important, because the project manager and his team must be respected by the user representatives and vice versa. In the first four years of the RDB development, there were two project managers and two senior user representatives. In each "replacement," the project manager and senior user representative were screened for selection by both the AFLC's Chief Information Office (CIO) and senior functional manager to ensure that the project manager and senior user representative would work together to accomplish the RDB goals. In addition, both knew they would eventually move to functional positions that relied on the RDB, knowledge that increased their commitment to the project.

Most of the PMO and user representatives have remained with the project, and AFLC senior management plans to keep the attrition of team members to a very low level. On the other hand, the project manager and senior user representative positions will probably continue to be "stepping stones" for the growth of senior managers within AFLC. This set-up emphasizes the importance of having an RDB background credential for up-and-coming senior management prospects, thus encouraging the best functional people to serve in the development.

The Procurement Contracting Officer

As indicated in Figure 1, after program manager approval for actions, the Air Force procurement contracting officer (PCO) provided all directions to the development contractor. The PCO has the actual directive authority to enforce or change the provisions of the development contract. Like the senior user representative, the PCO does not work directly for the program manager but for a centralized procurement officer of the same rank as the project manager and the Materiel Management Systems Division manager. Because of a shortage of experienced PCOs within the contracting organization, the PCOs assigned to the RDB were usually junior people. As a result of this—but also because of the importance of the RDB to AFLC—major contracting decisions would frequently be deferred to the most senior contract management personnel. This arrangement placed an added burden on the project manager to communicate project needs to senior contract management people who were not involved in the day-to-day operations of the development to gain their support for needed contract changes.

From a project perspective, it would have been more efficient for the contracting representative to work directly for the project manager. In this way, the senior contracting officer could have reviewed and approved the contracting officer's effectiveness report. However, the reality here was that the contracting organization did not have enough experienced PCOs to support all PMOs in this manner. Since not all projects required a full-time PCO, AFLC's matrix approach ensured that PCOs were used efficiently and helped expedite routine contracting functions.

Structure of the RDB PMO

As shown in Figure 1, the RDB PMO consisted of three organizations that reported directly to the project manager. The Business Management Division of the PMO was responsible for monitoring development contractor costs, schedules, and quality of contractor-delivered products and for reporting significant deviations from planned performance in these areas. The Operations Management Division was responsible for approving contractor-proposed operations procedures, operations manuals, and training programs for Air Force operations personnel who would operate contractor-delivered software at the AFLC sites. This division was also responsible for coordinating AFLC site-preparation activities to accept hardware at each site selected by the development contractor for RDB operations. The Information Engineering Division was responsible for approving detailed software designs and associated documents produced by the development contractor.

In addition, the PMO structure included an independent verification and validation (IVV) contractor, who reviewed the development contractor's documentation and software products to ensure that high-quality products were delivered. The IVV contractor reviewed acceptance test plans and conducted independent tests of software for the PMO. The project manager was responsible for providing technical direction to the IVV and development contractors.

The organizational approach used to develop the RDB placed a substantial communications and coordination burden on the project manager and other members of the PMO team to obtain the cooperation of people beyond their direct control; as a result, they needed strong communication and persuasion skills. Senior management took this burden into account when selecting the project manager and other PMO senior members. Locating the user representatives and the PMO at the development contractor's facility facilitated communications between these groups. Moreover, to facilitate coordination, the RDB PCO also spent two or three days each week with the PMO.

PROJECT RESPONSIBILITIES DURING EACH PHASE OF DEVELOPMENT

Specific RDB project responsibilities during each phase in the development cycle closely resembled those suggested by Synnott and Gruber for MIS project organizations (1981). To make steady progress on the RDB development, all the organizations involved in the development had to understand their roles and responsibilities clearly. Figure 2 outlines the responsibilities of the development contractor, users, and in-house systems analysts in the various phases of the RDB development. The figure explains how the major responsibilities shifted in the group depending on the particular phase of the life cycle of the development.

The Requirements Definition Phase

In the Synnott and Gruber model, the user is directly responsible for developing the functional requirements and for writing the functional description. The RDB contract, however, assigned this responsibility to the development contractor, assuming that the selected—rather than in-house—people would best understand the AFLC MRP process. However, it soon became apparent that in-house senior people were better suited to articulating a clear vision of the RDB. As a result, the PMO and users jointly developed a concept of operations that functionally described the "new world" the RDB was expected to achieve and how it would change current operations. Once the concept of operations was specified, the user representatives wrote descriptions that revised their functional processes accordingly.

FIGURE 2 RDB Responsibilities by Stage in Project Life Cycle

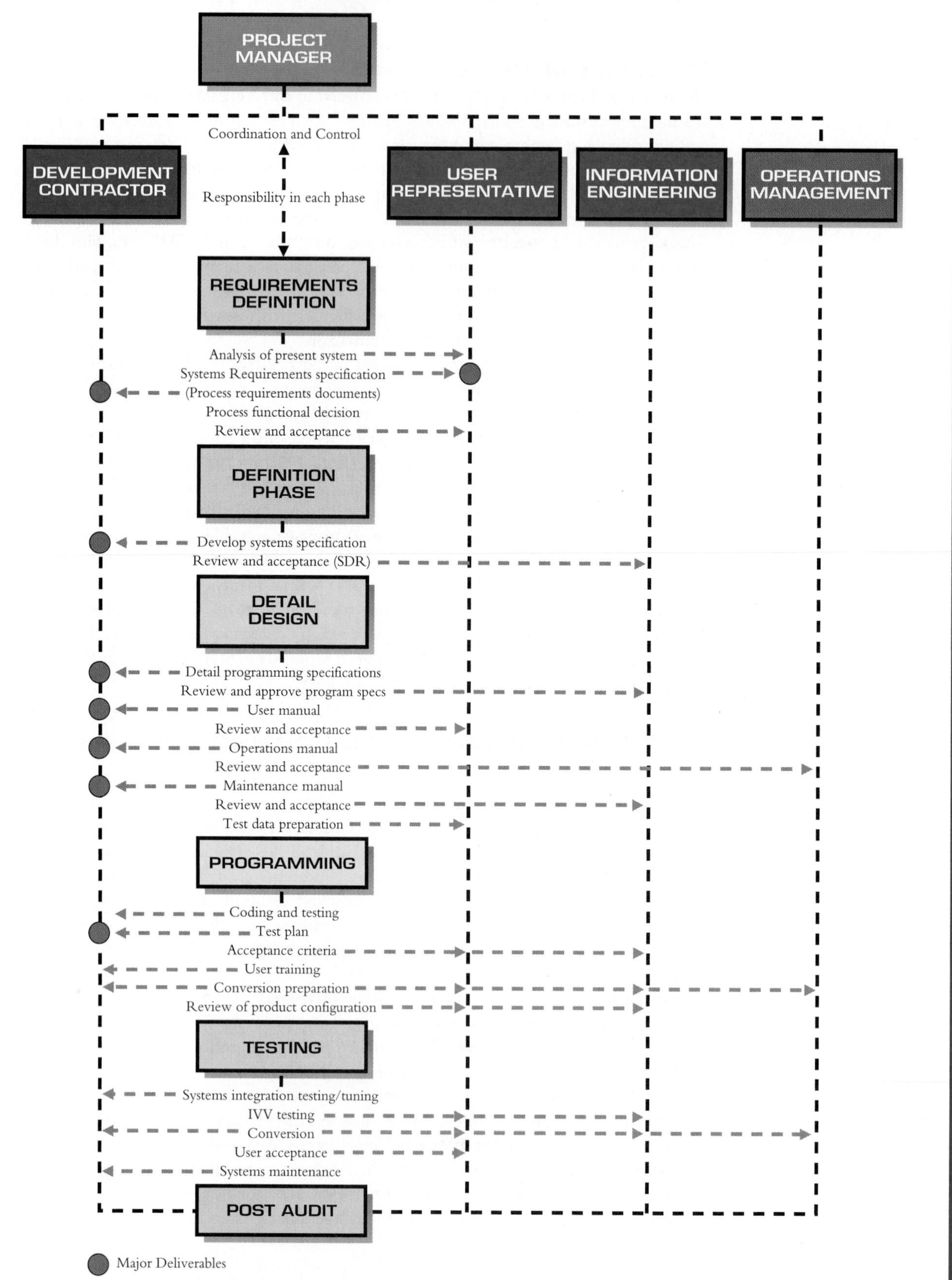

These descriptions, called process requirements documents, were delivered to the contractor, who then refined these documents and issued process functional descriptions (PFDs) that defined the details for all requirements of the RDB's sixteen segments. These PFDs had to be consistent with the concept of operations and the process requirements documents. The portfolio of sixteen completed PFDs were large and complex. They included over 6,500 pages, describing more than 2,200 processes.

The PFDs, which took over two years to develop, spelled out the functional requirements and offered details of all the process activities. The extra steps involved in this process paid off—the development contractor understood the requirement more fully, often helping to write the PFDs.

Traditional wisdom suggests that only the user can specify requirements. While this may be the case, the cost and political pressure associated with a large MIS development contract probably "forced" AFLC to specify the requirements sooner than would have been done without that pressure.

As indicated in Figure 2, the user organization has primary review and approval authority for the contractor-delivered PFDs. Formal mechanisms were established to provide direction to the contractor to correct deficiencies in the various documents and software products, as will be explained below.

The Definition Phase

The definition phase emphasizes how—rather than what—things are built in each RDB segment. The primary document in this phase was the systems specification. The primary responsibility for AFLC review and approval shifted from the users to the PMO systems analysts, who were housed in the Information Engineering Division.

The Detailed Design Phase

As the design for each segment progressed into detailed design, the contractor was required to submit several documents for review and approval before the next phase of development could proceed. The primary document during this phase was the program specifications, although the contractor also had to deliver drafts of the user's manual. Figure 2 indicates which PMO organization had primary responsibility for review and approval of each document.

The Programming Phase

During this phase, the development contractor coded the segments. The AFLC maintained a basically "hands off" role, except to answer questions.

The Testing Phase

During the test phase, AFLC activity was intense to ensure that the product met its requirements. Because the PMO had established good working relations with the development contractor, AFLC and IVV contract personnel were allowed to observe the development contractor integration testing activities. This practice helped build confidence that the system was meeting its objectives. Also, if problems were spotted by AFLC personnel, the contractor test department could document the problems before official AFLC acceptance testing started. This process helped shorten the process for making software changes when they were needed. The IVV contractor played a key role in this phase, as did the user. The user led the testing activity and was assisted by the IVV contractor. If problems were uncovered, which they invariably were, the user prioritized the problems that required software modifications. Usually, the highest-priority changes were made as soon as possible, while lower-priority changes were scheduled for later releases of the software.

The Post Audit

Six months after official acceptance of a segment, the user population was sent questionnaires to determine the extent of user satisfaction with the system and to determine if the segments met the requirement. If serious problems were found, software modifications would be developed for release to users.

ESTABLISHING AND MAINTAINING CONTROL: IMPORTANCE OF CONFIGURATION MANAGEMENT

Establishing control over any MIS development requires configuration management procedures—procedures that specify how the team members go about approving or modifying the contractor documents or software products during the MIS development cycle.

As discussed above, AFLC team members reviewed each of the contract documents and software products. Figure 2 shows who had the primary responsibility for accepting specific products during each phase of the development. Initial deliveries of documents and software products always required some correction or modification. To control the configuration of these documents, the appropriate members of the AFLC PMO wrote Design Problem Reports (DPRs) or Software Problem Reports (SPRs). DPRs were written against functional descriptions, systems specifications, users' manuals, operation manuals, maintenance manuals, data base specifications, and any other written document before these documents were accepted. SPRs were written against software deliveries, primarily in the test phase of development, before acceptance. Baseline Change Requests (BCRs) and Data Base Change Requests (DBCRs) were written after acceptance of products to change their configuration.

Because sixteen major segments were developed in RDB, the processes in Figure 2 had to be traversed at least sixteen times. (Actually, some of the segments were broken into several modules, so the process was repeated many more times). Thus, at any given time, several documents or software products were in process, involving different phases of development for the sixteen segments. To maintain control, AFLC provided written instructions to the contractor, using the appropriate configuration management documents described above.

Automated configuration management reports were developed to indicate the status of each document and software product, including information on how many problem reports were outstanding on each product. Using these reports, the project manager could determine where to focus management attention. Thus, a strong configuration management organization was needed just to track documents and software products and to correctly assign the products for corrective comments or acceptance.

The Business Management Division of the PMO handled configuration management, and because of its importance, configuration management was given special emphasis by the project manager.

Figure 3 illustrates the procedures used to propose and process BCRs. The procedures for processing other change requests and problem reports were similar. Users, PMO members, or the development contractor could initiate a change request. Upon receiving a change request, configuration management people within the Business Management Division of the PMO assigned the request a number for tracking purposes and prepared a letter for the project manager to forward the request to the development contractor for evaluation. The PCO endorsed the letter to the contractor to "authenticate" the request for evaluation. The development contractor then routes the change request to all potentially affected departments. After affected departments evaluate the proposed change, the contractor consolidates all responses and prepares a configuration change directive with the appropriate cost and schedule impacts of the change clearly specified. The contractor submits the change directive to configuration management, which logs the response and submits the change directive for user, PMO, and PCO coordination. If the change directive is submitted by the contractor

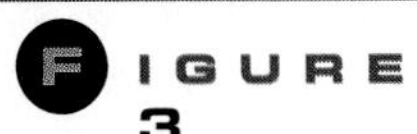

Configuration Management

AIR FORCE USER — GENERATES CHANGE REQUEST

PMO INFO ENGINEERING — GENERATES CHANGE REQUEST

DEVELOPMENT CONTRACTOR — ORIGINATES BCR ATTACHES DOCUMENT PAGES

DEVELOPMENT CONTRACTOR — ROUTES BCR FOR IMPACT

DEVELOPMENT CONTRACTOR — CONSOLIDATES RESPONSES IMPACT ON COST/SCHEDULE

DEVELOPMENT CONTRACTOR — INFO COPY OF EVALUATION TO PCO

PMO CONFIGURATION MANAGEMENT — PREPARES CCD FOR CCS ASSIGNS BCR # OF DC BCR

PMO INFO ENGINEERING — VERIFIES CHANGE IF SUBMITTED BY DC

PMO INFO ENGINEERING — OBTAINS COORDINATION OF USER REPRESENTATIVES

PMO PROGRAM MANAGER — APPROVES/ DISAPPROVES BCR

DEVELOPMENT CONTRACTOR — ACTS ON BCR

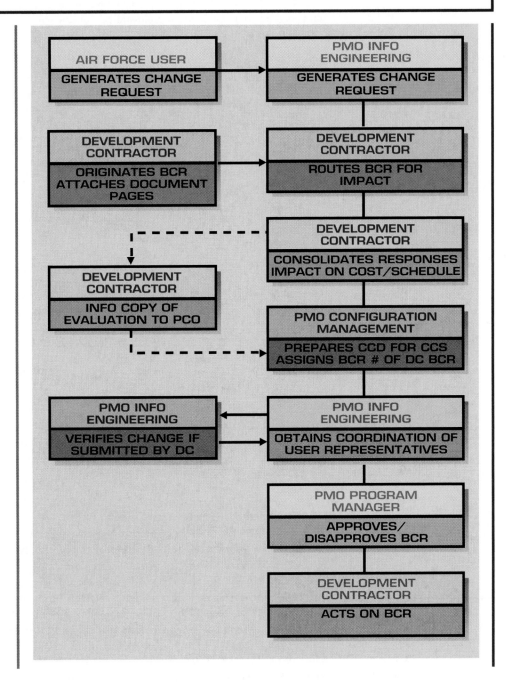

with no request from the AFLC team members, it receives a number and is routed to PMO and users for evaluation and approval. Finally, after the senior user representative has coordinated the change directive, it is approved or disapproved by the project manager. After the project manager's action, configuration management updates the BCR log and prepares a letter for the PCO to notify the contractor based on the outcome of the project manager's decision. The contractor then takes the appropriate action.

Although the procedures outlined above may seem bureaucratic, they are necessary to establish and maintain control in large-scale MIS developments. To be effective, users must support the process, the project manager must insist on following the procedures to the letter, and this discipline must be followed or control will be lost.

SOME LESSONS LEARNED

Initially, the roles and responsibilities of each group in the RDB development were not clearly defined (GAO 1986). The user representatives understood their role, but their perception of development goals differed from that of the development contractors. The users were accustomed to dealing informally with in-house developers, who traditionally pay little attention to the cost of information relative to its value. Users would request work through formal channels and the in-house developers would determine how many hours it would take to perform the work. If a conflict arose over resources, users and developers would sit down and prioritize the work to be done. In this environment, AFLC users had never been told that any job was impossible or beyond the project's scope. In short, the users had never worked in a formal, constrained environment where procedures were used to direct and modify MIS development efforts.

The development also faced a new situation. As mentioned earlier, the contractor was selected after prototypes of portions of two contractors' proposed designs were compared. (Several other contractors submitted proposals, but only two were selected to build design prototypes). During the prototype demonstrations, relations between AFLC personnel and the contractors were at arm's length. To prevent any possible favoritism to a single contractor, contractors received only information they specifically requested. Thus, normal customer relations were not established early in the program. As a result, the contractor developed the attitude—reinforced in the prototype competition—that there would be little feedback from users in the RDB development. This meant that contractors grew to feel their job was done when the product was delivered to the user. This attitude impaired necessary communications between users and development contractors. In a complex undertaking like the RDB, initial attempts to describe the system in any formal document are very likely to contain errors or inadequate descriptions that need modifications. In the early days of the RDB, the contractor was unprepared to engage in this dialogue in a controlled and disciplined manner.

PMO Coordination Failures

The initial RDB PMO was not prepared to coordinate these two groups or integrate their differing views of what was to be developed in the RDB. Disciplined configuration management procedures for directing and controlling the contractors' efforts were omitted, as were formal reviews for checking contractor progress at the critical design and development milestones. Too much informal dialogue between users and the contractor resulted in the contractor receiving conflicting and incomplete guidance. In addition, the PMO did not "preach" cost control or convince users that delays in decisions or incomplete disclosure of requirements lead to cost overruns and schedule slippages. Also, the PMO had former in-house systems people evaluating the proposed designs of the contractor. Some of these people resented having someone else work on a development they thought they should be doing. As a result, the contractor did not receive some information he needed to know.

Failing to control and manage these diverse cultures resulted in a large project with cost and schedule overruns projected barely six months after contract award. (The results of this failure have been documented [GAO 1986].) The root cause was a lack of understanding of roles and missions among the groups involved. As a result, a new PMO and senior contract staff were appointed to straighten out the situation.

Implementing Formal Procedures

Project management learned from initial problems and installed new leadership to correct them. The major task facing the new management team was to establish control over the project and clearly define the roles and responsibilities of each organization involved in the development. The new team explained the responsibilities of each group during the phases of development outlined above, emphasizing the importance of specifying requirements and minimizing changes, and implemented firm configuration management. The AFLC and contractor members of the design team were told flatly that contractor guidance must be in writing and must be approved by the project manager using appropriate configuration management procedures.

Users at first reacted negatively to these changes, expecting they would be criticized if several BCRs were written about their particular segment. When the project manager insisted upon implementation, he promised that no user representatives would be singled out for criticism based on number of BCRs. This promise induced the senior user representative to support the formal procedures.

Another problem about BCRs emerged. As indicated in the last section, each BCR had the schedule and cost to implement the change clearly identified on the bottom line. As a result, all PMO members became "independent cost estimators" and criticized the contractor estimates. Some of the criticisms were justified and were pursued through official channels. Most, however, resulted from failure to understand the full cost of changes. The project manager had to explain to PMO members that the contractor costs included not only direct costs for programming the changes but also charges for documentation changes and pro-rata charges for contractor overhead.

The RDB was the AFLC's first experience in contracting out MIS developments; as a result, users and in-house analysts had never seen the full cost associated with information system developments. (In-house resource requirements had shown only direct labor hours with changes.) To quell this uneasiness, functional people suggested that cost information be removed from the BCRs. The project manager vetoed this suggestion and insisted that the cost of each proposed change remain as the bottom line on the BCRs. He was supported by the senior user representative. Eventually, this problem disappeared, and users began to consider the value of the information versus the cost of the proposed change.

Figure 4 shows the cost of BCRs approved after the implementation of the procedures. After procedures to control informal talk were instituted, the number and cost of approved BCRs dropped dramatically, due in large part to the users' disapproving BCRs based on cost/benefit analyses before they reached the project manager for decision. While the costs of approved BCRs may appear to be large, they represent far less than 10 percent of the development costs during the periods shown. Figure 5 shows the cost of BCRs that users disapproved as a result of cost/benefit considerations during this period. As shown, users' cost considerations have introduced a good deal of restraint into the program. This form of self-control is the best form of discipline and is supported by all parties now.

CONCLUSIONS

Defining and controlling system requirements heavily depends on user attitudes and commitment to developing the system within the project's cost and schedule constraints. These user attitudes and this commitment can be directly affected and strengthened in turn by actions the project manager and corporate staff can take. This paper outlined some of those actions and pointed out that they are largely political and cultural in nature and, thus, should be managed accordingly.

Carefully selecting the lead user representative and organizationally placing user representatives in the MIS project team are key determinants of how successful the identification and

Costs of Approved Modification BCRs

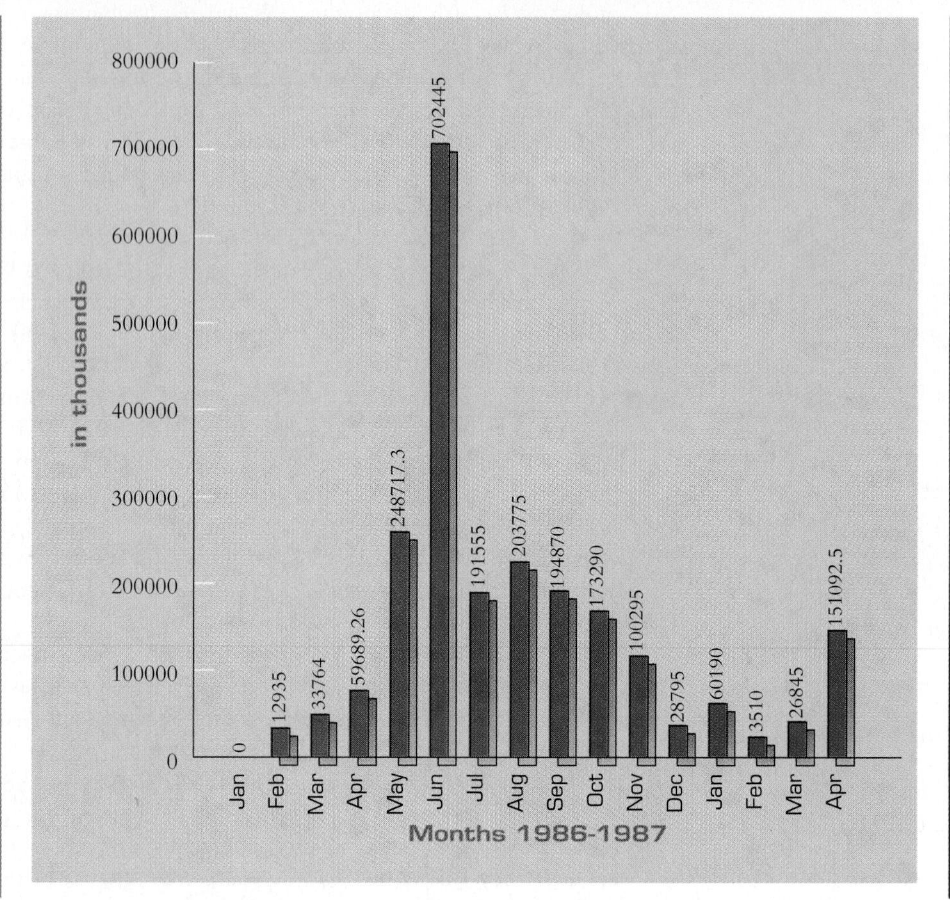

communication of requirements with the developer will be. Creating the proper organization and manning it with the right staff are political acts.

Once the requirements have been defined, user involvement in maintaining the requirements baseline is absolutely necessary. To make sure "requirements creep" is held to a minimum, the senior user must play a fundamental role in making sure the baseline is maintained. Specifically, he must be involved in the approval process during various steps in the design process and must participate in strict configuration management processes to review and approve all suggested changes before they are considered by the developer for cost and schedule effects. Making sure the requirement is maintained and not changed frequently is a cultural phenomenon that needs to be taught and nurtured.

References

Ahituv, Niv and Newmann, Seev (1984, June). A Flexible Approach to Information System Development. *MIS Quarterly,* 69–78.

Appleton, D. S. (1986, January 15). Very Large Projects. *Datamation,* 63–70.

BDM Corporation (1986). *The Air Force Requirements Data Bank Master Functional Description* (MFD), Revision B.

FIGURE 5 Costs of Disapproved BCRs

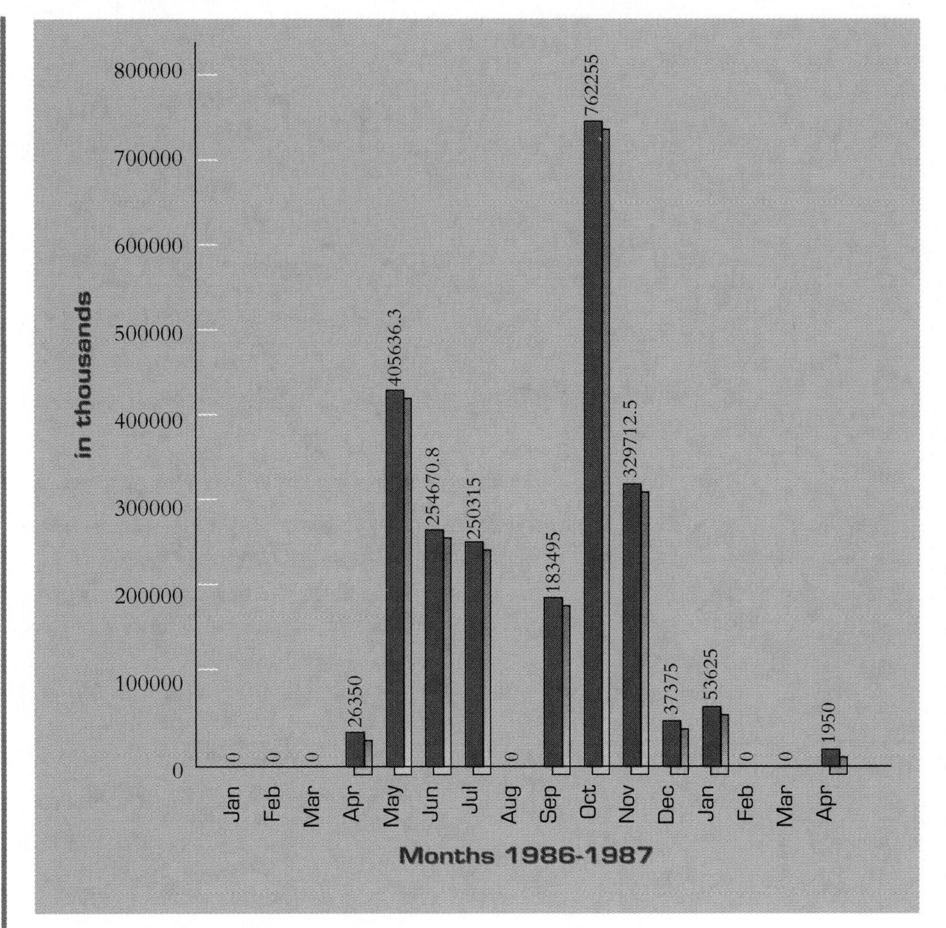

Doll, W. J. (1985, March). Avenues for Top Management Involvement in Successful MIS Development. *MIS Quarterly,* 17.

Hirscheim, R. A. (1985, December). User Experience With the Assessment of Participative Systems Design. *MIS Quarterly,* 295–304.

Juergens, Hugh F. (1977, June). Attributes of Information System Development. *MIS Quarterly,* 31–41.

King, William R. (1982). Alternative Designs in Information System Development. *MIS Quarterly,* 31–42.

Markus, M. L. (1983). Power, Politics, and MIS Implementation. *Communications of the ACM,* 26 (6), 430–444.

McFarlan, F. W. (1981). Portfolio Approach to Information Systems. *Harvard Business Review,* 59, 142–159.

Snow, Terry (1984). Use of Software Engineering Practices at a Small MIS Shop. *IEEE Transactions on Software Engineering,* SE-10 (4), 408–413.

Synnott, W. R. and Gruber, W. H. (1981). *Information Resource Management: Opportunities and Strategies for the 1980s.* New York: John Wiley and Sons.

Tait, P. and Vessey, L. (1988, March). The Effect of User Involvement on Systems Success: A Contingency Approach. *MIS Quarterly,* 91–108.

U.S. Department of the Air Force (HQ AFLC/LO[RDB]) (1982). *The Air Force Requirements Data Bank (RDB) Economic Analysis.* Wright-Patter AFB, OH.

U.S. General Accounting Office (GAO) (1986). Continued Oversight Crucial for Air Force's Requirements Data Bank. Report Number GAO/IMTEC-87-6. Washington, DC.

White, K. B. and Leifer, R. (1986, September). Information Systems Development Success: Perspectives from Project Team Participants. *MIS Quarterly,* 214–223.

Wong, Carolyn (1984). *A Successful Software Development. IEEE Transactions on Software Engineering,* SE-10 (6), 714–727.

STEP 2: Prepare the case for class discussion.

STEP 3: Answer each of the following questions, individually or in small groups, as directed by your instructor.

Diagnosis

1. What information needs did the Air Force have in the area of tracking materiel resources?
2. Why did the Air Force develop the RDB?

Evaluation

3. How well did existing systems meet the identified needs?

Design

4. What advantages did the proposed system offer?

Implementation

5. What steps in the SDLC did the Air Force follow?
6. What key decisions did they make in implementing such a large-scale MIS project?
7. What roles did the project manager, user representative, and procurement contracting officer play?
8. How were project responsibilities allocated during each phase of development?
9. How effective was project development?
10. What changes would you recommend if the Air Force implemented a similar MIS project?
11. What steps would comprise a quality development process for the Air Force?

STEP 4: In small groups, with the entire class, or in written form, share your answers to the questions above. Then answer the following questions:

1. What information needs did the Air Force have?
2. How did it attempt to meet these needs?
3. How effective were the resulting systems?
4. Did a quality systems development process exist?
5. What changes should be made in the development process? ●

Activity 22 It Won't Work in Kanji: The Case of Expert Systems Standardization at Global

STEP 1: Read the following case. (This activity is especially suited for use in conjunction with Chapter 14 of *Information Systems.*)

As Mr. Tanaka read Mr. Brown's memo, he could foresee many problems for Global Sekiyu's (GS's) Applications Development Group and for the company as a whole. The Applications Development Group, to which Tanaka belonged, was responsible for creating and maintaining computer programs to support GS's operations. The Group enjoyed a high level of success and status within GS and generally operated independently of GS's parent, Global Oil. Even so, GS often used software developed by Global, and vice versa. This strategy was possible because many software vendors produced products in both English and Kanji, the dominant Japanese language for business. Where this had not been the case, GS had developed programs on its own to meet its users' needs.

Brown's memo signaled a possible end to this happy state of affairs. Previously, Global Corporate had never exerted control over the application development of its subsidiaries. Now, Brown's memo asked GS to use a product called ADS for GS's Grease Project. As Brown and Tanaka both knew, ADS was not ideal from the Japanese perspective—it did not support Kanji on personal computers (PCs) and its vendor had no Japanese offices. However, the Grease Project was part of a larger effort that would involve Global Corporate and all its subsidiaries. For this reason, Global had insisted that all members of the "team" use a standard product. Global had selected ADS after an extensive evaluation procedure despite ADS's lack of Kanji support on the PC, despite the absence of other ADS customers and ADS vendor support in Japan, and despite the fact that GS had already begun its work on the Grease Project using a product called GURU, which supported Kanji. Tanaka had just completed an experiment to evaluate the difficulty of converting software from GURU to ADS and found that this took almost as much time as it had originally taken to develop the software from scratch!

Brown's memo had not taken Tanaka entirely by surprise. The Grease Project is an Expert Systems (ES) application (see Exhibit 1). Ever since the ES Subcommittee produced its enabling-strategy white-paper over a year and a half ago, Tanaka had foreseen the possibility that Global might issue ES standards that would be difficult for GS to endorse. As the ES Senior Supervisor, reporting directly to the Application Development Manager at GS, Tanaka had followed developments at Global, evaluated Global's policies as they related to GS, and given as much feedback to the Subcommittee as was diplomatically possible.

GLOBAL CORPORATION

Global Oil began in 1871 as Bearing Oil Company. Today, Global Oil Corporation is a large, integrated oil company that refines and sells petroleum products in over 100 countries. Global has centralized the management of its marketing, refining, and related operations at its headquarters in Virginia. The centralized Marketing and Refining Division (MRD) is divided into U.S. and international departments and is responsible for the foreign affiliates. Among the worldwide subsidiaries, Global Sekiyu is one of the strongest.

GS, founded in 1898, is a marketing and sales company. Although it owns no refineries, it does have partial shares in two, Keio Kabushiki Kaisha and Tohoku Petroleum Industries, Ltd. GS employs approximately 1,300 people in Japan, over 100 of whom are in the Information Systems (IS) department at the head office. Nearly half of the IS department are contractors from computer consulting companies.

Technical Note—Expert Systems

Introduction

An Expert System (ES) is a computer program that mimics the way a human expert in a given field uses his or her expertise to solve complex and ambiguous problems. To do this, the ES must first "capture" the knowledge and judgement that the expert has acquired through years of experience. Second, it must be able to generalize and reason from this experience to solve problems that are similar yet somewhat different from those that the expert has seen. Finally, it must be able to communicate its answer or decision in a way that laymen can understand and believe as if they were dealing with a human expert.

How Expert Systems Are Used

Human experts, in most fields, are in short supply. Typically, a person recognized as an expert has acquired his or her expertise through twenty or thirty years of experience beyond formal schooling. As their expertise peaks, such people tend to seek new challenges or perhaps to retire. As a result, at any time, the supply of experts in most companies is wanting.

The primary use of ES technology is to duplicate, rather than replace, an expert. An ES application, in effect, allows the expert to be in two places at once. For example, General Electric's DELTA helps maintenance personnel to find and repair problems with its diesel electric locomotives. Although all GE's repair people have been trained and are skilled, it takes many years for them to develop the experience that DELTA can provide. With DELTA, they have an expert immediately at hand to assist with problems that they cannot solve on their own. Similarly, medical ES applications assist physicians in making diagnoses and suggesting treatments, particularly at rural hospitals where specialists may be unavailable and time is critical. Legal ES applications advise lawyers in the formulation of trial strategies; financial ES applications assist traders and advisors in managing portfolios; manufacturing ES applications assist operations managers and designers in process control.

Occasionally, as with GS's Help Desk system, ES applications are used to replace an expert. The motivation for this is usually to reduce costs, although it often also improves service by increasing the availability of the expert. ES applications have also been built to capture the knowledge of an irreplaceable expert who is due to retire. Finally, ES applications have been built for the sole purpose of training novices.

How Expert Systems Are Built

Most ES applications start with an ES "shell." The shell is a computer program that knows how to reason, how to recognize patterns, and how to make judgements when given facts, rules-of-thumb, and representative situations; however, it lacks specific expertise, the facts, rules-of-thumb, etc., that are known to the human expert. It is normally equipped with a "knowledge engineer," along with a human expert, to train it in its intended expertise. Depending on the sophistication of the shell, it may also have the ability to learn from its own mistakes as it works side by side with the expert on the same problem. Finally, the ES shell has an "explanation module" which describes how the ES arrived at its decision. Therefore, the expert can determine where the ES thinking may have gone astray, and can train it to respond properly in the future. The explanation module is also important when the finished ES application is used to train novices and when it must convince a reticent human that its decision is reasonable.

The direct reporting relationship between GS and Global Oil is from Mr. Ozawa, President of GS, to Mr. Schiffman, Executive Vice-President of the MRD international division (see Exhibit 2). Although this relationship has the ultimate reporting responsibility, individuals within GS confer and report to their counterparts at Global Oil. Mr. Ozawa is the first Japanese to be the president of GS.

INFORMATION SYSTEMS

The IS department at GS communicates frequently with MRD via phone, video conferencing, and electronic mail. The electronic mail system spans all of Global's affiliates, allowing any Global employee to communicate with any other employee at any time despite time-zone differences. However, communication among divisions is primarily at the manager level or higher. GS guidelines state that company-related telecommunications must be approved by the IS director.

GS employees are rarely assigned to corporate headquarters for extended periods. Likewise, corporate employees are rarely transferred to GS. When employees are exchanged for project assignments, it is usually at the manager level or higher.

The Development and Technology Services (D&TS) is a division of the IS department. Its function is to develop and research new products and applications for use within GS. The Manager of D&TS, Mr. Kobayashi, has an MBA from a U.S. business school and has worked

EXHIBIT 2 Marketing and Refining Division—International

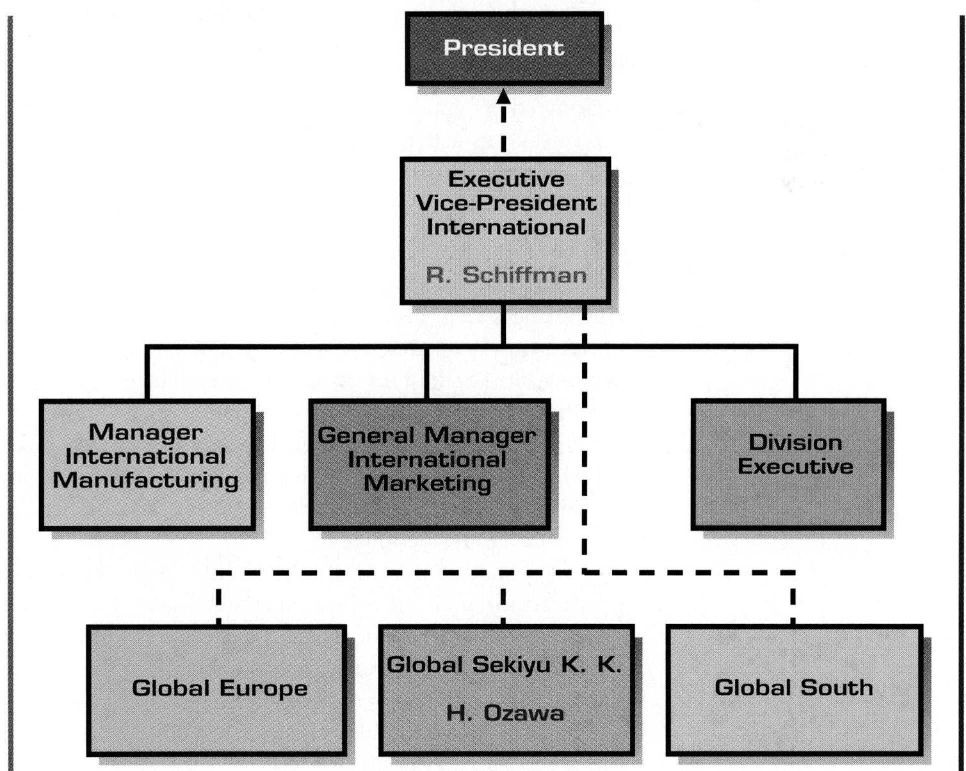

for several different departments within GS, as well as for other subsidiaries. He reports directly to the IS director (see Exhibit 3) and is responsible for everything that goes on in the division. Reporting to him is the Applications Development Manager, Mr. Matsui. Like Kobayashi, Matsui received an MBA from a U.S. business school, and has worked at many other divisions within GS. He supervises all development and research of new applications. Among the people he supervises is Tanaka, who also received an MBA from a U.S. business school and has worked in other divisions of GS. When Global decided to begin developing ES applications, Tanaka was selected to become GS's expert. He developed both ES applications currently in use at GS. The first application was for a computer help-desk, which allows users to find answers to their computer problems quickly and easily. The second, and larger, application is the Grease Project. When the project is completed, the Grease Expert System will allow engineers and salespeople to analyze customer problems and needs. Ultimately, it will be combined with a customer response center so that customers can call GS and get an immediate answer from the technician without having to wait for an engineer.

EXPERT SYSTEMS ENABLING STRATEGY

In early 1989, the steering committee for applications development at Global Corporate spun off an ES Subcommittee and charged it with the task of developing a strategy for enabling ES use within Global. The Subcommittee was composed primarily of managers from the Systems and Computer Services Group of the MRD. In June of 1989, the Subcommittee issued its report finding that

- ES technology had emerged as a valuable technique for providing cost-effective solutions to certain categories of business problems.
- The tools available for developing ES applications were evolving rapidly.
- Although Global's use of ES technology had been limited, various projects within Global and its subsidiaries confirmed the maturity and value of the technology. Five projects were cited.
- Competitors appeared to be increasingly active in ES; Global was behind and needed to accelerate its activity. The report cited statistics on staffing, etc., for 14 competitors.
- Many companies outside the oil industry had reported significant benefits of ES development. Nine well-known cases of strategic uses were summarized in the report.

The committee recommended a strategy of disbursing ES knowledge throughout the company while concurrently improving centralized support. To implement this strategy, specific changes were needed in the infrastructure supporting ES development. Among the recommendations was one to develop a guideline to "define a method for selecting the most appropriate (ES) tool for an identified application."

One section of the report was devoted to ES tool selection. It recommended that divisions with little or no experience in ES use one of several PC-based products to address small- to medium-sized problems. In addition, it recommended that an "interdivisional project be established to evaluate and recommend tools which can be used both on the mainframe and on the personal computer."

Tanaka had concurred wholeheartedly with the findings and recommendations of the report. At the time the white-paper was issued, Tanaka had just taken on the task of developing GS's first ES application. As part of this task, he had evaluated a variety of ES tools and settled on GURU, one of the products recommended in the white-paper, because of its support for Kanji and its support of image files (graphics). The development of this first system was highly successful and convinced Tanaka and others at GS that there was a greater role for ES in GS's future.

EXHIBIT 3 Information Systems at Global Sekiyu

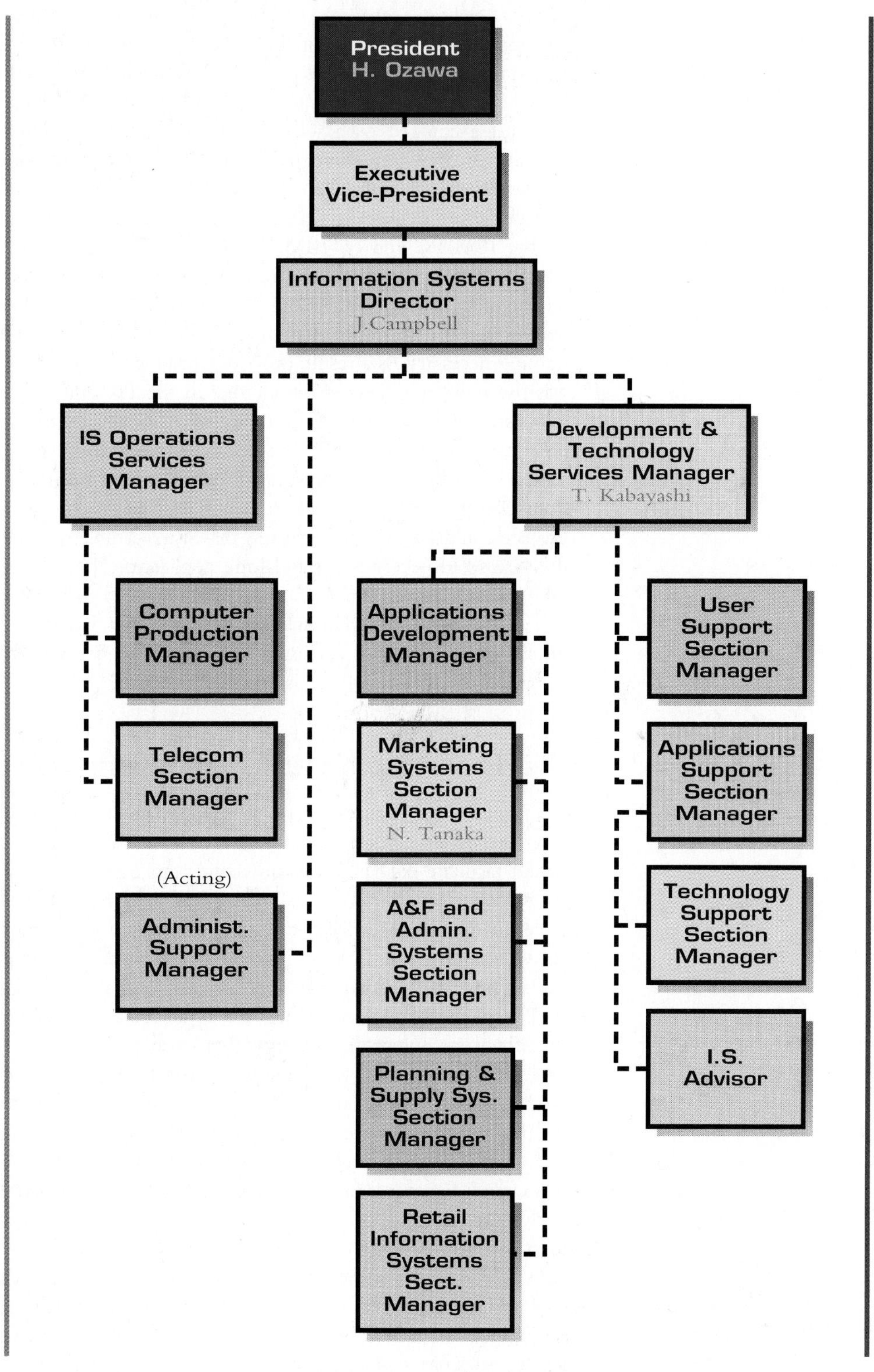

SELECTION OF ADS AS A STANDARD

On July 10, 1989, less than a month after the strategy report was published, the recommended ES evaluation project was initiated with a kick-off meeting at the MRD offices in Omaha, Nebraska. Prior to the meeting, Steven McKenzie, Tanaka's counterpart at Global Corporate, issued a memo identifying a preliminary list of factors that would be considered essential, important, and desirable in the selected ES product. Vendor support in Japan was listed as important but not essential, and support of Kanji was listed only as desirable. The committee charged with selecting the ES standard was composed of nine members from Global, six of whom were from MRD, including just one representative of International Applications Development.

After some deliberation, the committee limited its evaluation to programs that ran both on the IBM PC and on IBM mainframes. The purpose of this limitation was to minimize effort in transferring software from one platform to another, to increase the ability to share information among applications, and to reduce the number of products being used for ES development. This would maximize the availability of support and minimize the amount of training necessary. As a result, only four products were examined. Among these products, ADS was the only one deemed satisfactory in the PC environment. In April, 1990, the committee completed its report recommending ADS as a "standard-gap" product (one that should be considered the standard for the next one to three years).

Upon receipt of the Selection Report, Tanaka immediately undertook a review of ADS from GS's perspective. His report, issued less than three weeks later, confirmed that the Grease Project could be undertaken using ADS; nevertheless, based in part on the assumption that the Grease Project was a standalone application, he recommended that it be developed in GURU. As a caveat, Tanaka noted, "We will need to ask (MRD) whether ADS will be used as a tool for the Lube Knowledge Base and also whether GS should use the same tool for future integration with a master program. Even (if) that is the case, I will propose that GS postpone the investment decision (in ADS). . . ."

ISSUES FROM THE JAPANESE PERSPECTIVE

GS agreed with Global's policy to standardize the ES shell. It would eliminate duplication of effort by one or more subsidiaries as different ES applications were developed, and it would facilitate exchange of knowledge and expertise. However, GS had had no input into the selection of the standard; Tanaka was informed of the progress made by the U.S. task force. In turn, he had notified Global Corporate by memo that ADS would be difficult for GS to accept because of the following: 1. lack of Kanji support on the PC; 2. lack of vendor support; 3. lack of image support; and 4. absence of commercial sales in Japan.

The people who were to use ES applications at GS, while able to speak and read some English, were not proficient enough to use a program in English. In addition, the Grease Project in development was intended partly for the benefit of GS's customers, most of whom do not speak or read English.

The Japanese culture is highly visual. Most Japanese managers find that a picture is far clearer and easier to understand than its description in words. Therefore, graphics capability was crucial for any application at GS. ADS lacked support for graphics.

The lack of vendor support in Japan was also an obstacle. Who could Tanaka or other users call if there were problems? The vendor of ADS, Aion, is located in California. Because Tokyo is 11 hours ahead of the West Coast, support directly from Aion was impractical.

The fact that the product had never been sold in Japan also made GS uneasy. Also, with the absence of significant sales, Aion had little incentive to develop a Kanji interface or to create a support staff in Japan.

Worldwide Lube Expert Systems

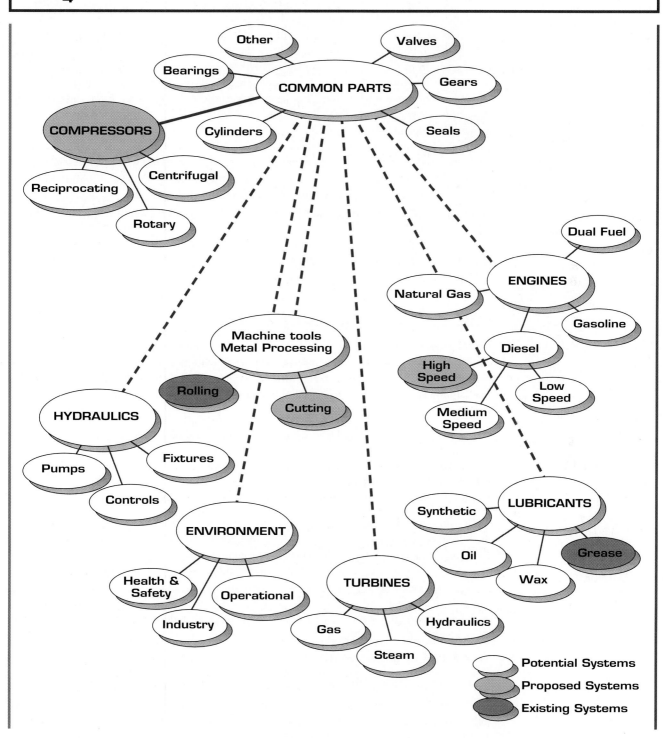

COMMON PARTS
Other
Valves
Bearings
Gears
Cylinders
Seals
COMPRESSORS
Centrifugal
Reciprocating
Rotary
Dual Fuel
ENGINES
Natural Gas
Gasoline
Diesel
High Speed
Low Speed
Medium Speed
Machine tools Metal Processing
Rolling
Cutting
HYDRAULICS
Pumps
Fixtures
Controls
ENVIRONMENT
Health & Safety
Operational
Industry
TURBINES
Gas
Steam
Hydraulics
LUBRICANTS
Synthetic
Oil
Wax
Grease

Potential Systems
Proposed Systems
Existing Systems

GS had few obvious alternatives, and none seemed very promising. It could switch its ES development to ADS, complying with the Global standard; it could use a program such as GURU that would be more useful for its own applications; or it could develop parallel systems in GURU and ADS satisfying both Corporate and local needs but incurring substantial "unnecessary" development costs and possible inconsistencies among the finished products. Mr. Campbell, the IS director, believes that given a valid reason and a solid case, GS can deviate from the corporate standards. However, everyone understands that this is a relatively short-term solution, and that whatever product(s) are chosen must be able to fit with long term corporate goals. Given that Japanese versions of software are often different from the original versions, with different features and capabilities, GS often has no choice than to go with a different product.

Tanaka had originally planned to develop the Grease Expert System in GURU so that it could be used by GS's engineers, technicians, and sales staff. This would satisfy GS's needs and would be extremely useful to its employees and customers. However, it would not help other Global affiliates, as very few people are fluent in reading Kanji.

The development of parallel systems is complex and costly. It is estimated that to convert one small portion of GURU to ADS would take over one man month and require a programmer or programmers fluent in ADS, GURU, English, and Japanese. Against these costs, GS must weigh the benefits of compatibility with Global Corporate and ease of use for its employees.

ISSUES FROM GLOBAL'S PERSPECTIVES

Global envisions the eventual development of a comprehensive, integrated, worldwide Lube Knowledge Base. As currently conceived, the Lube system would include components for compressors, hydraulics, environment, turbines, engines, lubricants (including GS's Grease system), and other common parts as well as machine tools metal processing (see Exhibit 4). The benefits of such a system include

- the ability to capture knowledge which would otherwise be lost through retirement, transfers and promotions;
- increasing the availability of knowledge and expertise to all field marketers;
- facilitation of knowledge sharing among affiliates; and
- reduction in duplication of common resource files and information.

By mid-1990, Brown began to realize that development of a Lube Expert System would be a long-term objective that would demand coordination on a worldwide bases. By late 1990, in conjunction with other managers throughout Global, he began to design an architecture that would encourage this development and enable it to flourish. The architecture laid out the various components of the system and began design of common systems such as the user interface and security system. It also laid out some ground rules for developers of other parts of the system. In particular, it required that development be done with the ADS ES shell.

STEP 2: Prepare the case for class discussion.

STEP 3: Answer each of the following questions, individually or in small groups, as directed by your instructor.

Diagnosis

1. What information needs did Global Sekiyu have?

2. How did these needs resemble and differ from the needs in other parts of Global Oil?

Evaluation

3. How well did the company's information systems meet those needs?
4. Why did Global Corporate want to introduce a standard application development in all subsidiaries?
5. What problems did such an introduction create for Global Sekiyu?

Design

6. What alternatives are available to Global Sekiyu?

Implementation

7. How did Global Sekiyu respond to Corporate's selection of the ADS standard?
8. What should Mr. Tanaka do now?
9. What challenges remain in defining IT policy?

STEP 4: In small groups, with the entire class, or in written form, share your answers to the questions above. Then answer the following questions:

1. What information needs did Global Sekiyu have?
2. How did Global Corporate attempt to meet this need?
3. What problems did the ADS standard pose for Global Sekiyu?
4. What should Global Sekiyu do now? ●

Activity 23 The Information Systems Infrastructure at AT&T

STEP 1: Read the AT&T Dream Team case. (This activity is especially suited for use in conjunction with Chapter 14 of *Information Systems.*)

THE AT&T DREAM TEAM

In July 1993, 60 of AT&T's top technology managers gathered nervously in a Berkeley Heights, N.J. conference room to meet their new chief information officer, Ron Ponder. "Morale was surging, anticipation was rising," recalls Rudolph Alexander, the company's VP of strategic information planning and the meeting's organizer. "It was like waiting on the arrival of the Messiah."

Ponder—lured away from Sprint, where he had also headed information systems (IS)—surprised his new colleagues with a talk that was decidedly nontechnical. "He said he was there to do two things," says Alexander. "Get customers and serve customers." Ponder, also a former CIO at Federal Express, made it clear he expected everyone else in the room to concentrate on customers, too.

In the nearly 28 months since that meeting, Ponder and AT&T, the third-largest company in the world, have embarked on what is probably the biggest, most ambitious information technology (IT) project under way anywhere.

To complete the project within his five-year deadline, Ponder is assembling a crack team of 26 CIOs, from within AT&T and from the outside. Of these, 23 have been assigned to AT&T business units, some of which are bigger than many corporations. They report directly to both Ponder and their business-unit managers, and all have technology projects of their own in the works.

In all, more than 50,000 AT&T employees—roughly one-sixth of the company's entire work force—report to Ponder and his all-star team of CIOs. At stake is nothing less than AT&T's ability to compete in the deregulated telecom marketplace.

The Problem Defined

Today, AT&T runs a hodgepodge of incompatible computer and communications systems. It allows each of its 23 business units to maintain customer records in forms that can't be shared with other units. Some business units can't even swap electronic mail with other business units without problems. "We've been like the shoemaker's children," says CEO Robert Allen. "We've been so focused on IT for the customer that we haven't spent enough time looking at our own operation. It's important to our cost structure to be able to make a connection between various business units." Ponder's project includes building a single, unified IT architecture around industry standards that will enable business units of the $75 billion telecom powerhouse to share selected data about customers.

At the heart of Ponder's vision is enabling AT&T to develop what he calls a "single view of the customer," from the time a company salesperson knocks on a customer's door throughout the life of their relationship. Or from the time teenagers get their first phones and computers, and even AT&T Universal Credit Cards. "I'm going to laser in, understand as much as I can about their buying habits, living habits, and lifestyles," says Ponder. "It's easy to invent

SOURCE: "The AT&T Dream Team" Mary Thyfault, *Information Week,* (March 6, 1995: pp 26–29, 34, 39.

the products if I can find the customer. Right now, we have the services but can't find the customers."

Company watchers, while admiring Ponder's talent and experience, warn that completing the IT project will be difficult. Sharing data is a challenge for a company that has its fingers in every slice of the communications-computing pie, including microchips, telephone systems, computers, and, of course, long-distance lines.

Ponder's vision of sharing data across the company runs counter to AT&T tradition. And the pressure is on to get it done. Even Ponder admits the clock is ticking. "We need to be well into this in the next three years because the marketplace won't wait on us, the customer won't wait on us," he worries. "Our enemy is time." In fact, according to Howard Anderson, managing director of the Yankee Group Inc., a consultancy in Boston, Ponder "faces the toughest and biggest job of any IT professional at any company in the world."

The Journey So Far

To appreciate how far Ponder and his team must travel, it helps to know where they started. When Ponder joined AT&T in June 1993, he found what he describes as a "disaggregated IT structure, operating in relatively low-level ways." Specifically, each business unit had its own IS structure, with William Osl, VP of new business development, overseeing information resources for AT&T's internal operations. "Overall, there was very little alignment of resources with the primary goals of the businesses and very little synergy between businesses," says Ponder. The Yankee Group's Anderson describes it more harshly: "They had very competent IT professionals that were being beat up by their divisions. And they've got every networking and operating system ever invented."

AT&T's technology structure made it difficult to get a single view of an AT&T customer, even within a business unit. Take AT&T's phone systems business—known as Global Business Communications Systems—where Bob Napier, the new CIO, found six IT organizations supporting different segments of the business. "If you wanted to get, say, a profitability statement by a customer prior to sitting for final negotiation on a deal," he says, "you'd have to go through some rather lengthy overnight batch jobs."

Customers weren't happy either. When Rino Bergonzi, now head of corporate IT services, was CIO at United Parcel Service, he used to get "very upset with AT&T," he says. "AT&T was an impossible company to deal with. Every time they visited me, they used to show up with 20 people. There was not one that knew my business." To change that, Ponder and his All-Stars will have to make great technical strides. For starters, Ponder has made a crucial breakthrough by convincing senior AT&T executives on the importance of merging the company's network and technology functions with the back-office billing and customer-care operations.

"This represents a whole new vision about the importance of information technology at AT&T," says Dan Elron, an analyst with Coopers & Lybrand in New York. "Traditionally in the telephone world, there was a definite wall between the two."

To further break down those walls, Ponder and his team have spent the last six months in heated debate over a crucial document known as the "foundation architecture." It will dictate technologies, standards, and products to all the company's CIOs. "When we get this fixed, we can move on the data in a very practical way," says Ponder. Already, the document calls for AT&T to use its own internal services and products where they make sense and where they are competitive. With that, the Yankee Group's Anderson estimates that AT&T may provide as much as 10% of sales for its Global Information Solutions (GIS) unit.

Back to Basics

The AT&T All-Stars are selecting a series of common industry standards on which to base their companywide systems. They've already decided to use TCP/IP to link 22 internal networks into one corporatewide frame-relay backbone that will eventually be migrated to asynchronous transfer mode (ATM) lines. Bergonzi estimates that standardized networks will save about $75 million and, more important, shave precious time spent cobbling together the business units' networks.

While Ponder refuses to provide additional details about the foundation architecture, a source close to the company says AT&T's networks will use Cisco and Wellfleet routers and Cabletron hubs. In the messaging arena, the source adds, AT&T will rely on the X.400 E-mail and X.500 directory standards. For enterprisewide computers, it will run client-server networks based on Unix VI.4. On desktop computers, AT&T will use DOS and Windows with a smattering of Unix VI.4.

Ponder also plans to regain control of billing from the local exchanges. While each business unit will be allowed to continue running its own systems, the difference is that those systems will all adhere to the common standards. "We want control of billing for time-to-market," he says. "Billing is key to databases, and databases allow you to become a market-facing organization."

The billing take-back and a move to client-server architecture centered around customers—as opposed to products—are enabling the consumer communications unit to add billing features 83% faster and improve order processing by 85% compared with previous measures, according to the company.

AT&T also hopes to use the companywide architecture to support common global applications for sales support, order entry, finance, and human resources. "People from Hong Kong to Pittsburgh can collaborate electronically rather than put their files in Federal Express," says Ponder. The architecture also enables AT&T to negotiate billions of dollars in volume discounts. "We saved millions of dollars already with just one vendor," Ponder adds.

People, of course, will make it all happen, and Ponder has done his best to recruit and promote the best business-technology managers he could find. Before he did, however, Ponder studied AT&T's business units. "Everybody kept looking for Ron in IS," says Alexander. "But he was spending his time with key business leaders and some of their customers, trying to understand all the needs of the businesses."

After Ponder got to know those needs, he recruited seven key CIOs. Jim Zucco, one of MCI's visionaries and key architects, left that company to be CIO and VP for AT&T's Business Communications Services (BCS). Jones of consumer long-distance was recruited from Tektronix. Bergonzi left UPS to become VP and division executive for Corporate Information Technology Services and run AT&T's internal operations. William Lewis joined from United Technologies' Pratt & Whitney division to run IT for Network Systems. Robert Napier came from Lockheed and is now CIO at Global Business Communications Systems. Gerald Corvino was recruited from mainframe maker Amdahl Corp. to be CIO at Microelectronics. Ronald Fowinkle left Sequent Computer Systems Inc. and is now the CIO at AT&T GIS.

Homegrown Talent

Ponder also recruited from within. His group of AT&T executives includes Judy Page, CIO and investment officer in the Network Services division, Robert Forte, CIO of Paradyne, and Norm Pancoast, CIO of Bell Labs. He also inherited Ingvar Peterson, CIO at newly acquired McCaw Cellular Communications Inc. in Kirkland, Washington.

"It's some pretty high-powered, impressive talent," says Jack Kelley, managing partner of the communications industry group, northeast region, for Andersen Consulting of Chicago. Adds Alexander, "Each one of these people is a contender to run one of our businesses in the future." Case in point: Zucco was promoted in January to chief of operations and general manager of BCS and was replaced by Les Lichter, formerly service engineering and development VP of BCS.

Each CIO sits at the senior management table of their business unit, with dual reporting responsibility. They report to the subsidiary president and to Ponder, who wants to keep the CIOs focused on meeting business needs, but at the same time create an infrastructure that enables AT&T to share customer information corporatewide. That dual reporting responsibility can be stressful, especially when Ponder and a business unit president call meetings at the same time. Microelectronics' CIO Corvino jokingly wishes for cloning technology "so that I can be in two places at once."

To finish arranging his team, Ponder came up with a way to segment the business-unit CIOs into four communities of interest—services, products, global, and support division—that meet monthly. "It brings a lot more focus and discipline to what we do," says Alexander. Additionally, all 26 CIOs meet quarterly, and a group of about 200 people from the company's IT community meets every six months. The interaction extends beyond the formal meetings. "I can pick up the phone and know I've got somebody I can talk to who understands the things I'm trying to do and is working the same issues," says Microelectronics' Corvino. Also, each AT&T business unit has its own consolidation and renewal initiatives. At AT&T GIS, for example, CIO Fowinkle is building teams to implement global ordering systems that are receiving high marks from users.

Network Systems, meanwhile, is creating the world's third-largest data warehouse—a terabyte in size—by year's end. Network Systems—the long-distance factory that manufactures goods for AT&T's business and consumer long-distance groups—isn't building from scratch: instead, it's cloning GIS's data warehouse. In the last year, Lewis has focused on an intensive training program for software developers while shifting his development budget from 80% legacy support to half the budget going to new projects. The legacy developers "pulled off a miracle to keep those running," he says.

Network Systems also is consolidating 150 systems to 30 or 40, deploying an online documentation system, and installing CAD/CAM (computer-aided design/manufacturing) systems that will enable real estate folks to see square footage and engineers to spot where equipment is stored.

Tracking Solutions

Corporate IT services is developing network-management tools that dynamically track a transaction through the network from the time it leaves a PC. "If something goes wrong with that individual transaction, we will know, whether it be a network, network node, or mainframe," says Bergonzi. "We can solve it immediately instead of having people constantly calling each other around the world."

McCaw is upgrading the network to meet regulatory demands that require it to offer customers a choice of any long-distance carrier to carry their cellular service. It is, they concede, a crucial project. In fact, until it's finally completed, regulators have legally separated McCaw's cellular company and AT&T.

In the consumer long-distance market, Jones will finish taking over the billing processes—and the wealth of billing data—from the local phone companies. In business long-distance, Lichter is upgrading the network so customers can share videoconferencing, spreadsheets, and Lotus Notes applications more easily and less expensively.

Several factors threaten to trip up Ponder and his All-Stars. For one, Ponder admits that other approaches to developing a corporatewide data warehouse haven't worked. "Many companies, including AT&T, have failed at this," he says. The most common mistake: "They get dozens of people together, and they do an enterprisewide data model, top down. Everybody would say, 'Yes sir, yes sir, you got it.' But you go back a year later and nothing's happened. The only thing you know when you start is it's going to fail—you just don't know how long it's going to take." Yankee Group's Anderson agrees: "If you build it right interoperability is free. If you build it wrong, you build black holes."

Laying the Groundwork

Even AT&T's brass knew Ponder's greatest challenge would be overcoming barriers within a company that has a very deeply embedded technology base. In the six months prior to Ponder's arrival, Alexander, acting as an emissary for then CFO Alex Mandl, began visiting senior executives within AT&T to sell them on the idea of bringing in a CIO. "We wanted to make sure Ponder landed on an undefended beach to the sounds of bands and music and would not have to fight his way in," says Alexander. "We wanted to make sure he was thought of as having value from Day One."

Naturally, AT&T's technologists were "probably the most resistant" to the CIO idea, explains Alexander. "I spent a half day in shirtsleeves tangling with that crew, and when I came out I had them convinced." The key: helping them understand the value of information—something quite different from technology. Once Alexander did that, he says, "there was an outcry. 'When is the CIO coming?' "

Another challenge: Ponder's counterparts at rival carriers aren't sitting still. Long-distance competitors such as MCI have already closely aligned their systems and operations. Quips one analyst, "The joke at MCI used to be 'Watch the television commercials in the morning, and program the service in the afternoon.' "

While MCI officials declined to comment, John Kresovsky, VP of IT services at Sprint, says his company is moving to distributed systems. But the comparison isn't exactly fair: Unlike AT&T, which competes in 23 businesses, MCI and Sprint are limiting themselves to just one—telephone services.

At times Ponder has felt overwhelmed by the enormity of his job, say associates. Alexander recalls him saying, "This is an impossible task. There is no one brain that can absorb all that has to be absorbed here. I need to think of this in bits and bytes and find a way to connect those." But it also helps that Ponder has support from the top.

Mandl, now executive VP and CEO of the Communications Services Group, says he's counting on Ponder to bring AT&T's information resources capabilities up several levels. "Building a robust information platform within AT&T is a very critical part of our strategy," he says. "It's the enabler for getting a bunch of other things done."

The complexity of it all threatens even the best. "It can get you confused, add to your costs, and slow your response," says Alexander. But he believes Ponder is leading the All-Stars' team meticulously. "He's walked very deliberately in the direction he needs to move," says Alexander. "He gains a lot of foresight and thought before he takes a step. When he puts that foot down, it's solid. He doesn't wiggle it; it doesn't move."

STEP 2: Prepare the case for class discussion.

STEP 3: Answer each of the following questions, individually or in small groups, as directed by your instructor.

Diagnosis

1. Describe AT&T's information infrastructure before the arrival of Ron Ponder.
2. What information needs did AT&T have?
3. How will AT&T's information needs change in the coming years?

Evaluation

4. How well did the company's information architecture support its needs?
5. How do the current information technology infrastructure and corporate culture at AT&T support or oppose a change in the architecture?

Design

6. How has Ponder proposed to streamline AT&T's technology structure and architecture?
7. What is the likely impact of the imposition of standards on the individual business units? What is its likely impact on the organization as a whole?
8. How has Ponder proposed to regain control of billing?

Implementation

9. What are the key elements of Ponder's restructuring plan?
10. Why did Ponder spend his time initially with key business leaders rather than with his CIOs?
11. What is the reporting structure for the CIOs? How does this reporting structure support Ponder's view of AT&T's information systems architecture? What problems does this reporting structure present?
12. How does the organizational structure support continued development of the architecture?
13. What challenges remain in defining IT policy at AT&T?

STEP 4: In small groups, with the entire class, or in written form, share your answers to the questions above. Then answer the following questions:

1. What information needs does AT&T have now and expect to have in the near future?
2. How did it attempt to meet these needs?
3. How effectively did the company manage the recent changes?
4. How effective are the changes likely to be?
5. What should AT&T do now? ●

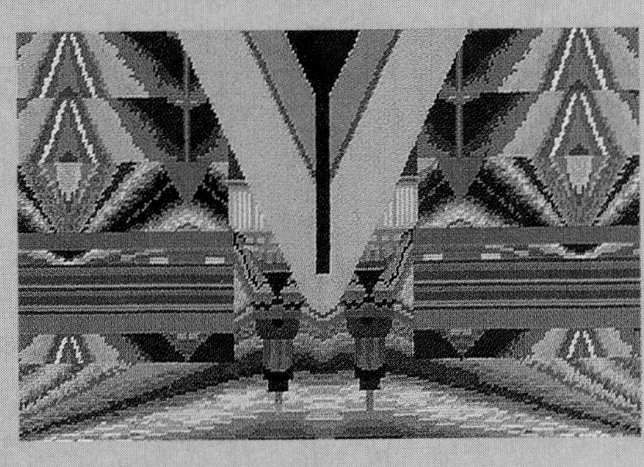

Readings

Reading 1 "Hot New PC Services," by David Kirkpatrick

(This reading is especially suited for use in conjunction with Chapter 2 of *Information Systems.*)

You're at the PC in your den, planning a weekend trip to San Francisco. First you call up airline schedules, pick the lowest fare, and type in a credit card number. Your ticket will arrive in tomorrow's mail. Next you check an up-to-the-minute hotel guide with ratings, select one, and make a reservation. What about an elegant restaurant to impress that important customer? Press a key to search the Zagat restaurant survey for San Francisco. If you have any doubts about your choice, type a public query asking if anyone has a better idea. Tomorrow or the next day you'll find responses from people you've never met. Send your customer a note inviting him to dine at that chic Italian place you picked. Take a peek at the weekend weather forecast for the Bay Area. Now get up and start packing.

All this and more can be done right now by subscribers to Prodigy, the interactive online service created by IBM and Sears Roebuck. But it's only the beginning. You'd better get your tongue around the term "interactive multimedia," because it's shorthand for a revolution. Sound, still photos, even video—anything that can be turned into bits of digital code—will zip in *and out* of your home and office, perhaps within three or four years. Information and entertainment will come to you when you want it, not when some TV network or pay-cable channel says you do. You will have far more control over what and when you watch. You'll be able to exchange video, pictures, and text with anybody.

This two-way communication with the world will have a profound impact on culture, markets, government, and daily life. Says Robert Stanzione, vice president for product development at AT&T Network Systems: "We are at the edge of a new age, where visual communication will be just as ubiquitous as voice communication is today." In this "new age," innovations in compressing and transmitting digital data will cause a vast upheaval in the way people receive and exchange information.

No one business will be able to create this brave new world single-handedly. Companies in a dizzying range of industries—including telecommunications, computing, print and broadcast media, entertainment, and consumer electronics—are jockeying and negotiating with one another for position in the interactive digital future. Says CEO Bill Gates of Microsoft, who is determined to play a central role in this evolving world: "We look at lists of those companies to see which ones we should be doing things with. A lot of guys are going to win and lose big." The most sought-after partners at the moment: cable television companies. Their coaxial links may be better suited than telephone wires for getting the new technology into the home.

A growing number of early voyagers are already testing the interactive future by logging on to today's relatively primitive services like Prodigy and CompuServe. Using PCs with modems attached to phone lines, these pioneers are defining a new kind of electronic connectedness. Consumer-oriented interactive services are now used in 3.3 million of the 92 million U.S. households, and the number is growing more than 30 percent a year, according to Arlen Communications, a Bethesda, Maryland, research company. These services will take in $473 million in 1992, predicts Link Resources, a New York City consulting firm, which projects a compound annual revenue growth rate of 28 percent for them. Some 9.6 million households have the requisite PCs with modems, Link figures; an additional 17.4 million have PCs but so far are modemless.

SOURCE: David Kirkpatrick, "Hot New PC Services" *Fortune* November 2, 1992, pp. 108–109, 112 and 114.

Today's services are limited mostly by their inability to display anything besides text and crude graphics. The services are also often annoyingly slow and difficult to operate. But subscribers are flocking to them anyway, simply for the rich variety of material they provide (see table). Most important, these services are *interactive,* meaning users within each service can talk to each other, through their keyboards, of course. They can communicate privately through electronic mail or publicly via bulletin boards and real-time gabfests. A huge percentage of the information available is created not by anonymous writers but by the actual users. This is not a passive medium. You are not a reader or a viewer, but an author and a contributor.

Users post more than 80,000 public messages on Prodigy's hundreds of bulletin boards each day, on topics ranging from heavy metal rock to vegetarian cooking to investment theory. At any given time over 500,000 messages are on tap for viewing. Says Esther Dyson, who publishes the technology newsletter *Release 1.0:* "If you go to a party and don't meet people you like, what's the point? When you go to the on-line party, you almost inevitably meet new people who share your interests."

Prodigy is merely the largest and most consumer-oriented of a burgeoning array of PC-based interactive services. It has jumped to 1.75 million users in 850,000 homes in the two years since it went national. Other top services include CompuServe, which offers the most data; America Online; General Electric's GEnie; and the Sierra Network, and independent all-game national network. Local and special-interest bulletin boards abound, including such offerings as GayCom and Christian Net.

Logging on to Prodigy for an hour or so a couple of times a week changed the life of Gayle Kinsey, 38, a part-time computer consultant, paralegal, and single mother in Corrales, New Mexico. When she wanted to start a newsletter to help promote her consulting business, she found about 15 others on the service who were eager to join the project. "We worked the whole concept through on Prodigy, even took a vote," she says. When she had an idea for a new kind of children's bed, she posted a query on Prodigy's Money Talk bulletin board and heard from several potential investors and a metallurgist in Pennsylvania who will build a prototype.

Of all Kinsey's adventures with Prodigy, probably none is more telling than what happened when she got angry with it. She didn't like the narrow focus of many of the bulletin boards, which are restricted to particular subjects; oddly, all health matters used to be discussed on the parenting board. So she posted critical notes on a number of the boards suggesting that users suspend their memberships in protest until Prodigy added more categories.

Several hundred other members responded. They began sharing the phone numbers of prodigy officials and discussing insurrectionary strategy. Here was a unique interactive phenomenon: using the service to change the service. The effort paid off in early September. Prodigy announced that in response to many member "requests" it was tripling its bulletin boards to 420. Kinsey pronounces herself very pleased.

Ross Glatzer, Prodigy's CEO, says he is awed by his customers' intensity. In midsummer he brought together 19 members from around the country, many of whom had become persistent on-line critics. Glatzer recalls: "One member said to me, 'I want you to understand that it may be your company, but it's *our* service.' How many companies would kill to have their customers embrace the product with such fervor?"

Besides Sears, Prodigy merchants that offer catalogues and individual items on-line include Hammacher Schlemmer, Lands' End, J.C. Penney, and Spiegel. Enthusiast Patricia Johnson of North Falmouth, Massachusetts, particularly appreciates the convenience: "I hate to shop. So sometimes when I don't want to waste time going to the store, I just call up Prodigy at 10 P.M. and buy basic items like sheets. They are delivered to my door two days later. That's a huge time saving for me." Johnson also cut through the crowds in June when air fares suddenly dropped and even many travel agents had a hard time grabbing tickets. She bought five cut-rate round trips to the West Coast for family members by logging on to Prodigy early in the morning.

Interactive Services You Can Use Now

All the services listed, except the Sierra Network, include late news, sports, weather, entertainment news and reviews, investing information, some games, shopping, on-line discount brokerage, electronic mail, and bulletin boards for discussions with other subscribers.

American Online 180,000 users	$7.95 a month for two hours, then 10 cents a minute; *800-827-6364.*	Specializes in live discussion and bulletin boards on all sorts of subjects. Relatively easy to use. A fast-growing startup that went public this year.
CompuServe 1,070,000 users	$49.95 initial charge plus $7.95 monthly for basic services. Other material available at $12.80 an hour and up; *800-848-8199.*	More data than other services but difficult for nontechies. Special strength: on-line computer hardware and software support. Owned by H&R Block.
GEnie 350,000 users	$4.95 a month for basic nonbusiness-day service, otherwise $6 an hour and up; *800-638-9636*	Lots of games, and bulletin boards on subjects including jokes, real estate, religion and ethics. Extensive computing information. Owned by General Electric.
Prodigy 1,750,000 users	$49.95 initial subscription, then $14.95 a month plus some charges for optional services; *800-776-3449.*	The easiest to use but sometimes very slow. Owned jointly by Sears and IBM.
The Sierra Network 12,000 users	$12.95 a month for 30 hours evenings and weekends, $2 to $7 an hour otherwise; *800-743-7721.*	All games and chat. Went national last year. Owned by Sierra On-Line, a publicly held computer games company.

One snag: Prodigy continues to lose money—$30 million to $50 million this year, according to Gary Arlen, president of Arlen Communications. He calculates that Sears and IBM have sunk well over $800 million into the service so far but projects a possible breakeven next year. (CompuServe, by contrast, has been profitable since 1979.)

Interactive services have broad implications for politics in particular. Ross Perot has proposed using them for electronic town meetings to resolve national issues. Already members debate political questions in a variety of forums on many of the services. Specially organized Prodigy events offer genuine interaction with politicians. During both nominating conventions this summer, Prodigy members who were also delegates (12 from each party) volunteered to answer specific questions from members. Want to know how your Congressman voted on family leave? On Prodigy, just type in your zip code for the voting record of your Representative and your Senators, and while you're at it check how much political action committees contributed to their latest campaigns.

The candidates have recognized the power of the on-line electorate. Both President Bush and Governor Clinton posted campaign statements on Prodigy in September and personally approved answers to questions from members. The spirited debate that ensued went on for weeks. Jerry Brown logged on to CompuServe in June, discussing his campaign, debating issues, and answering questions.

The new technologies also have intriguing potential in education. A study last spring at Northern Kentucky University suggests that in some situations on-line classes may be better than conventional ones. Students in six college courses in education, sociology, geology, and business law were divided into conventional sections and on-line sections that met only occasionally with teachers. The on-line section, used Macintosh computers and an educational interactive system called Olé, developed by Cincinnati Bell. In general, the on-line students got better grades and rate the course more highly than the control group did. Total costs per student are 30 percent lower with Olé than with traditional methods, the university says—a boon in the age of spiraling tuitions.

So how soon will you be able to add video, sound, and pictures to all this neat stuff? Bill Gates thinks such advanced systems may extend to a million homes within four years. In early October a consortium organized by Microelectronics & Computer Technology Corp. (MCC), a cooperative research group in Austin, Texas, announced that it hopes to deploy a multimedia interactive network by early 1995. The new venture, called First Cities, includes Apple Computer, Bellcore (the research arm of the Baby Bells), Corning, Eastman Kodak, North American Philips, Kaleida labs (an Apple joint venture with IBM), Tandem computer, and several telephone and cable companies. Says First Cities executive director Bruce Sidran: "Our vision is to provide multimedia information when, where, and how you want it—in your home, your car, an airplane, or while you're walking down the street."

Lucie Fjeldstad, IBM's general manager of multimedia, says Big Blue already has the technology to manage a nationwide system that would allow users anywhere to hold video conferences, collaborate on projects with people scattered in different cities, take a course from any university, and select from a cornucopia of entertainment options. Her notion of one way shopping interactively might work is striking: "Say you tell the system you need a new jacket. You can find one you like and have the machine call up a hologram that looks like you so you can try it on and order it if you like it."

Today's services are limited to text and graphics because phone lines, the only existing two-way connections between homes and offices and the outside world, have limited bandwidth—the capacity for carrying information. Technicians are making progress on several ways to expand it. First, telephone wires can be made to carry more data. A technology called ISDN, for Integrated Services Digital Network, expands the maximum bandwidth of conventional phone lines as much as sevenfold. It's widely used in Europe. In parts of Maine, Massachusetts, New York, and Vermont, ISDN is already available for roughly twice the cost of a conventional phone line; telephone companies plan a national rollout over the next two or three years.

Second, as the pipes are widening, the stuff that flows through them is getting smaller. Telecommunications standards-setting bodies are debating a number of methods for compressing digital data. Compression involves eliminating redundant or unnecessary parts of a signal—for example, the pauses in a conversation. By next year phone and cable companies in some test locations will be able to compress a video signal so that it takes up one-eighth the space on a wire it does today.

While telephone companies struggle to squeeze more stuff into their skinny little wires, the cable television industry is working to bypass the telephone system entirely. Cable's higher-capacity coaxial lines now run past more than 90 percent of American homes and connect to 65 percent of them. Any compression method that works on a phone line would open up even more usable space on cable. Today most big cable companies are installing fiber-optic strands as their systems' backbones, using coaxial cable only for the final link to consumers' homes.

A network combining fiber optics and coaxial cable could carry a gigabit of information per second—a billion digital bits, the equivalent of 30,000 single-spaced typewritten pages. That's roughly 500 times the capacity of a phone line. Until recently most experts believed that national interactive networks equipped for video would have to wait until millions of homes were strung individually with fiber-optic telephone lines, at the daunting cost of roughly $2,000 per home. (A cable connection costs an average of $500.) but since sufficient bandwidth already makes its way into homes via cable systems, the time frame has shortened drastically. The digital device you'll use to control all this interactive stuff will probably be some combination of a TV and a cable box rather than a supersmart telephone.

IBM and AT&T each claim to be best positioned to manage the vast digital networks that would feed material down the cable. Says IBM's Fjeldstad: "We believe we have the lead to establish this service over time." But at AT&T, Robert Stanzione isn't convinced: "It is our intention to be the leader in visual communication products and services. When it comes to networking, I know of no other company that has as much experience as AT&T." Other giants vying to manage future high-capacity networks include Alcatel Alsthom, Digital Equipment, Ericsson, Fujitsu, Hitachi, Matsushita, Northern Telecom, and Siemens.

Whoever ends up controlling the networks, cooperation between telephone and cable companies may be the best way to make interactive multimedia happen. Federal Communications Commission Chairman Alfred Sikes aims to break down the regulatory barriers that have kept companies in each industry from either cooperating or poaching on the other's turf. Says he: "I think competitive markets will deliver more quickly, just as increasingly competitive long-distance telephone markets have delivered better networks and services."

Following a favorable FCC decision, New York Telephone announced in early October that it would work with Liberty Cable Television to install a test system for interactive video in three Manhattan apartment buildings. It said it would replace the buildings' old-fashioned phone lines with coaxial cable—essentially adopting cable technology.

Phone companies have a crucial skill that the cable companies lack—experience in managing two-way communications. Says Eric Martin, a specialist at Gemini Consulting of Morristown, New Jersey: "Remember that the U.S. phone companies have built the most complex switched networks in the world and have a fantastic reputation for reliability and quality. And what's the bad rap on cable? That their service and transmission quality is relatively low."

Tele-Communications Inc., the largest cable system operator, is already a partner with US West, a major phone company. Their jointly owned system in Britain provides both telephone and television service on the same cable. In Denver the two companies have hooked up with AT&T to test "video on demand" over cable TV lines. Users can order from a catalogue of more than 1,000 movies and special events, watch them whenever they want, and stop each offering at will for up to ten minutes.

Cable companies will use their new capacity at first to offer a vastly expanded menu of movies and entertainment shows. Time Warner's experimental Quantum system in Queens already allows viewers to select from among 15 movies and special events at any one time; soon customers equipped with keyboards will be able to send each other messages. Within a few years Quantum will probably provide interactive classified ads, yellow pages, videogames, and retail catalogues with photographs, says Geoffrey Holmes, a Time Warner senior vice-president. IBM and others are especially interested in establishing a partnership with Time Warner. It is the nation's second-largest cable company, with 6.8 million subscribers, and it also produces and owns huge libraries of potential multimedia material—such as movies, music, and magazines (including *Fortune*). Holmes says recent FCC rulings mean he can quickly add long-distance phone service and, within five years, high-quality videophones.

Mitchell Kapor, founder of the computer software firm Lotus Development, left Lotus in 1986 and now heads the Electronic Frontier Foundation, which promotes a free and open flow of communication on information highways. It has won many influential ears, including those of FCC Chairman Sikes. Kapor worries that if cable companies control future multimedia networks, they will restrict access to them. "In print there are hundreds of thousands of publications with all shades of opinion," he says. "My dream is that we could get that same range of expression and ideas in this new interactive medium. But I fear that we'll just get more least-common-denominator, entertainment-oriented, advertiser-controlled stuff."

He points out that while the phone system is accessible to everyone, the cable system has been structured and regulated as a one-way flow controlled by the operators. "So either we need to change the policy regime under which cable is done, or we need to have phone companies do this," he says. Only if cable systems support independent origination of content, he believes, will nonprofit alternative information and entertainment sources flourish.

Replies Bob Thomson, a spokesman for Tele-Communications Inc.: "Nobody's going to make the huge investments necessary if that sort of model is imposed on them. We go out and buy our products wholesale and then retail them to our customers, and shape those offerings to best suit our marketplace. Some portions of our network may be totally open to all comers, just as public-access cable channels are today. If there's a market for that kind of service, it will have to be met."

The new industry that emerges could be a major force in the U.S. economy. Says Microsoft's Gates: "This is the information age, and we're talking about the deployment of a new generation of information technology to the homes of America. It's going to change things, big time. It will create a lot of wealth, and a lot of easier ways of doing things." Gates foresees more efficiency in virtually every market as companies develop ways to search quickly and easily through vast databases of available goods and services—including investments.

In pursuit of that vision, Gates has privately funded his own company, called Interactive Home Systems, in Redmond, Washington. Its 35 employees are trying to find and commercialize means of scanning through those huge databases of the future. Another project involves making digital representations of artworks for a high-quality on-line museum. Says Gates: "In the same way that Microsoft bet on the microprocessor, IHS is making bets on very, very broad-bandwidth and high-resolution screens connected to very intelligent interactive devices. It's the only company I know that's completely worthless unless this stuff all really happens."

The U.S. could gain a tremendous competitive advantage globally if it moves rapidly into on-line multimedia. No other country except Canada has a comparably sophisticated communications infrastructure that includes pervasive cable television. Says Brendan Clouston, chief operating officer of Tele-Communications Inc.: "One of the next great positives for America in the world community is that we are the leader in moving toward this kind of information network." See you on-line.

Discussion Questions

1. How do interactive information services affect the daily conduct of business and leisure activities?
2. How do interactive services help meet individuals' needs for information?
3. What role will the telephone and cable industries play in interactive services of the future? ▼

Reading 2 "Mrs. Fields' Secret Ingredient," by Tom Richman

(This reading is especially suited for use in conjunction with Chapter 3 of *Information Systems.*)

Part of the late Buckminister Fuller's genius was his capacity to transform a technology from the merely new to the truly useful by creating a new form to take advantage of its characteristics. Fuller's geodesic designs, for instance, endowed plastic with practical value as a building material. His structures, if not always eye-appealing, still achieved elegance—as mathematicians use the word to connote simplicity—of function. Once, reacting to someone's suggestion that a new technology be applied to an old process in a particularly awkward way, Fuller said dismissively, "That would be like putting an outboard motor on a skyscraper."

Introducing microcomputers with spreadsheet and word-processing software to a company originally designed around paper technology amounts to the same thing. If the form of the company doesn't change, the computer, like the outboard, is just a doodad. Faster long division and speedier typing don't move a company into the information age.

But Randy Fields has created something entirely new—*a* shape if not *the* shape, of business organizations to come. It gives top management a dimension of personal control over dispersed operations that small companies otherwise find impossible to achieve. It projects a founder's vision into parts of a company that have long ago outgrown his or her ability to reach in person.

In the structure that Fields is building, computers don't just speed up old administrative management processes. They alter the process. Management, in the Fields organizational paradigm, becomes less administration and more inspiration. The management hierarchy of the company *feels* almost flat.

What's the successful computer-age business going to look like in the not-very-distant future? something like Randy Fields's concept—which is, in a word, neat.

What makes it neat, right out of the oven, is where he's doing it. Randy Fields, age 40, is married to Debbi Fields, who turns 31 this month, and together they run Mrs. Fields Cookies, of Park City, Utah. They project that by year end, their business will comprise nearly 500 company-owned stores in 37 states selling what Debbi calls a "feel-good feeling." That sounds a little hokey. A lot of her cookie talk does. "Good enough never is," she likes to remind the people around her.

But there's nothing hokey about the 18.5 percent that Mrs. Fields Inc. earned on cookie sales of $87 million last year, up from $72.6 million a year earlier.

Won't the cookie craze pass? people often ask Debbi. "I think that's very doubtful . . . I mean," she says, "if [they are] fresh, warm, and wonderful and make you feel good, are you going to stop buying cookies?"

Maybe not, but the trick for her and her husband is to see that people keep buying them from Mrs. Fields, not David's Cookies, Blue Chip Cookies, The Original Great Chocolate Chip Cookie or the dozens of regional and local competitors. Keeping the cookies consistently fresh, warm, and wonderful at nearly 500 retail cookie stores spread over the United States and five other countries can't be simple or easy. Worse, keeping smiles on the faces of the nearly 4,500, mostly young, store employees—not to mention keeping them productive and honest—is a bigger chore than most companies would dare to take on alone.

Most don't; they franchise, which is one way to bring responsibility and accountability down to the store level in a far-flung, multi-store organization. For this, the franchiser trades off revenues and profits that would otherwise be his and a large measure of flexibility. Because its terms are defined by contract, the relationship between franchisor and franchisee is more static than dynamic, difficult to alter as the market and the business change.

Mrs. Fields Cookies, despite its size, has not franchised—persuasive evidence in itself that the Fieldses have built something unusual. Randy Fields believes that no other U.S. food retailer with so many outlets has dared to retain this degree of direct, day-to-day control of its stores. And Mrs. Fields Cookies does it with a headquarters staff of just 115 people. That's approximately one staffer to every five stores—piddling compared with other companies with far fewer stores to manage. When the company bought La Petite Boulangerie from PepsiCo earlier this year, for instance, the soft-drink giant had 53 headquarters staff people to administer the French bakery/sandwich shop chain's 119 stores. Randy needed just four weeks to cut the number to 3 people.

On paper, Mrs. Fields Cookies *looks* almost conventional. In action, however, because of the way information flows between levels, it *feels* almost flat.

On paper, between Richard Lui running the Pier 39 Mrs. Fields in San Francisco and Debbi herself in Park City, there are several apparently traditional layers of hierarchy: an area sales manager, a district sales manager, a regional director of operations, a vice-president of operations. In practice, though, Debbi is as handy to Lui—and to every other store manager—as the telephone and personal computer in the back room of his store.

On a typical morning at Pier 39, Lui unlocks the store, calls up the Day Planner program on his Tandy computer, plugs in today's sales projection (based on year-earlier sales adjusted for growth), and answers a couple of questions the programs puts to him. What day of the week is it? What type of day: normal day, sale day, school day, holiday, other?

Say, for instance, it's Tuesday, a school day. The computer goes back to the Pier 39 store's hour-by-hour, product-by-product performance on the last three school-day Tuesdays. Based on what you did then, the Day Planner tells him, here's what you'll have to do today, hour by hour, product by product, to meet your sales projection. It tells him how many customers he'll need each hour and how much he'll have to sell them. It tells him how many batches of cookie dough he'll have to mix and when to mix them to meet the demand and to minimize leftovers. He could make these estimates himself if he wanted to take the time. The computer makes them for him.

Each hour, as the day progresses, Lui keeps the computer informed of his progress. Currently he enters the numbers manually, but new cash registers that automatically feed hourly data to the computer, eliminating the manual update, are already in some stores. The computer in turn revises the hourly projections and makes suggestions. The customer count is OK, it might observe, but your average check is down. Are your crew members doing enough suggestive selling? If, on the other hand, the computer indicates that the customer count is down, that may suggest the manager will want to do some sampling—chum for customers up and down the pier with a tray of free cookie pieces or try something else, whatever he likes, to lure people into the store. Sometimes, if sales are just slightly down, the machine's revised projections will actually exceed the original on the assumption that greater selling effort will more than compensate for the small deficit. On the other hand, the program isn't blind to reality. It recognizes a bad day and diminishes its hourly sales projections and baking estimates accordingly.

Hourly sales goals?

Well, when Debbi was running *her* store, *she* set hourly sales goals. Her managers should, too, she thinks. Rather than enforce the practice through dicta, Randy has embedded the notion in the software that each store manager relies on. Do managers find the machine's suggestions intrusive? Not Lui. "It's a tool for me," he says.

Several times a week, Lui talks with Debbi. Well, he doesn't exactly talk *with* her, but he hears from her. He makes a daily phone call to Park City to check his computerized Phone-Mail messages, and as often as not there's something from Mrs. Fields herself. If she's upset about some problem, Lui hears her sounding upset. If it's something she's breathlessly exu-

FIGURE 1 The Information Flow

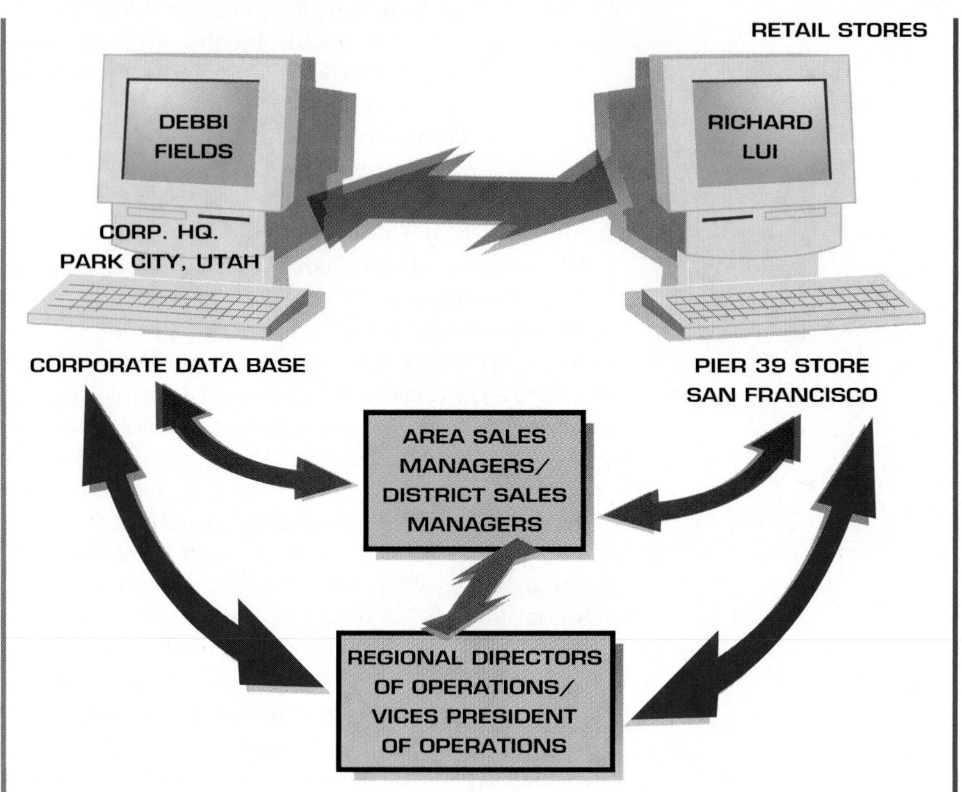

berant about, which is more often the case, he gets an earful of that, too. Whether the news is good or bad, how much better to hear it from the boss herself than to get a memo in the mail next week.

By the same token, if Lui has something to say to Debbi, he uses the computer. It's right there, handy. He calls up the Form-Mail program, types his message, and the next morning it's on Debbi's desk. She promises an answer, from her or her staff, within 48 hours. On the morning I spent with her, among the dozen or so messages she got was one from the crew at a Berkeley, Calif., store making their case for higher wages there and another from the manager of a store in Brookline, Mass., which has been struggling recently. We've finally gotten ourselves squared away, was the gist of the note, so please come visit. (Last year Debbi logged around 350,000 commercial air miles visiting stores.)

Here are some other things Lui's computer can do for him.

- Help him schedule crew. He plugs his daily sales projection for two weeks hence into a scheduling program that incorporates as its standards the times Debbi herself takes to perform the mixing, dropping, and baking chores. The program gives him back its best guess of how many people with which skill levels he'll need during which hours. A process that done manually consumed almost an hour now takes just a fraction of that time.
- Help him interview crew applicants. He calls up his interview program, seats the applicant at the keyboard, and has him or her answer a series of questions. Based on the answers given by past hirees, the machine suggests to Lui which candidates will succeed or fail. It's

still his choice. And any applicant, before a hire, will still get an audition—something to see how he or she performs in public. Maybe Lui will send the hopeful out on a sampling mission.

- Help with personnel administration. Say he hires the applicant. He informs the machine, which generates a personnel folder and a payroll entry in Park City, and a few months later comes back to remind Lui that he hasn't submitted the initial evaluation (also by computer), which is now slightly past due. It administers the written part of the skills test and updates the records with the results. The entire Mrs. Fields personnel manual will soon be on the computer so that 500 store managers won't forget to delete old pages and insert revised ones every time a change is made.
- Help with maintenance. A mixer isn't working, so the manager punches up the repair program on the computer. It asks him some questions, such as: is the plug in the wall? If the questions don't prompt a fix, the computer sends a repair request to Park City telling the staff there which machine is broken, its maintenance history, and which vendor to call. It sends a copy of the work order back to the store. When the work gets done, the store signs off by computer, and the vendor's bill gets paid.

That's a lot of technology applied to something as basic as a cookie store, but Randy had two objectives in mind.

He wanted to keep his wife in frequent, personal, two-way contact with hundreds of managers whose stores she couldn't possibly visit often enough. "The people who work in the stores," says Debbi, "are my customers. Staying in touch with them is the most important thing I can do."

It's no accident, even if Lui isn't consciously aware of why he does what he does, that he runs his store just about the same way that Debbi ran her first one 10 years ago. Even when she isn't there, she's there—in the standards built into his scheduling program, in the hourly goals, in the sampling and suggestive selling, on the phone. The technology has "leveraged," to use Randy's term, Debbi's ability to project her influence into more stores than she could ever reach effectively without it.

Second, Randy wanted to keep store managers managing, not sweating the paperwork. "In retailing," he says, "the goal is to keep people close to people. Whatever gets in the way of that—administration, telephones, ordering, and so on—is the enemy." If an administrative chore can be automated, it should be.

Store managers benefit from a continuing exchange of information. Of course, Park City learns what every store is doing daily—from sales to staffing to training to hires to repairs—and how it uses that information we'll get to in a minute. From the store managers' perspective, however, the important thing is that the information they provide keeps coming back to them, reorganized to make it useful. The hour-by-hour sales projections and projected customer counts that managers use to pace their days reflect their own experiences. Soon, for instance, the computer will take their weekly inventory reports and sales projections and generate supply orders that managers will only have to confirm or correct—more administrative time saved. With their little computers in the back room, store managers give, but they also receive.

What technology can do for operations it can also do for administration.

"We're all driven by Randy's philosophy that he wants the organization to be as flat as possible," says Paul Quinn, the company's director of management information systems (MIS).

"There are a few things," says controller Lynn Quilter, "that Randy dislikes about growth. . . . He hates the thought of drowning in people so that he can't walk in and know exactly what each person does. . . . The second thing that drives him nuts is paper."

"The objective," says Randy, "is to leverage people—to get them to act when we have 1,000 stores the same way they acted when we had 30."

He has this theory that large organizations, organizations with lots of people, are, per se, inferior to small ones. Good people join a growing business because it offers them an opportunity to be creative. As the company grows, these people find they're tied up managing the latest hires. Creativity suffers. Entropy sets in. Randy uses technology to keep entropy at bay.

He began by automating rote clerical chores and by minimizing date-entry effort. Machines can sort and file faster than people, and sorting and filing is deadly dull work, anyway. Lately he's pushed the organization toward automated exception reporting for the same reason. Machines can compare actual results with expected results and flag the anomalies, which are all management really cares about anyway. And within a few years, Randy expects to go much further in this battle against bureaucracy by developing artificial-intelligence aids to the running of the business.

Understand that it's not equipment advances—state-of-the-art hardware—that's pushing Mrs. Fields Cookies toward management frontiers. The machines the company uses are strictly off the shelf: an IBM minicomputer connected to inexpensive personal computers. It is, instead, Randy's ability to create an elegant, functional software architecture. He has, of course, had an advantage that the leader of an older, more established company would not have. Because Mrs. Fields is still a young enough company, he doesn't have to shape his automated management system to a preexisting structure. Every new idea doesn't confront the opposition of some bureaucratic fiefdom's survival instinct. Rather, the people part and the technology part of the Fields organization are developing simultaneously, each shaped by the same philosophy.

You see this congruence at corporate headquarters and in the company's operational management organization.

Between Debbi as chief executive officer and the individual store managers is what seems on paper to be a conventional reporting structure with several layers of management. But there's an additional box on the organization chart. It's not another management layer. It transcends layers, changing the way information flows between them and even changing the functions of the layers.

The box consists of a group of seven so-called store controllers, working in Park City from the daily store reports and weekly inventory reports. They ride herd on the numbers. If a store's sales are dramatically off, the store controller covering that geographical region will be the first to know it. If there's a discrepancy between the inventory report, the daily report of batches of cookies baked, and the sales report, the controller will be the first to find it. (It is possible for a smart thief to steal judiciously for about a week from a Mrs. Fields store.) "We're a check on operations," says store controller Wendy Phelps, but she's far more than just a check. She's the other half of a manager's head.

Since she's on top of the numbers, the area, district, and regional managers don't have to be—not to the same degree, at any rate. "We want managers to be with people, not with problems," says Debbi. It's hard, Randy says, to find managers who are good with both people and numbers. People people, he thinks, should be in the field, with numbers people backing them up—but not second-guessing them. Here's where the company takes a meaningful twist.

Problems aren't reported up the organization just so solutions can flow back down. Instead, store controllers work at levels as low as they can. They go to the store manager if he's the one to fix a discrepancy, a missing report, for instance. Forget chain of command. "I'm very efficiency minded," says Randy.

So the technology gives the company an almost real-time look at the minutiae of its operations, and the organizational structure—putting function ahead of conventional protocol—keeps it from choking on this abundance of data.

Some managers would have problems with a system that operates without their daily intervention. They wouldn't be comfortable, and they wouldn't stay at Mrs. Fields. Those who do stay can manage people instead of paper.

If administrative bureaucracies can grow out of control, so can technology bureaucracies. A couple of principles, ruthlessly adhered to, keep both simple at Mrs. Fields.

The first is that if a machine can do it, a machine *should* do it. "People," says Randy, "should do only that which people can do. It's demeaning for people to do what machines can do. . . . Can machines manage people? No. Machines have no feelie-touchies, none of that chemistry that flows between two people."

The other rule, the one that keeps the technological monster itself in check, is that the company will have but one data base. Everything—cookie sales, payroll records, suppliers' invoices, inventory reports, utility charges—goes into the same data base. And whatever anybody needs to know has to come out of it.

Don't enforce this rule, and, says Randy, "the next thing you know you have 48 different programs that can't talk to each other." Technology grown rampant.

Having a single data base means, first, that nobody has to waste time filing triplicate forms or answering the same questions twice. "We capture the data just once," says controller Quilter.

Second, it means that the system itself can do most of the rote work that people used to do. Take orders for chocolate, for instance. The computer gets the weekly inventory report. It already knows the sales projection. So let the computer order the chocolate chips. Give the store manager a copy of the order on his screen so he can correct any errors, but why take his time to generate the order when he's got better things to do—like teaching someone to sell. Or, take it further. The machine generates the order. The supplier delivers the chips to the store and bills the corporate office. A clerk in the office now has to compare the order, the invoice, and what the store says it got. Do they all match? Yes. She tells the computer to write a check. The more stores you have, the more clerks it takes. Why not let the computer do the matching? In fact, if everything fits, why get people involved at all? Let people handle the exceptions. Now, the clerk, says MIS director Quinn, instead of a processor becomes a mini-controller, someone who uses his brain.

The ordering process doesn't happen that way yet at Mrs. Fields, although it probably will soon as Randy continues to press for more exception reporting. You can see where he's going with this concept.

"Eventually," he says, "even the anomalies become normal." The exceptions themselves, and a person's response to them, assume a pattern. Why not, says Randy, have the computer watch the person for a while? "Then the machine can say, 'I have found an anomaly. I've been watching you, and I think this is what you would do. Shall I do it for you, yes or no. I yes, I'll do it, follow up, and so on. If no, what do you want me to do?' " It would work for the low-level function—administering accounts payable, for instance. And it would work at higher levels as well. "If," Randy says, "I can ask the computer now where are we making the most money and where are we making the least and then make a decision about where not to build new stores, why shouldn't that sort of thing be on automatic pilot too? 'Based on performance,' it will say, 'we shouldn't be building any more stores in East Jibip. Want me to tell [real-estate manager] Mike [Murphy]?' We're six months away from being able to do that."

The ability to look at the company, which is what the data base really is, at a level of abstraction appropriate to the looker is the third advantage of a single data base—even if it never moves into artificial-intelligence functions. It means that Debbi Fields and Richard Lui are both looking at the same world, but in ways that are meaningful to each of them.

The hurdle to be overcome before you can use technology to its best advantage—and that isn't equivalent to just hanging an outboard motor on a skyscraper, as Buckminster Fuller said—isn't technical in the hardware sense. Randy buys only what he calls plain vanilla hardware. And it isn't financial. For all its relative sophistication in computer systems, Mrs. Fields spends just 0.49 % of sales on data processing, much of which is returned in higher productivity.

Much more important, Randy says, is having a consistent vision of what you want to *accomplish* with the technology. Which functions do you want to control? What do you want your organization chart to look like? In what ways do you want to leverage the CEO's vision? "Imagination. We imagine what it is we want," says Randy. "We aren't constrained by the limits of what technology can do. We just say, 'What does your day look like? What would you *like* it to look like?'" He adds, "If you don't have your paradigm in mind, you have no way of knowing whether each little step is taking you closer to or further from your goal."

For instance, he inaugurated the daily store report with the opening of store number two in 1978. The important thing was the creation of the report—which is the fundamental data-gathering activity in the company—not its transmission mode. That can change, and has. First transmission was by Fax, then by telephone touch tone, and only recently by computer modem.

Having a consistent vision means, Randy says, that he could have described as far back as 1978, when he first began to create it, the system that exists today. But he doesn't mean the machines or how they're wired together. "MIS in this company," he says, "has always had to serve two masters. First, control. Rapid growth without control equals disaster. We needed to keep improving control over our stores. And second, information that leads to control also leads to better decision making. To the extent that the information is then provided to the store and field-management level, the decisions that are made there are better, and they are more easily made.

"That has been our consistent vision."

Discussion Questions

1. What information needs do the top executives of Mrs. Fields Cookies have?
2. What needs do the store managers have?
3. What systems exist to meet these needs?
4. How effective are these systems? ▼

"Prometheus Barely Unbound," by Tom Peters

(This reading is especially suited for use in conjunction with Chapter 4 of *Information Systems.*)

From Rutland, Vermont, to Timbuktu, business practice is being set upon its ear. Business and many general press publications chronicle the brave new world of commerce: There are tales of junk bonds and takeovers and LBOs, the so-called "market for corporate control." There were three consecutive days in mid-August 1989 when—ho-hum—Kodak, Digital Equipment, and Campbell Soup announced yet another round of thousands of staff reductions. No crisis triggered these decisions. Just business as usual. Or, as is increasingly the case, unusual.

More business as usual/unusual: A visit with the chief information officer (a new title/idea) at KG Stores, a 118-store menswear chain based in Denver. Using information technology, KG has reduced its order and replenishment cycle with Levi Strauss from about nine weeks in 1987 to three or four days.

Publications such as *Fortune, Industry Week, Business Week,* and *Business Month* often compile lists of competitive needs for managing the '90s. Such lists are helpful, but incomplete—they ignore the context which makes all this necessary. Competitive practices required to survive in the '90s—pursuit of "six sigma quality" (99.9997 percent perfect, a Motorola goal touted even in its ads), shrinking innovation and order cycles by orders of magnitude, the use of team-based organizations everywhere and the subcontracting of anything to anyone from anywhere—are downstream links in a chain of immutable forces sweeping the world's economy. Nothing less than "millennia change" is afoot, says Boston consultant and *Future Perfect* author, Stan Davis. Exhibit I (see chart) is primarily an effort to untangle the larger context.

PRIMARY FORCES AT WORK

The left side of the chart appears grossly oversimplified. But after much though, I am convinced that just *two* intertwined, primary forces are animating the massive economic transformation: globalization and information technology.

Globalization

Everybody talks about it. But what does it mean? For Americans—whether they run a multi-billion-dollar, old-line manufacturing outfit or the corner mom-and-pop shop—it means that any remnants of isolationism must go.

Consider the four top blocks under "Primary Forces at Work." Globalization concerns the recovered dominant economies—Japan and West Germany in particular. In simple terms, these big and great economies are every bit the match of the United States economy: witness Japan's high positive trade balance and the even higher positive trade balance from non-protectionist West Germany. Yet new sources of high-quality commodities and non-commodities are emerging from the Newly Industrialized Countries (NICs) like Korea, Taiwan, Singapore, and Hong Kong (assuming it's capitalist after the 1997 Chinese takeover). These "four dragons," along with other Asian growth nations such as Thailand, the Philippines, and Malaysia, now actually account for more trade with the United States than does Japan.

There's more. Italy continues to be the fastest-growing economy in the European Economic Community. And if you want to see electricity in the air, try Spain; real estate mar-

SOURCE: Tom Peters, "Prometheus Barely Unbound," reprinted with permission of Academy of Management Executive, 1990, Vol. 4, pp. 70–84.

EXHIBIT 1 Primary Forces at Work

Globalization
Results
Overall Impact
Impact at Company Personnel Level
Recovered Dominant Economies
• Japan
• Germany
• end of U.S. company dominance
• "value-added" competition among high-wage nations
Newly Industrialized Countries (NICs)
• Korea
• Taiwan
• Singapore
• Spain
• low-cost, high-quality commodities
• move toward "value-added"
Shift Toward Market Economies
• Eastern Europe
• Russia
• China
• more sources of goods
• enriched global network
• wild card
New Power Blocks
• EEC 1992
• "Yen Block"
• end of U.S. policy domination
Information Technology
• "age of intangibles"
• micro-markets
• "real-time" global/local linkages
• all products obsoleted/every product redefined
• entrepreneurial explosion
• all company relationships redefined
• economics of production and distribution scale challenged
• mixed-scale alliances
• markets over hierarchies
"Global Village" Realized
Economic Volatility
• oil
• currency
• trade flows
Lack of Cohesive Global Economic Leadership
Old Industry Restructuring
• LBOs
• mergers and break-ups
New Industry Emergence
Service Sector Dominance/"Service Added" in Manufacturing Brain-based Everything
New Organizational Forms
• no hierarchy
New Combinations of Organizations
• networks
Perpetual Change
Careers Redefined
• flexibility
Education Redefined
• lifelong
• creativity
Everyone (person/firm) a "Global Player"
Entrepreneurs Taking on Any Task
New Winners and New Losers
• jobs
• people
• firms
• industries
Search for New Bases for Competitive Advantage
• speed/time
• flexibility
• quality/design
• information technology
• alliances/networks
• fast innovation improvement
• skill upgrading
• "service added"
• "small within big"
• subcontracting
• globalization

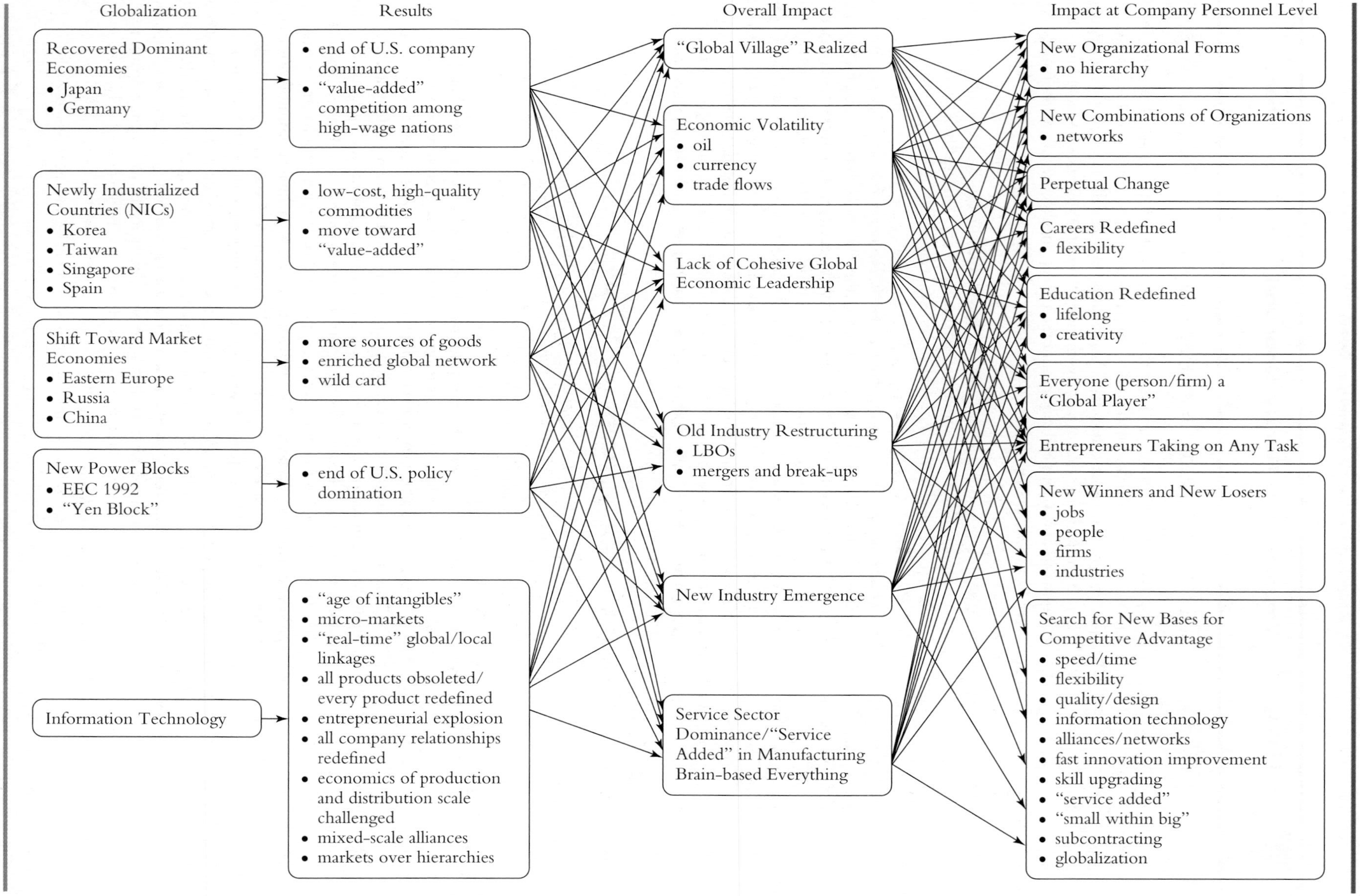

kets for plant sites are shooting toward the heavens as the Japanese and others race to enhance their "insider status" before 1992.

The growing market orientation of the planned economies throws a real spanner into the works. I don't expect the Soviet Lotta automobile to sweep North America off its feet the way VW Beetles, Honda Civics, and Hyundai Excels did. Nonetheless, the surge toward a market orientation in the Soviet Union, Eastern Europe and China—despite the latter's on-and-off gyrations—may profoundly affect the global economy by the late '90s.

Three balanced "power blocs" set the pace as the world economy charges headlong into the 21st century: North America (strengthened by the U.S.–Canada Free Trade Agreement), the European Single Market (today, more so post-1992 and still more as Eastern Europe becomes a partner) and the yen bloc, the more or less Japanese-led Asian powerhouse nations. It will never again be safe—or wise—to think of commerce in a local fashion. The rubble of the Berlin Wall is merely the most dramatic evidence of the movement to destroy borders that has begun in developed and developing nations.

Information Technology

While globalization has occurred somewhat autonomously, it has received a big boost from the new power of information technology. That doesn't just mean the transistor, microprocessor, computer, microwave relay, satellite dish, or fiber optic cable. It means all those things, increasingly woven together and abetted by thousands of networked systems and software packages tossed in for good measure.

The management and coordination of information have always driven economic change. The rise of the merchant class, which created the market economy, effectively broke feudalism's hold and ended the Dark Ages. What does information have to do with the Dark Ages? A Middle Ages crossroad, where a literal market stood, is nothing more than a dense knot of information (multiple buyers and multiple sellers). Another example: The Industrial Revolution was important for its smokestack technology and accompanying standardized production. But it blossomed in the United States, which had a rich transportation network in the world's biggest and most vigorous free-trade zone (the 48 contiguous states); in turn, the railroads' power to connect the nation was multiplied by the telegraph, which allowed timely market coordination. Then the telephone emerged (though routine long-distance calling is only 20 years old), and markets were once more compressed. Next came the computer, the definitive information processor, and along with it the arrival of fiber optic cable, microwave relays and satellites, creating the ultimate "information highways."

Information is power. Information technology allows us to instantly disperse power globally. It's not just economic power. Former Citicorp Chairman Walter Wriston and economist George Gilder are among those who argue that global computer-telecommunications networks destroy old political power blocs. This is no fantasy. Fax machines and television cameras played a leading role in Eastern Europe at the end of 1989.

Information technology (IT) affects a J.C. Penney store boss who sees a great sweater at Neiman Marcus. She buys it, photographs it, and faxes the reproduction to JCP buyers around the glob. In a day or two, a buyer finds a factory in Kuala Lumpur or Bangkok that can copy it. In a week or two, thousands of replicas are winging toward Penney stores. IT also means that CRSS, the giant Houston-based architectural firm, can exchange corrected drawings with client 3M on CAD machines almost instantly. IT permits an IBM engineer, stuck on a problem, to ask 70,000 expert colleagues around the globe for overnight help. IT causes GE to spend hundreds of millions of dollars to create a private global phone network to permit instant, seven-digit dialing from anywhere to anywhere. And IT makes the finance ministers of America and Germany and Japan almost powerless in the face of global financial trading networks. (In a symbolic watershed, the London Stock Exchange in 1989 replaced its trading floor with a computer-telecommunications network.)

RESULTS

What are the results of these primary forces (please look at the chart again)?

Globalization

Bid farewell to United States companies as peerless stars in the world economies; while Boeing and GE surely still play a big role, the "greats" today also include the world's 10 largest banks (9 are Japanese), Hitachi, Sony, Honda, Toyota, Nissan, and from West Germany, BASF, Bayer, BMW, and Bertelsmann.

Examine the recovered dominant economies of Japan and West Germany: Each giant and the entire manufacturing (and service) economies of the dominant nations shed commodities to swiftly climb the "value-added chain," as business strategist call it. There is little room for "commodity production" in the great economies if they wish to sustain high wages and continued growth. The battleground has shifted from "more, more, more for bigger, bigger, bigger markets" (the traditional American trump card) to "better, better, better for ever more finely diced markets." Note the growing role of the Japanese in upscale automobiles, where Honda (Acura), Nissan (Infiniti), and Toyota (Lexus) are altering the North American market. Superb quality, faster innovation (for individual firms and networks of firms), and "smarter" distribution (electronic data interchange networks) are hallmarks of these value-added economies.

There is a puff or two of air left in dominant and fully developed nations' commodity sails. Yet the big news is the burgeoning flow of increasingly fine goods pouring in from the newly industrialized countries. (Singapore's emphasis on education, value-added products and services and telecommunications networks is testimony to this.) Nonetheless, NICs and others like them have become, for reasons of relatively lower wages as well as mastery of advanced production techniques, the heartland for commodity production. However, "commodity" has a new meaning. In the past, "commodity" meant cheap—both inexpensive and far from the leading edge. Today commodity still means inexpensive, but the new technologies are equalizers. The *new* commodities (microwave ovens, television sets, and semiconductors from Korea, PCs from Taiwan, garments from Hong Kong) are of the highest quality and not far from state of the art technologically. Perhaps the most significant problem facing the exporters and partners is that commodity and low quality still go hand-in-glove in these nations.

(Among other things, this change turns up the competitive heat under the developed countries. Even superb quality is not enough to qualify as "high value added." High value added now hinges upon rapid distribution networks, service-added features, lightning-fast innovation—more on that later.)

The shift toward market economies by the Russians, Eastern Europeans, and Chinese is a wild card on the global game board. At the very least, it means more product choices for a world already choking on choices. (The *Economist* calls it "manic specialization.") If any of these undernourished areas can lick the infrastructure issue (computers, telecommunications networks—and basics such as highways, which are deficient in Russia and China), the global commercial network of nations will truly become the long-awaited little village.

Information Technology

Intangibles now dominate tangibles, a fact that is difficult for many to deal with. Matter doesn't matter so much anymore. "Lumps are out, brains are in," according to one colleague. It's the age of "no-mater," says consultant Stan Davis. Dun & Bradstreet sold the Official Airline Guide, a well-packaged compilation of publicly available information, for $750 million in 1987—twice what Donald Trump paid for the Eastern Shuttle. The ultimate intangible—well-packaged information—is more valuable than the aircraft, the pilots, the mechanics, the flight attendants, and the administrators of huge airlines!

A company's true worth increasingly bears little relationship to the lumps it owns. When Philip Morris shelled out $12.9 billion for Kraft, the accountants determined that the company had just $1.3 billion in "hard" assets (plants, equipment, cheese)—leaving a whopping $11.6 billion in "intangibles." Or consider Kimberly-Clark, which used IT to create a huge database for a Huggies diaper launch. With the names of 75 percent of the year's 3.5 million new American mothers in hand, the firm aimed direct mail barrages at the women. Each mother becomes a discrete market, catered to in a unique fashion. Kimberly-Clark officials insist that the database is as valuable as the trees that go into the product.

Then there is the "smart bathtub" from American Standard, priced at over $35,000—it includes a VCR, presettable bath temperatures, and a host of other features. And "smart" shopping carts which give shippers detailed information about specials, the location of goods and display interactive games or local news while shoppers wait in line. In short, "information-added" technology redefines and reconstructs every product, new or mature.

When it comes to IT, the changing nature of the links *within* and *among* organizations is as profound as the "smartening" of discrete products. Instant access to every corner of the globe is a 1990 reality. We're blasé as we read in David Lodge's novel on the industrial economy, *Nice Work,* about a London bond trader who always goes to bed with her remote, automatic price-quotation calculator stuffed under her pillow; instant information availability has redefined the entire financial services sector. Manufacturing is affected at least as much. Instant computerized order entry and instant interaction over product design issues are things of the present. Take Motorola's pager operation: Manufacture of a custom pager starts 17 *minutes* after the order is transmitted by a remote salesperson.

Or consider this discussion of Hitachi taken from the November–December 1989 *Harvard Business Review.* The story is not really about Hitachi; instead it's about the big firm's subcontractors and the subcontractors' subcontractors. In earlier times the task in question would have required weeks:

> There is a Japanese maker of high-precision dies that serves the burgeoning consumer electronics industry. . . . During the past five years, this small company has organized itself around an electronic network linking it to such giant electronics companies as Hitachi and to a highly specialized family of suppliers. Designers at Hitachi sketch a new part and sent it by fax to the diemaker. Die engineers review the sketch and, using computer-aided design (CAD) systems, generate the specifications for a new die in a matter of hours. The company then decides whether to make the die itself or subcontract it to one of the suppliers—all of whose skills, current capacity and work-in-progress have been logged. As often as not, it chooses a supplier and sends the specifications by fax, along with supplementary information about materials and stresses. The supplier, using advanced numerical control tools, makes the die, also in a matter of hours. It is not uncommon for Hitachi to get the die for some parts back in one day: the sketch arrives in the morning, the die is finished in the afternoon.

Another impact of monumental significance is the surge of entrepreneurs in the information age. With everything literally being reinvented and long production lines for mass widget-making dissolving, new players are entering all fields at an unprecedented pace. A prime example: the tens of thousands of software entrepreneurs who have recently sprung up. (What an industry: Microsoft's founder Bill Gates recently joined *Fortune's* list of billionaires.) But new entrepreneurial opportunities also arise in old-line industries, such as steel and packaged goods and financial services. Time-honored tenets of vertical integration just don't cut it anymore; businesses today go to whomever, wherever, of whatever size that can do this little bit of that little job best. Giant firms with 11- or 12-figure sales will probably still exist tomorrow. But beneath the surface, plant watering chores, cafeteria management, legal services, accounting, and even specialized R&D will be "outsourced" from a loose collection of small, efficient, and effective outfits gathered in a tight, electronically linked network. This shift is in its infancy; as global electronic highways proliferate in the next 10 to 15 years, we will see a much greater entrepreneurial surge.

Adversarial, arms-length dealing that have marked American companies' relations—with vendors, middlepersons, and customers—won't (*can't,* for survival's sake) exist in the new world. Recall the KG-Levi Strauss relationship: To cut an order cycle from nine weeks to four days, the two firms had to create intense technological links—*and they have to trust each other.* This increasingly commonplace "competing-in-time" (another new phrase) example is occurring again and again throughout the textile and garment industry: A 66-week cycle, which begins with design and ends with the production on the consumer's shelf, is shrinking to 11 weeks. For this to happen, the garment maker has to be closely tied to the fabric maker (as has happened with Levi Strauss and Milliken); the fabric maker needs tight links to its chemical suppliers (a Du Pont with a Milliken); and all must plug into even the fashion designer's curious world.

We can no longer think productively or profitably about "the company" alone. All models of "the firm" must include seamless global connections with vendors, vendors' vendors, middlepersons, customers, and customers' customers.

Embedded in all of the above is radical change to the economics of production and distribution scale. The biggest are losing out to the "bestest." And the new "bestest" will probably be alternative outfits that consist of *networks* of small, medium, and large firms gathered to do today's (and not necessarily tomorrow's) task as best they can. It is common to see a proud company like Digital Equipment make the following product announcements: Its top-of-the-line workstation (where Digital lags) contains a brain (a pioneering microprocessor) developed by relatively small MIPS computer of Sunnyvale, California. Efficient Tandy Corporation will manufacture Digital's personal computers. Ultimate sales end up on Digital's revenue line, but Digital itself adds unique value by providing the network, sales, and service skill, long-established customer relations, and an intellectual framework that ties the products together.

Markets will increasingly win out over hierarchies. We've favored hierarchies as a way to organize complex commercial affairs for the last several hundred years. In the late '50s, John Kenneth Galbraith labeled America's biggest corporations "perfect machines." Efficiency of coordination via massive, specialized staffs led to effectiveness on the bottom line. No more. Thanks to information technology (and numerous supply sources for everything), those specialists will most often be full-scale *outside* partners. Inside the firm, information readily available in sophisticated forms (via the use of expert systems, groupware, and networked PCs), dramatically reduces the need for management layers. After all, a hierarchy is only an information-processing machine. Formerly a firm needed a cast of thousands to collect receipts in hundreds of shoe boxes and a horde of senior financial analysts to count the shoe boxes. Not today.

OVERALL IMPACT

Look at the chart: Now the real mess begins! Each of the boxes and bullets under "Results" is a jumble of cause and effect leading to what I have labeled "Overall Impact." Sorting out the links is hopeless—and not particularly valuable. Each force impacts, and is impacted by, any number of other forces in a multiplicative way.

Begin with the "global village" that Marshall McLuhan predicted in the late 1950s. It's here, though we ain't seen nothing yet. Financial markets are globally connected 24 hours a day. No trader can afford to be out of touch at any time. Perhaps a more interesting window on tomorrow comes from assessing our and others' multinational companies. My daughter's IBM typewriter was made in West Germany, doubtless with components from a dozen nations. On the other hand, her Honda Accord, which sits in a sorority parking lot in Ithaca, NY, was made in Ohio. The issue of trade (and trade deficits) is no more about Japan's NEC competing with the United States' Cray in supercomputers than it is about Apple Japan and Apple Europe and Apple Singapore competing with Apple USA. Everyone is everyone else's subcontractor. Companies automatically scan the globe for the best solution to the make/buy decision. In *The Age of Unreason,* British professor Charles Handy even reports that London firms are sending their daily typing to Taipei, courtesy fax and global telecommunications networks!

The lack of cohesive economic leadership, also spurred by the homogenized effects of information technology networks, impacts our world and has destabilizing results. The Great Depression of 1930 is often attributed to Britain's loss of global economic leadership and America's hesitation to pick up the mantle. Subsequently, our cohesive global leadership contributed to the astonishing worldwide economic growth following World War II. Now we have the beginning of a leadership standoff among Japan and the yen bloc, the European Single Market and the United States. Though information technology networks have a homogenizing effect (feedback loops have been reduced from years in Columbus' time to nanoseconds today), the absence of firm leadership will most likely be destabilizing.

Can the absurd land values in Japan continue? Or the equally extraordinary valuation of the Tokyo and Taipei stock markets? Will oil cost $15 a barrel or $35? Will inflation run at 4 or 14 percent? This perpetual volatility on a previously unknown scale is especially significant. The reason: *All* modern business-planning techniques assume predictability. Capital budgeting methods using discounted cash flow analyses so popular the West depend on the ability to more or less accurately predict product supply and demand, competitors, technologies, interest rates, inflation, and raw material prices over a 10- to 25-year period. This was possible for a couple of decades following World War II, when such techniques took root. Such predictive accuracy is long gone.

The interaction of volatility, globalization, and information technology is leading to wholesale, speedy restructuring of *all* old industries, even in Japan. The changes (e.g., downsizing, shifting portfolios) in two successful Japanese industries—shipbuilding and steel—have been at least as dramatic as, and even quicker than, the highly touted United States Basic-industry restructuring. Historically, Japan has had no true multinationals, just exporters—the automakers first among them. Not today. Hardly a month passes without notice of a new Japanese automobile manufacturing operation to be opened on North American or Japanese automobile manufacturing operation to be opened on North American or European soil. The same is true in semiconductors and consumer electronics. Now the cycle is repeating itself in other countries: As wages soar, newly industrialized countries such as Korea and Taiwan are rapidly shipping their mundane textile and electronic assembly jobs offshore and pursuing higher value-added tasks at home.

Stir in the mergers and de-mergers sweeping the United States. Again cause and effect is impossible to sort out: While merger mania has been abetted by (some would say, caused by) such new financial instruments as junk bonds, it's equally fair to say that the instruments are a response to a deeper need for restructuring.

In fact, de-mergers (spinoffs, breakups, management-led LBOs) may turn out to be a bigger story than the mergers. Most often, after a merger, a massive sell-off of business bits to managers follows. Though some are frightened of this trend, LBO performance looks good overall. The failures lasso headlines; but the mounting empirical evidence suggests that most LBOs will readily weather a sizable recession. One recent study of the United States and British LBOs, for instance, observes that first- and second-year debt repayment exceeds plan by 400 and 500 percent respectively! Such success stems from the new owners' quick rationalization of hopelessly inefficient operations. Real value has been unlocked.

So old industries are restructuring wildly and new industries, especially information-related ones, are emerging just as fast. Already, information technology may contribute as much as 20 percent directly to the GNP; add indirect effects, like smart products and processes and networks, and that number easily could be doubled—and the IT age is still in diapers.

The direct role that silicon, microprocessors, computers, software codes, and fiber optic networks play is apparent. The less apparent role has just as great an impact. The young biotechnology revolution is as much a computer revolution as it is a biological sciences revolution; the ability of the computer to sort through and deal with billions of possible compound combinations is as important as the new theoretical scientific foundations. Information is changing and rearranging material sciences, too. Look at the massive array of new, customized compounds being developed by the chemical companies, and the overall shift among big firms from commodity to specialty production. Case in point: A decade ago, 70 percent of giant Monsanto's revenues flowed from commodity-grade chemicals; now that number is 2 percent.

Then there's the biggest shift of all—toward service-sector dominance. Consider these words from recently retired Motorola Chairman Bob Galvin: "The nation that masters the management of information for the service industries—along with owning the key parts of the service sector in the world's major developed markets—is destined for global economic leadership of historic proportion."

The service sector already directly employs 75 percent of Americans, a slightly lesser share of Europeans and about 60 percent of the Japanese. Moreover, service employees account for the lion's share of the payroll in what we still choose to call manufacturing companies. Take Hewlett-Packard: About 75 percent of its employees perform service tasks—accounting, MIS, research, marketing, sales, distribution, engineering, and design. The idea of a distinction between "manufacturing" firms and "service" firms is becoming useless or, worse, counterproductive. The most effective service firms today are those with the most sophisticated "factories": American Airlines' reservation system, the information systems and networks of a Federal Express or an American Express. The most effective manufacturers today, in turn, are those with the most extensive service operations—remember that huge General Electric investment in an independent, global telecommunications network.

Service is already the most sophisticated sector of the economy. Value-added and technology spending per employee stands above manufacturing. Via applications-pull, the service sector is dragging the manufacturing sector into the future.

Now look anew at the chart and reflect on all the "Overall Impact" elements: realization of the global village, economic volatility, lack of cohesive global economic leadership, old industry restructuring, new industry emergence, service-sector dominance, service-added strategies. It's an unmistakable snapshot of a world turning upside down. Yet, I cannot emphasize enough that we have barely begun to experience the impact of these multiplicative, intertwined forces. We are still largely "unwired," even with the explosive growth of global telecommunications networks. Globalization might appear to be well advanced, but the changes going on in the NICs and in Eastern Europe, and the radical transformation of Western European and Japanese companies, are also barely out the gate.

IMPACT AT COMPANY/PERSONAL LEVEL

This is the "meat and potatoes" of the seminars I normally conduct, and the heart of such revolutionary new management books as Charles Handy's *The Age of Unreason,* Stan Davis' *Future Perfect* and Harvard Professor Rosabeth Moss Kanter's *When Giants Learn to Dance.* The suggestions that spew forth from a Handy, Davis, Kanter or me are not "nifty-to-do" ideas. They are survival musts, driven by the interaction of all the destabilizing, youthful forces just reviewed.

New Organizational Forms

New ways of organizing are upending the applecart of about two millennia of management practice. Hierarchies—the only organizational format since the Chinese invented it 2,000 years ago (and the United States perfected it following World War II)—are being quickly dismantled. Multibillion-dollar, dozen-layer-deep organizations are being trampled in the global marketplace by multibillion-dollar, three-and four-layer organizations—witness Sears' trouncing by Wal-Mart in the '80s. Firms like Wal-Mart, The Limited, Nucor Corp., Federal Express, Compaq Computer, Quad/Graphics, and Cypress Semiconductor simply don't look like firms of old.

And firms of old are shedding *their* skins. In 1981, Jack Welch took over General Electric, the firm known in the '70s as *the* model for industrial excellence. Welch's predecessor, Reg Jones, was an "industrial statesman," spending as much time in Washington D.C. as in the corporate headquarters. When Welch took over, he dismantled corporate staffs including the fabled central strategic planing operation; and he tossed out many ill-fitting pieces in the business portfolio, such as Utah International, a natural resource company bought by Jones in the '70s to soothe earnings hiccups. He bought into the service sector with a vengeance—financial services, the media. GE of 1989 bears little resemblance to GE of 1981 in shape, attitude, or portfolio.

Other old-line firms are catching on. GM, Ford, and Chrysler are de-integrating and calling on subcontractors to make anything and everything. Thanks to the new information-technology linkups, the subcontracting relationship differs wildly from the past. After installing just-in-time inventory management schemes aided by electronic data interchange, companies like GM, for one, are now insisting that all supplier transactions soon be paperless!

New Combinations of Organizations

Little firms are signing up big firms to do this or that. Big firms are signing up little firms to do this or that. These relationships are creating additional new relationships. For example, the Ford Taurus development project brought outsiders into the design loop at the very beginning. The revolutionary aim was speed and more innovation from those who knew their business best. Makes sense? Of course. But it also wiped out a hundred years of conventional wisdom about product development.

Perpetual Change

"We eat change for breakfast," says Harry Quadracci, chairman of innovative Quad/Graphics, a half-billion-dollar revenue printing firm. "Our workers see change as survival," he adds. Dick Liebhaber, executive VP of $6 billion MCI, chimes in: "We don't shoot people who make mistakes; we shoot people who don't take risks."

Behaving in a "button-down fashion," "keeping one's nose clean" and acting as a "steward" were once the hallmarks of the climb up the corporate career ladder. Forget it. Firms that change—fast, constantly, and from bottom to top—have a chance at survival. Those that resist disorder and change don't.

I recall my doctoral studies at Stanford, examining the internal structures of organizations. The largest body of literature involved resistance to change at the company, small group, and individual level. Change *is* threatening. Yet those who welcome it will be the only contenders for survival, whether small or large, in an old industry or new one. How do we square characteristic resistance to change and the bedrock requirement to "eat change for breakfast?" Answer: It won't be easy. The attitudes and philosophies of the Quadraccis and

Liebhabers must become the norm. Perpetual change means perpetual retraining and worker reassignment, perpetual new alliances among companies of varying sizes, perpetual reorganization. The surviving organization will resemble a floating crap game of projects embedded amid networks of multiple companies.

Careers Redefined

The change process will redefine *every* career. Rosabeth Kanter claims that the only survivors will be those who "perpetually seek to add value." Her favorite word is "project." Everyone, janitor to vice president, must be "seeking out projects to add value."

So who's left to sweep the floor? A visit to a 3M facility in Austin, Texas, suggests that floor sweeping, food handling and security guarding are fast becoming almost as sophisticated as engineering. Computer-based floor sweepers and new security systems call for a sophisticated worker in virtually every job. A new, highly automated facility belonging to the huge drug distributor, Bergen Brunswig, is illustrative: Most manual work is done by machine. Work teams that dot the facility are not so much in the business of "doing" (by old standards), but in the business of improving the system. They are brain-involved, improvement-project creators, not muscle-driven lump shifters. There is no room on the staff for anyone who sees himself or herself as a pair of hands, punching a time clock.

Education Redefined

The nature of worker education must change. Employees have seldom loved "training"—as in second-rate instructors stuffing outdated material down throats. Yet Quad/Graphics is a university disguised as a company. Workers spend a day a week in the classroom—a "day a week, forever" as a leader in the firm's educational program puts it. "Training" is out. "Lifelong learning" is in. Every thriving firm, from bank to burger maker, will look like a university—period.

Besides training in the new technologies and techniques, like statistical process control and problem cause-and-effect analysis, there's a need for massive doses of "inter-firm relationship training," according to Stan Davis. It's a must if seamless links with "foreign" firms (suppliers, producers, middlepersons, customers from everywhere) are the norm.

Society's educational needs will differ too. Fads may stress a return to the three Rs (and that apple surely needs polishing), but the opposite is actually the more pressing requirement. Every viable worker will be required to think and create. Consider these words from Stan Davis:

> Mass production means meticulous attention to repetitive detail . . . Socialization in the industrial world was to make [children] capable of sustaining boredom in adult life. An example . . . is the way children who are naturally creative were punished in schools a few generations back. A not uncommon punishment was to write something like "I will not say _ again" one hundred times on the blackboard. The purpose . . . was to adapt them to carrying out repetitive detail in the industrial labor force. Perhaps today a more creativity-producing punishment for the same act would be to list a hundred different ways of saying the same "_" thing.

Every Person a "Global Player"

Recall Handy's description of London firms sending typing to Taipei. To survive, London typists must realize they are competing with Taipei typists. They must learn to "add value" (e.g., know more software programs, more languages than their Taiwanese counterparts) or else they'd better learn to love pounding the pavement. This is especially tough for xenophobic Americans, who grew up believing in the god-given invincibility of the United States economy. Every American work force survivor, receptionist to computer scientist, must become obsessed with Europe and Asia—and how to add more value than their counterpart at the big firm 6,000 miles away or the start-up next door.

Entrepreneurs Taking on any Task

As change accelerates, we will see more entrepreneurs like the software start-up, the biotech lab, the new financial services boutique, the specialty food maker, the personal-shopper outfit, the custom magazine producer (there were 491 new, customized magazines launched in the United States alone in 1988). But new *forms* of entrepreneurs will spring up, too. For example, middle managers at big firms will become "project creators," to use Kanter's term; smart ones will move quickly to create an independent skill base.

Let's fantasize for a moment about how the endangered middle manager might survive in the new "lean-and-mean" environment. Pretend you are a mid-level accounting boss in a $100 million division of a bigger firm. In the past, your job description was narrow: keep the books accurately. Bird dog (i.e. harass) those who don't get their numbers in on time. Stay in your office, ready to instantly answer queries from higher-ups.

Suppose your division has three factories, two distribution centers, a couple of sizable engineering groups, a marketing operation, and four sales branches. Your survival strategy today should begin with a wandering jag. Meet with your dozen groups' leaders: How can you and your gang help? You'll likely spark the enthusiasm of a couple of middle managers. Schedule a briefing session with each unit leader to talk about "the revolution in project accounting." Give your spiel quickly then discuss cooperative efforts. Volunteer one of your staff or yourself to work on an experimental project—e.g., a major modification to a costing system to accompany the next product launch. Aim to have a half-dozen pilot projects in various stages at any time; each of your people should be working on at least one, and 10 percent should be on full-time pilot assignment at any time.

Think like a consultant: Eventually, you should propose to sell your service to other divisions. This not only makes you and your team more valuable, it also prepares you for the next bold step: peddling your group's expert services for a profit *outside* the corporation. If later you are a victim of "pyramid flattening," you will have proven, marketable skills. You might even propose to cut the umbilical cord, go independent, incorporate, and then sell half your services back to the company. Of course, the story is no fantasy; it's practiced in outfit after outfit today.

So, "entrepreneur" means anybody from anywhere who can figure out some way to do *something* better. And the faster one can figure that out, and the quicker one is willing to become or consider becoming an independent purveyor of unique skills, the better the chances for continued participation in the work force.

New Winners and New Losers

New winners and new losers pop up every day. New losers include over 40 percent of the 1979 Fortune 500 that have disappeared from that list in the last decade. Losing means gone out of business, being swallowed up by another firm and reconfigured or dismantled, being supplanted by an up-start—Apple in computers, Nucor in steel. MCI CEO Bill McGowan may have described the new context best. The former "rags-to-riches-to-rags cycle," he says, was about three generations. Now it's down to five years. Never has an employee's, company's, industry's toehold been so precarious.

The same trauma even besets regions. The sluggishness of the Rust Belt versus the vitality of the Altanta-Tampa-Austin-Los Angeles-Portland "golden crescent," as I call it, is now old news. But the disparities will become more pronounced with time. In his superb book, *Job Creation in America,* economist David Birch comments that, "Most of the new firms taking the place of the older ones offer different kinds of locations and work forces, present different needs for capital, transportation, government services, education, recreation, and energy." A firm no longer gravitates to North Carolina for low wages, but for the prowess of Duke. Regions with skilled workers, great universities, a sound K–12 school system, a clean environment, and a ready flow of entrepreneurial capital will grab the lion's share of tomorrow's brain-based jobs and firms.

Search for New Bases for Competitive Advantage

Finally, all of the above comes down to the frantic pursuit of new bases for competitive advantage. Chief among them:

1. *Speed/time.* Time compression is becoming the principal basis for competitive advantage, according to one rapidly developing school of thought. Businesses are squeezing production cycles, slashing product development cycles, shrinking delivery time. Companies that can bring the "newest and most improved" to the market fastest, ensure instant delivery anywhere and everywhere, and then quickly upgrade the product stand a chance of surviving. Those that don't learn to play this very complicated game don't stand a chance. For example, KG Stores' chief information officer insists that soon his company will not accept orders from vendors that are not hooked up electronically. In another case, a mid-sized plumbing supply distributor in the deep South threatened mighty plumbing products manufacturer Kohler of Wisconsin: Speed up (a lot) or else. Kohler had to comply.
2. *Flexibility.* Quickly getting into and out of things is a necessity today, since "leap-frogging" takes place regularly in virtually any industry you can name. Quality improves dramatically overnight. New performance standards eclipse old ones in a flash. Rapidly forming new alliances is a parallel requirement. Thus the paradox: Flexibility means raw speed, but there is also an unprecedented need for patient investment in developing relationships and alliances, at home and in overseas markets.
3. *Quality/design.* Superb quality alone won't be enough for future survival. But superb quality is an absolute requisite for any developed (or developing) nation/firm in virtually every market. Quality moved atop the United States corporate priority list in the early 1980s. Now we are talking about other "top priorities," such as speed and service added. That's sensible. However, the average American firm has not "licked the quality issue." There is much more to be done in training and education, in employee involvement and adoption of self-managing teams to provide autonomy to those closest to the action. "World-class quality" may be a "given," as all my friends tell me, but it's a given at damn few of the firms I work with.

   Quality's handmaiden is design—aesthetics, user friendliness, functionality. Putting design "in the loop" from the start of the product development process, as a Ford now does and as a Herman Miller always has done, is one of the many new horizons that will distinguish tomorrow's winners from the losers.
4. *The astute—and pioneering—use of information technology.* Getting everyone to experiment brashly with information technology in every part of the organization, *and* in every "outside" business relationship, is a survival essential. "Fast followership" is not enough: Pioneering, scary or not, is required.
5. *Forming alliances and becoming a network partner.* Creating new temporary or permanent alliances and embedding the organization in tightly linked networks with suppliers, middlepersons, and customers are also absolute survival requirements. "Network management" skills will quickly become the most cherished in the firm.
6. *Fast innovation/perpetual improvement.* Dramatically compressing development cycles, tough as that job is, constitutes only a part of the emerging innovation equation. Most sizable firms still quake at the smallest failures, can't deal with obstreperous new-product champions, refuse to grant true autonomy and requisite spending authority to "low-level" units and overinvest in yesterday's winners. They are, in short, lousy innovators with a pronounced anti-innovation bias: It is tomorrow's kiss of death.

   The perpetual improvement of everything (another flavor of innovation) is also an absolute necessity that represents a stunning departure from the past. Fast-paced quality improvement can go on forever—and must. Fast-paced productivity improvement can go on forever—and must. Fast-paced organizational and business process improvement can go on forever—and must. Everyone, literally, must picture himself or herself in the "perpetual improvement business, full time," to quote one exec.

7. *Perpetual skill upgrading.* The skill package that the corporation and its network brings to the marketplace, and the pace at which that package increases compared to the skill package of its competitors and their networks, will determine competitiveness like no other factor. "World-class work force" must become a more common phrase than "world-class quality." Why? Because the former drives the latter.
8. *Service added.* Adding service—another form of intelligence—to every product and its distribution and marketing is yet another *survival* necessity. For example, Levi Strauss is betting the company on its ability to be responsive to customers, more than on its fashion design skills.
9. *Small within big.* Scale is changing. "New big" is neither beautiful nor ugly, just profoundly different from "old big." Big in the traditional sense—7,000 people under one auto factory's roof—is an almost guaranteed loser today. But big *networks* of various-sized firms is an oddball form that will likely survive and prosper.

   Other winners: Smallish, self-contained units within very big firms and big networks composed of specialist pieces of firms of various sizes. In fact, the successful "new big" outfit is probably best conceived as a "network/alliance manager," rather than a vertically integrated behemoth. Even goliath Boeing says its chief skill is "systems integration."
10. *Subcontracting.* In *The Age of Unreason* Charles Handy describes an exercise conducted by executives at a multibillion-pound British company; they aimed to determine what *couldn't* be subcontracted. They decided that everything could be farmed out "except for the chief executive officer and his car phone." That's a bit extreme, but only a bit. In the conservative publication *Business Month,* a wag recently predicted that "by the year 2010 there may be no CEOs" in the new, flat, network forms of organization.

    Consider what is perhaps today's ultimate example, the FI Group, one of Britain's largest software systems houses. FI employs about 1,100, most of who are part-time freelancers who need toil no more than 20 hours per week. More than two-thirds of the firm's work is done at home: All told, employees live in 800 sites and serve 400 clients at any time. Life at FI is captured in the November 1988 issue of *Business:* "Chris Eyles, project manager, sat down in her office in Esher, Surrey, and called up the electronic 'chit chat' mailbox. . . . The printer began to churn out messages. 'Help!' said [a message] from her secretary, based a few miles away in Weybridge. Somewhere in the Esher area, a computer analyst was in trouble. . . . Eyles checked the team diary and her wall plan, located the analyst and the problem and set up a meeting a FI's work center in Horley, 25 miles away."

    The benefits of FI's flexible configuration to employees are obvious. But clients benefit too. Talented specialists can be called upon at a moment's notice to perform almost any task. The firm has also developed an exceptional quality record, putting to rest the idea that dispersed part-timers can't turn out top-drawer, integrated systems. FI's business is booming because its clients are heading down the same path it has. FI chief executive Hilary Cropper observes, "Before, companies tended to use FI to fill. Now they want to off-load the whole show."
11. *Globalization.* "Thinking global" is/will be the province of virtually any would-be survivor of any size. "Global players" include the small flashlight maker Maglite in Los Angeles and the penmaker A.T. Cross in Lincoln, Rhode Island, as well as GE and IBM.

Review this article and you'll realize that not only will no stones be long left unturned, but no newly turned stones are likely to gather moss in the years ahead. Perhaps the best and only defense (or offense) is to broaden your interests and become a champion for change—whether you are a London typist, small-business owner, big-firm middle manager or chief executive officer. The forces foisting all this change upon us have barely been unleashed.

Discussion Questions

1. Briefly describe the forces of globalization and information technology that are affecting the massive economic transformation.
2. What are the results of these two forces?
3. What is the overall impact of these two forces? ▼

"Why Business Managers Are Empty-handed," by David Vaskevitch

(This reading is especially suited for use in conjunction with Chapter 5 of *Information Systems.*)

Do managers really spend most of their time processing words, building spreadsheets and maintaining simple databases? That's what you'd think, looking at today's software sales and the primary efforts of the PC software industry.

The dominant software categories are word processors, spreadsheets and databases, which account for 75% of the world's PC software purchasing dollars. The next tier of applications includes presentation graphics, project management and electronic mail.

But word processors never found their way into the hearts and minds of managers. Spreadsheets can be liberating for budget-building, but most managers spend little time calculating numbers other than at budget time. And while database software is quite powerful, it can also be quite complex.

In reality, most managers use their PCs for only a fraction of the day, instead preferring copiers, fax machines, telephones, filing cabinets, secretaries and personal interaction.

In fact, while the PC is supposed to represent an electronic desk, it doesn't even come close to replacing the piece of furniture on which the machine sits. That's because today's PC software doesn't fit with what today's managers really do.

During the '90s, the software industry has to gain a clearer picture of how managers work so it can deliver useful tools.

Managers tend to work through others instead of accomplishing tasks themselves. Rather than being generators of words and numbers, managers focus primarily on the three C's: communication, control and coordination.

The computer, particularly in a networked form, can help managers concentrate on communication, control and coordination, but only if new categories of software, as described in the following pages, emerge.

A new generation of applications that will finally support a manager's everyday tasks of communication, control and coordination will make its appearance before the decade is out. With a new set of software (described on these pages), the PC could become a tool managers use all day, every day. These machines will become—finally—a central part of every manager's job.

COMMUNICATE

Managers probably spend most of their time communicating. As new PC software becomes available that more directly supports this activity, the managerial workstation will become indispensable.

Today, most managers would hardly notice if the PC on their desks were taken away—except at budget time or while writing a key memo. However, in companies with active electronic-mail systems, managers notice and complain within minutes if the mail system or their PC stops working.

E-mail, in its ability to improve the informal communications process, is the first tool to change the underlying patterns that are implicit in a manager's everyday working life.

Yet in many ways, E-mail addresses only a small part of the real need. For one thing, most E-mail systems don't remember any history. In addition, they are limited in scope, best suited for directed communications among either individuals or small groups of people.

SOURCE: David Vaskevitch, "Why Business Managers are Empty-handed," *Computerworld,* April 5, 1993, pp. 93, 96, and 97.

Other types of communications software, namely bulletin board systems, markup packages and multiuser hypertext systems, start to address the rest of the need.

Bulletin board systems were specifically designed to remember lots of history, and they facilitate communication among medium and large groups of communicators. The system is organized around topics—that is, any subject a group of people is interested in discussing. Every message sent through a bulletin board is typically kept for subsequent display by all other interested users.

With a bulletin board system, a manager can confront an issue, come up to speed quickly, bring his longer term perspective to bear and make a decision that enables a deadlocked team to start making progress again.

A bulletin board system facilitates this process in three ways:

- The manager can stay on top of active topics by skimming the structure of the bulletin board to decide where he most needs to get involved.
- Once he has decided that an issue requires his involvement, the manager can quickly come up to speed on the context and background.
- Before making a decision, the manager can poll the team and others for additional input. The bulletin board provides both a mechanism for everyone involved in the decision to be equally up to speed and for contributors to add their input quickly, facilitating a rapid decision.

If bulletin boards are so useful, why aren't they more popular in the managerial community and among corporations in general? Part of the reason is that until recently, this technology did not really exist in a form that corporations could use internally. Lotus Development Corp.'s Notes is probably the first large-scale commercial product that is bringing bulletin board technology to commercial organizations.

But E-mail and bulletin boards are just the beginning. Waiting in the wings is an approach to communicating based on E-mail and bulletin boards that goes beyond those technologies.

To understand this communications environment, you need to understand the concept of multiuser hypertext. Whenever someone writes text, such as a memo, a story, a letter or a piece of E-mail, the author is taking a complex web of concepts and thoughts and reducing it to a linear, sentence-based form. Hypertext, on the other hand, enables users to store the original, nonlinear web of concepts directly in the computer.

Because the hypertext system maintains all the relationships between concepts, it is possible to jump from one concept to another.

Today, when a PC user communicates, he is forced to save his communication in one of three places: the traditional file system on his hard disk and network, his E-mail system or a bulletin board repository. Each of these meets a particular need, but they do not tie together very well.

Suppose you could replace all three with a single, organizationwide—or even worldwide—multiuser hypertext system?

In this new world, each time a manager communicates, what he writes would be stored in a universal shared information space. Each communication could be linked to all related communications.

Eventually, this system—in essence a synthesis of E-mail and bulletin board concepts—would be so powerful and ubiquitous that it could replace the current concept of a file system and become the underpinning of a PC-based information environment.

The file system is transformed from a passive, storage-based repository to an active communications environment that is visible to the user on a constant basis.

CONTROL

To be in control, a manager must be on top of his numbers; managers are expected to produce solid budgets and forecasts. Today's software not only falls short of supporting budget and forecasting needs, but it also fails to facilitate information access so managers can determine whether operations are on target.

You'd think budgeting and forecasting are well-served by existing tools, particularly the spreadsheet. Well, yes and no. Of course, the spreadsheet has become the primary tool used to develop budgets and forecasts, and, of course, it has simplified life tremendously compared with calculators. Yet the spreadsheet ignores two key components of budgeting: mathematical forecasting and data collection across the organization.

The standard spreadsheet leaves forecast model building, for instance, entirely up to the user. Because most people are notoriously bad at developing accurate forecasts, most business plans are based on some form of simple linear growth.

What managers need is access to some form of modeling tool that provides more sophisticated forecasting capabilities, along with built-in expert assistance in how to use them.

As for collecting data across the organization, spreadsheets again come up lacking. Most large organizations collect budget data from individuals and departments to get a corporatewide picture. Changes are then compared with overall profit targets, and managers are asked to redo their budgets. This process is repeated again and again.

The single-user spreadsheet tools available today cannot support this process. While limited facilities are provided for one spreadsheet to reference another, no spreadsheet available today has any understanding of how organizations are structured and how data is consolidated and controlled on an ongoing basis.

It is not hard to imagine a budgeting and control tool that would solve both of the problems described above. The system would start with an understanding of the organization's structure. It would also contain basic forecasting facilities, including a model for seasonal trends by product line as well as the company's master assumption about growth in the quarters ahead.

Individual managers would be able to use the system much as they use a spreadsheet today—in fact, the spreadsheet might be the basic mechanism for accessing the system. However, the underlying support structure would make all budgets and forecasts automatically part of the larger structure of organizationwide numbers without any need for copying spreadsheets or sending disks around by mail.

Such a system is not currently available. If it were, it would likely take the form of a spreadsheet front end to a database-oriented budgeting and accounting system.

Beyond sophisticated budget and forecasting, managers need to determine how their operations are doing against budget. Today—30 years after the introduction of the first computerized accounting systems—most managers have a hard time accessing that kind of performance information.

Understanding expenses often requires accessing more than accounting information; the manager must go back to the original memos, plans, proposals and status reports describing the project.

In theory, if this information is computer-based, it should be easy to find. Unfortunately, that's not the case.

Searching through multiple directories across several servors on a network is only slightly more likely to result in a retrieval than looking through file cabinets.

What managers need is a fast, friendly way of finding documents when they need them. This is an area that has received much attention during the last 20 years, yet the basic filing system most companies use continues to be based on DOS and its eight-character file names.

The kind of filing system managers need to make information access easier should have the following characteristics:

- Foldering facilities that enable documents to be filed in multiple places.
- Cross-document linking so that any document can refer to any number of other documents.
- Content-based retrieval so that documents can be located based on key words and phrases found anywhere in the text.

- Automatic archival both to migrate unused documents off the network and to bring these documents back.

Today, the only way to get the kind of filing system described here is to sweat through building it from scratch with third-party tools. Eventually, however, these types of facilities will likely become a basic part of operating systems.

COORDINATE

Coordinating the activities of a team is a time-consuming activity for most managers. This task largely involves goal-setting, schedule-setting and attending regular meetings to keep in sync with the team.

Superficially, project management software and personal information managers appear to address many of these coordination needs. Yet, even managers who depend on project management software tend to view it as a highly formal mechanism that they use only on the largest projects rather than as a vehicle for routine team coordination. Project software isn't suited for the kind of goal-setting important to the team environment.

Personal information managers, for their part, can establish and track goals and create to-do lists as well as coordinate multiple calendars to simplify meeting scheduling. But most are limited in a team setting, unable to manage the calendars of any group larger than about five to 10 people.

What business managers need is a combination of project manager and personal information manager features to yield what might be called a "team coordination system."

Such a system would include the following functions:

- **Goal manager:** *A shared forum to agree on goals, including unscheduled future objectives.*

How often have you thought of a future project that your team has no time for now and wondered how to keep track of that goal so it can be reconsidered periodically for eventual implementation? How about being able to see how all the goals for several groups, all part of a larger department, fit together?

A goal management system would deal with these kinds of problems, enabling goals set during an annual performance review to be reflected in quarterly, monthly and weekly objectives. The goal manager would enable a manager to see high-level objectives for himself, his managers and his team. He would be able to drill down to uncover the underlying details associated with accomplishing particular objectives within certain time frames.

Goal managers would be for team use. The software would provide a framework for group planning meetings, allowing the group to see high-level long-term goals or zero in on a particular area to plan a specific project.

Best of all, the system would provide a shared structure for all managers so they can share goals and coordinate activities.

- **Progress manager:** *A tracking mechanism for the timelines (strict and otherwise) associated with projects and goals.*

While the goal manager deals with the highest level planning and coordinating, a progress manager deals with the next level down. It tracks progress against objectives for a manager and his team.

Progress management software ensures that goals and schedules are in sync, it has no fixed beginning or ending date and it produces a fluid schedule that consists of multiple, unrelated activity networks. Goals, projects and tasks don't have to be part of a larger project.

Finally, progress management software has different types of output that are both simple and easy to annotate.

• **Schedule manager:** *A more detailed framework for sharing schedule information, including travel, meetings and activities related to goals.*

The final component of the team coordination system is a schedule manager. This component would include all the standard facilities of schedule, calendar and diary management, from scheduling meetings to keeping up on team travel and what project everyone is working on.

To make it all work, the system would have to exhibit some of these key characteristics:

- Fast and easy to use.
- Robust. Because calendar information, particularly for groups, is critical, it can't be lost. So a schedule manager would need the type of the integrity features found in transaction database systems.
- High throughput. Because the schedule manager has the potential for heavy use, it should be based on a highly distributed, scalable technology.

For large organizations, for instance, systems based on simple sharing of DOS files on a server would quickly run into critical performance limitations.

Some organizations have started to implement their own team coordination systems. One large government department, faced with a software project that will take eight years and involve thousands of programmers, is writing specifications for a comprehensive system. However, some companies can't afford the build-it-yourself approach.

In time, packaged software should emerge that marries personal information managers with the functionality in project management programs.

Discussion Questions

1. To what extent does currently existing software support the tasks of business managers?
2. How can managers use software to communicate, control, and coordinate more effectively?
3. What changes should be made in software to better support managers' tasks?. ▼

Reading 5 "Saving Time with New Technology," by Gene Bylinsky

(This reading is especially suited for use in conjunction with Chapter 6 of *Information Systems.*)

If you travel a lot, how can you possible keep in touch with everybody you need to talk to? How do you avoid getting trapped in endless time-wasting games of telephone tag?

Welcome to the world of bits, bauds, modems, laptops, faxes. E-mail, on-line data service, logon names, voice mail, pagers, cellular phones, and an electronic cornucopia of new hardware. An adventurous breed of top managers and professionals—call them the wired executives—stay on top of business wherever they are, anywhere in the world, with highly portable computers and telecommunications devices that liberate them from the constraints of the office. Universally, these peripatetic executives praise their newfound freedom. More than that, their use of electronic devices has made them enormously more productive and has saved them huge amounts of time in the office, on the road, and at home.

Kenneth Olsen, CEO of Digital Equipment Corp., calls what they're doing "nomadic computing." You don't have to be a Silicon Valley techie to practice it. While many of its adepts are men and women in the computer or telecommunications industries, some you will meet in these pages operate in unmistakably low-tech venues: marketing, public relations, journalism, local government, a university. You will discover how these pioneers deploy their supergadgets, and see some of their often spectacular results.

Philippe Kahn, 39, founder and CEO of Borland International, the fast-growing software company in Scotts Valley, California, had long been frustrated by old-fashioned hotel telephones. Wired permanently into the wall, they deprive portable computer users of their umbilical connection—a phone jack—to the rest of the world. Kahn, a born problem solver, decided to do something about it. He started carrying a kit containing a soldering iron, screwdrivers, pliers, and other tools to remedy that lapse.

A French-born mathematician, musician, sailor and software genius, Kahn is not your run-of-the-mill computer user. At any given time, Kahn may be testing his company's and competitors' software on many machines (they include a Mitsubishi mobile phone, a Poqet palmtop, Sporty's E6B flight navigation computer, a Sharp Wizard Palmtop, a Sharp graphics printer, a Dell System 320N laptop, and a Canon bubble-jet printer).

Four years ago, after checking into the Hôtel de Crillon, just across the rue Boissy d'Anglas from the U.S. Embassy in Paris, Kahn ordered a bottle of Perrier and dived under the table, tools in hand. The Perrier soon arrived. Ten minutes later, so did eight husky men who barged into Kahn's room without knocking, loudly demanding to know what he was doing. They were French and American security men. Says Kahn: "It took me half an hour to explain."

He arrived in the U.S. in 1982 with $2,000. Without a green card he couldn't get a job, so the next year he founded Borland International—a huge success from the start, thanks to his Turbo Pascal software that made it possible to write programs on PCs much faster than before. This October, Borland acquired rival Ashton-Tate (best known for its dBase software) for $439 million. That turned Borland overnight into one of the world's largest software companies, with estimated sales of $500 million this fiscal year.

Kahn runs Borland by E-mail from wherever he happens to be: Paris, New York City, or Auckland, New Zealand. Sometimes he runs it from a hilltop near his office. He drives up into the woods on his dirt bike to sit under a tree and transmit messages from his laptop via cellular phone.

SOURCE: Gene Bylinsky, "Serving Time with New Technology," *Fortune,* December 30, 1991, pp. 98–104.

He says he's fighting the "meetingomania" of American business. Managers from his 11 subsidiaries and three sales offices around the world rarely meet in person, but the are always on-line—electronically connected. Kahn spends as much as three hours a day answering up to 150 E-mail messages. A dynamo who gets by on an average of five hours' sleep, Kahn often sends E-mail as late as 2 a.m. and sometimes prepares slides on his laptop in the middle of the night aboard the red-eye or a leased corporate jet.

In 1988, he and a crew of 11, including his wife, Martine, sailed his 70-foot sloop *Kathmandu* in the biennial Pacific Cup race from San Francisco to Oahu in typically Kahnian fashion. Using a laptop, a fax machine, and a printer on board, Kahn calculated the advantages of different routes with a program he wrote and deliberately chose the longest course. By first heading nearly as far south as Los Angeles and then cutting west, he avoided a delaying weather system called the Pacific High. He won the race in record time.

Oh yes, those hoteliers in Paris and elsewhere need not worry about their phones. Kahn usually reconnects them carefully. Sometimes, though, he'll leave a temporary connection in place so when he returns he can ask for the same room to save himself trouble. Occasionally it even works.

When he set out on business trips a few years ago, Manville Corp. CEO W. Thomas Stephens, 49, often felt like a high-tech Himalayan porter, lugging around his heavy computer and mobile phone. Now as he glides in a limo through Manhattan traffic, Stephens works on a seven-pound Compaq notebook computer. An attachment, the JT Fax made by Quadram Corp., converts the computer into a fax receiver that pops incoming messages up on the screen. Aboard his company jet, Stephens also carries a small Kodak 150 printer. On overseas trips, he has with him an 11-ounce Hewlett-Packard palmtop. At his office in Denver, Stephens uses his Compaq as a desktop.

He employs all those computers and an Epson Equity III at home for much more than instant Access to financial and other data. He has always viewed the computer as an extension of his mind. Says he: "It gives you an opportunity to be a lot more powerful and to focus on being creative rather than spending your time making charts and that sort of thing."

Stephens used the power of the computers to help pull Manville out of bankruptcy. With spreadsheets and computer graphics, he prepared clear and convincing presentations for company directors and groups of people making asbestos health damage claims. He helped restore employee morale by answering letters on his PC. Now, as he hunts for acquisitions for his rejuvenated $2.2-billion-a-year company, Stephens finds he can analyze the possibilities with unmatched versatility and speed. But he still loses more computer chess games to his daughter Anne, 8, than he wins.

"Sir, you want to send a fax to *yourself*?" That question, with its implication that the customer is slightly daft, has been asked of wired executives in many parts of the world. James E. Clark, 39, a vice president for medium-size computers at AT&T's new NCR subsidiary, faced it recently in Bombay.

Clark wanted to print out a presentation by sending it as a message to his hotel's fax machine from his hotel room—a trick clever computer addicts use to save carting a printer along. But he encountered one of those telephones permanently wired into the wall. Knowing that fax machines usually have a phone jack he could plug his laptop into, Clark sauntered over to the hotel's business office. There sat two fax machines side by side. If Clark connected his computer to one of them, he could send a fax to its sibling. It took him some time to explain what he wanted to do, but he finally prevailed.

The phone jack problem, at least on the receiving end, has been solved for Clark and other users of AT&T's snazzy new Safari notebook computer. Introduced earlier this year, the Safari is equipped with the first "wireless mailbox" to hit the market. It's a small pager that can store at one time as many as 20 messages of about 40 words each bounced off a SkyTel satellite. The messages can be read off the pager's screen.

Wireless messaging should untether the workplace even further. Clark, on the road most of the time, practices it resolutely; he calls it "anytime, anywhere computing" using "a post office in the sky."

Inside Phoenix's Sky Harbor airport, a slightly built woman sits on the floor between two elevators. Another homeless person? No, she is well dressed and busily tapping away on her Safari notebook computer. Just another wired executive at work. "It's the only place I could find a plug," explains Patricia Seybold, 42, a much traveled Boston management consultant and computer newsletter publisher. She often walks to work with her seven-pound notebook machine and her 70-pound mutt, Garlic.

What Seybold likes is the instant interaction her electronic gear provides with both clients and the equally nomadic staff of analysts at her Office Computing Group. "We publish our information electronically for a select group of customers who choose to pay more for that," says Seybold. "The customers log on in their offices. They can get our publications on-line and they can ask questions. They can interact with me about the subject matter right on the computer screen."

Soon she plans to start using a computer she can write on with a pen. She will have it programmed to read the circles, triangles, and squares she draws to portray the flow of work—insurance claim processing, say, or readying a manuscript for publishing—at the companies she consults with, many of them Fortune 500 corporations. "You could project the image on an overhead screen so that a group could see it and work together to make that particular process more efficient."

At a recent meeting of some 40 media executives and academics at a Chicago hotel, John M. Lavine, 50, director of the Newspaper Management Center at Northwestern University, surprised some of the participants by whipping out on the spot printed drafts of rather complex standards for accrediting journalism schools even as the participants continued to polish the final version. Lavine did this with a Safari notebook computer and a four-pound Seikosha LT-20 printer, shown to his right in the picture at left. Both fit in his briefcase.

Lavine took advantage of a program feature that allows him to cross out portions of text to be deleted and to indicate proposed additions by underlining them. As the changes were agreed on, he incorporated them into the text and then used the hotel's Xerox machine to make enough copies of the paper for all the participants.

Lavine is the former publisher of a chain of eight Wisconsin dailies and weeklies; among other things, he does management counsulting for newspapers. He has some hard-earned advice for managers looking to become wired. "I'm not a computer hardware freak," he says. "The goal is to have electronics serve me, not for me to become a captive of it. Executives should guard against doing on computers what their assistants can do for them, such as some of the more menial computer work. Ask yourself, 'What's the best use of my time?' "

Accordingly, Lavine centers his electronic work on the creative side. "When I'm under pressure, I can compose and edit a proposal or a presentation on a computer. When I'm done, I push a button and the proposal comes out right in a newspaper or a consulting company's office." On the go, Lavine also uses a palmtop Wizard to take notes at meetings and to store his Rolodex, his appointment calendar, and outlines of some of the major projects he's thinking about. Concludes Lavine: "Computers and telecommunications have made possible much higher quality work."

When his mother became seriously ill recently, Bernard Krisher, 60, an American journalist-entrepreneur in Tokyo, took the next plane to New York. Armed with a vintage NEC 8201 laptop, Krisher flew off without hesitation. (He later added to his electronic arsenal a palmtop Sharp Wizard he bought in New York.) Says he: "I was able to stay at my mother's bedside for six weeks, until she passed away. I kept in touch with my clients via E-mail I sent from the hospital room, and I composed messages in taxicabs on the Wizard. Many of my clients didn't even know I wasn't in Tokyo."

Fax before breakfast. E-mail at lunch. Laptop after dinner. Krisher's days and nights center around computers and telecommunications. His friends and clients aren't surprised to get E-mail, faxes, or hardcopy letters that originated in such exotic places as an express train speeding across Germany or his vacation home near Japan's Mount Fuji. He is shown at right near that home, in the process of transmitting to Tokyo and New York City via cellular phone a message he has typed into his palmtop.

He connects a modem to his Wizard and then plugs the modem into a coupler that cradles the phone. The message will cross the Pacific via MCI Mail, an electronic messaging service Krisher subscribes to. One recipient in New York also subscribes to MCI Mail, so he will read the message on his computer screen. Another, a nonsubscriber, gets the message as a letter two days later; MCI prints it out at hard copy in New York and forwards it through the Postal Service. The Tokyo recipient will get it at his hotel by fax from New York.

After he returned to Tokyo recently, Krisher used a public phone equipped with a special jack that allows a computer modem to be plugged in for message sending over telephone lines. Unhappily for wired executives, those phones are rare in Japan and only a few are available in the U.S.—so far.

Electronic devices help Krisher do a prodigious amount of work. He is chief editorial adviser to *Focus,* a popular weekly he helped start; he set up a Harry Winston jewelry salon on the Ginza and acts as a company director in Japan; he writes speeches for Japanese executives; he advises a PC users network, similar to CompuServe, in Tokyo; and he operates a service he put together that retrieves information from databases for half a dozen top Japanese corporations. To do all that, Krisher employs not a single secretary—only electronic help. In addition to the NEC laptop and the Wizard, he has four Macintoshes, a Worldport modem, and a cellular phone.

When at home, Krisher is always at his Mac before breakfast sending faxes and E-mail. Says Krisher: "Often I get half a day's paperwork done—at 2400 baud—before getting dressed." He continues his on-line activities at the *Focus* office, tapping as needed into such electronic fact repositories as Nexis and Dow Jones. Back home in the evening, he sends more faxes and E-mail to clients.

"An on-line life has freed me from the straitjacket of being confined to any given place," says Krisher. "I've become totally self-reliant so that I can easily mix business and pleasure. I'm able to receive and send messages and manuscripts to and from practically anywhere. And no one even needs to know where I am."

If, as the adage has it, the difference between adults and children lies in the price of their toys, Regis and Dianne McKenna are seriously adult. The equipment and software in the spacious computer room of their house in Sunnyvale, California, are worth about $20,000. They include two Macintosh CX's, a Macintosh PowerBook notebook computer, two text scanners, Radius large-screen terminals, an Apple laser printer, two Hayes 9600 Smartmodems, and a fax machine.

The payoff has been overwhelming. Looking much like a lepidopterist scrutinizing a rare butterfly, Regis McKenna, 52, a Caere optical digital scanner in hand, captures a paragraph of text from the *Harvard Business Review.* The scanner reads the information into his Mac's memory by translating the letters into digital language. Later, as he composes a speech, McKenna retrieves the data and incorporates it into his talk. He then electronically transmits the draft to a freelance editor in Half Moon Bay, 50 miles away.

A few days later the editor electronically deposits her revised version into a computer server, a kind of information-storing traffic cop, at McKenna's Palo Alto office, ten miles from his house. At home soon thereafter McKenna retrieves the speech electronically from the office server, makes some changes on the screen, and prints it out on his laser printer—the first time the speech has appeared on paper.

McKenna is a Silicon Valley mover and shaker whose 100-person marketing consulting and public relations firm has put many a startup on the map. (He helped fledgling entrepreneurs Steve Jobs and Stephen Wozniak find venture capital to launch Apple Computer; a McKenna designer concocted the famous Apple logo.) McKenna is electronically linked not only to his five regional offices but also to the powerful Bay Area venture capital company Kleiner Perkins Caufield & Byers, of which he is a partner, and to a number of local high-tech companies he serves as a director.

Without the pervasive use of electronics at home, in the office, and on the road, McKenna says he could not have accomplished half as much. In pre-electronics days he would often hop into his Mercedes on weekends to fetch items from his office.

Now almost everything he needs is as near as the keyboards of his computers. When he travels, McKenna takes the new Macintosh notebook with him to stay in touch. He used an earlier portable Mac to write his latest book, *Relationship Marketing.*

McKenna and his wife, Dianne, 48, often work side by side on their his-and-hers Macs. Her domain is even larger than her husband's. She is chairwoman of the Santa Clara County board of supervisors, which is responsible for apportioning an annual budget of $1.3 billion to serve 1.5 million residents. She often writes letters on her computer at night to send electronically to her staff of eight in San Jose. Next morning, she rushes off at 7:30 for a meeting in San Francisco, 50 miles to the north, safe in the knowledge that her office is humming. She makes doubly sure of that over a cellular phone in *her* Mercedes. Out of town, she usually carries along a laptop. At home, she uses a computer to do the family banking and to operate a jukeboxlike 240-disk Phoenix System CD player, changing the music at the click of a mouse. Says she, in an understatement: "Electronics makes my work and my life a lot easier and more efficient."

Discussion Questions

1. What types of electronic equipment do executives who travel extensively use?
2. How does this equipment help them perform their jobs better?
3. Give three examples of executives' use of new hardware to help them perform their jobs better? ▼

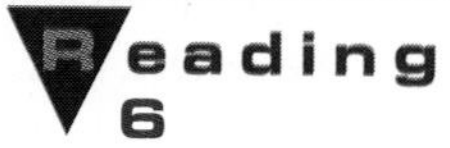

"In Search of the Perfect," by Steven Caniano

(This reading is especially suited for use in conjunction with Chapter 7 of *Information Systems.*)

Typically, one of the most difficult aspects of information systems engineering is selecting the software to manage the system's data. The success of a given system often hinges on the selection of DBMS software to store and control access to key business data properly.

Selecting this critical technology is very difficult. Many products are available, all claiming to be the premier DBMS. It is quite a challenge to understand each product's features, not to mention account for the differences among the many platforms and product releases.

People often find themselves in a maze of vendor hype and "expert" opinions and are left in the unenviable position of having to make a choice. This article will analyze the process of DBMS selection, presenting the key issues you should consider and questions you should ask. Obviously, as a reference guide, this article is much more generic than an application-specific analysis would be. Nevertheless, the issues presented will provide you with a solid foundation upon which to develop a more customized set of issues and, ultimately, help you make a selection.

Over time, I expect the key issues I will describe in this two-part series to evolve, as will the DBMS products' ability to address them. Readers must determine the levels at which the current portfolio of products address these key issues.

ISSUE CATEGORIES

This article defines dozens of issues that, for the purpose of clarity, I will structure into five general categories:

- System and application profile issues cover items that define the particulars of a given application. These factors are probably the most critical to consider since failure to meet application-specific needs typically outweighs the amount of features and functionality a product can provide.
- Management and vendor issues refer to items not specific to product features, but critical to understanding vendors and their services. Typical issues in this category are support, training, documentation, and financial health.
- Development and database administrator issues are those of particular concern to individuals who must use the product to design and build an application or database.
- System internals and architectural issues relate to the core components of a modern DBMS system and the implementation methods for the numerous "leading edge" features that compose it.
- Operations issues refer to the product's capabilities once it has been built in the DBMS technology and put into operation.

No one category is more important than another—that determination must be made according to the application in question. In some cases, however, issues that consider a range of product and vendor capabilities (such as vendor support) should be given more weight than a narrower product feature area. Nevertheless, the application must assign this order. Therefore, ordering these issues within a category is arbitrary and insignificant.

This list of issues is by no means a complete set for everyone who must select a DBMS product. Conceivably, you could consider hundreds of additional items, some of which

SOURCE: Steven Caniano, "In Search of the Perfect," reprinted with permission from *Data Base Programming & Design,* January 1992, Vol. 5, No. 1, pp. 44, 46–51, copyright Miller Freeman Inc., ALL RIGHTS RESERVED.

might make up new issue categories. Regardless, the issues I'll describe should help you identify potential problem areas or major weaknesses that you might have otherwise overlooked.

SIZE LIMITATIONS

The system and application profile category describes items that classify the DBMS's critical application needs. Although this category has the least number of issues, in many ways they are the most critical. You may prefer to think of them as "acid tests"—if a product cannot satisfy these needs, you should not consider using it, regardless of how well it evaluated against other issues.

The main issue here is size limitations. A critical variable in DBMS selection is how large a database (or tables) can be supported. Key questions to ask in this area are:

- What is the maximum number of tables. that can be supported in a database and a partition of a database?
- What is the maximum table size in theory versus practice? (You can check actual results by examining similar computing platforms.)
- What is/the maximum database size in theory versus practice?
- Can tables span physical storage devices (such as disk packs)? Can they span processors (in a distributed environment)?
- How will the product respond to potential database growth?

Perhaps the major point to evaluate is the difference between theory and practice. Often, theoretical limits are very large, if any exist at all. Ask your vendor for a reference list of other customers, preferable within your company, who have successfully built a database of a similar size to the one you are planning. If the vendor cannot produce a list, you are probably treading on new ground in terms of maximum database size for this product and should proceed with extreme caution.

BATCH PROCESSING SUPPORT

An application typically has batch processing requirements. To test how well the product meets needs in this area, you should ask the following questions:

- Does the product let you "turn off" the online system in lieu of batch processing?
- Can you execute batch jobs concurrently? (This feature may help you meet batch processing "window" requirements.)
- Are both queries and updates permitted in a batch mode?
- Can bulk data loads be performed in batch mode? Can the bulk load be segmented into pieces that are executed concurrently?
- Does batch processing support both static and dynamic SQL processing?

The major issue you should examine is whether the product will let all batch processing be performed within the window that can be allocated to batch. Of course, the product must support all types of required batch activities (such as updates, loads, queries, and so forth).

PERFORMANCE

One of the most critical aspects of any system is its ability to meet customer performance requirements. Unfortunately, this task is often the most difficult to analyze and predict. The following questions may help evaluate this category:

- What are the maximum transactions per second (TPS) ratios demonstrated on similar computing platforms?
- What types of transactions were ensured and how do they relate to the primary transactions included in the application? (Typically, vendors will cite high TPS figures that actually depict quite simple transactions. Customers must weigh these "benchmark" transactions against their actual workloads and weigh them accordingly.)
- How were the vendor benchmarks audited? (If they were not audited, the results are extremely suspect.)
- What metrics are available to describe full file scan performance; for example, time per MB and cost per MB? (This type of information will help you determine if such an activity can reasonably run within the batch window if necessary.)
- What metrics are available to measure data sorting performance?
- Is performance information available for workloads that range from online transaction processing to decision-support work, as well as combinations of the two? How closely does this resemble the applications environment?
- What is the maximum number of concurrent users supported in theory versus practice?

Obviously, performance is perhaps the most difficult area to quantify in the selection process. Nevertheless, it might be a fatal flaw to ignore it. Whenever possible, I recommend you benchmark a representative piece of the application with the product to determine the actual performance you can expect. Alternatives would be to translate other industry and company benchmarks into application terms and draw conclusions based on them.

The goal of analyzing the performance area is to feel satisfied that what needs to be done can be done. After being satisfied on this point, you can reassure yourself that work will be executed in a timely enough fashion to satisfy the application's customers.

MANAGEMENT AND VENDOR ISSUES

Management and vendor issues cover items that, while critical to DBMS selection, do not fall under any type of product feature category or classification. When you buy a product, you buy a vendor, and you must therefore consider key vendor issues, which are typically difficult, if not impossible, to quantify. In many cases, you must judge these areas by the vendor's reputation and the opinions of other customers. In some cases, however, an item is more credible if a vendor can cite examples of successes or provide supporting documentation.

QUALITY ASSURANCE

One of the major success factors for a company is its commitment to quality products and services. Many methods (called *quality assurance* [QA] *metrics*) measure product quality. These methods help better understand the vendor's level of commitment to product quality and the consistency of that quality. Some questions in this category include:

- What is the vendor's track record for quality products?
- What type of QA process is in place to assure the DBMS product's level of quality?
- Who is responsible for quality in the company? Is it a QA group that inspects the product after development or someone deeply involved in the development process?
- What metrics are in place to measure the level of customer satisfaction with the DBMS engine and the tool set? What is the ratio of closed- to open-reported problems? Will the vendor agree to time-committed fixes for severe problems?
- What test suites does the vendor currently use?
- Is the vendor willing to incorporate your test procedures into their test suites?

- What percentage of the product development staff is committed to QA of products?
- How does the vendor measure customer satisfaction?
- Does the vendor have any formal quality improvement programs in place with other customers and their suppliers?
- Does the vendor have a QA process in place with their original equipment manufacturer partners? Are they focused on a total quality solution for the customer?

The emphasis of this category is to determine how serious your vendor is about quality. Of course, they will all claim to be very serious, but unless vendors can answer a number of these questions satisfactorily, it is difficult to imagine how they will escape their "fire fighting" mode and focus on continuous quality improvements.

CUSTOMER REQUIREMENTS

Customer requirements gathering goes hand in hand with QA metrics. If you plan to deal with a vendor for a long period of time, you must understand how the vendor collects and reacts to the requirements and suggestions provided by customers. Several important questions in this category include:

- Does the vendor have a formal mechanism for collecting customer requirements?
- Who decides on the inclusion of a request? How is the response given to the customer? What measurements and time frames are included?
- What percentage of previous customer requests have been included in the product?
- How are new requirements balanced against reported problems for inclusion of product releases?
- Are past requests available for other customers to see?
- Do certain customers have priority in requests? How is the priority established?

Again, the emphasis is on determining the formality of the vendor's system for collecting and including customer requirements. This task may be a key requirement as your application evolves with the vendor.

VISION SYNERGY

Whether the application in question is critical to business operations or viewed as a strategic system, you want your vision of the future to match that of the vendor. For example, if you view distributed computing as the wave of the future and are designing architectures based on data sharing and connectivity, it would not be wise to select a vendor concentrating on traditional host-based, centralized processing and data management. Therefore, you must ask the following questions:

- Does the vendor's product architecture lend itself to processing in your current and planned architectural framework?
- Is the vendor a major player in the open systems arena or tied to a proprietary ancestry? If they are an open systems vendor, are they aligned with UNIX Software Labs (USL) or the Open Software Foundation (OSF)? How does their positioning relate to your direction?
- Can the vendor provide examples of successful partnering efforts with others in your company?
- Is the vendor willing to take extraordinary measures to guarantee success (for example, free on-site support, consulting, and so on)?
- If your company prefers a particular computer line, how well does it integrate with its current and evolving offerings?

I hope these points give you a basic idea of how well a vendor's view of the future might mesh with your own. Obviously, a long-term relationship will succeed only if both customer and supplier are moving in similar directions.

INVESTMENT PROTECTION

The vendor's historical track record in protecting the customer's software investment is often overlooked. If your company already uses this vendor, you have a leg up on getting this information. Does the vendor make their own products obsolete by regularly introducing the products that require you to purchase new licenses and convert from the "old" software? Those lacking personal experience with a vendor must rely on testimonials from other customers. Some questions to keep in mind for this category include:

- Does the vendor avoid functional discontinuity from release to release?
- When the vendor issues upgrades, do they work on the same hardware and operating system releases?
- Is the customer required to purchase new software for a new release?
- What type of database and application conversion is necessary for a typical new release?
- What is the vendor's release strategy? What is their target for quality and performance improvement from release to release? Are releases based on improving conformance to industry standards? What support commitment do they provide for older releases?

Ideally, a vendor will provide new releases on a fairly regular schedule at no charge to the customer, but keep in mind the pain involved in moving from release to release. Since it is not always possible to keep up with vendor releases, a strong support commitment for older releases is mandatory.

TEST BED FACILITY

The purpose of a test bed facility is to determine how capable the vendor is of assuring a quality product. The quality of the delivered product is very important, but the vendor's ability to recreate problems you experience in their environment is possibly even more important. To recreate these problems, they will need a similar (if not identical) test bed facility. Some important areas to consider include:

- Does the vendor have all of the processors (and their corresponding operating systems) that you use at their location?
- What priority do your computing platforms have in their porting schedules? (DBMS products tend to run in diverse environments, each of which must be ported and tested separately. If your environment is toward the bottom of the list, it can be years between the time when the vendor announces a product enhancement or release and when you actually receive it. Depending on your view, this wait can have positive or negative effects. On one hand, other customers may "shake the bugs out of a new release" so you won't have to, on the other hand, you might have to wait many months after their announcement before getting the new features.)
- What type of integration testing is performed? Does the vendor incorporate networking products and third-party software that you use in your environment into their tests? If they do not, the job of integration testing will be yours.
- Will the vendor commit to keeping their product current with your environment? As you upgrade components in your architecture, will they be working to assure efficient integration with these components? (If this testing is not performed, you may not be able to upgrade a component due to a lack of integration with the DBMS.)

In general, it is reassuring when the vendor can ensure your success because they've already demonstrated their product successfully on your equipment in their facility. Therefore, you should require a representative test bed.

SUPPORT CAPABILITY

Perhaps the single most important item in any evaluation is the vendor's ability to support the customer. Unfortunately, in today's data processing world, problems with products seem almost inevitable. The one differentiating factor among vendors is their ability to service customers in times of trouble.

Support is typically an intangible item bases on reputation and actual experience. One bad experience can often leave you with a bad impression of an entire company. Therefore, you must attempt to quantify customer support as much as possible. Ask yourself these key questions:

- What are the procedures for problem severity management? What are the hours of support? Is 24 × 7 service provided? If so, is this done through "live" coverage (for example, off-hours beepers, answering services, and so forth)?
- Are there limitations on whom can call the support line?
- Since many DBMS companies are headquartered on the West Coast, does the vendor also provide East Coast support? If so, what are the levels of expertise at each and what hours are they available?
- Is support customizable to the customer need?
- What is the procedure for obtaining on-site support during a crisis? Is there a cost to the customer? Is there a difference if it is a production versus a development problem?
- Is on-site support available on a full-time basis? If so, how is it arranged, at what cost, and what are the skill sets of the support person?
- Does the vendor provide consultation on demand? At what cost to the customer?
- Does the vendor maintain a "bug" tracking system, and is it available to customers?
- How many systems engineers are dedicated to your account? How many licenses do they cover?
- Can the vendor send granular fixes in a prompt time frame, or are fixes only available in maintenance releases?
- Will the vendor supply source code and debuggable object code for problem resolution and debugging?

Good support can be summed up in one statement: "The ability to do what is necessary to assure the customer's success." In many ways, good support is more of an impression than anything else until the customer actually needs to test it out. Hopefully, this article will help you form this impression before a crisis occurs.

DOCUMENTATION

Another nebulous but important area to consider is a product's documentation. Documentation can cover a broad spectrum of areas, and the quality in each of these areas can vary greatly as well. Although difficult to quantify, the following questions may help:

- Are product error messages documented? Are associated solutions provided?
- Are guides available that are tailored to specific user groups or functional areas (for example, DBA versus applications developer)?
- Are the guides tailored toward specific computing platforms? Is there a specialized platform-specific tuning guide?
- Is the documentation delivered prior to, in conjunction with, or later than the product?

- How accurate is the information in the documentation? (Unfortunately, this question can only be answered through experience—yours or that of other customers.)
- How is the documentation obtained, and what is its cost? Does a customer have the right to copy manuals for all interested parties or must you purchase "official" copies?
- Is there a product performance tuning guide?
- How timely and appropriate are documentation updates?
- What medium does the vendor use for documentation delivery (for example, paper, tape, online, and so forth)?

In general, successful documentation is timely, accurate, and geared toward specific functional groups and operating environments. If a vendor targets specific environments other than yours, you should be wary.

TRAINING

Training pertains to the formal education available from a vendor or a third party to build expertise in a product. Almost all vendors offer some level of training for their products, ranging from learning basic commands to full curriculums. The following points should help you evaluate training:

- What is the current curriculum offered by the vendor? Where are courses offered, how often, and at what cost?
- Can courses be tailored to meet the needs of specific customer groups? Will they "suitcase" a course to a customer location on demand?
- Is vendor training coordinated with other in-house training facilities? If not, would they be willing to move in this direction?
- Is computer-based training available? Is audio/visual (self-paced) training available?
- What are the skill levels of the instructors? How knowledgeable are they of your environment?
- Are the appropriate lab facilities available in the training sessions? (For example, if you are developing in UNIX, you don't want to do work exercises on Digital Equipment Corp.'s VAX/VMS.)
- What is the quality of the course materials? Do you have the right to copy these materials?
- Do the DBMS system and associated tools provide full "help" capabilities?
- Is there a prompted query capability in the product for the non-SQL literate?

Overall, you should look for flexible and dependable training that is customized as much as possible to the environments that concern you. Nontraditional training (computer-based and audio/visual) might be advantageous when budgets are tight.

BUSINESS HEALTH

The data processing industry is a volatile one. Technology changes at such a fast pace that a company on top today could find itself bankrupt tomorrow, unless it truly understands the marketplace and can exploit its products through continuous technological improvements. Similarly, a company with large technological advantages must not bury itself in technology, but create a business infrastructure that can support evolving customer demands and technological challenges.

Therefore, any vendor evaluation would be incomplete without a thorough analysis of the company as a business entity and its prospects for growth and continued success. Because when you purchase a product you purchase a company with it, you must believe that the company will support you as your business evolves. The following questions will give you valuable insights into the vendor's business health:

- What has the vendor's track record been over the last five to 10 years? Are they profitable? What are their revenue and profit patterns over time? What type of outstanding debts do they have? Do they have a large amount of receivables due?
- What are the vendor's plans to continue their success and improve upon it?
- What type of opinions do industry people have about this company? (Independent industry analysts and financial services companies are good sources of this type of information.)
- What is the company's investment in research and development (R&D)? What percentage of revenues does this figure represent? What percentage of R&D is put into computing platforms that affect you?
- What percentage of their revenue/income does the vendor generate from your computing platforms? How many licenses do they support per platform?
- Is the vendor having any known financial difficulties?

History has shown that you can never be certain regarding the future of a vendor in the data processing industry. Nevertheless, you must understand the business situation before deciding on a vendor in order to make an informed, intelligent decision. Remember to keep track of the vendor's situation closely throughout the life of the relationship.

THIRD-PARTY MARKETS

You might be interested in the third-party markets available for the products you are considering. Most third parties develop products for major DBMS players. Therefore, if none (or few) are available, the product may still be a minor or niche player.

Some users may prefer to not deal with third-party vendors since they are yet another variable in the equation of composing a total information solution. This point may be valid, but ignoring the third parties would overlook some of the best tools available for a product. As the third parties' main business is add-on tools, they often concentrate on the features of these tools more than the DBMS vendors (who tend to focus on the engine itself). Therefore, the best tools for a product are often marketed by a third party. In addition, you may want your DBMS to function as a server to many of your third party end-user tools. In this case, you will find more happening with the major players. If you are interested in the third-party market, the following questions should help:

- Is the engine viewed as a desirable server to many client applications? for example, does it support most of the major end-user front-end interfaces to access the DBMS as a server?
- What types of tools are available to augment and enhance the development and production environments? Who markets those tools, what is the relationship with the third party, and how successful are these companies?

A third-party market, if nothing else, usually provides a good perspective of who the major players are in the DBMS world. You should verify that the DBMS will integrate with your common front-end tools. Third-party tools may be desirable if the vendor's tools are lacking.

LICENSING ARRANGEMENTS

An area you should not overlook is the licensing arrangements in place and the flexibility of these arrangements. For example, many vendors offer volume purchase agreements to major customers. Special deals on maintenance contracts are also common. Anyone making a DBMS selection must examine these areas because the pricing available may be far different from the list prices. Some questions to ask include:

- What are the vendor's current licensing arrangements and how flexible are the terms?
- Will the vendor provide free evaluation copies to assist in the purchase decision?

- Are the licenses transportable? For example, if you purchase a license on one type of processor, can you move it to another type?
- Do you have the right to copy software? (This ability may be important if you are incorporating a vendor's product into a solution to sell to your customers.) Is a run-time license available for this purpose?

Licensing tends to be an item that is considered near the end of an evaluation. Looking at it closer to the beginning may prove valuable as the licensing restrictions may prove enlightening. This arrangement may make a very difficult decision quite simple.

STANDARDS SUPPORT

As open systems become more and more of a requirement for industry (and even more so for the federal government), standards conformance becomes a critical factor in the DBMS decision process. Those who want the flexibility of open systems require certain levels of conformance before they will do business with a vendor. If this area concerns you, you may want to consider standards support in the following areas:

- To what level of ANSI SQL (Level 1 and Level 2) does the vendor conform? Does the product also include proprietary extensions to SQL? If so, can they be "turned off" if you want to make use of ANSI SQL only?
- Is embedded SQL supported in the languages you require (for example, C, COBOL, and so on)? Is a preprocessor available for these languages? What type of limitations exist (for example, C on MVS)?
- Does the vendor participate in open standards committees working toward interoperability (ANSI SQL, X-Open, SQL Access, RDA, and so on)? Although such standards have not been agreed upon, these committees are actively pursuing them.

Although it is a new area, standards have entered the evaluation puzzle. This area may not be very important for customers who are not interested in distributed computing on multiple heterogeneous platforms with heterogeneous products. For those who care about such diverse environments, however, standards support quickly becomes one of the most important criteria.

Discussion Questions

1. What are the five categories of issues related to the selection of DBMS products?
2. What are the potential problem areas in selecting a DBMS?
3. What are three key questions to ask in each potential problem area? ▼

"The Race to Rewire America," by Andrew Kupfer

(This reading is especially suited for use in conjunction with Chapter 8 of *Information Systems.*)

Call it the first great business showdown of the 21st century: The giants of American communications are locked in a struggle to build and control a vast web of electronic networks. These so-called information highways will be of glass fiber and will deliver an abundance of services to offices and houses—video images, phone calls, helpful data in many guises. They promise to change the way people work and play. In the view of some technologists, they could affect American life as profoundly as railroads, interstate highways, telephones, and TV.

The risks are as colossal as the opportunities. Building a glass highway is moonshot expensive—by one estimate, extending the networks over the next 20 years may cost phone companies alone nearly $140 billion. Regulations are likely to change while the game is being played; technology is evolving so quickly that some highways could become obsolete before they are complete. The highways' success will depend on the revenues they generate. Yet no one knows how much consumers will pay to browse through movie libraries using their remote controls, play electronic games with far-off friends, or visit their doctors by video.

Since they control the information conduits feeding into households today, telephone and cable TV companies have the most at stake. The idea of receiving a phone call on a cable TV wire may sound as impossibly counterintuitive as, say, getting a cup of coffee out of an electrical socket. But the idea will soon be reality. New technology is breaking down the barriers between the industries. Telephone companies such as Bell Atlantic and GTE are eyeing the lucrative $20-billion-a-year cable TV business, while cable operators such as Tele-Communications Inc. and Time Warner (parent of *Fortune's* publisher) covet the vast $65-billion-a-year market for residential phone service.

The highways these rivals have started constructing are different from the electronic superhighway that Vice President Gore is promoting. His is a national network of supercomputers, linked by fiber optics, that will connect universities, hospitals, research centers, and other institutions that need to exchange vast amounts of data. Construction of this superhighway, an expansion of today's federally subsidized scientific networks, seems almost certain to proceed. But the Clinton Administration is counting on private enterprise to construct advanced networks that will serve the public generally. As a result, America's information system won't have a single owner: It will be a network of networks, controlled by many companies.

How government regulates the networks—or doesn't—will profoundly influence service and profits. Should regulators scrap rules that prevent cable TV and telephone companies from leaping into one another's businesses without constraint? Should government take the lead in ensuring that the networks all work together? If not government, who?

The most controversial question is whether business, without the help of Washington, will act quickly enough. Many people fear that the U.S. is lagging dangerously behind its trading partners in building information highways—a failing that could reduce America's competitiveness. Corning, the No. 1 maker of optical fiber, estimates that if telephone companies upgrade aging installations at their historical pace, the rewiring will take until 2037. But Japan is committed to completing a national fiber network by 2015 and believes that the resulting productivity gains will boost GNP by no less than 30%. Germany and France are not far behind in their plans. Observes Michael Morrison, manager of advanced operations testing at GTE: "These nations see how attracting and keeping companies with telecommunications helps them be competitive. We tend to trip over our own feet."

SOURCE: Andrew Kupfer, "The Race to Rewire," *Fortune* April 19, 1993, pp. 41–51.

Amid the debate and uncertainty, companies like Morrison's are placing billion-dollar bets. What follows is a look at the policies and technologies that will shape the new highways, the services they will make possible, and the competitive strategies of those who plan to build them.

NEW RULES OF THE ROAD

The Clinton Administration has put electronic highways on the national agenda but has yet to decide what Washington will do to get them built. One of the hottest debates is about how much the government should spend. Some people think zero. Brendan Clouston, chief operating officer of Tele-Communications Inc. (TCI), asks, "If multiple industries will create the architecture, why should taxpayers pay?"

But the highway builders face a chicken-and-egg problem that a sprinkling of government seed money could help solve. Unless fiber-optic networks can provide services that consumers want to buy, they will be just so many useless strands of glass. Useless, *expensive* strands. Meanwhile the businesses that might offer services such as movies on demand will need to invest in specialized hardware and software. Unless networks stand ready to carry their services, making these investments would be like putting up a motel before the road is built. Lee Camp, president of Pacific Bell Information Services, describes the dilemma his company faces: "Does one pursue a *Field of Dreams* strategy—'Build it and they will come'—or wait until there is proven demand?"

A modest investment of federal dollars could kick-start the industry, argues economist Eli Noam, a Columbia University professor and authority on telecommunications. Demonstration projects electronically linking, say, community libraries, schools, and universities could pique public interest and stimulate demand for high-capacity networks. Consultant Janice Obuchowski, a former Bush Administration official, advocates "applications funding," including grants to help entrepreneurs develop services to sell.

The Defense Department's Advanced Research Projects Agency or a civilian equivalent could also contribute to key technologies. In the 1980s the agency helped finance work on digital signal processing—the packing and unpacking of information for efficient transmission and reception. The technology still needs work. So does the science of translating video images into computerized form.

Regulators, meanwhile, could hurry the highway by loosening antiquated rules, especially those that hobble the telephone business. For instance, phone companies must depreciate their capital equipment over 20 years or more. That was the useful lifetime of telephone gear a decade ago, but today, when technology changes faster than governments in Bolivia, the rules deter investment.

The Federal Communications Commission and state utility commissions, which must arbitrate the networks' construction, are besieged by lobbyists from telephone and cable companies. Each side wants to gain an advantage. While the regulators deliberate, cable companies are getting into the phone companies' business and vice versa. Some cable operators have bought into companies that are laying fiber in city centers and stealing customers from the telephone network. A Bell company, in turn, just made an end run around rules barring it from the cable business in its service area by acquiring two big cable franchises out of state.

As cable and phone companies invade one another's markets, the government should dismantle the rules separating the industries carefully. So far the phone companies have won the right from the FCC to offer a "video dial tone" that enables other companies to use the phone network to transmit video programming. A few phone companies have also won relief from so-called rate-of-return regulations, which they say stifle innovation. The rules, administered by the states, limit the companies' return on assets, typically to 8% to 11%. If a company takes a chance on an ambitious new service and succeeds it must return any "excess" profits to customers in the form of rate rebates. Some states, such as New Jersey, have wisely begun to allow higher profits in exchange for guarantees that a new investment will lead to lower prices for basic phone service.

The most difficult issue government will face is how—and even whether—to make sure there is basic, low-cost service for every American who wants a phone and other essential services that the highway will provide. On the telephone network, that principle, known as universal service, has been the law of the land for 60 years. It reflects the belief that phones, like mail, electricity, and highways, unite the nation's people and make America strong.

The government achieves universal service through regulation. The phone companies are obliged to hook up everyone in their service area and charge each customer the same basic rate—even though this can mean stretching miles of wire to a customer whose payments won't cover the whole cost. High profits from some customers—such as those who pay for added services like call waiting—compensate for the money losers and enable the phone company to hit the rate of return the regulators allow.

But as competition and new technology galvanize local markets, universal service becomes harder to deliver in the traditional way. Cable companies aren't bound by universal service rules. Using leading-edge technology, a savvy cable operator could add phones to its system and target just those parts of the local market that produce the fattest profits. Indeed, Time Warner has asked the FCC to let subscribers on its advanced cable system in Orlando, Florida, use the cables to place long-distance calls. That would enable the company to claim a share of the lucrative fees that AT&T and other long-distance companies pay for connections to local customers. If the FCC approves Time Warner's plan, BellSouth would see its profits in Orlando erode—and might file for permission to raise basic rates.

What should the FCC do? Option A is to regulate local markets *more,* requiring newcomers to provide universal phone service. That would surely discourage competition and slow the development of information highways. Option B is to lift restrictions on phone companies just enough to let them counter, but not drive out, the invaders—say, by providing information services, including their own video programming, as long as such services are fairly priced. This approach involves a delicate balancing act that federal and state regulators would have to perform again and again as competing local networks pop up across the country during the coming decades. Still another option: Require new entrants to pay the phone company to help offset the cost of universal service.

Opening local markets to competition will be a difficult business because of the complex and interlocking nature of regulations affecting the industries—far trickier than opening up long distance, a process that has occupied the FCC and the courts for more than ten years. Eventually, in communities where competition flourishes, regulation may not be needed to ensure cheap and abundant telecommunications. In the meantime the government will have to be careful to modify its rules in a way that protects the public interest while giving neither industry an unfair advantage.

Letting many companies compete in building the information highway lessens the chance that the country will get married to the wrong technology. Competition will foster continuous innovation. But it also increases the risk that the U.S. will be dotted with networks that can't talk to one another.

Ah, for the simplicity of monopoly. When AT&T ran the Bell system, it kept everything working smoothly by setting detailed technical standards. When a new service appeared, it was sure to work everywhere. "But boy," says Bob Barada, chief strategist for Pacific Telesis, "was that process slow! This country can't wait for a standards body to cross every *t* before we get started."

Instead of defining standards in advance, regulators should jawbone companies into working out the details themselves. If a cable company and a telephone company operate competing networks in a community, residents should be able to reach each other no matter which network they use. But where should the physical connection between the networks occur? In a manhole? In a telephone company central office? And with what equipment? To be maintained by whom?

These are nuts-and-bolts questions that regulators aren't good at answering. Columbia University's Noam, who once served on the New York State Public Service Commission, advises regulators to bring all the parties into a room and tell them to work out their differences under threat of regulatory fiat. He says, "The arrangement works particularly well when it involves technologists—they're problem solvers." Once the rules are agreed on, regulators can codify and enforce them. If they do this job well and clear the way for competition, says Jim Chiddix, the chief technologist at Time Warner Cable, "it looks like all the forces are there for promoting tremendous innovation in technology: fear and greed."

THE GLASS HIGHWAY

"You'll be going to Cerritos, I hope," said the man from GTE. Cerritos is GTE's community of the future. Buried beneath the wide, straight roadways of the Los Angeles suburb, slender sheaths of glass guide pulses of infrared light from lasers in the switching center to two schools and 4,200 homes, bearing programs and telephone calls. A teacher summons up video lessons at the touch of a button. Some families on the network—brave Jetsons!—can call up movies on the system whenever they wish. The families can even converse with each other on the screen.

All two of them. "For years it was only one guy watching movies. It's a standing joke in the industry," says Danny Briere, president of TeleChoice, a New Jersey consulting firm, of the cautious pace at which GTE has pursued its five-year trial. But Cerritos is no joke to GTE. Billion-dollar decisions depend on what technologists and marketers learn there; other companies are conducting similar small-scale trials. They show the fitful and tentative way revolutions start.

The technology of the information highway is evolving at a furious pace. In December 1992 the FCC licensed CellularVision, a Freehold, New Jersey, startup company, to test an ultrahigh-frequency microwave radio system that may eliminate wires in some parts of urban networks. Such innovations could dramatically lower costs and reshape information networks even as they are being built.

The highways that cable and telephone companies currently envision will, in the words of GTE vice chairman John Segall, "tie the world together in a hush of photons." The network will be rich in fiber-optic cable, which has far greater carrying capacity than copper wire or coaxial cable.

Messages conveyed on the fibers will be encoded in the ones and zeros of computer language and compressed by sophisticated circuitry for easier storage and quicker transmission. Ultrafast switches will route video images as easily as ordinary phone calls. Special computers called video servers will store movies and TV programs in digital form.

These technologies will give the network its hallmark attributes. It will be "broadband." Just as a line painted with a broad brush contains more paint than a line traced with a narrow one, a broadband network can carry more information than its narrowband counterpart. Since signals on the network will all be digital, it will easily carry information of different kinds: It won't need to know whether a transmission describes a lark's song or a slasher movie. The network will also be two-way and interactive: Every user will be able to send all kinds of information—voice, video, data, and graphics—to anyone else.

Before this vision can become reality, phone and cable companies must each overcome innate weaknesses. Phone companies are experts at running networks linked by switches (powerful computers that let any customer dial any other) and at providing service with near-total reliability. But the system itself is narrowband, its thin-gauge copper wire unable to carry a high-quality video image. Cable systems, with their heavier-gauge coaxial cable, are broadband—a strength. But unlike telephone communication, which is two-way, cable signals flow in only one direction on the systems common today. They have no switches and can't relay phone calls.

GTE's experiment in Cerritos typifies the approach phone companies will probably adopt. A fiber strand runs from the phone company's central office to a curbside pedestal that can serve up to 20 houses. Inside the pedestal is an optical interface unit with a separate circuit card for each house. The card contains the subscriber's coded address and ensures that phone calls and video programs arriving on the shared fiber-optic line end up in the right place. The circuits also convert the incoming light pulses into electronic signals, which enter the household via coaxial and copper wires hooked to the TV and phone, respectively.

Cable companies, by contrast, don't need to take fiber all the way to the curb. They will run it to the edge of each neighborhood, where transmissions will feed into the coax network that is already in place. Each fiber link might serve as many as 2,000 families. By using the latest compression techniques, which can multiply tenfold the number of channels on a cable system, a company can assign channels to individual customers as needed—to deliver a movie, say, or relay a telephone call.

The fiber links are essential for two-way communication; coaxial networks alone can't handle it. In a coax system, signals pass through an amplifier every 2,000 feet or so. Each introduces a whisper of electronic interference to the line. In one-way transmission, the noise is manageable; but on the return path in two-way communication, it builds up, and the cacophony of the amplifiers drowns out the message. The introduction of fiber brings a measure of calm: Laser signals can travel for miles without a boost, so the total number of amplifiers in the system stays relatively low.

For both industries, the most expensive job will be laying down fiber. The work has barely begun. According to Corning, the U.S. now has some 12 million miles of fiber installed—compared with 1.2 *billion* of copper phone wire. Neither phone nor cable companies have put down much fiber in residential areas, which account for some 65% of the mileage of telephone networks and 75% of the mileage of cable systems.

It's hard to say how much rewiring for advanced networks will cost, partly because both industries are gradually switching to fiber anyway for their ordinary operations. Corning estimates that doubling the rate of conversion of the phone system—which would mean that the job would be finished by 2015—would increase spending over the period by $24 billion. Add the $63 billion that phone companies already plan to spend and $50 billion for new ultrafast switches to keep traffic flowing smoothly on the information highway, and the bill comes to $137 billion. That's just for the telephone network.

Until now, cable companies have held a theoretical advantage: They can make do with less fiber because they already own a broadband conduit into the home. By most estimates, a cable operator could add two-way services, including fiber to the neighborhood, for less than $1,000 per household. Installing a Cerritos-like system, including fiber to the curb, could cost its telephone rival hundreds of dollars more. That advantage will erode: As demand for two-way services increases, the cable operator will have to segment its network into smaller units and install more fiber. Eventually the two systems will look and cost just about the same. But in a developing market, the cable company's head start might be crucial.

Small wonder that Bellcore, the research arm of the seven regional Bell operating companies, has raced to find a practical way to transmit TV programs over ordinary copper telephone wire. In June 1991 it unveiled a digital compression system built to do just that. Known as ADSL (asynchronous digital subscriber line), the technology is still far from perfect. The longer the copper pathway the TV signal traverses the more the picture degrades; at best the picture quality is no better than that from an ordinary VCR. All the same, if regulations allow, phone companies can now look forward to offering video service as soon as they bring fiber to within a mile or so of a residential area.

Both industries need more breakthroughs. The greatest technical roadblock involves storage technology. In most electronic-highway plans, TV watchers will be able to scroll through menus of video libraries—Treasures of Columbia Pictures say—stocked by independent vendors. One push of a button on the remote control and the show will begin.

For such schemes to work, any company that wants to offer a video service should be able to buy a video server and hook it into the network. But servers that can store movies digitally and dish them out on command aren't ready yet. The task is crushing. Even a 95-minute film like *Wayne's World* requires billions of bits of memory. Ameritech is testing a system in Chicago that will enable Arthur Andersen, the consulting firm, to dispatch training films to clients.

Other developments, such as the evolution of wireless technology, could change the course of the highway race. In CellularVision's trial installation in Brooklyn, New York, subscribers with a decoder box receive 50 TV channels using a movable antenna only five inches square. Unlike ordinary microwave signals, which require a direct line of sight between transmitter and receiver, the ultrahigh-frequency signals bounce off concrete like a billiard ball off a felt rail, losing very little strength. So users need only move their antennas around until they get a good bounce. The system can also carry signals both ways; a test of telephone service will begin shortly.

Most telephone and cable executives dismiss the idea that any new technology, no matter how startling, will provide its owner with a sustainable edge. In the long run, the same technology will be available to all comers. TCI's Brendan Clouston gets downright testy when pressed on the pros and cons of competing schemes for an advanced network. "I don't like the way this conversation is going," he says. "Technology is not the issue. What do consumers want to buy? What do they want to pay, and when?"

THE KILLER APP

As they imagine the billions of dollars consumers might spend on electronic highways, telecommunications executives often exhibit the Pavlovian response of a gambling addict exposed to flashing neon lights. Listen to Arthur Bushkin, president of Bell Atlantic Information Services: "The marketplace is not the $20-billion-a-year cable market or the $12-billion-a-year movie rental market. It is into the hundreds of billions of dollars. It's for work force training, medical services, and shopping. It's the ability to see real estate before traveling there. It's videoconferencing and using multimedia. It's transmitting recipes. It's endless."

Maybe it will be, someday. But creating services that consumers will want to buy could make building networks seem as easy as running a string between two tin cans. Some applications are no-brainers—merely better ways of delivering services people already use. Others, the kind visionaries cite when they claim information highways will change the American way of life, pose obstacles to execution and problems in predicting how consumers will respond.

Almost without question, business demand will drive the market for advanced services at first. Manufacturers and their suppliers will use electronic highways to link their computers and collaborate on product development. Insurance companies could receive images of auto wrecks for claims processing. Video depositions and arraignments, which some law enforcement agencies already employ, would become common.

But to really cash in, communications companies will have to turn consumers on, says John Malone, president of Eastern Management Group, a Parsippany, New Jersey, consulting firm. Just as the personal computer industry languished until spreadsheet programs appeared, information highways need a "killer app"—software industry lingo for an application people are dying to use.

The No. 1 candidate for killer app status is video on demand, the armchair equivalent of a trip to the perfect video store. Viewers will be able to order movies and TV shows anytime, using remote control. TCI recently studied how such a service would compare with today's more cumbersome pay-per-view, which requires customers to phone in their orders. It found that viewers would increase movie spending three to five times.

Another likely hit: telecommuting. Despite the limitations of today's telephone networks, the number of employees working at home is rising at a startling rate. According to Malone, 14% of the FORTUNE 500 and Service 500 companies now have formal telecommuting policies; 870,000 employees work at home 35 hours or more each week, and 5.5 million do at least some home work. The numbers are growing by more than 35% a year.

The advent of information highways will accelerate the trend by increasing the number of jobs telecommuters can perform. An American Express service representative, for example, wouldn't have to leave home to field customer calls and tap into the company's immense databases. Telecommuting will get a lift in states like California, which requires companies to encourage the practice as a way of reducing auto pollution.

The educational possibilities of the advanced network are emerging in tests. Betty Hyatt, a teacher in Cerritos, uses the fiber-optic system to call up penmanship lessons for her third-grade class. That frees her from the chalkboard so she can roam the room and monitor her pupils' progress. Hyatt says, "It's changed the way I teach." Ameritech has begun a program in Warren, Michigan, that will link the homes of 115 fourth-graders to their classrooms, allowing the children to call up their homework electronically and do it on-screen. Advanced networks will eventually let students in remote areas attend college classes by wire. And they may matriculate not at Ohio State but at the Big Ten, mixing and matching video classes from any of the member universities.

For physicians, the house call may return, electronically. Using a video link on the network, a patient could see and talk to her doctor without leaving home; by placing a hand on an electronic sensor, she might relay vital readings the doctor could analyze.

The highway may be dangerous for debtaholics. Going on a buying spree will be as fun and easy as playing videogames, with no need to sit like a brass monkey before the Home Shopping Network. An armchair consumer will select a video catalogue from the on-screen menu and, by punching the remote control, ask to see a jacket in a certain size and color. A simulated three-dimensional model will rotate slowly on the screen. The subscriber can order by pushing a button; the network will have his address and credit card data on file.

Marc Porat, head of General Magic, a Silicon Valley software developer, believes the advanced network will change the way people buy information. He expects a form of publishing to emerge called electronic subscriptions. It will replace the sort of books that become obsolete as soon as you buy them—guides to New York City nightlife, for example. A broadband network could deliver an update every month by either displaying it on screen or transmitting data to the consumer's home printer.

Eventually the highway may deliver a lot more. A jovial, forward-thinking engineering colleague of Porat's predicts that people will don electronic gear and use the network to play virtual reality games. Players will have the illusion of moving through an artificial but lifelike 3-D landscape. That may put a new spin on humanity's oldest killer app. "The ultimate," says the engineer, "is when you'll be able to put on a visor and bodysuit that let you become anyone in the world having sex with anyone else in the world." Virtual reality enthusiasts call it teledildonics.

Virtual reality is the most extreme variant of so-called multimedia programming. In partnership with GTE, the Discovery Channel is already transmitting coded instructions in its TV signal that add graphics to the station's science and nature programs when they appear on the Cerritos system. Viewers may see a map superimposed on the screen, or a fact about an animal habitat. The information comes from a miniencyclopedia on a CD-ROM that plays in a device connected to the TV; the codes in the TV signal summon up relevant bits during the show. Only 50 or so families receive the disks now; nationwide rollout may begin next year. When advanced networks are ready, the disks will be unnecessary; the extra information can travel over fiber.

But like other services upon which the information highway will depend, multimedia is having trouble getting off the ground. Production is awkward and enormously expensive; most CD-ROM programs are as primitive as the *Groucho Marx Show* in TV's early days.

That's one reason network builders are having a tough time predicting customer interest. TCI's Clouston says: "Traditional marketing is done with products that exist. What we're doing now is like asking a horse-and-buggy driver whether he'd pay $100 more for a car with an air bag. He'll ask, 'What's a car?' Nobody knows what people will spend."

That leaves cable and phone companies with high hopes and gnawing doubts, like city leaders who erect a lavish sports dome in hopes of landing an expansion team. Are the network builders in for a nasty case of that queasy feeling you get when you wake up in a bad, bad place?

GIGADOLLAR GAMBLES

Gaining an advantage in 21st-century telecommunications won't be cheap. Stewart Personick, a networking information services executive at Bellcore, explains the cost of simply entering the race: "If you want to make a commitment, you have to have a million customers. The investment in optical fiber, network hardware and software, automated billing, and advertising is a minimum of $1,000 per customer. You've got to go for a billion dollars."

If technology, regulations, or business relationships change unexpectedly, that billion could vanish. Yet companies that hesitate could lose out completely. Even with imperfect technology, a big enough player making a big enough bet could stake out a dominant position. As a result, says Personick, the competition is like an Olympic bicycle sprint: "All of these guys are on their expensive racing bikes going five miles per hour, waiting for someone to make a break. And then they all go like mad."

The break has clearly begun. Last October, TCI announced it would soon begin offering some subscribers 500 channels. In January, Time Warner upped the ante with its Orlando plan to build a two-way network for 4,000 families. Then Cablevision promised a similar system in the New York metropolitan area—for over a million subscribers. Meanwhile, US West unveiled plans for fiber-to-the-curb systems in its 14-state region; Bell Atlantic won permission to replace with fiber all the copper wire in New Jersey by 2010. Virtually every other big communications company has an information highway plan in the works.

Among the contenders, Bell Atlantic stands out for aggressiveness and astute politicking. Its plan to rewire an entire state is a first. It convinced regulators that New Jersey needs the expensive new systems to maintain competitiveness. Bell Atlantic wants to time the installation of fiber to suit local markets in each of the seven states it serves. In a few neighborhoods, where marketers believe there is ready demand for interactive service, the company is extending fiber to the curb right away.

That has thrown a scare into at least one cable company. The owner of a housing development in northern Virginia says, "When the cable people found out Bell Atlantic was putting fiber optic in, they had a fit." Where the company thinks TV watchers will embrace an alternative to cable, it plans to take fiber to the neighborhood and send ADSL transmissions the rest of the way over existing copper wires.

US West is betting that the fastest way to roll out advanced networks is by cutting costs. The company has challenged suppliers to tighten their belts and help it build fiber-to-the-curb systems in new neighborhoods for no more money than a standard copper-wire system. (Right now putting in fiber costs about 30% more.)

TCI, the largest cable company, will switch to digital signal transmission in dozens of communities starting next year and has ordered one million state-of-the-art converter boxes to let customers tune in. The investment could serve as the foundation for two-way networks that can deliver video on demand. Archrival Time Warner has focused its attack more narrowly, concentrating on showcase projects designed to push network technology as far as it will go. The system planned for Orlando will have 600 digital channels for video on demand and phone calls, as well as 75 regular channels for ordinary TV. Construction is set for next year, even though crucial components such as video servers aren't yet available.

GTE, which owns local systems in 40 states, is maneuvering to cash in on a key advantage over other regional phone companies. Since it was never part of the Bell system, GTE is not bound by the federal consent decree that bars Bell companies from owning information businesses. GTE is testing interactive video services it can market through systems like the one in Cerritos. One lets customers pay bills by filling in on-screen checks; another helps students prep for SAT exams.

AT&T, finally, is poised at the edge of the field. It no longer owns a wire into the home, but with its proposed $3.8 billion investment in McCaw Cellular Communications, it could again be a powerful force in local markets, especially if wireless technology emerges as a way of delivering advanced information services.

As they circle one another warily, phone and cable companies are like predators at a jungle water hole, wondering, Will it try to eat me, or will it kill some other animal and let me share the meal? Conflicting motives leave them torn between competition and cooperation.

Phone companies could easily afford to put broadband wire into people's homes—regulators permitting. But the job would take a long time, and the companies lack experience in programming. Cable operators are in a position to skim off lucrative telephone business. But they have little experience with network management, and none with switching or billing phone calls. The industry's fragmentation also suggests a need to cooperate: Most metropolitan areas have several cable systems, which would probably have to work with the phone companies to provide local service.

Temporary alliances are taking shape. In Denver, for example, AT&T, US West, and TCI have teamed up to test-market video on demand. Viewers at home browse through a catalogue of 2,000 movies and punch in a code number on their remote controls. Exactly five minutes later the film starts playing, as if fetched from a computer's memory bank—though what actually happens is that a worker at the test center steps up, finds the proper videotape, and views it in a bank of VCRs. Customers pay $4.99 per showing, about $2 more than for a rental cassette.

Which companies clash will depend partly on the speed of deregulation. If state regulators move slowly, phone companies may move outside their service areas to get into other businesses, invading one another's areas. Southwestern Bell, for example, recently bought two cable systems near Washington, D.C., putting itself on a collision course with Bell Atlantic.

Where regulators are most flexible, phone companies will simply upgrade their own networks. They may even ally with local cable operators to economize. In such an arrangement the phone partner would handle switching and billing for calls and interactive services delivered through the cable system. Eli Noam of Columbia University thinks regulators should be leery of such plans, lest they give rise to powerful monopolies in local service: "Phone and cable companies should be beating each other over the head in their home service areas." But Clouston of TCI argues that alliances would speed network building.

In fact, technology is evolving so quickly that monopolies seem unlikely. Cellular-Vision, with its capable little antennas, has sent strategists scrambling at phone and cable companies alike. The household antenna and decoder box cost only $300 to install, much less than any glass highway hookup. Such innovations could alter the balance of power. Alarmed, several Bell companies tried to squelch Cellular-Vision's license application by filing objections with the FCC, saying the technology wouldn't work. But it does. During a recent demonstration in

Brooklyn, the picture quality was good, except when a moving crane passed before the window.

Among the would-be builders of information highways, it's too early to pick winners. At a recent press conference about Time Warner's ambition to build glass highways and fill them with photons bearing movies and recipes and homework, CEO Gerald Levin showed a flash of grim realism. Reflecting on the company's multimillion-dollar losses on Time Teletext, an early electronic information service, he said: "A lot of people are going to lose a lot of money." No doubt. But the bounty will be great for those who marry the right technology to the right services at the right time.

Discussion Questions

1. What is a telecommunications highway?
2. What technologies likely will make up a U.S. telecommunications highway?
3. What factors are hindering the developing of an effective U.S. telecommunications highway? ▼

Reading 8 "A Multimedia Solution to Productivity Gridlock: A Re-Engineered Jewelry Appraisal System at Zale Corporation,"[1] by Julie Newman and Kenneth A. Kozar

(This reading is especially suited for use in conjunction with Chapter 9 of *Information Systems.*)

ABSTRACT

Zale Corporation once melted down most of its damaged, returned, or repossessed jewelry, resulting in substantial lost revenues. It was determined that additional revenue could be produced from salvageable jewelry if the value of the items could be accurately determined. This meant the jewelry had to be appraised by experienced gemologists to determine the most profitable disposition. The gemologists' productivity suffered because the appraisal was extremely labor intensive. To address this problem, an automated multimedia system utilizing electronically linked measuring instruments, voice recognition, and interconnected LAN databases was developed. Although the unique voice recognition feature of the system was later abandoned, the use of the system enhanced productivity. This paper describes the systems development, its subsequent evolution, and the lessons learned from the process.

INTRODUCTION

The world of gems, jewelry, and diamonds is a fascinating one. Even though most of us at one time or another purchase these items, the jewelry industry has been given little attention in the business or information systems literature. Some problems of the jewelry industry are common to many businesses, but others are unique. Unlike many other products, the component parts of a piece of jewelry as well as the composite item have intrinsic market value. Not many items sold in retail outlets could be melted down and sold for their salvage value. This uniqueness creates both problems and opportunities for Zale Corporation.

THE PROBLEM/OPPORTUNITY

Zale Corporation, the world's largest jewelry retailer, has a jewelry processing center in its world headquarters building in Irving, Texas. Each year the center receives about 300,000 unsalable pieces of discontinued, damaged, or repossessed fine jewelry from its 1500 stores. In the past, a lack of sufficient processing ability forced Zale to ship these goods periodically to a local smelter to be melted down in acid baths. The smelter returned to Zale a check for the value of the recovered gold along with glass bottles containing the diamonds and other precious gemstones recovered from the melting process.

Almost all of the Corporation's so-called "surplus" jewelry was melted. Because the value of melted jewelry is far below its original cost, disposing of unsalable jewelry in this manner resulted in significant losses for Zale. Much of the original damage to this jewelry, if any, was slight—a loose prong or a scratch. However, determining a more profitable means of disposing of damaged jewelry is a very complex process. Experienced gemologists must perform a detailed appraisal of the jewelry. Scientific measuring devices, complex calculations, and subjective analysis are used to derive the current salvage value of each item and assess its potential for additional recovery. The gemologists also must look up current commodity prices for gold and gemstones to determine their salvage value. Since a good gemologist can

[1] Source: *MIS Quarterly* March 1994.

FIGURE 1 The Gemologists' World

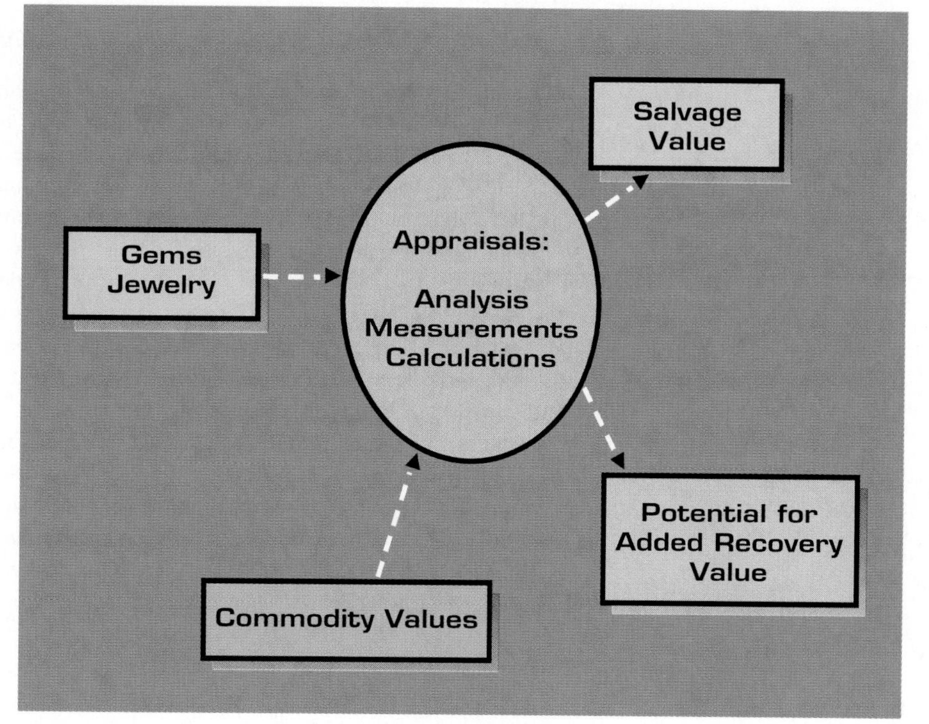

manually evaluate only about 25 pieces of jewelry per day, traditional methods are not a cost-effective process for appraising a high volume of jewelry.

In addition to the possibility of recovering additional revenue from intact damaged jewelry, there is an opportunity to recover more from the components of the jewelry that must be melted. Zale was paying "finders' fees" to various vendors for locating specific gems to satisfy insurance claims and customer repairs. Tens of thousands of dollars each month could be saved if Zale maintained an accurate inventory of the loose gemstones that were recovered when large quantities of jewelry were melted. The diamonds and gems recovered from the smelting process were being sold through brokers in large batches with little understanding of their individual size and quality. A perpetual inventory that identified the size, shape, and quality of precious gemstones would allow them to be reused, thus greatly enhancing their value to Zale.

The consequence of not knowing the actual value of salvaged jewelry was clearly illustrated when one of the authors was handed a bottle of loose diamonds and told that their total value was "probably about one million dollars." After appraisal, it was determined that the value of the diamonds in the bottle was closer to two million dollars.

A still greater potential for increasing the revenue produced by the disposition of distressed inventory came from refurbishing the jewelry and then retailing it at reduced margins through liquidation outlets. But first the rather daunting problem posed by the high volume of items that must be subjected to a gemologist's scrutiny had to be overcome.

To address the appraisal problem, Zale considered the possibility of automating the process in order to improve the productivity of the gemologists. At first glance, appraising jewelry appeared to be incompatible with automation. However, closer examination and revision of the gemologists' processes, combined with a concern for the end user, resulted in a creative and unique application of modern technology that led to dramatically increased productivity.

AN AUTOMATED SOLUTION TO JEWELRY APPRAISAL

An automated system to receive and appraise the unsalable inventory that accumulates in Zale Corporation jewelry stores was proposed. The end result was an intelligent, multimedia system named "MEDUSA."[2] MEDUSA was designed to run on a local area network and utilize voice recognition as the primary vehicle for capturing data. All of the activities performed by the gemologists were supported by voice commands, including the use of ancillary tools-of-the-trade such as calipers and diamond scales. Barcodes were used to track items as they made their way from receipt through a multitude of possible detours and destinations. This system allowed expert gemologists to increase their productivity by 600 percent, and Zale's recovery from distressed merchandise has increased by millions of dollars.

To build the system, three criteria were identified that in combination were expected to have the necessary impact on productivity: (1) allow the gemologists' hands and eyes to be used solely for evaluating jewelry, not for completing forms or performing keyboard data entry, (2) eliminate as much as possible the need to evaluate every item, and (3) provide decision support for the gemologists throughout the entire appraisal process. The first objective was realized to be of pivotal importance after conducting simulated evaluations and observing that the gemologists' hands and eyes were continually occupied with instruments and of course, the jewelry itself. Each objective was met by integrating new technology with leading-edge systems already in place at Zale Corporation.

The system has evolved since its original design—the gemologists no longer use the voice recognition feature. But the development and evolution process are nonetheless instructive. The following describes Zale Corporation's experiences with this new process for dealing with unsalable jewelry.

THE PROCESS OF EVALUATING UNSALABLE JEWELRY

The purpose of the gemologists' evaluation is to ascertain accurately the actual salvage value of each piece of jewelry. This value is used as the basis for determining the greatest revenue-producing disposition for each item by estimating the resulting profit or loss and accurately assigning the results to the appropriate cost center.

The merchandise that is processed through the MEDUSA system is comprised of four types of unsalable jewelry: (1) damaged or defective items, (2) discontinued items, (3) repossessed items, and (4) trade-ins. The 1500 retail stores periodically return these items to Zale Corporation headquarters in Irving, Texas. Store personnel produce a shipping document by entering a transaction into their point-of-sale system. This transaction also updates a host-based file with the details of the shipment.

When the jewelry is received in the processing center at Zale headquarters, a unique barcode is affixed to each item. A receiving auditor enters the number of the accompanying document into MEDUSA, and the shipment information is retrieved from the host-based file and displayed on the auditor's LAN-based workstation.

The auditor receives each line of the shipment by scanning barcodes until the quantity scanned equals the quantity shipped. For instance, if the quantity of an item on a shipping document is "3," the system expects the auditor to scan three different barcodes before proceeding to the next line. After all items in a shipment are received, they are sorted into common categories (watches, gold jewelry with stones, gold jewelry without stones, etc.) and staged for evaluation by the gemologists.

Another module of the application aids appraising and maintains a perpetual inventory of the loose diamonds that are returned from the smelter. This inventory, including stones that are removed prior to melting, is used to satisfy most diamond bond insurance claims and other repairs. (A diamond bond insures that a customer's diamond will be replaced if it is ever broken or lost from its mounting.)

When jewelry that needs a diamond replaced is received from one of the stores, a gemologist, determines the exact specifications of the stone needed to replace the customer's stone. With MEDUSA, the gemologist locates the diamond in the loose stone inventory and produces a barcoded label to keep track of the jewelry as it is circulated to the repair vendor and back to the store. At the end of each of step in the process, MEDUSA automatically sends a fax message to the store so that the current status of the repair is always available to satisfy customer inquiries.

MEDUSA also provides mechanisms for transferring evaluated items to various liquidation centers, repair vendors, and smelters. All necessary documents and reports are generated, and financial accountability for all activity is maintained at the cost-center level.

MULTIMEDIA JEWELRY EVALUATION

The jewelry evaluation module of MEDUSA utilizes unique processes and technology. (See Figure 2 for a view of the system inputs, outputs, and technological aids.) Voice recognition technology was chosen to satisfy the first productivity criterion of "keeping the gemologists' hands and eyes on the jewelry." To activate the voice processor, the gemologist uses a light-

FIGURE 2 An Overview of the MEDUSA Appraisal System

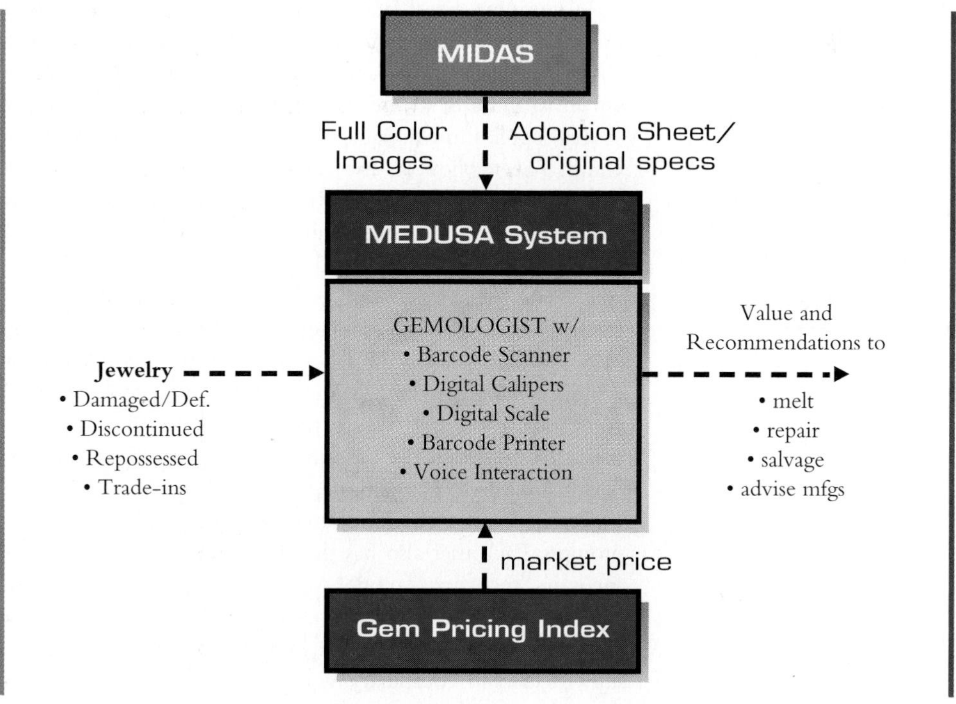

weight microphone headset plugged directly into a voice processing card located inside a 386-class workstation. Digital calipers and a highly sensitive digital scale are used to measure and weigh the jewelry. They are connected to the workstation through serial ports.

Positive identification of each item is ensured by its barcode label. When a gemologist is ready to evaluate an item, he or she scans the barcode with a fixed laser barcode scanner. The scanner utilizes a software interface to decode the scanner information for the workstation. If a repair is prescribed, a repair label is created with a barcode label printer that is attached to the workstation. If a stone is removed from a setting, the same printer produces a label for a "diamond paper" in which the diamond will be stored in inventory.

The second productivity criterion of eliminating the need to evaluate every item was met via an interconnected LAN environment that allows access to databases that reside on different LAN servers. A gemologist begins an evaluation by scanning the barcode on an item that has been received in MEDUSA. If the item originated as Zale-owned inventory, MEDUSA queries a database on another LAN called "MIDAS"[3] and retrieves a file containing its original manufacturing specifications. This file, known as an "adoption sheet," was created by a buyer at the time of the original purchase. Adoption sheet data includes the type and weight of the mounting metal, the cut, color and clarity of the diamonds, etc.—all of the information that a gemologist must ascertain during an appraisal.

If adoption sheet data is available, the gemologist modifies data elements that now differ from the original specifications because of the current condition of an item. For example, an adoption sheet for a multi-diamond ring specifies that the ring contains six identical sidestones, but one of the sidestones is now missing. The gemologist changes the quantity of sidestones to "5," reviews the rest of the specifications for discrepancies, and the evaluation is complete.

To confirm an evaluation, a gemologist can display a full-color image of an item on the workstation monitor. This image also is retrieved from a file on the MIDAS LAN. By referring to merchandise images, a gemologist can quickly verify whether the item being evaluated is the same item described on the adoption sheet and make the necessary corrections if an error in identifying an item has been made.

If adoption sheet data is not available, the gemologist must perform a complete evaluation. A typical, fully voice-supported appraisal for a simple diamond solitaire pendant with chain is scripted in Table 1. A "beep" sound is made after each data element appears on the screen to indicate to the user that the recognition was successful.

The application deduces the probable depth of the diamond from its shape, length, and width. The application uses the dimensions and the specific gravity to calculate the carat weight, because it is impossible to accurately weigh a mounted diamond. The application then uses the quality of the diamond (color and clarity) plus its shape and size to look up its current market price from a gem-pricing index that is downloaded to the system each week. The market price of gold also is maintained in the system and used to calculate the salvage of the gold in each item.

As each of these values is calculated, the gemologist either accepts the value by saying, "End," or speaks a new value digit by digit, followed by "End." After the values of all its components are derived, the system compiles the total salvage value of the item under evaluation and displays the amount for the gemologist's approval.

The interface was designed to be adaptable to the experience level of the end user. An experienced user who has memorized the evaluation scripts may choose to turn off the audio prompts. Each user also has the ability to adjust the intervals during which the voice processor is in "recognize" mode. As a gemologist becomes better at using the system, he or she can continually reduce the time required for an evaluation by turning off the voice prompts and then decreasing the time between beeps during which the voice recognizer is "listening" for a valid vocabulary word.

Table 1 An Example of A Voice-Supported Appraisal

Medusa Prompts:	**User Says:**	**Screen Displays:**
Type?	"Pendant"	Pendant
Metal?	"Gold"	
Karat?	"Fourteen"	14K
Weight?	(Puts pendant on scale) and says, "Read."	2.32gm
Stones?	"Yes"	
Type?	"Diamond"	Diamond
Shape?	"Oval"	Oval
Quantity?	"One"	1
Color	"H"	H
Clarity?	"SI2"	SI2
Length?	User measures length with caliper and says,"Read."	10.5mm
Width?	User measures width with caliper and says,"Read."	6.60mm
Depth?	"End," to accept the system calculated value.*	3.79mm
Carat?	"End," to accept the system calculated value.*	1.55ct
Value?	"End," to accept the system calculated value.*	$4,050.00
Type?	"Continue," to indicate that there are no more stones.	
Melt Value?	"End," to accept the system calculated value.*	$4,051.26
Disposition?	"Liquidation"	Liquidation
The application now returns to the "Enter barcode" prompt.		

*The user may override system-calculated values by speaking a new value, i.e., "three point eight five end."

The third criterion for increasing productivity was the availability of decision support for the gemologists throughout the evaluation process. In addition to deriving salvage values for a gemologist's approval, the application provides support for determining the costs of standard repairs and their impact on the potential profitability of reselling an item instead of melting it. After a gemologist has chosen a final disposition for an item, the application also recommends a retail price if the disposition is other than "Melt."

SPEAKER/INDEPENDENT VOICE RECOGNITION

The jewelry evaluators' workstations consist of a number of technical features that in combination provide an optimum environment for appraising jewelry. A focus on speaker-independent voice recognition in particular is included here because voice input is promoted as an interface feature that will be popular in the future (Bylinsky, 1993), yet has received little discussion in the information systems literature. The voice recognition feature was a highlight of the early implementation of the system. As the gemologists grew familiar with the system and sought greater productivity, the users sought alternative and faster methods. Nonetheless, an in-depth discussion of the development issues helps to reveal the strengths and weaknesses of the voice recognition system both in this case and for other potential applications.

Vocabulary size is one of the most important criteria to consider when evaluating the feasibility of using voice recognition in an application. The vocabulary should be relatively small and very stable since retraining a vocabulary to recognize a new word can be time intensive. The vocabulary used in MEDUSA consists of 127 words specific to the jewelry industry. To create the vocabulary, 40 volunteers—an approximately equal mix of men and women—were asked to record each of the words that the application had to recognize. Then the vocabulary was "trained," that is, a composite of all of the samples of each word in the vocabulary was created. Training is a batch process that can take many hours to complete, depending on the size of the vocabulary.

Each time an end user speaks a vocabulary word to the application, the word is stripped of all of the vocal characteristics that distinguish one speaker from another. The result is called a "token." The token contains only those auditory features that make a word unique. Since the information in the token is relevant to the speech rather than to the speaker, the token is said to be "speaker normalized." The normalized token is then compared to each of the templates in the vocabulary, and the template that is least different from the token is identified. The difference between the token and the closest template is scored; the score must be less than a specified value (called the acceptance threshold) for the application to recognize a vocabulary word.

The difference between the closest match and the second closest match also is calculated. This value must be greater than a specified value (called the delta threshold) in order for the application to proceed as though it has indeed recognized a vocabulary word correctly. If the delta threshold is too low, the user is asked to choose between the first and second matches:

System: "Did you say diamond?" User: "No"

System: "Did you say emerald?" User: "Yes"

At this point, the system can automatically untrain the word "diamond" and retrain the word "emerald." This user's token for the word "emerald" is subtracted from the template for diamond and added to the template for emerald. The vocabulary system thus is encouraged to learn from its own mistakes. It is interesting to note that one of the templates in the vocabulary is called the "garbage collector." The garbage collector is trained to recognize background noise, distortion, and conversation unrelated to the application so that the voice recognizer is not easily confused.

It is this adaptive training capability that is the key to accurate speaker-independent voice recognition. In the Zale application, using "on the fly" training has resulted in an accuracy rate that is better than 99 percent for a vocabulary that is considered large for this type of technology. Of course, productivity and user acceptance would be seriously impaired if the accuracy rate were poor.

MEDUSA SYSTEM BENEFITS

Since the first phase of MEDUSA implementation in November, 1991, the system has been accumulating data about the Zale Corporation's inventory of unsalable jewelry. The system is now yielding strategic information that is being used for much more sophisticated management of a valuable corporate asset. Executives now know the exact value of each commodity (gold, diamonds, etc.) in each of the disposition categories, and they have the flexibility to shift dispositions in response, to changing business demands. For instance, it is possible to ascertain exactly how much cash can be generated quickly by melting all items currently designated for repair as well as the loss that will be incurred by doing so. Zale can now verify that it is paid by the smelter for the correct amount of gold and that the correct number of diamonds is returned after a melt. Prior to MEDUSA, Zale was at the mercy of its vendors to perform these services accurately.

Another example of better asset management was related by one of the gemologists. Zale's National Diamond Bond Replacement Center, Zale's service center that satisfies insurance claims for lost or broken diamonds, was running low on .25 carat diamonds. Using MEDUSA, the gemologists were able to locate quickly all the one-quarter carat diamonds mounted in jewelry in Zale's inventory targeted to be melted. These stones were removed from their mountings, transferred to Diamond Bond and used to satisfy insurance claims. Over $100,000 worth of diamonds was supplied immediately, and the diamond bond center did not have to purchase additional stones.

In addition to financial control and increased revenue, MEDUSA is also contributing information that can be used to provide better quality merchandise to its customers. Zale's merchandisers now have the ability to identify chronically defective merchandise and advise manufacturers about defects. The MEDUSA gemologists are sensitizing the merchandisers to manufacturing techniques that should be avoided and are using information from MEDUSA to substantiate their advice. In one instance, the same defect was found repeatedly in a flexible tennis bracelet (it snapped in two instead of flexing). The item was recalled from all stores and returned to the vendor for credit.

MEDUSA also makes it possible to monitor shipments from the stores to the surplus processing center and ascertain whether abuse of corporate return and trade-in policies is occurring. Some stores grant excessive trade-in allowances in order to disguise unauthorized merchandise discounts. Now, when a trade-in is evaluated in MEDUSA, its appraised value is compared to the trade-in allowance granted to the customer, and significant discrepancies are reported to store management. Stores also used the practice of returning damaged merchandise to headquarters to relieve their inventories of admittedly undesirable, but definitely undamaged merchandise. These practices now can be identified and prevented.

ADAPTABILITY AND EVOLUTION OF MEDUSA

The MEDUSA system's "human factors" have had a positive influence on the morale and productivity of its end users.[4] In large part, MEDUSA and its users simply are a good match: creative individuals with a flexible multimedia computer system. But with this innovative technology, the users function as far more than an adjunct to a computer system.

First of all, the gemologists believe that they could not accomplish their job without the system due to the magnitude of the work to be done. Without MEDUSA, either they would be faced with an impossible task, or more likely, they would be forced to perform their work far below their personal standards. MEDUSA provides its users with the means to increase their productivity while meeting very high standards for quality.

Unforeseen flexibility in operating modes has also proven to be popular with the end users. The application was intended to be operated in a single context with a carefully controlled series of voice commands. However, because the gemologists have control over the audio portion of the interface and the option of keyboard entry (initially provided in case the voice processor failed), they have developed a great variety of techniques for capturing data. In fact, none of the gemologists operates the system exactly as originally envisioned.

The flexibility of the system proved fortuitous during changing business conditions—MEDUSA has evolved to adapt to new business needs. Soon after MEDUSA was implemented, Zale closed hundreds of its stores in an effort to adjust its business to the adverse economic conditions that have affected many retailers during the past few years. The entire jewelry inventory from each of these stores was returned to the Zale processing center for evaluation using MEDUSA. The quantity of goods received was many times greater than MEDUSA was originally expected to handle.

Decisions were made to change the gemologists' procedures to accommodate the extraordinary demand for expedited processing. Certain types of simple jewelry are no longer evaluated. The gemologists who have the most experience with MEDUSA can now make appropriate business decisions about the disposition of such things as "gold without stones" without relying on the system, because some decisions that were formerly supported by MEDUSA have now become automatic for the users. In this context, MEDUSA has trained the users' judgment over time and served as a bridge to an even more productive approach.

For more complex items, voice processing has been replaced for the most part in favor of short cuts like "hot keys" to read the digital instruments and bypassing certain data elements. The financial necessity of increasing the speed of the gemologists was deemed more important than the consequent sacrifice of some of the strategic information that MEDUSA provided. According to one of the gemologists, "Voice is still the preferable way to operate the system, because you get quality not possible without it."

The primary characteristic of voice recognition technology that impeded its use is the inherent delay that occurs after each word is spoken by the user. This is the time required for the voice processor to "recognize" a word. Not using the voice recognition feature eliminates this short delay. This elimination combined with modifying the evaluation procedures has increased the users' productivity by 16 to 18 percent.

It is possible that similar gains in productivity could have been achieved by improved technology. For instance, upgrading the workstations might have "recompensated" for the recognition delay, or changes made to the LAN infrastructure might have decreased the voice response time. Retraining the vocabulary may have improved response time and accuracy, or new versions of the technology might make recognition faster. However, no matter how well integrated and finely tuned a system might be, there will be an inherent delay in recognizing spoken input. In determining the feasibility of incorporating voice recognition in an application, the designer must consider whether the delay can be used productively to perform part of a process or whether the delay will simply amount to lost time.

Even without the voice recognition component, the MEDUSA system demonstrates synergy between a human and a machine. A number of complex algorithms in the application require minimal input from the gemologist to calculate or deduce most of the measurements and values that are required to appraise jewelry. This background processing is performing all of the "left brain" activity, leaving the gemologist free to evaluate the quality, design, and desirability of the jewelry—the "right brain" activity. The decisions of the gemologist are a synthesis between the left brain "value" of the jewelry and its right brain "appeal." MEDUSA thereby provides a satisfying experience for creative individuals who must perform subjective mental activity that cannot be performed by a computer but that requires computational support. Of course, even the calculations performed by the computer are scrutinized by the gemologist and can be overridden if the user's superior judgment so rules.

Finally, the novelty of the system itself is an obvious element of pride to its users. The gemologists each have from 10 to 20 years of experience and are dedicated to the jewelry industry. According to the gemologists, not only is MEDUSA a high-quality state-of-the-art system, but it is the only computer system in the world developed for appraising jewelry. "Driving" something unique and superior definitely contributes to the users' level of satisfaction with the system.

The above observations about MEDUSA could be applied in general terms to user-centric system design in any environment, regardless of the business or the technical platform. Some widely applicable lessons have been learned. A superior system will provide the users with the means to perform excellent-quality work; give them the flexibility to use the system in a variety of ways at their own discretion; and encourage the uniquely human contribution of the end user.

CONCLUSION

The development of the MEDUSA system was based on a need to manage the elimination of unsalable inventory from Zale Corporation's 1500 stores and recover as much revenue as possible from its final disposition. In order to accomplish this, a creative solution to facilitate processing the jewelry and improve the quality of information available to executives has been employed with impressive results, both tangible and intangible.

To begin with, Zale Corporation is now stocking 40 clearance stores with jewelry that would have been melted in the past. In fact, 58 percent of all jewelry processed through MEDUSA has been recycled for sale as finished goods. Although it still is advisable to melt a great deal of Zale's distressed inventory, the losses thus incurred are now more than offset by selling the majority of the jewelry in "off-price" retail outlets. Zale also is internally supplying loose diamonds for repairs and insurance claims from its own inventory, and all costs previously incurred by using outside vendors to provide this service have been eliminated. The total financial impact on the corporation will amount to millions of dollars each year.

The workstation architecture and application design have struck a very positive chord with the end users. Not only does the system give them the ability to meet a demanding need for productivity, but the unique nature of the integrated environment empowers their creativity.

Endnotes

1. An earlier version of this paper won second place in the 1992 Society for Information Management International Paper Awards Competition.
2. All Zale LAN-based systems are named after lesser known characters from Greek mythology.
3. MIDAS stands for Merchandise Imaging and Data Administration System.
4. For more details on human–computer interaction, see Card. S.K., Moran, T.P., and Newell, A. *The Psychology of Human-Computer Interaction,* Lawrence Erlbaum Associates, Hillsdale, N.J., 1983; Gerlach, J.H. and Kuo, F. "Understanding Human–Computer Interaction for Information Systems Design," *MIS Quarterly* (15:4), December 1991, pp. 526–549; Gould, J.D. and Lewis, C. "Designing for Usability: Key Principles and What Designers Think." *Communications of the ACM* (28:3), March 1985, pp. 300–311; and Norman, D.A. and Draper, S.W. (eds.) *User Centered System Design—New Perspectives on Human-Computer Interaction,* Lawrence Erlbaum Associates, Hillsdale, NJ, 1986.

Reference

Bylinsky, G. "At Last! Computers You Can Talk To," *Fortune* (127:9), May 3, 1993, pp. 88–91.

Discussion Questions

1. What problem did Zale Corporation face in dealing with unsalable pieces of fine jewelry?
2. What type of automated solution to jewelry appraisal was offered?
3. What were the components of the multimedia jewelry evaluation?
4. What were the benefits of the system? ▼

Reading 9

"Will Toys "B" Great?" by Subrata N. Chakravarty

(This reading is especially suited for use in conjunction with Chapter 10 of *Information Systems.*)

Helen Singer Kaplan, the noted psychiatrist and specialist in human sexuality, believes her husband suffers from an edifice complex. Her husband, Toys "R" Us founder and Chairman Charles Lazarus, does not disagree. "I like to have an expanding kind of business," Lazarus admits. "I like opening stores."

So do a lot of other people, but few with Lazarus' success. Since emerging from bankruptcy reorganization (where its parent, Interstate Stores, had taken it) in 1978, Toys "R" Us sales have compounded at close to 28% a year, to an estimated $3.17 billion for fiscal 1988 (ended Jan. 31). Earnings have more than kept pace, and Salomon Brothers' Bruce Missett thinks they hit a record $200 million ($1.60 per share) last year, and will grow to around $2.05 a share this year, even if there is a slump in overall consumer spending. Toys' net margins are nearly a couple of points ahead of margins at dynamic retailers like Wal-Mart and Nordstrom.

But nothing goes up forever. One need think only of Leslie Wexner's the Limited (*Forbes,* Apr. 6, 1987) to remember that great pride often goeth before a fall. A few months ago the Limited could do no wrong. Investors who believed that have since lost over half their capital. (Toys "R" Us is off around 20% from its precrash peak.) Retailing has a way of making those whom it would destroy magazine success stories first.

Will Lazarus and Toys "R" Us be different? Certainly, they are not taking success for granted. No hubris here. "The biggest danger to a retailer," Lazarus, 64, says, "is becoming complacent and saying, 'I've got it knocked, I know how this business works.' "

Say this for Lazarus' system: It is a wondrous thing. The thousands of cash registers in the company's 313 U.S. toy stores (there are 37 more overseas) transmit information on a daily basis to banks of central computers at the company's Rochelle Park, N.J. headquarters. Managers know every morning exactly how many of each item has been sold the day before, as well as how many were sold in the year to date, the prior year, and so on. All reordering is done automatically by the computers, without any communication by managers.

This sophisticated system allows Toys "R" Us to try out toys without committing to big orders in advance. Customers decide what gets reordered by their purchases. In December 1986, for example, Toys "R" Us tried out scooters—skateboards with handles—with a trial order of 10,000. They sold out in two days, a trend the computers immediately spotted and jumped on. Last year Toys sold over 1 million scooters.

When the computer conflicts with his own judgment, Lazarus will go with the computer. "I thought Cabbage Patch Kids dolls were ugly," Lazarus admits. "I didn't think my granddaughter would want to hold one." His computers, however, caught the craze early and reordered accordingly. They also warned him early that the Trivial Pursuit fad was fading.

Will Toys "R" Us, like the Limited, run into a ceiling on growth? Apart from Toys' 20%-plus market share, the $13 billion (retail sales) toy retailing business is highly fragmented. There are still many thousands of single-store outfits. It is a business, in short, that allows ample room for growth for a company as efficient as Toys. Last year Lazarus invested $35 million in scanning equipment to move customers through checkout lines faster—a major reason why Toys' stores open a year or longer increased sales by 12.3% on average last Christmas.

There are two other largish specialty toy chains. Lionel Corp., with 78 stores, has around 10% of Toys' sales volume and half its net margins. Child World, 81% owned by Cole National

Corp., has 152 stores. On sales of an estimated $840 million last year, Child World earned $14 million.

Lionel's and Child World's stores, says Lazarus, "don't do half our volume. They're not geared up for it. They don't have the variety or the backup systems. They don't have anything expect the advertising."

Toys' 46,000-square-foot warehouse-like stores are usually near shopping malls, not in them. That saves on real estate costs. Crammed with 18,000 items, the stores are open and fully stocked year-round—not just at Christmas—at prices that are 25% below list prices.

"When we started, the primary appeal was buying a brand-name toy at a lower price," Lazarus recalls. "As we developed, it became clear that, with mama going to work, there was no time to shop. So having it all became as important as the price, and now I'm not sure which is more important."

Toys "R" Us does not use temporary traffic-building promotions like sales, but it does sell the most popular toys at low markups and offers items like disposable diapers and infant formula near cost. Dennis Barron, head of Child World, publicly sneered at profitless diaper sales a few years ago. Now Child World, too, sells diapers.

Says Lazarus: "People will come out and buy all this stuff on which we make no money, but they will buy a few other things, too. How can you not buy your baby a toy when you're out there? Are you so mean? So, since everything is good value, you end up buying a lot more than you thought you were going to buy."

Where Toys sells popular items below list, it is not necessarily sacrificing profit margins. With its year-round operation and nose for trends, it is able to buy earlier in the year for better terms. "If you order in August, you pay in October," explains Lazarus. "But if you order in January, you know what? You pay next January." The manufacturers' cost of carrying the receivables gets passed on to those who order later.

Toys' cost advantages are a double-edged sword, and Lazarus uses both edges on his competitors' necks. When Toys "R" Us opened its first stores in the U.K. in late 1985, recalls Lazarus, "some very bright people said: 'Your prices could be 20% higher and you'd still undersell everybody in the marketplace.' No. That's not Toys "R" Us. The idea is to be preemptive, to sell at such low prices that no one will even try to compete."

A firm believer in the market-share approach to competition, Lazarus adds: "Don't ever bet on number two in anything. In any kind of product, the winners are going to take all if they are smart and aggressive."

If all this sounds simple, remember that the capital investment required to make it all work extends far beyond the computer system. To reap the advantages of early ordering, a retailer must have deep reserves of working capital and plenty of storage space. While all three toy supermarket chains have equivalent amounts of display space per store, Toys "R" Us has far more back-room storage space and many more central distribution warehouses than its competitors.

Recently 32 (off its high of 42), Toys' dividendless stock is selling at a slight premium to per-share sales and is priced at nearly 20 times last year's earnings and more than 15 times what Salomon's Missett thinks the chain will earn in the year ahead. Is it overpriced? The Limited sold for over 40 times trailing earnings before it crashed. Toys, for all its heralded success, has a far more modest multiple.

Besides the prospects of further growth in market share, Toys has plans for related growth in other markets. Kids "R" Us is a venture Lazarus launched in 1983 to do in children's clothing what he has done in toys. The approach is substantially similar: large stores (20,000 square feet on average) with enormous selections, stocked in depth, of good quality national brand name clothing, at prices about 25% below department store prices. There are currently 74 Kids "R" Us stores, with 31 more scheduled to open by July. The business, which made its first significant profit last year, is now doing roughly $300 million a year. "We intend this to be a very large business," Lazarus vows.

But in children's clothing, Lazarus faces a number of first-class competitors, not least of which is Macy's. Lazarus recently filed suit against Macy's, charging its management with using threats to stop suppliers from selling swimsuits to Kids "R" Us.

Whatever happens to him in kids' clothes, Lazarus probably has plenty of growth left in the toy business. He plans to open 60 Toys "R Us stores this year, 15 of them overseas, where he has been especially aggressive. With 37 stores now open in Canada, the U.K., West Germany, Singapore, Hong Kong and, next year, France, Toys "R" Us' international division, says Lazarus, moved into the black in fiscal 1987 and made a handsome profit last year.

In the U.S. Lazarus believes there is room for at least 700 Toys "R" Us outlets, vs. the 313 that exist now. Proclaims Lazarus: "We've barely scratched the surface.

"The one enormous advantage that we have over other retailers is that we are in a business that we love," Lazarus adds. Call it edifice complex, call it extraordinary drive, call it what you will, here is an extraordinary manager. If ever a company deserved its high reputation, this one does.

Discussion Questions

1. What was trend-setting about the computer system Charles Lazarus introduced at Toys "R" Us?
2. What types of information does the system generate?
3. How does the system increase sales? ▼

Reading 10 "An Appraisal of Executive Information and Decision Systems," by Brian McNamara, George Danziger, and Edwin Barton

(This reading is especially suited for use in conjunction with Chapter 11 of *Information Systems.*)

The necessity of compiling a clear and comprehensive summation of diffuse operational data to facilitate high-quality managerial decision making has become widely accepted. Toward this end, huge costs for hardware, software and training are willingly written off as strategic investments against anticipated—if unspecified—long-term returns. As a result, executive information and decision support systems have become a major growth area for computer applications.

Somehow, we have forgotten the fact that less-than-perfect information is all that can ever be made available. And in a system where the cost of information has increased in a way that is disproportional to the ever smaller increments in quality of information, it seems unlikely that even a computer can reverse the law of diminishing returns. And yet, despite this trend, ever growing in-house and external government and commercial databases are being tapped to produce a burgeoning grist for analytic mills in which, as a rule, canned statistical and graphics routines extract information for presentation to management. Meanwhile, the issue of whether or not management "knows" any more now than before all of this came to be has been conveniently brushed aside.

The information generated by these packages becomes the only reality that management ever sees. Managers who examine only abstracted information can easily lose touch with the real world processes that generate the data. Indeed, the analytic model often seems more real to the manager than reality itself. This reliance on a paradigmatic approach goes well beyond cases such as a fitted exponential sales growth curve masking an underlying "one-by-one" purchasing decision process.

ANALYZING THE DATA

The present system of analyzing business information systems seems analogous to the system that scientists have been accustomed to employing in analyzing their data. In his book *Structures of Scientific Revolution,* Thomas Khon explains that revolution in scientific knowledge and theory are systematically impeded by loyalty to (or reliance upon) the existing paradigm. All data collected from experiments is formulated and communicated according to the prevailing model. As a consequence, nothing that cannot be understood by—or fitted into—the dominant paradigm finds favor or is disseminated to the community at large. In particular, scientists operating under the assumptions of the prevailing model are likely to ignore or dismiss results that seem to contradict or deconstruct their paradigm. These, of course, may be precisely the results that will prove the prevailing model flawed or even invalid.

Business communities tend to share the empirical bias of science. Accompanying this empirical bias in business is the ever increasing availability of executive information and decision support systems (EIDS). Together they threaten the value of management decision making.

It is alleged that the computer has reached the stage of automated understanding. In any case, decision support now not only compels but directs decision making. The expert system is with us. The question is, are EIDS truly a new stage of computer development, or are they instead, merely another example of the familiar pattern of "two steps forward and one step back"?

SOURCE: Brian McNamara, George Danziger, and Edwin Barton, "An Appraisal of Executive Information and Decision Systems," *Journal of Systems Management,* May 1990, Volume 41 Issue 5, pp. 14–18. Permission granted by the Association for Systems Management.

THE PHASES OF COMPUTING VS. INDUSTRIAL PRODUCTION DEVELOPMENT

EIDS may best be understood as the first stage in the recapitulation of a cycle of growth in computer applications. Historically, in the first phase of the cycle, firms sacrificed flexibility for cost reduction via "mass production" automated transaction processing. In the second phase of the cycle, some flexibility was regained as the computer became a means of customizing products and markets. In the third phase, the personal computer boosted productivity of skilled workers in both office automation and analytical tasks despite the requisite heavy cost of investment in training.

These phases of development in computing are visible in the history of industrial production. The Taylor approach to scientific management emphasized the need for management to acquire control over diverse forms of knowledge. In the early stages of industrialization, skilled labor owned the knowledge of methods, and capital owned the physical means of production. One motive driving the introduction of mass production techniques was to reduce the skill level required of labor. Management succeeded in appropriating these methods, but only at the cost of flexibility and variety of product. The deskilled workers at Ford's River Rouge plant, for instance, could provide any color Model T desired, as long as it was black!

Gradually methods for re-introducing customized output into mass production environments were developed. These methods were not dependent upon higher skill levels on the production line. Instead, management made it possible, through data processing, for a customer to place an order for a particular combination of options and to receive delivery of a single designated "customized" unit out of a daily stream of thousands of slightly dissimilar units. Through standard cost techniques, the profit for each such custom unit was rendered predictable. In this way, managers conferred upon themselves the illusion of control, although the actual facts for any "real" single unit were unknown and unknowable.

Over time, statistical analyses of customer preferences and purchasing patterns led to the proliferation of standard models and options packages. This approach bypasses the expense and lead times associated with custom-building individual units. Improved data processing made possible control and marketing of a complex product mix coming off a single product line without the intervention of skilled labor, expensive management time, or special sales effort. In the service sector, the mass marketing of airline seats through virtually unlimited numbers of outlets run by largely unskilled personnel is perhaps the ultimate expression of computer-driven flexible mass production technology.

Of course, every solution engenders new problems. On the factor floor, the increase in product mix complexity has made it nearly impossible to compare input and output as a means to ascertain productivity and profitability. Standard cost systems have been reduced to dealing in pure fiction because there are no standards, only exceptions. In the office suites of top management, the bottom line outcomes in the near- and long-term of any particular strategic or tactical move have also become nearly impossible to predict. The causes of both these information overloads are similar and related.

The complexity of product mix optimization increases exponentially with the number of products and inputs. One may add to that problem variable yields tied to quality control difficulties and learning curve effects amplified by an ever changing product mix. The result is that prediction becomes impossible. The number of unknown variables exceeds the number of deterministic equations that can be generated from hard data based on actual experience. In the modern factory, the endless grind of the day-in and day-out sameness has been replaced by the constant change.

Management is caught between needing to be flexible in action and needing predictable outcomes. To managers who find themselves in this quandary, software houses offer the hope of executive information systems. Unable to gather sufficient numbers of observations from which stable patterns may be inferred, executives are driven to rely on simulations and hypothetical (speculative) models. Removed from both the factory and the sales floor, executives are drawn to systems that summarize the graphically present every larger collections of indicator variables that purport to reveal "what's going on." Finally, baffled by what all of the numbers mean in terms of choosing a concrete course of action, executives are grasping at the canned wisdom offered in expert systems.

TWO ILLUSTRATIONS

Just two reviews in the trade press of current offerings from the EIDS product genre will serve here to illustrate. In the May 15, 1989, issue of *Infoworld,* "The Politics of Executive Information Systems" by David Raths reports that top-level management in some large firms have authorized expenditures of $500,000 and more to acquire systems that reproduce the capabilities of previously installed software with more automated interfaces. The trade-off for reducing the skill required for the executives to operate the system is a corresponding reduction in the range of outputs and ability to construct novel analyses.

As Raths asserts, "What most of these products do is provide canned screens for an executive to look at. If he wants to go beyond that, somebody has to do a lot of work so that you can turn that next layer into a canned report." He apparently must depend on them to "make it look pretty before they pass it up the line." The thrust of the article is that data processing personnel "must educate top management about computer technology and its expanding capabilities to provide competitive advantage...," apparently without imposing upon top management the necessity of mastering the technology themselves.

At the small end of the business scale, Mike Falkner reviewed a $1,000 microcomputer package in a June 27, 1989, *PC Magazine* article called "CFO Advisor: Financial Analysis Beyond Spreadsheets." To use this package, substantial "manual" labor is required to get data into a form the program can handle. Thereafter, the program applied the "Du Pont return-on-net-assets-model" and provides goal-seeking and sensitivity analyses to compare alternative plans of action. "On three screens you get 15 analyses that show what a change to a key performance factor will do to six key-result areas."

The "...novice business user...may want to read the financial reference section...before getting started. It provides a good overview of the Du Pont theory..." An obvious fallacy here is that an analyst can proceed by just fiddling with numbers. An infinite number of monkeys seated at an infinite number of word processors would indeed eventually turn out all of the works of Shakespeare along with gigabytes of drivel and random nonsense. But the monkeys would have no way of knowing when to quit. CFO Advisor's advantage, then, is that it offers bells and whistles to signal success and to guide the novice in the right direction.

But the question remains: success at what? How is a novice to determine which of the many operating ratios should move in whatever direction to achieve what goals, and by when? Further, all of these manipulations imply (advise) real-world actions: the hiring and firing of real people, the buying and selling of real goods and services. How is the novice to know when the real world is being cantankerous, refusing to behave as theory predicts? Even more important, one wonders if goal-setting is covered as well as goal-seeking? Is the issue of to what to be sensitive covered in CFO Advisor's tutorial on sensitivity analysis? And what about effects that were never anticipated or intended by the designers of the expert system?

THE CASES OF FORD AND EASTERN

Consider whether, by using CFO Advisory, Eastern Airlines would have discovered that the public may be more concerned about flying in planes maintained by happy mechanics and flown by satisfied pilots than about the airline's bottom line to labor costs? Would Ford Motor Company have been warned when planning production of the Pinto about the potential of outraged public sensibilities, or would an EIDS system confine the analysis to the sensitivity of per-unit profit to closely shaved material and labor costs? In both cases, it is clear that the computer bean counter would reproduce the advice of the human bean counters.

The human cost-benefit analysis at Ford projected the per-unit cost of death benefits for customers "burned" to be less than a few dollars worth of protective hardware for the Pinto gas tank. This led to Ford's decision to forgo installation of minimal safety-enhancing features. The assumption by Ford's expert of no trend in the per-settlement cost over time was more than a technical error.

The experts at Ford and Eastern both failed to appreciate that the "inexpert" car-buying and flying public does not think stockastically. Each individual buyer makes an idiosyncratic purchasing decision. What in the aggregate means millions for the seller, amounts to only a few dollars either way to fly with happy crews and drive non-explosive cars for the consumer. It was the model of the customers' utility itself that was at fault. Had the risk benefit analysts from Ford left the office and gone down to a local dealership for just one evening, things would have gone very differently. They could have tried floating their cost-saving concept with a few customers. One can imagine the pitch:

> "I'm going to build two different cars. The Pinto will be priced at $1900 (late 1960s prices, remember) and the Nino will be $1910. Now these two will be exactly the same car except for one tiny detail. In order to bring the Pinto in at $10 less than the Nino, we will leave off a bracket and a few bolts that keep the bumper from folding in, causing the gas tank to explode if the car is hit from behind at relative speeds of 15 miles per hour or more. We will put this extra safety stuff on the Nino so it won't explode, although, we all know that if you are in a car that is hit from behind at relative speeds of much above 40 or 50 you likely won't survive even if you aren't fried. So, what do you think Mr. and Mrs. Average Customer, is an extra 25 or 30 miles an hour of survivability worth $10? Which car do you want, the Nino or the Pinto?"

Obviously, one evening of frank discussion at the local dealership might have averted disaster for Ford Motor Company, and saved some lives. It is hands-on knowledge of the material with which one is working—in this case, customer—that distinguishes craft from factory work.

Hands-on knowledge provides a means of judging the limits of models. What is addressed in this case is the issue raised earlier: that management must not confuse a model with reality. There is a price/volume relationship, no doubt. But neither customers' utility for money, nor what each added dollar buys, is uniform when the typical purchase is a single unit instead of so many pounds of potatoes at so much per pound. A model of the aggregated likelihood of sales of single units to many individual customers behaves on the computer screen much as a model of the likelihood of selling many units to a single customer does, but these two cases are fundamentally different. Leave out a critical component to reduce cost in the expectation of increasing volume, like the steering wheel or a few bolts and a bracket, and your marketing plan just might blow up in your face.

In computing, this means that an executive information system that isolates management from the underlying reality will inevitably lead management astray. When data are gathered for analyses and models built, the users of the models must possess the experience to identify critical aspects of the process under analyses that are not incorporated in the model.

Experience is also a guide to roughly what range of outcomes to expect before an analysis is run. Abstractions in models don't always act in the same way as are the real-world components they purport to represent. An unexpected analytical result leads an experienced manager to suspect the model first and their internal sense of the process last. The opposite tends to happen to an inexperienced manager. Prior knowledge of the processes producing the data being analyzed, and how well the indicators being tracked actually capture the fundamentals of those processes, helps an experienced manager to resituate the findings of an analysis in the real world. The significance of results must be evaluated on more than statistical grounds, and only hands-on experience can provide that "something extra."

Experience includes learning the jargon and nuances of categories: In order for analysis to proceed, the events of the real world must be scored and tallied into appropriate categories. This is perhaps the most critical step in any analysis, yet is one that top management typically leaves for others.

SUMMARY

It is hoped that the information presented here provides a sobering appraisal of executive and decision support systems. It is a poor craftworker who blames his tools for poor results. Above the minimal level of tool quality, it is clarity of purpose and conception, understanding of the material with which one works, and coordination of mind and hand that explain the bulk of the variance in the quality of results. If managers seek effective, efficient computer applications, they must themselves master the tools. If there are to be gains in productivity, there must be intimate knowledge of the tasks to be carried out. If systems are to stand and deliver, those who design and implement them must constantly observe, reflect upon and correct the methods of operation.

Discussion Questions

1. What is the quality of information that DSS and EIS can provide?
2. In what ways do business communities demonstrate the "empirical bias of science?"
3. How can managers judge the validity of models inherent in the information systems?
4. How can a manager improve the use of executive and decision support systems? ▼

Reading 11 "Networking with the Enemy," by Rochelle Garner

(This reading is especially suited for use in conjunction with Chapter 12 of *Information Systems.*)

Harry Brown was not amused. Word had gotten back to him that one of the companies invited into his carefully wrought network of suppliers and, yes, competitors wasn't playing fair. It was going after projects on its own instead of with the team.

"I said, 'If you can't abide by the rules, then you should leave.' They agreed and walked out."

Big mistake on its part.

The renegade manufacturer lost business because it didn't have the clout of Brown's network—an informal team of companies from around Erie, Pa., in the same small-parts business.

In contrast, Brown's EBC Industries, Inc. (Brown is its president) and all of its 11 allied suppliers and competitors have been growing at 12 percent to 15 percent every year since he cobbled together the network in 1988. EBC has grown from 68 employees to its current 93 and from less than $4 million in sales to $8.4 million expected by year's end.

That incident highlights the glories and potential pitfalls in the growing trend of "co-opetition."

Not familiar with the term? Get used to it—the word could become as prevalent as the phrase "virtual corporation."

Both embrace the concept of companies reaching across corporate boundaries to engage in mutually beneficial projects. But co-opetition, management pundits say, goes even further to include the notion of competitors working together toward a shared goal while continuing to compete.

For example, EBC gladly shares its electronic data interchange (EDI) expertise and inventory database with team members working on the same job. But should any member step on another one's territory, the members politely but firmly tell the violator to stop.

SOME UNSUCCESSFUL

Not everyone has had Brown's success. Others have ventured into collaborative waters only to find themselves mired in a swamp of distrust, churning through investment dollars without earning a single cent of return.

Take Electronic Joint Venture (EJV) Partners. Like the Erie network, New York-based EJV Partners embodied the shared vision of competitors. But rather than laid-back, small-parts manufacturers from the green valleys of Pennsylvania and Ohio, these companies were six of Wall Street's leading bond-trading firms.

Their goal was enormous profit. The result so far has been an industry joke.

Three years ago, the bond-trading market hungered for data and analytical tools to more confidently buy and sell bonds. Sure, Bloomberg Financial Services, a financial news service, provided some information. But only some.

London's Reuters Holdings PLC, one of the largest market data companies in the world, approached New York-based Goldman, Sachs & Co.'s senior bond traders with a deal. Help us start a service to compete against Bloomberg. The business side called in James K. Burns, then Goldman, Sachs's chief information officer, to evaluate the prospect.

SOURCE: Rochelle Garner, "Networking with the Enemy," *Computerworld,* November 29, 1993: pp. 83–85.

The idea looked great. So great, in fact, that Burns, along with Salomon Brothers, Inc.'s Mark Sternberg, with whom he discussed the project, decided to eliminate the middleman.

"We both agreed: Why share this with Reuters?" said Burns, now president and CIO of SHL Systemhouse, Inc., a systems integration and outsourcing organization based in Canada and New York. "But we also said whatever we would do would start off behind Bloomberg, so we needed more partners."

Eventually, Goldman and Salomon recruited CitiBank NA in New York, The First Boston Corp. in New York, Morgan Stanley & Co. in New York, and Lehman Brothers, Inc. in New Haven, Conn. Each partner would donate data and software that the resulting service company—EJV Partners—would turn into a data and analytics system powerhouse certain to lure business away from Bloomberg.

Only it hasn't turned out that way. Every partner had a different idea of how to deliver the information: with a cutting-edge system that would take time to build or with a "reasonable" package that it could sell almost immediately. Cutting-edge won, and Bloomberg continued to gain ground with more customers.

But the problems ran deeper. While EJV Partners won't confirm or deny it, word throughout the halls of Wall Street hold that the six partners continually bickered over what facts, analytics, and software they would give to the venture, holding out the best information for themselves.

Whatever the reason, the initial bond-trading system sucked eggs.

"When we evaluated EJV's system, it became clear that the marginal benefit for Bloomberg just wasn't worth the rest," says Tony Coffey, portfolio manager at Franklin Resources, Inc. in San Mateo, Calif.

In more than a year and a half, not one customer bought the system. Zip. EJV Partners employment fell from 180 to its current 110. The firm's chief executive officer also felt the ax and was replaced last summer by Thomas Wendel. However, EJV Partners released a new, more capable system last summer that is finally winning customers.

"We've gone from [having] no paying customers to between 15 and 20 in the past four months," says Dick MacWilliams, EJV Partners' head of sales and marketing. Six of those paying customers are EJV Partners' original partners. What went wrong?

AGREEING TO AGREE

"It's always difficult getting competitors to agree on common goals, common standards, and common methodologies," MacWilliams says. "And when you have partners contribute more than just money, decision-making becomes even more complex."

EJV Partners management operated like the multiheaded Hydra, each with its own idea of how things should work.

That, maintains Jessica Lipnack, co-author of *The Team-Net Factor,* can be a common source of failure. Lipnack, who actively promotes the idea of co-opetition, says participants must define with hard-edged clarity the purpose of their project. "That purpose is the glue holding the teamnet together," Lipnack says. "Without it, the project will fail."

Her point transcends mere platitude. After all, a traditional hierarchy contains rules, regulations and policies that people can follow. "But in a [teamnet] network, all you have is the shared agreement of what needs to be done," she says.

Perhaps one way to ensure clarity of purpose is with a disinterested arbitrator. That's one role Electronic Data Systems Corp. is playing as it helps four California managed-care plans develop the California Health Information Network (CHIN).

Initially, Dallas-based EDS and its partner, Health Information Technologies in Princeton, N.J., were setting up an EDI system to transmit uniformly formatted claims/encounters, eligibility information and referral authorizations among health care plans, independent physicians associations (IPA), and medical groups. For the competitors—PruCare, HealthNet, TakeCare, and Blue Cross/Blue Shield of California—the challenge is to discover what they have in common without revealing proprietary data.

"I constantly have to weigh in the back of my mind what is competitive information," says Joseph Sinsangkeo, manager of information systems technology at HealthNet in Woodland Hills, Calif. "That's where EDS and [Health Information Technologies] play a role—as keepers of company-specific information. And a lot of times they'll come back and say, "You all have a lot more in common than you realized. Are you willing to share?"

And while EDS's role as information broker is important, so is the relationship among the four partners. Every week, IS representatives from the four, along with representatives from EDS and Health Information Technologies, hold conference calls to work out implementation concerns.

Every month, CIOs and top business executives meet to hash out larger issues, such as choosing where the January pilot will roll out. Each member has an equal voice, which it exercises loudly and clearly. It's as if the project leaders had read Lipnack's book, with its admonition to meet regularly, push information both up and down the hierarchy, and create more leaders (and fewer bosses) throughout the team.

FEWER THE BETTER

It is also wise to limit the number of partners in the group at the outset and let the membership increase as it learns to work together.

For example, when CHIN finally goes on-line, partners will pay per transaction. And since volume will lead to volume discounts, participants hope to recruit as many competitors, IPAs, and medical groups as possible.

That, however, will be much later. For now, the aim is to keep the process running, which means limiting the players to four.

"I think the difficulty of reaching agreement increases exponentially as you add people," says Linda Hutchinson, senior systems consultant at PruCare. "But the nature of the project is that by having four of us cooperating, we will accomplish more than any one company could do alone."

This kind of openness and lack of formality among members is what's so intriguing about a network of erstwhile enemies, says Brown at EMC. "We all just call, ask to come over, and discuss the topic."

TAKING THE TEAM APPROACH

Interested in a particular job? Just tell the other players; they might want to vie for it, too. Want a new computer-numeric control program for your milling machine? No problem. EBC's programming staff will send one over.

The team approach has helped each member reach independent goals in ways otherwise not possible. In Brown's case, his goal was big, lucrative contracts that were beyond his reach. Brown, quite simply, needed help.

When he first took over what was then called Erie Bolt Corp., the manufacturer of parts for the transportation and defense industries was losing $100,000 a year.

Worse, much of the shop floor equipment had been cannibalized to keep other machines operating. Then an order came in that EBC couldn't fill.

"So I went to my competitors, explained my dilemma, and proposed that we go after contracts together," he says.

As it happened, one of those competitors, Joseph Dyson & Son in Painesville, Ohio, saw this as the opportunity to expand. It was the beginning of a beautiful relationship—one that eventually grew to include up to 12 suppliers and competitors that team up against much larger forces bidding on the same contract.

"We still compete. But we cooperate on areas where individually we couldn't do it alone, either because of equipment or capacity reasons," Brown explains.

THAT'S THE TICKET

That attitude is just the ticket needed to succeed and one that is obviously not being lost on the CHIN group. Chances are, the four players in the CHIN group will succeed. Somehow, whether through common sense or just plain luck, they've established a way of interacting that promotes trust, open communication and a constant eye on the project's objective.

Those ingredients—crucial for any co-opetitive venture—are damnably difficult to instill among allied competitors. Just ask EJV Partners' members.

So before you enter the oh-so-brave world of collaboration, ask your gut if you and your potential partners can work together. If the answer's yes, prepare to work long and hard. If it's no, back out.

Discussion Questions

1. Define and illustrate *co-opetition*.
2. What are the benefits and pitfalls of co-opetition?
3. What problems did EJF Partners experience?
4. What factors contribute to effective cooperation among competitors? ▼

Reading 12 "The End-user Developer: Friend or Foe?" by Jeff Papows and Joe King

(This reading is especially suited for use in conjunction with Chapter 13 of *Information Systems.*)

USER DEVELOPERS BUILD BETTER BUSINESS SYSTEMS

It's too late to debate whether end users should be invited into the application development process. They have already arrived.

Groupware, with the power it gives to end users, is the phenomenon that is forcing the development rules to change. Groupware products are both technologically and dynamically in tune with the user developer: The level of complexity varies with users' needs and knowledge. Entry-level users can whip built-in templates and examples into simple applications, while power users can take advantage of macros to help develop more sophisticated tracking and work-flow applications.

In this way, end users can become the most effective weapon against an applications backlog that can mount up to several years at the typical Fortune 1,000 company. And people who work in glass houses shouldn't be throwing stones at this idea: Information systems needs to stop hoarding development and realize the best thing that could happen to an organization is for users to develop what they need.

The benefits of harnessing user power in to the development process are clear. For starters, no one has a keener insight into what makes an efficient and effective business application. It stands to reason that end-user developers will create—or quickly add—a necessary function once they know they need it.

There is no opportunity for the messy and costly miscommunication that sometimes occurs in the typical development life cycle when users hand in their requirements and pass system specs to programmers, who hand applications back to users and so on.

Even more importantly, as users develop these systems, they can discover flaws in work flows the applications address.

At one New York-based advertising company, for instance, a cross-functional team of businesspeople, with little help from IS, planned to develop an automated traffic control system for projects. The groupware-based system was to replace the company's manual, nine-step time- and paper-intensive work-flow process. As the team mapped the work flow, it realized the process was a mess. It would be a mistake merely to automate it. For instance, there was no formal way to specify who would be a member of which project, to assign team duties or to set up teamwide briefings.

Because the developers were professionals integrally involved in the business, they picked up on the poor processes. IS would never have been able to.

This is heady—and empowering—stuff for users. "Suddenly, they see their own information needs being met and quickly envision myriad specific applications to be implemented," says the IS director at an accounting and consulting firm. He says the appeal of this kind of development is "almost visceral."

As users, excited and enabled by groupware, flock to the application development party, business organizations are starting to see quantifiable results in terms of reduced time to action and improved quality in business processes, including product development, account management and customer service.

SOURCE: Jeff Papows and Joe King, "The End User Developer: Friend or Foe?" *Computerworld,* November 15, 1993, pp. 180–182.

One leading scientific equipment manufacturer I know of got a 20% increase in response after putting in a prospects and sales tracking system that an applications engineer and the company's director of training created.

On the basis of this improved response, the company estimates that if each rep makes one additional sales call per week it can bring in $4.3 million more in revenue annually.

As users are brought into the development mix, the loudest applause should come from savvy IS professionals. Only those with their eyes on the past will bemoan the rise of groupware as the fall of the IS profession. There's a chance for users and IS to work together.

That's because, as Mark LaRow, a consultant at the Ernst & Young Center for Technology Strategy, points out, there is a shift occurring. Command, control and communications are no longer the driving forces in companies.

Users in the development process can't be ignored anymore.

IF YOU WANT TROUBLE, THEN LET USERS DEVELOP

Don't be swayed by the popular myth that users are your programming resources of the future.

With the PC applications backlog what it is—at least three years, by my reckoning—it would be great to think that end users are the answer to the information technology group's prayers. What information systems manager would turn down a bunch of extra helping hands if it meant faster development?

But getting end users involved will do more harm than good.

I'm not talking about end-user development with personal productivity tools, such as spreadsheets, word processors and personal databases. That's baby stuff, stand-alone and isolated development that rarely has any ripple effect on applications and communications companywide.

Rather, the danger is letting end users go wild with new enterprisewide multiuser application systems of which Notes, Objectvision and Visual Basic are all a part. Combine user-controlled development and the workgroup computing nature of such tools and you have the makings of a technological Molotov cocktail.

Such products are a siren song to end users. They promise simplicity and ease. (Perhaps a new Dale Carnegie course is in order—"Yes, You, Too, Can Be an Application Developer.") Users don't have to wait around with their hair turning gray to get an application built. But are you prepared to have your users "simply" and "easily" handle complex communications software, administer a client/server environment, ensure security over multi-platform systems, distribute databases over a wide-area network and master multiple programming languages?

Yet these are all part and parcel of what it means to develop applications with Notes or Visual Basic or whatever. It's been my observation that the learning curve for Notes—and I'm talking about the learning curve for technical professionals—is long: about six months. Users take twice that time to come up to speed—if they ever do. Can your organization afford to have your users spend up to a year learning to be competent developers?

I'm not kidding when I say development can get complicated. Notes, for instance, doesn't sit there by itself; building a complete application often requires, say, Visual Basic or Objectvision. I know of one project that needed as many as seven separate products to build a single system.

You can't really expect users to master all of these tools. Even if they did, issues of design, data integrity, and quality come into play.

I know one company whose business users built a slick shared database application on a LAN. But it took so much effort to maintain that the support staff doubled. And then it doubled again. The system duplicated the existing corporate systems' data entry functions, and the company was left with data that did not balance. Data integrity has become a major issue.

While the rigors of design, analysis, testing and methods are second nature to professional developers, users haven't been versed in these areas. And you can kiss documentation good-bye.

Also, when companies let their users take on development, users quickly discover that for their applications to have value (surprise!) they either have to get data from or talk to older systems. So it ends up spending a good chunk of its time figuring out how to integrate new and legacy systems. What starts out as a way to shorten an applications backlog ends up adding to it instead.

I don't want to give the impressions that I'm not a big fan of these new development tools. Quite the contrary. The tools can have a profound impact on the development life cycle. But *only if* development is in the right hands.

It's not like users won't be involved in development at all; in fact, one of the things these tools have going for them is iterative and rapid development, which brings users and developers together in a real-time "conversation." Users participate actively, but control stays with IS.

I can't see why companies want to create more development headaches than they already have.

Discussion Questions

1. What advantages do user developers offer?
2. What role does groupware play in users' developing software?
3. What disadvantages do user developers create?
4. How can an organization achieve balance in the involvement of users in systems development? ▼

Reading 13 "No Set Rules for Systems Design," by Kathleen A. Gow

(This reading is especially suited for use in conjunction with Chapter 14 of *Information Systems.*)

Many factors, including geographic origins and locations of foreign sites, influence the manner in which multinational corporations handle systems planning and acquisition.

Japanese companies, for example, tend to encourage local autonomy wherever they operate as a means of staying close to local markets, according to Christopher Bartlett, professor of business administration at Harvard Business School and author of *Managing Across Borders, the Transnational Solution*. "If you shook a Japanese manager out of sleep today, he would be mumbling 'localization,' not globalization," Bartlett says.

In other instances, multinationals allow greater latitude for local decision-making in certain areas of the world. Many, for example, give Latin American business units and subsidiaries much more local control over systems planning and acquisitions than their North American or European counterparts. There are a number of reasons why Central and South American sites are accorded this special treatment. One is that systems and communications software used in other parts of the world are either unavailable in these areas or incompatible with the local standards. Another is that stringent government regulations frequently restrict the flow of information across borders.

Bartlett describes the challenge for multinational firms as being able to balance the need for local differentiation with the seemingly contrary objective of achieving integration and coordination on a worldwide basis.

Achieving this balance calls for a certain amount of flexibility in weighing the cost and efficiency advantages of centralization and standardization against the requirements of individual areas.

At Gillette Co., for example, David Lawless, assistant director of international systems, says Gillette Europe is handled very differently from Gillette Latin America. Europe has centralized planning and direction coming out of the Isleworth, UK, facillity for every function, including IS. Latin America, on the other hand, looks like Europe did seven years ago: Although the region adheres to the framework of centrally developed hardware, organizational and procedural standards, there is much more local autonomy.

"Local control is useful to the degree that business requires resident systems, but it can mean higher costs and the risk of mismanagement," Lawless says.

At Stockholm-based Alfa Laval AB, local control is encouraged but within certain limits. In the early 1980s, Alfa Laval sought to counter a structure that was too cumbersome by decentralizing control of its business units, which are arranged by product area. The only requirement imposed on these units, says John Tower, a rate manager of MIS at Alfa Laval, Inc. in Park Ridge, NJ, is that they maintain systems compatibility with headquarters.

Alfa Laval uses an IBM communications network and range systems that vary locally. The seven business areas use different processes and manufacturing equipment, but some systems have come out of headquarters, such as electronic mail and the in-house-developed Global Inventory File.

Corning, Inc., takes a very broad view of IS diversity. "We're opportunistic," Harvey Shrednick, vice-president of information services, says of the Corning, N.Y.-based conglomerate's approach to IS. "We share where we can and manage by prevention."

SOURCE: Kathleen A. Gow, "No Set Rules for Systems Design." *Computerworld,* October 1, 1990, pp. 98–99.

Shrednick holds overall responsibility for corporate IS worldwide. He says Corning has not come up with a global strategy that it can use across the board. Rather, the strategy varies depending on the needs of the industry and the people involved in each unit.

In North America, IS operations are centralized and report directly to Shrednick. In Latin America and Europe, however, systems control for the consumer products groups is much more local. The central IS function provides advice and guidance, but decision-making authority for hardware and applications software rests locally. "We have chosen not to legislate what people use," Shrednick says. It is each group's responsibility to purchase equipment and software that will communicate with headquarters.

Although achieving worldwide coordination in this type of an environment is not easy, Shrednick says he stresses that individual freedom does not always lead to a choice to be different. He gives the example of a U.S. plant floor reporting system that was taken to Japan and adapted for Japanese plants, complete with a hot key between English and Japanese versions.

MANAGING BY CONSENSUS

Many multinationals have set up international IS management groups to help achieve coordination through consensus. At Xerox Corp., for example, the Corporate Information Management (CIM) group brings together senior information managers from business units worldwide to make decisions on issues such as architectures, operating system software and primary database modules.

According to Judi Campbell, manager of strategic technology deployment at Xerox in Rochester, N.Y., the CIM group can also serve as a catalyst for resource sharing. In one instance, she says, a member—the liaison for Latin America—was able to identify an opportunity for adapting a set of systems developed for a European region to the requirements of a Mexican unit.

Bartlett says it is impossible to overemphasize the value of forums that permit face-to-face meetings. Globalization is not just to gain access to markets, he says, but also to gain information such as competitors' activities and government regulations.

"In the old role, the subsidiary served as a delivery pipeline, essentially acting as a dumb terminal," he says. "Now, they capture and transfer knowledge—not just raw data processing, but information" and, for that reason, "it is better to manage through socialization," he maintains.

Bartlett stresses that this transfer shouldn't just be between headquarters and subsidiaries but from one subsidiary to another: "That's what drives transnational innovation."

Discussion Questions

1. What factors influence the way multinational corporations handle systems planning and acquisition?
2. Do multinational companies have uniform systems architectures and sites in different continents?
3. What advantages and disadvantages does localized versus corporate control create?
4. Offer three illustrations of decisions about systems architecture by multinational companies. ▼

GLOSSARY

4GL. *See* fourth-generation language.

Access control technique. A method such as token passing or CSMA/CD used to determine which device or devices can put a signal on the network.

Accounting. The process of recording, classifying, and summarizing the financial activities of an organization.

Accounts payable system. A transaction processing system that tracks money owed by an organization and deals with transactions associated with purchasing, including generating purchase orders, producing checks, and authorizing payments; an accounting system for keeping track of money an organization owes to individuals or other organizations.

Accounts receivable system. A transaction processing system that tracks monies and other debts owed to the organization and deals with transactions associated with sales, including checking consumer credit, monitoring bad debts, and pursuing overdue accounts; an accounting system for providing information about money owed to a company.

Acoustic coupler. An early type of modem consisting of a cradle in which a telephone headset could be placed and electronics to produce an analog tone from a digital signal and vice versa.

Active data entry. Actions taken by a user to enter data into a computer.

Ad-hoc query. A request that has not been preprogrammed for information from a database, generally one made by a nonprogramming user who is using a user-friendly language.

Address. A location in the computer's memory.

AGV. *See* automated guided vehicle.

Allocated cost center. An accounting scheme in which the IS department allocates and charges its costs to the departments that use its services.

Alpha testing. *See* system testing.

Alternative analysis. The second stage of the systems development life cycle, in which alternative systems are proposed and their feasibility analyzed.

Analog signal. An electrical signal that changes smoothly.

Architecture. The long-term structural plan for investing in and organizing information technology; it acts as the blueprint for the technology portion of an organization's information systems infrastructure.

Arrow key. A special key on the computer keyboard that usually controls the position of the cursor on the screen.

Artificial intelligence. A branch of computer science that emulates human behavior and thought in computer hardware and software.

ASCII. A code used by most microcomputers to represent characters.

Aspect ratio. The relationship between the length and width of a graphics design.

Assembly language. A programming language whose commands correspond to commands understood by the computer, requiring programmers to specify in painstaking detail every step they want the computer to perform.

Asset. The property of a person or an organization that is used to produce an output.

Asynchronous communication. Along with synchronous communication, one of the two most common technologies for sending and receiving data.

Attribute. A characteristic of an entity, such as phone number, hair color, height, or weight of the entity "person"; a column of a relation in the relational model.

Audit trail. A permanent record of transactions that auditors use to verify corporate information reported by the company.

Authorware. Software that trainers use to develop courseware.

Automated guided vehicle. Also known as AGV, a computer-controlled vehicle that moves along a guidance system built into a factory or warehouse floor.

Automatic forwarding. A feature of electronic mail that allows all messages, or all messages that meet certain criteria, to be forwarded to another mailbox.

Automation. The use of computers to perform tasks previously performed by people.

Automation system. A system that uses information technology to perform tasks that would otherwise be done manually.

Backup. Duplicate copies of data, often kept at another location, to protect firms against the loss of data due to systems malfunction, fire, or natural disaster.

Band printer. A type of impact printer often used on minicomputers and mainframes.

Bandwidth. A measure of the information-carrying capacity of a communication channel; its unit is the hertz.

Baseband. Along with broadband, one of two major signaling technologies for local area networks.

Batch processing. A system of data processing in which transactions are not processed singly as they occur but batched for processing at some later time.

Benchmark. When pertaining to a database management system, a test to measure its effective speed while controlling for the type of hardware used.

Beta testing. *See* pilot implementation; also, a phase of software testing in which the software is tested in a real environment before its official release to paid users.

Billing system. Part of an accounts receivable transaction processing system that generates account statements and bills for customers.

Bit. Short for binary digit, the smallest amount of data that can be stored; it has one of two possible values—on or off—zero or one.

BITNET. A supernetwork among research universities throughout the world.

Bits per second. Abbreviated bps, the maximum number of bits of data that a channel can accept in one second without losing information.

Blind carbon copy. A copy of a mail message sent to a third party in such a way that the designated recipient does not know that the third party has received a copy.

BPR. *See* business process redesign.

Branch. In the hierarchical model, one of potentially many data items that relate to an item higher in the hierarchy.

Broadband. Along with baseband, one of two major signaling technologies for local area networks.

Budgeting. The process of planning expenses and revenues for the future.

Bug. An error in the way that a system operates.

Bus. A common topology for local area networks that exists when all workstations and devices are connected to a single communication medium without any repeaters.

Bus width. The number of bits a computer can move at one time from one area of memory to another.

Business growth rate. The speed of industry growth.

Business process redesign. Also known as business process reengineering and BPR, the breaking of traditional notions of how an organization accomplishes its work to redesign the work processes, generally taking maximum advantage of information technology.

Business process reengineering. *See* business process redesign.

Byte. A unit of storage capacity equal to eight bits; the amount of memory that stores a single character in the most popular coding schemes.

Cache memory. A small amount of primary storage that is faster than the rest of the primary storage in a computer.

CAD. *See* computer-aided design.

CAM. *See* computer-aided manufacturing.

Capacity planning. The process of determining or sizing organizational resources for production in the short and long run.

Carbon copying. Sending a message to someone in addition to the designated recipient.

Cartridge tape. A data storage device that resembles cartridge tapes used to record music.

CASE. *See* computer-assisted software engineering.

CASE workbench. A software package that provides a set of CASE tools that address a significant part of or an entire systems development methodology.

Cash management system. A system that processes transactions related to the receipt and distribution of cash.

CBT. *See* computer-based training.

CD-ROM. An optical disk used for data storage similar to a compact disk used to play music.

Centralized architecture. A design that calls for database management system operations to be centralized on a single computer.

Chain printer. A type of character impact printer used primarily with minicomputers and mainframes.

Character impact printer. A printer that, like a typewriter, operates one character at a time and produces an image on the output medium by having a solid object with an image of each character strike through a ribbon or carbon.

Chief information officer. Also known as the CIO, a person responsible for managing the information-related resources and activities of an organization.

Chip. A small wafer of silicon holding electronic circuitry equivalent to millions of transistors.

CIM. *See* computer-integrated manufacturing.

CIO. *See* chief information officer.

Circuit board. A rigid board with etched wiring connecting electronic chips.

CISC processor. *See* complex instruction set computer.

Client. In a client/server architecture, a computer, typically dedicated to a single user, that relies on other computers called servers to perform special services, such as database services or printer services, on their behalf.

Client/server architecture. A plan for running a network of computers such that one or more participants are designated to perform specialized services for others. For database management systems, a design that divides the functions among connected computers on a network, while centralizing permanent storage for all data on one or more computers known as the database servers.

Clip art. Graphics designs or pictures that can be purchased in a library form for use with a variety of horizontal application software packages.

Clock. An electronic circuit that emits a regular electronic beat or pulse to synchronize the operation of the processor.

Clock speed. The number of times per second that the clock emits a pulse.

Cluster. A tightly coupled network between two or more computers, generally minicomputers and mainframes, that allows them to appear to the user as a single computer and often act as a single computer, sharing secondary storage, printers, and jointly providing output to a single screen; also the computers so networked.

Coaxial cable. The type of wire that cable television companies use to bring television signals into the home.

Code generator. Software that can generate complete and working programs based on designer specifications.

Code key. A key of the keyboard, such as the letter *B,* the *Backspace* key, or an arrow key, that sends a specific code to the computer.

Collision. An attempt to send two messages over a local area network at the same time.

Command/data-oriented programming language. A computer programming language such as FORTRAN, COBOL, or Pascal that separates data storage from procedural parts of a program.

Command-driven interface. Operating system software that requires users to direct a computer's next action by entering a command, typically by typing it at a keyboard.

Commodity. A saleable item indistinguishable from others of its types.

Communication channel. A path that data follow as they move from their source to a destination computer.

Communication hardware. Devices that obtain data from and send data to other computers.

Compensation design and administration. Activities to determine wages, benefits, and other forms of compensation, such as bonuses or stock options.

Competitive advantage. An advantage held by one company in an industry that cannot be easily duplicated by its competitors.

Competitive necessity. A change in the way that one company in an industry does business that forces its competitors to follow its lead.

Compiler. A type of language translator that translates a file of computer code into a language that can be understood directly by the target computer.

Complex instruction set computer. Computer whose processor understands a rich and varied instruction set.

Compression software. Software to compress or shorten messages so that they require less capacity for data communication, along with the software to reconstruct the messages at the receiving end.

Computer-aided design. Also known as CAD, a system that helps transcribe designers' ideas into engineering drawings, redraws designs from different angles, evaluates the technical characteristics of alternative designs, and performs other noncreative tasks associated with manufacturing design.

Computer-aided manufacturing. Also known as CAM, a system that automates or partially automates monitoring and control functions during manufacturing.

Computer-assisted software engineering. Also known as CASE, the application of engineering principles to the design and maintenance of software products.

Computer-based training. Also known as CBT, training programs that use courseware.

Computer fax. A circuit board that can be installed in a computer for transmitting computer files or screen images to a facsimile machine and that can receive a fax for direct processing by the computer.

Computer hardware. The physical equipment that handles electronic information.

Computer-integrated manufacturing. Also known as CIM, the coordination of CAD and CAM automation systems with each other and with information systems that depend on or relate to design and manufacturing.

Computer-supported cooperative work. *See* groupware; also known as CSCW.

Computer virus. A program that inserts a copy of itself into other programs.

Computerized database. A database stored on computer-readable media such as tape, disk, or CD-ROM.

Computerized reservation system. Also known as CRS, an order entry system used by airlines, hotels, car rental agencies, and other companies that sell, rent, or otherwise allocate a limited and typically perishable capacity to provide a service or use of an asset.

Concurrency control. Procedures and techniques for properly managing simultaneous updates and access to data.

Content. The elements of data that appear on an output report or screen.

Contextual inquiry. A way of collecting information about how users perform their work by watching them working or working alongside them.

Control. Activities and systems to ensure that performance meets established standards, workers' activities occur as planned, and the organization proceeds toward its established goals.

Controller. An intelligent device, more complex than a multiplexor, that can combine and route messages over an organized multicomputer network.

Cooperative processing. The use of local area networks to connect PCs with larger computers so that each type of equipment can be used for what it does best.

Coordination system. Groupware for project management that helps coordinate the scheduling of project activities and team member participation.

Copyright. The right of an author of an original work to receive payment from those who copy or use it.

Copyright Act of 1976. The U.S. law that explicitly extended copyright protection to software.

Cost leadership. The strategy that seeks to achieve competitive advantage by allowing a business unit, by keeping its costs low, to make more profit than its competitors at the same price.

Courseware. Software that automates education and training.

CRS. *See* computerized reservation system.

CSCW. Computer-supported cooperative work. *See* groupware.

CSMA/CD. A technique to detect message collisions on a local area network.

Cursor. The position marker on the computer screen.

Customized software. Software that has been modified after purchase.

Cycle. A circular activity or chain of events, such as the emergence of newer systems from older ones.

Daisy-wheel printer. A type of character-impact printer that has a wheel on whose spokes are raised character images.

Data. Raw facts whose uses and application are undefined.

Data administration. The tasks and functions of ensuring the integrity of the data resource in an organization. These include identifying data collected by the organization; determining where they are to be stored and how they are to be named; establishing security and access controls; minimizing data redundancy; and maximizing ease of data access.

Data administrator. A person who performs data administration functions (*see* data administration).

Data communication. The transfer of data between two or more computers.

Data design. The process of identifying and formalizing the relationships among the elements of data that will form an organization's database.

Data dictionary. Also known as a data repository or data encyclopedia, a database about all the data used within an organization.

Data element. In the network model, an object such as a person, event, or thing about which data are collected.

Data encyclopedia. *See* data dictionary.

Data entry clerk. A relatively low-skill, low-pay job position with the responsibility of entering data into a computerized system.

Data-flow diagram. Also known as a DFD, a diagram that graphically illustrates the creation and use of data by system processes and provides a complete picture of the relationship between inputs and outputs.

Data integrity. Self-consistency among data in a database.

Data model. An approach to treating the relationships among data.

Data pollution. Faulty, flawed, or unreliable data or data processing.

Data redundancy. Duplication of data within a database.

Data repository. *See* data dictionary.

Database. An organized collection of related data.

Database administration. Technical tasks and functions associated with monitoring, tuning, and servicing the DBMS or DBMSs running in a given environment, including performing database backups, managing database recovery upon system crashes, and installing DBMS updates and software tools. It may also include the task of modifying a data design to correct performance problems.

Database administrator. A person who performs database administration functions (*see* database administration).

Database management system. Also known as a *DBMS,* software comprising programs to store, retrieve, and otherwise manage a computerized database and provide interfaces to application programs and to nonprogramming users, as well as provide a host of other data creation, manipulation, and security features.

Database manager. *See* database management system.

Database server. In a *client/server architecture,* a computer that stores data and runs the software to access its data in response to requests from client computers.

DBMS. *See* database management system and database manager.

DDE. *See* dynamic data exchange.

Decentralized architecture. A design in which databases are developed on an ad-hoc basis as required by individual applications, without central planning and without central control.

Decision support system. Also known as *DSS,* an information system designed to assist managers in evaluating the impact of alternative decisions and in making the best possible choice, usually integrating information from a variety of internal and external information sources and incorporating models, analytical tools, and the support of ad-hoc queries.

Decode. Determine the meaning of a computer instruction.

Delayed delivery. A feature of electronic mail systems that allows users to specify that a message should not be delivered until a specified time and date in the future.

Delivery control. Features of electronic mail that include priority delivery, receipt verification, failure notification, and delayed delivery.

Density. The number of dots a device produces per inch horizontally and vertically.

Design. Part of the information management model involved with correcting deficiencies in existing systems and integrating state-of-the-art practices and technology into them. Also, the third stage of the systems development life cycle; the creation of a detailed specification of the proposed system. Also, the creation of a concept and specification for a finished good or service and/or the creation and specification of equipment and procedures for manufacturing or producing it.

Design specification. A document prepared by systems designers that communicates the specifics of a design to the programmers who will implement it.

Desktop conferencing. A method of conferencing featuring the use of sophisticated workstations incorporating a video camera connected over a network or high-capacity conference line that transmits text, graphics, voice, and video.

Desktop publishing software. Also known as DTP, software that helps users lay out text and graphics in a form suitable for publication.

Detail report. A report produced by a management reporting system that is used primarily by low-level managers and that provides data about individual transactions.

Development. The fourth stage of the systems development life cycle, which includes the procurement of hardware, the development or purchase of software, and testing to ensure that the developed systems meets the specifications formulated in the design phase.

Development environment. A computing environment (hardware, software, and data) that appears to be real but that is separate from the production environment in which software developers develop new programs or modify old programs.

DFD. *See* data-flow diagram.

Diagnosis. Part of the information management model requiring a description of the existing problem, the context in which it occurs, the type of information available, the type of information required to solve it, and the possible ways of securing the needed information.

Differentiation. The strategy that seeks to distinguish the products and services of a business unit from those of its competitors through unique design, features, quality, or other characteristics, allowing it to charge a premium for its product or service.

Digital signal. An electrical signal whose voltage takes on one of only two possible values at any time, or an electrical signal approximating this ideal.

Digital signal processor. A device, also known as a DSP, that converts an electronic wave signal, such as one arising from sound or other sensory inputs, to a stream of digital bits, and vice versa.

Direct cut-over. An implementation strategy in which the old system is removed and the new system put into place overnight, over a weekend, or over some other period of time when the company does not operate.

Disk controller. A device that provides the interfaces to removable and/or permanent disk drives.

Disk duplexing. A process for preventing data loss by using hardware that passes data destined for storage to two separate controllers with two separate disks.

Disk mirroring. An operating systems feature to prevent data loss by sending all requests to store data to two or more disk devices.

Disk pack. A storage medium consisting of a stack of magnetic-coated metal disks connected by a central spindle.

Diskette. A storage medium consisting of a circle of mylar or similar material coated with a magnetic film and protected with a cardboard or hard plastic cover.

Diskette drive. A device that spins diskettes rapidly, exposing and reading any part of the storage surface within a few hundredths of a second.

Distance education. The application of data communication technology to bring education resources to students at distant locations.

Distributed DBMS architecture. A design that allows data to reside on any or some subset of networked computers.

Distribution architecture. A plan that specifies how data and database processing are physically distributed among the computers in a typical organization.

Distribution list. Also known as a mailing list, a list of electronic mailboxes that computer users can create, name, and use to identify recipients of their messages.

Document DBMS. A class of DBMS that operates on text documents and includes intra-document DBMS and inter-document DBMS.

Dot matrix impact printer. A printer with a print head that typically contains 9 or 24 wires that can be fired individually at a print ribbon.

Dot pitch. A measure of resolution specifying the space between adjacent dots on a computer screen.

Downsizing. The process of moving some or all of an organization's computing to a larger number of less powerful computers, generally to PCs connected by a network. Also, the process of replacing minicomputers and mainframes with microcomputer networks.

Downstream. Relative to a given company, the direction on the value chain of companies such as customers, distributors, and repackagers who add value to a product or service after the company has added its value.

Drill down. A capability provided by most executive information systems that allows a user to easily reveal the details behind aggregated data.

Drum. The cylinder in a laser printer that, when heated by the laser, attracts dots of toner, which then are transferred to the paper.

DSP. *See* digital signal processor.

DSS. *See* decision support system.

DTP. *See* desktop publishing software.

Dynamic data exchange. Also known as DDE, an industry standard accepted by most horizontal application software for exchanging data among different software programs.

E/R model. *See* entity-relationship model.

EBCDIC. A code IBM and some other mainframe manufacturers use to represent a character in eight bits.

EDI. *See* electronic data interchange.

EDIfact. The European and Asian standard for EDI.

EIM. *See* electronic imaging management.

EIS. *See* executive information system.

Electronic address. Also known as an electronic mailbox, the address by which recipients of electronic mail are known to electronic mail software.

Electronic bulletin board. A system for electronic conversation and messaging controlled by a central manager that uses a central repository to store messages.

Electronic data interchange. Also known as EDI, the electronic exchange of data (usually transactions) between two business organizations using a standard electronic format.

Electronic desk. The area of a screen in which a GUI operating system presents the user with icons for starting office automation functions such as electronic mail, word processing, and spreadsheets.

Electronic imaging management. Also known as EIM, systems that store documents on computers instead of in filing cabinets.

Electronic list. A distribution list for electronic mail.

Electronic mail. A message sent electronically between two users on a computer system or on networked computers; also, the software that supports the sending of electronic mail.

Electronic mailbox. *See* electronic address.

Electronic market system. Component of an interorganizational information system that provides information about industry players so as to increase competition and efficiency in vertical markets, reducing a seller's power and creating lower prices for buyers.

Electronic notes. Software that organizes electronic messages by topic or group and provides support for sending and reading such messages.

Encapsulation. A bundling of data and methods that is closed from the view of users and other programs in an object-oriented environment.

End user. A consumer of IS services; he or she uses a computer to accomplish such tasks as word processing, electronic mail, statistical analysis, and report generation.

Entity. A data object such as a person, event, or thing about which data are collected.

Entity-relationship model. Also known as the E/R model, a pictorial way of showing the interrelationships among various types of data.

ES. *See* expert system.

ESS. *See* executive support system.

Evaluation. Part of the management information model concerned with assessment of the methods, techniques, and systems for handling both manual and computerized information.

Event-initiated report. A report generated by a management reporting system in response to the occurrence of a prespecified event, typically either a milestone or an expected problem.

Exception report. A report generated by a management reporting system that is designed to alert managers to potential problems by showing only data that fall outside an accepted or expected range.

Executable module. Also called a load module, software, already translated into the language of a computer, that can be loaded into the computer and run.

Execute. Perform an instruction.

Executive information system. *See* executive support system.

Executive support system. Also known as an ESS, executive information system, or EIS, software that supports executive activities, often specifically designed for a particular executive, reflecting his or her style and information requirements.

Expected value of information. The difference between (1) the expected value of a sequence of optimal decisions when information is obtained; and (2) the expected value of a sequence of optimal decisions made without the benefit of information.

Expert system. Also known as ES, computer software that automates the role of an expert in a given field; a system that automates functions requiring highly specialized knowledge, such as product design, medical diagnosis, or equipment repair.

Expert system user interface. The component of an expert system that acquires and modifies the rules and knowledge in the knowledge base, accepts a description of the user's problem, asks the user for additional information if necessary or desirable to address the problem, and presents its conclusions, recommendations, and explanations in an understandable fashion.

Expert systems shell. Off-the-shelf expert systems software that provides all the components of an expert system except the knowledge base.

Explanation module. The component of an expert system that tells the user how the inference engine applied the rules and facts to reach its conclusion.

Explode. To reveal the detail behind aggregated data (*see* drill down).

External modem. A stand-alone modem having its own power, a connection for a telephone cord, and a connection for a cable to a computer's serial port.

Facsimile machine. An electromechanical device, also known as a fax, that transmits and receives documents and images almost instantaneously over telephone lines.

Failure notification. A feature of electronic mail that alerts the sender to a message that could not be delivered.

Fair use doctrine. The aspect of patent law that permits the legal production of copies in a variety of circumstances that either encourage the progress of arts and science or cause no substantial diminution of the author's market; it limits the scope of a copyright.

Fault-tolerant system. A system that achieves high reliability by using hardware incorporating redundancy and software designed to take advantage of this redundancy.

Fax. *See* facsimile machine. Also, a document sent by facsimile machine.

Fetch. Retrieve an instruction from memory.

Fiber optic cable. A cable made of glass fibers that carries messages on a beam of light rather than using an electrical signal.

File manager. A simple database manager that deals with only a single set of related records at a time.

File server. A computer in a client/server architecture that is used to store and retrieve data and programs for the clients.

Financial accounting. Activities dealing with preparing accounting information for users outside the organization, such as regulatory bodies, investors, shareholders, and tax assessors.

Fixed asset system. A system to organize the information about a firm's assets and any funds maintained for their renewal.

Flat-bed scanner. A device used to scan into a computer a graphics image of books, magazines, and other media that cannot be fed through a sheet feeder.

Flexible manufacturing. A system of manufacturing requiring that all machinery be adaptable and potentially have multiple uses.

Floating point accelerator. A special fast-calculating device that performs complex arithmetic computations faster than the computer's main processor.

Floating point arithmetic. Calculations with numbers having a decimal point and stored in exponential format.

Focus. The strategy that achieves competitive advantage by concentrating the organization's resources on a single market segment, allowing it to become a big player in a small market rather than a small player in a larger market.

Form. Regarding output, the way information is presented.

Formal sources of information. Sources that provide information in a relatively organized and predictable fashion, such as business forms, electronic monitoring equipment, digital thermometers, and an encyclopedia on a compact disc.

Formatting. Changing the appearance of a document to make it more readable or more attractive without changing its wording.

Fourth-generation language. Also known as a 4GL, a computer language whose commands convey a great deal of meaning and that generally operates in conjunction with a database management system.

Frame. A historical or hypothetical scenario that an expert system shell can use as knowledge about a specific environment.

Function key. Any of several keys on the keyboard, typically marked with the letter *F* and a number, whose codes are interpreted by software as instructions to perform a particular function.

Fuzzy logic. The ability to recognize a pattern or predict a result using data that are incomplete or not entirely accurate.

Gateway. A computer that accepts data from one network, processes it into a format for another network, and retransmits it.

GDSS. *See* group decision support system.

General ledger system. An accounting system for classifying expenses and revenues in ways that allow managers to attribute profits and losses to departments or individual products.

Geographical information system. Also known as GIS, software with the ability to examine and manipulate geographical information, along with associated databases containing geographical information.

GIS. *See* geographical information system.

Global corporation. A corporation that has rationalized its international operations to achieve greater efficiencies through central control.

Goal-seeking software. Software that applies a variety of tools to quickly determine the best or optimal solution after users specify the criteria for evaluating the outcomes of different decisions.

Graphical user interface. Also known as GUI, software that uses menus and icons to interface with a user.

Graphics processor. A device that rapidly manipulates images—rotating them, zooming in and out, presenting appropriate views of three-dimensional objects, coloring regions, and detecting and drawing edges.

Graphics scanner. A device that inputs pictures and other graphics into a computer after first converting them into a numeric format that computers can process.

Group decision support system. Also known as GDSS, software that supports group decision making.

Group mailbox. A repository for electronic mail or notes that can be accessed by anyone within an authorized group.

Groupware. Also known as computer-supported cooperative work (CSCW), information technology that facilitates the sharing or communication of information among members of a group and helps the group to perform common tasks and to accomplish its goals, including such products as electronic mail, electronic notes, bulletin board systems, and electronic meeting systems.

GUI. *See* graphical user interface; pronounced "goo-ey."

Hacker. An individual who accesses computer systems without authorization, often solely for the challenge of doing so.

Hard disk. The most common type of fixed medium, consisting of magnetic-coated metal platters arranged on a spindle, encased in a vacuum chamber, and packaged with a device (motor, electronics, and magnetic sensors) that positions, reads, and writes data on the medium.

Hardcopy. Output that can be removed from the computer on a medium such as paper.

Hardware. The physical equipment used in electronic information processing.

Hedging. Investing in financial instruments to protect against unexpected reductions in income or increases in expenses.

Help desk. Also known as an information center, the IS staff and associated systems that help end users solve immediate problems with their equipment or software.

Hertz. A clock rate of one pulse per second; also a unit of bandwidth equal to the number of times a signal (normally in the form of a wave) can be repeated in one second.

Hierarchial model. *See* hierarchical model.

Hierarchical model. A data model in which data items are related to one another in a hierarchy resembling an inverted tree.

Hold key. A key, such as the *Shift, Ctrl,* or *Alt* key, that affects the code sent by other keys pressed at the same time.

Home-grown software. Software that is not for commercial resale.

Homonym. A name for an item that is the same as the name for a different item.

Horizontal application software. Software that performs generic tasks common to many types of problems and applications across and within industries.

Host. A computer, typically multiuser, that accepts connections via modem from remote devices such as terminals or computers running terminal emulation software and performs processing for the remote user.

Host computer. *See* host.

Human resource management. The deployment, development, assessment, reward, and management of individual organizational members and worker groups.

Hypertext. A type of intra-document DBMS that allows database designers to build cross-references, or linkages within a database that users can traverse interactively.

Icon. A pictorial representation of the resources of a computer or its potential operations.

Image compressor. A specialized processor that reduces the number of bytes needed to store an image by recognizing similarities among parts of a single digitized image or among sequential frames of a moving image.

Implementation. The fifth stage of the systems development life cycle, in which the old system is deactivated and the new one activated.

Inbound logistics. The transport of raw goods to a company from its suppliers.

Infected. Adjective describing a program that harbors a computer virus.

Inference engine. The component of an expert systems shell that processes the knowledge base supplied by users to reach conclusions, answer questions, and give advice.

Infoglut. An overload of information.

Informal sources of information. Sources that provide information in a less structured way, such as conversations with customers and the observation of personal and organizational activities.

Information. (1) most commonly, processed data that influence choice—that is, data that have somehow been formatted, filtered, and summarized; (2) according to economic theory, the negative measure of uncertainty; (3) according to *information theory,* inputs and outputs of communication.

Information center. *See* help desk.

Information leadership. The strategy of increasing the value of a product or service by infusing it with expertise and information.

Information link. An interorganizational information system's function of providing coordination between individual organizations and their customers or suppliers.

Information management model. The four-step model incorporating diagnosis, evaluation, design, and implementation used in this book as a pedagogical tool to demonstrate the effective use of information in managerial decision making.

Information system. The combination of information technology, data, procedures for processing data, and people who collect and use the data.

Information theory. A branch of statistics concerned with measuring the efficiency of communication between people and/or machines.

Informationalizing. The strategy of using information-based enhancements to revitalize mature businesses by their creating or selling information as a core product.

Infrared signal. An electromagnetic signal that can carry data for short distances, such as within a building, but only within a line of sight.

Infrastructure. The underlying structure or features of an organization's information systems and technology.

Ink jet printer. A printer that operates by spraying streams of ink at the paper.

Input analysis. A formal cataloguing and review of the information an organization collects, stores, and uses.

Input hardware. A device or devices that send signals to a computer; devices used to capture information electronically.

Instruction counter. *See* instruction register.

Instruction register. A hardware device that contains the address of a location in the computer's memory that holds the next instruction the computer will execute.

Instructions per second. The average number of instructions a processor performs in a second.

Integrated package. Accounting software that combines all accounting functions into a single package with seamless interactions and central files for all accounting functions.

Integrated services digital network. Also known as ISDN, a set of standards for integrating voice, computer data, and video transmission on the same telephone line.

Integration testing. Testing that addresses the interaction between large, independently developed components of a new system.

Integrator. A company that packages hardware and software to meet a customer's specification.

Intelligent agent. Expert systems software often included within a GDSS, in which the computer becomes an active participant in decision making through contributions in both process and content.

Inter-document DBMS. A DBMS specialized for organizing, managing, searching, and retrieving groups of related documents.

Interactive dialogue. The discourse between a computer and its user.

Interface design. The specification of the form and methods of data output and entry.

Interface device. A device that sends data from a computer onto a communications medium or processes signals from a communications medium for input into a computer.

Internal modem. A circuit board that acts as a modem and resides inside a computer with a connector, extending through the back of the computer, for a telephone cord.

International corporation. A corporation that exports the expertise and knowledge of the parent company to its subsidiaries.

Internet. A worldwide supernetwork.

Interorganizational information system. *See* interorganizational system.

Interorganizational system. Also known as IOS, an automated information system that two or more companies share to support the linkage of their businesses.

Interpreter. Software that translates a computer program into code that the computer can understand, one instruction at a time, and then executes each instruction before translating the next instruction.

Intra-document DBMS. A DBMS specialized for searching and retrieving parts of a document based on its words, images, and other components.

Inventory control. The management of partially completed goods and services.

IOS. *See* interorganizational system.

IS steering committee. A committee of top business managers, selected users, MIS managers, and technical specialists who provide direction and vision about the use and development of the IS infrastructure.

ISDN. *See* integrated services digital network.

ISO 9000. A set of five related quality management standards adopted by the International Standards Organization and many businesses that ensure complete documentation and rigorous business practices in manufacturing.

JIT. *See* just-in-time inventory.

Just-in-time inventory. Also known as JIT, the practice of obtaining inventory precisely as needed, neither too early nor too late.

Keiretsu. Financial and operating agreements among a family of Japanese companies, along with cross-ownership, that allow the parties to operate as a closely knit team.

Kernel. The basic part of an operating system, as distinguished from the utilities packaged with the operating system.

Keyboard. An input device like a typewriter keyboard that consists of a plastic or metal housing containing keys that when pressed send a signal to the computer.

Knowledge. An understanding that is derived from information.

Knowledge base. Facts, rules-of-thumb, relationships, frames, and other information that an expert knows and might use to solve problems in a particular area or domain; the component of an expert system or decision support system that contains facts, rules, and other relationships among data.

Knowledge engineer. A professional trained to probe experts on how they know, understand, or suspect their diagnoses to be true.

Labor-management relations. The interactions between union and management.

LAN. *See* local area network.

Language translator. Software that translates computer programs written in a language conducive to software development into a language that the computer understands.

Laptop computer. Also known as a notebook, portable processing hardware that generally weighs less than 5 pounds and can be battery operated.

Laser printer. A printer that produces high-quality text and graphics output (typically 300 dpi or better) at a fast rate (typically 4 pages per minute or better) using a laser-driven xerographic process.

Layout. The physical shape of a network.

Leased line. Transmission capacity provided by telephone companies between two points, generally charged per period rather than by usage.

Legacy system. A system that by virtue of its lack of documentation, degree of complexity, and/or importance to the organization cannot easily be changed or replaced.

Light pen. An input device consisting of an item shaped like a pen that emits a small light whose position relative to a computer screen can be detected by electronics on or within the screen.

Line printer. A character impact printer such as a band printer or chain printer, used most often with minicomputers and mainframes, that prints a line of characters at a time.

Linear. A network layout that seeks to minimize the amount of cable used by connecting nearby devices to one another so that they all line up along the cable.

Link-loader. Software that links object modules into one complete program.

Linkage. The strategy of obtaining a competitive advantage by establishing special, exclusive relationships with customers, suppliers, and competitors.

Load. To copy software from secondary storage into primary storage.

Load module. *See* executable module.

Local area network. Also known as a LAN, a network that connects parties in the same building or in clusters of buildings within a few miles of one another using media, typically cable, dedicated especially to it.

Local computer. When using data communication software, the user's computer.

Log. A record of transactions processed by a DBMS and used to trace and recover transactions after a computer hardware or systems failure.

Logical view. A view of data based on a data model that is independent of the way in which the data are physically stored.

Logistics. The transport of goods and associated activities, such as warehousing.

Low-cost leadership. The strategy that seeks to achieve competitive advantage by allowing a business unit, by keeping its costs low, to make more profit than its competitors at the same price.

Macro. A series of recorded keystrokes, often with the addition of more sophisticated programming commands, that users can invoke with ease; most horizontal application software provides the facility to record, edit, and use macros.

Mail server. In a client/server architecture, a computer that acts as the postmaster and sometimes as the post office in electronic mail applications.

Mailbox. A repository for electronic messages.

Mailing list. *See* distribution list.

Mainframe. A computer designed and marketed to handle the largest processing tasks of an organization, typically costing at least several hundred thousand dollars and usually requiring a separate, air-conditioned room and a staff of trained professionals to support its use.

Maintenance. The sixth and final stage of the systems development life cycle, it encompasses the processes associated with fixing software that does not operate properly and adding features to systems to improve them and respond to user demands.

MAN. *See* metropolitan area network.

Management reporting system. Also known as MRS, a system that helps managers monitor the operations and resources of an organization and the environment in which the organization operates.

Management system. Information system that has been designed and developed to facilitate the management of an organization by supplying the information management needs to function better or by assisting managers to communicate more effectively.

Managerial accounting. Provision of financial information that managers within the organization need for their decision making.

Manufacturing. The process of transforming raw materials into finished products.

Many-to-many relationship. A relationship between two entities, such as "stored in" for the entities *product* and *warehouse,* in which an instance of one entity can be related to many instances of the second, and vice versa.

Mapping software. Software that translates the output produced by other software into an acceptable EDI format and translates standard EDI formats into the input format required by the other software.

Market research. The process of gathering information about what consumers want and need.

Market share. The portion of the industry market captured by the business unit or organization of interest.

Marketing. A social process involving the activities necessary to enable individuals and organizations to obtain the products and services they need and want through exchanges with others.

Math coprocessor. *See* floating point accelerator.

Medium of transmission. The carrier of a data signal between two or more computers.

Megaflop. Millions of floating point operations per second.

Megahertz. One million hertz.

Member. In the network model, a set on the "many" side of a one-to-many relationship.

Memory board. A circuit board containing the circuitry to control RAM.

Menu-driven interface. Operating system software that presents a list of possible commands for the user to select.

Message. A communication between objects in an object-oriented program or database; also the medium in an object-oriented language through which objects communicate with one another.

Metadata. Data about data.

Method. An action or program performed by an object in an object-oriented program or database.

Metropolitan area network. Also known as MAN, a network spanning a metropolitan region.

Microcomputer. *See* personal computer.

Microwave signal. An electromagnetic signal that can carry data without cables over long distances using a series of relay stations or a communication satellite.

Middleware. Software that operates between a PC client and mainframe or minicomputer servers to translate client requests into traditional or standard minicomputer and mainframe packages.

Minicomputer. A computer designed and marketed to be used simultaneously by a small to moderate number of people, generally an entire department.

MIPS. Millions of instructions per second.

Model base. A component of a decision support system that provides analysis tools, including spreadsheets, simulation packages, forecasting tools, and statistical packages.

Modem. A device that converts a digital signal to an analog signal and an analog signal to a digital signal for communication between computers over telephone lines.

Monitor. A video output device that receives an analog electrical signal similar to that received by a television set from the video adaptor and shows a display of text or graphics.

Motherboard. A circuit board that contains a computer's processor as well as other chips central to the computer's operation. The motherboard may also contain slots for connections to other circuit boards, especially those that control the input, output, and storage devices.

Motion-sensing device. An input device that responds to the direction a user moves it.

Mouse. A motion-sensing input device shaped like a mouse that fits into the hand and has one to three buttons used to send special signals to the computer.

MRS. *See* management reporting system.

Multinational corporation. A corporation that has built or acquired a portfolio of national companies that it operates and manages with sensitivity to its subsidiaries' local environments.

Multiplexor. A device that combines the signals from several computers or multiple signals from a multiuser computer into a signal that can be sent over a single phone line for long-distance transmission to another multiplexor that separates the signals at the receiving end.

Multiuser editor. A type of groupware, software that allows multiple users to access and modify a common document.

Navigating. In the network model, the process of specifying a path through a database to find desired data.

Needs analysis. The first stage in the systems development life cycle, a formal, integrated, and usually time-limited process of gathering data about the needs and opportunities of end users and their managers; evaluating and ranking the importance of these needs; and addressing the possibility that they cannot be satisfied by continuous improvement of the existing systems.

Net value of information. The difference between the value and cost of information.

Network. A collection of individuals, work groups, departments, divisions, or organizations that agree to communicate with one another, together with the computers, communication devices, and media that enable such communication. Also, the hardware connections between computers that coordinate operations and allow them to share data with one another.

Network architecture. The relationship that network designers intend to establish among a network's participants.

Network management server. In a client/server architecture, a computer that handles such network management tasks as adding new clients to a network and providing authorization for users upon logging in.

Network model. A data model in which all entities are related to one another through one-to-many relationships.

Network operating system. Also known as NOS, software that manages and controls the joint or shared resources of a group of computers connected by a network.

Neural network. A class of self-teaching expert systems that operate by mimicking the human brain.

Nonprocedural language. Computer language such as SQL and many expert system shells that can operate without step-by-step instructions.

Nonstop system. *See* fault-tolerant system.

Nonvolatile storage. Data storage that does not require electricity to retain its memory.

Normalization. A formal procedure for organizing data into a normalized form.

Normalized form. A relational design that organizes that data elements of a database into tables in such a way as to simplify retrieval, reduce data entry and storage, and minimize the likelihood of data inconsistencies.

NOS. *See* network operating system.

Notebook. *See* laptop computer.

Numeric keypad. An area of the keyboard that contains keys for numbers and simple calculation signs (plus, minus, times, and divide).

Object. A structure consisting of data and procedures that operate on that data.

Object class. Also called an object type, a group of objects that share the same attributes and methods.

Object linking and embedding. Also known as OLE, an industry standard accepted by most horizontal application software that allows objects created in one software program to be included (embedded) within the data created by a different software program.

Object model. A data model derived from object-oriented programming that encapsulates data and methods and organizes objects into object classes, among which there can be a hierarchical relationship.

Object module. Computer code to perform a particular task after it has been translated by a compiler; these may be linked together into an executable module.

Object-oriented language. A computer language such as Smalltalk or C++ that merges procedures and data into a structure called an object.

Object-oriented user interface. A user interface featuring icons and a mouse-controlled cursor often used for decision support and executive information systems.

Object type. *See* object class.

OCR. *See* optical character recognition software *and* optical character reader.

Off-the-shelf software. Also known as packaged software, vertical software sold for installation without modification; its license often prohibits any modification.

OLE. *See* object linking and embedding.

On-demand report. Any report that a management reporting system provides for authorized users upon request.

On-line data entry. Data entry process in which computers capture transactions directly, eliminating the need for source documents.

One-to-many relationship. A relationship between two entities, such as "represents" for the entities *sales rep* and *customer,* in which an instance of one entity, a sales rep in this case, can be related to many instances of the second, but in which an instance of the second entity can be related to only one instance of the first entity.

One-to-one relationship. A relationship between two entities in which an instance of one entity can be related to one instance of the second, and vice versa.

Open operating system. An operating system that adheres to industry standards, whose specifications are not owned by one vendor, and for which a set of tests that check for conformance to the standard is available.

Open system interconnection model. *See* OSI model.

Operating system. Programs that perform the most basic housekeeping, resource allocation, and resource monitoring functions for a computer with a minimum of input or control by the user.

Operational capability demonstration. Also known as OCD, a simulation performed before software development that allows users to judge how rapidly the system will perform under the expected processing loads and illustrates various features of the system to be developed.

Operational planning. Planning for the issues of implementation.

Operations management. The processes of planning, organizing, directing, and controlling the physical operations of an organization.

Optical character reader. An input device that recognizes and reads numbers and letters written in a special font.

Optical character recognition software. Software that recognizes and processes text characters appearing within a graphic image.

Order entry system. A transaction processing system that records and processes the taking of an order.

Organizing. Establishing a formal reporting structure and a system of accountability among workers, including forming employees into meaningful work groups with appropriate supervision; defining the hierarchy of authority; determining the location of decision making; and providing for coordination.

OSI model. Also known as the open system interconnection model, a model of the communication process that divides it into seven layers for which standards have been independently created.

Outbound logistics. The transport of finished products from a company to its customers.

Output analysis. The systematic identification of ways that people in an organization use information.

Output hardware. Devices used by a computer to present information to its users.

Outsourcing. Purchasing from another company services, such as software development, that could have been performed in-house; the contracting of a service, such as information processing and applications development, to a party outside the organization.

Owner. In the network model, a set on the "one" side of a one-to-many relationship.

P-code. An intermediate code that preserves much of the source language in a highly compact, incomprehensible form, yet still allows an interpreter to be run.

Packaged software. *See* off-the-shelf software.

Packet. A division of data used by communication software; for example, many data communication software packages send data in a packet of a fixed number of bytes.

Parallel implementation. An implementation strategy in which users employ both new and old systems for a period of time.

Parallel interface. A standard interface for input and output devices that deals with data eight bits at a time.

Parallel processor. A processor often used for scientific computers that includes hundreds of smaller processors connected to one another in complex and programmable ways.

Passive data entry. Methods of entering data into a computer without the active participation of a user.

Patent. A legal document that protects an idea from being copied.

Payroll system. A transaction processing system that tracks employee hours, wages, and other benefits and that generates paychecks and records of additional benefits or payments to employees on a prescribed schedule.

PC. *See* personal computer.

Peer-to-peer architecture. A plan for running a network of computers such that no hierarchical relationships exist among the network participants, and data and program elements are treated as sharable resources for authorized network participants.

Perception. The active process by which an individual attends to certain stimuli and then organizes them in a meaningful way.

Performance appraisal. The tasks of providing evaluation data about employee performance for administrative and training and development decisions.

Performance testing. The first stage of system testing, during which developers identify and correct problems that might cause the system to become inoperative or cause it to create and save erroneous information.

Periodic report. Any report that a management reporting system produces on a periodic basis for delivery to a prespecified list of employees.

Personal computer. A computer designed and marketed to be used by an individual or a small number of people and to be owned and managed by an individual.

Personal information manager. An electronic device and associated software, also known as a PIM, that automates many personal information functions and may include such features as a personal telephone directory, phone dialer, diary maintenance, note taking, outlining capability, office appointment scheduling with "alarm clocks" to remind users of appointments, calculator abilities, and generic "card" files that can be organized by topic and searched in a variety of ways.

Phased implementation. An implementation strategy that introduces a new system one component at a time.

Physical design. Decision making about the hardware used to deliver a system.

Physical view. A view of data that expresses the way in which they are physically stored on a storage medium, or the way in which their physical addresses are assigned.

Pilot implementation. An implementation strategy, also called beta testing, that requires one or more segments of the company to use a new system before the entire company uses it.

PIM. *See* personal information manager.

Pipelining. The overlapping of fetching, decoding, and executing of different instructions by a processor.

Pixel. A dot on the computer screen.

Planning. Activities involved in the specification of goals and in the design of the blueprint for achieving them.

Platen. *See* drum.

Plotter. An output device that operates by moving a pen or pens over paper, much in the same way as a person writes, to produce drawings.

Point-of-sale system. Also know as a POS, a transaction processing system that records the sale of a product or service and updates company records related to or affected by the sale.

Pointing device. An input device used to identify a location on a computer screen by sensing either motion or position.

Port. A socket usually located at the back of a computer through which the monitor, keyboard, and other input and output devices are connected via cables to interface cards inside the computer.

Portability. The ability of software to be used by different types of computers.

POS. *See* point-of-sale system.

Position sensing device. A device such as a touch screen or light pen that allows the user to identify a specific point on the output screen.

Positioning key. A key on the keyboard, such as *Home* or *PageUp,* normally interpreted by computer software as an instruction to move the cursor.

Postimplementation review. The processes of evaluating how well a system meets user needs, setting priorities for new development, and determining when to re-initiate a needs analysis.

Presentation graphics software. Software that allows users with little graphics training to produce professional-looking slides, overheads, or prints to support their presentations.

Primary storage. Electronic data storage that can be accessed rapidly, and often directly, by the computer processor.

Print server. In a client/server architecture, a computer that allocates and controls the network's printing devices.

Priority delivery. A feature of electronic mail software that allows the message sender to attach a priority, such as urgent, regular, or low, to each message.

Procedural language. Computer language, such as C, COBOL, or FORTRAN, that forces a software developer to give step-by-step instructions to the computer.

Procedure analysis. The process of diagnosing whether or not an organization collects the information it needs, uses the information it collects effectively, and has efficient processes to address its information needs.

Process design. The creation and specification of equipment and procedures for manufacturing a finished good. Also, the design of both the computational and logical processes underlying a system; the tasks of identifying the technologies to be used in producing a product or service; selecting specific equipment, software, etc. to be used in production; specifying how the product or service should flow through the production system; selecting facilities and locations where the product is to be manufactured or the services rendered; making decisions about how to arrange the layout of the facilities so as to maximize throughput and minimize nonproductive activities; and designing the jobs that need to be performed in carrying out production plans.

Processing hardware. Computer chips and other devices that manipulate information according to instructions encoded into software.

Product and service planning and design. The process of generating ideas, testing them for feasibility, and finalizing them into the design of a product or service.

Product design. The creation of a concept and specifications for a finished good.

Product information manager. Software that controls a database of engineering information, including metadata about drawings and documents such as part numbers, date of last revision, storage location, and acceptable viewers.

Production environment. An environment consisting of hardware, the most recent releases of software, and current transaction data, and that emphasizes high system reliability.

Profit center. An organization of an IS department that requires it to bid for the work of internal users, to seek work from other organizations, and to charge internal users what it would charge external users.

Programmer. A job position describing the work of those who produce custom software.

Project manager. A manager who supervises teams of workers who together must accomplish a specific goal. Also, the person responsible for directing a software development project and ensuring that the project meets user requirements within a specified budget and time frame.

Proofing tool. A feature of word processing programs, such as a spell checker or grammar checker, that helps users reduce the number of errors in the documents they create.

Protocol. Any of several standard procedures that data communication software and devices follow to establish acceptable connections between devices, ensure the integrity of data transmission, and protect against the simultaneous transmission of data by two or more computers sharing the same transmission medium.

Purchase order. A document that authorizes and documents the purchase of goods or services from a supplier.

Purchasing system. A transaction processing system that supports and documents transactions associated with the purchasing of goods and services.

Quality control. The management of the production process to minimize or eliminate defects and errors. Also, the process of ensuring that a newly developed system works as designed.

RAD. *See* rapid application development.

Radio signal. An electromagnetic signal that can carry data for short distances, such as within a building, and can penetrate walls.

RAID. An acronym for redundant arrays of inexpensive disks, a storage device that uses a large number of relatively small hard disks to create what appears to be a single storage device and that, because of these redundancies, can continue to operate even when one or more of these disks fail.

RAM. *See* random access memory.

Random access memory. Volatile primary storage.

Range. A region of a spreadsheet.

Rapid application development. Also known as rapid prototyping and RAD, the condensation of the design and development stages of the systems development life cycle using an iterative process and special software tools that enable the development, in a few hours, of systems that appear to be real.

Rapid prototyping. *See* rapid application development. Also, the production of three-dimensional output from CAD designs.

Read-only memory. Nonvolatile primary storage; ROM holds the instructions that a computer uses when it is first turned on.

Reader of formatted input. An input device that reads text specifically formatted for its use.

Real-time conferencing. Hardware and software that allow people to hold meetings electronically by typing their comments into networked computers.

Real-time processing. The processing of data upon their entry, resulting in the immediate update of affected databases and the immediate availability of transaction data to authorized users.

Receipt verification. A feature of electronic mail software that notifies a sender when the receiver reads a message.

Receiving document. A document that verifies the receipt of purchased goods.

Receiving system. A transaction processing system that documents the shipment of goods by suppliers and their receipt and acceptance by the organization.

Record. A group of data items that logically belong together, such as the data maintained for a single customer; a DBMS organizes data into such records.

Recruiting. The component of staffing involving the communication of information about job openings and the hiring organization to those best qualified for the positions.

Reduced instruction set computer. Processor that responds to relatively few instructions, as opposed to a complex instruction set computer.

Redundant arrays of inexpensive disks. *See* RAID.

Reel tape. A nonvolatile secondary storage device that resembles a reel of movie film.

Relation. In the relational model, a table.

Relational model. First proposed in 1970, a data model in which each type of object is described by a table whose rows correspond to individual instances of the object and whose columns correspond to object attributes.

Remote computer. A computer running terminal-emulation software connected via a communication device, typically a modem, to a host computer.

Repeater. An electronic device that boosts, or strengthens, a signal.

Report generator. Software that creates report programs directly from the report design.

Request for proposal. Also known as RFP, a document that clearly identifies its information processing requirements and information needs of an organization and requests software developers to submit bids for software development responding to these needs.

Requirement analysis. *See* needs analysis.

Resolution. Any measure of the fineness with which an output device can be controlled.

Resource. Input used in the production of output.

Reverse engineering. The process of analyzing the software that implements an existing system to identify and document exactly what it does and how it does it.

RFP. *See* request for proposal.

Right-sizing. The process of determining what overall architecture to employ for individual systems or for an organization as a whole.

Ring. A common network topology consisting of a series of repeaters, each connected to a workstation, joined point to point into a closed loop or a pair of closed loops.

RISC processor. *See* reduced instruction set computer.

Risk analysis. The process of identifying where risks might arise and analyzing the tradeoff of risk against costs and benefits.

RJ-11 jack. A standard wall connector for telephone cable.

Robot. A computer-controlled machine that has humanlike characteristics, such as intelligence, movement, and limbs or appendages.

Robotic output device. A device that moves physically in response to signals from a computer.

Robotics. The study of robots and their use; the application of robots in manufacturing.

ROM. *See* read-only memory.

Root. The base of the hierarchy of data modeled in a hierarchical model.

Router. An electronic device that connects two or more similar networks, passing data between them with minimal or no format conversion and without apparent delay.

Rule base. The component of an expert system that expresses rules that generally are rarely changed.

Satellite office. An office established away from the city center and near employee residences offering an alternative to the home office.

Scheduling. The process of matching equipment and employees to work processes.

Screen generator. Software that allows designers with little or no programming experience to use standard text and drawing tools to generate programs for screen-based data entry or screen-based queries.

Screen-saver. A systems utility that blanks out a computer screen or shows a pattern on the screen if the computer has not been used for a certain period of time.

Script. A language in which a user having minimal training can write small programs for an application software product; a language for writing macros.

SDLC. *See* systems development life cycle.

Second-mover. A company that follows the innovations of another.

Secondary storage. Data storage, usually magnetic or optical, from which data must first be transferred into primary storage before they can be accessed by the processor.

Segment. In a hierarchical model, a group of related records.

Selection. The component of staffing involving the matching of job candidates to job openings.

Serial interface. A standard interface for input and output devices that deals with data one bit at a time.

Server. In a client/server architecture, a computer dedicated to performing special services for client computers on the network.

Set. In the network model, the combinations of owners and members in a one-to-many relationship.

Simulation. The process of representing real processes with analytic models.

Site license. A license giving an organization the right to use a specified number of copies of a specific software product or the right to give a specified number of users access to a single copy of that software at a discount relative to the price of an individual license.

Situational analysis. Also known as SWOT, the process of collecting and analyzing information about a company's strengths, weaknesses, opportunities, and threats.

Smart house. A house that includes computer systems to automatically lock doors, turn on outside lights at dusk, or sprinkle the yard; emergency alert systems to check on children or the elderly; appliance systems that monitor appliance usage; and voice-activated communication and entertainment systems.

Smart hub. A router residing on several local area networks that accepts and responds to commands to connect two or more of these networks.

Snapping. A feature of desktop publishing software that allows users to move text or graphics onto some type of coordinate system.

Softcopy. Output on a medium such as a computer screen that cannot be detached from the computer.

Software. The instructions, in the form of computer code and its accompanying documentation, for processing data electronically.

Software developer. A specialist in one or more software development tools.

Software development tool. Software that helps people create new software.

Software engineer. A person trained in the use of one or more CASE workbenches.

Source document. A predesigned form for capturing transactions on paper, along with the data on that form.

Spatial DBMS. A DBMS designed to enable users to analyze and change the spatial relationship among objects stored in its databases.

Spreadsheet software. Horizontal software that imitates an accountant's spreadsheet, facilitating the calculation of tabular information whose values are dependent on one another, and automates the process of performing repeated calculations.

SQL. An easy-to-use nonprocedural language that has been adopted as a standard for the relational model.

Staffing. The recruiting and selecting of individuals for job positions.

Standard. A set of rules governing the types of investments an organization may make in information technology.

Star. A layout for a local network that uses an individual cable from a central point to each device on the network; also a topology for a local area network that exists when all workstations and devices are connected to a single central repeater/switch that reads the address of any message it receives and forwards it directly to the intended recipient.

Statistical report. *See* summary report.

Steering committee. *See* IS steering committee.

Storage hardware. Any device used to save or store information.

Strategic alignment. A congruence and synergy between an organization's strategic goals and objectives and its information systems.

Strategic planning. The long-term planning for accomplishing an organization's mission.

Strategic system. Information system that implements or strongly supports the implementation of an organizational strategy, often by extending the systems concept beyond organizational borders, to include customers, suppliers, distributors, and strategic partners.

Strategy. The long-term direction or intended set of activities for an organization to attain its goals.

String testing. Testing that examines the interaction of a series of programs that likely will be used in concert within a system, such as those that process a transaction.

Structure. The division of labor, coordination of positions, and formal reporting relationships that exist in an organization.

Structure chart. A diagram that shows the relationship among the programs and subprograms that will make up a finished system.

Structured analysis. The process of diagramming existing and proposed systems so that users can understand and critique an analyst's perception of information relationships.

Style sheet. A feature of word processing software that permits users to create a document that follows a template with variations in different parts of the document.

Summary report. A report that shows totals, averages, maximums, minimums, or other statistical data aggregated over time, personnel, products, or some other quantity.

Supercomputer. A computer designed and marketed to support scientific research.

Supernetwork. A networks of networks.

SWOT. *See* situational analysis.

Synchronous communication. Along with asynchronous communication, one of the two most common technologies for sending and receiving data.

Synonym. One of two or more names of a given data item.

Sysop. The central manager of an electronic bulletin board.

System testing. Also known as alpha testing, the testing of an entire system under realistic conditions.

Systems analyst. The job title of a person who provides the interface between information systems users and information systems developers.

Systems development life cycle. Also known as SDLC, the analysis of user needs and the selection, design, development, implementation, and maintenance of application systems to meet such needs.

Systems development methodology. An approach, such as the systems development life cycle, for analyzing, developing, and maintaining systems, usually supported by CASE tools.

Systems software. Software that provides the functions a computer needs to manage its various parts, such as its printers, keyboards, video screens, and data storage devices.

Systems utilities. Programs that operate primarily under user control and provide basic resource management functions, such as the ability to copy files or sort data.

Tactical decision. Also known as tactics, medium- or short-term decision that helps organizations achieve their strategic objectives.

Tactical planning. The medium- and short-term planning performed in most organizations by middle managers.

Tactics. *See* tactical decisions.

Tape. Data storage medium on which information is encoded onto the magnetic coating of a thin mylar tape.

Telecommuting. Using electronic communication technology to work primarily from home or an office in the home rather than at an office owned or rented by one's employer.

Teleconferencing. A meeting among people in different locations using specially designed rooms with video and sound equipment to enable interactive conversation as if the participants were in the same room.

Temporal DBMS. A database management system designed to store and retrieve historical changes to information.

Terminal. A video output device that receives a digital signal representing characters or cursor positioning commands from the computer and modifies its display accordingly.

Terminal emulation. Software that makes a user's keyboard and screen appear connected to a computer other than the user's computer.

Terminator. A device at the end of a bus layout that absorbs all signals to remove them from the network.

Testing environment. A computing environment (hardware, software, and data) similar to the production environment in which software developers can themselves test or have users test new software or modified software that is ready to be moved into the production environment.

Testing plan. A plan, typically introduced during the design stage of the systems development life cycle, to ensure the quality of software development.

Thimble printer. A character impact printer whose print head consists of a plastic or metal piece shaped like a sphere or a thimble containing the raised image of each character.

Toggle key. A key on the keyboard such as *Caps Lock* or *Scroll Lock* that functions in one or two states and changes states each time it is pressed.

Token. A special signal used in certain collision avoidance techniques that a computer must receive before it can send a message.

Token passing. A technique for avoiding collisions on a local area network by passing a token.

Toner. Particles of a dark powder used as ink in a laser printer.

Topic mailbox. A repository for messages related to a single topic or hierarchy of topics and managed by electronic notes software.

Topology. The structure of interconnections among workstations and devices attached to a local area network.

Touch screen. An input device usually placed over or built into an output screen that can detect where the screen is touched.

TPS. *See* transaction processing system.

Trackball. A motion-sensing input device consisting of a ball that can be rotated by the user in any of several directions.

Training and development. Addressing and removing deficiencies in skills, knowledge, or experience required for quality job performance or advancement in the organization.

Transaction. A business event that affects an organization conducting its business, such as the sale of a product, receipt of a payment, hiring of an employee, or taking of a reservation.

Transaction processing. The manual or computerized recording of the transactions of a business.

Transaction processing system. Also known as TPS, an information system that records and processes an organization's routine business activities.

Transnational corporation. A company that incorporates and integrates multinational, global, and international strategies.

Tree. A hierarchical layout for a local area network in which branches emanate as in a biological tree.

Tuple. A row of a relation in the relational model.

Turn-key system. Hardware and software bundled for sale as a single product.

Twisted-pair wire. The wire used in most homes to connect a telephone to its telephone jack.

Unallocated cost center. An accounting scheme in which end users and their managers are not held financially accountable for the costs of the information systems department.

Uninterrupted power supply. A secondary source of power for computer equipment, such as a battery or electric generator, along with circuitry that can recognize and react to a loss of power from the primary supply before it can affect the computer.

Unit testing. The testing of each small component of the system to guarantee its proper operation.

Unstructured architecture. A network architecture that places few, if any, restrictions upon the participants.

Upstream. Relative to a given company, the direction on the value chain of companies such as suppliers who add value to a product or service before the company has added its value.

Usability lab. A place where developers can observe and record for later analysis user reactions to a new or revised system.

Usability testing. An evaluation of a new or revised system on the basis of how well it meets users' expectations and needs.

User mailbox. A repository for electronic messages destined for a single individual.

Value-added network. A reseller of telephone and/or satellite transmission capacity.

Value-added reseller. Also known as VAR, a software manufacturer's representative authorized to customize its software.

Value-adding partnership. Also known as VAP, the linkage of companies that view the whole value system, not just the value chain, as their competitive unit and who share information freely with others in the value system so that they can compete successfully in this environment.

Value chain. A system of generic interconnected activities, such as design, engineering, manufacturing, distribution, and sales, that a company performs to add value to its products or services.

Value system. A model of product development and delivery in which value is built through a sequence of steps (*see* value chain) such as design, engineering, manufacturing, distribution, and sales.

VAP. *See* value-adding partnership.

VAR. *See* value-added reseller.

Vertical application software. Software that performs tasks that are common to a specific industry.

Video adaptor. A circuit board inside the computer, also known as a video controller, that supports and controls the monitor.

Video controller. *See* video adapter.

View. A subset of the database that can be made available to certain classes of users or to certain applications.

Virtual device. A feature of an operating system that simulates a real device.

Virus. *See* computer virus.

Voice mail. Computer and communication technology that can record and store the voice of a telephone caller and from which caller and recipient can execute commands via a touch-tone phone.

Voice processor. A device that can translate sound-wave inputs into sound groups called phonemes and then into written words.

Volatile storage. Storage that loses whatever data it has if the power is turned off.

WAN. *See* wide area network.

Wide area network. Also known as WAN, a network that spans one or more cities and usually uses third-party services to connect its sites.

Word processing software. Software that assists users in creating, editing, formatting, and printing documents.

Workgroup editor. Software that screens, edits, and consolidates messages, especially with those delivered by electronic lists and notes.

Workstation. A powerful microcomputer that is used for engineering and for executive support systems.

WORM. *See* write-once read-many.

Write-once read-many. A storage technology, also known as WORM, in which a laser burns microscopic holes in optical disks to represent data.

NAME INDEX

BUSINESS INDEX

SUBJECT INDEX